COMPANION TO
THE UNITED METHODIST
HYMNAL

COMPANION TO THE UNITED METHODIST HYMNAL

CARLTON R. YOUNG

ABINGDON PRESS
NASHVILLE

COMPANION TO THE UNITED METHODIST HYMNAL

Copyright © 1993 by Abingdon Press

This book is printed on acid-free recycled paper.

ISBN 0-687-09260-4

03 04 05 06 07 - 10 9 8 7 6

Scripture quotations noted RSV are from the Revised Standard Version of the Bible, copyright 1946, 1952, 1971 by the Division of Christian Education of the National Council of Churches of Christ in the USA. Used by permission.

Scripture quotations noted NRSV are from the New Revised Standard Version Bible, copyright © 1989, by the Division of Christian Education of the National Council of Churches of Christ in the United States of America.

Young, Carlton Raymond, 1926–
    Companion to The United Methodist Hymnal/Carlton R. Young
        p. cm.
    Includes bibliographical references and index.
    ISBN 0-687-09260-4 (alk. paper)
    1. United Methodist Church (U.S.) — Hymns—History and criticism.
2. Hymns. English—United States—History and criticism.   I. United Methodist hymnal.
1989. II. Title.
ML3170.Y68   1993
264' .07602—dc20   93-4115
                                                                              CIP
                                                                              MN

MANUFACTURED IN THE UNITED STATES OF AMERICA

Dedicated to

Marjorie Lindner Young

PREFACE

Nothing is more integral to worship in the Methodist tradition than hymn singing, for Methodists have been producing hymnbooks from their very beginnings.

The idea of the first *United Methodist Hymnal* began in 1980 when the General Conference meeting in Indianapolis authorized The United Methodist Publishing House and the General Board of Discipleship to conduct research about the need for a new hymnal and to report their findings to the General Conference that met in Baltimore in 1984.

The statement of need was clear, and the 1984 General Conference authorized the formation of a Hymnal Revision Committee whose report was made to the 1988 General Conference in St. Louis. The Hymnal Revision Committee presented a 1,141-page report with diverse content, rich music, and innovative worship resources that quickly won the hearts of the voting delegates of the General Conference, and immediate publication was authorized.

Production of the *The United Methodist Hymnal* required unprecedented financial resources, but the overwhelming acceptance by The United Methodist Church and the widespread critical acclaim following the hymnal's 1989 publication proved the wisdom of the investment. Within four years after publication, sales of *The United Methodist Hymnal* passed the four million mark.

Undoubtedly a principle factor in the new hymnal's success was the review and feedback process that was established by the Hymnal Revision Committee during its earliest meetings. Thousands of reader-consultants in local churches were given opportunities at every milestone to express their feelings about the proposed contents of the new book. Additionally, numerous consultants made presentations to subcommittees and to the full Hymnal Revision Committee about various concerns for the new hymnal. In short, the Hymnal Revision Committee listened to the membership of The United Methodist Church and responded as well as, and probably better than, any similar body in history. The result is a hymnal of and for the church.

The publisher was privileged to serve as a member of the Hymnal Revision Committee and experienced, as few publishers are able to, the historic responsibility of providing this most basic worship resource to the church, since hymnals are rarely published more often that once in twenty-five years. The experience deepened an individual sense of personal and professional mission and spurred a consciousness of the committee's and the publishing house's place in the historic stream of those who have attempted "to serve the present age."

The Hymnal Revision Committee was a talented, dedicated collection of people committed to doing their best for their church. They met often and worked diligently and intelligently. The publisher, as well as the whole membership of The United Methodist Church, owes this committee much for its devoted labor. Particular thanks is due to Bishop Reuben P. Job, the most patient and caring chair any committee could hope for, and to Dr. Carlton R. Young, the consummately professional editor of *The United Methodist Hymnal* and probably the only person ever to serve as editor of two of his denomination's official hymnals.

The hymnal was presented for the glory of God in a service of thanksgiving and consecration at the Edenton Street United Methodist Church in Raleigh, North Carolina, on May 4, 1989. It stands in the great historic tradition of Methodist and Evangelical United Brethren hymnals published over the centuries.

ROBERT K. FEASTER, Publisher
The United Methodist Church

FOREWORD

Worship is humankind's most profound act. It is our response to God's call to be in community with God and all of God's people. Consequently, the creation of a resource that is meant to sustain and promote worship is a significant undertaking, a challenge and opportunity of which the Hymnal Revision Committee quickly became aware.

It was clear from the beginning of our work that each person brought unique strengths and distinct expectations to the assigned task. One member remarked, "I would like to see our work become an icon, a resource through which United Methodist Christians will see and experience God's grace and presence as they are led to ever greater levels of faithfulness." This hope became a reality as the committee engaged in an intensive process of listening to the people and knowing that this was one way of hearing the voice of God. We listened to poets, musicians, theologians, the young, old, evangelical, catholic, charismatic, traditional, nontraditional, minority, and majority— and took each voice seriously.

As members of the Hymnal Revision Committee, we experienced freedom and openness to explore new ways of life in Christ, new sources of strength and joy, and a new depth and breadth to our work and our individual lives. As a consequence, we became a continually renewed community, enabled to hear and value the contribution of each. As our work became worship, we were increasingly aware that we were gathered in the searching and sustaining light of God's presence. Within that renewing experience a hymnal was formed to invite and enable United Methodists to sing and pray the story of God's redemptive act in Christ Jesus and to express the joy of that gift in a multitude of voices that reflects the human rainbow of God's global community. *The United Methodist Hymnal* reflects our past, offers guidance for the present, and points towards the promising future offered to God's people.

The *Companion to the United Methodist Hymnal* is the story about the most widely acclaimed and used worship resource of the second half of the twentieth century, and it is commended to the church for study, reflection, and guidance.

RUEBEN P. JOB, Chair
The Hymnal Revision Committee

INTRODUCTION

The publishing of companions to our authorized hymnals began with David Creamer's *Methodist Hymnology*, 1848, and continued with Charles S. Nutter's *Hymn Studies*, 1884. In the twentieth century Wilber F. Tillett produced *Our Hymns and Their Authors*, 1900; Charles S. Nutter and Wilbur F. Tillett, *The Hymns and Hymn Writers of the Church*, 1911; Carl F. Price, *The Music and Hymnody of the Methodist Hymnal* [1905], 1911; Robert G. McCutchan, *Our Hymnody* [1935], 1937; and Fred D. Gealy, Austin C. Lovelace, and Carlton R. Young, *Companion to the Hymnal* [1966], 1970. The *Companion to The United Methodist Hymnal* [1989] continues that tradition. It follows the tripart format of the 1970 volume: General Articles, Commentaries on Texts and Tunes, and Biographies.

The general articles are greatly expanded in order to provide both an overview of the history of Christian song and the development of USA-Wesleyan style congregational song: the gospel hymn, the social gospel hymn, the religious song of Native Americans, African Americans, Hispanic Americans, and Asian Americans; and the history and development of the hymnals of the former Evangelical United Brethren and the former Methodist churches. A significant portion of this section is devoted to the process that produced the first hymnal for The United Methodist Church.

The second section includes commentary on each hymn and its tune and the acts of praise, prayer, and psalm response. It is organized alphabetically by first line or common title and provides a brief history, interpretation, and scriptural references of the words cross-referenced to other hymns. The sources of the tune are included with suggestions on the musical style and performance practice, cross-referenced to *The United Methodist Hymnal Music Supplement*, volume 1, and recent hymnals. Where appropriate, the commentary also provides the circumstances whereby the Hymnal Revision Committee included the words or music and this writer's and others' opinions about the worth and usefulness of a text or tune.

In the third section are brief biographies of the poets, authors, and composers. These are followed by a bibliography of works referred to in the volume, including hymnic collections, a general index, and an index of hymn tunes.

The writer wishes to express his appreciation to those who have assisted in various aspects of the preparation of this work. William J. Reynolds read the articles on ecumenical and USA hymnody, and eighteenth-century Wesleyan hymnic traditions were read by the late Roger Deschner. The overviews of specific ethnic traditions were read in part or in whole by the following: Native American—Marilyn Hofstra; Hispanic American—Raquel Mora Martínez, Pablo Sosa, Gertrude Suppe, and Eradio Valverde, Jr.; African American—William B. McClain, Cyntha Wilson-Felder, and J. LaVon Wilson; Asian American—I-to Loh. Barbara Day, Beryl Ingram-Ward, and Laurence Hull Stookey read the final draft of the general articles.

The commentaries were critiqued by my colleague and the preeminent hymnologist, Austin C. Lovelace. The late John Wilson, Guildford, England, patiently and thoroughly responded to numerous inquiries about sources, bibliography, and musical and textual variants. Robin A. Leaver, a contributor to *The Hymnal 1982 Companion*, verified the dates and sources of a number of historic texts and tunes. The commentaries on prayers and service music were read by Hoyt L. Hickman. S T Kimbrough, Jr., verified the dates and source of each Wesley text or translation, read my commentary, and in some instances provided previously unpublished commentary, included here with his permission. In each instance valuable suggestions were made, and their inclusion greatly enriched the text.

This companion, as most, has used the information base of John Julian's monumental *Dictionary of Hymnody*, revised 1907. Other companions and handbooks that are frequently cited include Percy Dearmer's and Archibald Jacob's *Songs of Praise Discussed*, 1952, Robert G. McCutchan's *Our Hymnody*, 1942, Leonard Ellinwood's *Hymnal 1940 Companion*, 1956, Maurice Frost, ed., *Historical Companion to Hymns Ancient and Modern*, 1962, and William J. Reynolds' *Hymns of Our Faith*, 1964, and *Companion to the Baptist Hymnal*, 1976. Stanley L. Osborne's *If Such Holy Song*, 1976, Wesley Milgate's *Songs of the People of God: A Companion to the Australian Hymn Book/With One Voice*, revised 1985, and *A Companion to Sing Alleluia*, 1988; Marilyn Stulken's *Hymnal Companion to the Lutheran Book of Worship*, 1981, and Richard Watson and Kenneth Trickett, eds., *Companion to Hymns and Psalms*, 1988, have proved helpful in tracing recent hymns, tunes, and biographies.

William C. Rice's unpublished doctoral thesis "A Century of Methodist Music: 1859-1950," 1953, was very helpful in tracing turn-of-the-century developments of the former churches: The Methodist Episcopal Church, The Methodist Episcopal Church, South, and The Methodist Protestant Church. It is unfortunate that the volume was never published since it is the only reliable source for one hundred years of bibliography and commentary on USA Methodist hymnody and worship music performance practice.

In preparing the hymn commentaries I have in some instances adapted Fred D. Gealy's work in *Companion to the Hymnal*, 1970. In addition, Gealy's research files of correspondence, photocopies of pages of rare hymnals and original texts, exhaustive notes, and unedited copy that he carefully organized before his death were made available via microfiche by the Bridwell Library, Perkins School of Theology, Southern Methodist University, Richard P. Heitzenrater, interim librarian. These files have provided much new information and insight. Items from the research files are designated by file box and item number—for example, Gealy 557/224.

I wish to thank Abingdon Press for permission to use material from *The Hymns of The United Hymnal*, Diana Sanchez, editor; and *The Worship Resources of The United Methodist Hymnal*, Hoyt L. Hickman, editor. Hope Publishing has graciously granted permission to incorporate material from *A Year of Grace*, *Faith Looking Forward*, *Fill Us with Your Love*, *The Hymns and Ballads of Fred Pratt*

Green, The Hymn Texts of Fred Kaan, Later Hymns and Ballads and Fifty Poems, Lift Every Heart, Praising a Mystery, and *Welsh Hymns and Their Tunes.* I am also grateful to United Theological Seminary and the General Commission on Archives and History of The United Methodist Church, Madison, New Jersey, respectively, for permission to incorporate material from "The Hymnody of the Evangelical United Brethren Church," by Ellen Jane Lorenz Porter from the 1987 *Journal of Theology* of United Theological Seminary; and "Singet Hallelujah!: Music in the Evangelical Association, 1800-1894," by Terry Heisey, from the July 1990 issue of *Methodist History.*

The Benson Collection in the Speer Library of Princeton Theological Seminary was the place of primary research by Fred D. Gealy in 1966. Photocopies of that work are the foundation of his research files. I have been privileged to renew the relationship with that bibliography through the courtesy of William Harris, director of Special Collections and its cataloger, Paul R. Powell, who have generously provided access to the collection's treasures.

The following have responded quickly and thoroughly to my requests for information and verification: Cindy G. Runyon, Pitts Theological Library, Candler School of Theology, Emory University, Atlanta, Georgia; David Himrod, Garrett-Evangelical Theological Library, Evanston, Illinois; the Peabody Library, Johns Hopkins University, Baltimore, Maryland; Rosalyn Lewis and Hazel Luna, librarians of The United Methodist Publishing House, Nashville, Tennessee; J. Samuel Hammond, rare book librarian of the William R. Perkins Library, Duke University, Durham, North Carolina; Marion J. Hatchett, School of Theology, University of the South, Sewanee, Tennessee; Mary Lou Moore, librarian, Scarritt-Bennett Center, Nashville, Tennessee; William J. Reynolds and J. Stanley Moore, Southwestern Baptist Theological Seminary, Fort Worth, Texas; Paul A. Richardson and Roger Walworth, the Southern Baptist Seminary, Louisville, Kentucky; Kenneth E. Rowe, director of the Archives and History Center of The United Methodist Church, Drew University, Madison, New Jersey; and Page Thomas, Bridwell Library, Perkins School of Theology, Southern Methodist University, Dallas, Texas.

I am grateful to Maxine Clarke Beach, executive director, the Scarritt-Bennett Center, Nashville, Tennessee, for her encouragement and for allowing me time away from my responsibilities at the center.

I am indebted to Kenneth E. Rowe, director of the Archives and History Center of The United Methodist Church, Drew University, Madison, New Jersey, who compiled for this volume the first listing with annotations of the hymnals of the former United Brethren Church and who has granted permission for its inclusion. Beth McCoy has verified the first appearance of English texts in these hymnals using copies that were made available on loan by Paul Schrodt, librarian, United Seminary, Dayton, Ohio.

Thomas Remenschneider prepared the reduction and update of biographies of composers and authors from the 1970 *Companion,* and new biographic entries were researched and drafted by Beth McCoy. In some instances after repeated research and written requests, no information was available at the time of publication.

The copyeditor for this volume is Sylvia Mills, who also copyedited *The Methodist Hymnal* [*The Book of Hymns*], 1966, and *Companion to the Hymnal* [1966], 1970. Once again I have had the good fortune to be associated with one of the most talented, knowledgeable, and competent copyeditors of hymnic commentary and bibliography. Gayl Hinton, electronic-copy specialist, Gary Alan Smith, music editor, and Donna Nowels, music assistant, The United Methodist Publishing House, carefully guided the manuscript from my computer to publication.

The commentaries on Hymns, Canticles, and Acts of Worship are arranged alphabetically by first line and cross referenced when necessary. The commentaries are also cross referenced to other hymnal companions and *The United Methodist Hymnal Music Supplement,* vol. 1, 1991. Complete bibliographical information for references cited in the general articles and commentaries is found in **References**.

I wish to thank Robert K. Feaster and Reuben P. Job for providing appropriate introductions to this volume from their perspectives as publisher of The United Methodist Church and chair of the Hymnal Revision Committee, respectively. Their wise council and strong support, present throughout the process, are acknowledged with great appreciation.

Since the subject is complex and comprehensive, this one-volume work is incomplete and may inadvertently contain some errors. Regarding the former, the reader is referred to the bibliography and those companions and handbooks of recent hymnals. As for the latter, the writer will incorporate the appropriate corrections in future printings.

The volume is dedicated to my wife, Marjorie Lindner Young, whose encouragement, understanding, and love have sustained me in its preparation.

> Nun danket alle Gott,
>   mit Herzen, Mund und Händen,
> der grosse Dinge tut
>   an uns und allen Enden;
> der uns von Mutterleib
>   und Kindesbeinen an
> un zählig viel zugut
>   bis hieher hat getan.

"Nun danket alle Gott" ("Now thank we all our God")
Martin Rinkart, *Jesu Hertz-Büchlein*, 1663

CARLTON R. YOUNG
"The Owl's Nest"
Advent 1992
Nashville, Tennessee

CONTENTS

GENERAL ARTICLES

A SURVEY OF CHRISTIAN HYMNODY

INTRODUCTION

HYMN comes from the Greek *hymnos*, a poem usually sung to heroes or to the gods. Ancient Greece produced a variety of these monodic and choral songs as well as individual and group epic narratives, incantations, and marriage songs, sometimes combined with dance within a liturgical setting.

Non-Western hymns of both the pre-Christian and Christian eras include those from Mesopotamia dating from 1200 B.C.; Indian *Vedic* hymns dating from at least 1500 B.C.; Buddhist hymns, *gatha*, in performance practice similar to early Christian chant; and Egyptian hymns to Amon-Re and Ikhnaton's great Aton-hymn, which some cite as the basis of Psalm 104 **(826)**, dating from 1300 B.C. Chinese hymns are extant as early as the T'ang dynasty, 618-907, and imitated in the thirteenth-century Jin Twelve Hymns. In Korea, the "Hymn for the Sacrifice to Confucius" dates from the fourteenth century.

Hebrew scripture contains numerous hymns. For example: Exod. 15:1-18 **(135)**, a tripart hymn (invitation to praise, accounting God's mighty acts, and closing verses of praise); Deut. 32:1-43, the Song of Moses; Judg. 5, the Song of Deborah; 2 Sam. 22 (Ps. 18:1-50), David's Song of Thanksgiving; 1 Sam. 2:1-10, Hannah's Prayer, with its parallel in Mary's Song of Praise, Luke 1:46-55; Isa. 26:9-20, the Prayer of Isaiah, and 42:10-13, a Hymn of Praise; Jon. 2:2-9, the Prayer of Jonah; Hab. 3:2-19, the Prayer of Habakkuk; and Dan. 2:20-23, Daniel's Blessing of the God of Heaven.

The Psalms contain the greatest concentration of hymns. *Hymns of Praise* are found in Psalm 100 **(74, 821)** and Psalm 117 **(838)**, the latter a festival-opening hymn of praise, quoted by Paul in Rom. 15:11. Psalms 103 **(824),** 135 **(851),** and 146 **(858)** draw on cultic traditions, and Psalms 147 **(847),** 148 **(861),** 149, and 150 **(862),** on the Psalter's concluding doxology. Psalm 46 **(780)** is a *hymn of faith*. Psalms 104 **(826)** and 134-135:19-20 **(850-52)** are *creation hymns*. Psalm 103 **(824)** addresses the poet's own soul; Psalm 104 **(826)** sings of the soul in praise of God. Psalm 149 (see also Isa. 42:10, above) joins God's power at creation with the eschaton.

For commentary on early Christian use of psalms, see Massey H. Shepherd, *The Psalms in Christian Worship*.

EARLY CHRISTIAN HYMNS

Paul's often-quoted delineation of Christian song as psalms, hymns, and spiritual songs (Col. 3:16c) does not describe or distinguish their independent or collective functions, characteristics, or contents. Psalms, for example, can be performed as a solo or by a choir, in antiphonal, responsoral, plain, or ornate settings. Their flexibility proved very useful in the varieties of geographic, linguistic, and ethnic contexts in which early Christians worshipped. The form as well as the content of psalmody linked temple/synagogue worship practice with that of early Christians, but psalms do not constitute the sole repertory, as is evidenced by the presence of complete as well as fragments of Christian hymns in the New Testament. These hymns were composed for use in Christian contexts. They contain functional and teachable christological images and apocalyptic descriptions and metaphors. Some were composed in response to the Gnostics' successful use of the hymn in teaching and praise (see Wainwright 1980, 255). In their overall style they maintained both Hellenistic poetic form (1 Tim. 3:16) as well as Semitic/Hebrew characteristics of parallelism and accentual rhythm. For the development of hymns and hymn singing in Christian worship, see "Creeds and Hymns," pages 182-217 in Geoffrey Wainwright, *Doxology,* "Hymn and Cognate Forms," pages 207-62 in Eric Werner, *Sacred Bridge,* and Charles M. Mountain, "The New Testament Christ-Hymn," *The Hymn,* January 1993, 44:20-28.

Fred Gealy observes:

> Many New Testament phrases sound so hymnlike that one is tempted to see a veritable ground swell of hymnody underlying the prose of its praise and to conclude that the hymn form, whether doxological, a hymn to God or to Christ, was and is the most potent form of Christian speech. Therefore hymns may have formed a basic part of the catechetical instruction given to converts. (Gealy, Lovelace, Young 1970, 16)

There are at least six categories of early Christian hymns to be found in scripture: (1) *doxological,* addressed to God or Christ, or an ambiguous ascription, Rom. 11:36; Gal. 1:5; Eph. 3:20-21; Phil. 4:20; 1 Tim. 1:17 **(103)**, 6:16; 2 Tim. 4:18; Heb. 13:21; 1 Pet. 4:11, 5:11; Jude 24-25; Rev. 1:6, 5:14 **(674)**, 7:10 **(655)**, 7:12 **(181)**, 19:1, 4; (2) *baptismal,* Eph. 5:14; (3) *creedal,* 1 Tim. 3:16; John 1:1-18; (4) *Phrases from hymns addressing God,* Acts 4:24-26; Rom. 11:33-36; 2 Cor. 1:3-4; Eph. 1:3-14; Col. 1:13-14; 1 Pet. 1:35; Rev. 4:8 **(64, 65);** Rev. 11:17, 15:3-4, 19:5, 6b-8 **(623);** (5) *phrases from hymns addressing Christ,* Phil. 2:5-11 **(166, 167, 168, 177, 193, 536, 692);** Eph. 5:14; Col. 1:15-20; 1 Tim. 1:15 and 3:16; 2 Tim. 2:11-13; Heb. 1:3; Rev. 5:9; and (6) *Lukean hymns in the style of Hebrew psalms,* Song of Mary, 1:46-55 **(198, 199, 200);** Song of Zechariah, 1:68-79 **(208, 209),** and Song of Simeon, 2:29-32 **(225, 226, 665, 668).**

An example of an early eucharistic prayer is found in "Let all mortal flesh keep silence" **(626)** from the fourth-century *Liturgy of St. James of Jerusalem.* For commentary on early Christian hymns, see John Ferguson, "Hymns in the Early Church," *Bulletin: The Hymn Society of Great Britain and Ireland,* 1989.

GREEK HYMNS

Greek hymnody, according to Eric Werner, is grouped in four periods: (1) *Gnostic-Hellenistic*, second and third centuries; "Father, we thank you, for you have planted the grain on the hillside" **(563, 565)** is a paraphrase from the second-century *Didache*, or "teachings"; (2) *Judeo-Hellenistic*, third through fifth centuries, with examples of the morning hymn "Glory be to God on high" **(82)** and its abridged form, the lesser doxology **(70, 71)**; the evening hymn "O gladsome light" **(686)**; "Holy, Holy, Holy" **(9, 13, 16, 17, 19, 21, 23, 25, 28, 755)** from the Hebrew *kodosh* (Isa. 6), when combined with the *Benedictus* (Matt. 21:9), forms the hymn that is sung at the beginning of the Great Thanksgiving in "A Service of Word and Table" **(13)**. During this period the biblical songs or *canticles*, e.g., the Prayer of Zacharias (Luke 1:68-79), were also introduced into the liturgy; (3) *Syrian-Hellenistic*, sixth to the ninth centuries, sees the flowering of classic Greek hymnody, e.g., "The day of resurrection" **(303)** by John of Damascus and the anonymous evening hymn "The day is past and over" **(683)**; and (4) *Iconoclasm and schism*, ninth through fourteenth centuries, an unproductive period marked by a decline of the empire, the iconoclasts, and the final break with Rome. (Werner 1959, 221-26)

LATIN HYMNS

Latin hymns also had their beginnings in the church's struggle with Gnosticism. Representative Latin hymns come from three periods: (1) Latin and early monasticism, fourth through ninth centuries; (2) monastic hymnody of the tenth through the sixteenth centuries; and (3) the Roman Catholic hymnody of the seventeenth and eighteenth centuries.

The first period is described by Augustine in his *Confessions*, ix. 7: "[In] the church of Milan . . . all sing together with great earnestness of voice and heart," indicating that the hymns must have been easily taught to, remembered and sung by even those who were not literate. Hymns of this period include Ambrose of Milan's "Splendor paternae gloriae," "O splendor of God's glory bright" **(679)**, "Veni redemptor gentium," "Savior of the nations, come" **(214)**, and fourteen others of disputed authorship. The Spaniard Aurelius Clemens Prudentius is represented by "Corde natus ex Parentis," "Of the Father's [heart] love begotten" **(184)**; Venatius Fortunatus by his passion processional, "Pange, lingua, gloriosi corporis mysterium," "Sing, my tongue, the glorious battle" **(296)**; "Veni creator spiritus," "Come, Holy Ghost, our souls inspire" **(651)**, is attributed to Rabanus Maurus; Theodulph of Orleans is represented by "Gloria, laus et honor," "All glory, laud, and honor" **(280)**. During this same period emerged the Mozarabic "Christ, mighty Savior" **(684)** and the Latin form of the Te Deum, "We praise thee, O God" **(80)**.

Western *monastic hymnody* of the tenth through the sixteenth centuries marked the climax of monastic devotional literature from which hymns have been extracted and paraphrased, as in Peter Abelard's "O quanta, qualia sunt illa sabbata," "O what their joy and glory must be" **(727)**; the anonymous "O amor quam exstaticus," "O love, how deep, how broad" **(267)**; and Jean Tisserand's "O filii et filiae," "O sons and daughters" **(317)**. During this same time occurred two unrelated and perhaps contradictory contributions to Western hymnody: in the thirteenth century Frances of Assisi **(62, 481)** composed hymns in the vernacular, and in the sixteenth century as an early response to Luther, hymn singing was admitted into the liturgy of the Roman mass. Two historic Roman Catholic hymnals were published, Vehe's *Ein Neue Gesangbuchlein Geistlicher Lieder*, 1537, and Johann Leisentritt's *Geistliche Lieder und Psalmen*, 1567.

Examples of seventeenth-and eighteenth-century Roman Catholic hymnody are "Veni, veni Emmanuel," "O come, O come Emmanuel" **(211),** and "Adeste fideles," "O come, all ye faithful" **(234)**. Consistent with post-Council of Trent efforts towards simplicity and singability, tunes in the French diocesan hymnals, such as CHRISTE SANCTORUM **(188)**, *Paris Antiphoner*, 1681, are patterned after English adaptations of the metrical *psalm tune*; other melodies are composed in a neo-plainsong style. For the congregation these proved to be viable alternatives to traditional chant and were so successful that Anglicans included them in their late nineteenth-and early twentieth-century hymnals, e.g., *The English Hymnal*, 1906, revised 1933.

In England, Roman Catholic hymn singing had been restricted to the chapels of the foreign embassies. With the reestablishment of the Roman hierarchy in 1850, the needs of parish worship, and the activity of the Tractarians, English Roman Catholicism began to produce its own brand of hymns, e.g., the translations of Edward Caswall **(175, 185, 470)** and the hymns of Frederick W. Faber, "Faith of our Fathers" **(710)**.

GERMAN HYMNS

A century before the German Reformation, the Bohemian Brethren, after the reformer John Huss, 1369?-1415, taught that scriptures should be translated, taught, and preached in the vernacular and that worship should be congregationally centered by the use of the common cup and the singing of hymns. (See John H. Johansen, *Moravian Hymnody*, 1979, and Andrew P. Slabey, "John Huss and Congregational Singing," *The Hymn*.) The violence of the Hussite revolution and the force of the sixteenth-century German Reformation all but set aside this unique body of hymns, some 400 of which were published in *Kancional*, 1505. According to Jaroslav J. Vajda in *Hymnal Companion to the Lutheran Book of Worship*, they were to influence the development of the German chorale:

> Luther drew upon these sources as he rewrote the Czech reformers' Latin originals in German, and later Lutheran hymnodists and hymnal compilers drew upon the compositions of [these] Bohemian or Silesian hymnwriters. (Stulken 1981, 51)

Our hymnal may have one tune from these sources, MIT FREUDEN ZART **(126),** first printed in German hymnody in Vetter's *Kirchengesäng*, 1566, its roots most likely in the Middle Ages folk song. When making reference to the Moravians one must clearly distinguish between the fifteenth-century Slavic Moravians and the eighteenth-century German pietistic Moravians under Nicolaus Ludwig Count Von Zinzendorf, who later greatly influenced Charles and John Wesley.

The German reformer Martin Luther was a skilled dilettante musician and an articulate writer, translator, and preacher. His creation of the chorale embodied the essence of late fifteenth-century liturgical reform. Following his own injunction in *Order of Mass and Communion for the Church at Wittenberg* (1523) he wrote:

> I also wish that we had as many songs as possible in the vernacular which the people could sing during mass, immediately after the gradual and also after the Sanctus and Agnus Dei. For who doubts that originally all the people sang these which now only the choir sings. . . . But poets are wanting among us, or not yet known, who could compose evangelical and spiritual songs, as Paul calls them. (Luther 1965, 36)

In 1524 Luther composed four hymns for the *Etlich Christlich lider (Achtlieder-buch)*, one of which is "Aus tiefer Not," "Out of the depths I cry to you" **(515)**. Luther stands in the tradition of the meistersinger, combining the talents and insight of the poet and the tune writer. In the chorale he joined doxa (praise) with dogma (belief). He is the paradigm of the Protestant preacher/poet.

The sources of the sixteenth-century Lutheran chorale are (1) the *sequence* and *office hymn*, e.g., "Nun komm, der Heiden Heiland," "Savior of the nations, come" **(214)**; (2) the *leisen*, in which the melodies of the pre-Reformation German folk hymn "Christ ist erstanden" and the Latin *sequence* "Victimae paschali laudes" are joined in the chorale tune CHRIST LAG IN TODESBANDEN **(319)**; (3) the Latin *cantios*, IN DULCI JUBILO **(224)**. According to Keith Falconer, "In Germany, and Bohemia especially, the *cantio* was often translated into the vernacular and performed antiphonally with the Latin original" (Glover 1990, 172); (4) the *contrafacta*, setting a sacred text to a secular melody, O WELT, ICH MUSS DICH LASSEN **(631)**; and (5) original texts (hymns and psalms in metrical paraphrase) and rhythmic, vigorous, and memorable unison tunes composed to be sung without accompaniment, sometimes in *alternatum* by choir and congregation. To enhance the memorable qualities of the texts, many were composed in bar form, after the meistersingers: "stollen, stollen, abgesang," i.e., A(ab), A(ab), B(cde), as in "Ein' feste Burg ist unser Gott," "A mighty fortress is our God" **(110)**.

Two decades after Luther's death a second generation of poets turned towards a more devotional and reflective style. "Wachet auf, ruft uns die Stimme," "Wake, awake, for night is flying" **(720),** and "Wie schön leuchtet der Morgenstern," "O Morning Star, how fair and bright" **(247)**, are often cited as the "king and queen" of the chorales. The earlier performance style, *contrapunctum simplex*, was simplified into the cantional style by Lucas Osiander in *Fuenfzig geistliche Lieder und Psalmen*, 1585, "Fifty sacred songs and psalms." The popular collection made possible in one setting the participation of choir, organ, instruments, and congregation in any combination including *alternatum*. The chorale's further development during the the Thirty Years' War, 1618-1648, and the three decades that followed is characterized on the one hand by "cross and comfort hymns," set to major and minor rather than modal tunes, and by masterpieces of devotional poetry including Paul Gerhardt's "O Jesu Christ, mein Schöntes Licht," "Jesu, thy boundless love to me" **(183)**; Johann Franck's "Schmücke dich, O liebe Seele," "Deck thyself, my soul, with gladness" **(612)**; Martin Rinkart's "Nun danket alle Gott," "Now thank we all our God" **(102)**; and Johann Heermann's "Herzliebster Jesu, was hast du verbrochen," "Ah, holy Jesus, how hast thou offended" **(289)**.

During the Pietist movement, 1675-1750, which began with Philip Jacob Spener's *Pia desideria*, the chorale tune form shifted from the earlier rhythmic version to isorhythmic; and in this format it was imported in England by William Henry Havergal in *Old Church Psalmody*, 1847, and F. D. Maurice in *Choral Harmony*, 1854. The most important German hymnals of this time are J. A. Freyling-hausen's *Geistreiches Gesangbuch*, 1704, and *Neues Geistreiches Gesangbuch*, 1714. J. S. Bach was music editor of Georg Christian Schemelli's *Musikalisches Gesangbuch*, 1736, an important book of spiritual songs for the home. Though the hymnic output was spotty, two of the stronger hymns are Joachim Neander's "Lobe den Herren, den mächtigen," "Praise to the Lord, the almighty" **(139)**, and Johann Jakob Schütz's "Sei Lob und Ehr dem höchsten Gut," "Sing praise to God who reigns above" **(126)**. A few hymns were added to the repertory from eighteenth-century rationalism and the nineteenth-century confessional revival. The older chorale tradition was sustained until after World War II.

Among the first hymns to emerge from Germany since the publication of *Wehr und Waffen*, 1934, by the Confessional church, were those of the martyr Dietrich Bonhoeffer, e.g., "By gracious powers so wonderfully sheltered" **(517)**. By an ironic set of circumstances a melody, not a hymn tune, commissioned by the Nazi government and composed in 1938 by Hugo Distler, was set to a text lauding the annexation (invasion) of Austria. That same tune is found in several recent USA hymnals without the triumphal war text, perfectly wedded to Martin Franzmann's "Weary of all trumpeting, weary of all killing" **(442)**. From the postwar church movement, *Kirchentag*, emerges the first sustained effort to compose a new brand of hymnody and a viable alternative to the chorale tradition. The tunes of Heinz Werner Zimmermann and his pupil Rolf Schweizer represent schooled and academic alternatives to the widely distributed strictly pop and disposable music. The texts on the whole reject the pietistic traditions of the past and stress topics such as the care of the earth and the environment and nonviolent approaches to solving conflicts.

See Robin A. Leaver, "English and German Hymnody: Imports and Exports," *Bulletin: The Hymn Society of Great Britain and Ireland;* Karl Christian Thust's article in *Music and Kirche*, "Das Kirchen-Lied der Gegenwart" ("The Hymns of the Present Day"), a comprehensive coverage of recent German hymnody, its liturgical, theological, and stylistic development as well as the contributions of important poets and musicians with extensive documentation, discography, and bibliography; and Hans-Jörg Njieden, "Zur Beurteilung neuer Kirchenliedmelodien" ("A critical review of recent musical settings of hymns"), *Music und Kirche.*

SCANDINAVIAN HYMNS

Scandinavian hymnody, from its beginning profoundly influenced by the parent Lutheran chorale tradition, in the nineteenth and twentieth centuries developed into two distinct streams: (1) Danish, Norwegian, and Icelandic; and (2) Swedish **(141)**, **(502)**, and Finnish. Within each of these five components are remarkably unique features. The most comprehensive review in English of this body of hymnody is by Edward A. Hansen in *Hymnal Companion to the Lutheran Book of Worship.* (Stulken 1981) The current revitalization of Scandinavian hymnody is seen in two hymnals, *Andlig Visa,* 1964, and *Psalmer och Visor,* 1975, and in the works of composer Sven-Erik Bäck and poets Oliv Hartmann and Anders Frostenson, "Guds kärlek är som stranden och som gräset," translated by Fred Kaan, "Your love, O God, is broad like beach and meadow" **(120)**; and "Tron sig sträcker efter frukten när i vlomning trädet går," translated by Kaan, "Faith, while trees are still in blossom, plans the picking of the fruit" **(508)**.

GENEVAN/ANGLO METRICAL PSALMODY

John Calvin developed a second stream of Reformation hymnody, metrical psalmody, as a by-product of his radical reform of Christian worship, a reform that attempted to bring it into strict conformity with the norms of New Testament worship, i.e., praying, preaching, and singing. Congregation song was limited to the metrical paraphrase of the book of Psalms, but was later expanded to include the Lord's Prayer, the Song of Simeon, the Ten Commandments, and the Summary of the Law. Calvin enlisted the services of poets Clement Marot and Theodore de Bèze to compose metrical psalter texts in a variety of meters. By 1562 the material totaled 125 meters and 110 different tunes, e.g., the sturdy GENEVA 124 **(670)**. His composers, including Louis Bourgeois **(75, 686)** who was also music editor, carefully crafted their psalm tunes in a unique style that showed little influence of the chorale, folk hymnody, or the emerging Roman Catholic congregational melodies. Robin A. Leaver has provided the first comprehensive study of the sources of British metrical psalms in *Goostly Psalmes and Spirituall Songes.*

BRITISH HYMNS

The ideals of continental Reformed worship were transmitted to England and Scotland during the reign of Queen Mary I when clergy, who had fled to the continent and had heard the singing of metrical psalms, returned to present the ideals of Genevan psalmody to an English audience in the Anglo-Genevan Psalter, 1560-61. A century later the extensive publication of psalters for public worship had established psalm singing as the norm of English congregational song. In contrast to the Genevan practice of only unison, unaccompanied congregational singing, in English practice tunes were often harmonized for the choir and accompanied by the organ and/or a single viol on the bass line. For the most part, metrical patterns were limited to iambic variants of 8's and 6's, for example: Common Meter, 86.86; Short Meter, 66.86; Long Meter, 88.88. The sturdy, rhythmic Genevan tunes were abridged and adapted as in ST. MICHAEL **(372)** to fit into these basic meters. Our hymnal includes paraphrased psalms and other scripture from the following psalters: William Kethe's "All people that on earth do dwell" **(75)** from Sternhold and Hopkins, *The Whole Book of Psalms Collected into English Meter*, 1562; "The Lord's my shepherd" **(136)**, Scottish Psalter, 1650; and Nahum Tate's "While shepherds watched their flocks by night" **(236)** from Tate and Brady, *The New Version of the Psalms of David*, 1696. A complete list of hymns based on psalms and other scripture is given in the "Index of Scripture" **(923-26)**. For commentary on the development of English and Scottish psalmody, see "English Metrical Psalmody" in *The Hymnal 1982 Companion*, 1990.

The repertory and performance practice of congregational song developed in very dissimilar places and circumstances—the Chapel Royal, cathedrals, parish churches, abbeys, and academic chapels. For commentary on these developments, see Nicholas Temperly, *The Music of the English Parish Church*, 1979; Peter Le Huray, *Music and the Reformation in England*, 1967; and Christopher Dearnley, *English Church Music 1650–1750*, 1970.

The language base of most English hymns through the middle of the twentieth century is the King James Version of the Bible, 1611 **(137)**, and the liturgies **(26-31)**, prayers **(76)**, and psalms **(91)** in the *Book of Common Prayer*, 1559-1561. Seventeenth-century English hymns include Thomas Ken's "All praise to thee, my God, this night" **(682)**; John Cosin's translation of "Veni, Creator Spiritus," "Come, Holy Ghost, our souls inspire" **(651)**; and the poetry of George Herbert, in the eighteenth century adapted as hymns, e.g., "Let all the world in every corner sing" **(93)**.

For a survey of English translations of the Bible, see Bruce M. Metzger and Luther A. Weigle, "English versions of the Bible" (Metzger and Murphy 1991, 400-06).

The Hymns of Isaac Watts

The modern English hymn has its beginnings in the early eighteenth century in the work of Isaac Watts, often referred to as the "father of the English hymn." Watts's hymns and psalm paraphrases mark the transition of English Protestant worship song from strictly psalmody to a mixture of psalmody and hymnody. In paraphrasing his sermons into easily learned and sung congregational hymns he established for English evangelical hymnody that distinctive and compelling interplay between the "word preached" and the "word sung." The congregation sings what is preached, and the minister preaches what is sung. Fred D. Gealy makes this assessment of Watts's legacy:

> The epoch-making work of Watts rests, first upon his bold repudiation of the Calvinist principle that only scripture should be sung in church and that the psalter alone was adequate for Christian worship. Second, being a

better poet than previous psalm versifiers, he rejected the practice of making the psalm paraphrases "close-fitting" to the Hebrew. And third, of chief importance was his theological boldness in rejecting portions of the psalms as unfit for Christian use, in christianizing ["Jesus shall reign" **(157)**] some psalms by teaching David "to speak like a Christian," and even more important, in writing hymns ["When I survey the wondrous cross" **(298)**] which made no pretense to being psalm paraphrases. Thus his insistence was that the church's song should be fully evangelical and not just a supplement to the psalms, that it should be freely composed and not just hold to the letter of scripture and that it should give straightforward expression to the thoughts and feelings of the singers and not merely recall events of the distant past. . . . Their simple, direct language, their plain words of one syllable, their glad healthful faith in God as Creator and Redeemer have given them enduring value. (Gealy, Lovelace, Young 1970, 26)

The Wesleys

The greatest figure in English hymnody in the mid- and late-eighteenth century is John Wesley, translator, compiler, editor, and distributor. While in Georgia as a missionary priest, he compiled *A Collection of Psalms and Hymns*, 1737, the prototype of the modern English hymnal, including in one format a variety of selections: translations, metrical psalms, and English devotional poetry. (See also "John Wesley and the Music of Hymns," pages 49-52.) The career of his brother Charles, the most prominent hymn writer of the eighteenth century (he composed over 6,500 hymns; some claim as many as 9,000!), parallels the brothers' preaching of God's prevenient, justifying, santifying and perfecting grace: invitation, **(339)**, repentance, **(355)**, pardon, **(363)**, assurance, **(372)**, rebirth-new creature, **(385)**, personal holiness, **(384)**, social holiness, **(449)**. Charles's repertory also includes the church, its unity and fellowship **(332)**, Holy Communion, **(613)**, the greater festivals, e.g., All Saints', **(709)**; and the Christian Year: Advent, **(196)**, Christmas, **(240)**, Passion, **(282)**, Easter, **(302)**, Enthronement, **(716)**, Pentecost, **(603)**, The Second Advent, **(718)**. Fred D. Gealy writes that the Wesleys

are credited with bringing into existence two kinds of hymns, the evangelistic hymn and the hymn of Christian experience. If Watts's hymns were consistently and gloriously objective, free from introspection, the Wesley hymns were often autobiographical, bringing to moving expression the rapture of the soul in its response to the wonder and love of God as proclaimed in the gospel. (Gealy, Lovelace, Young 1970, 32)

The substance of Wesleyan theology is not found in a systematic ordering of belief but primarily in the sixty-four separate collections that the Wesleys published between 1738 and 1785. The Wesleys' successful establishment of a disciplined organization for perpetuating their teachings and activity assured, by way of an inherit pragmatism and flexibility, its spread and acceptance regardless of racial identity, language, or geography. For Methodists, that uniquely evangelical interplay of preaching and song (see Watts, above) became both a means of praise and a confessional act. The hymnbook was and continues to be their prayerbook; revivalism was and continues to be their most compelling liturgical form. See "Wesley Hymns," page 159.

John Wesley sets forth in his preface to his final hymnal, *A Collection of Hymns for the Use of the People called Methodists*, 1780, an articulate and persuasive argument as to how a hymnal ought to function within the context of evangelical Christianity. Bernard L. Manning summarized the preface's literary import in his address to the University Methodist Society at Wesley Church, Cambridge, November 20, 1932:

> They robbed you in 1904 of what, as the children of John Wesley, you should regard as one of your priceless heirlooms. I use strong language, but the Preface is, to begin with, one of the noblest pieces of eighteenth-century prose extant. . . . Apart altogether from Methodist interest, it is a first-rate introduction to the mind of the eighteenth century, a stimulating bit of literary criticism, and a model of plain, forceful, and at times sarcastic prose. (Manning 1942, 10-11)

An extensive discussion and detailed elaboration of Wesley's articulate and persuasive argument are found in F. Hildebrandt's and O. A. Beckerlegge's commentary in *A Collection of Hymns for the Use of the People called Methodists*, "Introduction," pages 1-75.

The full text of Wesley's preface to the *Collection* follows:

> 1. For many years I have been importuned to publish such a hymn-book as might be generally used in all our congregations throughout Great Britain and Ireland. I have hitherto withstood the importunity, as I believed such a publication was needless, considering the various hymn-books which my brother and I have published within these forty years last past; so that it may be doubted whether any religious community in the world has a greater variety of them.

> 2. But it has been answered, 'Such a publication is highly needful upon this very account; for the greater part of the people, being poor, are not able to purchase so many books: and those that have purchased them are, as it were, bewildered in the immense variety. A proper collection of hymns for general use, carefully made out of all these books, is therefore still wanting; and one comprised in so moderate a compass, as to be neither cumbersome nor expensive.

> 3. It has been replied, 'You have such a collection already, (entitled "Hymns and Spiritual Songs,")—which I extracted several years ago from a variety of hymn-books.' But it is objected—'This is in the other extreme; it is abundantly small. It does not, it cannot, in so narrow a compass,

contain variety enough—not so much as we want, among whom singing makes so considerable a part of the public service. What we want is, a collection not too large, that it may be cheap and portable; not too small, that it may contain a sufficient variety for all ordinary occasions.'

4. Such a Hymn-Book you have now before you. It is not so large as to be either cumbersome, or expensive: and it is large enough to contain such a variety of hymns, as will not soon be worn threadbare. It is large enough to contain all the important truths of our most holy religion, whether speculative or practical; yea, to illustrate them all, and to prove them both by Scripture and reason. And this is done in a regular order. The hymns are not carelessly jumbled together, but carefully ranged under proper heads, according to the experience of real Christians. So that this book is, in effect, a little body of experimental and practical divinity.

5. As but a small part of these hymns is of my own composing, I do not think it inconsistent with modesty to declare, that I am persuaded no such hymn-book as this has yet been published in the English language. In what other publication of the kind have you so distinct and full an account of scriptural Christianity? Such a declaration of the heights and depths of religion, speculative and practical? So strong cautions against the most plausible errors; particularly those that are now most prevalent? And so clear directions for making your calling and election sure; for perfecting holiness in the fear of God?

6. May I be permitted to add a few words with regard to the *poetry*? Then I will speak to those who are judges thereof, with all freedom and unreserve. To these I may say, without offence, 1. In these hymns there is no doggerel; no botches; nothing put in to patch up the rhyme; no feeble expletives. 2. Here is nothing turgid or bombast, on the one hand, or low and creeping, on the other. 3. Here are no *cant* expressions; no words without meaning. Those who impute this to us know not what they say. We talk common sense (whether they understand it or not) both in prose and verse, and use no word but in a fixed and determinate sense. 4. Here are (allow me to say) both the purity, the strength, and the elegance of the English language— and, at the same time, the utmost simplicity and plainness, suited to every capacity. Lastly, I desire men of taste to judge—these are the only competent judges, whether there be not in some of the following hymns the true spirit of poetry, such as cannot be acquired by art and labour, but must be the gift of nature. By labour a man may become a tolerable imitator of Spenser, Shakespeare, or Milton, and may heap together pretty compound epithets, as pale-eyed, meek-eyed, and the like; but unless he be *born* a poet, he will never attain the genuine *spirit of poetry*.

7. And here I beg leave to mention a thought which has been long upon my mind, and which I should long ago have inserted in the public papers, had I not been unwilling to stir up a nest of hornets. Many gentlemen

have done my brother and me (though without naming us) the honour to reprint many of our hymns. Now they are perfectly welcome so to do, provided they print them just as they are. But I desire, they would not attempt to mend them—for they really are not able. None of them is able to mend either the sense or the verse. Therefore, I must beg of them one of these two favours: either to let them stand just as they are, to take them for better or worse; or to add the true reading in the margin, or at the bottom of the page; that we may no longer be accountable either for the nonsense or for the doggerel of other men.

8. But to return. That which is of infinitely more moment that the spirit of poetry, is the spirit of piety. And I trust, all persons of real judgment will find *this* breathing through the whole *Collection*. It is in this view chiefly, that I would recommend it to every truly pious reader: as a means of raising or quickening the spirit of devotion, of confirming his faith, of enlivening his hope, and of kindling and increasing his love to God and man. When poetry thus keeps its place, as the handmaid of piety, it shall attain, not a poor perishable wreath, but a crown that fadeth not away.

John Wesley

London, Oct. 20, 1779

Other evangelical hymn writers of the late-eighteenth and early-nineteenth centuries include James Montgomery, "Hail to the Lord's Anointed" **(203)**; Philip Doddridge, "O happy day, that fixed my choice" **(391)**; John Cennick, "Be present at our table, Lord" **(621)**; Edward Perronet, "All hail the power of Jesus' name" **(154)**; Augustus M. Toplady, "Rock of Ages, cleft for me" **(361)**; Thomas Kelly, "The head that once was crowned with thorns" **(326)**; and Anglicans John Newton, "Amazing grace" **(378)**, and William Cowper, "Heal us, Emmanuel" **(266)**. For further commentary on the development of evangelical song in Great Britain in the eighteenth-century see Lionel Adey, "Revival Hymnody and the People" in *Class and Idol in the English Hymn*, 1988. Bishop Robert Lowth's discoveries of the patterns of Hebrew poetry in the Old Testament during his professorship at Oxford, 1741-50, produced *De sacra poesi Hebraeorum*, 1753 (*Lectures on Hebrew Poetry*, 1787). While his writings influenced a generation of biblical scholars, his text when translated into metrical hymns resulted in "stiff and stately odes." (Julian 1907, 921)

Although hymn singing was not officially sanctioned for Anglican worship until early in the nineteenth century, its practice was already widespread in parish worship when Reginald Heber, "Holy, holy, holy" **(64)**, supplied the first alternative to the evangelical topical/doctrinal organization of hymnals in his posthumously published *Hymns Written and Adapted to the Weekly Services of the Church Year*, 1827. The further revitalization of Anglican hymnody came later in the century, in part by way of the Oxford movement's search for the church's "catholic roots," and resulted in the writing and translation of hymns concerned with the church's history, mission, ministry, and sacraments, e.g., "The church's one foundation" **(545)**; translations of Greek and Latin hymns, John M. Neale's "Of the Father's love begotten" **(184)** and "The day of resurrection" **(303)**; and the translation of German hymns by Catherine Winkworth, "We believe in one true God" **(85)**. In addition to Winkworth other female hymn writers of Great Britain, all of them evangelicals, include Charlotte Elliot, "Just as I am, without one plea" **(357)**; Elizabeth Clephane, "Beneath the cross of Jesus" **(297)**; and Frances Ridley Havergal, "Take my life, and let it be" **(399)**.

Hymns Ancient and Modern, 1861, is the culmination of nineteenth-century Anglican hymnic activity and is characterized by Erik Routley:

> [It] gathered up the discoveries of previous [nineteenth-century] editors; combin[ed] church dogma and easily accessible musical style for parish family participation, led by the choir and organ [and] translated into parish practice the principles of the Tractarians . . . [and] express[ed] and propagate[d] the principles of the new-style Church of England. 1. The arrangement of the book corresponds very closely to that of the *Book of Common Prayer*, 1662, thus laying stress on the <u>centrality of its use in liturgy</u>; 2. It incorporated into parish worship the <u>hymns of the ancient Offices</u>, matched them to easily learned and sung tunes. (Routley 1957, 92)

The English Hymnal, 1906 (rev. 1933), was to become the single most important literary and musical reaction to *Hymns Ancient and Modern*. The latter by the turn of the century had become the paradigm of inbred popular and comfortable Victorian parish worship practice. Today *The English Hymnal* is still the most influential single volume of English hymns for use in Anglo-Catholic worship, primarily because of the quality of its musical content: plainsong, Roman Catholic hymn tunes, carols, folk tunes, tunes and arrangements by its musical editor Ralph Vaughan Williams, and Joseph Parry, C. V. Stanford, Gustav Holst, and John Ireland; and its texts, including the standard translations by Robert S. Bridges, "O splendor of God's glory bright" **(679)**, which were carefully selected by its literary editor, Percy Dearmer, "Draw us in the Spirit's tether" **(632)**. The same team produced a successful "national" hymnal for use in church and school, *Songs of Praise*, 1925. The compilation of the folk music of Great Britain, which began in the late-nineteenth century with the work of compilers H. R. Bramley and John Stainer in *Christmas Carols New and Old*, 1871, was continued early in this century by George Ratcliff Woodward and culminated in the publication of *The Oxford Book of Carols*, 1928. Other influential early- and mid-twentieth-century hymnals from Great Britain include the *Public School Hymn Book*, 1903, revised, 1919, 1949 and 1964, the latter as *Hymns for Church and School*, *The Church Hymnary*, 1927; *The Methodist Hymn Book*, 1933; *Congregational Praise*, 1951; the *BBC Hymn Book*, 1951; and *Hymns for Church and School*, 1964.

In spite of the wide popularity of gospel hymns (see USA hymnody, pages 27-30), for most of the twentieth century only a few were included in standard

Anglican and Methodist hymnals. In *The English Hymnal*, 1906, gospel hymns and songs of "the revival," the Sunday school and the Salvation Army mission, are relegated to the section titled "For Mission Services" with the stern subtitle "Not for ordinary use"!

Recent British Hymnody

In the "hymnic explosion" of English language hymns, which began in the mid 1960's, hymn writers, composers, compilers, and publishers have produced a large number of congregational songs on a great variety of topics and in a wide range of musical styles. The results are fair to good with more than a few items comparing very favorably with the best in the standard repertory. The texts (1) demonstrate the shift in the language base of the church away from that in the *Book of Common Prayer* and the King James Version of the Bible towards the metaphors and descriptions found in more recent translations of the Bible and revisions of the church's language of liturgy; (2) reflect the impact of twentieth-century science and technology, including space travel; (3) often name the church as servant and its people as pilgrims in a world in which the environment as well as its human family face extinction; and (4) show the influence of Vatican II and other gestures of Christian unity and depict the sacraments, particularly the Eucharist, in a global and ecumenical setting.

This period's most articulate and important influence was Erik Routley, "All who love and serve your city" **(433)**. In interviews with the celebrated hymn writers Fred Pratt Green, Fred Kaan, and Brian Wren, Robin A. Leaver in his article "New Hymnody: Some Problems and Prospects" in *Duty and Delight* (1985, 217-28) documents that Routley's critique and review of their early efforts continued until his death in 1982. Particularly important for the development of USA hymnody, Routley from the period of the Dunblane Workshops, 1963-1967, until his death was the vital link between the "explosion" in Great Britain and the resulting aftershocks felt as the "hymnbook explosion" of the 1980's in North America. *The Hymn,* January 1983, contains tributes to Routley by his colleagues and an account of the memorial service held at Westminster Choir College, Princeton, New Jersey, October 12, 1982. The February 8, 1983 memorial service in Westminster Abbey is noted in *The Hymn,* 34 (2): 110-11.

Representative hymn writers of the explosion are Albert Bayly, "What does the Lord require" **(441)**; Fred Pratt Green, who did not begin to write hymns until age 65, "When in our music God is glorified" **(68)**; evangelical Anglican Timothy Dudley-Smith, "Behold a broken world" **(426)**; Congregationalists Fred Kaan, "Help us accept each other" **(560)**, and Brian Wren, "God of many names" **(105)**; Anglican priest Sydney Carter, "Lord of the dance" **(261)**; and Roman Catholics James Quinn, "Word of God, come down on earth" **(182)**, and [William] Brian Foley, "Holy Spirit, come, confirm us" **(331)**. Important supplements and hymnals from this time are the supplements to *Hymns Ancient and Modern, 100 Hymns for Today,* 1969, and *More Hymns for Today,*

1980; the supplement to *Congregational Praise, New Church Praise*, 1975; *Hymns for Today's Church*, 1982; the Roman Catholic *New Catholic Hymnal*, 1971; the British Methodist supplement, *Partners in Praise*, 1980, and the revision of its 1933 hymnal, *Hymns and Psalms*, 1983.

Robin A. Leaver in *The Hymnal 1982 Companion* has provided the most recent and comprehensive coverage of British hymnody. He cites two influences in addition to the "hymnic explosion":

> [1] the charismatic movement which moved into virtually all mainline denominations [represented] in three collections edited by Betty Pulkingham, *Sound of Living Waters*, London, 1970, and *Fresh Sounds: A Companion Volume to Sound of Living Waters*, London, 1976; and *Cry Hosanna*, London, 1980; [(2) another] . . . movement that has had an increasing effect on British hymnody since the mid-1970's is the ecumenical movement.— One of the most influential [hymnals] was *Cantate Domino*, Kassel, 1974— a vigorous, multi-confessional, multi-language ecumenical hymnal. (Glover 1990, 1:593-94)

Another ecumenical hymnal of this period is *The Australian Hymn Book*, 1977, issued in Britain as *With One Voice: A Hymn Book for All Churches*, 1978. Wesley Milgate has provided excellent companions to this hymnal in *Songs of the People of God*, 1985 rev. ed., and *A Companion to Sing Alleluia*, 1988, for the supplement *Sing Alleluia*, 1987. For a summary of recent English hymns and hymnals, see Eric Sharp, "Developments in English Hymnody in the Eighties," *The Hymn*, 1991.

TAIZÉ AND GELINEAU PSALMODY

Psalmody, choruses, and rounds from the French ecumenical lay community of Taizé, e.g., "Gloria, gloria, in excelsis Deo" **(72),** are attractive and memorable contributions to our hymnal. Joseph Gelineau's enormous contribution to sung psalmody is represented in his antiphon (response) "My shepherd is the Lord" **(137).**

USA HYMNODY

Early USA hymnody is divided into two periods: 1640-1721 and 1721-1793. In 1640 the *Bay Psalm Book* was introduced two decades after the Pilgrims established their first settlement. This period culminated with the publication of the first standard tune book by John Tufts, *An Introduction to the Singing of Psalm-Tunes*, ca. 1721. The age from 1721-1793 heralded the Great Awakening in New England and was marked by the preaching of Jonathan Edwards and George Whitefield. This period produced the rise of the singing schools, the music of William Billings, the fuging tune, and Dutch, Lutheran, and Moravian hymnody, and saw the publication of the earliest United States tune still in common use, CORONATION **(154),** in *Union Harmony*, 1793.

For a reliable overview of the development of the imported as well as early indigenous USA hymnody, see William J. Reynolds and Milbern Price, *A Survey of Christian Hymnody*; Frank J. Metcalf, *American Writers and Compilers of Sacred Music*; and Irving Lowens, *Music and Musicians in Early America*.

Introduction

In the late-eighteenth century and during the nineteenth century hymnals and songbooks developed in both content and format into two distinct but related tracks: (1) *denominational*—Methodists, Baptists, and others, including those denominations with European ethnic roots, such as German-speaking Lutherans and Mennonites, whose products were usually, but not exclusively, compiled, published, and distributed for a limited constituency by church-owned publishing houses. The varied contents reflect each church's struggle to perpetuate its distinct traditions while at the same time accommodating to always developing and sometimes hostile social settings (see Reynolds and Price 1987, 95-98 and 103-105); and (2) *private/commercial*, a diversified output paralleling that of the secular music markets, e.g., Stephen Foster's popular ballads and love songs, Civil War ballads and marches, and minstrel songs. The product lines of this music publishing followed the quick opening and distinct church markets: namely, Sunday school, temperance, revival, home recreational-social singing, and educational. Its repertory ranged from camp-meeting choruses, choir anthems, folk hymns, collections of modified "European" tunes by Lowell Mason, keyboard arrangements and service music for the organist, to the first collections of African American religious song and the gospel hymn collections, perennial products of Reconstruction's urban revival.

For further reading see Reynolds and Price (1987, 86-89) and James Warrington, *Short Titles of Books Relating to or Illustrating the History and Practice of Psalmody in the United States 1620-1820*. Irving Lowens tells the story of his "discovery" of the Warrington collection (1964, 272-78), an extensive bibliography that with the Silas H. Paine, Waldo Selden Pratt collections is housed in Pitts Theological Library, Candler School of Theology, Emory University, Atlanta, Georgia. For the progression of United States hymnody in the late-nineteenth and early-twentieth centuries, see the sections "British Hymns," pages 9-17; "Hymnals of The Methodist Church," pages 91-122; "Music of the [United Methodist] Hymnal," pages 164-70; and "Recent United States Hymnody," pages 43-47.

Another contribution of the USA was the repertory taught and performed in the singing schools of the late-eighteenth and early-to-mid-nineteenth centuries. For a comprehensive review of this contribution, see Lowens (1964, 115-55 and 237-48) and Routley (1981, 125-34).

While the singing school along with its "fuging tune" was imported into USA hymnody, its development in colonial New England and a century later in the mid-Atlantic and southern states provided a distinctive way of transmitting and assimilating the standard English evangelical texts by Charles Wesley, Isaac Watts, John Newton, William Cowper, and James Montgomery. See George Pullen Jackson, *White Spirituals of the Southern Uplands* and *The Story of the Sacred Harp, 1844-1944*, Buell Cobb, *The Sacred Harp: A Tradition and Its Music*, and the section in this book, "Music of the [United Methodist] Hymnal," pages 164-70.

Asian hymnody and Hispanic hymnody developed in their separate, unique, and multicultural settings in the USA as well as in nationalistic, regional, global, and ecumenical contexts. In addition to discussing Asian and Hispanic hymnody, this section will survey the five unique contributions of USA hymnody: the song of the USA and Canadian Native American; the slave songs, spirituals, and urban gospel song of the African American; the gospel hymn; the social gospel hymn; and recent developments in USA hymnody.

Native American Hymns

Research and recordings of Native American music began late in the nineteenth century and initiated the continuing documentation, showing that for centuries music has been integral to Native American life and its celebration in unique story and ceremony. An example of how music is traditionally revered by Native Americans is found in the creation story of the Piwa people of the southwestern USA in *The New Oxford Companion to Music*: "When the Earth was newly created, then the first time came the songs." (Arnold 1983, 52) Other creation narratives tell of Creator as actually singing the first song. Another expression of this importance is in D. Donald Donalto's preface to a collection of Native American hymns and prayers, *Voices: Native American Hymns and Worship Resources*, 1992:

> Native Americans have traditions which stress that because life is a gift from God, everything one does with life is a gift back to God and, thus, a communication with God. . . . Because the Creator formed human beings to feel the emotions which accompany the songs, and because all of life is a prayer, so too is music. Such has been the belief among Native Americans since the oral traditions began thousands of years ago.

In order to communicate with Native Americans, most without a written language, missionaries first had to learn the sounds and the sense of the language and then compile a dictionary of key words and phrases when their ministry began among the Native Americans of the USA and Canada. Christian prayers, scripture, and hymns in the language of the missionary were then taught through crude systems of communication or "aids to memory"; these included the *quipii*, the sequencing of ideas and concepts by weaving together colored and knotted strings; *order of songs*, sequential pictures depicting the story in a verse of the hymn or scripture; *notched stick*, "gesture speech," a form of speech transmitted by burnt and colored characters fashioned on notched sticks; and *rebus*, a form of hieroglyphics or ideograms. Early in the nineteenth century the invention of the *syllabary* allowed the sounds of an Indian language to be transmitted syllable by syllable. One of the most widely used *syllabaries* was prepared by Wesleyan Methodist minister James Evans in 1840 for use with the Cree people.

J. Vincent Higginson describes the process in which the Indians learned hymns:

> At first instruction by rote was the only solution until the missionaries had learned the language. This was the approach in New France as well as the Spanish missions. In the latter the Indians lived in closely established communities which lightened the task. Evidence from early mission manuscripts used by the missionaries to teach the Indians shows that hymns formed a part of these early instructions. Slow as the process was, it had the advantage of having the the prayers learned and the hymns sung and passed from one group to another. (Higginson 1954, 6)

Discussing the missionaries' use of indigenous music, Higginson continues:

> However they [the Indians] did learn tunes as well as words. Lota Spell, from her study of the *Jesuit Relations* points out that at first Indian melodies were used for the hymns and after they had become familiar with the Christian words, European melodies were introduced. (Higginson 1954, 6)

The history of Native American Christian hymnody has been almost exclusively that of the process of translating Euro-Anglo hymns and liturgy into one of the languages of the Native American. The reverse of this translating process has been slow, however, primarily because Native Americans were and continue to be viewed by some as inferior, and according to Donalto in *Voices*, their music and hymns are viewed as inferior:

> Quite simply, they were not able to distinguish between the power or presence of Christ and the European cultural soil in which their own faith had first taken root. Native Americans lived differently and had, for the most part, no written language. Europeans were primarily a written-language people and tended to judge the degree of civilization and the religious capacity of other peoples by this standard. It did not occur to them that people could be highly intelligent "civilized," open to God, and indeed, ready to follow Christ, with an oral-language-based culture. (*Voices* 1992, ix)

Yet in the instance of at least one seventeenth-century Indian hymn just the opposite occurred. The nativity story, which had been taught by a Jesuit priest to the Hurons, was reformed by them and expressed in their words and descriptions. The result has been called the first Native American Christmas carol, "Jesous Ahatonhia," " 'Twas in the moon of wintertime" **(244)**.

Today in the USA there are between 250 and 400 Native American language groups, depending upon how the groups are defined, and relatively few have a written language. Only within the past half century have Native American hymns in any number been translated and formed to English equivalent sounds, the tunes transcribed and set to an approximation of the melodic line. The work of the Mennonite Indian Leaders' Council, in Busby, Montana, has been particularly significant in this area.

In the nineteenth century the Methodist Episcopal Church produced several hymnals and songbooks for use in Indian missionary activity, including *Indian Melodies*, 1845, by Thomas Connuck, a Narragansett Indian, harmonized by Thomas Hastings, Esq.; *Chippeway-English Hymnal*, 1851, translated by Peter Jones; and *A Collection of Hymns for the Use of Native Christians of the Mohawk Language*.

Homer Noley in *First White Frost*, 1991, has contributed a brief and well written history of Christian missions among Native Americans in North America and within The United Methodist Church. See chapter 4, "Exile from the Ancient Domain," for a discussion of Native Americans and the nineteenth-century camp meeting. The volume does not trace the roots of Native American religious song or recent developments that have led to their inclusion in this hymnal.

The Methodist Hymnal, 1966, was the first of any major hymnal to include a Native American hymn, "Many and great" **(148)**. Some selections in our present hymnal are printed in a "complete" format, that is, texts interlined with music, e.g., "DAW-KEE, AIM DAW-TSI TAW," "Great Spirit, now I pray to you" **(330)**; others are printed only in phonetic transcription, "TSISA A KI KE Y HA" **(191)**, one Cherokee's rendering of the first stanza and chorus of "Jesus loves me! This I know." The inherit problems in transmission and the absence of any other texts for comparison sometimes make first attempts incomplete and only approximations. See, for example, the text and the melody of "HELELUYAN" **(78)**. As we shall see in the commentary on hymn texts, some texts, as printed, are not the literal equivalent Native American words for the English, and as often occurs in translation, some are far from the original, e.g., "Silent night" **(239)**.

African American Hymns

The history of African American sacred song includes both that song as it originated and continues to be sung in the mother continent and the newer song described by Thea Bowman in her article "The Gift of African American Sacred Song":

> African men and women brought sacred songs and chants that reminded them of their homelands and that sustained them in separation and in captivity, songs to respond to all life situations, and the ability to create

new songs to answer new needs, . . . preserving a holistic African spirituality, of rhythms and tones and harmonies that communicated their deep-
est feelings across barriers of region and language.—in fields and quarters, at work, in secret meetings, in slave festivals, in churches, camp
meets and revivals, wherever they met or congregated, consoled and
strengthened themselves and one another with sacred song—moans,
chants, shouts, psalms, hymns, and jubilees—in the crucible of separation
and suffering, African American sacred song was formed. (Preface to *Lead
Me, Guide Me* 1987)

This sacred song is generally identified as the African American spiritual, but
Wyatt Tee Walker identifies it as but one genre of "Black Sacred Music" developed since 1619:

1619-1800	SLAVE UTTERANCES: Moans, Chants, Cries for Deliverance
1760-1875	SPIRITUALS: Faith-Songs, Sorrow Songs, Plantation Hymns, etc.
1810-1900	METER MUSIC: Watts, Wesley, Sankey, et al.
1875-1950	HYMNS OF IMPROVISATION: Euro-American hymns with "beat"
1920-1975	GOSPEL MUSIC: Music of Hard Times (Cross-fertilization with secular)

(Walker 1979, 380)

For a detailed discussion of the development of distinctive African American
religious music, see Dena J. Epstein, "Distinctive Black Religious Music" in
Sinful Tunes and Spirituals and Jon Michael Spencer, *Protest & Praise: Sacred
Music of Black America.*

John Wesley, as an Anglican missionary-priest in Georgia, made contact with
African Americans in South Carolina. In his *Journal* he relates that on Sunday,
August 1, 1736, in Charles Town (now Charleston, South Carolina), he
preached and administered the Eucharist to fifty communicants including one
Negro woman. In another entry he records that [in England] on November 29,
1758, he baptized his first two black converts, one of whom was a woman. "By
the mid-eighteenth century the Wesleyan movement had spread to colonies,
and large numbers of slaves were among those who responded to the
Methodist preacher, exhorting the revivals and camp meetings of the First
Great Awakening in the 1740's." (Lincoln and Mamiya 1990, 50)

The African American's early response to Methodism has been traced by
Lewis V. Baldwin:

Several reasons account for the strong support given by Negroes to
Methodism. . . . First, the Methodist style and ethos of revivalism allowed
for a freedom of expression that was similar to what many Negroes had

experienced in African traditional religions. They were free to sing, pray, preach, testify, groan, weep, shout, and dance with an intensity of emotion that was unacceptable in many religious communions in America at that time. (Shockley 1991, 26)

For further discussion regarding the Methodist movement and African Americans, see William B. McClain, "The Appeal of Methodism to Black Americans," in *Black People in The Methodist Church,* 1984. For the documentation of the development of Methodist and other evangelical African American religious song in the nineteenth century see Dena J. Epstein, "Sacred Black Folk Music, 1801-67," in *Sinful Tunes and Spirituals.*

Grant S. Shockley has commented on the beginnings of distinctive Methodist African American worship forms in churches and institutions that were established for ex-slaves by Northern Methodist missionaries: "Negro folk religion and spirituals merged with a somewhat more restrained Methodist Episcopal worship tradition to produce a unique black Methodist Episcopal religious ethos." (Shockley 1991, 42)

Eileen Southern provides a significant history and commentary on African American music in *The Music of Black Americans.* Southern supplies an account of the first African American hymnal developed for black Methodists, *A Collection of Hymns and Spiritual Songs Selected from Various Authors by Richard Allen, African Minister,* 1801 (Reprinted with introduction by J. Roland Braithwaite, 1987, A.M.E.C. Sunday School Union). Allen was one of two blacks present at the Baltimore Christmas Conference, 1784, and later the first black to be ordained deacon. In 1786 after he and other blacks were directed to sit only in the galley and on the side benches of Old St. George's Methodist Episcopal Church, Philadelphia, Allen and his followers left that church and in 1787 founded the African Methodist Episcopal Church. Southern recounts that Allen's collection

> consists of fifty-four hymn texts, without tunes, drawn chiefly from the collection of Dr. Watts, the Wesleys, and other hymn writers favored by the Methodists of that period, but also including hymns popular with the Baptists. . . . As was customary at the time, Allen neither provided author's names nor indicated appropriate melodies for his hymns. (Southern 1971, 86)

Allen's contributions to African American hymnody are further discussed:

> In addition to writing hymns especially for the 1801 collection, Allen (or one of his associates) made alterations or introduced supplementary lines into some of the orthodox hymns that he included. In some instances sophisticated words or phrases were replaced by simpler ones that would have more meaning for the illiterate worshippers in the Bethel congregation. More important, refrain lines or choruses were added to the orthodox stanza forms—this, at a time when the hymn-with-chorus was not yet admitted into the repertory of official Protestant hymnody. (Southern 1971, 89)

For additional commentary on Richard Allen's hymnal, see Jon Michael Spencer, "The African Methodist Episcopal Church" in *Black Hymnody: A Hymnological History of the African-American Church*.

Baptists further "blackened" the classic hymns of Watts and Wesley, and according to Wendell P. Whalum, "They virtually threw out the meter signature and rhythm and before 1875 had begun a new system which, though based on the style of singing coming from England to America, was drastically different from it. (Whalum 1973, 347-48) "Blackening" hymns meant to modify European hymn tunes and classic evangelical texts in CM, SM, and LM by performing them in a stye of unaccompanied responsoral singing between leader (deacon or preacher) and group; this practice was known as "meter music" or "Deaconing out" a hymn. In this performance practice the leader lined out a couplet of the metered hymn in a slow extended elaboration on a familiar hymn tune, and the group, allowing for individual improvisations, sings it back. See 11 in *Songs of Zion*, 1981, "Father, I stretch my hands to thee" for an example of a lined out hymn in this style.

Besides this distinct development of African American song in northern urban churches, Southern also cites African American contributions of the spiritual, chorus, and shout to the song repertory of the northern rural camp meeting. Ellen Jane Lorenz Porter has demonstrated this latter point in her study of the unique stylistic contributions of African Americans:

a. The chorus comes first much more often.
b. There is more frequent use of modes, syncopation, and free melody.
c. The words are more imaginative, more poetic, more dramatic, more humorous.
d. There is the same kind of repetition [as in the whole of the repertory] but more variety of shouting words.
e. There is almost never a mother-hymn.
f. There are fewer refrains in the aaab form, but with more freedom. (Porter 1980, 66)

The end to the Civil War brought new problems to blacks and these problems were reflected in their music:

> In keeping with his traditions, the ex-slave sang about his experiences—his new freedom, his new occupations, the strange ways of the city, current events, and his feelings of rootlessness and loneliness. Above all he sought a self-identity. Slavery had deprived him of a name, a homeland, and a family. The original African names of his forbears had long ago been forgotten, the land of Africa no longer beckoned after almost two hundred years and fifty years of exile, and his relatives had been dispersed, for the slave auction block had separated husband from wife, mother from child, brother from sister, and lover from lover. (Southern 1971, 245)

The struggle for identity resulted, in part, in the post-war spiritual.

> Like the social songs, [the spiritual] employed the old forms and musical idioms of the slave songs, but the content of these songs reflected the new status of the singers and the different circumstances under which they lived. (Southern 1971, 249)

Part of that new status was the African American's struggle for new educational opportunities, including a college education. In 1866 Fisk University was established in Nashville "using the one story frame buildings, which had been erected and used for hospital barracks by the Union Army." (Marsh 1897, 10) George L. White, the university's treasurer who "had a special love for music, though he never had any musical instruction," organized a group of students for informal and recreational singing. Their repertory consisted entirely of their "music," the spiritual. Within a short time he had recruited a large chorus, from which he "began to pick the most promising voices and give them that special training" forming them into the "Singers." (Marsh 1897, 12-15) When the Singers went public, their success was immediate and convincing, extending to the Midwest, New England, and eventually to England and Europe.

Nevertheless, Southern writes that an important by-product of that success, and with it the wide acceptance of the spiritual, was the concertized spiritual, not the genuine product:

> When the spirituals were removed from the original setting of the plantation or the Negro Church and sung by persons who had not directly experienced slavery, these songs no longer served their primary function. Concert singers could present to the public only an approximation of how the spirituals had been sung by the slaves. (Southern 1971, 245)

For the documentation of the development of distinctive African American religious song in the nineteenth century see Dena J. Epstein, "Sacred Black Folk Music, 1801-67," in *Sinful Tunes and Spirituals*.

For most of a century the heritage of African American song, outside of its use in African American worship, has been sustained in the repertory of school and church choirs, the unofficial hymnals and songbooks but not in the official mainline hymnals. During the antiwar and civil rights movements of the 1960's, African American songs emerged from the oral worship tradition and were sung in white churches as well as in the streets. "We shall overcome" **(533)** remains the most popular and enduring from that time. For a survey of the music of the civil right movements see, Jon Michael Spencer, "We shall overcome" in *Protest and Praise: Sacred Music of Black America*. Another genre, the urban black gospel hymn, originated by Charles Albert Tindley and later popularized by Thomas A. Dorsey, centers on unique "black" liberation themes and improvisational performance practice, and is distinctly set apart from the "other" gospel hymn (see comments on the gospel hymn, pages 27-30).

African American music was considered by some as inferior music (see discussion on Native American Hymns, pages 19-21). African American spirituals were included in the 1957 *Hymnal* of the Evangelical United Brethren, where they were cited as Negro spirituals. In former Methodist hymnals no spirituals were included until the 1966 edition of *The Methodist Hymnal*, where at the request of the African American members of the revision committee, they were cited as American Folk Hymns.

This general citation for African American music was deeply resented by the next generation, and its inadequacy became, in part, the rallying point for the publication of *Songs of Zion*. As William B. McClain writes:

> This urgent recommendation was made . . . after we carefully surveyed the present *Book of Hymns* [*The Methodist Hymnal*, 1966] only to find it contains only one hymn by a Black composer and a mere five Negro spirituals, listed simply as "American Folk Hymns." (Preface to *Songs of Zion* 1981, ix)

The African American songs and prayers in our hymnal are from several repertories: traditional gospel hymn, "Precious Lord, take my hand" **(474)**, choruses, "To God be the glory" **(99)**, prayer responses, "Kum ba yah" **(494)**, contemporary gospel, "Soon and very soon" **(706)**; and spirituals. The spirituals fall into three styles: call-and-response, leader or soloist and group, "Come out the wilderness" **(416)**, repeated, syncopated phrases, usually fast-moving rhythms with instrumental accompaniment, hand clapping, and body movement, "I'm goin' a sing when the Spirit says sing" **(333)**, and long sustained phrases in a slow tempo, that may be accompanied, "Oh, fix me" **(655)**.

Most of the adaptations and arrangements of African American music in our hymnal are by William Farley Smith. They breathe the spirit of African American keyboard and vocal styles and are written in a mid-stream performance style that makes them accessible to a wide audience. For suggestions on the performance practice of African American Music, e.g., rhythms, dialect, and tempo, see "Keys to Musical Interpretation, Performance, and Meaningful Worship" by the late J. Jefferson Cleveland, in *Songs of Zion*, pages xiii-xvii. In other articles in the collection he discusses the several genres of African American Worship Music: "A Historical Account of the Hymn in the Black Worship Experience"; "A Historical Account of the Negro Spiritual"; "A Historical Account of the Black Gospel Song," in the latter providing an account of the gospel hymn, particularly as it was developed by Charles Albert Tindley, "Nothing between my soul and my Savior" **(373)**, and Thomas A. Dorsey, "Precious Lord, take my hand" **(474)**. For a survey and critique of African American urban gospel hymnody see Jon Michael Spencer, "Christ Against Culture" in *Protest and Praise: Sacred Music of Black America*.

Other selections from African Americans include "Easter people, raise your voices" **(305)** by William James; "How like a gentle spirit" **(115)** by C. Eric Lincoln; BURLEIGH **(548)**, an arrangement of a spiritual by Harry T. Burleigh; the "Black National Anthem," "Lift every voice and sing" **(519)**, by James

Weldon Johnson and J. Rosamond Johnson; Duke Ellington's "Come Sunday" **(728)**; and poetry and prayers by Martin Luther King, Jr., **(106)** and Howard Thurman **(401, 489)**.

The first scholar to present the contributions of African American religious song so as to lay claim on its unique repertory, performance practice, and cultural setting was Professor John W. Work, Jr., of Fisk University, in *Folk Song of American Negro Spirituals*, 1915. His son, Professor John W. Work, III, also of Fisk University, in his address "The Negro Spiritual" to the International Hymnological Conference, New York City, September 1961, continued his father's lifelong effort by debunking George Pullen Jackson's claim in *White Spirituals of the Southern Uplands*, chapter 19, "Tunes of the White Man's Spirituals Preserved in the Negro's Religious Songs," that the Negro spiritual is derived from white spirituals and gospel songs. A generation later that issue has not been settled as Dena J. Epstein comments, "The assumption that the blacks learned all their songs from the whites has not been proved, nor has documentation been found to prove the opposite. (Epstein 1981, 199)

William B. McClain in *Come Sunday* has made a substantive contribution to the understanding of African American song, worship, and preaching within The United Methodist Church; see chapter 3, "The Black Church: A Mirror of Tragedy and a Vision of Hope"; chapter 4, "The Liturgy of Zion: The Soul of Black Worship"; and chapter 5, "Black Preaching and Its Message: 'Is There Any Word from the Lord?'"

See also C. Eric Lincoln and Lawrence H. Mamiya, "The Black Methodists: The Institutionalization of Black Religious Independence," and "Music and the Black Church"; *The Black Church and the African American Experience*; John Lovell, Jr., *Black Song; The Forge and the Flame*; Dena Epstein, *Sinful Tunes and Spirituals*; Jon Michael Spencer, "The Hymnody of Black Methodists," *Theology Today* (1991, 373-85); Jon Michael Spencer, *Black Hymnody*; and "West Indian Music" (Arnold 1983, 1979).

Gospel Hymns

Precursors of the gospel hymn are the camp-meeting melodies, spirituals songs and choruses of the Great Awakening, shaped-note hymnody of the "singing schools," and the songs and songbooks of the Sunday school, Salvation Army, YMCA, and Temperance movements. The gospel song's simple repetitive music and words complemented late-nineteenth-century revival preaching in England and the United States. Its harmonies, rhythms, and melodies are derived from and reflect the popular military marches, the waltz and other dance steps, the minstrel songs, and the parlor ballads of Stephen Foster.

The gospel hymn of Reconstruction days remains as Protestantism's most characteristic and popular hymnody in the United States of the nineteenth century. Its appeal has been discussed by Robert M. Stevenson:

Gospel hymnody has been a plough digging up the hardened surfaces of pavemented minds. Its very obviousness has been its strength. Where delicacy or dignity can make no impress, gospel hymnody stands up triumphing. In an age when religion must win mass approval in order to survive, in an age when religion must at least win a majority vote from the electorate, gospel hymnody is inevitable. Sankey's songs are true folk music of the people. Dan Emmett and Stephen Foster only did in secular music what Ira D. Sankey and P. P. Bliss did as validly and effectively in sacred music. (Stevenson 1953, 162)

The first use of the term "gospel hymn" appears to be in the subtitle of Philip P. Bliss's *Gospel Songs, A Choice Collection of Hymns and Tunes, New and Old, for Gospel Meetings, Sunday School*, Cincinnati, 1874, begging the distinction between a "gospel song" and a "gospel hymn." The development of the gospel hymn is further described by this writer in "Gospel Song" in *Key Words in Church Music*:

Beginning with Bliss and excluding only the more recent revivals of Graham-Shea, most—if not all—"revivalism" directed, maintained and recycled the gospel-song style through the means of exclusive copyright. The direct effect of this [monopoly] was to bring into sharp contrast the music and words of traditional hymnody as found in the hymnals of the major denominations on the one hand, and the songbooks used in other than the main worship services on the other—which is to say that the gospel song became "**the** song" [for] recreation, education and evangelism, and for many it still is. Although viewed by many as America's unique religious song, [the gospel song] . . . has at the same time been criticized as being inadequate in the explicit verbal proclamation of the social demands of the Gospel, [and] has provided a much too friendly musical setting for words [expressing] the life, death and resurrection of Jesus Christ. (Schalk 1978, 176-77)

Only very recently have mainline denominational hymnals included much of this optimistic religious folk hymnody, having included instead "standard" texts and tunes from late-nineteenth- and early-twentieth-century English hymnals, or the "social gospel hymn" (see discussion, pages 30-33). This reluctance to include the gospel hymn was evident in our hymnals as recently as the 1935 *Methodist Hymnal*, when the editors placed all of the gospel hymns in the section titled "Songs of Salvation."

The reasons for excluding or limiting the number of gospel hymns are not solely based on matters of musical taste and adequacy of theology, although there is still considerable complaint registered in these areas by professional church musicians and seminary-trained clergy. One of the prominent contributing factors in the continuing controversy was that the gospel hymn was not only organically related to the continuing and successful urban revival, but prior to radio and television its proliferation was tied to that relationship. As copyrighted material owned by private publishers essentially business and profit oriented, it was a commodity to be sold or licensed. Exorbitant permission fees proposed by the owners of these popular songs resulted in their being excluded from denominational hymnals, since church-owned publishers were viewed by the owners of these copyrights as competitors; yet at the same time the product's market value of the gospel hymns was enhanced as "alternative" songs to the foreign content in the church's "formal" hymnals.

Since all of the gospel hymns of last century and most of those written early in this century are now in the public domain, and those most recently written are available for a licensing fee, usually a prorated royalty, the arguments for and against including them remain musical and theological. Those arguments notwithstanding, their inclusion in greater number in this present hymnal is certainly one of the factors in its wide acceptance.

William J. Reynolds describes the story of the development of these easy, singable, memorable songs by Ira Sankey and a host of others including Fanny Crosby, "To God be the glory" **(98),** and William B. Bradbury, "He leadeth me: O blessed thought" **(128).** He traces the development of recent gospel publishing from the Singing Convention, an outgrowth of the singing schools, to the Gospel Sing, an enterprise that connected mass singing, sometimes all-night singing, to that part of the entertainment industry called gospel music, a billion-and-a-half-dollar industry housed along Music Row in Nashville, Tennessee. Reynolds comments on the industry:

> As [rental, travel, and fees] went up, admission fees were charged. Promoters appeared on the scene to handle the details of facilities, schedules, equipment, and so on, and to free the musicians to be artists and performers. Fancy attire, custom buses, elaborate sound equipment, instrumental rhythm groups for accompaniment and high professional promotional techniques are the rule.

> Ironically, since the vast public following of this music has little need for seeing the printed songs sung by gospel music groups, the identification of shaped-notation with this music has greatly diminished. The printed page is not important to the listener and he cares not whether the song is printed in round or shaped notation. He is interested only in what he hears. The sound of the music [of] the Speer Family, the Imperials, the Oak Ridge Boys, the Happy Goodmans and other groups has roots in that traditionally associated with Stamps, Bartlett, Vaughan, Showalter, Kieffer, Funk and others. . . . But the distinctive technique for teaching music reading so long identified with this musical tradition in America has all but disappeared. (Reynolds, 1987, 93-98)

The immense popularity of this most recent gospel music, its shear volume, and its ability to change and adapt to the fast-moving market and get on the "charts" limit its potential for inclusion in any great number in hardbound hymnals intended for two decades or more of use by a given denomination. Several "standards," some "contemporary Christian" in style and audience, are included in this hymnal, including those by Amy Grant, "Thy Word is a lamp" **(601)**; Michael Card and John Thompson, "El Shaddai" **(123)**; and a cross-over "black gospel" chorus by Andraé Crouch, "To God be the glory" **(99)**. (See page 170 for further discussion.) Carol Doran has contributed a thoughtful survey of popular hymnody in "Popular Religious Song," *The Hymnal 1982 Companion*, 1990, 1:13-28.

Social Gospel Hymns

The social gospel hymn is as optimistic about the perfectibility of humankind as the gospel hymn, with the city replacing heaven as the work place of God's grace. Along with the urban black gospel hymn, it is this century's contribution to ecumenical hymnody from the United States. Its precursors are in the nineteenth-century works of esteemed poets such as John Greenleaf Whittier, "Dear Lord and Father of mankind" **(358)**, and the hymns of pastor-poets: Unitarians Edmund H. Sears, in his Christmas carol of 1849, "It came upon the midnight clear" **(218)**, probably the first of this genre, and Samuel Longfellow, "Holy Spirit, Truth divine" **(465)**; Congregationalist Washington Gladden, "O Master, let me walk with thee" **(430)**; Methodist Frank Mason North, "Where cross the crowded ways of life" **(427)**; and Episcopalian Walter Russell Bowie, "O holy city, seen of John" **(726)**.

Theologically the social gospel hymn is grounded in the writings and teachings of Walter Rauschenbusch. Rauschenbusch, while not the first, was certainly the most articulate and convincing exponent of the social implications of the gospel of Jesus Christ as implemented by "Christian social action." His book, *Christianity and the Social Crisis*, written in 1907, was the social gospel's most influential single volume, serving for half a century as the manifesto for the theological reconstruction of the mainline church—its worship, mission, education, and indirectly its hymnody.

Rauschenbusch's words are a clear call to action:

> In a few years all our restless and angry hearts will be quiet in death, but those who come after us will live in the world which our sins have blighted or which our love of right has redeemed. Let us do our thinking on these great questions, not with our eyes fixed on our bank account, but with a wise outlook on the fields of the future and with the consciousness that the spirit of the Eternal is seeking to distill from our lives some essence of righteousness before they pass away. (Rauschenbusch 1908, xv)

He continues with astonishing aptness for a church preparing to enter the twenty-first century:

The insistence on religious morality as the only thing God cares about is of fundamental importance for the question before us. The social problems are moral problems on a large scale. Religion is a tremendous generator of self-sacrificing action. Under its impulse men have burned up their animals they had laboriously raised; they have sacrificed their first-born whom they loved and prized; they have tapped their own veins and died with a shout of triumph. But its unparalleled force has been largely diverted to ceremonial actions which wasted property and labor, and were either useless to social health or injurious to it. In so far as men believed that the traditional ceremonial was what God wanted of them, they would be indifferent to the reformation of social ethics. If the hydraulic force of religion could be turned toward conduct, there is nothing which it could not accomplish. (Rauschenbusch 1908, 6)

And as the prophets of Hebrew Scripture called Israel to national perfection, Rauschenbusch sees a parallel in the Christians of the twentieth century:

In our personal Christian life every call to duty is immensely strengthened by the large hope of ultimately attaining a Christlike character and the eternal life. That creates the atmosphere for the details of the religious life. In the social movement of our time the singly reformatory demands are drawing a new and remarkable power from the larger conception of a reconstitution of social life on a coöperative basis. It takes a great and comprehensive hope to kindle the full power of enthusiasm in human lives. Their [the prophets] demands for justice were reënforced by the conviction that these were at the same time an approximation to that wider national regeneration and a condition of its final completion. (Rauschenbusch 1908, 32)

These hymns of social action are, according to Fred Gealy, "concerned with the redemption of the social order—'we'- hymns rather than 'I'-hymns; hymns of the Christian community, and this-worldly, rather than other-worldly." (Gealy, Lovelace, Young 1970, 40)

By the 1930's the social gospel hymn had become the marching song of liberal Protestantism in the United States, and with it came the declaration from its theologians that salvation comes in part by abstaining from the seductive embrace and cheap grace afforded in the singing of the nonsocial and "other-worldly" gospel hymns. Classically trained church musicians joined in, following the lead of Ralph Vaughan Williams who wrote in his preface to the music of *The English Hymnal*, 1906.

The usual argument in favour of bad music is that the fine tunes are doubtless 'musically correct,' but that the people want 'something simple.' Now the expression 'musically correct' has no meaning; the only 'correct' music is that which is beautiful and noble.

It is indeed a moral rather than a musical issue. No doubt it requires a certain effort to tune oneself to the moral atmosphere implied by a fine melody; and it is far easier to dwell in the miasma of the languishing and sentimental hymn tunes which so often disfigure our services. Such poverty of heart may not be uncommon, but at least it should not be encouraged by those who direct the services of the Church; it ought no longer to be true anywhere that the most exalted moments of a church-goer's week are associated with music that would not be tolerated in any place of secular entertainment.

Deeming gospel music as aesthetically unworthy as an offering to God, schools of sacred music have trained church musicians to have complete disdain for it. Mainline USA Protestant worship along with the hymnals it produced became, and still is, a continuing battleground for prolonging the alliance of liberal theology's teaching of freedom and inclusively, with Vaughan Williams, the view that good taste is more pleasing to God than bad taste; i.e., good taste is a moral imperative. This stance has been with apparent disregard of the perceived indifference and condescension towards the unwashed, a stance that remains in fundamental conflict with Rauschenbusch's critique of ceremonial actions (see above).

The musical settings for these hymns advocating radical social change were many times the sweet and staid Victorian tunes, achieving little more than an accommodation of the meter of the poem and seldom characterizing and expressing systemic evil or its cure via radical Christian social action, e.g., BLAIRGOWRIE **(444)**. In the present hymnal the Victorian part-song has been replaced with sturdy, challenging, and memorable tunes that more aptly reflect the urgency, passion, and consequences of Christian social concern and reform. (See hymns in the section "Social Holiness," **425-450**.)

Ironically, unlike the gospel hymn with its gentle, nurturing, and caring metaphors and descriptions of God in Christ, many social gospel hymns are militant, sexist, and noninclusive. In this latter regard, for example, the entire first stanza of John Haynes Holmes's "The voice of God is calling" **(436)** was completely rewritten, and the fourth stanza of "God of grace and God of glory" (see comments on Fosdick, below) was dropped (see commentary on these hymns). In the instance of a hymn from the liberal tradition of the former Methodist church, "O young and fearless prophet" **(444)** by S. Ralph Harlow has been restored. The original text, which expressed distrust of wealth, both inherited or acquired, and the categorical rejection of war as a means of solving international disputes, had been altered by the 1966 revision committee because of its lack of patriotic zeal and harsh indictment of the wealthy.

A few classic social gospel hymns are now standard fare for most if not all denominational hymnals, even included in hymnals of churches for whom "social action" has been traditionally characterized as "work done in vain," and which hold to the teaching, belief, and practice of biblical inerrancy and baptism by immersion as conditions for joining and continuing in the church. This anomaly is illustrated in the apparently deliberate inclusion in the hymnals of "conservative" churches that paradigm of the "liberal" hymn, "God of grace and God of glory" **(577)**, written by the liberal preacher, teacher, ecumenist, pacifist, "northern" Baptist minister, and social activist Harry Emerson Fosdick.

Since World War II and continuing through the Watergate and the end of the Vietnam War eras, the theological climate in mainline Protestantism has modified towards a more realistic appraisal of the varied successes of the human endeavor in overcoming systemic and surd evil. As a consequence most of the early overly optimistic social gospel hymns have been dropped from our hymnals in favor of more recent attempts to express the social imperatives of the gospel, such as Fred Kaan's "For the healing of the nations" **(428)** and "We utter our cry: that peace may prevail" **(439)**.

For additional reading, see Victor E. Gebauer, "Problems in the History of American Church Music," *The Hymn,* 1990; the unpublished paper by James R. Sydnor presented to the Hymn Society of America, April 1979, "Hymns of the Social Gospel, Including Such Concerns as Ecology, Non-Sexist Language and Elimination of Hunger and Poverty"; Jon Michael Spencer, "Songs of the Free," a discussion of abolitionist hymnody, and "The Kingdom come," commentary on Rauschenbusch and his times, in *Protest and Praise: Sacred Music of Black America;* and Paul Westermeyer, "Hymnody in the United States from the Civil War to World War I," *The Hymnal 1982 Companion,* 1990, 1:447-73.

Asian American Hymns

The development of a supplement of Asian hymns, *Hymns from the Four Winds,* 1983, was the first attempt of any major denomination to bring together the repertory that had developed mostly outside the United States over the past three decades and to make it available to serve the emerging needs of Asian American Christian communities.

I-to Loh describes the context in which Asian Christian contributions to the supplement were formed:

> After so many continually tragic war experiences in Asia, the 1970's saw new hope of peace and prosperity. However, the United States, being located on the eastern end of the Pacific Ocean, again is getting more and more deeply involved with the other side of the "basin." Asians in exodus gave threatening impressions of refugees, unending waves of immigration, new religious and economic invasions, counteracting any appreciation of culture or expression of faith and Christian living that the Asian Christians brought to the worshipping community here on the American scene.

Asian expressions of worship through music evolved throughout three
stages. In the first stage . . . the sharing was strictly one way . . . from
Euro-American to Asian hymnals. The tunes sounded entirely foreign
and the messages appeared primitive to Asians. Next came the stage of
imitation and adaptation. During this stage Asians learned to attune
themselves to the Christian West. . . . But now, the end of the twentieth
century ushers in the . . . [third] stage, [led by] . . . liberated Asians . . .
who dare to test the [premise] that vehicles developed by Euro-Ameri-
cans are no longer adequate or capable to . . . carry the breadth of Christian life and the depth of the Christian message to human hearts everywhere. (Preface to *Hymns from the Four Winds* 1983, vii)

The selection of representative hymns for use in a predominantly Anglo-European church hymnal and from such a diversity of languages, musical styles, and
cultural traditions, some with inherent antagonisms toward the history and culture of other peoples, was not without its problems. Foremost proved to be the
convening of representatives from the seven cultural/geographic regions for the
purpose of developing an inclusive list of hymns and recommending them to the
full Hymnal Revision Committee: Chinese (678), Filipino (411), Taiwanese (151),
Indochinese, Laotian (350), Cambodian, Vietnamese (498), Japanese (552), Korean (343), and Southern Asian (521). Convening such a group proved much easier
than developing a list of hymns. Simply put, the qualitative selection of representative hymns quickly gave way to the inherent political struggle of each
group for visibility within both the National Federation of Asian-American United Methodists (NFAAUM) and the general church. While this type of tension
provides the impetus for the revision processes, it can and must be sustained and
dealt with creatively within the framework of the entire contents of a hymnal if
the product is to have wide use. Political processes are meant to further political
ends, and quality may or may not flow from that process.

The task of choosing what hymns, from where, and how many was in time
made the responsibility of a representative group of pastors and lay persons
within NFAAUM, none of whom had been members of the editorial committee of *Hymns from the Four Winds*, yet some of whom had made contributions
of music or words. This group, meeting in San Francisco in April 1987, decided that six of the seven regions would be allowed three selections and that the
other larger and growing Korean would be allowed four, with the understanding that this ratio would be sustained by the full Hymnal Revision Committee if the total number of twenty-two had to be reduced because of space
limitations in the new hymnal.

In the final revision process the full Hymnal Revision Committee selected two
hymns each from six groups and three from the Korean repertory. In our hymnal original texts and melodies from the seven groups are gathered in the
index (922) under "traditional hymns, melodies, and prayers"; others will be
found, listed irrespective of national origin, under the individual author,
and/or composer; for example, Timothy Tingfang Lew is the author of "The

bread of life for all is broken" **(633)**; its setting is to an original tune, SHENG EN, composed in a traditional style by Su Yin-Lan.

A second concern addressed by the committee centered on matters of musical style, or rather, whose musical style? As in the struggle of the African Americans, Native Americans, and Hispanic Americans to express their religious belief through their own music and performance styles, the same issue applied when Asian hymns were considered for inclusion in the hymnal of a church whose music is predominantly Anglo-European. For a discussion of the styles of Chinese hymn tunes, see Bliss Wiant, "What Music Means to the Chinese," *The Hymn,* 1974, and "Chinese Artifacts Inspire Christian Hymns," *The Hymn,* 1974.

The eminent scholar, I-to Loh, editor of *Hymns from the Four Winds* as well as the recent CCA (Christian Conference of Asia) hymnal *Sound the Bamboo,* lists six musical styles within the greater Asian hymnic repertory:

1. Traditional melodies from the respective cultures with or without foreign influences.
2. Imitations of Western gospel song styles as taught by early missionaries.
3. Adaptations from folk and/or newly created melodies with Western harmony.
4. Native or original melodies with harmonic idioms different from those of the West.
5. Contemporary Western musical styles.
6. Combination of more than one style in a single hymn.

(Preface to Hymns from the Four Winds 1983, x)

When the hymn tunes committee received from the Hymnal Revision Committee the approved list of Asian hymns, it agreed that in most instances Western harmonic settings of tunes should be used, an example of which is "Rise to greet the sun" **(678),** harmonized in 1936 by Methodist missionary-musician to China, Bliss Wiant. In other instances the committee agreed to include selections characterized as distinctly "Asian":

We would like to point out, however, that a major difference among some Asian musics is their monophonic nature, i.e., melody without harmony; their music generally emphasizes the beauty in melody, rhythm, and color or timbre. This is why so many hymns are to be sung in unison. Although harmony is foreign to some of them, Asian music can be effectively contextualized for our modern use, with proper understanding of their musical styles, and with skillful handling of multipart techniques without destroying their integrity and beauty. (Preface to *Hymns from the Four Winds* 1983, xi)

Two distinctly Asian examples are "God created heaven and earth" **(151),** the traditional Taiwanese melody harmonized by I-to Loh; and "Jaya Ho" **(478),** the Hindi melody arranged by Victor Sherring.

The third concern, that of language, seemed on the surface easily solved since English is the common second or third language of Asian Americans as well as the primary language of The United Methodist Church. The revision committee's report to the 1988 General Conference that bilingual settings of Spanish, French, and German texts would be included prompted NFAAUM in the summer of 1988 (after the content of the hymnal had been approved) to raise the question that while the sense of an Asian text may be transmitted into English, it is impossible to communicate the original sounds of Asian hymns. The whole matter of producing the sounds of a hymn in its original language is made possible with varying results as regards the Spanish, French, and German texts, all of which are printed in a common script. Yet many Asian hymns are written in "character"-based script, and unless the singer is able to read/sing the language, the unique sounds of the Asian hymns may be lost. To provide a means for singing the original sounds, Dr. Loh has provided phonetic transcriptions of stanzas from representative hymns. The first stanza of "Here, O Lord, your servants gather" (552) is printed in both the English translation and the sounds of the text transcribed into English equivalents as "Sekai no tomo to."

On the whole, the repertory of Asian American hymns in our hymnal, while representative in the political sense, is very Western and conservative within that characterization. Disappointly, it does not represent in any substantial way the striking originality and charm of the recent contributions that were the focus of *Hymns from the Four Winds*, 1983. Both the political process that selected the repertory and the essentially "Western" ear of the Hymnal Revision Committee limited an even-handed consideration of the fullness of that recent part of Asian hymnic repertory.

The contributions of Asian Americans to The United Methodist Church are reviewed in Artemio R. Guillermo, editor, *Churches Aflame: Asian Americans and United Methodism*, 1991. Disappointingly the volume fails to mention developments in Asian American hymnody, including *Hymns from the Four Winds*, 1983, or the contributions that Asian Americans made to the forming of *The United Methodist Hymnal*, 1989. Ironically the front cover of the book pictures six persons, presumably Asian Americans, singing from *The United Methodist Hymnal*.

Hispanic American Hymns

Franciscan Spanish Roman Catholic missionary priests, who were the first to teach the native Indians Roman-Spanish liturgy and Western musical notation, style, form, and vocal technique, also encouraged the collecting and performance of the Indians' indigenous religious expressions—folk music, with elements of dance, instruments, and folk lore; as a consequence, in time folk music was brought into the church's liturgies and festivals. In some regions the task of musical instruction was aided by the Aztecs' highly developed musicality and musicianship.

The other religious orders, Dominican, Augustinian, and Jesuit, also taught music in their efforts to convert the Indians. The most comprehensive account of this activity is Robert Stevenson's *Music in Aztec & Inca Territory*:

> The Society of Jesus entered Mexico in 1572. Andrés Pérez de Ribas (1576-1655), a Jesuit, testified a century after the conquest that in his experience music instruction and performance were still one of the best means of attracting and holding the Indians. Wherever they worked in Sinoloa and Sonora, they founded schools for apt Indian children; "reading, writing, and music" were always the three R's. [footnote: Ribas reprehends trying to teach music merely "by ear"; the child must begin by learning to read and write.] But music in the villages was rustic compared with that in the capital. Each year at Mexico City the privileged Indian youths enrolled in San Gregorio staged several big entertainments of the kind that would today be called "folklore festivals." (Stevenson 1968, 164-66)

Stevenson summarizes and cites the musical excellence and extensive activity of sixteenth-century Indian choirs as stated by Juan de Torquemada in his *Monarquía Indiana*, published in 1615:

(1) Without receiving any lavish gifts of choirbooks, the Indians nevertheless were able to create splendid libraries of Church music by painstakingly copying books brought over by Zumárraga and his deputies.

(2) By sharing among themselves the teaching that certain privileged ones were able to get from Spanish masters, musical culture of the European type became sufficiently diffused for them to develop polyphonic choirs, even in their smaller villages. . . . "Competent instrumentalists are also found everywhere. The small towns have their supply of instruments, and even the smallest hamlets have three or four Indians who sing every day in church."

(3) Because the Indians, in addition to making their own instruments, soon developed among themselves the art of fabricating clever imitations of European instruments brought over by the invaders, they were able to develop instrumental accompanying ensembles with unique and unforeseen tone color possibilities. . . . "In all Christendom there is nowhere a greater abundance of flutes, sackbuts, trumpets, and drums, than here in New Spain. The Indians make the organs under supervision, and they play the organs in our monasteries and convents. The other instruments which serve for solace or delight on secular occasions are all made here by the Indians, who also play them: rebecs, guitars, trebles, viols, harps, spinets."

(4) Indian musical accomplishment was by no means limited to clever imitation of European performance, but included also a certain amount of original creative activity in the European idiom. . . . "Only a

few years after the Indians began to learn to chant, they also began to compose. Their [works] have been adjudged superior when shown Spanish masters of composition. Indeed the Spanish masters often thought they could not have been written by Indians." (Stevenson 1968, 171-72)

Leonard Ellinwood also traces this activity in *The History of American Church Music*:

The first activity [of this sort] within the present limits of the United States of America was at the Mission of San Felipe in New Mexico, where Father Cristóbal de Quiñones installed a small organ and began to teach the San Felipe Indians to sing the music of the liturgy sometime between 1598 and 1604. During the following century and a half, through the many Franciscan missions there was laid a love of the Church and its music, especially that of a folk character, that even the extensive deprivations of the nineteenth century failed to erase from Indian hearts.

Typical of the religious folk-hymns were the *alabados* (Songs of Praise). These were simple folk-hymns in the form of the Spanish *romance*, which could be used on all occasions. The texts were summaries of the essential tenets of the Christian religion, an important means of propagation of the faith among illiterate natives. Many *alabados* were either composed in, or translated into the different Indian languages. (Ellinwood 1953, 5)

In addition to discussing the *alabados*, John Donald Robb in *Hispanic Folk Music of New Mexico and the Southwest: A Self-Portrait of a People* also identifies the *alabanza, decima a lo divino, himno*, familiar country hymns sung in village churches, *rogativa*, and *despedimento*. (Robb 1980, 690-701) He also traces the influence of plainsong and songs from religious drama (see the following discussion) on the folk songs of this region.

Religious pageants, *Comedia de Adán y Eva* and *Los Pastores* (*Adam and Eve* and *The Shepherds*), combined Spanish and Indian melody, the latter moving in sequence to the drama from a room in the village to the church chancel. By the late-eighteenth century composers used parodies of folk melodies in the choral settings of the mass.

When the Roman church was forced to close its missions at the time of Mexican independence in 1822, it also brought an end to both the teaching of the traditional liturgical music and the church's assimilation of folk music into its liturgical music. By the final decades of the nineteenth century that vital interplay was all but lost, but in the twentieth century its repertory was unearthed by musicological research.

Shortly after Mexican independence and particularly after the war between Mexico and the United States (1846-48) in most of the southwestern United

States, English-speaking Protestants began proselytizing the Indian population. They preached conversion and release from the world, sin, Rome and
the Pope, and all the trappings of "anti-Christ" Roman worship, including its
music. They used with their preaching the enthusiastic, simple, and memorable camp-meeting hallelujahs and choruses of the United States and, later,
the gospel hymn in translation. Revival "spiritual music" also displaced the
worldly music of "pagan" Indian folk music and dance. By the 1870's,
revivalistic music and worship style were solidly in place and together
remain the most characteristic musical/liturgical style in Protestant churches
of the Americas, including that part of The United Methodist Church identified as the Rio Grande Annual Conference.

The beginnings of Protestant, and indirectly Methodist, worship in the southwestern United States is summarized by Alfredo Náñez (Náñez's hymnal collection is housed in Bridwell Library, Perkins School of Theology, Southern
Methodist University, Dallas) in his *History of the Rio Grande Conference of The
United Methodist Church*:

> Protestant services were held among the colonists in Texas prior to 1836;
> but such services were illegal and the leaders of the colonies discouraged
> them because they did not want to get in trouble with the Mexican
> authorities. Soon after freedom of religion came to Texas and New Mexi-
> co, the chief Protestant denominations (Baptists, Methodists and Presby-
> terians) became interested in proclaiming their message to the Spanish-
> speaking population. (Náñez 1981, 42)

While it is true that gospel hymns and choruses were and continue to be the
most characteristic song of Spanish-speaking evangelical Protestants in the
Americas, there is some evidence that European styles persisted in the education of young people in mission schools. In describing the daily routine of a
mission's boys' school in Albuquerque, ca. 1880, Náñez writes:

> The assistant teacher for the regular school work now calls the school to
> order, by a short Scripture reading, prayer and singing, one of the boys
> always presiding at the chapel's organ. (Náñez 1981, 43)

The significant influence of "traditional Anglo music" is described by Alejo
Hernández, often called the "first Mexican missionary of the Methodist Epis-
copal Church, South," in the account of his conversion in a chapel setting in
Brownsville, Texas, ca. 1865:

> I was seated where I could see the congregation but few could see me. I
> felt that God's spirit was there, although I could not understand a word
> that was being said, I felt my heart strangely warmed. . . . Never did I hear
> an organ play so sweetly, never did human voices sound so lovely to me,
> never did people look so beautiful as on that occasion. I went away weep-
> ing for joy. (Náñez 1981, 43)

In 1875 the Methodist Publishing House of the Methodist Episcopal Church, South, published its first Spanish hymnal, *Himnos para el uso de la Iglesia Metodista, del Sur, en Mexico*, a modest book that found wide use in Mexico and Texas. The production of hymnals for Spanish-speaking Methodists continued, according to Náñez, in the work of Primitivo A. Rodríguez, an instructor of Spanish, Vanderbilt University, and the first to be employed by the Methodist Publishing House, 1888-1909, as a translator of English language resources into Spanish, including a Spanish hymnal. No title is provided in Náñez text, but it probably was *Himnario Christiano*, 1908, described as "a very attractive [words only edition] hymnal which at the time of publication was the best hymnal in the Spanish-speaking field." (Náñez 1981, 113)

Other Methodists of this period who were active in hymn writing, translation, and publishing include musician-translator William Butler, d. 1889, and pastor-musician Thomás García, d. 1906. Later contributions were made by pastor-compiler Pedro Grado Valdés, 1862-1923, and composer Epigmentio Velasco, 1880-1940, the associate of Vincente Mendoza, 1875-1955 (see "Jesús es mi Rey soberano," page 438-39).

As early as 1939 when the newly organized Spanish language annual conference, the Rio Grande Conference, was established by the Uniting Conference of The Methodist Church, Náñez writes that the conference expressed concern that they had no common hymnal: "All through these years (1940-1950), again and again the matter of the publication of a hymnal was brought up, but nothing was done due to the prohibitive cost." The complaint continued into the next decade:

> The long pressing matter of unifying the worship services through the use of a common hymnal and the use of the basic ritual of the church was faced. . . . More than ten different hymnals were being used throughout the conference and no ritual of the church was available for the people. (Náñez 1981, 111)

The cost effectiveness of publishing a hardback hymnal for such a small constituency proved too much, even with the argument that there was a great need for such a hymnal and that the church's publisher ought to provide the funding consistent with the general church's commitment to the Rio Grande Conference. In a gesture of cooperation one of the church's publishers, Arthur "Ben" Whitmore, offered to provide for reprint purposes the plates of *Himnario Christiano* published in 1909. To the chagrin of all, however, the plates had been melted down during World War II.

Faced with the seemingly endless obstacles associated with finding a publisher for the hymnal, Náñez devised a workable plan. He recalls:

> This avenue for the publication of the hymnal being closed, the writer [Dr. Náñez] who had been named editor of the hymnal, approached the

Baptist Publishing House of El Paso, Texas, about the possibility of publishing the hymnal. Since they had published several hymnals already and had the plates of what could serve as the basis of a hymnal suitable for our needs, a contract was made with them.

In 1955 *Himnario Metodista* came off the press, and immediately the churches began to use it. More than 10,000 copies of the hymnal were sold during the first six months. By 1956 it was being used by all the churches in the conference, most of the Methodist Spanish-speaking churches in this country and also in Cuba and Puerto Rico. In Cuba a special edition with only the words was made. This lowered the price and enhanced the sales. In all more than 24,000 copies of this hymnal were sold. It is significant that no outside subsidy was received for its publication, and at the end more than $6,000.00 in profit was realized. (Náñez 1981, 113)

The "hymnal issue" was once again raised in October of 1964 after the 1964 General Conference of The Methodist Church had approved the revision of *The Methodist Hymnal*, without a single item in Spanish. Náñez writes that a hymnal committee was appointed to start work on the publication of a new

hymnal to replace the one published in 1955. The following were the members of the committee: Alfredo Náñez, editor; Anita González, secretary; Roy Barton, treasurer; Noé Gonzales, A. T. Grout, Daniel Cortez, Albert López, Jr. and Robert Wolfe. . . . The editor immediately began to work on the project . . . [and] after long negotiations the publishing house taking over the project. (Náñez 1981, 134)

After nine years and with the Rio Grande Conference contributing the materials and paying for the copyrighted material that was included, the book was published. At the 1973 annual conference special mention was made of the work of Robert L. Hoffelt, music editor of Abingdon Press: "For untold months [he] gave the finest expert care and advice to the composition of *Himnario Metodista*." (Náñez 1981, 135)

Nevertheless, potential dissatisfaction with the content of that hymnal as being "too Anglo-Saxon" had been expressed three years earlier at the 1970 annual conference in that conference's "message of confession":

We have adopted the worship, the customs, the norms and values of our spiritual ancestors, the Anglo-Saxon missionaries of the 19th century who originally brought us the Gospel, and we have denied ourselves a development strictly our own, genuinely representative of the spirit of our people. (Náñez 1981, 136)

At that juncture it appeared that the time had arrived for the production of a songbook, or supplement to *Himnario Metodista*, for Hispanic Protestants with a broad ecumenical/global content and appeal. The production of such a hymn-book was assigned to the newly formed Section on Worship within the General Board of Discipleship, which had already begun to publish supplemental worship resources for what had been identified as "four ethnic-minority churches." The first effort of the Section on Worship was to produce a supplement to *Himnario Metodista*, 1973. A project task force, Celebremos, was formed, consisting of Roberto Escamilla, project director; Elise Shoemaker Eslinger, music editor; Raquel Gutiérrez-Achón, chair; Mary Lou Santillán Baert, Roger Deschner, Esther Frances, George Lockwood, Raquel Martínez, Dolores Márquez, and Gertrude Suppe. The purpose of Celebremos was stated:

> To respond to [the] recommendation of MARCHA [Methodists Associated Representing Concerns of Hispanic Americans] that greater use be made of indigenous music in Hispanic worship, and to gather and distribute a variety of such materials throughout the church. (Preface to *Celebremos II*)

The Celebremos project produced *Celebremos. Primera Parte, Colección de Coritos*, 1979, a collection of familiar choruses; and *Celebremos Segunda Parte, Colección de Himnos, Salmos y Cánticos*, 1983, a more global and ecumenical content with selections from Latin America, Spain, Puerto Rico, and the United States.

Some Hispanic material was informally presented at the beginning of the work on *The United Methodist Hymnal*, but it was referred to a "Hispanic Consultation," comprised of both Hispanic and Anglo translators, editors, and composers, some of whom served on the committees that formed *Celebremos* and *Himnario Metodista*. The consultation's work was funded entirely by The United Methodist Publishing House; its task was described in *The Report of the Hymnal Revision Committee to the 1988 General Conference of The United Methodist Church*, page 22:

> The Spanish language is commonly spoken throughout the United States, second only to English. There are certain diversities within its general musical style. Resources under consideration came from the churches of Spain [North America, Mexico], Latin America [South America], and various Hispanic communities across the nation. . . . Both new and traditional hymns and other resources of high quality deemed most likely to enhance . . . [a] new English-language hymnal. In addition, Spanish translations of several traditional English hymns which might be used in bilingual ecumenical services have been recommended for placement alongside English hymns—a first in [United] Methodist hymnals.

The consultation many times split concerning the overall repertory that it should recommend for inclusion in the new hymnal. From those representing the needs of the Rio Grande Conference, the repertory and performance practice that would serve that majority of Hispanics within The United Methodist Church comprised the gospel hymn, both those written in Spanish, "Jesús es mi Rey soberano," "O Jesus, my King and my Sovereign" **(180)**, and translations of traditional English language gospel hymns; praise choruses (*coritos/estribillos*); and standard English hymns in translation, with congregational singing supported by the traditional instruments of the church. Others with a view of serving the new diversity of USA Hispanics, few of whom are United Methodists, wanted to cast their nets wider and include the emerging repertory and performance practice of the global Hispanic community, allowing a future revision of *Himnario Metodista* to serve the needs of the Rio Grande Conference.

At the close of nearly two years of work the consultation recommended that forty-three items be considered for inclusion in the revised hymnal. The full Hymnal Revision Committee, following the lead of those advocating the broader repertory, voted to include eighteen selections in the revised hymnal. All but three were from the contemporary global and ecumenical repertory of Hispanic religious song: "Mil voces para celebrar," "O for a thousand tongues to sing" **(59)**; "Santo, Santo, Santo," "Holy, Holy, Holy" **(65)**; and "Jesús es mi Rey soberano," "O Jesus, my King and my Sovereign" **(180)**. Many of the selections are well suited to be accompanied by tambourine, maracas, drums, and guitar, as for example, "De tierra lejana venimos," "From a distant home the Savior we come seeking" **(243)**, from Puerto Rico, traditionally used in the "Service of Las Posadas," a Christmas musical drama about Joseph and Mary attempting to find lodging in Bethlehem.

With an aroused conscience of the oppression and dehumanizing aspects of contemporary society, Spanish-speaking musicians and hymn writers in both Spain and the Americas have composed hymns of liberation and hope, including Cesáreo Gebaráin's "Tú has venido a la orilla," "Lord, you have come to the lakeshore" **(344)**, and "Camina, pueblo de Dios," "Walk on, O people of God"**(305)**; and the magnificent tune CENTRAL by Pablo D. Sosa, the setting for the Nicolás Martínez text, "¡Cristo vive, fuera el llanto," translated by Fred Kaan, "Christ is risen, Christ is living" **(313)**.

The eighteen items finally included in the new hymnal are about a fourth of the total of that which was carefully selected, much of it translated and arranged for keyboard. The Celebremos project in *Celebremos* used only 44 of a total of 150 items that it had developed.

At this writing the General Board of Discipleship and the United Methodist Publishing House have formed a committee to produce a successor to *Himnario Metodista*, 1973. Raquel Mora Martínez has been named editor. See also Justo L. González, general editor, *Each in Our Own Tongue, A History of Hispanic United Methodism;* and Cecilio M. McConnell, *La Historia del Himno en Castellano*, 1987 3d ed.

Recent USA Hymnody

With the exception of the inclusion of the social gospel hymn, mainline Protestant hymnals for the first part of this century shunned the other unique contributions of USA hymnody, the African American religious song as well as hymns and psalms from the "singing school" tradition, while they reluctantly included a few gospel hymns. By mid-century a few new texts from Britain had found their way into our hymnals. Robin A. Leaver in "British Hymnody Since 1950" in *The Hymnal 1982 Companion* quotes Erik Routley's remark made in the 1940's about the quality of new British hymns: "Well do I remember how difficult it was to find any new texts that were fit to use: we reckoned we were clever to find about a dozen." (Glover 1990, 1:556)

The 1957 and 1966 hymnal committees reviewed very few quality new hymns. In his survey Fred D. Gealy cites only one (then) recent USA hymn, Georgia Harkness's "Hope of the world" **(178)**. (Gealy, Lovelace, Young 1970, 15-40)

The exception to the generally low quality of USA hymns and an important source for our 1966 and 1989 revision committees was the repertory developed by the Hymn Society of America, renamed in 1989 the Hymn Society in the United States and Canada. The society was founded in 1922 to encourage the writing of hymns in general, and from time to time the organization put out the call for poets to write hymns on particular selected topics, namely, family, peace, education, city, ecumenicity, and the Bible. Its efforts have produced several important texts, including Georgia Harkness, "Hope of the world" **(178)**; George W. Briggs, "God hath spoken by the prophets" **(108)**; Frederick B. Morley, "O church of God, united" **(547)**; and F. Pratt Green, "How blest are they who trust in Christ" **(654)**. Through its papers and the periodical *The Hymn*, the society continues to foster important hymnological research of USA hymns, hymnals, and hymn writers. In addition the church music departments of several Southern Baptist seminaries, through doctoral programs, have recently provided important leadership in hymnological research and have significantly extended hymnic bibliography. The three-decade contributions of Southern Baptist hymnologist William J. Reynolds place him foremost in recent USA hymnic research and commentary.

Another exception to the paucity of quality hymns is in the work of F. Bland Tucker, one of the USA's most important translators and hymn writers, who contributed six items to the Protestant Episcopal *Hymnal 1940*. Included from that list in the present hymnal are "All praise to thee, for thou, O King divine" **(166)**; "Our Parent [orig. Father], by whose name" **(447)**; and "Father, we thank you, for you planted" **(563)**. From Tucker's last efforts, *The Hymnal 1982*, are his translation of stanzas 5-7 of "Holy God, we praise thy name" **(79)**, and his paraphrase of Romans 13:11-14 and Ephesians 4:4-6 in "Awake, O sleeper" **(551)**.

In our 1957 and 1966 hymnals traditional British-American hymnody was supplemented with the addition of several non-Western hymns with metaphors, musical style, and performance practice significantly distinct from those in Euro-USA standard hymnody (see the section on "Asian American Hymns," pages 33-36). The present hymnal greatly expands that emerging repertory, for example, the African "At the birth of a child" **(146)** and "Send me, Lord" **(497)**; the Hindi "Jaya ho" **(478)**; and the Vietnamese "My prayer rises to heaven" **(498)**. For additional non-Western hymns and tunes see also the ecumenical hymnal produced by the World Council of Churches, *Cantate Domino*, 1974, and the listing under "Traditional hymns, melodies, and prayers" in Index of Composers, Authors, and Sources **(922)**.

The importance of the work and witness of the late Erik Routley to the development of hymnody in the USA has already been cited in the section "Recent British Hymnody," page 16. Particularly significant was his work as coeditor, with Austin C. Lovelace, Alec Wyton, and Carlton R. Young, of *Ecumenical Praise*, 1977, a very influential supplemental collection with a wide range of contemporary, largely English hymnic content to which he generously contributed his editorial services. Twenty-three recent hymns that first appeared in this collection are included in our hymnal. His enormous activity as teacher, author, lecturer, and consultant to hymnal committees had by 1980 vitally connected the hymnody of Great Britain to that of the USA so that as Russell Schulz-Widmar has written,"It is increasingly difficult to speak [as one might have a generation ago] of English hymnody and American hymnody as two different things." (Leaver and Litton 1985, 191)

An important exception to Schulz-Widmar's characterization is the so-called "language controversy." The issue of contemporary language in hymns and liturgy began in the USA, as it did in Britain, with the modification of the three-century-old King James Version of the Bible, the sixteenth-century *Book of Common Prayer* language base by way of new liturgies and new translations of the Bible, including the Revised Standard Version, 1946, 1952, Phillips, *New Testament in Modern English*, 1958, and *The New English Bible*, 1962. The issue of "people language" was advanced in the USA, but not in Britain, within the larger struggle for equal rights. The former accepted rendering of "men" and "man" as "everyone" had by the mid-1970's become exclusive and therefore obsolete for an increasing number of women. The *Lutheran Book of Worship*, 1978, was the first USA mainline hymnal to deal with this issue; where possible, its editors changed "men" to "all" or "mankind" to "humankind."

The Protestant Episcopal *Hymnal 1982* in "O for a thousand tongues to sing" and elsewhere advanced the "issue" beyond "people language" to deal with traditional words that in the early 1980's had become discriminatory, as for example, Charles Wesley's original first line of stanza 12, "Glory to God, and praise and love" **(58)** which he obviously quoted from the New Testament (Luke 7:22) and expressed in guileless eighteenth-century Wesleyan evangelical hyperbole: "hear him, ye deaf, his praise, ye dumb." In deference to the recent shift in meaning of "dumb" from a person who cannot speak to one who is "stupid," *The Hymnal 1982* changed Wesley's line: "Hear him, ye deaf; ye voiceless ones," but avoided, as did the present hymnal, dealing with the equally discriminatory invitation for "the deaf to hear," "the blind to see," and "the lame to leap."

Recent British hymnals, including *Hymns and Psalms*, 1983, have followed to a lesser extent these practices of changing or eliminating archaic, sexist, and discriminatory words and phrases. For the principles that guided the Hymnal Revision Committee in formulating its language guidelines for both old as well as new hymns, see pages 131-34 in the chapter *"The United Methodist Hymnal, 1989."*

The final language issue to emerge is that of "God language." It began in England with Bishop John Robinson's *Honest to God*, 1963, in which he advocated the rejection and the restatement of traditional metaphors, descriptions, and forms of address for deity, heaven, and earthly things in terms that could be understood and restated with integrity by the average person. Leaver writes in *The Hymnal 1982 Companion*:

> Bishop Robinson was also concerned with God-language, an issue that [became] a major preoccupation in the 1980's, but for different reasons. His concern was to debunk the popular imagery for God as an old man in the sky with a long white beard. He argued that all traditional names for God carried at least something of this caricature, and therefore proposed to substitute instead the phrase "the Ground of Our Being." (Glover 1990, 1:562)

In the USA, the nonsexist rendering of the forms of address, descriptions, and metaphors for deity began on seminary campuses in the mid 1980's. There were two foci to the rationale: (1) it was believed to be consistent with the Old Testament view of God as neither male nor female; and (2) there was a widening and deepening demand by women that church authority be shared, resulting in the beginnings of the empowerment of women first to voice a concern and then to claim and assume vital leadership roles at both local and denominational levels of activity. The modification of the church's political structures from exclusively male to shared female/male in some places has resulted in a profound change in how its authority and God's nature and authority and the resurrected Christ are characterized and described in nonmasculine and nonhierarchical language. For two opposite views of this issue, see Donald G. Bloesch, "The Battle of the Trinity," *The Debate over Inclusive God Language*, and Brian Wren, "What Language Shall I Borrow?" in *God Talk in Worship: A Male Response to Feminist Theology*.

Not all hymnal revision committees have dealt with the language issues with equal energy or insight; some have ignored it. For a description of the work of the Hymnal Revision Committee concerning language, see pages 131-34 and 138-43 in the chapter *"The United Methodist Hymnal, 1989."*

Several USA hymn writers have not only maintained a stance equal with their counterparts in Great Britain, but have made unique contributions to recent hymnals. In addition to the contributions by F. Bland Tucker, nine others, among a growing number of talented and productive writers, should be recognized: Martin H. Franzmann, "Weary of all trumpeting" **(442)**; Jaroslav Vajda, "Now" [Now the silence] **(619)**, and the translation of the Czech nativity carol, "Rock-a-bye, my dear little boy" **(235)**; Gracia Grindal, who served as a language consultant to the Hymnal Revision Committee, "To a maid engaged to Joseph" **(215)**; Carl Daw, "Like the murmur of the dove's song" **(544)**; and Jeffery Rowthorn, "Creating God, your fingers trace" **(109)**.

Texts by USA writers commissioned by the Hymnal Revision Committee include Ruth Duck, "Wash, O God, our sons and daughters" **(605)**, William W. Reid, Jr., "O God who shaped creation" **(443)**, Miriam Therese Winter, "Wellspring of Wisdom" **(506)**; and Thomas H. Troeger, "Source and Sovereign, Rock and Cloud" **(113)**.

USA hymnody has been enriched by two decades of contributions from Roman Catholic poets, namely, Omer Westendorf, "You satisfy the hungry heart" (Gift of finest wheat) **(629)**, and his translation from the Latin, "Ubi caritas," "Where charity and love prevail" **(549)**. An important dimension of the Roman Catholic hymnody is in its "folk" and "pop" eucharistic hymns, including Joe Wise's "Take our bread" **(640)** from the 1960's and the more recent "One bread, one body" **(620)** by John B. Foley. For other references to pop and folk hymnody, see pages 166-70 in the chapter *"The United Methodist Hymnal, 1989."* For a history of Roman Catholic hymnody in the United States, refer to J. Vincent Higginson, *History of American Catholic Hymnals: Survey and Background,* 1982; and for a commentary on Roman Catholic hymnic repertory, see Thomas Day, *Why Catholics Can't Sing,* 1990. For a review of Roman Catholic music and liturgy in the 1980's, see *The Hymn* 37 (1): 7-18.

The most recent addition to USA hymnic repertory in our hymnal comes from the chorus and scripture songs of the "charismatic" communities, e.g., Bob McGee's "Emmanuel, Emmanuel" **(204)** and Jack Hayford's "Majesty, worship his majesty" **(176)**.

THE MUSIC OF HYMNS, WESLEYAN STYLE

JOHN WESLEY AND THE MUSIC OF HYMNS

A review of John Wesley's seven "Directions for Singing" (vii) from his *Select Hymns*, 1761, which in some regard are complaints about "why don't we do things the way we used to," provides us with valuable insights into his vital interest in, if not his preoccupation with, the power of music to promote or prevent the people's sung praise and prayer. (See commentary on pages 320-21.)

Wesley's interest and expertise in music, which came by way of his upbringing in psalm and hymn singing in the Epworth rectory and parish church, and evangelical hymn singing as a member of the Holy Club at Oxford, were fully expressed while he was in Georgia as missionary-priest with the publication of *A Collection of Psalms and Hymns*, Charleston, South Carolina, 1737. It took him about a year and a half to produce the collection, and in the process he selected, translated, and reduced all seventy texts to five basic iambic meters so that he could more easily teach his parishioners its contents page by page, perhaps playing his flute to set the tune. (For a review of the consequences of Wesley's musical editorship of this, the first hymnbook, compiled and printed in the USA and intended for use in Anglican worship, see Carlton R. Young, "John Wesley's 1737 Charlestown *Collection of Psalms and Hymns*," *The Hymn*, 1990.)

In Georgia, Wesley not only began his fifty-year career as text editor and publisher of hymnals, but by testing the contents of his first hymnal as to their singability he began his parallel activity of compiling and publishing tune books and initiated that unique aspect of the Wesleyan ethos, "singing what was preached, and preaching what was sung." His first tune book was the 1742 *Foundery Collection*, and his last in 1780, *Sacred Harmony*. From our church's beginnings vital preaching and congregational singing have been the core of our worship tradition, a tradition passed on in part each time official hymnals are revised, which is approximately once each generation. (See "Hymnals of The Evangelical United Brethren Church," pages 75-89, and "Hymnals of The Methodist Church," pages 91-122.)

John Wesley expanded the Methodist tune's repertory to include new tunes composed or adapted to accommodate the increasing number of meters in Charles Wesley's enormous output of sacred texts: folk tunes and their imitations, vocal and instrumental melodies from Italian opera, and sacred and secular oratorio, much of it Handelian. This latter occasionally highly ornamented melody, hardly the simple unison congregational song that John Wesley championed in his writings, was scored in basso-continuo solo social style and accompanied by a viol, or string bass; in some places organ or harpsichord were added. In some Wesley chapels, modeled after the practice of evangelical chapels, precentors or leaders of congregational song were recruited to teach and direct the hymns.

John's Wesley's ability to select solid tunes in a variety of meters is seen in these tunes that are still included in our hymnal from his *Foundery Collection*, 1742:

AMSTERDAM (76.76.77.76) **96**, CAREY'S (SURREY) (88.88.88) **579**, EASTER HYMN (77.77D) **302**, HANOVER (10.10.11) **181**, OLD 113TH (888.888) **60**, SAVANNAH (77.77) **385**, TALLIS' CANON (LM) **682**, UFFINGHAM (LM) **450**, VATER UNSER (88.88.88) **414**, WER NUR DEN LIEBEN GOTT (98.98.88) **142**.

For additional commentary on John Wesley and hymn tunes, see Fred Kimball Graham, "John Wesley's Choice of Hymn Tunes," *The Hymn*, 1988.

Wesley expressed concern for the standardization of hymn singing performance practice under the broader topic of formality in worship. This is seen in this excerpt from the "Large" *Minutes*.

Q 39. How shall we guard against formality in public worship; particularly in singing?

A. (1) By preaching frequently on the head. (2) By taking care to speak only what we feel. (3) By choosing such hymns as are proper for the congregation. (4) By not singing too much at once; seldom more than five or six verses. (5) By suiting the tune to the words. (6) By often stopping short and asking the people, "Now, do you know what you said last? Did you speak no more than you felt?"

Is not this formality creeping in already, by those complex [anthems and fuging] tunes, which it is scarcely possible to sing with devotion? Such is, "Praise the Lord, ye blessed ones:" such the long quavering hallelujah annexed to the morning-song tune, which I defy any man living to sing devoutly. The repeating the same words so often (but especially while another repeats different words, the horrid abuse which runs through the modern church-music), as it shocks all common sense, so it necessarily brings in dead formality, and has no more of religion in it than a Lancashire hornpipe. Besides, it is a flat contradiction to our Lord's command, "Use not vain repetitions." For what is a vain repetition, if this is not? What end of devotion does it serve? Sing no anthems. (7) Do not suffer the people to sing too slow. This naturally tends to formality, and is brought in by them who have either very strong or very weak voices. (8) In every large society let them learn to sing; and let them always learn our own tunes first. (9) Let the women constantly sing their parts alone. Let no man sing with them, unless he understands the notes, and sings the bass, as it is pricked down in the book. (10) Introduce no new tunes, till they are perfect in the old. (11) Let no organ be placed anywhere, till proposed in the Conference. (12) Recommend our tune-book everywhere; and if you cannot sing yourself choose a person or two in each place to pitch the tune for you. (13) Exhort every one in the congregation to sing, not one in ten only. (14) If a Preacher be present, let no singer give out the words. (15) When they would teach a tune to the congregation, they must sing only the tenor. After the preaching, take a little lemonade, mild ale, or candied orange-peel. All spirituous liquors, at that time especially, are deadly poison. (Mason 1862, 1:529-33)

While solo voices occasionally sang ornamented versions of hymns at the time of the invitation from collections such as J. F. Lampe's *Hymns on the Great Festivals and Other Occasions*, 1746, it was the large repertory of simple unadorned psalm tunes and evangelical melody held in common by evangelicals of all persuasions that was the foundation of congregational song that functioned in the compelling Wesleyan (evangelical) model of praise, prayer, and proclamation. See commentary on pages 49-50, 108, 201, 310, 426, 428, 441, 557, 565, 602, and 659.

The performance practice of hymn singing varied from the two centers, John Wesley's City Road Chapel in London and the New Room in Bristol, to the Anglican parish churches, evangelical chapels, and meetinghouses in the small towns and villages in the hundreds of circuits maintained by a network of trained lay preachers who were the conveners and leaders of the preaching services. Wesley hymns, probably those in meters in variants of 8's and 6's, functioned in these services as an integral part of the proclamation to the unconverted of God's saving grace in Jesus Christ, as well as a reminder to the converted of having fallen short. The recitation and study of hymns were used in class meetings as devotional poetry to form the members' faith and prayer. This practice also served to sustain the hymns' meanings and impact in the intervals between preaching services (see "Directions for Singing," **vii**).

John Wesley's authority in music and its performance practice was self-assumed within his general oversight of a disciplined itinerancy, and this authority was seldom open for review or modification. He maintained this domination in part as the sole publisher and distributor of publications. In this latter regard he consulted and used the services of those recognized musicians who were in general agreement with his views and tastes. In some regard his proclamations and opinions expressed during his last two decades, 1770-91, along with the increased latitude of tunes in his collections, e.g., operatic and oratorio airs and choruses, were his response to the growing encroachment of local social singing groups and their repertory of fuging tunes and anthems on the worship life of the societies' classic evangelical worship form of praise, prayer, and proclamation.

Wesley had some qualified appreciation for organs and the organist's ability to express appropriate moods of quiet meditation or exultation in Anglican worship, as well as the society's preaching services sometimes held in Anglican parishes. He was particularly attracted to the effects of the newly invented swell box that had been installed in the organ of Exeter Cathedral. He expressed concern for the congregation not to become dependent upon the organ or the choir for support.

Charles Wesley's influence in defining the proper music for the societies is seldom evidenced, but it may be surmised that his increasing interest in the musical education and introduction to London society of his precocious sons Charles and Samuel, along with his allegiance to the worship and liturgical music of the Anglican cathedral and parish, caused him to be somewhat distanced from John's restricted views. However, in stanza five of a poem in *Hymns and Sacred Poems*, 1749, he echoes his brother's warning against the power of music to distract the faithful:

> Still let us on our guard be found,
> And watch against the power of sound
>   With sacred jealousy;
> Lest haply sense should damp our zeal.
> And music's charms bewitch and steal
>   Our hearts away from thee.

Wesley's 1779 tract "On the Power of Music" impressively summarizes his mature understanding concerning the importance of music in worship. For further discussion of Wesley and music, see Erik Routley's commentary on this tract, pages 20-26 in *The Musical Wesleys*; and Franz Hildebrandt's and Oliver A. Beckerlegge's commentary on the 1780 *Collection*: Appendix E, a reprint of Wesley's preface to *Select Hymns with Tunes Annext*, 1761; Appendix F, Wesley's twelve-page course in reading music, *The Gamut, or Scale of Music*, 1761; Appendix G, lessons in music theory and note reading, *The Grounds of Vocal Music*, 1765; Appendix H, Wesley's tract, *Thoughts on the Power of Music*, 1779; Appendix I, critical notes by Hildebrandt and Beckerlegge on each of the 104 tunes that Wesley selected for the 1786 edition of the 1780 *Collection* with titles included at the head of each text.

THE MUSIC OF CHRISTIAN HYMNS IN USA-WESLEYAN TRADITIONS

British Roots

James F. White has characterized the Wesleyan revival and its worship life as an countercultural movement in the midst of the English Enlightenment. . . [that was] denounced for producing Spirit-filled Christians or "enthusiasts" rather than staid pewholders [and] reached out primarily to the poor. . . in an era that placed so much emphasis on power and prestige. . . . To reach the poor urban masses [of Bristol, Birmingham and London], one had to go beyond the parish system and develop a whole new form of mission. This outreach shaped Methodist worship in definite ways. (White 1989, 152)

During the post-Revolutionary era and into the early nineteenth century much of British Wesleyan worship life, including hymnic repertory, was modified. Much of that modification, some would say rejection, was simply because the vast majority of the population of the fledging expanding nation, apart from some who resided in its seaboard "European" urban communities, was illiterate. In contrast, not only was British Methodism founded and served primarily by Anglican priests and lay persons with roots in the educated privileged class exemplified by John and Charles Wesley, but at the center of the Wesleyan movement is an educational work ethic. Both of Methodism's organizational pillars, the class meeting and the annual conference, were essentially "adult learning experiences": important questions of faith and witness were posed by the leader, then stated and memorized answers recited by its members. As young itinerants replaced older Anglican preachers and younger lay class leaders replaced their elders, they were instructed to study Wesley's fifty-six volume *Christian Library* in addition to his tracts and essays.

As late as 1790 John Wesley stated his concern for literacy in a letter to George Holder, quoted by David C. Shipley in "The European Heritage," *The History of American Methodism*:

> It cannot be that the people should grow in grace unless they give themselves to reading. A reading people will always be a knowing people. A people who talk too much will know little. Press this upon them with all your might. (Bucke 1964, 1: 24)

As for the "formal" education of ministers, British Methodism in the nineteenth century established educational standards for its clergy under the rubric that "Education *for* the ministry is a function *of* ministry."

Concerning lay education, Shipley explains that Methodist lay persons

> shared responsibility for [the] education of [his/her] . . . neighbor as a dimension of the ministry shared by all Christians. . . . This was seen not only through the discussions [in] the class meetings—and the prescribed program of reading enforced through the discipline of the society—but also in the instruction of children deprived of every opportunity for an education. Methodist orphanages were noted for their educational concern and accomplishment, though the discipline of the children, according to standards of the present day, was positively cruel. . . . The [education] of children [was also] manifested—in the Methodist promotion of the Sunday School, which was, in the eighteenth century, a school for children on Sunday (since they worked the other six days of the week) where the basic skills of reading, writing, arithmetic, and geography were taught. Significantly, Methodist women first discerned this responsibility. (Bucke 1964, 1:26-27)

USA Frontier Religion

Characteristically, in the United States as in Britain, Methodism's "good news of acceptance in Christ" took hold irrespective of education or class: among the literate as well as the illiterate, in the city as well as on the frontier. While it is true that many if not most of its first leaders had been educated in England and that their work had begun among the literate in urban settings, their activity through the societies soon became focused on the illiterate migrants, including recruitment of them as "traveling ministers." The educational standards established by Wesley and so vital to the sustaining power of the Wesleyan movement in Britain did not always apply to United States Methodists, who, as Nathan Bangs complained, were perceived as "enemies to learning," a trait apparently supported in Bishop Francis Asbury's so-called Valedictory Address to Bishop McKendree that is quoted by Richard M. Cameron in "The New Church Takes Root," *The History of American Methodism:* "I have not spoken against learning. I have only said that it cannot be said to be an essential qualification to preach the gospel." (Bucke 1964, 1:265)

Authority in matters hymnic and musical were implicitly transmitted by Wesley to superintendents Coke and Asbury in 1784. As bishops they in turn passed it along to clergy who they ordained to an itinerate ministry of Word, Sacrament and Order. At the urging of Bishops Coke and Asbury the all-ministerial 1798 (General) Conference first expressed its role as the arbiter of appropriate musical style by stating in the *Discipline* that fuging tunes "puff up with vanity" those who sing them"—ignoring the characteristic product of the New England school of composers, e.g., Billings, as well as the growing popularity of the singing schools.

The lack of an educated clergy and people contributed to the modification of the textual as well as the musical content of hymns, which resulted in a new repertory, much of which still divides USA and British Methodists. For instance, British Methodists sing "O for a thousand tongues," *Hymns and Psalms,* 744, to three eighteenth-century tunes, not to our nineteenth-century AZMON (**57**).

Part of this new repertory developed on the frontier by the unique joining of music and dance with preaching in the social-religious phenomenon, the camp meeting. Song and dance, innate human musical and kinesthetic expressions, were the convert's free and natural response in a setting devoid of standards of the literate and sophisticated upon hearing and experiencing the Wesleyan doctrine of "free Grace." By the second decade of the nineteenth century the hymnody and worship performance practice of the frontier camp meetings and improvised meetinghouses had spread from their beginnings in Kentucky, to the Carolinas, Ohio, Georgia, Virginia, Maryland, Delaware, Pennsylvania, New York, Massachusetts, Connecticut, Vermont, and New Hampshire.

Reynolds and Price give this description of the appeal of the camp-meeting music:

[The hymns] were in ballad style, couched in the simplest language, mainly concerned with the salvation of the sinner. The tunes were simple and folk like in character. The refrain, which was the most important, was sometimes appended to an existing [familiar] hymn and tune. Collections of these camp-meeting hymns were not plentiful in the early camp meetings, and those available usually contained words without any tunes. The teaching of these hymns by rote demanded that the tunes be easy, singable, and instantly contagious. Under these circumstances, a popular catchy repetitious refrain was of invaluable assistance. (Reynolds and Price 1987, 86)

An example of a camp-meeting tune is CLEANSING FOUNTAIN (**622**) and a camp-meeting chorus, the refrain of CLEANSING FOUNTAIN or CAMPMEETING (**492**). The spirit of the camp-meeting hymn is perpetuated in the gospel hymn, particular its chorus, for example, "He is Lord" (**177**), and in the choruses and scripture songs of the charismatic communities, such as, "Majesty, worship his majesty" (**176**).

As a historical footnote Reynolds and Price document:

By 1825, the outdoor camp meeting was almost exclusively a Methodist institution. [Their] . . . camp meeting activity continued, particularly among the Pentecostal Holiness branch of Methodism, into the beginning of the twentieth century. (Reynolds and Price 1987, 87)

The most readable, reliable, and concise coverage of the developments in nineteenth-century USA Wesleyan worship forms is found in the chapters "Frontier Worship" and "Methodist Worship," in James F. White, *Protestant Worship, Traditions in Transition*. White describes the function of frontier worship music as essentially "to prepare people for preaching that was to bring them to repentance and conversion. . . . To unite the congregation to act as one body . . . to create a sense of unity . . . and as a softening-up technique for what was to come. . . . By using a form more elevated and participatory than ordinary speech, it heightened the sense of expectancy that made the suitable matrix for the sermon. (White 1989, 184)

Dena J. Epstein has traced the involvement and contributions of African Americans to the style and song of the camp meeting in "Sacred Black Folk Music, 1801-67" in *Sinful Tunes and Spirituals*, including this insight from Lucius Bellinger, an itinerant Methodist preacher

who recalled a quarterly meeting at Pine Grove, South Carolina, about 1830: "Old Pine Grove had never seen such a turn out for many years . . . . The people . . . came in crowds . . . singing as the old-time Methodists used to sing. . . . The negroes are out in great crowds, and sing with voices that make the woods ring. (Epstein 1981, 198)

One of the early Wesleyan collections to reflect the modification of standard English hymns for use in camp-meetings and revivals is *A Collection of Hymns and Spiritual Songs*, 1801, by Richard Allen, the famous African American preacher and founder of the African Methodist Episcopal Church. See "African American Hymns" page 23.

Concerning the church's official acceptance of this type of activity Ellen Jane Lorenz in *Glory Hallelujah! The Story of the Campmeeting Spiritual* states:

> It is hard to believe, but true, that officially, the Methodists never accepted the campmeeting and never sanctioned a single revival songbook. [It is] . . . inexplicable in view of the Methodists' resounding success in holding campmeetings and singing campmeeting songs.
>
> There were rules and warnings [against these revival songbooks]. But despite them all, Methodist songsters began to appear in the early years of the nineteenth century, and Methodist revival songbooks poured from the presses in the fifties and sixties, and nobody but the bishops [who made the rules against them] seemed to pay any attention to the rules. (Lorenz 1980, 73)

Unlike the Methodists, the leaders of the United Brethren in Christ "welcomed the inclusion of revival hymns in their [authorized] books." (Lorenz 1980, 76). This distinctive song continues to be endemic to that worship style, flowing within and emerging from it, and, as celebrated in the contemporary church, appears to be in lineage with the rural camp meeting and its counterpart, the urban tent or indoor revival.

In addition to these rousing frontier hymns another repertory, the part song composed in "dispersed," sometimes dissonant harmony, and the "fuging tune" of the literate singing school also competed with the standard British tune. (Lowens 1964, 248) Its structured performance practice, consistent with Wesley's disdain of it, was deemed divisive and completely foreign to the improvisational and spontaneous style of the revival. Fuging tunes in their original form, printed in round rather than "shaped notes," were included as music for the choir in our official hymnals and tune books as late as 1878. Later attempts to introduce this vigorous music to congregations have usually resulted in "cooled down" and staid four-part "European" arrangements, after the style of Lowell Mason, e.g., LENOX **(379)**, CORONATION **(154)**, and FOUNDATION **(529)** from R. M. McIntosh *Tabor*, 1867.

Music Leadership

The early followers of Wesley, urban or frontier, were rightly called a singing people, though relatively few could read either words or music. In the colonial period and extending well into the nineteenth century, preachers were the teachers of both word and song. As the repertory of tunes expanded along with the number of tune books, preachers who could not read music of necessity delegated the selection, teaching, and leading of a "new" congregational song to the musically literate, usually a song leader, sometimes referred to as "precentor."

Not all texts, even those with the same meter, can and ought to be sung to the same tune. For instance, try singing "O for a thousand tongues to sing" (**57**) to CHRISTMAS, which is the tune for "While shepherds watched their flocks by night" (**236**). Thus the task of the song leader was soon expanded to include the selection of the appropriate tune for a given text.

Some song leaders were trained instrumentalists whose performing abilities were in constant demand in the sparse artistic developing urban cultures such as Boston and New York. Others were the products of the singing schools, which had thrived in New England in the last decades of the eighteenth century and later spread along the Atlantic coast, then to the South and the West. Both types recognized, taught, promoted, and replicated musical excellence in performance. With the noted exceptions of Joshua Leavitt in New York, Benjamin Carr in Philadelphia, and Lowell Mason in Boston, most song leaders lacked the pedagogical expertise or patience needed to train those who were musically illiterate to sing hymns in worship settings. The qualitative and operational distinctions between the musician as enabler and the musician as performer soon became a problem area. In the nineteenth century the problem developed into a deep controversy about music and musical leadership, a controversy enlivened and sustained by the proliferation of tunes and tune books and the rise of the song leader.

Consistent with British evangelical practice, USA hymnbooks were initially printed in a "words-only" format. The tunes, with a stanza of a particular hymn interlined, were printed in a separate tune book for the benefit of the song leader. With the expansion of the repertory of tunes it was not always possible to assume that all who gathered would know the same tunes. As the tune repertory was expanded to accommodate the wider range of poetic meters, particularly the hymns of Charles Wesley, simple recall on the part of the singers was replaced by rote teaching from a tune book by a song leader.

The notion of the worshipper having or in any profound sense using a hymnal with tunes had little impact on the standard words-only format, except in some few instances where tunes were appended in a small section at the back of the book. To facilitate the recall of the tune by other than its melody, names were provided for each tune. Tunes were named for cities, AMSTERDAM (**96**); streets, BOYLSTON (**413**); persons, ACKLEY (**310**); and countless other categories (see "Index of Tune Names," **931**). With tune names listed alphabetically it was possible for the song leader to call out the tune name to the singers who would respond on hearing the name of the tune by telling the song leader whether or not it was familiar. This practice became very complicated when in time the same name was used for one or more tunes. (For more information see Robert Guy McCutchan, *Hymn Tune Names.*)

THE METERS OF TUNES AND TEXTS

In addition to being listed by names, tunes were cross-referenced by meter (see "Metrical Index," **926**). The initials CM, for example, were used as an abbreviation of the term Common Meter, meaning 8 6. 8 6, or four lines of poetry with eight syllables or words on the first and third lines, and six on the second and fourth, as in the first stanza of "O for a thousand tongues" (57):

O **for** a **thous**and **tongues** to **sing**	(eight)
my **great** Redeemer's **praise,**	(six)
the **glories of** my **God** and **King,**	(eight)
the **triumphs of** his **grace!**	(six)

For a succinct review of meter and poetic foot, see Austin C. Lovelace, "A Survey of Tunes," *Companion to the Hymnal*, 1970, excerpts of which follow:

The most common metrical designs are Common Meter (listed in the hymnal as CM [86.86]), Short Meter (SM [66.86]), and Long Meter (LM [88.88]). When "D" is added to any of these (or any series of numbers), it stands for "Double" and means that the pattern is repeated. . . . All of these meters, along with numerous others, use *iambic* movement [or foot]; that is, the first syllable is unaccented, and the second is accented in any pair of syllables [see above]. . . . The reverse of this pattern is called *trochaic* and begins with an accented syllable followed by a weak syllable. (Gealy, Lovelace, Young 1970, 41, italics added)

In our hymnal, an example is found at 400:

Come, thou **Fount** of **every blessing,**

Lovelace continues with an explanation of the remaining two patterns:

All hymns in 77.77 are *trochaic*, along with other meters which are based on the "falling foot." When an accent is followed by two weak syllables, the pattern is called "dactyllic." (Gealy, Lovelace, and Young 1970, 41)

For example:

Immor**tal, in**visi**ble, God** only **wise (103).**

When the two weak syllables precede the strong accent, the movement is called "anapestic.". . . A wide variety of meters is possible in poetry using only these four patterns because of the varying number of syllables in each line of poetry. It takes fourteen syllables to sing the first line of "Praise to the Lord, the Almighty" [139]. (Gealy, Lovelace, Young 1970, 41)

For example, look at the following:

1	2	3	4	5	6	7	8	9	10	11	12	13	14

"Praise to the Lord, the Al-might-y, the King of cre-a-tion"

In our hymnal, when none of the three basic patterns of Common Meter, Short Meter, or Long Meter are used, numbers indicating the meter are placed at the lower right hand of the page under the tune name. See, for example, "Immortal, invisible, God only wise" **(103)**:

> ST. DENIO
>
> 11 11.11 11

Lovelace continues:

> A period is used to indicate which lines go together to make up a rhyme scheme or a group of lines which carry a single thought. For example, OLD 113TH [the tune for "I'll praise my Maker while I've breath" **(60)**, see below] is listed as 888.888 since the rhyme scheme is AA B CC B (breath-death, powers; past-last, endures–which is a false rhyme with "powers"). (Gealy, Lovelace, Young 1970, 42)

I'll praise my Maker while I've breath;	[A]
and when my voice is lost in death,	[A]
praise shall employ my nobler powers.	[B]
My days of praise shall ne'er be past,	[C]
while life, and thought, and being last,	[C]
or immortality endures.	[B]

Yet, Lovelace points out that ST. PETERSBURG ("Thou hidden source of calm repose," 153), even though with six lines of poetry, is listed as 88.88.88 because of its rhyme scheme:

Thou hidden source of calm repose,	[A]
thou all—sufficient love divine,	[B]
my help and refuge from my foes,	[A]
secure I am if thou art mine;	[B]
and lo! from sin and grief and shame	[C]
I hide me, Jesus, in thy name.	[C]

In conclusion, Lovelace states:

> Therefore the text of hymn **[60]** . . . cannot be sung conveniently with the tune for hymn . . . **[153]** although there are the same number of syllables and the same number of lines. Likewise, an *iambic* tune such as AURELIA ["The church's one foundation" **(545)**] cannot be substituted for ST. KEVIN ["Come ye faithful raise the strain" **(315)**] which is *trochaic*, though both are 76.76.D. (Gealy, Lovelace, Young 1970, 41, italics added)

As a result of the complex problems related to the expanding repertory, to facilitate teaching the hymns, tune books were produced for use with a particular hymnal or hymnals, and conversely, tune names were placed under or near the title or first line of the hymn and were cross-referenced to several separate tune books. This practice of separate tune books was still used a century later when the (Northern) Methodist Episcopal Church in 1857 produced *Tunes for Congregational Worship* as a supplement to its 1849 official hymnal, containing 300 hundred tunes, most in the five basic meters, with fifty indicated as PM or peculiar meter, e.g., 87.87.87. (*The United Methodist Hymnal* has over 500 tunes in 340 meters, including 115 in irregular meters.)

CONGREGATIONAL SONG AT MID-CENTURY

Developments in the leadership of congregational song through mid-century may be summarized as follows:

1. The general conference of ordained clergy received and began to express authority in matters hymnic and musical. The official hymnal emerged as the province of the General Conference, and unofficial hymnals and songbooks were remanded to the church's publishing interests and private music publishers.
2. Some clergy who could not deal with the proliferation and complications of music-hymnic resources hired trained musicians to lead congregational singing.
3. Music leaders also emerged as skilled compilers, editors, and publishers of tune and anthem books. See "Hymnals of The Methodist Church: Authorized Hymnals," page 96.
4. The competition of the secular singing school, with its repertory of standard hymns of Watts and Wesley set to engaging anthems and fuging tunes, caused local church choirs and choruses to be hastily formed to perform in Methodist worship. This development not only expanded the task of the song leader to choir director, in time the musician's primary task, but eventually divided the congregation and its function and repertory from the choir's.
5. Qualitative and operational distinctions emerged between the musician as enabler and the musician as performer. The pastor-in-charge, who was preacher-performer, and the singer-performer choir and its leader began to vie for performance times and spaces.

The preface to the 1857 tune book, while illustrating the problems posed by the expanding musical repertory, states that the desired role of song leaders should be as enablers rather than lecturers:

Now, if the friends of the enterprise [i.e., the long awaited tunebook], especially our ministers and leading singers, will interest themselves in bringing the work before the people, we have little doubt of its success. It would be desirable for the congregations to meet occasionally to *practice* —that is, to *sing* the tunes, rather than study the principles upon which they are constructed. Though it may be impossible to induce them to learn the science of music, many will learn to sing, if they are properly encouraged.

Frequent examples given by the leader, of the proper manner of singing, will be found to be very serviceable. Good-natured perseverance will surmount all difficulties, and insure good earnest congregational singing, both where there are choirs and where there are none. (Preface to *Tunes for Congregational Worship*, 1857)

By mid-century, by any measurement, the musical aspects of Wesleyan hymnody at the applied level had become nearly chaotic. William C. Rice in his unpublished doctoral dissertation, "A Century of Methodist Music: 1859-1950," paraphrases Erastus Wentworth's "Methodism and Music" (1865):

The flood of new books and new methods that went with the "singing school" fad of the preceding generation was responsible for the purchase and rapid discarding of numerous tune collections until every group owned an embarrassingly large stack of slightly used books. (Rice 1953, 26)

The solution was to replace the many tune books, which a "tune-smith," precentor, or song leader had to have in hand to lead effectively in congregational song, with a single volume hymnal with words and music on the same page. This trend was quickened during Reconstruction times with the advent of the privately published gospel songbook with simple, easily learned tunes interlined for each text. By 1870 the publishing interests of the churches keenly felt the competition of the unified music and words format of the popular gospel hymn collection. With the assistance of the church's hymnal revision committee, the publication of the 1878 hymnal invoked a dramatic and lasting change in the format of our hymnals. (See the seventy-six-page report, *The Revision of the Hymn Book of the Methodist Episcopal Church.*)

THE 1878 HYMNAL OF THE METHODIST EPISCOPAL CHURCH

The 1878 book set the pace for all succeeding hymnals, including *The Hymnal*, 1957, and *The Methodist Hymnal*, 1966. This book succeeded in setting aside the established practice of printing separate tune books for use by the song leader and accompanist by "wedding" particular tunes with texts of the same meter and printing them on the same page in four-part harmony. The fixing of the appropriate tune was justified by the hymnal committee:

We have sought to make the *actual adaptation* of tunes to hymns, and not merely to print the music within reach, and then leave the particular selection to the choristers. For the chorister to practice disregarding or changing the adaptations, is, in our judgment, fatal to the success of such a book, and hence in our plan we have intended to make them definite, providing, however, whenever practicable, for an alternative choice between the old tune and one newer and fresher. (*Revision* 1878, 71)

Thus a unified "full music edition" was produced to be used by the singer in the pew, the choir, and the accompanist. The results of this new format established, in fact, mandated, one and sometimes two tunes for each text. With the practice of textual interlining it modified and in some instances significantly reduced, but more often than not destroyed, the expressive power of metaphor, sentence structure, and word accent. Words became subservient to music. The essential character of the strophic hymn ceased to be poetic, the prosody set aside as in an anthem or part song. The hymnal became a powerful advocate for music at the expense of poetry and was intended for singers not readers.

In *An English-Speaking Hymnal Guide*, Erik Routley has commented on the subsequently lost pleasure of reading hymns:

> That is the godly and sensible pleasure of *reading* hymns. I do not mean reading them communally in church, which strikes me as a miserable substitute for that cheerful song which is now the delight of all Christian communions. I mean reading them in solitude, reading them as lyric poetry. When one does this, their crudities and roughness, which any literary critic must observe, which the lover of hymns must admit, and which some Christians (among them my revered C. S. Lewis) have openly despised, become softened by the associations of communal song which these texts must inevitably carry. . . . I simply grieve to think that this particular pleasure and religious nourishment is withheld from so many or ignored by so many in these later days. (Routley 1979, v-vi)

The hymnal greatly expanded the repertory, placing side by side standard evangelical tunes of the eighteenth and early nineteenth centuries, USA fuging tunes from shaped-note songbooks, and Lowell Mason's tunes and his adaptations of tunes by Handel and Haydn. Folk melodies of Great Britain, northern Europe, and the USA were placed alongside Lutheran chorales (in isorhythmic form), Anglican chants (forty single and double chants), and "new and popular" four-part English parish hymn tunes by Dykes and Barnby. Missing was the African American spiritual, even though some of that repertory had been in print for most of the decade. (For examples of the above, see "Music of *the* United Methodist *Hymnal*," pages 166-70; and for an annotation of hymns in the 1878 hymnal and the first attempt to list the official hymnals of The Methodist Church, see Charles S. Nutter, *Hymn Studies*, 1897 3d ed.)

The selection of ecumenical and historic texts, also seen in the contents of the Presbyterian and Episcopal hymnals of that decade, was greatly influenced by *Hymns Ancient and Modern*, 1861. (See "Hymnals of The Methodist Church," pages 91-122, and page 15 in the discussion of "British Hymns.")

HYMNALS AND WORSHIP FORMS

The 1878 hymnal and its counterparts, the hymnals of the Methodist Episcopal Church, South, 1889, the Methodist Church, 1872, and the Methodist Protestant Church, 1882, defined USA Methodist congregational song more than any previous books within the style of worship that for two decades had been developing in the urban establishment churches of the eastern seaboard, the East, and the Northeast. If one were to classify this type of worship within the Wesleyan tradition, it would be more catholic than evangelical, more formal than spontaneous. And most significant, its congregations perceived themselves as more educated and sophisticated than their counterparts in rural settings:

> For our Methodism is not now, as it was at first, struggling for a foothold and recognition, or simply carrying the Gospel to the ignorant and degraded; but it sustains pastoral relations to millions, among whom are the prosperous, the cultured and the influential. (*Revision* 1878, 42)

This liturgical reform was in essence a return by Methodists to their Anglican roots in *The Sunday Service of the Methodists in North America, with Other Occasional Services,* which John Wesley in 1784 had sent to American Methodists. Harmon discusses the importance of these services:

> Thus in 1784 from the English *Book of Common Prayer,* whose history we have followed to this point, John Wesley, founder of the people called Methodists, framed a Liturgy which he intrusted to Thomas Coke, Richard Whatcoat, and Thomas Vasey to bring to America. This Liturgy was intitled: "The Sunday Service of the Methodists in North America, with Other Occasional Services"; London: Printed in the year 1784. It was an abridgment of the *Book of Common Prayer* of the Church of England, including twenty-four of the thirty-nine Articles of that Church; and for ordination—which last were for the perpetuation of ministerial orders in Methodism. This was the "Prayer Book" or "American Liturgy" which Mr. Wesley evidently intended should be the Ark of the Covenant for American Methodism, just as the parent Book had been for the Church of England. (Harmon 1926, 39)

The fate of the services during the nineteenth century is described by James. F. White:

> Wesley's service was little used, the Americans being convinced that they could pray better with their books and eyes shut than with them open. In 1792 the 305 pages of *The Sunday Service* were reduced to eight services in 37 pages in the back of the *Discipline.* Morning prayer and evening prayer were not among them. For more than a century Methodist ministers concocted their own order of worship without assistance from official forms. Due to revivalism, evangelistic preaching often dominated the entire service. (White 1970, 16)

For further commentary on Wesley's *Sunday Service* see *John Wesley's Prayer Book* with introduction, notes, and commentary by James F. White; and White 1989, 153-57. For a survey of nineteenth-century Methodist worship practice, see William N. Wade, "A History of Public Worship in the Methodist Episcopal Tradition."

In implementing the return to Wesley's liturgy the reformers also affirmed the fundamentals of order and authority in church government as stated by Richard Whatcoat, one of the founders of the USA church:

> We agreed [in 1784] to form a Methodist Episcopal Church in which the liturgy (as presented by the Rev. John Wesley) should be read, and the sacraments be administered by a superintendent, elders, and deacons, who shall be ordained by a presbytery, using the Episcopal form, as prescribed in the Rev. Mr. Wesley's prayer book. (Harmon 1926, 44)

The reformers also attempted to strike a balance between the freedom of the Brush Arbor camp meeting and the structured formal worship of the urban Gothic structures. Bishop Nolan Harmon quotes R. J. Cooke:

> It is not the genius of Methodism to be confined to forms. With Christian art and ceremony as such, Methodism can have no conflict. To her thought there would be nothing incongruous in holding a "revival" service under the dome of St. Peter's, in the aisles of Cologne, or under the spires of Milan, in which the joyful shouts of new-born souls and the sobbings of the penitent would take the place of the swelling organ and Gregorian chant. A cathedral, or a leafy bower in the forest—she is at home in either. (Harmon 1926, 48)

As Sunday morning worship moved away from the traditional evangelical revival-preaching format, the hymnal-songbook that had served that setting for eight decades was set aside in favor of a worshipbook that was thought could more adequately serve the urban church's emerging liturgical-hymnic needs. A footnote at viii in the preface of the 1873 edition of the Methodist Church, *The Voice of Praise*, 1871, demonstrates one of the desired qualities of a hymnal for the emerging urban worship setting:

> The hymns in this book are so arranged as, in no instance, to cross over from the right-hand page to the next page forward. The foot of every right-hand page ends the hymn. Hence no rustling of leaves by turning during service.

The same hymnal of the Methodist Church (formally part of the Methodist Protestant Church) appears to be the first general hymnal to provide worship forms, aids to worship, and musical settings of the traditional and occasional chants:

SIX CHANTS WITH POINTING:
1. Gloria Patri
2. Psalm 23
3. Lukean account of shepherds, "There were shepherds abiding in the field," etc.
4. The Lord's Prayer
5. Baptismal Chant, "The mercy of the Lord is from everlasting to everlasting upon them that fear him, and his righteousness unto children's children, etc., mixed with Isaiah, "He shall feed his flock," "Suffer the little children"; the Matthewian postscript: "Go ye, therefore, and teach all nations, baptizing them," etc.
6. Funeral Chant: "If a man die, shall he live again?", ending with Job, "I know that my Redeemer liveth"

22 DOXOLOGIES (most of them carried over from previous hymnals)

RITUALISTIC SERVICES (beginning on page 717)

ADMISSION TO MEMBERSHIP

THE LORD'S SUPPER
(Some additional rubrics are offered in a four-paragraph postscript, including one that may be the first documentation of the practice of table dismissals via hymns sung.)

"While administering the Supper, one of the ministers should occasionally give out an appropriate verse or two of a hymn, to be sung by the congregation. This might be so timed as to serve for a signal for those who have communed, to rise and retire to their places in the church, and give opportunity for the remaining communicants to repair to the table."

BAPTISM OF INFANTS
BAPTISM OF ADULTS

MARRIAGE

THE DEAD (Burial Service)

THE APOSTLES' CREED, with "he descended into the grave"; and "Holy Catholic" (cap "C")

SCRIPTURE SENTENCES APPROPRIATE TO OPENING PUBLIC SERVICES (13 selections)

The 1878 book included, in addition to hymns, the rituals of "Baptism," "Reception of Members," and "The Lord's Supper" (ending with the "Gloria In Excelsis," the setting identical to **82**). To demonstrate the increasing influence of liturgical reform the church's official order for public worship was printed on the inside front cover of the 1896 edition. This marks the first appearance in a Methodist hymnal of an official order of worship—a service of word, song and prayer.

ORDER OF PUBLIC WORSHIP
OF THE METHODIST EPISCOPAL CHURCH
ADOPTED BY THE GENERAL CONFERENCE,
MAY 1896
[Parts in brackets may be omitted.]*

1. [VOLUNTARY.]
2. SINGING FROM THE HYMNAL, the people standing.
3. [THE APOSTLES CREED.] (The complete text was included, minus "he descended into hell.")
4. PRAYER, the minister and people kneeling, concluding with the Lord's Prayer, repeated audibly by all.
5. [ANTHEM.]
6. LESSON FROM THE OLD TESTAMENT, which if from the Psalms, may be read responsively. (No readings are included in the hymnal.)
7. [THE GLORIA PATRI.] (Meineke **(70)** was printed and scored for two voices: soprano and alto.)
8. LESSON FROM THE NEW TESTAMENT.
9. COLLECTION AND NOTICES.
10. SINGING FROM THE HYMNAL, the people standing.
11. SERMON.
12. SHORT PRAYER, for a blessing on the Word.
13. SINGING, closing with a doxology. (19 doxologies are included in the hymnal.)
14. THE APOSTOLIC BENEDICTION.

* Comments within the parentheses are the present writer's.

Expectations for the use of the hymnal in the liturgy are described by Nolan Harmon in his comprehensive *Rites and Rituals of Episcopal Methodism*. Harmon comments on the singing of hymns during Holy Communion:

> The singing of a hymn, as called for in the Southern Book [Methodist Episcopal Church, South], is in line with Christian consciousness as well as with the spirit and atmosphere of this act. The minister should have the hymn ready and there should be no overtures nor interludes in singing it. Dr. Summers [in his 1874 Commentary] advises that there should be no singing during the distribution of the elements, but only at intervals. "Sing the hymns for the Lord's Supper in the Hymn book—there are none like them." (Harmon 1926, 146)

Concerning congregational singing of the service, Harmon continues:

> Bishop Cooke declares that if this prayer [the Gloria] is to be said it should be said by all; if sung, then sung by all. "But it is more in harmony with the first

Communion service to sing the *Gloria in Excelsis* than to say it. . . . No Liturgy in the world comes to a more solemn or majestic conclusion . . . and it is fitting that all who have partaken of the holy institution should sing their gratitude in the peerless Hymn of the Universal Church." (Harmon 1926, 150)

Harmon concludes with Summers's instruction for music for "The Service of the Burial of the Dead": "Dr. Summers in explanation of this rubric in the Southern Book states: 'It (the hymn) should be judiciously selected by the Minister from the rich variety of funeral hymns in our hymnal.'" (Harmon 1926, 302)

URBAN METHODIST WORSHIP AND MUSIC

Although espousing the ideals and programs of the urban revival, the temperance movement, local and world missions, and the Sunday school, the urban church also competed with other mid-stream Protestant churches in attracting middle and upper class professionals. Some of these churches became preoccupied with applying good taste to worship practice, architecture, music, and even the dress of their ushers. Sunday morning worship focused on quality preaching and musical performance in a formal setting with the literate and sophisticated the intended audience. For the most part the popular music of the revival was relegated to missions, rallies, revivals, and the Sunday school.

New and larger worship spaces were constructed to accommodate the burgeoning congregations. To support congregational singing and undergird the congregation's learning the new hymnic repertory, chorus choirs were formed, and organs were installed.

There should be a choir or a precentor, and an organ, if possible, to lead the people. The best arrangement is to have the choir and organ in front of the congregation. (*The Methodist Hymnal* 1878, vii)

Eben Tourjée, prominent USA music educator who had studied in Germany and in 1867 with Robert Goldbeck founded the New England Conservatory of Music, was the most influential voice in church music of his day. He served as one of the music editors of the 1878 Methodist Episcopal Church hymnal and was the compiler and general editor of the 1882 Methodist Protestant Church hymnal, *The Tribute of Praise*. His introduction to the latter hymnal (printed below) ranks in influence in the music of USA hymnody with Ralph Vaughan Williams's preface to the music of the 1906 *English Hymnal* (revised 1933). Its comprehensive statement of urban American musical taste influenced for nearly a century the development of the music and worship spaces of Protestant worship, the performance practice and repertory for organ, brass, and choir, the professional standards for church musicians including their relationships with clergy, and the emerging roles for choir and congregation.

INTRODUCTION

The publication of this present work will, it is hoped and believed, greatly facilitate the more general adoption in our churches and social meetings, of song as an element of worship. In its production, extensive researches have been made made in both European and American psalmody, from which the best tunes have been carefully selected. Above the fifty of the most popular and useful German and English chorals, the singing of which has delighted and edified Christian hearts in all lands since the day of Luther, have been added.

Prepared with special reference to encouraging and assisting *the people* to engage in choral worship, it will be found replete with those standard familiar congregational tunes so precious for many years to the hearts of all denomination of believers, together with an extensive collection of the best and most popular production of modern composers. Trashy and sentimental compositions have been discarded.

The Department for the Choir will be found especially rich in English and Gregorian Chants, Sentences, and Chorals, with a very choice selection of tunes. The Te Deum, Gloria in Excelsis, Gloria Patri, and Responses for the Commandments are also included.

An important feature of the work is its collection of hymns and tunes for the use of social meetings. It comprises a large number of those most extensively known, with many others which have been greatly admired wherever introduced, and which promise to achieve an enduring popularity. Great pains have been taken to make this department complete, and it is believed that it embraces all that is essential for the musical service of prayer and conference meetings. While some of its hymns and and tunes may not fulfil the requirements of the most fastidious taste, their inherent usefulness, and the devotional spirit they breathe, have secured their introduction. No hymn or tune should be discarded on account of defects in its structure, if upon trial it is found to enkindle, or give utterance to, the devotional fervor of the church of Christ.

A number of attractive Sunday School hymns and tunes have been added, to give completeness to the work.

The following suggestions must be carefully observed, in order to secure successful

CHOIR AND CONGREGATIONAL SINGING.

They embody the results of a long experience, and it is believed that wherever adopted, they will be followed by gratifying results.

1. An organ and a choir are essential to the proper maintenance of singing as an element of worship in church service.

2. The organ should be of sufficient power to sustain and lead the congregation in the general song; and should contain such a variety of registers as will furnish a suitable accompaniment to the choir, and at the same time give the organist proper scope for the voluntaries. Its appropriate position is in the rear of the pulpit, or divided and placed on each side of it.

3. The organist and chorister should be well fitted for their respective position, both by their musical knowledge, and by their religious character.

4. The first organ voluntary should be dignified, devout, bringing the first offerings of adoration and prayer which arise from the assembled multitude: all mere displays of execution are out of place and inconsistent with the impressive services of the house of God. It should seldom exceed five minutes in length, and ought to be brought to a close with the softest stops as soon as the congregation are seated and the minister is ready to commence the services. In the concluding voluntary the desires and aspirations for a holier life awakened in the hearts of the people by the sermon should be deepened by the sympathetic tones of the organ. Otherwise it had better be dispensed with altogether.

5. The choir*, where practicable, may be arranged in two divisions, one composed principally of children, with men's voices for the tenor and bass parts, another of adults, including the solo voices. It should be located on each side of the pulpit, or in front of the body pews, *upon a level with the congregation*, its divisions facing each other. It should consist of at least twenty-four trained voices (sixty would be much better), whose duty it will be, —

First: To sing music bequeathed to us by the great masters, ancient and modern, the correct rendering of which will serve to impress the minds of the people with the sacredness and beauty of divine worship, and prepare their hearts for the prayers and songs which are to follow. A secular music should be rigorously excluded; long solos and *virtuoso* display should seldom be permitted, as their tendency is rather to produce a critical rather than a devotional frame of mind; in fact, each hymn, chant, or anthem should be given as an individual act of worship by every participant.

Second: To assist and lead the congregation in the general song. Here all must remember that choir and congregation are now to become an

---

*Called, respectively, the "Cantores" and "Decani" choir.

assembly of devout worshippers, raising heart and voice in one united song of praise to a common Father and Redeemer.

6. CHANTING, which is not only the most ancient but also the most devotional method of worshipping by song, has of late years been entirely abandoned in most churches. The Psalms of David were thus sung nearly three thousand years ago, and it was the only kind of music known to the church during the first six centuries of the Christian era. A revival of this primitive, simple style of worship is highly desirable.

The chants in this work furnish a suitable variety both for choir and congregational use. The double chant, from its resemblance to the ornamental style of church psalmody, is particularly adapted to the choir, and should rarely be attempted by the congregation, while the simplicity and dignity of the Gregorian and other single chants best adapt them as a means by which "a congregation may, in a pleasing and devotional manner, read together the words of God."

The single chant consists of two divisions or strains, the first containing three and the second four bars. The double chant consists of four divisions of three and four bars arranged alternately. . . .

7. Congregational singing should be introduced at least twice in each service. In order to prepare the people for joining generally in this exercise, "Praise Meetings" should be frequently held under the joint direction of the pastor and chorister [chorister=music director] in which the congregation may join in singing familiar tunes. The choir should always be present at these occasions, and lend their assistance by singing with the congregation; by introducing from time to time new tunes which may be sung by the congregation at subsequent meetings; and also by occasionally singing appropriate select pieces. The pastor should frequently intersperse the singing exercise with short addresses, containing incidents concerning the hymns or tunes, and other remarks appropriate to the occasion. As far as practicable, they should be divested of all formality, and rendered social and attractive.

When properly conducted, such meetings cannot fail to awaken the people to a new interest in church music, infuse them with the spirit of song, quicken their religious life, and give a new impetus to every department of church labor. Indeed, so great has been their influence, that, in several instances, powerful revivals have resulted from their introduction. The regular weekly prayer meeting may be most appropriately and profitably prefaced by a half hour's service of this character.

8. The tunes which the congregation are expected to sing should be selected by the chorister with reference to their adaptation to the hymn and to their familiarity to the people. If the tune set to the hymn is not

generally known, another which is familiar should be chosen, and its name, and the page where it may be found, announced by the minister.

Fugue tunes [fuging tunes] are quite unsuited for congregational use. A few have, however, been introduced into this volume in deference to the earnest wish of friends to whom they are exceedingly precious. In general, the tune upon the opposite page may be substituted.

9. The minister and chorister ought to mutually confer with each other with reference to the selections to be used, and all the arrangements should be completed beforehand, so that the utmost promptness may be secured in the commencement and progress of the service. A grave responsibility rests upon the minister in connection with the musical exercises of the church, which he should be competent to direct, if necessary. If he is indifferent or unsympathetic, they will rarely be carried on with efficiency.

10. The organist should give out the tune by playing the melody upon the great organ with loud stops, and the harmony upon the swell or choir organ. The *tempo* must never be taken so fast but that the congregation can easily join.

11. *The minister and congregation should rise while the organist is playing the last line of the prelude*, the congregation always facing the pulpit.

12. At the conclusion of the prelude, let the organist begin the tune upon the great organ with full harmony, giving the first chord as an arpeggio from the pedal note upwards, and the choir and congregation immediately join together upon the first note of the tune.

   The choir may sing either the harmony or the melody, but *the congregation should invariably sing the melody*. In order to facilitate this, the key of the tunes has been arranged, wherever practicable, so that the melody shall not ascend above E. The organist should accompany the choir and congregation generally with the full organ, and confine himself solely to the notes of the tune.

13. The last note of each line should be sustained whenever the musical structure of the tunes will admit.

14. Interludes savor of display, and divert the attention of the worshipper, and should be omitted, the pedal note being continued between the verses.

15. At the conclusion of the hymn the organist may play a few chords, giving a *decrescendo* effect while the congregation are being seated.

16. The congregation should be invited, encouraged, and exhorted, if necessary, to join with heart and voice in this delightful service. *All* should sing, and sing "lustily"; and all endeavors to produce artistic effects should be avoided.

17. Wherever practicable, it is desirable that the singing should be accompanied by one or more brass instruments. The congregation are thereby sustained and borne along, and the devotional effect is very greatly improved.

18. FINALLY, it is indispensable to the success of congregation singing, that each pew should be liberally supplied with tune books.

The subscriber records, with profound gratitude, the increasing favor with which congregation singing is everywhere regarded. If this work shall hasten on the day, when from every church in the land shall ascend one general song of praise from the united voices of choir and congregation entire, we shall feel that our labor has not been in vain.   (Tourjée 1884, pages iii-vi)

Tourjée's philosophy united congregation and choir into one "general song of praise." It was a way for urban churches to continue, for different theological and liturgical reasons, the unity of song and word that was the compelling and integrating force of revivalism's fourfold worship model: praise, prayer, proclamation, and conversion.

The implementation of Tourjée's music program by urban Methodist churches was part of the return to Wesley's worship ways begun in the 1870's. According to Gerald O. McCulloh in "The Theology and Practice of Methodism, 1876-1919," by 1919 the character of Methodist worship was fundamentally changed:

Methodism had passed through its period of greatest informality in worship. In 1881 [at the ecumenical Methodist conference] "formality" had been classed with "worldliness" and "improper amusements" as a peril to Methodism. The proper place for the "rags of ritualism" was then said to be "in the wastebasket." But now, in the first two decades of the twentieth century, liturgy and the established ritual were being restored to use in Methodist churches. (Bucke 1964, 2:636)

During the passage, worship, formerly the means of converting the illiterate and unchurched, moved away from an evangelical revival-preaching format to "aestheticism and worship as social crusade." (White 1990, 166) Sunday morning worship allied the orator-preacher with musical performance in a programmed appeal to the educated upward-bound middle and upper classes for social action, benevolent giving, and charitable acts. Those who had been saved from sins of poverty and illiteracy gladly returned for Sunday vesper and evening services to hear their own success stories retold in vibrant biblical images reinforced by organ, vocal, and choir music.

The song leader, a position stemming from the Reconstruction-times revival, was replaced by the choir and organ. The revival chorus-choir gave way to an ensemble of paid singers whose stated purpose was the support of congregational song. In most places, however, the roar of the almighty pipe organ sufficed, and choirs performed in Anglo-Catholic fashion as an offering on behalf of the congregation. Congregational song was redefined within a tripart worship paradigm: hymn singing, choral music, and preaching. The traditional hymnal-songbook was set aside in favor of a worshipbook, and hymnals became a proving ground for literacy and sophistication. The substantial and familiar repertory of "other worldly" and "nonsocial" folk hymnody and gospel hymns was supplanted by mission hymns, the forerunners of the social gospel hymn, and the ecumenical repertory from *Hymns Ancient and Modern*, 1861.

Since the 1870's each revision of our church's official hymnals has been the battleground for the opposing forces of this change. At the local level the music program was increasingly referred to as the "War Department." In 1914 Ruth W. Alexander complained of the

> rivalries, the jealousies, the fractions, the factions, the insubordinations, and the quarrels that are born in, and fostered by, this department.

> In the music of our churches today the spiritual and ethical elements are almost completely ignored, and, what is worse, our taste and capacity for specifically religious music are being destroyed. . . . Church music in our day has been popularized but debased. . . . And many . . . of the hymn writers of today do not stop to consider what kind of emotion their songs excite, just so it be emotion. . . . From our choirs and soloists we usually get sensational quasi operatic selections and displays of vocal pyrotechnics; and from our congregation, loose, flimsy renditions of sentimental songs. (Alexander 1914, 60:53-66)

Kenneth E. Rowe comments that as urban churches designed worship spaces to accommodate the rural revival tradition they contributed to the development of the Akron-plan sanctuary:

> Evangelists liked sloping floors and semicircular pews to bring the people near. They liked a stage to pace across. Revival choirs left their traditional gallery over the entrance to mount the stage with the evangelist as part of the act. The people, settled down in their cushioned pews as an audience settles in the theater, passively, to watch the professionals perform. (Rowe 1993, 18)

For additional commentary see "Social Gospel Hymns," pages 30-33, Arthur L. Stevenson, *The Story of Southern Hymnody*, and these vintage resources: Waldo Selden Pratt, *Musical Ministries in the Church*, 1901; Edward Dickinson, *Music in the History of the Western Church*, 1908; Edmund S. Lorenz, *Practical Church Music*, 1909; Peter C. Lutkin, *Music in the Church*, 1910; and Carl F. Price, *The Music and Hymnody of the Methodist Hymnal*, 1911.

HYMNALS OF THE EVANGELICAL UNITED BRETHREN CHURCH

THE HYMNODY OF THE UNITED BRETHREN IN CHRIST

According to Ellen Jane Lorenz Porter, "The history of Evangelical United Brethren hymnody is yet to be written." (Porter 1987, 74) While it is true that there is no composite history, there has been recent significant research and commentary including *Pennsylvania Spirituals* by Don Yoder, 1961 (Yoder's hymn collection is housed in the music library of the University of North Carolina at Chapel Hill); "Singet Hallelujah!" by Terry Heisey in *Methodist History*, 1990; Kenneth E. Rowe's unpublished listing, "Authorized United Brethren Hymnals"; and Porter's work in *Journal of Theology*, 1987. In addition, James I. Warren in *O for a Thousand Tongues* provides a linkage of the hymnic traditions of the two branches of United Methodism.

The Book of Discipline of The United Methodist Church, 1988, discusses the origins of this branch of United Methodism:

> The Evangelical United Brethren Church had its roots in the spiritual quick-ening which emerged in the United States in the late eighteenth and early nineteenth centuries. This movement challenged not only religious indiffer-ence, but all the contemporary tendency to substitute "religion" for a vital and experiential relationship with God. (*The Book of Discipline 1988*, 11)

A history of the background of this movement is provided by J. Bruce Behney and Paul H. Eller:

> The German revival movements, which culminated in the United Brethren and Evangelical Churches, antedated the Second Awakening, but coin-cided with it as they entered their denominational phase. The beginnings of the United Brethren and Evangelical Churches were the result of several causative factors: religious (theological-pietistic), nationalistic (German), and cultural (pioneer-agricultural). (Behney and Eller 1979, 31)

The founder of the United Brethren Church was Philip William Otterbein, 1726-1813, who came to America in 1752 and served pastorates in the German Reformed Church in Pennsylvania and Maryland. In 1773 he was called to the German Reformed Church in Baltimore where he met Francis Asbury. Behney and Eller note the results of this meeting:

> The intimacy of Otterbein and Asbury led to many occasions when they and their respective colleagues joined forces in evangelistic work—one

group preaching in German, the other in English. However, in spite of this close fellowship in purpose and labor, the German and the English Methodist movements did not coalesce. Two reasons are given: the difference in language and the difference in concepts of authority. (Behney and Eller 1979, 55)

The traditional hymnody of the German Reformed Church did not adequately serve Otterbein's evangelicals any more than did John Wesley's 1780 classic hymnal suit the needs of American Methodists. The earliest hymnal, *Das Aller Neuste Harfenspiel*, published in 1795, was produced to serve the needs of the Bush-Meeting Dutch, before "the camp-meeting retreaded their hymnody into something completely American." (Yoder 1961, 388-89) Along with revival hymns, its contents included many standard seventeenth- and eighteenth-century German hymns, including "O Haupt! voll blut und wunden," "O sacred Head, now wounded" **(286)**. This pattern continued into the early nineteenth century as revival, Mennonite, and Moravian hymns as well as translations of Watts and Wesley were placed alongside the older German hymns.

THE HYMNODY OF THE EVANGELICAL ASSOCIATION

The second major branch of the former Evangelical United Brethren Church was the *Evangelische Gemeinschaft*, the Evangelical Association, founded by Jacob Albright, 1759-1808:

Albright was attracted to the Methodists by their preaching and their *Discipline*, not their singing. In all the hagiographies there is no mention, with all the testimonies to his forceful preaching and radiant spirituality, of his singing voice. His call was to preach to an indifferent, even hostile, people, the Pennsylvania Germans. Only after his preaching had born fruit in little Methodist classes could his disciples join in praise and song. Yet, Albright surely sang the English hymns of Wesley and Watts in Isaac Davis' Methodist class, which he joined after his conversion in 1791. From the very first, the meetings of the Albright People including [*sic*] singing, mostly the seventeenth-century Pietist chorales (hymns) of their Lutheran and Reformed heritage.

Soon, however, a new century brought a new form of worship and outreach, the camp meeting, and a new form of sacred song, the camp meeting or "bush-meeting" spiritual, ideally suited to the Methodist and Evangelical spirit. The Methodists quickly spread the new ways from the Kentucky frontier (1800-1801), where they started, to southeastern Pennsylvania (1804), and the third (1810) Annual Conference of the Albright People organized the first two German camp meetings in the world. Just as quickly, the simple yet rhythmic choruses and songs with choruses sung around the camp fires were translated, adapted, and extended by the Evangelicals. (Heisey 1990, 237-38)

Yoder recounts how the texts of the camp-meeting songs found their way into the worship of German-speaking Evangelicals:

> The cultural transfer of revivalism into the German-speaking areas of Pennsylvania and adjacent states involved the translation or adaptation of the camp-meeting hymns into the German language and its more commonplace daughter, Pennsylvania Dutch. This transfer began to take place in the decade 1800-1810. At that time the camp-meeting arrived in Pennsylvania, the first songs were translated or adapted. While the pattern of transfer was set by 1810, the transfer was to continue—English to German, general American to local Pennsylvanian—until after the Civil War. (Yoder 1961, 388)

The publication in 1825 of the book of camp-meeting hymns represented a milestone in the transferral process:

> To [John] Winebrenner is due the honor of publishing the first English camp-meeting songster to appear among the Bush-Meeting Dutch. His *Revival Hymn Book* [1825] has historical importance in revealing to us the originals, in English, of the Wesleyan and American camp-meeting hymns which were translated and sung in German by the Evangelicals and United Brethren. The Winebrennerian songsters are in a sense the intermediate version of the bush-meeting songs, in the transition from the English-language Methodist originals to the fully developed Pennsylvania Dutch spiritual. (Yoder 1961, 397)

The outgrowth of the development of the hymnody of the Evangelicals produced two separate books:

> As time went on, the German hymnal situation in Evangelical circles standardized into two volumes. The more churchly hymns, the great majority of them inherited from the general body of Lutheran and Reformed hymnody, were channeled into the *Geistliches Saitenspiel* which in 1850 was renamed the *Evangelisches Gesangbuch*. The bush-meeting favorites, many of them translations of the English Methodist hymns, or original German productions by the bush-meeting evangelists themselves, found their way into the *Geistliche Viole*. In the 1855 edition, published at Cleveland, Ohio, these two volumes were bound together, with separate pagination and indices. (Yoder 1961, 393)

The history of hymn singing and its performance practice, as presented by both Yoder and Heisey, is not without controversy. The older Lutheran and Reformed practice of "lining out" a hymn persisted until the 1870's, but in time was set aside in favor of singing choruses, which in time also came under criticism because the fundamental question was raised as to the purpose of having a songbook in the hands of the worshipper:

> "Lining out" was never a good solution to the lack of hymnals. Most Evangelicals relied, instead, on memory to sing the few hymns they thought

worth memorizing. By mid-century the singing of the old choruses had become lifeless and "formal," and the repertoire of hymns had dwindled to a very few favorites, sung week after week and sometimes more than once in the same service. (Heisey 1990, 243)

Others raised the issues of taste and decorum (see, for comparison, a discussion of the 1878 *Methodist Hymnal* in the chapter "The Music of Hymns, Wesleyan Style," pages 61-62):

At the same time, a new generation of wealthier, better-educated, more urbanized Evangelicals were beginning to place a greater emphasis on decorum and propriety than the "animal excitement" of the early years. "As society advances," explained the *Evangelical Messenger*, "decorum chastens our exhibition of emotion and the cultivation of the intellect, and the refinement of taste, while they deepen our better feelings, soften their expression." One Evangelical compared the "disgusting" singing of "unintelligible choruses" to the braying of a mule or the music of a farce. (Heisey 1990, 244)

Heisey continues, citing the 1863 "Episcopal Message to the General Conference of the Evangelical Association":

In reference to singing in our congregations, there is still in many places, a great defect apparent, at many places but few hymns are used. . . . Many take no part in this part of the service. . . . Barely the one-hundredth part of our [repertory of] richly spiritual song [is] used. . . . There is [also] a custom prevalent in many places, of allowing almost any one who desires to do so, to select the hymns. And the singing of senseless or absurd choruses, to irreverent tunes, we are sorry to say, is still prevailing in many places, to an extent that seriously disturbs the solemnity of the worship. (Heisey 1990, 244)

Heisey states that the German language became firmly established as the favored language for worship:

A few of the Evangelical classes did begin using the English language in the 1820's and 1830's and English-speaking ministers were accepted into the itinerancy, causing dissension in the young church. The 1830 General Conference acted to prohibit the acceptance of any more non-German-speaking preachers and within a year the English-language work was dead. (Heisey 1990, 242)

The struggle between German and English continued in the publication of English language hymnals:

The hymns in the English hymnbook were not translations of those in the German hymnals. When individuals and congregations changed language and hymnal, they effectively left German sectarianism for the American Protestant mainstream. (Heisey 1990, 243)

Another issue faced by the German Evangelicals was in the challenge, as noted also in the discussion of nineteenth-century Methodism, of sustaining a rural evangelistic worship experience in an increasingly urban setting. Porter observes that the growing use of the Sunday school song and the gospel hymn was an aid in maintaining revivalistic roots:

> Both the United Brethren and the Evangelicals turned naturally to the singing of gospel songs. These began to take over the church services of the less formal congregations in the last third of the nineteenth century. Most of their native hymn writers strongly emphasized the gospel song style. (Porter 1987, 75)

Heisey notes that the use of instruments in worship services did not introduce major differences within the body of worshippers:

> The Evangelical Association never officially opposed the use of instruments in worship, but the spontaneous chorus singing and hymn "lining out" of the early church did not lend themselves to instrumental involvement. In the prosperous Gilded Age, however, Evangelicals began purchasing reed organs for their parlors and having their children taught to play them. Soon, fine new churches began to list organs among their rich appointments, and reports of Sunday School Christmas programs casually extended credit to the "expert performer on the organ." Or [sic] course, conservatives fought the introduction of organs into Sunday Schools. . . . [In time] the regular church service, and pianos were still too closely associated with the saloon to pass muster in the house of God, but the latter years of the century even saw the organization of orchestras in larger Evangelical churches, and instruments were never a major source of contention. (Heisey 1990, 248)

However, one prominent hymn pastor and hymn writer, Benjamin R. Hanby, who wrote "Who is he in yonder stall," see pages 705-06, and the abolitionist song "Darling Nellie Gray" and the Christmas song "Up on the House Top," had difficulty in introducing instruments into worship: "During his ministry at New Paris, Ohio, Hanby's use of musical instruments in church and his liberal theology aroused opposition sufficient to force him from the pastorate." (Harmon 1974, 1:1067)

The presence and the use of choirs in worship did evolve into a major controversy. Those who insisted on incorporating the trappings of middle and upper class respectability into evangelical worship pressured "for permission to organize 'mixed' choirs . . . when many congregations did not even allow men and women to sit 'mixed' on the same side of the church." (Heisey 1990, 248)

Yet, with the success of the leader-soloist of the Reconstruction-day revival song, Heisey writes that a positive force developed within the controversy:

> Some Evangelicals, impressed by D. L. Moody's soloist, Ira D. Sankey (1840-1908), even advocated vocal soloists to root out choirs. Yet, Sankey himself was an advocate of choirs, not as performers of sentimental ballads or replacements for the congregation, but as leaders and enablers of congregational song. . . . In time, church leaders, while rightly condemning inattentive choir members, "fashionable, mincing, lisping, mouthing performances," and compensation for choir to perform in place of the congregation, came to see choirs as a key ingredient, with pipe organs and the new generation of hymnals, in a revitalization of Evangelical worship. (Heisey 1990, 249)

Not unlike Methodism, several former Evangelical United Brethren colleges and universities in the late nineteenth and early twentieth centuries placed high priority on the establishment and maintenance of European conservatory models of music education with strong emphases on choral, vocal, organ, and instrumental performance. With these emphases also came the qualitative distinctions of music "made in school" and "made in church," distinctions persisting to this day. See "The Music of Christian Hymns in USA-Wesleyan Traditions," pages 52-57, and "USA Hymnody," pages 17-19.

Yet Porter observes that both the Evangelicals and the United Brethren had their own native hymnists:

> The Evangelicals had native hymn writers from their beginning. The United Brethren, after borrowing German hymns from the Evangelicals, developed their own hymn writers from the middle of the nineteenth century in the persons of Isaac Baltzell, William Mittendorf, and Edmund S. Lorenz. (Porter 1987, 75)

Porter goes on to point out that the folk traditions of Evangelical United Brethren hymnody were all but dismissed in the formation of the the 1957 *Hymnal*:

> It disappointed some hymnologists on the grounds that it failed to reflect the parental hymnals. Hymn writers, especially from the former United Brethren Church, seemed virtually unrepresented, and the former folk hymn elements were almost entirely lacking. (Porter 1987, 75)

Porter also raised the question if any of the folk traditions of the Evangelical United Brethren hymnody would be included in the present hymnal. For a response to this question, see the article *"The United Methodist Hymnal, 1989,"* pages 129-31.

Kenneth E. Rowe has prepared the following chart and annotations for the authorized hymnals of the former United Brethren Church and the Evangelical Association.

AUTHORIZED HYMNALS OF THE EVANGELICAL UNITED BRETHREN CHURCH

United Brethren Church in Christ

Evangelical Association

1795 *Das Aller Neuste Harfenspiel*

1808 *Lobegesange zu Ehren dem Heiligen und Gerechten in Israel*

1810 *Eine Kleine Sammlung alter und neuer Geistricher Lieder*

1816 *Herzens Opfer; eine Sammlung Geistreicher Lieder*

1817 *Das Geistliche Saitenspiel*

1818 *Die Kleine Geistliche Viole*

1821 *Eine Sammlung neuer Geistlicher Lieder*

1824 *Zwen Geistreiche Leider*

1826 *The Sacrifice of the Heart; or, A Choice Selection of Hymns*

1829 *The Sacrifice of the Heart*; 2d ed.

1830 *Eine Sammlung von Geistlichen, Lieblichen Liedern*

1835 *A Collection of Hymns, For the Use of the United Brethren in Christ*; and *Union Songster*

1835 *A Collection of Hymns*

1842 *The Church Harp*

1846 *Hymns Selected From Various Authors*

1847 *Die Kirchen-Harfe*

1848 *A Collection of Hymns*, for the use of *The United Brethren in Christ*

1850 *Evangelisches Gesangbuch*

1854 *Das Gesangbuch der Vereinigten Bruder in Christo*

1857 *The Evangelical Hymn-Book*

1858 *A Collection of Hymns, for the Use of the United Brethren in Christ*

1865 *Das Gesangbuch, der Vereinigten Bruder in Christo*

1867 *The New Evangelical Hymn-Book*

United Brethren Church

1874 *Hymns for the Sanctuary and
  Social Worship*

1878 *Gesangbuch der Ver.
  Brüder in Christo* [New Edition]

1888 *Deutsches Gesangbuch der
  Vereinigten Brüder in Christo*

1890 *The Otterbein Hymnal* [also published
  as *The People's Hymnal*]

1914 *The Sanctuary Hymnal*

1935 *The Church Hymnal*

Evangelical Association

1877 *Evangelisches Gesangbuch*

1881 *Hymn-Book of the Evangelical
  Association*

1882 *The Evangelical Hymn and
  Tune Book*

1887 *Gesangbuch der Evangelischen
  Gemeinschaft*

1910 *Gesangbuch der Evangelischen
  Gemeinschaft* (new ed.)

1921 *The Evangelical Hymnal*

United Evangelical Church (1894-1922)

1897 *Evangelisches Gesangbuch*

1897 *Hymn Book of the United
  Evangelical Church*

The Evangelical United Brethren Church

1957 *The Hymnal*

Hymnals of the United Brethren in Christ

1795 *Das Aller Neuste Harfenspiel*, oder Zugabe einiger Lieder; auf Begehren von J. Engel, P. Eby, C. Grosch und anderer Mitgleider der Vereinigten Bruderschaft in Pennsylvania. [The very latest play of the Harp or supplement of several hymns, by request of J. Engel, P. Eby, and C. Grosch and other members of the United Brotherhood in Pennsylvania.] Ephrata, PA: Salomon Meyer, 1795. 45 pages.

39 unnumbered hymns, without music but with suggested "melodies." A mixture of revival hymns and standard German hymns from Mennonite hymnals. Published as appendix to Salomon Meyer's 1795 Ephrata printing of *Das kleine Davidische Psalterspiel*, popular among Dunkers and Mennonites in Pennsylvania since its first Pennsylvania printing in 1744.

1808   *Lobegesang zu Ehren dem Heiligen und Gerechten in Israel*, und zur Erbauung des Volkes Gottes; wie auch Zu Gebrauch fur Jederman, der gerne selig werden mochte. [Hymns to honor the Saints and Righteous of Israel and for the Devotion of the People of God as well as for the use of Everyone who wants to be saved.] Hagerstown, MD: John Gruber, 1808. 212 pages.

200 hymns, without music. Compiled by George Güthing (Geeting) at the request of the 1807 United Brethren conference. Includes first translations of several Moravian hymns.

1816   *Herzens Opfer, eine Sammlung Geistreicher Lieder*, aus dem mehrsten jetzt üblichen Gesangbücher gessammlet [*sic*]; zum öffentlichen und privat Gebrauch für Liebhaber des Göttlichen Lebens. Lancaster, Ohio: Gedruckt bei Eduard Schaeffer, 1816. [ca. 1815] iv, 352 [28] pages.

266 hymns, without music. Based on Henry Evinger and Thomas Winters, *Herzens Opfer, eine Sammlung Geistreicher Lieder*, 1814.

1826   *The Sacrifice of the Heart; or, A Choice Selection of Hymns*, from the Most Approved Authors For the Use of the United Brethren in Christ. Compiled by Rev. James T. Stewart, and approved of by the General Conference. Cincinnati, Ohio: Printed and Published by S. J. Browne, Emporium Office, 1826. [ii], 366 pages.

335 hymns, without music. **The first English hymnal**.

1829   *The Sacrifice of the Heart; or, A Choice Collection of Hymns* [etc.]. Published by Rev. Jacob Antrim, second edition, Enlarged and Improved. Dayton, Ohio: Printed by Regans and Van Cleve, 1829. 380 pages.

332 hymns, without music.

1830   *Eine Sammlung von Geistlichen, Lieblichen Liedern*, aus verschiedenen Gesangbücher gesammelt, zum Gebrauch des Oeffentlichen und privat wahren Gottesdienstes [by Jacob Erb]. Harrisburg, [PA]: Gedruckt bei Jacob Baab, 1830. [ii], 365 pages.

274 hymns, without music. A modest revision of *Herzens Opfer*, 1816.

1835   *A Collection of Hymns,* For the Use of the United Brethren in Christ; and *Union Songster;* taken from the Most Approved Authors and Adapted to Public and Private Worship. Circleville, [Ohio]: Printed at the Conference Office, 1835. 349 pages.

393 hymns, without music. The first United Brethren "Church" book (?).

1842   *The Church Harp;* or, Latest compilation of sacred songs suitable for private, prayer, sanctuary, camp, revival and anniversary meetings: designed for the sweet singers in Israel of every denomination. Compiled by Rev. Wm. Hanby. Circleville, OH: Conference Office of the United Brethren in Christ, 1842. 144 pages.

155 hymns, with choruses, without music.

1847   *Die Kirchen-Harfe;* oder Eine kleine Sammlung alter und neuer Geistreicher Lieder, zum Gebrauch des Privat Gottes-Dienstes. Erste Auflage. Lebanon, [PA]: Gedruckt bei J. Hartman ü. Sohn, 1847. 225 pages.

156 hymns without music. Edited by Heinrich Staub and Jacob Scholler. Many hymns borrowed from the Evangelical *Die geistliche Viole*, 1842, without choruses.

1848   *A Collection of Hymns,* For the use of the United Brethren in Christ, taken from the Most Approved Authors, and Adapted to Public and Private Worship. Circleville, Ohio: Published at the Conference of the United Brethren in Christ, 1848. 432 pages.

577 hymns, without music. A revision of *A Collection of Hymns*, 1835, which was ordered by the 1845 General Conference. Compiled by H. G. Spayth, William Hanby, and George Hiskey?

1854   *Das Gesangbuch der Vereinigten Brüder in Christo*, zum Gebrauch Des Öffentlichen und Privat-Gottesdienstes. Dayton, O[hio]: Gebruckt in der Druck- und Buch-Anstalt der Vereinigten Brüder in Christo, 1854. 576 pages.

512 hymns, without music. The original hymns are mostly borrowed from hymnals of the Evangelical Association.

1858   *A Collection of Hymns,* For the Use of the United Brethren in Christ, taken from the Most Approved Authors, and Adapted to Public and Private Worship. Dayton, Ohio: Vonnieda and Sowers, Agents, 1858. 764 pages.

1,078 hymns, without music. Reprinted in 1862 and 1867.

1865   *Das Gesangbuch, der Vereinigten Brüder in Christo*, zum Gebrauch des Öffentlichen und Privat-Gottesdienstes. Zweite verbesserte Auflage. Dayton, O[hio]: Gedruckt in der Buch-Anstalt der Vereinigten Brüder in Christo, 1865. 512 pages.

503 hymns, without music.

1874   *Hymns for the Sanctuary and Social Worship*, with Tunes. Dayton, Ohio: United Brethren Publishing House, 1874. 502 pages.

484 hymns, with music. Ordered by the General Conference of 1873; committee: W. H. Lanthurn, W. J. Shuey, S. E. Kumler, I. Baltzell, and D. Berger. "Special thanks are due E. S. Lorenz for original contributions."

1878   *Gesangbuch der Ver. Brüder in Christo*, Eine Auswahl geistlicher Lieder für Kirchlichen und häuslichen Gebrauch. Dayton, Ohio: Verlegt von Rev. W. J. Shuey, 1878. [x], 750 pages.

615 hymns, without music.

1888   *Deutsches Gesangbuch der Vereinigten Brüder in Christo*; Eine Auswahl geistlicher Lieder für Kirchlichen und Häuslichen Gebrauch. Dayton, Ohio: United Brethren Publishing House, Rev. W. R. Funk, agent. [x], 724 pages.

780 hymns, without music. **The final German hymnal**.

1890   *The Otterbein Hymnal* for use in Public and Social Worship. Prepared by Edmund S. Lorenz. Dayton, Ohio: United Brethren Publishing House, 1890. 304, 55 pages.

548 hymns, with music. A reissue of *The People's Hymnal*, 1890.

1914   *The Sanctuary Hymnal*. Published by order of General Conference of the United Brethren in Christ. Edited by J. P. Landis. Dayton, Ohio: United Brethren Printing Establishment, W. R. Funk, Publisher, 1914. [xxiv], 425, 67 pages.

605 hymns with music.

1935   *The Church Hymnal*. The Official Hymnal of the Church of United Brethren in Christ. Prepared by Edmund S. Lorenz, under the direction of the Board of Bishops. Dayton: Ohio: The United Brethren Publishing House. J. Balmer Showers, Publishing Agent, 1935. 496 pages.

579 hymns, with music. For churches with more formal worship.

Hymnals of the Evangelical Association

1810   *Eine Kleine Sammlung alter und neuer Geistreicher Lieder* [A brief collection of Old and New Spiritual Songs] zur Erbauung und Gebrauch aller GOTT-liebenden Seelen. Zusammengetragen und zum Druck befordert von Johannes Walter Prediger. Reading, [PA]: Gedruckt bei Johann Ritter und Comp., für den Verfasser, 1810. 73 pages.

56 hymns, without music. For use in class meetings, prayer meetings, and revivals. Probably the first of its kind for German Americans. Contains Walter's translation of Isaac Watts's "My God the spring of all my joys" ("Mein Gott, du Brunnen aller Freud") along with a number of his own hymns highly esteemed by later Evangelicals. Contains two of Walter's best-known hymns: "Kommt Bruder, kommt, wir eilen fort" ("Come brethren come, we'll journey on") and "Wer will mit uns nach Zion gehen?" ("Who will go with us to Zion?").

1817 *Das Geistliche Saitenspiel* [The Spiritual Lyre or Psalter]; oder, eine Sammlung auserlesener, erbaulicher, geistreicher Lieder, Zum Gebrauch aller Gottliebenden Seelen, insonderheit für die Gemeinen der Evangelischen Gemeinschaft, Gessammelt, und zum Druck befördert Erste Verordnung ihrer Prediger Conferenz. Erst Auflage. Neu-Berlin, (Penns.): Gedruckt durch Salomon Miller und Henrich Niebel, für die Evangelische Gemeinschaft, 1817. [viii], 436 [8] pages.

487 hymns, many of them German translations of standard English hymns, without music; however, the tune name of suggested tunes appropriate for each text was placed above the first line. **The first official hymnal.** Compiled by Dreisbach and Niebel; mostly traditional German Lutheran and Reformed chorales. *The Church Book.*

1818 *Die kleine Geistliche Viole* [The little Spiritual Viol]; oder, eine kleine Sammlung alter und neuer Geistreicher Lieder zum Gebrauch und Erbauung der Evangelischen Gemeinschaft und Aller Gott-liebenden Seelen, zusammengetragen von Johannes Dreisbach und Henrich Niebel. Erste auflage. Neu-Berlin, (Penns.): Gedruckt durch Sal. Miller und Henr. Niebel für die Evangelische Gemeinschaft, 1818. [3] 186 [6] pages.

115 hymns, without music, but matched to 33 mostly popular or folk melodies; includes translation of USA camp-meeting songs and and original compositions from *Eine kleine Sammlung*, 1810. This hymnal filled the need for a smaller, less expensive hymnal. It was the most popular of the early Evangelical hymnals and went through 13 editions in 37 years, including, according to Porter, 5 European editions. It is the most important camp-meeting hymnal of the German revivalist groups before the rise of German chorus-books after the Civil War.

1821 *Eine Sammlung neuer Geistlicher Lieder,* für alle Säuglinge der Wahrheit, wie auch für alle Liebhaber. Neu-Berlin, [PA]: Gedruckt durch Joh. Dreisbach, für die Evangelische Gemeinschaft, 1821. 41 pages

23 hymns without music, but matched to popular tunes. Mostly translations and original compositions by Dreisbach and Reading layman Daniel Bertolet; first to include choruses with hymns.

1824 *Zwen Geistreiche Leider.* Ueber verschiedene Gegenstande. Zum erstenmal in Amerkia zum Druckt befordert Durch Carl Betz, Schullehrer. Neu-Berlin: Gedruckt und zu haben bei G. Miller, 1824. 12 pages.

Contains two hymns on perseverance in the Christian life. The first, "Auf, ihr Christen Christi Glieder" ("Rise, ye children of God"), in 27 stanzas was written by Justus Falckner (1672-1723), pioneer Lutheran minister in Pennsylvania. The hymn was first published in the *Geistreiches Gesangbuch*, Halle, 1697. The "Zwentes" hymn, "O selige Stunden, die Jesu uns schenk," in 23 stanzas, may be by the same author.

1835 *A Collection of Hymns,* Selected from Various Authors for the use of the Evangelical Association and all lovers of pious devotion. New Berlin, PA: Printed by Geo. Miller, 1835. 340 pages.

333 hymns without music. **The first English hymnal.**

1846 *Hymns Selected From Various Authors* for the use of the Evangelical Association, and All Lovers of Pious Devotion. Fourth edition, enlarged and improved. New Berlin, PA: Published by J. C. Reisner for the Evangelical Association. W. Tea, Printer, 1846. 480 pages.

566 hymns, without music. **The second English hymnal.**

1850 *Evangelisches Gesangbuch;* oder, Eine Sammlung Geistreicher Lieder zum Gebrauch der Evangelischen Gemeinschaft und aller heilsuchenden Seelen. Vierte und verbesserte Auflage. Neu-Berlin, PA: Verlegt von Heinrich Fischer für die Evangelische Gemeinschaft, 1850. 600 pages.

506 hymns, without music (19 more than the old *Geistliche Saitenspiel*). Preface signed: Joh. Dreisbach Saitenspiel, renamed, reprinted several times, often undated. **The second formal German collection.**

1857 *The Evangelical Hymn-Book;* adapted to public, social, and family devotion, and designed for the members of the Evangelical Association and all lovers of Jesus. Cleveland, OH: Charles Hammer for the Evangelical Association, 1857. 854 pages.

716 hymns without music. **The third English hymnal**.

1867 *The New Evangelical Hymn-Book,* Adapted to Public, Social, and Family Devotion, And Designed For the Members of the Evangelical Association and All Lovers of Jesus. Cleveland, Ohio: Published by Charles Hammer for the Evangelical Association, 1867. 860 pages.

1,262 hymns, without music. **The fourth English hymnal**.

1877 *Evangelisches Gesangbuch mit Vierstimmigen Melodien* für den öffentlichen und häuslichen Gottesdienst. Cleveland, Ohio: Verlegt von W. F. Schneider für die Evangelische Gemeinschaft, 1877. 600 pages.

585 hymns, with music. A new German collection edited by Bishop J. J. Escher, William Horn, and Martin Lauer. Includes important hymns from the *Geistliche Viole*. **The third formal German hymnal** and the first German hymnal with music. The texts are set on the left page interlined with four-part tunes, and other texts with the same meter are printed on the facing pages.

1881 *Hymn-Book of the Evangelical Association*. Cleveland, Ohio: Publishing House of the Evangelical Association, 1881. [ii], 549 pages.

875 hymns, 16 doxologies, without music.

1882 *The Evangelical Hymn and Tune Book*. Cleveland, Ohio: Publishing House of the Evangelical Association, Lauer and Yost, agents, 1882. [vi], 446 pages.

875 hymns, with music. The music edition of the 1881 book.

1887 *Gesangbuch der Evangelischen Gemeinschaft* für öffentlichen und häuslichen Gottesdienst. Cleveland, Ohio: Verlagshaus der Evang. Gemeinschaft, M. Lauer, Verleger, 1887. 826 pages.

985 hymns, without music.

1910 *Gesangbuch der Evangelischen Gemeinschaft fur öffentlichen and häuslichen Gottesdienst*. Cleveland, Ohio: Verlagshaus der Evangelischen Gemeinschaft, C. House, Agent, 1910. 670 pages.

740 hymns and 12 choruses without music; "Vorwort" signed W. Horn, G. Heinmiller and Chr. Stabler. Available with music, 1915. **The last German hymnal**, it was in print through 1921.

1921 *The Evangelical Hymnal*. Harrisburg, PA: The Evangelical Publishing House, 1921. [xxv], 453 pages.

589 hymns, with music.

Authorized Hymnals of the United Evangelical Church

1897 *Hymn Book of the United Evangelical Church*. Harrisburg, PA: Publishing House of the United Evangelical Church, S. L. Wiest, Publisher, 1897. Second printing under revised title: *Hymnal of the United Evangelical Church*. Harrisburg, PA.: Publishing House of the United Evangelical Church, J. J. Nungesser, Publisher, 1897. [vi] 408 pages.

723 hymns, with music. According to Ellen Jane Lorenz Porter, [The 1897 hymnal] "contained many gospel songs and camp-meeting choruses."

1897 *Evangelisches Gesangbuch, die Kleine Palme, mit Anhang.* Harrisburg, PA: Verlag der Vereinigten Evangelischen Kirche, 1897.

318 hymns, with music.

Authorized Hymnal of The Evangelical United Brethren Church

1957 *The Hymnal.* Dayton, Ohio: Published by the Board of Publication, The Evangelical United Brethren Church, 1957.

481 hymns, with music, psalter, and ritual.

In contrast to Porter's negative comments about this hymnal (see page 80), another perspective is provided by Paul H. Eller:

Likewise serving to fuse the two church traditions into the Evangelical United Brethren Church was *The Hymnal* which was published in 1957. In this book were 455 hymns expressive of many cultural, theological, and ecclesiastical traditions, a broad lectionary, and a modest collection of aids to worship. *The Hymnal* was greeted with unanticipated cordiality, and three editions, totaling 225,000 copies, were printed. (Behney and Eller 1979, 374)

HYMNALS OF THE METHODIST CHURCH

REPRINTS OF WESLEY HYMNS

John Julian has written about the importance of hymns and hymn singing to John Wesley:

> With that wonderful instinct for gauging the popular mind, which was one element in his success, [John] saw at once that hymns might be utilized, not only for raising the devotion, but also for instructing and establishing the faith of his disciples. He intended the hymns to be not merely a constituent part of public worship, but they were also a kind of creed in verse. (Julian 1907, 1257)

Wesley apparently did not use his first hymnbook, *A Collection of Psalms and Hymns*, Charleston, 1737, except in his Anglican parish in Savannah. In England his leadership of the evangelical movement engaged his abilities as editor, compiler, and distributor of hymnals. This leadership, along with his brother's remarkable ability as hymn writer, resulted in the publication of sixty-four hymnbooks over the span of fifty-three years.

Wesley's *Hymns and Sacred Poems*, 1739, was brought over by George Whitefield for use in his meetings in the colonies. Whitefield had it reprinted in Philadelphia by A. Bradford in 1740, the first Wesley hymnal to be reprinted in the USA. The 1769 reprint in Philadelphia of *Hymns for the Nativity of Our Lord*, 1745, by Robert Williams, "seems to have been one of the first books commissioned by and published for a continuing society of Methodists in America." (Pilkington 1968, 28) In 1770 John Dunlap reprinted Wesley's *Hymns and Spiritual Songs, Intended for the Use of Real Christians of All Denominations*, 1753. In 1781 three Wesley collections, *Hymns and Spiritual Songs*, 1753, *Hymns for those that seek and those that have Redemption in the Blood of Jesus Christ*, 1747, and *A Collection of Psalms and Hymns*, 1741, were reprinted by Melchior Steiner for use in St. George's Church, Philadelphia.

An accounting of the official hymnals of the former Methodist Church that began in the 1878 *Report* was continued by Carl F. Price, *The Music and Hymnody of the Methodist Hymnal*, in his account of the production of *The Methodist Hymnal*, 1905, the joint hymnal of the Northern and Southern churches. Robert Guy McCutchan in "The Antecedents of *The Methodist Hymnal*" in *Our Hymnody*, 1937, used Price's work, factored in the events surrounding the publishing of *The Methodist Hymnal*, 1935, and added the hymnals of the former Methodist Protestant Church. McCutchan's work was updated by the present writer and included in "American Methodist Hymnbooks," *Companion to the Hymnal*, 1970.

GERMAN METHODIST HYMNALS

The hymnody of German Methodists in the United States was not included by McCutchan or the present writer. This movement, unrelated to either the former United Brethren or Evangelical churches, centered in the activity of the former Methodist Episcopal Church during the mid-nineteenth century among German-speaking immigrants in the Ohio valley, the Midwest, South, and Southwest. The movement was led by William Nast, 1807-99. Three German-speaking conferences, Pittsburgh, Cincinnati, and St. Louis, were formed by the 1844 General Conference. The movement peaked at the turn of the century and was looked upon with suspicion during World War I and in its aftermath, as were Germans and Germanic culture, including German-language churches. In the third decade German Methodist churches began to decline in membership, and by 1932 its last ministers were ordained to serve exclusively German congregations. At the time of unification of the three branches of Methodism in 1939, most of the German-speaking churches had been assimilated into the main English language church.

Concerning the hymnals of German Methodism Paul F. Douglas writes in *The Story of German Methodism* that "for the first four years of Nast's work, 1835-39, the people sang without aid of a hymnal." (Douglas 1939, 230) Their first hymnal was published in 1839 and furnished the foundation for subsequent editions that were published each generation:

1839   *Sammlung von geistlichen Liedern*, für kirchlichen und häuslichen Gottesdienst, mit Beifügung deutscher und englischer Melodien. Cincinnati: J. F. Wright & L. Swormstodt, 1839, 480 pages.

The book resulted from the collaboration of Nast and Peter Schumucker, the former choosing the words and the latter selecting tunes which were "partial to the English taste, which preferred four lines to six, and livelier songs to the slower chorales." (Douglas 1939, 230)

1868   *Deutsches Gesangbuch, der bischöfliche Methodisten Kirche*. Eine neue Auswaht geistlicher Lieder für Kirche, Haus und Schule. Cincinnati: Hitchcock and Walden. 768 pages.

Douglas dates this edition 1865. (Douglas 1939, 230)

1871   *Gemeinschaftliches Gesangbuch;* Herausgegeben zum Gebrauch der deutschen erweckten Gemeinden von Baltimore, enthaltend eine Auswahl von geistlichen Liedern aus den verschiedenen Gesangbuchern der drei vereinigten Gemeinschaft, und Ver. Bruder in Christo. Baltimore: Gedrucht bei Th. Kroh, 1871. 70 pages.

A publishing venture of the three German-American Wesleyan churches: Methodist Episcopal Church, Evangelical Association, and United Brethren Church.

1888   *Deutsches gesang- und melodienbuch der Bischöflichen Methodisten-kirche*. Cincinnati, Chicago [etc.]: Cranston & Stowe; New York: Phillips & Hunt, 1888. 447 pages.

780 hymns; 12 benedictions.

According to Douglas, this was "the first time so that the words and music appeared on the same page." (Douglas 1939, 230) He writes that the last hymnal of this movement (in 1905) was edited by Munz:

> The fact that the notes were so belatedly added to the hymnals, according to the German custom, placed special emphasis on a usable memory knowledge of tunes. German Methodists knew their hymns. (Douglas 1939, 230)

NATIVE AMERICAN HYMNALS

See "Native American Hymns," pages 19-21.

PORTUGUESE LANGUAGE HYMNALS

Hymnario da Egreja Methodista Episcopal, compilado pelo Rev.do Sr. George B. Nind, sob a direicção do Rev.do Sr. Bispo J. C. Hartzell, was published by the Methodist Episcopal Church in 1906. Its intended use was probably by Bishop Hartzell in the missionary activity of the Northern church in Africa (Mozambique?) or among Portuguese immigrants to the USA at the turn of the century.

SPANISH LANGUAGE HYMNALS

See "Hispanic American Hymns," pages 36-43.

HYMNALS OF OTHER LANGUAGES AND ETHNIC GROUPS

The relationship of hymns, hymn singing, hymnals, and hymnody to the global missionary activity of both the Northern and Southern churches, which by 1921, according to H. Richey Hogg in "The Missions of the Methodist Church," saw "nearly 2,300 overseas missionaries" (Bucke 1964, 3:125), has yet to be documented.

AUTHORIZED METHODIST HYMNALS

1780 (London) *A Collection of Hymns for Use of the People called Methodists* ("large hymnbook")

The solid lines on this chart show a direct relationship and influence between the hymnals. The dotted lines indicate indirect or questionable influences.

1784 (London) *A Collection of Psalms and Hymns for the Lord's Day* (attached to *The Sunday Service of the Methodists in North America*)

1785 (London) *A Pocket Hymn Book for the Use of Christians of all Denominations*, John Wesley.

1785 (York) *A Pocket Hymn Book, designed as a constant companion for the pious; collected from various authors* (compiled by Robert Spence)

1786 (New York) *A Pocket Hymn Book: Designed as a Constant Companion for the Pious. Collected from various authors.* 5th ed.; printed by W. Ross.

1802 (Philadelphia) *The Methodist Pocket Hymn Book, revised and improved: designed as a constant Companion for the pious of all denominations* (Revised and published by Ezekiel Cooper)

1808 (New York) *A Selection of Hymns from various authors, designed as a Supplement to the Methodist Pocket Hymn Book, compiled under the direction of Bishop Asbury and published by order of the General Conference.* (The "Double Hymn Book" J. C. Totter, printer, 1810)

1821 (New York) *A Collection of Hymns for the use of the Methodist Episcopal Church, principally from the Collection of the Reverend John Wesley, M.A., late Fellow of Lincoln College, Oxford* (slightly revised in 1835 and tunes cross-referenced with *The Methodist Harmonist*, 1821)

1836 (New York) *A Collection of Hymns* . . . (prepared by Nathan Bangs, a supplement of 90 hymns to the 1821 Collection).

The Methodist
Protestant Church

1829 (Baltimore) *A compilation of Hymns, adapted to public and social Divine Worship* (compiled by John Harrod in 1828(?); adopted by the 1834 General Conference)

1837 (Baltimore) *Hymn Book of the Methodist Protestant Church* (compiled by Thomas H. Stockton; adapted by the 1838 General Conference)

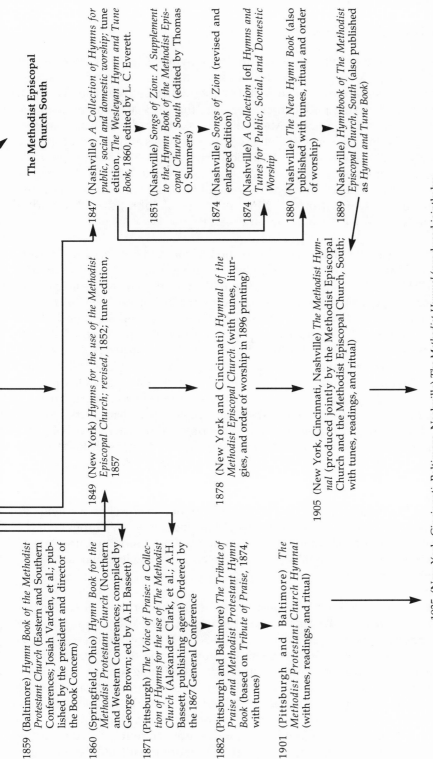

**The Methodist Episcopal
Church South**

1847 (Nashville) *A Collection of Hymns for public, social and domestic worship;* tune edition, *The Wesleyan Hymn and Tune Book,* 1860, edited by L. C. Everett.

1851 (Nashville) *Songs of Zion: A Supplement to the Hymn Book of the Methodist Episcopal Church, South* (edited by Thomas O. Summers)

1874 (Nashville) *Songs of Zion* (revised and enlarged edition)

1874 (Nashville) *A Collection [of] Hymns and Tunes for Public, Social, and Domestic Worship*

1880 (Nashville) *The New Hymn Book* (also published with tunes, ritual, and order of worship)

1889 (Nashville) *Hymnbook of The Methodist Episcopal Church, South* (also published as *Hymn and Tune Book*)

1849 (New York) *Hymns for the use of the Methodist Episcopal Church; revised,* 1852; tune edition, 1857

1878 (New York and Cincinnati) *Hymnal of the Methodist Episcopal Church* (with tunes, liturgies, and order of worship in 1896 printing)

1905 (New York, Cincinnati, Nashville) *The Methodist Hymnal* (produced jointly by the Methodist Episcopal Church and the Methodist Episcopal Church, South; with tunes, readings, and ritual)

1935 (New York, Cincinnati; Baltimore, Nashville) *The Methodist Hymnal* (produced jointly by the three churches; texts only; and with tunes, readings, and ritual)

1966 (Nashville) *The Methodist Hymnal* (with tunes, readings, and ritual)

1859 (Baltimore) *Hymn Book of the Methodist Protestant Church* (Eastern and Southern Conferences; Josiah Varden, et al.; published by the president and director of the Book Concern)

1860 (Springfield, Ohio) *Hymn Book for the Methodist Protestant Church* (Northern and Western Conferences; compiled by George Brown; ed. by A.H. Bassett)

1871 (Pittsburgh) *The Voice of Praise: a Collection of Hymns for the use of The Methodist Church* (Alexander Clark, et al.; A.H. Bassett, publishing agent) Ordered by the 1867 General Conference

1882 (Pittsburgh and Baltimore) *The Tribute of Praise and Methodist Protestant Hymn Book* (based on *Tribute of Praise,* 1874, with tunes)

1901 (Pittsburgh and Baltimore) *The Methodist Protestant Church Hymnal* (with tunes, readings, and ritual)

AUTHORIZED HYMNALS

The previous chart of hymnals identifies those hymnals that have been either authorized or approved, or both, and in some instances received by a general conference of the various branches of The Methodist Church. The Wesleyan tradition of authorizing publications began in the work and authority of the mid-eighteenth-century English Methodism book steward who was responsible for maintaining considerable inventory of books and tracts for the use of local Methodist societies. The local book steward in turn was responsible to the general book steward, John Wesley, leader of the Methodist movement. USA Methodists did not have a general book steward until 1789 when the conference elected John Dickins, minister of John Street Methodist Church in New York City. (Pilkington 1968, 80)

One of Dickins's first tasks, "at the direction of the conference," was to oversee the reprinting of the *Pocket HymnBook*, already in use (see "Methodist Episcopal Hymnals," pages 97-108). The editorial prerogative, as it had earlier rested with John Wesley, was assumed by the bishops of the USA church and later was extended to bishops and committees acting on behalf of the General Conference. The musical aspects of revision were handled ad hoc until late in the nineteenth century, but not without controversy (see "The Music of Hymns, Wesleyan Style," page 54). Notable exceptions to this practice were Methodist Protestant Eben Tourjee, the Southern church's Rigdon M. McIntosh, and others, who were either on the revision committees or were hired by them for specific tasks, e.g., Episcopalian Peter Lutkin as co-music editor of the 1905 joint hymnal. This process ultimately evolved into the current practice of a musician being named as editor, with Robert Guy McCutchan named editor of the 1935 book and Carlton R. Young, editor of the 1966 and 1989 hymnals.

According to Pilkington the printing and distribution of the church's hymnals have long been a source of income for its publishing interests: "Throughout the history of Methodist publishing, seldom is any publication more important to the denomination and its publishers than the current 'new hymnbook.'" (Pilkington 1968, 385)

The publication of hymnals has resulted in a number of best sellers, beginning with Dickins's *Pocket Hymn Book* (Pilkington 1968, 101) to the 1966 and 1989 hymnals, both with sales in excess of 4,500,000 copies. It has resulted as well in gross failures such as the shaped-note edition of the 1935 hymnal. With instructions from the general church, its publishing houses, unlike private publishers, can declare former editions out-of-print and can produce and distribute the church's authorized or official hymnals. At the same time the publishing interests, particularly those of the former Methodist Episcopal Church, South, have maintained, though not without objection on the part of some worship leaders, that to be competitive with publishers, most of whom sell directly to local churches, they must retain the right, some would say the responsibility, to publish and sell unauthorized hymnals and songbooks. The most notable example is *The Cokesbury Hymnal*, 1923, and its successive editions, e.g., *The Cokesbury Worship Hymnal*, first produced as the needed alternative to the 1905 hymnal and later to the 1935 and 1966 hymnals, with approximately 4,000,000 sales to date.

Methodist Episcopal Hymnals

The first USA Methodist collection of congregational song authorized by the general church is the 118 metrical paraphrases and hymns bound by John Wesley with *The Sunday Service of the Methodists in North America*, 1784, and approved for use by the 1784 Baltimore Christmas Conference. It was bound and sold in England, but it was not reprinted in the USA. The first collection to be compiled at the direction of the General Conference and distributed by its publishing house was the *Pocket Hymn Book*, 1790, presumed to be the tenth edition of a collection compiled in 1785 by Robert Spence, the York, England, bookseller and friend of Francis Asbury and Thomas Coke.

The first Methodist body to show interest in the precursors of our hymnals was the committee that produced our 1878 hymnal who included the following in their report to the General Conference:

> The origin of the first collection of hymns in use among the Methodists of this country cannot be satisfactorily ascertained. [Although] . . . there is extant a copy of the "Pocket Hymn Book: ninth edition, published in Philadelphia, Pa., 1788." This contains two hundred and fifty hymns. We may infer from the number of Methodists in the country that the first edition may have been published about 1785 or 1786, say twenty years after Embury began to preach. (*Revision* 1878)

Louis F. Benson in *The English Hymn* cites the existence of an edition (see item 8 below) of a pocket hymnbook that had been published in New York, not York, England, in 1786. With his characteristic thoroughness Benson states, "The book itself cannot at present be found; . . . there is evidently something interesting here, if only we knew what it was. . . . A link has dropped out of the early history of American Methodist Hymnody." (Benson 1915, 287)

Twentieth-century Methodist hymnologists Carl F. Price (1911, 18-19) and Robert G. McCutchan (1942, 10) traced the lineage of authorized hymnals without being able to examine their contents. They both assumed that our first hymnals, including the first hymnal authorized by the general church and compiled by its first book steward, were essentially reprints of Spence's collection, with additional hymns added by the USA bishops to serve the underdeveloped tastes and short-term needs of the fledging USA church. This writer's "Chart of Methodist Hymnals" prepared for *The History of American Methodism*, 1964, did not significantly move the study beyond that assumption.

Since the earliest collections have never been compared with Spence or Wesley's pocket hymnbooks, a comparison can establish the link between British and USA Methodist hymnic repertory. That study shows that our first hymnals were excerpted from Spence's 1785 *Collection and* John Wesley's 1785 follow-up to his 1780 *Collection,* and that both the large 1780 *Collection* and the 118 psalms and hymns that were appended to *The Sunday Service* were ignored by a USA Methodist editorial force, probably Bishops Thomas Coke and Francis Asbury. It is they who probably produced the first volume for USA Methodists from a diverse and expanding repertory, and in doing so expressed the USA church's independence from British Wesleyan repertories, an independence that continued well into the nineteenth century.

The following eight collections are the possible sources**** of the first USA hymnals. See chart of "Authorized Methodist Hymnals," pages 94-95.

1. **A Collection of Hymns for the Use of the People called Methodists,* London, 1780. Wesley' definitive collection (with changes, some by Wesley), served British Methodists until 1831 when it was issued with a *Supplement.* This collection was imported and apparently used by some USA societies, though subject to the criticism expressed in the forewords to the pocket hymnbooks: "admirable indeed, but. . . too expensive for the poor, who have little time and less money." While its broad content came to USA hymnals through the Spence pocket hymnbook that was adapted and enlarged by the USA church (see below), it did not directly influence the mainstream of USA Wesleyan hymnody until the publication of *A Collection of Hymns for the use of the Methodist Episcopal Church,* principally from the Collection of the Reverend John Wesley. M. A. late Fellow of Lincoln College, Oxford, New York, 1821.

2. *A Collection of Hymns from Various Authors,* Designed for General Use. In Three Parts. York: Printed for R. Spence Bookseller, in High Ousegate. 1781. There are 174 selections in 154 pages. This is Robert Spence's collection marketed shortly after the release of Wesley's 1780 *Collection.* Although it plagiarizes that volume and is editorially flawed, its popularity eventually prompted Spence to issue an abridgement in the form of a pocket hymnbook. There is a copy in the Garrett-Evangelical Library, Evanston, Illinois.

3. One hundred and eighteen metrical paraphrases and hymns from *A Collection of Psalms and Hymns,* 1741, enlarged 1743, were bound by Wesley with *The Sunday Service of the Methodists in North America,* 1784. These were separately printed as *A Collection of Psalms and Hymns for the Lord's Day,* London, 1784. Frank Baker comments that this collection was "enlarged by Dr. Thomas Coke after Wesley's death, [and] it became the authorized 'Morning Hymn Book' for use where Methodists held a liturgical service." (Baker 1962, 384) Its use in USA Methodism has not been documented, though it is assumed, as was the *Sunday Service* and the abridged prayer book.

4.* *A Pocket Hymn Book for the Use of Christians of all Denominations,* John Wesley, London, 1785. It was published by Wesley to make available some of the hymns that were not included in his 1780 *Collection.* The contents of the book were determined by the fall of 1784, the preface is dated October 1, 1784, and the contents may have been shared with Bishops Coke and Asbury. The chart below shows that of the thirty-four new items in the 1786 USA edition, thirteen are from Wesley's 1785 book, while only five are from the 1780 *Collection,* and one is from the psalms and hymns appended to the 1784 *Sunday Service.*

The 200 selections in 208 pages are organized in the same way as the parent 1780 *Collection:* with slight modification.

CONTENTS

PART I
Containing Introductory Hymns

Sect. I. Exhorting and beseeching Sinners to turn to God
    II. Describing
                  1. The goodness of God
        _____2. Death
        _____3. Judgment
        _____4. Heaven
        _____5. Hell

PART II
Describing true religion

PART III
Sect. I. For Mourners convinced of Sin
    II. _____ Backsliding

PART IV
Sect. I. For Believers
                  1. Rejoicing and praising God
        _____2. Fighting
        _____3. Praying
        _____4. Watching
        _____5. Working
        _____6. Suffering
        _____7. Longing for full Redemption
        _____8. Saved
        _____9. Interceding

PART V

Sect. I. For the Society 1. Meeting
_____2. Prayer
_____3. Parting
Funeral Hymns

5. ** *A Pocket Hymn-Book, designed as a constant companion for the pious; collected from various authors.* York. Sixth Edition. Printed for and sold by R. Spence, in Ousegate; and sold also by T. Scollick in the City Road, London. 1786 [1785]. This is a revision by Spence of his 1781 *Collection* and the volume that became popular in Great Britain and the USA. There are 232 selections in 206 pages organized as follows:

Awakening and inviting
Penitential
Rejoicing
Praise
Trusting in Providence
Suffering
Funeral
For Persons joined in Fellowship
    On admitting a new Member
    On visiting a Friend
    Parting
Strife in Heaven
A Dialogue
Birth Day
Backslider
For the King
A Parent's Prayer
Nativity
New-Year's Day
Good-Friday

For additional commentary on Spence's collection, see "From all that dwell below the skies, pages 350-51.

6. ** *A Pocket Hymn Book Designed As A Constant Companion for the Pious. Collected from Various Authors.* Fifth Edition. New York: Printed by W. Ross, in Broadway, and sold at No. 20, John Street. 1786. The book's 230 selections in 224 pages are organized as follows:

Awakening and inviting
Penitential
Rejoicing
Praise

    Trusting in Providence
    Suffering
    Funeral
    For Persons joined in Fellowship
       On admitting a new Member
       On visiting a Friend
       Parting
    Strife in Heaven
    Birth Day
    Backslider
    A Parent's Prayer
    Nativity
    New-Year's Day
    Good-Friday
    Sacramental

This collection, referred to in this discussion as "USA 1786," and the implied antecedent printings that probably date as early as 1785 appear to be the earliest hymnic repertory compiled and printed for the USA Methodist church. There are two extant copies of USA 1786: the one housed at the American Antiquarian Society, Worcester, Massachusetts was not allowed to be copied; a second copy in the Peabody Music Library, Johns Hopkins University, Baltimore, was copied and supplied to this writer.

The type in USA 1786 is a little larger than the Spence book. There is distinctive spelling and copyediting, e.g., "Rejoice the Lord is King" is printed without a comma after "Rejoice" in the text and with a comma in the index, and in the first line of the text there is a comma after "King" instead of the original exclamation mark. There is no introduction or advertising. Even though its general context and format are patterned after Spence's book, the 1786 collection's distinctive editorial direction is clear, and its contents demonstrate a developing alternative USA hymnic repertory and a distinctive editorial direction, presumably that of bishops Coke and Asbury. For example, it is interesting that the second stanza of "Love divine, all love's excelling," excluded from the 1780 *Collection* by John Wesley, is included in USA 1786 with Charles Wesley's original wording of the fifth line: "Take away our pow'r of sinning." There are these additional distinguishing traits:

The editors deleted thirty-eight selections from Spence and made thirty-four substitutions, most of them from the contents of Wesley's 1785 pocket hymnbook.

Some of Spence's selections with choruses are retained while others are omitted including "Encouraged by thy word" (Beggar's Prayer); "Jesus, and shall it ever be" with the instruction "Spoken extemporary." Other omitted selections are "A Dialogue," "Tell us, O women, we would know," a dialogue interspersed with a chorus; "For the King," inappropriately for USA Methodists addressed to the British throne; and "A Master's Prayer," apparently written for the head of the household.

The section titled "Sacramental" contains nine communion hymns by Charles Wesley from *Hymns on the Lord's Supper*, 1745. Other eucharistic hymns from that collection are found elsewhere in the volume. The editors of the hymnal were apparently expressing the new church's ministry that, unlike its British counterpart, combined Word and Sacrament. The category "Sacramental" in the 1786 collection is distinct from the pocket hymnbooks of both Spence and Wesley.

After deleting thirty-eight selections from Spence** 1785, the USA editors apparently substituted hymns from John Wesley's 1785 *Pocket Hymnbook*, instead of his 1780 *Collection*. The thirty-eight selections deleted from Spence are shown on the following chart. Note that seventeen hymns included by Spence from the 1780 *Collection* are dropped.

Hymns from Spence 1785 not included in USA 1786
Those in *italics* are included in Wesley's 1780 *Collection*

First Line

A Christ I have, O what a Christ have I
And am I born to die
Cast on the fidelity
Come all, whoe'er have set
Come, and let us sweetly join
Come, let us anew (in JW '85 incorrectly indexed to "Come let us ascend")
Encouraged by thy word (Begger's Prayer)
Far above yon glorious ceiling
Father, in the name I pray
For ever here my rest shall be
God moves in a mysterious way
Hail happy day, a day of holy rest
Hark! how the gospel-trumpet sounds
Holy lamb, who thee receive
How shall a lost sinner in pain
If to Jesus for relief
Jesu, let thy pitying eye
Jesu, my life, thyself apply
Jesu, the weary wand'rer's rest
Jesu, great shepherd of the sheep
Jesus, and shall it ever be/Spoken extemporary
Lord, how divine thy comforts are
Lord, I adore thy gracious will

Lord, in the strength of grace
Lord, thou hast bid thy people pray/For the King
Master supreme, I look to thee
O glorious hope of perfect love
See, Jesu, thy disciples see
Tell us, O women, we would know (dialogue with chorus)
The despised Nazarene
The one thing needful, that good part
Tho' strait be the way, with dangers beset
Thou lamb of God, thou Prince of Peace
Thou, my God, art good and wise
Thy daily mercies, O my God
'Tis a point I long to know
Two are better far than one
Ye happy pilgrims, come (with chorus)

These thirty hymns were selected by the USA 1786 compilers to replace those deleted from Spence.

Hymns in USA 1786 not in Spence 1785

First Line

All praise to him who dwells in bliss
All ye that pass by
Almighty Maker God
Author of our salvation, thee
Come, let us anew, our journey pursue, with vigor arise
Come, let us sweetly join
Come, Lord and help me to rejoice
Father, I stretch my hands to thee
God of my salvation, hear
How happy every child of grace
How tedious and tasteless the hours
In that sad memorable night
Jesu, at whose supreme command
Jesu, dear, redeeming Lord,
Jesu, great shepherd of the sheep
Jesu, we thus obey
Jesus, redeemer of mankind
Jesus, thy wandering sheep behold
Let all who truly bear
Lord Jesu, when, when shall it be
Lord of the harvest hear
Lord, I believe a rest remains
O God, of good the unfathom'd sea
O Jesus, my rest

O thou, who this mysterious bread
Rejoice, the Lord is king
Rock of Israel, cleft for me
See gracious Lord, with pitying eyes
We lift our hearts to thee (John Wesley author?)
When gracious Lord, when shall it be
Where is my God, my joy, my hope
Who is this that comes from far
Whom man forsakes thou wilt not leave
Ye heavens rejoice in Jesus's grace

This final chart demonstrates that the USA compilers in replacing the thirty-eight items deleted from Spence continued to shun the 1780 *Collection* (Coll '80) by adding only five selections from it. They all but rejected the 118 psalm paraphrases and hymns (SS '84) that Wesley appended to the 1784 *Sunday Service*. They apparently turned to Wesley's 1785 *Pocket Hymn Book* (JW '85) for thirteen of the thirty-four new items. The contents of that collection had been determined by the fall of 1784; the preface is dated October 1, 1784.

The consequence of these choices for succeeding editions of our hymnals is shown in the right-hand column where twenty-four of the thirty-four replacements were maintained through the 1849 hymnal.

First lines, USA '86	Coll '80	SS '84	JW '85	METH '49
All praise to him who dwells in bliss				√
All ye that pass by			√	
Almighty Maker God		√		√
Author of our salvation, thee				√
Come, let us anew (in BRPH85 incorrectly indexed)				
Come, let us anew, our Journey pursue, with vigor arise			√	
Come, let us sweetly join	√		√	√
Come, Lord and help me to rejoice				
Father, I stretch my hands to thee				√
God of my salvation, hear	√			√
How happy every child of grace			√	√
How tedious and tasteless the hours				√
In that sad memorable night				√
Jesu, at whose supreme command				√
Jesu, dear, redeeming Lord,				
Jesu, great shepherd of the sheep	√			√
Jesu, we thus obey				√
Jesus, redeemer of mankind			√	√
Jesus, thy wandering sheep behold			√	√
Let all who truly bear				√

First lines, USA '86	Coll '80	SS '84	JW '85	METH '49
Lord Jesu, when, when shall it be				
Lord of the harvest hear			√	√
Lord, I believe a rest remains	√			√
O God, of good the unfathom'd sea			√	√
O Jesus, my rest			√	
O thou, who this mysterious bread				√
Rejoice, the Lord is king			√	√
Rock of Israel, cleft for me				√
See gracious Lord, with pitying eyes			√	
We lift our hearts to thee				√
When gracious Lord, when shall it be	√		√	
Where is my God, my joy, my hope				
Who is this that comes from far			√	
Whom man forsakes thou wilt not leave			√	√
Ye heavens rejoice in Jesus's grace			√	

34 selections in US '86 are not in Spence '85

Key to sources

Coll '80 =JW's 1780 *Collection*	5/34	
SS '84=the psalms and hymns with 1784 *Sunday Service*	1/34	
JW '85=JW's 1785 *Pocket Hymn Book*		13/34
METH '49=retained in the 1849 *Methodist Hymnal*		24/34

Summary:

1. While the 1786 collection has the same format and content of Spence's collection, the USA church probably as early as the spring of 1785 through bishops Coke and Asbury began a separate course for USA Methodist hymnals.

2. Of the thirty-eight hymns dropped from Spence, seventeen are found in the 1780 *Collection*.

3. The balance of the new content of the 1786 USA collection is found in Wesley's 1785 *Pocket Hymn Book* rather than his 1780 *Collection*.

4. The 1786 collection contains the first USA printing of some of Charles Wesley's most important hymns, e.g., the enthronement hymn, "Rejoice! The Lord is King," and the eucharistic hymn, "O thou, who this mysterious bread." There is preliminary indication that these Charles Wesley texts in the 1786 collection are included in variants from the parent British collections.

7. *A Pocket Hymn Book for the Use of Christians of all Denominations*, John Wesley, London, 1787. This collection was published to counter the popularity of Spence's 1785 *Pocket Hymn-Book* and is based on that collection.

Spence's publishing activity is the butt of John Wesley's complaint in his preface to this collection.

A few years ago I was desired by many of our preachers to prepare and publish a small Pocket hymn-book, to be used in common in our Societies. This I promised to do, as soon as I had finished some other business which was then on my hands. But before I could do this, a Bookseller stepped in, and without my consent or knowledge, extracted such a Hymn-book chiefly from our works, and spread several editions of it throughout the kingdom. Two years ago I published a Pocket Hymn-book according to my promise. But most of our people were supplied already with the other Hymns. And these are largely circulated still. To cut off all pretence from the Methodists for buying them, our Brethren in the late Conference at Bristol advised me to print the same Hymn-book which had been printed at York. This I have done in the present volume. (Julian 1907, 398)

It has not been established when this collection began to influence the content of USA *pocket* hymnbooks.

8. *A Pocket Hymn Book: Designed as a Constant Companion for the Pious, Collected from various authors*, Eighth Edition. Philadelphia: Printed by Prichard and Hall, in Market Street, 1788.

This is a reprint of the 1786 or possibly earlier edition. The foreword, essentially the same as found in later printings, is addressed "To the Members of Friends of the Methodist Episcopal Church," and signed, "We are, Dear Brethren, Your Faithful Pastors in Christ." With its publication the compilers apparently meant to supersede some of the hymnals and collections listed above.

The Hymn Books which have been already published among us, are truly excellent. The Select Hymns, the double collection of Hymns and psalms, . . . (which we promise to publish with a third and more complete edition of our Prayer Book) and the Redemption Hymns. . . . The large Congregational Hymn Book [probably John Wesley's 1780 *Collection*] is admirable indeed, but is too expensive for the poor, who have little time and less money. The Pocket Hymn Book [either Wesley's or Spence's or combinations of both] lately sent abroad in these States is a most valuable performance for those who are deeply spiritual, but it is better suited to the European Methodists. (Preface to *A Pocket Hymn Book*, eighth edition 1788)

The foreword also states, "We intend to strike off an impression of twenty or thirty thousand copies," which suggests that this is the eighth printing of an existing collection that had been published by USA Methodists, perhaps as early as late 1785.

9.* *A Pocket Hymn Book: Designed as a Constant Companion for the Pious Collected from Various Authors*. Ninth Edition. Philadelphia: Printed by Joseph James,

Chestnut-Street, 1788. It includes the 230 hymns in the eighth edition, and 27 additional hymns in part 2, nos. 233-57. Tune names are placed above the hymns in part 2, a first for USA collections. There is no preface.

In 1789 the conference instructed its first book steward, John Dickens, as his first task to continue the printing of this collection. These 1790, *"tenth" and *"eleventh" editions are reprints of the 1788 ninth edition, reprinted from the 1786 edition. They include the original 230 hymns, 27 hymns from part 2 of the ninth edition, and 26 new hymns. Coke's and Asbury's names are at the end of the preface, which is identical to the 1788 eighth edition preface except in the former preface the bishops' names were not included. This appears to be the first collection to include the meter of the hymn with each selection. These printings are the third revision of a collection dating from at least 1786.

This collection was revised in either 1802 or 1803 as *The Methodist Pocket Hymn Book, revised and improved*, containing over four hundred hymns, and signed by Bishops Coke, Asbury, and Richard Whatcoat on behalf of a revision committee whose members were selected from each annual conference.

In the preface bishops Coke and Whatcoat disclaim any profit motive for publishing of the hymnal:

> We are the more delighted with this design, as no personal advantage is concerned, but the public good alone—For after the necessary expenses of publication are discharged, we shall make it a noble charity, by applying the profits, arising therefrom, to religious and charitable purpose.

Having made this statement of intent, the bishops continue:

> We must therefore earnestly entreat you, if you have any respect for the authority of the Conferences, or of us, or any regard for the prosperity of the Connection, to purchase no Hymn-Books, but what are signed with the names of your Bishops. And as we intend to keep a constant supply, the complaint of our congregations, "that they cannot procure our Hymn-Books," will be stopped.

In 1808 *A Selection of Hymns* was published as a supplement to the *Pocket Hymn Book*. In 1810 they were bound together as the "Double Hymn Book" with an appropriate statement in the preface about its price: "We think you will not complain of the additional price, seeing that the two bound together will be much lower than if they were separate."

The 1821 and 1836 hymnals more fully reflect the content of John Wesley's 1780 *Collection* than previous editions. The variants of texts prompted David Creamer of Baltimore to publish *Methodist Hymnology*, 1848, the first Methodist commentary on Wesleyan hymnody and hymnal companion, produced in either Great Britain or the USA.

For a survey of Wesley hymns included in early USA hymnals, see David W. Music, "Wesley Hymns in Early American Hymnals and Tunebooks," *The Hymn*, 1988.

* Items in the Benson Collection, Speer Library, Princeton Theological Seminary, Princeton, New Jersey, that to date have been examined by the writer.

** Photo print of the 1786 sixth edition with no contents or index pages obtained from Garrett-Evangelical Library, Evanston, Illinois. The United Methodist Publishing House in Nashville, Tennessee, has a 1785 fourth edition in poor condition that was the copy used by the second book steward, Ezekiel Cooper, in preparing later editions of pocket hymn-books. The contents and index pages were copied and compare page for page with the sixth edition.

*** Photoprint obtained from Peabody Library, Johns Hopkins University, Baltimore, Maryland.

**** Frank Baker has kindly shared the in-progress revisions of the *Union Catalog of Wesley Publications*.

Early Tune Collections

Wesley did not limit his publishing activity to texts, but he also published tune books to demonstrate his view that the power of music and its performance practice can be either a complement or a detriment to the central purpose of worship and preaching. (See "John Wesley and the Music of Hymns," pages 49-52.) Following Wesley, USA Methodists early on made limited use of the *Foundery Collection*, 1742, and Thomas Butts, *Harmonia Sacra*, ca. 1754, which was reprinted with additional tunes at Andover in 1816.

Tune names that suggested the appropriate tune for a given text were printed over the first lines of hymns as early as the 1788 *Pocket Hymn Book*. *David's Companion*, 1808, was the first attempt to produce an authorized and standardized tune book. In 1808 the conference gave it tacit approval even though it contained the fuging tunes so repugnate to John Wesley. Reflecting the musical activity of the John Street Methodist Church, New York City, it was revised in 1810 and 1817 but was never officially sanctioned.

The first authorized tune book appears to be *The Methodist Harmonist*, 1821, which was cross-referenced to the 1821 hymnal and revised in 1833 and 1837. Another tune book, *The Devotional Harmonist*, 1849, was also referenced to official hymnals. Other unofficial tune collections published by the church greatly expanded the repertory of tunes, including *Select Melodies*, 1843; *The Harmonist*, 1844; *Sacred Harmony*, 1848; and *Musical Gems*, 1849. See "The Music of Christian Hymns in USA-Wesleyan Traditions," pages 52-57.

The Methodist Episcopal Church continued to expand the content and use of a common hymnal. The 1849 book contained 1,148 hymns, and in 1858 a companion tune book was issued. The size of the hymnal raised anew the criticism that it was more an anthology of devotional poetry than a practical congregational hymnal. The next two decades saw a flood of songbooks published to please those who so strongly objected to both the size and the content of the official hymnal. The General Conference of 1876 finally opened the canon of the official hymnal and authorized a new edition; see "The 1878 Hymnal of the Methodist Episcopal Church," pages 61-62, for a discussion of the 1878 book.

Methodist Protestant Hymnals

At the time of their separation the Methodist Protestants adopted John Harrod's 1828 collection, already in common use. Their next collection issued in 1837 served as the basic source for several hymnals that followed, including the three books produced by both the Methodist Protestant Church and the Methodist Church. An interesting feature in the appendix of the 1859 book is the cross-reference of a dozen tune books with the name of a tune suggested for each hymn, apparently for the convenience of the song leader in selecting a familiar and appropriate tune for a given text.

At the first General Conference of the reunited Methodist Protestant Church, Tourjee's popular *Tribute of Praise* was adopted as the official hymnal according to Walter Newton Vernon, since "the denomination was unable to compile a hymnbook with music when one was called for in 1880 because of the expense." (Vernon 1988, 113) See pages 68-72 for Tourjée's introduction to this hymnal. The 1901 hymnal was the last published by this church and in many respects was more forward-looking in its design and format than most hymnals of that time. The book was published in only one edition, tunes and texts together on a page, one hymn for one tune, with most of the text between the lines of music. A large section before the hymns was devoted to scripture readings and ritual. A comparison of this book with its contemporary, the 1905 hymnal jointly produced by the Northern and Southern churches, shows the Methodist Protestants' successful efforts in producing a small handsome volume with inclusive content.

Vernon describes the church's reception of the book:

> Both directories [branches of the church] were to see better days before the decade was out, due principally to sales of the new hymnal ordered by General Conference at this time. The reason for the new hymnal was simply that the plates of the old one, *Tribute of Praise*, were worn out. The reception of the hymnal by the church was more than gratifying. By 1902 the third edition was on the press and the Pittsburgh Directory reported the most prosperous year in its history . . . [and] by 1904 sales were above the 50,000 mark . . . which was more than the old [hymnal] had sold in its first fifteen years. (Vernon 1988, 113)

Hymnals of the Methodist Episcopal Church, South

Nolan B. Harmon in "The Organization of the Methodist Episcopal Church, South" in *The History of American Methodism* has written that upon separation of the Methodist Episcopal Church into northern and southern branches, the Southern church in its first General Conference, 1846, after some debate, "finally decided that a committee be appointed to compile and publish [a new hymnbook] without reporting back to the conference." (Bucke 1964, 2:141) The committee was assisted in that task by David Creamer of Baltimore who among other distinguished accomplishments put together the first commentary on Wesleyan hymns, *Methodist Hymnology*, 1848. Creamer also assisted in the preparation of the 1859 hymnbook for the 1859 Methodist Protestants.

The Southern church's first hymnal was published late in 1847. (Pilkington 1968, 385) The popular *Songs of Zion*, 1851, which had been compiled by the church's book editor T. O. Summers, became an unofficial supplement to the authorized book, serving a large section of the church that would have nothing to do with the larger collection of 1,047 selections, including 600 by the Wesleys and 150 by Watts. *Songs of Zion*, enlarged in 1873, is the paradigm of the Southern church's publishing house policy of promoting unofficial books as alternatives to the official book. This practice was carried into the merger of the three churches in 1939 and remains in some quarters a misunderstood and controversial policy in marketing worship resources for use by a diverse constituency.

The need for a standardized tune book, according to Robert G. McCutchan, was discussed by the General Conference of 1858:

> [The publishers were authorized to] provide a book which would contain the hymns of the *Collection* of 1847 with musical settings. Such a book had already been prepared by Lemuel C. Everett, from whom the Book agent secured exclusive rights for its publication as *The Wesleyan Hymn and Tune Book:* comprising the Entire Collection of Hymns in the Hymn Book of the Methodist Episcopal Church, South, with Appropriate Music Adapted to each Hymn. It was issued in 1859. (McCutchan 1942, 11)

This music edition appears to have been published in 1860, not 1859 as McCutchan indicates. Its four-page preface stands in contrast to the few instructions that were included in the preface of its counterpart published by the Northern church, *Hymns for the use of The Methodist Episcopal Church and Tunes for Congregational Singing*, 1858. L. C. Everett, the music editor of the 1860 collection, articulates the importance of music in worship and congregational participation:

> Sacred music should be universally cultivated; it is an essential part of divine worship, and, as such, that it is the bounden duty of *all*, not a mere choir of twelve or fifteen persons, but the *entire* congregation, to engage in it.

To implement this principle Everett suggests that

> a permanent congregational singing class be formed for the purpose of meet-
> ing together frequently, say one evening each week, to practice the tunes
> under the direction of a suitable qualified chorister or leader. . . . [Thomas O.
> Summers addressing clergy states] it would also be well for every minister,
> in whose church a congregational singing class may be formed, to supply the
> leader of the music, previous to each weekly rehearsal, with the hymns to be
> used on the following Sabbath. (L. C. Everett and Thomas O. Summers, Pref-
> ace to *Wesleyan Hymn and Tune Book* 1860)

The short-lived 1874 edition with tunes did not prove as successful as had been
hoped, though it did initiate, through the work of Rigdon M. McIntosh as music
editor, the practice of printing the tunes on the page with the words, a practice
that in time became the standard full music edition.

Vernon has provided an account of the reception of the new format:

> Southern Methodists got their first hymnal with the music included on the
> page [with the hymns] in 1874. . . . [The book had] been authorized by the
> 1870 General Conference. The inclusion of hymn *tunes* was a distinctive
> step forward, and this addition was widely acclaimed. One critic, however,
> expressed the feeling that here was one "sad defect" in the volume: a great
> number of new tunes were attached to the old and familiar hymns. While
> the critic (simply signed "L") praised the book as "the best collection of
> church-music ever issued," he also begged "to hope that should another
> edition be prepared, your compilers will be careful to put old tunes to old
> hymns, and new tunes to new hymns." (Vernon 1988, 87)

For further discussion of the development of the hymnals from a words-only
format to a full music edition, see "The Music of Hymns, Wesleyan Style,"
pages 56-57.

According to McCutchan, *"The New Hymn Book*, authorized by the General Conference of 1878, was issued in 1881" (this writer has dated it 1880):

> [The book was issued] in response to a general appeal from certain
> churches of the denomination for a smaller and less expensive hymnal. It
> proved to be an abridgement of *Songs of Zion*, which is referred to in the
> Preface of the *New Hymn and Tune Book* as "the standard Hymn Book."
> (McCutchan 1942, 11)

The action of the 1886 General Conference requested the publishers to produce a
book of not more than 800 selections. The result was the 1889 book patterned after
the 1878 hymnal of the Northern church which included 918 hymns, 11 doxologies,
14 chants, printed in a full music edition as *Hymn and Tune Book*. It was the final
hymnal produced by the Southern church. Perhaps in response to the encroach-

ment of "formal worship" on more informal revivalistic settings, the preface force-fully states that the Wesleyan tradition is best taught through congregational song since Charles Wesley's hymns "hold the essence of sermons and serve as the liturgy of our Churches." (Preface to *The Methodist Hymnal*, 1889, 4)

The Pan-Methodist Hymnal of 1905

Louis Benson in *The English Hymn*, 1905, identifies the hymnal jointly pre-pared by the Northern and Southern churches as a "Pan-Methodist" hymn-book. The move towards a joint hymnbook began with the Southern church's General Conference of 1886 as part of the efforts of both churches to move in concert in matters of common interest. Both were unhappy with the large size of their hymnals, and both had been hard pressed to compete with the mass appeal of revival and Sunday school songbooks. The process of producing this hymnal began with the establishment in 1896 of a joint commission on federation, which in 1898 recommended the joint publication of a joint hym-nal, as well as a common catechism and a common order of public worship. (Vernon 1988, 199)

In *The Music and Hymnody of the Methodist Hymnal*, 1911, Carl F. Price has care-fully reconstructed the path that led to the production of this joint hymnal in 1905, followed the same year by an annotated edition of the hymnal by Charles S. Nutter and Wilbur F. Tillett. According to Walter N. Vernon the files of the secretary of the committee, Charles M. Stuart, and a record of the revision com-mittee's work are housed in the library at Garrett-Evangelical Theological Semi-nary:

> [It] was a splendid book, everyone agreed. Seven hundred and forty-eight hymns new and old which [as described in its preface were an] . . . "expres-sion of sound doctrine and healthful Christian experience" [with] alternate tunes provided for some hymns either with a view to please both branches of the church or to secure a better musical expression for the words than is given by the tune now familiar. It was a big book, 602 pages, and the size of present-day hymnals. It was very much a more scholarly selection of classi-cal church music than previous hymnals of either church: a goodly number of the nineteenth century gospel songs were missing and many new compo-sitions by modern composers were introduced. (Vernon 1988, 200)

The introduction of responsive readings in the hymnal was "an innovation in congregational participation." These readings were printed in sequence for use in fifty-two morning and evening Sunday services during the year. They were comprised of selections from the Psalms and other scripture, many times synthe-sized and printed as one reading and cross-referenced to topics, particular occa-sions, and special days. This worship practice was so popular that "by 1919 the Old Testament lesson in the Sunday service in many Methodist churches was read responsively by the congregation." (Vernon 1988, 200)

In spite of widespread promotion and positive acceptance of the hymnal as both a songbook and a worshipbook, there was still criticism:

All this briefing didn't cut down on the opposition. It was perhaps more southern than northern, more rural than urban; but even these generalizations are weakened by hundreds of exceptions. Where, the voices demanded, was "Shall We Gather at the River," "Softly and Tenderly Jesus Is Calling," "I Am Thine, O Lord," "Let the Lower Lights Be Burning," "Throw Out the Lifeline," "When the Roll is Called Up Yonder," and a dozen favorites? (Vernon 1988, 200)

The Order of Worship as adopted by both churches and carried in the front of the new hymnal gave more trouble. It was quite a change for many congregations that were used to a freer extemporaneous type of service. A sore point was the recitation of the Apostles' Creed and the "I believe in the . . . holy catholic church" (offensive to both churches, apparently, for it was subject to tinkering by General Conferences since 1836). Catholic meant "papist" to a lot of people, not "universal." (Vernon 1988, 201)

Some in the church would express that the troublesome phrase in the Apostles' Creed was the result of a misunderstanding since according to Hoyt L. Hickman: "The word 'catholic' means simply 'universal' and does not refer in particular to the Roman Catholic Church. " (Hickman 1989, 200) The objection was carried over into the consideration of the present hymnal by the 1988 General Conference: "In an amendment to the hymnal report [it] voted to include a footnote explaining this wherever the Apostles' Creed occurs in the hymnal [e.g., **881**]." (Hickman 1989, 200)

Regardless of its imperfections, the 1905 joint *Hymnal* was indispensable:

[It] remained the book no congregation could do without, even if they did sing at times out of the little song books [e.g.] . . . *Songs of Faith and Hope* [1906 and 1909]. Nearly a million copies of these little books had been sold by 1912, when the Book Concern issued a third song book, *Sacred Praise*, which explained in its preface that it was well fitted to serve the prayer and gospel meetings, young people's meetings, Sunday schools, and revival meetings. (Vernon 1988, 201)

For further discussion of the process and content of this hymnal see Arthur L. Stevenson "The Present Methodist Hymnal" [1905], and "Controversy Over Methodist Hymnal," in *The Story of Southern Hymnology*.

The 1935 *Methodist Hymnal*

The 1905 book was for many a beloved book, serving as the official hymnal of the two churches until their union in 1939 with the former Methodist Protestant Church to form The Methodist Church. The editorial process of the 1935 hymnal was begun by the Northern church in 1928 with the creation of a revision committee. This committee was later expanded to include representatives of the Methodist Protestant and the Methodist Episcopal churches.

If anyone has ever doubted the earnestness of the committee's desire to produce a representative hymnal, consider that the entire revision was accomplished at a time when the three branches of the the church were still separate entities and the country was in the throes of economic disaster. A review of the papers and correspondence of the hymnal's remarkable general editor, Robert Guy McCutchan, and the book editor, John W. Langdale, confirms that the editorial process was carried out under the most trying and frustrating conditions to face a hymnal committee since the pre-Civil War efforts of the Methodist Protestants. When one is fully aware of their task and accomplishments, it is apparent that the 1935 hymnal was much better in every detail than might have been expected. McCutchan's files, in part, are housed in the Bridwell Library, Perkins School of Theology, Southern Methodist University; Langdale's files were at one time in the records of The United Methodist Publishing House where they were studied by the present writer in 1969. John W. Langdale prepared a twelve-page description of the revision process and an overview of the hymnal's contents, *The New Methodist Hymnal*, that was distributed by the Methodist book Concern with the publication of the hymnal.

The hymnal's responsive readings and aids to worship were published in 1932 for trial use. The readings followed the form of the previous book and with few exceptions, the book's 562 texts were fully interlined. The hymnal's content was influenced by the leading British hymnals of the first quarter of the century, in particular the 1906 *English Hymnal*. Representative selections from the rich heritage of the United States as well as universal folk hymnody were included. The confining of all gospel hymns to one section titled "Songs of Salvation" appeared to one group as putting them in a second-class relationship with other hymns; others complained, according to Vernon, that their inclusion was to waste space that could have been given over to "much better hymns that have been crowded out." (Vernon 1988, 339) A related issue concerned the so-called liberal bias of the committee who, according to critics, deleted and/or altered too many hymns to make them fit their theology at the expense of traditional biblical symbols and metaphors, and evangelical rhetoric.

In 1935 the publishing houses of the three churches concurrently published the completed hymnal; each church printed its own liturgies in the back of the book and a common form of public worship in the front. In spite of the recession, the hymnal was an economic success:

> In the first year of publication [the Northern church's] Methodist Book Concern reported 200,000 copies in use; by 1938 the Southern Publishing House had sold 300,000 copies. But it was a different story with the Methodist Protestants. [They reported in 1936:] We have been disappointed in the failure of our churches to respond to the appeal in the interest of the new Methodist hymnal. (Vernon 1988, 268-69)

Vernon relates the importance of hymnal sales to the Northern publishing house:

In the late 1930's the Book Concern agents were reporting on the wide acceptance and general use of the *Hymnal*. Forty-two per cent of the total merchandise sales of the Book Concern were from sales of the *Hymnal* in 1936; in 1937 the percentage was 36 1/2; and in 1938 it was 21 per cent. In terms of dollars, three months in 1935 brought in $214,000; 1936 was the big year with $394,000 in *Hymnal* sales; in 1937 $191,000 worth were sold; and sales in 1938 totalled $155,000. (Vernon 1988, 337)

Concerning the sales of the hymnal in the Southern church, Vernon writes that "in the first year [1935] its sales amounted to $114,851. In the second year sales reached $98,581, [which greatly] . . . helped to reduce the annual deficit on the *Christian Advocate.*"

The hymnal was also promoted extensively by the Southern publishing house:

One feature arranged by [E. M.] McNeill and [Walter L.] Seaman was a radio program over Station WSM, Nashville, called "Hymns of the Ages," on which hymns were sung from the *Hymnal* by the Chapel Choir [probably comprised of publishing house personnel]. (Vernon 1988, 373-74)

Frederick E. Maser in "The Story of Unification," *The History of American Methodism*, writes, "On a motion by Robert G. McCutchan [hymnal editor], former dean of the School of Music of DePauw University *The Methodist Hymnal*, already adopted officially by the three churches, became the official hymnal for The Methodist Church." (Bucke 1964, 3:473) In 1939 at its first General Conference in an unparalleled action, the newly formed church, responding to thousands of complaints from church members, ordered the harmonizations by Van Denman Thompson of three tunes (including "What a friend we have in Jesus") removed from the 1935 hymnal and restored to their original and traditional harmonies. In addition the new church also experienced the confusion of having three different rituals in three printings of the "official" hymnal. At unification still a fourth ritual was authorized and incorporated in hymnals printed after 1939. This hymnal was also the last to be printed in shaped-notes.

The 1966 *Methodist Hymnal*

The revision of the 1935 hymnal was set in motion by the 1960 General Conference by a narrow margin of 375-343. The committee, authorized by that conference and named in the jurisdictional conferences, was the first to reflect the church's inclusive constituency, and for the first time a woman and African Americans were voting members. The total revision committee was comprised of twenty-nine members: six bishops, five general board secretaries and staff members, and the eighteen members of the Commission on Worship, in addition to twelve consultants. The age and experiences of the revision committee members, three of whom had served on the committee that produced the 1935 hymnal, effectively linked the music of the hymnal to the past.

Shortly after the publication of the hymnal Erik Routley, who had met with the committee in 1962, sent this writer a hymn-by-hymn critique, prefaced by a letter showing his uneasiness with the book:

> It is obvious how much ground you have had to concede to people who worship mediocrity. . . . I don't think your folk were all that clever in finding new words: I recognize one or two from the outpourings of the Hymn Society, and all I can say about those is that they show you why we don't run hymn-writing sprees over here! But you have your moments of inspiration, and there are enough of them to make me feel that if I had to live with this book I could be a lot worse off." (Correspondence with Carlton R. Young, August 1966)

Routley commends the revision committee for the increase of chorales, USA folk and shaped-note hymnody, and hymns from the Third World, including the Nigerian hymn "Jesus, we want to meet" **(661)**.

Routley later made this additional comment:

> The *Methodist Hymnal* of 1966 . . . was edited by a very large committee representing the various religious interests . . . whose acute consciousness of the need to please many diverse cultural traditions inhibited their inventiveness. Among the new tunes in it we may certainly mention [those] by Lloyd Pfautsch and V. Earle Copes. One wishes that this hymnal's editors had been a little less injudicious in their selection of English tunes—in which field they seem to have backed many losers—but this was the first hymn book to include a tune by Peter Cutts, WYLDE GREEN, and it also includes, uniquely in America, Kenneth Finlay's AYRSHIRE. (Routley 1981, 173)

The leadership and consummate knowledge of the subject area by the celebrated hymnologist and church musician Austin C. Lovelace, chair of the tunes subcommittee, greatly influenced the content of the book. While the committee's efforts, during the years 1960-62, to find new texts came before the hymnic explosion, the book did contain several important new hymns, including those by USA Methodists: Leon Adkins, "Go, make of all disciples" **(571)**, and Georgia Harkness, "Hope of the world" **(178)**, both of which became very popular. (See the article "Recent USA Hymnody," pages 44.)

There was an increase in the number of hymns by the Wesleys and other eighteenth-century evangelicals. Our hymnals' connections with classic English hymnody were maintained and strengthened, for example, with the inclusion of Gilbert K. Chesterton's provocative "O God of earth and altar." The number of gospel hymns was increased, and contrary to the 1935 book, they were spread throughout the hymnal by category or topic. Guy Snavely has described the hymnal's organization:

> An important departure from the historic topical format of American Methodist hymnals is the inclusion of the Christian Year as one of the major sections of the hymnic portion of the book. Other sections are The Gospel and Christian Experience; The Church; and Times, Seasons and Occasions. (Harmon 1974, 2:1190)

The Psalter proved controversial. Fifty psalms from the Revised Standard Version of the Bible were included in whole or in part, but they were printed in short phrases that for the most part destroyed their characteristic parallelism. As in previous hymnals other readings from the Bible and canticles, both spoken and sung, were included. The section on service music was expanded with the intention that it be more accessible to the congregation as well as to the choir.

A worship service in full and brief form was printed in the front of the hymnal. According to James F. White the service was adapted from John Wesley's *Sunday Service* of 1784:

> In returning to Wesley (and what is almost the same, the 1552 *BCP*), the service is tied directly to its origins in the medieval monastic hours, the offices of the early church, and the synagogue service. At the same time, it includes many developments characteristic of nineteenth-century Methodism: extempore prayer, invitation to Christian discipleship, and hymn singing. Thus it is a curious, though workable, fusion of the ancient Christian tradition of the offices plus nineteenth-century evangelical Protestantism. (Dunkle and Quillian 1970, 17)

John Wesley's "Directions for Singing" was included for the first time in a USA Methodist hymnal. The rituals of baptism, confirmation, and holy communion and aids to worship were included in the back. The liturgical reforms initiated with the 1878 hymnal continued to be implemented, with the inclusion of Wesley's abridgement of the Cranmerian eucharistic text from the 1562 *Book of Common Prayer* in both its full form, with John Merbecke's musical responses, and in a four-page reduction. The service's penitential mood, along with its archaic and sexist language, caused it to be set aside in the next decade for leaner and less reflective rhetoric and more upbeat music. One of the finest contributions to the hymnal was Philip R. Dietterich's "Communion Service in E Minor," but because it was printed outside the full service, it was seldom used. A continuing complaint from the church was the lack of consecutive numbering in the ritual section of early editions of the book, making it next to impossible for either worship leaders or the average person to find, follow, or perform the liturgy.

Funding for the revision process came from general church funds allocated for the travel expenses of scheduled meetings of the full and subcommittees.

In addition The Methodist Publishing House funded the expenses of the executive-editorial subcommittee that carried on the day-by-day work of revision through the editor Carlton R. Young, music editor of Abingdon Press. Meetings of the full committee were twice a year, February and October. In between the meetings of the full panel the four subcommittees met: Psalter and ritual/service music; tunes; texts; and executive-editorial. Simple majority rule passed or rejected recommendations; a two-thirds rule prevailed in matters of reconsideration. Walter N. Vernon has characterized the revision process as "not a 'cut and paste' job. It was truly a reconstructed *Hymnal*." (Vernon 1988, 487)

This writer has described the revision process in *Companion to the Hymnal*, 1970:

> Sixty-five hymnbooks were studied. Manuscripts and suggestions were received from thousands of Methodists. An eighty-nine point questionnaire was sent to 22,000 pastors in charge of local churches. Eleven thousand of these questionnaires were returned; the results were tabulated and made available to the hymnal committee at its February, 1961 meeting. The membership of the [then] National Fellowship of Methodist Musicians also received a questionnaire dealing with the music of the 1935 hymnal.

> The results of the hymnal committee's work were recorded in an unprecedented 515 page report* [*most United Methodist college and seminary libraries have copies of the report] and sent in January to the delegates of the 1964 General Conference which met in Pittsburgh in April. The first major business session of the conference was devoted to the hymnal committee's report. After an hour's presentation and discussion, the conference adopted the report without a negative vote. (Gealy, Lovelace, Young 1970, 60-61)

The Methodist Publishing House, while sustaining the substantial expenses of the executive-editorial subcommittee, was also responsible for funding the publishing costs of the hymnal, including permission to use copyrighted material. Vernon has documented the tortuous negotiations and the very high cost, $2,000.00, for permission to use "How great thou art" **(77)**. (Vernon 1988, 488-89) The payment of that fee caused a great stir in denominational publishing and probably initiated the gradual and substantial increase in the cost of permissions experienced by the denominations in the 1980's, including the cost of production of the 1989 hymnal. In May 1977 Robert O. Hoffelt documented the production and promotion of the book in a report titled "The Development of *The Methodist Hymnal*, 1964." The editor's correspondence and working files and Fred D. Gealy's research for his contribution to *Companion to the Hymnal* are housed in Bridwell Library, Perkins School of Theology, Southern Methodist University, Dallas, Texas.

Emory S. Bucke, book editor of The Methodist Church, wrote of the production of the hymnal:

The new hymnal went into production at once, and by the time it was ready for delivery [July 1966], more than two and one-half million copies had been ordered. Five years after publication approximately four million copies were in use throughout [the church]. (Gealy, Lovelace, Young 1970, ix)

Vernon comments on the hymnal's wide acceptance:

Ruth Nighswonger called the appearance of the *Hymnal* "the greatest church music publishing event of this century." V. Earle Copes, editor of *Music Ministry*, emphasized (September 1966) the "important opportunities" of "helping our people learn to love and value the vast repertoire of hymns and other worship resources in their new book." Egon W. Gerdes of Vanderbilt Divinity School examined "Theological Trends in the New Hymnal" in which he concluded that certain of the Wesleyan hymns (such as "Author of faith, eternal Word") help to keep clearly before us the understanding that salvation is of God and not man's achievement: "Here lies the secret of Wesleyan holiness; it is not self-made." . . . *Time* magazine (July 22) [1966] reported that the new *Hymnal* "really balances tradition and innovation." (Vernon 1988, 490)

This wide acceptance was accompanied by unprecedented sales. Yet The Methodist Publishing House discovered that it lacked the labor force, experience, and equipment necessary to produce, print, and distribute well over two million books in a brief period of time and also continue its normal publishing schedule. Enormous problems were encountered, not the least of which was the challenge of printing, binding, and shipping the hymnal.

For a decade the publishing house had been under pressure to upgrade its printing facilities in order to stay competitive with publishers and printers, including those who compiled and printed hymnals and songbooks. Reprints in the 1960's of the 1935 hymnal reflected the printing standards of the late 1920's since for three decades they had been produced from metal plates on letterpress. At the 1964 General Conference the publishing house was asked how the new hymnal would compare in print quality to the 1935 book. According to Vernon, the publisher "promised the 1960 [actually the 1964] General Conference to produce a hymnal that would be the best one possible from the standpoint of materials and printing." (Vernon 1988, 490)

The commitment was made in good faith, and careful research and preparations were initiated to ensure the fulfillment of the promise, a commitment made in part to justify the publishing house's anticipated huge expenditure in purchasing a Cottrell web offset press. Paper by the boxcar-loads was special ordered from a Canadian supplier, but when the paper arrived in Nashville, it had not been prepared for use on the new offset press. Probably without the firsthand knowledge of the publisher and without notification to the hymnal committee and the editor, the first signature (the first forty-eight pages) was printed on the old letterpress, a process that effectively canceled out, by literally pounding out, the subtleties of musical notation and type that had been perfected so painstakingly in two years of editorial and production efforts. The executive-editorial subcommittee of the hymnal committee, the ongoing contact between the general conference and the publisher, met with the publisher. At the conclusion of the meeting the publisher agreed to set aside the first signature of the hymnal, already printed at a cost of $123,000, and print the hymnal according to the original specifications. (For the specifications, see Vernon 1988, 490)

In addition the huge pre-publication sale of the new hymnal brought great pressure upon The Methodist Publishing House to get the book off the press and into the hands of the worshipper. As soon as the book began to roll off the press, the churches who had placed orders and made pre-publication payments for the over two million copies wanted their books to be in the pews by the fall of 1966. Fulfilling the huge print orders and storing the printed sheets slowed down the publishing house's normal extensive printing activity and used all available extra storage space in the Nashville plant. The bindery worked around the clock. Salaried executives were pressed into duty to assist plant personnel in boxing and moving the huge inventory towards shipment to local churches who were eager to be the first to sing from the new book. Most of the hymnals were in the pews by Advent. Unfortunately, after a few months of use in some churches, the books began to fall apart because of the faulty design and construction whereby the pages (signatures) pulled away from the spine when the books were set upright in the pew racks. The publishers replaced all defective books and developed a more sturdy binding that held up well in future printings.

THE FATE OF THE 1966 HYMNAL

In spite of its initial acceptance and wide use, with over 4,500,000 sales, the new hymnal failed to become the single worship resource for The United Methodist Church, formed by the merger of the former Evangelical United Brethren and the former Methodist Church two years after the hymnal's publication. The Evangelical United Brethren Church had published its last hymnal in 1957 (see "Hymnals of the Former Evangelical United Brethren Church," page 89). As the negotiations towards merger proceeded, the churches who had purchased that hymnal, as well as the denomination's publishing interests, pondered the future of their investment in what was an essentially new hymnal.

The process that produced the content of the 1966 hymnal occurred at the same time that the merger negotiations were in process. Questions about the advisability of continuing with the revision of the Methodist hymnal were raised by leaders in both denominations. In response, two consultants were named from the former Evangelical United Brethren Church, Paul H. Eller, an editor of the 1957 hymnal, and Paul A. Washburn, who became one of the last bishops elected by the former Evangelical United Brethren Church. Their presence in the work of the Methodist revision committee did little to shape the contents of the Methodist book, but it was politically astute to include the consultants since it allowed the committee to state to the 1964 General Conference that it had consulted with The Evangelical United Brethren Church. Publishing a hymnal by the former Methodist Church while in the process of merger was an arrogant and futile demonstration of dominance. For a discussion of the influence of the 1957 hymnal on the content of the 1989 hymnal, see *"The United Methodist Hymnal, 1989,"* pages 129-31.

The future of the 1957 *Hymnal* was again raised with the closing of the former Evangelical United Brethren printing facilities in Dayton and Harrisburg, and all printing was consolidated in Nashville. In response to this concern the 1970 called session of the General Conference meeting in St. Louis, at the publisher's request through the book editor, retitled *The Methodist Hymnal* as *The Book of Hymns,* with the assurance that the 1957 hymnal would be kept in print for an unspecified period.

The committee, certainly not its editor, could hardly have foreseen the combination of forces that would prevent the hymnal's being used for less than the three-decade average life of its predecessors this century. This writer has traced these forces in the forthcoming *Music of the Heart: Church Music from a Wesleyan Perspective:*

First was Vatican II, 1963 forward, with its startling reforms in leadership, language and music in time embracing and influencing the entire ecumenical and global Christian community.

Second, the music of the civil rights and anti-war movements was on the tube every night at 5:30 and 6:00. In terms of hymnic repertoire, the European musical styles and rhetoric in *The Methodist Hymnal* (1966) simply were out of sync with what was going on outside the church. As the message and energy of these movements were replicated in traditional worship settings, the style and content of standard hymns were challenged by the song of the slave and the urban black, [and] the guitar strumming war protestor. For many teenagers and young adults John Lennon's "Imagine" was more relevant than Fanny Crosby's "Blessed Assurance."

Third, Christian worship became a segment of the entertainment industry as religious television programs and commercial recordings refashion it, particularly its music, into a popular and saleable commodity. Local churches in their attempts to incorporate the repertory of the then called "electric church' into their worship services began to set aside traditional hymns, and sang the new repertory from paperback songbooks accompanied by guitar, piano and drums.

Fourth, from the hymnic explosion [see "Recent British Hymnody," pages 16-17] there emerged more than 1,200 new hymns expressing current topics and concerns, written in the emerging language base, set to singable tunes, and printed in paperback supplements which were used along with the traditional hymnal as well as the pop paperbacks.

Fifth, the development, compiling and publishing of the hymnody of ethnicity: African American, Asian American, Native American, and Hispanic American. [See the discussion in "USA Hymnody," pages 19-27.]

Sixth, the modification of the language base of hymns and liturgy in North American churches away from the King James Version of the Bible and *Book of Common Prayer*. [See "Recent USA Hymnody," pages 45-46.]

Seventh, the elimination of hymnody, worship, and preaching as requirements in seminary curricula contributed to an unqualified use by worship leaders of questionable alternative hymnody, and the narrowing of a congregation's repertory to the predictable and familiar. (Young 1993)

These forces coalesced, and the contents of the hardbound hymnal were regarded as inadequate for worship. The hymnal's perceived lack of relevance and the development and proliferation of supplemental materials began in seminary worshipping communities and in the programs and publications of the church's bureaucracy. Throw-away supplemental worship materials and music, much of it illegally reproduced by photocopying, became the *sine qua non* for introducing alternative styles of music, liturgy, poetry, and performance practice. Local churches filled their pew racks with songbooks from private publishers, prompting fundamental questions to be raised: what is an authorized hymnal, who is it meant to serve, and who should determine its content? These questions were restated and answered through the process that produced The United Methodist Church's first hymnal.

THE UNITED METHODIST HYMNAL, 1989

Well into the 1980's The United Methodist Publishing House had maintained a cautious and conservative attitude towards publishing supplements to the church's two official hymnals, the 1957 *Hymnal* and *The Methodist Hymnal*, 1966. Its first attempt was the songbook *Ventures in Song*, 1972, compiled by the denomination's Commission on Worship, later titled the Section on Worship, a part of the new General Board of Discipleship. While the songbook's content reflected alternative religious song, its cluttered format, poor print quality, price, and lack of marketing strategy made it one of the best-kept secrets in the music trade.

Hoyt L. Hickman writes that the publishing of alternative religious song was advanced by the general church in its concern for ethnic minority persons and their churches:

> [The 1976 General Conference made] ethnic local church ministries one of the missional priorities for 1977-80. As a result, moneys became available to enable the Section on Worship to work with ethnic caucuses and to fund the task forces, consultations, and editors needed to produce ethnic hymn and songbooks. (Sanchez 1989, 10)

Action by the conference also mandated the preparation of a "supplemental contemporary Hymnal." The task of supervising the preparation of supplements to the authorized hymnals was remanded to the Section on Worship. The following supplements have been developed in cooperation with Abingdon Press: *Songs of Zion*, 1981; *Supplement to the Book of Hymns*, 1982; and *Hymns from the Four Winds*, 1983. *Celebremos I* and *II* and *Voices: Native American Hymns and Worship Resources*, 1992, were developed and distributed by Discipleship Resources. For a discussion of the religious song from these traditions see the appropriate section in "USA Hymnody," pages 17-47.

SUPPLEMENT TO THE BOOK OF HYMNS

The 1976 General Conference presented the Section on Worship and The United Methodist Publishing House with a joint mandate:

> [To produce] a supplemental contemporary Hymnal, possibly loose-leaf in form for additions and deletions, for local church use. It should reflect our

contemporary religious climate, as well as the heritage of many diverse groups in The United Methodist Church. (*Daily Christian Advocate* 1976, 614)

The volunteer task force named by the Section on Worship with the approval of the publishing house was Jane Marshall, chair, Sara Collins, and James A. Rogers. Consultants were Roger N. Deschner, Ellen Jane Lorenz Porter, and John Erickson. Carlton R. Young served as editor. At the conclusion of three years the task force's recommendations were submitted to the Section on Worship and The United Methodist Publishing House.

After the contents of the *Supplement* were reviewed and approved, the publishing house began manuscript preparation, cleared copyright permissions, including the approval of textual changes, and arranged for the music to be set. As proofs were circulated, the elected members of the Section on Worship, who throughout the process had pressed for a more populist collection, declared the collection's contents too elitist. Without consulting with the task force, the staffs of the the two agencies gathered at the publishing house and in a protracted meeting significantly changed the proposed contents, ironically, working in a room adjacent to the one where the *Supplement's* editor, who had been hurriedly summoned, was checking "final proofs." When the proposed changes were presented to the chair and editor as nonnegotiable, they resigned. They returned to complete the editorial task after the original content was restored.

The *Supplement* contained 123 hymns and songs that were selected by the task force, complying with the instructions from the General Conference:

> The *Supplement to the Book of Hymns* is a collection of congregational song . . . which has been used in The United Methodist Church and the wider Christian community since the canon of *The Book of Hymns* was closed in 1963 . . . [with] selections from The Evangelical United Brethren Church; the old and new gospel traditions; that [have been] . . . identified as representative song by task forces from four ethnic minority groups within United Methodism. . . . In its editorial work, which spanned three years, the *Supplement* task force received from the general church and reviewed approximately fifteen hundred texts, some already with appropriate music settings. (Preface to *Supplement to the Book of Hymns*, 1982)

The work of the task force anticipated the debates concerning language later experienced by the church in the preparation of *The United Methodist Hymnal*:

> The task force [was] sensitive to the importance that United Methodists place on inclusive, nonsexist, and nondiscriminatory language. Accordingly, some word changes have been made in texts. (Preface to *Supplement to the Book of Hymns*, 1982)

Even though it went through several printings, the *Supplement to the Book of Hymns* was viewed by the church as a whole as too "far out" for sustained Sunday-by-Sunday use because of its broad content and inclusive approach to language that had been mandated by the General Conference. The alphabetical arrangement of the hymns seemed to emphasize the lack of cohesion topically or by liturgical season.

From another perspective Erik Routley in an article about supplements to major hymnals, which proved to be his final published writing on USA hymnody, gave this evaluation of the *Supplement*: "All I can say is that on the whole the editors of this book . . . went for what they were advised would cause them to be well thought of by women, by ethnic groups, and by progressive ministers. . . . By reading this *Supplement* through I am left in some doubt about what Methodists really stand for in the 1980s." (Routley 1982, 510)

United Methodists in the early 1980's were ill at ease with multiethnic and multilanguage hymns, and professional musicians were surprised by, if not disappointed with, the juxtaposition of Bill Gaither, "Because He lives" **(364)**, with Dietrich Bonhoeffer, "By gracious powers" **(517)**. The church's musical and liturgical leadership seemed to lack the creative and informed skills necessary to teach and use effectively such a rich variety of material in a congregational setting. Pastors who were in charge of planning the worship and selecting the hymns, except for recent seminary graduates, were particularly ill equipped to deal with the *Supplement* even after purchasing it, preferring instead other supplements or the standard hymnal. The main use of the *Supplement* was in seminaries, choirs, and alternative worshipping communities. Those from the Section on Worship who had insisted on a more populist and friendly content appeared to have made their point. Music and worship leaders who affirmed the content of the *Supplement* braced for what appeared to be in store for the committee, although yet to be formed, charged with the revision of the hymnal.

Of the four supplements, *Songs of Zion* with its generous fare of teachable and singable spirituals, standard evangelical hymns, and gospel songs proved to be the most popular. *Celebremos* fared well in the Hispanic community but elsewhere had very little use. *Hymns from the Four Winds* had a similar fate outside the Asian American community.

STUDY AND RESEARCH

In addition to the mandate for the Section on Worship and The United Methodist Publishing House to develop a "supplemental contemporary Hymnal," the 1976 General Conference also "remanded all matters of changes in the *Book of Worship* and Hymnal to the Board of Discipleship for study." Hoyt L. Hickman has summarized the results of this study:

> In response to the second action, the General Board of Discipleship asked The United Methodist Publishing House to join it in setting up a joint task force for a four-year study. This was done; the resulting study found that

(1) the need for a new hymnal was growing but not yet urgent enough to require immediate action, and (2) the existing psalter and service music sections of the hymnal were seriously deficient, and research and field testing were needed to determine what psalter and service music would be suitable for United Methodists.

On petition from the General Board of Discipleship, the 1980 General Conference (*Daily Christian Advocate*, pp. 476, 983-84) authorized the board to do research, preparatory work, editing, and design, in cooperation with The United Methodist Publishing House, toward a new official United Methodist hymn and worshipbook and to make a report to the 1984 General Conference. (Sanchez 1989, 11)

This preparatory work included research to determine what content of the church's two official hymnals were being used; what use had been made of the supplements and other like materials; and what United Methodists wanted in a proposed new hymnal, including content, format, size, and price. In addition it mandated the Section on Worship to develop and test a new version of the Psalter; to pursue the suitable research and publish a collection of service music; to develop recommendations about the general design of the proposed hymnal; and to prepare all of these recommendations in a report to go to the 1984 General Conference.

Hickman continues on the work of the Section on Worship:

For the next four years this work was carried out. Surveys were taken, which yielded much specific information as to what United Methodists were and were not singing, and what they wanted. Study of needs relating to the psalter resulted in the commissioning of a new translation of the Psalms by Gary Chamberlain, which The Upper Room published in *The Psalms* (1984) and *Psalms for Singing* (1984). Study of needs relating to service music resulted in a Service Music Project, which commissioned and tested a variety of new service music.

Two findings emerged from this work:
1) The need for a new official United Methodist hymn and worshipbook had grown to the point where full-scale development of such a book should begin.
2) More time was needed for developing and testing a suitable psalter and service music, and for developing the specifications and outline of the book as a whole. (Sanchez 1989, 12)

The findings were incorporated into the larger report presented to the 1984 General Conference. The Discipleship Legislative committee, after discussing the report, recommended to the plenary that there be authorized a quadrennial Hymnal Revision Committee "to prepare a single volume hymn and worship book for congregational use in The United Methodist Church and to submit the contents of this book to the 1988 General Conference for adoption as the official hymnal of The United Methodist Church." (Sanchez 1989, 12)

THE REVISION IS AUTHORIZED

The conference considered the matter of revision immediately following heated debate on the report *Words that Hurt and Words that Heal*, which was presented by the conference's study commission on language. Debate concerning the hymnal centered on two issues: language and the use of general church funds to finance the expenses of the revision process. After extended discussion both issues were remanded to the Discipleship Legislative committee, who in turn met with the committees on Publishing Interests and Finance and Administration. The next day the revised proposal was brought back to the conference, and at the close of debate the conference voted by a margin of three to one to authorize the revision.

In the final action, bowing to pressure that no general church funds be used in the revision of the hymnal, The United Methodist Publishing House agreed to fund the process of revision, which in the end amounted to over two million dollars.

ENABLING PETITION

As amended by Action of the 1984 General Conference
(DCA pp. 402, 567, 610-613, 718)
and Enacted by That Body

Enabling Petition

Disciplinary Reference: Para. 1314.3

The Board of Discipleship, in cooperation with The United Methodist Publishing House, petitions the General Conference to enact the following:

A quadrennial Hymnal Revision Committee is hereby constituted and authorized to prepare a single volume hymn and worship book for congregational use in The United Methodist Church and to submit the contents of this book to the 1988 General Conference for adoption as the official hymnal of The United Methodist Church.

It is recommended that the committee be sensitive to 1) inclusion of hymns from the EUB tradition; 2) inclusion of hymns representing ethnic minorities; 3) inclusive and non-discriminatory language; and 4) the needs of small membership churches.

The hymnal committee shall be instructed to respect the language of traditional hymns contained in the 1964-66 United Methodist [sic] hymnal, but may also include alternate texts for the same hymn tunes in instances determined by the committee.

The committee shall consist of the following voting membership:

1) Three bishops from different Colleges of Bishops, elected by the Council of Bishops.

2) Ten at-large representatives, two from each jurisdiction, including three laymen, three laywomen, and four clergy, at least one to be a clergywoman. These to be selected by the Council of Bishops from a pool chosen from each jurisdiction—a pool of one layman, one laywoman, one ethnic, one clergyman, one clergywoman and balanced by the Council of Bishops.

3) Three representatives of The United Methodist Publishing house, including the Editor of the hymnal.

4) Five representatives of the Board of Discipleship, not more than two to be staff members.

5) One voting representative of the Fellowship of United Methodists in Worship, Music, and Other Arts.

6) No more than three additional representatives to provide that the overall committee shall have at least one ethnic from each of the four ethnic groups, two clergywomen, one small church rural member or clergy, and one young adult.

One of the three bishops shall be the convenor and shall supervise the election of the chairperson and other officers at the first meeting.

The United Methodist Publishing House shall be the publisher in accordance with Para. 1314.3 of *The Book of Discipline* and shall be responsible for the employment of the hymnal editor. The Board of Discipleship shall "provide editorial supervision of the contents" in accordance with Para. 1214.3 through its representatives on the committee and by supplying staff support to the developmental process.

The enabling petition affirmed the editorial prerogative of the Board of Discipleship, which "shall provide editorial supervision of the contents," as per *The Book of Discipline*, Para. 1214.3; but at the same time it diluted that responsibility (and in practice during the process of revision it was set aside) by providing that editorial supervision of the revision would take place "through its representatives on the committee and by supplying staff support to the developmental process."

In reality, several factors worked together to make it impossible for any significant alteration of the work of the Hymnal Revision Committee other than by the 1988 General Conference.

The revision process was coordinated from the editor's office housed in The United Methodist Publishing House in accordance with Para. 1313.3 of *The Book of Discipline* ("The United Methodist Publishing House shall be the publisher [and] shall be responsible for the employment of the hymnal editor"); and the contents of the new book was determined in the very brief period of two and one half years by a politically inclusive twenty-five-member revision committee. The political reality expressed in the petition is that power flows from those who pay the bills. As the political aspects of the revision process developed, it became evident that there probably would have been no report to the 1988 General Conference, except one of progress, if the coordination of the editorial process had been housed outside The United Methodist Publishing House.

THE EVANGELICAL UNITED BRETHREN ISSUE

Another recommendation in the petition was for "the inclusion of hymns from the EUB tradition." Ellen Jane Lorenz Porter had earlier expressed her concern on this issue:

In 1968 The Evangelical United Brethren Church merged with The Methodist Church to form The United Methodist Church. It was the hope and expectation that the strong emphasis on hymn singing in the EUB church would have a positive impact on the equally strong Methodist love of hymns. Although the first hymnal to be published since the union will not be issued for about four years, it is perhaps pertinent here to offer a few opinions from one who has been involved directly in the discussion of the future hymnal in its formation.

Earlier in her capacity as one of the representatives of the former Evangelical United Brethren denomination and as a consultant to the committee for the compilation of the 1982 *Supplement to the Book of Hymns* and to the Hymnal Revision Committee for the forthcoming new hymnal (in 1991?), the present writer attended meetings in Nashville and Bethlehem, Pennsylvania, and furnished the committees with listings of hymns written by Evangelical and United Brethren writers which have continued to be used in the churches. In her considered opinion, the inclusions in the *Supplement* are somewhat disappointing, and the inclusions in the proposed new hymnal could be equally disappointing.

Hanby's "Who is He in Yonder Stall" can be found in both. Arranged by a former United Brethren, "Near to the Heart of God," by Cleland B. McAfee, a Presbyterian clergyman, will be found in the new hymnal [472]. It is considered to be representative of The Evangelical United Brethren Church because it was contained in the last United Brethren hymnal and the Evangelical United Brethren hymnal.

Some of us, however, still hope for the inclusion of United Brethren clergyman Frank Cross's "Go Forth, Strong World of God," which won a prize in a Hymn Society contest. Also, some of us would include E. S. Lorenz's "Come, Let Us All Unite to Sing." (Lorenz's "The Name of Jesus Is So Sweet" can be found in the recently published *Songs of Zion*.) The Evangelical writer Elisha Hoffman, who wrote gospel songs that are found in the Evangelical United Brethren hymnal and others, is best known for his "Christ Has For Sin Atonement Made," and this should probably also be included. It is not yet known whether some or all of these will appear in the final version of the hymnal. If they do not, some former Evangelical United Brethren may be tempted to suspect the compilers of tokenism. The new hymnal's primary purpose, we were given to understand, was to represent *United* Methodism. Along with these hymns it is also hoped that the new hymnal retains or even enlarges the admirable number of folk hymns found in the 1966 *Book of Hymns*. Such folk hymns would help many former Evangelical United Brethren to feel at home in the hymnal. (Porter 1987, 75-76)

The General Conference's unqualified recommendation to include hymns from Evangelical United Brethren sources was interpreted in two ways by the Hymnal Revision Committee: hymns should be considered from the hymnic tradition of the former Evangelical United Brethren Church, and consideration ought to be given also to hymns written by members of the former church.

Concerning the first issue, the action of the 1980 General Conference had made provisions for gathering information on the use of these hymnals, but that research was conducted solely to determine the use of the 1966 Methodist book. Without a research tool such as the study involving the 1966 book, the texts subcommittee studied the 1957 book and found that there was much overlapping with the 1966 book: about 300 hymns in whole or part were in common between the two books. Specific suggestions for the inclusion of hymns in the Evangelical United Brethren tradition came chiefly from revision committee members who had been members of the former Evangelical United Brethren Church, and for the most part their suggestions duplicated Porter's.

The second issue concerned the consideration of hymns composed by hymn writers from the Evangelical United Brethren tradition. Ellen Jane Lorenz Porter, who had served as consultant to the task force that compiled the *Supplement to the Book of Hymns*, met with the texts subcommittee in the summer of 1985 to make recommendations. These recommendations and additional materials that were later sent to the editor in time were considered by the texts subcommittee. As she had feared, Ms. Porter's suggestions from Evangelical United Brethren Sunday school and revival hymnody were rejected by the texts subcommittee, primarily because of their similarity in style to the evangelical hymnody from the Methodist side of that tradition and also because the larger committee lacked an advocate for the cause of preserving the evangelical hymnody of the former church.

The texts subcommittee recommended to the full committee Evangelical United Brethren favorites, such as "Who is he in yonder stall" **(190)**, written by Benjamin Russell Hanby, who was a nineteenth-century Evangelical Association minister; "Great is thy faithfulness" **(140)**, composed by Methodist minister William Marion Runyan; and "Forward through the ages" **(555)** by Unitarian minister Frederick Hosmer. Yet it became apparent to the editor that none of the hymns that were recommended by Porter from the former church's revival and Sunday school tradition would be included in the 1,144-page report to the delegates of the General Conference; therefore, on the editor's initiative and with the approval of the full committee at the site of the 1988 General Conference, Porter's transcription of a camp-meeting hymn, "O the Lamb" **(300)**, which had been included in the *Supplement*, was added as an amendment to the report. The intent of this action was twofold: to perpetuate the name of Lorenz, which is synonymous with late nineteenth- and early twentieth-century evangelical hymnody and publishing; and to include an additional contribution from the camp-meeting traditions, important factors in the development of hymnody in both the former Evangelical United Brethren and Methodist churches. Nevertheless, it was tokenism and demonstrated that the 1980-84 research, which dealt only with the 1966 Methodist book, tipped the entire revision process towards the perpetuation of that body of hymnody; even that part of the petition concerning language (see below) cites the 1966 *Book of Hymns* as normative, with no mention of the 1957 *Hymnal*. The omission of a significant number of Evangelical United Brethren hymns also confirmed the revision committee's chronic difficulty in identifying Sunday school and revival hymnody for what it really is—folk hymnody—and revealed a lack of perception by committee members concerning the former Evangelical United Brethren Church that their hymnody, as part of their heritage, was worth perpetuating. The present hymnal as well as USA hymnic bibliography is poorer for these errors in judgment.

THE LANGUAGE ISSUE

Establishing Guidelines

The "Enabling Petition" expressed the language issue in classic political doubletalk:

> It is recommended that the committee be sensitive to . . . inclusive and non-discriminatory language. The hymnal committee shall be instructed to respect the language of traditional hymns contained in the 1964-66 [*sic*] United Methodist hymnal, but may also include alternate texts for the same hymn tunes in instances determined by the committee.

The Hymnal Revision Committee at the very beginning of its task attempted to understand the curious if not contradictory set of directions: "be sensitive to inclusive language, but respect the language of traditional hymns." As the revision process proceeded, it became apparent that the task of the committee was made easier by having no official rules about language; consequently, it was free to produce its own rules and test them against the church's perception of how the language issue should be approached.

Because the committee's "Language Guidelines" are the first to be developed by any official body of the church, they are included below.

A. Guidelines for making specific changes in hymns written in traditional language:

1. All texts shall be tested by the Wesleyan quadrilateral of *Scripture, tradition, experience* and *reason*, which includes sensitivity to our participation in the ecumenical church. (These are the same criteria applied to selection by the Texts Subcommittee before reference to the Language Subcommittee.)

2. In traditional hymns or in new hymns written in traditional language we can and should employ inclusive forms of address for persons in the assembly, in the community and the world. "Traditional language" is defined as language used in devotional poetry either in [the] original or in [a] translation based on Cranmer and/or the King James Version until the time of World War II.

3. In traditional hymns or new hymns written in traditional language, it should, in most instances, be possible to retain the poet's original forms of address, descriptions, and metaphors for God, all three persons, but to substitute for unnecessarily repeated gender metaphors, nouns, and pronouns.

4. Texts shall be carefully examined to determine what they state or imply with regard to: care of God's creation; human rights with respect for all races and cultures and both sexes, and with equal opportunity and dignity for all persons; international understanding and cooperation; the eradication of war and the establishment of justice and peace.

   Therefore, language that is discriminatory or not otherwise in accord with the Social Principles of *The Book of Discipline* should be altered or deleted.

5. Substitutions may be made for gender descriptions, and forms of address for church, nation, nature, objects, and virtues.

B. Editorial considerations when dealing with hymns written in traditional language with a view toward alterations and changes.

1. *Belief*: determine that a given text *as is* constitutes a statement of faith and belief for significant numbers of United Methodists; and determine that if the text is substantially altered, it *would* or *would not* remain a statement of faith or belief for significant numbers of United Methodists.

2. *Syntax*: changes in texts that are quotations or paraphrases of biblical texts ought to be done in the language base of the original text. The above ought to apply also in instances of English translations and

devotional poetry. [The committee should] avoid rewording of word order and substituting words that change the poet's original intention.

3. Substitutions for words and phrases ought not change the essential message of the hymn.

Guidelines for "New Hymns"

[Note: These were based on guidelines suggested by S. Paul Schilling]

1. The hymn text should be in accord with the basic faith of the Christian community, consistent with biblical teachings and the highest experience and insight.

2. The poetic and often metaphorical language of the hymn should express convictions that are consonant with Christian truth and have a recognizable relation to the psalms, parables, or worship tradition (s).

3. The hymn text should be inclusive and universal in outlook, free from divisive elements and phrases which convey attitudes of superiority or indifference toward people outside the circle of singers.

4. The entire hymn should be structurally sound and have a central theme or organic unity of ideas.

5. The use of language should be simple, concrete, and direct with an emphasis upon clarity and coherence.

6. The specific words and phrases should be put together in an orderly, connected fashion, while following accepted laws of grammar and syntax.

7. The hymn's lines should be poetic, euphonious, and aesthetic. The accented syllables should conform to a rhythm suitable for singing.

Definition of a "New" Hymn

1. When it is *not* written in what we are calling the "traditional English language" associated with the King James Version of the Bible or the *Book of Common Prayer*, and in common use in the church till about the mid-twentieth century. This language includes syntax, grammar, words for God and people, and other vocabulary not in common use today.

2. When the hymn text was written after 1962, at which time the corpus of our present *Book of Hymns* was closed.

Note: For editing purposes, some hymns written after 1962 would, because of their use of the traditional English language, be treated as traditional hymns. Likewise, some hymns written earlier in the twentieth century may, because of language usage, be treated as "new" hymns. But in most cases, the definitions in paragraphs 1 and 2 above should prevail as the basis for a distinction between "new" and "traditional" hymns.

In applying these guidelines, the changes in people language was the least of the committee's problem since there had already been significant progress in education and communication by the late 1980's (see "Recent USA Hymnody," pages 43-47). While there was considerable grumbling in the church about the proposed changes (e.g., with reference to the human family "men" was changed to "all"), early in the process these changes were generally accepted as *fait accompli* and posed little threat that this part of the issue would prevent the acceptance of the committee's report at the 1988 General Conference or the sale of the hymnal after approval.

Another issue the committee faced concerned anachronistic or old language, for example in the hymn "Come, thou Fount of every blessing" **(400)** in stanza 2:1, "Here I raise mine Ebenezer." Here and in most instances unless the entire hymn could be rendered in contemporary language, there was no change. Therefore "thou" was not changed to "you"; "mine" was not changed to "my"; and "Ebenezer," which literally means "a pile of rocks or other marker designating the length of a day's journey," was retained (see page 301). An example of a hymn that was recast in contemporary English is Albert F. Bayly's "Lord, whose love through humble service" **(581).** In stanza 1:2 "who didst on the cross" is changed to "who upon the cross," and in the balance of the hymn "thine" and "thy" changed to "your." The committee's work in this area of language was very conservative and for the most part preserved the lyric and memorable qualities of traditional hymns.

In 1985 Fred Pratt Green dedicated this poem to the Hymnal Revision Committee upon learning of their struggles, some of it related to his hymns.

For Editors and Committees of a New Hymn Book

The Lord have mercy on you, gentlemen
(And you, dear ladies, I make haste to
    add):
For what's a Hymn? Come, tell us, why
    and when.
Some say a Hymn must be addressed to
    God.
Which means it must not be *about* him: so
Mine eyes have seen the glory has to go!
Cantate Domino!

How quickly language changes meaning,
    dates:
So Wesley's *motions* are a proper gaff!
Jehovah on his shining seat creates
In schoolboy circles an excuse to laugh;
Even behest is obsolescent: so,
The day Thou gavest, Lord, will have to go!
Cantate Domino!

From sexist language, Lord, deliver us;
As from the wrath of Woman when she's
    vexed;
To us, mere males, it matters not a cuss.

Let no one maul a long-accepted text,
A pity Whittier knew no better; so,
Dear Lord and Father of mankind must go!
Cantate domino!

Emotional excess must be avoided;
It turns religion, we are told, to dope;
Beware its side-effects as Marx and Freud
    did,
Preferring solid fact to sloppy hope,
Sentiment, yes! the sentimental, no!
Tell me the old, old story has to go!
Cantate Domino!

When choosing tunes a chill runs down
    the spine
(It's music makes nice people much less
    nice):
'Either AURELIA's out, or I resign!'
Printing too many tunes puts up the price;
Best keep the peace and leave the hymn
    out: so,
The Church's one foundation has to go!
Cantate Domino!

When all is done, the critics will complain
You've left out all the hymns they wanted in;
And those who never go to church will rain

Abuse upon you, making such a din
Appreciation will be silenced: so
Why not let other suckers have a go?
Cantate Domino!

Onward, Christian Soldiers!

The committee's real difficulties with dealing with the language problem came with attempts to change the texts of hymns perceived as contrary to the social concerns of the church, particularly as these concerns had been historically expressed in its Social Principles (see guideline no. 4, above).

Early in the language/theology discussions militaristic images became a matter of concern, and the committee focused on dropping "Am I a soldier of the cross?" in the first round of deletions, October 1985. Much protest was subsequently heard, via mail to the office, so much in fact that on May 17, 1986, the hymn was restored. May 17 is also the date when the committee by a split vote of 11-10 deleted "Onward Christian soldiers" from the approved list and modified the text of "The battle hymn of the republic." According to the majority, this action was consistent with the Social Principles of the church. The decision was also greatly influenced by the April 1986 nuclear disaster at Chernobyl, USSR, and "In Defense of Creation," a position paper by the bishops of The United Methodist Church on the futility of nuclear armaments. On the next day, Sunday, May 18, Ray Waddle's front-page story in the Nashville *Tennessean* had the headline "Hymnal Committee Axes Two Favorites." And the war was on!

The story was picked up by CBS TV Sunday evening news; NBC Sunday news mentioned it. On Monday, May 19, all local television stations were covering the story. The ABC network flew in a crew to interview the editor. On Tuesday ABC ran about thirty seconds of the interview, juxtapositioning it with an interview of an African American youth standing outside the US Supreme Court building in Washington, DC, who lamented, "I wish they hadn't done that."

Members of the the full committee received phone calls and letters, including an anonymous caller on the Memorial Day weekend who told the editor, "I've got a lot on you." The Reader Consultant sessions at the annual conferences, which had been planned to get information about the revision process to the church and to receive suggestions, for the most part turned into angry, foot-stomping, shouting matches between the conveners, and the pros and cons. Most of these sessions were covered by television, radio, and print media. Many annual conferences could not get on with their stated agendas until comment had been made, and in some instances debate held, relating to the reported actions of the Hymnal Revision Committee.

By June 6, 200 letters and petitions began each day's routine in the revision office. The daily mail warranted the attention of ten staff members who opened and sorted all the correspondence. By July 1 over 11,000 pieces of mail, 44 in support of the committee's action, had been processed, and replies were sent to each person, church, or group. The office had to make outgoing calls from a pay phone in the lobby because all lines were jammed.

The correspondence expressed four concerns: (1) no changes should be made in traditional hymnody; (2) hymns using military metaphors should be retained as an affirmation of the implied assumption that Christian duty carries an inherent obligation toward civic duty as well. Related to this was the acknowledgement that peace may be gained by a "just war." There was strong resentment to the implication perceived in the committee's action of "dishonoring the memories of those who died for God and country"; (3) militaristic metaphors within hymns should be construed in reference to spiritual warfare, which has a firm biblical base; and (4) just as other special interests were apparently being taken seriously by the committee, e.g., ethnic hymns, hymns with accepted usage from the majority ought to be considered in equal measure.

On July 1, 1986, at the height and in the heat of the controversy Brian Wren wrote this satirical poem, and dedicated it to the Hymnal Revision Committee:

Battle-Cry of the (Spiritual) Republic

Onward, Christian Rambos,
   spoiling for a fight!
Wave the flag for Jesus,
   knowing that we're right!
Spread the gospel nerve-gas,
   throw grenades of prayer,
blast the Spirit's napalm:
   evil's ever there—

Refrain:
Onward, Christian Rambos
   spoiling for a fight!
Wave the flag for Jesus,
   knowing that we're right!

Like a panzer army
   we shall blitz the foe.
Rugged Cross, old glory,
   lead us as we go!

Hail or heil your leader,
   Christians, do or die,
schooled and drilled for combat
   never asking why—

(Refrain)

Feel the thrill of bloodshed,
   guns and holy wars.
We don't really mean it:
   it's all metaphors.
Nuke the Devil's Empire,
   for in God we trust.
We will love our en-e-mies,
   when they bite the dust—

(Refrain)

The poet comments on his poem and the hymn in "Onward Christian Rambos? The Case Against Battle Symbolism in Hymns," *The Hymn* 38(3):13-15. For responses to this poem see *The Hymn* 38(4):36-38.

On July 7, in special session the committee restored "Onward, Christian soldiers" to the list of approved hymns, adding the original second stanza with the reference to Christians fighting the forces of Satan. The full text of "The battle hymn of the republic" was also approved. (See the commentary on these hymns, pages 546-47, 621-22, and Lionel Adey, "Soldiers of Christ and the Sovereign" in *Class and Idol in the English Hymn*, 1988.)

In reversing itself the committee was perceived as responsive to the will of the majority, a view in sharp contrast to the way that the multitudes regarded some church agencies and the church's general political structure. From that time forward the committee was for the multifarious majority a trusted and responsive ally in the war against United Methodism's repressive and impervious bureaucratic superstructure. The committee's work was applauded as an open and an honest attempt to do the will of the church. The New York *Times*, Manchester *Guardian*, *Time*, and scores of others ran feature stories and angry letters to the editor, the end result of which was that there were few United Methodists who had not heard of the revision of their hymnal.The resolution of this controversy in favor of "the people" contributed to the ongoing approval of the work of the Hymnal Revision Committee, its acceptance at General Conference, and in turn the sale and acceptance of the hymnal. Ironically, the entire incident was played out in the misunderstanding, perpetuated as misinformation by the news media, that the committee actually had the power either to prohibit or enable the inclusion of certain hymns, a power reserved to the General Conference, as seen in the Enabling Petition.

In further expressing the church's Social Principles the committee examined traditional hymns that had been claimed to be discriminatory to those persons of color or handicapping conditions. It purged from traditional hymns words, metaphors, and expressions viewed as discriminatory. For example, "white as snow" was removed from line three of the second stanza of "Have thine own way, Lord" **(382)**, in deference to the objections from those of color. During the debate on this hymn one African American member of the committee exclaimed, "You can wash me all you want, but I'll still be as black as I am right now! My blackness is beautiful!" Other familiar hymns viewed as discriminatory, such as those with language describing handicapping conditions, were either changed (see the discussion of "O for a thousand tongues to sing" **(57)** in "Recent USA Hymnody," page 45, and in the commentary pages 510-11) or allowed to stand with the understanding that to change the text, particularly in the first stanza, might prevent the singing of the hymn in many churches.

Other social principles, "concerns for peace, justice, the care of the planet Earth, hunger, and the reconciling ministry of Christ's church to the world" (Preface to *The United Methodist Hymnal*, vi), were expressed in new hymns, e.g., Fred

Kaan's "For the healing of the nations" **(428)** and Timothy Dudley-Smith's "Behold a broken world" **(426)**, both hymns appearing for the first time in any hymnal. Regrettably no hymns with more than passing reference to hunger or the environment were included.

God Language

A second task for the Hymnal Revision Committee dealt with the issue of God language. (For a discussion of God language, see "Recent USA Hymnody," page 46) While the 1984 General Conference's mandate made no explicit reference to God language, the committee responded to the implicit directive of the conference's third instruction: "be sensitive to . . . inclusive and non-discriminatory language."

This task proved as controversial as that dealing with militaristic and discriminatory language as seen in this typical sample unsigned opinion received by the revision office:

> Judgment day is coming. Pray. The Trinity, God the Father, Son and Holy Ghost. I oppose very deeply to any removable of my God and father from any hymn. God is a MAN. Jesus and God are one. Believe the bible not some women's group. No wonder the Methodists are loosing members. Shame on we Methodist. [*sic*]

Initial discussion about God language (i.e., the preponderance of masculine descriptions, metaphors, and addresses to God in many traditional hymns) was led by Beryl Ingram-Ward in the full committee. Its introduction quickly produced sharp negative reaction from conservative members of the committee, especially the articulate William Randolph (Randy) Smith. As a consequence, the matter was quickly remanded to the special language/theology subcommittee comprised of consultants who along with members from the committee approached their task from divergent views: Riley B. Case, United Methodist pastor prominent in evangelical circles; Gracia Grindal, poet and teacher who had served as a language consultant on the committee that produced the 1978 *Lutheran Book of Worship*; Diedra Kriewald, seminary teacher; Jane Marshall, composer; Carolyn Henninger Oehler, annual conference program council director; S. Paul Schilling, theologian and author of *The Faith We Sing*, which became required reading for the group; and John Yarrington, church musician. That group developed the above guidelines that were approved by the parent committee.

The following excerpts from the editor's notes presented during the December 19, 1985, meeting of the subcommittee represent the quality that the subcommittee strived for in textual alteration:

> Our task of altering texts is a practice that has continued in our tradition since 1737 when John Wesley altered/adapted all seventy texts he included in his Charleston *Collection*, a practice he continued for fifty years in his work as

editor-compiler/publisher. One of the least-appreciated aspects of hymnbook editing is the responsibility, if not the necessity, of modifying/changing anachronistic words, phrases, metaphors, descriptions, and forms of address to God and the human family; and selecting, from long poems, the appropriate stanzas to be included. In this regard it is comforting to note that only twenty percent of the hymns in the 1966 book came to us without change from the author's original text. Change is apparently the least desired part of revising a hymnal as expressed by the average person, yet in historic perspective it remains the most compelling aspect of revising a hymnal. Here are some issues I want to raise about changes and alterations.

1. "The alteration must not produce something that labels the original author as a bad poet, a shoddy thinker, or an indifferent stylist." (Routley, *Worship* (1979) 53:1)
2. "Alterations should be confined to places where the offending words are used lightly." (Routley, *Worship* (1979) 53:1)
3. Alterations should avoid simplistic solutions; for example, the inflexible substitution of God for the author's use of "he," "his," and "him."
4. Alterations must be at least as singable as the original text.
5. Some stanzas and in some instances whole hymns ought to be recommended to the parent committee for deletion .
6. With the exception of the end of prayers and doxological stanzas or where the composer has written the music for an "amen," the amen is recommended for deletion. The hint of that action has already brought this response from Chicago:

Dear Dr. Young:

This is the LAST STRAW! If Methodists drop the Amen, I am ready to leave [the] UMC. Then you wonder why the church is losing members. When you even consider doing such a thing as this what do you expect members to do ? I'd rather we keep the old hymnal as it is than do such a ridiculous thing as drop the Amen.

PLEASE KEEP THE AMEN. Worship via the hymns in many instances is more meaningful than the sermons so we NEED TO KEEP THE AMEN.

(Note: The action of the parent committee deleted all amens from all hymns; the only exception is found in the amen to "Praise God, from whom all blessings flow" **(95)**. The committee also placed all the amens in all major and minor keys in the Keyboard Edition of the hymnal.) (For further discussion of amens, see "Amen," pages 581-82, and Routley 1976, 96-99.)

In all our work we should be aware that we are the custodians, the keepers of a tradition of faith language that will continue to be used in evangelical churches well into the next century. . . .We must allow those who are strengthened and counseled with the traditional language to continue in that relationship. At the same time we want, through this hymnal, to introduce young people and others to that same tradition, knowing that textual redefinition and alteration are important so that the church—particularly The United Methodist Church—does not seem too distant from the language base of the everyday world.

In the language subcommittee's work reported through the hymns subcommittee on to the full committee, as a general principle the first lines of hymns were not altered, e.g., "Dear Lord and Father of Mankind" **(358)**. Changes were usually made further along in the text, and then subtilely so as not to jar the memory of the singer. Nevertheless in some hymns changes were made throughout the text.

For example, in "If thou but suffer God to guide thee" **(142)**:

1:2	"him" to "God"
1:3	"he'll" to God"
2:1	"his" to "God"
2:3	"Father" to "Maker"
2:5-6	"nor doubt our inmost wants are known to him who chose us to his own." changed to "we know our inmost wants are known, for we are called to be God's own"
3:1	"his" to "God"
3:3	"his" to "God"
3:6	"him" to "God"

These changes are out of character with the masculine language of the hymn's roots in German pietistic theology. Yet in the opinion of the committee the hymn in its traditional form would have had little continuing use by succeeding generations of those educated and informed within the context of inclusive language.

Another approach to making changes in the God language of traditional hymns was to render phrases in the vocative "who."

Stanza 2 of "I sing the almighty power of God" **(152),**

> I sing the goodness of the Lord,
>   **That** filled the earth with food;
> **He** formed the creatures **with his** Word,
>   And then pronounced them good,

was changed to

> I sing the goodness of the Lord,
>   **who** filled the earth with food,
> **who** formed the creatures **through the** Word,
>   And then pronounced them good.

The language guidelines were also applied when the committee considered traditional language texts written by living poets. A case in point is Timothy Dudley-

Smith's metrical paraphrase of Mary's Song of Praise (Luke 1:46b-55), "Tell out my soul" **(200)**. When compared to the lyricism of the poet's original, the changes are infelicitous, yet the hymn would not have not been included if it were not for the eight instances in which the committee changed "his" to "God." While the changes were cleared with the publisher, who was the author's agent, they were not forwarded to the author. A copy of the author's letter is stored in the editor's asbestos-lined file!

The attribution of God as mother-like is found in a number of traditional hymns. In line 2:5 of "Sing praise to God who reigns above" the imagery in the English translation of the seventeenth-century German pietistic hymn has been changed from female/male,

> As with a mother's tender hand,
> **He** gently leads **his** chosen band,

to female/neuter,

> As with a mother's tender hand,
> **God** gently leads **the** chosen band.

Rupert E. Davies's 4:3 of "Praise to the Lord, the almighty" **(139)**,

> Then to thy need God as a mother doth speed,
> spreading the wings of grace o'er thee,

is set in contrast to the eight masculine descriptions found in previous stanzas, including the caring male(?) eagle of 2:2.

Several new hymns offer the freshness of female imagery and metaphor, among them the well-constructed and singable hymn by R. Deane Postlethwaite, "The care the eagle gives her young" **(118),** and Brian Wren's "How can we name a Love" **(111)**. In 2:4 of the latter hymn, "A father kind, a mother strong and sure," the poet names God as Love and, in a reversal of traditional depictions of male and female parents, describes the father, i.e., God, as "kind" and the mother, i.e., God, as "strong and sure."

More explicit female metaphors are found in 1:3 of Wren's text, "God of many names" **(105):** "God of hovering wings, **womb** and **birth** of time." Another text by Wren, "Bring many names," was significantly reworked at the request of the committee, but was rejected at the committee's final meeting because of the reference at 2:1: "Strong mother God, working night and day."

Because of the fear that extensive reworking of the language of traditional hymns might also be brought into question by the 1988 General Conference if hymns that addressed God as "she" or described God as "mother" were included in the revision, the committee backed away from recommending more provocative hymns, e.g., Brian Wren's "Who is She" (stanza one follows).

> Who is She,
> neither male nor female,
>   maker of all things,
> only glimpsed or hinted,
> source of life and gender?
> She is God,
> mother, sister, lover;
>   in her love we wake,
> move and grow, are daunted,
> triumph and surrender.

As a consequence, the church's general hymnal is isolated from the significant and fresh contributions that in 1988 had just begun to emerge from academic and alternative worshipping communities and are being compared with and in some instances are setting aside some of the five-century-old forms of address and descriptions of deity. The book is less on the growing edge than it might have been and, according to some, should have been.

For additional comments on hymns with female imagery and attributes, see the commentary on the hymns "Wash, O God, our sons and daughters" **(605)**, "O God who shaped creation" **(443)**, "Sing of Mary, pure and lowly" **(272)**, "The first one ever" **(276)**, "Woman in the night" **(274)**, and "Ye who claim the faith of Jesus" **(197)**

The work of the psalms text subcommittee did produce a people-inclusive and deity-neuter text and is the hymnal's significant language contribution. A review of the language guidelines developed by the psalms text subcommittee, Harrell Beck, John Holbert, S T Kimbrough, Jr., and Alan Luff, shows how their work extended beyond that of the parent committee:

Guidelines of the Psalms Text Committee's Adoption of the *New Revised Standard Version Bible*, the "Book of Psalms," in Preparation of The United Methodist Liturgical Psalter.

The . . . United Methodist Liturgical Psalter Guidelines reflect the principles set forth in the inclusive language guidelines adopted by the HRC integrated with a serious regard for the integrity of the Hebrew text. The following integrating principles have been adopted by the PTC in the course of its work: [The traditional rendering of the text is shown in parentheses; the texts cited are from the Psalter, **736-862**, *The United Methodist Hymnal*.]

1. As a general rule, the English neuter is used for inanimate objects regardless of the Hebrew gender. See Ps. 46:5;

(she)
God is in the midst of the city which shall not be moved

2. The third-person masculine singular is retained when translating the third-person masculine singular Hebrew pronoun which refers to the psalmist. See Ps. 22:8:

> He committed his cause to the Lord;
>> let the Lord deliver him.
> Let the Lord rescue him,
>> for the Lord delights in him.

3. The third-person singular generic nouns and pronouns usually are rendered in the plural. See Ps. 1:1:

> (is the man)
> Blessed are those
> (does)
> who do not walk in the counsel of the wicked;

4. When the third-person masculine singular Hebrew pronouns appear as a suffix or in a prepositional phrase referring to God and the antecedent is clear, the pronouns are rendered by the definite article or the demonstrative pronoun.

[Because the biblical text does refer to God in the third-person masculine singular pronoun, objections were raised by some delegates, resulting in the setting aside of this guideline by the 1988 General Conference and the restoration of the masculine reference "his" in forty-six psalms, e.g., Ps. 28:8b:

> The Lord is the strength of the people
> (the)
> the saving refuge of **his** anointed

For additional discussion of this aspect of the work of the psalms text committee see pages 114-115, *Worship Resources of the United Methodist Hymnal.*]

5. When the word "king" refers to God metaphorically, it is translated "Ruler." When an earthly ruler is intended, it is translated "king." See Ps. 44:4a,

> You are my Ruler and my God.

and Ps. 135:11,

> Sihon, king of the Amorites.

6. In North American English language usage the words for "Lord" and "God" are essentially synonymous; therefore, they have been used interchangeably in the PTC's work. (*Report* 1989, 66-67)

ADMINISTRATIVE CHART OF THE REVISION PROCESS

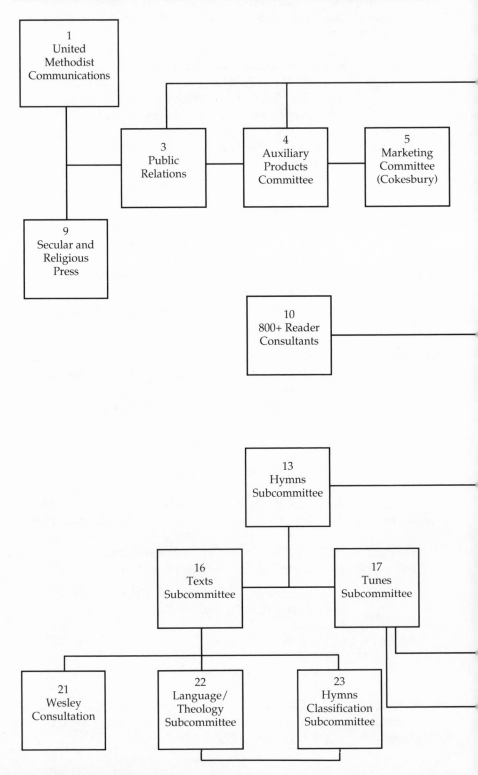

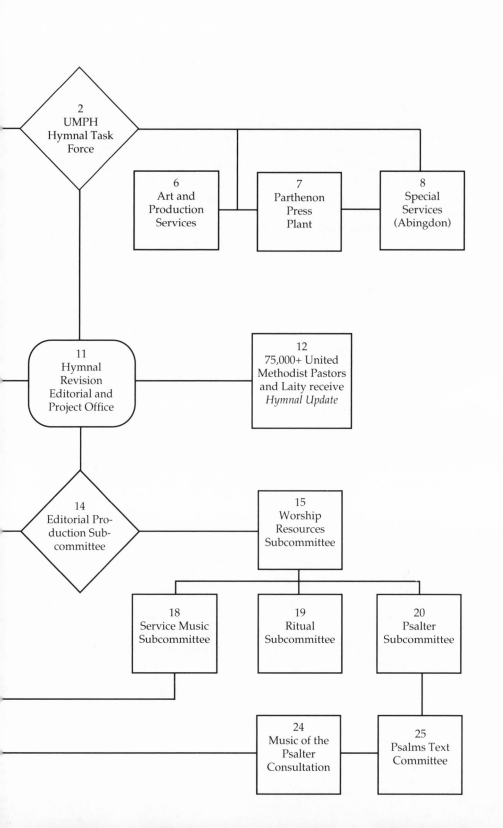

HYMNAL REVISION COMMITTEE MEMBERS, STAFF, CONSULTANTS, PRESENTERS, AND READERS

Sally Ahner, SM
Frank Baker, WC
Tammy Baker, P
Roy D. Barton, HIS
GEORGE W. BASHORE, PC
Harrell F. Beck, PS, PTC
ROBERT C. BENNETT, HY, TU*, CL
Donald G. Bloesch, P
Nancy Regen Bozeman, Design/Production
Ted Campbell, WC
MARY BROOKE CASAD, HY, TX
Riley B. Case, LT, WC
Jonah Chang, P, AC
HELEN GRAY CROTWELL, WR, RI
L. E. Crowson, P
ROGER DESCHNER, secretary, HRC, HY, TU, LT, CL, WC
Carol Doran, P
Agnes H. Fair, Research
Harold Fair, Recording Secretary
ROBERT K. FEASTER, WR, PS, EP*
Ben Fong, P, AC
Don Ford, HY, TU
Craig B. Gallaway, WC
Ira Gallaway, P
BONNIE JONES GEHWEILER, HY*, TX, TU, LT*, CL, WC*, EP
Ray Glover, P, R
Bill Gnegy, Recording Secretary
Anita González, HIS
Gracia Grindal, LT
Eileen Gunther, R
RAQUEL GUTIÉRREZ-ACHON, Vice-chair, HRC, HY, TU, EP
W. T. HANDY, JR., HY, TX, EP
Nobuaki Hanaoka, P, AC
Nolan B. Harmon, P
Charles Hawkins, R
James V. Heidinger II, P
Richard P. Heitzenrater, WC
Betty Henderson, P
JACK HOLLAND HENTON, WR, RI, WC
Hoyt L. Hickman, HY, WR, LT, WC
John C. Holbert, PS, PTC
Denise Hopkins, R

Sharon Howell, P
J. EDWARD HOY, HY, TU, CL
Don Hustad, R
BERYL INGRAM-WARD, WR, RI*, LT, CL, WC
HAROLD DEAN JACOBS, HY, TU, SM
Victor Jacobs, P
REUBEN P. JOB, Chair, HRC, WR, RI, CL, WC, EP
EZRA EARL JONES, HY TX, EP
Ivor Jones, P
Scott Jameson Jones, WC
S T Kimbrough, Jr., PS, PTC, WC
Diedra Kriewald, LT
Arthur J. Landwehr, LT
Thomas A. Langford, III, WR
James E. Leath, Design/Production
Robin Leaver, R
George F. Lockwood, HIS
Judy L. Loehr, PS
I-to Loh, P, R
Alan Luff, P, PTC
Kendall Kane McCabe, WC, R
William Bobby McClain, HY, TX
Jane Manton Marshall, LT
Rex D. Matthews, WC
Frances Merritt, HRC office
Floyd Mevis, HRC office
Donna Nowels, HRC Office
Carolyn Henninger Oehler, LT
HOPE OMACHI-KAWASHIMA, HY, TU, SM, AS
Albert C. Outler, WC
RONALD P. PATTERSON, HY, TX, CL*, EP
Ellen Jane Lorenz Porter, P
Jeanne Audrey Powers, P
Marjorie Proctor-Smith, R
Richard Proulx, PS
William Watkins Reid, Jr., R
William J. Reynolds, R
Don E. Saliers, PS
Diana Sanchez, SM
Lyle Schaller, P
S. Paul Schilling, LT
Russell Schulz-Widmar, R
CHARLES M. SMITH, WR, PS*, LT, CL

Gary Alan Smith, HRC Project Director, TU, SM
William Farley Smith, HY, TU
WILLIAM RANDOLPH SMITH, HY, TX, LT
Jim Snead, P
Naomi Southard, P, AS
NANCY STARNES, WR, PS
Laurel Steinhice, HRC office
LAURENCE H. STOOKEY, WR*, RI, SM, PS, EP, WC, CL, LT
Gertrude Suppe, HIS
Becky Thompson, P
Sibley Towner, R

Thomas H. Troeger, P
MARJORIE BEADLES TUELL, HY, TX*, LT, CL, WC
Dwight Vogel, R
Linda Vogel, R
CHARLES H. WEBB, HY, TU, WR, SM*
Ross Whetstone, P
J. LAVON WILSON, HY, TX, LT
Brian Wren, P
John Yarrington, LT
CARLTON R. YOUNG, Editor, HRC, HY, TX, TU, WR, RI, SM, PS, PTC, LT, CL, EP, WC

KEY TO SYMBOLS AND ABBREVIATIONS:

*	Chair or Convener
AC	Asian Consultation
CL	Hymns Classification Subcommittee
EP	Editorial Production Subcommittee
HIS	Hispanic Consultation
HRC	Hymnal Revision Committee
HY	Hymns Subcommittee
LT	Language/Theology Subcommittee, merged with Classification
P	Presenter of paper to committees
PS	Psalter Subcommittee
PTC	Psalm Text Subcommittee
R	Reader of whole or parts of revision text
RI	Ritual Subcommittee
SM	Service Music Subcommittee, merged with Tunes
TU	Tunes Subcommittee
TX	Texts Subcommittee
WC	Wesley Consultation
WR	Worship Resources Subcommittee

Italic Capitals—Member of HRC
Italic Capitals and Lower Case—Staff
Roman Type—Consultants

ORGANIZATION OF THE REVISION PROCESS

The United Methodist Publishing House

The revision process was organized at two levels, one within The United Methodist Publishing House and the other within the editorial process. Groups 1-8 on the organizational chart were coordinated by a central United Methodist Publishing House Hymnal Task Force. Public relations (3) was led by Martha Pilcher, assisted by Garlinda Burton, United Methodist Communications reporter, both of whom attended every meeting of the Hymnal Revision Committee and monitored and initiated day-by-day communication with the various audiences. Media reporters were invited to meetings of the Hymnal Revision Committee and its subcommittees. Press releases were prepared to inform United Methodists as well as the general public about the content and process of revision. Much time and effort were spent in reacting to negative and uninformed media coverage. (See the controversy surrounding "Onward, Christian Soldiers," pages 135-37.)

The auxiliary products group (4) formulated plans for producing products related to the parent book, e.g., *The United Methodist Hymnal Music Supplement*. The marketing committee (5), working with members from the revision committee including Charles M. Smith, developed a strategy for merchandising the hymnal after its approval by the General Conference. The page design and production of the proposed hymnal were provided by groups 6 and 7. The printing plant (7), while providing important information during the revision process about the printing, binding, and distribution of hymnals, was closed in December 1989. For the first time this century the official hymnal was not produced in one of the church's printing plants. The book was printed and shipped from Kingsport, Tennessee. Research and special services (8) were supplied by Abingdon Press personnel.

The hymnal revision office (11) was divided into editorial and project units. Regarding public/church relations the former was responsible for maintaining contact through the public relations group with the 800 Reader Consultants who represented each annual conference, school of theology, and the Council of Bishops. The project director, G. Alan Smith, processed the results of the consultants' responses and produced the twice yearly updates on the progress of revision, which were sent to 75,000 lay persons and pastors.

Hoyt L. Hickman has described this aspect of the process:

> The needs, concerns, and preferences of local congregations were identified and clearly defined, so that the new hymnal would meet the needs of the average person in the pew. A continuing opinion research sampling called the Reader Consultant Network, numbering over 800 lay persons, clergy, musicians, and teachers, was established by [in] the hymnal revision project office. Nine surveys were conducted at intervals throughout the revision

process. Hymnal updates were sent twice a year to 75,000 United Methodist pastors and lay persons. . . . In response, more than 20,000 letters were received [and answered] by the committee. All this combined to provide an understanding of what United Methodists wanted, an understanding which was taken with the greatest seriousness by the committee. (Sanchez 1989, 15)

In this regard the hymnal was marketed from within the revision process. Most United Methodists knew about the revision of their hymnal and had an opinion about its projected contents and could thus claim some ownership of the product before its publication.

The Hymnal Revision Committee

The editorial component also included the oversight of the Hymnal Revision Committee's thirteen subcommittees and consultations whose work resulted in the content of the revised hymnal.

Hickman has written how the work of the revision committee was structured:

The [revision committee] formed a series of subcommittees [worship resources (15) and hymns (13)], by which the detailed preliminary and follow-through work was done. In this way, all proposals and materials were prepared carefully before being considered by the full committee, and the decisions of the full committee could be implemented efficiently. In addition to twelve meetings of the full committee and the subcommittee meetings which took place during those meetings, there were more than eighty subcommittee and consultation meetings. (Sanchez 1989, 14)

The basic principles that guided the committee's work are summarized in the preface to the hymnal:

The Hymnal Revision Committee has taken a commonsense approach to the preparation of a new hymnal and worship book: seeking the middle ground of evangelical hymnody held in common by the various traditions and constituencies, and identifying and retaining that "traditional core" of hymns that has the strongest potential value and usefulness to most local United Methodist congregations. . . .

The committee began by recognizing a common problem: it is not possible to accede to all wishes in a single volume! Having shown a willingness to listen to the constituency, early in our work we made a firm commitment that this would be the people's hymnal, belonging to the whole United Methodist Church—a church uniquely inclusive in membership, episcopal and itinerate in government, and global and ecumenical in ministry. (Preface to *The United Methodist Hymnal*, vi)

The Report of the Hymnal Revision Committee to the General Conference of The United Methodist Church outlines the significant amount of time spent on the revision process:

> Voting members of the committee and continuing consultants to the committee spent an average of 1,250 hours per person on the revision project in a period of just over two and one-half years. [See the list of committee members, consultants, and presenters, pages 146-47.] In the same time frame [revision] office staff members devoted an average of 4,675 hours per person on the project, not including time spent by additional United Methodist Publishing House staff members who maintained a significant level of part-time involvement. The editor spent an estimated 6, 875 hours on the hymnal revision project through its editorial content phase. (*Report* 1988, 15)

The members and leaders of the hymnal committees who edited our 1957 and 1966 hymnals and worshipbooks with few exceptions were men, a precondition routinely applied when local or general church decision-making bodies were convened. Two women served on the thirteen-member Evangelical United Brethren committee, in addition to Ellen Jane Lorenz who was the music editor. Of the twenty-nine members on the Methodist hymnal committee there was only one woman.

The Enabling Petition of the 1984 General Conference mandated a significant increase in the number of laywomen and clergywomen elected to serve as voting members of the Hymnal Revision Committee. The nine women selected made distinctive and significant contributions: Bonnie Jones Gehweiler, church musician and author, Waynesville, North Carolina; Marjorie Beadles Tuell, hymnologist and musician, Los Angeles; and Beryl Ingram-Ward, pastor and author, Tacoma, Washington. All were tireless, productive, insightful, and competent chairs of subcommittees. Raquel Gutiérrez-Achon, Los Angeles, California, ably served as vice-chair of the full committee and as the primary consultant for Hispanic American hymns. Mary Brooke Casad, Valley View, Texas, made a significant contribution from the repertory of hymns and songs for children and young people. Helen Gray Crotwell, Fayetteville, North Carolina, provided pastoral insight to the work of the ritual subcommittee. Hope Omachi-Kawashima, Los Angeles, California, provided her qualified interpretation of the Asian American repertory. Nancy Starnes, Sparta, New Jersey, brought a particular and personal understanding of the power of hymns and liturgy in the lives and witness of the disabled and disenfranchised, and J. Lavon Wilson, Springfield, Illinois, a third generation African American United Methodist, convincingly shared her heritage and brought important insight to contemporary hymnic repertory.

During the nineteenth century the bishops and the publishing interests of our church were the *de facto* hymnal revision committees. During the twentieth century increasing numbers of clergy were named by the general church and joined the bishops and the publishing interests in controlling the process and dictating the contents of our hymnals. As recently as our 1966 hymnal clergy, including bishops, accounted for twenty-one of the twenty-nine members of the revision committee. Only two clergy were pastors of local churches; the balance were bishops, district superintendents, and denominational board and agency executives. An illustration of that clergy-centered revision process was evident in the committee's effort to ascertain what hymns were sung from the 1935 hymnal, what hymnals were in use, and what hymns should be included in a new hymnal. Even though millions of Methodists would presumably be purchasing and singing from the proposed hymnal, no general lay opinion of consequence was solicited. On the contrary, reflecting the mind-set of the church, the revision committee authorized the publishing house to send opinion questionnaires to 22,000 Methodist ministers of local churches. Because the questionnaire was cleverly written to elicit little specific or new information, the massive response from 11,000 pastors was received by the committee, still uneasy about the General Conference's narrow thirty-two vote mandate as a "popular mandate" for a new hymnal. Lay persons from across the church, angry at being ignored, inundated the church's state, regional, and national newspapers, as well as the hymnal editor's office, with petitions, letters, and postcards! The committee proceeded in the established tradition to revise the hymnal on *behalf* of the church, only incidentally *for* the church (see "The 1966 *Methodist Hymnal*," page 116).

The naming of twelve lay persons, from a total of twenty-five, to the Hymnal Revision Committee for the 1989 hymnal resulted from the 1984 General Conference mandate along with considerable pressure from lay groups. The steadfast commitment of these lay persons to the work of revising our hymnals called for spending an enormous amount of time away from their primary responsibilities as spouse, parent, teacher, lawyer, and church musician. Their sustained presence and participation in the revision process resulted in the most populist hymnal of this century and a metaphor for the remembering and renewal of the Body of Christ.

Of the thirteen clergy persons on the Hymnal Revision Committee only one, Beryl Ingram-Ward, was a local church pastor during the entire revision process. Three others, Helen Gray Crotwell, who had been a local pastor, was named a district superintendent; Charles M. Smith and Jack Holland Henton, who had been district superintendents, were appointed pastors. The balance of the clergy included were bishops, district superintendents, teachers and denominational agency personnel. The present writer in over four decades of ministry has seldom experienced from the clergy such sensitivities to individual differences, deep and abiding pastoral care, unchallenged personal integrity, thoroughgoing theological insight, and a willingness to learn, as evidenced in the work of the clergy persons on the committee.

Three bishops were assigned to the Hymnal Revision Committee. Reference has already been made regarding the skilled chair of the full committee, Reuben P. Job, whose applied pastoral instincts kept the work of the full committee focused on the church and its expectation to be served by the committee's efforts. George W. Bashore brought a wealth of experience as a singer and pastor. In the latter regard if a hymn seemed to be on the verge of being dropped or was on the borderline of acceptance, the bishop's sure and sonorous baritone voice could and often made a difference in the full committee's vote. W. T. Handy eloquently represented the "average person in the pew." The committee's more erudite and elitist gestures and actions were constantly questioned by the bishop, who looking over the top of his glasses would casually utter mezzo-forte, "But who's going to sing this, the choir or the folk!"

Supported by the wise and pastoral guidance of Reuben P. Job, the strong encouragement of Robert K. Feaster and Ezra Earl Jones, and the unprecedented cooperation of their two agencies charged with the responsibility of revision—the United Methodist Publishing House and the General Board of Discipleship—and the dedication and skill of the subcommittees' chairs, members and consultants applied themselves in a spirit of cooperation and concern to serve the entire United Methodist Church.

Hickman has summed the spirit of the entire committee:

> They shared differing and often opposing points of view, some in vigorous debate but always showing due respect for each of the advocates and the constituencies represented. In the process the committee became a working community [this writer would describe it as family] with very high levels of trust and support. (Sanchez 1989, 15)

Worship Resources

The explicit mandate from the General Conference called for the Hymnal Revision Committee to bring to the 1988 General Conference its recommendations for the contents of a combination hymnal and worshipbook. The work of revising the church's liturgies and worship resources had for the most part been accomplished during 1968-84 in the work of the Section on Worship, the General Board of Discipleship, ably guided by Hoyt L. Hickman. These new services and resources, along with "the *Book of Ritual* of The Evangelical United Brethren Church, 1959, and *The Book of Worship for Church and Home* [1965] of The Methodist Church," formed the church's official ritual. (*The Book of Discipline* 1968, Par. 1388) (See *The Book of Services*, 1985, and *Companion to the Book of Services*, 1988, for a description of the development and interpretation of these resources.)

Hickman described the subcommittee's procedures in the following report:

> The Worship Resources Subcommittee and its subcommittees—Ritual, Service Music, Psalter, Psalms, Text, and Music of the Psalter Consultation—

screened and evaluated these materials before presenting them to the full committee. An introduction to this material is found in *The Worship Resources of The United Methodist Hymnal*. (Sanchez 1989, 14)

The preface to the hymnal provides this summary of the subcommittee's work:

[The] Hymnal provides what the congregation needs for Sunday and other times of worship (including the sacraments): the rites of marriage and burial, and morning and evening prayer and praise. Additional worship materials are topically placed among the hymns; other prayers, litanies, and creeds follow the occasional services. . . .

The psalms, with spoken or sung responses, occupy a more prominent position than in previous editions. One hundred psalms prescribed by the lectionary of the Consultation on Common Texts as well as psalms for special occasions are included. (Preface to *The United Methodist Hymnal*, v)

The work of the worship resources subcommittee, led by its indefatigable and talented chairs Laurence Hull Stookey and Beryl Ingram Ward, and secretaries Jack H. Henton and Hoyt L. Hickman, who kept precise records, is outlined below. The liturgy for generations had been buried in the back of Methodist books without benefit of a consecutive numbering system. Placing it in the front of the hymnal had been under consideration for two years. The recommendation to place the eucharistic and baptismal services preceding the hymns came very late in the revision process following the committee's receiving the results of a reader consultant survey indicating that half of those surveyed wanted the change, while the other half did not. The debate in the committee centered on how congregations might react to "O for a thousand tongues to sing" usually the first selection, placed after the liturgy.

In the final meeting of the full revision committee, fall 1987, a compromise was reached, and two services were placed in the front of the hymnal along with distinctive congregational musical responses. The new format begins with the "Basic Pattern of Worship," page 2, continues with its elaboration into "An Order of Sunday Worship Using the Basic Pattern," and concludes with three settings of "A Service of Word and Table" with five different and distinctive musical responses.

Hickman has summarized the historical importance of the third setting of "A Service of Word and Table":

[The third service is adapted] from the rituals of the former Methodist and Evangelical United Brethren churches. These [latter] services were all adapted from the service of Holy Communion in *The Book of Common Prayer* of the Church of England, which John Wesley sent to the American Methodists and which preserves the majestic sixteenth-century language style of Thomas Cranmer [and the music of John Merbecke]. (Hickman 1989, 78)

These additional worship resources follow the Psalter: "Service of Christian Marriage," **864**, "Service of Death and Resurrection," **870**, and orders for "Morning Praise and Prayer" and "Evening Praise and Praise," **876-79**. These latter services were prepared by the Section on Worship under the direction of Thomas A. Langford, III, and constitute a unique contribution to the work of this subcommittee. (Langford provides an informative introduction in Hoyt L. Hickman's *Worship Resources of the United Methodist Hymnal*," 177-98.) This section concludes with prayer, creeds, and litanies.

Another striking and well-received feature of the new book has been the sixty-five poems, prayers, litanies, prose selected by Laurence Hull Stookey and biblical songs (canticles), which are topically integrated within the hymns section, a format that was borrowed from *Hymns for the Family of God*, 1976. "Service music" was brought from the back of the book and topically and functionally integrated with the other items in the hymns section. The work of Diana Sanchez in selecting and integrating appropriate service music from both the former churches, hymnals, and the incomplete and unequal results of the Service Music Project (suggested by the 1980 General Conference) was a significant contribution.

As noted previously, the most compelling and unique aspect of our hymnal is the Psalter. The psalms text subcommittee also provided the texts and responses for the eighteen canticles. The work of this energetic, dedicated, and talented group of scholars, pastors, and musicians is described in pages 110-26 in *The Worship Resources of the United Methodist Hymnal* by its chair Charles M. Smith who brought to the editorial process both his musical and pastoral insights.

One of the most dramatic and compelling work sessions of the psalms text subcommittee was held in February 1987 in the Jerusalem Room of Westminster Abbey, the room where the King James Version of the Bible was translated. During the four-day session this writer made audio tapes for his research files of the singing, conversation, aural editing, and other interactions of Professor Harrell F. Beck (since deceased) of Boston University School of Theology; Dr. S T Kimbrough, Jr., biblical scholar and singer, Princeton, New Jersey; Professor John C. Holbert, Perkins School of Theology, Southern Methodist University; the Reverend Alan Luff, Precentor of Westminster Abbey chairperson, Charles M. Smith; and editor Carlton R. Young. The entire United Methodist Liturgical Psalter was published in 1992 as *Psalms for Praise and Worship: A Complete Liturgical Psalter*, edited by John Holbert, S T Kimbrough, Jr., and Carlton R. Young, with a foreword by Walter Brueggemann.

The "Baptismal Covenant" service, **32-54**, which attempts to provide in one format the ritual for Holy Baptism, Confirmation, Reaffirmation of Faith, Reception into The United Methodist Church, and Reception in a Local Congregation, has received mixed reactions, many of them negative comments from pastors who are overwhelmed by the seemingly cumbersome format. Other assessments from pastors indicate that they have both read and followed the introduction to the service "Concerning the Services of the Baptismal Covenant" **(32)** and Laurence H. Stookey's step-by-step explanation, pages 86-109, in Hoyt L. Hickman's *Worship Resources of the United Methodist Hymnal.*

Hymns Subcommittee

Hickman writes concerning the work of the hymns subcommittee:

> The hymns . . . were the responsibility of the Hymns Subcommittee [chaired by Bonnie Jones Gehweiler] and its subcommittees—Texts [Marjorie B. Tuell, chair], Tunes [Robert C. Bennett, chair], Language/Theology—and the Wesley and ethnic consultations [chaired by Bonnie Jones Gehweiler]. They screened, evaluated, and in some cases recommended changes in hymns to be presented to the full committee. The Hymns Subcommittee invited and heard presentations by representatives of several United Methodist organizations and constituencies with distinctive viewpoints and concerns. They also commissioned thirteen poets to create new texts and four composers to create new tunes. In all, they examined the texts and tunes of more than 3,500 hymns. (Sanchez 1989, 14)

An important contribution of the texts subcommittee (Marjorie Tuell, chair; Bonnie Jones Gehweiler, Ezra Earl Jones, Ronald P. Patterson, J. LaVon Wilson, Mary Brooke Casad, W. T. Handy, and consultant William B. McLain) was its urgent concern that the revised book have sufficient popular, singable, and memorable hymns to ensure that children, youth, and adults might once again have access to our hymnal.

The task of the hymns subcommittee was greatly aided by those members of the tunes subcommittee who had expertise in both the music and the texts of traditional as well as contemporary hymns. (See pages 164-66 for a review of the work of the tunes subcommittee.) Throughout the entire process the efforts of musicians Raquel Gutiérrez-Achón, Robert C. Bennett, chair, J. Edward Hoy, Roger Deschner, and Charles H. Webb, with Laurence Hull Stookey were the heart of the revision process which produced, in the words of Charles H. Webb, "a quality product." Their contributions made the difference between a distinctive hymnic resource, rather than an average, pedestrian, or commonplace one.

Classification Subcommittee

Concurrent with the work of the hymns subcommittee the hymns classification subcommittee, chaired by Ronald P. Patterson, organized hymns, canticles, and acts of praise from diverse traditions and sources into five classifications from a proposal devised by Laurence Hull Stookey in consultation with James C. Logan, both members of the faculty of Wesley Seminary, Washington, DC.

Craig Gallaway has elaborated on this organizational structure (outlined below):

[The structure] reflects two basic and interlocking patterns: doctrine and experience.

Explicitly, [it] reflects the pattern of the Apostles' Creed. The first three sections focus on the persons of the Trinity; the fourth, upon the doctrine of the Church; and the fifth, on "the last things.". . . Not [in] a dry enumeration of doctrines but a living invocation of the Triune God, whose love touches every reach of human joy, suffering, struggle, and hope. (Sanchez 1989, 249)

I. THE GLORY OF THE TRIUNE GOD
  Praise and Thanksgiving
  God's Nature
  Providence
  Creation

II. THE GRACE OF JESUS CHRIST
  In Praise of Christ
  Christ's Gracious Life
      Promised Coming
      Birth and Baptism
      Life and Teaching
      Passion and Death
      Resurrection and Exaltation

III. THE POWER OF THE HOLY SPIRIT
  In Praise of the Holy Spirit
  Prevenient Grace
      Invitation
      Repentance
  Justifying Grace
      Pardon
      Assurance
  Sanctifying and Perfecting Grace
      Rebirth of the New Creature
      Personal Holiness
      Social Holiness
      Prayer, Trust, and Hope
      Strength in Tribulation

IV. THE COMMUNITY OF FAITH
  The Nature of the Church
      Born of the Spirit
      United in Christ
      Called to God's Mission

The Book of the Church: Holy Scripture
The Sacraments and Rites of the Church
    Baptism, Confirmation, and Reaffirmation
    Eucharist (Holy Communion or the Lord's Supper)
    Marriage
    Ordination
    Funeral and Memorial Service
Particular Times of Worship
    Opening of Worship
    Closing of Worship
    Morning
    Evening
    Special Days

V. A NEW HEAVEN AND A NEW EARTH
    Death and Eternal Life
    Communion of the Saints
    Return and Reign of the Lord
    The Completion of Creation (The City of God)

Laurence Hull Stookey has provided further clarification:

The organizational scheme follows the patterns of the historic ecumenical creeds (Trinity, church, eschatological hope) and also reflects emphases distinctive to the Wesleyan understanding of ecumenical theology.

This Wesleyan focus is particularly evident in the third division. Prevenient grace, justifying grace, and sanctifying and perfecting grace reflect Wesley's understanding of salvation. So also, for example, does the juxtaposition of personal holiness and social holiness.

What will seem strange at first to casual observers is that few of two hundred items (337-536) actually mention the Spirit. So why place them in the section headed "The Power of the Holy Spirit"? The answer lies in the distinctive experiential emphasis of Wesleyanism: Our experience of grace is the work of the Spirit, even though the role of the Spirit is often hidden and unacknowledged.

A crucial illustration of the organizational principle at work here is this: The basic text of Isaac Watts's "Alas and did my Savior bleed" appears twice in the collection: First, [at number 294] in the "passion and death" portion of the division "The Grace of Jesus Christ"; second, [at number 359] in the "repentance" section of the division "The Power of the Holy Spirit."

This wide separation of the same basic text is no oversight. For in the first appearance of the text, the believer is essentially recounting the events of the cross—a historical consideration of Jesus' suffering and death. But in the second appearance of the text a refrain has been added:

> At the cross, at the cross,
> where I first saw the light,
> and the burden of my heart was rolled away,
> there it was by faith
> I received my sight,
> and now I am happy all the day.

The refrain moves the text out of the historical sphere into the experiential sphere. And while the Holy Spirit is nowhere mentioned, Wesleyans understand that this personal experiential appropriation of saving history is one of the gifts of the Spirit in our lives. It is only through the Spirit's power that history unburdens us and gives us insight into the ways of God.

Many hymnal organizations run on two separate tracks—the first theological, usually based on trinitarianism; and the second liturgical, based on the events commemorated in the observance of the Christian year. Such an organization characteristic of the 1966 *Book of Hymns* was carefully considered and rejected for two reasons:

1. Typically such a pattern results in confusion resulting from an artificial separation of texts on the same subject. Thus some hymns about the Holy Spirit, for example, go into the theological section (under the Third Person of the Trinity) and others into the liturgical section (for the Day of Pentecost). Persons planning a Pentecost Sunday service may well overlook the first set of resources.

2. Recent revisions in the liturgical calendar have made the old categories obsolete and new categories difficult to maintain. Once, for example, Lent was considered to be exclusively about Jesus' passion and death. But now Lent is understood much more broadly: the many apt hymns reflect a great variety of themes that are more appropriately scattered throughout the hymnal. So also, some aspects of Advent [195-216] while others have to do with the church's hope of God's triumph at the end of time [714-735]. Therefore it was decided that liturgical year concerns are better dealt with through topical index entries, see below, than in the primary organizational scheme of the hymns section. Far from devaluing the use of the liturgical year in worship, this preserves its richness and encourages flexibility in planning worship. (Correspondence with Carlton R. Young, March 1991)

To provide an alternative organizational pattern of the hymnal, a topical organization of the hymns, canticles, and acts of praise was prepared by Marjorie B. Tuell, "Index of Topics and Categories" (934), later supplemented with extensive listings by "Christian Year" and "Service Music," prepared by Diana Sanchez and Thomas A. Langford, III. The scriptural references for the entire book were supplied by Hoyt L. Hickman and are gathered in "Index of Scripture: Services, Psalter, Acts of Worship" **(923)** and "Index of Scripture: Hymns, Canticles, Prayers & Poems" **(924)**. Austin C. Lovelace prepared the "Metrical Index" **(926)** and "Index of Tune Names **(931)**.

Consultations to the Hymnal Revision Committee

In addition to the voluminous amount of material, much of it unsolicited, studied by the text and tunes groups, three distinct consultations were convened to deal with Wesley texts, evangelical hymns, and ethnic hymns:

> A special Wesley Consultation (21) was formed to study the Wesley texts as a body—a formidable task, since Charles Wesley alone wrote over 9,000 poems, many of them hymn texts. From this distinguished panel of internationally recognized authorities and its extensive pool of individual and collective research came two significant accomplishments: 1) a recommendation for the ecumenical and creedal ordering of the new hymnal, with Section III structured on the basis of John Wesley's *ordo salutis* (order of salvation). . . . 2) recommendations for the inclusion of 99 Wesley texts, some set as hymn texts and others to be printed as poetry. (*Report* 1988, 20)

Wesley Hymns

The presence and contributions of outstanding scholars such as Frank Baker, Richard P. Heitzenrater, S T Kimbrough, Jr., along with the valuable research shared by Rex D. Matthews and Craig B. Gallaway, resulted in the most thorough work to be accomplished by any revision task force or consultation. The primary contribution of the consultation was to make the case, both historically and theologically, for the inclusion of a significant number of Wesleyan hymns in the hymnal of a church whose members seldom sing over a dozen Wesley hymns per year and who would probably recall only half that number as Wesleyan. The outstanding work of the tunes subcommittee, primarily through the efforts of the late Roger Deschner, resulted in a more singable base for what is essentially a mostly unsingable hymnic repertory, at least for USA congregations. The inclusion of several texts as poems, some in their complete form along with a brief historic footnote prepared by Dr. Baker, e.g., "Come, O thou traveler unknown" **(387)**, introduces the greatness of Wesleyan hymnody in a user friendly format. In spite of these positive factors, this may be the final USA Methodist hymnal to accommodate Wesley hymns in any appreciable number, and along with them the distinct Wesleyan theology, due in large part to the almost total lack of coverage of the Wesleyan tradition in United Methodist seminary education.

Gospel Hymns

The need to bring into the hymnal an increased number of gospel songs and hymns was an agenda left over from the work of the committee that produced the

1966 book. In addition to that need was the new repertory of choruses and scripture songs from the charismatic communities. Related to the consideration of these repertories was the claim, some of it substantiated, that theologically mainline United Methodist churches were on the decline, and evangelical and charismatic churches were increasing in membership. (See the January 1987 issue of *The Hymn* 38 (1):7-30, for a survey of the latter repertory.) To the consternation of the classically trained, the solution early on was expressed in simplistic terms of "how many and which ones," rather than "should we?" The whole matter of popular religious song was potentially so divisive that, as with language, it was given to a special group of experts and practitioners to name, frame, and suggest the repertory in a proposal that would be considered by the hymns subcommittee. The committee's work was greatly aided by consultant Riley B. Case who had already conducted a survey in the churches in his mid-Indiana rural-small town district of the most popular religious songs found in five widely used hymnals and songbooks other than the 1957 Evangelical United Brethren and the 1966 Methodist hymnals.

This survey resulted in a list of 300 selections circulated and evaluated by outside consultants along two criteria: which of the hymns and songs are already classic within the genre of gospel music, and which have the potential to enter the standard repertory. That process narrowed the field down to about 150 selections, in time to the approximately 85 that are in the present book, an increase of 50 over the previous Methodist hymnal. This accommodation to the popular and familiar, combined with the 28 singable selections from the African American repertory, brought the official hymnal of the church for the first time within the range of the needs of small membership churches and fulfilled another mandate of the 1984 General Conference: "be sensitive to the needs of small membership churches."

Only time will tell if that accommodation was too little too late to meet the needs of the emerging United Methodist Church, a church whose music, theology, and worship practice over three decades has become more evangelical, conservative, and culturally exclusive, its hymnic repertory and singing performance practice evoking minimal cognitive response from the worshipper.

Ethnic Hymns

Hymns from ethnic sources were also the responsibility of the hymns subcommittee. A discussion of the general historic developments is found in the appropriate sections of the article "USA Hymnody," pages 17-47. The Hymnal Revision Committee members and consultants collected and, in some instances, created repertories from the four ethnic groups for possible inclusion in the 1989 hymnal. The product of their work is not only unique in that United Methodist hymnody represents a wide spectrum of God's rainbow of humanity and faith as expressed in religious song, but it is unparalleled in USA denominational hymnody. The scope of their efforts is described in the *Report* sent to the delegates of the 1988 General Conference:

In order to preserve authenticity and ensure potential maximum use of minorities and majority constituencies alike, special translators, consultants, and [representative] material have been brought to bear upon the committee's work with regard to hymnody reflective of the [four] traditions. . . . Rather than relying solely upon current publication and/or setting up quota-based apportionment of time and other resources allotted to each [group], the committee [funded by The United Methodist Publishing House] chose to take important initiatives. In some instances a particular hymnic tradition . . . required more research and deliberation than others. To this end special consultations were called and visits were made by HRC members to all ethnic caucuses to develop the repertories firsthand. (*Report* 1988, 22)

HISPANIC AMERICAN

The *Report* includes a brief account of the work of the consultations that developed the four repertories. First, Hispanic hymns:

The Spanish language is commonly spoken throughout the United States, second only to English. There are certain diversities within its general musical style. Resources under consideration came from the churches of Spain, Latin America, and various [other] Hispanic communities across the nation; the consultation's task and challenge was to sift through the wealth of available material and bring to the attention of the full [committee] both new and traditional hymns and other resources of high quality deemed most likely to enhance the new hymnal. . . .

HRC member Raquel Gutiérrez-Achon's previous experience in the preparation of Spanish-language hymnals and supplements and general expertise with regard to Hispanic hymnody were of strong benefit to the full committee. In order to also involve persons from a broad geographical and performance practice range and hear additional concerns and suggestions, a separate Consultation, working with the vital assistance of Professor Roy Barton, was established to compile, translate, and fine-tune Hispanic texts before they were brought before the full committee. [The work of translators George F. Lockwood and Gertrude Suppe is significant. The consultation read, sang, and critiqued the repertory three times.] (*Report* 1988, 22)

An important feature of the consultation's work was the recommendation that all hymns originally in Spanish would be translated, and both Spanish and English texts should be interlined within the music, the titles across the page appearing first in Spanish, then in English. The musically sensitive and stylistically apt arrangements of Hispanic melodies by Skinner Chávez-Melo greatly enhance this repertory.

AFRICAN AMERICAN

According to the *Report* the contributions to the present hymnal from African American sources were developed from three guidelines. Additional instructions were framed by full committee members W. T. Handy, LaVon Wilson, and J. Edward Hoy from an extensive study and presentation by consultant William B. McClain who had chaired the work of the significant and successful collection of African American religious song, *Songs of Zion*:

1) The character and "soul" of the selections must be preserved. 2) Certain characteristics indigenous to the Afro-American spirituals must be dealt with in such a way as to render them understandable to the uninitiated. 3) The poetry of these songs must be put in such a way that it is comprehensible to the church at large. (*Report* 1988, 23)

The *Report* cites additional instructions from the committee:

Regional variations were [to be] collected, compared, evaluated, and standardized; stanzas from diverse sources were scrutinized for stylistic authenticity and theological integrity. Symbolic phrases and imagery with subtle religious meanings commonly understood within the Black Methodist experience were [to be] clarified so that they would have promise of substantial use across United Methodism. (*Report* 1988, 22)

The full committee commissioned William Farley Smith, director of music at St. Mark's United Methodist Church, New York City, to research and develop this distinct repertory within the above guidelines, as part of the general responsibility of the tunes committee. Dr. Smith's research and findings extended over a period of two years and resulted in carefully crafted musical arrangements that are a distinctive contribution to the 1989 hymnal as well as general USA hymnic repertory. Despite some criticism that some of Dr. Smith's selections are "over-arranged" and more suitable for choirs than congregations, for the most part his work maintains the integrity of improvised African American keyboard and vocal style, and at the same time makes this genre of religious song accessible to congregations whose training and experience are outside the African American worship tradition. For a discussion of the African American worship, see *Come Sunday* by William B. McClain and sources cited in "African American Hymns," pages 21-27.

ASIAN AMERICAN

Through committee member Hope Omachi-Kawashima, and Naomi Southard, executive director of the National Federation of Asian American United Methodists, NFAAUM, contact was made with Asian American hymnic sources. The *Report* continues:

In selecting hymns from the various Asian traditions, the committee was faced with challenges and balances of tension unique to the seven cultural heritages designated as Asian American. [NFAAUM] . . . is a coalition of seven major cultures: Chinese, Filipino, Taiwanese, Indochinese (Lao, Cambodian, Vietnamese), Japanese, Korean, and Southern Asian. Unlike hymnody from the Black tradition, much of which is already quite familiar to many non-Blacks, Asian hymnody (with the exception of four hymns from Asian sources in the 1966 *Book of Hymns*) has had little familiarity within the non-Asian mainstream of the denomination. Faced with a myriad of language bases, dialects, and alphabets, the committee had little opportunity to fine-tune texts rendered into English and necessarily relied on existing material, much of it more paraphrase than translation.

[Unlike Hispanic hymns] the musical forms and harmonies of each of the several Asian traditions are often quite different from those commonly found in non-Asian congregations [as well as predominantly Asian congregations] who use Western music exclusively. The introduction of music which differs substantially from anything previously heard may encounter great resistance. (*Report* 1988, 23-24)

The development of this repertory was greatly aided by the work of editors and scholars Dal Joon Won and Sang E. Chun, who perfected the English texts of the three Korean hymns and provided an inclusive translation for the "Statement of Faith of the Korean Methodist Church" **(884)**. The phonetic transcriptions supplied by internationally acclaimed ethno-musicologist I-to Loh make it possible for the sounds of Asian hymns to be experienced by occidental as well as Asian American congregations. See "Asian American Hymns," pages 33-36, for an evaluation of this repertory.

NATIVE AMERICAN

In the May 1985 meeting of the full committee, committee member Harold Dean Jacobs of the Lumbee tribe, Cherokee tradition stated that the lines from "O beautiful for spacious skies,"

> O beautiful for pilgrim feet,
>   whose stern, impassioned stress
> a thoroughfare for freedom beat
>   across the wilderness!

were to Native Americans a poignant reminder of the cruel and racist treatment of their forebears by nineteenth-century white settlers, who had forced them from their land under the guise of manifest destiny. "Native Americans have feet, too, and they were here before the Pilgrims," Jacobs said. (See the comments on this hymn for interpretation.) The committee moved to set aside the offensive parts of the hymn, and this action resulted in a public response that was both negative and forceful, as seen in the following note from a United Methodist from Pennsylvania:

WHY DO YOU INSIST ON AIDING, ABETTING AND SPREADING THE COMMUNIST CONSPIRACY BY CREATING CONFUSION AND CONTROVERSY?

NOW: - TO ALL PASTORS, BISHOPS, DO-GOODERS AND ALL OTHER ECCLESIASTICAL BIG-WIGS: GET OUT OF THE DRIVER'S SEAT, LET GO AND LET A MUCH GREATER POWER THAN YOU TAKE CONTROL, MANAGE AND RUN THE SHOW!!!

Similar to the development of the Asian American (see pages 33-36) and Hispanic American (see pages 36-43) repertories, the gathering of representative Native American hymns was also treated by their representatives as a political consideration. The *Report* contained a euphoric description of the committee's success in bringing together representative hymns from the Native American traditions:

Members of the Native American community have responded enthusiastically to the HRC's call for hymnic recommendations and suggestions, and have shown a keen interest in the new hymnal as a whole. (*Report* 1988, 24-25)

In reality, with the exception of a presentation by Becky Thompson in early 1986 to the full committee, there was little response by other representatives of that constituency to the committee's repeated requests to frame a recommendation of hymns. At the conclusion of almost three years of effort to obtain recommendations, the task was given over to committee member Roger Deschner whose research resulted in the hymns that were included from Native American sources. The Native American prayers were recommended by Laurence Hull Stookey. For the development of Native American hymns see the article, pages 19-21.

MUSIC OF THE HYMNAL

Beginning with the 1878 hymnal, church musicians, professional and lay, have provided insight, energy, and comprehensive understanding of how hymns have functioned in worship, education, and recreation, and these musicians have been at the center of shaping the content and design of our hymnals. No less crucial was the work of the church musician in the development of the 1989 hymnal. As stated on page 155:

The task of the hymns subcommittee was greatly aided by those members of the tunes subcommittee who had expertise in both the music and the texts of traditional as well as contemporary hymns. . . . Their [efforts] made the difference between a distinctive hymnic resource, rather than an average, pedestrian, or commonplace one.

Work of the Tunes Subcommittee

The dramatic change in the musical content demonstrated in the 1989 hymnal was made possible by the hard work of an already overcommitted group of professional and paraprofessional church musicians. The chair of the tunes subcommittee, Robert C. Bennett, concert organist and minister of music at St. Luke's United Methodist Church, Houston, Texas, hosted the group in that church on repeated occasions. Other members of the subcommittee were Raquel Gutiérrez-Achon, vice-chair of the full committee and primary consultant for Hispanic American hymns; J. Edward Hoy, minister of music at historic Tindley Temple, Philadelphia; Roger Deschner, hymnologist, Wesley scholar, and professor of church music, Perkins School of Theology, Southern Methodist University, Dallas, Texas; Charles H. Webb, concert pianist, composer, chair of the service music subcommittee, and dean of the School of Music, Indiana University, Bloomington, Indiana; and Carlton R. Young, editor. Midpoint in the revision process with the work of the service music subcommittee having been completed, Harold Dean Jacobs, Native American church musician, Maxton, North Carolina, and Hope Omachi-Kawashima, Asian American church musician, Los Angeles, California, were added to the tunes group. Staff members Diana Sanchez and Gary Alan Smith made significant contributions and kept thorough subcommittee records and minutes.

The breadth of musical content in *The United Methodist Hymnal*, 1989, is the single most dramatic change in the hymnals of the former Methodist Church since the 1878 book. But it is less dramatic than the hymnals of the former Evangelical United Brethren Church: *The Evangelical Hymn and Tune Book*, 1882, and *Hymns for the Sanctuary and Social Worship*, 1874, culminating in the Evangelical United Brethren *Hymnal*, 1957, linked classic and popular religious song in an attempt to put it "all" into one official book. The musical content of *The United Methodist Hymnal*, 1989, follows in that inclusive tradition. (See "Hymnals of the Evangelical United Brethren Church," pages 75-89, and "Hymnals of the Methodist Church," pages 91-122.)

In preparing the musical content of this hymnal the tunes committee studied the leading hymnals of Great Britain: *Hymns Ancient and Modern*, 1861, and its succeeding editions and supplements; *The English Hymnal*, 1906 and 1933; *The Church Hymnary*, 1927; *The Oxford Book of Carols*, 1928; *Songs of Praise*, 1931; *BBC Hymn Book*, 1951; *Congregational Praise*, 1951; *Hymns for Church and School*, 1975, and a great number of supplements, including *New Church Praise*, 1975, and the British Methodist *Hymns and Psalms*, 1983.

USA denominational hymnals were consulted, with their supplements: Presbyterian US, *The Hymnal*, 1933; Protestant Episcopal, *The Hymnal 1940* and its successor *The Hymnal 1982*; Congregational, *Pilgrim Hymnal*, 1958; *The Baptist Hymnal*, 1975; *Lutheran Book of Worship*, 1978; Reformed Church in America, *Rejoice in the Lord*, 1985; Roman Catholic, *Worship III*, 1986, and the independently produced *Hymns for the Living Church*, 1974; *Ecumenical Praise*, 1977;

Hymns for the Family of God, 1976, as well as all recent former Evangelical United Brethren and former Methodist official and unofficial hymnal supplements. The most popular of all supplements to our hymnals is *The Cokesbury Worship Hymnal*, 1938, with four million sales to date.

Specialists in Native American, African American, Hispanic American, and Asian American religious song recommended the repertory that was considered by the revision committee. Much of it came from *Songs of Zion*, 1981; *Supplement to the Book of Hymns*, 1982; *Celebremos II*, 1983; and *Hymns from the Four Winds*, 1983. (For a discussion of the hymns from these traditions, see "USA Hymnody," pages 19-27.)

Another illustration of the dramatic change in our hymnal's musical content is found in the breadth of its musical offerings: e.g., Bach and Charles Ives; Beethoven and Amy Grant; Ralph Vaughan Williams and Duke Ellington—a breadth of content meant to serve the worship needs of a church that professes to be both catholic and evangelical, inclusive in membership, episcopal and itinerant in government, and global and ecumenical in ministry.

Sources of the Music

Psalm Tones

Probably the most ancient of all musical forms, the psalm tone consists of a single pitch for monotony with the text, followed by a half cadence; a second pitch for monotoning, followed by an ending cadence. There are five single chant settings adapted from *Lutheran Book of Worship* for use with all 100 psalms in our Psalter. On pages **736-37** are instructions for chanting the psalms.

Plainsong

Plainsong is unaccompanied melody based on one of the ancient modes. In modern hymnals an accompaniment is usually provided **(692, 184)**.

Folk Carols

The texts may be either sacred or secular, and usually are of unknown authorship. The sacred texts in the English and continental traditions are for the most part about the nativity of Jesus and other major feasts and days in the Christian calendar. The anonymous tunes are typically in two-part form: the chorus or refrain is sung by the group and may precede or be a response to the story that is sung by a solo voice or soli voices, "Sing we now of Christmas" **(237)**. Other carols, "The friendly beasts" **(227),** are without a refrain and in this instance may have been sung by solo voices depicting the various animals, followed by an improvised instrumental interlude with a ring dance led by the storyteller. Most authorities link dance to the folk carol (see Erik Routley, *The English Carol*).

A distinct folk song tradition developed in the early-nineteenth century in the mountain regions of the southeastern USA with roots in British forms of the carol, some composed without a refrain but with a reiterated last line, e.g., "What wondrous love is this" **(292)**. Much of this song entered the common repertory by way of the singing school.

The folk carol without its medieval performance practice may also be seen in the modern English carol, "The first Noel" **(245)**, the gospel hymn, "Pass me not, O gentle Savior" **(351)**, the Hispanic Epiphany carol, "De tierra lejana venimos" ("From a distant land") **(243)**, the African American Christmas spiritual, "Go, tell it on the mountain" **(251)**, the first Native American Christmas carol, "'Twas in the moon of wintertime" **(244)**, and the Pakistani hymn, "Saranam, Saranam" **(523)**.

Traditional Melodies

Of the total of 507 tunes in our hymnal, 179 traditional melodies come from 32 countries and 4 inclusive ethnic sources: Native American, African American, Hispanic American, and Asian American. (See Index of Topics and Categories, **934,** and Index of Tune Names, **931**.)

Native American melody is scored with harmony (KIOWA, **330**) and without harmony (HELELUYAN, **78**). In Hispanic hymns the melodic line is supported by light but traditional harmonies (CARACAS, **222**), and the indigenous 3-against-2 rhythms are maintained (NELSON, **107**). Asian tunes are harmonized in both Western (LE P'ING, **678**) and quasi-traditional parallel harmonies (SHENG EN, **633**). The African American gospel hymn and spirituals are for the most part set in a "midstream" style that, while retaining many of the indigenous melodic and rhythmic characteristics, allows them to be played either as is or serves as the basis of an improvised accompaniment.

Chorales

The chorale is an original genre of sacred song from the Lutheran tradition (see "German Hymns," pages 7-8), usually wedded to one text, but since the mid-nineteenth-century English language hymnals they have often been used with more than one text. Some chorales are composed melody (AUS TIEFER NOT, **515**); some melodies are taken directly from secular usage **(286)**; and others are derived from the medieval carol, plainsong, and sequence **(319)**, imitating the melodies of the troubadours, trouvères, and meistersingers. Many were composed in the meistersinger bar form (repetition of the first two lines of music, occasionally also used in the final line) for the purpose of teaching powerful doctrinal texts. Later chorales are found at UNSER HERRSCHER **(578)**, WER NUR DEN LIEBEN GOTT **(142)**, RATISBON **(173)**, and LOBE DEN HERREN **(139)**. The chorales in our hymnal are scored in both their rhythmic versions (SCHMÜCKE DICH, **612**), as well as their later isorhythmic versions (EIN' FESTE BURG, **110**). J. S. Bach's harmonizations (for example, ERMUNTRE DICH, **223**) are used for twelve of the twenty-nine chorale melodies found in our hymnal. See "German Hymns," pages 6-8; and Carl Schalk, "German Church Song," *The Hymnal 1982 Companion.*

Psalter Tunes

Melodies composed for use in Calvin's Genevan Psalter are included in their rhythmic form (OLD 100TH, **75**) and in their anglicized adaptation (ST. MICHAEL, **372**). See "Genevan/Anglo Metrical Psalmody," page 9, and Robin A. Leaver, "English Metrical Psalmody," *The Hymnal 1982 Companion.*

Anglican Chant

An exclusively British four-part choral form, Anglican chant developed from the seventeenth-century practice of accompanying the chanting of psalm tones. It is usually accompanied by lightly doubling the voices at the organ, but in addition, a solo stop may be played over the voices and/or various tonal colors and levels of amplitude employed in "tone painting" the meaning of the text. Late in the nineteenth century in Anglican and Methodist practice, the congregation was invited to join with the choir in singing a limited number of familiar chants. In the 1878 *Methodist Hymnal* there were twenty-one settings; in the 1966 book the number had been reduced to nine. Because most of the canticles in our present hymnal are formatted for reading, rather than chanting, we have only two settings: OLD SCOTTISH CHANT **(82)** and WILLIAM BOYCE **(91)**. For ease of singing they are reduced to the style of a hymn. Austin C. Lovelace provides a brief introduction to the performance of both the psalm tone and Anglican chant at page 662 in *The Methodist Hymnal,* 1966. A more recent and extensive introduction is provided by James H. Litton and Russell Schulz-Widmar in "General Performance Notes," pages 11-17, *The Hymnal 1982 Service Music.* See also Ruth M. Wilson, "Harmonized Chant," *The Hymnal 1982 Companion.*

English Hymn Tunes

The greatest number of tunes in our hymnal are from Great Britain: sixteenth century, Thomas Tallis, TALLIS' CANON **(682)**; seventeenth century, Orlando Gibbons, CANTERBURY **(550)**, and arranged from Henry Purcell, WESTMINSTER ABBEY **(559)**. From the eighteenth century included are Jeremiah Clark's UFFINGHAM **(450)**; ST. ANNE **(117)**, attributed to William Croft; adaptations of Moravian tunes (by John Wesley?), AMSTERDAM **(96)** and SAVANNAH **(385)**; Henry Carey, CAREY'S (SURREY) **(579)**; William Knapp, WAREHAM **(258)**; George F. Handel, GOPSAL **(716)**; Aaron Williams, ST. THOMAS **(732)**; and John Hatton, DUKE STREET **(438)**. Nineteenth-century evangelical tunes are by James Ellor, DIADEM **(155)**; and from *Hymns Ancient and Modern,* 1861, and its Appendix, 1868, tunes by John B. Dykes, NICAEA **(64)**, Joseph Barnby, LAUDES DOMINI **(185)**, and harmonizations by W. H. Monk, ELLACOMBE **(203)**. Samuel Sebastian Wesley, the grandson of the hymn writer, contributed LEAD ME, LORD **(473)**, HEREFORD **(501)**, and AURELIA **(545)**. Other nineteenth-century English contributions are by John Goss, LAUDA ANIMA **(66)**, and Arthur S. Sullivan, ST. KEVIN **(315)**; from Scotland, Jesse Seymour Irvine, CRIMOND **(136)**; from Wales, Joseph Parry, ABERYSTWYTH **(479)**.

Tunes by early twentieth-century composers include Charles Hubert Hastings Parry, JERUSALEM **(729)**, Charles Villiers Stanford, ENGELBERG **(68)**, and Ralph Vaughan Williams, music editor of *The English Hymnal*, 1906, revised 1933, and author of its remarkable preface to its music, SINE NOMINE **(711)**. Tunes are contributed by Sydney Hugo Nicholson, CRUCIFER **(159)**, and Gustav Holst, CRANHAM **(221)**, with arrangements of folk tunes by Ralph Vaughan Williams, KINGSFOLD **(606)**, and Martin Shaw, ROYAL OAK **(147)**. From later in this century are settings by Herbert Howells, MICHAEL **(132)**, Sydney Carter, LORD OF THE DANCE **(261)**, Cyril V. Taylor, ABBOT'S LEIGH **(660)**, Peter Cutts, BRIDEGROOM **(544)**, Erik Routley, SHARPTHORNE **(441)**, William Mathias, Word and Table "Musical Setting E" **(25)**, and John Rutter, "Amen" **(902)**.

USA Hymn Tunes

In addition to traditional melodies, our hymnal includes tunes written late in the eighteenth century by the "first" American school of composers, some of them fuging tunes with similarities to the simple imitative sections of sixteenth-century English motets: KEDRON **(109)**, CORONATION **(154)**, and LENOX **(379)**. Other tunes composed in the early nineteenth century are found in most hymnals: MORNING SONG **(198)**, NETTLETON **(400)**, and DAVIS **(518)**. Some traditional melodies, such as WONDROUS LOVE **(292)** and some imported by settlers from Great Britain, were arranged for and included along with the above original tunes in the singing school's oblong books printed in shaped notes. Others remained in the oral tradition and became the core of rural camp-meeting melody. (See the entry "Traditional hymns, melodies, and prayers," in the Index of Composers, Authors, and Sources **(922)** for additional examples.) Lowell Mason, pioneer music educator and hymn and anthem book compiler, also arranged for use in his hymnals selections from the folk music repertory cast in an Anglo-European style but printed in round notes, e.g., CLEANSING FOUNTAIN **(622)**.

Until very recently, the music of our hymnals has been selected from the Germanic/Anglo repertory and performance practice, with scant reference to our own significant contributions. More recent hymnals, including the present hymnal, have included an increasing number of USA tunes from the eighteenth and nineteenth centuries. (See "USA Hymnody," pages 18-19, for a discussion of this repertory.) In order to find room for them (since many texts come with the tunes) there has been a decrease in tunes written in the late nineteenth-century Victorian style.

Recent hymnals have also begun to include tunes that modestly reflect twentieth-century compositional techniques: Peter Cutts, SHILLINGFORD **(260)**; Jane

M. Marshall, HIGH STREET **(590)**; David Hurd, MIGHTY SAVIOR **(684)**; Carl Schalk, NOW **(619)**; Natalie Sleeth, PROMISE **(707)**; Hugo Distler, TRUMPETS **(442)**; William Albright, ALBRIGHT **(563)**; Richard Wayne Dirksen, VINEYARD HAVEN **(161)**; Austin C. Lovelace, MUSTARD SEED **(275)**; Max Miller, MARSH CHAPEL **(426)**; and Earle V. Copes, VICAR **(178)**. Charles Ives's SERENITY **(499)** is a solo and an exception to the hymnal's basic congregational content. Duke Ellington's "Come Sunday," ELLINGTON **(728)**, is also a solo, but is gaining wide acceptance as a congregational hymn.

The revision committee commissioned new tunes by Carlton R. Young, STOOKEY **(627)**, for the Charles Wesley eucharistic text, "O the depth of love divine"; David Ashley White's BISHOP POWELL **(543)** for Bessie Porter Head's "O breath of life"; Carol Doran's GOD'S NAMES **(113)**, the tune with Thomas H. Troeger's commissioned text, "Source and Sovereign, Rock and Cloud"; Charles H. Webb's HAIZ **(274)** for Brian Wren's compelling text, "Woman in the night"; and numerous harmonizations of standard tunes, e.g., LAND OF REST **(269)** and LO DESEMBRE CONGELAT **(233)**. Many of the psalm and canticle sung responses were composed especially for this hymnal by Richard Proulx **(738)**, Gary Allan Smith **(748)**, Jane Marshall **(760)**, Don E. Saliers **(828)**, Alan Luff **(814)**, Timothy E. Kimbrough **(74)**, and Carlton R. Young **(742)**.

The recent gospel music of Andraé Crouch, MY TRIBUTE **(99)**, or Bill Gaither, RESURRECTION **(364)**, as well as the contemporary Christian music of Amy Grant, THY WORD **(601)**, should not be dismissed, as was its counterpart in the last century, as inferior because it is popular if our church is to continue with integrity its claim as being both evangelical *and* catholic.

See James I. Warren, *O for a Thousand Tongues*, for relating hymnody to the development of Methodism in the United States; Erik Routley, *The Music of Christian Hymns*, for a comprehensive review of the musical content and performance practice of hymns from earliest times to the present; and companions to major hymnals, e.g., *The Hymnal 1982 Companion*.

THE 1988 GENERAL CONFERENCE APPROVES THE HYMNAL

The Hymnal Revision Committee finished its work in October 1987, and after review and acceptance by the General Board of Discipleship, the hymnal revision office produced the 1,144-page *Report of the Hymnal Revision Committee*. A recording of selected hymns and interviews of committee members was produced, and on February 1, 1988, it was mailed with the report to delegates of the General Conference.

Hickman, who with the editor and chair Reuben P. Job, guided the progress of the committee's *Report* through the legislative committee, describes its progress at the conference:

At the conference the report went first to the [legislative] Committee on Discipleship [Rex Bivens chair]. It was evident that the committee members already had given much study to the report, and they discussed it at length, first in subcommittees [Edward L. Duncan, chair] and then in the full committee. One hymn was added: "Lord of the Dance" [probably after its being sung earlier that morning in response to a sermon by Bishop Woodie W. White]. Several other amendments were adopted [Baptismal Covenant and the Psalter. See Hickman 1989, 115, for a discussion of this action]. The report was adopted by the committee by a vote of 99 to 0.

The report as amended by the committee then went to the full General Conference, where on May 3 [at 11:45 a.m.] it was debated and passed by a vote of 893 to 69 accompanied by a sustained standing ovation. (Sanchez 1989, 16)

The importance of that moment was recorded in the editor's calendar and included in the sermon he preached almost a year later in the service of dedication, Raleigh, North Carolina, May 4, 1989 (see pages 174-77 for a portion of that service.):

The giant screen on either side of the platform came alive with the vote— 92% for, 8% opposing the content of the first United Methodist Hymnal. For a full five minutes the delegates and visitors joined in sustained applause, unprecedented in my experiences of seven previous general conferences. Tears swelled from their eyes, rolling down the cheeks onto their sleeves. The call from the floor requested that we sing "O for a thousand tongues" in both English and the Spanish translation prepared for the hymnal by Bishop Frederico J. Pagura. As we stood singing those words of faith and fulfillment written by our forebear Charles Wesley at the first anniversary of his giving himself to Christ and receiving Christ's gracious and redemptive gift of life—as we witnessed to each other, all of us experienced afresh the unity and strength which God in Christ can and is witnessing through The United Methodist Church: evangelical, ecumenical, and global.

That moment of unity in spirit and song in time gave way to this reflection on the meaning of revising a hymnal. The first is that we are a church of law, i.e., discipline and order. The vote on the hymnal was the occasion for the highest legal authority in our church to receive and approve its contents. That vote came at the conclusion of the ordered and orderly process whereby one General Conference initiates revision and a succeeding General Conference approves the revised contents of the church's book of prayer and praise.

Second, as our forebears passed on to us the Gospel of Jesus Christ in dialect and gesture, in story set to music, by way of this hymnal we passed from our generation to the present and to those yet unborn the spiritual ethos embodied in our song and sacred texts, a passing on of our heartfelt expressions for grace freely given and grace freely accepted. I can state without equivocation that the work of this your Hymnal Revision Committee stands in clear contrast to any former revision committee of my knowledge. It addressed all the issues: what, whose, which, how much ethos would be transmitted by simply asking United Methodists what they would like to have included in their hymnal and worshipbook—now that's worth an Amen and a Hallelujah!

Third, with that moment marked by unity in spirit and song came the perception that successfully completing the task of revising a hymnal inexorably leads to the fulfillment of the church's implicit obligation for introducing and interpreting the book to those for whom it was intended to be a tool of piety, prayer, and praise; and in time to receive back from the church based on its estimation of its usefulness, which in turn will embark the church on yet another revision. (Carlton R. Young notes, May 3, 1989)

PRODUCTION

The progress of the hymnal after its acceptance at the conference has been traced by the editor:

The Hymnal Revision Committee early on had approved the specifications and colors of the bindings, the page size, the style and size of the typeface, the musical [notation] styles and sizes. General Conference action remanded to the Editorial production subcommittee of the Hymnal Revision Committee the responsibility to oversee production of the hymnal, including the possible cutting of content should the music-setting process lead to a book that would be beyond the desired length, which was 960 pages. When enough of the music had been set to make an estimate, the book was projected to contain 1,014 pages rather than the desired 960 pages. That meant that 54 pages, or 5 percent, had to be cut across the board—hymns, prayers, worship resources, and psalter. This was accomplished in unanimous action by the Editorial Production Committee in September 1988. (Sanchez 1989, 17)

In the fall of 1988, it was determined that The United Methodist Publishing House printing facility would not be able to print, bind, and distribute the hymnal. This decision was based on three factors: first, the disappointing experience of the printing plant in producing the 1966 book was reviewed (see "Hymnals of The Methodist Church," pages 118-19); second, in order to do the job, the necessary investment in new or replacement equipment would have to be forthcoming at a time of limited resources; and third, the determination had already been made that within twelve months the plant would be closed. As a consequence, the administrative task of producing the book outside The United Methodist Publishing House fell to James E. Leath and Nancy Regen Bozeman.

Since none of the 1,144 *Report* could be used in the production of the hymnal, the type and music setting of the 960-page hymnal was begun. Each page of music and text was copyedited, individually designed, set, and proofed a minimum of four times by eight readers, including committee members Robert C. Bennett, Charles H. Webb, and Marjorie B. Tuell. Hoyt L. Hickman and Laurence H. Stookey aided in the page design and proofed the worship resources.

Concurrent with the design and in some cases the redesign and proofing of each page was the task of determining the ownership of approximately 1,000 items, securing permission for their use, and researching correct spelling and dates of each translator, composer, arranger, and source for about 3,000 different entries. Prior to the actual printing of the hymnal, the efforts of twenty-four staff plus five members of the Hymnal Revision Committee were involved in the editorial/production effort as follows:

Manuscript preparation	5
Music setting	3
Proofing	10
Research, permission, credits	6
Design, production	5
Support staff	2

Particularly noteworthy was the performance of project director Gary Alan Smith, who brought his unique and mature musical and theological judgment and computer skills to the project. Over the five years that the revision office was in operation the editor and the committee were blessed with an abundance of talented and dedicated personnel, including Laurel Steinhice, Floyd Mevis, Frances Merritt, Donna Nowels, and Alice Fischer. Christine Benagh was research specialist. Jean Hager copyedited the text. Sarah Huffman copied and set up all of the music pages. Robert J. Hill, Jr., who also worked on the 1966 book, made a substantive contribution to the editorial process, including preparing contracts and clearing copyright permissions.

Early in the revision process and continuing through the printing and distribution of the hymnal the editors and publishers of other hymnals provided invaluable insight into every facet of our work. The editor had frequent contact with the following: Fred Bock, editor of *Hymns for the Family of God*, 1976; Ray Glover, general editor of the Protestant Episcopal Church *Hymnal 1982*, who generously gave of his time and expertise to the editor and his staff on numerous occasions during the crowded final months of his work on *The Hymnal 1982*, and who presented to the Hymnal Revision Committee the concept of the Reader Consultant network; Ann MacKensie who completed Erik Routley's work on the Reformed Church in America hymnal *Rejoice in the Lord*, 1985; Emily Brink, general editor of the Christian Reformed Church's *Psalter Hymnal*, 1987; Robert J. Batastini, general editor of the Roman Catholic hymnal *Worship*, 1986 (3d ed.); George H. Shorney and William G. Shorney of Hope Publishing Company; and members of the Church Music Publishers Association.

In 1985 conversations were initiated with the committee that produced the *Presbyterian Hymnal*, 1990, for the Presbyterian Church (USA), a denomination whose worship practice, hymnody, and sociological patterns, particularly in the South-east, overlap those of United Methodism. We shared our files on language and process, a member of their committee visited a series of our meetings at our expense, and their editor attended two of our crucial language/theology subcommittee meetings and the hymnal marketing meetings of The United Methodist Publishing House. To the disappointment of the Hymnal Revision Committee there was no reciprocation.

DEDICATION

The concluding event of the revision process was the impressive, formal presentation of the new hymnal to the church through its Council of Bishops, who were in session, in a "Service of Thanksgiving and Consecration," held at historic Edenton Street United Methodist Church, Raleigh, North Carolina, May 4, 1989. For the Hymnal Revision Committee this service of celebration and commitment was to share with a wider group the essence of their work, not from a mere content/process orientation, but from that which was at the vital core of their work—prayer and hymn singing.

The service was written and designed by Laurence Hull Stookey. Members of the Hymnal Revision Committee and staff led in the liturgy of Word and Table. Music was written and directed by Charles H. Webb, Robert C. Bennett, and Carlton R. Young. The sermon, "United in Spirit, United in Song," was preached by the editor. The hymnal was presented by members of the revision committee to their counterparts in the general church: bishops, pastors, musicians, educators, lay persons, and youth. At the Eucharist representative hymns were sung, including "Let us break bread together" **(618)**, "O thou who this mysterious bread" **(613)**, "The bread of life for all is broken" **(633)**, "Precious Lord, take my hand" **(474)**, and "Jesus loves me" **(191)**.

Included below is that section of the service used when the new hymnals were presented and dedicated:

RECOGNITION OF THE HYMNAL REVISION COMMITTEE
Bishop Ernest T. Dixon, Jr.
President, The Council of Bishops
Members of the Hymnal Revision Committee:
We welcome you with joy and thanksgiving,
as we prepare to dedicate to the glory of God
and the service of God's people
the book which you have prepared for our use.
Your diligent and careful work has been warmly commended
by the action of the 1988 General Conference,
and we eagerly await use of this book in our church.

THE ACTS OF PRESENTATION
Bishop Rueben P. Job
Chair, The Hymnal Revision Committee
Members of the Council of Bishops,
we present *The United Methodist Hymnal*:
Book of United Methodist Worship to you,
and through you to the whole church
of which we are a part.
As its title implies,
this is the first official hymnal
of the denomination formed more than two decades ago.
As its subtitle indicates,
this is more than a collection of hymns;
it is the book of worship for our denomination.

Robert K. Feaster
President and Publisher, The United Methodist Publishing House
This book has been prepared with immense care
and concern for our church.
We have sought to include within it
resources for everyone in our diverse denomination,
both for public and for private use.
We have incorporated materials old and new,
Wesleyan and ecumenical.
We have brought before United Methodist people
a diversity of musical styles, cultural traditions,
and ethnic heritages
unprecedented in our history and, perhaps,
unprecedented in the history of the whole church catholic.
We believe that we have both listened to the church
and been prophetic for the church.

Bishop Job:
I now ask the other members of the committee
to join us in this act of presentation.

Hymnal Revision Committee Members:
With humble and immense joy,
we present this book to you
and commend it to all United Methodist people.
Throughout the process of revision
we have prayed earnestly that this book might be
a gift to the church
and an instrument of profound spiritual renewal
within the church.
In this hope, we offer to God
The United Methodist Hymnal:
Book of United Methodist Worship.

Bishop Job presents the first book to Bishop Dixon.

Bishop Dixon:
On behalf of the Council of Bishops and General Church,
I accept this book now
to be dedicated to the glory of God.

PRAYER OF DEDICATION   **Bishop Judith Craig**

The Lord be with you.
And also with you.
Lift up your hearts.
We lift them up to the Lord.
Let us give thanks to the Lord our God.
It is right to give our thanks and praise.
Gracious God:
You are the source of all joy and delight,
the fount of all consolation and hope.
Thus we laud and honor you
in every circumstance of life.
As your people redeemed by Christ,
we gather in congregations of your church
to praise you in word and song
as the Scriptures are read and expounded,
as the Sacraments are celebrated for our benefit.
There we offer to you *The United Methodist Hymnal*
as a testimony to your goodness,
as a guide to your people at prayer,
as a source of strength and help to all.
Receive this from our hands,
the gift of a multitude of labors.
By the Holy Spirit who filled the hearts
of authors, poets, and composers,
of translators, editors, and revisers:
Fill the whole people of United Methodism,
that millions of voices in one accord
may tell your good works from generation to generation.

Blessed be your name for ever.
In your goodness, hear our prayer.

(All holding their hymnals high:)

O God, before whose throne
praise and worship continually are offered,
where trumpets sound
and saints and angels sing:

Accept this, *The United Methodist Hymnal,*
which we offer to your great glory
   in praise of our risen and ascended Lord.
Amen! Alleluia!

FESTIVAL FANFARE ON THE HYMN TUNE "AZMON" Carlton R. Young

During the fanfare you may remove the paper band and open your Hymnal.

Then we join in singing the hymn which stands first in our collection of hymns, as it has since the time of the Wesleys:

HYMN 57: "O for a thousand tongues to sing," Brass and Organ setting: Charles H. Webb

Stanza 1—All
Stanza 2—Hymnal Revision Committee Members
Stanza 3—Choir
Stanza 5—Council of Bishops
Stanza 6—All

DISTRIBUTION

"A book is not published until it is in the hands of the consumer," chided the late Pat Beaird to another generation of editors, writers, and retailers. This admonition by Beaird, who was the force in The Methodist Publishing House behind projects such as *The Interpreter's Bible,* prompted the program for the successful marketing of the 1966 hymnal. The products of its sale were used by the publishing house to shore up its shaky finances, set up an elaborate regional-national retail distribution system, and make important investments in real estate (see "The 1966 *Methodist Hymnal,*" page 119). The book received euphoric acclaim from the former Methodist Church, but in less than a decade its usefulness had been overshadowed by unanticipated occurrences, its life span far short of the average three decades of its immediate predecessors (see the section "Fate of the 1966 Hymnal," pages 120-22).

The promotion and sale of the 1989 hymnal stemmed from a comprehensive marketing plan developed concurrently with the revision process by Marc Lewis, Cokesbury Division of The United Methodist Publishing House, in consultation with the Hymnal Revision Committee (see page 148). In the fall of 1989 the plan was set in motion through the efforts of Cokesbury staff members led by Bill Gnegy. A myriad of promotional devices and purchase incentives resulted in prepublication orders in excess of 3,000,000, a record for USA denominational hymnal publishing.

Currently, The United Methodist Publishing House has distributed in excess of 4,000,000 hymnals in addition to several auxiliary products, e.g., *Large Type Edition,*

The United Methodist Hymnal. The product from these sales is appropriately and responsibly being applied to ensure the future of the church's investment in proliferating Christian knowledge through its publishing arm, The United Methodist Publishing House.

The phenomenal sale and wide acceptance of the hymnal were followed by its interpretation in a cooperative effort of the Cokesbury Division of The United Methodist Publishing House and the Section on Worship of the General Board of Discipleship. In November 1989, a national training event was held in Nashville for some 400 leaders in music, education, and worship, who in the spring of 1990 led day-long conference and regional TV satellite training events. In this group were a few members of the Hymnal Revision Committee, but for the most part the timely, informed insights and perspectives by the majority of the Hymnal Revision Committee and consultants were unprofessionally and insensitively ignored. Some members of Hymnal Revision Committee and consultants contributed to *The Hymns of The United Methodist Hymnal,* Diana Sanchez, volume editor; and *The Worship Resources of The United Methodist Hymnal,* Hoyt L. Hickman, volume editor.

The church has once again enthusiastically received its new hymnal. Many can vividly remember the euphoria that attended the impressive sale and initial use of the 1966 book and its premature eclipse. What will be the fate of this hymnal as we approach the third millennium?

Computer technology is already available that may in this decade render obsolete the practical need for publishing a nineteenth-century style, single volume, bound hymnal. In this age of computer data storage and instant recall and publishing, given the enormous extant hymnic repertory that cannot be contained in one or even a dozen books in the pew racks, will church leaders continue to insist that worshippers hold a book rather than a worship leaflet; or sing and pray from hand-held hymnals rather than from images projected on a bigger-than-life screen? Time will tell whether the church has compiled and sold the last hardbound hymnal in any quantity except as a reference book on a library shelf.

In addition to the possible impending technological obsolescence of hardbound hymnals, ethical and pragmatic considerations have emerged. Should the church perpetuate a nineteenth-century formatted hymnal whose sale extracts enormous dollar investments from local churches, and indirectly from the general church, as we prepare to frame and fund an increasing role in serving the hungry, homeless, and parentless?

Within a growing ecumenism and an emerging consensus of worship forms as well as a common core of hymns and tunes, can The United Methodist Church, in faithfulness to its historic claim as an agent in the restoration and remembering of the body of Christ, continue to publish a separate but equal hymnal for a separate church? In the final decade of the twentieth century will United Methodism be the first to remove this vintage icon of ecclesial exclusivity from the pew and commend it to our libraries and museums to be researched by hymnologists, and occasionally dusted off for public display?

This hymnal's future, like its predecessors, is also tangential to developments in our church's worship, education, mission, ministry, and publishing. The 1984 General Conference in mandating a "single volume hymnal and worshipbook" tipped its hand to the past and, consequently, placed very practical limits on the Hymnal Revision Committee's attempts to serve the future with today's unproven products and alternative performance practices. In that context the new hymnal is, as were its predecessors, a very conservative offering that will in time, perhaps within this decade, be supplemented by viable and marketable alternatives. Our church needs to move from its dependence on replicating past methods of revision of the church's hymnal each generation—and the excessive costs of using other publishers' or authors' copyrighted material—and initiate an ongoing strategy that encourages the writing, compiling, publishing, and ownership of hymnic and liturgical resources, which can be distributed effectively through low-cost computer technology.

Finally, our hymnal's future is inextricably tied to the future of The United Methodist Church whose unique heritage and commitment to social witness, global/ecumenical mission and ministry, pragmatic theology, and flexible worship forms will continue to be tested. As the church encounters the seductive passive models of entertainment masquerading as vital worship and the success-oriented evangelical predilection that "bigger is better," we face the same challenges and opportunities to be faithful to the gospel of Jesus Christ as those that confronted our forebears.

> Sois una llama que ha de encender
> *You are the flame that will lighten the dark,*
> resplandores de fey caridad.
> *sending sparkles of hope, faith, and love;*
> Sois los pastores que han de llevar
> *you are the shepherds to lead the whole world*
> al mundo por sendas de paz.
> *through valleys and pastures of peace.*
> Sois los amigos que quise escoger,
> *You are the friends that I chose for myself,*
> sois palabra que intento esparcir.
> *the word that I want to proclaim.*
> Sois reino nuevo que empieza a engendrar
> *You are the new kingdom built on a rock*
> justicia, amor y verdad.
> *where justice and truth always reign.*

Estribillo/Refrain

Id, amigos, por el mundo,
Go, my friends, go to the world
anunciando el amor,
proclaiming love to all,
mensajeros de la vida,
messengers of my forgiving
de la paz y el perdón.
peace, eternal love.
Sed, amigos, mis tesigos de mi resurrección.
Be, my friends, a loyal witness,
from the dead I arose;
Id llevando mi presencia;
"Lo, I'll be with you forever,
con vosotros estoy.
till the end of the world."

"Sois la Semilla," stanza 2, *The United Methodist Hymnal*, **583**; Cesareo Gabaraín, 1979; translated by Raquel Gutiérrez-Achon and Skinner Chávez-Melo.

HYMNS, CANTICLES & ACTS OF WORSHIP

A charge to keep I have (413)

Charles Wesley, 1762 (Lev. 8:35)

The text was first published as a two-stanza SMD text in vol. 1 at 58-59 under the title "Keep the charge of the Lord, that ye die not, [Leviticus] 8:36" in *Short Hymns on Select Passages of Holy Scripture*, 1762, a two-volume work of 2,030 biblical texts from Genesis to Revelation. (Baker 1962, 135) F. Hildebrandt and O. A. Beckerlegge in their commentary on the 1780 *Collection* suggest that Wesley's text is more than likely based on Matthew Henry's *Commentary on Leviticus:*

> We have every one of us a charge to keep, an eternal God to glorify, an immortal soul to provide for, needful duty to be done, our generation to serve; and it must be our daily care to keep this charge, for it is the charge of the Lord our Master, who will shortly call us to an account about it, and it is our peril if we neglect it. Keep it 'that ye die not'; it is death, eternal death, to betray the truth we are charged with. (Wesley 1983, 7:465.)

Other scriptural references are 2 Peter 1:10, Hosea 6:2, and Matthew 25:30 and 26:41. Lines 3 and 4 of stanza 4, uncharacteristically for Wesley, state a finality of judgment (4:4), "I shall forever die," and have been altered. The most recent attempt is found in *Hymns and Psalms*, 785:

> So shall I not my trust betray,
> nor love within me die.

Fred D. Gealy evaluates similar attempts to change these lines: "The alteration weakens the intensity of the hymn. The Gospel always comes with threat and [as well as] promise." (Gealy 555/1) The hymn entered our hymnals in 1786.

According to William Farley Smith, in the African American tradition this hymn is often sung at the close of worship and during Holy Communion. (Smith 1991, 1 (3):7)

Additional scriptural references for this and other hymns may be found in "Index of Scripture: Hymns, Canticles, Prayers and Poems," *The United Methodist Hymnal*; and Robert D. Ingram, *Scriptural and Seasonal Indexes of The United Methodist Hymnal.*

Boylston

Lowell Mason, 1832

Boylston is one of Mason's several tunes that reflect his attraction to chant, probably psalm tones (see page 166 and hymn **373**). The tune first appeared in *The Choir, or Union Collection of Church Music*, 1832. Boylston is the name of a street in Boston.

A mighty fortress is our God (110)
Ein' feste Burg ist unser Gott

Martin Luther, 1527-29; trans. by Frederick H. Hedge, 1853 (Ps. 46)

Luther's stirring hymn, which was probably written in response to the martyrdom of his friend Leonhard Kaiser, has been translated into 53 languages including 100 English versions, the first of which appeared in 5 stanzas in Miles Coverdale's *Goostly Psalmes and Spirituall Songes*, ca. 1535.

Further information on Coverdale's version is found in the research files of Fred D. Gealy (555/2):

> Since Coverdale's early attempt is an important artifact of English hymnody, the first stanza is printed below from George Pearson, ed., *The Remains of Myles Coverdale* (1846, 569-70).

> The xlvi. Psalme of David
> Deus noster refugium

> Oure God is a defence and towre,
> A good armoure and good weape;
> He hath been ever oure helpe and succoure,
> In all the troubles that we have ben in.
> Therefore wyl we never drede,
> For any wonderous dede
> By water or by londe,
> In hilles or the see dōse;
> Oure God hath them all in his hod.

Further information on Coverdale's version is found in Robin A. Leaver, *'Goostly Psalmes and Spirituall Songes,'* Maurice Frost, *English & Scottish Psalms & Hymns Tunes, ca. 1543-1677*, and the research files of Fred D. Gealy (555/2).

English language churches generally use either or combinations and variants of two translations: Thomas Carlyle, 1831, "A safe stronghold our God is still"; and Hedge's that appeared in *Hymns for the Church of Christ*, 1853. (See Jaroslav Vajda, "Translations of 'Ein' Feste Burg,'" *The Hymn*, 1983.) Our hymnals have used the Hedge translation without alteration since 1878. A comparison of Luther's text (stanza 2:5-9), the composite English text, and Hedge's illustrates the difficulty in translating the hymn's idiomatic expressions and forceful homiletical style into a singable English text:

Luther:

> Fragst du, Wer der ist?
> Er heißt Jesus Christ,
> der Herr Zebaoth;
> und ist kein andrer Gott,
> das Feld muß er behalten.

Composite:

> Ask ye, who is this?
> Jesus Christ it is,

of Sabaoth Lord,
and there's none other God;
he holds the field forever.

Hedge:

Dost ask who that may be?
Christ Jesus, it is he;
Lord Sabaoth, his name,
from age to age the same,
and he must win the battle.

Ulrich Leupold dates the text as between 1527 and 1529. It was apparently printed in Joseph Klug's *Geistliche Lieder*, Wittenberg, 1529, although no copy is extant. (Luther 1965, 53:283)

Ein feste Burg

Martin Luther, 1527-29

The earliest printing of the tune is in *Kirche gesang, mit vil schönen Psalmen vnnd Melodey, gantz geendert un gemert,* Nürnberg, 1531. (Stulken 1981, 307) Our harmonization is from *The New Hymnal for American Youth,* 1930, and was first used in our hymnals in the 1935 *Methodist Hymnal.* It is one of many adapted from J. S. Bach's harmonization of the isorhythmic version of the melody as found in the final movement of his chorale cantata *Ein Feste Burg,* S. 80. A rhythmic setting of the chorale, a descant, and an alternate harmonization are found at 111-13 in *The United Methodist Hymnal Music Supplement.* In the tradition of identifying chorale tunes, the tune name is from the first line of the German text. See also pages 7-8 for a discussion of the chorale.

A covenant prayer in the Wesleyan tradition (607)

The Rev. Dr. David Tripp has supplied this information:

[This prayer is] a twentieth-century adaptation of prayers adopted from Puritan writings by John Wesley in connection with the Renewal of the Covenant. The last 5 lines are from the close of the main Covenanting prayer which was composed by Joseph Alleine, 1662, the preceding lines from a preparatory prayer (one of a series set in a long meditation on various aspects of God's relationship with us) written by Richard Alleine. John Wesley, from 1755, developed a regular Renewal of the Covenant at his main centers of work in England, at his main times of visitation. After his death, British Methodists standardized on the New Year, which had been his usual time for his observance when in London. This combination of elements borrowed from Alleine is the work of George B. Robson, 1922, British Methodist minister and author. (Correspondence with Carlton R. Young, July 1991)

For further discussion see David Tripp, *The Renewal of the Covenant in the Methodist Tradition,* 1969. See also "Come, let us use the grace divine," page 293, and "Covenant Renewal Service," pages 288-94 in *The United Methodist Book of Worship,* 1992.

A refuge amid distraction (535)

Trad., India

This traditional prayer from India may be used effectively with other hymns and prayers in the section "Strength in Tribulation" and "Prayer, Trust, Hope." For example, it can be used with "Not so in haste, my heart" **(455)** and "Stand by me" **(512)**.

Abide with me (700)

Henry Francis Lyte, 1847 (Luke 24:29)

The text first appeared in leaflet in 1847 and was included in *Hymns Ancient and Modern,* 1861. The occasion of its writing seems to be Lyte's failing health, which forced him to give up his parish in Lower Brixham. The circumstances of Lyte's writing the hymn, according to Fred D. Gealy, produced the imagery of eventide linked with low tide and death:

> [Lyte] rallied to preach one last sermon and to celebrate one last Holy Communion, September 4, 1847. On the evening of that day, before seeking health in the milder climate of France, he walked out to the cliffs overlooking the sea at the end of his garden. There the setting sun reminded him of Luke 24:29: "Abide with us, for it is toward evening, the day is far spent." . . . In less than an hour he had written the hymn. (Gealy, Lovelace, Young 1970, 68)

Stanza 1:2 originally was "The darkness <u>thickens</u>"; 3:4, "<u>O</u> bide with me"; and 5:1-2, "Hold <u>then</u> thy cross" and "<u>Speak</u> through the gloom." Most hymnals since *Hymns Ancient and Modern* omit stanzas 3, 4, and 5. They are included here since they complete the poet's compelling invitation:

> Not a brief glance, I beg, a passing word;
> but as thou dwell'st with thy disciples, Lord,
> familiar, condescending, patient, free,
> come not to sojourn, but abide with me.
>
> Come not in terrors as the King of kings,
> but kind and good, with healing in thy wings,
> tears for all woes, a heart for every plea,—
> come, Friend of sinners, and thus bide with me.

> Thou on my head in early youth didst smile;
> and, though rebellious and perverse meanwhile,
> thou hast not left me, oft as I left thee,
> on to the close, O Lord, abide with me.

The hymn entered our hymnals in 1874 in five stanzas.

Eventide

William Henry Monk, 1861

Lyte wrote a tune for his hymn, which is included in *Musical Times*, February 1, 1908, and *Historical Companion to Hymns Ancients and Modern*, page 142. Monk's tune, according to legend, was composed at the intermission of a meeting of the *Hymns Ancient and Modern* editorial committee. The tune first appeared with the text in *Hymns Ancient and Modern*, 1861. Erik Routley calls EVENTIDE Monk's one "universal" tune, "and perhaps for all its modesty, it is his most characteristic tune." (Routley 1981, 98)

Advent (201)

Book of Common Prayer; alt. 1988 by Laurence Hull Stookey, 1987

Stookey interprets this seasonal prayer:

> During the season of Advent we recall the role of the prophets in preparing for the coming of Messiah, particularly their teaching and exhortation. We look ahead to the celebration of Christmas Day and to the time when the Lord, who came in humility to Bethlehem, will come in glory. (Sanchez 1989, 80)

Ah, holy Jesus, how hast thou offended (289)
Herzliebster Jesu, was hast du verbrochen

Johann Heermann, 1630; trans. by Robert S. Bridges, 1899

Heermann's text was written during the Thirty Years' war, 1618-48, and is based on the pseudo-Augustinian *Meditationes*, attributed to Jean de Fécamp, d. 1071, whose writings were influential during the Middle Ages. "The sentiment and the style of the hymn, so similar to the twelfth-century 'Reproaches' (see Methodist *Book of Worship*, pages 109-10), could easily if mistakenly be identified with Anselm or Augustine." (Gealy 555/5) The German text was first published in fifteen stanzas in Heermann's *Devoti Musica Cordis*, 1630, as "the cause of bitter sufferings of Jesus Christ and consolation from his love and grace." Bridges's brilliant translation "with the nobility of phrase [that] recaptures both the sense and the spirit of the Latin and German texts" (Gealy 555/5) entered our hymnals in 1966. Our version is unaltered except for 1:2, "man" to "we" and "hath" to "have"; 3:3, "man's" to "our," "he" to "we," and "heedest" to "heeded"; and 3:4, "intercedeth" to "interceded."

Herzliebster Jesu

Johann Crüger, 1640
The tune first appeared in a harmonized setting by the composer in his *Newes vollkömliches Gesangbuch Augburgischer Confession*, Berlin, 1640. It is apparently adapted from the Louis Bourgeois tune for Psalm 23 in the Genevan Psalter, 1543, and Johann Hermann Schein's tune, "Gelieben Freund," in his *Cantional oder Gesangbuch Augsburgischer Konfession*, Leipzig, 1627. The harmonization is the composer's modified for *The Chorale Book for England*, London, 1863, with the original cross-relationship restored in the alto and bass parts, measures 12 and 13. J. S. Bach used the melody in *St. Matthew Passion* and *St. John Passion*.

Alas! and did my Savior bleed (294)

Isaac Watts, 1707
This passion text was printed in six stanzas in *Hymns and Spiritual Songs*, book 2, "Composed on Divine Subjects," July 1707, under the heading "Godly Sorrow arising from the Sufferings of Christ." (Gealy 555/6) Even though the hymn found limited use in Great Britain, its inclusion in early nineteenth-century USA shaped-note books, where it was sung to five different tunes, assured its wide introduction and use among evangelicals. Fanny J. Crosby states in her autobiography that upon hearing it sung at the time of her conversion, "my soul flooded with celestial light."

The hymn's strong metaphors caused even the author to place a bracket on the second stanza in the 1709 edition,

> Thy body slain, sweet Jesus Thine—
> And bath'd in its own blood—
> While the firm mark of Wrath Divine
> His Soul in anguish stood,

with the suggestion that its vivid imagery might be omitted when the hymn was sung:

> Those parts are also included in crotchets which contain words too poetical for meaner understandings, or too particular for whole congregations to sing. But after all, 'tis best in publick Psalmody for the minister to chuse [*sic*] the particular parts or verses of the Psalm or Hymn that is to be sung, rather than leave it to the judgment or casual determination of him that leads the tune. (Watts 1709, 14)

Apparently not entirely satisfied with lines 2:3-4, he also made these changes:

> While all exposed to Wrath Divine,
> the glorious Suff'rer stood!

Several additional changes have been made in the text since its first appearance in our hymnals in 1786. In 1935 stanza 1:4, "For such a worm as I" was changed to "For sinners such as I"; 2:1, "crimes" to "sins" and "groaned upon" to "suffered on." Line 3:3, "When God, the mighty maker, died," while intended figuratively, became a problem to hymnal editors who feared that the words might be taken literally as the untimely death of God. Thus, in the 1821 hymnal "God" was changed to "Christ"; in the 1935 hymnal the line was altered to "When Christ, the great Redeemer, died." The original line was restored in the 1966 hymnal, and it is included in this hymnal. In stanza 3:2, "his" has been changed to "its." The change in 3:4, from "for man the creatures sin" to "for his own creature's sin," renders the text people inclusive, but detracts from Watts's simple and direct style.

Martyrdom

Hugh Wilson; arr: by R. A. Smith, 1825

The tune, also called "Avon," "Fenwick," "Drumclog," "Inverness," and "All Saints," was apparently arranged late in the eighteenth century by Wilson in CM (4/4) from a Scottish traditional melody. He printed it in leaflets for his village music classes. R. A. Smith, precentor at St. George's, arranged it in triple meter (3/4) in *Sacred Harmony*, Edinburgh, 1825, calling it an "old Scottish melody." Wilson's heirs brought suit and proved that Wilson had copyrighted the CM tune, but no conclusion was reached concerning its probable folk origin. Erik Routley has described the tune as "one the finest, most dignified, and most celebrated of all psalm-tunes. In Scotland its associations are invariably penitential: it is marked for Psalm 130 in the *Scottish Psalter*." (Parry 1953, 189-90)

Alas! and did my Savior bleed (359)

Isaac Watts, 1707; refrain by Ralph E. Hudson, 1885

Ralph E. Hudson added a familiar camp-meeting refrain "At the cross" to Watts's text. This version entered our hymnals in 1898.

Hudson

Ralph E. Hudson, 1885

The form of the tune in our hymnal was first printed in Hudson's compilation, *Songs of Peace, Love and Joy*, Alliance, Ohio, 1885. William J. Reynolds in

Companion to the Baptist Hymnal has shown that Hudson probably wrote the music for the body of the text and then added the refrain from the repertory of camp-meeting choruses:

> Because of the difference in character of the music for the stanzas and that of the refrain, it is quite likely that the refrain melody was a familiar one at that time and was used by Hudson in completing this hymn. . . . A comparison of the central theme of the stanzas with that of the refrain text is most revealing. (Reynolds 1976, 28)

Ernest K. Emurian suggests that the melody and first line of the refrain were borrowed by Eugene Raymond for the Civil War song published in 1864, "Take me home to the place where I first saw the light." (Emurian 1980, 195)

The hymn is set in two tunes, one Euro-Anglo and the other gospel/frontier. These tunes, used for over a century in contrasting and distinct worshipping communities as well as separate social and racial settings, clearly demonstrate USA Methodism's wide divergence—some would state schizophrenia—in musical taste.

All creatures of our God and King (62)

Francis of Assisi, ca. 1225; trans. by William H. Draper, 1919; revised 1987
Saint Francis's "Canticle of the Sun," or the "Song of Brother Sun and of All Creatures," is one of several *laude*, a popular Italian form of religious songs, which he composed for use in nonliturgical praise gatherings.

Fred D. Gealy has written that Francis wrote the hymn

> in the last months of his life from July, 1225, to October, 1226, in times of intense pain and prolonged suffering and in the presence of death. The st. on forgiving others derives from Francis' distress over the quarrels between the secular and spiritual powers in Assisi and Perugia. (Gealy, Lovelace, Young 1970, 72)

The adaption and paraphrase by Draper was written

> while he was rector of Adel, near Leeds, for a Whitsuntide festival for children. The exact date of writing is not known, but must have been between 1906 (the date of publication of *The English Hymnal*) and 1919 . . . [when it was] first published in the *Public School Hymn Book*. (Watson and Trickett 1988, 213-14)

In his adaptation and paraphrase of Francis's poem as a hymn, Draper personifies all creatures and calls on them to praise God.

Considered to be one of the first genuine religious poems in the Italian language, the text entered our hymnals in the 1935 *Methodist Hymnal* without the final stanza, our stanza 6, which was restored in the 1966 book. Our text was adapted and revised by Gracia Grindal, a consultant to the language/theology subcommittee. Her adaptation changes the refrain's reiterated "him" to "ye" and renders male and female attributions more consistent with Francis's text.

Francis's final stanza, in the original Italian "Laudato si, Misignore, per sora nostra morte corporale," was probably written after his return to Assisi when he was informed that his illness was incurable.

> Praised be thou, My Lord, for our sister bodily Death,
> from whom no living man can ever 'scape.
> Woe unto those who die in mortal sin.
> Blessed are those who are found in thy most holy will;
> to them the second death will bring no ill.
> Praise and bless my Lord, render thanks to him
> and serve him with great humility. (Petry 1957, 125)

Draper composed the concluding stanza from lines 6 and 7 and added a doxology.

Lasst uns erfreuen

Ausserlesene Catholische, Geistliche Kirchengesänge, Cologne, 1623
Arr. and harm. by Ralph Vaughan Williams, 1906

Vaughan Williams prepared his harmonization of one of the strongest German Catholic tunes in the repertory for *The English Hymnal*, 1906, as a setting for the text "Ye watchers and ye holy ones" **(89)**. Erik Routley evaluates the contributions to hymnody by Vaughan Williams in this and other harmonizations of Roman Catholic tunes:

> [He brings] into the present the treasures of the past. It was in the exercise of editorial skill, that special virtue of the good hymnologist, that the book [*The English Hymnal*] got its message through. This is the skill which knows where to find a fresh tune in the existing repertory and knows to what text it should be set. (Routley 1981, 142)

The tune and harmonization first entered our hymnals in 1935, where Vaughan Williams was not cited as arranger, and it was printed without identifying the contrasting textures of unison melody supported by an organ accompaniment with five- and six-part harmony, and the four-part harmony of the Alleluias. These elements have been restored in our hymnal. The hymn's length makes it suitable for a festival procession, with alternate groups singing the stanzas and everyone singing the Alleluias in four-part harmony. The harmonization can be found in a lower key at page 199 *The United Methodist Hymnal Music Supplement.*

John Wilson has provided a full discussion of the development of the tune in the article "The Tune 'Lasst uns erfreuen' as We Know It," *Bulletin: Hymn Society of Great Britain and Ireland*, January 1981.

All earth is waiting to see the Promised One (210)

See "Toda la tierra," pages 667-68.

All glory, laud, and honor (280)
Gloria, laus et honor

> *Theodulph of Orleans, 8-9th cent.; trans. by John Mason Neale, 1851*
> *(Zech. 9:9; Matt. 21:8-15; Mark. 11:8-10; Luke 19:36-38; John 12:12-13)*

Fred D. Gealy has summarized the charming legend of the origin of this traditional Palm Sunday processional:

According to the legend as told by Clichtoveus, in his *Elucidatorium*, 1516, the hymn was composed and first sung on a certain Sunday when Theodulph was in prison in Angers. The Emperor Louis was present that day as the procession moved through the city and halted beneath the tower where the saint was imprisoned. Suddenly, to his astonishment, the Emperor heard from above the *Gloria, laus*, chanted loudly and melodiously. Being charmed he asked the name of the singer and was told that it was his own prisoner, Theodulph. Moved with compassion for him, the Emperor pardoned the saint, returned him to his see, and ordered that henceforth the hymn which Theodulph had composed be sung on Palm Sunday. Ancient Palm Sunday use of the hymn is well attested in the French, Roman, and English rites. (Gealy, Lovelace, Young 1970, 73)

Eight translations of the hymn were made between 1849 and 1874. Neale made two translations, one in *Mediaeval Hymns and Sequences*, 1851, consisting of unmetered elegiac couplets in six stanzas plus the antiphon, "O savior of the world." For example, the first couplet,

> Gloria, laus, et honor tibi sit, rex
>   Christe redemptor,
> cui puerile decus prompsit Hosanna pium,

was translated:

> Glory and honor and laud be to thee, Christ, King and Redeemer,
> Children before whose steps raised their Hosannas of Praise.

The second version is from his *Hymnal Noted*, part 2, 1854, in eight stanzas of 76.76, with the first stanza used as a refrain. The first six stanzas have been used in our hymnals since 1905 with little change from the version that was adapted from *The Hymnal Noted* for the trial edition of *Hymns Ancient and Modern*, 1859. The first line originally began "Glory, and laud, and honour," but was altered for the first edition of *Hymns Ancient and Modern*, 1861, to "All glory," with Neale's approval, to accommodate the upbeat. Neale also retranslated stanza five, orginally written in multi-meter. In our hymnal 2:4 was altered from "and mortal men and all things created make reply" to "and we with all creation in chorus make reply"; and the first stanza becomes the refrain, as in Neale's original text.

Neale observes in the second edition of *Mediaeval Hymns*, 1863, page 26 (Gealy 555/9), that "another [seventh] verse was usually sung, till the 17th century; at the pious quaintness of which we can scarcely avoid a smile:"

> sis pius ascensor tu, nos quoque simus asellus;
> tecum nos capiat urbs veneranda Dei.

Neale translated it as follows:

> Be Thou, O Lord, the Rider,
> And we the little ass,
> That to God's Holy City
> Together we may pass.

An interesting typographical error occurred in stanza 3:2 in our hymnal's first printing rendering it "with psalms" instead of "with palms."

St. Theodulph

Melchior Teschner, 1615

The tune, also called "Valet Will Ich Dir Geben" after a funeral hymn, was one of two five-part settings for that hymn in *Ein andächtiges Gebet*, Leipzig, 1615. The form of the tune, as well as the harmonization that is used in most hymnals, follows W. H. Monk's version in *Hymns Ancient and Modern*, 1861. J. S. Bach used the tune in his *St. John Passion* as a interlude sung by the choir.

All hail the power of Jesus' name (154)

Edward Perronet, 1780; alt. by John Rippon, 1787

The first stanza only of the hymn was printed interlined with the tune "Miles' Lane" without attribution, facing page 584 in the November 1779 issue of Augustus M. Toplady's *Gospel Magazine*. (Gealy 555/10) In the April 1880 issue, page 185, it appeared with the first and seven additional stanzas under the title "On the Resurrection, The Lord is King." The hymn has seldom been printed in its original form since John Rippon in his *Selection of Hymns from the Best Authors, intended to be an Appendix to Dr. Watts' Psalms and Hymns*, 1787, essentially rewrote the hymn by omitting Perronet's stanzas 2, 3, and 6:

> Let high-born seraphs tune the lyre,
>   and, as they tune it, fall
> before his face who tunes their choir,
>   and crown him Lord of all.

> Crown him, ye morning stars of light,
>   who fix'd this floating ball;
> now hail the strength of Israel's might,
>   and crown him Lord of All.

> Hail him, ye heirs of David's line,
>   whom David Lord did call;
> the God incarnate, Man divine,
>   and crown him Lord of all.

He titled the remaining stanzas "Angels," "Martyrs," "Converted Jews," "Believing Gentiles," "Sinners of every Nation," and added two new stanzas with titles:

> Sinners of every Age

> Babes, Men, and Sires, who know his love,
>   who feel your sin and thrall,
> now join with all the hosts above,
>   and crown him Lord of all.

The second new stanza is the final stanza of most versions of this hymn:

> Ourselves

> O that with yonder sacred throng,
>   we at his feet may fall!
> We'll join the everlasting song,
>   and crown him Lord of all.

One of most felicitous changes by Rippon was to alter the original,

> Let every tribe and every tongue,
>   that bound creation's call,
> now shout, in universal song,
>   the crowned Lord of all,

to that used in most versions of the text since the early nineteenth century:

> Let every kindred, every tribe
> on this terrestrial ball,
> to him all majesty ascribe,
> and crown him Lord of all.

Perronet's original third stanza, omitted from our hymnals since early in the nineteenth century, has been restored in our hymnal as stanza five. The hymn entered Methodist hymnals in the Methodist Protestant book of 1837.

Coronation

Oliver Holden, 1792

The tune was first printed in *Union Harmony or Universal Collection of Sacred Music,* published in Boston in 1793. The delightful two-measure duet in the middle of the tune between bass and soprano in the original setting was probably first put into our collections in four-part harmony in *Hermon, A New Collection of Sacred Music,* New York, 1873, either by Rigdon M. McIntosh or Thomas O. Summers, the latter credited on the cover of the collection as having "Assisted in the hymn-tune department." All of our hymnals since 1878 have included the tune without further alteration. A free hamonization and instrumental descant are included at 67 in *The United Methodist Hymnal Music Supplement.*

Diadem

James Ellor, 1838

Ellor composed this tune at the age of nineteen on the occasion of the anniversary of a Wesleyan Sunday school in his hometown of Droylsden, Manchester. It was reprinted and distributed in single sheets to Methodists and other evangelical groups where for generations it has been the source of vigorous part-singing. Erik Routley suggests that the composer may have introduced the tune in the USA. Routley also proposes that the tune with its repeated "Crown him" tossed back and forth between male and female voice is really a short anthem. (Routley 1981, 84) Whether it is a hymn tune or an anthem, the robust and enthusiastic singing of this typical early nineteenth-century evangelical tune, very similar in style to SAGINA **(363)**, has transformed many congregations into instant choirs. It was first included in our hymnals in the 1935 *Methodist Hymnal.*

In *The United Methodist Hymnal Music Supplement,* two modulations are provided at 69 and 70 between the keys of the two tunes so that both may be used: e.g., stanzas 1-3, CORONATION, and stanzas 4-6, DIADEM. Stanzas may also be sung in other sequences using both tunes.

All my hope is firmly grounded (132)
Meine Hoffnung stehet feste

Joachim Neander, 1680; trans. by Fred Pratt Green, 1986 (1 Tim. 6:17b)
Neander's hymn of praise to the all-providing God, titled "Grace after meat," was first published in five stanzas of seven lines in A *und W Joachimi Neandri Glaub- und Liebesübung*, Bremen, 1680. The hymn is apparently based on 1 Timothy 6:17b:

> As for those who in the present age are rich, command them not to be haughty, or to set their hopes on the uncertainty of riches, but rather on God who richly provides us with everything for our enjoyment.

Our hymnal is the first to include Green's translation. Bernard Braley has written of the circumstances concerning its creation:

> When in 1986 John Wilson asked Fred to do another, and closer, translation of Joachim Neander's text, he wondered what was wrong with Robert Bridges's "All my hope on God is founded" [*The Yattingdon Hymnal*, 1899], surely one of the noblest of hymns. But when he read not only a literal translation of the German original but translations by J. Jacobi and Catherine Winkworth, it became clear that Bridges's hymn, noble as it is, is not a translation of the original. Rather it may be said to be inspired by it. . . .[The creation of] the text involved creative consultation between Fred and John Wilson. He accepted John's advice to telescope verses 3 and 4; but rejected the use of Bridges's first line.

> In attempting a more accurate translation, Fred has kept as strictly as possible to Neander's use of imagery and has tried not to introduce his own ideas, however spiritually attractive. (Green 1989, 106)

Some alterations were made in Green's text for this hymnal with his permission: 1:2, "our" to "the"; 1:5, "Him" to "God"; 3:7 and 4:2, "his" to "God's"; 4:3, "He" to "God"; and 4:7, "his" to "God."

Michael

Herbert Howells, 1930, 1977
Companion to Hymns and Psalms provides the historical background of the hymn tune:

> [In 1930] at the request of Dr. Thomas Fielden, then Director of Music at Charterhouse, for use at that school. On receiving the request, Howells wrote the tune while still at the breakfast table opening his mail. It was published in the *Clarendon Hymn Book*, 1936. The present version, with the

composer's slight revision of the bass line, was made for *Hymns for Church and School*, 1964. The composer named the tune after his son, Michael, who died in childhood [age 9]. (Watson and Trickett 1988, 70)

This expressive and singable tune composed by one of the most celebrated twentieth-century composers of church music is a welcome addition to our hymnals.

All people that on earth do dwell (75)

William Kethe, 1561 (Ps. 100)

John Wilson in "The Sources of the 'Old Hundreth' Paraphrase," *Bulletin: Hymn Society of Great Britain and Ireland*, 1962, renewed interest in the origins and variants of this text. Nicholas Temperley has shown that this earliest English metrical paraphrase probably first appeared in the fourth edition of "the Geneva service book (*Short Title Catalogue* No. 16561a.5) issued in 1560 [with] twenty-five new psalm versions signed 'W. Ke.' (William Kethe), among which is Ps. 100. . . . It is possible that the text was first issued in 1559." (Glover 1993, 1233)

Robin A. Leaver in *'Goostly Psalmes and Spirituall Songes'* states that Kethe's text was also included in an expanded version of the 1560 collection, *Psalms of David in Englishe Metre, by Thomas Sterneholde and others . . .* , 1561. (Leaver 1991, 247) The text has been included in most psalters and hymnbooks since then.

The archives of Fred D. Gealy's research (Gealy 555/13) provide extensive documentation of the historic contexts of the Anglo-Genevan psalters and the authorship, date, and textual variants of this text. Gealy describes the basic alterations that have been made in Kethe's text:

In 1:3 the original read "Him serve with fear." "Fear" is not a correct rendition of Psalm 100:2, which is properly translated "gladness." The Scottish Psalter of 1650 altered "fear" to "mirth." In our hymnals "mirth" was first printed in 1935 [*The Methodist Hymnal*].

The first line of st. 2 originally read "The Lord, ye know, is God indeed." Here, too, the Scottish Psalter of 1650 altered the text to "Know that the Lord is God indeed," introduced into our hymnal in 1935 [*The Methodist Hymnal*]. Though this rendering is a more accurate translation of the psalm, Kethe's version is frequently retained.

Very early in the transmission of 2:3 "flock" replaced "folk (e)." Though the British Museum exemplar reads "folke," it is spelled "folck" in the Day Psalter of 1561. "Folck" gets altered to "flock (e)," which is the usual text in the Sternhold-Hopkins and Scottish psalters. That Kethe wrote "folke" now seems proved by the text of the British Museum copy referred to above and by the Geneva Bible which in Psalm 100:3 read "people." "Flock" was printed in our 1878 [where it was included in our hymnals for the first time] and 1905 hymnals, but was replaced by "folk" in 1935. Most modern editors prefer "folk." (Gealy, Lovelace, Young 1970, 80)

Kethe's text is mentioned in Shakespeare's *Merry Wives of Windsor* (act 2, scene 1): "They do no more adhere and keep peace together than the Hundredth Psalm to the tune of 'Greensleeves.'" A setting of the hymn by Ralph Vaughan Williams for choir and congregation was performed at the coronation of Elizabeth II, June 2, 1953. John Wesley preferred Watts's paraphrase, "Before Jehovah's awful throne," which was included in our hymnals until this revision when it was decided to include only Kethe's paraphrase along with Psalm 100 from the King James Version and the New Revised Standard Version of the Bible.

Old 100TH

Louis Bourgeois, 1551

Bourgeois either adapted/arranged or composed this tune as a setting for Psalm 134 in the Genevan Psalter, 1551. Its designation "old" was used to identify its inclusion in the "older" psalter, Sternhold and Hopkins's *Whole Book of Psalms*, 1562, as opposed to the "newer" psalter by Tate and Brady, *New Version of the Psalms*, 1696. Its setting for Kethe's paraphrase firmly established it in the repertory where it has also been used with other paraphrases of the psalm, including two by Watts (see above), and for the doxological stanza of Ken's evening hymn, "All praise to thee my God this night," incorrectly cited in church bulletins and in common practice as "the doxology." (There are hundreds more; see **951** under "Service Music.") The amen has been added in deference to its use as the final cadence of "the doxology" sung by USA Methodists and many others as part of the choreography for the procession of ushers with the morning offering.

Until the 1966 edition of our hymnals two versions of the tune, rhythmic and isorhythmic **(621)**, both with long documented use in English hymnody, were included. Both versions are included in this edition. The version used with this text is close to Bourgeois's original shape of the tune. Our harmonization, except measures 9 and 10, is from 365 in *The English Hymnal*. Another harmonization is by John Dowland, with melody in the voice above the bass, composed for Thomas Ravenscroft's *Whole Booke of Psalmes*, 1621. Vaughan Williams used this in his anthem, (see comments on the text above); it is number 365 in *The English Hymnal*, 1906. See also 257, 258, and 259, *The United Methodist Hymnal Music Supplement*.

All praise to our redeeming Lord (554)

Charles Wesley, 1747 (1 Cor. 1:3-10; 12:3-12; Eph. 4:1-16)

With the title "At Meeting of Friends" the text was first included at 42 in three stanzas of CMD in *Hymns for those that seek and those that have Redemption in the Blood of Jesus Christ*, 1747. Even though John Wesley did not include it in his

1780 *Collection,* early in the nineteenth century it was used by Wesleyan groups as a hymn of parting and fellowship. Since our 1810 hymnal the double stanzas have been printed in CM, probably because of the full supply of CM tunes and the shortage of CMD tunes. In our hymnal the full text is printed for the first time since the 1878 hymnal. Craig B. Gallaway suggests the varieties of usage for the text:

[Since the hymn is] a celebration of the goal and process of Christian community (what John Wesley called "social religion"), it may be used in services commemorating the role of spiritual gifts in the body of Christ (1 Cor. 12; Eph. 4), or in the recognition and dedication of small group ministries. (Sanchez 1989, 189)

Armenia

Sylvanus B. Pond, 1836; harm. Austin C. Lovelace, 1963

Austin C. Lovelace writes of the tune's origin:

The tune first appeared in *The Musical Miscellany,* which comprised the music published in the *Musical Magazine,* edited by Thomas Hastings (Vol. I, No. 16) and published by Ezra Collier, New York, 1836. It was set there to "Let the sweet hope that thou art mine." It later appeared in Pond's *United States Psalmody* in 1841, the same year that it was printed in Thomas Hastings, *The Manhattan Collection,* published by Daniel Fanshaw in New York. (Gealy, Lovelace, Young 1970, 81-82)

Hastings is acknowledged in the preface to *Tunes for Congregational Worship,* 1857, the tune edition of the 1849 hymnal, as one of several who assisted its compilers, "two of our most experienced and popular choristers Sylvester Main, of New York, and William C. Brown, of Boston." On page 278 ARMENIA is interlined with the first stanza of "Lord, while for all mankind we pray," and suggested as the tune for eight additional CM hymns that are printed on facing pages. On page 52 "All praise to our redeeming Lord" appears as a CMD hymn with one stanza interlined with the tune GIARDINI.

The first wedding of the the text with ARMENIA in our hymnals was in 1878. Lovelace's harmonization was prepared for the 1966 hymnal.

All praise to thee, for thou, O King divine (166)

F. Bland Tucker, 1938 (Phil. 2:5-11)

One of the hymns the distinguished author wrote while a member of the commission that prepared *The Hymnal 1940,* the text was first published in that hymnal. In a letter of March 30, 1966, to Fred Gealy the poet states that "the hymn was written because I wanted alternative [meditative] words for the tune

SINE NOMINE." (Gealy 555/16) But copyright restrictions did not allow the use of that tune with any text other than "For all the saints" and caused that hymnal committee to set this text to ENGELBERG.

The committee that produced our 1966 book, being unaware of that limitation, set the text according to the author's original intent, and there is no doubt that the popularity of this hymn in United Methodism is primarily because of its setting with Vaughan Williams's tune. Vaughan Williams's tune is now in the public domain in the USA, which allows the text to continue to appear, in this instance without challenge, in our hymnals with the tune intended by the writer.

Tucker's text is based on Philippians 2:5-11. Jane Marshall suggests that "the combination of this text with Ralph Vaughan Williams's tune SINE NOMINE, the author's own preference, is excellent, for the concluding Alleluias in each stanza affirm the Christian's ecstatic confession that Jesus Christ is Lord." (Sanchez 1989, 70)

For a comparison of this text and "At the name of Jesus," see Mark Alan Filbert, "An Analysis of 'All praise to Thee, For thou, O King Divine' and 'At the Name of Jesus' in Relation to Philippians 2:6-11," *The Hymn* 40 (3):12-15.

Other settings of the text appear in our hymnal: "Canticle of Christ's obedience" **(167)** is the full text in the style of a psalm; "At the name of Jesus" **(168)** is another metrical paraphrase; and hymns **193, 536,** and **692** paraphrase parts of the biblical source.

Sine nomine

Ralph Vaughan Williams, 1906

This tune name literally means "without name," and it is one of four tunes the composer contributed without attribution to the first edition of *The English Hymnal*, 1906. It remains one of the most widely used tunes from the repertory of unison tunes composed in Great Britain in the early part of the twentieth century. Vaughan Williams's brilliant tune is composed in the style of a baroque trio: an independent and moving bass line, the harmonic realization on the manual in the left hand, and the melody in the third and upper voice. The composer slightly revised the tune for the 1933 edition. A four-part choral setting is found at **711**, making it possible for the choir to sing alternate stanzas in parts. The tune is lowered one whole step at 314 in *The United Methodist Hymnal Music Supplement*, followed by free harmonizations with descants at 315-18 in the original key.

All praise to thee, my God, this night (682)

Thomas Ken, ca. 1694

Bishop Ken probably had in mind both his evening hymn as well as the morning hymn, "Awake my soul, and with the sun," when in 1674 he published his manual of prayers for the students of Winchester College, admonishing them to "be sure to sing the Morning and Evening hymn in your chamber devoutly." (Unfortunately his morning hymn is not included in our hymnal.) In 1695 he printed both in the manual, describing them as "newly revised," probably with reference to pirated versions published in 1694. He revised the text in 1709. Many hymnals use versions of the first five stanzas and "the doxology," stanza six. Our hymnal omits the compelling fifth stanza,

> When in the night I sleepless lie
> my soul with heavenly thoughts supply;
> let no ill dreams disturb my rest,
> no powers of darkness me molest.

The full text of the twelve stanzas in the 1695 and the 1709 versions is printed in John Julian (1907, 619-20). Fred D. Gealy (1970, 82-83) discusses the textual variants and the use of the hymn in our hymnals. Concerning Ken's doxology, (see commentary, pages 555-56) he states that it has "been sung more often than any other lines ever written" and cites James Montgomery's eloquent assessment in *The Christian Psalmist*, Glasgow, 1825, supplied from Gealy's research.

> The well-known doxology is a masterpiece at once of amplification and compression;—amplification, in the burthen, "Praise God," repeated in each line;—compression, by exhibiting God as the object of praise in every view we can imagine praise due to Him;—praise for all *His* blessings, yea, for *all* blessings, none coming from any other source,—praise, by every creature, specifically invoked "here below," and in heaven "above"; praise, to Him in each of the characters where in He has revealed Himself in his word—"Father, Son, and Holy Ghost." (Gealy 555/16)

The hymn entered our hymnals in 1847. Hymnals of the Methodist Episcopal Church changed the first line to "Glory to thee, my God, this night."

Tallis' canon

Thomas Tallis, published 1561-67

This is the eighth of nine tunes that Tallis composed for Matthew Parker's *Whole Psalter translated into English Metre*, 1561-67. In its original version as a setting for Psalm 67, the tenor led the canon and was answered by the treble before continuing the next phrase. The canon was reduced to four parts with the melody in the tenor in Thomas Ravenscroft's *Whole Booke of Psalmes*, 1621. That harmonization was adapted for use in nineteenth-century hymnals. Our hymnals since the 1880's have used the form from *Hymns Ancient and Modern*, 1861. According to *Historical Companion to Hymns Ancient and Modern*, page 139, the tune was first printed with Ken's evening text in *The Harmonious Companion*, 1732, by Smith and Prelluer. John Wesley printed a version of the tune,

"Cannon Tune," in his *Foundery Collection*, 1742, with his translation of N. L. Zinzendorf's "Jesu, thy blood and righteousness," which he probably began in Georgia, ca. 1736. A version of the tune, probably adapted after "Brentwood" in George Whitefield's *Divine Musical Miscellany*, 1754, was used in the music edition of our 1849 hymnal.

The hymn may be performed by congregation and choir in canon at the octave between male and female voices with or without the harmonization. *The United Methodist Hymnal Music Supplement* includes a vocal or instrumental descant at 325.

All Saints (713)

After the Book of Common Prayer
This prayer adapted by Laurence H. Stookey from the *Book of Common Prayer* links past, present, and future. It is suggested for use on All Saints' Day (November 1), during the eight days encompassed from the Sunday previous to the day to the following Sunday, or anytime that the "cloud of witnesses" is remembered and celebrated.

All things bright and beautiful (147)

Cecil Frances Alexander, 1848 (Gen. 1:31)
The poem, originally in seven stanzas without the refrain that is the first stanza, is an exposition of the article "Maker of heaven and earth" in the Apostles' Creed **(881)**, number 9 in Mrs. Alexander's *Hymns for Little Children*. It is one of three hymns she wrote on the creed to make it interesting and intelligible to children. Our hymnal also contains the second of the three, "Once in royal David's city" **(250)**. Gealy has described her verse: "The innocent childlike quality of her verses has indeared them to young and old alike and has assured them a place in most hymnals." (Gealy, Lovelace, Young 1970, 85)

The charm of this hymn is described by Percy Dearmer:

> Lines like "The ripe fruits in the garden" [3:2] are perfect examples of good poetry in its simplest form. The poem is written in 76. 76 and refrain. But not really a simple metre: in the refrain which opens the song the first line is trochaic, but the second changes to iambic; and so with the last couplet of the refrain. The rest, however, is purely iambic; hence the peculiar swing round as the refrain keeps coming in. Unique. (Dearmer and Jacob 1933, 239)

Two stanzas are omitted in our present hymnal: stanza 3, a Calvinistic view of the social order that even the editors of *The English Hymnal*, 1933 new ed., could not abide:

> The rich man in his castle,
>   the poor men at his gate,
>   God made them, high or lowly,
>   and ordered their estate;

and stanza 7, deemed nostalgic by older urbanites, unimaginable by others raised in the city:

> The tall trees in the greenwood
>   the meadows where we play;
>   the rushes by the water
>   we gather every day.

The hymn entered our hymnals in 1935. Alterations made for this hymnal are stanza 1:3, "he" to "God"; 1:4, "he" to "and"; and 3:4 and 4:1, "he" to "God."

Royal Oak

English traditional melody; arr. by Martin Shaw, 1915

The first setting of this text was in *Home Hymn Book*, 1887, to W. H. Monk's tune with a refrain, "All Things Bright and Beautiful." The text has been very popular since that time. The hymn has been in our hymnals since 1935, with refrain. The traditional melody ROYAL OAK was arranged by Martin Shaw and was published in 1915. It was included at 444 in *Songs of Praise Enlarged*, 1931:

> [The tune] has been associated with a loyalist song titled "The Twenty-ninth of May," celebrating the restoration of Charles on May 29th, 1660 and was first printed in 1686. The name of the tune refers to the tree at Boscobel, Shropshire, in which Charles II is supposed to have hidden during his flight after the Battle of Worcester in 1651. (Watson and Trickett 1988, 214)

The tune, arranged by William H. Hewlett, was used in the 1935 hymnal. In the 1957 hymnal it was set to a tune attributed to Louis Spohr, arranged by Ellen Jane Lorenz. The 1966 book used Shaw's harmonization of ROYAL OAK in a simplified setting by V. Earle Copes. This is our first hymnal to use Shaw's original version of the tune.

All things come of thee (588)

1 Chron. 29:14b

This response is adapted from a portion of David's prayer of farewell that states that all human offerings give back to God that which has been provided "from your hand and is all your own."

But who am I, and what is my people, that we should be able to make this freewill offering: For all things come from you, and of your own have we given you. (1 Chronicles 29:14)

Offering

Anon.

This offertory response entered our hymnals at number 754 in *The Methodist Hymnal*, 1905, without attribution. Robert Guy McCutchan cites the music as "arranged" from Beethoven (McCutchan 1942, 552), and Austin C. Lovelace attributes the music to him in *Companion to the Hymnal* (Gealy, Lovelace, Young 1970, 441). When one compares the chant with the hymn tune ARLINGTON, it appears the former was arranged as a single line of chant from the hymn tune (see "Am I a soldier of the cross," **511**), using Ralph Harrison's harmonies and adaptation of Thomas Arne's melody in measure 1, the penultimate measure, and the final cadence. The practice of arranging choral sentences or chants from existing tunes and attributing them to famous composers or to one's self was a common practice in nineteenth-century USA tune books. The source of this possible adaptation has not been discovered.

All to Jesus I surrender (354)

See "I surrender all," page 421.

All who love and serve your city (433)

Erik Routley, 1966 (Luke 19:41; Ezek. 48:35)
The author has written about the circumstances of his writing this hymn:

> Though of British origin, this text owes something to America. It was written in October 1966 at a workshop in Dunblane, Scotland, where musicians and writers gathered to discover, or to compose, new hymns and canticles. The author of the text, who had never composed an original text before was trying to compose a tune; but in the next room to him another composer [Alan Luff] was at work who was unable to compose otherwise than by raising his voice in song. Thus frustrated, the composer turned author; his mind went in two directions—towards a beautiful tune by Peter Cutts [BIRABUS] which had no text, and towards the special griefs of the American cities which at the time were suffering from riots (Oakland, California had been in trouble about that time). The contrast between the peacefulness of the Scottish country town [Dunblane] and the condition of the cities in America and elsewhere evoked this text, which was published in the second volume of *Dunblane Praises II* (1967) [number 4], and [later in the USA

Presbyterian's *Worshipbook*, 1972, number 293] where the editors allied the text with this beautiful American folk hymn which Carlton Young had arranged for *The Methodist Hymnal*, 1966. (Routley 1977, 56)

The text is a significant contribution to the genre of twentieth-century hymns about the city, as contrasted with traditional agrarian settings, as a place for the redemptive witness of God in Christ. Ray Glover has commented on the text:

> The poet sees the city as a place over which the Risen Lord reigns as Judge and Glory. He challenges the city dweller, in the midst of strife and stress, to seek the Lord, the source of life. Though surrounded by "wealth and plenty, wasted work and wasted play" he reminds us that, in the words of Jesus, "I must work while it is day." (Glover 1987, 96)

The hymn's final line "Come today, our Judge, our Glory, be its name, 'The Lord is there!'" is a powerful summary.

For further reading on the 1961-69 Dunblane creative workshops for worship leaders, composers, and poets, see "Beginnings at Dunblane" by its key enabler Ian M. Fraser in *Duty and Delight, Routley Remembered* (Leaver and Litton 1985, 171-90). For commentary on other hymns on the city see "O holy city seen of John," page 516, and "Where cross the crowded ways of life," page 701.

Charlestown

Amos Pilsbury, The United States Sacred Harmony, 1799
harm. by Carlton R. Young, 1964

The tune's name comes from Charlestown, South Carolina, the birthplace of Pilsbury. The harmonization, made for *The Methodist Hymnal*, 1966, is the first use of the tune in our hymnals since 1889. A vocal descant is found in 62 in *The United Methodist Hymnal Music Supplement*.

Alleluia (186)

Words and music: Jerry Sinclair, 1972

Alleluia is the Latin form of Hallelujah, an acclamation formed by joining "Hallelu" (to praise) with the first syllable in a Hebrew name for God, Yahweh. The use of Hallelujah as an interjection is replete in the Psalms, particularly the so-called Hallelujah Psalms, 146-150, which, as Johannes Hempel notes in "Alleluia," "combine[s] all these motives in a general praise of all that God did, does, and will do." (Bucke 1962, 2:515) The word was taken into Christian worship in both the Eastern and Western churches. (Werner 1959, 302) Hallelujah was introduced into German usage with Luther's translation of the Bible. English language churches since the eighteenth-century evangelical revivals have used both the Germanic and Anglo-Catholic forms of this vital word of praise.

Claims and counterclaims about the ownership of this scripture song, widely used for decades without attribution, were concluded with the determination by the courts that Sinclair's version of the song was standard and other forms were derived. Simple, improvised, repetitive scripture songs in the 1960's became the *sine qua non* of "charismatic" worship. The acceptance of the performance style and the repertory of this song into mainstream worship practice has been slow, but in some instances their projection on large overhead screens and use in "free-form" worship have allowed them to become an alternative to classic evangelical hymnody traditionally learned and sung from bound hymnals.

Alleluia (486)

Chant Mode VI; arr. by John Schiavone, 1978
The Mode VI setting of Alleluia is widely used in Christian worship, generally before and after the Gospel reading. It may be sung with or without accompaniment, introduced by a solo voice and answered by the congregation, or used as an antiphon within a chant for a day or season, e.g., Easter, "Christ our passover."

Alleluia, Alleluia! Give thanks to the risen Lord (162)

Alleluia No. 1
Words and music: Donald Fishel, 1973
These paraphrased Pauline scripture sentences were set to music in 1971 and arranged by Betty Pulkingham, Charles Mallary, and George Mims for publication in *The Word of God*, 1973. The song has been included in most recent USA hymnals. A simplified version of the accompaniment is found at 170 in *The Baptist Hymnal*, 1991. *The United Methodist Hymnal Music Supplement* includes a vocal descant at 14.

Am I a soldier of the cross (511)

Isaac Watts, Sermons, 1721-24
Watts, the paradigm of the British evangelical preacher-pastor-poet, composed this hymn "For Sermon XXXI, Holy fortitude, or remedies against fear" based on 1 Corinthians 16:13, "Stand fast in the faith, quit you like men, be strong." The preface to the hymn makes clear that the intent of both the sermon and the hymn is to bolster sagging faith and enthusiasm:

Art thou ready to face the king of terrors, and to descend into that dark valley? Thou must meet this adversary shortly, O my soul: Labour therefore daily to get courage and victory over death, by faith in a dying and a rising saviour.

Happy is that faith that has no carnal fear attending it, but is got above the frowns and smiles of this world. My soul longs after it, and reaches at it, as something within the power of her present attainment through the grace of *Christ*! I long to be armed with this sacred courage, and to have my heart fortified all round with these divine munitions. I would fain be calm and serene in the midst of buffetings and reproaches, and pursue my course steadily toward heaven, under the banner of faith, through all the arrows of slander and malice. Lord *Jesus*, I wait for thy divine influence, to bestow this grace, and thy divine teachings, to put me in the way to obtain it. (Gealy 555/21)

The text, although not included in British hymnals, has been included in USA evangelical hymnals, including ours, since 1803. In the fall of 1985 the Hymnal Revision Committee deleted this text, deeming it too militant, but after a public outcry it was restored in May of 1986 at the same meeting in which "Onward Christian soldiers" was deleted—but later restored.

Arlington

Thomas A. Arne, 1762; arr. by Ralph Harrison, 1784

This tune was a favorite CM tune in early nineteenth-century USA tune books. According to Leonard Ellinwood,

ARLINGTON is a theme from the Overture to Thomas Arne's *Artaxerxes*, an opera produced in London in 1762. The arrangement as a hymn-tune was made by Ralph Harrison, and first published in Vol. I of his *Sacred Harmony*, 1784. (Ellinwood 1956, 212)

See 22-23 in *The United Methodist Hymnal Music Supplement* for a vocal descant and an alternative harmonization.

Amazing grace! How sweet the sound (378)

John Newton, 1779; stanza 6 anon.
Navajo phonetic trans. by Albert Tsosi (1 Chron. 17:16-17)

Newton's autobiographical hymn of Christian experience reveals a deeply felt conversion and transformation from his former wretched life as a slave trader. It was first printed at XLI in *Olney Hymns*, 1779, under the superscription "I Chronicles xvii. 16-17, Faith's review and expectation." The *Olney* collection was one of the first collections of evangelical hymns produced for use in an Anglican parish (Newton was curate in the Olney parish, 1764-80), and its importance has been described in J. H. Johansen's article (Gealy 555/22):

When you have picked out of Watts and Doddridge their best hymns, you find it a wearisome and profitless task to plod through the remainder. An outrageous rhyme is a pleasing break in the dull monotony of the sentiment, but the *Olney Hymns*, even at their feeblest, have life and vigour, and are often provokingly easy to remember. Their influence on modern hymnody has been all in favour of the expression of personal, individual experience, in which regard they may not unfairly be compared with many of the sublimest psalms. (Johansen 1956, 23)

The hymn entered our songbooks early in the nineteenth century through *Zion Songster*, 1829, but it was not included in our official books until the 1847 hymnal of the Southern church. Since then it has been included in all our hymnals, usually in five stanzas, omitting the original sixth,

> The earth shall soon dissolve like snow,
> the sun forbear to shine;
> But God, who called me here below,
> will be for ever mine.

The English text of the first five stanzas appears without alteration. Our sixth stanza, beginning "When we've been there ten thousand years," is not Newton's and is printed as the final stanza to "Jerusalem, my happy home" in early nineteenth century collections. According to William J. Reynolds the earliest appearance of the stanza is in Richard and Andrew Broaddus, *A Collection of Sacred Ballads*, 1790. (Adams 1992, 92) The first Methodist collection to include the stanza appears to be *A Collection of Hymns and Spiritual Songs*, 1801, by Richard Allen, the famous African American Methodist preacher. (See "African American Hymns," page 23.) Its connection with the fuller text does not come until E. O. Excell's *Coronation Hymns*, Chicago, 1910, where "together with the first three stanzas of Newton's hymn . . . this anonymous quatrain appears as the fourth and final stanza." (Reynolds 1976, 165)

The text is unknown in British hymnals, including Methodist books, until C. Kemble's *Collection of Hymns*, 1864. The hymn matched with the USA tune did not come until the 1960's when it hit the pop charts of British recorded hits, bagpipes and all! The Cherokee, Kiowa, Creek, and Choctaw phonetic transcriptions are from hymns that are sung to the tune AMAZING GRACE, but not to this text. Instead they are stanzas from anonymous hymns on the Second Coming of Christ. The Reverend Fred Yazzi of Shipwreck, New Mexico, supplied the Navajo text.

Amazing grace

Anon. 19th-cent. USA melody; arr. by Edwin O. Excell, 1900
Marion J. Hatchett has traced this tune to two versions named "St. Mary's" and "Gallaher" in Benjamin Shaw's and Charles H. Spilman's *Columbian Harmony*, 1829. (*The Hymn*, January 1991) The text and tune first come together matched to the tune name "New Britain" (one of five nineteenth-century names for the tune) on page 8 in William Walker's *Southern Harmony*, 1835. The melody is in

the voice above the bass (men and women both sing the melody in the shaped-note singing tradition); a third voice is above the melody and is also sung by both men and women. The shape of the melody and the harmonization in our hymnal come from E. O. Excell's *Make His Praise Glorious*, 1900.

Amens (898-904)

See "Service Music," pages 581-83.

America (My country, 'tis of thee) 697

Samuel F. Smith, 1831

The author's account of the writing of the most sung of our patriotic hymns (because the nation's anthem is unsingable) has been the subject of much research.

Leonard Ellinwood has provided the traditional version:

> The author . . . frequently told that story that Lowell Mason had loaned him a number of collections of German songs with the request that he translate or adapt poems from them for Mason's use, at his own convenience. Accordingly one afternoon at his home in Andover, Massachusetts, coming upon this particular tune [AMERICA], Smith wrote out this text. (Ellinwood 1956, 101)

Gealy continues the story in Smith's words:

> I instantly felt the impulse to write a patriotic hymn of my own adapted to the tune. Picking up a scrap of waste paper which lay near me, I wrote at once, probably within half an hour, the hymn "America" as it is now known everywhere. (Gealy, Lovelace, Young 1970, 289)

The five-stanza hymn was first performed by a children's choir at Park Congregational Church, Boston, July 8, 1831. Mason's *Choir, or Union Collection of Church Music*, Boston, 1832, is the first collection to print the hymn, including four stanzas. (Reynolds 1976, 145) The third stanza of the original, omitted since its first performance, rejoices in a tyrant-free land:

> No more shall tyrants here
> with haughty steps appear,
>   and soldier bands;
> no more shall tyrants tread
> above the patriot dead—
> no more our blood be shed
>   by alien hands.

America

Anon., Thesaurus Musicus, 1744-45

Of British origin, perhaps as early as the late sixteenth century, the tune in the USA has been set to many texts, including "God save America," God save George Washington," "God save the Thirteen States," and "My country, 'tis of thee." For a history of the tune and its quotation and settings by various composers including Charles Ives's *Variations on God Save the Queen*, see Percy Scholes, *God Save the Queen* (London: Oxford University Press, 1954), and *The Oxford Companion to Music* (Ward 1970, 408-13).

America the Beautiful (696)

Katharine Lee Bates, 1904

The hymn was composed at the close of a summer school held at Colorado Springs, Colorado, probably July 22, 1893, where the author was teaching English religious drama. On her trip west she had stopped off in Chicago to visit the Columbian World Exposition, where the exposition's "White City" stood in celebration of the 400th anniversary of America's discovery, inspiring the metaphor "alabaster cities" in the hymn's fourth stanza. In 1918 the author wrote a special history of the hymn for the *Boston Athenæum*, an informative and delightful account of the circumstances of the writing of the hymn.

> We strangers [teachers from Eastern schools] celebrated the close of the session by a merry expedition to the top of Pike's Peak, making the ascent by the only method then available for people not vigorous enough to achieve the climb on foot nor adventurous enough for burrow riding. Prairie wagons, their tail-board emblazoned with the traditional slogan, "Pike's Peak or Bust," were pulled by horses up to the half-way house, where the horses were relieved by mules. We were hoping for half an hour on the summit, but two of our party became so faint in the rarified air that we were bundled into the wagons again and started on our downward plunge so speedily that our sojourn on the peak remains in memory hardly more than one ecstatic gaze. It was then and there, as I was looking out over the sea-like expanse of fertile country spreading away so far under those ample skies, that the opening line of the hymn floated into my mind. When we left Colorado Springs, the four stanzas were pencilled in my notebook, together with other memoranda, in verse and prose, of the trip. The Wellesley work [she was a teacher at Wellesley] soon absorbed time and attention again, the note-book was laid aside, and I do not remember paying heed to these verses until the second summer following, when I copied them out and sent them to *The Congregationalist*, where they first appeared in print July 4, 1895. (Gealy 555/321)

Various changes were made in the text by the author until it was published in its final form probably in 1918 when the above article was published. It entered our hymnals in 1935 in four stanzas. In the present hymnal, the hymn was reduced to three stanzas in deference to complaints about "white manifest destiny" suggested in the second stanza (see pages 163-64):

> O beautiful for pilgrim feet,
>   whose stern, impassioned stress
> a thoroughfare for freedom beat
>   across the wilderness!

The hymn remains a classic social gospel hymn with with the use of phrases "God mend thy every flaw," "liberty in law," and the "self control" of nationalistic warring instincts.

Materna

Samuel A. Ward, 1882

After decades of seeking a suitable tune for the text, Bates wrote in 1918 that of the over sixty tunes written for the hymn, Ward's was the most popular. The tune first appeared in *The Parish Choir*, 1888, where it was set to "O mother dear, Jerusalem" (thus the name of the tune, MATERNA); with permission of Ward's widow the tune was wedded with Bates's poem in 1912. Willam J. Reynolds has provided additional background on Ward:

> The union of words and music became immensely popular during World War I. Ward, a highly respected church organist in Newark, New Jersey, had also established a successful music store there. In 1934, because his hymn tune had become so popular, Ward was memorialized by a brass plaque erected to his memory at Grace Episcopal Church in Newark where he had served as organist. (Reynolds 1990, 193)

An invitation to Christ (466)

Dimitri of Rostov, Russia, 17th cent.

This is a petition for God in Christ to enter one's life as Light, Life, Physician, Flame, King, and Lord. It first appeared in English in *The Orthodox Way*, 1979, compiled by Kallistos Ware.

An invitation to the Holy Spirit (335)

Eric Milner-White, England, 20th cent.

This prayer is an invitation to the Holy Spirit to enter our lives actively as wind, fire, and dew, to cleanse, refine, and refresh us. It may be spoken as a call to worship or read before one of the hymns on the Holy Spirit, for example, "Holy Spirit, come, confirm us" (331). The prayer was included in George Appleton, ed., *The Oxford Book of Prayer*, 1986.

And are we yet alive (553)

Charles Wesley, 1749

John Wesley included the hymn in his 1780 *Collection* as the first hymn of section 5, part 1, "For the Society. . . at meeting." He also began the practice of opening the annual meeting of Methodists with the singing of this hymn, a practice followed by Methodists around the world. The words speak directly to itinerate ministers and lay persons and the experiences each may have had since they last met. The text appeared at 2:321 in *Hymns and Sacred Poems*, 1749, in the section on "Hymns for Christian Friends" under the heading "At meeting of friends." Originally a SMD hymn of four stanzas, it has rarely been sung in that form; most hymnals include it as a SM hymn and print at least four stanzas.

John Wesley made changes in the hymn for his 1780 hymnal that were maintained in USA Methodist hymnals from 1803 until our 1966 edition. The 1966 hymnal restored our stanza 6, our 1989 hymnal restored what is our stanza 2; and with the exception of the two omitted stanzas, below, and "hides" for "hide" at 4:4, the text appears in its original form. Wesley's final CMD is as follows:

> Jesus, to thee we bow,
> And for thy coming wait:
> Give us for good some token now
> In our imperfect state;
> Apply the hallowing word,
> Tell each who looks for thee,
> Thou shalt be perfect as thy Lord,
> Thou shalt be all like me!

Typically, as in most Charles Wesley hymns, there are numerous scriptural references: 1:2, Genesis 46:30; 2:1, 1 Peter 1:5; 3:3, 2 Corinthians 7:5; 4:1-2, 1 Timothy 3:11; 4:4, Colossians 3:2; 5:1, Psalms 34:2; 5:3, Hebrews 7:25; 6:1, Mark 8:34; 6:2, James 1:12; 6:3, Philippians 3:8.

According to William Farley Smith, in the African American worship experience this hymn is often sung at the opening of local church meetings and services of Holy Communion, and at watch night and covenant services. (Smith 1991, 1 (3):7) John Wesley introduced the singing of hymns during Holy Communion to his Savannah parish, probably following Moravian practice. (Young 1990, 21)

Dennis

Johann G. Nägeli; arr. by Lowell Mason, 1845

Lowell Mason published this tune in *The Psaltery*, which he compiled in 1845 with George J. Webb, with the text "How gentle God's commands." Although Mason cites the tune as "Arranged from J. G. Nägeli," the source is unknown.

And can it be that I should gain (363)

Charles Wesley, 1739 (Acts 16:26)

This is one of two autobiographical hymns that Wesley composed at or near his conversion; the other is "Where shall my wondering soul begin" **(342)**. The hymn is in 88.88.88, a meter often employed by Charles Wesley for the exposition of a major statement of faith.

Frank Baker has commented on Wesley's metrical preference:

> The most prolific of all was his favourite form of six 8's—8.8.8.8.8.8., rhyming ABABCC. In this metre he composed over 1,100 poems [a tenth of his entire output], a total of nearly 23,000 lines, most of them with a vigour, a flexibility, yet a disciplined compactness, that proved this to be the instrument fittest for his hand. (Baker 1962, 45)

It is not known to which of the two hymns Charles makes reference in his journal entry of May 23, 1738, "At nine I began a hymn on my conversion but was persuaded to break off for fear of pride. . . . I prayed Christ to stand by me and finished the hymn."

The hymn was published in six stanzas in *Hymns and Sacred Poems*, 1739, under the heading "Free Grace." It has been included in most Methodist (but not Evangelical United Brethren) hymnals, using either four or five stanzas; it is included in our hymnal in five stanzas. In stanza 1:6 "God" has been changed from "Lord." The original stanza 5 has been omitted since John Wesley excluded it from his 1780 *Collection*:

> Still the small inward voice I hear,
>   That whispers all my sins forgiven;
> Still the atoning blood is near,
>   That quench'd the wrath of hostile heaven:
> I feel the life his wounds impart;
> I feel my Savior in my heart.

Five questions are posed at the hymn's opening, which establish a feeling of urgency that proceeds unrelentingly through this remarkable confession that is "an extraordinary and daring tour-de-force, both poetically and theologically." (Watson and Trickett 1988, 152) Oliver A. Beckerlegge states that the whole kenosis doctrine (emptying of self, see Philippians 2:5-11 and hymns **166-167**) is condensed into a single line at 3:3. (Wesley 1983, 7:323)

John Wilson has commented in *Bulletin: Hymn Society of Great Britain and Ireland:*

> "And can it be" immediately deepens the questioning, so that in the suffering and the sacrifice we also become aware of the Amazing Love, the Mercy and the Mystery, the promise of Sins forgiven and a Crown to be claimed." (Wilson 1992, 104)

Scriptural references include 1:1-2, Matthew 26:28; 1:3-6, Romans 5:6-8; 2:3-6, I Peter 1:12; 3:1-4, Philippians 2:5-8; 3:4, Romans 5:14, I Corinthians 15:22; 3:5-6, Psalm 85:7-7, Romans 5:15-18; stanza 4, Acts 12:7, 16:23-32; 5:1, Romans 8:1, 5:3, Ephesians 4:15; 5:4, Ephesians 6:14; 5:5, Hebrews 4:16; 5:6, 2 Timothy 4:8.

Sagina

Thomas Campbell, 1825

Although Wesley's text has been in Methodist hymnals for over two hundred years, as far as USA Methodists are concerned it was seldom sung until SAGINA was introduced in the 1960's, and then with the complaint from some as to the tune's fitness for the words and its inherit musical worth. Erik Routley has stated that while SAGINA "is certainly about the best tune available for that majestic but intractable text" (Routley 1981, 156), nevertheless, "there is little inspiration in melody or harmony, and what there is has to be beaten out very thin in order to accommodate a word-repetition, which, associated with a text so monumentally intense, come near profanity." (Routley 1981, 84)

The tune first appeared in Campbell's *Bouquet*, 1825, a book of twenty-three original tunes, all with botanical names after the title of the collection. *Sagina* is a Latin word meaning nourishment, or fattening when related to the circumstance that the sagina plant "grew in profusion on the Roman Campagna and provided abundant spring fodder for flocks of sheep pastured there for fattening." (Milgate 1985, 73) Although the tune was printed in *Supplement to the Book of Hymns*, 1982, this is the first use of the tune in either a Methodist or Evangelical United Brethren authorized hymnal.

And God will raise you up on eagle's wings

See "On eagle's wings" pages 541-42.

Angels from the realms of glory (220)

James Montgomery, 1816 (Luke 2:8-20; Matt. 2:1-12; Mal. 3:1)

The hymn first appeared in the 1816 Christmas Eve edition of the Sheffield *Iris*, a newspaper edited by Montgomery. Three years later the hymn was included in *The Christian Psalmist*, 1825, where the author provided the title "Good tidings of great joy to all people." The hymn entered our hymnals in 1837 with all five stanzas, including the following lines that reveal the author's evangelical grounding, excluded since the 1935 *Methodist Hymnal*:

> Sinners, wrung with true repentance,
>   doomed for guilt to endless pains,
> justice now revokes the sentence,
>   mercy calls you; break your chains.

For the performance of the hymn Jane Marshall suggests:

[As a Christmas processional] the stanzas may be sung by a choir, with the congregation joining in the refrain. In a Christmas pageant, the angels may enter as stanza one is sung; the shepherds may process during stanza two; the wise men may enter on stanza three, and finally Anna and Simeon may join the assembly during stanza four. (Sanchez 1989, 86)

Regent Square

Henry T. Smart, 1867

Smart's brilliant four-voice hymn tune was composed for *Psalms and Hymns for Divine Worship*, London, 1867. It was first matched with Montgomery's words in our songbooks at page 194 in Rigdon M. McIntosh's *Hermon*, 1873. The 1905 hymnal appears to be the first authorized hymnal to put text and tune together. The tune's name comes from the square in London, the site of St. Philip's Presbyterian Church where the composer was organist 1839-44. In *The United Methodist Hymnal Music Supplement*, 280-81, there is an alternate harmonization and a vocal or instrumental descant.

Angels we have heard on high (238)
Les anges dans nos campagnes

Trad. French carol; trans. in Crown of Jesus, 1862; alt. (Luke 2:6-20)

This carol, a favorite of all ages, according to Jan R. H. de Smidt, *Les Noëls et la tradition populaire*, 1932, was first published in *Nouveau reçueil de cantiques*, 1855, with the first stanza:

> Les anges dans nos campagnes
> Ont entonné l'hymne de cieux,
> Et l'echo de nos montagnes
> Redit ce chant mélodieux:
> Gloria in excelsis Deo.

The several versions of the text all evidently stem from the same source, i.e., "The Angels we have heard on high," *Holy Family Hymnal*, 1860; "Bright angels we have heard on high," *The Parochial Hymnbook*, 1880; and "Bright angel hosts are heard on high," R. R. Chope, *Carols for Use in the Church During Christmas and Epiphany*, 1875. The carol entered our hymnals in 1935 in an anonymous version from a mystery play, *The Nativity*, 1922. In the 1966 hymnal, because of the popularity of another version of the text printed in anthems, the form of the translation beginning "Angels we have heard on high" in *Crown of Jesus*, 1862, (Gealy 555/29), was included. Stanza 1:4 originally read "Echo still their joyous strains"; 2:2, "Why your rapturous strain prolong?"; 2:3, "Say what may the tidings be?"; 3:1, "Come to Bethlehem, come and see"; 3:4, "The Infant Christ, the new-born King." Stanza 4 originally read:

> See within a manger laid,
>   Jesus, Lord of heaven and earth!
> Mary, Joseph, lend your aid
>   To celebrate our Saviour's birth.

In this hymnal "him" in stanza 3:2 has been changed to "Christ."

Gloria

French carol melody; arr. by Edward Shippen Barnes, 1937
harm. by Austin C. Lovelace, 1964

According to Erik Routley,

> The first appearance of [this] tune was with [this] French noel, and the first
> appearance of the tune in an English book carried an English tr. of that
> carol by the Rev. G. Crenthem, "When the crimson sun had set." (Routley
> 1956, 206-7)

Austin C. Lovelace slightly modified Barnes's setting from *The New Church Hymnal*, New York, 1937, for the 1966 hymnal. A additional harmonization by Martin Shaw in the key of G may be found in *The Oxford Book of Carols*, 1964, at page 250.

Apostolic Blessing (669)

See "The Apostolic Blessing," page 620.

Are ye able, said the Master (530)

Earl Marlatt, 1926

The six-stanza hymn was written for the consecration service of the Boston University School of Religious Education, 1926, under the title "Challenge." It first appeared in five stanzas as number 174 in *American Student Hymnal*, 1928.

The usually omitted stanzas 2 and 3 are found in the poet's original broadsheet:
(Gealy 555/30)

> Are ye able to relinquish
>   Purple dreams of power and fame,
> To go down into the Garden,
>   Or to die a death of shame?

> Are ye able, when the anguish
>   Racks your mind and heart with pain,
> To forgive the souls who wrong you,
>   Who would make your striving vain?

Four stanzas have been used since the hymn's first inclusion in our 1935 hymnal. The hymn was widely sung in Methodist and Evangelical United Brethren youth rallies in the 1930's and through the 1950's. During the past three decades Methodists and Evangelical United Brethren have both rejected and embraced the hymn. Its rejection has been in part a matter of musical taste, but primarily because of the suggestion reiterated in the hymn's refrain that Christ's followers can at any point affirm that they "are able," i.e., without qualification, to drink the bitter cup of disappointment. Those who affirm the hymn like to sing the music, pointing out that the poet's words are scriptural, and assert that our spirits, in Christ, can be reformed and shaped in God's image.

A portion of Marlatt's account of the writing of the hymn is in Robert Guy McCutchan's *Our Hymnody*, page 306 (the entire article is found in Gealy's research, 555/30), and explains the poet's intent to join in this hymn two scenes from the passion of Christ. The first is from Mark 10:35-40, when James and John, the sons of Zebedee asked Jesus to allow them to sit at his right and left. Jesus asks if they are able to drink or be baptized with the baptism (impending crucifixion) with which he is to baptized, to which they reply, "We are able." Jesus promises them that baptism but states it is not within his ability to place them at his side. The second scene is from Luke 23:39-43, which recounts Jesus' affirmation that the two thieves would be with him today in Paradise.

The hymn has not been included in any recent hymnals except those of the former Methodist and the former Evangelical United Brethren churches.

Beacon Hill

Harry S. Mason, 1924

The tune was composed by Mason while he was a student at Boston University School of Religious Education. One of the objections to using the hymn is its length caused by the extended refrain. The hymn's stanza-refrain form invites the stanzas to be sung by solo voices or the choir, and the refrain answered by the congregation.

Arise, shine out, your light has come (725)

Brian Wren, 1987 (Isa. 60:1-3, 11a, 14c, 18-19)

The hymn was written at the request of the Hymnal Revision Committee as it sought to include metrical paraphrases for three portions of Isaiah traditionally titled "Songs of Isaiah." Our hymnal contains paraphrases of portions of two of the three songs. One is F. Pratt Green's "Seek the Lord who now is present" **(124)**, based on Isaiah 55:6-11. The second is the present hymn in which Wren paraphrases Isaiah 60:1-3, 11a, 14c, and 18-19 from the New English Bible. The text was completed April 9, 1987, and first appeared as number 6 in *Bring Many Names,* 1989, a collection of thirty-five of Wren's texts with musical settings (five of them his) and three doxologies. The poet suggested using the tune DUNEDIN for his text.

Dunedin

Thomas V. Griffiths

The tune is named after the site of the King Edward Technical College, Dunedin, New Zealand, where the composer served as director of music 1933-42. According to Wesley Milgate the tune first appeared in *New Catholic Hymnal*, 1971. (Milgate 1988, 18) Composed in the unison voice style reminiscent of C. H. H. Parry, it is one of the finest of twentieth-century LM tunes, with stanzas designed to be sung in alternation between choir and congregation.

As man and woman we were made (642)

Brian Wren, 1973

This wedding text first appeared in four stanzas as "Wedding Carol," number 24 in the poet's *Mainly Hymns*, 1980, and later in *Faith Looking Forward: The Hymns and Songs of Brian Wren with many Tunes by Peter Cutts*, 1983, number 27, with a change in 1:6, "man and wife" to "husband, wife." Each stanza is titled after the Pauline "fruits of the spirit," Galatians 5:22: stanza 1, "Love"; stanza 2, "Joy"; stanza 3, "Hope"; stanza 4, "Peace." Scriptural references include stanza 1, Genesis 1:27-28, Matthew 19:5-6; stanza 2, John 2:3-10; stanza 3, Romans 8:24; stanza 4, Revelation 7:17. The text celebrates our creation, redemption, and resurrection in Christ in the context of the wedding feast (see John 2:1-11 and Matthew 9:15 and 22:1-10).

Sussex carol

Trad. English melody; arr. and harm by Ralph Vaughan Williams, 1919

Vaughan Williams's pioneer efforts in collecting and arranging English folk melody began in the first decade of this century and culminated in *The Oxford Book of Carols*, 1928. "SUSSEX CAROL was sung to the composer by Mrs. Harriet Verrall, of Monk's Gate, Horsham, Sussex, on May 24, 1904." (Watson and Trickett 1988, 101) This tune was first set by Vaughan Williams in his *Fantasia on Christmas Carols*, 1912. In *Eight Traditional English Carols*, 1919, the composer scored the version used in our hymnal. Later he supplied a version for unaccompanied four-part mixed voices in *The Oxford Book of Carols*, page 49, which may be sung by the choir on alternate verses or as light accompaniment or humming under a solo voice. Another performance suggestion is to include a tambourine on counts 1 and 4 in stanzas 2 and 4.

As the sun doth daily rise (675)

Matutinus altiora
Latin hymn; trans. by J. Masters; adapt. by Horatio Nelson, 1864

The only other USA hymnal in which this hymn has been included seems to be the *Pilgrim Hymnal*, 1958. The information on the text comes from the handbook to that hymnal:

Nephew of the renowned and celebrated Admiral Viscount Nelson, Horatio Nelson, 1823-1913, recast and included this hymn in his *Hymns for Saints' Days, and other Hymns*, 1864. Based on a Latin hymn, beginning with the words "Matutinus altiora" (Morning), it was first published in translated form, according to John Julian (1907, 1579), by J. Masters (no date) who referred to it as "King Alfred's hymn" and credited the words to "O.B.C." and the music to "Dr. Smith." There is no evidence that King Alfred wrote the Latin text, and the author is unknown. (Ronander and Porter 1966, 31) Julian states that the hymn also appeared in the *Sarum Hymnal*, 1864.

Jane Marshall suggests that this is

> an excellent hymn for children to learn and introduce to the congregation; stanza 3 may be sung by the choir in harmony, all singing stanza 4 a cappella, and stanza 5 with full accompaniment. (Sanchez 1989, 226)

The choir may also sing the first stanza as a joyous call to worship.

Innocents

The Parish Choir, 1850; harm. by W. H. Monk, 1861
The tune's name comes from the occasion of the tune's first use with the text "Little flowers of martyrdom," sung at the Feast of the Holy Innocents. That text and tune appeared together in the November 1850 edition of *The Parish Choir*, an important Anglo-Catholic church music periodical that lasted only three years. The source of the tune may be Joseph Smith's unpublished song "The Sun," ca. 1850, at 61 in *The English Hymnal*, 1906 (the editors used Monk's harmonization without citation). The Smith source is also suggested by James T. Lightwood in *The Music of the Methodist Hymn-Book* (1935, 448). W. H. Monk harmonized the tune for *Hymns Ancient and Modern*, 1861, where it is set to "Conquering kings their titles take," page 106. His harmonization was altered for use in the 1966 hymnal and was, unfortunately, continued in our present hymnal.

Ascension

See "The Ascension," pages 620-21.

Ash Wednesday (353)

Laurence Hull Stookey, 1987
The author has written a brief commentary on this prayer:

> [It draws] upon scriptural themes for the beginning of Lent: Gen. 3:19; Ps. 51:10; and 1 Th. 2:12. It identifies the cross as the center of redeeming

and reactivating power for our broken lives. Although specifically written for Ash Wednesday, the prayer may be used publicly or privately on any occasion when sin, repentance, and renewal are the pertinent themes. (Sanchez 1989, 127)

Ask ye what great thing I know (163)
Wollt ihr wissen, was mein Preis?

Johann C. Schwedler, 1741; trans. by Benjamin H. Kennedy, 1863
(2 Cor. 2:2; Gal 6:14)

The hymn was published in six stanzas with refrain in *Hirschberger Gesangbuch*, 1741, eleven years after the author's death. The text, which poses a series of questions with a single answer, expresses the author's firm belief in the all-sufficiency of Christ Jesus, the crucified Savior. In German language hymnals the one-line refrain is repeated, sometimes dictated by the tune (see, for example, number 362 in *Evangelisches Gesangbuch fuer Brandenburg*, 1931):

> Wollt ihr wissen, was mein Preis?
> Wollt ihr lerlnen, was ich weiß?
> Wollt ihr sehn mein Eigentum?
> Wollt ihr hören, was mein Ruhm?
> Jesus, der Gekreuzigte,
> Jesus, der Gekreuzigte.

Two translations were made in the nineteenth century. One with the first line "Do you ask what most I prize?" was prepared for Moravian hymnals. (Julian 1907, 1019) Most hymnals, however, use four of five stanzas from Kennedy's translation included in his *Hymnologia Christiana, or Psalms and Hymns Selected and Arranged in the order of the Christian Seasons*, 1863. It was first published as a hymn in *Hymns of the Church*, 1869, in five stanzas. Four stanzas of the text entered in our hymnals in 1935.

In our hymnal stanzas 2 and 3 are omitted.

> What is faith's foundation strong?
> What awakes my heart to song?
> He who bore my sinful load,
> Purchased for me peace with God,
>   Jesus Christ the crucified.

> Who is He that makes me wize
> To discern where duty lies?
> Who is He that makes me true
> Duty, when discerned to do,
>   Jesus Christ the crucified.

Hendon

H. A. César Malan, 1823

The first appearance of this, the surviving tune of the many written by Malan, was probably in 1823, but some writers cite his 1827 *Chants de Zion* as the source. It is a typical tune composed for use in evangelical circles in the early nineteenth century. Lowell Mason brought it back from one of his trips to Europe and included it in his *Carmina Sacra*, 1841.

The tune can be found in most evangelical songbooks of the mid-nineteenth century; for example, on page 145 in *Tabor*, 1867, R. M. McIntosh matches it with "To thy pastures, fair and large." It first appeared with this text in *Hymns of the Church*, 1869. This hymn can be effectively performed with the questions sung by the choir or a soloist, and the congregation joining on the one-line affirmation at the refrain, "Jesus Christ, the crucified."

Hendon was a village in Middlesex, England, now a London suburb, where it is believed that Malan visited.

At the birth of a child (146)

From the rituals of African peoples: the Massai and the Akamba

This act of worship is intended for use when the birth of a child is to be announced. The name of the child (or children) should be inserted in the first sentence, and the names of the parents and the birth date may be added. It was included in John S. Mbiti, *The Prayers of African Religion*, 1975.

At the close of day (689)

Dietrich Bonhoeffer, 1943-45

This evening prayer, suitable for use in either personal or group devotions, was written by the German Christian theologian and martyr Dietrich Bonhoeffer. It was shared with friends and relatives in one of his many letters written in the Nazi prison camp where he was executed April 9, 1945. The letters were posthumously published as *Letters and Papers from Prison*, 1962.

At the name of Jesus every knee shall bow (168)

Caroline M. Noel, 1870 (Phil. 2:5-11)

Noel, like Charlotte Elliott ("Just as I am," 357), was a great sufferer. She included this hymn in eight stanzas in her book *The Name of Jesus, and other Verses for the Sick and Lonely*, 1870 enlarged ed. At one point the first word was changed from "At" to "In" to conform to the text of the Revised Version of the Bible, 1881. Most twentieth-century hymnals use the original. Various commentaries state that there were seven stanzas in the original hymn.

In 1991 the British hymnologist Bernard S. Massey verified that the 1873 edition of the author's collection contains eight stanzas. This information, the order of stanzas, and the text of the original stanzas 4 and 6 were supplied by the hymnologist and hymnal editor John Wilson, Guildford, Surrey. Wilson's delightful demurrer was included with his research and is printed with his permission.

> This is a hymn for which I have not the slightest use! Yards of glib theology in doggerel verse! I'm quite proud to have discouraged its inclusion in two hymnals. How many people understand "Bore it up triumphant"—Christ carrying his own name up to heaven as a sort of exhibit. (Correspondence with Carlton R. Young, September 1991)

Erik Routley in *A Panorama of Christian Hymnody* describes the text:

> [It is] the only completely objective theological hymn to come from the hand of a nineteenth-century woman writer. No hymnal includes all the stanzas, and yet, which can really be spared without damaging the shape of the whole? (Routley 1979, 116)

The omitted stanzas are printed below:

Stanza 2

> Mighty and mysterious
>   in the highest height,
> God from everlasting,
>   Very Light of Light;
> in the Father's bosom,
>   with the Spirit blest,
> Love, in Love eternal,
>   rest, in perfect rest.

Stanza 3

> At his voice creation
>   sprang at once to sight,
> all the angel faces,
>   all the hosts of light,
> thrones and domination,
>   stars upon their way,
> all the heavenly orders,
>   in their great array.

Stanza 6

> Name him, brothers, name him,
>   with love as strong as death,
> but humbly and with wonder,
>   and with bated breath;
> he is God the Savior,
>   he is Christ the Lord,

ever to be worshipped,
trusted, and adored.

Stanza 8

Brothers, this Lord Jesus
shall return again,
with his Father's glory,
with his angel-train;
for all wreaths of empire
meet upon his brow
and our hearts confess him
King of glory now.

The hymn entered our hymnals in 1966 using stanzas 1, 4, 5, and 7. The original stanza 2:4 read "amount whom he came."

King's Weston

Ralph Vaughan Williams, 1925

The tune was composed for this text at number 392 in *Songs of Praise Enlarged*, 1931. It is included in that hymnal in the section on processionals, presumably as the opening hymn for Ascension and Christ's enthronement. It is also suitable as a general hymn of praise to Christ. In our hymnal it is placed with other settings of the Philippians text, "All praise to thee, for thou, O King divine" **(166)**, and "Canticle of Christ's obedience" **(167)**. Archibald Jacob, who wrote the comments on the music of *Songs of Praise* in *Songs of Praise Discussed*, states that KING'S WESTON "is a solid tune, in triple time, with a strongly stressed rhythm, and a characteristic exchange of accent in the last two lines. It is a dignified, but not a solemn tune, and must not be sung too slowly." (Dearmer and Jacob 1933, 213)

John Wilson has commented on this tune:

A comparison of the style of KING'S WESTON with that of SINE NOMINE and DOWN AMPNEY—written years earlier—shows the effect on [Vaughan Williams's] creative mind of his profound study of English folk song. (Correspondence with Carlton R. Young, October 1991)

The tune is named after the beautiful country home of Philip Napier Miles, built by Vanbough and overlooking the Bristol Channel. Here Ralph Vaughan Williams spent many happy weekends, often with other musicians.

Awake, O sleeper (551)

F. Bland Tucker, 1980 (Rom. 13:11-14; Eph. 4:4-6)

The history of the text comes from Ray Glover in *A Commentary on New Hymns*:

The author wrote of this text, "The first two lines (Eph. 5:14) are a quotation from a very ancient Christian hymn, probably. There is no known copy of it in existence; so I filled it out with quotations from other verses in the same epistle."

Taking chapters three, four and five of the epistle as his source, Dr. Tucker encapsulates important themes from each to create a credal statement of God's redemptive acts in Christ combined with a charge to all people to follow the way of Christ. He frames the entire text with an antiphon-like device. Stanza one opens with the call,

> Awake, O sleeper, rise from death,
> and Christ shall give you life.

The closing two lines of stanza 4 reflect a similar theme but, as if Dr. Tucker engaged in a subtle play on words, "rise from death" becomes "arise, go forth," and "Light" becomes "life":

> Awake, arise, go forth in faith,
> and Christ shall give you life. (Glover 1987, 94)

The hymn was commissioned February 1980 by the late David N. Johnson and served as the text for his anthem setting released the same year by Augsburg Publishing House. Its first appearance in a hymnal was *The Hymnal 1982*. Our hymnal prints the hymn without alteration except stanza 3 where in the original text "body," "faith," and "baptism" are capitalized.

Marsh Chapel

Max Miller, 1984

The tune was composed for this text and first appeared in *The Hymnal 1982*. It ranks among the finest contributions to the repertory by a late twentieth-century composer. The composer writes of his tune, "Since I have been at the University Chapel so long, and in all likelihood will finish my "time" there, I would like to call the tune, 'Marsh Chapel.' The Chapel lies at the heart of the [Boston] University." (Glover 1987, 95)

Away in a manger (217)

Anonymous, USA; stanzas 1-2, 1885; stanza 3, 1892 (Luke 2:7)

Fred D. Gealy has provided a summary of the interesting and complicated story of this delightful Christmas carol:

All that can be said confidently about the origin of this carol is that Martin Luther himself had nothing to do with it. The evidence suggests that it is wholly an American product. The original 2-st. form probably originated among German Lutherans in Pennsylvania about 1885.

The earliest extant printing of [the text in] this form derives from [its inclusion as a "Nursery" hymn in J. C. File's *Little children's book: for schools and families. By authority of the general council of the Evangelical Lutheran Church in North America*] Philadelphia in 1885. St. 3 appears first in 1892 in a Louisville, Ky., imprint and may have been contributed by an editor or publisher who thought the 2 narrative sts. needed to be supplemented by a prayer.

Richard S. Hill, in a painstaking and brilliant article ["Not so far away in a manger: Forty-one settings of an American Carol," pages 12-36] in Music Library Association *Notes* (December 1945) [series 2, 3, no. 1; a complete copy of the article is found in Gealy 555/46] conjectures that the association of the carol with Luther is the product of a series of illicit inferences. The decisive one was the association of the carol with the glorification of Luther's family life as depicted in a series of sentimental engravings done in the early nineteenth century by G. F. L. König, beloved by Lutherans everywhere and reproduced in Philadelphia in 1855, with the picture portraying Luther with his family on Christmas Eve as frontispiece. In 1872, the author of the 1855 publication, T[heophilus] B[aker] Stork [1814-1874], in a book called *Luther at Home* (sponsored by the Lutheran Board of Publication, Philadelphia), in commenting on this picture, states that "Luther's carol for Christmas, written for his own child Hans, is still sung," etc. Since Stork does not name the carol, opportunity to supply the deficiency was wide open. Either "Away in a manger" was written to fill the gap, or, as a popular anonymous carol, was associated with the picture and the cherished concept of Luther as a kindly family man in such a way that, for example, James R. Murray, in *Dainty Songs for Little Lads and Lasses*, 1887, could easily call the hymn "Luther's Cradle Hymn, composed by Martin Luther for his children, and still sung by German mothers to their little ones." But unfortunately for this latter statement, no German original can be found in Luther's writings.

The earliest extant printed text has "his" bed, 1885; "a" bed appears in 1887. "The poor baby wakes" becomes "the baby awakes" in 1895. "In the hay," 1885, becomes "on the hay," 1887. The original last line of st. 2, "And stay by my crib watching my lullaby," 1885, became "And stay by my cradle till morning is nigh" in 1895. St. 3 seems never to have been altered since its first printing. (Gealy, Lovelace, Young 1970, 107-08)

There is only one German version of the carol. It was included in Herbert W. Wernecke, *Christmas Songs and Weihnachts-Lieder* (privately published by the compiler), Webster Groves, 1934. Printed below is the first stanza in English and German, of which Hill writes, "Half an ear for natural prosody is sufficient to tell that the German is the translation, not the English."

So arm in der Krippe	Away in a manger,
Keine wiege zum Bett	No crib for a bed,
Der liebe Herr Jesus,	The little Lord Jesus
Da schlief er so nett,	Lay down His sweet head.
Die Sterne am Himmel	The stars in the sky
Sahen auf ihn so froh—	Looked down where he lay,—
Der liebe Herr Jesus,	The little Lord Jesus
Er schlief nur auf Stroh.	Asleep on the hay.

The third stanza first appeared, without authorship, in Charles H. Gabriel, *Gabriel's Vineyard Songs*, Louisville, 1892.

William J. Reynolds has commented on the carol:

> For sheer beauty and childlike simplicity the carol claims special attention. It is a gentle lullaby, tender and warm, especially loved by children; and when adults of any age sing it, they become children again. (Reynolds 1990, 33)

Away in a manger

James R. Murray, 1887

The tune was incorrectly attributed to Martin Luther by Murray, and after Robert Guy McCutchan in *Our Hymnody* cast doubt upon Luther's authorship of the text by stating that "the whole [matter of authorship] presents an interesting problem for research" (McCutchan 1942, 436), scholars began to question the authorship of the text, as well as the source of the tune, MUELLER, to which the text has been set since 1887. (Hill in his 1945 article incorporates a lengthy excerpt from McCutchan.)

Austin C. Lovelace writes regarding the source of the tune:

> Murray himself [caused the problem] when he first published the tune, attributing it to Luther, in *Dainty Songs for Little Lads and Lasses* [Cincinnati, 1887]. . . .

> The [tune] name "Mueller" [used in our 1957 and 1966 hymnals] comes from the incorrect ascription of the tune to a "Carl Mueller" in *Worship and Song* 1921. . . .

> In 1888 the tune appeared in a new collection, *Royal Praise for the Sunday School* by John Murray . . . (Cincinnati, April 25), with the music slightly altered, put in the key of G, and with the heading "Music by J. R. M." Murray published a third collection in 1892 with the tune back in the original key of F. (Gealy, Lovelace, Young 1970, 109)

The tune with its simple harmonization has been included in our hymnal without alteration. *The United Methodist Hymnal Music Supplement* at 30-32 has an arrangement for handbells in the key of G, with the tune as it appears in the hymnal in the key of G.

Baptism of the Lord (253)

After the Book of Common Prayer (Matt. 3:13-17; Mark. 1:9-11; Luke 3:21-22)
Laurence H. Stookey, who adapted this prayer, has commented:

> While appropriate at any Baptism or the Reaffirmation of the Baptismal Covenant [26-54], this prayer is especially intended for use on the Sunday of the Baptism of the Lord (the Sunday following January 6). The prayer first presents meanings of Jesus' own baptism; he was thus proclaimed God's Son and anointed with the Holy Spirit. The prayer then connects our baptism with his: We are baptized into his name and are joined in covenant with him. We are called to confess him boldly, and for this task of faithful witness we ask God's help. (Sanchez 1989, 96-97)

Battle Hymn of the Republic (717)

See "The Battle Hymn of the Republic," pages 621-24.

Be not dismayed whate'er betide (130)

See "God will take care of you," pages 376-77.

Be present at our table, Lord (621)

John Cennick, 1741
Cennick's (pronounced Ṣennick) table grace is included without alteration, except for capitalizations and contractions, as it appears at number 130, page 198, with the title "Before Meat" in his *Sacred Hymns for the Children of God, in the Days of their Pilgrimage*, 1741 (London, 2d ed.). A tradition, now discredited, held that the grace was engraved on teapots made by Josiah Wedgewood and used by John Wesley. The grace is sung throughout United Methodism to both the isorhythmic (quarter note) setting of OLD 100TH **(621)** as well as its rhythmic setting **(95)**. Variations from the original text, "mercies" for "creatures" and "fellowship" for "paradise," tend to weaken the hymn:

> "Creatures" means "anything created" and is a reminder that both we and the food and drink on our table are God's creatures. The word "paradise" reminds us that not only Holy Communion but all eating and drinking together should be for Christians a foretaste of the heavenly "supper of the Lamb," Rev. 19:9. (Sanchez 1989, 210)

The text entered our hymnals in 1935 without change under the title "The Wesley Graces."

Cennick provides another grace, "After Meat," at number 131 in his 1741 collection:

> We bless Thee, Lord, for this our Food;
> But more for Jesu's Flesh and Blood;
> The *Manna* to our Spirit's giv'n,
> The Living Bread sent down from Heav'n;
> Praise shall our Grateful Lips employ,
> While Life and Plenty we enjoy;
> 'Till worthy, we adore thy Name,
> While banqueting with Christ, the Lamb!

Old 100th

See "All people that on earth do dwell," page 197.

Be still, my soul (534)
Stille, mein Wille! Dein Jesus hilft siegen

Katharina von Schlegel, 1752; trans. by Jane Borthwick, 1855 (Ps. 46:10; 1 Tim.)
The hymn first appeared in *Neue Sammlung geistlicher Lieder*, 1752, in six stanzas, and five of the six stanzas were translated by Borthwick for *Hymns from the Land of Luther*, second series, 1855. *The Handbook to the Lutheran Hymnal*, 1958 (pages 462-63), prints four stanzas in parallel English and German.

The third and fifth stanzas are usually omitted:

> Be still, my soul: when dearest friends depart,
>   and all is darkened in the vale of tears,
> then shalt thou better know his love, his heart,
>   who comes to soothe thy sorrow and thy fears.
> Be still, my soul: thy Jesus can repay
>   from his own fondness all he takes away.
>
> Be still, my soul: begin the song of praise
>   on earth, be leaving, to thy Lord on high;
> acknowledge him in all thy words and ways,
>   so shall he view thee with a well-pleased eye.
> Be still, my soul: the Sun of life divine
>   through passing clouds shall but more brightly shine.

The hymn entered our hymnals in 1935 in three stanzas. Changes made in the text for our present hymnal are 1:1 and 1:3, "thy" to "your"; 1:4, "he" to "God"; 1:5, "thy best, thy" to "your best, your"; 2:1, "thy" to "your"; 2:2, "he has the" to "in ages"; 2:3, "thy hope, thy" to "your hope, your"; and 2:6, "his voice" to "the Christ."

Finlandia

Jean Sibelius, 1899; arr. from The Hymnal, 1933

This section of Sibelius's tone poem *Finlandia* was adapted as the setting for this text in the 1933 hymnal of the Presbyterian Church, U.S.A.

Be thou my vision (451)

Trans. by Mary E. Byrne, 1905; versed by Eleanor H. Hull, 1912; alt.

The authors of *Companion to Hymns and Psalms* provide the historical context of the hymn:

> This hymn appears in two eighth-century manuscripts in the Royal Irish Academy Library, one of which is copied from the other, beginning 'Rob tu mo bhoile, a Comdi cride'. It was translated into [sixteen couplets of literal] prose by Maire ni Bhroin (Mary Bryne) and so published in *Eriú*, the *Journal of the School of Irish Learning*, Vol. ii, Part 1 (1905). (Watson and Trickett, 1988, 237)

Bryne's literal, prose translation is printed here as found in *Companion to the School Hymn Book of The Methodist Church*, 1950, pages 366-67.

A PRAYER

(1)   Be thou my vision,   O Lord of my heart.
      None other is aught   but the King of the seven heavens.
(2)   Be thou my meditation   by day and night;
      May it be thou that I behold   even in my sleep.
(3)   Be thou my speech,   be thou my understanding,
      Be thou with me,   be I with thee.
(4)   Be thou my father,   be I thy son.
      Mayst thou be mine,   may I be thine.
(5)   Be thou my battle-shield,   be thou my sword.
      Be thou my dignity,   be thou my delight.
(6)   Be thou my shelter,   be thou my stronghold.
      Mayst thou raise me up   to the company of the angels.
(7)   Be thou every good   to my body and soul.
      Be thou my kingdom   in heaven and on earth.
(8)   Be thou solely   chief love of my heart.
      Let there be none other,   O high King of Heaven.
(9)   Till I am able   to pass into thy hands,
      My treasure, my beloved,   through the greatness of thy love.
(10) Be thou alone   my noble and wondrous estate.
      I seek not men,   nor lifeless wealth.
(11) Be thou the constant guardian   of every possession and every life.
      For our corrupt desires are dead   at the mere sight of thee.
(12) Thy love in my soul   and in my heart—
      Grant this to me,   O King of the seven heavens.

(13)	O king of the seven heavens	grant me this—
	Thy love to be in my heart	and in my soul.
(14)	With the King of all,	with Him after victory won by piety
	May I be in the kingdom of heaven	O brightness of the sun.
(15)	Beloved Father,	hear, hear my lamentations;
	Timely is the cry of woe	of this miserable wretch.
(16)	O heart of my heart,	whate'er befall me,
	O ruler of all,	be thou my vision.

A metrical version of Byrne's text, arranged in twelve couplets, was made by E. H. Hull and published in her *Poem-Book of the Gael*, 1912. It is interesting to compare the two versions of the text.

The first adaptation of Hull's text as a hymn with the tune SLANE was in the Irish *Church Hymnal*, 1919. Its appearance in a great number of British hymnals brought it to the attention of USA editors after World War II, and it is a standard item in most hymnals today. Editors have usually arranged Hull's sixteen couplets down to four stanzas, seldom printing them as found in her text.

The hymn entered our hymnals in 1957. The selection of the couplets that are included in our present hymnal was made to render the text nonsexist. In the present hymnal, the former 2:3/3:21 are omitted; 3:3-4 becomes 2:3-4; and in 2:3 and 3:1, "high King God of heaven" becomes "great God of heaven."

The hymn, a prayer for the vision of God to be sustained throughout one's life, may be sung or read antiphonally by lines or stanzas.

Slane

Trad. Irish melody; harm. by Carlton R. Young, 1963

This traditional Irish melody is from Patrick Weston Joyce's *Old Irish Folk Music and Songs: A Collection of 842 Irish Airs and Songs hitherto unpublished*, 1909. It was arranged by Leopold McC. L. Dix and set with the text in the Irish *Church Hymnal*, 1919. The harmonization in our hymnal is adapted from Erik Routley's harmonization in *Congregational Praise*, 1951. A setting of stanza 3 for voices in canon at the octave with free accompaniment is found at 319 in *The United Methodist Hymnal Music Supplement*.

Beams of heaven as I go (524)

Words and music: Charles Albert Tindley, ca. 1906
arr. by J. Edward Hoy, 1984

Titled "Someday," this is one of forty seven hymns of the famous African American preacher Charles Albert Tindley in his *New Songs of Paradise*, No. 6 (meaning sixth edition), Philadelphia, 1916 (reprinted 1984).

C. Eric Lincoln and Lawrence H. Mamiya describe the social context in which Tindley wrote his hymns of hope and faith for his congregation at Tindley Temple in Philadelphia:

> Tindley wrote songs incorporating the black folk imagery which attempted to interpret the oppression African Americans faced as they settled in the cities of the North, an experience not essentially different from that which produced the spirituals. The Tindley hymns (which are congregational songs) admonish those who suffer the storms of life to stand fast in Christ. . . . They are also addressed to helping the oppressed to survive *this* world. (Lincoln and Mamiya 1990, 360)

William B. McClain in *Come Sunday*, the companion to *Songs of Zion*, describes the important contribution of Tindley:

> [His] gospel hymns comprised an entirely new genre as he allowed the Negro spirituals to heavily influence the words he produced. Incorporating proverbs, folk images, biblical allusions well-known to black Christians, he had considerable influence on black hymnody and a universal appeal to the human heart with words of hope, grace, love and pity. (McClain 1990, 75)

McClain comments on the performance practice of the African American gospel hymn:

> "Some Day," also known as "Beams of Heaven" should be sung slowly with great expression. Do not perform it in a cut and dried manner; *elongate the quick and short-value notes.* Improvise, both vocally and instrumentally. (McClain 1990, 129)

Someday

See commentary above.

Because he lives (364)

Words: Gloria and William J. Gaither, 1971 (John 14:19)
Music: William J. Gaither, 1971

This gospel hymn is one of the five most requested by United Methodists to be included in this hymnal. John 14:19c, "because I live, you also will live," appears to be the scriptural allusion for the central point of the hymn, particularly stanza 2 and the refrain. The authors have provided this background for the writing of the hymn:

> "Because he lives" was written in the midst of social upheaval, threats of war, and betrayals of national and personal trust. It was into this world at such a time that we were bringing our third little baby. Assassinations,

riots, drug traffic, and war monopolized the headlines. It was in the midst of this kind of uncertainty that the assurance of the Lordship of the risen Christ blew across our troubled minds like a cooling breeze in the parched desert. Holding our tiny son in our arms we were able to write:

> How sweet to hold our newborn baby,
> And feel the pride, and joy he gives;
> But greater still the calm assurance,
> This child can face uncertain days
> Because he lives.

(Correspondence with Carlton R. Young, October 1992)

Concerning the pronoun "he" in 2:2 and 2:4, the authors now state that the former refers to their newborn son and the latter to Jesus. If their view had been known at the time that the hymn was under consideration by the Hymnal Revision Committee, it is doubtful that the exclusive reference to a male baby in 2:1-2 would have been acceptable, and the hymn would probably not have been included. In the reference to Jesus in 2:4, "he" is not capitalized since the revision committee had agreed to continue the copyediting procedures of the 1966 hymnal, which in turn had followed the practice of the Revised Standard Version of the Bible, 1946, and the King James Version of the Bible, 1611, in which the pronouns, "he," "him," "his," "thou," "thine," etc., when referring to persons of the Trinity, are not capitalized. It appears that the asterisk at 2:2, related to the footnote "Jesus," should be moved to "he" in 2:4.

Resurrection

The refrain may be sung as a response to prayer or at the close of the service.

Because thou hast said (635)

Charles Wesley, 1745 (Luke 22:19; 1 Cor. 11:24-25)

The text is titled "Thou meetest those that remember Thee in Thy Ways," with the heading "Isaiah. 64:5," page 19 in *A Short View of the Difference between the Moravian Brethren, Lately in England; And the Reverend Mr. John and Charles Wesley,* 1745, London. There are two other printings, Dublin, 1747, and Bristol, 1748 (2d ed.), that include the hymn. *Companion to Hymns and Psalms* provides the history of the tract:

> *A Short View. . .* was a tract written to combat the quietism of some extreme Moravians in England, which was beginning to gain ground among Methodist societies. It contains fourteen pages at the conclusion of which the names of John and Charles Wesley appear with the date May 20, 1745, followed by six hymns of Charles Wesley. (Watson and Trickett 1988, 347)

The hymn was not included in any hymnal until the 1983 British Methodist book that uses stanzas 3 and 4, altering "we" to "I" throughout, changing "here only I hope" to "'tis here that we hope," and placing Christ's words of remembrance, "Do this for my sake," in quotes. We follow those changes in our present hymnal and include the hymn among the eucharistic hymns.

The omitted first and second stanzas:

> Come, Lord to a Soul
>   That waits in thy Ways,
> That stays at the Pool
>   Expecting thy Grace:
> To see thy Salvation,
>   And prove all thy Will,
> With sure Expectation
>   I calmly stand still.
>
> With Fasting and Prayer
>   My Savior I seek,
> And listen to hear
>   The Comforter speak;
> In Searching and Hearing
>   The Life-giving Word
> I wait thy Appearing,
>   I look for my Lord.

S T Kimbrough, Jr., has commented that the "hymn expresses the anticipation of Christ's followers who do his will and partake of the sacred meal in all its mystery and promise." (Correspondence with Carlton R. Young, September 1992)

Paderborn

Catholisch-Paderbornisches Gesangbuch, 1765
harm. by Sydney Hugo Nicholson, 1916

There are two tunes in the repertory that bear the name PADERBORN. One, according to Erik Routley, is from N. Beuttner's *Catholisches Gesangbuch [sic]*, Gratz, 1602, found in *The English Hymnal*, number 176 (Routley 1981, 19); and the second, the tune in our hymnal, is from *The English Hymnal*, number 568, cited as "Melody from a French Paroissien."

According to *Companion to Hymns and Psalms*,

> this [latter] tune is derived from a folksong noted in 1742 and printed in a collection of German songs published in Berlin by Buschnig and Von der Hagen in 1807. [Brahms used the tune in number 9 of his collection of forty-nine folk songs.]

In a modified form it appeared as a hymn tune in *Catholisch-Paderbornisches Gesangbuch*, 1765 [as a setting for "Maria zu lieben"]. In England it became known [in Roman Catholic churches] in two versions in the *Westminster Hymnal*, 1912. (Watson and Trickett 1988, 348)

The English Hymnal uses the "corrupt" version. The other version, closer to its folk roots, was arranged in its present form by Sydney H. Nicholson at number 704 in *Hymns Ancient and Modern*, 1916 Second Supplement.

Nicholson named the tune PADERBORN after hearing the tune sung in the Cathedral of Paderborn, the city located between Hanover and Essen, where the tune was first published, and a center for Roman Catholic theological education. This is the first appearance of the tune in our hymnals.

Become to us the living bread (630)

Miriam Drury, 1970 (John 6:35-58)

H. Myron Braun has described this expressive communion hymn:

> With artistic simplicity, brevity, and clarity, several meanings of the Lord's supper are lifted up, especially that of the sustaining and supporting presence of Christ that enables us to take up our tasks as the covenant people. Though written by a Presbyterian, this text surely would have gladdened the heart of John Wesley, with his doctrine of the mystical, or spiritual, yet real presence of Christ in the sacrament. (Braun 1982, 9)

The hymn was first included in *The Worshipbook*, 1970.

Gelobt sei Gott

Ein schön geistlich Gesangbuch, 1609

The tune is also called VULPIUS for Melchior Vulpius, famous Lutheran cantor and composer and the compiler of the above collection in which this folk melody was used for Michael Weisse's "Gelobt sei Gott im höchsten Thron." It entered English hymnals in *Songs of Praise*, 1925, in an arrangement by Henry G. Ley (Dearmer and Jacob 1933, 100-101), whose anthem setting became a standard in USA church choirs in the mid-twentieth century. The tune entered the *Pilgrim Hymnal*, 1958, in a setting presumably made by its music editor Hugh Porter. The tune with that harmonization entered our hymnals in 1966.

Suggestions for performance include to allow the rollicking melody to dance in one strong beat per measure, with everyone singing stanzas 1 and 3 in unison. The choir may sing the second stanza in parts, with everyone joining on the Alleluias. For an effective variation use a less restricted harmonization in 6/4 meter, for example number 205 in *The Hymnal 1982*. *The United Methodist Hymnal Music Supplement* has a vocal descant at 137. For comment on accompanying "dance tunes," see "The first Noel," pages 633-34.

Behold a broken world (426)

Timothy Dudley-Smith, 1985 (Isa. 2:1-4; Micah 4:1-4)

This moving prayer for peace skillfully elaborates and combines the metaphors and imagery of the two excerpts from Hebrew prophetic scripture with the Christian affirmation of Jesus Christ as "the Prince of Peace." A reference to Psalm 46:9a, "[God] makes wars cease to the end of the earth," is found at 3:3, and a phrase from the introductory chapter of in T. E. Lawrence's *Pillars of Wisdom* is echoed at 4:4, "the dreamers of the day."

> All men dream: but not equally. Those who dream by night in the dusty recesses of their minds wake in the day to find that it was vanity: but the dreamers of the day are dangerous men, for they may act their dream with open eyes, to make it possible. (Lawrence 1935, 23)

The text was one of the five chosen entries in the Hymn Society of America's search for hymns with the theme of "Peace," 1984-85, and was first printed in the society's journal *The Hymn*, July 1985, and appeared in *Singing for Peace*, 1986. It may be used effectively as a spoken prayer, read responsively by two groups or by leader and congregation, or the stanzas may be alternately sung and spoken. The hymn may also be used as the theme hymn for an entire service or celebration that emphasizes peace, combining the reading of scripture, other prayers, and preaching.

Marsh Chapel

See "Awake, O sleeper," page 223.

Behold the Savior of mankind (293)

Samuel Wesley, ca. 1709

This hymn on the passion of Christ was one of the few relics of Samuel Wesley's papers that survived the the fire that destroyed the Epworth rectory the night of February 9, 1709. George John Stevenson provides the traditional account of the hymn's origin:

> [It was] probably written shortly before the fire at the Rectory at Epworth, 1709. Immediately after the fire, the original MS, blown by the wind out of the window, was found partly burned in the garden by the author. Probably a lately finished MS. (Stevenson 1883, 29)

The fire was also the occasion when the rector's son, young John Wesley, was rescued, and John later made reference to the event as a "brand plucked out of the burning." John included four stanzas of the hymn in his *Collection of Psalms and Hymns*, Charleston, 1737, pages 46-47, number 8, with the heading "On the crucifixion" in the section "For Wednesday or Friday." The hymn later appeared at 131-32 in *Hymns and Sacred Poems*, 1739, and in his 1780 *Collection*, number 22, under "Describing the Goodness of God." Wesley's mainly historic interest in his father's hymn has been continued by its inclusion in USA Methodist hymnals since 1786.

The power of this hymn is related in Thomas Jackson's *Lives of Early Methodist Preachers* (2 [1871]: 4-5):

> The Irish Roman Catholic, Thomas Walsh, told how a Methodist opening prayer was reinforced by Samuel Wesley's hymn, "Behold the Saviour of mankind": "The former words in the prayer, and those in the hymn, came with such power to my heart that I was constrained to cry out, "Bless the Lord, O my soul! . . ." And now was I divinely assured that God, for Christ's sake, had forgiven me all my sins. (Wesley 1983, 7:65)

Charles Wesley relates in his *Journal* that when Mr. Bray and he were locked in a cell with prisoners at Newgate on July 18, 1778, they sang "Behold the Savior of Mankind" and that the calm that ensued "was the most blessed hour of my life." (Wesley 1:123)

Stanzas 2 and 6 have been omitted from our hymnal:

> Though far unequal our low praise
> To thy vast sufferings prove,
> O Lamb of God, thus all our days,
> Thus will we grieve and love.

> Thy loss our ruin did repair;
> Death by thy death is slain;
> Thou wilt at length exalt us where
> Thou dost in glory reign.

Although no tune has been provided for this hymn, MARTYRDOM on the next page (**294**) is an appropriate and easily sung setting. Craig B. Gallaway suggests that the hymn might be read antiphonally in the Service of Tenebrae on Holy Thursday, or on Good Friday. (Sanchez 1989, 109)

Beneath the cross of Jesus (297)

Elizabeth Cecilia Clephane, 1872

This meditation on the meaning of the cross was published anonymously three years after the death of the poet under the heading "Breathings on the Border," in the Scottish Presbyterian magazine *Family Treasury*, 1872. Eight of Clephane's hymns were published in the periodical 1872-74, the last, "There were ninety and nine," made famous by Sankey in the Moody revivals in England, 1873-74. The magazine's editor, William Arnot, tells of publishing the first of these hymns:

These lines express the experiences, the hopes, and the longings of a young Christian lately released. Written on the very edge of this life, with the better land fully in view of faith, they seem to us footsteps printed on the sands of Time, where these sands touch the ocean of Eternity. These footprints of one whom the Good Shepherd led through the wilderness into rest, may, with God's blessing, contribute to comfort and direct succeeding pilgrims. (McCutchan 1942, 180)

The hymn entered our hymnal in 1935. In spite of the escapist stanza 3:3, "Content to let the world go by," it remains a standard hymn for the Lenten season and Holy Week. In the omitted stanzas 2 and 3, the poet further elaborates on the comfort and strength she has found in the cross's shadow:

> O safe and happy shelter!
>   O refuge tried and sweet!
> O trysting-place where heaven's love
>   and heaven's justice meet!
> As to the exiled patriarch
>   that wonderous dream was given,
> so seems my Savior's cross to me
>   a ladder up to heaven.
>
> There lies beneath its shadow,
>   but on the further side,
> the darkness of an open grave
>   that gapes both deep and wide;
> and there between us stands the cross,
>   two arms outstretched to save,
> like a watchman set to guard the way
>   from that eternal grave.

St. Christopher

Frederick C. Maker, 1881

The tune was written for this text and first appeared in the 1881 *Supplement* to the *Bristol Tune Book*. It is not known why the composer chose to name the tune after the third-century patron saint of travel and travelers.

Benedictus

See "Canticle of Zechariah," page 268.

Bless thou the gifts (587)

Samuel Longfellow, ca. 1886

According to *Guide to the Pilgrim Hymnal* this offertory response is stanza 4 of Longfellow's hymn beginning "Thou Lord of life, our saving health," composed ca. 1886 and first published in his *Hymns and Verses*, 1894. (Ronander and Porter 1966, 396) It entered our hymnals in 1935 in its present form as an offertory sung response, but it was not included in the 1966 book. The setting to DEUS TUORUM MILITUM began with our 1957 book.

Deus tuorum militum

> *Grenoble Antiphoner, 1753; adapt. by Ralph Vaughan Williams, 1906*
> *harm. by Basil Harwood, 1908*

The name of this vigorous tune is from the first line of the Latin in the office hymn for martyrs, "God, the portion, the crown and reward of thy soldiers," to which it was set in the 1753 antiphoner. M. Stulken has succinctly traced the development of this genre of hymn tune:

> During the sixteenth and seventeenth centuries, concurrent with the "modernization" of the Breviaries, there arose in France a new kind of church tune. Although generally not clearly cast in a regular rhythmic meter, these tunes were more measured than the older plain-chant and were also in the modern major and minor modes. Some of the tunes were adapted from older plainsong melodies, others from secular tunes; but the origins of most of the melodies have not as yet been discovered. These French melodies made their way into England when a number of them were taken from La Feillée's *Méthode de Plain-Chant* (1750, 1782 and 1808) into *The Hymnal Noted*, 1851, a work prepared by John Mason Neale and Thomas Helmore. From there they entered *The English Hymnal*, 1906, and later English collections. (Stulken 1981, 185)

The tune entered our hymnals in 1957 in a harmonization from *The Hymnal 1940*, number 344, where it had probably been adapted from a four-part setting by Basil Harwood in *The Oxford Hymn Book*, 1908 (suggested by Routley 1981, 113), in contrast to Vaughan Williams's unison setting at 181 in *The English Hymnal*, 1906.

Blessed assurance, Jesus is mine (369)

> *Fanny Jane Crosby, 1873*

This hymn is among the ten most popular sung by United Methodists. In form, content, and circumstance of writing it is a paradigm of a successful gospel hymn. In her autobiography, *Memories of Eighty Years*, Boston, 1906 (Gealy 555/57), the author provides insight about the power of music and her collaborative hymn-writing technique used in the composition of this, no doubt, the most sung of all of her more than 8,000 hymns.

> In a successful song words and music must harmonize, not only in number of syllables, but in subject matter and especially accent. In nine cases out of ten the success of a hymn depends directly upon these qualities. Thus,

melodies tell their own tale, and it is the purpose of the poet to interpret this musical story into language. Not infrequently a composer asks, "What does that melody say to you?" And if it says nothing to you the probability is that your words will not agree with the music when an attempt is made to join them. "Blessed Assurance" was written to a melody composed by my friend, Mrs. Joseph F. Knapp [Phoebe P. Knapp]; she played it over once or twice on the piano and then asked me what it said to me. I replied,

> Blessed assurance, Jesus is mine!
> O what a foretaste of glory divine!
> Heir of salvation, purchase of God,
> Born of His spirit, washed in His blood.

The hymn thus written seemed to express the experience of both Mrs. Knapp and myself. (Crosby 1906, 168-69)

It was included in Ira Sankey's *Gospel Hymns, No. 5*, 1887, and used extensively in Britain and the USA in the Moody and Sankey revivals. The hymn has been included unaltered in all our hymnals since its first appearance as number 860 in the "Supplement" section of the 1889 hymnal.

Assurance

Phoebe P. Knapp, 1873

The tune and text were apparently first printed as number 66 in *Gems of Praise, Choice Collection of Sacred Melodies*, 1873, by John R. Sweney, Methodist Episcopal Book Room, Philadelphia. Compared to the musical setting used in our hymnals since 1889 in the 1876 printing of Sweney's collection, the hymn is written in 3/4 meter rather than 9/8, and in the refrain the harmonies are different in measures 3 and 6. *The United Methodist Hymnal Music Supplement* provides an alternate harmonization at number 24.

Blessed be the God of Israel (209)

Michael Perry, 1973 (Luke 1:68-79)

This metrical paraphrase of the "Canticle of Zechariah" (Benedictus) **(208)** falls short (as do most paraphrases because of their less than faithful transmission of metaphor and meaning and the Hebraic parallelism) in its portrayal of the human/divine drama that is unfolding as God's promise (covenant) to Abraham is about to be fulfilled in the liberating presence of God in Christ. God is portrayed as the mighty Savior anticipated in Psalms 18:1-3, 92: 10-11; 132:17-18; the one who comes as a child in Malachi 4:5 and Luke 7:26; the one who shows the way of salvation in Mark 1:4; the one who is God's blessing in the breaking of dawn from on high, Malachi 4:2 and Ephesians 5:14; and the one who is the light for those in darkness, Isaiah 9:2, Matthew 4:16, and Luke 4:18.

Our hymnal's text retains the poet's stronger original words at 3:1 and 2:4, where some editors prefer "messenger" for "harbinger," and "Where once was fear and darkness" for "On prisoners of darkness." In stanza 2:4 "day" should probably be capitalized "Day," i.e., the day of the Lord (Isaiah 2:1, 2:12, and 22:5-8a, and other references in Hebrew and Christian scripture). The hymn first appeared as "O bless the God of Israel" in *Psalm Praise*, 1973.

Merle's tune

Hal H. Hopson, 1983

According to the composer, this tune

> [was] written in 1983 for the text "Blessed be the God of Israel" by Michael A. Perry. It was first published in *The Upper Room Worshipbook*, 1985. The tune is named for Hopson's elder sister Merle who was his first piano teacher. (Correspondence with Carlton R. Young, June 1991)

Blessed be the name (63)

USA camp-meeting chorus Ps. 72:19

William J. Reynolds has traced this anonymous chorus as a 66.8 phrase of folk and camp-meeting origin that in the nineteenth century was often inserted between lines of text and used as the refrain for familiar standard hymns, e.g., "O for a thousand tongues." (Reynolds 1976, 156-57)

> O for a thousand tongues to sing,
> *Blessed be the name of the Lord!*
> The glories of my God and King,
> *Blessed be the name of the Lord!*
> (*Refrain*)

This is the first inclusion of this chorus in our hymnals.

Blessed be the name

Arr. by Ralph E. Hudson, 1887

According to William J. Reynolds, Hudson arranged this refrain from folk and camp-meeting sources for his *Songs for the Ransomed*, Alliance, Ohio, 1887. It is one of a number of choruses included in our hymnal for occasional use as brief, joyous affirmations to prayer or as a sung response to the reading of scripture. These choruses may also be blended into a medley of other choruses or refrains from larger hymns connected with keyboard modulations (see "Modulation Formulas," Appendix F, 391, in *The United Methodist Hymnal Music Supplement*).

Blessed be the Lord (208)

See "Canticle of Zechariah" (Benedictus), page 268.

Blessed Jesus, at thy word (596)
Leibster Jesu, wir sind hier

Tobias Clausnitzer, 1663; trans. by Catherine Winkworth, 1858

The hymn, whose first line reads,

> Liebster Jesu, wir sind hier,
> Dich und dein Wort anzuhören,

was written to be sung before the sermon. It was published anonymously in *Altdorffisches Gesang-Büchlein*, 1663. In the 1671 edition Clausnitzer's name appeared as author.

John Julian cites eleven translations of the text. (Julian 1907, 235-36) Of these Winkworth's has been the most popular. It was first included in her *Lyra Germanica*, 1858, and reprinted in *The Chorale Book for England*, 1863. The hymn entered our hymnals in 1935.

Leibster Jesu

Johann R. Ahle, 1664

Ahle included this tune for the advent hymn "Ja er ist's, das Heil der Welt" in his *Neue geistliche auf die Sontage*, Mülhausen, 1664. That form of the melody is included by Robert Guy McCutchan in *Our Hymnody* (1942, 332). The tune was later set to Clausnitzer's hymn, and its marriage with that text has been standard for most German hymnals since that time.

The tune entered our hymnals in 1935 in two harmonizations, numbers 310 and 390, the latter by J. S. Bach. The source of the former harmonization, that continued with slight alteration in 1957 and 1966, has not been found. Further changes were made for use in the present hymnal. The tune is also known as "Nuremberg," "Dessau," and "St. Mark."

Blest be the dear uniting love (566)

Charles Wesley, 1742

This hymn of Christian fellowship is found on pages 159-60 in *Hymns and Sacred Poems*, Bristol, 1742, with the title "At Parting." It is immediately preceded by another fellowship hymn, "Glory be to God above," titled "At the Meeting of Christian Friends," and is followed by a committal hymn for the departed, "Let the World lament and grieve," titled "The Commendation." In 1780 John Wesley included six of the eight stanzas in his *Collection*, number 520 in the section "For the Society, Parting." Five original stanzas are included in our present hymnal. They are unaltered with one exception: stanza 3:1, "O let us ever," following John Wesley, has been changed to "O may we ever." The omitted stanzas 4, 5, and 8 are printed as follows:

Closer, and closer let us cleave
  To His belov'd Embrace,
Expect His Fulness to receive,
  And Grace to answer Grace.

While thus we walk with Christ in Light
  Who shall our Souls disjoin,
Souls, which Himself vouchsafes t'unite
  In Fellowship Divine!

But let us hasten to the Day
  Which shall our Flesh restore,
When Death shall all be done away,
  And Bodies part no more.

The hymn was first included in our hymnals in 1786. It has traditionally been sung at the close of worship and to conclude other gatherings for prayer and praise. If the original stanza 8 is sung as a final stanza, it could also be an appropriate hymn for a Christian funeral. Scriptural references include stanza 2:1, 1 Corinthians 6:17; 2:3, 1 Peter 2:21; 3:2, 1 Corinthians 2:2; 4:1, Acts 11:23; 4:3-4, John 1:16; 5:2, Acts 4:32; and 5:3-4, Romans 8:38-39:

For I am convinced that neither death, nor life, nor angels, nor rulers, nor things present, nor things to come, nor powers, nor height, nor depth, nor anything else in all creation, will be able to separate us from the love of God in Christ Jesus our Lord.

Evan

William Havergal, 1847; arr. by Lowell Mason, 1850
Mason's arrangement of Havergal's tune first appeared in *New Carmina Sacra*, 1850, under the name of EVA. Havergal so disapproved of Mason's adaptation that he called it "a sad estrangement." Mason changed the tune's name to EVAN perhaps to avoid indexing problems with a popular LM tune with the same name by A. B. Everett, but more likely to be able to claim ownership of his adaptation of Havergal's tune, a flowing setting for a poem by Robert Burns, into another simple, memorable, and popular 3/2 tune. Our 1966 hymnal was the first to match this tune and text.

Jane Marshall has suggested that the choir sing a stanza of the hymn without accompaniment and "exchange the tenor and alto parts or have men sing the melody with women singing the tenor part up an octave." (Sanchez 1989, 193)

Blest be the tie that binds (557)

John Fawcett, 1782

The hymn of Christian love, concern, and fellowship first appeared as hymn 104 under the title of "Brotherly Love," page 188, in the author's *Hymns Adapted to the Circumstances of Public Worship and Private Devotion*, Leeds, 1782. The collection contained 166 hymns, most of them to be sung as a congregational response to the sermon. The story concerning Fawcett's writing the hymn as a response to his long ministry at Wainsgate is interesting but no doubt apocryphal. Most of our hymnals have included the hymn since its first inclusion in *A Selection of Hymns*, 1810. We use four of the six stanzas as they appear in the author's collection. Stanzas 5 and 6 are included herein:

> This glorious hope revives
> Our courage by the way;
> While each in expectation lives,
> And longs to see the day.
>
> From sorrow, toil and pain,
> and sin we shall be free;
> And perfect love and friendship reign
> Thro' all eternity.

Dennis

See "And are we yet alive" page 211.

Our 1878 hymnal seems to be first to wed this text to the tune DENNIS.

Blow ye the trumpet, blow (379)

Charles Wesley, 1750 (Lev. 25:8-17)

The hymn was first published on pages 12-13 in *Hymns for New-Year's Day*, London, 1750, under the title "The Year of Jubilee" from Leviticus 25:9 where after seven sabbatical years (7 X 7), the next, the fiftieth year, is to be a year of jubilee. The blowing of the ram's horn ushered in the year in which the Israelites returned to their ancestral homes.

> Then you shall have the trumpet sounded loud; on the tenth day of the seventh month—on the day of atonement—you shall have the trumpet sounded throughout all your land. . . .It shall be a jubilee for you: you shall return, every one of you, to your property and every one of you to your family. (Lev. 25:9, 10b)

Craig B. Gallaway has commented on the power of Wesley's text:

In this great hymn of justifying grace the biblical themes of atonement and the year of jubilee become an invitation to the whole world to receive through "the precious blood of Christ" [like that of a lamb without defect or blemish] (I Peter 1:19) a salvation that cannot be bought or earned. (Sanchez 1989, 134)

While it was printed in several eighteenth-century collections of evangelical songs, such as Augustus Toplady's *Psalms and Hymns for Public and Private Worship*, London, 1776, and *A Select Collection of Hymns, Universally sung in all the Countess of Huntingdon's Chapels*, London, 1786, the hymn apparently was not popular in the Methodist revival. John Wesley did not include it in his 1780 *Collection*.

All six stanzas were printed when the hymn was first included in our 1786 hymnal. Stanzas 4 and 5 appear in our hymnal for the first time in a twentieth-century USA Methodist hymnal. In stanza 6:7, "return, ye, ransomed sinners, home" has been restored to "return, to your eternal home."

Lenox

Lewis Edson, ca. 1782

The tune, also called TRUMPET, was first published in *The Chorister's Companion*, New Haven, 1782 or 1783. In the USA the hymn's inclusion in standard shaped-note books matched to Edson's fuging tune (one of the earliest) brought it into the repertory of the singing schools, and from there into the standard hymnals of Methodism. The tune was printed as a fuging tune as late as the 1857 tune edition of the 1847 Methodist Episcopal hymnal. The shape of the tune mandates that the sixth line of the poem be repeated. The arrangement of the tune in four-part hymn style was probably the work of Rigdon M. McIntosh in *The Gem*, Nashville, 1876, page 145, along with another of Wesley's "Hallelujah meter hymns" (6666. 88), "Arise, my soul, arise."

Bread and justice

Rubem Alves

Laurence H. Stookey has written on the prayer's significance:

This is a prayer to be studied with care and prayed with deliberation. Images such as coffee, an open door, and shouts of children in the first half of the prayer contrast sharply with images such as lack of bread, closed doors, and sad children in the second half. The prayer is intended particularly for private or group use at a service of Holy Communion; we ask that the sacramental signs of God's goodness may make us more aware of the world around us, with both its gifts and its pain. (Sanchez 1989, 215)

The prayer is from the author's *I Believe in the Resurrection of the Body*, 1986.

Bread of the world in mercy broken (624)

Reginald Heber, 1827 (John 6:35-58)
This brief communion hymn, with an unknown date of composition, was included at pages 124-25 under the title "Before the Sacrament" in the author's *Hymns Written and Adapted to the Weekly Service of the Church Year*, 1827, published by his widow a year after his death. The hymn is composed in the emerging literary style of hymn writing and is a prayer of awe and adoration in simple and understandable words to the consecrated host, i.e., Christ, the sacrificial Lamb of God. The hymn entered our hymnals in 1874.

Eucharistic hymn

John Sebastian Bach Hodges, 1868
The tune was written for this hymn by Hodges, who was rector of Grace Episcopal Church, Newark, New Jersey. It first appeared in the Protestant Episcopal *Book of Common Praise*, 1869. While the hymn has been set to several tunes, some in 98. 98. D (e.g., RENDEZ Á DIEU in *Book of Hymns*, 323), only EUCHARISTIC HYMN seems to complement the text's beautiful simplicity. It should be sung in a direct and unhurried style.

Break forth, O beauteous heavenly light (223)
Ermuntre dich, mein schwacher Geist

Johann Rist, 1641; st. 1, trans. by John Troutbeck, ca. 1885
sts. 2, 3, Fred Pratt Green, 1986 (Luke 2:8-14)
The hymn appeared first in eleven stanzas in Rist's *Himmlische Lieder*, Leipzig, 1641. It came into our hymnals in 1966 in the translation of Rist's stanza 9 which Troutbeck had provided for the Novello English text edition of J. S. Bach's *Christmas Oratorio*:

> Brich an du schönes Morgenlicht
> Und lass den Himmeltagen,
> Du Hirten-volk erstaune nicht
> Weil dir die Engel sagen;
> Dass dieses schwache Knäbelein
> Soll unser Trost und Freude sein,
> Dazu den Satan zwingen
> Und alles wieder bringen.

The hymn was not widely used primarily because of its setting to the intricate harmonies of J. S. Bach, but also because it had only one stanza. To explore the possibility of including additional stanzas the committee approached Fred Pratt

Green who had been working with German pastor Friedrich Hofmann in the translation of Green's hymns into German. Hofmann supplied a literal translation of Rist's eleven-stanza hymn, and the poet adapted the translator's words into the stanzas he submitted to the committee with the understanding that they were based on a translation but not *his* translation. The translations were accepted with only two minor changes: in 3:1, "sweetest" to "dearest" and 3:3, "a new life" to "the new life."

Fred Pratt Green also composed two original additional stanzas, which he later withdrew. They demonstrate the poet's propensity for creatively pursuing a project to its conclusion and to his satisfaction.

> Shine on, O bright prophetic star,
>   Reveal the place of meeting:
> You magi, hastening from afar,
>   Beware of Herod's greeting.
> This child, who comes to set us free
> From sin and sin's malignity,
>   To human guile a stranger,
>   Is born—how soon?—to danger.
>
> Then let us, we who are his Church,
>   Be like those shepherds watching,
> Those magi, patient in research,
>   Their prompt obedience matching:
> And moved by Christ's nativity
> Offer him gifts and bow the knee,
>   And in his Incarnation
>   Proclaim the world's salvation.
>
> © 1993 Hope Publishing Co.

(From the poet's correspondence with Carlton R. Young, October 1, 1986)

In 1:1, "beauteous" is retained, although the poet preferred the change to "celestial," and at 1:3, "ye" was changed to "you."

Ermuntre dich

Johann Schop, 1641; harm. by J. S. Bach, 1734

Schop, the music editor of Rist's collections, composed this tune in triple meter for *Himmlische Lieder*, 1641. It was included in an altered form in Johann Crüger's *Praxis Pietatis Melica*, 1647, which is probably the source for J. S. Bach who further arranged the tune for his choral setting in part 2 of *Christmas Oratorio*, 1737. A slight reduction of Bach's setting was included at number 25 in *The Hymnal 1940*, and reprinted in our 1966 hymnal. Since Bach's extraordinary part writing was not intended to be used as the setting for a three-stanza strophic hymn, it would be appropriate to allow the second stanza to be sung by a soloist, unison men or women, or an unaccompanied mixed choir. When the hymn is sung at a slow pace, the moving harmonies in the tenor and alto can more effectively be realized.

Break thou the bread of life (599)

Mary A. Lathbury, 1877

The hymn was written by Mary A. Lathbury, "the Laureate of Chautauqua," at the request of its founder and longtime manager John H. Vincent, for use in Bible study and with other groups that were sponsored by Chautauqua's Literary and Scientific Circle. The two-stanza text, apparently inspired by Jesus' feeding of the five thousand (Mark 6:39-44), was completed in the summer of 1877, and according to William J. Reynolds it was first included in *The Chautauqua Carols*, 1877. (Adams 1992, 102). It is still sung at the institute's Sunday evening vesper services. The hymn entered our hymnals in 1905 with the original text.

Fred D. Gealy received additional information about the circumstances of the hymn's composition in a letter dated November 7, 1967, from Gladys E. Gray, Geneva, New York:

"Break Thou the bread of life" was written as a "study hymn" for the Normal Classes. The Chautauqua movement started for the sole purpose of providing opportunity for Sunday School teachers to come apart and do some intensive studying in the preparation for better work in their local churches. . . . One of the mis-statements given wide publication has been that this hymn was written particularly for the famous Chautauqua Literary and Scientific Circle. However, the hymn was written in 1877, and Mr. Vincent did not inaugurate the Circles until 1878. Dr. [Jesse L.] Hurlbut explains:

"Originally composed for the Normal Class, then the most prominent feature of the program, after the Chautauqua Circle arose to greatness in 1878, they ["Day is dying in the west" and "Break thou the bread of life"] were adopted as the songs of the widespread organization." (Gealy 556/67)

The hymn with Sherwin's tune BREAD OF LIFE was first printed in leaflets published by the institution. The first hymnal to include the hymn was Charles S. Robinson's and Robert S. MacArthur's *Calvary Selection of Spiritual Songs*, New York, 1878, page 66 in the section of hymns for "Close of Worship." It was introduced into Great Britain via W. Garrett Horder's *Congregational Hymns*, 1884. In 1904 two additional stanzas by Alexander Groves were included in the British Methodist hymnal:

> Thou art the bread of life,
> O Lord, to me,

Thy holy Word the truth
    That saveth me;
Give me to eat and live
    With Thee above;
Teach me to love thy truth,
    For Thou art love.

O send Thy Spirit, Lord,
    Now unto me,
That He may touch mine eyes,
    And make me see:
Show me the truth concealed
    Within Thy Word,
And in thy Book revealed
    I see the Lord.

Since that time the hymn has been included in British Methodist hymnals using the original first stanza and Groves's two stanzas and sung to "Bethsaida," at best a distraction from the poet's simple rhetorical style. The stanzas have also appeared in some USA hymnals.

Bread of life

William Fiske Sherwin, 1877
The tune was written for the text by Sherwin who was Chautauqua's director of music. It first appeared with the hymn in *The Calvary Selection of Spiritual Songs*, 1878.

Breathe on me, Breath of God (420)

Edwin Hatch, 1878 (John 20:22)
Fred D. Gealy has traced the appearance of the text in various publications:

The hymn was first published privately in the pamphlet *Between Doubt and Prayer*, 1878; then in Henry Allon, *The Congregational Psalmist [Hymnal]*, 1886; and then in 1890 in a posthumous collection of Hatch's poems, *Towards Fields of Light*. (Gealy, Lovelace, Young 1970, 124)

The hymn is a meditation on "born of the Spirit," which, in turn, rests upon the images of the creation story:

Jesus answered, "Very truly, I tell you, no one can enter the kingdom of God without being born of water and Spirit." (John 3:5)

When he [Jesus] had said this, he breathed on them and said to them, "Receive the Holy Spirit." (John 20:33)

Then the Lord God formed man from the dust of the ground, and breathed into his nostrils the breath of life; and the man became a living being. (Genesis 2:7)

Companion to Hymns and Psalms provides this further interpretation:

In stanza one the Spirit brings new life: Galatians 2:20 and 5:22; in stanza two, purity and obedience, Psalm 51:10, Mark 13:13; in stanza three surrender and inspiration, Acts 2:3-4; and in stanza four, eternal life, 1 Peter 5:10. (Watson and Trickett 1988, 189)

The hymn entered our hymnals in 1905.

Trentham

Robert Jackson, 1888

According to James T. Lightwood the tune was written for Henry W. Baker's "O perfect life of love" in *Fifty Sacred Leaflets*, 1888. (Lightwood 1935, 509) In the USA it is usually used as the setting for Hatch's text.

By gracious powers
Von guten Mächten wunderbar geborgen

Dietrich Bonhoeffer, 1944; trans. by Fred Pratt Green, 1972

Wesley Milgate has supplied this information about the writing of this text:

From the Gestapo bunker in Prinz-Albrecht-Strasse, Berlin, to which he had been transferred to Tegel on 8 October 1944, Dietrich Bonhoeffer wrote this New Year message to his friends on the last New Year's Eve of his life, 31 December 1944; it was smuggled out of the prison, and has become one of Bonhoeffer's best-known compositions. (Milgate 1988, 33)

The English text appeared in seven stanzas under the title "New Year 1945" in *The Cost of Discipleship*, 1959 2d ed. In 1972 Erik Routley, who was the general editor of *Cantate Domino*, 1974, invited Fred Pratt Green to versify five stanzas of the English text for use in that forthcoming hymnal of the World Council of Churches. Four stanzas of Green's text were included in *Supplement to the Book of Hymns* to the tune "Le Cenacle" (named after a house in Geneva), composed by Joseph Gelineau for *Cantate Domino*.

The fifth stanza is usually omitted:

> Now, when your silence deeply spreads around us,
>   O let us hear all your creation says—

That world of sound which soundlessly invades us,
And all your children's highest hymns of praise.

Ray Glover has described the importance of Bonhoeffer's letters and poems:

This poem and his letters to family and friends are filled with the hope and assurance of the Gospel. These expressions, found throughout the hymn, are not pious platitudes but statements founded on biblical truth and on the wisdom gained from writers, artists and musicians of the ages. (Glover 1987, 130)

Intercessor

Charles Hubert Hastings Parry, 1904
The tune was commissioned for Ada Rundall Greenway's "O word of pity, for our pardon pleading," number 129 in *Hymns Ancient and Modern*, 1904. Erik Routley has commented on Parry's tune.

In 1904 he [Parry] was drafted by the editors of that year's *Hymns Ancient and Modern*, and wrote a number of tunes on commission, some of which are conventional and blameless, but one or two of which. . . and supremely INTERCESSOR (HAM 115) show a quite new kind of melodic genius. (Routley 1981, 111)

Archibald Jacob in *Songs of Praise Discussed* says that INTERCESSOR "is a grave Aeolian tune, of a broad, solid type, very characteristic of this composer." (Jacob 1933, 174) The tune takes its name from the second word in stanza 4:1, "O Intercessor, who art ever living." This is its first appearance in our hymnals.

Camina, pueblo de Dios (305)
Walk on, O people of God

Cesareo Gabaraín; trans. by George Lockwood, 1987
In this contemporary Spanish hymn Christ's resurrection is expressed as the "new creation": a new birth, a new people, a new joy, the reconciliation of all people, and the reunion of heaven and earth. The hymn is summarized in 3:7-8:

Christ's resurrection has freed us.
There are new worlds to explore.

When the hymn is introduced, the choir or solo voice should sing the refrain in either Spanish or English, and the congregation may sing in either or both languages. Stanzas should be sung in a free expressive style in either language by a children's choir or a solo voice, with the compelling refrain sung in a steady, slightly accented slow two counts per measure. The song was first included in *Dios con nosotros,* ca. 1978.

George Lockwood was a member of the Hispanic Consultation responsible for the selection and the translations of Spanish language hymns in the present hymnal.

Nueva creación

Cesareo Gabaraín; harm. by Juan Luis García, 1987

The tune's name comes from the last line of stanza 2: "all creation is reborn."

¡Canta, Débora, canta! (81)
Sing, Debora, sing!

Words and music: Luiza Cruz, 1973
English trans. by Gertrude C. Suppe, 1987
Spanish trans. by Raquel Gutiérrez-Achon, 1987 (Judg. 5)

The Song of Deborah is from the oldest part of the Hebrew Bible, perhaps dating as early as the twelfth century B.C. A prose version of the poem, repeated in Judges 4:2-24, recounts the victory of the Hebrew armies led by the prophetess Deborah over Sisera. "The [story] celebrates the Lord's victory over Sisera, won because of a sudden downpour that made it impossible for [the enemy's superior] chariots to maneuver." (Metzger and Murphy 1991, 306)

Dorothea Ward Harvey has described Deborah:

An outstanding person, able to arouse the scattered tribes of Israel to a sense of unity and loyalty to Yahweh in their early struggles against the Canaanites. This sense of religious unity was of crucial importance for the establishment and continuing life of the nation of Israel. (Buttrick 1962, 1:809)

At one point in the deliberations of the Hymnal Revision Committee, consideration of the the hymn sparked a lively discussion about militaristic images and the role and status of women portrayed in hymns.

Luiza Cruz, pen name of Norah Buyers, composed this compelling victory hymn in Portuguese, the language of her native Brazil. "In 1973 and it became the theme for that conference. It has been popular in Brazil and also in Guatemala, where Raquel Achon introduced it to a national meeting of Methodist Women in 1980-81." (Correspondence with Carlton R. Young, August 1992) The hymn was first included in *A Nova Cancâo,* 1975, edited by Cruz. The translations were made as part of the work of the Hispanic Consultation.

Débora

Luiza Cruz, 1973

Sing this hymn with great spirit accompanied by keyboard, guitar, and string bass. Let a solo voice or unison choir sing the stanzas with light accompaniment. On the refrain add trumpet, hand clapping, and traditional rhythm instruments.

Cantemos al Señor (149)
Let's sing unto the Lord

Trans. by Roberto Escamilla, Elise S. Eslinger
and George Lockwood, 1983, 1987 (Ps. 19:1)

This joyous entrance hymn is the second movement, titled "Alleluya," from the composer's *Rosas Del Tepeyac,* a setting of the mass *Díez Çanciones Para la Misa,* 1976. The text was apparently suggested by verse 1 of Psalm 19 (**750**):

> The heavens are telling the glory of God;
> and the firmament proclaims
> his handiwork.

It first appeared in this arrangement at number 16 in *Celebremos. Segunda Parte,* 1983, with the title "Alleluia." George Lockwood's modification of the English text assists in bringing it closer to Spanish meaning and prosody.

Rosas

Carlos Rosas; arr. by Raquel Mora Martínez, 1980

The simplified keyboard arrangement was made for *Celebremos. Segunda Parte,* 1983. Suggestions for performance practice include its use as a processional hymn accompanied by maracas and hand clapping, with the choir or leader singing the stanzas alternately in Spanish and English, and the congregation joining on the chorus in both languages. Ritard and reinforce the second ending, and add choir voices ad lib above the melody for a forceful ending. Throughout, encourage the keyboard instrument(s), guitar, and rhythm instruments to bring out the rhythmic figures 2 against 3 where they occur in the left hand of the accompaniment against the melody.

Gertrude Suppe, who attended a workshop by the composer, April 1991, writes that he "used a simple, rather lyrical type of guitar accompaniment at a metronome speed of 160 for an eighth note, much slower than we had sung it at home. It gave a very different feeling." (Correspondence with Carlton R. Young, July 1991)

Cantemus Domino (135)

See "Canticle of Moses and Miriam," page 258.

Canticle of Christ's obedience (167)
Christ Jesus, though he was

Phil. 2:5-11

This early Christian song is the centerpiece of Paul's letter from prison to the Christian community at Philippi (see Acts 16:11-40), the first established by Paul in what is now Europe. The canticle begins at 2:6 after the introduction of 2:5, "Let the same mind be in you that was in Christ Jesus," and proclaims Paul's understanding of Christ, and by inference Christ's followers if they are to be Christlike, as obedient to God's will to the point of self-emptying, "kenosis," and ultimately death. Only through this obedience can one expect the exaltation of the Resurrection. Settings of this text in contrasting metrical paraphrases are found at **166** and **168**.

Response 1

Words: Phil. 2:5
Music: Gary Alan Smith, 1987

Response 2

Words: Caroline M. Noel, 1870
Music: Ralph Vaughan Williams, 1925

The two sung responses express the themes of the mind of Christ and the name of Jesus.

All canticles are pointed for singing beginning on page 374 in *The United Methodist Hymnal Music Supplement*. The canticle may be sung to Tone 5 in D minor, as pointed at page 381 in *The United Methodist Hymnal Music Supplement*.

Canticle of covenant faithfulness (125)
Seek the Lord
Quaerite Dominum

Isa. 55:6-11

Isaiah's hymn, traditionally called the "Second Song of Isaiah," is a call to repentance and return to God's ways, the promise of God's forgiveness, and the assurance that the Lord's salvation will be accomplished as assuredly as snow and rain from heaven replenish the earth to nourish the seed and provide our daily bread.

Response

Words: Isa. 55:6
Music: Thomas Hastings

The sung response uses the familiar tune TOPLADY **(361)**. Worship leaders are encouraged to use phrases from other familiar hymns as sung responses. The canticle may be read in unison without its response before it is sung in metrical paraphrase in hymn **124**. The canticle may be sung to Tone 4 in G minor, as pointed on page 378 in *The United Methodist Hymnal Music Supplement*. In the same publication, 367-70, the five psalm tones are transposed to seven adjacent keys for ease in making the appropriate adjustments in pitch in order to accommodate the sung response and the sung text.

Canticle of God's glory (82, 83)
Gloria in excelsis

Luke 2:14; John 1:29

Glory be to God on high (82)

Book of Common Prayer, 1549
Fred D. Gealy has provided this background information about this canticle:

The 2 great doxological prayers of the Western Church as we now know them, the Lesser Doxology ["Glory be to the Father," **71, 72**] and the Greater Doxology [Canticle of God's glory], were formed in the third and fourth centuries under the pressure of Arianism and other Gnostic sects. The pattern of praise, however, goes far back to Jewish antecedents, as may be seen, for example, in the responses [concluding doxologies] to the 5 books of the psalter: psalms 41:13, 72:18-19, 89:52, 106:48, and 150 [the concluding doxology for the entire Psalter].

The simpler New Testament antecedents may be seen in Romans 16:27, Ephesians 3:21, II Peter 3:18, Jude 25, and Revelation 5:13 [see "Early Christian Hymns," page 4].

[The] Greater Doxology . . . is an expansion of Luke 2:14, originally a Jewish Messianic song (see Psalm 118:26) acclaiming the coming salvation. The second st., addressed to Jesus Christ in his passion and exaltation, is built on the *Kyrie* **[482, 483, 484, 485]** and *Agnus Dei* ["O Lamb of God," **30**].

St. 3 reflects the acclamation in the Eastern liturgies by which the people respond to the celebrant just before Communion, "One holy, One Lord Jesus Christ, to the glory of God the Father."

Used first in the daily offices of the Eastern Church, since at least the fourth century it was introduced into the Roman Mass by Pope Symmachus (498-

514) as an extension of the *Kyrie* at the beginning of the service. Archbishop Thomas Cranmer kept the position of the *Gloria* at the beginning of the service in 1549, but in 1552 removed it to its traditional English place as part of the Post-Communion thanksgiving. It remained in this position in our liturgy until [our 1966 hymnal] returned . . . it to its original location in the Roman mass and in the First Prayer Book of Edward VI, 1549, at the beginning of the service. (Gealy, Lovelace, Young 1970, 445-46)

The canticle was included in the chant section of our 1873 hymnal. In our hymnal it appears in both traditional and modern English and set apart from its former place in the communion liturgy to encourage its use as a general hymn of praise. It would be appropriate to sing either setting at the entrance or opening of the services of Word and Table, **6, 12, 15,** and **26.** In line 1 of **82,** "men" has been changed to "all."

Old Scottish chant

Anon.

Our musical setting entered our hymnals in 1878. In *The Hymn* (31 (3):174-82) Ruth M. Wilson traces this anonymous Anglican chart to Robert Bremner's *Rudiments of Music,* ca. 1763, and the chant and the canticle printed together in William Smith, *The Churchman's Choral Companion to his Prayerbook,* 1809.

Glory to God in the highest (83)

ICET, 1975; rev. ELLC, 1987

For commentary, see "Glory be to God on high," pages 253-54.

Response

Alexander Peloquin, 1972

The congregational response is from Alexander Peloquin's "Gloria" from *Mass of the Bells,* 1972. The response should be sung first by the leader, then answered by the congregation. The sung response is transposed to the key of F major, **54** in *The United Methodist Hymnal Music Supplement.* On 367 the text is pointed for singing and may be sung to Tone 3 in G major.

Canticle of hope (734)
We shall see a new heaven

Rev. 22:1-6; 23-24; 22:5, 12, 20, adapt. by S T Kimbrough, Jr., 1987

This canticle is described by its author, S T Kimbrough, Jr., as follows:

This composite biblical song is based on the description of the new Jerusalem in Revelation 21 and 22. It expresses hope in God's new cre-

ation of life, where earthly fear of darkness vanishes before God's perpetual light. It also emphasizes the eternal hope of the faithful in three
affirmations of God: "God's dwelling is with mortals" [21:3b]; "I make all
things new" [21:5a]; and "I am coming soon" [22:7a]. This canticle is particularly appropriate for services of death and resurrection, memorials,
renewal, watch night, and the new year. (Sanchez 1989, 245)

Response

Words: Rev. 21:23; 22:5, adapt.
Music: Carlton R. Young, 1987

The sung response in its shift of tonality contrasts earthly light with perpetual
heavenly light. The canticle may be sung using Tone 4, F minor, 389 in *The
United Methodist Hymnal Music Supplement.*

Canticle of light and darkness (205)
We look for light

Isa. 9:2; 59:9-10; Ps. 139:11-12; Dan. 2:20a, 22
1 John 1:5, adapt. by Alan Luff, 1987

This "synthetic canticle," i.e., a composite thematic reading usually formed with
materials from one or more books of the Bible, expresses light in darkness, one
of the traditional themes of Advent and Christmas. In this canticle biblical passages are selected from Hebrew psalms, prophetic and apocalyptic literature,
and Christian scripture, John 1:9 and 1 John 1:5.

The author's original text used all of Isaiah 59:10 with its poignant description
of the human condition as blind and helpless prior to receiving God's light in
Christ.

> We grope like the blind along a wall,
> > groping like those who have no eyes;
> we stumble at noon as in the twilight,
> > among the vigorous as though we were dead.

Even though the canticle is printed to be read in unison, it would be effective to
read the lines of the text in alternation, with everyone joining on the sung
response. The canticle may be sung as follows: Response 1, Tone 4 in F minor;
Response 2, Tone 2 in D minor; and Response 3, Tone 3 in E minor. See 383, in
The United Methodist Hymnal Music Supplement for the pointed text.

Although the canticle was prepared for *Hymns and Psalms*, 1983, it appears
not to have been included in that collection.

Response 1

Words: Isa. 9:2, adapt.
Music: Carlton R. Young, 1987

This first response may be sung as a choir processional in a canon with voices entering every two measures.

Response 2

Words: Alan Luff, 1987
Music: Richard Proulx, 1987

Response 3

Words: trans. by Frederick Oakeley and others, 1841
Music: John F. Wade, ca. 1743

Canticle of love (646)
Let love be genuine

Rom. 12:9, 16; Song of Sol. 8:6-7
1 Cor. 13:4-8; Col. 3:12-14; 1 John. 3:18
Tob. 8:7; Pss. 127:1, 34:8
adapt. by S T Kimbrough, Jr.

S T Kimbrough, Jr. has described this canticle:

> [It stresses] the continuity of the biblical ideas of love that culminate in the love of Christ, [who] alone binds each heart and every relationship . . . [and] is the foundation of enduring relationships. While appropriate for marriages, the canticle emphasizes the inclusiveness of God's love for all persons in all relationships. (Sanchez 1989, 218)

Response 1

Words: John 15:12
Music: Gary Alan Smith, 1987

Response 2

Words: Eph. 5:30, 31b, adapt.
Music: Gary Alan Smith, 1987

Gary Alan Smith's second response may be played on the guitar/and or keyboard.

When using the printed sung response and singing the pointed text, the appropriate keys for them are as follows: Response 1, Tone 1 in Eb major; Response 2, Tone 5 in E minor. *The United Methodist Hymnal Keyboard Edition* contains the full accompaniment of this and all sung responses for psalms and canticles.

Canticle of Mary (199)
My soul proclaims the greatness of the Lord
Magnificat anima mea Dominum

Luke 1:46b-55, ICET, 1975; rev. ELLC, 1987

The canticle is about Mary, "a virgin engaged to a man whose name was Joseph," Luke 1:27a, who sings this hymn of joy and promise in response to the angel Gabriel's announcement in Luke 1:31-32,

> And now, you will conceive in your womb and bear a son, and you will name him Jesus. He will be great, and will be called the Son of the most High, and the Lord God will give him the throne of his ancestor David,

and Elizabeth's blessing in Luke 1:42b,

> Blessed are you among women, and blessed is the fruit of your womb.

The literary form and the text of the canticle come largely from Hannah's prayer in 1 Samuel 2:1-10. Fred D. Gealy writes:

> Because of the influence of the Mary cultus of the Middle Ages, it was the text most frequently set to music, next to the mass. Therefore its very powerful lines became widely known.

> In the Eastern Church it was used at early Morning Prayer at least from the fourth century. St. Benedict, sixth century, appointed it for Vespers, probably following Roman usage. This determined its place in *The Book of Common Prayer*, 1549, in the office of Evening Prayer, between the Old and New Testament lessons. (Gealy, Lovelace, Young 1970, 454-55)

This New Testament hymn summarizes the Hebrew scripture's declaration that God is seen and experienced in the humble, poor, homeless, parentless, and hungry. As a liturgical text it has been set for congregation and choir to both plainsong and Anglican chant. Since the seventeenth century it has been set as an extended choral work by Dunstable, Dufay, Binchois, Lassus, Palestrina, and Schütz. Monteverdi, J. S. Bach, and others into the nineteenth and twentieth centuries have composed it in concerted style for choir, soloists, and instruments. Anglican composers have used it with its companion the "Song of Simeon" in choral settings of the Full Service.

The canticle entered our hymnals in traditional language in 1905. The text for this hymnal is from the Ecumenical Liturgical Language Consultation (ELLC) who modified an earlier text developed by the International Consultation on English Texts to make it inclusive of persons and deity nonsexist. The canticle is found in metrical paraphrase in "Tell out my soul" **(200)** and "My soul gives glory to my God" **(198)**. Other hymns that relate to the canticle are "To a maid engaged to Joseph" **(215)**, "Ye who claim the faith of Jesus" **(197)**, "That boy-child of Mary" **(241)**, and stanza 1 of "The first one ever" **(276)**. Mary's Song along with Simeon's Song, "Lord, now let your servant depart in peace" **(225)**, are traditionally sung or read at evening services of praise and prayer. The canticle may be sung to Tone 3 in F major. See 382 in *The United Methodist Hymnal Music Supplement* for the pointed text.

Response

Words: Isa. 40:5, adapt.
Music: Richard Proulx, 1987

Canticle of Moses and Miriam (135)
Cantemus Domino

Exod. 15:1-6, 11-13, 17-18, 20, 21
This is one of the oldest of scripture songs. It celebrates God's victory in the deliverance of Israel from Egyptian bondage and death. In a Christian setting it is particularly appropriate, along with Psalm 150 **(862)**, for the Easter vigil, Easter Day, the Easter season, and for general use whenever the community is celebrating God's and our saving acts of liberation and reconciliation. The song begins and ends with Miriam's song of victory, which tradition teaches might have been composed by an eyewitness to the event:

> Sing to the Lord, for he has
> triumphed gloriously;
> horse and rider he has thrown into
> the sea.

The canticle is set on a facing page to the African American spiritual "O Mary, don't you weep, don't you mourn," proclaiming the God in the Hebrew song of triumph is the same God revealed in Christ's mighty resurrection and the source of the Christian's songs of hope both now and at the apocalypse. The "new Miriam" is both Mary at the foot of the cross (John 19:25) and Mary Magdalena at the tomb (John 20:11-18).

Concerning this text Maxine Clarke Beach has written: "The Hebrew word 'israre,' the root for dancing, is similar to the one used for giving birth." Beach also states that "Miriam had a near cult following in part of the early church. The community would eat, and then dance—singing songs of Miriam." (Unpublished research furnished to Carlton R. Young, 1990)

Response

Words: Ps. 21:13
Music: Carlton R. Young, 1987
The response should be sung with force and vigor, adding instruments and dance in the spirit of verse 20:

Then the prophet Miriam, Aaron's sister, took a tambourine in her hand; and all the women went out after her with tambourines and with dancing.

The refrain of "O Mary, don't you weep, don't you mourn" and the response to Psalm 150, "Alleluia," are also appropriate sung responses. All canticles have been pointed for chanting in *The United Methodist Hymnal Music Supplement*, 373-89. This canticle may be sung using Tone 2 in C minor; see 379 in *The United Methodist Hymnal Music Supplement*.

Canticle of praise to God (91)
Venite Exultemus

Pss. 95:1-7b; 96:9, 13

Massie H. Shepherd, Jr., has described this canticle:

> The Venite is a jubilant summons to the whole world of nature and man to worship its Creator, Provider, and Judge, with joy and with thanksgiving, in beauty and in awe. With consummate art it weaves together the principal themes of all true worship: the majesty and glory of God manifest in the created order which [God] has made and over which [God] presides, [God's] tender care and providence for his people as of a shepherd for his flock and the stern but just demands of righteousness and truth that he makes upon them as their final Judge. This last, ethical note is particularly characteristic of Jewish and Christian worship, and saves it from both sentimentality and irresponsibility. (Shepherd 1955, 10)

Psalm 95 was taken into Christian worship as a hymn of praise celebrating God who is creator, sustainer, sovereign, and judge. It was first prescribed for daily use by the Benedictine Rule, sixth century, for the "vigil," or matins, a service of praise and prayer held after midnight. According to Fred D. Gealy:

> From this use it entered the Roman (1568) and Sarum [Anglo] (pre-Reformation) breviaries. In 1549 it was set in its familiar place [using the version from the Great Bible of 1539] in *The Book of Common Prayer* of the Church of England, after the Prayer of Absolution and the Lord's Prayer. (Gealy, Lovelace, Young 1970, 455-56)

Verses 7c-11 of the psalm were set aside by the USA Episcopal Church in its prayer book of 1789 as harsh and judgmental, lacking the essential spirit of praise in the balance of the psalm. Verses 9 and 13 were substituted from Psalm 96. Verse 9 continues the sense of awe in Psalm 95:1-7b, and verse 13 substitutes the universal qualities of judgment for God's particular complaint against [the Hebrew] people,

> whose hearts go astray,
> and they do not regard my ways.
> Therefore in my anger I swore,
> "They shall not enter my rest."
>
> (Psalm 95:10b-11)

In Anglican worship practice the synthesized canticle is often called "the Venite" (usually pronounced in its anglicized form, *Veh-nahee-tee*) from the opening Latin word of Psalm 95. The "Glory be to the Father" (see comments, page 355) is a Christian doxology to the Trinity and is not verse 10, as might be inferred. Its inclusion as an option after the canticle expresses the traditional linkage of Hebrew and Christian worship traditions, in common praising the one God of all people. It is not an improvement or purification of "inferior" Hebrew scripture with "superior" Christian scripture.

Boyce chant

Attr. to William Boyce, 1770

This chant, according to Robert Guy McCutchan, is from William Boyce's *Divine Harmony, Being a Collection of Two Hundred and Seven Double and Single Chants in Score, Ancient and Modern*, London, 1770. In this book the chant is accredited to "Mr. David." (McCutchan 1942, 561) The chant was included in Wesleyan songbooks as early as Rigdon M. McIntosh's *Tabor*, 1867, chant number 15, page 287. With a slight harmonic alteration it entered our hymnals in 1878. In 1905 the harmonies were again slightly altered, and the text was pointed for chanting. The 1935 hymnal maintained these changes and transposed it from D down to C. In the 1966 book the pointing was slightly changed after the version in *The Hymnal 1940*. The present hymnal returns to the 1905 pointing. Austin C. Lovelace has provided "Instructions for Chanting" at number 662, *The Methodist Hymnal*, 1966. See Anglican chant in "Music of the Hymnal," page 168. Note that the music for verse 8 is also used for verse 9.

The canticle may be sung as a call to worship, as a gathering, or as a general hymn of praise. There are many choral settings of the canticle from Latin, German, and English choral traditions.

Canticle of prayer (406)
We do not know how to pray

Alan Luff, 1962 (Rom. 8:26; Luke 11:9-10)

This canticle is a product of the Dunblane Scottish Churches' Consultation on Church Music, begun in 1962, and is a collaboration of two of the most prominent and creative forces in the British hymnic explosion (see "British Hymns," pages 16-17). The text is from the Revised Standard Version of the Bible and with the tune was first published under the title "Prayer Canticle" in *New Songs for the Church: Book 2, Canticles,* 1969, edited by Erik Routley and Reginald Barrett-Ayers.

The text has been altered for this hymnal as follows: in the antiphon, "but the Spirit himself intercedes for us" has been changed to "but the Spirit intercedes for us"; verse 2 originally read:

> For everyone who asks receives,
> And he who seeks finds,
> And to him who knocks it will be opened.

In order to render the text inclusive regarding persons it was changed:

> For all who ask receive,
> and all who seek find;
> and to those who knock it will be opened.

Prayer canticle

Erik Routley, 1969

The canticle may be sung as a call to prayer with soloists or a group singing the verses, and the congregation joining on the response. The tune is composed in the style of Gelineau psalms with one slow pulse per measure in both the antiphon and the verses (see the notational equivalents printed under the second score on the hymn). The canticle first appeared in USA hymnals in *Ecumenical Praise,* 1977, number 110, and, except for this hymnal, it has not been used in any denominational hymnal to date. John Wilson composed a tasteful six-measure intonation for *Sixteen Hymns of To-day for Use as Simple Anthems,* 1978. It is included at number 545 in the British Methodist *Hymns and Psalms.*

The canticle was sung in Westminster Abbey at the memorial service of the composer, February 8, 1983.

Canticle of redemption (516)
Out of the deep
De Profundis

Ps. 130

S T Kimbrough, Jr., has described the psalm:

> [It] is the cry of a sincerely penitent person . . . [to whom] God's grace and forgiveness give strength and assurance to rise from despair. The psalm declares that forgiveness is a reality because God is with us. . . . It ends with a testimony to God's unfailing mercy. (Sanchez 1989, 176)

Fred D. Gealy has written about the canticle from a Wesleyan perspective:

Psalm 130 is a [personal as well as a national] penitential psalm which issues from a confident trust and joyful assurance of salvation. It is of special interest to Methodists because of its association with John Wesley's search for "justifying, saving faith." On the afternoon of May 24, 1738, he was asked to go to St. Paul's, London, where "the anthem [usually attributed to William Croft] was 'Out of the deep have I called unto Thee, O Lord: Lord, hear my voice. . . . O Israel, trust in the Lord: for with the Lord there is mercy, and with Him is plenteous redemption.'" It was that evening when he went "very unwillingly" to the Aldersgate Street society, where his heart was "strangely warmed." (Gealy, Lovelace, Young 1970, 458)

The psalm first appeared in our hymnals in 1905 coupled with Psalm 131 as the second reading for the evening of the forty-fifth Sunday, page 66. In the 1935 hymnal it was included as the second reading for church anniversaries and as an "Ancient Canticle" in a chant setting, number 640. Our 1966 hymnal continued the psalm in formats for speaking and reading. After the determination was made that only a few churches regularly sang the canticles, the Hymnal Revision Committee opted for taking them from the back of the hymnal where they had been ensconced since 1878 and spreading them within the classification scheme of the hymnal. With one exception, they are set in the same read/sung format of the psalms.

There are three versions of the psalm text in our hymnal: this canticle in the Great Bible version; the version included in the Psalter as Psalm 130 **(848)** in the New Revised Standard Version; and the psalm at **873** in the "Service of Death and Resurrection," slightly altered from the Revised Standard Version of the Bible, 1946. The psalm is also included in metrical paraphrase in "Out of the depths I cry to you" **(515)**. The canticle is appropriate for Easter vigil, evening, funeral, memorial, and healing services.

Response

Words: Ps. 120:1-2, adapt.
Music: Jane Marshall, 1987
Jane Marshall's simple and plaintive response may be sung without accompaniment. The canticle may also be sung using Tone 4 in G minor. See *The United Methodist Hymnal Music Supplement*, 386.

Canticle of remembrance (652)

Wisd. of Sol. 3:1-9, adapt.
The canticle is from a teaching attributed to King Solomon, contrasting the blessed state of the righteous at peace with God and enjoying immortality, and the punishment to be meted out to the ungodly; the former, according to

Floyd V. Filson in *The New Oxford Annotated Bible*, "[will enjoy] a gift of God to the righteous, not [as] the result of having an immortal or spiritual 'soul.'" (Metzger and Murphy 1991, 58)

S T Kimbrough, Jr., has described the canticle:

> [It affirms] what the Bible says from beginning to end: "Those who trust in God will understand truth, and the faithful will abide in love" [verse 9a], because God's grace and mercy reign over the faithful. (Sanchez 1989, 220)

The text appears to have entered our hymnals in 1935, page 633, as the second reading for use in commemorative services. It was also included in the 1966 hymnal with a different selection of verses. The text in our present hymnal was prepared by Harrell Beck who was noted for his depth of understanding and appreciation for the wisdom literature in Hebrew scripture. The canticle is appropriate for services of death and resurrection, All Saints, and Heritage Sunday.

Response 1

Words: Wisd. of Sol. 3:1-9, adapt.
Music: Gesangbuch, Meiningen, 1693
adapt. by Timothy E. Kimbrough, 1987

Response 2

Words: Ps. 28:7
Music: Jane Marshall

There are two contrasting settings for the canticle; both need to be sung accompanied. The entire canticle may also be sung. For Response 1 use Tone 1 in D major; Response 2, Tone 4 in A minor. See 338 in *The United Methodist Hymnal Music Supplement*.

Canticle of Simeon (225)
Lord, now let your servant go in peace
Nunc Dimittis

Luke 2:29-32; ICET, 1975; rev. ICEL

Simeon, a "righteous and devout" man living in Jerusalem at the time of the birth of Jesus, proclaims that Jewish messianic hope, i.e., the consolation and redemption of Israel, has been fulfilled in the child Jesus. The occasion is the act of purification (see Leviticus 12:1-8 and Exodus 13:2, 12) usually referred to as the presentation of Jesus at the temple.

> Guided by the Spirit, Simeon came into the temple; and when the parents brought in the child Jesus, to do for him what was customary under the law, Simeon took him in his arms and praised God, saying

> Master, now you are dismissing your servant in peace,
>   according to your word;
> for my eyes have seen your salvation,
>   which you have prepared in the presence of all peoples,
> a light for revelation to the Gentiles
>   and for glory to your people Israel.   (Luke 2:27-32)

At the conclusion of his song Simeon blesses the parents and prophesies:

> This child is destined for the falling and the rising of many in Israel, and to
> be a sign that will be opposed so that the inner thoughts of many will be
> revealed—and a sword will pierce your soul too.   (Luke 2:34-35)

This canticle is one of the earliest biblical songs with continuous use in Christian worship, having been sung or read at the evening offices of the Western church since the fourth century. It became the canticle for compline in Roman and Sarum breviaries, and was also sung in procession before the mass on the Feast of Purification. In evening services of praise and prayer it is placed between the reading from Christian scripture and the Apostles' Creed. Massie Shepherd has written, "As the Magnificat [see pages 257-58] looks forward to the Incarnation, this canticle looks back upon it as an accomplished fact." (Shepherd 1955, 29) The song was sung by Calvinists at the conclusion of Holy Communion and, according to Fred D. Gealy (557/misc.), was included in metrical paraphrase in the Genevan Psalter. Martin Luther in 1524 composed an extended hymn from the canticle, "Mit Fried und Freud ich fahr dahin" (translated by Catherine Winkworth, 1863, "In peace and joy I now depart").

Johann Walther's tune was arranged by J. S. Bach for his *Orgelbüchlein (Little Organ Book)* and may be appropriately performed in conjunction with the singing or reading of the canticle in a service that celebrates "The Presentation of Our Lord" each year on February 2.

The canticle is pointed for chanting in *The United Methodist Hymnal Music Supplement*, page 386. When it is sung at evening prayer, Tone 1 in D major is suggested; at Christmas or other occasions, Tone 1 in Bb major is suggested. Our hymnal also includes the canticle in paraphrase, "My master, see, the time has come" **(226)**

Response

Words: Ps. 72:11
Music: Richard Proulx, 1975

Canticle of thanksgiving (74)
Make a joyful noise unto the Lord
Jubilate Deo

Ps. 100, Book of Common Prayer, 1552

Psalm 100 is a psalm of praise that some scholars suggest may be a doxology and/or a summary of the preceding psalms, 93-99, that celebrate God's rule over all the earth and its peoples. According to Fred D. Gealy,

> Psalm 100 was used in both Temple and synagogue services from ancient times, from which it entered Morning Prayer services of the Church. The psalm was introduced into the 1552 *Book of Common Prayer* as an alternative to the Benedictus [because Puritans disliked New Testament psalms]. It has been included in our hymnals since 1878, and according to tradition in the version of the Great Bible, 1539. (Gealy, Lovelace, Young 1970, 455)

The text appears in three translations in our present hymnal: the canticle in the version from the 1552 *Book of Common Prayer*; **821** in the Psalter from the New Revised Standard Version of the Bible; and in metrical paraphrase, "All people that on earth do dwell" **(75)**. The canticle may be used by the choir and congregation as a call to worship or as a general act of praise.

Response 1

Words: Charles Wesley, adapt.
Music: Timothy E. Kimbrough, 1987

Response 2

Words: Edward H. Plumptre, 1865
Music: Arthur H. Messiter, 1889

Keys suggested for chanting the psalm are F minor when using Response 1, and F major when using Response 2. See page 374 in *The United Methodist Hymnal Music Supplement.*

Canticle of the Holy Trinity (80)
We praise you, O God
Te Deum Laudamus

4th-5th cent. hymn, ICET, 1975; rev. ELLC, 1987

Millar Patrick in *The Story of the Church's Song* has provided this description of the Te Deum:

> It is unsurpassed as a confession of the church's faith and a testimony of its thanksgiving. Its comprehensiveness, the grandeur of its conceptions, the incomparable dignity of its language, the moving transition from adoration to confession and supplication, and the final mounting of its confidence to the quiet but firm assertion of the faith that a soul settled on the rock of these triumphant certainties will never be confounded—*In te, Domine, speravi: non confundar in aeternum*—combine to give it an unchallenged place as the greatest of all the hymns of "the Holy church throughout the world." (Patrick 1927, 28)

Both hymns of praise to God: Father, Son, and Spirit—the Te Deum and the Gloria in Excelsis, "Glory to God in the Highest" **(82, 83)**—stem in part from anonymous second-century Greek sources according to M. Alfred Bichsel:

> The *hymnos eothinos*, or morning hymn, is an expansion of the greater doxology, *Doxa en ypsistis theo* (Glory to God in the highest). Closer examination reveals that one verse is later found toward the end of the *Te Deum*. [See discussion of part 3, below.] (Stulken 1981, 5)

John Julian in *A Dictionary of Hymnology* (1907, 1119-34), provides an extensive article on the Te Deum. The most thorough recent coverage of this hymn is by Wesley Milgate:

> The hymn properly consists of two parts. Part I is a praise to the Trinity from earth and heaven, with the *tersanctus* of angels (Isaiah 6:3, Revelation 4:8) in its Latin, or Western, form followed by a "confession" of the Church on earth (reminiscent of phrases used in chapter 26 of St. Cyprian's *De Mortalitate*, ca. 252 AD) and ending with a trinitarian acclamation. Part II is a continuous hymn to Christ which probably, by its trinitarian emphasis, reflects the combatting of Arianism in the 4th cent., and which closes with an antiphon, "Come then, Lord." Later a third part was added to the hymn, being a litany made up of two antiphons ["Save your people, Lord" (Psalm 28:9) and "Day by day we bless you"], followed by suffrages (versicles and responses) taken almost entirely from Psalms 123:3; 33:22; 31:1 (71:1). This litany probably originated in part from an early addition to the Great Doxology (*Gloria in excelsis*) [see above]; it appears to make use of St. Jerome's second revision of the Psalter (the "Gallican" Psalter) 388 A.D. (Milgate 1985, 19)

The earliest extant version of the hymn is contained in the late seventh-century antiphonary of the Celtic church monastery at Bennchar (Bangor), Ireland. Scholars have usually attributed the first use of parts 1 and 2 to southeast Gaul and Milan, and its authorship to Nicetas, Bishop of Remesiana, Dacia (Yugoslavia), from 392 until 414. Milgate cites the recent work of Ernst Kähler (*Studien zum Te Deum* 1958), who has posed the possibility that the hymn was probably written in North Africa in the middle of the fourth century. (Milgate 1985, 19) In the Roman rite it has been used in both the Saturday evening office as well as Sundays at matins along with the Gloria Patri.

The English text was prepared by Thomas Cranmer for the 1549 *Book of Common Prayer* where it was prescribed for daily use except during Lent; but the 1552 *Book of Common Prayer* removed this exception. (Shepherd 1955, 10-11) Today it is generally used at morning prayer. It was first included in our hymnals in 1878 in sixteen verses set to an Anglican chant in the back of the book where with the other canticles for over a century it has remained separated from the main body of Christian hymnody represented in our hymnals. The text of the canticle used in this present hymnal was prepared by the International Commission on English Texts, revised in 1987 by the English Language Liturgical Consultation.

The fourth line, part 2, "you humbly accepted the Virgin's womb," is reflected in stanza 4 of "O come, all ye faithful" **(234)**:

> True God of true God,
> Light from Light Eternal,
>   lo, he shuns not the Virgin's womb.

In 1744 the Latin text was translated and metricized into German. An English translation of that hymn by Clarence Walworth, with additional stanzas by F. Bland Tucker, is found at **79**, "Holy God, we praise thy name." The canticle is pointed for singing on page 375 in *The United Methodist Hymnal Music Supplement*, using Tone 1 in A$^\flat$ major.

Response

Words: Johann J. Schütz, 1675; trans. by Frances E. Cox, 1864
Music: Kirchengesänge, 1566

Canticle of wisdom (112)

Wisd. of Sol. 7:15, 24-30, adapt. by Harrell Beck, 1987

This prayer for wisdom, attributed to Solomon (see antecedents in 1 Kings 3:11a, 12b, "Indeed I give you a wise and discerning mind; and 2 Chronicles 1:10, "Give me now wisdom and knowledge"), was adapted by Harrell Beck who selected portions to construct a synthetic canticle. Solomon's prayer reflects other prayers and pleas for wisdom found in Job, Psalms, and Ecclesiastes. The psalms text subcommittee of the 1989 hymnal attributed female gender to wisdom, citing Solomon's prayer as well as Proverbs 1:20-33 that personifies wisdom as a prophetess. In chapter 8 "Lady Wisdom" is described as being of divine origin before anything was created, and in Sirach 24:1, 3, "Wisdom praises herself and tells of her glory in the midst of her people. . . . 'I came forth from the mouth of the Most high, and covered the earth like a mist.'" The presentation to the full committee occurred in the midst of its continuing heated discussions about the political "wisdom" of including female attributions and forms of address to deity in hymns (see *"The United Methodist Hymnal*, 1989," pages 141-42). The full committee entered into considerable debate and in the end agreed to accept the psalms text subcommittee's recommendation, as well as that of Hebrew Scripture!

The canticle is pointed for singing on page 375, *The United Methodist Hymnal Music Supplement*; and E$^\flat$ major is recommended as the key for Response 1, Tone 3; and E minor for Response 2, Tone 5.

Response 1

Words: Harrell Beck, 1987
Music: Carlton R. Young, 1987

Response 2

Words: Henry Sloane Coffin, 1916
Music: 15th cent. French

Canticle of Zechariah (208)
Blessed be the Lord
Benedictus

Luke 1:68-79: ICET, 1975; rev. ELLC, 1987

Fred D. Gealy has written about this canticle as follows:

> The *Benedictus* . . . is a Messianic hymn, made up largely of Old Testament passages. It may have been independently composed in Aramaic or Hebrew, then used with reference to John the Baptist, and then adapted for Christian use.
>
> Its medieval use was as the canticle for Lauds, the service at dawn at which psalms 148-50, in which *laudate* (praise ye) often occurs, were sung. In *The Book of Common Prayer*, 1549, when parts of Lauds and Matins were combined to form the office of Morning Prayer, the Benedictus was assigned to a place after the New Testament lesson. The version is that of the Great Bible, 1539. (Gealy, Lovelace, Young 1970, 443)

An abridged version of the canticle was included in our 1878 hymnal, page 435, verses 68-71, plus the Gloria Patri, pointed and set to a chant. The full text of the canticle was first included in our 1935 hymnal. It was also in our 1966 book. For further commentary on the biblical text, see "Blessed be the God of Israel" **(209)**. Our text is an inclusive rendering by the psalms text subcommittee of the revision of the text that had been prepared the International Consultation on English Texts and revised by the English Language Liturgical Consultation. The canticle is pointed for singing using Tone 5 in F major. See page 384, *The United Methodist Hymnal Music Supplement*.

Response

Words: James Montgomery, 1821
Music: Gesangbuch der H. W. k. Hofkapelle, 1784

See "Hail to the Lord's Anointed," page 385.

Child of blessing, child of promise (611)

Ronald S. Cole-Turner, 1981

The hymn first appeared in *Everflowing Streams*, 1981, page 51, and was sung at the baptism of the author's daughter, Rachel Elizabeth, June 13, 1982. The text appears without alteration with one exception: in stanza 4:1, "the loving Parent" has been changed to "your loving Parent." The author has suggested a change in stanza 1 when the hymn is used in a service of infant dedication.

Since this is a rite outside the parameters of United Methodist sacramental theology, the committee did not include this version of stanza 1:2-3:

> Child of blessing, child of promise,
> Consecrated and assigned,
> To the care of God who claims you
> Unto love and grace divine.

This is one of several hymns in the "Baptism, Confirmation, Reaffirmation" section of the hymnal, **604-11,** suggested for use with the Baptismal Covenant II,
"Holy baptism for children and others unable to answer for themselves," pages
39-43. The first two stanzas of the hymn may be sung by the congregation and
choir following the pastor's invitation and as the child, parents, family, and
friends approach the font. Stanzas 3 and 4 may be sung at the conclusion of the
service, page **43,** following the pastor's address to those who have been baptized.

Stuttgart

Attrib. to C. F. Witt, 1715; adapt. by Henry J. Gauntlett, 1861

The source of the tune is *Psalmodia Sacra, oder, Andächtige und schöne Gesange,*
Gotha, 1715, edited by A. C. Ludwig and C. F. Witt. The original melody,
attributed to Witt, is reproduced on page 174 of *Historical Companion to Hymns
Ancient and Modern.* The tune was adapted in its present form, harmonized, and
named "Stutgard" by Henry J. Gauntlett for *Hymns Ancient and Modern,* 1861,
page 47. Gauntlett's harmonization was altered, and new material, usually
attributed to Vaughan Williams, was added for *The English Hymnal,* 1906.
Another harmonization, presumed to be the work of David Evans, was prepared for the 1927 rev. ed. of *The Church Hymnary.* Another harmonization is
found without citation, number 13, in *The Hymnary,* United Church of Canada,
1930. This latter harmonization entered our hymnals without attribution in 1935
for hymn 75. The 1966 hymnal used the tune five times. Portions of the 1861,
1906, 1927, and 1930 harmonizations were excerpted and appear in four slightly
different settings. The harmonization from *The Hymnary,* hymn 334, is included
in our present hymnal. There is a vocal descant by Lois Fyfe at number 324 in
The United Methodist Hymnal Music Supplement.

Child so lovely (222)

See "Niño lindo," pages 493-94.

Children of the heavenly Father (141)
Tryggare kan ingen vara

Caroline Wilhelmina Sandell-Berg, 1855
trans. by Ernst W. Olson, 1925

Marilyn Kay Stulken in *Hymnal Companion to the Lutheran Book of Worship* provides the most recent information about this hymn and its tune, including the

date of its composition. Most commentaries state that the hymn was written by Sandell, "the Fanny Crosby of Sweden," in 1858 in a time of grief caused by the death of her father by drowning. Stulken presents new information in this regard: "The present text was written while [Karolina] was still in her teens and [first] appeared in her *Andeliga daggdroppar* in 1855." (Stulken 1981, 496)

The translation, titled "A Hymn Born of a Broken Heart,"was made by Ernst William Olson for *The Hymnal*, 1925, published by the Augustana Synod. Most hymnals include four of the original six stanzas. The two omitted stanzas are as follows:

> Lo, their very hairs he numbers,
> And no daily care encumbers
> Them that share his every blessing,
> And his help in woes distressing.
>
> Praise the Lord in joyful numbers:
> Your Protector never slumbers.
> At the will of your Defender
> Every foeman must surrender.

The English words in stanza 2:3, "For all evil things he spares us," fly in the face of those in pain or grief, believer or unbeliever. The literal translation provided by Gracia Grindal is a better expression of the mystery of God's providence: "No one can be safer than the children of God who holds us faster than the stars or the birds in heaven." (See An Interpretation: "'Children of the Heavenly Father.'" *The Hymn*, October 1988.)

The hymn entered our hymnals in 1957 in five stanzas. Four stanzas were printed in our 1966 hymnal; the text is included in our present book without alteration.

Tryggare kan ingen vara

Swedish Melody

The name of this folk melody is from the first line of the Swedish, literally, "No one can be safer." The first wedding of the tune and text in Sweden was in Fredrik Engelke's *Lofsånger och andeliga wisor*, 1873. In the USA they were printed together in the Augustana Lutheran Synod's edition of *Hemlandssånger*, 1890. (The latter information was first supplied by Joel W. Lundeen in a letter to Austin C. Lovelace, September 1965. [Gealy 556/73])

Stulken cites the research of Oscar Lövgren in *Den Segrande Sången*, which states that the tune is a Swedish folk song discovered by Fredrik Engelke, with German origins. She concludes:

> With so many variants in at least two countries at the beginning of the nineteenth century, it seems very possible that the tune has antecedents in the 1700's, which perhaps remain to be discovered. (Stulken 1981, 496)

Christ for the world we sing (568)

Samuel Wolcott, 1869

The theme of a convention in Cleveland, Ohio, of the YMCA, February 7, 1869, was "Christ for the world, and the world for Christ." The words of the theme were constructed with evergreen branches and displayed above the speaker's platform. After reflecting on the theme and immediately upon returning to the parsonage of the Plymouth Congregational Church, where he was pastor, the author wrote this hymn. It first appeared in W. H. Doane's *Songs of Devotion for Christian Associations*, 1870, entered our hymnals in 1889 and most evangelical hymnals in Great Britain by the 1920's. The text appears in our present hymnal with the author's original four stanzas.

Italian hymn

Felice de Giardini, 1769

Our 1957 hymnal was the first to match this tune and text. The tune was written for the anonymous hymn "Come, thou almighty King" (**61**) and was first published in Martin Madan's *Collection of Psalm-Tunes never published before*, 1769, sold for the benefit of the Lock Hospital where Madan served as chaplain. The composer contributed four tunes to that collection. It was reprinted several times including once in the USA in Boston, 1809. In Great Britain where the tune is also named "Moscow," it is sung in a slightly different form from the version in our hymnal, one that is closer to the original melody. Other names for the tune are "Trinity," "Fairford," "Florence," "Hermon," and "Giardini's."

The tune in another harmonization and one step lower in F major is found at 185 in *The United Methodist Hymnal Music Supplement*, followed at 186 with a vocal descant in G major.

Christ, from whom all blessings flow (550)

Charles Wesley, 1740

This hymn is an eloquent statement on the unity within our diversity we seek and already have in Christ, and our interdependence on one another as members in the body of Christ. The poem entitled "Communion of Saints" originally consists of six parts with thirty-nine stanzas of eight lines, and first appeared in five eight-line stanzas in the section "Communion of Saints," under part four, page 194, in *Hymns and Sacred Poems*, 1740. In 1780 John Wesley sectioned the hymn into ten four-line stanzas. The stanzas selected for this present hymnal are 1, 2, 5, 6, 9, 10.

Wesley uses Paul's listing of the virtues and attributes of and the arguments for the unity in Christ, which he expounded on in 1 Corinthians 12:4-31 and

Ephesians 4:1-15. Hildebrandt and Beckerlegge have noted the parallel between our stanza 6 and Matthew Prior's *Solomon*, 2, 241-42 (Wesley 1983, 7:694):

> Or grant, thy passion has these names destroyed;
> That love, like death, makes all distinctions void.

The hymn was first included in our hymnals in *A Selection of Hymns*, 1810, dropped from our 1905 and 1955 books and restored in 1966. Our hymnal has added stanzas 4 and 5. In our stanza 4:1-2, "Never from our office move, needful to the others prove" has been changed to "Never from thy service move, needful to each other prove."

Canterbury

Adapt. from Orlando Gibbons, 1623

Orlando Gibbons composed his complete output of sixteen tunes to be appended to George Wither's *Hymns and Songs of the Church*, 1623. Gibbons marked each tune with the number of the song in the collection for which it was written. This tune, "Song 13," was intended to be sung to Wither's metrical paraphrase of the Song of Solomon beginning at chapter 4, "Oh, my Love! How comely now, And how beautiful art thou!"

Wither's collection is significant, according to Erik Routley in *Companion to Congregational Praise*, 1953, because it is one of only a few collections of congregational song published between 1551 and 1700 that is a book of songs rather than a psalter. Wither's appraisal of Gibbons's tunes is stated in preface to the collection:

> [He] hath chosen to make his music agreeable to the matter, and what the common apprehension can best admit, rather than the curious fancies of the time. (Lightwood 1935, 30)

Gibbons's tunes were reintroduced in 1856 by Edward Farr in the foreword to the reprint in which he discusses the great controversy that Wither's collection had aroused in the essentially psalm-singing English church. Gibbons's tunes were scored for melody and bass, and were set in a rhythmic and modal style that was maintained by Ralph Vaughan Williams in *The English Hymnal*, 1906, hymn 413. Nevertheless, the several adaptations of his arrangement have made the tune sound like a traditional but good devotional Victorian setting. The tune entered our hymnals in 1966 in this style.

Of all the new tunes introduced in the 1966 hymnal CANTERBURY has been the most widely accepted. Ralph Vaughan Williams's harmonization is included in *The Hymnal 1982*, number 670. A vocal descant may be found at number 53, *The United Methodist Hymnal Music Supplement*. Marilyn Kay Stulken discusses the tune in "The Hymn Tunes of Orlando Gibbons," in the October 1982 volume of *The Hymn*.

Christ is alive (318)

Brian Wren, 1968, alt.

Brian Wren composed this hymn under the title "The crucified Lord" while he was the minister of Hockley Congregation Church, Essex, England. The following is the poet's account of the hymn's composition and the significant changes in the text:

(April 1968; last stanza revised 1978) Ten days after the assassination of Dr. Martin Luther King [Jr.], I and my congregation at Hockley, Essex, met to celebrate Easter. The hymn tried to do so with truth and integrity, in words that could be more widely applied. It also tries to reinterpret the biblical imagery of Christ 'reigning at the right hand of God.' Intended originally to suggest his majestic and universal sovereignty, and thus Christ's universal sovereign *presence* with the believer, the idea of Christ reigning 'above' now connotes remoteness, and lack of involvement with everyday life. Hence stanzas 3-4, which try to redress the balance. The final stanza (see *New Church Praise* [1975], no. 9) was rewritten to remove the masculine metaphors in the original (he rules . . . to every man displayed), but, more particularly to catch the dynamism of the Holy Spirit. (Wren 1983, commentary on hymn 20)

Further changes were made by our Hymnal Revision Committee: stanza 3:1, "above" to "afar"; 3:4, "with the Father reigns" to "in the Godhead reigns." The final stanza was significantly changed from

> Christ is alive! His Spirit burns
>   through this, and every future age,
> till all creation lives and learns
>   his joy, his justice, love and praise.

The study of the chronology and the theology of the changes that have occurred in this text for more than two decades shows both the maturing and accommodation of one of our most important hymn writers of the "hymnic explosion" (see "British Hymns," pages 16-17), the impact on British hymn writing by the USA "market," and the insistence that texts should be inclusive in regard to people. It also reflects the beginnings of a concern in the USA for the nonsexist rendering of forms of address and metaphors for deity (see *"The United Methodist Hymnal*, 1989" pages 138-43).

Truro

Anon. in Psalmodia Evangelica, 1789

The tune first appeared without citation in part 2 of Thomas Williams's *Psalmodia Evangelica: A Collection of Psalms and Hymns in Three Parts for Public Worship*, 1789. British hymnals use versions of the tune closer to the original, while USA hymnals, according to Erik Routley, include "a corrupt text which was in currency in England in the 19th century." (Routley 1981, 72) A version very close to the original may be found at hymn 99 in Routley's *Rejoice in the Lord*, 1985. The tune entered our hymnals in the 1857 tune edition of the 1849 hymnal in the original key of D major. An alternate harmonization and vocal descant can be found at 334-35 in *The United Methodist Hymnal Music Supplement*.

Christ is made the sure foundation (559)
Angularis fundamentum

Ca. 7th cent. Latin; trans. by John Mason Neale, 1851

Fred D. Gealy has provided this commentary:

> Neale's translation of the ancient Latin hymn, variously dated from the sixth to the ninth century, was first published in his *Mediaeval Hymns and Sequences*, 1851, in 9 sts., the first line being "Blessed city, heavenly Salem." For *The Hymnal Noted*, 1851, it was revised and divided into 2 parts, the second beginning with stanza 5: "Christ is made the sure foundation." The hymn was subjected to a variety of alterations. The most lasting is the one made by the compilers of *Hymns Ancient and Modern*, 1861. . . . The Latin hymn occurs in the oldest extant hymnals and in many medieval breviaries was widely used for the dedication of a church. (Gealy, Lovelace, Young 1970, 131)

The Gealy research files (556/77) also include Neale's text in a plainsong setting, 44-45 in *The Hymnal Noted*, 1856; an English text with the translator's commentary, 18-21 in *Mediaeval Hymn and Sequences*, 1863; and 242-44 in the first edition of *Hymns Ancient and Modern*, 1861.

The text entered our hymnals in 1878 with three of the four stanzas from *Hymns Ancient and Modern*, 1861, hymn 244, without the doxology. Our present hymnal retains those three stanzas and the doxology that was restored in 1957. In stanza 2:3, "wonted" is changed to "faithful."

Westminster Abbey

Henry Purcell, ca. 1680; adapt. by Ernest Hawkins, 1843

The final Alleluias from Purcell's "O God, thou art my God," a verse anthem composed ca. 1680 and later included in William Boyce's *Cathedral Music*, 1760, were arranged by Ernest Hawkins as the hymn tune "Belleville" for *The Psalmist: A Collection of Psalm and Hymn Tunes*, 1843, and included in several nineteenth-century English hymnals. In 1939 Sydney Nicholson, music consultant for the revisions of *Hymns Ancient and Modern*, included the tune in the *Shortened Music Edition*, renaming it WESTMINSTER ABBEY, remembering Purcell who had served as organist, as had Nicholson, 1919-28. It was included in *Congregational Praise*, 1951, and other British hymnals, but it became more widely known after it was sung at the wedding of Princess Margaret in 1960. Erik Routley introduced the tune to the USA in his hymn festivals held during the late 1960's and early 1970's, and included it in *Westminster Praise*, 1977. In *Rejoice in the Lord*, hymn 392, there is vocal descant; and in hymn 599 Purcell's original harmonies are used. There is a vocal descant in *The United Methodist Hymnal Music Supplement*, 346.

Christ is risen (313)

See "Cristo Vive," page 311.

Christ is risen (307)

Brian Wren, 1984

The author composed this text to a tune by William P. Rowan and after the meter of a resurrection text by Frank von Christierson. "In writing, the rhythms and melody line of the music shaped the flow of the words, which then had to be looked at and finalized as a text." (Wren 1986, Notes on hymn 5)

The author introduced this and other hymns he had written in manuscript form at an early meeting of the hymns subcommittee of the 1989 hymnal. The text was approved for further consideration and sent to the tunes subcommittee who recommended setting it to Beethoven's rousing HYMN TO JOY **(89)**, rather than the tune to which the author wrote the hymn. This decision was communicated to the poet as part of a process assiduously maintained by the editor; the response was predictably negative, "Not my text with that tune!" Wren suggested using the Polish carol W ZLOBIE LEZY ("Infant holy, infant lowly," **229**) with its reflective qualities and musical connection of Christ's nativity and resurrection, a tune that aptly expresses the metaphors of a tree growing in the desert with "healing leaves of grace"; walking from "caverns of despair" into a morning of gladness"; and the triumph song "get you gone" sounding over the "demonic chorus."

A postscript: *The Presbyterian Hymnal*, 1990, set this text to HYMN TO JOY.

W zlobie lezy

Polish carol, arr. by Edith M. G. Reed, 1926
harm. by Austin C. Lovelace, 1963

The tune name means literally "In manger lying." Milgate has traced its first use in English hymnody to the 1877 edition of *The Hymnal Companion*, where it was called "Noel and given in equal notes in common time as the tune for 'Angels, from the realms of glory.'" (Milgate 1985, 104) It was first printed in a USA hymnal in our 1935 hymnal, number 105, in the version that appeared at number 39 in *School Worship*, 1926, published by the Congregational Union of England and Wales, George Thalben-Ball, editor. The photocopy of these pages from *School Worship* in Fred D. Gealy's research file (556/227) shows that each line begins on a downbeat, as it was in our 1935 hymnal and was maintained in Austin C. Lovelace's harmonization prepared for the 1966 hymnal. The music editor of the Presbyterian *Hymnbook*, 1955, David Hugh Jones, ignored the tune's subtle dance qualities and scored the tune with upbeats throughout, substituting a four-part choral setting, which negates the intimacy and innocence of the Polish carol. This version was included in our 1957 book as well as in our present hymnal. Our version of the tune, hymn **229**, also eliminates the arranger's appoggiatura and suspended cadence in the interludes. For further commentary, see "Infant holy, infant lowly," pages 433-34. Number 345 in *The United Methodist Hymnal Music Supplement* is an alternate harmonization of measures 8-16 scored for handbells and/or keyboard.

Christ is the world's light (188)

Fred Pratt Green, 1968, alt.

Fred Pratt Green was asked by the committee that produced *Hymns and Songs*, 1969, to write a text to the stirring tune CHRISTE SANCTORUM. Bernard Braley describes the poet's work in *The Hymns and Ballads of Fred Pratt Green:*

> [The meter of CHRISTE SANCTORUM calls for] Sapphic verse form which, excellent in Latin, is not suitable to the English language owing to its feminine line endings,
>
> Chri-ste, sanc-tor-um de-cus an-ge-lor-*um*
>
> To overcome this technical problem, Fred found a way of fitting words to the tune, strengthening the weak endings by the effective device of repeating the final words of lines 1, 2, and 3 in each verse and adding an emphatic last line. The metre adopted is in fact 10.11.11.6 rather than the Sapphic 11.11.11.5. (Green 1982, 5)

The hymn, titled "The Uniqueness of Christ," is based on John 8:12, Ephesians 2:14, John 1:4 and particularly 14:9, "The one who has seen me has seen the Father." It was first sung at a harvest thanksgiving service at Vale Royal Methodist Church, Tunbridge Wells, Kent, September 1968. First printed in *Hymns and Songs*, 1969, the hymn has been widely used in British and USA hymnals. Textual changes to avoid exclusive and male imagery were pressed upon the author, first by the USA Protestant Episcopal Church as it prepared the report to the General Assembly of 1982, containing the texts recommended for the proposed hymnal, then by other USA hymnal committees including our own.

Christe sanctorum

Paris Antiphoner, 1681; harm. by David Evans, 1927
For a discussion of the source of this tune see "Latin Hymns," page 6. The tune's name is literally "Christ, the fair glory of the holy angels." It was introduced to English hymnody by Ralph Vaughan Williams in his unison setting in E^b for *The English Hymnal*. This setting is also at hymn 1, *The Hymnal 1982*. The tune is used three times in this present hymnal with the harmonization by David Evans from *The Church Hymnary*, 1927 rev. ed. Number 64 in *The United Methodist Hymnal Music Supplement* is a vocal descant.

Christ Jesus lay in death's strong bands (319)
Christ lag in Todesbanden

Martin Luther, 1524; trans. by Richard Massie, 1854
Luther's mighty Easter hymn first appeared in seven stanzas of seven lines each in *Enchiridion*, Erfurt, 1524. Massie published his translation of the full hymn in *Martin Luther's Spiritual Songs*, 1854; it was later reduced to four stanzas for *Church Hymns*, 1871, and the first line changed from "Christ lay awhile in Death's strong bands" to its present form. The hymn entered our hymnals in 1966 in the version found in the 1882 edition of Godfrey Thring's *Church of England Hymn Book*.

The omitted stanzas:

2. No man from death could victory win,
     O'er all mankind he reigned;
   Alas! that cometh of our sin,
      There was not one unstained;
      Wherefore Death in triumph came,
   And over us a right did claim;
      He held us all in thraldom. Hallelujah!

3. Christ Jesus, God's own Son, came down
      That he might us deliver,
   And in destroying, took his crown
      From Death's pale brows for ever:
      Stript of power, no more he reigns:
   Empty shape alone remains;
      His sting is lost for ever. Hallelujah!

5. Here the true Paschal Lamb we see,
      Whom God so freely gave us;
   He died on the accursed tree
      So strong his Love!—to save us.
      See! his blood doth mark our door,

> Faith points to it; Death passes o'er,
> The Murderer cannot harm us. Hallelujah!

In our hymnal's stanza 2:7, "his" has been changed to "death."

Christ lag in Todesbanden

Geistliches Gesangbuchlein, 1524
harm. by J. S. Bach, 1724

See "Chorales," page 167. The chorale tune was adapted from the plainsong melody of the sequence for Easter, "Victimae Paschali laudes," probably by Johann Walther, editor of the Wittenberg *Geistliches Gesangbuchlein*. The setting in our present hymnal is the final movement of J. S. Bach's chorale cantata *Christ lag in Todesbanden*, S. 4. There are numerous other harmonizations including a rhythmic setting by Hans Leo Hassler, number 185 in *The Hymnal 1982*, and Erik Routley in *Rejoice in the Lord*, number 324. These may be sung in unison or in parts by the choir on either stanza 2 or 3. There are many settings of the chorale for organ including J. S. Bach's in his *Orgelbüchlein*.

Christ Jesus, though he was in the form of God (167)

See "Canticle of Christ's Obedience," page 252.

Christ loves the church (590)

Brian Wren, 1985

The author has written about this hymn:

> For Church/Anniversaries/Mission/Confirmation/Ordination. [Completed] July 3, 1985. Commissioned by High Street United Methodist church, Muncie, Indiana, for its 150th Anniversary Year, 1986. When we give thanks for the Church of Christ, we praise not ourselves, but God's grace, presence, and mission. We can't afford to be self-indulgent, nor yet refrain from being thankful. (Wren 1986, Notes on hymn 6)

In this instance the poet's imagery ("spinning gold from straw"), the skillful use of contrast ("the world's respect, or opposition"), alliteration ("Christ bears the Church, corrupted or conforming"), and economy of words (in stanza 1, of the 36 words only 6 have more than 1 syllable) tend to be diminished when set to music—any music. The hymn appears in our hymnal with only one change, in stanza 4:1, "so" to "to."

High Street

Jane Marshall's tune was approved by the committee at the same time as the text. The tunes subcommittee altered the bass line of her sturdy four-part tune in measures 2, 8, and 15, but unfortunately the composer never saw the changes until the hymnal was published. Because the first printing was 1,400,000 copies, it was agreed that the changes would remain to avoid the possible confusion of trying to sing or play from two different versions. The composer's tune in its original form may be found at number 6 in *Praising a Mystery*, 1986.

Christ, mighty Savior (684)
Christe, Lux mundi

Anon. 10th cent. Mozarabic; trans. by Alan G. McDougall, 1916
rev. by Anne K. LeCroy, 1982
Ray F. Glover, general editor of *The Hymnal 1982*, comments on this hymn:

The church's vast and rich treasury of ancient Latin office hymns is the source of the beautiful hymn for the third Sunday after Epiphany, "Christ, mighty Savior." Dr. Anne K. LeCroy . . . wrote this text which is based on an earlier translation of Alan G. McDougall of a nine-stanza anonymous 10th century Mozarabic evening hymn, "Christe, Lux mundi" in *Pange Lingue*, 1916. Both Dr. LeCroy and Mr. McDougall retained the metrical structure of the original, but the 1982 revision in contemporary English casts the text into a work of particular poetic beauty.

In this hymn, we, the faithful gathered at day's end, first give praise to the Creator who lights the day with brilliant sunlight and graces the evening with shimmering stars. We then pray for pardon, strength and rest. The hymn closes with a clear assurance that, even in our body's slumber (often a metaphor for death), our spirits will continue in this assurance of the peace of Jesus. (Glover 1987, 1)

Mighty Savior

David Hurd, 1983
[This tune] imparts . . . a quality of serenity. Particularly arresting is the rhythm of the last four measures which expands and emphasizes the verbal climax of each stanza. (Glover 1987, 2)

The tune and text first appeared in *The Hymnal 1982*, 1985. The composer has provided a vocal descant for stanza 4 at number 191 in *The United Methodist Hymnal Music Supplement*.

Christ the King (721)

Adapt. from the Book of Common Prayer, 1987

This prayer for God's restoration of all things through Christ, the sovereign of all creation, was adapted by the worship resources subcommittee from the *Book of Common Prayer*. It is placed in our hymnal with those hymns and acts of praise that proclaim the return and reign of the Lord, for example, "Rejoice, the Lord is King" **(715)**. The prayer is appropriate in the annual celebration of Christ the King, usually the Sunday just before Advent, within Advent, and for general use.

Christ the Lord is risen today (302)

Charles Wesley, 1739; and others

The text was first published under the title "Hymn for Easterday" in eleven four-line stanzas of 7's, page 149 in *Hymns and Sacred Poems*, 1739. In 1760 Martin Madan, *A Collection of Psalms and Hymns*, reduced the number of stanzas to eight. Because John Wesley did not include the hymn in his 1780 *Collection*, it did not come into use until 1831 in British Methodist hymnals, although it had been reprinted with "Hallelujah's" added in other collections, including T. Cotterill's *Selection of Psalms and Hymns*, 1823. The text entered our hymnals in 1849, hymn 152, with the first five of the original eleven stanzas. The hymn was sung to a variety of tunes until our 1905 book, number 156, matched it with the present tune and altered each line with the addition of the Hallelujah's. Hallelujah was changed to "Alleluia" in the 1935 hymnal. Our present hymnal includes seven stanzas; the second is the first couplet of Wesley's second and the second couplet of his third. The omitted couplets:

> Lo! our Sun's Eclipse is o'er,
> Lo! He sets in Blood no more.
>
> Vain the Stone, the Watch, the Seal;
> Christ has burst the Gates of Hell!

S T Kimbrough, Jr., has commented that "most versions conclude this hymn with the line 'Ours the cross, the grave the skies,'" the last line of original stanza 5. Our version restores the final two stanzas (original 10 and 11) and provides Wesley's "actualized definition of eternal life as here and now." (Correspondence with Carlton R. Young, September 1992)

In stanza 1:2, "sons of men and angels" has been changed to "earth and heaven in chorus."

In the research files of Fred D. Gealy are photocopies of the hymn from its first printing through the mid-nineteenth century. (Gealy 556/80)

Easter hymn

Anon. Lyra Davidica, 1708; alt. The Compleat Psalmodist, 1741
harm. anon. 19th cent.

James T. Lightwood in *The Music of the Methodist Hymn-Book* (1935, 149-50) provides an overview of the music and texts in John Walsh's *Lyra Davidica*, including a photocopy of the tune, melody and bass, as it appeared under the title "The Resurrection," set to the anonymous Latin Easter text "Jesus Christ is risen today." The melismatic and exuberant tune lives up to the compiler's purpose as stated in his preface:

> [To introduce] a little freer air than the grave movement of the Psalm-tunes . . . [as in] Germany, where they have abundance of divine songs and hymns, set to short and pleasant tunes . . . and have no such custom as we unhappily labour under, of ballads and profane songs. (Lightwood 1935, 150)

It is among the first of the hymn tunes composed in the emerging evangelical style that culminates in Thomas Campbell's SAGINA, 1835. The tune was altered and brought to its present form in succeeding editions of John Arnold's *Compleat Psalmodist*, 1741. John Wesley included the melody as "Salisbury Tune" in his 1742 *Foundery Collection*. S T Kimbrough, Jr. has commented: "Although Wesley did not include the text in his 1780 *Collection*, his apparent long-standing interest in the hymn is seen in his autographed copy of *Sacred Harmony*, 1780, where 'he crossed out G. F. Handel's tune 'Maccabes' and wrote 'Easter' (meaning "Easter Hymn") in the margin.'" (Correspondence with Carlton R. Young, September 1992)

Thomas Butts in his *Harmonia Sacra*, ca. 1754, named the tune "Christmas Day" and set it to Charles Wesley's "Hark, how all the welkin rings," later altered to "Hark, the herald angels sing" (**240**). In USA hymnals the tune was also linked to the Christmas hymn. A futile attempt was made to restore this relationship in the 1966 hymnal, hymn 387, where it was printed as the first tune with "Mendelssohn" the second tune, hymn 388. The tune is also called "Anglia," "Easter Morn," "The Resurrection," and "Worgan."

The tune first appeared in our hymnals in 1905 in D major using the harmonization in *Hymns Ancient and Modern*, 1861, second tune, number 171. The tune in its original form with Butts's modified bass is printed at number 108 in *The United Methodist Hymnal Music Supplement*. Vocal and instrumental descants are also included at number 107. The seven stanzas may be performed as an extended Easter processional, with the Alleluias sung alternately by the congregation, the choir, female, or male voices.

Christ the victorious (653)

Carl P. Daw, Jr., 1982

This text was prepared for *The Hymnal 1982* from the Eastern Orthodox Memorial Service as it appears in the Order for Burial in the *Book of Common Prayer*, 1990, pages 483-99. The author has provided this description:

This paraphrase [of the Kontakion for the Departed] was written specifically for the tune "Russia" in order to preserve some of the flavor of the original text for congregations unable to sing the traditional Kiev melody for the Kontakion.

1. "Victorious" is an intentional allusion to the Christus Victor view of atonement, most notably set forth by Gustav Aulen . . . and echoes the traditional exchange at prayers for the departed: "Rest eternal grant to them, O Lord; and let light perpetual shine upon them."

2. . . . The mystery of humanity's creation in the image of God (Genesis 1:26-27) is recalled by the expansion of the Kontakion text to include the adjective "glorious."

3. The second line of the third stanza quotes God's words to Adam (Genesis 3:19), which are also used on Ash Wednesday at the Imposition of Ashes. This language is further employed in the Burial Office. (Daw 1990, 148)

The hymn is appropriate for funerals, memorial services, and All Saints' Day.

Russian hymn

Alexis R. Lvov, 1833

In 1833 Emperor Nicholas decreed that Russia would have a new national anthem, "Bozhe, tsarya khrani" ("God save the Tsar"), replacing the one that had traditionally been sung to "God save the Queen." Lvov was commissioned to write the music and provides this account of its composition in his memoirs:

> I felt the necessity of composing what would be majestic, powerful, full of sentiment, comprehensible to all, suitable to the army and suitable to the people, from the learned to the illiterate. (Ellinwood 1956, 314)

It was first performed and officially adopted by the Russian army in 1833. As a hymn tune it was first printed in John Hullah's *Part Music*, 1842, to Henry F. Chorley's "God the all-terrible," a text that was written for the tune, as was Daw's text. It entered our hymnals with Chorley's text in 1878, hymn 1093. A vocal or instrumental descant for stanza 4 is printed at 289 in *The United Methodist Hymnal Music Supplement*.

Tschaikowsky used the tune in his *1812 Overture*.

Christ, upon the mountain peak (260)

Brian Wren, 1962

Brian Wren's second hymn, written in June 1962, retells the story of Jesus' mystical and nonearthly transfiguration, and his naming by God as "my Son, my

Chosen." The event probably took place on Mount Hermon, near Caesarea Philippi, and was witnessed by Peter, John, and James (see Matthew 17:1-8, Mark 9:2-8, Luke 9:28-36). Fulfilling the promise of Malachi 4:4-6, the Mark account links teaching and prophecy in the appearance of Moses, the lawgiver and foundation of Hebrew scripture, and Elijah, the charismatic prophet:

> Remember the teaching of my servant Moses, the statutes and ordinances that I commanded him at Horeb for all Israel.
> Lo, I will send you the prophet Elijah before the great and terrible day of the Lord comes.   (Malachi 4:4-5)

The hymn first appeared in *English Praise*, 1975, number 52. For our hymnal in stanza 3:3, "his" is changed to "the."

Shillingford

Peter Cutts, 1962

The tune, skillfully composed in the characteristic manner of the music of Paul Hindemith in a distinctly twentieth-century harmonic context, eloquently captures the journey to the Mount of Transfiguration and the otherworldliness of its setting. The text and tune first appeared together in 1977 in *Ecumenical Praise*, 67, and *Westminster Praise*, 42. The tune was named after a community near Oxford.

Since the musical setting is challenging and the Transfiguration is celebrated annually, the choir or soloists might sing the stanzas, with the congregation joining on the Alleluia. The alternate tune LIEBSTER JESU, **182**, is suggested for the faint of heart.

Christ, whose glory fills the skies (173)

Charles Wesley, 1740

The hymn first appeared in three stanzas on pages 24-25 in *Hymns and Sacred Poems*, 1740, under the title "Morning Hymn." It was included without citation in Augustus Toplady's *Psalms and Hymns*, 1776. John Wesley in his 1780 *Collection*, number 150, included only stanzas 2 and 3 of the hymn, preceding them with a stanza from another one of Charles's hymns beginning, "O disclose thy lovely face"; he added further complication by including another hymn by Charles, number 517, with the identical first line, "Christ, whose glory fills the skies." It was included in a number of nineteenth-century English hymnals, including *Hymns Ancient and Modern*, 1861, where the text was first matched with RATISBON. British Methodist hymnals did not include the full hymn until the early twentieth century. It was not included in USA Methodist hymnals until 1878, but was dropped from our 1905 book, and restored in 1935. In our present hymnal the text is printed without alteration.

The first stanza is alive with bright messianic metaphors for Christ, "The true light which enlightens everyone, was coming into the world," John 1:9; "Sun of Righteousness," Isaiah 2:6 and Malachi 4:2; and "Day-star," Isaiah 14:12 and 2 Peter 1:19. Stanza 2 describes the beginning of the day without Christ as dark and cheerless. Stanza 3 invites Christ, "Radiancy divine," to enter our lives.

Ratisbon

German melody arr. in Johann G. Werner's Choralbuch, 1815
alt. and harm. by William H. Havergal, 1861

The tune entered our hymnals in 1935 in the version found in hymn 5 in *Hymns Ancient and Modern*, 1861. Wesley Milgate in *Songs of the People of God*, page 74, has provided the most accurate and recent information about this exceedingly dull "grey" tune that seldom complements Wesley's dynamic, exciting, and contrasting metaphors. Two additional harmonizations are found at 278-79 in *The United Methodist Hymnal Music Supplement*. Ratisbon is the old name for Regensburg, a lovely Bavarian city on the Danube.

Christian people, raise your song (636)

Colin P. Thompson, 1975
(1 Cor. 15:22)

The poet composed this hymn to encourage the singing of the tune AVE VIRGO VIRGINUM from a concern that there were few hymns suitable for use at the offering of bread and wine, and from a desire to say something simple about the gifts of creation in the communion service. (Braun 1982, 13-14). It appeared in *New Church Praise*, 1975, number 11.

Changes made in the text for this present hymn are 2:3, "he" to "who"; 2:5, "him" to "the"; and 2:7, "men" to "we."

Ave virgo virginum

J. Horn's Gesangbuch, 1544
harm. by Ralph Vaughan Williams, 1906

This cheerful German tune apparently was first published in J. Horn's *Ein Gesangbuch der Brüder im Bohemen and Merherrn*, Nürnberg, 1544. It was introduced to English language hymnals in *Hymns Ancient and Modern*, 1904, sufficiently modified to render it bland and harmless. Vaughan Williams harmonized the tune for *The English Hymnal*, 1906, but did not fully restore its original rhythms. *Hymns Ancient and Modern,* Revised 1950, restored the shape of the tune, and that version entered our hymnals in 1966 with Vaughan Williams's harmonization, except for the penultimate measure. It can be sung in two-part canon at the octave, the second voice entering after one measure. The tune is transposed down one step to F major in *The United Methodist Hymnal Music Supplement*, number 29.

Christmas (231)

The Book of Hymns, 1966; alt. by Laurence Hull Stookey

This prayer links Jesus' birth with our rebirth and continues the theme of stanza 4:3-4 of the Christmas hymn "O little town of Bethlehem" **(230)**: "Cast out our sin, and enter in, be born in us today."

Close to thee (407)
Thou my everlasting portion

Fanny Crosby, 1874

In the poet's words in *Memories of Eighty Years*, this hymn was composed after the composer had brought her one of his new tunes:

> Toward the close of a day in the year 1874 I was sitting in my room thinking of the nearness of God through Christ as the constant companion of my pilgrim journey, when my heart burst out with the words. (Gealy 557/489)

The words and music were first published the same year in *Songs of Grace and Glory*, number 17. (Gealy 557/489-b) It entered our hymnals in 1889. In 1966 only the refrain was included. The entire hymn is included in our present hymnal.

Close to thee

Silas J. Vail, 1874

The composer took this tune to the poet and asked her to write a text for it. It was first published with the text as indicated above. In the first printing the dotted eighth- and sixteenth-note figure was used throughout. As with many gospel hymns, matters of tempo, dialect, and singing the tune as written are dictated by their common use as folk hymns.

Cold December flies away (233)

See "En el frio invernal," pages 326-27.

Come, all of you (350)
Choen thaan thang-lai, thang-ying thang-chai

Sook Pongnoi; trans. by Cher Lue Vang, 1987
(Rev. 22:17; Matt. 11:28; John 14:27; Isa. 55:1-2)

According to I-to Loh this is "actually a Thai hymn ["Come, take the water of life"], but the text is transliterated into Laotian." Dr. Loh's interpretation follows:

[The hymn calls] for those who are thirsty to come and drink freely. The author has also incorporated the New Testament images, Jesus calling for the "bearers of burden" to find rest (Mt. 11:28), for the "troubled minds" to receive peace (Jn. 14:27), and the "hungry and poor" (Isa. 55:1-2; Rev. 22:17) to accept the bread and water of life. (Correspondence with Carlton R. Young, April 1988)

The translation was made in 1987 at the request of Naomi Southard by Reverend Cher Lue Vang, then living in Piscataway, New Jersey, and chairperson of the Indo-Chinese caucus of the National Federation of Asian American United Methodists (NFAAUM). The translation is in a slightly different paraphrase at number 209 in *Sound the Bamboo*, 1990.

Soi Son Tad

Thai traditional melody; harm. anon.

As with most Asian vocal music the strength and charm of this tune are lost when burdened with Western harmonies, voice leadings, and cadences. Pages 16-18 in *Sound the Bamboo* contain notes on performance practice to assist in singing the glides up and down (notated by grace notes) and occasional quarter tones. The instruments and their performance appropriate for accompanying subtle Asian melodies are also described.

Come, and let us sweetly join (699)

Charles Wesley, 1740

Our hymnal follows the selection in the British Methodist *Hymns and Psalms*, 1983 (hymn 756, part 1), of stanzas and alterations from parts one, two, and three of Wesley's original five-part hymn titled "The Love-Feast" at 181-82 in *Hymns and Sacred Poems*, 1740 (see also "Let us plead for faith alone," (**385**). Four of the parts are printed in the 1780 *Collection*, numbers 505-08. The love feast was adapted from Moravian practice, and like the Moravians, Methodists have made a clear distinction between the human feast and Holy Communion (see stanza 3). Hildebrandt and Beckerlegge have written about the Methodist practice of the love feast:

The love-feast, not unlike but to be distinguished from the Lord's Supper, goes back to the *agape* of the early church [Jude :12a], and had been revived by the Moravians, from whom John Wesley adopted it. Usually held in an evening during his time, it sometimes lasted from 7 until 10 p.m. Bread or plain cake, and water in a loving cup, were passed around, and the token meal became an occasion for religious testimonies by those present. (Wesley 1983, 7:695)

The hymn was included in our hymnals until it was dropped in 1905. It was restored in the 1966 hymnal with one stanza printed as a call to worship.

Stanzas 1 and 4 may be used as a table grace. Another hymn on the love feast is "Christ, from whom all blessings flow" (**550**).

Canterbury

See "Christ from whom all blessings flow," pages 271-72.

Come back quickly to the Lord (343)
Uhsuh-do-oh rah-oh-oh

Young Taik Chun, 1943
trans. by Sang E. Chun and Ivy G. Chun, 1988 (Luke 15:11-32)
This hymn on the parable of the prodigal son was written during World War II by Young Taik Chun, a pastor in the Korean Methodist Church and the editor of the Korean Christian Literature Society. The translation was made for our hymnal by the author's son, Sang G. Chun, and his granddaughter, Ivy G. Chun.

Korea

Jae Hoon Park, 1943
The author's son has written of the circumstances of the composition of the tune:

One day in 1943 when the composer visited the author, he was handed a poem that Rev. Chun had cut out from a page of his Christian literary magazine. (Sang E. Chun correspondence with Carlton R. Young, August 1991)

Come, Christians, join to sing (158)

Christian Henry Bateman, 1843
According to Wesley Milgate the hymn did not originate with Bateman but was rewritten by him from "Join now in praise, and sing" by William Edward Hickson, and included in his *Singing Master*, 1836. (Milgate 1985, 83)

Fred D. Gealy has provided additional information:

[The hymn was] first published [in five stanzas, number 4] in the author's *Sacred Melodies for Children*, 1843 [Edinburgh], . . . but Bateman reduced it to 3 in his new and enlarged edition called *Sacred Melodies for Sabbath Schools and Families*, 1854. These 3 make up the hymn in our hymnal. . . . The original line 1 . . . has been altered [and the "Hallelujahs" changed to "Alleluias" in USA Presbyterian books beginning with *The Hymnal*, 1933] to make the hymn available to all age groups. (Gealy, Lovelace, Young 1970, 136)

It entered our hymnals in 1966 and has become one of our most popular "new" hymns.

Spanish hymn

Trad. melody; arr. by Benjamin Carr, 1824
harm. by Austin C. Lovelace, 1963

Austin C. Lovelace has supplied the following information about this tune, also called "Spanish," "Chant," "Spain," and "Madrid."

> In 1825 Carr copyrighted variations for pianoforte of a popular parlor piece of the period. In 1826 it was published with the title *Spanish Hymn Arranged and Composed for the Concerts of the Musical Fund Society of Philadelphia by Benjamin Carr, The Air From an Ancient Spanish Melody* (Philadelphia, 1826), arranged for solo, quartet, and full chorus. The fly-leaf indicates that its first performance was on December 29, 1824. Montague Burgoyne published it in *A Collection of Metrical Versions*, London, 1827, which indicates that the tune was rather generally known. (Gealy, Lovelace, Young 1970, 137)

Additional research is included in *"Spanish Chant: An Intruder's Adventures into Hymnology"* by R. T. Boehm, *The Hymn*, January 1981. Nothing has been substantiated that connects the tune with Spain.

The tune first appeared in our hymnals in 1889. Austin C. Lovelace's harmonization was prepared for our 1966 hymnal. Number 321 in *The United Methodist Hymnal Music Supplement* is a vocal descant.

Come, divine Interpreter (594)

Charles Wesley, 1762 (Rev. 1:3)

First printed in vol. 2, number 412 in *Short Hymns on Select Passages of Holy Scripture*, 1762, it appropriately heads the section in our present hymnal "The Book of the Church: Holy Scripture." The text is based on the first of seven blessings found in John's Revelation:

> Blessed is the one who reads aloud the words of the prophecy, and blessed are those who hear and who keep what is written in it; for the time is near.
> (Revelation 1:3)

S T Kimbrough, Jr., comments:

> Wesley wrote many hymns and poems for the reading of scripture. [See also "Whether the Word be preached or read" **(595)**.] They were often enti-

tled "Before Reading the Scriptures" and stressed the virtue, power, blessing, and strength gained from reading them. "Come, divine interpreter" epitomizes his many poems on this theme in one. (Correspondence with Carlton R. Young, September 1992)

The poem is included for the first time in our hymnals. It may be sung to RED-HEAD 76, **290**.

Come down, O Love divine (475)
Discendi, amor santo

Bianco of Siena, 15th cent.; trans. by Richard F. Littledale, 1867, alt.
The hymn is a translation of four of the original eight stanzas from Bianco's *Laudi Spirituali del Bianco da Siena*, Lucca, 1851. The English stanzas were included by Littledale in *The People's Hymnal*, 1867, but the hymn was not widely used until it appeared in *The English Hymnal*, 1906, set to Vaughan Williams's tune DOWN AMPNEY. The hymn has been included in most major hymnals of the twentieth century. It entered our hymnals in 1966 with stanzas 1, 2, and 4.

The omitted stanza 3:

> Let holy charity,
> Mine outward vesture be,
> And lowliness become mine inner clothing;
> True lowliness of heart,
> Which takes the humbler part,
> And o'er its own shortcomings weeps with loathing.

In our stanza 3:5, "he become" is changed to "they become."

Gracia Grindal comments that "the entire hymn is an invocation to the Holy Spirit [to] 'kindle' the heart so that it burns with the ardor of the Spirit" in "An Interpretation: Come Down, O Love Divine," *The Hymn*, 1988.

Down Ampney

Ralph Vaughan Williams, 1906
Erik Routley, seldom remembered for expressing undeserved praise, describes the tune in *Companion to Congregational Praise* as "perhaps the most beautiful hymn-tune composed since the Old Hundreth." (Parry 1953, 118) The tune was composed for the text and included in *The English Hymnal*, 1906. Austin Lovelace states, "Its quietly rising and falling pattern fits both the unusual meter (66. 11. D) and the introspective nature of the text." (Gealy, Lovelace, Young 1970, 137)

The tune is named after the composer's birthplace near Cirencester, Gloustershire. Number 98 in *The United Methodist Hymnal Music Supplement* is a vocal descant.

Come, every soul by sin oppressed (337)

See "Only trust him," pages 545-46.

Come, Holy Ghost, our hearts inspire (603)

Charles Wesley, 1740

The hymn was first published in *Hymns and Sacred Poems*, 1740, as one of three hymns under "Before Reading the Scriptures." It entered our hymnals in *A Selection of Hymns*, 1810, in four stanzas with the alterations made by John Wesley for his 1780 *Collection*, which include stanza 1:2, "thy" to "thine," and 3:1, "prolific" to "celestial." Stanza 2:2 has been changed to "the prophets" from "thy prophets," and 4:1, "God, through himself, we then shall know" has been changed to "God, through the Spirit we shall know." Watson and Trickett have commented on the extraordinary language of the hymn:

> The hymn is remarkable for its employment of metaphorical language [fountain, fire, key, dove] even by the standards of such a fine and imaginative writer as Charles Wesley. [And it] is one of the most comprehensive and yet succinct statements of the person and work of the Holy Spirit. (Watson and Trickett 1988, 284)

Winchester Old

Est's Whole Booke of Psalmes, 1592
harm. from Hymns Ancient and Modern, 1861

This melody is similar to Christopher Tye's in chapter 8 of his *Acts of the Apostles*, 1553, and may have been transcribed by George Kirbye, 1560-1634, and set to Psalm 84 in Est's 1592 collection. The tune in the version from *Hymns Ancient and Modern*, 1861, was used in our 1878 hymnal. The harmonization from *Hymns Ancient and Modern*, 1861, number 44, appeared in our 1889 hymnal and has been used in all our hymnals to date.

Come, Holy Ghost, our souls inspire (651)

Attr. to Rhabanus Maurus, 9th cent.
trans. by John Cosin, 1625

Latin and English versions of this hymn have been used in Christian worship for ten centuries. Its Latin roots are unknown and its authorship unverifiable but generally attributed to Rhabanus Maurus, abbot of the monastery at Fulda, later Archbishop of Mainz. As early as the eleventh century it was sung in ordination services and in English coronations beginning in the fourteenth century. Cosin's translation, the most widely used English version, was composed for the coronation of Charles I, 1625, and first published, pages 75-76, in Cosin's *Collection of Private Devotions in the Practice of the Ancient Church, called the Hours of Prayer*, 1627. (Gealy 556/87) The hymn was prescribed for use in "Praiers for The Third Hour" (Terce or 9 A.M.) at the beginning of the service following the Lord's Prayer, Gloria Patri, and versicles. It was included in the 1662 *Book of Common Prayer* along with the older version from the 1549 prayer book, "Come, Holy Ghost, eternal God." Fred D. Gealy has commented:

> Though Cosin's translation condensed the original 24 lines into 18, its simplicity and restraint together with its secure position in the liturgy have enabled it to subordinate other, perhaps better, translations to itself. (Gealy, Lovelace, Young 1970, 141)

Cosin's version was selected by John Wesley for inclusion in his abridged version of the ordinal he sent in 1784 for use by the USA church. Since that time it has been included in our services of ordination of elders and consecration of bishops. The hymn entered our hymnals in 1878, was dropped in 1905 and restored in 1935.

Donald P. Hustad provides a helpful commentary on the hymn's archaic images in "An Interpretation: Come, Holy Ghost, Our Souls Inspire," the April 1986 volume of *The Hymn*.

Veni Creator

Plainsong, Vesperale Romanum, Mechlin, 1848
harm. adapt. from Hymns for Church and School, 1964

This version of the melody is a product of the nineteenth-century revival of plainsong in simplified versions for the French-speaking Roman Catholic Church. Our 1935 hymnal, number 636, was the first of our hymnals to use this melody, placing it with "Ancient Hymns and Canticles." It was continued there with another harmonization in our 1966 book. The topical inclusion of the hymn within the body of our present hymnal brings with it the hymnal committee's anticipation of its introduction and use at ordination services and morning prayer.

Singing lines of the hymn alternately between soloist and the choir and congregation will aid its learning. The imaginative might follow the medieval practice of using "incense, lights, bells and the richest vestments." (Milgate 1985, 133) In a procession it may be sung in unison accompanied by two handbells, A and E, played indeterminately. The slimmer harmonization included in our present hymnal was prepared by the music editors of *Hymns for Church and School*, 1964, and appeared at number 146.

Come, let us eat (625)
A va de laa mioo

Sts. 1-3, Billema Kwillia, 1970; trans. by Margaret D. Miller, 1970
st. 4, Gilbert E. Doan, 1970 (1 Cor. 5:7-8)

Billema Kwillia's Loma language communion text with her tune first appeared in the fourth edition of *Laudamus*, 1974, number 77a, along with the translation at number 77b. It is based on 1 Corinthians 5:7b-8:

> For our paschal lamb, Christ, has been sacrificed. Therefore, let us celebrate the festival, not with the old yeast, the yeast of malice and evil, but with the unleavened bread of sincerity and truth.

The hymn was composed by Kwillia, a Liberian convert and literacy teacher-evangelist, who sang this hymn for a meeting where it was first recorded. (Stulken 1981, 294) The poet's original text was in three lines: two 8's, one 10. The translator's four staid lines of 10's corrupt the form of the hymn as well as its charming original accents:

A va de | laa me - oo, | dii - | oo |.

A va de

Billema Kwillia, 1970; alt. and harm. by Leland Sateren, 1972

The tune first appeared with the text at number 77a in *Laudamus*. At 77b it has been changed from triple to duple meter and two counts added to the end of each line. The adaptation and harmonization in our present hymnal are by Leland Sateren from the *Lutheran Book of Worship*, 1978, number 214. It is difficult to find a more blatant recent example of the emasculation of an indigenous hymn. These performance suggestions will help restore the hymn's original qualities. Never use the keyboard harmonies provided. Sing in unison as a call-and-response; add hand clapping and rhythm instruments. Sing the hymn in the offertory procession of the bread and wine; accompany with two handbells, F and C, on the downbeats of measures 1, 5, 9, and 13. The tune may also be sung as a two-part canon with entrances at two-measure intervals. See *The United Methodist Hymnal Music Supplement*, 2 and 3.

Come, let us join our friends above (709)

Charles Wesley, 1759

The text first appeared as "Hymn 1" in five CMD stanzas in the second series of *Funeral Hymns*, 1759. It was not included by John Wesley in the 1780 *Collection*, but by the mid-nineteenth century it appeared in both British and USA hymnals, entering our books in 1847.

The hymn is acclaimed as among Wesley's finest. John Wesley is said to have had it sung in Dublin, July 12, 1789, when preaching a funeral sermon for his brother, commenting that "it was the sweetest hymn his brother ever wrote." J. Ernest Rattenbury has written about the poet's "sense of the one-ness of all Christian people in Heaven and on earth [that] is best expressed in the superb hymn which some think his masterpiece." (Rattenbury 1941, 333) Concerning Wesley's use of militaristic imagery and metaphor Bernard Manning says, "Not a word wasted. It is as spare and taut as the warriors it describes. . . . No distant triumph song stealing in the ear or countless hosts streaming through gates of pearl, but 'Shout to see our Captain's sign, To hear His trumpet sound.'" (Manning 1942, 36-7)

Stanza 3 in our hymnal is a composite of 3:1-4 and 4:5-8 of the original. Stanza 1:5, "Let saints on earth unite to sing" differs from the original "Let all the saints terrestrial sing." Our version follows the versification of *Hymns and Psalms*, 1983.

Forest Green

Trad. English Melody; arr. by Ralph Vaughan Williams, 1906
The harmonization was made for *The English Hymnal*, 1906, and was first included in our hymnals in 1957. The tune's ballad meter, AABA form, simple and attractive melody, and skillful harmonization combine to make it the sturdiest of all CMD tunes in the repertory. Forest Green is the village in Surrey where Vaughan Williams heard "The Ploughboy's Dream." He transcribed and renamed it.

Come, let us use the grace divine (606)

Charles Wesley, 1762 (Jer. 50:5)
The hymn is from vol. 2:36-37 of *Short Hymns on Select Passages of Holy Scripture*, 1762, based on Jeremiah 50:5, "Come, and let us join ourselves to the Lord in a perpetual covenant that shall not be forgotten." The hymn originally consisted of three stanzas of eight lines each. Our version mainly differs from the original at 2:5-6 that read "We never will throw off his fear, who hears our solemn vow"; 3:5 read "the covenant-blood apply."

It entered our hymnals in the *Pocket Hymn-Book*, 1788, 9th ed. John Wesley and his followers in Britain and the USA used the hymn in conjunction with the service "The Renewal of the Covenant," which he originated but did not write, usually held on the first Sunday of every year. See also "A covenant prayer in the Wesleyan tradition" **(607)**.

Kingsfold

English melody; arr. by Ralph Vaughan Williams, 1906

The melody is given in *English County Songs* by Lucy E. Broadwood and J. A. Fuller Maitland, 1893, as noted down by Alfred J. Hopkins in Westminster; he knew no words for the tune . . . but associated it with "Dives and Lazarus" (*The Oxford Book of Carols*, 57). (Milgate 1985, 183)

Vaughan Williams first heard the tune at Kingsfold in Sussex and named the tune accordingly. His skillful arrangement for *The English Hymnal*, 1906, number 574, was first included in our hymnals in 1957, number 101. The composer used the tune in his *Five Variants on Dives and Lazarus* for harp and strings, written for the 1939 New York World's Fair. Erik Routley traces variants of the tune at pages 94-96 in *The English Carol*, 1958.

See "O sing a song of Bethlehem," pages 527-28, for suggestions on using this tune as a hymn anthem.

Come, my Way, my Truth, my Life (164)

George Herbert, 1633 (John 14:6)

This poem, "The Call," is part of the extended work *The Temple* that was published the year following the author's death. Herbert was a favorite of John Wesley, who included the poet's "(O) King of Glory, King of Peace," page 21, in his very first *Collection*, Charleston, 1737, and "The Call" in his *Hymns and Sacred Poems*, 1739. In both instances Wesley smoothed out, some say botched, the poetry to make it conform to the foot and meter of a familiar tune.

Herbert's poem is based on Jesus' words in John 14:6b-c: "I am the way, and the truth, and the life. No one comes to the Father except through me." He expands the text by employing metaphors, e.g., Feast, Strength, Joy, Love, Heart, in escalating importance to form a unique invitatory hymn to Christ. Watson and Trickett have commented on the hymn's structure: "The three-fold structure of the first verse is repeated in the other two: there is a trinity in each verse, and three verses, making a trinity of trinities. (Watson and Trickett 1988, 173)

The text first appeared as a hymn in *The Oxford Hymn Book*, 1908.

The call

Ralph Vaughan Williams, 1911; adapt. by E. Harold Geer

E. Harold Geer's arrangement of Vaughan Williams's setting of the Herbert text in his *Five Mystical Songs*, 1911, appeared in *Hymnal for Colleges and Schools*, 1956, number 156. It appears that his is the first attempt to unite author and composer in a hymnal setting.

Come, O thou traveler unknown (386) (387)

Charles Wesley, 1742

First published in *Hymns and Sacred Poems*, 1742, pages 115-18, under the title "Wrestling Jacob," the text is widely regarded as Charles's greatest hymn. The hymn's central theme is the intense struggle attendant in the changing of one's own heart and being. The struggle is imaged through the story of Jacob wrestling with the angel of God at Peniel (Genesis 32:24-32) and in the end receiving a new name. The hymn, described by Isaac Watts as "worth all the verses that he himself had written," is divided into two parts: stanzas 1-8 that contain the questions of one who seeks to know God's nature, and stanzas 9-14 that affirm that God's "nature and name is love." Wesley's faith journey, as told through his hymn, ends with the revelation that God is "pure universal Love." Watson and Trickett have contributed an extended commentary on this text for *Companion to Hymns and Psalms* (1988, 264-65).

This is one of Wesley's hymns in our hymnal in which the full text as poetry has been included. All fourteen stanzas are printed with few alterations: stanza 4:5, hymn **386**, was originally "To me, to all, thy bowels move." In hymn **387**, through an error in page design in the first three printings of the present hymnal, the stanza beginning "Contented now upon my Thigh" was incorrectly printed as the seventh stanza. It should be printed as the thirteenth or penultimate stanza. Dr. Frank Baker has contributed notes on this hymn that are found at the end of the full text.

The hymn entered our hymnals in the *Pocket Hymn-Book*, 1790, 11th ed.

Candler

Trad. Scottish Melody; arr. by Carlton R. Young, 1963

The tune entered our hymnals in the 1935 *Methodist Hymnal*. Its original name was the first line of Robert Burn's poem, the poet having set it to the tune of "Ye banks and braes o' Bonnie Doon." Its name was changed by the 1935 hymnal committee to CANDLER in recognition of Bishop Warren A. Candler, the chief advocate for retaining the hymn, who suggested the tune. (Pierce 1948, 179) The tune's pentatonic melodic line was restored and harmonized for the 1966 hymnal.

Richard L. Burns has supplied the following information. According to *Scots Musical Museum*, the tune has a curious origin:

> A good many years ago, Mr. James Miller, writer in your good town . . . was in company with our friend Clarke; and talking of Scottish music, Miller expressed an ardent ambition to be able to compose a Scots air. Mr. Clarke, partly by way of joke, told him to keep to the black keys . . . and he would infallibly compose a Scots air . . . . In a few days, Mr. Miller produced the rudiments of an air, which Mr. Clarke, with some touches and corrections, fashioned into the tune in question. (*Scots Musical Museum*, 346)

The melody was widely used in early nineteenth-century USA tune books, including *The Christian Lyre*, 1830, and *The Hesperian Harp*, 1848. The selection of this tune by the 1935 hymnal committee and its subsequent wide use, even though demonstratively unsuited for the narrative text, is responsible for the retention of this text interlined with a tune.

Among the alternative tunes that provide a better matching of the poem's sense and feeling are Erik Routley's "Woodbury" in *Ecumenical Praise*, 1977; and the nineteenth-century USA folk melody "Vernon" in *Christian Harmony*, 1873 rev. ed.

Come out the wilderness (416)

African American Spiritual
adapt. and arr. by William Farley Smith, 1986

William B. McClain has provided this commentary:

> The wilderness experience has always been a popular motif in black religious thought, often referring to the experience of the Hebrews and of Jesus. In either case, the focus was on *leaving* the wilderness. This song is another example of the dualism in the Negro spiritual. It reflected on the conversion experience as coming out of the wilderness of sin, and to the freedom experience as coming out of the wilderness of bondage. This lively and spirited song is useful with the confirmation and reception of adult members into the church, particularly when the congregation extends to these individuals the "right hand of Christian fellowship." (McClain 1990, 111)

William Farley Smith states that the words of the refrain, "leaning on the Lord," come from the phrase "leaning on de lawd" from the preaching of Nat Turner, the mystic who, like John the Baptist, was "preaching in the wilderness." Turner was the leader of the 1831 slave rebellion in Southampton County, Virginia. "The calls and responses in this text are unique among Afro-American spirituals in that they were first printed [from interviews with Turner] in the local newspaper." (Sanchez 1989, 146)

A simpler version of the spiritual is found in *Songs of Zion*, 1981, number 136.

Turner

See commentary above.

Come, sinners to the gospel feast (616, Communion)
Come, sinners to the gospel feast (339, Invitation)

Charles Wesley, 1747 (Luke 14:16-24)

The subtle double interpretation of the parable in the hymn's first line prompted the Wesley Consultation to construct two separate hymns, communion and/or invitation, from Wesley's original 24-stanza hymn found at 50 in

Hymns for those that seek and those that have Redemption in the Blood of Jesus Christ, 1747. The full hymn appeared under the title "The Great Supper, Luke xiv. 16-24." John Wesley selected nine stanzas and included them at number 2 in his 1780 *Collection.*

Both hymns represent the openness, force, and integrity of traditional invitation extended in Wesleyan-style gatherings of word and/or sacrament that vitally celebrate the redemptive and wholistic gospel of Jesus Christ. An account of the first sermon preached by the early Methodist leader Jesse Lee in Boston, July 1790, illustrates this distinctly United Methodist doctrine:

> At the appointed time [in Boston Common], with only a few people standing by to see what the stranger would do he gave out the hymn beginning: "Come, sinner, to the gospel feast." Then, himself starting the tune, he made Boston Common vocal with his sonorous voice, as it called the people together by holy song. . . . The new preacher preached what were to them new doctrines, such as free grace, full salvation, and blessed assurance of it after it is obtained. It is said that, as he was reading the couplet which says,

> > There need not one be left behind,
> > For God hath bidden all mankind,

> a Calvinist present shouted, "That isn't true! It is only for the elect!" or some such utterance. But Jesse Lee and the Methodist Church he represented believed that "whosoever will" are the elect, and whosoever will *not,* and they alone, are the non-elect. (Meredith 1909, 77-78) (Gealy 556/98)

Stanza 1:4 has been changed from "all mankind," to "all humankind." The hymn entered our hymnals in 1786 in seven stanzas. Beginning in 1821 the number of stanzas was reduced to either four or five.

Hursley

Katholisches Gesangbuch, ca. 1774
adapt. from Metrical Psalter, 1855

The tune is a variant of GROSSER GOTT **(79)**, first published in Vienna to the German paraphrase of the Te Deum, "Grosser Gott, wir loben dich." The abridged version of the tune from William Josiah Irons and Henry Lahee, *Metrical Psalter,* 1855, as harmonized in *Hymns Ancient and Modern,* 1861, number 11, entered our hymnals in 1878. The tune's name is the parish near Winchester that was served for thirty years by the poet John Keble, to whose text "Sun of my soul" the tune is set in *Hymns Ancient and Modern.* The Hymnal Revision Committee wisely chose this familiar, singable, memorable, and teachable tune for both invitation texts. The tune is transposed down to E^b in *The United Methodist Hymnal Music Supplement,* 164, and an alternative harmonization in E^b is found at 165-66.

Come Sunday (728)

Words and Music: Duke Ellington, 1943

This sacred song is a set piece from the composer's 1943 jazz suite *Black, Brown and Beige* that he reduced into a four-movement concert piece for his big band, solo saxophone, and jazz violin that was recorded at Carnegie Hall, December 19, 1944. In the recorded introduction the composer commented that the suite's title, *Black, Brown and Beige*, was the tone parallel to the history of the American Negro. The success of the 1943 and 1944 Carnegie Hall concerts, repeated annually, was a significant step in establishing the "Duke," whose remarkable career linked jazz, club shows, recordings, and movies, as a first-ranked composer. "Come Sunday" became an Ellington standard. In 1958 Ellington added lyrics to the instrumental theme and recorded it in Hollywood, California, February, 1958, under the title *Black, Brown and Beige*. The recording (COL 468401 2) featured the gospel singer Mahalia Jackson. It was included as a vocal along with other gospel, spiritual, jazz, and blues set pieces, some written especially for the event including its performance in Ellington's First Sacred Concert, recorded in its second performance in the Fifth Avenue Presbyterian Church, New York, December 26, 1965.

Duke Ellington's biographer James Lincoln Collier describes the composer's religious beliefs:

> [They were] like his music, to some extent home brewed, but basically they were typical of the time and place he had come from: God is unknowable, love is central to his message, people ought to be kind and caring and considerate of one another, forgiveness is one the greatest virtues, prayer is the way to God. He [Ellington] said, "I believe because believing is believable, and no one can prove it unbelievable." (Collier 1987, 292)

William B. McClain describes the meaning of Sunday in today's society:

> The importance of Sunday is seen in almost every aspect of black life. Secular music reflects the importance of Sunday. One can hear a deeply serious Nina Simone crooning "One More Sunday Morning in Savannah," and hear her add to the song, "in Savannah, in Atlanta, it's the same thing"; or Lou Rawls singing, "The eagle flies on Friday, and Saturday I go out to play. But Sunday, I go to church and pray: 'Lord, have mercy'"; or a hundred blues singers intoning: "I want a *Sunday* kind of love." Sunday is a special day, every week, every month, every year. (McClain 1990, 57)

McClain goes on to describe the special meaning of Sunday in the African American community.

To the Christian Sunday is, or should be, another Easter, in which God's victory in Christ over sin and death are celebrated in work, word, song, prayer, and preaching. After all, even master and owners tried to be more human on Sunday . . . [unlike Christmas] Sunday came every week; and that day was special—a regular time to anticipate." (McClain 1990, 28)

Our setting of this slow and sustained pop-style optimistic religious song is the standard sheet-music version arranged from the recording. The words are excerpted from a number of improvised, personal witness, and Christian stanzas. The first hymnic collection to include this song was *Ecumenical Praise*, 1977. While most of the Hymnal Revision Committee welcomed the song into our hymnal, it was generally perceived as a choir and solo work that would need a skilled accompanist, choir, and soloist to recast it as congregational song.

Ellington

While Ellington's Sunday services were not the first to bring jazz into worship, they did contribute to the postwar introduction of pop, jazz, and blues as viable alternatives in traditional worship.

During the First Sacred Concert the composer made these comments about sacred music:

Sacred music in all of its forms offers a universal point of meeting. But what makes music sacred is not a rigid category nor a fixed pattern of taste. The sole criterion is whether or not the hearts of the musician and the listener are offered in response and devotion to God. (Ellington 1965, COL 468401 2)

Come, thou almighty King (61)

Anon., ca. 1755

Until our 1905 hymnal this anonymous hymn was ascribed to Charles Wesley because of its inclusion with six stanzas of his "Jesus, let thy pitying eye" in a tract that was bound with the widely used 1757, 1759, and 1760 editions of George Whitefield's *Collection of Hymns for Social Worship*. In the Fred D. Gealy research files (556/104) is a photocopy of the hymn from the twenty-second edition of Whitefield's collection. The hymn was composed ca. 1755 in 664.666.4 meter, one never used by Charles Wesley and the meter of the tune for "God save the King" (see comments on AMERICA, page 209). Perhaps sensing that this attractive and straightforward trinitarian hymn, now considered the oldest English language Christian hymn in 664. 666.4, would never have continued use in British social or religious settings while matched to that tune, Martin Madan set it to ITALIAN HYMN in his 1769 *Collection of Psalm-Tunes never published before* (see page 271).

The hymn entered our hymnals in 1814 but has never been included in British Methodists books. By the middle of the nineteenth century it was sung only to ITALIAN HYMN. It continues to be one of our most singable hymns of praise, now freed from the aphorism that hymns in triple meter should not be selected as processional hymns because choir members, incapable of walking irrespective of the meter or the tempo of the hymn as a result of their training to tramp in a martial lock-step, might attempt to waltz down the aisle in a bright one-step.

Not unusual for its time, but counter to the claims that the only masculine metaphors for God are "authentic and inspired," the author skillfully integrates gender and nongender biblical metaphors for deity: 1:1, "King"; 1:4, "Father"; 1:7, "Ancient of Days"; 2:1, "incarnate Word"; 2:6, "Spirit of holiness"; 3:1, "holy Comforter"; 3:7, "Spirit of Power"; 4:1, "the great One in Three."

Contrary to its usual description as "one of the best examples of a text's trinitarian organization" (see page 38 in Diana Sanchez, *The Hymns of the United Methodist Hymnal*), the hymn is trinitarian only when the second person of the Trinity is included, as in the omitted stanza 2:

> Jesus, our Lord, arise,
> Scatter our enemies,
>   And make them fall.
> Let thine Almighty aid
> Our sure defense be made,
> Our souls on Thee be stay'e:
>   Lord, hear our call.

Italian Hymn

See "Christ for the world we sing," page 271.

Come, thou Fount of every blessing (400)

Robert Robinson, 1758 (1 Sam. 7:12)

The earliest printing of this hymn was as hymn 1 in *A Collection of Hymns for the use of the Church of Christ, Meeting in Angel-Alley, Whitechappel, Margaret-Street, near Oxford-market, and other Churches in Fellowship with Them*, 1759. Martin Madan included stanzas 1, 2, and 3 in his 1760 *Collection of Psalms and Hymns*, a practice followed by most hymnals in Britain and the USA that unfortunately eliminates the apocalyptic climax of the author's invitatory prayer to the Holy Spirit:

O that Day when freed from sinning,
  I shall see thy lovely Face;
Clothed then in blood-washed Linnen [*sic*]
  How I'll sing thy sovereign grace;
Come, my Lord, no longer tarry,
  Take my ransom'd Soul away;
Send thine Angels now to carry
Me to realms of endless Day.
             (1759 text; Gealy 556/101)

The hymn entered our hymnals in the thirtieth edition of the *Pocket Hymn-Book*, 1803. It was also a favorite hymn of the singing schools, where it was set to three tunes other than NETTLETON in their oblong songbooks. The hymn has been included in our hymnals since 1822 with the text version in our present hymnal. The Hymnal Revision Committee for the 1989 hymnal, responding to suggestions that "Ebenezer" meaning "Stone of Help" in stanza 2 be eliminated, was not able to supply any alternative that was consistent with the language and meter of the hymn, and 1 Samuel 7:12:

Then Samuel took a stone and set it up between Mizpah and Jeshanah, and named it Ebenezer; for he said, "Thus far the Lord has helped us."

The hymn's strong evangelical themes and its singable and rousing tune have made this one of our most beloved hymns.

Nettleton

Anon. in Wyeth's Repository of Sacred Music, Part Second, 1813
The tune first appeared as HALLELUJAH on page 112 of Wyeth's collection, where it is one of two tunes for "Come, thou fount of every blessing." It is scored for melody and bass, four counts per measure usually in F major, but also in D minor. Elkanah Kelsay Dare, Methodist minister and the music editor and compiler of Wyeth's collection, may have been responsible for adapting this tune from the camp-meeting repertory of Methodists and Baptists, the primary market for supplemental songbooks. Our harmonization first appeared in our 1878 hymnal, where it was apparently adapted from the setting in our 1857 music edition of the 1849 hymnal. The name of the tune is after the famous nineteenth-century evangelist, Ahasel Nettleton, 1783-1844, but there is no evidence that he was the composer. For commentary on the sources and variants of the text and tune, see Jack L. Ralston, "Come, Thou Fount of Every Blessing," *The Hymn*, 1965.

There is a vocal descant at 244 in *The United Methodist Hymnal Music Supplement* and another harmonization in *Hymns and Psalms,* number 517 (i).

Come, thou long-expected Jesus (196)

Charles Wesley, 1744
This familiar Advent hymn is number 10 in Charles Wesley's *Hymns for the Nativity of our Lord*, 1744. The collection was reprinted twenty times in Wesley's lifetime, yet the hymn does not appear in any British Methodist hymnal until 1876. It was first included in our hymnals in 1847. It has been printed in both its original two stanzas of eight lines and four stanzas of four lines.

The central themes in Wesley's hymn are Hebraic messianic expectation— long-expected freedom, release, rest, and consolation, and hope—and Christian fulfillment of that expectation in the birth of a child whose birth brought and continues to bring deliverance from the bondage of sin for the whole human family and the establishment of God's gracious reign in our hearts.

According to William Farley Smith, this hymn has particular meaning for many African Americans who affirm the essential mission of Jesus Christ and his church as setting free the prisoner and the slave. (Smith 1 (3):7)

Hyfrydol

Rowland H. Prichard, 1844
"Hyfrydol" literally means pleasant, melodious. In USA English the "y" is pronounced a soft "i" as in "him." The tune was first included in the composer's *Cyfaill y Cantorion* (*The Singer's Friend*), 1844, which according to Alan Luff in *Welsh Hymns and Their Tunes*, was published "for the use of the Sunday Schools, to wean them from 'empty and defiling songs' to those that are devotional and moral." (Luff 1990, 177) On page 178 Luff also includes the original three-part setting of the tune.

The tune entered our hymnals in 1935 in two harmonizations, including the version from *The English Hymnal*, 1906, number 301, which appears in our present hymnal. The hymn is an excellent choral call to worship for the four Sundays in Advent. A transposition of the tune one step higher to G major, a vocal descant, an organ descant, two alternate harmonizations, and a keyboard interlude are included at 167-72 in *The United Methodist Hymnal Music Supplement*.

Come, we that love the Lord (732)
Marching to Zion (733)

Isaac Watts, 1707; refrain, Robert Lowry, 1867
This joyous and optimistic song of praise first appeared in Watts's *Hymns and Spiritual Songs*, Book 2, 1707, "Composed on Divine Subjects," in ten stanzas,

page 105, entitled "Heavenly Joy on Earth." A photocopy of the text from the first edition is in the Fred D. Gealy research files (556/109). Watts made slight alterations in the second edition, 1709. For his 1737 Charleston *Collection*, pages 28-29, John Wesley selected from Watts's two versions of the hymn the eight stanzas with some modifications including "Come, ye" from the original, "Come, we," that made up the eight SM stanzas for our hymnals until the 1935 edition when the number was reduced to four. Wesley also qualified the hymn's title to read "Heaven begun on Earth." For his 1780 *Collection* Wesley included the hymn in four SMD stanzas at number 12 in the section "Describing the Pleasantness of Religion." Yet the hymn has never found a place in Wesleyan hymnals. "Given the grimness of much eighteenth-century nonconformist piety it is a delight to read the original st. 2" [never included in our hymnals]. (Gealy, Lovelace, Young 1970, 159)

> The Sorrows of the Mind
> Be banish'd from the place;
> Religion never was design'd
> To make our pleasures less.

Our present hymnal includes stanzas 1, 3, 9, and 10 from Watts's text. To make the text consistent with hymn 3 in *Songs of Zion*, 1981, the following changes were made: 1:2, "your" from "our"; 1:4, "and thus surround his throne" from "while ye surround his throne." Robert Lowry composed a new tune and added the refrain that was published as "Marching to Zion" in *Silver Spray*, 1868. (Reynolds 1976, 56)

St. Thomas

Aaron Williams, The New Universal Psalmodist, 1770

See comments below in "Marching to Zion."

Marching to Zion

Robert Lowry, 1868

Watts's text was a favorite of the singing schools in at least five different settings to fuging tunes, some incorporated in our hymnals as late as 1857. Various attempts to match the enthusiasm of the text with tunes suitable for congregational singing continued without success into the twentieth century. The sturdy ST. THOMAS had been included in our hymnals and tune books beginning with *The Methodist Harmonist*, 1821; however, it was not matched to Watts's text until our 1905 hymnal. The hymn was continued in our hymnals in this sedate and proper setting expressing its music editor's doctrine of "good taste" through our 1966 book, even though Lowry's gospel hymn setting was a perennial favorite of United Methodists whose roots were in Sunday school and revival traditions and the African American worship experience.

The appearance of these tunes side by side in our hymnal exemplifies United Methodism's inured struggle to serve its multiethnic, national, intergenerational, and intercultural constituencies with a single and inclusive worship resource reflecting their diversity of musical taste and worship practices.

Come, ye disconsolate (510)

Thomas Moore, 1816; alt. by Thomas Hastings, 1831

These words of comfort and consolation are the author's only enduring poetry aside from his popular "Believe me, if all those endearing young charms" and "The last rose of summer." The three-stanza poem was written for "a German air," so Moore states in *Sacred Songs*, 1816. (Gealy, Lovelace, Young 1970, 156) Hastings altered the poem as a hymn for his *Spiritual Songs for Social Worship*, 1831.

> He gave [stanza] 1:2 its permanent hymn form: "Come to the mercy seat." In 2:2 he altered "Hope, when all others die" to "Hope of the penitent." In 2:3 "in mercy saying" replaced "in God's name saying," which in turn gave way to "tenderly saying." But more radically Hastings omitted Moore's st. 3 and in its stead composed a st. of his own. (Gealy, Lovelace, Young 1970, 155)

The omitted stanza 3 is a reminder that within evangelical Christianity there lurks the tacit understanding that God's comforting, hopeful words and deeds are for the exclusive benefit of believing Christians:

> Go, ask the infidel, what boon he brings us,
>   What charm for aching hearts he can reveal,
> Sweet as that heavenly promise Hope sings us—
>   "Earth has no sorrow that God cannot heal."

Consolator

Samuel Webbe, Sr., 1792
arr. by Thomas Hastings and Lowell Mason, 1831

The tune was probably arranged from folk sources by Samuel Webbe, Sr., and his son Samuel for his *Collection of Motets or Antiphons*, 1792. Thomas Hastings and Lowell Mason adapted the tune for *Spiritual Songs for Social Worship*, 1831. A photocopy of page 42, number 57, from the collection is in Fred D. Gealy's research files (556/103) and is dated by Gealy as 1833. A footnote on the page provides this insight about early nineteenth-century USA vocal performance practice and the relationship of that repertory in social and church settings:

> Arranged as a Solo and Duet. This arrangement is intended for families, and for small praying circles; but is also suitable for choir, where there is, in general, more talent, and better advantages for executing small notes to be sung in repeating.

The tune was retained in this format until our 1878 hymnal where it was har-monized in the style of a dull four-part Victorian hymn tune. These practices were continued by the music editors of our 1905 and 1935 hymnals who suc-ceeded in nullifying the tune's original lyrical charm and with it Moore's gentle dactyllic lines. Attempts by the last two revision committees to provide a new tune for this text have not prevailed.

Come, ye faithful, raise the strain (315)
᾿Αἰσωμεν πάντεζ λαοί

John of Damascus, 8th cent.; trans. by John Mason Neale, 1859 (Exod. 15)
John of Damascus is considered the most important of the Greek hymn writers, and his finest work, the "Golden Canon," composed on the Song of Moses, Exo-dus 15, links the mighty acts of God: the Hebrews' exodus and Jesus' resurrec-tion. (See "Canticle of Moses and Miriam" page 258, and "The day of resurrec-tion," pages 630-31.) For the text of the "Golden Canon" and a commentary, see pages 223-29 in Egon Wellesz's *History of Byzantine Music and Hymnography,* 1949.

This hymn was written on the Exodus text, the lesson for St. Thomas's Sunday, the Sunday after Easter, also called Low Sunday. Neale's translation first appeared in the *Christian Remembrancer,* April 1859, and then in his *Hymns of the Eastern Church,* 1862. It entered *Hymns Ancient and Modern,* 1868 Appendix to the first edition, at number 291 in three stanzas, with a doxology that is not Neale's, substituted for his original stanza 3. The hymn entered our hymnals in 1905, number 163, with the same number of stanzas, set to ST. KEVIN. In addition to these three stanzas, our 1966 hymnal included Neale's original stanza 3, and the doxological stanza, all of which are continued in our present hymnal. In Neale's original stanza 3 is one of a scant number of references in hymns to the postresurrection appearance of Jesus among the twelve and Jesus' encounter with Thomas (see John 20:24-26). Two textual changes have been made for this hymnal: stanza 1:3, "his" to "forth"; 5:3, "triumphant" to "in triumph."

St. Kevin

Arthur S. Sullivan, 1872
The tune was written for this text and included in *The Hymnary,* 1872, for which Sullivan was music editor. In his *Church Hymns with Tunes,* 1903, he named it after "St. Kevin (Coemgen), whose name means 'fair begotten,' [who] was a [seventh-century] hermit in the Vale of Glendalough (Valley of the Two Lakes), Ireland." (Gealy, Lovelace, Young 1970, 157)

It is difficult to imagine a more unsuitable tune for this historic dynamic resur-rection paen. This is one of the worst of Sullivan's tunes, which in Erik Rout-ley's words, taken as a group are by far the worst, the least sincere, the most pretentious and misconceived, of any written by a major Victorian composer. . . . It is a misfortune of the church that the Easter season brings his unmeritable work into so much prominence. (Routley 1981, 104-05)

The more appropriate tune AVE VIRGO VIRGINUM **(636)** is suggested as the alternate tune with the understanding that it will be difficult for Easter visitors to sing.

Come, ye sinners, poor and needy (340)

Joseph Hart, 1759
refrain anon. in P. P. Bliss's Gospel Songs, 1874
This invitation hymn was first published in the author's *Hymns Composed on Various Subjects*, 1759, page 133, under the title "Come, and welcome, to Jesus Christ." The text was altered, mostly by A. Toplady and R. Conyers, changing the original first line from "Come, ye sinners, poor and wretched." John Wesley did not use it in any of his collections; however, it was included in Spence's 1785 *Pocket Hymn-Book,* and from there it entered our *Pocket Hymn-Book* in 1786. Its popularity extended into Sunday school and revival repertory, including Ira D. Sankey's *Gospel Hymns, Nos. 1 to 6 Complete*, 1894, number 670.

The hymn's reiterated invitation to unbelievers is an elaboration of the evangelical themes of free and undeserved grace, the unmerited gift of new life through the all-atoning death of God's only son, and Jesus Christ risen and ascended, our advocate and friend, the *sine qua non* of revivalist preaching and worship practice. The omitted stanza 3 is reminiscent of the Thai hymn "Come, all of you" **(350)** (see also Isaiah 55:1-2, and Revelation 22:17):

> Come, ye thirsty, come and welcome;
> God's free bounty glorify:
> True belief, and true repentance,
> Every grace that brings us nigh—
> Without money
> Come to Jesus Christ, and buy.

The selection of stanzas and the text is from *The Baptist Hymnal*, 1975, number 197. According to Ellen Jane Lorenz the anonymous refrain with reference to the parable of the prodigal son was "found in Southern hymnbooks as early as 1811. . . . [Its] first appearance in the North seems to have been in Joseph Hillman's *The Revivalist*, 1868." (Lorenz 1978, 109) It is included at number 111 in P. P. Bliss's *Gospel Songs*, 1874, with this footnote:

This chorus may be sung after each of the following stanzas, or as a response to "Come, ye sinners, poor and needy," "Jesus sought me when a stranger," etc. It is one of the old-fashioned camp-meeting "spirituals," and well deserves a place among *Gospel Songs*. P.P.B. (Reynolds 1976, 58)

Restoration

The Southern Harmony, 1835; harm. Charles H. Webb, 1987
The tune, appearing for the first time in our hymnals, is from William Walker's *Southern Harmony and Musical Companion*, 1835, page 5. A transcription of the original setting for high voices, melody, and bass is found at 283, *The United Methodist Hymnal Music Supplement*. The four-part harmonization was made for our present hymnal by Charles H. Webb, chair of the service music subcommittee of the Hymnal Revision Committee.

Come, ye thankful people, come (694)

Henry Alford, 1844, alt. (Mark 4:26-29; Matt. 13:36-43)
One of the most popular of all our harvest hymns, the text first appeared in four stanzas in the author's *Psalms and Hymns Adapted to the Sundays and Holydays*, 1844, hymn 16, under the heading "After Harvest." Various revisions of the text made in the next two decades, including the version in *Hymns Ancient and Modern*, 1861, brought this response from the author in a footnote to the hymn in the 1865 edition of his *Works*:

> This hymn having been in various collections much disfigured by alterations made without the author's consent, he gives notice that he is responsible for this form of it only. (Gealy 556/106)

Alford again revised the text in 1867. The hymn entered our hymnals in 1878, with Elvey's tune, in four stanzas of the author's 1867 version.

In practice this hymn is sung joyously and enthusiastically at the annual ingathering of crops celebrated in the USA on or near Thanksgiving Day. The incongruity of this practice is revealed when upon closer examination of the author's text the annual harvest is presented as a metaphor for the final future harvest, i.e., the second advent so vividly presented in Jesus' parable of the weeds of the field in Matthew 13:36-43:

> And his disciples approached him, saying,

> "Explain to us the parable of the weeds of the field."

> He answered, "The one who sows the good seed is the Son of Man; the field is the world, and the good seed are the children of the kingdom; the weeds are the children of the evil one, and the enemy who sowed them is the devil; the harvest is the end of the age, and the reapers are angels.

> Just as the weeds are collected and burned up with fire, so will it be at the end of the age. The Son of man will send his angels, and they will collect out of his kingdom all causes of sin and all evildoers, and they will throw them into the furnace of fire, where there will be weeping and gnashing of teeth.

Then the righteous will shine like the sun in the kingdom of their Father. Let anyone with ears listen!

Several changes have been made rendering this hymn gender inclusive when referring to people: stanza 2:2, "fruit unto his praise to yield" to "fruit as praise to God we yield"; 2:4, "unto" to "are to"; 3:2 and 3:3, "his" to "the"; 3:5, "give his angels" to "giving angels"; 3:8, "his" to "the."

St. George's Windsor

George J. Elvey, 1858

The tune first appeared in E. H. Thorne's *Selection of Psalm and Hymn Tunes*, 1858, and was matched to this text in *Hymns Ancient and Modern*, 1861, number 223. It is named after St. George's Chapel Royal, located at Windsor Castle, one of the alternative residences for the British crown, where Elvey served as organist from 1835 to 1882. The organ descant and alternative harmonization at 302-03, in *The United Methodist Hymnal Music Supplement* tend to exacerbate the joyous misappropriation of the text (see the above commentary on this hymn).

Concerning the Scriptures (602)

After the Book of Common Prayer

This prayer was adapted from the *Book of Common Prayer* as included in *The Lutheran Book of Worship*, 1978, page 47, titled "Grace to receive the Word." The worship resources subcommittee of the Hymnal Revision Committee made additional changes for our hymnal. It is intended for use in worship services, Sunday school classes, and other study groups as a prayer for illumination to be read by a worship leader or in unison before the reading of scripture.

Covenant prayer in the Wesleyan tradition (607)

See "A covenant prayer in the Wesleyan tradition," page 184, and "Come, let us use the grace divine," page 293.

Creating God, your fingers trace (109)

Jeffery Rowthorn, 1974 (Ps. 148)

This psalm paraphrase was one of two winning texts in the 1979 Hymn Society of America's "New Psalms for Today" competition. It first appeared as a hymn in *The Hymnal 1982*. That hymnal's general editor, Ray Glover, has written about Bishop Rowthorn's text:

The poet has recast this ancient Old Testament hymn in a form that speaks directly to the modern worshiper while retaining the spirit and intent of the original. . . . Each stanza [opens] with an address to God who is: "creating," "sustaining," "redeeming" and "indwelling." (Glover 1987, 54)

Stanza 2 is one of few references in our hymnal that speak to our obligation to protect the earth's environment. The text is printed without alteration.

Kedron

The United States Sacred Harmony, 1799
attr. to Elkanah Kelsay Dare

The tune first appeared in Amos Pilsbury's *United States Sacred Harmony*, 1799, and became one of the most popular tunes in early nineteenth-century USA folk hymnody. Elkanah Kelsay Dare, Methodist minister and music editor for Wyeth's *Repository of Sacred Music, Part Second*, 1813, is named in the tune index of that collection as the composer of KEDRON, page 43, the setting for Charles Wesley's text "Thou man of grief, remember me," identical to its use in Pilsbury's 1799 book. The fact that most later collections credit Dare as the composer of the tune raises the distinct possibility that the young Wesleyan musician Dare, who would have been seventeen years of age when Pilsbury's collection was published, is the composer.

KEDRON entered twentieth-century hymnals in *The Hymnal 1940*, number 81, in an arrangement by Hilton Rufty from *Twelve Folk Hymns*, 1934. The arranger set aside the tune's "dispersed" harmony (see "The Music of Hymns, Wesleyan Style," page 56) for an early twentieth-century English "school chorus" setting for unison voices and eliminated the poignant flatted ninth (D^b in the key of C minor) in measure 3 in the melody. The tune, in the setting from the *Pilgrim Hymnal*, 1958, adapted from *Hymnal for Colleges and Schools*, 1956, entered our hymnals in 1966 and is continued in this present hymnal without alteration.

Creator of the earth and skies (450)

Donald Hughes, 1964, 1969, alt.

This hymn by the late British Methodist minister and educator is an eloquent prayer for wisdom and strength in the face of humanity's unrelenting pride, folly, misery, hatred, and war. It was first included in six stanzas in *Hymns for Church and School*, 1964. The hymn was shortened and altered for *Hymns and Songs*, 1969. A slight alteration was made on the final couplet of stanza 4 for *Hymns and Psalms*, 1983, and this version is included in our hymnal.

Erik Routley has commented on the hymn:

Hughes has . . . produced a perfect lyric, serious but hopeful, not a word out of place, with a Wesley-like balance between the massive words and the small ones. (Routley 1979, 189)

The two omitted stanzas 2 and 5:

> Like theirs of old, our life is death,
>   our light is darkness, till we see
> the eternal Word made flesh and breath,
>   the God who walked by Galilee.

> For this, our foolish confidence,
>   our pride of knowledge, and our sin
> we come to you in penitence;
>   in us the work of grace begin.

Uffingham

Jeremiah Clark, 1701

The melody and bass of this tune first appeared in *The Divine Companion, or David's Harp New Tun'd*, 1701, page 27, set to an evening hymn:

> Sleep downey sleep, come close mine eyes
> Tired with beholding vanities.
> Welcome, sweet sleep, that driv'st away
> The toils and follies of the day.

Erik Routley describes Clark's work as the continuation of Henry Purcell's highly individualistic "Restoration" vocal style:

> [Clark was] one of the supreme melodists of that school. . . . [The tune] Uffingham combines a constant downward movement by step with periodic lifts by wide leap, and is one of the finest of all tunes in the intimate and contemplative manner. (Routley 1981, 55)

John Wesley included the tune in his *Foundery Collection*, 1742, page 28, calling it "Clark's Tune" and setting it to "Jesu, to thee my heart I bow," his translation of N. L. Zinzendorf's "Reiner bräutgam meiner seelen," earlier published in his 1737 Charleston *Collection*, page 26. The tune was included in Thomas Butts's *Harmonia Sacra*, ca. 1754, number 80, and named "Uffington." In the 1786 edition of his 1780 *Collection* John Wesley began indicating the appropriate tune for each hymn, and he recommended UFFINGHAM, then named "Bradford," for five hymns. The tune was included in *Hymns Ancient and Modern*, 1875, Standard Version, number 658, and a four-part harmonization appeared in *The English Hymnal*, 1906, number 434. This latter setting was adapted and included in *Songs for Liturgy and More Hymns and Spiritual Songs*, 1971, and is the setting that is included in our present hymnal. Ethel K. Porter in *Guide to The Pilgrim Hymnal*, page 74, states that the tune first appeared in a USA collection in Aaron Williams's *American Harmony or Universal Psalmodist*, 1771. This is the first appearance of the tune in our hymnals.

Creator of the stars of night (692)

Anon. Latin, 9th cent.
trans. from The Hymnal 1940 (Phil. 2:10-11)

The hymn's five stanzas and doxology translated from the Sarum breviary text in its plainsong setting is included in J. M. Neale's *Hymnal Noted*, 1864, page 33, under the title "Evening Hymn in Advent." A photocopy of page 33 from this hymnal is found in Fred D. Gealy's research files (556/108). The hymn entered our hymnals in 1966 in four stanzas from the version in *The Hymnal 1940*. When it became apparent to the hymns subcommittee that the hymn might not be included in the revised hymnal because of a record of low usage, stanzas 3 and 4 were omitted, and it was proposed and accepted as an evening hymn. The full text is in *The Hymnal 1982*, number 60, including stanza 6, considered to be the first extant concluding doxology to a Christian hymn.

Conditor alme

Plainsong, Mode IV; harm. by C. Winfred Douglas, 1943, alt.

This tune with one word or syllable per note is one of the simplest of all hymn melodies and is traditionally associated with this text. A simpler accompaniment is found in *The Hymnal 1982*, number 60.

Cristo vive (313)
Christ is risen

Nicholás Martínez, 1960; trans. by Fred Kaan, 1972 (1 Cor. 15)

This resurrection hymn by Argentinean, Disciples of Christ poet, and translator Nicholás Martínez is a paraphrase of verses from 1 Corinthians 15:12-23. It was written in 1960 for *Cántico Nuevo*, 1962, and translated in 1972 by Fred Kaan for the text edition of *Cantate Domino*, 1974, number 89; melody line edition, 1974, full music edition, 1980. Erik Routley served as general editor of this ecumenical hymnal produced by the World Council of Churches, Geneva, Switzerland. Fred Kaan was a member of the council's Geneva staff and assisted the editors of the project.

Central

Pablo D. Sosa, 1960

Pablo D. Sosa composed this distinctive tune for the text in 1960 for *Cántico Nuevo*, 1962. It is named after Central Methodist church, Buenos Aires, Argentina.

Crown him with many crowns (327)

Matthew Bridges, 1851, and Godfrey Thring, 1874 (Rev. 19:12)

This stirring hymn of praise to the ascended and reigning Christ is composed of portions and whole stanzas, and the cumulative alterations from two poems. Bridges's text first appeared in six stanzas in *Hymns of the Heart*, 1851, under the title "In capite ejus, diamemata multa, Apoc. xix. 12 ("His [the rider of the white horse] eyes are like a flame of fire, and on his head are many diadems; and he has a name inscribed that no one knows but himself." (Gealy 556/110) Each stanza is an elaboration on one of the names for Christ: 1, "the Lamb upon the throne"; 2, "the Virgin's Son"; 3, "the Lord of Love"; 4, "the Lord of Peace"; 5, "the Lord of Years"; 6, "the Lord of Heaven." All except stanzas 5:6-8 and 6:1-4 were included in *Hymns Ancient and Modern*, 1868 Appendix, number 318.

Godfrey Thring and others did not approve of Bridges's text, and he was encouraged to arrange a new hymn using some of his own new stanzas along with some of Bridges's. The new configuration appeared in six stanzas in *Hymns and Sacred Lyrics*, 1874. A selection of stanzas from both hymns entered our hymnals in 1905, and was altered in 1935 and 1966. The 1966 version is included in our present hymnal.

Diademata

George J. Elvey, 1868

This well-constructed and stirring tune was written for Bridges's text and first appeared in the 1868 *Appendix* to *Hymns Ancient and Modern*. It is named after the Greek word for "crowns." Instrumental and vocal descants and an alternate harmonization are found at 86-91 in *The United Methodist Hymnal Music Supplement*.

Cuando el Pobre (434)
When the poor ones

Spanish words and music: J. A. Olivar and Miguel Manzano, 1971
trans. by George Lockwood, 1980 (Matt. 25:31-46)

The theme of the hymn is the parable of the great judgment, Matthew 25:31-46, particularly verses 34-36:

> Then the king will say to those at his right hand, "Come, you that are blessed by my Father, inherit the kingdom prepared for you from the foundation of the world; for I was hungry and you gave me food, I was thirsty and you gave me something to drink, I was a stranger and you welcomed me, I was naked and you gave me clothing, I was sick and you took care of me, I was in prison and you visited me.

Its setting is the Emmaus story, Luke 24:13-35, "While they were talking and discussing, Jesus himself came near and went with them" (24:15). The central teaching is the classic liberation motif that God in Christ is seen and experienced in the plight of the rejected of society: the homeless, the poor, and the parentless. In life's journey we are closer to God when we love them and share from our abundance of food, clothing, and shelter. Those who choose the alternatives—greed, hate, and war—will "go away into eternal punishment" (Matthew 25:46a).

The hymn and its translation were included in *Celebremos, Segunda Parte*, 1983, number 32, under the title "Va Dios Mismo en Nuestro Caminar" ("God Still Goes That Road with Us"). (For the history of the development of *Celebremos* see "Hispanic American Hymns" page 42.)

For this present hymnal stanza 1:1 has been changed from "when a poor man" to "when the poor ones."

El Camino

Arr. by Alvin Schutmaat, 1971

There is no information to date about the arrangement of this tune.

To express fully the subtlety of the typically Spanish rhythmic pattern of a downbeat eighth followed by a quarter note, the tune needs to be performed on either the piano or the guitar. Chord symbols are provided in this and several hymns to encourage improvised accompaniments.

Daw-Kee, aim daw-tsi-taw (330)
Great Spirit, now I pray

Traditional Kiowa prayer; phonetic transcription,
translation, and paraphrase by Libby Littlechief, 1980

To an Indian, however, music is prayer; even love songs and songs full of humor are prayer, because Creator formed humans to feel the emotions which accompany such songs, and because all of life is a prayer, so, too is music. (Donalto, Preface to *Voices*, 1992)

This prayer is from the Kiowa nation, a Native American people who for centuries have inhabited the region designated as Colorado, Kansas, New Mexico, Oklahoma, and Texas. Libby Littlechief phonetically transcribed, translated, and paraphrased this ancient prayer in 1980 for *Supplement to the Book of Hymns*, 1982. It first appeared as number 876 in that collection. It is apparently the first Kiowa prayer with musical setting to be successfully transmitted from the oral tradition into a written form.

There is another version of the tune and text at 43 in *Voices*, 1992.

Libby Littlechief has commented on Kiowa hymns: Most songs are very old and since the Kiowa people have no written language songs must be committed to memory and passed from generation to generation. Kiowa hymns were usually made early Christian converts. (Correspondence with Carlton R. Young, July 1992)

Kiowa

Native American melody; arr. by Charles Boynton, 1981
Charles Boynton, the son of Libby Littlechief, arranged this traditional melody using the harmonies that are sung by Native Americans gathered in regional meetings including the Oklahoma Indian Missionary Conference of The United Methodist Church. The prayer in this setting first appeared in *Supplement to the Book of Hymns*, 1982.

The prayer may be sung as a call to or a response to prayer. In the latter regard it may be used as a response to the Native American prayer "Prayer to the Holy Spirit" **(329)**. Suggestions for performance practice include the introduction of the tune during the prayer with a solo recorder or flute, then a solo voice or a section of the choir singing the phonetic transcription, followed by the congregation singing the hymn either in unison or parts. The prayer should be sung very slowly and deliberately without accompaniment.

Day is dying in the west (687)

Mary A. Lathbury, sts. 1, 2, 1877; sts. 3, 4, 1890 (Isa. 6:3b)
In November 1967 Gladys E. Gray wrote to Fred D. Gealy concerning the origin of this favorite evening hymn indicating that this hymn along with "Break thou the bread of life" **(599)** had been written at the request of Bishop Vincent, founder of the Chautauqua Institution for its opening session, August 7, 1877.

> *The Assembly Herald* . . . [stated] "(after . . . the reading of Isaiah 55), the congregation joined in singing of the following hymns, written expressly for the occasion" and then goes to quote "Day is dying in the west . . ." (first two stanzas only.) This has become the traditional opening for each Sunday Vesper Service at 5 p.m., and the Sacred Music Service at 8 p.m. [held in the amphitheater] and, as such, has become a permanent part of each participant. (Gealy 556/111)

The first two stanzas were first included in *The Calvary Selection of Spiritual Songs*, edited by Charles S. Robinson and Robert S. MacArthur, 1878, number 1072, under the title "Day is dying" in 6/4 meter without dynamic markings. The circumstances of added stanzas 3 and 4 are provided by Gray:

After the hymn had come into use in the churches, regrets at the shortness of the hymn were expressed by many, and the two following stanzas were added, about 1890, at the desire of the Rev. C. S. Harrower, D.D. of New York—a Methodist hymnologist. (Gealy 556/111)

The hymn entered our hymnals in 1905, number 57, in two stanzas with the dynamic markings added to song sheets printed by the assembly. Stanzas 3 and 4 were added in our 1957 hymnal. It is one of twelve hymns and prayers appropriate for evening services of prayer and praise. The poet skillfully expresses the cosmic in gentle, nurturing, nature and deity metaphors: "evening lamps," "dome of the universe," "fold of thy embrace," and "heart of Love enfolding all." In stanza 1:4 "her" has been changed to "the."

Chautauqua

William F. Sherwin, 1877

This tune was composed for the hymn by William F. Sherwin, the director of music at Chautauqua, and it was first included in *The Calvary Selection of Spiritual Songs*, 1878.

The tune should be sung in the style of a lullaby—gentle, rocking, and reflective—to complement the poem's quiet and nurturing metaphors and symbols, not as in a waltz.

Day of Pentecost (542)

Laurence Hull Stookey, 1987 (Acts 1:4, 13-14; 2:3, 11, 21)

The author skillfully blends the accounts of two post-Resurrection events, the disciples with women followers gathered in the Upper Room in Jerusalem (Acts 1:4, 13-14) and the Day of Pentecost (Acts 2:3, 11, 21). Stookey states that the sixth line of the prayer based on Acts 2:3 ("Divided tongues, as of fire, appeared among them, and a tongue rested on each of them") "reminds us of Wesley's 'heart strangely warmed' and the flame that is a part of the official symbol of The United Methodist Church." (Sanchez 1989, 185)

De Profundis (516)

See "Canticle of redemption" pages 261-62.

De tierra lejana venimos (243)
From a distant home

Trad. Puerto Rican carol; trans. by George K. Evans, 1963 (Matt. 2:1-12)

This traditional Epiphany carol from Puerto Rico retells the story of the wise men, some texts call them magi or astrologers, who came to worship the

"Child who has been born King of the Jews" (Matthew 2:2a). George K. Evans's translation first appeared at 288 in *The International Book of Christmas Carols*, 1963.

Isla del encanto

Trad. Puerto Rican melody; arr. by Walter Ehret, 1963
The tune's name means literally "enchanted island." The arrangement was made by Walter Ehret for *The International Book of Christmas Carols*, 1963, and retains the traditional parallel thirds in the upper voices, and the dotted eighth and sixteenth rhythm in the bass.

The carol might be included as a set piece in a nativity or Epiphany service. Stanza 1 may be sung in procession by three male and/or female solo voices in either Spanish or English. Add tambourine and other traditional rhythm instruments as the congregation begins the estribillo (chorus). As in all bilingual settings, the congregation may sing in either the original language, the translation, or both. Assign the remaining stanzas to one of the soloists as they lay the appropriate gifts of gold, frankincense, and myrrh at the baby Jesus' crib.

Dear Jesus, in whose life I see (468)

John Hunter, 1889
This two-stanza prayer was first included in the author's collection *Hymns of Faith and Life*, 1889, number 263. The text entered our hymnals in 1935 in its original form. In the present hymnal in stanza 1:1, "Master" was changed to "Jesus" as part of the Hymnal Revision Committee's endeavor to minimize the magnitude of masculine metaphors. In 1:3, "forever" was originally "for ever."

Hursley

See "Come, sinners to the Gospel feast," page 297.

Dear Lord and Father of Mankind (358)

John Greenleaf Whittier, 1872
Whittier's seventeen-stanza poem sharply contrasts the efforts to achieve unity with Deity through ecstasies induced by either drug-centered ritual or revival preaching and song, with the Quakers' quiet yet fervent prayer. It first appeared in *Atlantic Monthly*, April 1872, pages 473-74, under the title "The Brewing of Soma." (Gealy 556/112) Stanzas 1-11 describe in vivid images and compelling metaphors the rites of

the priests of Indra [who] had brewed from honey and milk a "drink of the gods" which when drunk by the worshipers produced a frenzy, a sacred madness, an ecstatic storm of drunken joy, the beginning of a "new, glad life." Offended by the noisy and hysterical camp meetings and neighborhood revivals, Whittier recalled [in stanza 8] how age

> after age has striven
> By music, incense, vigils drear,
> And trance, to bring the skies more near
> Or lift men up to heaven. (Gealy 1970, 163)

Stanzas 12-17 are Whittier's exquisite six-stanza Quaker Christian hymn that W. Garrett Horder included, except for stanza 13, in his *Worship Song*, 1884, in a section marked "Speech," under the title "'And after the fire a still small voice,' I Kings xix. 12," number 440. Horder's dynamic markings "m" and "p" for some lines and stanzas became the standard, albeit perplexing, performance practice for many organists and singers. In stanza 5:1 "the pulses of desire" is replaced by the poet's original "the heats of our desire." See SERENITY, pages 587-88, for commentary on Charles Ives's setting of stanzas 3 and 4.

Rest

Frederick C. Maker, 1887

The tune was written for this text and was first included in G. S. Barrett's *Congregational Church Hymnal*, 1887. It entered our hymnals in 1905, number 543, in C major. Appropriately named REST, in contrast to Whittier's dynamic and fervent prayer, the tune begins in lethargy, continues in monotony, and ends in a soothing spiritual snooze. See 282 in *The United Methodist Hymnal Music Supplement* for suggestions for performing a vocal or instrumental descant.

Dear Lord, for all in pain (458)

Amy W. Carmichael, 1931

This intercessory prayer for the sick and those who serve them was composed in 1931 following the author's crippling accident and was included in *Rose from Briar*, 1933. It is one of five hymns and prayers, **457-61**, set on facing pages for use in healing services or at the bedside of those who suffer illness and pain.

Raphael

Kenneth Donald Smith, 1965

The tune was written for these words and first included in *The Anglican Hymnal*, 1965. According to the composer: "The melody is wholly stepwise, save for the one upward leap of a minor 7th. The angel of healing (John 5:4) is traditionally known as Raphael [the tune's name], after the angel in the Book of Tobit [6:1-9]." (Correspondence from the composer to Joyce Horn, Oxford University Press, London, September 1991)

Dear Lord, lead me day by day (411)

Words and music adapt. from a trad. Philippine folk song
by Francisca Asuncion, 1976

I-to Loh gives the origin of this lively hymn:

Adapted from a very popular Filipino folk song, "Planting Rice Is Never Fun." . . . The original phrase "bent from morn till the set of sun" . . . [was transformed by Francisca Asuncion] into "praise from morn till the set of sun," suggesting the intimate relationship between work and celebration. (Sanchez 1989, 144)

The hymn was written in August 1976, while the author was recuperating in her sister's home in Cottage Grove, Minnesota, from an auto accident. It first appeared in *Hymns from the Four Winds*, 1983, in the section for "Children," number 96. It might be introduced by a children's choir accompanied by guitar and string bass or piano with the congregation joining on the refrain.

Cottage Grove

Adapt. from a trad. Philippine folk song by Francisca Asuncion, 1976

This tune is adapted from a traditional Filipino melody and was arranged by I-to Loh for *Hymns from the Four Winds*, 1983. The tune's name comes from Cottage Grove, Minnesota, where the hymn was first sung in the Community Church by the author's eight nephews and nieces, accompanied by guitar, recorder, and piano.

Deck thyself, my soul, with gladness (612)
Schmücke dich, O liebe Selle

Johann Franck, 1649, 1653
trans. by Catherine Winkworth, 1858, alt. 1863 (John 6:35-58)

The first of nine stanzas of this superb communion hymn appeared in Johann Crüger's *Geistliche Kirchen-Melodien*, 1649, with the melody with which it has always been associated. The full hymn appeared in the composer's *Crüger-Runge Gesangbuch*, 1653. Catherine Winkworth translated six stanzas of the hymn as poetry in 88.88.77.77 meter for her *Lyra Germanica*, 1858, second series, pages 133-34. In her *Chorale Book for England*, 1863, number 93, she interlined stanza 1 with the chorale melody and altered her original text to conform to the tune's and the hymn's original LMD meter. (Gealy 556/114)

The hymn entered our hymnals in 1966 using stanzas 1, 5, and 6 from Winkworth's 1863 version. United Methodism's penchant for uncelestial rhetoric and compressed liturgies has thus far conspired to restrict to the choir loft the singing of this reflective, understated, yet joyous anticipation of the heavenly banquet. Textual changes for this present hymnal are stanza 1:5, "him" to "Christ"; 2:3, "Joy, the sweetest man e'er knoweth" to "Joy, the best that any knoweth." The Hymnal Revision Committee resisted revisionists' attempts to render the hymn's opening line, "Deck yourself, my soul."

Schmücke dich

Johann Crüger, 1653
harm. from The Service Book and Hymnal, 1958; adapt. 1964
The tune first appeared in the composer's *Geistliche Kirchen-Melodien*, 1649, with one stanza of the hymn interlined. The tune, particularly its rhythmic middle portion—measures 12-18—demonstrates Crüger's debt to the Genevan psalm tune. The chorale came into English hymnals by way of Winkworth's *Chorale Book for England*, 1863, where its dance rhythms were smoothed over. The original rhythm of the middle section is included as a footnote at number 306 in *The English Hymnal*, 1906. The harmonization in our present hymnal first appeared in our 1966 hymnal. It was adapted from *The Service Book and Hymnal*, 1958, number 262. There are numerous settings of the chorale melody, including those in Johannes Brahms's and J. S. Bach's organ preludes, and the latter's chorale cantata number 180, *Schmücke Dich*.

Depth of mercy! Can there be (355)

Charles Wesley, 1740
The text first appeared at pages 82-84 in *Hymns and Sacred Poems*, 1740, in thirteen stanzas under the title "After a Relapse into Sin." (Gealy 556/115) It is a reflection on John 20:20a, "He showed them his hands and his side," and upon the meaning to the sinner of the broken body of Jesus, God's sacrificial gift of life. The hymn is both Charles Wesley's spiritual autobiography (see also "Come, O thou traveller unknown," page 295) and his prayer for repentance, acceptance, and assurance. Wesley's text is based on two biblical themes: Paul's confession, in 1 Timothy 1:15,

> The saying is sure and worthy of full acceptance, that Christ Jesus came into the world to save sinners—of whom I am the foremost,

and Hebrews 6:6b, "Since on their own they are crucifying again the Son of God and are holding him up to contempt."

John Wesley included twelve of the thirteen stanzas as the first hymn in section 4, "Convinced of Backsliding," number 162 in his 1780 *Collection*, and in stanza 1 changed the original exclamation marks to question marks. Hildebrandt and Beckerlegge in their commentary on this section of the *Collection* (1983, 290-91) trace its theme to Wesley's sermon "The Lord our Righteousness":

> These things must necessarily go together in our justification: upon God's part his great mercy and grace, upon Christ's part the satisfaction of God's justice, and on our part faith in the merits of Christ.

Our stanza 4 is an eloquent summary of Wesleyan piety:

> There for me the Savior stands,
> shows his wounds and spreads his hands.
> God is love! I know, I feel;
> Jesus weeps and loves me still.

The hymn was first included in our hymnals in *A Selection of Hymns,* 1810. Our present hymnal includes stanzas 1, 2, 3, 9, and 13 of the original text. In our stanza 5:2, "sins" has replaced the original "fall."

Canterbury

See "Christ, from whom all blessings flow," page 272.

Directions for singing (vii)

John Wesley, 1761

These seven directions were printed on one page following the tunes index in Wesley's *Select Hymns with Tunes Annext,* 1761, a collection of texts and tunes, the latter described by Wesley in the preface as "all the tunes which are in *common use* among us. They are pricked *true,* exactly as I desire all our congregations may sing them."

The directions are addressed to members of the societies and demonstrate Wesley's concerns for the standardization of hymn singing performance practice, and are prefaced by the following:

> That this Part of Divine Worship may be the more acceptable to God, as well as the more profitable to yourself and others, be careful to observe the following Directions.

The directions parallel similar concerns printed as questions and answers in his "Large" *Minutes;* see "John Wesley and the Music of Hymns," page 50.

S T Kimbrough, Jr., has commented:

> Why were these major points in the Directions made at this time? (1761):

1. Learn these tunes
2. Sing them exactly
3. Sing all
4. Sing lustily
5. Sing modestly
6. Sing in time
7. Sing spiritually

Why these seven? What is cardinal about them? . . . I suspect that part of what is behind the directions is that with a core of good tunes in prevalent meters one could sing many different hymns. . . . For example, in *Select Hymns,* 1761, most tunes are assigned to more than one hymn. Above all, I think the Wesleys had come to understand the power of the wedding of text and tune as the most vital way of celebrating and remembering faith, scripture, theology, and the task of social service. The hymns had become the "theological memory" of the Methodist movement, and if the singing of them were imprecise and nonchalant, so would be the theology of the church. One could perhaps find directions 1-6 in any good book on hymn or choral singing, but No. 7 is the crowning direction of John Wesley and the Methodist movement. (Correspondence with Carlton R. Young, June 1992)

John M. Walker apparently introduced these directions to USA Methodists in the preface to *Better Music in Our Churches,* 1923. In the early 1950's they were brought to the attention of a broader audience by Ruth Krehbiel Jacobs, founder of the Chorister's Guild, in her workshops on children and youth music and through her newsletters to friends and associates. They were first included in our hymnals in 1966.

Do, Lord, remember me (527)

African American spiritual
adapt. and arr. by William Farley Smith, 1986 (Luke 23:42)
William B. McClain has provided this commentary:

Quoting the words of the thief on the cross, recorded in Luke 23:42 ["Jesus, remember me when you come into your kingdom"], the slaves realized that even in the face of death, the last word belongs to God. . . . As oppressed people today continue to feel despised and rejected by the individuals, systems, and structures of this world, the cry remains, "Lord remember me." This song is especially useful in memorial services and funerals. (McClain 1990, 105)

The Hymnal Revision Committee was divided on which of several versions of this widely sung spiritual should be included. It recommended that two settings be printed; however, considerations of space prevented this.

Ditmus

The tune's name comes from St. Ditmus, the thief on the cross, who was named and sainted in the third century. Additional stanzas and a simpler melodic line are found in *Songs of Zion*, number 119. Add tambourine, hand clapping, and movement. Dr. Smith's four-voice arrangement is essentially for choirs..It should be accompanied in a bright and steady subdivided four.

Dona nobis pacem (376)

Trad. round

These Latin words meaning "grant us peace" are set in an ancient two- or three-part canon or round. The number in the circle indicates where the second or third voices begin to sing the entire melody. An effective use of the round would be to have the congregation and choir sing the entire tune in unison as the choir moves into the congregation. Begin the round with female voices, have the male voices enter at circle two, and a third voice join at circle three. Have each voice sing the melody four times, including the unison introduction. As each voice finishes the fourth time, signal them to hold the final note as a pedal point until all voices have finished singing. Hand-bells, guitar/autoharp may be added ad lib; see 97, *The United Methodist Hymnal Music Supplement*. The suggested English sounds for the Latin words, DOH-nah NOH-bees PAH-chem, are from the "Pronunciation Guide," page 390, in the *Music Supplement*.

The round was first included in our 1957 hymnal set to an English text, "Father, Father, grant thy blessing."

Draw us in the Spirit's tether (632)

Percy Dearmer, 1931 (Matt. 18:20)

This text has an interesting history. In 1874 George H. Bourn privately published *Seven Post-Communion Hymns* for use in the chapel at St. Edmund's College, Salisbury. One of the hymns, "Lord, enthroned in heavenly splendor," was included in *Supplement* to *Hymns Ancient and Modern*, 1889, and later in *The English Hymnal*, 1906, set to the powerful Welsh tune "Bryn Calfaria" (sadly missing from our hymnal). Percy Dearmer thought this popular tune lacked the desired quiet devotional qualities for a postcommunion hymn. Consequently, he composed three new stanzas and set them to an ancient melody "said to be from the Tour Breviary." (Dearmer and Jacob 1933, 160) Apparently for reasons related to his task as editor Dearmer printed his text under the nom de plume "B. R.," curiously calling it part 2 of Bourn's hymn, now reduced to stanzas 1 and 2, and printed them side by side in *Songs of Praise Enlarged*, 1931, number 274. The first USA hymnal to include the hymn is apparently *Hymnbook for Christian Worship*, 1970.

"Tether" is an archaic, albeit felicitous and ingratiating word for "tying" or "joining together." Stanza 1 reminds us of Christ's presence ("Where two or three are gathered in my name, I am there among them," Matthew 18:20); and the hemorrhaging woman's fervent affirmation ("If I only touch his cloak, I will be made well," Matthew 9:20b). Stanzas 2 and 3 paraphrase the simple ancient Christian eucharistic rite of gathering, giving thanks, and sharing over the cup and loaf, and sending forth into the world as Christ's disciples called to render all our meals and living as a sacrament and a means of God's grace. See "The Basic Pattern [of Worship] Explained," in Hoyt L. Hickman, *Worship Resources of the United Methodist Hymnal*, pages 17-26. Our text is unchanged from Dearmer's original with the exception of stanza 2:1, "the brethren" to "disciples."

Union Seminary

Harold Friedell, 1957; adapt. by Jet E. Turner, 1968

The tune is a section of a communion anthem on this text by Harold Friedell published in 1957. The adaptation was made by Jet E. Turner and first appeared in *Hymnbook for Christian Worship*, 1970, number 316. The tune is named after the School of Sacred Music, Union Theological Seminary, New York City, where Friedell taught theory and composition, and from where Jet E. Turner graduated.

This is one of the strictly choral pieces in the hymnal. While it may be performed in four parts by some congregations, its main use is intended for accompanied or unaccompanied choirs. The three stanzas may be performed as an anthem during the distribution or as follows: stanza 1 as a call to prayer; stanza 2 as the offering of bread and wine is brought to the communion table; stanza 3 as a closing response. The performance note in *The United Methodist Hymnal Music Supplement*, 337, suggests that a flute may double the melody an octave higher.

Easter people, raise your voices (304)

William M. James, 1979

This bright resurrection and liberation hymn celebrates Christ's victory and ours over sin and death. It was first sung at Community United Methodist Church, New York City, where the author was pastor. Stanzas 1, 3, and 5 of the original 5 were included in *Songs of Zion*, 1981, number 6. They appear in our hymnal without alteration.

Regent Square

See "Angels from the realms of glory," pages 213-14.

Easter Vigil or Day (320)

The Book of Worship, 1944

This anonymous collect was adapted for our 1966 hymnal, number 699 from *The Book of Worship*, 1944, page 177. It was slightly modified for this hymnal.

Eat this bread (628)

Words: Robert Batastini and the Taizé Community, 1982 (John 6:35)
Music: Jacques Berthier, 1982

This communion response is based on John 6:35:

> Jesus said to them, "I am the bread of life. Whoever comes to me will never be hungry, and whoever believes in me will never be thirsty."

The response comes from the ecumenical lay community of Taizé, a village in eastern France near Cluny, Burgundy. Since its founding in 1940 the community has dedicated its efforts to the renewal of the devotional life of the Christian church through the rediscovery and composition of simple songs and rounds. As Taizé developed from its French roots into an international and ecumenical worshipping community, the need for a common language emerged. The need was met in part by the composition of extended canticles and other liturgical texts in a form whereby the chorus or antiphon is sung in Latin, and the body of the text is performed in a living language by the cantor or song leader. To meet the particular needs of USA worshipping communities the entire repertory has been translated into English.

The Taizé community has a unique way of developing new worship music. The community leaders first identify the particular topic, then find a biblical or traditional text that expresses the topic and set it in paraphrase. The text is forwarded to the composer, Paris organist Jacques Berthier, who skillfully sets it in a traditional harmonic idiom with sufficient musical interest so that it will still be fresh after being sung for ten or more minutes. United Methodists have readily accepted the music of Taizé since the short repeated chorus is scarcely a new idea.

Robert J. Batastini has supplied this information about the composing of this response:

> Batastini (representing GIA) and Jacques Berthier met at Taizé the week of October 2-7, 1983, to prepare the new American edition of *Music from Taizé* Vol. 2. [At the end of the week] Taizé musician Brother Robert ask Batastini if he had any additional texts to propose. [Expressing the need] for easily memorized music that communicants can sing as they approach the table, Batastini prepared this text from three English language Bibles. Since Berthier does not speak English, Batastini also chose the meter and wrote the rhythms above the text. Berthier wrote the music within the next

several hours. Thus, in the course of one long afternoon, this incredibly popular piece was conceived and written. (Correspondence with Carlton R. Young, July 1992)

Berthier

Jacques Berthier, 1982

"Eat this bread" may be sung with or without accompaniment several times by the congregation as as it gathers around the communion table. It may also be performed in the above expanded form with congregation, cantor, and optional instruments. The full music edition and vocal and instrumental parts for this and other songs from Taizé are available from GIA Publications, Inc., 7404 S. Mason Ave., Chicago, IL 60638.

El Shaddai (123)

Words and music: Michael Card and John Thompson, 1981

This is the chorus of a religious pop song recorded and made famous in the late 1980's by the contemporary Christian singer Amy Grant. The laid-back song provides alternative metaphors and names for deity, i.e., *El Shaddai, El Elyon, Adonai*, and *Erkahmka*, and singing it may open the way to more substantial and equally provocative texts such as Brian Wren's "God of many names" **(105)**. This song is one of several in our hymnal for which only the refrain is included in order to save space. Anthem and solo settings are available for the choir or soloist. Add keyboard and rhythm backup, and invite the congregation to join in the refrain.

El Shaddai (123)

The song received the Dove award as the "Song of the Year" for 1983.

Emmanuel, Emmanuel (204)

Words and music: Bob McGee, 1976

The name "Emmanuel" comes from Matthew 1:22-23. This passage follows Matthew 1:18-21 where the angel of the Lord explains to a disturbed Joseph that Mary, to whom he was engaged, has been made pregnant by the Holy Spirit in order for Jesus (who will save us) to be born.

All this took place to fulfill what had been spoken by the Lord through the prophet:

> "Look, the virgin shall conceive
> and bear a son,
> and they shall name him
> Emmanuel,
> which means, "God is with us."
> (Matthew 1:22-23)

Matthew's text is adapted from Isaiah 7:14:

> Therefore the Lord himself will give you a sign. Look, the young woman is with child and shall bear a son, and shall name him Immanuel.

Matthew offers this as proof that the dead and risen Jesus of Nazareth is "the Messiah" and the fulfillment of God's promise to Israel. Some scholars, attempting to maintain the integrity of the Hebrew scripture, show that Isaiah delivered his message to King Ahaz's court as both a threat and a promise, and that his words were fulfilled within a short time in the birth of Ahaz's son, Hezekiah. While there is no general agreement on this view, it points toward the underlying truth that the import of Jesus's ministry, death, resurrection, and his promised coming cannot be contained in one word or one verse of scripture, but forcibly flows from God's repeated promises in the Hebrew Bible. Christian scripture records the fulfillment of that promise in Jesus Christ. "Emmanuel, God with us" will be and is the mighty savior (Psalms 18:1-3; 92:10-11; 132:17-18), came and still comes as a child (Malachi 4:5, Luke 7:26), shows the way of salvation (Mark 1:4), is God's blessing in the breaking of dawn from on high (Malachi 4:2, Ephesians 5:14), and is the one who is the light for those in darkness (Isaiah 9:2, Matthew 4:16, and Luke 4:18).

McGee

This chorus should be accompanied at the piano, and it may be repeated ad lib as a gathering song during Advent or as a congregational response to prayer or scripture. The inclusion of chord symbols with a suggested harmonic realization communicates the notation but hardly the tempo, improvised "fills," right and left-hand arpeggios, occasional rubato, and over-all style of this loquacious love song. Classically trained keyboard musicians may want to defer to those who are more at home with Broadway ballads.

En el frío invernal (233)
Cold December flies away

> *Catalonian carol; trans. by Howard Hawhee, 1978*
> *Spanish trans. by Skinner Chávez-Melo, 1987 (Isa. 35:1-2)*
> The wilderness and the dry land shall be glad,
>   the desert shall rejoice and blossom;
> like the crocus, it shall blossom abundantly.
>   (Isaiah 35:1-2)

The origin of this delightful carol from Catalonia is unknown. The carol's theme is God's promise given to Isaiah to restore Zion from a wilderness of frustration, oppression, and despair to a garden of hope, justice, joy, and gladness. This transformation is mirrored in the metaphors of Christ's nativity and resurrection: the cold of winter is dispelled, and the sleeping world awakes as the unseen power and warmth of spring prompt the tree to bear a fragrant rose. Howard Hawhee prepared the English text from the original Catalan, a language spoken in both Spanish and French Catalonia and derived from French with attributes of Spanish and Latin, for the *Lutheran Book of Worship*, 1978, number 53.

Catalonia is a fiercely independent region of northeastern Spain with a unique heritage of art, architecture, literature, folklore, dance, and religious festivals and processions. The Spanish text by Skinner Chávez-Melo first appeared in *Albricias*, 1987, number 5, a collection of thirty-eight hymns in Spanish edited for the Protestant Episcopal Church by Chávez-Melo.

Lo desembre congelat

Catalonian carol; harm. by Skinner Chávez-Melo, 1987
Skinner Chávez-Melo's setting first appeared with his Spanish text in *Albricias*, 1987, number 5. In *The United Methodist Hymnal Music Supplement* there is an introduction or harmonization and flute descant at 216 and 217. Walter Ehret prepared a simpler harmonization for *The International Book of Christmas Carols*, 1963, which may be found at number 53, the *Lutheran Book of Worship*.

Epiphany (255)

Laurence Hull Stookey, 1987
This prayer incorporates biblical themes from Acts 17:26, Matthew 2:2 and 1:23, Ephesians 34:6, and Isaiah 60:3 that are appropriate to the Feast of the Epiphany. Epiphany, from the Greek word meaning appearance or manifestation, celebrates the journey of the Gentile magi to the infant's crib and is an eloquent metaphor for the human family's unity in Christ. It is observed on January 6 and may be celebrated on the Sunday closest to that date. See also hymns "De tierra lejana venimos" (From a distant land), pages 315-16, and "We three kings," page 681.

Every time I feel the Spirit (404)

African American spiritual
adapt. and arr. by William Farley Smith, 1986 (Rom. 8:15-17)
There is little evidence in the text that this spiritual had its roots in Paul's understanding of the Spirit (Rom. 8:15-17), but rather, as described by William B. McClain,

[this] spiritual describes the power and energy released in black devotion to the God of emotion. Black people have never had any concept of a God

who could not be felt. It is this *feeling* of the spirit of God that renders the black religious experience [given its distinctive spontaneity] incomparable to any other. (McClain 1990, 105)

James H. Cone in *The Spirituals and the Blues* makes further comment:

This song invites the believer to move close to the very sources of black being, and to experience the black community's power to endure and the will to survive. The mountains may be high and the valleys low, but "my Lord spoke" and "out of his mouth came fire and smoke." All the believer has to do is to respond to the divine apocalyptic disclosure of God's revelation and cry, "Have mercy, please." This cry is not a cry of passivity, but a faithful, free response to the movement of the Black Spirit. (Cone 1972, 5)

According to William Farley Smith, "shine" in stanza 1:3 means brightness, and the imagery of "train" is often found in spirituals. "Here, a train has been substituted for Elijah's chariot." (Sanchez 1989, 142)

Pentecost

This setting is one of Dr. Smith's better efforts to express the spiritual's style, simplicity, and accessibility to the average singer and pianist. The use of the "blue note" and subtle harmonic shifts are tasteful and effective. This upbeat music cries out for movement, hand clapping, and additional improvised stanzas. Members of the congregation whose hands are tightly attached to their hymnals will discover clapping to be a spirited challenge!

Fairest Lord Jesus (189)

> *Anon. in Münster Gesangbuch, 1677; st. 1-3, trans. anon., 1850*
> *st. 4, trans. by Joseph August Seiss, 1873*

Fred D. Gealy writes:

The hymn first came to be widely used when A. H. Hoffman von Fallersleben, author of *Deutschland über alles*, and E. F. Richter, director of the choir school at St. Thomas' Church in Leipzig, found a new tune for [the text] in Glaz, Silesia, and included the hymn, greatly altered, in their compilation *Schlesische Volkslieder* (Leipzig 1842), a collection of Silesian folk songs. (Gealy, Lovelace, Young 1970, 171)

The hymn's three anonymous stanzas from Richard Storrs Willis's *Church Chorals and Choir Studies*, 1850, entered our hymnals in 1905. Our fourth stanza is new to our hymnals. It is stanza 1 of J. A. Seiss's translation first published in *The Sunday School Book for the Use of Evangelical Lutheran Congregations*, 1873. His four-stanza translation is used almost exclusively in Lutheran hymnals. As is the consequence of most translations and paraphrases, when compared with the German text, both English texts have lost some of the word-for-word meaning, idiomatic expressions are stilted, and the hymn's essential charm is reduced. The hymn was arranged for the St. Olaf Choir by F. Melius Christiansen and is widely performed in churches and schools.

St. Elizabeth

Schlesische Volkslieder, 1842
arr. by Richard Storrs Willis, 1850

Austin C. Lovelace has traced the first printing of this tune to the above Fallersleben and Richter collection. (Gealy, Lovelace, Young 1970, 171) The form of the melody and harmonization in our hymnal are by Richard Storrs Willis, and first appeared in his *Church Chorals and Choir Studies*, 1850, number 193, under the title "Crusader's Hymn." (Gealy 556/122). It was first included in our hymnals in 1905. The tune's name comes from its use by Franz Liszt in his oratorio about John the Baptist's mother, *The Legend of St. Elizabeth*, 1862. As Willis had done in a footnote to his 1850 version, the composer placed erroneous information in the score's appendix that this tune dated from the crusades of the twelfth century. A form of the melody called "Ascalon" has been in British Methodist use since 1877, but not with this text. The tune is also called "Schönster Herr Jesu" and "Crusader's Hymn." There is a vocal descant at 301 in *The United Methodist Hymnal Music Supplement*.

Faith of our fathers (710)

Frederick W. Faber, 1849

Shortly after Faber followed J. H. Newman out of the Church of England into the Roman Catholic Church, he published a collection of hymns, *Jesus and Mary—Catholic Hymns for Singing and Reading*, 1849. "Faith of our fathers" appeared in 4 sts. [number 29], the first and fourth (our third) being identical with the text as always printed in [our hymnals], beginning with the 1878 hymnal [number 608]. Very early the hymn was published in 2 forms, one for Ireland [seven stanzas] and one for England. (Gealy, Lovelace, Young 1970, 172)

Perhaps most who sing this hymn are unaware that it was written to be sung by Roman Catholic parishioners who in their newly granted freedom of political expression in the parliamentary acts of 1833 and 1850 were calling for the conversion of England and the return of Roman rule to the Church of England. In the original second stanza "Fathers" meant those faithful to Rome who had suffered martyrdom and who should be our example:

> Our Fathers, chained in prisons dark,
>   Were still in heart and conscience free:
> How sweet would be their children's fate,
>   If they, like them, could die for thee!

For an English audience our third stanza originally read:

> Faith of our Fathers! Mary's prayers
>   Shall win our country back to thee;
> And through the truth that comes from God
>   England shall then indeed be free.

And according to Ellinwood, this version for Irish Catholics:

> Faith of our Fathers! Mary's prayers
>   Shall keep our country fast to thee;
> And through the truth that comes from God
>   O we shall prosper and be free.
>   (Ellinwood 1956, 251)

While the hymn in some form is included in a few British hymnals, the memory of its original intended use, combined with the perceived shortcomings of its tune, characterized by Erik Routley as "a melody of the Salvation Army" (Routley 1953, 69), has kept it out of all editions of *The English Hymnal* and *Hymns Ancient and Modern*. The hymn has been altered and abridged by USA Protestant and Roman Catholic hymnal committees into a non-Christian hymn. And ironically, given its ancestry, it has become a popular, sentimental, feel-good expression of our nineteenth-century folk-patriotic-militaristic-religious roots. In our hymnal "Fathers" is footnoted: *"The martyrs" may be substituted for "our fathers."* In stanza 2:4, "mankind" has been changed to "we all."

St. Catherine

Henri R. Hemy, 1846; adapt. by James G. Walton, 1874

The tune was first included in the Roman Catholic revival movement collection Part 2, *The Crown of Jesus Music*, 1864, edited by Hemy. It was set to the text beginning "Sweet Saint Catherine, maid most pure, Teach us to meditate and pray." The tune is named after St. Catherine of Alexandria, a fourth-century Christian martyr.

James G. Walton adapted Hemy's tune and added the final eight measures. He included it in his *Plain Song Music for the Holy Communion Office*, 1874. It enjoyed immediate and wide use in British and USA Methodist hymnals. In our 1878 hymnal, in addition to its setting for this text, it was also the tune for standard Wesley hymns such as "Come, O thou Traveler unknown" **(386)** and "I'll praise my Maker" **(60)**. In recent hymnals its identification with the essentially patriotic "Faith of our Fathers" (see above) has all but ruled out its use with any other words.

Faith, while trees are still in blossom (508)
Tron sig sträcker efter frukten när i blomning trädet går

Anders Frostenson, 1960; trans. by Fred Kaan, 1972 (Heb. 11)
Fred Kaan translated Anders Frostenson's poetic exegesis on faith for *Cantate Domino*, text edition, 1972, number 44. The text is replete with biblical images, many with parallels in Hebrew and Christian scripture. The main text is Hebrews 11, beginning with verse 1: "Now faith is the assurance of things hoped for." Others are "the thrill of harvest" (John 4:35); Noah and the ark (Hebrews 11:7); Abraham's faith (Hebrews 11:8); the crossing of the Red Sea (Hebrews 11:29, Exodus 14:21-23); Isaiah's response to the call of God (Isa. 6:8c). For our hymnal stanza 5, "He will be who He will be" was changed to "God will be what God will be!" and "faith accepts his call" to "faith accepts the call."

For the bread

V. Earle Copes, 1960; harm. 1989
This tune was composed in 1959 for Louis F. Benson's communion text "For the bread which thou hast broken" and first performed at the National Con-vocation of Methodist Youth, 1960. That same year the composer developed the tune into a hymn anthem and changed the "E" in the downbeat of the second full measure to a "G." The first version was included in our 1966 hymnal, number 314. The tune had been named KINGDOM after the last line of the communion hymn, "Let thy kingdom come, O Lord." At the end of the first term of copyright, twenty-eight years, the publisher neglected to renew the copyright of the 1959 form of the tune, and it entered the public domain. The composer reharmonized the 1960 version, renaming it FOR THE BREAD from the first line of the same communion hymn for which it was composed, "For the bread which you have broken" **(614)**. Regrettably there are two ver-sions of the tune in common use. Copes's tune is one of the best and most durable tunes contributed by a recent USA composer and has enjoyed wide use in a variety of hymnals.

Farewell, dear friends (667)

See "Shalom," p.age 593.

Father, we praise thee, now the night is over (680)
Nocte surgentes vigilemus omnes

Attr. to Gregory the Great, 6th cent.; trans. by Percy Dearmer, 1906
The office hymn (See "Latin Hymns," pages 5-6) is a distinct contribution of Western monastic communities that began in the fourth century and continued into the thirteenth. These hymns were composed for, sung at, and appropriate

to a particular and fixed time for worship called "offices" or duties. The author of the hymn is unknown, and its attribution to Gregory the Great cannot be substantiated since the first manuscript dates from the tenth century.

The hymn's first line, "Nocte surgentes vigilemus omnes," literally "getting up from sleep, and staying awake," indicates that it was probably sung at the before dawn vigil office of matins. Dearmer's English text was intended for parish worship, and he rightly places the worshipper's act of praise well into the morning hours, "now the night is over." The beauty of the unrhymed Latin text and its classic Sapphic meter are skillfully transmitted by Dearmer, as seen in these opening lines:

> Father we | **praise** thee | **now** the | **night** is | over;
> active and | **watchful** | **stand** we | **all** be- | **fore** thee;

The hymn was first included in *The English Hymnal*, 1906, number 165, in the section "Trinity to Advent." It entered our hymnal in 1966.

The words "active and watchful, stand we all before thee; singing" are the vital heart of prayer and praise. A more perfect match of words and music is not to be found in our hymnal.

Christe sanctorum

See "Christ is the world's light," pages 276-77.

Father, we thank you (563) (565)

Greek, 2nd cent.; trans. by F. Bland Tucker and others, 1939, 1982; alt. This hymn is a paraphrase of a composite of very early Christian writings called *The Teaching of the Twelve Apostles*, or *Didache*, in two sections, one a manual of moral catechism (chapters 1-5), the other a manual of church order (chapters 6-15). The text is believed to have originated in the Church of Antioch, Syria perhaps as early as 110. There has been exhaustive research on its date and authorship since the only extant manuscript, dating from the middle of the eleventh century, was discovered in Constantinople in 1875 by the Greek scholar Bryennios. Fred D. Gealy has provided this additional background:

> The [manual of church order provides] rules for baptism, fasting, prayer, visiting teachers and prophets, and the Lord's Supper, and containing the fine prayers which F. Bland Tucker has effectively paraphrased, appears to reflect the practices of the rural churches of Syria toward the end of the first century. (Gealy, Lovelace, Young 1970, 176)

The first three stanzas of F. Bland Tucker's paraphrase are postcommunion prayers of thanksgiving for the gifts of life through Jesus Christ. The fourth is a prayer at the distribution for God to gather all Christians into one body, just as the grain gathered from the harvest that was made into one loaf is shared in the eucharistic rite. Tucker prepared his text for *The Hymnal 1940*, number 195. It was slightly altered by the poet for *The Hymnal 1982*. In our hymnal "thy" and "thine" have been changed to "you" and "yours." In stanza 1:1, "who hast planted" has been changed to "for you planted." The hymn entered our hymnals in 1966 in the section "The Lord's Supper." In this hymnal it is included in the section "United In Christ" and crossreferenced in "Eucharist" (Holy Communion or the Lord's Supper"), where it more likely will be used.

Albright

William Albright, 1973

The tune named after the composer is one of several late twentieth-century compositions in our hymnal. (See pages 169-70) It was commissioned by Alec Wyton and first performed in a Eucharist during the 1973 meeting of the Anglican Choirmasters Association, Cathedral of St. John the Divine, New York City. The composer taught the broad unison tune to the congregation, added the impressionistic and optional instrumental "ostinato" for harp, glockenspiel, celesta, vibraphone, chimes, glass harmonica, handbells, etc., supplied performance suggestions, and conducted the piece in the service. The optional performance suggestions are not included in our hymnal; yet they were included in the first publication of the work, its first appearance in a congregational format in *Ecumenical Praise*, 1977, numbers 4-5. The instructions are also included in *The Hymnal 1982, Accompaniment Edition*, Vol 2. When introducing this setting, first teach the melody to the congregation (half-note = ca. 60), then add the accompaniment tying all repeated notes in the hands.

Rendez à Dieu

Attr. to Louis Bourgeois, 1551; harm. by John Wilson, 1979

The tune in this form was included in the Genevan Psalter, 1551, and the Scottish Psalter, 1564. The name of the tune is from its use with the French paraphrase of the final Hallel psalm, Psalm 118, "Rendez à Dieu louange et gloire" ("Give to the Lord all praise and honor"). It entered our hymnal in 1966 as an alternate tune to "Bread of the world in mercy broken." It was seldom sung, however, in part because of the perception of United Methodist worship leaders that all hymns should "sing themselves" and that the necessary rehearsal and introduction are an intrusion into worship. The consequence of this paucity of pastoral leadership is the relegating of those chorale and psalm tunes that "do not sing themselves" on first hearing and singing to the choir to sing on behalf of the congregation. John Wilson's harmonization first appeared in a USA hymnal in *Rejoice in the Lord*, 1985, number 119. Suggested alternate tunes are BEGINNINGS **(383)** and EUCHARISTIC HYMN **(624)**.

Fill my cup, Lord (641)

Words and music: Richard E. Blanchard, 1958

This song was composed [when the author] "was not in a mood to be used by God, but God was in a mood to use him." I was waiting for a couple [who were late] to counsel them in marriage. . . . I went to a Sunday School room . . . and to soothe my frustrated feelings sat down to an old up-right piano . . . . In about a half hour the total song came to me. (Correspondence with Carlton R. Young, July 1992)

Only the chorus is provided in our hymnal. As with several other selections, for example "El Shaddai" **(123)**, the full score will be needed for the choir or soloist. The song reflects Jesus' words: "But those who drink of the water that I will give them will never be thirsty" (John 4:14); "I am the bread of life. Whoever comes to me will never be hungry, and whoever believes in me will never be thirsty" (John 6:35); and the psalmist's "my cup overflows" (Ps. 23:5b). The chorus may be sung by the congregation as a prayer to be made whole, or as a response in Holy Communion.

Fill my cup

Arr. by Eugene Clark, 1971

The chorus is excerpted from a setting for solo voice arranged by Eugene Clark in 1971.

Filled with excitement (279)

See "Mantos y palmas," pages 479-80.

Filled with the Spirit's power (537)

John R. Peacey, 1969 (Acts 2)

The hymn was first included in *100 Hymns for Today*, 1969. Unlike many hymns on the Holy Spirit that tell of its witness to the individual Christian, Canon Peacey's poem is about the witness of God's Spirit as we our extend our circle of care and concern to include the whole human family. The author's widow, the late Mildred Peacey, has written of her husband's activity in the cause of union between the Church of England and the Methodist Church. In an August 1988 letter granting permission for his hymn to be included in this hymnal, she told this writer that its inclusion "would certainly have pleased my husband. He was so keen on reunion." In stanza 3:2, "in your strong care the men of every race" has been changed to "in your strong care all those of every race."

Sheldonian

Cyril V. Taylor, 1943

The tune first appeared in a leaflet in 1943 with the hymn "Lead us, O Father, in the paths of peace," "a hymn frequently used in the broadcast daily service during the Second World War." (Watson and Trickett 1988, 206) It was included in the *BBC Hymn Book*, 1951, and named after the Sheldonian Theater next door to the University Music School, Oxford, and the meeting place of that hymnal committee. It is one of the best recent four-part tunes in 10 10. 10 10 meter.

Finding rest in God (423)

Augustine of Hippo, North Africa, 4th cent. (Matt. 11:28)
Sundar Singh, India, 20th cent.

These are two prayers on the same topic: humankind's reliance upon God and the human soul's incompleteness without God.

The first is the familiar prayer from the opening of St. Augustine's *Confessions*. (See also "Latin Hymns," page 5.) The second prayer was written by Sundar Singh of India and is from this century. Laurence H. Stookey has suggested that these prayers may be used in private devotion and in public worship:

> In corporate worship they may be used in a variety of ways. One such way is for the congregation to speak the prayer of St. Augustine in unison, with the leader then reading the commentary by Singh. This could be a preparatory act before prayer, or an act to open the entire service of worship, whether on the Lord's Day or a weekday. These acts may also be used in conjunction with the singing of the hymn "Thou hidden love of God" [414], for the close of that hymn's first stanza alludes to this prayer of St. Augustine ["My heart is pained, nor can it be at rest, till it finds rest in thee"]. (Sanchez 1989, 148)

The text by Sundar Singh, a Christian sadhu (holy man), is from *With and Without Christ*, 1929, and was included by Thomas S. Kepler in *The Fellowship of the Saints*, 1948.

Fix me, Jesus (655)

African American Spiritual
adapt. and arr. by William Farley Smith, 1986 (Rev. 6:11; 7:9-14)

Dr. Smith has described this spiritual as the identification of the slave with the slain martyrs:

> They found biblical expression for their views in Revelation 6:11 and 7:9-14. . . . Here, slave-poets long for elevation to saintly status replete with

"white" tribulation robes that have been "washed in the blood of the lamb." (Sanchez 1989, 221)

William B. McClain has also commented on this spiritual:

Black folks have always had a sense of being chosen people of God; and have always been confident that they would, individually and collectively, spend eternity in heaven . . . . "Fix Me, Jesus" expresses the earnest desire of the slaves to be fit for their ultimate destination. The somber, reverent, almost pleading melody has made it a favorite for devotional services, testimony service, altar call, and invitational selections. (McClain 1990, 106)

Fix me, Jesus

The spiritual must be sung very slowly at no more than quarter note = 48. The glides should be performed as moaning prayers. There is a setting for choirs in *Songs of Zion*, number 122.

For a new day (676)

Eastern Orthodox Prayer

This prayer may be used in personal or family devotions, as one of the prayers for "Morning Prayer and Praise" **(876)**, or duplicated in the bulletin as opening prayer for Sunday morning worship.

The prayer was included in Paul Simpson McElroy, ed., *Prayers and Graces of Thanksgiving*, 1966.

For a peaceful night (693)

Trad. prayer of the Boran people

The key word in this traditional African prayer is "pass." We give thanks for passing the day in peace, ask to pass into sleep in peace, and as we pass the night in sleep, we rest assured that God, both Mother and Father, is caring for us.

For all the saints (711)

William W. How, 1864 (Heb. 12:1)

The hymn first appeared in Horatio Nelson's *Hymns for Saints' Days and Other Hymns*, 1864, page 40, in eleven stanzas under the title "Saints'-Day Hymn" and "A cloud of witnesses.—Heb. xii.1." (Gealy 556-132) (See "As the sun doth daily rise," page 217.) The original first line read "For all thy saints"; with the author's permission "thy" was changed to "the."

Reminiscent of the "Canticle of the Holy Trinity" **(80)**, Te Deum, the omitted stanzas complete the ongoing parade of the faithful:

> The golden evening brightens in the west;
> Soon, soon to faithful warriors cometh rest:
> Sweet is the calm of Paradise the blest.
>   Alleluia.

> But lo! there breaks a yet more glorious day;
> Th Saints triumphant rise in bright array:
> The King of glory passes on his way.
>   Alleluia.

> For the Apostles' glorious company
> Who, bearing forth the cross o'er land and sea,
> Shook all the mighty world, we sing to thee,
>   Alleluia.

> For the Evangelists, by whose blest word
> Like fourfold streams, the garden of the Lord
> Is fair and fruitful, be thy name adored,
>   Alleluia.

> For martyrs, who with rapture-kindled eye
> Saw the bright crown descending from the sky,
> And died to grasp it, thee we glorify,
>   Alleluia.

The hymn entered our hymnals in 1905 in eight stanzas in the section titled "Trials and Triumphs," set to Joseph Barnby's tune "Sarum." It was reduced to six stanzas in the 1935 Methodist book.

Only four stanzas were included in the 1957 Evangelical United Brethren *Hymnal* where it was set to Barnby's "Sarum." Both tunes were included in our 1935 and 1966 books.

For decades the singing of this hymn was for the most part limited to the memorial services of annual, jurisdictional, and general conferences. There are several reasons for this isolation. First, few local churches observed the Roman Catholic All Saints' Day; instead, on or near November 1, they promoted and attended Reformation Day observances, militantly singing "A mighty fortress is our God" in commemoration of Martin Luther's posting of his Ninety-five Theses on All Saints' Eve, 1517. Further, the Christian funeral, the likely occasion for singing this hymn, was removed from the church to the nondescript and sanitized funeral parlor (later called home) sans liturgy, choirs, and vital congregational singing.

During World War II the hymn began to be introduced in local churches' memorial services, a development coincidental with the recovery of All Saints' Day, prompted by the 1944 *Book of Worship* that had included one prayer for All Saints', listed All Saint's as a day in "Kingdomtide," and provided one proper preface for Holy Communion if observed on All Saints' Day.

In the 1950's when the hymn was used in either conferences or in local churches, it was invariably sung to Barnby's "Sarum." Young seminary-trained clergy and church musicians opined that Ralph Vaughan Williams's tune SINE NOMINE was superior, Barnby's Victorian tune was inferior, and thus began a war of tunes that extended into the 1970's (see "The Social Gospel Hymn," pages 31-32). The controversy over the proper tune was not limited to the USA. In the mid-1930's Bernard Manning, who had dismissed Vaughan Williams's tunes as "jazz music," said, "Until it was set to a feeble dance tune [SINE NOMINE] by Vaughan Williams, Bishop How's 'For all the saints' was a hymn with merit." Manning continues with this critique of Bishop How's hymn:

There is more than a touch of King Arthur and the Round Table about the distant triumph song, the golden evening brightening in the West, and Paradise the blest. But that is nothing. When we reach the last two verses, they ring dreadfully false and thin. The exactness of the geography of earth's bounds and ocean's coast does not fit the apocalyptic gates of pearl, and then with this unreal picture of the saints rising from land and sea, and entering the gates of pearl we come suddenly on what should be no Arthurian romantic stuff: the doxology to the Holy Trinity. (Manning 1942, 36)

Using the alternate harmonization for several stanzas will underscore the reflective qualities of this hymn and help mitigate the tendency of strong unison singing to caricature the Christian church and its mission and ministry, as unqualifiedly optimistic, militaristic, and triumphal.

Sine nomine

See "All praise to thee, for thou, O King divine," pages 198-99.

For courage to do justice (456)

Alan Paton, South Africa, 20th cent.
The prayer by the social reformer Alan Paton is akin to the peaceful "Prayer of St. Francis" **(481)**. It may be prayed in private or used in conjunction with one of the hymns in the section "Social Holiness," for example, Fred Kaan's "We utter our cry that peace may prevail" **(439)**.

The prayer was included in the author's *Instrument of Thy Peace*, 1968.

For direction (705)

After the Book of Common Prayer
This prayer for guidance and direction is a traditional collect from the *Book of Common Prayer*. It first appeared in our hymnals in 1935, titled "For God's continual help" in "Prayers and Collects," page 513. For this hymnal "thy" and "thee" have been changed to "you" and "your." Laurence H. Stookey comments that the plural pronouns in the prayer "should not prevent us from [using this prayer] in personal devotion, even as we do not hesitate to pray 'Our Father, who art in heaven' when we are alone." (Sanchez 1989, 235)

For God's gifts (489)

Howard Thurman, 1953
This exquisite prayer by the late African American Howard Thurman may be used in either private or corporate devotions. Each petition may be preceded by group singing of a chorus, e.g., "Move me" **(471)** or "Lead me, Lord" **(473)**. After each petition the leader may invite individual silent or spoken prayers; when these have been offered, the chorus is repeated. The prayer was included in Thurman's *Meditations of the Heart*, 1953.

For grace to labor (409)

Thomas More, England, 16th cent.
This brief petition for God's grace to cause us to labor for the particulars of our prayers is by Sir Thomas More, a central figure in the opposition to Henry VIII's church reforms and the author of *Dialogue Concerning Herecies and Matters of Religion*, 1529, written in opposition to William Tyndale.

The prayer was included by George Appleton, ed., in *The Oxford Book of Prayer*, 1986.

For guidance (366)

Anon. Korean, 20th cent.
This translation of an anonymous petition for God to dwell and guide our lives is from Korea and first appeared in *The World at One in Prayer*, 1942, compiled by Daniel Fleming.

For help for the forthcoming day (681)

After the Book of Common Prayer
alt. by Laurence Hull Stookey, 1987
This prayer of thanksgiving for the past night and the promise of new day is an adaptation of "A collect for Grace," which follows the creed in the service of Morning Prayer, the *Book of Common Prayer*. A slightly altered text was prepared for *The Book of Worship*, 1944, page 123, as a "Prayer for use upon entering

church." Stookey's alteration follows this text. He restores "almighty and everlasting God" to the first line, omits the original ascription, "O Lord, our heavenly Father," and replaces "thee" and "thy" with "you" and "your."

For holiness of heart (401)

Howard Thurman, 1953

This petition for a pure heart may be used with the chorus or stanzas of the spiritual "Lord, I want to be a Christian" **(402)** or the chorus of "Spirit of the living God" **(539)**. The text first appeared in *Meditations of the Heart*, 1953.

For illumination (477)

Christina G. Rossetti, England, 19th cent.

This prayer for the indwelling presence of God was included in Robert N. Rodenmayer, ed., *The Pastor's Prayerbook*, 1960.

For our country (429)

Toyohiko Kagawa, 1950

This prayer, titled "Our Lord of Light," was included in the author's *Meditations*, 1950, a collection of prayers and reflections by Japan's Toyohiko Kagawa, whose articulated pacifism in the 1930's and 1940's ran counter to his country's militaristic mind-set. The poet's prayer for his country is the believer's prayer for all governments and peoples. The words are particularly appropriate for services of worship on or near national celebrations such as the Fourth of July, Thanksgiving, and Memorial Day. It may be used effectively in this context with the following hymns: "O God of every nation" **(435)**, "We utter our cry" **(439)**, "Weary of all trumpeting" **(442)**, "O God who shaped creation" **(443)**, and Charles Wesley's prayer "Our earth we now lament to see" **(449)**.

For overcoming adversity (531)

Girolamo Savonarola, Italy, 15th cent.

Laurence H. Stookey suggests that this prayer for strength and grace to overcome adversity from a political reformer of the sixteenth century has an affinity with the witness and words of Martin Luther King, Jr. (Sanchez 1989, 181)

The prayer is from Selina Fitzherbert, ed., *A Chain of Prayer Across the Ages*, 1916.

For protection at night (691)

Trad. India (Matt. 23:37; Luke 13:34)

The metaphor of the nurturing mother hen in this evening prayer for protection recalls Jesus' words:

Jerusalem, Jerusalem, the city that kills the prophets and stones those who are sent to it! How often have I desired to gather your children together as a hen gathers her brood under her wings, and you were not willing. (Matthew 23:37 and Luke 13:34)

The prayer is from George Appleton, ed., in *The Oxford Book of Prayer*, 1986.

For renewal of the church (574)

Anon. South Africa, 20th cent.
This congregational prayer of intercession, confession, and renewal was included in John de Gruchy's collection of worship resources *Cry Justice*, 1986.

For the beauty of the earth (92)

Folliot S. Pierpoint, 1864
This hymn is one of the most popular, singable, and durable selections in the repertory. The text came to the author as he sat on a hill overlooking Bath and recounted the gifts of God that were displayed in a panoramic view of that elegant city and its environs.

The text was published in eight stanzas in Orby Shipley's *Lyra Eucharistica* (1864 2d ed.) under the title "The sacrifice of Praise." The operative words in the hymn, "praise," "offering," and "sacrifice," come from the 1662 *Book of Common Prayer* postcommunion prayer. This prayer, now inappropriately placed before the distribution on page 29 in our hymnal, has been included in our communion services since 1784 when it was received by the American societies from John Wesley.

The hymn entered our hymnals in 1905, number 28, in six stanzas, some altered, as a hymn of praise with the refrain: "Christ, our God, to thee we raise this our hymn of praise." In our 1935 hymnal in deference to those squeamish about singing "Christ our God," this metaphor, based on teaching found in early Christian hymns that address Christ as God, was changed to "Lord of all." Our hymnal includes the original refrain for optional use in the Eucharist.

The hymn in its original form has been included in only one hymnal in this century, *The English Hymnal*, 1906. The original sixth stanza has troubled hymnal committees on several counts. It originally read:

> For each perfect gift of thine
> To our race so freely given,
> Graces human and divine,
> Flowers of earth and buds of Heaven.

The generally accepted altered version of this stanza is included in our hymnal with a further modification to avoid the possible hint of racial exclusivity; in stanza 6:2, "our race" has been changed to "the world."

The change in stanza 5, "For thy Bride" to "For thy church," was included in our 1905 version. The poet's orthodox upbringing is seen in the two omitted concluding stanzas. The final line, "Jesus, Victim undefiled," is from the opening phrase of the sequence *Victimae Paschali laudes* (Christian, to the Paschal victim offer your thankful praises!):

> For thy Martyr's crown of light,
>   For thy Prophets' eagle eye,
> For thy bold Confessors' might,
>   For the lips of infancy:

> For thy Virgins' robes of snow,
>   For thy Maiden-mother mild,
> For thyself, with hearts aglow,
>   Jesus, Victim undefiled:

Dix

Conrad Kocher, 1838; harm. by William H. Monk, 1861
This sturdy adaptation and harmonization of Kocher's melody was made by W. H. Monk for *Hymns Ancient and Modern*, 1861, number 64, and the tune first appeared in this form in our 1878 hymnal. The harmony in measure 2 was modified by the editors of *The English Hymnal*, 1906, and the balance of Monk's setting is included without attribution. That version has been included without alteration in our hymnals since 1905.

The tune's name is the last name of the author of "As with gladness men of old," the Epiphany hymn to which it was originally set, a hymn that was excluded from our hymnal because of space limitations, not by reason of its sexist language, e.g., "men of old." There are three descants and two alternate harmonizations at 93-96 in *The United Methodist Hymnal Music Supplement*.

For the bread which you have broken (614)

Louis F. Benson, 1924 (Matt. 26:26-29; Mark 14:22-25; Luke 22:15-20)
Robert G. McCutchan has provided this account of the hymn.

[It] was first published [at 41] in Doctor Benson's private collection entitled *Hymns [Original and Translated]* in 1925 . . . [where the poet states on the page] that the first stanza of the hymn "was suggested by Bonar's 'For the bread and for the wine,' and was written to fill the place of the post-communion hymn." The first draft seems to have been made on November 21, 1924. . . . "Dr. Henry Sloane Coffin [read the draft] but wanted an additional verse bringing in Service and Kingdom. . . . The next day I sat down and wrote the verse." (McCutchan, 1942, 420)

The hymn effectively draws upon the Gospels' accounts of Christ's institution of his board of remembrance to unite our earthly celebrations with the Lamb's high feast. It entered our hymnals in 1935 unaltered. Alterations were made for the *Lutheran Book of Worship*, 1978, *Hymns from the Four Winds*, 1983, and our hymnal. The eight changes in the text from seventeenth-century century English combine to blur the imagery, lessen its directness, and diminish its literary and singing qualities (e.g., the first line "which thou hast" to "which you have" and the de-gendering of "our Father's board" to "the Lord God's board").

Beng-Li

I-to Loh, 1970

The composer sensitively combines his melody, composed in the style of traditional Asian vocal music, with a contemporary three-part accompaniment. It was written in 1970 to be sung in the scene in a passion play that depicts the Last Supper and first appeared in *Hymns from the Four Winds*, 1983, number 36. Performance notes are found at 43 in *The United Methodist Hymnal Music Supplement*.

More specific suggestions for playing and singing Asian music are found in the preface to *Hymns from the Four Winds*, number xii. See also "Asian American Hymns," pages 35-36.

For the bread

See "Faith, while trees are still in blossom," page 331.

For the fruits of this creation (97)

Fred Pratt Green, 1970

The text was written in response to a suggestion by John Wilson that Francis Jackson's tune EAST ACKLAM, composed as an alternate to AR HYD Y NOS **(688)**, needed a new text, preferably on a harvest theme. Dr. Green obliged, and the text was first printed in the *Methodist Recorder*, August 1970, under the title "Harvest Hymn." (Green 1982, 20) The hymn was included in most hymnals produced in Great Britain during the 1970's. The *Lutheran Book of Worship*, 1978, was the first USA hymnal to include it and introduced the first of several alterations that have made it an inclusive text.

The poet skillfully employs the motif of thanksgiving for God's bounteous gifts as the continuum for an eloquent and forceful social gospel hymn, advocating adequate compensation to the laborer and chiding the Western world and its church as ungrateful for God's gifts of food and unable and unwilling to share these gifts with the rest of God's family.

In our first line the change of "his creation" to "this creation" conveys a suggestion of many creations and creators.

East Acklam

Francis Jackson, 1957

This tune was written while the composer was organist at York Minster. It was composed as an alternate tune to the Welsh melody AR HYD Y NOS, a popular setting for "God, that madest earth and heaven" **(688)**, but a union that had perplexed Anglican organists and choirmasters since its inclusion in *The English Hymnal*, 1906. According to *Companion to Hymns and Psalms*, Jackson's tune "was first sung at a reunion service of old choristers there [York Minster] in October of 1957." (Watson and Trickett 1988, 220) The first setting of this tune with Fred Pratt Green's text was in the Roman Catholic hymnal *Praise the Lord*, 1972.

For the healing of the nations (428)

Fred Kaan, 1965 (Rev. 21:1-22:5)

The author has commented about this text:

Of all the hymns I have written, this is the text that has been more widely reprinted and incorporated in major hymnbooks than any other. It was first used in 1965 in a worship service at the Pilgrim Church, Plymouth, to mark Human Rights Day (December 10). Subsequently, it has been used on many official occasions, such as the 25th anniversary of the United Nations organization. (Kaan 1985, 35)

In stanza 2:1, "Father," has been changed to "forward." Otherwise the text is included as it appears in the author's 1985 version.

Cwm Rhondda

John Hughes, 1907

The tune's name CWM RHONDDA literally means Rhondda Valley, the name for a coal mining district in South Wales. According to William J. Reynolds (1975, 77), it was composed for the 1907 Baptist Cymanfa Ganu (A Gathering for Song) at

Pontypridd; and by 1930 it had been sung at over 3,000 such gatherings. It appeared in the *Salvation Army Tune Book*, 1931, where it was set to the hymn "Jesus, give thy blood-washed Army/Universal liberty." (Watson and Trickett, *Supplemental Notes* to *Companion to Hymns and Psalms*, 1990.) In the USA it first appeared in the Presbyterian *Hymnal*, 1933, and entered our hymnals in 1935. Alan Luff has commented on this tune:

> [It] was resisted by the main hymn book editors in both Welsh and English for many years, no doubt because of the tune's great vigour and, what can best be called its vulgar appeal—not necessarily a bad thing. . . . It should be sung for its full worth, in harmony, and not too fast, with the bass striding through the first four lines and rising, with the repetition of the words in both bass and alto, to the dominant seventh chord at the end of the fifth line. (Luff 1990, 223).

Singing the hymn to EBENEZER **(108)** or GRAFTON **(505)** will avoid the vain repetition of the final seven syllables of each stanza. There is a descant and alternate harmonization in *The United Methodist Hymnal Music Supplement*, 76-77.

For the sick (457)

Book of Common Prayer; alt. by Laurence Hull Stookey, 1987

This prayer is one of fifteen hymns and prayers for the sick listed under "Healing" in the "Index of Topics and Categories," **943**. The prayer was adapted by Dr. Stookey from "For strength and confidence" in the section "Prayers for the Sick," the *Book of Common Prayer*, 1979, page 459. In a corporate setting the ill may be named. It is also a prayer for those who, like Jesus the great physician, minister to persons ill of mind and body.

For the spirit of truth (597)

Prayer from Kenya

This prayer is for deliverance from those particular attributes that prevent us from stating and acting out the truth.

The prayer is from George Appleton, ed., *The Oxford Book of Prayer*, 1986.

For the unity of Christ's body (564)

Chinese Prayer

The centerpiece of this prayer for Christian unity are Paul's account of Jesus' words to his disciples at the Passover meal, "And when he had given thanks, he broke it and said, "This is my body that is for [some ancient authorities read *broken for*] you" (1 Corinthians 11:24); and the apostle's description of the church as Christ's body, "And he has put all things under his feet and has made him the head over all things for the church, which is his body, the fullness of him who fills all in all" (Ephesians 1:22-23). This prayer is a petition that Christ will never be able to attribute his and the church's brokenness to our divisive thoughts and acts.

The prayer is from George Appleton, ed., *The Oxford Book of Prayer*, 1986.

For those who mourn (461)

Laurence Hull Stookey, 1987 (James 11:35; Matt. 5:4)
The author has commented on his text:

> Perhaps the greatest gift to those who mourn is an insight into the heart of God who weeps. Jesus' tears [of sorrow and sympathy] at the tomb of Lazarus [John 11:35] give us permission not to hide our anguish but to express it, knowing that God accepts and understands human sorrow, and strengthens those who mourn. [Blessed are those who mourn, for they will be comforted. (Matthew 5:4)] (Sanchez 1989, 160)

For true life (403)

Teresa of Avila, Spain, 16th cent.
Laurence Hull Stookey has provided this commentary:

> At the heart of this prayer there is a striking request: "Do not punish me . . . by granting that which I wish or ask." The great Spanish mystic Teresa of Avila knew it could be—should God grant our foolish requests. The prayer is clearly an expansion of Jesus' petition in Gethsemane: "Not my will, but thine, be done" (Lk. 22:42). (Sanchez 1989, 142)

The prayer is from Barbara Greene and Victor Gollancz, eds., *God of a Hundred Names*, 1962.

For true singing (69)

Fred D. Gealy, 1965; alt. by Laurence Hull Stookey, 1987 (James 1:22)
This prayer is appropriate for use at any occasion that gathers choirs and congregations for singing. At its heart is this passage from the letter of James:

> But be doers of the word, and not merely hearers who deceive themselves. For if any are hearers of the word and not doers, they are like those who

look at themselves in a mirror; for they look at themselves and, on going away, immediately forget what they were like. But those who look into the perfect law, the law of liberty, and persevere, being not hearers who forget but doers who act—they will be blessed in their doing. (James 1:22-25)

Dr. Gealy composed the prayer for the Seminary Singers of Perkins School of Theology, Southern Methodist University, and adapted it for *The Book of Worship*, 1965, page 167. Stookey has altered the original first line from "Almighty God, at whose right hand are pleasures evermore" and modified the language of the prayer to contemporary USA English.

Forgive our sins as we forgive (390)

Rosamond E. Herklots, 1966 (Matt. 6:12)

This text is an elaboration of a verse of the Lord's Prayer, Matthew 6:12, "And forgive us our debts, as we also have forgiven our debtors," and Paul's admonition in Colossians 3:13, "Bear with one another and, if anyone has a complaint against another, forgive each other; just as the Lord has forgiven you, so you also must forgive." According to *Companion to Hymns and Psalms*,

> This hymn was written in June 1966 and printed soon afterward in the parish magazine of St. Mary's Church, Bromley, Kent. The idea of the hymn had occurred to Miss Herklots when she was digging out weeds in her nephew's garden; she reasoned that their deep roots, obstructing the growth of the flowers near them, resembled the bitterness and resentment that can become intrenched and hinder the Christian's growth in grace. (Watson and Trickett 1988, 110)

It was revised by the author for *Hymns & Songs*, 1969, where it appeared under the heading "The Unforgiving Heart." Alterations have been made for our hymnal in stanza 3:3, "How small the debts men owe to us" to "what trivial debts are owed to us," and 4:3, "Then, reconciled to God and man" to "then, bound to all in bonds of love."

Detroit

Attrib. to Bradshaw in Supplement to Kentucky Harmony, 1820
harm. by Gerald H. Knight, 1979

Austin C. Lovelace cites the similarity of the tune to "The wife of Usher's well," an English folk song collected by Cecil Sharp. (Gealy, Lovelace, Young 1970, 397) The tune was very popular in the nineteenth century, appearing in a dozen or more USA tune books. It has also been included in several recent British collections. Our harmonization with an unfortunate suspension at midpoint is by Gerald H. Knight and appeared in *More Hymns for Today*, 1980. Since there was no credit on the page, it was included in our hymnal without citation. The tune is set in a singing school style for three voices at 85 in *The United Methodist Hymnal Music Supplement*.

Forth in thy name, O Lord (438)

Charles Wesley, 1749

This hymn is titled "Before Work," number 32 in the section of "Hymns for Believers," *Hymns and Sacred Poems*, 1749. The hymn was first included in our hymnals in 1838 with a selection of five stanzas of the original six. The four stanzas in our hymnal appear as in the original text with only one change: stanza 2:4 originally read "And prove thine acceptable will."

In the omitted stanza 3 the poet warns against busyness for its own sake:

> Preserve me from my Calling's Snare,
>   And hide my simple Heart above,
> Above the Thorns of Choaking [*sic*] Care,
>   The guided Baits of Worldly Love.

And in stanza 5, work in the name of Christ, like worship, is the duty and delight of the faithful as they journey toward that eternal and glorious day:

> Give me to bear thy Easy Yoke,
>   And every Moment watch and pray,
> And still to things Eternal look,
>   And hasten to thy Glorious Day.

Erik Routley's comment that this is "perhaps the first and greatest of weekday hymns" (Routley 1979, 27) is a casual understanding of this text as an expression of the Protestant work ethic. On the contrary, this hymn is a prayer that our work *everyday*, including Sundays for church workers, may be done in faithful response to the stirring within us of God's Holy Spirit. The text was included in John Wesley's 1780 *Collection* in the section "For Believers Working," hymns that distinguish "inward" religion from "formal" religion. As Hildebrandt and Beckerlegge remind us,

> it should not be forgotten that the early Methodist Conferences were "Conversations about the work *of* God, not the work of man for God!" The flame of faith can be lit only from outside and above—it is the gift of the Holy Spirit. Christ is the subject and agent [as in the hymn omitted from our hymnal "Author of faith, eternal Word"].

> Increase in us the kindled fire,
> In us the work of faith fulfil.

To the question, "What shall we do that we might work the works of God?" the answer is "This is the work of God, that ye believe," John 6:28-29. (Wesley 1983, 7:474)

The hymn is not, as stated by Craig B. Gallaway, "a natural hymn for Labor Day Sunday." (Sanchez 1989, 153) Underachievers, overachievers, the unsuccessful, and the unemployed ought to be spared its inclusion in this and other ill-advised Sabbath services convened to extol the virtues of the Protestant work ethic and to inventory the harvest of righteous works.

Duke Street

John Hatton, 1793

According to *Companion to Hymns and Psalms,*

> [This tune first appeared] anonymously in *A Select Collection of Psalm and Hymn Tunes . . . By the late Henry Boyd, Teacher of Psalmody* (Glasgow, 1793), with the heading 'Addison's 19th Psalm' ["The spacious firmament on high," not included in our hymnal]. It was later ascribed to John Hatton and named DUKE STREET in *Euphonia, containing Sixty-Two Psalm and Hymn tunes . . . Harmonized, Arranged and Composed . . . by W. Dixon* (Liverpool, c. 1805). (Watson and Trickett 1988, 51)

Hatton lived for a short time on Duke Street in St. Helens, formerly Lancashire, now Merseyside, thus the tune's name. According to Robert G. McCutchan, this sturdy LM melody entered our hymnals as "Newry" in *The Methodist Harmonist,* 1821. (McCutchan 1942, 41) Vocal descants and alternate harmonizations may be found at 100-103 in *The United Methodist Hymnal Music Supplement.*

Forward through the ages (555)

Frederick Lucian Hosmer, 1908

This is a turn-of-the-century, forward-looking social gospel hymn (see "Social Gospel Hymns," page 30). Its Unitarian theology is optimistic ("wider grows the kingdom"), vague ("shining goal"), without a Christology. The hymn was written in 1908 for the installation of a minister for the First Unitarian Church, Berkeley, California, and according to William J. Reynolds, it was included in the author's *Thought of God in Hymns and Poems,* 1918, third series. (Reynolds 1976, 68) It was first included in our 1957 hymnal and was recommended for our present hymnal as one of the favorite hymns of the former Evangelical United Brethren Church. Setting it to the tune ST. GERTRUDE, the setting for the equally optimistic "Onward Christian Soldiers," reflects the Hymnal Revision Committee's intention for the tune to be sung to a less controversial text.

St. Gertrude

See "Onward, Christian soldiers," pages 546-47.

Freedom in Christ (360)

Rubem Alves, Brazil, 20th cent.

This prayer by the contemporary Brazilian theologian and teacher Rubem Alves is a petition to be freed from the fear of our death so that we may live the good life that God has intended for each of us.

It is from the author's *I Believe in the Resurrection of the Body*, 1986.

Freely, freely (389)

Words and music: Carol Owens, 1972 (Matt. 10: 8; 28: 18-20)

This gospel hymn expresses the obligation of those who have been forgiven and made new creatures in Christ to share freely (Matthew 6:12) that graceful gift to the lost and needy in the spirit of the great commission, "Go therefore and make disciples of all nations, baptizing them in the name of the Father and of the Son and of the Holy Spirit." (Matthew 28:19)

The hymn was arranged by Jimmy Owens for the author's musical *Come Together*, 1972. (Adams 1992, 126)

Freely, freely

The tune reflects the easy, singable, and memorable qualities of the traditional gospel hymn.

From a distant home (243)

See "De tierra lejana venimos," page 315-16.

From all that dwell below the skies (101)

Sts. 1-2, Isaac Watts, 1719; sts. 3-4, anon., 1781 (Ps. 117)

Praise the Lord, all you nations!
    Extol him, all you peoples!
For great is his steadfast love toward us,
    and the faithfulness of the Lord endures forever.
Praise the Lord! (Psalm 117)

The first two stanzas are Watts's paraphrase of Psalm 117 from his *Psalms of David Imitated, in the Language of the New Testament*, 1719, page 305. (Gealy 556/137) The brevity of the hymn has caused most editors to print additional stanzas. Our stanzas 3-4 are from *A Pocket Hymn-Book, Designed as a Constant Companion for the Pious. Collected from Various Authors*, ca. 1781, where they were included at 153 without attribution by its editor Robert Spence, Methodist class leader and bookseller. Spence's publishing activity is the butt of John Wesley's complaint in his preface to his 1787 *Pocket Hymn-Book*, which he printed to drive Spence's book off the market. See "Methodist Episcopal Hymnals," pages 97-108.

The four stanzas entered our hymnals at 150 in *A Pocket Hymn-Book*, 1788, taken over from Spence's book; see the chart of official hymnals in "Authorized Methodist Hymnals," pages 94-95.

Duke Street

See "Forth in thy name, O Lord, I go," pages 348-49.

Gift of love (408)

See "The gift of Love," page 636.

Give me the faith which can remove (650)

Charles Wesley, 1749

The hymn first appeared at vol. 1:188 in *Hymns and Sacred Poems*, 1749, titled "For a Preacher of the Gospel" in eight stanzas. The hymn was seldom reprinted in its entirety because, as seen in its first stanza printed below, it reveals the poet and co-leader of the revival struggling to express a positive word during a particularly dry and uninspired moment. Hear this longing for the former days of strength, insight, and energy!

> O that I was as heretofore
> When first sent forth in Jesu's Name.
> I rush'd thro' every open Door,
>   And cried to All, 'Behold the Lamb!'
> Seiz'd the poor trembling Slaves of Sin,
>   And forc'd the Outcasts to come in.

"Clearly by 1749 CW felt some cooling off of his zeal. [In the 1780 *Collection*] his brother removed [the record of] this depression by his choice of verses." (Hildebrandt and Beckerlegge 1983, 596-97)

John Wesley included five of the original eight stanzas in his 1780 *Collection*. The text entered our hymnals in 1821. This is the first of our hymnals to include the hymn since the 1836 *Collection*. Our four stanzas (original 3, 5, 6, 7), appropriate for any occasion when ministry is celebrated, are identical to those in the British Methodist *Hymns and Psalms*, 1983, number 767, except that in 4:4, "their Shepherd" has been changed to "the Shepherd," and the original 1:4-5 read

That love which one may Heart o'erpower'd
And all my simple Soul devour'd.

Carey's (Surrey)

Henry Carey, ca. 1732; harm. from The English Hymnal, 1906
This tune was composed for solo voice and continuo, and first appeared in
John Church's *Introduction to Psalmody*, ca. 1723, set to Joseph Addison's "The
Lord my pasture shall prepare." The melody is found in several tune books
used by Methodist societies during John Wesley's time. Wesley included it in
both *Sacred Melody*, 1761, and *Sacred Harmony*, 1780. The form of the melody
and the harmony are from *The English Hymnal*, 1906, number 491. This is the
first appearance of the tune in our hymnals and a welcome addition to the
scant repertory of singable 88.88.88 melodies, a favorite meter of Charles
Wesley in which he composed over 1,100 poems and a total of 23,000 lines.
(Baker 1962, xlv) The tune is also named "Surrey." A descant, three alternate
harmonizations, and the setting from Thomas Butts's *Harmonia Sacra*, ca.
1754, number 133, are found at 57-61 in *The United Methodist Hymnal Music
Supplement*.

Give to the winds thy fears (129)
Befiehl du deine Wege

Paul Gerhardt, 1653; trans. by John Wesley, 1739 (Ps. 37:5)
Gerhardt's hymn, according to Theodore B. Hewitt in *Paul Gerhardt as a Hymn
Writer and His Influence on English Hymnody* (1976, 114), was first published in
Johann Crüger's *Praxis Pietatis Melica*, 1656, number 333, in twelve stanzas of
76. 76 D. It is an acrostic on Luther's version of Psalm 37:5, "Befiehl dem Herren deine Wege und hoffe auf ihn, er wirds wohl machen." Each word of the
verse, except "dem Herren" which begins the second verse, is the first word of
successive stanzas.

John Wesley's journal shows that by October 17, 1735, while on board the *Sim-
mons* bound for Georgia, he began to learn German by singing with the Moravians in their *Singstunde* (singing meetings), probably from J. A. Freylinghausen's *Geist-reiches Gesang-Buch*, 1704 and 1714. The first stanza (see below)
may have been a comfort to Wesley during the stormy voyage to Georgia. This
and other occasions may have introduced him to Gerhardt's classic hymn of
consolation and trust and other German hymns in translation that he included
in his 1737 *Collection*. (Curnock 1909, 114)

Wesley's work on Gerhardt's text was probably in progress and may have been
completed while he was still in Georgia. (For further commentary about Wesley
in Georgia, see Carlton R. Young, "John Wesley's 1737 Charlestown *Collection of
Psalms and Hymns*," *The Hymn*, October 1990.)

The translation that first appeared in *Hymns and Sacred Poems*, 1739, pages 141-44 in sixteen stanzas of four lines under the heading "Trust in Providence. From the German" (Gealy 556/142), is widely held to be the most faithful to the meaning and the spirit of the original. (Hewitt 1976, 115) A comparison of the first stanza in German with Wesley's translation of the original first and second stanzas demonstrates his sensitive modification of the original 76's into SM (66.8.6).

Befiehl du deine Wege	Commit thou all thy Griefs
und was dein Herze kränkt,	And Ways into his Hands;
der allertreusten Pflege	To his sure Truth and tender Care
des, der den Himmel lenkt.	Who earth and Heav'n commands.
Der Wolken, Luft und Winden	Who points the Clouds their Course,
gibt Wege, Lauf and Bahn,	Whom Winds and Seas obey;
der wird auch Wege finden,	He shall direct thy wand'ring Feet,
da dein Fuß gehen kann.	He shall prepare thy Way.

Wesley's text entered our hymnals in 1786 in two hymns, "Give to the winds thy fears" and "Commit thou all thy griefs." The entire hymn was dropped from our 1935 hymnal, but four stanzas were included in the 1957 book. Our 1966 hymnal printed the four stanzas, which correspond to original stanzas 9, 10, 13, 16 as published in 1739, that are carried over into our present hymnal. In stanzas 3:1, "he" is changed to "God," in 2:3, "he" to "God's," and in 3:4, "his" to "this." For the full German and English texts see *The Handbook to the Lutheran Hymnal*. (Polack 1942, 362-65)

Festal song

William H. Walter, 1894

The tune first appeared in J. I. Tucker and W. W. Rousseau's *Hymnal Revised and Enlarged*, 1894, a popular music edition of the 1892 Protestant Episcopal hymnal. The matching of this slick and predictable tune to this solid hymn is unfortunate and continues the futile efforts to find a suitable and singable setting. There is a vocal descant at 129 in *The United Methodist Hymnal Music Supplement*.

Gloria in excelsis (BCP) (82)

Gloria in excelsis (ICET) (83)

See "Canticle of God's glory," pages 253-54.

Gloria, gloria, in excelsis Deo (72)

Luke 2:14

For commentary on this text, see "Canticle of God's glory," pages 253-54.

Gloria canon

Jacques Berthier and the Community of Taizé, 1979
This joyous song of the angels may be used as a call to worship or as a Christmas Eve processional. It may be sung in unison, or as a two-, three-, or four-voice round with a different group beginning as indicated by the number in the circle. For commentary on the music of Taizé, see "Eat this bread," pages 324-25. See 390, *The United Methodist Hymnal Music Supplement* for suggested English sounds for the Latin words.

Glorious things of thee are spoken (731)

John Newton, 1779 (Ps. 87:3; Isa. 33:20-21; Exod. 13:22)
This is one of the most sung hymns in the repertory. It first appeared in John Newton and William Cowper's *Olney Hymns*, 1779, Book 1, pages 75-77, number 60, in five stanzas under the title "Zion, or the city of God. [Isaiah] Chap. 33: 27-28." (Gealy 556/143) The hymn first appeared in our hymnals in 1847 with three stanzas. The present hymnal includes the first four stanzas with one alteration: stanza 1:3, "He" to "God."

In the first edition of the hymn the poet footnotes these scriptural references to selected lines: the title, Psalm 87:3; stanza 1:1, Psalm 132:13-14; 1:4, Matthew 16:18; 1:7, Isaiah 26:1; 2:2, Psalm 46:4; 3:2, Isaiah 4:5-6; 4:4, Revelation 1:5-6.

Austria

Croatian folk song; arr. by Franz Joseph Haydn, 1797
The famous Austrian composer used the first four measures of the Croatian folk hymn "Vjatvo rano se ja vstanem" (see *The New Oxford Companion to Music*, page 464) as the basis of this ingratiating melody that has been performed in such disparate circumstances as the Austrian national anthem, "Gott erhalte Franz den Kaiser," for which it was composed; as the theme for the variation he scored for each instrument in the slow movement of string quartet in C, Op. 70, No. 5, "The Emperor"; as a hymn tune in Edward Miller's *Sacred Music*, 1802; and as the tune sung by Hitler's mobs and storm troopers in Nazi Germany during World War II to "Deutschland über alles." In this latter regard this writer shall never forget the puzzled and pained expression on the face of Elie Wiesel, famed survivor of Hitler's death camps, as the audience gathered in the spring of 1983 at Cannon Chapel, Emory University, and spiritedly sang the insensitively selected Newton hymn, prior to his receiving an honorary degree and giving a paper on "Remembering the Holocaust." Music, like words, may hurt as well as heal.

The tune entered our hymnals in 1878. In 1966 measure 14 was restored to Haydn's original. There is a vocal descant and an alternate harmonization in F major at 27-28, *The United Methodist Hymnal Music Supplement*.

Glory be to God on high

See "Canticle of God's glory," pages 253-54.

Glory be to the Father (70, 71)

This pattern of praise is rooted in Jewish traditions, for example the blessings and doxological verses found at the close each of the five sections of the Psalter: 41:13; 72:18-19; 89:52; 106:48, and the climactic concluding Psalm 150. Early Christian doxologies are found at Matthew 28:19, "Go therefore and make disciples of all nations, baptizing them in the name [i.e., the possession and protection] of the Father and of the Son and of the Holy Spirit," Romans 16:27, Philippians 4:20, and Revelation 5:13. See also "Early Christian Hymns," page 4.

Massie H. Shepherd has written on the origins of the "Lesser Doxology," as distinguished from the "Greater Doxology" ("Glory be to God on high," **82** and **83**):

[The origins] go back to the beginnings of antiphonal psalmody at Antioch. Though its purpose was to give a Christian ending to the Psalms, its earliest forms were a matter of dispute with the Arian heretics, who preferred "Glory to the Father through the Son in the Holy Spirit." In order to stress the equality of the three Persons of the Trinity the orthodox form in the Eastern Churches came to be:

> Glory to the Father and to the Son
>   and to the Holy Spirit,
> Now and always and to the ages of ages.

To emphasize the eternity of the three Persons, again in opposition to the Arians, the Western Churches [Vaison Council, 529] added to the second part of the *Gloria*: "As it was in the Beginning." (Shepherd 1976, 43)

The purpose for singing a Christian doxology at the close of a canticle or psalm or other occasions must never be to declare Hebrew scripture and tradition as inferior, but rather to affirm that the God of Jewish life and witness is "the same as the God manifested in Christ . . . and that the [consubstantiality] unity and equality of the three Persons of the Trinity are eternal." (Gealy, Lovelace, Young 1970, 447)

For further commentary see Geoffrey Wainwright, *Doxology* (1980, 257-59); "Canticle of God's glory" ("Glory be to God on high"), pages 253-54; "Holy, holy, holy," pages 400-01; and "All praise to thee, my God, this night," pages 199-200. See "Doxology" and "Gloria Patri" in the "Index of Topics and Categories," **951**, for additional settings.

Greatorex (71)

Henry W. Greatorex, 1851
This setting first appeared as "Gloria Patri No. 1" at 146 in the composer's *Psalm and Hymn Tunes*, 1851.

Meineke (70)

Charles Meineke, 1844
This setting is from "Evening Prayer" in the composer's *Music for the Church*, 1844, and was first included in our hymnals in 1878, page 442. On the page facing the title page of the 1896 printing the soprano and alto parts are interlined in the "Order of Public Worship." For commentary on this service see pages 65-66.

Glory to God, and praise and love (58)

See page 511.

Glory to God in the highest (82, 83)

See "Canticle of God's glory," pages 253-54.

Go down, Moses (448)

African American Spiritual
Adapt and arr. by William Farley Smith, 1986 (Exod. 3:7-12)
John W. Work, III, classified this as the first of three types of spirituals: "call and response chant; the slow, sustained long-phrase melody; and the syncopated segmented melody." (Sydnor 1962, 24)

Dr. Smith states that this widely sung spiritual may have been "sung first by the Hutchingson Brothers, a black quartet, at Cooper Union in New York City on the occasion of an emancipation speech delivered by President Lincoln in 1863." (Sanchez 1989, 156)

Wyatt Tee Walker elaborates on the structure of the spiritual:

[It is] the classic illustration of a Spiritual that possessed a double [or coded] meaning. . . . Perceptive and intuitive spiritual insights of the New World Africans saw instantly the parallel between their circumstance in this alien land and that of the house of Israel in the Land of Egypt. This Spiritual hymn with its majestic cadences was the expressed hope and desire that God would send a "Moses" into the Egypt land of slavery and command the Pharaohs of the slavocracy to "let [his] people go." (Walker 1979, 56-57)

A simple call-and-response setting for solo voice and four parts is found at 112, *Songs of Zion*, 1981. The spiritual appeared in twenty-five stanzas in "Jubilee Songs," a supplement of 139 selections compiled by F. J. Loudin for *The Story of the Jubilee Singers*, 1896.

The earliest published version of the text and two variants, "The Song of the Contrabands" and "The Lord Doth Now to This Nation Speak," are included at 363-74 in Dena J. Epstein, *Sinful Tunes and Spirituals*.

Tubman

The tune's name comes from the ex-slave and underground railroad conductor Harriet Tubman, who, according to Dr. Smith, was known as "the Moses of her People." (Sanchez 1989, 156)

Go forth for God (670)

John R. Peacey, 1975

This hymn was first included in five stanzas at number 77 in *English Praise*, the supplement to *The English Hymnal*, by "J. R. Peacy and editors." The consistency of the the first four stanzas indicates that they are principally if not completely Canon Peacy's. The fifth stanza illustrates why hymnal committees and their editors should get more sleep!

> Sing praise to him who brought us on our way;
> > Sing praise to him who bought us with his blood;
> Sing praise to him who sanctifies each day;
> > Sing praise to him who reigns, one God, above.

The sources of the hymn are discussed in "Go Forth for God," *Bulletin: The Hymn Society of Great Britain and Ireland.* 1987.

Ray Glover has provided this commentary on the four stanzas included in *The Hymnal 1982*:

> [It is] a hymn that amplifies the admonitions of the Eucharistic post-communion prayer, "send us now into the world in peace . . . to love and serve you." . . . The text is also suitable for Confirmation and for Commitment to Christian Service. . . . [In this latter regard we are directed] to go forth in strength, in love, and in joy [Romans 12:9-21]. (Glover 1987, 44)

Our hymnal, following *The Hymnal 1982*, transposes stanzas 2 and 3. Since the text is 10 10. 10 10. and our tune, GENEVA 124, is 10 10. 10 10. 10., the last line of each stanza and the key words of the hymn, "peace," "love," "strength," and "joy," are restated, a wholly satisfactory outcome serving to surmount the problem posed by the poet's use of enjambment (overlapping) of the third and fourth phrases in stanzas 2 and 3. Other changes are in stanza 1:4, "behold his face" to "see face to face"; 2:4, "His" to "God's"; 3:3, "man" to "one"; 4:2, "brethren" to "people." The Hymnal Revision Committee made a wise choice in setting this impressive text to GENEVA 124, and it has become one of the most compelling new hymns in our hymnal.

Geneva 124

Genevan Psalter, 1551; harm. by C. Winfred Douglas, 1940, alt.
This tune from the French-Genevan Psalter *(Pseaumes octante trois de David)* of 1551 has been slightly modified during its four centuries of use in Anglo psalters and hymnals. The tune entered our hymnals in 1966 set to "Turn back, O man, forswear thy foolish ways," one of the very few texts, along with paraphrase of Psalm 124, to match the tune's unique meter.

In a sense this tune has for many years been looking for a text. Its new association with Canon Peacy's fine hymn may be its most felicitous liaison to date. The shape of the tune and the harmonization, the latter with some alteration, are from *The Hymnal 1940*. An intriguing harmonization from John Day's sixteenth-century Anglo psalter is found at 23 in *With One Voice*. See 138-40 in *The United Methodist Hymnal Music Supplement* for a vocal descant and two alternate harmonizations.

Go, make of all disciples (571)

Leon M. Adkins, 1955, alt. (Matt. 28:19-20)
The hymn was first sung at the commissioning of teachers and church school officials during Christian Education Week, 1955, at University Methodist Church, Syracuse, where the author was pastor. It was first printed in the *Church School*, February, 1956. The author made several alterations for its first appearance at 342 in our 1966 hymnal, and the hymn remains one of the most widely used "new" hymns in the repertory. The "going forth" theme makes it an ideal choice for revivals, ordinations, consecrations, dedications, and commissionings.

In 1966 the author provided Fred D. Gealy with an extended commentary that is summarized:

> The first stanza suggests that to make disciples of all is not man's idea but God's . . . who calls us to this task . . . with whom we communicate through prayer, and understand that daily living obscures or reveals God's intent for us.

The second stanza emphasizes the church's ministry in continuity as we baptize and redeem in the name of Christ.

The third stanza is about Christian vocation, learning, work, and witness. The roots of discipleship are "implanted in the soul" by God at our birth, and by cultivating in others that God-given nature we reflect the Master Teacher's art.

The concluding stanza is our commitment to and our assurance from the One who stays by "to the close of the age," Matthew 28:20. "Calling" is not merely to perform an assembly of many chores, rather it should invoke enthusiasm and continuing growth within an understanding that the completion of God's task in establishing the Kingdom depends not on us alone. (Gealy 556/144)

The hymn appears in the same form as in the 1966 hymnal with one change, "alway" to "always" in stanza 4:3.

Lancashire

Henry T. Smart, 1835

The tune was composed for the three-hundredth anniversary of the English Reformation set to Reginald Heber's "From Greenland's icy mountain," and was first sung from leaflets during a festival held at Blackburn, Lancashire, October 4, 1835. It was later included in the composer's *Psalms and Hymns for Divine Worship*, 1867, published by the Presbyterian Church of England. Following the lead of *Hymns Ancient and Modern* and *The English Hymnal*, most British hymnals have not included this tune. However, it has been widely used in the USA, usually with the text "Lead on, O King eternal" **(580)**, entering our hymnals with that text in 1905. There are two alternate harmonizations and a vocal descant at 195-97 in *The United Methodist Hymnal Music Supplement*.

Go now in peace (665)

Words and music: Natalie Sleeth, 1976 (Luke 2:29)

This delightful dismissal response was first included in the composer's *Sunday Songbook*, 1976. It may be sung a number of times by the congregation and choir in unison or as a two-, three-, or four-part round with a different group entering as indicated by the number in the circle.

Go in peace

Orff and other instruments may be used for the melody and the accompaniment figure in other octaves. See 146 in *The United Methodist Hymnal Music Supplement* for additional instrumental patterns for Orff instruments.

Go tell it on the mountain (251)

African American spiritual
adapt. by John W. Work, Jr., ca. 1907 (Luke 2:8-20)

This spiritual in the typical call-and-response pattern is a simple, compelling, and straightforward retelling of the Lukean natal narrative. The words and perhaps the music were adapted from traditional sources by John W. Work, II. According to Edith McFall Work, widow of John Work, III,

> the verses of these songs were published by John Work, II in place of the original ones which could not be found. In 1940 John Work, III, had the songs copyrighted and published [at 215] in his book *American Negro Songs*. (Correspondence with Carlton R. Young, December 1987)

William J. Reynolds relates:

> [John Work, III] took pleasure in recalling his early days as a child on the campus of Fisk University where his father was a teacher. Very early on Christmas morning, long before sunrise, it was then the custom for students to gather and walk together from building to building singing [this spiritual]. (Reynolds 1976, 71)

James H. Cone has commented that the birth of Jesus announces the ministry of "the conquering King, and the crucified Lord who has come to bring peace and justice to the dispossessed of the land. That is why the slave wanted to "go tell it on de mountain." (Cone 1972, 49)

The *Pilgrim Hymnal*, 1958, was the first mainline denominational hymnal to include this or any African American spiritual. While the permissions section of the hymnal included proper credit, there was no attribution on the hymn page to the Work family. It is a matter of record that while pop, jazz, and classical composers and performing and publishing rights have increasingly been protected and recognized, the hymnic efforts and rights of African American composers and authors have been slighted.

The spiritual entered our hymnals in 1966, number 404, with words by John W. Work, II, with an adaptation from Work's 1940 arrangement for solo voice and four-part choir (Gealy 556/145) into a four-voice European hymn setting by Hugh Porter, music editor of the *Pilgrim Hymnal*, 1958.

Go tell it on the mountain

African American spiritual
adapt. and arr. by William Farley Smith, 1986

Dr. Smith's adaptation of Work's setting tastefully embellishes the chorus and the end of the verses with the blue note, chromatic turns, and turn-of-the-century male quartet textures and voice leadings. It improves but does not abandon Porter's European setting.

Go to dark Gethsemane (290)

James Montgomery, 1820, 1825, alt.

The author wrote two versions of this passion and resurrection hymn, which appeared in Thomas Cotterill's *Selection of Psalms and Hymns for Public and Private Use*, 1820, and the author's *Christian Psalmist*, 1825. (Gealy 556/146) The latter was included in our 1878 hymnal. Evangelical United Brethren hymnals continued the hymn, while Methodists dropped it from their 1905 and 1935 Methodist hymnals, restoring it in 1966. Our present hymnal includes the hymn without change from the 1822 version with the exception of stanza 2:2, "Beaten, bound, reviled, arraigned," from the 1820 text (see Julian 1907, 430); and 4:4, "hath" to "has."

The poet's bidding verbs, "go," "see," "adore," and "hasten," make this an ideal congregational hymn for Holy Week or other occasions celebrating Jesus's passion, death, and promised resurrection. Redhead's expressive setting can be an effective call to worship, a response to prayer and to scripture, particular the passion narratives.

Redhead 76

Richard Redhead, 1853

This tune, also called "Ajalon," "Gethsemane," and "Petra," is number 76 in the composer's *Church Hymn Tunes, Ancient and Modern*, 1853. Composed by a composer-clergyman who was at the center of Tractarian music, the tune expresses prevailing mid-nineteenth-century Anglo-Catholic perceptions that to recapture the spirit of antiquity is to compose reserved, understated, if not cheerless, hymn tunes. Routley's opinion that "Redhead did better work when he was not composing" (Routley 1981, 91) may not be an overstatement.

The matching of this tune to "Rock of ages, cleft for me," page 108, *Hymns Ancient and Modern*, 1861, there named "Petra" (Latin for rock), introduced it into broad Anglican use and from there to USA hymnals including our 1878 hymnal, page 407. Here it was the setting for "When this passing world is done." "Rock of ages," following late eighteenth-century evangelical practice, was already inseparably joined to TOPLADY **(361)**. With the exception of our 1878 book, where the tune awkwardly began on the third count of the measure, it has always been included in its original form. It was first matched with the above text in our 1957 hymnal.

God be with you will we meet again (672, 673)

Jeremiah E. Rankin, 1880

During the nineteenth century in the USA, refrains and final stanzas were often sung at the conclusion of camp meetings, revivals, annual homecoming services and at the departure of the minister, musician, or missionary to another assignment. In another tradition shaped-note singing schools and annual singings still conclude with a good-bye or farewell selection, with the singers exchanging a handshake or hug. In both traditions this can be a tearful moment for the elderly and their families and friends.

Today many churches conclude worship services with the singing of "Shalom" **(666, 667)**, other selections from the section "Closing of Worship" **(663-672)**, or J. E. Rankin's good-bye ("God be with you") hymn. The hymn first appeared in *Gospel Bells*, 1880, number 50, under the heading "The grace of our Lord Jesus Christ be with you.—Rom. 16:20" (Gealy 556/147), and was first sung at a revival in the First Congregational Church, Washington, DC, where the author was pastor. It was popularized among Methodists who attended the summer ingatherings at the Ocean Grove Campmeeting Association on the Jersey shore. Moody and Sankey used it at countless meetings around the world, and it was sung as Protestant missionaries embarked for Africa and Asia.

The hymn was first included in our hymnals in 1889. In 1966 the refrain was dropped; it is restored in this hymnal.

God be with you (672)

William G. Towner, 1880

Rankin sent one stanza of his hymn to two composers. He selected W. G. Towner's tune and included the additional stanzas. The tune was revised by J. W. Bischoff, music editor of *Gospel Bells*, 1880, where it first appeared.

The tune, as most gospel hymnody, has not received high marks from trained church musicians. Several hymnal committees, including our 1966 committee hoping to discourage its singing, dropped the refrain. The sound of the congregation singing the refrain a cappella from memory and with great feeling has bewildered organists who, following the score, have just begun the next stanza. Those unhappy with the change dispatched disagreeable letters to the Hymnal Revision Committee and the editor. Thus far the restoration of the refrain has not produced letters of either congratulation or condemnation.

Randolph (673)

Ralph Vaughan Williams, 1906

The tune was first included in *The English Hymnal*, 1906, number 524. Its ABCA form is a perfect match for the text and successfully combines simple unison and part singing in a setting accessible to choirs as well as congregations. It was first included in our hymnals in 1966. According to *Companion to Hymns and Psalms*, "'Randolph' was the name used in the composer's family for his cousin and great friend Ralph Wedgwood, to whom the *Sea Symphony* is dedicated." (Watson and Trickett 1988, 372)

God created heaven and earth (151)
Chin Chú Sióng-té chó thiⁿ tóe

Trad. Taiwanese hymn
trans. by Boris and Clare Anderson, 1983 (Gen. 1:1-5, Acts 4:24)

This translation of a popular Taiwanese creation hymn was revised in 1981 and first included in *Hymns from the Four Winds*, 1983, number 3. The hymn is printed in both Chinese and English in *Sound the Bamboo*, 1990, number 173.

Toa-sia

Trad. Taiwanese melody; harm. by I-to Loh, 1983

The tune is described in *Sound the Bamboo* as a Piⁿ-po melody from Taiwanese Sèng-si. I-to Loh's setting preserves the distinctiveness of the tune and at the same time supplies interesting counterpoint and counter rhythms. Solo or soli voices doubled by flute or recorder can be effectively used to introduce this hymn. For additional performance practice suggestions see "Asian American Hymns" pages 35-36.

God forgave my sin (389)

See "Freely, freely," page 350.

God hath spoken by the prophets (108)

George W. Briggs, 1952, alt.

This is one of *Ten New Hymns on the Bible* published in 1953 by the Hymn Society of America to celebrate the printing in 1952 of the complete text of the Revised Standard Version of the Bible. (Gealy 556/149) Our 1966 hymnal was the first USA book to include the hymn. It is one of a few hymns from this period that successfully sustains a single theme, employs a minimum of forced rhymes, avoids a shallow optimistic appraisal of history, and is only three stanzas long. The hymn chronicles the active, creative, righteous, eternal God of Hebrew and Christian scripture as speaking in and through human experience *by* prophets who proclaimed God's righteous reign, *by* Jesus Christ, God with us, and *by* the ever-renewing and sustaining Spirit.

Several textual changes were made to avoid sexist and exclusive language: stanza 1:1, "his prophets" to "the prophets"; 1:7, "is King, his throne eternal" to "eternal reigns forever"; 2:6, "began" to "was born"; 2:8, "man revealing God to man" to "Christ, as God in human form"; 3:1, "his" to "the"; 3:2, "the hearts of men" to "the hearts again"; and 3:7, "his word" to "the Word."

Ebenezer

Thomas J. Williams, 1890

This is one of several Welsh tunes with harmonizations from *The English Hymnal*, 1906, that entered our hymnals in 1935. Most commentators, following Archibald Jacob in *Songs of Praise Discussed*, page 174, date this tune as 1890. Alan Luff provides this new information in *Welsh Hymns and Their Tunes*:

> The date of 1896 was given for its composition in an article on the composer in *Trysorfa's Plant* (The Children's Treasury) of 1940, when the composer was still alive. The composer included it in an anthem "Golau yn y glyn" (Light in the valley). It became well known during the 1904-5 revival [led by Evan Roberts], and from that became known in England. It was first published in a book in the *Baptist Book of Praise* (probably 1901), and it was after its appearance there that the story was spread that it had been found washed up in a bottle on the coast of North Wales. Thus it came to be called "Ton' Y Botel" (The Bottle Tune) [the name used when it entered our 1935 hymnal]. The proper name [EBENEZER] comes in fact from the chapel in Rhos, Pontardawe of which the composer was a member at the time the tune was composed. (Luff 1990, 222-23)

The tune should be sung slowly enough to allow the triplet figure to be distinctly articulated. The dotted quarter/eighth-note pattern is performed as a triplet. It is presumed, since Luff gives no citation, that the harmonization at 223 in *Welsh Hymns and Their Tunes* is the earliest form. Most hymnals use the setting from *The English Hymnal*, 1906. There is a vocal descant and alternate harmonization at 109-10 in *The United Methodist Hymnal Music Supplement*.

God is able (106)

Martin Luther King, Jr., USA 20th cent.

This litany was adapted by Laurence Hull Stookey from a sermon, "Our God is able," by Martin Luther King, Jr. The sermon was first preached at the Dexter Avenue Baptist Church, Montgomery, Alabama, later at the Ebenezer Baptist Church, Atlanta, Georgia. It was included in his *Strength to Love*, 1963, a collection of sermons and statements that provide insight about the martyred human rights leader as pastor-preacher.

God is here (660)

Fred Pratt Green, 1978

The circumstances of the writing of this hymn are provided in correspondence between Russell Schulz-Widmar, co-director of music at University United Methodist Church, Austin, Texas, and the poet:

We are in need of a hymn. It would be sung for the first time at the closing service of an eight-month long festival centering round the themes of Worship, Music and the Arts. . . . The closing Service of this festival will center around the dedication of new reading desks, communion table, and font, and finally, the rededication of the people to the life commanded of us and given through Jesus Christ. . . . We would prefer a metre of 8.7.8.7.D. since we could then use your text to introduce the tune ABBOT'S LEIGH to our congregation. (Letter from Russell Schulz-Widmar to Fred Pratt Green, December 1977)

The exchange also illustrates Green's extraordinary gift to craft a text within the guidelines of a commissioning. The hymn was sung for the first time on April 30, 1978, set to an arrangement of ABBOTTS'S LEIGH for congregation, choir, organ, and brass quintet composed for the service by Austin C. Lovelace. The hymn first appeared in Schulz-Widmar's *Songs of Thanks and Praise*, 1980. There is one change in our hymnal: stanza 1:1, "As we his people" to "As we your people."

Abbot's Leigh

Cyril V. Taylor, 1941

According to *Companion to Hymns and Psalms*,

this tune was composed one Sunday morning in [the spring of] 1941 for the hymn "Glorious things of thee are spoken" at Abbot's Leigh, [a village near] Bristol, where the composer was serving [as assistant to head] in the wartime headquarters of the Religious Broadcasting Department of the BBC. It was printed that year on a leaflet [by Oxford University Press] for use at the BBC services. . . . It was popularized by being used (with other tunes) in orchestral form before and after [the radio program] "Lift up your hearts" on the BBC Home Service. It was set in its original key of D major . . . in *Hymns Ancient and Modern Revised* [number 257]. (Watson and Trickett 1988, 440)

The composer states in *Hymns for Today Discussed*:

People have assured me . . . that it was written in response to feelings of disgust expressed in some letters to the BBC's Religious Broadcasting Department that we should go on using a German tune [Austria] not only for "Praise the Lord! Ye heavens, adore him" but also for "Glorious things." (Taylor 1984, 9)

Erik Routley describes the tune as "the archetypal example of a hymn tune taught to the whole of Britain through broadcasting. . . . It has exactly the kind of universal appeal that one attributes to Dykes's NICAEA." (Routley 1981, 152)

The range of the tune (D-E, a 9th) has prompted most hymnal committees, including ours, to lower it to the key of C. While solving the problem of range, lowering the tune's pitch dulls the inner harmonies, makes the low bass notes inarticulate, and makes singing it an arduous journey. The vital singing of this stately (not a waltz!) 87. 87. D tune need not be limited to academic settings or festival occasions replete with multiple choirs, descants (*The United Methodist Hymnal Music Supplement*, 4-5), instruments, and organ accompaniment. In most local churches this tune, as others in our hymnal, must be taught to the congregation phrase by phrase, interval by interval, and line by line.

Have everyone sing the first stanza with the melody doubled by a solo wind or reed, or organ stop. Divide stanzas 2 and 3 into two parts: the first four lines (87.87) and the final four lines (87.87). These four half-stanzas may be sung by the congregation in alternation with these suggested vocal ensembles: female and male voices; full SATB choir; soli SATB choir; unison mixed voices; children's voices; or youth choir. In stanza 4, modulate to D major using the directions for "Whole-step Modulations," page 392 of *The United Methodist Music Supplement*. The tune with the identical harmonies is printed in D major in *The Hymnal 1982*, number 511. In *Hymns and Psalms*, 1983, number 817, it appears with an alternate harmonization and descant by John Wilson.

God of change and glory (114)

See "Many gifts, one Spirit," pages 481-82.

God of grace and God of glory (577)

Harry Emerson Fosdick, 1930

The hymn was one of three written by the author in 1930 at his summer home in Boothbay Harbor, Maine, and was first published in H. Augustine Smith's *Praise and Service*, 1932. During the depression the three texts were reprinted from that hymnal and pasted into existing hymnals. (Gealy 556/155)

"God of grace and God of glory" was written as the processional hymn for the opening service of Riverside Church, New York City, October 5, 1930. It was also sung at the service of dedication, February 8, 1931. This impressive $5,000,000 edifice seating 1,800 worshippers, replete with educational and administrative units, was situated overlooking the Hudson River, as stipulated by Fosdick, "in a less swank district" than Park Avenue. The area was later named Morningside Heights, distinguishing it from nearby Harlem.

Fosdick's stirring radio sermons, books, and public pronouncements established Riverside as a forum for the critique of the same wealth and privilege whose gifts had made possible the building of the church. Under his leadership Riverside Church was interdenominational, interracial, without a creed, and, astonishingly for Baptists, required no specific mode of baptism. At the center of Fosdick's ministry was urban social service.

This paradigmatic hymn of early twentieth-century USA liberal Christianity is in essence a prayer that this new congregation may once more experience Pentecost; that God will grant it the wisdom and courage to embody Christ's teachings of peace and liberation; that it and its pastor may be freed from the bondage of fear and doubt (anticipating Franklin D. Roosevelt's famous fireside chat of 1933, "We have no fear but fear itself"); and that it be reformed into social service units dedicated to the eradication of suffering, hunger, poverty, and war. The first four lines of each stanza are specific prayers and petitions. Each stanza concludes with a plea for wisdom and courage to be faithful witnesses for Christ.

Stanza 4, which was omitted because of its sexist language, demonstrates the author's skillful and peaceful use of biblical militaristic imagery:

> Set our feet on lofty places;
>> gird our lives that they may be
> armored with all Christ-like graces
>> in the fight to set men free.
> Grant us wisdom, grant us courage,
>> that we fail not man nor thee.

For additional commentary, see "Social Gospel Hymns," pages 32-33.

Cwm Rhondda

For commentary on this tune, see "For the healing of the nations," pages 344-45.

This tune was first matched to this text in our 1935 hymnal, number 279, apparently at the suggestion of hymnal editor Robert Guy McCutchan. (Reynolds 1976, 77) Its immediate success in Methodism recommended it to other denominational groups and hymnals. The author opposed the tune on literary grounds because he had consciously composed the text to be sung to REGENT SQUARE, a tune in ABC form that allowed each stanza to conclude succinctly with a brief petition for wisdom and courage sung on one phrase of music. When the Welsh tune is used, the petition is vainly repeated!

In 1968 this writer asked the author why he continued to object to the Welsh tune for his hymn in spite of the tune's wide use. Dr. Fosdick replied, "My views are well known—you Methodists have always been a bunch of wise guys." (Correspondence with the Carlton R. Young, February 1968)

While USA hymnals generally use the Welsh tune, most British hymnals still include a more straightforward 87. 87. 87 setting.

God of love and God of power (578)

Gerald H. Kennedy, ca. 1939

The author commented on his text in correspondence with Fred D. Gealy in 1966:

> At my first church after seminary which was the Calvary Methodist Church in San Jose, California, I became acquainted with a man who was head of one of the music departments in one of the junior high schools. He said to me one day that he would like to write a hymn tune if I would write the words. . . . I was a young preacher just starting out and tried to express my feeling of the main Christian theme of that particular period. The young people here and there began to get a hold of it and it became a fairly popular hymn in California. Then it spread here and there and I was quite thrilled when they sang it one night in Australia at a youth rally where I spoke a couple of years ago. (Gealy 556/156)

The author's text has many similarities to Fosdick's "God of grace and God of glory." It was set in a typically Epworth League turn-of-the-century Sunday school march in 4/4 time, complete with this rousing chorus (the accompaniment figure is shown in brackets):

> God of love, [*dum de dum*] God of power, [*dum de dum*]
> Thou hast called us for this hour.
> We are not afraid of the choice we've made,
> Triumphantly we march with thee.

When this hymn was considered for inclusion in the 1966 hymnal, most musicians on the hymnal committee recommended that it be matched to a more stately tune. During the deliberations Daniel L. Ridout said to Bishop Kennedy, also a member of the committee, "Bishop, we want this hymn to have a future, which it doesn't have with the original tune." The author and committee members who had sung his hymn at youth rallies across the church were nonplussed. However, after long deliberation it became apparent that the text would not be approved with the original tune, and the hymn's advocates reluctantly accepted the seventeenth-century melody UNSER HERRSCHER, converted to 77. 77. 77 to accommodate the text. When the new hymnal was issued, those in the church who wished to continue singing the original version pasted it in the back of their new hymnals.

A quarter of a century later those who still sang the hymn in its original version petitioned the Hymnal Revision Committee for its inclusion along with the altered setting. A four-year effort to restore the original version, led by Marjorie B. Tuell, prevailed until the final meetings of the Hymnal Revision Committee when it was dropped from the *Report* by a substantial majority. The hymn has not been included in other hymnals, but it is once again in our hymnal, and in its original form—glued on a blank page.

Unser Herrscher

Joachim Neander, 1680

This tune, also known as "Neander," "Magdeburg," and "Ephesus," is adapted from Joachim Neander's *Alpha und Omega, Glaub-und Liebesübung*, 1680. Its present form comes from the late seventeenth and early eighteenth century, particularly J. A. Freylinghausen's *Gesangbuch*, 1704. It was first included in our 1966 hymnal in the harmonization from the *Pilgrim Hymnal*, 1958. *Guide to the Pilgrim Hymnal*, page 380, cites this setting as from *The Chorale Book for England*, 1863, although there is little difference from the version in *Hymns Ancient and Modern*, 1868 Appendix, page 36. The tune's form, AAB, allows phrases of 77. to be sung in alternation by combinations of the following: sections of the congregation, male and female voices, choir and congregation. All voices sing the final phrase. Vocal and instrumental descants for the final stanza are found in both B^b and C at 338-41 in *The United Methodist Hymnal Music Supplement*.

God of many names (105)

Brian Wren, 1985

According to the author the text and the tune, which had been completed in February of that year, were submitted unsuccessfully to the 1985 Hymn Society of America/American Guild of Organists' search for new hymns on "Music and Praise."

> The hymn prays for an encounter with the holy mystery of God. The Hebrew of Exodus 4:13 inspires the conviction of God, "moving, endlessly becoming," who cannot be defined and labelled. (Notes to *Praising a Mystery*, 1986)

In his introduction to the same collection, Wren writes:

> The living God is a mystery, not a secret: secrets puzzle us, but lose their fascination when they are revealed. A mystery deepens the more it is pondered and known. At their best, worship, thinking and action are attempts to praise that mystery, to know God, and be known. (Wren 1986, "Introduction")

In this hymn of praise to the God who is love incarnate, the poet effectively uses biblical images that expand the hymnic repertory of metaphor, forms of address, and descriptions of God. The author retells the story of creation within an understanding of God who is "endless, but yet becoming." The poem describes the moving and becoming One whose womb birthed time; the One of all people who chose a particular people, the Hebrews, to manifest liberation and law; the God of Jesus Christ, the carpenter's son and advocate of the poor, wounded, suffering, crucified, and the author of new creation. The congregation responds in troubadourian style with a circle dance of praise affirming "God is love."

The story may be effectively told by using solo voices or soli choir on the verses, with the congregation responding in the joyous refrain; add tambourine, hand clapping, and circle dance in the style of bar mitzvah. The text is included without change from the author's 1986 version, except these metaphors and descriptions of deity that were not capitalized: Names, Moving, Becoming, Hovering Wings, Womb, Birth, Breath, Exodus, Law, Wounded Hands, Web, Loom, Carpenter.

Many names

William P. Rowan, 1985, alt.

The composer originally set this text for unison voices. It was first included in *Praising a Mystery*, 1986. In 1988 at the request of Mary Oyer, for Mennonite congregational singing he re-scored the refrain for SATB, and at the request of the Hymnal Revision Committee he altered measure 5 in the refrain to provide an eighth- and sixteenth-note pattern throughout. See 227 in *The United Methodist Hymnal Music Supplement* for additional performance notes.

God of the ages (698)

Daniel C. Roberts, 1876

This widely sung patriotic hymn was written for a 1876 centennial Fourth of July celebration and was first sung at Brandon, Vermont, to "Russian Hymn." The hymn was first included in the 1892 hymnal of the Protestant Episcopal Church. The text with the tune NATIONAL HYMN entered our hymnals in 1905.

Stanza 1 praises the eternal and transcendent God of our forbears. Stanza 2 is a selective and optimistic recounting of the nation's past under God. Stanza 3, written between the Civil War and World War I, is a prayer for peace. Stanza 4 enumerates the future blessings under God of a nation steeped in the false optimism of manifest destiny, a refreshed people, a land transformed from night to day, a land filled with love and divine grace.

In following their own guidelines, the Hymnal Revision Committee attempted to reduce where possible the predominance of masculine pronouns and images. When the first line of this hymn was changed from "fathers" to "ages," some on the committee took issue, stating that the author's use of "fathers" refers to George Washington, Thomas Jefferson, etc., "fathers of the USA," obviously male, and that the change slights the fact that these "fathers" were "believers." In stanza 2:2, "by" has been changed to "with."

National hymn

George W. Warren, 1894

Austin C. Lovelace has provided this information about the tune:

After [this text] had been accepted for inclusion in the revised Protestant Episcopal *Hymnal*, 1892, Warren composed a tune [for the New York

City 1894 centennial celebration of the adoption of the USA Constitution] which first appeared in J. I. Tucker and W. W. Rousseau's 1984 musical edition of the 1892 Protestant Episcopal *Hymnal*. (Gealy, Lovelace, Young 1970, 197)

Concerning the trumpet fanfare that precedes each stanza, *Guide to the Pilgrim Hymnal* provides this needed caution:

Too often the trumpet interludes dominate to such an extent that worshippers hardly think of the words they are singing and the music is cheapened. Organists should remember that a little trumpet goes a long way. (Ronander and Porter 1966, 334)

God of the sparrow God of the whale (122)

Jaroslav J. Vajda, 1983

The author has provided this commentary:

Having been fascinated for more than 40 years in the ministry by the proper and effective motivation for Christian service, a request from the Concordia Lutheran Church of Kirkwood, Missouri, provided an opportunity to compose a hymn text that would provide answers from the users of the hymn as to why and how God's creatures (and children) are to serve him. The Law of God demands perfect love from every creature; the love of God and the Gospel coax a willing response of love as an expression of gratitude. "We love because he first loved us." God's adopted family responds both as creatures and as children, thus fulfilling the expectation of the Law with the fruits of the Spirit, and in doing so "saying" with action something of significance to God and the world. (Vajda 1987, 152)

The text is included in its original form except in stanza 4:3 with the deletion of "wayward Child" following "prodigal," and in 5:3 the deletion of "olive branch," following "pruning hook." Although these changes were approved by the author for singing, he prefers the original text.

Roeder

Carl Schalk, 1983

This tune was composed for the text. It was first included in *Hymnal Supplement II* (1987), and was initially performed at the annual meeting of the Hymn Society of America, Ft. Worth, Texas, July 1987.

The hymn may be sung effectively by alternating the stanzas between children and adults. At ending six on the word "home," let everyone choose a note of the C major chord and hold it ad lib.

The tune's name is the composer's spouse's maiden name. Its use with this intriguing hymn recalls the creative ministry of her father, Reverend Paul J. Roeder, pastor in the Lutheran Church, Missouri Synod.

God sent his son (364)

See "Because he lives," pages 230-31.

God, that madest earth and heaven (688)

St. 1, Reginald Heber, 1827
st. 2, Frederick Lucian Hosmer, 1912 (Gen. 1:1-15)

Bishop Heber's evening hymn first appeared as one stanza, our first, number 128 under "Another" in *Hymns Written and Adapted to the Weekly Service of the Church Year*, 1827, published a year after his death. (Gealy 556/163) The text's unique meter, 84. 84. 888, gives credence to the account that Heber immediately wrote the words to the melody after hearing a harp playing "Ar hyd y nos" in his host's home one evening in Wales. Our second stanza was written in 1912 by the USA Unitarian minister Frederick L. Hosmer and was first included in *Hymn and Tune Book*, 1914.

Other stanzas that have been joined with Heber's one stanza include Richard Whately's translation and rhymed paraphrase of the antiphon "Salve nos, Domine, vigilantes" for the Nunc Dimittis at compline, which first appeared in *Sacred Poetry Adapted to the Understanding of Children and Youth*, 1836:

> Guard us waking, guard us sleeping:
>   And when we die,
> May we, in Thy mighty keeping,
>   All peaceful lie.
> When the last dread trump shall wake us,
> Do not Thou, our Lord, forsake us,
> But to reign in glory take us
>   With Thee on high.

The two stanzas entered our hymnals in 1935 and are included without alteration.

Ar hyd y nos

Trad. Welsh melody; harm. by Luther Orlando Emerson, 1906

"Ar hyd y nos" means "the livelong night." *The English Hymnal*, 1906, was the first to match this popular melody to this text, but not without controversy. Erik Routley comments that this was one of that hymnal's "boldest strokes." (Routley

1953, 271) Leonard Ellinwood in *The Hymnal 1940 Companion*, page 126, has included an excerpt from Edward Jones's *Musical Relicks*, 1784, for solo voice, chorus, and harp. The tune was included in several popular nineteenth-century USA sacred collections with the texts "There's a friend above all others" and "When the spark of life is waning." (Ronander and Porter 1966, 51)

L. O. Emerson's harmonization entered our hymnals in 1935, apparently taken from the 1933 *Hymnal* of the Presbyterian Church, number 41, by editor Robert G. McCutchan. No further information about the source of the harmonization is available. For additional comment, see "For the fruits of this creation," pages 343-44.

God the Spirit, guide and guardian (648)

Carl P. Daw, Jr., 1987

This hymn on ministry was the final new text approved for this hymnal. It was written for the consecration of Jeffery Rowthorn as bishop suffragan of the diocese of Connecticut, the Protestant Episcopal Church, September 19, 1987. Immediately following the consecration service the poet and the editor, who were attending separate meetings in New York City, were introduced to each other, and the poet shared his text. Since the Hymnal Revision Committee had been unsuccessful in finding a suitable new text on ministry and the final committee meeting was two weeks hence, Daw's hymn was immediately conveyed to them. It was approved with the footnote for stanza 2:5: "When appropriate, 'ministers' may be substituted for 'pastors.'"

The poet writes that the hymn begins "with an address to the Third Person of the Trinity rather than the First because the traditional prayers and hymns of the ordination rites . . . are so addressed." (Daw 1990, 126)

The poet's commentary continues:

> [The text continues with a] paraphrase of the Greek term *Paraklete* (John 14:26); "wind-sped flame" recalls the first Christian Pentecost (Acts 2:1-4); "hovering dove" alludes to the Baptism of Christ (Matthew 3:14-17; Mark 1:9-11; Luke 3:21-22; John 1:32-33); "breath of life" refers to creation (Genesis 2:7); "voice of prophets" echoes the Nicene Creed, which is part of the consecration rite (BCP, p. 520); "sign of blessing" refers to the gift of the Holy Spirit at Baptism (BCP, p. 308); "power of love" pulls together Jesus's words to the disciples (Acts 1:8) and the well-known hymn "Come down, O Love divine" **[475]**. (Daw 1990, 126)

The central image of stanza 2 is Christ the Good Shepherd (John 10:11-16). In the fifth line the original reading "all bishops" was changed to "all pastors" to be consistent with the shepherd image. At the request of the Hymnal Revision Committee the author permitted the above footnote to be included to allow the text to be used in the United Methodist consecration of layministers.

Stanza 3 recasts traditional forms of address to deity in gender-free language: "Life-bestower" and "Womb of mercy." The former is a substitute for "calling the First Person our Father" which sufficed until the nineteenth century under the assumption "that the male provided all the life-bearing substance needed for pro-creation." The latter reflects "the fact that the Hebrew and Aramaic words for mercy are derived from a root meaning 'womb.'" (Daw 1990, 128)

Daw elaborates further on the theme of the text:

> The final stanza calls on the undivided Trinity to bless the full range of ministries entrusted to the Church. The diversity of lay and ordained ministries is a reflection of the plenitude of God, yet even the sum of them falls far short of God's full glory. (Daw 1990, 128)

The hymn enters our hymnals at a crucial time when the General Conference of The United Methodist Church is redefining the "ordering" and "naming" of ministry, and annual conference boards of ordained ministry are mediating the growing concerns of lay persons for the apparent contradiction in the life-styles and careers of some clergy-persons between their "exaltation," i.e., their being setting apart for the work of ministry, and their "accountability" for a disciplined and productive ministry.

Hyfrydol

See "Come, thou long-expected Jesus," page 302.

The author suggests IN BABILONE (325) and NETTLETON (400) as alternate tunes. (Correspondence with Carlton R. Young, November 1987)

God, who stretched the spangled heavens (150)

Catherine Arnott Cameron, 1967

This widely used hymn is among the first to employ space age imagery, and it is one of the most imaginative, provocative texts of that genre. The author notes that "the hymn was written [to the tune AUSTRIA] over a period of several months at a time when I was experiencing a new sense of direction, growth, and creativity in my life." It was first included in *Contemporary Worship-1*, 1969. (Stulken 1981, 488)

Lutheran Book of Worship, 1978, used stanzas 1, 3, and 4, rewriting the original last stanza that had read:

> As thy new horizons beckon,
> Father, give us strength to be

children of creative purpose,
  thinking thy thoughts after thee,
till our dreams are rich with meaning,
  each endeavor, thy design:
great Creator, lead us onward
  till our work is one with thine.

One of the most poignant moments in contemporary hymnody is found in the compelling lines of stanzas 2 and 3 as the author contrasts the human endeavor, imagination, and skill expended in space exploration with our seeming inability to deal with the earthly realities of lifeless, faceless, and lonely cities, and the possibility that we will terminate God's gift of life in a nuclear holocaust.

Holy manna

Attr. to William Moore, 1825
The delightful AABA tune is easily taught. It is generally attributed to William Moore, compiler of *The Columbian Harmony*, 1825, and was included in a number of shaped-note songbooks including *The Southern Harmony* (see below). The source of the Sunday school style harmonization is unknown, but it apparently dates from Reconstruction days.

Although the author wrote the text to be sung to AUSTRIA and still prefers that tune, most major hymnals since the *Lutheran Book of Worship*, 1978, have used the present tune to express more adequately the hymn's rich and expansive metaphors and descriptions: "spangled heavens," "silent fields of space," "winging through untraveled realms of space," and "probed the secrets of the the atom, yielding unimagined power." According to Marion J. Hatchett our harmonization has been in common use in Methodist and Baptist hymnals since it appeared in Rivert H. Coleman, *The Modern Hymnal*, 1926. (Correspondence with Carlton R. Young, August 1992)

A vocal descant, alternate harmonization, and an arrangement for Orff instruments are found at 160-62 in *The United Methodist Hymnal Music Supplement*. Number 580 in the *Accompaniment Edition of the Hymnal 1982* is a transcription of the three-part, shaped-note setting from *The Southern Harmony*, 1835, page 103.

God, whose love is reigning o'er us (100)

William Boyd Grove, 1980
The text was written for the marriage of Susan Jane Grove and Alan Douglas DeJarnett, November 29, 1980. It was first included in *The Upper Room Worshipbook*, 1985, number 4a, as an alternate text for "Praise, my soul, the God of heaven."

This hymn begins with praise to the Creator for the creation (Genesis 1:1-21). Stanza 3 remembers God's covenant with Abram (Genesis 15:12), and stanza four recounts the new covenant in Jesus Christ (2 Corinthians 3:7-18). The hymn closes with an invitation to live responsibly and harmoniously, joining our voices in songs of faith and love.

The one change in the text (stanza 4:1), "Jahweh" to "Holy," avoids rendering the Divine Name, the "Tetragrammaton" (YHWH), "as though there were other gods from whom the true God had to be distinguished, [a practice that] began to be discontinued in Judaism before the Christian era and is inappropriate for the universal faith of the Christian Church." (Metzger and Murphy 1991, xiii) Yet the rendering of the Divine Name as the proper name "Jehovah," e.g., "Guide me, O thou great Jehovah" (127), according to this view is equally offensive to our Jewish neighbors.

Lauda anima

John Goss, 1869

From the Latin meaning "Praise, my soul," the tune is also called "Praise my soul" after the first line of the hymn by H. F. Lyte, "Praise my soul, the King of heaven" **(66)**, for which the tune was written. It was included in *Supplemental Hymn and Tune Book, compiled by the Rev. R. Brown-Borthwick. Third edition with new Appendix*, 1869. It entered our hymnals in 1966 as the setting for R. T. Brooks's "Thanks to God whose word was spoken" and precluded this excellent text from ever being sung. Its inclusion in both *Hymns Ancient and Modern*, 1875 Standard Edition, and *The English Hymnal*, 1906, aided it in becoming one of the most widely sung Victorian tunes. Erik Routley offers this faint praise: "Who can deny the inspired simplicity and effectiveness of "Praise my soul" . . . the only tune of Sir John Goss that has remained in currency? What a masterpiece of inspired obviousness!" (Routley 1981, 107)

There are two vocal descants and an alternate harmonization at 205-207 in *The United Methodist Hymnal Music Supplement*. Number 410 in *The Accompaniment Edition of the Hymnal 1982* includes Goss's harmonization for each of the four stanzas. Goss also harmonized a stanza in $F^{\#}$ minor, included at number 30 in *The Hymn Book of the United Church of Canada*, 1971.

The setting included in our hymnal is an adaptation by Ralph Vaughan Williams, 1906?, of the first seventeen measures of Goss's harmonization for stanza 2, and the second section of yet another setting by Goss for four voices in E major with uncharacteristic parallel fourths in the upper voices of the last four measures.

God will take care of you (130)

Civilla D. Martin, 1904

This hymn of assurance in God's loving care, especially for those bearing burdens of illness and hardship, was first published in John A. Davis, *Songs of*

Redemption and Praise, 1905. The poet has provided the following account of the composition of the words and music:

> I was confined to a sick bed in a Bible school in Lestershire, New York. My husband was spending several weeks at the school, making a songbook for the president of the school. "God will take care of you" was written one Sunday afternoon while my husband went to a preaching appointment. When he returned I gave the words to him. He immediately sat down to his little Bilhorn organ and wrote the music. That evening he and two of the teachers sang the completed song. It was then printed in the songbook [which has never been identified] he was compiling for the school. (Reynolds 1976, 219)

The hymn first appeared in our hymnals in 1966.

Martin

W. Stillman Martin, 1904
The tune was composed by the author's husband for this text and was included with it in the 1905 collection.

Good Christian friends, rejoice (224)
In dulci jubilo
Nun singet und seyt fro!

14th cent. Latin; trans. by John Mason Neale, 1855
J. M. Neale's paraphrase of this fourteenth-century German-Latin (macaronic) carol was first included in his *Carols for Christmas-tide*, 1853, pages 17-19, number 6. Neale began each line with "Good Christian men rejoice" although it is not in the original text. Thomas Helmore, music editor of the collection, incorrectly transcribed the tune from the old notation and added two notes after each third phrase. To accommodate the change in meter Neale added "News, news," "Joy, joy," and "Peace, peace." With the text, this version of the tune was incorporated into Gustav Holst's widely performed anthem "Christmas Day," which resulted in choirs and congregations singing two versions of the carol.

The carol is included in our hymnal with these changes from Neale: stanza 1:1, "men" to "friends"; 2:6, "oped the heavenly" to "opened heaven's," and "man is blessed evermore" to "ye are blest forevermore."

In dulci jubilo

German melody; harm. by Gary Alan Smith, 1988
Literally meaning "in sweet shouting, or jubilation," the melody of folk origin was included with the text in Joseph Klug's *Geistliche Lieder*, 1533. There is a

setting with triangle and finger cymbal accompaniment at 180 in *The United Methodist Hymnal Music Supplement*. Other possibilities are to double the melody with flute or recorder and use V. Earle Copes's harmonization from the 1966 hymnal on the second stanza, adding the "News, news" notes in each stanza.

There are extensive notes on the sources of this carol and harmonizations by Bartholomew Gesius and J. S. Bach in *The Oxford Book of Carols*, pages 186-88.

Good Friday (284)

After the Book of Common Prayer

This prayer, adapted from the "Proper Liturgy for Good Friday," the *Book of Common Prayer*, was first included in our worship resources in *The Book of Worship*, 1944, page 64, "Good Friday—Three-Hour Service." It petitions God to look with favor upon the human family for whom Jesus suffered and died. The prayer may be combined with other prayers and hymns on the atoning work of God through Christ in "Passion and Death," **278-301**. For other selections see "Atonement," **944**, in the "Index of Topics and Categories" and hymns and prayers in "Prevenient Grace" and "Justifying Grace," **337-381**.

Grace greater than our sin (365)

Julia H. Johnston, 1911 (Rom. 5:20)

This hymn on the abundant grace of God through Jesus Christ was composed ca. 1910 and reflects Paul's teaching of justification by faith:

> But the free gift [of grace] is not like the trespass. For if the many died through the one man's [Adam's] trespass, much more surely have the grace of God and the free gift in the grace of the one man, Jesus Christ, abounded for the many. (Romans 5:15)

> But law came in, with the result that the trespass multiplied; but where sin increased, grace abounded all the more. (Romans 5:20)

Those who engage in "feel-good" preaching and singing about God's grace frequently ignore Paul's probing question that follows:

> Should we continue in sin in order that grace may abound? By no means! How can we who died to sin go on living in it? (Romans 6:1b-2)

The hymn is appropriate for invitation or Holy Communion.

Moody

Daniel B. Towner, 1910

According to William J. Reynolds this text and tune first appeared in the composer's *Hymns Tried and True*, 1911. The hymnal committee for the *Baptist*

Hymnal, 1956, named the tune MOODY to recognize the composer, a distinguished Methodist musician, for his dedicated service as head of the music department of Moody Bible Institute, Chicago, Illinois. (Reynolds 1976, 140)

The original harmonization did not have a G$^\sharp$ in measures 13-14 and 29-30, and the bass and alto sang "Marvelous grace, infinite grace" under the melody and tenor in measures 17-20, 25-28.

Great is thy faithfulness (140)

Thomas O. Chisholm, 1923 (Lam. 3:22-23)

In 1923 the author, a writer, Methodist minister, and later an insurance agent, sent a number of his poems to his friend William M. Runyan, a lifelong friend, composer, and Methodist minister. Runyan composed the tune and included the hymn in his *Songs of Salvation and Service*, 1923. According to Don P. Hustad, the hymn "is the unofficial 'school hymn' of Moody Bible Institute in Chicago, with which Dr. Runyan was associated for a number of years." (Hustad 1978, 33; see also Reynolds 1976, 80-81, for his correspondence with the author and the composer and their accounts of the writing of the hymn.)

The central theme of this popular hymn of praise to an unchanging God in a changing world is a line from an extended "Job-like" lament cried out in Jerusalem, leveled in 586-87 B.C. by the Babylonians:

> The thought of my affliction and my homelessness
> is wormwood and gall!
> My soul continually thinks of it and is bowed down within me.
> But this I call to mind,
> and therefore I have hope:
>
> The steadfast love of the Lord never ceases,
> his mercies never come to an end;
> they are new every morning;
> great is your faithfulness.
>
> "The Lord is my portion," says my soul,
> "therefore I will hope in him." (Lamentations 3:19-24)

William J. Reynolds (1990, 98) cites the alternate reading of James 1:17c as the source of stanza 1:2:

> Every generous act of giving, with every perfect gift, is from above, coming down from the Father of lights, with whom there is no variation due to a shadow of turning.

Although authored by Methodists and included in most evangelical hymnals and songbooks since its publication in 1923, the hymn was never published in an official Methodist hymnal. Many members of the former Evangelical United Brethren Church, whose hymnals did include it, in requesting its inclusion in this hymnal often cited it as "from their tradition." The hymn was second only to "In the garden" **(314)** as the most requested hymn.

Faithfulness

William M. Runyan, 1923

The composer has commented on the writing of the tune:

> This particular poem held such an appeal that I prayed most earnestly that my tune might carry its message in a worthy way, and the subsequent history of its use indicates that God answered prayer. (Reynolds 1976, 81)

The tune was named by the composer at the request of the committee that produced the *Baptist Hymnal*, 1956. It is common practice to sing the first two phrases of the refrain in alternation between female and male voices. The hymn may be found in E^b, number 68, *The Hymnal*, 1957, of The Evangelical United Brethren Church.

Great Spirit, now I pray (330)

See "Daw-Kee, Aim Daw-Tsi-Taw," pages 313-14.

Guide me, O thou great Jehovah (127)
Arglwydd, arwain trwy'r anialwch

William Williams, 1745
trans. from the Welsh by Peter Williams and the author, 1771

This hymn was originally published in Welsh by William Williams, Pantycelyn, in five stanzas in his *Alleluia*, 1745, titled "Nerth i fyned trwy'r Anialwch" ("Strength to pass through the Wilderness").

> Peter Williams translated stanzas 1, 3 and 5 into English for his *Hymns on Various Subjects*, 1771. A year later, the original author—or his son John—made another version, retaining Peter Williams' first st., then translating anew 3 and 4 of the original and adding a new fourth. (Gealy, Lovelace, Young, 1970, 205)

The hymn entered our hymnals in 1847 with the first three of the four stanzas that were included in a leaflet titled *A Favourite Hymn, sung by Lady Hunt*ing*don's*

Young Collegians [i.e., in the college at Trevecca]. *Printed by the desire of many Christian friends. Lord, give it Thy blessing!* c. 1771-72. (Milgate 1985, 177) The hymn was included in the collections of hymns by Countess Huntingdon. *A Select Collection of Hymns, Universally sung in all the Countess of Huntingdon's Chapels. Collected by her Ladyship*, 1786, is in the Gealy research papers (556, 171).

Stanza 1:6 originally read "feed me now and evermore"; stanza 2:3, "Let the fiery cloudy pillar."

Stanza 4 is seldom included:

> Musing on my habitation,
>   Musing on my heavenly home
> Fills my soul with holy longing,
>   Come, my Jesus, quickly come,
> Vanity is all I see,
>   Lord, I long to be with Thee.

The hymn draws upon strong biblical metaphors, especially from Exodus 13 and 16: "manna," "crystal fountain," "fire and cloudy pillar," "crossing the river Jordan to Canaan's side." Some commentators, this writer not among them, point to the text as an example of biblical typology prefiguring Jesus Christ.

Alan Luff in his *Welsh Hymns and Their Tunes*, pages 93-103, has provided the most recent and reliable account of Williams's career as the forceful preacher/poet of the Welsh Methodists, 1744 until his death in 1791. In commenting on this hymn, Luff describes the world of Williams:

> [It] is a mixture of his own Wales and the land of the Bible. So a preaching journey can become both the toiling of the Israelites through the wilderness and Everyman's pilgrimage through life to the eternal home. The best known of his hymns in English, "Guide me, O thou great Jehovah," shows the truth of this; in it we are the Israelites seeking food and water in the wilderness and at the end we are passing through the waters of the Jordan to reach final safety on the other side. (Luff 1990, 99-100)

Cwm Rhondda

See "For the healing of the nations," pages 344-45.

Alan Luff makes an interest comment about the use of this tune with this text:

> Though it is not often used in Wales, least of all for the original of the William Williams' hymn ["Guide me, O thou great Jehovah"], it is almost the invariable choice for Ann Griffith's great love song to her Saviour,

"Wele'n sefyll rhwng y myrtwydd" [There he stands among the myrtles, worthiest object of my love], which has nothing to do with CWM RHONDDA's martial tread. (Luff 1990, 224)

Hail the day that sees him rise (312)

Charles Wesley, 1739
This Ascension text first appeared at 211-13 in *Hymns and Sacred Poems*, 1739, in ten stanzas with the title "Hymn for Ascension-Day." The four stanzas in our hymnal are the original 1, 2, 4, and 5.

Various changes were made in the text including those by Thomas Cotterill for his *Selection of Psalms and Hymns*, 1820. In our version stanza 1:2 originally read "ravished from our wishful eyes"; in stanza 2:1, "pompous" has been changed to "glorious"; 2:3 was originally "wide unfold the radiant scene"; 3:1, "Him tho' highest heaven receives"; in 3:2, "yet" is changed to "still"; and in 3:4, "mankind" to "the world." The hymn entered our hymnals in 1838.

The hymn as a whole is an elaboration of the accounts of Christ's ascension in Mark 16:19 and Luke 24:15. Stanza 2 is an allusion to the ruler's entry into the Temple, Psalm 24:7-10; and stanza 4 reflects Luke 24:51, "While he was blessing them, he withdrew from them and was carried up into heaven." Alleluias were added to the end of each line in G. C. White's *Hymns and Introits*, 1852. (Watson and Trickett 1988, 142)

Llanfair

Robert Williams, 1817; harm. by David Evans, 1927
The melody is attributed to Robert Williams, though it is doubtful that he set it down since he was blind from birth. It was first included in John Parry's *Peroriaeth Hyfryd (Sweet Music)*, 1837, as one of a number of tunes suggested and harmonized by John Roberts, Henllan. (Luff 1990, 169) *The English Hymnal*, 1906, was the first to set this tune with this hymn. Our setting by David Evans from *The Church Hymnary*, 1927 rev. ed., entered our hymnals in 1935. Llanfair is the anglicized form of "Llanfechell," the composer's home, Mynydd Ithel, Llanfechell, Anglesey.

The lines of the text and the Alleluias may be sung in alternation. A vocal descant with the tune transposed down one step to F major is found at 213-24 in *The United Methodist Hymnal Music Supplement*.

Hail thee, festival day (324)
Salve festa dies

Venantius Honorius Fortunatus, ca. 582

The opening of the twentieth couplet of Fortunatus's "Tempora florigero ruti-
lant distincts sereno,"

> Salve festa dies toto venerabilis aevo
> Qua Deus infernum vicit et astra tenet,

formed the first line of many seasonal processionals in the Middle Ages. Versions of these processionals were included in *York Processional*, 1530. John
Henry Newman included eight stanzas in his *Hymni Ecclesiae*, 1838, 1865. The
first English translation was apparently by Thomas Cranmer in 1544.
(Dearmer and Jacob, 1933, ix) Translations of centos for Dedication, Whitsun,
Easter, and Ascension were made by Arthur James Mason for *Hymns Ancient
and Modern*, 1904. (Frost 1962, 560) Our hymnal uses with slight alteration the
translation and settings appropriate for Easter, Ascension, Pentecost, and general use from *The English Hymnal*, 1906, number 625, in the sequence and format of the *Lutheran Book of Worship*, 1978, number 142. For a definitive study of
this text, see Ruth Messenger's "Salve festa dies," *Transactions of the American
Philological Association*, 1947, 208-22.

The form of the processional suggests that the congregation sing the refrain
and the choir the stanzas. Youth and children's choirs may sing alternate stanzas with adults. The melody of the refrain may be doubled by a solo trumpet.
The stanzas for Easter and all seasons are appropriate for general use.

Salve festa dies

Ralph Vaughan Williams, 1906

The tune was composed for *The English Hymnal*, 1906. The syncopation in
measure 15 that was parallel to that in measure 3 has been eliminated. *The
Hymnal 1982*, number 216, includes the tune one step higher in G.

Hail, thou once despised Jesus (325)

Attr. to John Bakewell, 1757, and Martin Madan, 1760, alt.
(Rev. 4:2-11)

Fred D. Gealy has provided this commentary on this stirring Ascension hymn:

> The hymn first appeared in 2 sts. in *A Collection of Hymns Addressed to the
> Holy, Holy, Triune God, in the Person of Christ Jesus, Our Mediator and Advo-
> cate*, 1757. . . . When the hymn next appeared, in Madan's *Collection of*

Psalms and Hymns, 1760 [Gealy 556/172], it was expanded to four sts. St. 1 was retained without alteration. A new st. 2 beginning "Paschal Lamb by God appointed" appeared. The 1757 [original] second st. was split, each half becoming the first quatrain of sts. 3 and 4 respectively, and 2 new quatrains were introduced to complete sts. 3 and 4. (Gealy, Lovelace, Young 1970, 206)

There is no evidence that Bakewell wrote the original hymn, nor is the reviser known.

Additional changes were made by A. M. Toplady for his *Psalms and Hymns for Public and Private Worship*, 1776, "to reflect his Calvinistic views . . . [and a] fifth stanza was added, now known to be from a 1757 collection [James Allen's *Collection of Hymns*] and no longer printed." (Gealy, Lovelace, Young 1970, 206)

The Toplady version was included in our first hymnals and was maintained until our 1966 hymnal when the Madan text was restored. Changes from our 1966 text are in stanza 2:3, "appointed" to "anointed"; 2:8, "peace is made twixt man and God" to "reconciled are we with God"; and 4:4, "meet" to "right."

The hymn's basic themes of salvation and atonement are from Romans 5:8-12, Hebrews 8:1, 7:25. The triumphant final stanza paraphrases Revelation 4:11 and 5:12-13.

In Babilone

Trad. Dutch melody; arr. by Julius Roentgen, 1906
The tune is from *Oude en nieuwe Hollantse Boerenlities en Contradanseu* (*Old and New Dutch Peasant Songs and Country Dances*), ca. 1710. Ralph Vaughan Williams came across several arrangements of these tunes by the Dutch educator Julius Roentgen, and he included this one in *The English Hymnal*, 1906. There is an alternate harmonization at 178, *The United Methodist Hymnal Music Supplement*, and two additional harmonizations are in *The Hymnal 1982* at 215 and 495.

Unfortunately, this winsome diatonic melody in its academically proper harmonization so restrains the hymn's evangelical rhetoric and fervor that in the end it is rendered as unexciting as most preaching on the Ascension and enthronement of Christ. Suggested alternative tunes are EBENEZER **(108)** and HOLY MANNA **(150)**.

Hail to the Lord's anointed (203)

James Montgomery, 1821 (Ps. 72)
This paraphrase of Psalm 72, considered by many as Montgomery's greatest hymn, was written for a Christmas Day Moravian convocation in Fulneck,

Yorkshire, 1821. Montgomery recited the hymn at the close of his lecture to a missionary conference in Pitt Street Wesleyan Chapel, Liverpool, April 4, 1822. Adam Clarke, who was presiding, was so impressed with the hymn that he included its eight stanzas at the end of his commentary and exposition on Psalm 72 in his *Commentary on the Bible*, 1822 (Gealy 556/173), with this introduction:

> I need not tell the author that he has seized the spirit and exhibited some of the principal beauties of the Hebrew bard; though (to use his own words in a letter to me) his "hand trembled to touch the harp of Zion." (Gealy 556, 174)

The complete hymn was first published in the author's *Songs of Zion, Being Imitations of the Psalms*, 1822, pages 59-63. It entered our hymnals in 1847. Most editions have included the four stanzas that are in our present hymnal, which are the original 1, 2, 4, and a stanza composed of the first half of 7 and the last half of 8.

Montgomery, one of the most striking figures in social reform and liberation of early nineteenth-century England, breathes that passion for righteousness and justice in stanzas 1 and 2. This hymn is appropriate for Advent and Palm/Passion Sunday and other occasions that celebrate the righteous reign of Christ.

Ellacombe

Gesangbuch der H. W. k. Hofkapelle, 1784, alt.
adapt. and harm. by W. H. Monk, 1868

This rousing tune of German Roman Catholic origin was first printed in a book used in the chapel of the Duke of Würtemberg. "Many variants appeared in nineteenth century books, and it reached virtually the present form in Oehler's *Katholisches Gesangbuch zum Gebrauch bei dem offentlichen Gottesdienste*, 1863, the revised edition of an older hymn book of St. Gall, a Benedictine monastery." (Watson and Trickett 1988, 147) Its present form and harmonization are that of W. H. Monk for *Hymns Ancient and Modern*, 1868 Appendix, number 366. Descants and alternate harmonizations are found at 114-16, *The United Methodist Hymnal Music Supplement*.

Hallelujah! What a Savior (165)

Words and music: Philip P. Bliss, 1875 (Isa. 53)

This gospel hymn on the Atonement of Christ first appeared in *The International Lessons Monthly*, 1875, under the title "Redemption." (Reynolds 1964, 119) The hymn and tune were first included in *Gospel Hymns No. 2*, 1876. This is the hymn's first appearance in our hymnals.

Hallelujah! What a Savior

Ira Sankey in *My Life and the Story of the Gospel Hymns* describes how he performed the hymn:

> When Mr. Moody and I were in Paris, holding meeting in the old church which Napoleon had granted to the Evangelicals, I frequently sang this hymn as a solo, asking the congregation to join in the single phrase, "Hallelujah, what a Saviour." (Sankey 1906, 96)

Bliss's setting is typical of the reflective, chordal, quasi-choral music of the Reconstruction era's revival that has been all but lost in the mounds of frivolous and repetitious dance tunes in the gospel hymn repertory. In SATB performance, preferably without accompaniment and following Sankey's practice, each statement about Christ's passion may be sung slowly with deep devotion, followed ad lib with a rousing "Hallelujah! What a Savior!"

Happy the home when God is there (445)

Henry Ware, Jr., 1846

This hymn was published three years after the author's death under the title "The Happy Home" in *Selection of Hymns and Poetry for Use of Infants and Juvenile Schools and Families*, 3d. ed., 1846. (Julian 1907, 1569) The hymn entered our hymnals in 1878 as an anonymous poem, but it was dropped in 1905. It was reinstated in our 1935 hymnal with Ware's authorship. (See Robert G. McCutchan, *Our Hymnody*, page 431.) Our hymnal makes one change: stanza 2:3, "lisp" to "speak."

In this hymn the Christian home is described and extolled as the place of God's indwelling where children learn from parental example that prayer, Bible reading, and study are routines leading to happiness. The Hymnal Revision Committee reluctantly included this hymn with lingering questions as to its relevance for our day, including: "does it teach that unhappiness in a home, i.e., physical or mental impairment and illness, death, estrangement, violence, necessarily demonstrates a family's lack of Christian commitment and God's absence?" See other hymns under "Home and Family," **943**, in the "Index of Topics and Categories."

St. Agnes

John B. Dykes, 1866

The tune was first printed in John Grey's *Hymnal for Use in the English Church* with accompanying tunes, 1866. The composer named the tune after Agnes, a Roman girl who was "martyred at the age of 13 on January 21, 304, for refusing to marry a young nobleman. She is the patron saint of young girls." (Gealy, Lovelace, Young 1970, 208)

The tune is also called "St. Agnes, Durham" and "St. Agnes, Dykes" to distinguish it from another tune with the same name by James Langran. There is a vocal descant and an alternative harmonization at 291-92 in *The United Methodist Hymnal Music Supplement*.

Hark! the herald angels sing (240)

> *Charles Wesley, 1739; alt. by George Whitefield, 1753, and others (Luke 2:8-14)*

The text first appeared at 206-08 in *Hymns and Sacred Poems*, 1739, in ten 77.77 stanzas under the title "Hymn for Christmas Day." (Gealy 556/176) Alterations and selection of stanzas were made by George Whitefield in his 1753 *Collection*, including changing the first line to "Hark the herald angels sing" from "Hark, how all the welkin rings." "Martin Madan in *A Collection of Psalms and Hymns extracted from various authors*, 1760, also made alterations that have survived until this day, notably our 1:7-8 to its present form." (Gealy, Lovelace, Young 1970, 209)

In *Psalms of David*, the 1782 edition of Nahum Tate's and Nicolaus Brady's *New Version*, Madan's alterations were used, the stanzas were doubled, and the opening lines were set as a refrain. John Wesley did not include the hymn in his 1780 *Collection*. It was first included in our hymnals in 1786. Later editions suggested that it be sung to "Salisbury Tune" (EASTER HYMN). (See "Christ the Lord is risen today" page 281, for comments on the use of EASTER HYMN **(302)** with this text.)

A great controversy arose when the 1935 hymnal set aside the reference to the virgin birth of Jesus with the following changes in 2:3-4: "Late in time behold him come, offspring of a Virgin's womb" to "Long desired, behold him come, finding here his humble home." The 1966 hymnal restored the original text, except Whitefield's "the virgin" was substituted for "a virgin." Our hymn restores "a virgin." Other changes are in stanza 2:7, "as man with men" to "with us in flesh"; 3:6, "man" to "we"; 3:7, "born to raise the sons of earth" to "born to raise us from the earth."

The full text is included to show the many other changes that have been made over the years in this extraordinary hymn on humankind's recreation, reformation, and reconciliation in the life and witness of Jesus Christ.

Hark how all the welkin rings!   Christ by highest heaven adored,
"Glory to the King of kings,   Christ, the everlasting Lord,
Peace on earth and mercy mild,   Late in time behold him come,
God and sinners reconciled."   Offspring of a Virgin's womb.

Joyful, all ye nations, rise,   Veiled in flesh the Godhead see!
Join the triumph of the skies;   Hail the incarnate deity!
Universal nature say: Pleased as man with men to appear,
"Christ the Lord is born to Day."   Jesus! Our Immanuel here!

Hail the heavenly Prince of Peace!
Hail the Sun of Righteousness!
Light and life to all he brings,
Risen with healing in his wings.

Mild he lays his glory by,
Born that man no more may die,
Born to raise the sons of earth,
Born to give them second birth.

Come, Desire of nations, come,
Fix in us thy humble home;
Rise, the woman's conquering seed,
Bruise in us the serpent's head.

Now display thy saving power,
Ruined nature now restore,
Now in mystic union join
Thine to ours, and ours to thine.

Adam's likeness, Lord, efface;
Stamp Thy image in its place;
Second Adam from above,
Reinstate us in thy love.

Let us Thee, though lost, regain,
Thee the life, the inner Man;
O! to all Thyself impart,
Form'd in each believing heart.

Mendelssohn

Felix Mendelssohn, 1840; arr. by William H. Cummings, 1856

This melody is from the second chorus of Mendelssohn's cantata *Festgesang* composed in 1840 for male chorus and brass to celebrate the 400th anniversary of Johannes Gutenberg's invention of printing by moveable type. "Mendelssohn's melody appeared unadapted in *The Congregational Psalmist*, ed. Henry Allon and H. J. Gauntlett, 1858." (Milgate 1982, 105) W. H. Cummings's adaptation and arrangement was first included in R. R. Chope's *Congregational Hymn and Tune Book*, 1857. It forms the basis of all succeeding versions, including that in *Hymns Ancient and Modern*, 1861, number 43 (in the key of G), where, apparently in deference to altos and basses, a footnote indicates that the tune is to be sung in unison "except the 9th line." The tune in this arrangement was included in private collections in the USA in the mid-nineteenth century and first appeared in our hymnals in 1878. Two alternate harmonizations and a descant are included 234-36 in *The United Methodist Hymnal Music Supplement*.

Have thine own way, Lord (382)

Adelaide A. Pollard, 1902 (Jer. 18:5-6)

The author of this invitation hymn, a religious activist chronically frail and ill in mind and body, wrote this hymn during the distressful aftermath of an unsuccessful campaign to raise funds for a missionary trip to Africa. Following a prayer meeting she felt peace and a renewed relationship to God through her complete abandonment to do God's will. She expressed that new relationship in the potter-clay imagery from Jeremiah:

> Then the word of the Lord came to me: Can I not do with you, O house of Israel, just as this potter has done? says the Lord. Just like the clay in the potter's hand, so are you in my hand, O house of Israel. (Jeremiah 18:5-6)

The text with the tune first appeared in *Northfield Hymnal with Alexander's Supplement*, 1907. There are two changes in the hymn: stanza 2:4, "Master" to "Savior"; 2:5, "whiter than snow" to "wash me just now." The Hymnal Revision Committee debate on the latter change was intense and sustained. Those proposing the change stated that one does not have to be white, a North European, or Anglo Caucasian to be perceived as spiritually pure and socially acceptable. An African American member said, "You can wash me as much as you wish, but after you've finished I'll be just as black, which is beautiful." Those who wished to retain the original argued that the reference to washing was not about the pigmentation of human skin, but to the soul as in Psalm 51:7, "Purge me with hyssop, and I shall be clean; wash me, and I shall be whiter than snow." See the discussion of language, *"The United Methodist Hymnal*, 1989," page 137.

Adelaide

George C. Stebbins, 1907

The tune was composed for this text, and it first appeared in the above hymnal.

He is born (228)
Il est né

Trad. French carol; trans. by George K. Evans, 1963

George K. Evans's translation of this delightful French carol first appeared in *The International Book of Christmas Carols*, 1963, page 94, titled "He is born, the holy Child."

Il est né

Trad. French melody; harm. by Carlton R. Young, 1988

The harmonization was prepared for this hymnal. Individual solo voices or a duet may sing the stanzas ad lib, with melody instruments and tambourine supporting the congregation on the refrain. For an arrangment for Orff instruments see 177 in *The United Methodist Hymnal Music Supplement*.

He is Lord (177)

Words and music: 19th cent. USA trad. refrain (Phil. 2:9-11)

This chorus was reintroduced in the repertory in the 1960's in churches that use choruses and hymn stanzas and fragments for gathering in worship. See "Canticle of Christ's obedience" for the biblical text that may be read before singing this chorus. There are three additional stanzas which begin "He is King," "He is love," "He is life," page 256, in *Hymns and Psalms*, 1983.

He is Lord

Trad. chorus; arr. by Tom Fettke, 1986

This setting first appeared in *The Hymnal for Worship and Celebration*, 1986, number 105, in the refrain for "Emptied of his glory." Another harmonization is found at number 234 in *Hymns for the Family of God*, 1976.

He leadeth me: O blessed thought (128)

Joseph H. Gilmore, 1862 (Ps. 23)

This hymn was composed during the uncertainties of the Civil War following a preaching mission conducted by the author at the First Baptist Church, Philadelphia, in 1862. The author has commented on the writing of the hymn:

> I set out to give the people an exposition of the 23rd Psalm, which I had given before on three or four occasions, but this time I did not get further than the words "He Leadeth Me." Those words took hold of me as they had never done before. I saw in them a significance and beauty of which I had never dreamed." . . .

> The hymn first appeared in the *Watchman and Reflector* (December 4, 1862, p. 4) in four six-line stanzas, entitled, "He Leadeth Me Beside Still Waters: and is signed CONTOOCOOK. . . . The text and tune appeared in W. B. Bradbury's *The Golden Censer*, 1864, number 105." (Reynolds 1976, 85)

The hymn entered our hymnals in 1875. One alteration was made in 1935 that has been incorporated in the present hymnal: stanza 3:1 "clasp thy hand in mine" to "place my hand in thine."

Other scriptural and hymnic versions of Psalm 23 are found at **136, 137, 138, 518**, and **754**.

He leadeth me

William B. Bradbury, 1864

The tune was first included with Gilmore's text in *The Golden Censer*, 1864. Bradbury modified the refrain by adding "His faithful follower I would be" and included a performance note "Four to each measure," apparently to suggest that it be sung in a tempo much slower than a bright subdivided two that characterizes the superficial and insensitive accompaniment of most organists and pianists. Three hairpin accent marks and four fermatas were included in the original score (Gealy 556/179); the latter remain in performance practice though long since deleted from the printed score. Our hymnals have included the tune without alteration.

In his preface to *The Golden Censer* the composer includes an interesting comment on the form of the Sunday school song:

The most popular and appropriate modern feature, the ever-recurring "Refrain" and "Chorus," sung as children only *can* sing them, tend to fasten like "a nail in a sure place" the sentiment of the hymns. (Ronander and Porter 1966, 289)

He lives (310)

Words and music: Alfred H. Ackley, 1933

This hymn was written following the author's exchange with a young Jewish man who, after being invited to receive Christ, asked Ackley, "Why should I worship a dead Jew?" Ackley replied, "He lives!" The exchange is echoed in the final line of the refrain:

> You ask me how I know he lives?
> He lives within my heart.

The couplet suggests that Christ's work in the world, e.g., "I see his hand of mercy," "I see his loving care," is insufficient evidence of the Resurrection until verified by those who claim to have experienced Christ in their hearts. Fortunately, the section of hymns on the Resurrection and exaltation of Christ **(302-327)** provides many alternatives that are more gospel centered, theologically convincing, and musically substantial.

The hymn first appeared in *Triumphant Service Songs*, 1934. It entered our hymnals in 1957. In stanza 1:4, "whatever men may say" has been changed to "whatever foes may say."

Ackley

The tune was named after the composer by the committee responsible for the *Baptist Hymnal*, 1956.

He never said a mumbalin' word (291)

African American spiritual
adapt. and arr. by William Farley Smith, 1986

William B. McClain has commented on this spiritual:

> Here again, the Crucifixion motif dominates the imagination of the slave. James Cone [Cone 1972, 52] notes that the slaves were "impressed by the Passion because they too had been rejected, beaten, and shot without a chance to say a word in defense of their humanity." The message and the slow, haunting, and reverent tone of this song make it ideal for the most somber of days in the Christian year, Good Friday. (McClain 1990, 97)

Cone continues his commentary with a variant of the first stanza:

> Oh, dey whupped him up de hill, up de hill, up de hill,
> Oh, dey whupped him up de hill, an' he never said a
>   mumbalin' word,
> Oh, dey whupped him up de hill, an' he never said a
>   mumbalin' word,
> He jes' hung down his head an' he cried. (Cone 1972, 52)

In *Songs of Zion*, 1981, page 101, "and" and "never" appear in dialect "an'" and "nevuh." The Hymnal Revision Committee, acting on the recommendation of African American committee members and consultants, rendered texts in dialect only in instances where rhythmic nuance and articulation called for its use, for example "mumbalin'" in the the first line of this spiritual, and in "O Mary, don't you weep" **(134)**, stanza 2:

> When I get to heaven goin'a sing and shout,
> ain't nobody there goin'a turn me out.

Sufferer

William Farley Smith's setting lends itself to the choir or a soloist singing the Good Friday account with the congregation answering "and he never said a mumbalin' word." A simpler harmonization with another variant of the melody is found at 95 in *The Presbyterian Hymnal*, 1990.

He rose (316)

African American spiritual
adapt. and arr. by William Farley Smith, 1986

William B. McClain makes this commentary:

> The Resurrection is the divine guarantee that black people's lives are in the hands of the Conqueror of Death. "He Arose" might appear simply to be a chronicle of the events surrounding the death and Resurrection of Christ, but its refrain, "And the Lord will bear my spirit home," implies that through the Resurrection of Jesus, God has done something personal for each of us. What God has done is to free us to "do what is necessary to remain obedient to the Father . . ." and to enable us to "bear the trouble and endure the pain of loneliness in oppression." "He Arose" (or He 'Rose) remains a standard in the black church for Easter Sunday services. (McClain 1990, 122-23)

George Pullen Jackson in *White Spirituals of the Southern Uplands* demonstrates the probability of a common source for this text by citing stanzas 1 and 3 in another musical setting in *The Sacred Harp*, 1844. (Jackson 1933, 269)

Ascensius

The name was given by Dr. Smith, who has provided names for other spirituals that are prompted by the central meaning of the text or are the name of a leader or a significant event in the African American's struggle for freedom and justice. ASCENSIUS is a corruption of *ascensus*, meaning to climb or rise. William Farley Smith suggests that the spiritual should be sung "with unrestrained joy . . . [as] an effective opening for Easter Sunday worship." (Sanchez 1989, 116) As in some other settings by Dr. Smith, this is essentially a choral piece to be taught to the choir and "caught" by the congregation. Number 168, *Songs of Zion*, 1981, is a more traditional arrangement utilizing three chords: tonic, subdominant, dominant.

He touched me (367)

Words and music: William J. Gaither, 1963
(Matt. 8:3; Mark 1:41; Luke 5:13)

The immediate, widespread, and sutained popularity of this hymn among former Evangelical United Brethren and Methodists was demonstrated in its being one of the most requested "new hymns" for inclusion in this hymnal. The hymn's main theme is the joy experienced when Jesus cleanses the sinner from sin's "guilt and shame" and restores wholeness in the same way that he cleansed the leper—by touching him.

> A leper came to him begging him, and kneeling he said to him, "If you choose, you can make me clean." Moved with pity, Jesus stretched out his hand and touched him, and said to him, "I do choose. Be made clean!" Immediately the leprosy left him, and he was made clean. (Mark 1:40-42; also Matthew 8:1-3 and Luke 5:12-13)

William J. Gaither recalls that this song was prompted by a discussion with Doug Oldham in 1963 in Huntington, Indiana. "Dale simply suggested to me, 'Bill, you should write a song with the phrase 'He Touched me' in it.' There is something about the 'touch of God—to know that we can be touched by God at our place of need. It was first included in *Hymns for the Family of God*, 1976." (Correspondence with Carlton R. Young, October 1992)

See also Gloria Gaither's reflection on this text at 19-25 in *Fully Alive!*

When affirming the power of Christ's healing in his "touching" the sinner as like that of his healing of the leper, one should be careful not to confuse the causes and cure of human sin with the causes and cures of physical or mental impairment.

He touched me

See commentary above.

Heal me, hands of Jesus (262)

Michael Perry, 1982

This prayer to be healed, restored, cleansed, forgiven, released from pain, guilt, and anxiety, and given peace through the "hands," "blood," "mind," and "joy" of Jesus first appeared in *Hymns for Today's Church*, 1982, page 319.

The author comments that the text "was first written when we were compiling *Hymns for Today's Church*—specifically to fill the tremendous gap in hymns about healing. And as a response to my own pastoral experience with people (including myself!)." (Correspondence with Carlton R. Young, September 1991)

The poet's unusual use of a trochaic foot in the first line brings emphasis to the first, third, and fifth words in this line in each stanza. The composer of the tune altered the poem from 5 6. 8 6 to SM by changing "Christ" to "Jesus" in the first line of each stanza. Other changes that were made with the permission of the poet and incorporated in the hymn's first appearance are in stanza 3:2, "replace the love of sin" to "and show me all my sin," and stanza 4:4, "for Christ shall bring me peace!" to "for Jesus brings me peace!"

Sutton Common

Norman L. Warren, 1982

The tune was composed for this text and first appeared in *Hymns for Today's Church*, 1982.

Heal us, Emmanuel, hear our prayer (266)

William Cowper, 1779 (Mark 9:14-27, Matt. 9:20-22
Mark 5:25-34, Luke 8:43-48)

The hymn was first included in *Olney Hymns*, 1779, under the title "Jehovah-Raphi, I am the Lord that healeth thee. Exod. xv." The healing touch of Jesus was a constant need in Cowper's daily life, for he suffered from periodic deep depressions, and he felt that he would die if God did not spare him.

Our text follows the version of the text in *Hymns and Psalms*, 1983, but omits the fifth stanza that Erik Routley commented should not be used because "the last line we are bound to call bathos, and 'firm and strong' is the kind of needless reduplication that we find nowhere else in the *Olney Hymns*. (Routley 1951, 131)

> Concealed amid the gathering throng,
> She would have shunned thy view;
> And if her faith was firm and strong,
> Had strong misgivings too.

The several scriptural references might form the basis of a sermon based on healing, with stanzas of the hymn sung and scripture read before, during, and after preaching. This is the hymn's first appearance in our hymnals.

Gräfenberg

Johann Crüger, 1647; harm. from The English Hymnal, 1906

The tune first appeared in Crüger's *Praxis Pietatis Melica*, 1647. This harmonization from *The English Hymnal*, 1906, entered our hymnals in 1935, without citation and minus the rhythmic form of measures 6 and 10. The 1966 hymnal tunes subcommittee's restoration of those rhythms is continued in this hymnal. In Great Britain the tune is also named "Nun Danket All," which is the first line of the hymn to which it was set in *Praxis Pietatis Melica*, 1647. There is a vocal descant at 149 in *The United Methodist Hymnal Music Supplement*.

Hear us, O God (490)

Trad. prayer petition

This is a traditional petition to God to hear the prayer of the faithful, e.g., Psalm 54:2a, "Hear my prayer, O God."

Hear us

Sally Ahner, 1983

This prayer response first appeared in the Service Music Project, 1983, sponsored and distributed by the Section on Worship of the General Board of Discipleship.

Heleluyan (78)
Alleluia

Words and music: Trad. Muscogee (Creek) Indian
transcription by Charles H. Webb, 1987

According to Harold D. Jacobs, Native American member of the Hymnal Revision Committee,

> this is a Muscogee (Creek) hymn that originated before or during the Trail of Tears and has been kept familiar in the Muscogee (Creek Indians) through the Oral Tradition. (Correspondence with Christine Benagh, November 1987)

Dr. Webb made this transcription from a video tape of the opening stanza of this hymn as sung by a Muscogee (Creek) United Methodist family in New York state. In the second measure "Yah-hay-ka-thei" ("I will be singing") should be substituted for "Heleluyan" to form the original opening phrase "Alleluia, I will be singing." This is the first time this tribal melody has appeared in print.

Heleluyan

See comments above.

Help us accept each other (560)

Fred Kaan, 1974

The author has commented on the origin of the hymn:

> This text was set in motion upon reading a Bible study article Mrs. Jackie Mattonen had written for the Cumberland Presbyterian Church in the USA. . . . It was almost accidentally and at the last moment included in the fourth edition of *Cantate Domino* [1974, with the author's German and Dutch translation when the editors were forced to drop a particular text], . . . and it so happened that my "Hymn on acceptance" was just the right length to fill the two blank pages that needed filling. (Kaan 1985, 55)

The text was introduced in the USA in *Break Not the Circle,* 1975, to the tune "Baronita." It was not widely sung until it appeared in an anthem setting with a new tune by John Ness Beck. Scriptural references include stanza 1:2, Romans 15:7; stanza 3:4, John 3:21, Ephesians 4:15; and stanza 3:7, Matthew 18:21.

It was included with Beck's tune in *Supplement to the Book of Hymns* and became a favorite hymn for services and times of reconciliation, including Christian ecumenical services.

Acceptance

John Ness Beck, 1977

The composer made this hymn setting from his anthem "Help us accept each other," 1977, and it was first included in *Supplement to the Book of Hymns,* 1982, number 899.

Heralds of Christ (567)

Laura S. Copenhaver, 1915

The poet describes how the metaphor of the highway links her own thirty years of mission work in the mountains of Virginia to the more visible missionary activity in Africa and India, and expresses the determined, dynamic, energetic, and expansive attributes of nineteenth-century Christian missions:

> In writing "Heralds of Christ" for one of the Summer Conferences at which I used to lecture, I was moved with a deep sense of unity with the builders of the King's Highway in far lands, next door to me in America, and even with those great ones I had known as a child now gone on with the immortals by way of Africa and India. . . . Today in every land Christians are uniting to build a Kingdom which shall have no geographical bounds, no limitations of race, no barriers of cast or class. (McCutchan 1942, 466-67)

The hymn appeared in H. Augustine Smith's *Hymns for the Living Age*, 1923, number 401, in the section "Foreign Missions," set to NATIONAL HYMN. (Gealy 556/182) Stanzas 1, 2, and 4 entered our hymnals in 1935. As early as the third decade of this century the omitted third stanza was for some a questionable characterization of foreign missions:

> Where once the twisting trail in darkness wound,
> let marching feet and joyous song resound,
> where burn the funeral pyres, and censers swing,
> make straight, make straight the highway of the King.

In stanza 1:3 "ye" is changed to "you"; stanza 2:3, "ye" to "now."

National hymn

See "God of the ages," pages 370-71.

Here I am, Lord (593)

Words and music: Daniel L. Schutte, 1981 (Isa. 6:8)

This song of commitment and sending forth is sung in both denominational and ecumenical worshipping communities in the USA. Schutte's setting contrasts the Hebrew psalmic transcendent characterizations of God as Lord of sea, sky, snow, rain, wind, and flame, with compelling prophetic and pietistic themes of the caring God who is intimately involved in the struggles of the poor and oppressed and is concerned for the well-being of each member of the human family—the witness of that struggle and concern being those, like Isaiah, who positively respond to the call:

> Then I heard the voice of the Lord saying, "Whom shall I send, and who will go for us?" And I said, "Here am I; send me!" (Isaiah 6:8)

Its lack of Christian rhetoric makes the hymn an ideal song for use in interfaith worshipping communities and similar occasions.

Here I am, Lord

Adapt. by Carlton R. Young, 1988

Light folk/pop rhythmic accompaniment may be added under the melody and chords. The stanzas may be sung by solo or soli voices, with the congregation joining on the refrain. The refrain is scored for SATB voices and may be sung without accompaniment as a closing or dedication response.

Here, O Lord, your servants gather (552)
Sekai no tomo to te o tsuna gi

Tokuo Yamaguchi, 1958; trans. by Everett M. Stowe, 1958
phonetic transcription from the Japanese by I-to Loh, 1988

This hymn and tune were composed for the fourteenth World Council of

Christian Education Convention, Japan, 1958. The text first appeared in Japanese and in English translation in the convention's program booklet *Christian Shimpo*, 1958, in the section of the church's "Nature and Unity." The English text also included these scriptural references: Ephesians 2:13-19, 3:20, 21; John 14:6, 12; Psalm 102:25-27. According to Paul A. Richardson in *Handbook to the Baptist Hymnal*, "Its first inclusion in a hymnal was in United Church of Christ in Japan's hymnal, *Hymns of the Church*, 1963. The first USA hymnal to include it was *The Mennonite Hymnal*, 1969." (Adams 1992, 139)

The hymn was written during the uncertainties of the decade that followed the USA's atomic destruction of Hiroshima and Nagasaki, and saw the advent of space exploration in the USSR's launching of Sputnik. It is a prayer for the church to unite in a common effort for peace under the leadership of Jesus Christ who is the "Way," "Truth," and "Life."

Tokyo

Isao Koizumi, 1958

The tune was composed for this text in the *Gagaku* mode, which originated in China and was used in traditional Japanese court music. Isao Koizumi's use of traditional scales supported by open parallel harmonies is typical of that employed by a school of post-World War II Japanese composers. The hymn may be sung by alternating stanzas with solo voices and congregation and choir. It first appeared in the program booklet of the convention with a metronomic marking of quarter note = ca. 88.

Here, O my Lord, I see thee (623)

Horatius Bonar, 1857 (Rev. 19:6-9)

This communion hymn was written at the request of John James Bonar, minister of St. Andrew's Free Church, Greenock, Scotland, the elder brother of the author:

It was the custom of the church to distribute parish notices and a hymn after each communion service. In October 1855 he asked his brother to supply a hymn, and in a day or two received this one (possibly composed beforehand); it was read at Communion in the Greenock church and was then printed with the church notices. (Julian 1907, 513)

The hymn was revised and first appeared in the first series of Bonar's *Hymns of Faith and Hope*, 1857, pages 118-19, under the heading "Do This In Remembrance Of Me." (Gealy 556/183) It entered our hymnals in 1905 in six stanzas, using the original stanzas 1, 2, 4, 5, 6, and 10. This selection was reduced to four in 1935 and 1957, increased to five in 1966, and retained in this hymnal.

The omitted stanza 5 is included in some hymnals:

> I have no help but thine; nor do I need
> another arm save thine to lean upon;
> it is enough, my Lord, enough indeed;
> my strength is in thy might, thy might alone.

Scriptural allusions to the marriage feast of the Lamb and his bride, the church, are found throughout the hymn (particularly stanza 5:4):

And the angel said to me, "Write this: Blessed are those
who are invited to the marriage supper of the Lamb." (Revelation 19:9)

The form of the abridged hymn suggests that it may be sung in two sections: stanzas 1-3 before communion and stanzas 4-5 after.

Penitentia

Edward Dearle, 1874

This tune from Arthur Sullivan's *Church Hymns with Tunes*, 1874, entered our hymnals with this text in 1905. Our 1957 hymnal set the hymn to MORECAMBE **(500)**. The hymn appeared in two settings in the 1966 hymnal, PENITENTIA and the exquisite, although seldom sung plainsong, "Adoro te." A vocal descant and alternate harmonization are found at 265 and 266 in *The United Methodist Hymnal Music Supplement.*

His name is wonderful (174)

Words and music: Audrey Mieir, 1959

This popular chorus was written on the flyleaf of the author's Bible after she heard the minister speak the opening scriptural sentence "His name shall be called Wonderful" (Isaiah 9:6) at a family Christmas service, Bethel Union Church, Duarte, California. It was first published in 1959. (Reynolds 1976, 88)

This chorus that extols the names of Christ, "wonderful, King, Master, Lord, Shepherd, Rock of ages, almighty God," may be combined with the singing of the first stanzas of other selections in "In Praise of Christ" **153-94**, or the prayer "Praising God of many names" **(104)** and the hymn "God of many names" **(105)**.

His name is wonderful

The tune is also called "Mieir."

Holy God, we praise thy name (79)
Grosser Gott, wir loben dich

Sts. 1-4, anon. 18th cent.; trans. by Clarence Walworth, 1853
sts. 5-7, F. Bland Tucker, 1982

Robin A. Leaver has written of the historical background of the text:

[This paraphrase of the portions of the Te Deum] has been attributed to Ignaz Franz. It was published in *Katholisches Gesangbuch, ca.* 1774. (Glover 1993, vol. 2)

Walworth's translation and paraphrase first appeared in a Redemptorist mission hymnal, ca. 1853, and in the USA in *Evangelical Hymnal*, 1880. It entered our hymnals in 1966 in four stanzas.

The hymn follows the two-part form of the Te Deum, "Canticle of the Holy Trinity" **(80)**. See page 265-67 for commentary on this canticle. Stanzas 5-7, praising Christ as "King, Savior, Son of God, and judge," were made by F. Bland Tucker for *The Hymnal 1982*; their addition makes for a more complete paraphrase of the canticle.

Grosser Gott

Katholisches Gesangbuch, 1774

The tune first appeared in *Katholisches Gesang-Buch* of Maria Theresa of Austria (undated, but 1774-80, probably 1774). (Ellinwood 1956, 180) It became a favorite hymn in both German and French Roman Catholic hymnals. In England it was introduced in an abridged form in long meter as HURSLEY **(468)** (see page 297). "Its earliest appearance in the USA was in Philip Rohr's *Favorite Catholic Melodies*, 1854, p. 81, set to the text 'Thee, Sovereign God, we grateful praise.'" (Milgate 1982, 56)

The tune entered our hymnals in 1964 with an anonymous harmonization from the *Pilgrim Hymnal*, 1958, number 247, that appears to be from *The Hymnal 1940*. The tune is also known as "Framingham," "Halle," and "Te Deum." There are vocal descants and an alternative harmonization at 151-53, *The United Methodist Hymnal Music Supplement*.

Holy, holy, holy! Lord God Almighty (64)

Reginald Heber, 1826 (Rev. 4:8-11)

The author was a leading figure of those Anglicans who, knowing firsthand the vitality of evangelical and independent church singing, urged the lifting of the church's restrictions on the singing of hymns in worship. In consequence, Heber, who as a student at Oxford had been a prize-winning poet, wrote hymns based on the lectionary to be sung between the sermon and the creed by his parish in Hodnet, Salop.

This is the author's best known hymn. It was written for Trinity Sunday, the first Sunday after Pentecost, and is based in part on the epistle printed in the *Book of Common Prayer*, Revelation 4:6-11. It was first included in *Selection of Hymns for the Parish Church of Banbury*, published in 1826 shortly after Heber's death.

This hymn on the transcendence and praiseworthiness of the Holy Trinity is widely acclaimed as the paradigm of a singable and memorable hymn composed on a single theme. Percy Dearmer has commented: "In Victorian times there were so few hymns about God, and this hymn, free from all subjectivity, filled a large gap, expressing the pure spirit of worship in stately language." (Dearmer and Jacob 1933, 115) The hymn was a favorite of Tennyson and was sung at his funeral in Westminster Abbey, 1892. Its unique meter, 11 12. 12 10, prompts the question as to what tune it was sung before *Hymns Ancient and Modern*, 1861, matched it with Dykes's NICAEA. Robin A. Leaver, "Dykes' Nicaea: An Original Hymn Tune or the Reworking of Another," *The Hymn*, April 1987, John Wilson's response to Leaver in *The Hymn*, July 1987, and Marilyn Stulken in *Hymnal Companion to the Lutheran Book of Worship*, tend to demonstrate that Dykes's tune was in part formed from tunes already in print in England and the USA.

The hymn entered our hymnals in 1878 and has been retained in all editions without alteration. Its exclusive use in many churches as the processional in services of Holy Communion stems from the instruction found at the beginning of the liturgy in the 1935 hymnal, page 523: "The People shall stand and join in singing the hymn 'Holy, holy, holy, Lord God Almighty,' or other suitable hymn."

Victorian hymns with their tunes still tend to image the gathered church as a successful middle-class family at worship in a protected and clean environment sheltered from worldly concerns, an attribute that may preoccupy some congregations and worship leaders who, contrary to the compelling transcendental rhetoric of this hymn, in time render the worship setting—its decor, music, lighting, carpeting, and preaching—as both the means and the end of worship.

For commentary on the Spanish version of this hymn, see "¡Santo! ¡Santo! ¡Santo!" page 573.

Nicaea

John B. Dykes, 1861

This is Dykes's finest, most sung tune and a perfect match for the romantic yet refined literary qualities of Heber's text. In naming the tune NICAEA Dykes has cleverly interrelated its opening and reiterated triadic (three-tone) motif (after WACHET AUF, **720** ?) with the doctrine of the Trinity formulated at the Council of Nicaea, 325, and the subject of the hymn.

The tune's range, counterpoint, subtle chromaticism, well-crafted voice leadings, so "perfectly" (see stanza 3:4) matched to express the refined, reverent yet impersonal qualities of the text, suggest that a congregation of amateur singers should not even attempt to sing the hymn, but that it should only be performed as an offering by a trained choir accompanied by a pipe organ in the original key of E major. (See "British Hymns," page 15, for comments by

Erik Routley on Victorian parish performance practice.) Attempts since 1950 in the USA to make this and other Victorian tunes accessible to the average singer have unfortunately resulted in their transposition downward as much as a minor third for unison singing in three octaves (one each for the intentional, casual, and non-singer), occasionally beefed up with descants and free accompaniments. There are alternative harmonizations and a vocal descant at 245-48 in *The United Methodist Hymnal Music Supplement.*

Holy Spirit, come, confirm us (331)

Brian Foley, 1971

The text is Foley's hymn on the work of the Holy Spirit within each of us to "confirm," "console," "renew," and "possess." It is one of fourteen hymns included in *New Catholic Hymnal*, 1971, from those that the author had revised from a group of seventy-two written since the 1950's. Like the ideas in most of his hymns, they "come out of prayer or out of wrestling with the modern problems of theology." (Milgate 1982, 122) Scriptural references include stanza 1:3-4, 1 Corinthians 2:12-13; stanza 2, Romans 8:26-27; and stanza 4, Ephesians 3:16-17.

Cyril Taylor comments that the poem also expresses "the Spirit as Strengthener, Advocate, and Life of the Christian Community." (Taylor 1984, 39-40)

For the bread

See "Faith, while trees are still in blossom," page 331.

Holy Spirit, Truth divine (465)

Samuel Longfellow, 1864

This hymn first appeared in six stanzas under the heading "Prayer for Inspiration," number 407 in *Hymns of the Spirit*, 1864, edited by the author and Samuel Johnson. (Gealy 556, 188) It is one of a number of excellent hymns composed by New England Unitarian pastor-poets and introduced to USA hymnody by way of their inclusion in late nineteenth- and early twentieth-century British hymnals. The poet's listing and elaborations on the gifts and attributes of the Holy Spirit that are inspired, i.e., breathed, within each believer, are completed in the omitted stanzas 5 and 6:

> Holy Spirit, Peace divine!
> Still this restless heart of mine;
> Speak to calm this tossing sea,
> Stayed in Thy tranquility.

Holy Spirit, Joy Divine!
Gladden Thou this heart of mine;
In the desert ways I sing
'Spring, O Well! forever spring.'

Stanza 4:1, "Holy Spirit, Right divine, King," may be the author's unintentional but instinctive gibe at the anathematized "divine right of kings." In stanza 3:3, "by thee may I" has been changed to "grant that I may."

Canterbury

See "Christ, from whom all blessings flow," pages 271-72.

Holy Thursday (283)

After the Book of Common Prayer
(Matt. 26:26-29; Mark 14:22-25; Luke 22:17-20; 1 Cor. 11:23-26
Laurence Hull Stookey has provided this commentary on this prayer for Holy or Maundy Thursday.

Even as we remember the suffering and death of Jesus, we look beyond his anguish to the bread and wine with their promise of eternal life through Christ, whose resurrection we will celebrate three days hence. (Sanchez 1989, 106)

The prayer's address was originally "Almighty Father, whose dear Son," and the final sentence ended with "and who now lives and reigns with you and the Holy Spirit, one God, for ever and ever. Amen."

Hope of the world (178)

Georgia Harkness, 1954
Fred D. Gealy has provided this commentary:

The hymn was written for and selected as the winning hymn by the Hymn Society of America from among nearly 500 hymns submitted for use at the Second Assembly of the World Council of Churches, meeting at Evanston [USA, October], 1954. It was first published in the July issue of *The Hymn* and in "Eleven Ecumenical Hymns," 1954. (Gealy, Lovelace, Young 1970, 218)

The hymn was written in 1953 on the theme of the assembly, "Jesus Christ, hope of the world," and was first printed in the Hymn Society's "President's Message" in the July 1954 issue of *The Hymn*. (Gealy 556/189) It was one of eleven hymns selected to be offered for use at the assembly. Today it seems inconceivable that anyone would have questioned the assembly's theme. But its challenge to the assumption that human endeavor was sufficient to bring in the kingdom caused a stir within USA liberal Protestantism that was only partly assuaged with the announcement that the winning hymn had been written by one of the USA's leading liberal theologians and ecumenists.

The first four stanzas recall the compassionate, healing, and reconciling ministry of Jesus. The final stanza calls us to be faithful to the gospel and tells of the conquering power of the risen and reigning Christ. The hymn entered our hymnals in 1957. In stanza 2:4, "end her" has been changed to "end all."

Vicar

V. Earle Copes, 1963

The Second Assembly of the World Council of Churches was held at First Methodist Church, Evanston, and its minister of music, Austin C. Lovelace, accompanied the hymn's premiere sung to the Dorian mode psalm tune "Donne Secours." In "Eleven Ecumenical Hymns" it was set to both "Donne Secours" and "Ancient of Days."

VICAR, the first name of the composer's father, was written for our 1966 hymnal as an alternative to the lightweight but nevertheless singable "Ancient of Days" and the sturdy "Donne Secours," judged not upbeat enough for Harkness's hopeful hymn.

Copes's tune is composed in the style of the unison English public school (meaning private school) hymn tunes of Geoffrey Shaw, George Dyson, and C. S. Lang. The melody for the most part is diatonic and scored in the middle and upper range and supported by a strong moving bass line. Although it has been included in a number of hymnals as a welcome addition to the meager repertory of 11 10. 11 10. tunes, VICAR is yet to be accepted by some United Methodists who prefer singing less demanding four-part evangelical tunes and reject the challenges and rewards of singing unison tunes such as ENGELBERG **(68)** and ABBOT'S LEIGH **(584)**.

Hosanna, loud hosanna (278)

Jeanette Threlfall, 1873 (Matt 21:8-9; Mark 11:8-10; John 12:12-13)

Jesus' entry into Jerusalem accompanied by the joyous songs of children is depicted in this Palm Sunday hymn, the one item still sung of the seventy poems collected in the author's *Sunshine and Shadow*, 1873.

In stanza 2:5, "men and angels" has been changed to "earth and heaven."

Ellacombe

See "Hail to the Lord's anointed," pages 384-85.

How blest are they who trust in Christ (654)

Fred Pratt Green, 1972

Bernard Braley has traced the origin of the text:

> This hymn . . . was first written and published [under the title "For a
> Memorial Service"] in the *Methodist Recorder*, 1972. It was submitted in 1976
> to the Roman Catholic Commission on English in the Liturgy, accepted by
> them, and then rejected as theologically inadequate. In 1980, with the omis-
> sion of a verse and one small change in text, it was one of the four (out of
> 475) entries accepted by the Hymn Society of America for new texts on the
> Christian life. Despite its title, it is suitable for general use.
>
> The original third verse:
>
> > They journey on! While we must stay,
> > Our work not done, our time unspent;
> > What baffles us to them grows clear.
> > In Christ the Truth they are content.
>
> A later version of this verse has as its last two lines:
>
> > May we, each day, rejoice in grace,
> > Each day our stubborn sins repent.   (Green 1982, 49-50)

The author's four-decade experience as a pastor to the grieving is embodied in
this hymn about the strength and blessing that come in times of death and
remembrance to those who have trusted and witnessed to the death and resurrection of Jesus Christ.

Maryton

H. Percy Smith, 1874

One of the most durable of all LM Victorian tunes, Smith's tune was composed for John Keble's "Sun of my soul" in *Church Hymns with Tunes*, 1874,
music edition by Arthur Sullivan. The tune entered our hymnals in 1905
where it was used four times. Robert G. McCutchan states without elaboration
that "Maryton" is "a farm, or manor, name." (McCutchan 1957, 100)

How can we name a Love (111)

Brian Wren, 1973

The author has commented on the writing of this hymn, which first appeared
in the form that was initially considered by the Hymnal Revision Committee:

[It was written September 1973 while serving] on the Committee that compiled *New Church Praise*, (published in 1975) for the United Reformed Church. Malcom Williamson's tune "Mercer Street" (1973) came to our ears and was well received. This [was] an attempt to put new words to it. It also marks the beginning of an attempt to break out from the heavy masculinity of traditional metaphors and images of God. (Wren "Notes" in *Faith Looking Forward*, 1983)

The text came to the attention of the Hymnal Revision Committee in the form that appeared as selection two under the heading "The Beyond in the midst of life" in *Faith Looking Forward*, 1983.

It was the Hymnal Revision Committee's intention (see pages 138-43) to include a number of hymns that went beyond the repertory of traditional metaphors and images of God. On the surface this hymn appeared to be one that might represent that cause, with the exception that the poet addressed God as "our Mother strong and sure" in parallel with God as "our Father kind." The hymn caused problems with the committee at other points; e.g., stanza 3 was judged too intimate for a United Methodist hymnal and was set aside.

> If in another's arms
> closeness and joy astound
> and as we take and give
> we die and live,
> are lost and found,
> or if by others' trust
> shyness and pride unbend
> we glimpse God's ways
> and hush to praise
> our Lover and our Friend.

Letters of negotiation were exchanged over an eighteenth-month period, 1987-88, between the poet and editor Carlton R. Young. The latter on behalf of the Hymnal Revision Committee attempted to deal with the committee's perceived potentially political problem at the 1988 General Conference if the original text were included. The text in our hymnal is the poet's recasting of his original stanzas 1, 2, 4, and 5.

Terra Beata

Trad. English melody; adapt. by Franklin L. Sheppard, 1915

Translated "blessed earth," TERRA BEATA, according to Ethel K. Porter in *Guide to the Pilgrim Hymnal*, page 366, is arranged from the traditional English melody "Rusper" and first appeared in Franklin L. Sheppard's hymnal *Alleluia*, 1915. Since the number of SMD tunes is limited and the Hymnal Revision Committee desired to set this "controversial" text to a familiar tune, the result is a less than perfect wedding and ironically the tune for "This is my Father's world." The tune is transposed to D major at 326 in *The United Methodist Hymnal Music Supplement.* An alternate harmonization by Edward Shippen Barnes, 1926, is included in *The Presbyterian Hymnal,* 1990.

How can we sinners know (372)

Charles Wesley, 1749

Fred D. Gealy has provided this commentary:

> The hymn first appeared in *Hymns and Sacred Poems*, 1749 [2:220-21], in eight 8-line [66. 66. 86. 86] sts., beginning a series under the title "The Marks of Faith. (Gealy 556/194) When John [Wesley] printed the hymn in his 1780 *Collection* he omitted the original stanzas 4 and 5 [added 2 syllables to each third line], and removed 2 syllables from each fifth line, thus reducing the entire hymn to Short Meter [Double]. (Gealy, Lovelace, Young 1970, 221)

This hymn on God's justifying and sanctifying grace through Jesus Christ was first included in our hymnals in 1821 with stanzas selected from John Wesley's 1780 revisions. In addition to adding two stanzas, other changes from our 1966 hymnal include stanza 1:1, "a sinner" to "we sinners"; 1:2, "his sins" to "our sins"; 2:3, "sons of men" to "ends of earth"; and 5:3, "his Spirit" to "that Spirit."

In the extensive commentary on this hymn in *Companion to Hymns and Psalms,* Charles Wesley's original poem is called "a great Methodist manifesto."

> It describes a Christian's experience of assurance through the inward witness of the Spirit. John Wesley defined this as an inward impression on the soul that "I am a child of God," that "Jesus Christ has loved me and given himself for me"; and that "all my sins are blotted out.' This experience is confirmed by the believer's own awareness that in some measure he shows the marks of the Spirit. (Trickett and Watson 1988, 414)

St. Michael

Genevan Psalter, 1551; adapt. by William Crotch, 1836

This is one of several Genevan tunes (this one set to Psalm 134 and barely recognizable from the original; see *Historic Companion to Hymns Ancient and Modern,* pages 219-20) that came into the English repertory from the Anglo-Genevan Psalter, 1560-61 (see commentary on "All people that on earth do dwell," pages 196-97; "British Hymns," pages 9-10; and Robin Leaver, "English Metrical Psalmody," Vol. 1, *The Hymnal 1982 Companion*).

The tune was neglected during the seventeenth century. It was reintroduced in an abbreviated form with a new ending, harmonized, and probably named ST. MICHAEL by William Crotch for his *Psalm Tunes*, 1836. The tune entered our hymnals in 1935 in a setting that combined the rhythm of *Hymns Ancient and Modern*, 1861, number 55, with the harmonization from *The English Hymnal*, 1906, number 48. There is an alternate harmonization, a vocal descant, and transposition to F major at 306-08 in *The United Methodist Hymnal Music Supplement*.

How firm a foundation (529)

"K" in Rippon's Selection of Hymns, 1787
(2 Tim. 2:19; Heb. 13:5; Isa. 43:1-2)

Fred D. Gealy has provided this commentary:

> The hymn in 7 sts. first appeared [as hymn 128] in John Rippon, *A Selection of Hymns from the Best Authors*, 1787 [13th ed., Gealy 556/190], under the title "Exceeding Great and Precious Promises." Authorship was ascribed to "K." As early as 1822, "K" [became "Kn," in 1835, "Keen" after] . . . Richard Keen, precentor in the London Baptist church where Rippon was minister. (Gealy, Lovelace, Young 1970, 221)

Included above the text is the scriptural reference 2 Peter 1:4:

> Thus he has given us, through these things, his precious and very great promises, so that through them you may escape from the corruption that is in the world because of lust, and may become participants of the divine nature.

These promises flow from the word of God as contained in the scriptural references and are closed in quotation marks. The final line of the hymn, "I'll *never*, no *never*, no never forsake," is followed by a footnote: "Agreeable to Dr. Doddridge's Translation of Heb. xiii. 5:"

> Keep your lives free from the love of money, and be content with what you have; for he has said, "I will never leave you or forsake you." (Hebrews 13:5)

William J. Reynolds in *Companion to the Baptist Hymnal*, 1976, pages 90-91, has traced the sources and the variants of this text. The hymn has been included in most of our hymnals since 1847 in five, six or seven stanzas

In our hymnal in stanza 2:3, "thee, help" has been changed to "and help."

Foundation

Early USA melody; harm. from Tabor, 1866

This tune was used exclusively with this text in the hymnals of the Methodist Episcopal Church, South. Yet as late as 1935, following Ira Sankey's *Gospel*

Hymns, 1896, with a hint of cultural bias our hymnal committees still named FOUNDATION as the second tune, ADESTE FIDELES the first. According to William J. Reynolds, who has documented the sources and variants of this tune in *Companion to the Baptist Hymnal*, pages 91-92, this early nineteenth-century USA melody was first included in Joseph Funk's *Genuine Church Music*, 1832.

This version of the tune with the harmonization is from Rigdon M. McIntosh's *Tabor*, 1867, a tune book popular in the South. It is the setting that has been used in most Baptist and Methodist hymnals. The tune appears in another setting in the style of shaped-note "dispersed harmony," 133 in *The United Methodist Hymnal Music Supplement*. (For a discussion of this style, see "The Music of Christian Hymns-USA Wesleyan Traditions," page 56.) The melody may be sung as a round at the octave with the second voice entering on the second half of the second measure. There is an alternate setting at 636 in *The Hymnal 1982*.

How great thou art (77)
O store Gud

Words and music: Stuart K. Hine, 1953
At the beginning of the work on this hymnal a poll taken by *The United Methodist Reporter* revealed that this hymn was at the top of the list of hymns that should be retained in the revised hymnal. "What no previous survey had found, though, is that 'How Great Thou Art' may also be United Methodist's least liked hymn." (John A. Lovelace, *The United Methodist Reporter*, August 23, 1985)

As the most requested hymn for our 1966 hymnal, its inclusion sparked a controversy that continues today. The 1966 revision committee reluctantly included the hymn, arguing that including this, the most popular of all recent gospel hymns, would necessitate few others in the genre being added. Upon hearing of the committee's decision to include the hymn, many church musicians and pastors expressed dismay that the church's official hymnal would bring respectability to the theme song of the Billy Graham crusades. Others brought equally uninformed and unfair criticism on the Methodist Publishing House for presumably dictating editorial policy and cheapening the church's official hymnal. The very high permission fee for that day that was paid received bad press. Walter Vernon has documented the tortuous negotiations of the $2,000.00 fee. (Vernon 1988, 488-89) See also "The 1966 *Methodist Hymnal*," page 118.

From another perspective Erik Routley made this deleterious comparison:

> The remarkable resemblance between this tune and that of Hitler's *Horst Wessel Song*, the theme-song of the Nazi Youth Movement, may be judged anything from curious to sinister. (Routley 1981, 138)

Ironically, a year later in deference to the clamor from members of the Reformed Church in America to include the hymn in their forthcoming hymnal, Routley, its chief editor, wrote a new text, "O mighty God!" based on Psalm 93, Mark 4:35, Matthew 8:23-27, Acts 2:2, and John 14:26, and set it to his reharmonization of the Swedish tune. This was one of his last works, and it was included as hymn 466 in *Rejoice in the Lord*, 1985.

There are two accounts of the writing of this hymn: Stuart K. Hine, "The Story of 'How Great Thou Art,'" 1958 (Gealy 557/352), and George Beverly Shea in *Crusade Hymn Stories*, 1967, reprinted pages 161-62 in *Companion to the Baptist Hymnal*. The hymn was composed ca. 1885 by Carl Boberg. He published it as an interlined hymn in 1891 after hearing it sung to the delightful anonymous Swedish folk tune in its original subtle dancing triple-time setting. In 1925 in the USA, E. Gustav Johnson translated four of the nine stanzas as "O mighty God," but it did not become popular. The text was translated into German, "Wie gross bist Du," by Manfred von Glehn in 1907, and this text was translated into Russian in 1927 by L. S. Prokhanoff in *Kimvali (Cymbals)* published by the Baptist Kompas Press, Lodz, Poland. (Adams 1992, 204). It is this Russian text, not Boberg's original, that Hine heard and sang in the western Ukraine, where amid "unforgettable experiences" in the Carpathian mountains he was prompted to translate three stanzas into English. In 1939 he used them in his preaching campaigns in England. A fourth stanza was added in 1948 as he heard the repeated question from refugees who had fled to England to escape the Nazi terror ask, "When are we going home?"

The hymn with Russian and English words was printed in 1949 in four stanzas with the Swedish tune in 4/4 time harmonized in four parts in C major. It was distributed gratis in Hine's Russian gospel magazine *Grace and Peace*, and within the year it became known throughout the Christian mission fields of the world where it was translated into most languages. In 1958 Hine added two optional stanzas.

The hymn's fame in the USA came by way of the Billy Graham crusades. George Beverly Shea writes:

> We first sang [it] in the Toronto, Canada, Crusade of 1955. Cliff Barrows and his large volunteer choir assisted in the majestic refrains. Soon after, we used it in the "Hour of Decision" [radio broadcasts] and in American crusades. In the New York meetings of 1957 the choir joined me in singing it ninety-three times! It became a keynote of praise each evening. (Reynolds 1976, 162)

An extended court battle as to whether the hymn was properly and legally copyrighted was resolved in favor of Manna Music who successfully demonstrated that Hine's English words in his musical setting, dated 1953 (Gealy 557/352), was the first, final, and fixed form of the hymn. See also Byron E. Underwood, "'How Great Thou Art' (More Facts About Its Evolution)," *The Hymn*, 1973, 1974.

The appeal of this hymn to those who love it and are sustained by singing it or hearing it sung is in the tuneful retelling of the salvation story: the almighty, majestic, and transcendent God described and worshiped in stanzas 1 and 2 has given us new life through the Crucifixion and death (no mention of his powerful Resurrection) of the Son, Jesus Christ, who at the second advent will take us home to worship God eternally by singing with the heavenly choir "How great thou art." The apocalyptic hope of those who shun this hymn is to live in one of the many dwelling places in our Father's house (John 14:2a) eternally free from its hearing.

How great thou art

Stuart K. Hine, 1953

At the request of the copyright owner, Stuart K. Hine is cited as the source of the music. In "The Story of How Great Thou Art" Hine states that the origin of the melody of his hymn tune is "the original Swedish folk melody, to which Boberg heard his poem being sung." He prints it with the citation "(reconstructed by S. K. H. from a faded and partly illegible 1891 copy.)" (Hine 1958, 4)

Austin C. Lovelace states that "the tune first appeared "in *Sanningsvittnet*, 1891, set in 3/4 time for piano and guitar by Ad. Edgren. In 1894 it was included in the hymnbook of the Swedish Missionary Alliance set in 4/4, much as it is sung now." (Gealy, Lovelace, Young 1970, 323)

There is an alternative harmonization at 163 in *The United Methodist Hymnal Music Supplement*.

How like a gentle spirit (115)

C. Eric Lincoln, 1987

Originally titled "Let God be God," the hymn is one of three provided by the author in response to the texts subcommittee's invitation to thirteen poets to submit hymns using alternatives to the traditional repertory of metaphors and images of God. When Dr. Lincoln received word that this text had been accepted, he wrote:

> I am extremely gratified that [this hymn] found favor with the Committee. I wanted so much to make a contribution to the uniqueness and the universality of the the Divine Being as it should be expressed in worship. (Correspondence with Carlton R. Young, 1987)

"Fretful" in stanza 5:2 was originally "Noxious." In the author's gracious response to the committee's request for alternatives to "noxious," he suggested five other adjectives, with this pointed comment: "'noxious' represents my lack of patience with both sex and race as qualifications of the religious enterprise, or of religious commitment."

Sursum corda

Alfred M. Smith, 1941

This tune was composed and submitted anonymously for the text "Lift up your hearts!" in *The Hymnal 1940*. (Ellinwood 1956, 298) This is its first appearance in our hymnals.

How shall they hear the word of God (649)

Michael Perry, 1982 (Rom. 10:14-15)

This hymn for dedications, missions, ordinations, and consecrations is based on Paul's summons to his followers to preach the word of God in order that Israel should never be able to claim that it has never heard the gospel of Jesus Christ, "And how are they to hear without someone to proclaim him?" (Romans 10:14a)

The author has provided this information about the hymn:

> The text was written in November 1980 as a commission from BBC Radio Solent to mark the 10th anniversary of the opening of their radio station. It was first sung with my tune "Solent" in Winchester Cathedral (to the accompaniment of a Salvation Army band), January 4, 1981. (Correspondence with Carlton R. Young, October, 1991)

It first appeared in *Hymns for Today's Church*, 1982, number 507. In stanza 1:2, "his" has been changed to "the"; 3:2, "if heralds are not sent?" to "that sinners may repent?"; 3:4, "if we are negligent?" to "if heralds are not sent?"

Auch jetzt macht Gott

Choralbuch (Koch), 1816

This chorale tune with this harmonization is from *The English Hymnal*, 1906, number 550, and appears not to have been used in any USA collections until it was matched with this text in *Worship*, 3d ed. 1986, with slight harmonic changes in measure 7.

The author's arresting and rhythmic tune "Solent," composed for the hymn's premier, is more in character with Paul's urgent call to preach the word of God than either the proper "Pembroke" in *Hymns for Today's Church*, 1982, or the harmless AUCH JETZT MACHT GOTT.

Hymn of promise (707)

Words and music: Natalie Sleeth, 1985

The author has commented on the text in *Adventures for the Soul*, 1987:

> This was created after "Happy Are They" (Spring of '85), and I seem to have been much involved in pondering the ideas of life, and death, spring and winter (which Denver weather was exhibiting about then on alternate days!), Good Friday and Easter, and the whole reawakening of the world

that happens every spring. . . . One evening we entertained a friend for supper, and he, too, had been pondering such themes, and, even shared a work by T. S. Eliot in which there was a phrase something like "In our end is our beginning." That was virtually the catalyst for the form of the text of "Hymn of Promise" which I wrote the next day or two. . . .

I worked on the words very carefully, choosing just the right "pairings," attempting to get across the idea of something inherent in something else even though unseen, and I even bought a tulip plant (though it was in bloom and bright yellow) to contemplate the idea of the "bulb" leading to the flower even though the bulb itself seems "dead." (Sleeth 1987, 113-15)

"Hymn of promise" was first performed in anthem form at the Pasadena Community Church, St. Petersburg, Florida, March 1985, during a festival weekend and concert of the author's music. Since the word "hymn" is in the title, this "suggests that perhaps a congregation could sing it, and since it is basically a unison number (with Alleluia descant on the last verse) that is possible." (Sleeth 1987, 115)

Following this suggestion by the author, the hymn was brought to the attention of the Hymnal Revision Committee by her friend Bonnie Jones Gehweiler, chair of the hymns subcommittee. Its introduction and singing instilled quiet reflection and affirmation.

The author includes this epilogue:

Soon after writing "Hymn of Promise," my husband [Ronald] became ill with what turned out to be a terminal malignancy. As the end neared he asked me to use "Hymn of Promise" as one of the anthems at his funeral service—which was done—and I subsequently (at publication) dedicated the piece to him. Again, a "mysterious" set of circumstances, but—perhaps again—a sort of "preparation." (Sleeth 1987, 115)

Promise

Jane Marshall has suggested:

This is a fitting hymn for funerals and memorial services. Children can introduce the hymn to the congregation with choir or congregation singing stanza 2 and all singing stanza 3. A fitting intergenerational hymn, you may combine children and older adult choirs in introducing it to the congregation. (Sanchez 1989, 236)

I am leaning on the Lord (416)

See "Come out the wilderness," pages 296-97.

I am the church (558)

See "We are the church," pages 675-76.

I am thine, O Lord (419)

Fanny J. Crosby, 1875 (Heb. 10:22)
This hymn was written in 1874 during a visit to Cincinnati by the poet where she was the house guest of William H. Doane, an amateur musician with whom she had often collaborated. William J. Reynolds has provided this commentary about the writing of the hymn:

> One evening she and Doane talked at length about the nearness of God in their lives. When Fanny went to her room, her mind and heart were flooded with ideas from their conversation. Before she went to sleep, the lines of "I am thine, O Lord" were in her mind. . . .

> The next morning she recited the words to Doane, who wrote down the stanzas and composed the tune. (Reynolds 1990, 110)

The hymn first appeared as selection twenty-two with the title "Draw Me Nearer" in *Brightest and Best*, 1875. (Gealy 556/202)

Above the text is the scriptural reference "Heb. 10:22":

> Let us approach [draw near to the sanctuary] with a true heart in full assurance of faith, with our hearts sprinkled clean from an evil conscience and our bodies washed with pure water. (Hebrews 10:22)

The mixing of the metaphors for cleansing, "pure water" and "bleeding side," was apparently prompted by the preceding verses:

> Therefore, my friends, since we have confidence to enter the sanctuary by the blood of Jesus, by the new and living way that he opened for us through the curtain (that is, through his flesh), and since we have a great high priest over the house of God. (Hebrews 10:19-21)

The hymn entered our hymnals in 1889.

I am thine

William H. Doane, 1875
The tune was composed as related above.

I can hear my Savior calling (338)

See "Where he leads me," page 702.

I come to the garden alone (314)

See "In the garden," pages 432-33.

I come with joy (617)

Brian Wren, 1968 (1 Cor. 10:16-17)

The author has provided this commentary:

> [The hymn was] written for the congregation at Hockley, to sum up a series
> of sermons on the meaning of communion. The hymn tries to use simple
> words to suggest important theological themes. It begins with the individ-
> ual ("I come") and moves gradually into the corporate, with which it ends
> ("together met, together bound, we'll go"), while v. 4 relates Christ's "real
> presence" to the communal nature of the occasion. (Wren "Notes" on
> *Mainly Hymns* 1980, hymn 22)

This is one of a very few hymns written during the early years of the British
"hymnic explosion" that has not been substantially altered by USA hymnal
committees and later their British counterparts to accommodate inclusive
forms of address for people. The original text read at 3:3, "man's true communion bread," and at 3:1, "for men to share." Otherwise, the text is included
without alteration. It was first included in *The Hymn Book* of the Anglican
Church of Canada and the United Church of Canada, 1971. As the author suggests, the hymn may be sung in three parts— for gathering, sharing, and
departing.

Dove of peace

The Southern Harmony, 1835; harm. by Charles H. Webb, 1987

This tune was first set to this text in *Ecumenical Praise*, 1977, by Austin C.
Lovelace. Charles H. Webb prepared this harmonization for this hymnal. It is
one of the most singable additions to the repertory of communion hymns.

The tune with its name first appeared on page 89 in T*he Southern Harmony* as
the setting for this hymn on the search for inward peace:

> O tell me where the Dove has flown
> To build her downy nest
> And I will rove this world all o'er,
> To win her to my breast,
> To win her to my breast.

Our version of the tune has a slight change in the melody of measure 6.

The writer is indebted to Harry Eskew, New Orleans Baptist Theological Seminary, for information about this tune.

I danced in the morning (261)

See "Lord of the dance," pages 472-73.

I heard an old, old story (370)

See "Victory in Jesus," page 673.

I know not why God's wondrous grace (714)

See below, "I know whom I have believed," pages 416-17.

I know whom I have believed (714)

Daniel W. Whittle, 1883 (2 Tim. 1:12)

The refrain of the hymn is from Paul's second letter to Timothy:

> For this gospel I was appointed a herald and an apostle and a teacher, and for this reason I suffer as I do. But I am not ashamed, for I know the one in whom I have put my trust ["whom I have believed," KJV], and I am sure ["persuaded," KJV] that he is able to guard until ["against," KJV] that day what I have entrusted ["committed," KJV] in him. (2 Timothy 1:11-12)

The stanzas of the hymn go beyond Paul's words to express a sure faith in God through the Son and Holy Spirit, and within human limitations to foresee perfectly the future and to have full understanding of God's redemptive and graceful acts. The hymn first appeared at number 7 in Ira Sankey's *Gospel Hymns*, No. 5, 1887.

El Nathan

James McGranahan, 1883

The tune's name is the pseudonym of the revival preacher Daniel W. Whittle. The composer was Whittle's music director.

I love thy kingdom, Lord (540)

Timothy Dwight, 1801

E. Harold Geer has commented on this hymn in *Hymnal for Colleges and Schools (The Yale Hymnal)*, 1956:

> Before assuming the presidency of Yale College in 1795, Timothy Dwight (1752-1817) had been an army chaplain, farmer, teacher, legislator, and parish minister. Under his dynamic leadership the college experienced a notable development, particularly in its religious life. His famous revision of Isaac Watts' *The Psalms of David* published in 1800 [*sic*], was done

at the request of the General Association (Congregational) of Connecticut and was widely used in this country, being known familiarly as "Dwight's Watts." This is one of the 33 original hymns he added to the revision. (Geer 1956, 27)

The author extends a portion of Psalm 137, the poignant song of the exiled Jews, beginning "How could we sing the Lord's song in a foreign land?" (Psalm 137:4), into a Christian hymn that extols the virtues of the church. As a hymn distinguished from a metrical paraphrase, this may be the oldest contribution by a USA citizen to remain in continuous use. The hymn was first published in Dwight's 1801 revision of Watts's *Psalms of David Imitated*, 1719, on page 317 in 8 stanzas under the heading: "Psalm 137. Short Metre, Third Part, 'Love to the Church.'" (Gealy 556/208)

"The first 6 [stanzas] . . . were used in the Methodist Episcopal, South hymnals of 1847 and 1889. The 1849 Methodist Episcopal hymnal printed 1, 2, 5, 6, and 8, a cento now generally used." (Gealy 1970, 228)

St. Thomas

See "Come, we that love the Lord," pages 302-03.

I love to tell the story (156)

Katherine Hankey, ca. 1868

According to research on the use of the 1966 hymnal (see *"The United Methodist Hymnal*, 1989," pages 130-31), this hymn, which entered our hymnals in 1878, is still a great favorite of United Methodists.

Information concerning the source of the words and music was first provided by Robert G. McCutchan in *Our Hymnody*, 1942, and in collaboration with William J. Reynolds was updated by Fred D. Gealy in *Companion to the Hymnal*, 1970. Gealy's exhaustive research on both the words and music is housed in Gealy 556/209.

Reynolds has provided this summary in *Companion to the Baptist Hymnal*, 1976:

This hymn is taken from a long poem by Katherine Hankey, written in 1866 and based on the life of Christ. The first section of the poem is entitled "The Story Wanted," and was written on January 29. The hymn, "Tell Me the Old, Old Story" [222 in *The Baptist Hymnal*] is from this first section. The second section—written in November, 1866, and entitled "The Story Told"—contained the stanzas used in this hymn. The text of the refrain was written by the composer of the tune. (Reynolds 1976, 104-05)

Hankey

William G. Fischer, 1869

[The tune] was first published in a pamphlet, entitled *Joyful Songs*, Nos. 1 to 3 (Philadelphia: 1869, Methodist Episcopal Book Room). Twenty-four of the forty-one tunes in this pamphlet were composed or arranged by Fischer. Five years later it appeared in Bliss's *Gospel Songs* (Cincinnati, 1874), and in 1875 it was included in Bliss's and Sankey's *Gospel Hymns and Sacred Songs*. These two collections brought the hymn to the attention of multitudes, and it became extremely popular. (Reynolds 1976, 104)

I need thee every hour (397)

Annie S. Hawkes, 1872 (John 15:5)

According to Ira Sankey, this hymn was first sung in 1872 at a convention of the National Baptist Sunday School Association Convention. (Sankey 1907, 116) It first appeared with Lowry's refrain at number 35 under the scripture sentence from John 15:5, "Without me, ye can do nothing," in *Royal Diadem for the Sunday School*, 1873. (Gealy, Lovelace, Young 1970, 229-30) Moody and Sankey used the hymn in their meetings in both England and the USA.

McCutchan includes this background from the poet about her hymn:

> I remember well the morning . . . when in the midst of the daily cares of my home . . . I was so filled with the sense of nearness to the Master that, wondering how one could live without Him either in joy or pain, these words, "I need Thee every hour," were ushered into my mind, the thought at once taking full possession of me. (McCutchan 1942, 272)

The hymn entered our hymnals in 1875.

Need

Robert Lowry, 1873

The tune was written shortly after the words were presented to the composer by his parishioner, Annie S. Hawkes.

I serve a risen Savior (310)

See "He lives," page 391.

I sing a song of the saints of God (712)

Lesbia Scott, 1929

This song was written by the poet to help her own children understand that saints not only lived and witnessed for Christ in the distant past, but they also live and work among us in everyday life. It was included with a number of her poems in *Everyday Hymns for Little Children*, 1929. In the USA it first appeared in *The Hymnal 1940* with the tune GRAND ISLE.

Discussion by the Hymnal Revision Committee on this hymn whose roots are in the gentility of British living of half a century ago centered on its efficacy for today's children in the USA. How many children have met a saint in lanes (bowling or freeways?), on trains, at tea, or at sea; or have seen a queen or a shepherdess on the green! For many United Methodists hearing or singing this hymn is little more than a delightful and irrelevant diversion.

Stanza 3:5-7 originally read:

> You can meet them in school, or in lanes, or at sea,
> In a church, or in trains, or in shops, or at tea,
> For the saints of God are just folk like me.

Grand Isle

John H. Hopkins, 1940

The tune was written for these words and first appeared in *The Layman's Magazine of the Living Church*, November 1940. The tune's name comes from the community on the island of the same name in Lake Champlain, Vermont, where the composer was living in retirement. (Ellinwood 1956, 164)

I sing the almighty power of God (152)

Isaac Watts, 1715

Our hymn is stanzas 1, 3, and 5 of "Praise for Creation and Providence," one of 8 texts that Watts included in *Divine Songs Attempted in Easy Language, for the Use of Children*, 1715. This was the first hymnal intended for use by children. In his preface to the collection Watts expresses the desire that children of all social and religious distinctions "may all join together in these songs . . . as I have endeavoured to sink the language to the level of a child's understanding." Watts concludes with a prayer that the children of Great Britain "may be a glory among the nation, a pattern to the christian [sic] world, and a blessing to the earth." (Gealy 556/211)

Excerpts from this collection became the mainstay for the moral upbringing of children with parents teaching their offspring to memorize verses such as the following, titled "Against quarreling":

> Let dogs delight to bark and bite,
> For God hath made them so;

> Let bears and lions growl and fight,
> For 'tis their nature to.
>
> But children, you should never let
> Such angry passions rise;
> Your little hands were never made
> To tear each other's eyes.

Recent hymnals seldom include a section of "Hymns for Children" since compilers view these selections as condescending and sentimental verse composed by adults writing about children rather than for children. Wesley Milgate believes Watts's hymn is an exception:

> Watts shows in this hymn a readiness rare in his time to credit children with some intelligence and imagination, so that it is a fine hymn for adults also. (Milgate 1985, 37)

In stanza 1:7, "his" has been changed to "God's"; stanza 2:2, "that" to "who"; 2:3, "he" to "who"; 2:3, "with his" to "through the"; and stanza 3:7, "man" to "we."

Forest Green

See "Come, let us join our friends above," pages 292-93.

I sought the Lord (341)

Anon. USA, ca. 1880

This anonymous hymn on God's prior claim on our lives first appeared as number 142 entitled "He first loved us" in *Holy Songs, Carols, and Sacred Ballads*, 1880. (Gealy 556/212) It entered our hymnals in 1935 in the form from the *Pilgrim Hymnal*, 1904, where these changes from the original text were apparently made: stanza 1:2, "it who sought for me" to "seek him, seeking me"; stanza 2:4, "as by thy hand of me" to "as thou, dear Lord, on me"; stanza 3:1, "but ah, the whole" to "but oh, the whole"; and 3:3, "Lord thou wert" to "For thou wert."

Stanzas 2 and 3 refer to Peter walking on the sea, Matthew 14:22-32.

Peace

George W. Chadwick, 1880

According to Robert G. McCutchan, "'Peace' was written in 1890, but its first publication date has not been ascertained." (McCutchan 1942, 343)

I stand amazed in the presence (371)

Words and music: Charles H. Gabriel, 1905 (Luke 22:41-44)

The words and music first appeared in E. O. Excell's *Praises*, 1905. This song of gratitude and praise for the atoning death of Jesus is a personal and adventist

interpretation of Luke's account of Jesus' sweating blood in the Garden of Gethsemane, a portion of the passion narrative not included in the other Gospels. It
entered our hymnals in 1957.

My Savior's love

The music was included with the text in *Praises*, 1905.

I surrender all (354)

Judson W. Van DeVenter, 1896

William J. Reynolds has provided this account in *Hymns of Faith*:

> According to the account of the author "this hymn was written in memory
> of the time when, after a long struggle, I had surrendered and dedicated
> my life to active Christian service. The song was written while I was con-
> ducting a meeting at East Palestine, Ohio, and in the home of George
> Sebring, who later founded the city of Sebring, Florida." The Sebring camp
> meeting at Sebring, Ohio, was also founded by him. (Reynolds 1964, 13)

Surrender

Winfield S. Weeden, 1896

According to Reynolds (1964, 13), the tune was first published with this text in
Gospel Songs of Grace and Glory, 1896, compiled by Weeden, Van DeVenter, and
Leonard Weaver. Our hymnal retains the original gospel vocal quartet texture:
a duet between soprano and tenor in the stanzas, and SA and TB voices in echo
on the refrain.

I, the Lord of sea and sky (593)

See "Here I am, Lord," page 397.

I want a principle within (410)

Charles Wesley, 1749

This text was included in vol. 2:230-31 in five CMD stanzas under the title "For a
Tender Conscience" in *Hymns and Sacred Poems*, 1749. (Gealy 556/213) The
hymn was first included in our hymnals in 1788 in CMD as John had printed in
his 1780 *Collection*. Later editions printed it in SMD.

In stanza 1:5, "help me" is restored to "I want." Charles Wesley's particularly
personal eighteenth-century evangelical vocabulary, e.g., "help me to feel an

idle thought as actual wickedness," proved too much for the Hymnal Revision Committee, and stanza 2 was dropped. In stanza 3:3, "burden" is restored to "mountain"; in 3:7, "grace" to "blood."

One phrase that was retained, "Quick as the apple of an eye," is a metaphor for spiritual sensitivity and a prayer that one's conscience may be as sensitive to sin as the pupil of the eye is to light. The reference to the "apple of the eye" is also found in Psalm 17:8, "Guard me as the apple of the eye" (see Psalm Response **749**).

Gerald

Louis Spohr, 1834; adapt. by J. Stimpson

Austin C. Lovelace has provide background on this tune:

> The tune is adapted from a solo, with chorus, in Spohr's oratorio written in 1834, called *Das Heiland's letzte Stunde* (*The last Hours of the Savior*) and first performed at Cassell, Germany, on Good Friday, 1835. The solo given to Mary, "Though all thy friends prove faithless," was adapted to "As pants the hart," by J. Stimpson and published as an anthem which became popular.

> The tune was originally called "Spohr," but another tune by this name created confusion. The name GERALD was chosen by the 1935 hymnal editorial committee to include parts of the name of Dr. Fitzgerald Sale Parker, a member of the 1905 as well as the 1935 hymnal committees, and Miss Geraldine Reid Sherrill, secretary to the [hymnal's] editor. (Gealy, Lovelace, Young 1970, 232)

Our hymnal is apparently alone in matching this trivial tune to Wesley's resolute text.

I want Jesus to walk with me (521)

African American spiritual
adapt. and arr. by William Farley Smith, 1986

William Farley Smith has provided commentary on this spiritual:

> Afro-American slaves converted to Christianity sought comfort in a real and personal Savior who would be available to them as they made their pilgrimage out of bondage to the promised land. (Sanchez 1989, 178)

According to William B. McClain:

> This song is not so much a request as it is an affirmation that the Jesus of their salvation would be with them. They could look "back to the historical-

divine experiences and the reports of their predecessors" and assert "He walked with my mother, he'll walk with me." (McClain 1990, 95)

The source of this and most spirituals is unknown. Don Hustad in *Dictionary-Handbook to Hymns for the Living Church* writes that "I want Jesus to walk with me" is "probably one of the 'white spirituals' which thrived for more than two hundred years in the rural Appalachian culture." (Hustad 1978, 152) If Hustad's assumption is correct, this and other "journey songs," e.g., "Jesus walked this lonesome valley" and "We shall walk thro' the valley and the shadow of death," may have roots in early nineteenth-century camp meetings that were attended and led by Native Americans, African Americans, and Euro/Anglos. See commentary on "I will trust in the Lord," pages 424-25.

Sojourner

William Farley Smith named this tune after Sojourner Truth, "the courageous freed slave woman who took to the dangerous byways of antebellum America preaching the abolition of slavery and equality for 'all o' Gawd's chillun's.' " (Sanchez 1989, 178)

There is a setting for SATB voices in D minor at 95 in *Songs of Zion*, 1981.

I want to be ready (722)

African American spiritual
adapt. and arr. by William Farley Smith, 1986 (Rev. 21:2, 16)
William Farley Smith has provided this commentary:

Rev. 21:10-27 inspired this widely sung spiritual. In a vision John "saw the holy city, new Jerusalem, coming down out of heaven from God." Slaves envisioned themselves as residents of this new city and thought it to be their promised land. In many songs, they celebrated their longing for such a city and expressed a desire to enter through one of its "twelve gates." Here, the slave-poets draw on the theme "get yo' house in order" to point out an obligation and need for special preparation to gain entrance into such gates. (Sanchez 1989, 241)

I want to be ready

William Farley Smith has suggested that this "jubilee style" spiritual be performed in a lively "foot-pattin'" manner in a call-and-response between leader and the group. Add tambourine and hand clapping. There is another setting in F major at 151 in *Songs of Zion*, 1981.

I want to walk as a child of the light (206)

Words and music: Kathleen Thomerson, 1966

This hymn was first sung in the summer of 1966 in the Church of the Redeemer, Houston, Texas, the home of Mrs. Thomerson's family and "the location of . . . [the church] to which the composer has deep emotional ties." (Glover 1987, 84)

The gospel song chorus style with a refrain of strong musical phrases and memorable biblical images ties together the scriptural allusions that range from Isaiah 42:6c, "I have given you as a covenant to the people, a light to the nations"; Malachi 4:2, "But for you who revere my name the sun of righteousness shall rise, with healing in its wings"; Hebrews 12:1b, "And let us run with perseverance the race that is set before us"; Ephesians 5:8b-9a, "For once you were darkness, but now in the Lord you are light. Live as children of light"; to Revelation 21:25b, "And there will be no night there," and 22:5b, "They need no light of lamp or sun."

This hymn first came to the attention of a wider ecumenical audience with the supplement to *The Hymnal 1940*, *Songs for Celebration*, 1980, edited by George E. Mims, then organist and director of music, Church of the Redeemer, Houston, Texas. Under Mims's leadership this church's music was distinguished for its evangelical fervor and breadth of styles—incorporating in its liturgical forms rock, pop, folk, as well as traditional hymns and chant.

Houston

Russell Schulz-Widmar in *The Hymnal 1982 Companion* places this hymn within the genre of "contemporary folk music—the kind of music that evolved in the 1960's and 1970's." Thomerson's song is "a good example of the heights to which this genre can be brought. . . . It has a tender pathos and loveliness that has made it a popular addition to the repertoire."(Glover 1990, 624)

A gospel hymn by any other name is still a gospel hymn. For many on the Hymnal Revision Committee this gospel hymn was more acceptable than many others because of its inclusion in *The Hymnal 1982*.

I will trust in the Lord (464)

African American spiritual
adapt. and arr. by William Farley Smith, 1987

William Farley Smith states this spiritual

is one of those . . . oddities that points an accusing finger at the congregation and seeks to exact testimony concerning the immediate intentions of the accused. . . . Those questioned should always respond by singing stanza l. (Sanchez 1989, 161)

Dr. Smith also notes the similarities of this tune to the shaped-note melody "Pisgah," remarking that both melodies may come from

> camp meetings of frontier U.S.A. [that] allowed interracial attendance, resulting in many shared, borrowed, and adapted tunes and texts. . . . [It should be] sung moderately slowly with heavy rhythmic accents, [accompanied by] . . . a dignified swaying body motion. (Sanchez 1989, 161)

There is another setting of this spiritual at number 14 in *Songs of Zion*, 1981.

I will trust

See comments above.

If death my friend and me divide (656)

Charles Wesley, 1762

This hymn first appeared in vol. 2:324-25 in *Short Hymns*, 1762. The original three stanzas are included. The scriptural reference is 1 Thessalonians 4:13b, "Sorrow not, even as others which have no hope" (Authorized Version).

Wesley's text came very close to being set aside for lack of space when at the final meeting of the Hymnal Revision Committee the late Roger Deschner successfully argued that it uniquely expressed God's promise to the believer, through Christ, of the continuity of friendship beyond death.

Although the hymn is included as poetry, it may be sung; yet there are no 886.D tunes in our hymnal. The British Methodist *Hymns and Psalms* has several choices including William Boyce's "Chapel Royal" at number 385 (ii). The hymn entered our hymnals in 1838 and last appeared in 1878.

The hymn was read by this writer at Roger Deschner's memorial service, October 25, 1991, in the chapel of Perkins School of Theology, Southern Methodist University, Dallas, Texas.

If the world from you withhold (522)

See "Leave it there," page 459.

If thou but suffer God to guide thee (142)
Wer nur den lieben Gott läßt walten

Words and music: Georg Neumark, 1657
trans. by Catherine Winkworth, 1863 (Ps. 55:22)

Fred D. Gealy has written concerning this hymn:

The German text was written in 1640 or 1641 after Neumark had had the bitter experience of being robbed by highwaymen of all but a prayer book and a few coins, and was long without work and almost destitute, when unexpectedly he was employed as a tutor in the home of a wealthy judge in Kiel. Then and there, he wrote this hymn based on Psalm 55:22 and entitled it "A Song of Comfort: God will care for and help everyone in His own time."

The [text and tune were] . . . first published [in Jena] in Neumark's *Fortgepflanzter musikalisch-poetischer Lustwald* (Jena, 1657), in 7 sts. (Gealy, Lovelace, Young 1970, 233-34)

Neumark's hymn entered our hymnals in 1905 in the translation from Winkworth's *Lyra Germanica*, 1855, "Leave God to order all thy ways." (Gealy 556/216). Our hymnal prints stanzas 1, 3, and 7 from her second translation in *The Chorale Book for England*, 1863.

In the first line "suffer" means to "allow" or "let" God to *walten*, i.e., govern or control one's life.

Changes have been made as follows: stanza 1:2, "him" to "God"; 1:3, "he'll give thee" to "God will give"; 2:1, "his" to "God's"; 2:4, "all-deserving" to "all-discerning"; 2:6, "him" to "God"; 3:1 and 3:3, "his" to "God's"; 3:6, "him" to "God."

Wer nur den lieben Gott

Georg Neumark, 1657

This is one of the tunes that John Wesley apparently learned from the Moravians, and he included a version at page 30 in his *Foundery Collection*, 1742, calling it "Slow German Tune." (For commentary on the Moravians see "German Hymns," pages 6-7; and for Wesley's contact with the Moravians see "Give to the winds thy fears," page 352.) J. S. Bach included settings of the tune in his cantatas and organ literature, and Mendelssohn used it in his oratorio *St. Paul*.

The tune entered our hymnals in 1905 in a 4/4 version that was continued in the 1935 edition. Our version of the tune combines Mendelssohn's harmonization, slightly altered, with the tune's original triple meter. It was taken from the *Pilgrim Hymnal*, 1958, and was included in our 1966 hymnal.

The tune is also called "Neumark" and "Bremen."

Il est né, le divin Enfant (228)

See "He is born," page 389.

I'll praise my Maker while I've breath (60)

Isaac Watts, 1719; alt. by John Wesley, 1737; alt. 1989 (Ps. 146)
This is the first of two paraphrase of Psalm 146, entitled "Praise to God for his
Goodness and Truth" at 384-82 in Isaac Watts's *Psalms of David, Imitated in the
Language of the New Testament*, 1719. (Gealy 556/217) John Wesley made slight
changes in stanzas 1, 2, 4, and 6 of the 6, and included them at page 9 in the section of hymns and psalms for "Sunday" in his Charlestown *Collection*, 1737. The
hymn remained a favorite of Wesley, who included it in his collections from
1741 until 1780. It has been included in all our hymnals since 1786.

As stated in the preface to the 1933 British *Methodist Hymn Book*,

Watts's great hymn . . . has found a place in every Methodist hymn-book
since 1737. It was on Wesley's lips as he lay dying, and its message is one
of the heirlooms of Methodism. (Preface, iv)

The evangelical theme of endless praise in stanza 4,

and when my voice is lost in death,
praise shall employ my nobler powers,

is echoed in stanza 4 of William Cowper's "There is a fountain filled with blood"
(622),

Then in a nobler, sweeter song,
I'll sing thy power to save,
when this poor lisping, stammering tongue
lies silent in the grave.

Our version follows Wesley's 1780 text, with these changes: stanza 2:1, "the
man" to "are they"; 2:2, "he" to "who"; 2:4, "his" to "whose"; 2:5, "he" to "who,"
and "he" to "and"; 2:6, "his" to "God's"; 3:3, "he" to "and"; 3:4, "he" to "God";
and 4:1, "him while he" to "my God who."

Old 113TH

Attr. to Matthäus Greiter, 1525; harm. by V. Earle Copes, 1963
The tune is attributed to Matthäus Greiter, who set it to his paraphrase of Psalm
119, "Es sind doch selig alle," in his *Strassburger Kirchenamt*, 1525. In Germany in
the sixteenth and seventeenth centuries it was set to the penitential text "O Mensch,
bewein' dein Sünde gross" ("O man, thy grievous sin bemoan") and sung during
Holy Week as Christ's passion is recalled in word and song. J. S. Bach set it as the
concluding chorus of part 1 of his *St. Matthew Passion* and included a setting in his
Orgelbüchlein. It appeared in Genevan psalters as settings of both Psalms 36 and 68.
The tune entered the English repertory by way of the Anglo-Genevan Psalter, 1560-

61, set to William Kethe's paraphrase of Psalm 113, thus the tune's name, OLD 113TH. The British use of "Old" in assigning names for tunes may refer to either a tune taken over from the Genevan psalters using the number of the psalm to which it was set, or a tune in Thomas Sternhold and John Hopkins, *The Whole Book of Psalms Collected into English Metre*, 1562.

John Wesley included it in his *Foundery Collection*, 1742, and *Select Hymns*, 1765; in the latter it was printed with Watts's "I'll praise my maker" in 888.888 D, taking two full stanzas to sing the entire tune. Several variants of the tune were made in the eighteenth and nineteenth centuries, including its reduction to 888.888 by deleting the repeated first section and omitting much of the third. In this abbreviated form it entered our 1935 hymnal with Ernest MacMillan's harmonization, number 10 in *The Hymnary*, 1930. V. Earle Copes modified MacMillian's setting for our 1966 hymnal. The tune is also called "Es sind doch selig alle," "Geneva 36," and "Que Dieu se monstre seulement."

There is a tympani part at 260 in *The United Methodist Hymnal Music Supplement*.

I'm goin' a sing when the spirit says sing (333)

African American spiritual;
adapt. by William Farley Smith, 1986

Dr. Smith states that this spiritual is "well known in the United States with regional variations" and might have arisen as "a reaction to formal worship patterns that did not allow for spontaneous expression." (Sanchez 1989, 121) William B. McClain comments that "this spiritual may have its roots in the slave choosing to obey the Spirit of the Lord, rather than the slave owner." (McClain 1990, 91)

For comment on the use of dialect, e.g., "goin'a," see "He never said a mumbalin' word," pages 391-92.

I'm goin' a sing

Dr. Smith' s adaptation of this jubilee-type spiritual is taken from a recording made in 1986 by several veteran singers at St. Mark's United Methodist Church, Harlem, New York City. (Sanchez 1989, 121) This arrangement skillfully integrates blue notes and vocal slides and glides. As the spirit builds, add hand clapping, tambourine, and body movement. Additional stanzas may be added, e.g., "I'm goin' a preach." This spiritual is appropriate for Pentecost or other times celebrating the gifts of God's Spirit.

Immortal, invisible, God only wise (103)

Walter Chalmers Smith, 1867 (1 Tim. 1:17)

The original text first appeared on pages 210-11 in six 11 11. 11 11 stanzas under the title "Now unto the King eternal, immortal, invisible, the only wise God, &c.—1 Tim. i, 17" in Walter C. Smith's *Hymns of Christ and the Christian Life*, 1867. (Gealy 556, 218) After undergoing several revisions it was included in four stanzas in *The English Hymnal*, 1906, where it was first set to the Welsh hymn tune ST. DENIO. The hymn entered our hymnals in 1935 using the 1906 version.

The author skillfully combines images of God as "invisible," "unchanging," and "hidden," yet a God visible in creation both "great and small," and a God of righteousness whose "justice [is] like mountains high soaring above."

Changes in the text have been made for our hymnal in stanza 4:1, "great Father of glory, pure Father of light" to "thou reignest in glory; thou dwellest in light"; and 4:3, restoring the original "laud" for "praise."

St. Denio

Welsh melody adapt. from Caniadaeth y Cysegr, 1839
harm. from The Hymnal 1940

This melody known in Wales as "Joanna" first appeared as a hymn tune in John Robert's *Caniadaeth y Cysegr* (*Songs of the Sanctuary*), 1839.

Alan Luff has made this comment on the tune:

> It has a considerable resemblance to the ballad entitled "Can mlynedd i nawr" ("A hundred years from now"). . . . As will be seen, many of the Welsh tunes in the major [key] make great use of the notes of the major chord based on the keynote of the tune. This tune begins as though in a different key and only reaches the notes of the home key at the end of the first line. This thrusts into prominence the fifth note of the tune which signals that the first expectation is wrong. Without recognizing the technical reason the singer appreciates the additional impetus that this gives to the tune—a quality that has justly made it popular, though the words with which it is associated now begin to look somewhat tired and dated. (Luff 1990, 154-55)

The tune entered our hymnals in 1935 with a harmonization by Van Denman Thompson. Our 1966 hymnal substituted the harmonization from *The Hymnal 1940*, an adaption from *The English Hymnal*, 1906.

The AABA form makes this tune one of the most singable and teachable tunes in the repertory. There is an alternate harmonization at 300 in *The United Methodist Hymnal Music Supplement*.

In Christ there is no east or west (548)

Sts. 1, 2, 4, John Oxenham, 1913
st. 3, Laurence Hull Stookey, 1987 (Gal. 3:28)

This text was originally part of the author's libretto composed for *The Pageant of Darkness and Light*, produced in 1908 for the London Missionary Society's exhibition, whose theme was "The Orient in London." In 1913 the poet included it in his book of verses, *Bees in Amber*. (Gealy 556/221) The theme of Oxenham's hymn, one of the most durable hymnic statements of Christian unity in the twentieth century, is from Galatians 3:28:

> There is no longer Jew or Greek, there is no longer slave or free, there is no longer male and female; for all of you are one in Christ.

The hymn has been included in most USA hymnals since the 1920's to the tune ST. PETER **(549)**. It entered our hymnals in 1935. In our hymnal in stanza 2:1, "him" has been changed to "Christ"; 2:4, "all mankind" to "humankind"; and stanza 3 has been replaced with a new stanza by Laurence Hull Stookey that extends the hymn to include Galatians 3:29, "And if you belong to Christ, then you are Abraham's offspring, heirs according to the promise."

Laurence Hull Stookey has commented on the circumstances of composing the new stanza 3:

> While serving on the language and theology subcommittee, [I] became frustrated with the assignment given [me] to revise the words. . . . After numerous unsatisfactory attempts to make Oxenham's language inclusive, [I] decided to write a replacement stanza based on Galatians 3:28. (Correspondence with Carlton R. Young, September 1992)

McKee

African American spiritual
adapt. and harm. by Harry T. Burleigh, 1939

In 1939 the African American singer and composer Harry T. Burleigh arranged this tune from the chorus "Done changed my name for the coming day" of the spiritual "The angels changed my name," number 104 in "Jubilee Songs," in *The Story of the Jubilee Singers*, new edition, 1897. It was first included in *The Hymnal 1940*. The tune was named after Elmer M. McKee, rector of St. George's Episcopal Church, New York City, where for over fifty years Burleigh was baritone soloist. See Charlotte W. Murray, "The Story of Harry T. Burleigh," *The Hymn*, 1966.

This is the first appearance of this tune in our hymnals. A performance note, a vocal descant, and alternate harmonization may be found at 231-33 in *The United Methodist Hymnal Music Supplement*.

In the bleak midwinter (221)

Christina G. Rossetti, 1872 (Luke 2:8-14)

In this nativity poem Jesus' birth is imaged in the cold and snow of a British winter. *Companion to Hymns and Psalms* suggests that the poet, after Milton in

"On the Morning of Christ's Nativity," connects her verse to "the nativity tradition that it snowed at the birth of Christ to cover the fallen world with a pure whiteness." (Trickett and Watson 1988, 96)

Rossetti's poem was first published as "A Christmas Carol," page 278, in *Scribner's Monthly*, January 1872. (Gealy 556/224) It first appeared as a hymn in *The English Hymnal*, 1906, with Holst's tune and entered our hymnals in 1935 in four stanzas. The omitted stanza 3 continues the contrast of earthly and heavenly metaphors:

> Enough for Him whom Cherubim
> Worship night and day,
> A breastful of milk
> And a mangerful of hay;
> Enough for Him whom Angels
> Fall down before,
> The ox and ass and camel
> Which adore.

Fred D. Gealy has written about this hymn:

"In the bleak midwinter" is not a prayer; it is not a "song with praise to God" (*pace* Augustine); it is a proclamation, a declaration, a witness to the amazing mystery of what the church when it spoke Latin called "incarnation," the Word becoming flesh, God becoming man, yet so that God remains God and man remains man. (Gealy 556/224)

The poet's evangelical piety is exquisitely expressed in the final line, "what can I give him: give my heart."

Cranham

Gustav Holst, 1906

The tune was composed for the poem and first appeared in *The English Hymnal*, 1906. Cranham is a village near Cheltenham, the composer's birthplace.

In the bulb there is a flower (707)

See "Hymn of promise," pages 412-13.

In the cross of Christ I glory (295)

John Bowring, 1825

This hymn first appeared under the title "The Cross of Christ," page 60 in the author's *Hymns by John Bowring*, 1825. (Gealy 556/225) Most commentators follow John Julian in *Dictionary of Hymnody* and state that the hymn is based on the words of Paul, "Far be it for me to glory except in the cross of our Lord Jesus Christ." (Galatians 6:14, KJV)

While the the hymn's theme is the cross, it is not so much Christ crucified as in Isaac Watts's "When I survey the wondrous cross" **(298)**, but the author's personal testimony to the comforting divine light that eternally shines through as well as from an empty cross, towering above human tragedy, beaming comfort and solace, a theme that reflects Bowring's long service in social and political causes.

The hymn has been printed without change since it was included in our 1878 hymnal.

Rathbun

Ithamar Conkey, 1849

According to Leonard Ellinwood the tune first appeared in Henry Greatorex's *Collection of Psalm and Hymn Tunes*, 1851. (Ellinwood 1956, 219) Robert G. McCutchan, citing a story in the *Norwich Bulletin*, June 24, 1907, states that the tune was named in tribute to Mrs. Beriah S. Rathbun, the soprano soloist in the composer's choir at the Central Baptist Church, Norwich, Connecticut, who was the only one to show up one rainy Sunday morning. (McCutchan 1942, 186)

See 276-77 in *The United Methodist Hymnal Music Supplement* for an alternate harmonization and vocal descant.

In the garden (314)
(I come to the garden alone)

Words and music: C. Austin Miles, 1913 (John 20:11-18)

This gospel hymn was inspired by the dialogue at the garden tomb between the risen Christ and Mary, John 20:11-18. (Reynolds 1990, 111) It invites the singer to experience Jesus in the unique way as Mary did as the risen Savior and Lord. It is appropriately included in the selection of Easter hymns and may be effectively performed without accompaniment by a female voice singing the stanzas, answered by the congregation in four-part harmony and/or unison on the refrain, optionally supported by keyboard.

This was one of the most requested of hymns to be included in this hymnal; and it is also one of the least liked, often denounced as erotic and egocentric. For an interpretation of this hymn, see Donald P. Hustad, "In the Garden," in the October 1983 volume of *The Hymn*.

The hymn was first included in *The Gospel Message No. 2,* 1912, and appears for the first time in our hymnals.

Garden

Adapt. by Charles H. Webb, 1987

The tune was adapted into four-part choral style for this hymnal by Charles H. Webb.

In thee is gladness (169)
In dir ist Freude

Johann Lindemann, 1598
trans. by Catherine Winkworth, 1858

Information about this text and music is from the *Hymnal Companion to the Lutheran Book of Worship*, 1981. This text first appeared in the author's *Amorum Filii Dei Decades Duae*, 1598. Catherine Winkworth's translation was first included in her *Lyra Germanica*, second series, 1858.

In dir ist Freude

Giovanni Giacomo Gastoldi, 1593

The tune is an adaptation of the madrigal "Alieta vita" from *Balletti a cinque voci*, 1593, and was first included in Lindemann's *Amorum Filii Dei Decades Duae*, 1598, where the author may have adapted it as a hymn tune. Our harmonization is from the Albert Riemenschneider edition of J. S. Bach's *Orgelbüchlein* and is probably by Bach.

Hymnal Companion to the Lutheran Book of Worship, page 558, has included the title pages and text pages of the Gastoldi and Winkworth collections.

In time of illness (460)

Georgia Harkness, 1943

Laurence Hull Stookey has described this prayer as "characterized by honesty and asks not for miracles of extraordinary healing but for confidence and grace to accept whatever must be endured." (Sanchez 1989, 160) It was first included by the author in her work *The Glory of God*, 1943.

Infant holy, infant lowly (229)

Polish carol; trans. by Edith M. G. Reed, 1926 (Luke 2:6-20)

Wesley Milgate writes:

> This traditional Polish carol is found in *Spiewniczek Piesni Koscielne*, 1908 . . . where the guess is hazarded that it belongs to the 13th or 14th cent. . . . [It] was [first] printed in *Music and Youth*, vol. 1, no. 12 (December 1921). (Milgate 1985, 104)

The text was first printed in a hymnal as number 39 in *School Worship*, 1926, edited by George Thalben-Ball (Gealy 556/227) and first appeared in a USA hymnal in our 1935 edition. The carol quickly entered the standard repertory of nativity hymns for both children and adults owing in no small measure to its simplicity and unique, compelling form—two opening sections in 447, followed by lines of 44447 sung in short ascending and sequential phrases.

Ẉ zlobie lezy

See "Christ is risen," pages 275-76.

It came upon the midnight clear (218)

Edmund H. Sears, 1849 (Luke 2:8-14)

Scarcely a nativity hymn, the text is among the first USA social gospel hymns (see "Social Gospel Hymns," page 30). The hymn's central theme contrasts the scourge of war with the song of the angels' "peace to God's people on earth." (Luke 2:14b) It embodies the witness of Unitarians in the time of political and social unrest preceding the Civil War. The text first appeared in the Boston *Christian Register* for December 29, 1849, volume 28, number 52, page 206. (Gealy 556/228)

The hymn entered our hymnals in 1878 in the five original stanzas; it was reduced to four in our 1935 hymnal and to three in 1966 and in the *Report* to the 1988 General Conference. A month after the hymnal had been approved, it was discovered that our fourth stanza, the core of one of very few Christmas social gospel hymns, was missing. Its restoration by the Hymnal Revision Committee is the only instance of an addition to the 1988 General Conference authorized text.

The omitted stanza 3 continues to contrast the song of peace with the din of war:

> But with the woes of sin and strife
>   The world has suffered long;
> Beneath the angel-strain have rolled
>   Two thousand years of wrong;
> And man, at war with man, hears not
>   The love-song which they bring:
> O hush the noise, ye men of strife,
>   And hear the angels sing!

In 1966 with the century-long "age of gold" promise still unfulfilled, stanza 4:1, "prophet-bards foretold" was changed to "by prophets seen of old"; and 4:2, "comes round the age of gold" to "shall come the time foretold."

Carol

Richard Storrs Willis, 1850, alt.

According to Leonard H. Ellinwood the music first appeared in the composer's *Church Chorals and Choir Studies*, 1850, set to Philip Doddridge's baptism hymn "See Israel's gentle Shepherd stands." In a letter written in 1887 Willis states that as a vestryman ca. 1860 at Church of the Transfiguration (The Little Church Around the Corner) he altered his tune from CM to CMD by repeating the last line as the second and adding a new third line. In this form it was included in Protestant Episcopal Church collections as the setting for "While shepherds watched their flocks by night." (Ellinwood 1956, 13)

Our 1878 hymnal seems to be the first to wed the tune to Sears's social gospel hymn. It is usually sung in the style of a gospel hymn.

It is well with my soul (377)

Horatio G. Spafford, 1873

This hymn of faith was written in the aftermath of the tragic loss of the author's four daughters in the sinking of the *S. S. Ville du Havre*, November 22, 1873.

The hymn entered our hymnals in 1957.

Ville du Havre

Philip P. Bliss, 1876

The tune was composed for the text and was first included in *Gospel Hymns No. 2*, 1876, compiled by the composer and Ira Sankey. In some hymnals it was called "It is well," and in others it bore the name of the ill-fated ship *Ville du Havre*.

It only takes a spark

See "Pass it on," page 552.

It's me, it's me, O Lord (352)
(Standing in the need of prayer)

African American Spiritual
arr. by William Farley Smith, 1986

William B. McClain has commented on this widely known spiritual:

> The slaves saw the assurance of salvation as largely a personal responsibility. Realizing imperfection, the people affirmed in this song a total and complete reliance upon the grace of God. . . . [It is] an obvious choice for an altar call song in most any church service. (McClain 1990, 101)

James H. Cone has written about this spiritual from the perspective of God's liberating us from sin and death:

> Sin is . . . a universal concept that defines the human condition as separation from God. If God is known as the liberator of the oppressed from bondage, and Jesus is his Son who is still present today, then the "Sinner Man" is everyman who is in need of divine liberation. He is the person who needs "dat ol' time religion" or the one "standin' in the need of prayer." (Cone 1972, 82)

Penitent

To get into the spirit of this arrangement sing the refrain several times, add hand clapping on the afterbeats and tambourine. The stanzas are set for solo voice at 110 in *Songs of Zion*, 1981, and may be substituted for those in this SATB setting.

Jaya Ho (478)
Victory be to you

Anon. Hindi; trans. by Katherine R. Rohrbough, 1958
phonetic transcription from the Hindi by I-to Loh, 1988

This traditional Hindi hymn was brought to the USA by the Centennial Choir of India, Victor C. Sherring, director, and in 1955-56 was performed by them in concerts and worship services in seventy cities that celebrated the centenary of Methodist missions in that country. Victor C. Sherring has written: "The hymn was first included in *Jaya Ho, Songs of Joy from India*, 1955-56, a collection of songs in Indian and Western musical notation published in Lucknow by the Centenary Music Committee; and in *Joyful Songs of India*, 1955-56, a collection of songs in translation from Southeast Asia." (Correspondence with Carlton R. Young, June 1992) The translation was made for Cooperative Recreational Services, Delaware, Ohio.

I-to Loh has written about this hymn:

> To "bow in quiet reverence" is a typical posture of humility as is paying homage to the great and Holy God; praying for forgiveness and protection from harm and evil are primary concerns of the faithful. (Sanchez 1989, 165)

Victory hymn

Trad. Hindi melody; arr. by Victor Sherring, 1955

The tune was arranged by Victor Sherring for the Centennial Choir of India and was first included at 15 in *Jaya Ho, Songs of Joy from India*, 1955-56. The small grace notes indicate where optional ornamentation may be added. Except for the solo sections, men's voices may drone the tonic note (Low B^b) with the fifth above (F). For other suggestions on the performance practice for Asian hymns see "Asian American Hymns," pages 35-36.

Jesu, Jesu (432)

Tom Colvin, 1968 (John 13:1-17)

This simple and memorable folk hymn from Ghana has been included in most recent USA hymnals. It was written for a meeting of evangelists at Chereponi, and it is a statement of both commitment and servanthood. The hymn is particularly appropriate for Holy Week services including those that observe Jesus' washing the feet of his disciples, recalling his words: "Very truly, I tell you, servants are not greater than their master, nor are messengers greater than the one who sent them." (John 13:16) Other parts of the hymn were suggested by Jesus' words to the lawyer: "You shall love . . . your neighbor as yourself." (Luke 10:27)

The text was composed at Chereponi, Ghana, and was first included in the author's *Free to Serve*, 1968, a collection of twenty-four Ghanaian hymns published through the Iona community. Stanza 2 originally read "Neighbors are rich men and poor, Neighbors are black men and white."

Chereponi

Ghana folk song; adapt. by Tom Colvin, 1968
harm. by Charles H. Webb, 1988

This tune was collected by the author at Chereponi in northern Ghana. The harmonization was prepared for our hymnal.

Jesu, thy boundless love to me (183)
O Jesu Christ, mein schönstes Licht

Paul Gerhardt, 1653; trans. by John Wesley, 1739

These are stanzas 1, 2, 3, and 16 of John Wesley's translation of Paul Gerhardt's "O Jesus Christ, mein schönstes Licht" ("O Jesus Christ, my beautiful light"), a sixteen-stanza hymn on the love of Christ based on "Prayer V" in Johann Arndt's *Paradiszgärtlein*, 1612. Wesley prepared his translation while in Georgia using the text from Count Nicolaus Ludwig Von Zinzendorf's Moravian hymnal, *GesangBuch*, Herrnhut, 1735. He included sixteen stanzas at 156-59 in *Hymns and Sacred Poems*, 1739, under the title "Living by Christ. From the German." [(Gealy 556/250)] "He later quoted stanza two at the end of his sermon 'A Plain Account of Christian Perfection' as 'the cry of my heart' upon leaving Georgia, rejected and disillusioned." (Frank Baker notes on hymn 183, *The United Methodist Hymnal*, 1989)

For a discussion of Wesley's translations of Gerhardt's hymns, see Theodore Brown Hewitt, *Paul Gerhardt as a Hymn Writer and His Influence on English Hymnody*, 1918.

The hymn entered our hymnals in 1786. Our version of the text is identical to the nine stanzas of the original that were included by John Wesley in his 1780 *Collection*. It may be sung using ST. CATHERINE **(710)** or other 88. 88. 88 tunes, including VATER UNSER **(414)**.

Jesus calls us (398)

Cecil Frances Alexander, 1852 (Matt. 4:18-22)
This hymn of discipleship and commitment was included in *Hymns for Public Worship*, 1852, under the title of "St. Andrew's Day." (Gealy 556/231) Leonard Ellinwood in *The Hymnal 1940 Companion* has remarked that the author "has caught the spirit of the collect, Epistle, and Gospel for St. Andrew's Day to a remarkable degree." (Ellinwood 1956, 332) Although the first line of the original stanza 2 was appropriately "As, of old, St. Andrew heard it," it was omitted when it entered our hymnals in 1905. When that stanza was restored in our 1966 hymnal, that line was changed by those afflicted with *allergios Evangelicus sancticus.*

Galilee

William H. Jude, 1874
According to Leonard Ellinwood this tune was composed for this text and was first included in *Congregational Church Hymns*, 1888. (Ellinwood 1956, 332)

Jesús es mi Rey soberano (180)
O Jesus, my King and my Sovereign

Words and music: Vicente Mendoza, ca. 1921
trans. by Esther Frances, 1982, and George Lockwood, 1988
Gertrude Suppe has supplied information about this hymn from page 39 in Cecilio McConnell's *Conozcamos Neustro Himnario*, and pages 54-55 in *Comentario Sobre Los Himnos Que Cantamos*:

> This hymn was first sung in 1921 in Mexico City at the Gantes Metodista Iglesia, and shortly after that was included in a revision of the author's *Himnos Selectos*, first published in 1901. Beginning with the first edition Mendoza included some of his own words and melodies, although still using the style of his North American antecedents. They are pioneer examples of Latin American hymnody.

Dr. Mendoza wrote this hymn in 1921 when he was living in California. While waiting for a rain storm to slow he began to play the piano, resulting in the melody we now have. He wrote the stanzas that same day. The final stanza was composed under a street light as he waited for his daughter's train. The author has commented that "this was the easiest and most natural song that has come to my heart and mind, making me think with humble reverence that it was truly inspired from above."

The hymn was inspired by the author's reflection on the paradox of Jesus Christ who not only reigned over Mendoza's life, but who also accepted him as one would a family member. Jesus is both King and friend. (Correspondence with Carlton R. Young, July 1991)

Esther Frances translated this hymn for the *Supplement to the Book of Hymns*, 1982. Portions of her text were included in the translation George Lockwood prepared for this hymnal.

Mi Rey y mi amigo

Information about this tune is included above.

Jesus is all the world to me (469)

Words and music: Will L. Thompson, 1904

The words and music first appeared in the author's *New Century Hymnal*, 1904. The author's use of "friend" to describe his relationship with Jesus Christ is reminiscent of "What a friend we have in Jesus" **(526)** and "Jesús es mi Rey soberano" ("O Jesus, my King and my Sovereign"), **(180)**. Intimate metaphors such as friend and lover, e.g., "Jesus, lover of my soul" **(479)**, are distinctive and compelling characteristics from seventeenth-century German pietistic hymnody that John Wesley could not abide, and he often deleted, these hymns or strengthened their intimate metaphors; for example, in the first line of "O for a thousand tongues to sing" **(57)**, he changed "dear Redeemer" to "great Redeemer."

The hymn entered our hymnals in 1966.

Elizabeth

The compilers of *Baptist Hymnal*, 1956, named the tune after the author's wife Elizabeth Johnson.

Jesus, Jesus, Jesus! There's something about that name (171)

See "There's something about that name," page 650.

Jesus, joy of our desiring (644)

Martin Janus, 1661; trans. probably by Robert S. Bridges

The English text is based on Martin Janus's hymn "Jesus bleibet meine Freude, meines Herzens Trost und Saft" ("Jesus remains my joy, of my heart comfort and sap") and was set by J. S. Bach for the closing chorus of his Cantata 147, *Herz und Mund und Tat und Leben*. The English text is thought to be by Robert S. Bridges. A close reading of the text tends to show that its performance at weddings is essentially a musical matter, and appropriately so.

Jesu, joy of man's desiring

Johann Schop, arr. by J. S. Bach, 1723

This tune is excerpted from the chorus that J. S. Bach composed to close each of the two sections of Cantata 147. Bach shaped this famous chorus by harmonizing a melody by Schop and cleverly integrating it with the well-known triplet-figured obbligato. A number of adaptions have been made for voice, choir, and instruments.

The first line of the hymn and the tune name are an interesting anomaly. The tune is also called "Werde munter," the first words of a text by Johann Rist. Gary Alan Smith has adapted J. S. Bach's instrumental obbligato figure into a psalm response **(771)**.

Jesus, keep me near the cross (301)

Fanny J. Crosby, 1869

The author composed this hymn to fit a tune as she did on other occasions. It is one of many texts by Crosby that combine vivid imagery (the author was blinded in her childhood) and powerful biblical and evangelical metaphors: the cross, a fountain of healing streams, free grace, the daily walk of faith, God's pursuing love and mercy, Jesus, the Lamb of God, beyond the river of death—heaven with its golden streets—and rest for the postraptured soul.

The hymn first appeared with the tune entitled "Near the cross," number 130 in *Bright Jewels*, 1869. (Gealy 556/236) It entered our hymnals in 1882, was dropped in 1905, and was restored in 1935.

Near the cross

William H. Doane, 1869

When the hymn reentered our hymnal in 1935, this gospel tune was altered in an attempt to strengthen the harmonies and smooth out its voice leadings. Our hymnal retains this editorial fussiness.

Jesus, Lord, we look to thee (562)

Charles Wesley, 1749

This hymn on Christian forbearance first appeared in six stanzas in volume 1, page 248, entitled "For a Family" in *Hymns and Sacred Poems*, 1749. (Gealy 556/237) It was first included in our hymnals in 1786. Our version of the text is the same as that included by John Wesley in the section "For the Society, Praying" in his 1780 *Collection*. For our hymnal changes have been made in stanza 1:4, "jars" to "strife"; 3:2, "courteous, pitiful" to "gentle, courteous"; 4:2, "each his brother's burdens bear" to "each the other's burdens bear."

S T Kimbrough, Jr. has provided this commentary:

> The hymn provides an excellent picture of living as Christians in family stressing Christ as the mediator of peace, living in love and unity, caring for one another, freedom from strife and anger, holiness, how to live and how to die. (Correspondence with Carlton R. Young, September 1992)

Savannah

Foundery Collection, 1742

In their notes on the tunes in *Sacred Harmony*, 1780, F. Hildebrandt and O. A. Beckerlegge state that the tune "was composed about 1690 by G. C. Strattner, who died in 1705." (Wesley 1983, 7:778) According to *Companion to Hymns and Psalms*, "this tune is of Moravian origin, and has been traced to a manuscript collection dated c. 1735." (Watson and Trickett 1988, 323)

John Wesley apparently learned the tune from the Moravians either en route or during his stay in Georgia where he served as missionary priest in charge of the Anglican parish in Savannah. For a discussion of the Moravians and Wesley's interaction with them, see "German Hymns," pages 6-7, and "Come, and let us sweetly join," page 286. Wesley included the tune on page 10 under the name "Herrnhuth Tune" in his *Foundery Collection*, 1742. On pages 8-9 in the collection there is a totally different Moravian tune named "Savannah Tune," later renamed "Irene."

Jesus, lover of my soul (479)

Charles Wesley, 1740 (Wis. 11:26)

The hymn first appeared in five stanzas under the title "In Temptation" in *Hymns and Sacred Poems*, 1740. (Gealy 556/238) The hymn was written shortly after Wesley's conversion and may have been prompted by a passage from the wisdom literature: "But thou sparest all, for they are thine, O Lord, thou lover of souls." (Wisdom of Solomon, 11:26, KJV) Another possibility of a source is

Thomas à Kempis's *Imitation of Christ*, "Most mighty God of Israel, zealous Lover of faithful souls." (Watson and Trickett, 1988, 312)

Charles Wesley's powerful intimate images, e.g., "lover" and "bosom," may have prevented the hymn's inclusion in his brother's definitive 1780 *Collection* until the 1797 edition issued eight years after his death. Wesley did include it in his *Hymns and Spiritual Songs*, 1753, and in the 1785 *Pocket Hymn-Book*, without stanza 3. It was first included in our hymnals in 1786. For commentary on the *Pocket Hymn-Book*, see "From all that dwell below the skies," page 350. For other comments on John Wesley's editorial treatment of intimate metaphors and terms of endearment, see "Jesus is all the world to me," page 439.

Concerning the hymn's great appeal, Erik Routley has commented that this "is a hymn for the crises of life." (Routley 1956, 176) From another perspective William Farley Smith has written:

> [This hymn] had particular meaning to slaves who without names, parents, or status could claim Jesus as their provider, parent, and safe haven in the storms of life. Stanza 1:6 is often sung, "till the storms of life be passed," affirming Jesus' sustaining power in both the past and present tense." (Smith 1991, 1 (3):7)

Aberystwyth

Joseph Parry, 1879

Alan Luff has written in *Welsh Hymns and Their Tunes* that the composer records that the tune was composed in 1876. It first appeared in *Ail Lyfr Tonau ac Emynau*, 1879, "and has proved to be the most widely used of all the Welsh hymn tunes . . . [and usually set to] Charles Wesley's 'Jesus, Lover of my Soul' where its mounting phrases in the second half of the tune, sinking finally to a sombre close, admirably match the words." (Luff 1990, 213)

The tune is named after the city in North Wales where the composer was a professor of music. It entered our hymnals in 1935.

Jesus loves me (191)

St. 1, Anna B. Warner, 1860; Sts. 2-3, David Rutherford McGuire
trans.: Cherokee, Robert Bushyhead, 1987; German, Psalter und Harfe, 1876
Japanese phonetic transcription, Mas Kawashima, 1988
Spanish anon., Himnario Metodista, 1973

According to William J. Reynolds,

> Anna B. Warner's hymn was included in her sister's novel, *Say and Seal*, 1860. At one point in the story a sick little boy, Johnny Fax, is comforted by

his Sunday school teacher, John Linden. He rocks the child in his arms, and when Johnny asks him to sing, he begins a new song, and Anna B. Warner provides the four stanzas of this hymn. It first appeared in *Golden Shower*, 1862. (Reynolds 1976, 124)

The revised stanzas 2 and 3 were prepared by David R. McGuire, a member of the revision committee for the United Church of Canada, in *The Hymn Book*, 1971. Stanza 2 reflects the story in Matthew 19:13-14, where Jesus gathers the children around him.

Early in its work, the Hymnal Revision Committee determined that since the central theme of this hymn is the love of Jesus transcending boundaries of race, language, and place, the hymn would appear in several languages. Roger Deschner was responsible for gathering the translations and phonetic transcriptions.

An effective use of this hymn is to teach the non-English stanzas to children and have them share them with adults in worship and informal settings.

Jesus loves me

William B. Bradbury, 1862

The tune was composed for the hymn, with the composer adding the refrain. It first appeared in *Golden Shower*, 1862.

Jesus, our brother, strong and good (227)

See "The friendly beasts," page 635.

Jesus our friend and brother (659)

Attr. to Ova'hehe; trans. by David Graber and others, 1982
(John 15:14-15)

This may be the earliest Christian hymn from the Cheyenne oral tradition. (For comment on transcriptions from oral traditions see "Native American Hymns," pages 19-21.) According to David Graber in *Tsese-Ma'heone-Nemeototse (Cheyenne Spiritual Songs)* it may be an adaptation of "What a friend we have in Jesus." Three somewhat related traditions trace the song's origins to Ova'hehe (Mrs. Bear Bow), 1880-1934, Watan, an Arapaho leader, and Ho'evoo'otse (Buffalo Meat) of Kingfisher, Oklahoma, who used it as a "gathering song." (Graber 1982, 156, 164)

David Graber has also commented,

This song, like many in the Cheyenne tradition, does not distinguish ownership from origins. Apparently it was owned by (originated?) by

Ho'evoo'otse (Buffalo Meat) as well as Ova'hehe. Since Ova'hehe died in 1936, and Ho'evoo'otse died in 1920, 14 years earlier, it is possible Ho'evoo'otse is the authentic originator of the hymn. Cheyenne people remember Ova'h'ehe better than Ho'evoo'otse; hence Ova'hehe is my choice of source of the hymn. The story of Ho'evoo'otse is a dramatic, fascinating story. Chief Lawrence Hart of Clinton, Oklahoma, knows this story. The story of this hymn was also gathered from Mr. and Mrs. Moses Stair of Custer, Oklahoma. (Correspondence with Carlton R. Young, September 1992)

Esenehane Jesus

Attr. to Ova'hehe; transcribed by David Graber, 1982

This transcription was first included in *Cheyenne Spiritual Songs*, 1982.

Jesus, priceless treasure (532)
Jesu, meine Freude

Johann Franck, 1653; trans. by Catherine Winkworth, 1863

Fred D. Gealy in *Companion to the Hymnal* has provided an account of the source of the hymn:

> The text, patterned after a love song by Heinrich Alberti, "Flora, meine Freude, meiner Seele Weide," 1641, was first published in Johann Crüger, *Praxis Pietatis Melica*, 1653.
>
> Catherine Winkworth made 2 translations of the hymn, 1 in her *Chorale Book for England* (London, 1863), in 5 sts.; 1 in *Christian Singers of Germany*, 1869, in 6 sts. (Gealy, Lovelace, Young 1970, 248-49)

The hymn entered our hymnals in 1964 with three stanzas from Winkworth's 1869 translation. (Gealy 556/240) Two ill-advised alterations, made in stanzas 2:8 and 3:7 to render the personal pronouns plural, are retained in our hymnal. Although the hymn shares the personal pietistic imagery of Charles Wesley's "Jesus, lover of my soul" (479), see pages 441-42, its peculiar meter, metaphors, and melodic line tend to restrict its use in worship to performances of J. S. Bach's motet *Jesu, meine Freude* and various settings for organ.

Jesu, meine Freude

Praxis Pietatis Melica, 1653

Ethel K. Porter in *Guide to the Pilgrim Hymnal* provides extensive coverage of this tune. Concerning its source she writes:

[The tune] appeared with Franck's hymn in *Praxis pietatis melica*, 1563 [*sic*], edited by Johann Crüger to whom it is attributed. Parts of it seem to be adapted from older traditional material. . . . The first two measures of this melody are almost identical with a phrase that appears three times in "Kyrie, Gott Vater in Ewigkeit," which was sung to an adaptation of the Latin plainsong "Kyrie, fons bonitatis." (Ronander and Porter 1966, 178)

Our harmonization is the first movement of J. S. Bach's six-movement motet *Jesus, meine Freude*, composed for a memorial service in 1723 and which Albert Schweitzer has described as Bach's "sermon upon life and death."

Jesus, remember me (488)

Luke 23:42
This is the request of one of two criminals who were crucified with Jesus and placed on crosses "one on his right and one on his left." (Luke 23:33b) Jesus responds: "Truly, I tell you, today you will be with me in Paradise." (Luke 23:43)

Remember me

Jacques Berthier and the Community of Taizé, 1981
This chorus may be sung in response to prayer or during Holy Communion. For commentary on the music of Taizé see "Eat this bread," pages 324-25.

Jesus, Savior, Lord, lo, to thee I fly

See "Saranam, Saranam," page 573.

Jesus, Savior, pilot me (509)

Edward Hopper, 1871 (Matt. 8:23-27; Mark 4:35-41; Luke 8:22-25)
This hymn is based on the Gospel account of Jesus stilling the waves, "He got up and rebuked the winds and the sea; and there was a dead calm," (Matthew 8:26b). It was written by Edward Hopper, pastor of the Church of the sea and land, New York City, for sailors who attended the church (Reynolds 1964, 104), and was first included with the author's name and under the citation "For the Sailor's Magazine" in *The Sailor's Magazine and Seamen's Friend*, vol. 43, no. 4:119, April 1871. I am indebted to Charles A. Green for this information. The same year it appeared in the section of occasional hymns, page 516 (Gealy 556/2141) in *The Baptist Praise Book*.

The description of Jesus as a mother caring for her child demonstrates the tender and intimate qualities found in many gospel hymns. With the recent attempts to balance female and male images and descriptions these hymns compare very favorably with social gospel hymns that tend to accentuate militant and masculine metaphors.

With the dropping of "Let the lower lights be burning" this remains the only hymn in our hymnal with a preponderance of seafaring metaphors, images, and descriptions. The hymn entered our hymnals in 1901 with one, five, and six of the original six stanzas.

Pilot

John E. Gould, 1871

The tune was composed for this text and first appeared in *The Baptist Praise Book*, 1871 (Gealy 556/241), with the tune name "Saviour, pilot me."

Jesus shall reign (157)

Isaac Watts, 1719 (Ps. 72)

This paraphrase of the second part of Psalm 72 first appeared in eight stanzas on page 186 under the title "Christ's Kingdom among the Gentiles" in Watts's *Psalms of David, Imitated in the Language of the New Testament*, 1719. Watts's Christianization of this psalm is in character with his resolve, as stated in the preface to his 1719 collection, to make David and Asaph "always speak the Common Sense and Language of a Christian."

The omitted stanzas 2 and 3 demonstrate the poet's hyperbolic departure from the biblical text. They are bracketed apparently as optional stanzas, in the copy of the hymn in Gealy's research (556/242) :

> Behold the Islands with their Kings,
>   And Europe her best Tribute brings;
> From North to South the Princes meet
>   To pay their Homage at his Feet.
>
> There Persia glorious to behold,
>   There India shines in Eastern Gold;
> And barbarous Nations at his Word
>   Submit and bow and own their Lord.

For commentary on using Hebrew scripture in Christian worship see "Canticle of praise to God," pages 259-60.

While it is often described as the earliest of mission hymns, the text did not come into general use until the greatly expanded missionary activity of the nineteenth century. Even though John Wesley apparently did not include it in any of his collections, early on the hymn was included in our hymnals. Sometimes it was printed in seven stanzas as in the 1847 edition, more often in four or five stanzas, some made with centos formed from portions of stanzas. Our hymnal includes stanzas one, four, five, six, and eight of the original. Changes occur in stanza 1:3, "stretch" to "spread"; 2:1, "For him shall" to "To Jesus"; 4:2, "the prisoner leaps to loose his chains" to "all prisoners leap and loose their chains"; 4:4, "the sons of" to "who suffer"; and 5:2, "peculiar honors" to "honors peculiar."

Duke Street

See "Forth in thy name, O Lord," pages 348-49.

Jesus! the name high over all (193)

Charles Wesley, 1749 (Phil. 2:9-11)

This hymn is comprised of stanzas 9, 10, 13, 8, 18, and 22, in that order, from a 22-stanza hymn in vol. 1:305-08 under the title "After Preaching (in a Church)" in *Hymns and Sacred Poems*, 1749. (Gealy 556/244) John Wesley selected seven stanzas for his 1780 *Collection* and made it into a very serviceable hymn of praise ending with John the Baptist's confession "Behold the Lamb of God," John 1:29.

By including the original stanza 14 in his *Collection*, John demonstrates his occasional lapse from a preoccupation for modifying, though more often deleting, what he perceived as his brother's intimate pietistic rhetoric:

> O that my Jesu's Heavenly Charms
> Might every Bosom move!
> Fly Sinners, fly into those Arms
> Of everlasting Love.

The text was first included in our hymnals in *A Selection of Hymns*, 1810. In our hymnal changes occur at stanza 1:3, "men before it fall" to "mortals prostrate fall"; 3:4, "mankind" to "the world"; and 5:2, "his saving grace proclaim" to "his saving truth proclaim."

S T Kimbrough, Jr. has commented:

> John Wesley averred in *Plain Account of Kingswood School*, 1781: "I have nothing to hope for, here; only to finish my course with joy." Then he quoted the last stanza of this hymn. (Correspondence with Carlton R. Young, September 1992)

For additional commentary on other hymns based on passages from Philippians 2:5-11, see "All praise to thee, for thou, O King," pages 198-99, and "At the name of Jesus," pages 220-22.

Gräfenberg

See "Heal us, Emmanuel, hear our prayer," page 395.

Jesus, the very thought of thee (175)
Dulcis Jesu memoria

Attr. to Bernard of Clairvaux, 12th cent.
trans. by Edward Caswall, 1849

Fred D. Gealy cites the basic reason for attributing this joyous hymn of praise to Jesus to Bernard of Clairvaux:

> The chief support of the tradition ascribing the poem to Bernard is its place in the great devotional movement of the Middle Ages in which mystical piety centers in personal devotion for Jesus . . . [and imbues] the spirit of [Bernard's] prose writings. . . . A study by F. J. E. Raby in the *Bulletin* of the Hymn Society of Great Britain and Ireland, October, 1945, [concludes] . . . that the poem "is the work of an Englishman and was written about the end of the twelfth century." (Gealy, Lovelace, Young 1970, 253)

Earlier Stephen A. Hurlbut summarized the manuscript evidence in *Hortus Conclusus*, VII, 1933. (Gealy 556/246) For comment on monastic hymns, see "Latin Hymns," pages 5-6.

In 1858 Edward Caswall translated the text in fifty four-line stanzas under the title "St. Bernard's Hymn, or, the Loving Soul's Jubilation" in *The Masque of Mary and Other Poems*. (Gealy 556/246) Caswall selected five stanzas, one through four and forty, to form a vesper hymn for the Feast of the Most Holy Name of Jesus, the Second Sunday after Epiphany, in the section "Hymns from the Proper of the Season" in his *Lyra Catholica*, 1849. (Gealy 556/246) This selection entered our hymnals in 1878.

The original stanza 2 that eloquently unites heart, voice, and memory has regrettably been dropped in this hymnal:

> Nor voice can sing, nor heart can frame,
>   Nor can the memory find,
> A sweeter sound than thy blest name,
>   O Saviour of mankind!

In stanza 4:2, "wilt" is changed to "will."

St. Agnes

See "Happy the home when God is there," pages 386-87.

Jesus, thine all-victorious love (422)

Charles Wesley, 1740

This text is comprised of stanzas 4, 7, 8, and 9 from a 12-stanza hymn titled "Against Hope, believing in Hope" with the first line "My God! I know, I feel thee mine" that first appeared at 156-58 in *Hymns and Sacred Poems*, 1740. (Gealy 556/247) John Wesley printed all twelve stanzas in his 1780 *Collection*, and from there it passed into our 1849 hymnal. In the 1935 *Methodist Hymnal* the holiness-perfection stanzas 11 and 12 in the original text were deleted, but unfortunately, they were not restored in our hymnal.

> No longer then my heart shall mourn,
>   While purified by Grace,
> I only for His Glory burn,
>   And always see his Face.
>
> My steadfast Soul, from falling free,
>   Can now no longer move;
> Jesus is all the World to me,
>   And all my Heart is Love.

Azmon

Carl G. Gläser; arr. by Lowell Mason, 1839
William J. Reynolds has provided the source for the tune:

> [It] first appeared anonymously in Lowell Mason's *Modern Psalmist*, 1839. In the preface of this book, Mason states that his recent European tour was primarily "to obtain materials for a work like this . . . from distinguished composers of different nations . . . which had not before reached this country." The list of names in this preface includes "Gläser, J. M., German, 1780." (Reynolds 1976, 112)

There are descants, alternate harmonizations for keyboard and brass, and a transposition to F at 33-38 in *The United Methodist Hymnal Music Supplement*.

Jesus, united by thy grace (561)

Charles Wesley, 1742
This hymn on Christian unity is excerpted from a four-part hymn with twenty-nine stanzas entitled "A Prayer for Persons joined in Fellowship," which first appeared at 139-40 in *Hymns and Sacred Poems*, 1742. (Gealy 556/251) The hymn, following Wesley's 1780 *Collection*, entered our hymnals in 1788 in nine CM stanzas. Our cento is comprised of stanzas 1/IV, 3/I, 5/I, 4-6/IV.

The hymn's central theme seen in its opening lines, "Try us, O God and search the ground of every sinful heart!," is our unity in Christ as grounded in our common confession as sinners in need of forgiveness. Other portions of the hymn, including these from section 2, often confront and penetrate our shallow, incomplete, and qualified confessions:

> Our fig-leaves all be cast aside;
>   Let no self-soothing art
> Conceal the lust, to' indulge the pride
>   Of a foul hellish heart.
>
> Open a window in our breast,
>   That each our heart may see,
> And let no secret be supprest,
>   Since all are known to Thee.

In stanza 2:3, "each his" has been changed to "all their," and in 2:4, "his brother's" to "each other's."

St. Agnes

See "Happy the home when God is there," pages 386-87.

Jesus, we want to meet (661)

Words and music: A. T. Olajide Olude, 1949
trans. by Biodun Adebesin; versed by Austin C. Lovelace, 1962
This magnificent hymn of praise and and confession was brought to the attention of the 1966 hymnal revision committee as described in *Companion to the Hymnal*:

> While Adebesin was serving at the United Nations, he and his family became members of Christ Methodist Church in New York City. . . . [The committee] was meeting at the church the day Adebesin joined, . . . and Austin C. Lovelace, then minister of music at Christ Church, and Carlton R. Young, editor of the hymnal, spent the evening with Adebesin when he translated the Nigerian hymn that he had learned during the 1950's. [Lovelace's work sheet and notes are in Gealy 556/253.] It was his suggestion that the drumbeat be added for optional use. (Gealy, Lovelace, Young 1970, 258)

> The words and music were written in 1949 for a musical monthly service at Abeokuta to popularize Yoruba music in Christian worship. (Gealy, Lovelace, Young 1970, 258)

In stanza 2:7, "and" has been changed to "let."

In 1978 Austin C. Lovelace learned about an almost identical text to ours by the British poet Elizabeth Parson (born 5 June 1812, Tavistock; died 1873, Plymouth) that was written, with others, for her "willing class," a group of young men and women that from 1840 to 1844 she gathered for instruction on Sunday evenings in the vestry of her father's church. For additional information about Parson and her works, see page 882-83 in John Julian's *Dictionary of Hymnody*.

The hymn was probably introduced to Nigerian Christians by British missionaries late in the nineteenth century or early in the twentieth century. It is not known when or from whom A. T. Olajide Olude learned the hymn. Austin C. Lovelace has contrasted Parson's and Olude's texts:

> Olude's treatment . . . (although in the same meter) adds several new dimensions to the text. For example, in the first line it is not "love to meet" but "want to meet," which is a more profound understanding of Sunday worship. He also had an additional stanza [an expansion of her stanza 3] and several different metaphors and poetic ideas . . . that he had absorbed but presented in a fresh, more profound text with the added dimension of a tune which moves back and forth between 3/4 and 6/8, which is purely African in style. Parson's text is included at 245 in *Psalter Hymnal*, 1987. A comparison of her text with ours is revealing:

Elizabeth Parson, ca. 1842

Jesus, we love to meet
On this, Thy holy day;
We worship round Thy seat
On this, Thy holy day;
Thou tender, heavenly Friend,
To Thee our prayers ascend;
Over our spirits bend
   (orig: O'er our young spirits bend)
On this, Thy holy day.

We dare not trifle now,
On this, Thy holy day;
In silent awe we bow
On this, Thy holy day;
Check every wandering thought,
And let us all be taught
To serve Thee as we ought
On this, Thy holy day.

We listen to Thy word
On this, Thy holy day;
Bless all that we have heard
On this, Thy holy day;
Go with us when we part,
And to each loving (orig: youthful) heart
Thy saving grace impart
   On this, thy holy Day.

(Correspondence with Carlton R. Young, July 1992)

Nigeria

In the 1966 hymnal this hymn was set to traditional Anglo hymnal harmonies. In this hymnal it is scored for unison voices in a clearer call-and-response pattern. As an introduction in the accompaniment for voices and in interludes between stanzas, use the suggested drumbeat patterns, combining them with other instruments playing these cross rhythms:

$$\text{♪} = 200 \quad ♪♪ \quad ♪♪ \quad ♪♪ \quad \| \quad ♩♩♩ \quad \| \quad ♪♪♪ \quad ♪♪♪$$

There is an arrangement for Orff instruments at 249 in *The United Methodist Hymnal Music Supplement*.

Jesus' hands were kind hands (273)

Margaret Cropper, 1926

According to *Companion to Hymns and Psalms*, this hymn was written ca. 1926 (Watson and Trickett 1988, 246) and appeared in the authoress's *Hymns and Songs for the Church Kindergarten* (SPCK, ca. 1937, Milgate 1985, 88)

The poem cleverly combines images and experiences of Jesus using his hands as healer and helper, and ends with an offering of our hands in his name in our daily lives. It is an ideal hymn for children to learn and share with adults.

Au clair de la lune

Old French melody; harm. by Carlton R. Young, 1988

This delightful tune and the words from which the tune is named are sometimes attributed to Jean-Baptiste Lully. It was first set to this text in *School Hymn-Book of the Methodist Church*, 1950. This harmonization was prepared for our hymnal.

Joy to the world (246)

Isaac Watts, 1719 (Ps. 98:4-9)

This standard Christmas hymn is a paraphrase of Psalm 98:4-9. The entire psalm is found at **818,** and in *The New Oxford Annotated Bible* it is described:

> Hymn proclaiming the future establishment of God's kingship on the earth . . . . [Verses 4-9] summons to all nations and to the physical universe to join in God's praise. (Metzger and Murphy 1991, 758)

The entire psalm was paraphrased in two parts in *The Psalms of David, Imitated in the Language of the New Testament*, 1719; the first part, verses 1-3, is titled "Praise for the Gospel"; our hymn was the second part and is titled "The Messiah's Coming and Kingdom." (Gealy 556/256)

In a note between the hymns, the poet describes the importance of the two hymns as expressing the messianic fulfillment of Hebrew scripture in Jesus Christ:

> In these two Hymns which I have formed out of the 98th Psalm I have fully exprest what I esteem to be the first and chief Sense of the Holy Scriptures, both in this and the 96:b Psalm, whose Conclusions are both alike. (*The Psalms of David*, 253)

The original first line "Joy to the earth" was included in our hymnals until 1878 when "earth" was changed to "world." In our hymnal, stanza 2:2, "men" is changed to "all."

Antioch

Arr. from G. F. Handel, 1741, by William Holford, 1834, and others
The tune is the piecing together of themes in Handel's *Messiah* found in the chorus and in the instrumental interludes in "Lift up your heads" and the introduction and interludes of the recitative "Comfort ye." John Wilson in "Handel and the Hymn Tune: II, Some Hymn Tune Arrangements," in the January 1986 volume of *The Hymn* has traced the tune's origins to *A Collection of Tunes*, ed. T. Hawkes, 1833, and *Voce de Melodia*, ed. W. Holford, ca. 1835. It was popularized in the USA by Lowell Mason who included our version in *Occasional Psalm and Hymn Tunes*, 1836, and for no stated reason named it ANTIOCH (see Henry L. Mason, *Hymn-Tunes of Lowell Mason*, 1944).

The original SA middle section was later filled out in fuging tune style causing purists to deride the setting as further confusing the sense of the text, reflected in John Wesley's stern criticism of fuging tunes in *The Power of Music*, 1779, and continued by USA Methodist bishops Thomas Coke and Francis Asbury in the 1792 *Discipline,* where this genre is characterized: "They 'puff up with vanity' those who sing them." See also "The Music of Christian Hymns in USA-Wesleyan Style," page 54. There are two trumpet descants at 19-20 in *The United Methodist Hymnal Music Supplement*.

Joyful, joyful, we adore thee (89)

Henry Van Dyke, 1907; st. 4 alt. 1989
This favorite hymn of praise was composed in 1907 and was inspired by the beauty of the Berkshire mountains. It was written to be sung to Beethoven's tune.

In September 1992, J. Michael Walker discovered the author's manuscript copy of the hymn dated November 27, 1907, in the Benson Collection, Speer Library, Princeton Theological Seminary. It was attached to correspondence from the poet to Louis F. Benson requesting the latter to review the text and suggest changes. The poem is titled "'A Hymn to Joy' (Beethoven's Ninth Symphony)." Stanza 4 begins "Blend your voices in the chorus, Millions of the mortal clan"; 4:6, reads "Out of darkness, out of strife"; and 4:8, "this triumphant-song" instead of "the." Benson suggested the changes in these stanzas that have been included in all hymnals.

Fred D. Gealy has commented on the hymn:

> Van Dyke countered [the doom prior to World War I] by speaking a gay cheery all's-right-with-the-world note which was in complete harmony with the widely held belief in an easy if not inevitable progress. His theophany, unlike those of the Psalms, does not take place in the might of God's terrible acts, earthquake and storm, but in the gentle face of nature . . . . The daintiness of phrase and the lilt of rhythm suggest Elysium or Eden before the Fall. (Gealy 556/257)

The hymn entered our hymnals in 1935 from the 1933 Presbyterian *Hymnal* with its slight modifications from the original. (Gealy 556/257) In our hymnal in stanza 4:3, "Father love" is changed to "love divine," and in 4:4, "brother love binds man to man" to "binding all within its span."

Hymn to joy

Ludwig Van Beethoven, 1824; arr. by Edward Hodges, 1864
W. A. Mozart used this motif as instrumental interludes in his motet *Misericordias Domine*, K. 222. Beethoven employed the theme in his early works including *Fantasy*, 1808, for piano, chorus, and orchestra, and more impressively in the finale of his Ninth or *Choral* Symphony, 1824, published in 1826. Our version of the theme is by Edward Hodges named "Joy" at 254 and 255 in *Trinity Collection of Church Music*, 1864, apparently drawn from an adaptation at 183 in Elam Ives, Jr.'s *Mozart Collection*, 1846. The latter version retained the syncopation at the beginning of the fourth line.

Its use as a hymn tune has not been without some complaining—most concerning why Beethoven's syncopation at the beginning of the fourth line is flattened out. Its restoration in our hymnal has spawned complaints from those for whom congregational song is devoid of surprises—and resurrection!

There is a transposition to F, a descant, and two performance notes at 172-76 in *The United Methodist Hymnal Music Supplement*.

Jubilate (74)

See "Canticle of Thanksgiving," pages 264-65.

Just as I am, without one plea (357)

Charlotte Elliott, 1835

The poet, a complete invalid, was so overcome by her anguish as to her purpose in life and the reality of her faith in God that

> she restated for herself the essentials of her faith [the gospel of pardon, peace, and heaven] in the text of this hymn. First published in a leaflet in 1835, it was included in [her] *Hours of Sorrow, Cheered and Comforted (or Thoughts in Verse)*, 1835. (Gealy, Lovelace, Young 1970, 262)

The first hymnal to include the text was *The Invalid's Hymn Book* (2d rev. ed. 1841), where it appeared under the scripture "Him that cometh unto me, I will in no wise cast out.—John 6:37." (Gealy 556/260) The hymn entered our hymnals in 1878 with the original six stanzas. In 1935 stanza 3:3, "Fightings within, and fears without" became " Fightings and fears within, without."

The hymn has been widely used in churches for a century as a response to the preacher's call to accept Christ. More recently at the conclusion of public television staged events of witness, song, and preaching held in sports complexes, such as the Billy Graham Crusades, it is the Pavlovian musical cue, then the relentless accompaniment, for hundreds as they file from their seats and assemble on the playing field.

There is a gospel-style alternate harmonization at 208 in *Songs of Zion*, 1981.

Woodworth

William B. Bradbury, 1849

This tune first appeared in *Mendelssohn Collection, or Third Book of Psalmody*, 1849. It is not known when it was first set with this text. While singing this amalgam of musical simplicity, sentiment, religiosity, spiritual epigrams, and key evangelical words, one may be reminded of the gospel song's impressive ability to masquerade as vital piety.

Kum ba yah (494)
Come by here

African American spiritual

William Farley Smith has provided this commentary:

> "Kum ba yah" originated in the South Carolina low country, U.S.A, and the title phrase is from the Gullah language used there. In many coastal

regions of the South, words and idiomatic expressions that appear to be of African origin are used. The simple utterance "Come by here, my Lord" is universally appealing and has found popularity wherever Christians gather for worship. (Sanchez 1988, 169)

William B. McClain adds this comment:

As the slaves met for worship, often under the cover of darkness, first on their agenda was to invoke the presence of the Lord by softly and reverently chanting "Kum Ba Yah." (McClain 1990, 113)

Desmond

African American Spiritual; harm. by Carlton R. Young, 1988
The tune was named by William Farley Smith after Desmond Tutu, social activist and Anglican archbishop of Capetown, South Africa. The harmonization was prepared for this hymnal.

Kyrie eleison (483, 484)

Lord, have mercy (482)

Let us pray to the Lord (485)

"Lord, have mercy upon us" is one of the oldest forms of prayer and liturgical response in Christian worship. It is "a half-biblical, half-pagan acclamation" (Werner 1959, 268) that entered the Western church from the East and in the sixth century was altered by Gregory the Great to include a second petition to Jesus Christ, Kyrie eleison. As it entered the Anglican tradition, it was used by Thomas Cranmer at the beginning and after the Prayer for Purity, and before the Gloria in excelsis. When the Ten Commandments were introduced, they were followed by the Kyrie. (Gealy, Lovelace, Young 1970, 452-53)

Wesley's incorporation of the Ten Commandments into our liturgies of Holy Communion and the Burial Service brought them into our *Disciplines*, but as noted by James F. White, they were not included in our formative worship patterns of song, prayer, scripture, and preaching. (White 1990, 153)

With the renewal of interest in our Anglican roots (see the discussion in "The 1878 Methodist Episcopal Hymnal," page 62), our hymnals, beginning in 1905 with numbers 738-39, included the Ten Commandments and sung responses— "Lord, have mercy upon us, and incline our hearts to keep this law." This practice was continued in our 1935 and 1966 hymnals. In our 1957 hymnal they were included with only spoken responses. The Ten Commandments are not included in our present hymnal, and the Kyrie has been removed from our liturgies. Thus, it functions primarily as a call or response to prayer—joyous as well as penitential.

An interesting comment is supplied by Nolan B. Harmon:

> Anyone reading Wesley's Journal in its account of his earlier years will be struck with the frequent "K. E." in his crabbed hand, with which he closed, to him, poor record of a day. (Harmon 1926, 133)

Orthodox kyrie (483)

Russian Orthodox Liturgy
This setting is adapted from the sung liturgy of the Eastern church and may be sung in three parts by men or women, or together in six parts. See Pronunciation Guide, 390 in *The United Methodist Hymnal Music Supplement*.

Taizé kyrie (484)

Jacques Berthier and the Community of Taizé, 1979
This music is a setting from the worship music of Taizé. For commentary on this music, see "Eat this bread," pages 324-25.

Kriewald kyrie (482)

James A. Kriewald, 1985
This is from the composer's setting of the service of Holy Communion that first appeared in *Alive Now*, July 1985.

Petitions Litany (485)

Byzantine Chant; harm. by Robert Batistini, 1984
This prayer response, incorporating the English words of the Kyrie eleison, Christe eleison, first appeared as "Petitions Litany" in *Praise God in Song*, 1979.

La palabra del Señor es recta (107)
Righteous and just is the word of our Lord
Words and Music: Juan Luis García, 1986
trans. by George Lockwood, 1987 (Ps. 33:4-11)
This hymn invites all creation to dance in celebration of God's liberating and just word.

Nelson

The Cuban style *Punto Guajiro*, two-against-three rhythms, may be accentuated by adding traditional rhythm instruments to double the rhythm of the melody and the bass line. At the verses (*a la Estrofa*) as the tune shifts from minor to parallel major, let solo or soli voices sing the story of praise and liberation with lighter accompaniment; add the full instruments on the Refrain (*Estribillo*) with the shift back to minor.

Lead me, Lord (473)

Samuel S. Wesley, 1861

This is the final movement of "Praise the Lord, O my soul," 1861, a large scale organ and choral work composed to celebrate the new organ at Holy Trinity Church, Winchester. (Routley 1968, 174-75) It was first included in our hymnals in 1957.

Lead on, O King eternal (580)

Ernest W. Shurtleff, 1887

This favorite dedication hymn was written for the all-male 1887 graduating class of Andover Theological Seminary, of which the author was a member. It was included the same year in the author's *Hymns of the Faith*. (Reynolds 1964, 110) This hymn, not unlike "Onward, Christian soldiers" (575), calls the faithful to fight in a war against sin to establish God's kingdom of peace and love. The conclusion of worship in the social gospel tradition replaces graduation as "the day of march" that follows "days of preparation" into "fields of conquest."

The hymn entered our hymnals in 1901.

Lancashire

See "Go, make of all disciples," page 359.

Leaning on the everlasting arms (133)

Elisha A. Hoffman, 1887 (Deut. 33:27)

Upon hearing from two friends who lost their wives in death, Anthony J. Showalter wrote them letters of consolation quoting the passage from Deuteronomy, "The eternal God is thy refuge, and underneath are the everlasting arms." (Deuteronomy 33:27, KJV; the primary NRSV text is very different)

The scripture suggested the refrain "leaning, leaning on the everlasting arms," and Showalter asked Elisha A. Hoffman to write the stanzas. According to Harry Eskew, "The hymn was first included in two collections which are identical in all aspects except for the words 'Glad' and 'Song' in their titles:" *The Glad [Song] Evangel for Revival, Camp and Evangelistic Meetings,* 1887. (Adams 1992, 269) Showalter's account of the writing of this hymn is included at 280-81 in Lester Hostetler's *Handbook to the Mennonite Hymnary,* 1949. The hymn entered our hymnals in 1897.

Showalter

Anthony J. Showalter, 1887
The tune is appropriately named for the composer who prompted the hymn and supplied the refrain.

Leave it there (522)

Words and music: Charles Albert Tindley, ca. 1906
William Farley Smith has commented:

> The entire hymn bears out God's promise never to leave us alone. The theme of the poem puts to use sentiments of slave-poets who declared, "Mah lawd done jes' whut he say'd." (Sanchez 1989, 179)

This is the hymn's first appearance in our hymnals.

Leave it there

Arr. by Charles A. Tindley, Jr.
This arrangement appears at 30 in *New Songs of Paradise,* 1941. Verolga Nix's arrangement at 23 in *Songs of Zion,* 1981, uses a version of the tune with even eighth notes replacing the dotted eighth and sixteenths with some syncopation.

The music of the stanzas is similar to Tindley's "God will provide for me," 3 in *New Songs of Paradise,* No. 6, 1941. The music of the entire hymn was so similar to James M. Black's "When the roll is called up yonder" that its copyright owner, Tabernacle Publishing, to prevent a public airing of claims of authorship of the tune by these two prominent Methodist ministers, bought Tindley's "Leave it there" and licensed both hymns for use in essentially mutually exclusive racial constituencies.

Lent (268)

Lutheran Book of Worship, 1978
This prayer links our observance of Lent to the Hebrews' journey in the wilderness and of Jesus' wilderness temptation. It appeared on page 17 in the *Lutheran Book of Worship,* 1978.

Let all mortal flesh keep silence (626)
Σιγησάτο πᾶρα σάρξ

Liturgy of St. James, 4th cent.
trans. by Gerard Moultrie, 1864 (John 6:35-58; Rev. 4)

Fred D. Gealy has written about the source of this hymn:

> In the Liturgy of St. James of Jerusalem—the Syrian rite—while the Communion elements are being brought into the sanctuary at the beginning of the Liturgy of the Faithful, the readers sing "the thrice-holy hymn to the quickening Trinity," and the priest chants the prayer: "Let all mortal flesh keep silence, and stand with fear and trembling . . . for the King of Kings, and Lord of Lords, Christ our God, comes forward to be sacrificed and to be given for food to the faithful." (Gealy, Lovelace, Young 1970, 265)

Moultrie's metrical paraphrase was included in *Lyra Eucharistica* (2d ed. 1864) and appeared under the title "Prayer of the Cherubic Hymn" at 169 in *The People's Hymnal*, 1867. The Greek text in F. E. Brightman's *Liturgies, Eastern and Western*, 1896, and the prose translation of the entire rite from J. M. Neale and R. F. Littledale, *A Translation of the Primitive Liturgies*, 1868-69, are found in Gealy 556/265.

The hymn entered our 1935 hymnal as a one-stanza Call to Worship; in 1966 the four original stanzas were included. The hymn's rich eucharistic metaphorical prose and the eucharistic prose of John 6:52-59 can be effectively combined in sermon and song.

Picardy

Harm. from The English Hymnal, 1906

This French melody, "probably of the 17th century" (Dearmer and Jacob 1933, 157), was first matched with this text in this form in *The English Hymnal*, 1906, in a harmonization probably by Ralph Vaughan Williams. Gustav Holst's 1921 festival choral setting helped to bring the combination into the repertory. There is an arrangement for handbells and a vocal descant at 268-69 in *The United Methodist Hymnal Music Supplement*.

Let all the world in every corner sing (93)

George Herbert, 1633

This poem was published shortly after the author's death in his collection *The Temple*, where it is titled "Antiphon (I)." Unlike Herbert's other verse, its form suggests that he might have meant it to be said or sung. The text entered our hymnals in 1935.

Augustine

Erik Routley, 1960

The tune was named after the Augustine-Bristo Congregational Church, Edinburgh, where Routley served as minister 1960-67. It was first included at 237 in *Hymns for Church and School*, 1964.

The composer has written about his tune:

> The present tune happens to be the only one in circulation which preserves the original form of the text [antiphon, stanza, antiphon, stanza, antiphon] and, written in 1960 in Edinburgh, was first published in *Hymns for Church and School*, 1964. (Routley 1977, 6)

This tune replaces "All the World" by Robert G. McCutchan, which was included in our 1935, 1957, and 1966 hymnals. When AUGUSTINE was approved, many members of the Hymnal Revision Committee, comparing it to McCutchan's tune, commented, "That'll never be sung."

Let it breathe on me (503)

Words and music: Magnolia Lewis-Butts, 1942 (John 20:22)

This is the chorus from a hymn that was composed for the Metropolitan Community Gospel Church, Chicago, Illinois. The church's pastor, Theodore Richardson, has provided the following information about this chorus: "This hymn or gospel song was written and immediately became the hymn most used following the Prayer of Invocation in our services." (Correspondence with Carlton R. Young, August 1992)

Let it breathe

The original hymn is included at 224 in *Songs of Zion*, 1981. Our harmonization was made by William Farley Smith for our hymnal

Let my people seek their freedom (586)

T. Herbert O'Driscoll, 1971 (Deut. 8:14-18)

H. Myron Braun has commented on this hymn:

> We have here a powerful hymn emphasizing at least two concepts deep-rooted in the history of the people of God—covenant and pilgrim. At no point in the history of Israel or of Christianity has our covenant with the Almighty allowed us ease or the backward look. We cannot avoid the storm of change. (Braun 1982, 24)

The hymn appeared in the United Church of Canada, *The Hymn Book*, 1971. Fearing that the original first line, "From the slave pens of the Delta," would prevent the hymn's selection, the Hymnal Revision Committee made it the second line. Lines 1 and 2 in stanza 2 were also inverted. There are no other changes in this challenging hymn that mirrors the Hebrew exodus in contemporary images.

Ebenezer

See "God hath spoken by the prophets," page 364.

Let there be light (440)

Frances W. Davis, 1968

This hymn, first included in a collection of hymns published for St. George's Anglican Church, Quebec, is a prayer for peace, freedom, and understanding among all people. The author's original text was formed as a continuing prayer with the beginning word in each stanza lowercased, and each stanza, except the final, ending with a semicolon. "Thy" has been changed to "your" in the allusions to the Lord's Prayer in stanzas 4 and 5.

Concord

Robert J. B. Fleming, 1968

The tune was composed for this text with its unique meter and was included in *The Hymn Book*, 1971. The hymn may be sung more effectively as a continuing prayer by alternating stanzas between female and male voices, with everyone joining on the final and summary stanza.

Let there be peace on earth (431)

Words and music: Sy Miller and Jill Jackson, 1955

This popular prayer for world peace affirms that as children of God peace begins with each of us in our everyday lives. It was first performed in the summer of 1955 at the national convention of Christians and Jews, Ilyllwide Pines, California.

World peace

Harm. by Charles H. Webb, 1987

A piano-vocal score of the song was simplified for our hymnal.

Let us break bread together (618)

African American spiritual
adapt. and arr. by William Farley Smith, 1986

According to Miles Clark Fisher in *Negro Slave Songs in the United States*, this spiritual is apparently derived from the gathering song "Let us praise God together on our knees," used in Virginia by slaves to convene secret meetings when law prohibited them to assemble by drumbeat. After the Civil War with the addition of the metaphors of bread and wine, it became a communion hymn, though still retaining the slave's allusion to facing the rising sun and with it the question of its relationship to the celebration of Holy Communion at times other than sunrise. (Fisher 1953, 29)

John Lovell, Jr., has commented on the origin of this allusion as the slave poet's appropriation of the compelling folk symbol of the sun as an agency of spiritual light:

Turning one's face to the sun is a sign of looking upward in one's own life and of being ready to receive the bounty. (Lovell 1972, 263-64)

The earliest published version seems to be in James Weldon Johnson, *The Second Book of Negro Spirituals*, 1927. It was included in the United States Air Force *Chapel Conference Songbook*, ca. 1955. The text was first included in our hymnals in 1966.

Let us break bread

The arranger, William Farley Smith, has commented on this setting:

Here, an effort has been made to restore the spiritual to a traditional performance practice uniting voices with keyboard. This restoration has been dressed in "black harmonies," including the traditional musical variant for the fourth stanza. . . . The 2/2 meter indicates that the spiritual should be sung throughout in a rocking manner, without interruption between stanzas. (Sanchez 1989, 209)

Let us now depart in thy peace (668)

Lee Hastings Bristol, Jr., 1953 (Luke 2:29)

The opening line of this dismissal is from Simeon's Song offered to God in praise for having seen and held the baby Jesus, the Messiah. (Luke 2:29) It first appeared at number 11 in *Hymns for Children and Grownups to Use Together*, 1953, edited by Lee Hastings Bristol, Jr., and Harold William Friedell.

A la puerta

New Mexican folk song
adapt. and harm. by Lee Hastings Bristol, Jr.
and Harold William Friedell

This tune appeared in the 1953 collection with the citation "Folk Song from New Mexico believed to be of Spanish origin." The response may be sung by both congregation and choir. There is an optional threefold choral amen **(903)** that may be substituted for the amen. The hymn and amen are included at 1 in *The United Methodist Hymnal Music Supplement.*

Let us plead for faith alone (385)

Charles Wesley, 1740 (Eph. 2:8-10)

This text is part of a long five-part poem entitled "The Love Feast," 181-87 in *Hymns and Sacred Poems*, 1740, from which "Come, and let us sweetly join" **(699)** is also excerpted. Our hymn is comprised of sections 3 and 4 of Part 3, and eloquently elaborates on Paul's teaching that good works result from salvation and not the reverse. (Ephesians 5:b, 8-10) The first line of our hymn originally read "Plead we thus for Faith *alone.*" In stanza 2:2, "is its end" has been changed to "is the end." This is the first appearance of this text in our hymnals.

S T Kimbrough, Jr. has commented:

This is one of Charles Wesley's most succinct summaries of "justification by faith alone." Martin Luther's explication of this teaching greatly influenced Wesley through the former's commentary on Galatians, although the poet later found the teaching to be firmly rooted in the Articles of Religion of The Church of England. It is also interesting that in the first edition "alone" at the end of stanza 1:1 is italicized for emphasis, as is "applies" at the end of 1:4. (Correspondence with Carlton R. Young, September 1992)

Savannah

See "Jesus, Lord, we look to thee," page 441.

Let us pray to the Lord (485)

See "Kyrie," pages 456-57.

Let's sing unto the Lord (149)

See "Cantemos al Señor," page 251.

Lift every voice and sing (519)

James Weldon Johnson, 1921

The poet relates the story of the writing of this stirring song of faith, freedom, and hope in his autobiography *Along This Way*, 1933. It first appeared in sheet music in 1921. In recent years it has been called the "Negro national anthem" or "Black national anthem."

Lift every voice

J. Rosamond Johnson, 1921

Apparently quoting the author, Harry Eskew writes that the hymn was "first sung by a chorus of Black schoolchildren in Jacksonville, Florida, in celebration of the birthday of Abraham Lincoln." (Adams 1992, 179-80) William Farley Smith reduced our arrangement for congregational singing from a setting for piano and voice. A version of this song for congregation and choir by Verolga Nix is at 210 in *Songs of Zion*, 1981.

Lift high the cross (159)

George William Kitchin and Michael Robert Newbolt, 1916, alt.

This hymn in eleven stanzas with the refrain first appeared at number 745 under the title "Jesus Christ, and Him crucified" in *Hymns Ancient and Modern*, 1916 Second Supplement. Wesley Milgate has traced the hymn's origin as based on a hymn Kitchin had written for a Society for the Propagation of the Gospel festival in Winchester Cathedral, June 1887. "It probably owes something to the words in [the Emperor] Constantine's vision, as related in Eusebius's *Life of Constantine*: "In hoc signo vinces" ("In this sign—i.e., of the cross—thou shalt conquer.") (Milgate 1985, 121)

Stanley Osborne has commented:

> [The hymn] has no room for weak resignation. It summons the mightiest and leaves them gazing upon a Love that gave its life to achieve life. (Osborne 1976, hymn 321)

A new first stanza intended to reduce sexist and militaristic images was provided by the Hymnal Revision Committee. The original stanza 1 read:

> Come, brethren, follow where our Captain trod,
> Our King victorious, Christ the Son of God.

Stanzas 3, 7, and 11 are included from the original text with these alterations: 2:1, "soldier" to "servant"; 2:2, "his" to "the"; 3:2, "all men" to "the world."

More than half a century after its publication the hymn was introduced in the USA in *Hymns for the Living Church*, 1974, which led to its inclusion in all recent hymnals. Our hymnal's version provides the opportunity to express the spirit of "Onward Christian soldiers" without singing militaristic metaphors.

Crucifer

Sydney Hugo Nicholson, 1916
The tune was written for this text and was first included in *Hymns Ancient and Modern*, 1916 Second Supplement. The tune's name means literally "Cross-bearer." Three descants and a setting for brass and timpani are included at 71-75 in *The United Methodist Hymnal Music Supplement*.

Lift up your heads, ye mighty gates (213)
Macht hoch die Tür, die Tor' macht weit

Georg Weissel, 1642; trans. by Catherine Winkworth, 1855 (Ps. 24)
This hymn, composed for the First Sunday in Advent, first appeared in five eight-line 88.88.88.66 stanzas in *Preussische Festlieder*, 1642. Catherine Winkworth translated the hymn in five eight-line stanzas for her *Lyra Germanica*, first series, 1855, from which the first four lines of stanzas 1, 4, and 5 were selected for our 1935 hymnal. In stanza 3 the singular pronouns were changed to plural. The final four lines of Winkworth's text are included in our hymnal as stanza 4. In order to bring the text into LM, in line 3 the original "eternal praise and fame" has been extended to "eternal praise, eternal fame."

Faithful to its pietistic roots, the hymn in stanza 2:2-3 exchanges the imagery of the temple procession for the entrance of Christ into the heart of the faithful, a place "set apart from earthly use."

Stanzas of the hymn may be used as responses to the reading of Psalm 24 at **212** or **755** in an act of praise suitable for Advent, Passion/Palm Sunday, or any occasion celebrating the coming of Christ.

Truro

See "Christ is alive," pages 274-75.

Like the murmur of the dove's song (544)

Carl P. Daw, Jr., 1981
The poet states that the text was written expressly for Peter Cutts's tune BRIDEGROOM. The first stanza portrays *how* the Spirit comes as moaning dove and at

the first Pentecost as wind and flame (see Louis Evely in *A Religion for Our Time*). Stanza 2 is about the *where* or *to whom* of the Spirit's coming—as a gift of divine empowerment to the church gathered in the name of Christ. Stanza 3 "is concerned with the purposes for which the Spirit is given (the *why*): for reconciliation, prayer (Romans 8:26), divine power (Acts 1:8), and quiet confidence." (Daw 1990, 84)

Ray Glover has commented:

> Like the ancient hymn "Veni Sancte Spiritus," this new text pulls together diverse images of both the Holy Spirit and the People of God in an attempt to suggest the scope of divine power and the depth of human need. (Glover 1987, 88)

Bridegroom

Peter Cutts, 1968

At the suggestion of Erik Routley the tune was composed for the text "As the bridegroom to his chosen" and first appeared in *100 Hymns for Today*, 1969. Lines of the stanzas may be sung antiphonally between groups or solo voices, with everyone joining on the closing phrase "Come, Holy Spirit, come." The diatonic melody and subtle chromaticism combine to make this one of Peter Cutts's most successful tunes.

Listen, Lord (A Prayer) (677)

James Weldon Johnson, 1927

This prayer for use at the beginning of morning worship is an excerpt from the poet's African American style poetic sermons in *God's Trombones*, 1927.

Litany for Christian Unity (556)

Karol Wojtyla (Pope John Paul II), 20th cent.

This prayer for Christian unity was composed by the author while he was a bishop in Poland. It may effectively be used before any of the hymns in the section "United in Christ." It is also appropriate as a prayer at ecumenical gatherings of Christians. The prayer is from Karol Wojtyla, *Prayers of Pope John Paull II*, 1982.

Lo, he comes with clouds descending (718)

Charles Wesley, 1758 (Rev. 1:7)

John Julian in *Dictionary of Hymnody* has traced the complicated history of this hymn and shows that Wesley apparently wrote this hymn after John Cennick's "Lo! he cometh, countless trumpets" from his *Collection of Sacred Hymns*, 1752.

The text is based upon Revelation 1:7:

> Look! He is coming with the clouds;
> every eye will see him,
> even those who pierced him;
> and on his account all the tribes of the earth will wail.
> So it is to be. Amen.

The hymn first appeared at 32-33 in Wesley's *Hymns of Intercession for All Mankind*, 1758, "the second of a trilogy of hymns in this metre; they are preceded by two other hymns under the same title [Thy Kingdom Come!]." (Baker 1962, 130) The hymn was first included in our hymnals in 1788 and has been in all our hymnals except the 1935 edition, which dropped many hymns and references to the Second Advent of Christ following a doctrinaire application of the social gospel. The original four stanzas are printed with minor alterations—in each stanza "Hallelujah" is repeated as an accommodation to the tune; in stanza 4:2, "thine" is changed to "thy," and in 4:5, "Jah Jehovah" to "Hallelujah."

Helmsley

Thomas Olivers, 1765
harm. from The English Hymnal, 1906

Maurice Frost has traced the complicated history of this tune at pages 156-57 in *Historical Companion to Hymns Ancient and Modern*, 1962, and states that the tune was composed by Thomas Olivers and appeared under the name "Olivers" in Wesley's *Select Hymns with Tunes Annext*, 1765. Olivers may have based it on other tunes including one with a similar first line found in Thomas Arne's *Thomas and Sally*, 1761, or one in Martin Madan's *Collection of Hymn and Psalm Tunes*, 1769, issued in sections over a period of time. For other possible sources, see Wesley Milgate (1985, 96).

Erik Routley has provided this commentary:

> [The tune's] dubious ancestry, and its varied history ending in association with one of the most solemn hymns in the language, show the universality of really great melody. Dr. Richard Conyers, vicar of Helmsley . . . proba-bly received from Wesley the tune composed in its original form . . . and gave it the new name, *Helmsley*. (Routley 1953, 97)

The tune entered our hymnals in 1878. Our harmonization except for measure 23 is from *The English Hymnal*, 1906. John Wilson has provided a stirring setting of stanza 4 for SATB choir, congregation, and organ at 241 in *Hymns and Psalms*, 1983. There is a vocal descant at 157 in *The United Methodist Hymnal Music Supplement*.

Lo, how a Rose e'er blooming (216)
Es ist ein Ros entsprungen

Sts. 1-2, 15th cent. German; trans. by Theodore Baker, 1894
st. 3 from The Hymnal 1940 (Isa. 35:1-2)

The origins of this German advent hymn that employs the symbol of a blooming rose for the coming of Christ may date as early as the fifteenth century. Marilyn Stulken has written in *Hymnal Companion to the Lutheran Book of Worship*:

> The earliest source of the text is a manuscript from St. Alban's Carthusian monastery in Trier, which is preserved in the municipal library of Trier . . . [and] was written down between 1582 and 1588. As first published in the *Alte Catholische Geistliche Kirchengeseng* [sic]*(Speierischen Gesangbuch)*, Cologne, 1599, the text consisted of twenty-two stanzas and related the events of Luke 1 and 2, and Matthew 2. (Stulken 1981, 160-61)

Stanzas 1 and 2 are from Theodore Baker's 1894 translation (see 76 in *The Oxford Book of Carols*, 1972, for the German text). Stanza 3 is from *The Hymnal 1940* version that apparently was adapted from a translation by Harriet Reynolds Spaeth of a nineteenth-century German text by Friedrich Layritz.

Es ist ein Ros

Michael Praetorius, 1609

Our version was adapted for congregational singing from *The Hymnal 1940* from Praetorius's setting of this old German melody in *Musae Sionae*, 1609. The composer's original harmonization with the poignant alto part is number 81 in *The Hymnal 1982* and may be used by choirs in alternation with our setting that is slightly more suited to congregational singing.

Lonely the boat (476)
Kam-kam-han bam

Helen Kim, 1921; trans. by Hae Jong Kim, 1980
versed by Linda and Doug Sugano, 1981
and Hope Omachi-Kawashima, 1987 (Matt. 8:23-27)

This Korean hymn is based on the account of Jesus' stilling the storm in Matthew 8:23-27 with parallels in Mark 4:35-41 and Luke 8:22-25 and effectively transfers the story's metaphors into a personal testimony of the abiding support, love, and peace afforded by God in Christ for the Christian on "life's cruel sea." The English text first appeared in *Hymns from the Four Winds*, 1983. The complete Korean text is found at 253 in *Sound the Bamboo*, 1990.

Bai

Dong Hoon Lee, 1967

The tune was adapted in 1981 by the Asian American Hymnbook Project and was first included in *Hymns from the Four Winds*, 1983.

Lord, dismiss us with thy blessing (671)

Attr. to John Fawcett, 1773

Our two-stanza hymn is a version of a text that appeared without attribution under the title "Close of Service" in *A Supplement to the Shawbury Hymn Book*, 1773. After extensive research John Julian concludes that the hymn's "author is very probably Dr. Fawcett." (Julian 1907, 687) The hymn entered our hymnals in 1837 in three stanzas. Our version of the text is as it appears in Richard Conyers, *A Collection of Psalms and Hymns from Various Authors*, 1774.

The omitted stanza 3 ends the hymn and the worship service on an apocalyptic note:

> So where'er the signal's given
>   Us from earth to call away,
> Borne on angels' wings to heaven,
>   Glad the summons to obey,
> May we ever
>   Reign with Christ in endless day!

Sicilian Mariners

The European Magazine and London Review, 1792

Maurice Frost in *Historical Companion to Hymns Ancient and Modern*, 1962, writes that the tune is of late-eighteenth-century Italian origin where it is associated with a hymn to the Virgin, "O sanctissima, O piissima." (Frost 1962, 355) Wesley Milgate (1985, 84) has produced the fullest account of the tune's history.

The tune became very popular in the USA after its appearance in William Smith and William Little's *Easy Instructor*, 1798, set to "Lord, dismiss us." (Gealy, Lovelace, Young 1970, 273) According to Robert Guy McCutchan the tune entered our repertory in an edition (1832?) of *The Methodist Harmonist*, 1821. (McCutchan 1942, 51) It entered our hymnals in the 1857 tune edition of the 1847 hymnal, appeared in our 1878 and 1889 hymnals, and was dropped in 1905. Our harmonization was apparently made by McCutchan for the 1935 hymnal.

Lord God, your love has called us here (579)

Brian Wren, 1973

The poet wrote this text in April 1973 under the heading "And can it be" to Erik Routley's tune "Abingdon," with the dedication to the composer "in love and appreciation." Brian Wren has written about the hymn:

[It is] a restatement (but not a replacement) of Wesley's hymn, "And can it be that I should gain an interest in the Saviour's blood?" **[363]**. It sees God's gracious love in the context of sin built into socio-economic structures, but also of Christian hope. (Wren "Notes" in *Faith Looking Forward*, 1983)

The hymn was first included in *New Church Praise*, 1975.

Carey's (Surrey)

See "Give me the faith which can remove," page 352.

Lord, have mercy (482)

See "Kyrie," pages 456-57.

Lord, I want to be a Christian (402)

African American spiritual
adapt. and arr. by William Farley Smith, 1986

This spiritual embodies one of the fundamental teachings of evangelical Christianity as desiring and intending ("Lord I want") to have a pure heart, i.e., to be Christlike in thought and deed. It is also an ironic commentary of the slave poet on the dehumanizing institution of human slavery practiced by Christians and defended by their churches.

A third stanza included in early versions, "I don't want to be like Judas, in my heart," prompted this comment from John Lovell, Jr.:

> [The slave] did not want to be like Judas. Overseers and other managers of the slave felt it necessary to play slaves off against one another; they offered premiums to members of the group who would tattle and betray. Regardless of the material benefits he could gain from betraying and regardless of the lack of material benefit in being "more loving" and "more holy," the slave firmly chose the latter. . . . It was more than a prayer; it was a declaration that, from this point, he was going to follow the man-god he admired." (Lovell 1972, 288)

This spiritual has been widely sung during this century within and without the African American worship traditions. Our text follows the version at 258 in *Folk Songs of the American Negro,* 1907, compiled by J. W. Work, Jr., and Frederick J. Work. It entered our hymnals in 1957.

I want to be a Christian

William B. McClain suggests this performance practice:

One particularly powerful rendition is to have the music played through without singing after the third verse, and have the singing resume at a slightly faster tempo in the fourth verse and chorus. (McClain 1990, 90)

There is an adaptation of the standard 1907 harmonization by J. W. Work, Jr., and Frederick J. Work at 258 in *The Cokesbury Worship Hymnal*, 1938, that retains the dialect "in-a-my" and avoids the fussy chromaticism that tends to discourage congregational singing.

Lord of the dance (261)

Words and music: Sydney Carter, ca. 1963

In this song Jesus invites humankind to join him in the dance of salvation. Carter obviously parodied his setting after the eleven-stanza, seventeenth-century Cornish carol "Tomorrow shall be my dancing-day," 158 in *The Oxford Book of Carols*, 1972, described by Erik Routley as "world-affirming, not world-denying." (Routley 1958, 78) The phrase "Lord of the dance" may have roots in English folklore whereas the convener of the annual fair was the "Lord of the dance" or Lord or, i.e., "provider," creation. The song first appeared in *Nine Songs or Ballads*, 1964.

This was the only hymnic addition to the *Report of the Hymnal Revision Committee to the 1988 General Conference of the Methodist Church*, and its inclusion was prompted by Bishop Woodie W. White's use of the song as the centerpiece of his sermon preached in the opening worship service of that conference.

Lord of the dance

19th cent. Shaker tune; adapt. by Sydney Carter, ca. 1963
harm. by Gary Alan Smith, 1988

This melody is the author's variant of "Simple Gifts" from the USA Shaker repertory, presumably of British origin as was the sect. The tune was uniquely used by that Utopian group in their formation-dances.

Dancing in early Shaker tradition was a spontaneous response to the spirit. In the foreword to *A Shaker Hymnal*, Cheryl Anderson has described how dancing functioned in early Shaker worship as a spontaneous response to the Spirit and gradually evolved into formal group dance patterns known as

"holy order" or "square order shuffle," that consisted of Brothers and Sisters in lines on opposite sides of the meeting room, stepping forward and back three steps . . . more of a moving meditation than a dance. . . .

[In time] dancing occurred after the opening hymn and an exhortation by an elder or eldress [Shakers believed in a female-male Godhead, and a female second advented Christ], then dancing, or "laboring" as it was called by the believers, commenced. For laboring, a group of the best singers—four or five Brothers and four or five Sisters—would stand in the center of the worshippers to accompany the dancing with unison, vocal music. . . . Laboring songs, as a rule, have only one verse, which was repeated again and again for as long as the "Gift" lasted [see 1 Corinthians 12:1-11] to continue the particular dance. (Anderson 1990, iv, vi-ii)

Daniel Patterson in *The Shaker Spiritual*, 1979, has traced the tune to a "quick dance" that may have originated in the Alfred (Maine) Ministry, June 28, 1848. (Patterson 1979, 373-73) The tune was included in E. D. Andrews, *The Gift to Be Simple: Songs, Dances and Rituals of the American Shakers*, 1940. Aaron Copland used it in his ballet *Appalachian Spring*, 1944, and set it for voice and piano in *Old American Songs*, 1950. For a discussion of Shaker tunes see Donald E. Christenson, "A History of the Early Shakers and Their Music," in the January 1988 issue of *The Hymn*.

Stanzas may be danced as they are sung by solo or soli voices. Accompany with a trap set, bass, and piano for a nostalgic trip to the 1960s. The harmonization was prepared for this hymnal.

Lord, speak to me (463)

Frances R. Havergal, 1872 (Rom. 14:7)
The hymn first appeared in seven stanzas in *Under the Surface*, 1874, under the heading "A Worker's Prayer. None of us liveth unto himself, Romans 14:7." (Gealy 556/288) It entered our hymnals in 1901.

Canonbury

Adapt. from Robert Schumann, 1839
This adaptation is from the composer's "Nachtstücke," Op. 23, No. 4; it was first included in J. Ireland Tucker's *Hymnal with Tunes, Old and New*, 1872. Erik Routley comments that "this is a particularly bad example of a poor tune being made out of a beautiful original." (Routley 1981, 86-87)

Lord, who throughout these forty days (269)

Claudia F. Hernaman, 1873
(Matt. 4:1-11; Mark 1:12-13; Luke 4:1-13)
This hymn on the temptation of Jesus first appeared in the poet's *Child's Book of Praise; A Manual of Devotion in Simple Verse*, 1873. It is the author's only hymn still in common use and one of a very few that relates to that part of the Christian Year from Ash Wednesday to Easter.

Land of rest

USA folk melody; arr. by Annabel Morris Buchanan, 1938
harm. by Charles H. Webb, 1988

Marion J. Hatchett has traced this tune to *The Christian Harp,* 1832, 1836 ed. (Glover 1993) The version of the melody in our hymnal is from Annabel Morris Buchanan's *Folk Hymns of America,* 1938, and was based on the compiler's recollection of the tune as sung by her grandmother to the words of the folk hymn "O land of rest, for thee I sigh." Our harmonization was prepared for the 1989 hymnal.

Lord, whose love through humble service (581)

Albert F. Bayly, 1961, alt.

The hymn was written in response to an invitation by the Hymn Society of America for hymns on social concerns. It was published in the society's *Seven New Social Welfare Hymns,* 1961, and was the conference hymn for the Second National Conference on the Churches and Social Welfare, Cleveland, Ohio, October 1961.

There are several minor changes in the text: stanza 1:3, "didst on" to "did on"; 1:4, "work thy" to "offered"; 1:5, "thy" to "your"; 1:8, "thou dost" to "that you"; 2:1, "the" to "your"; 2:4, "Men mourn their" to "we mourn our"; 2:5 and 2:7, "thy" to "your"; 2:8, "men" to "us"; 3:2 and 3:6, "thy" to "your"; 3:8, "thine" to "your"; 4:1, "unto" to "to your"; 4:2, 4:7, and 4:8, "thy" to "your"; 4:7, "thy children" to "your servants."

Beach Spring

Attr. to B. F. White, 1844; harm. by Ronald A. Nelson, 1978

The tune first appeared in *The Sacred Harp,* 1844, attributed to its co-compiler, Major Benjamin Franklin White. The harmonization and setting for unison voices were made for the *Lutheran Book of Worship,* 1978. The arranger adapted his setting for SATB singing for our hymnal.

Lord, you give the great commission (584)

Jeffery Rowthorn, 1978 (Luke 9:2; Matt. 28:19-20; Luke 23:24)

This hymn on Christ's commission was written for the tune ABBOT'S LEIGH and first appeared in *Laudamus,* 1984, a supplemental hymnal for use at Yale Divinity School, for which the poet served as general editor.

Ray Glover has provided this commentary:

> [Stanza one] speaks directly to the call that we, as the body of Christ, the Church, witness to God's purpose "with renewed integrity." In succeeding

stanzas we are called to mission, to a life of sharing, to forgiveness and to servanthood. (Glover 1987, 90)

The hymn, although similar to the direct and more easily sung "Go, make of all disciples" **(571)**, based on the same text, is distinctive in that the closing petition in each stanza calls forth the Holy Spirit for empowerment for ministry, and the Eucharist is yoked with baptism as a means of sharing God's saving act in Christ. The church is also reminded of the social imperatives of the gospel—the sharing of wealth and the establishment of a just society.

In stanza 3:3, "Let your priests" has been changed to "Let us all."

Abbot's Leigh

See "God is here," page 365.

Lord, you have come to the lakeshore (344)

See "Tú has venido a la orilla," pages 669-70.

Lord's Prayer (GREGORIAN) (270)

See "The Lord's prayer" (GREGORIAN), pages 641-42.

Lord's Prayer (WEST INDIAN) (271)

See "The Lord's Prayer" (WEST INDIAN), page 642.

Love came down at Christmas (242)

Christina G. Rossetti, 1885
"Love" is used by the poet eleven times in this succinct yet expressive Christmas hymn and prompts this commentary in *Companion to Hymns and Psalms*:

> The Incarnation of the Godhead, Love divine, is echoed by love in human form, which is our plea to God, our gift to the world, and our sign to all that Christ has come as Redeemer. (Watson and Trickett 1988, 94)

The text first appeared in the poet's *Time Flies: a Reading Diary*, 1885, under the date of December 29. Stanza 3:4 originally read "Love the universal sign"; later it was changed by the author to its present form in *Verses*, 1893. (Osborne 1976, 422) It entered our hymnals in 1935.

The footnote at the bottom of our hymn page—"'neighbor' may be substituted for 'all men'"—illustrates the Hymnal Revision Committee's ambivalence towards altering, i.e., maiming, classic texts.

Gartan

Trad. Irish melody; harm. by David Evans, 1927; alt.

This melody is from "the *Petrie Collection* of Irish melodies, ed. C. V. Stanford, Part 2, 1902, where it is described as a 'Chant, or Hymn.'" (Milgate 1985, 112) Our harmonization is from *The Church Hymnary*, revised 1927, with measure 3 slightly altered. The tune takes its name from "Lough Gartan, a small lake in County Donegal, Ireland." (McCutchan 1957, 72)

Love divine, all loves excelling (384)

Charles Wesley, 1747

This Wesley hymn is included in all major hymnals. The text first appeared in four stanzas in *Hymns for those that seek and those that have Redemption in the Blood of Jesus Christ*, 1747. Frank Baker in *Representative Verse of Charles Wesley*, page 94, has noted Wesley's apparent spiritual parody of the poem by John Dryden set by Henry Purcell in his opera *King Arthur*, 1691:

> Fairest Isle, all isles Excelling
> Seat of Pleasures, and of Loves;
> Venus here will chuse her Dwelling,
> And forsake her Cyprian Groves. (Gealy 556/292)

John Wesley was apparently taken with his brother's parody of Dryden and its setting in Purcell's opera, and he set the hymn to Purcell's melody, altered as "Westminster," hymn 128, *in Select Hymns with Tunes Annext*, 1761. This setting is included by F. Hildebrandt and O. A. Beckerlegge on page 546 in their 1983 commentary on John Wesley's 1780 *Collection* and in *Our Hymnody*, pages 388-89.

Baker comments on the controversial line in stanza 2:5, "Take away our power of sinning":

> It was this line particularly which impelled John Wesley and others to omit the second verse from their hymn-books, since it implies an extreme view of Christian perfection—a subject on which Charles Wesley himself was very scathing in some of his later poems. The Rev. John Fletcher of Madeley suggested its alteration to 'Take away the love of sinning,' pertinently asking: 'Can God take away from us our *power of sinning* without taking away our power of free obedience?' (Baker 1962, 95)

Beginning in the eighteenth century and continuing to this day, changes have been made in other words and phrases and punctuation, some of which are included in our text. In stanza 1:1, changing "love" to "loves" has made for stylistic consistency but little more; in stanza 1:2, by substituting a comma for a semicolon at the end of the line and placing a comma after "heaven," John Wesley in his 1780 *Collection* changed this line from a declaration of faith into a prayer; in stanza 2:4, our 1935 hymnal changed "second rest" to "promised rest" (see comment on Christ's Second Coming, "Lo, he comes with clouds descending," pages 467-68); in stanza 3:2, John Wesley for his 1780 *Collection* changed "life" to "grace"; and in 4:2, "sinless" has been unconvincingly altered in countless hymnals, including our own, to "unspotted," "holy," and "spotless."

The hymn was first included in our hymnals in 1786. Its theme is that troublesome attribute of Wesley's theology of holiness—variously subtitled entire sanctification, perfecting grace, perfect love, or Christian perfection. In USA Methodism holiness has primarily been taught and practiced as either individualist or social, with the hymns of the social gospel reflecting the latter emphasis (see "Social Gospel Hymns," pages 30-33). With an appreciation of Wesley's emphasis on our wholistic response to the gospel, Geoffrey Wainwright writes that "positively formulated, perfection meant for Wesley the pure love of God and Neighbour." (Wainwright 1980, 461) In our hymnal the hymns of "Personal Holiness," **396-424**, and "Social Holiness," **225-450**, are placed within the general classification of "Sanctifying and Perfecting Grace."

Beecher

John Zundel, 1870

This lightweight tune, also called "Zundel" and "Love Divine," was composed for these words and included in the composer's *Christian Heart Songs*, 1870. "In the index Zundel attempted to indicate the right tempo for each tune by giving the number of seconds required for singing one stanza. The time indicated for this tune is sixty-five seconds." (Reynolds 1976, 138)

An alternate harmonization and vocal descant are found at 41-42 in *The United Methodist Hymnal Music Supplement*. The alternate tune HYFRYDOL is a more appropriate setting.

Low in the grave he lay (322)

See "Up from the grave he arose," page 672.

Magnificat (199)

See "Canticle of Mary," pages 257-58.

Majesty, worship his majesty (176)

Words and music: Jack W. Hayford, 1981

Gordon L. Borror has provided information on this hymn in *The Worshiping Church*, Worship Leaders' Edition:

Author Jack Hayford says that in 1977 while he was traveling in Great Britain he developed special interest in the actions and symbols of the royal family, relating them to Christ and his kingdom. We need to cultivate a sense of the *majestic* presence of God. He is a close friend, by his grace; but he is also the majestic, holy, awesome God of the universe and we need constant reminding not to take His royal presence lightly. In this short song we are called to recognize His majesty and then ascribe the glory due His name. (Hustad 1991, hymn 99)

The hymn was first included in *The Hymnal for Worship and Celebration*, 1986.

Majesty

Eugene Thomas, 1981

Although it was known to only a few of the Hymnal Revision Committee, the reported wide acceptance and use of this chorus in our churches commended its inclusion in our hymnal, thus attesting to the committee's cultural isolation as well as its flexibility and pastoral concern.

Make a joyful noise unto the Lord (74)

See "Canticle of thanksgiving," pages 264-65.

Make me a captive, Lord (421)

George Matheson, 1890

The hymn first appeared under the title "Christian Freedom" with the heading "'Paul, the prisoner of Jesus Christ,' Ephesians 3:1," page 172 in the author's *Sacred Songs*, 1890. (Gealy 556/295) The paradox—to be a prisoner of Christ is to attain perfect freedom—is expressed eleven times in the text, including "captive-free," "sink-stand," "my own-thine." The hymn entered our hymnals in 1935 and is included without change.

Diademata

George J. Elvey, 1868

This tune is one of the most sturdy SMD tunes in the repertory and was composed for and first appeared at 318 in *Hymns Ancient and Modern*, 1868 Appendix. It entered our hymnals in 1878 and has been reprinted without change.

There are instrumental and vocal descants and alternate harmonizations at 86-91 in *The United Methodist Hymnal Music Supplement*.

Maker, in whom we live (88)

Charles Wesley, 1747

This hymn first appeared under the title "To the Trinity" in *Hymns for those that seek and those that have Redemption in the Blood of Jesus Christ*, 1747. Charles Wesley is apparently among the first to exploit the trinitarian form; the first three stanzas are devoted to a person of the Trinity with the final stanza in praise to the undivided Trinity. Wesley also published two collections of hymns to the Trinity in 1746 and 1767.

Craig B. Gallaway has provided this commentary:

> The distribution of address in the first three stanzas sketches the panorama of trinitarian history—grounded in creation (Acts 17:28 and Lk. 2:14), centered in Christ (Rev. 7:10), carried forward by the Spirit (Tit. 3:5)—rising finally to the communal adoration of stanza 4. (Sanchez 1988, 47)

The hymn entered our hymnals in 1821 in eight SM stanzas. It was omitted from the 1905 and 1935 editions and restored in our 1966 hymnal in a four-stanza hymn comprised of the first quatrain of each of the original eight-line stanzas. The original first line was "Father, in whom we live," and 4:2 was "Let all the sons of men."

Diademata

See above "Make me a captive, Lord," page 478.

Man of Sorrows! what a name (165)

See "Hallelujah! What a Savior," pages 385-86.

Mantos y palmas (279)
(Filled with excitement)

Rubén Ruíz Avila, 1972
trans. by Gertrude C. Suppe, 1979, 1987 (Matt. 21:8-9)

This Palm/Passion Sunday hymn is based on the account of Jesus' entry into Jerusalem in Matthew 21:8-9, with parallels in Mark 11:8-10, Luke 19:36-38, and John 12:12-13. Two stanzas and the refrain were composed ca. 1972. Variants of the second stanza and other stanzas have appeared since its publication in *Canciones de Fe y Compromiso*, 1978, arranged and published by Alvin Schutmaat, director of the Christian Performing Arts Association, Centro Christian Internacional par lós Artes. The author has commented that the song was composed for the choir of the United Methodist Church in Covington, Virginia, where the author and his two sons were members for a period of time. (Correspondence with Carlton R. Young, September 1992)

The first and presumed only composition by Avila, the hymn was acclaimed at the Festival Internacional de Coros Evangélicos (International Festival of Evangelical Choirs), Gante Methodist Church, Mexico City, 1980.

In 1979 Gertrude C. Suppe completed the translation for the Celebremos project (see "Hispanic Hymns," page 42). It was first included as "Mantles and branches," at 900 in *Supplement to the Book of Hymns*, 1982. For our hymnal the translator made slight changes in her text to accommodate a more literal rendering of the Spanish.

Hosanna

Rubén Ruíz Avila, 1972; arr. by Alvin Schutmaat, 1978

The transcription of the melody was made by Javier Arjona for Alvin Schutmaat who arranged it for *Canciones de Fe y Compromiso*, 1978. (Pauline Schutmaat correspondence 1988)

When the hymn is used as a processional, the choir may enter singing the "Hosannas" accompanied by rhythm instruments, with a soloist or soli voices singing the stanzas in either Spanish or English. The congregation may join on the refrain after the first stanza.

Myron Braun has commented:

We are told that Rubén Ruíz uses this hymn at a stately, dignified pace, in the manner of a solemn procession. The combined effect of words and tune is delightfully attractive, yet with just a bit of the feeling of gravity that hovers over the Palm Sunday procession. (Braun 1982, 33-34)

Many and great, O God (148)
Wakantanka taku nitawa

Joseph R. Renville, ca. 1846
para. by Philip Frazier, 1929 (Ps. 104:24-30; Jer. 10:12-13)

This hymn was composed in the Dakota language between 1835-42 by Joseph R. Renville, a French-Dakota fur trader and Bible translator, at Lac qui Parle Indian Mission, now in western Minnesota. The original seven-stanza hymn is a paraphrase of the creation hymn in Jeremiah 10:12-13, which begins, "It is he who made the earth by his power, who established the world by his wisdom." It was first included on page 98 in the words-only edition of *Dakota Odowan* (*Dakota Hymnal*), 1842, a songbook that served Congregational and Presbyterian Indian churches in the Dakotas, Nebraska, and Montana. The collection was a joint product of missionaries: a minister, Stephen R. Riggs; John P. Williamson, a physician; and composer James R. Murray.

In 1929 Philip Frazier was requested to paraphrase the hymn for the 1930 national meeting of the YWCA "because for years this hymn had appeared in camp songbooks and young people had been singing the Indian words, not knowing what they meant, but they loved to sing it for the lovely native tune." (Susie M. Frazier correspondence ca. 1969, Gealy 556/296) Frazier's paraphrase reflects Psalms 104:24 and 8:3-4; it was published in a number of songbooks including *Hymns of the Rural Spirit*, 1947.

The religious traditions of the Dakota Native Americans were described in *Lift Every Voice*, a publication of the Methodist Church:

> The Dakotas had always believed in a Power greater than themselves, manifesting itself in the universe. They referred to it as Wakan, sought to understand it and worshipped it through its various revelations. A flowing river, a growing plant, the sun which warmed them, even fire, were kindly manifestations. Thunder they feared and sought to appease, but it meant one aspect of Wakan to them. The great social idea of giving was also deeply a part of Dakota culture; in fact, they made almost a fetish of giving. (*Lift Every Voice*, 1953)

Many times the hymn is sung in the original language by the Dakota people for general worship as well as for births, communion services, funerals, and burials. According to Sidney Byrd, a Dakota Presbyterian pastor of Santa Fe, New Mexico, "the hymn was sung at the hanging [during the Dakota uprising] of the 38 Dakota men at Mankato on December 26, 1862." The hymn's appearance in our 1966 hymnal marked its first inclusion in a major hymnal.

Lois C. Willand's unpublished research has been used with permission for much of this information.

Lacquiparle

Native American Melody; harm. by Richard Proulx, 1986
The tune name in French means "lake that speaks." The hymn was set to this traditional Native American melody by Renville. The tune was harmonized by James R. Murray (see "Away in a manger," pages 223-25) and first appeared with the words at 141 in the 1879 edition of *Dakota Odowan*. Our harmonization is from *Worship III*, 1986.

Many gifts, one Spirit (114)

Words and music: Al Carmines, 1973
This song was commissioned for the 1973 Assembly of the Women's Division, General Board of Global Ministries, The United Methodist Church, and is widely sung in their meetings. It is one of the first texts to express the unity, creativity, and witness of the Spirit within our diversity of human gifts and conditions in completely inclusive language with respect to both people and deity. It was first included in *Go to Galilee: Songs by Al Carmines*, 1974.

The Hymnal Revision Committee in its consideration of this favorite song of women's groups tended to pair it with "Rise up, O men of God" **(576)**, a hymn sung at the national convocations of United Methodist Men, but seldom elsewhere.

Katherine

The tune is named for the composer's mother, Katherine Elizabeth Graham Carmines. The accompaniment, presumably the composer's, accommodates the tune in the stanzas. The refrain, however, suffers from a crude unimaginative bass line and occasional minor second collisions of the right hand and melody. Improvements might have been suggested to the composer by members of the tunes committee, but since the members were fundamentally opposed to the hymn's inclusion, they stipulated that it be included without change. Chord symbols are provided for those who can improvise and wish to add guitar and drums.

Marching to Zion (733)

See "Come, we that love the Lord," pages 302-03.

Marvelous grace of our loving Lord (365)

See "Grace greater than our sin," pages 378-79.

May God grant that I may speak (112)

See "Canticle of wisdom," page 267.

Mil voices para celebrar (59)
O for a thousand tongues to sing

Charles Wesley, 1739
trans. by Federico J. Pagura; sts. 1, 3, 5, 1962; sts. 2, 4, 6, 7, 1987
Stanzas 1, 3, and 5 first appeared in *Cántico Nuevo*, 1962, and stanzas 2, 4, 6, and 7 were commissioned for our hymnal.

Azmon

See "Jesus, thine all-victorious love," page 449.

Mine eyes have seen the glory (717)

See "The Battle Hymn of the Republic," pages 621-24.

More love to thee, O Christ (453)

Elizabeth P. Prentiss, 1869
This hymn was composed as a prayer ca. 1856 during a time of physical and mental distress. The poet kept it to herself for many years. It was published in a leaflet in 1869 and was first included in a hymnal in *Songs of Devotion for Christian Associations*, 1870. (McCutchan 1942, 382) The hymn entered our hymnals in 1878.

The essence of the hymn is found in stanza 3 with the poet's affirmation that God's sweet messengers sing within her sorrow, grief, and pain.

More love to thee

William H. Doane, 1870

The tune was composed for this text and first appeared in the composer's *Songs of Devotion for Christian Associations*, 1870.

Morning glory, starlit sky (194)

W. H. Vanstone, 1980 (1 Cor. 13:7)

Canon Vanstone included this poem on the paradoxical nature of the love of God revealed in Christ's passion and death at the conclusion of his book *The Risk of Love*, 1980.

Ray Glover has commented on the hymn:

> [It] opens with a listing of some of God's gifts open to and easily grasped by our intellect and senses, but almost immediately the poet presents, in an almost shocking starkness, the hidden nature of love—"love's agony, love's endeavor, love's expense" . . . reaching a climax in the final two [stanzas] which recount the ultimate act of love in which God gave his Son "whose arms of love, aching, spent, the world sustain." (Glover 1987, 106)

J. W. Shore of Rochdale, Lancashire, the owner of the text, has written:

> These words [were] passed on to me by Canon Vanstone in recognition of voluntary services rendered as choirmaster for 27 years at the local parish church. (Correspondence with Carlton R. Young, 1988)

Monkland

Attr. to John Antes, ca. 1800
arr. by John Lees, 1824; harm. attr. to John B. Wilkes, 1861

John Wilson in "The Tune 'Monkland' and John Antes," *Bulletin: Hymn Society of Great Britian and Ireland*, 1987, indicates that the tune was included with a figured bass in a manuscript book, *A Collection of Hymn Tunes Chiefly Composed for Private Amusement by John Antes*, ca. 1800. John Lees probably harmonized the tune for *Hymn Tunes of the Church of the Brethren*, 1824, and his harmonization was included with little change in *Hymns, Ancient and Modern*, 1861. (Watson and Trickett 1988, 52) The tune entered our hymnals in 1878 in the latter version and has been included in succeeding hymnals without change. Monkland is a village in Herefordshire, England. The harmonizer and arranger are discussed by Bernard S. Massey in "John Wilkes and Monkland," *Bulletin: Hymn Society of Great Britain and Ireland*, 1987.

There are vocal and organ descants at 238-39 in *The United Methodist Hymnal Music Supplement*. CANTERBURY **(355)** may be used as an alternate tune to reflect the passion of Christ, the focus of the hymn.

Morning has broken (145)

Eleanor Farjeon, 1931 (Lam. 3:22-23)

The poet was requested by Percy Dearmer, editor of *Enlarged Songs of Praise*, 1931, to write a short dactylic hymn on the theme of thanksgiving to the tune BUNESSAN. (Dearmer and Jacob 1933, 16) Apparently its first inclusion in a major USA denominational hymnal was in the Presbyterian *Hymnbook*, 1955. The hymn's popularity as a pop song in the 1970's has brought about its wide use and has led to its inclusion in other major hymnals.

The text effectively links and expresses the creation stories in Genesis 1 and John 1, and reminds us that each new day is a gift from God. In stanza 3:7 God's graceful acts of "re-creation" are not divine recreational activity.

Bunessan

Trad. Gaelic melody; harm. by Carlton R. Young, 1988

This melody was first printed in Lachlan MacBean's *Songs and Hymns of the Gael*, 1888, and appeared with the nativity text "Child in the manger'" in the Irish *Church Hymnal*, 1919. In the 1970's the hymn was recorded by the pop singer Cat Stevens and hit the top 40 charts. It has been included in most recent hymnals since that time without Stevens's melodic alterations and vocal slides.

Our harmonization reflects the spirit of Farjeon's hymn of praise and is an alternative to David Evans's gentle rocking lullaby in *The Church Hymnary*, 1927 rev. ed. Other harmonizations are by Martin Shaw in *Enlarged Songs of Praise*, 1931, and John Wilson, with an SA descant, in *Hymns and Psalms*, 1983. There are two descants at 50-51 in *The United Methodist Hymnal Music Supplement*.

Mountains are all aglow (86)
San-ma-da bu-ri-tan-da

Ok-In Lim, 1967; trans. by Hae Jong Kim, 1988
(Ps. 65:9-13; Acts 14:17)

The hymn was composed for the 1967 *Korean Hymnal*. Paul Park, a leader of the Methodist Church in Korea and member of the committees that produced the 1967 and 1989 collections, has commented that the former collection that was published "to meet the modern trend of the time" caused much reaction in the Church that led to the publishing of the *United Korean Hymnal*, 1989. (Correspondence with Carlton R. Young, April, 1992)

The hymn was translated in 1980 by Hae Jong Kim under the title "Harvest Thanksgiving" for *Hymns from the Four Winds*, 1983. In 1988 Kim prepared a new translation for our hymnal, and it was versified by Hope Omachi-Kawashima, who was a member of the Hymnal Revision Committee.

The hymn may be preceded by the unison or individual reading of verses 9-13 of the thanksgiving Psalm 65 **(789-90)**.

Kahm-sah

Jae Hoon Park, 1967

The tune name means thanksgiving. It first appeared in *The Korean Hymnal*, 1967. I-to Loh comments that the tune's "triple rhythm and syncopations ("is from our God") are typical of Korean folk styles, and Koreans find special excitement in singing it. Add drum (*changgo*) accompaniment to enliven the spirit of praise." (Sanchez 1989, 46)

Move me (471)

Words and music: Richard Alan Henderson, 1978

This congregational chorus is excerpted from an elaborate setting for choir, soloist, and keyboard at 185 in *Songs of Zion*, 1981.

Move me

This chorus was adapted for our hymnal by William Farley Smith.

Musical Responses for Baptismal Covenant (53-54)

See "Service Music," pages 583-84.

Musical Settings for Word and Table I, II, III (17, 25); IV (28-31)

See "Service Music," pages 589-91.

Must Jesus bear the cross alone (424)

Thomas Shepherd and others, 1693

Fred D. Gealy in *Companion to the Hymnal*, 1970, was the first to provide complete research on this hymn.

The text probably stems from three sources. Stanza 1 is from an altered form of a quatrain which originally appeared in Shepherd's *Penitential Cries*, dated 1693 by John Julian. Its original form was:

> Shall Simon bear the cross alone,
>   And other saints be free?
> Each saint of thine shall find his own
>   And there is one for me.
>
> (Gealy, Lovelace, Young 1970, 287-88)

Our st. 2, according to Julian, is first found in a missionary collection published in Norwich, England, c. 1810, author unknown. However, both our sts. 2 and 3 were taken from *The Oberlin Social and Sabbath School Hymn Book*, compiled by George N. Allen, variously dated 1844 and 1849. [See Gealy 556/304.] The edition available to us is dated 1846. (Gealy, Lovelace, Young 1970, 288)

The hymn entered our hymnals in 1878 in three stanzas from H. W. Beecher, *Plymouth Collection of Hymns*, 1855. It has been retained without alteration.

Maitland

George N. Allen, 1844

Composed for the text, the tune first appeared in the composer's *Oberlin Social and Sabbath School Hymn Book*, 1844-1849. Thomas A. Dorsey's tune for "Precious Lord, take my hand" **(474)** is the same as Allen's except for slight changes in measures 5 and 6.

My country, tis of thee (697)

See "America," pages 208-09.

My faith looks up to thee (452)

Ray Palmer, 1830

The author's account of the writing of this hymn is found in the appendix to *The Poetical Works of Ray Palmer*, 1876. (Gealy 556/306) In it the author states that the hymn's final line, especially "a ransomed soul," summarizes the whole work of redemption and salvation of God in Christ.

The hymn was composed in six stanzas in September 1830 in New York while the author was teaching at a private women's school prior to returning to Yale to complete his preordination studies. Lowell Mason met the poet in Boston, set the hymn to the tune OLIVET in a matter of a few days, and included it in *Spiritual Songs for Social Worship*. (Gealy 556/306) The collection is variously dated 1831, 1832, and 1833, perhaps owing to the different dates of the copyright notices and the prefaces. The Dictionary of American Hymnology Project traces it to Lowell Mason's *Manual of Christian Psalmody*, 1832.

The hymn entered our hymnals in four stanzas in 1849 and thereafter has been included unaltered.

Olivet

Lowell Mason, 1831
The tune was composed for SAB voices in G major. (Gealy 556/306) Various attempts have been made to displace Mason's simple period piece of choir music that matches the simplicity and directness of the the poet's petition for grace and support with another more sophisticated choral setting that relieves the presumed monotonous bass line, and fills in interesting alto and tenor parts. None is more graceful than Ralph Vaughan Williams's(?) setting at 58 in the appendix to *The English Hymnal*, 1906.

My God, I love thee (470)
O Deus, ego amo te

Latin, 17th cent.; trans. by Edward Caswall, 1849
In this hymn we examine our motives for loving God. Its origins have been traced by John Julian to an anonymous seventeenth-century Spanish sonnet at one time attributed to St. Francis Xavier, which begins "No me mueue, mi Dios, para quererte." The full text may be found in Ellinwood (1956, 282). Both Ellinwood and Milgate 1985, 70-71, have significantly added to the information about the hymn as it was translated into Latin, German, and English.

Caswall's translation under the title "Hymn of St. Francis Xavier" was made for his *Lyra Catholica*, 1849, and is from a Latin version of the text in *Coeleste Palmetum*, 1669. (Milgate 1985, 70)

The hymn entered our hymnals in 1905 with stanzas 1, 2, 4, 5, and 6 from the version of Caswall's text in *Hymns Ancient and Modern*, 1861. In stanza 1:4, "Must burn eternally" was changed to "I must forever die." The omitted stanza follows:

> And griefs and torments numberless,
>> And sweat of agony;
> Yea, death itself; and all for me
>> Who was Thine enemy.

The hymn was dropped from our 1935 hymnal. Its restoration was in part because of the lobbying by Casa View United Methodist Church, Dallas, Texas, Wil Bailey, pastor, where in the 1960's the hymn had become a favorite having been introduced from the 1935 hymnal by Fred D. Gealy.

Winchester Old

See "Come, Holy Ghost, our hearts inspire," page 290.

My hope is built (368)

Edward Mote, 1834

Robert G. McCutchan has provided this information about the hymn:

This "grand hymn of faith" in six stanzas of four lines each, with a refrain, in its original form beginning "Nor earth, nor hell, my soul can move" entitled "Jesus, my All in All" was written by Edward Mote probably in 1834. His story of the writing and first publication of it appeared in an issue of *The Gospel Magazine*, London: "One morning it came into my mind as I went to labour, to write an hymn on the 'Gracious Experience of a Christian.' As I went up to Holborn I had the chorus,

> On Christ the solid Rock I stand,
> All other ground is sinking sand.

In the day I had four first verses [*sic*] complete, and wrote them off. . . . On the Sabbath following . . . by the fireside [I] composed the last two verses. . . . Brother Rees of Crown Street, Soho, brought out an edition of hymns (1836) and this hymn was in it." (McCutchan 1942, 283)

In 1836 the hymn also appeared under the title "The Immutable Basis of a Sinner's Hope" in Mote's *Hymns of Praise, A New Selection of Gospel Hymns*, 1836. (Gealy 556/308) It entered our hymnals in 1878 with three altered stanzas from the latter version set to "Evanston" in 88. 88. 88. In the 1905 hymnal a fourth stanza was added, and the hymn was set to Bradbury's tune, which repeats the final line of the refrain.

A critical review of the original text reveals it as characteristic nineteenth-century evangelical doggerel (see page 148 in William J. Reynolds's *Companion to the Baptist Hymnal*, 1976). Nevertheless, its compelling topic—the parable about the security of building a house on rock, as opposed to sand (Matthew 7:24-27)—and subsequent redaction and setting to a simple, repetitious, foot-stomping tune have merged to form a hymn of faith that over the generations has proved useful and comforting to many in their daily spiritual journey.

The solid rock

William B. Bradbury, 1863

The tune was composed for this text and first appeared in the composer's *Devotional Hymn and Tune Book*, 1864. McCutchan cites this collection as the only new Baptist hymnal to be printed in the USA during the Civil War. (McCutchan 1942, 284)

My Jesus, I love thee (172)

William R. Featherstone, 1864
This hymn of dedication to and praise of Jesus Christ was written possibly at the conversion of the author sometime between 1858 and its first appearance in *The London Hymn Book*, 1864. It entered our hymnals in 1901 in four stanzas including the usually omitted stanza:

> I will love Thee in life, I will love Thee in death,
> And praise Thee as long as Thou lendest me breath;
> And say when the deathdew lies cold on my brow,
> If ever I loved Thee, my Jesus, 'tis now.

"Lord Jesus" has been replaced by the original words "My Jesus."

Gordon

Adoniram J. Gordon, 1876
According to William J. Reynolds, "The text had appeared in at least eight collections before its first appearance with Gordon's tune . . . [composed by the co-compiler for] the 1876 edition of *The Service of Song for Baptist Churches*." (Reynolds 1976, 149)

My Lord, what a morning (719)

African American spiritual
adapt. and arr. by William Farley Smith (1 Cor. 15:51-52; Rev. 6:12-17)
This slave song of hope about the Second Coming of Christ, the resurrection of the dead, and the coming of the Day of the Lord may be derived from Isaac Watts's "When I can read my title clear," a selection in Richard Allen's 1801 hymnal, *A Collection of Hymns and Spiritual Songs.* (Southern 1971, 218) Its apocalyptic symbols and metaphors come from Paul's letter to the Corinthians,

> Listen, I will tell you a mystery! We shall not all die, but we will all be changed, in a moment, in the twinkling of an eye, at the last trumpet. For the trumpet will sound, and the dead will be raised imperishable, and we will be changed. (1 Corinthians 15:51-52),

and from Revelation 6:12-17, when at the opening of the fifth and sixth seals there will occur an earthquake, the sun will become black, the moon will appear as blood, and the stars will fall. These events "represent social upheavals and divine judgment on the Day of the Lord (Isa. 34:4; Joel 2:30-31; Amos 8:9) [when] . . . all classes of society seek to escape from God (Isa. 2:10)." (Metzger and Murphy 1991, 371 NT)

This spiritual, as others, may convey a double meaning depending on how the fifth word of the text is spelled. William Farley Smith has traced the confusion to the conflicting spellings used by the early compilers of spirituals, T. P. Fenner in 1874 and Theo. F. Seward in 1882. (Sanchez 1989, 240)

If the word is spelled "morning," it may mean the dawning of a new day of righteousness and liberty, the Day of the Lord, "the 'great gettin' up morning,' in which Christ would return to earth . . . an apocalyptic cosmic expectation which would accompany the ending of this present age just preceding the sound of the first trumpet (see 1 Thessalonians 4:16)." (McClain 1990, 115)

If it is spelled "mourning" as it is in *Songs of Zion*, 1981, and at number 79 in "Jubilee Songs," a supplement with 139 selections compiled by F. J. Loudin for *The Story of the Jubilee Singers*, 1896, the slave poet was probably singing about a day of mourning and judgment when God "will turn [the wicked's] feasts into mourning, and all [their] songs into lamentation. . . . I will make it like the mourning for an only son, and the end of it like a bitter day." (Amos 8:10) William Farley Smith comments that "slave-poets viewed judgment as a happy event for the survivors—the righteous." (Sanchez 1989, 240)

Burleigh

William Farley Smith comments that he named the tune for Harry T. Burleigh, (see comment on McKee, page 430) who "adopted Seward's spelling for his arrangement of this text." (Sanchez 1989, 240) There is an alternate setting in call and response style at 145 in *Songs of Zion*, 1981.

My Master, see, the time has come (226)

Luke 2:29-32

This metrical paraphrase of Simeon's Song is from *The Psalms: A New Translation*, 1980. It is appropriate for services of evening praise and prayer. See "Canticle of Simeon," pages 264-65.

Morning song

Sixteen Tune Settings, 1812
harm. by Charles H. Webb, 1988

Marion J. Hatchett has traced this tune to John Logan's *Sixteen Tune Settings*, 1812, where it is named "Consolation" and printed in a four-part setting. (Glover 1993) The next year it was included in Wyeth's *Repository of Sacred Music, Part Second* in a three-part setting without the alto. The tune was included in numerous nineteenth century collections and is one of a very few early USA melodies to be included in recent British hymnals. The harmonization was made for our hymnal. There is an arrangement for Orff instruments and flute, and a vocal descant at 241-42 in *The United Methodist Hymnal Music Supplement*.

My prayer rises to heaven (498)
Ca Khuc Tram Huong

Dao Kim

This prayer in praise of God's power and majesty is the first hymn from Vietnam to enter a USA denominational hymnal. The opening line is a paraphrase of Psalm 141:2, "Let my prayer be counted as incense before you"—"My prayer rises . . . as the smoke ascends when the precious incense burns." Like the night bird singing at the dawning of the day, the prayer becomes a morning song of praise to the Lord God, petitioning for protection from harm's way in this new day and remembering the Lord's love and justice.

Several paraphrases from the psalms are included: "so I raise my hands high in prayer"— "Lift up your hands to the holy place, and bless the Lord," Psalm 134:2; and "How I wish I could live with you for the rest of my life"—"I shall dwell in the house of the Lord my whole life long," Psalm 23:6c.

Vietnam

Dao Kim; arr. by Margret S. Meier

The melody should be supported by the keyboard's steady half-note chords. Each stanza may be sung by a soloist or soli voices with the congregation responding on the refrain.

My soul gives glory to my God (198)

Miriam Therese Winter, 1987 (Luke 1:46b-55)

This metrical paraphrase of the "Canticle of Mary," see pages 257-58, was first included in the author's *God with Us, Resources for Prayer and Praise*, 1979. It was revised using fully inclusive forms of address and descriptions of people and deity for *Woman Prayer, Woman Song*, 1987.

Morning Song

See above "My Master, see, the time has come," page 490.

My tribute (99)
To God be the Glory

Words and music: Andraé Crouch, 1971

This refrain may be sung by the congregation as a response to the stanzas performed by a soloist, as a prayer or praise chorus, an introit, or an offertory response. The full hymn is included at 153 in *The Baptist Hymnal*, 1991.

My tribute

The gospel hymn was first recorded in *Singin' a New Song*, 1971, and has been widely performed by the composer in concerts and praise gatherings. William Farley Smith has commented that the song "usually is sung very slow, the singer holding the right hand high, index finger pointed up, and swaying in a left to right 'praising' motion on beats 1 and 3." (Sanchez 1989, 51)

Near to the heart of God (472)

Words and music: Cleland B. McAfee, 1903

William J. Reynolds in *Companion to the Baptist Hymnal*, 1976, cites the author's daughter's account in her book *Near to the Heart of God* that the hymn was written in response to the death from diphtheria of the author's two infant nieces.

> The [Park College, Parkville, Missouri] family and town were stricken with grief. My father [who was the campus Presbyterian church preacher and choir director] often told us how he sat long and late thinking of what could be said in word and song on the coming Sunday. . . . So he wrote the little song. The choir learned it at the regular Saturday night rehearsal, and afterward they went to the Howard McAfee's home and sang it as they stood under the sky outside the darkened, quarantined house. It was sung again on Sunday morning at the communion service. . . . The hymn was first included in *The Choir Leader*, October, 1903. (Reynolds 1976, 220-21)

The stanzas affirm that near to God's heart is a meeting place with the Savior, a place of "quiet rest," "comfort," "full release," and "joy and peace." The refrain petitions Jesus to sustain us near to God's heart. The hymn entered our hymnals in *The Church Hymnal*, 1935.

McAfee

This was one of several hymns often requested by members of the former Evangelical United Brethren Church to be included in the hymnal (see "The Evangelical United Brethren Issue," pages 129-31). When this hymn along with five others, including "When in our music God is glorified" **(68),** was circulated to 85,000 pastors and lay leaders for evaluation, the overwhelming response affirmed the musical style of McAFEE as normative congregational music, and ENGELBERG, the tune for "When in our music God is glorified," as choir music. See discussion on page 160.

In the refrain the alto part may be sung up one octave as a descant.

Nearer, my God, to thee (528)

Sarah F. Adams, 1841 (Gen. 28:10-22)

The text was included at 85 in William J. Fox's *Hymns and Anthems*, 1841. The first USA collection to include it was James F. Clarke, *The Disciples' Hymn Book*, 1844, selection 378, under the title "Nearer to God." (Gealy 556/311)

Erik Routley comments that the hymn is a meditation on the story of Jacob's ladder, a means and a metaphor for communication between God and humans.

> At Bethel when Jacob had his dream about the ladder going up to heaven from earth, all his life at once took shape. He was enabled to see more clearly than he had ever seen or was like to see again, the pattern of his life. He saw what he had taken on in assuming the birthright. He was exalted and frightened and humbled. . . . Jacob came "near to God" in that night. He was, for a brief space, a whole man, a sane man, a man who knew where God meant him to go, a man who could stand up straight and talk with his God. (Routley 1956, 166)

The hymn entered our hymnals in 1878, and since that time there has occurred only one alteration: in stanza 5:4, "upwards" was changed to "upward."

Bethany

Lowell Mason, 1856

The tune was written for the text and first appeared in *Sabbath Hymn and Tune Book*, 1859. Robert G. McCutchan suggests that it may have been suggested to Mason by the melody sung to "Oft in the stilly night." (McCutchan 1942, 381) The tune repeats line 6 of each stanza, thus altering the meter of the poem from 64. 64. 664 to 64. 64. 6664.

The account of the text of the hymn's being sung to this tune by the passengers and crew of the sinking British ship *Titanic* cannot be substantiated for several reasons. The tune was unlikely to have been played by English musicians in the ship's band since in Britain this text has never been associated with Mason's tune.

Niño lindo (222)
Child so lovely

Trad. Venezuelan carol; trans. by George Lockwood, 1987

This translation was made for our hymnal by George Lockwood who has commented:

[This carol] is an *Aguinaldo,* a song sung by carolers hoping to receive little treats or gifts called *aguinaldos.* The text represents the devotion inspired in a youngster viewing the Christ Child. (Sanchez 1989, 87)

A soloist or soli voices may sing the stanzas, and the congregation may join on the refrain. Add claves and maracas to double the alternating two eighth notes and triplets.

Caracas

Trad. Venezuelan melody; arr. by Vicente E. Sojo
This keyboard setting from *Aguinaldos Populares Venozolanos* reflects the harmonies and chord progressions in guitar performance practice. The tune is named after the city in Venezuela near the Caribbean coast.

Nobody knows the trouble I see (520)

African American spiritual
adapt. and arr. by William Farley Smith, 1986
The form of the spiritual is from "Nobody knows de trouble I've had," Ex. VII.21 in *Slave Songs of the United States,* ca. 1867, cited by Eileen Southern in *The Music of Black Americans.* The opening interval of the refrain is different from our version; nevertheless, the words are the same. In the first two stanzas the slave-poet rejoices:

> One morning I was a-walking down,
> O yes Lord!
> I saw some berries a-hanging down,
> O yes Lord!
>
> I pick de berry and I suck de juice,
> O yes, Lord!
> Just as sweet as the honey in de comb,
> O yes Lord!   (Southern 1971, 207)

The final two stanzas are as they appear in our hymnal.

William Farley Smith has commented that the first line reads "I see" rather than "I've seen" because the spiritual is addressed to the slaves' immediate future, rather than their past suffering, and the song may have originated in the fields as a "caution signal, alerting work gangs to cease inappropriate activities in view of approaching 'trouble'—an overseer or some other authority." (Sanchez 1989, 178) This plausible historic footnote does not restrict our singing about past sorrows and disappointments. The appeal of the spiritual is its poignant expression of the pain of everyday life experienced in past, present, and future.

Du Bois

The tune was named by William Farley Smith after W. E. B. Du Bois, 1863-1963, educator, editor, and sociologist, who was a chief chronicler and commentator on African Americans, their history and destiny. His studies and books include *The Souls of Black Folk*, 1903.

A quartet or SATB choir may sing the stanzas with the congregation joining on the refrain. There is a simpler harmonization at 170 in *Songs of Zion*, 1981.

Not so in haste, my heart (455)

Bradford Torrey, ca. 1875

This hymn first appeared in *The Boston Transcript*, ca. 1875, signed "B.T.," and at its inclusion in the *Pilgrim Hymnal*, 1904, it was incorrectly credited to W. Garrett Horder. In that hymnal's 1912 edition the poem's authorship was properly cited as Bradford Torrey. (McCutchan 1937, 348) The author employs the poetic device anadiplosis, "using words or ideas which end one stanza as the start of the next. [This hymn is] . . . a poor example because the device is overused to the point of annoyance." (Lovelace 1965, 94)

The hymn entered our hymnals in *The Methodist Hymnal*, 1935. It was dropped from our 1966 edition and is restored in this hymnal.

Dolomite chant

Austrian melody; harm. by Joseph T. Cooper, 1879

Robert G. McCutchan has traced this setting of an Austrian traditional melody to the 1877 revision of *The Hymnal Companion to the Book of Common Prayer*, 1858. (McCutchan 1941, 348) The Presbyterian *Hymnal*, 1933, credits the harmonization to Joseph T. Cooper, 1819-70. The melody's charming change from duple to triple rhythm is unique to our hymnals.

Nothing between (373)

Words and music: Charles Albert Tindley, ca. 1906

This is one of eight hymns, including "Stand by me" (**512**), written during a difficult period of Tindley's life when negotiations were underway for the purchase of the Westminster Presbyterian Church on Broad Street. These hymns "reflect Tindley's religious and philosophical beliefs, as well as some emotional joys and, in some instances, disappointments." (Jones 1982, 40).

William Farley Smith comments that "in this hymn of Christian perfection, Charles A. Tindley teaches us how to clear the path in order to make the soul and Savior one. Worldly ways must be renounced even if friends and the world may turn against you. . . . The hymn is especially appropriate . . . during the serving of Holy Communion." (Sanchez 1989, 132) The hymn is included as it appears at 6 in *New Songs of Paradise*, 1916, reprinted 1984.

Nothing between

Arr. by F. A. Clark

Horace Clarence Boyer has commented that this tune is "extremely well formed . . . [and] F. A. Clark's simple harmonies only add to the beauty of one of the most moving of Tindley's hymns." (Correspondence with Carlton R. Young, January 1992) There is an alternate harmonization by J. Edward Hoy at 21 in *Songs of Zion*, 1981.

Nothing but the blood of Jesus (362)

Words and music: Robert Lowry, 1876

This hymn on the sacrificial redeeming and pardoning blood of Jesus was near the top of the list, compiled by Riley B. Case on the most popular religious songs found in five widely used hymnals and songbooks other than the 1957 Evangelical United Brethren and 1966 Methodist hymnals. (See *"The United Methodist Hymnal*, 1989," page 160.)

The hymn first appeared under the heading "Without the shedding of blood there is no remission of sin" (Heb. 9:22) in William H. Doane's and the composer's *Gospel Music*, 1876. (Reynolds 1964, 225) It entered our hymnals in United Brethren Church's *Church Hymnal*, 1935.

Plainfield

The revision committee for the 1956 *Baptist Hymnal* named this tune after the city in New Jersey in which Robert Lowry served as pastor of Park Avenue Baptist Church and lived in retirement until his death. (Reynolds 1976, 239)

Now let us from this table rise (634)

Fred Kaan, 1964

This postcommunion hymn was composed for the Pilgrim Church, Plymouth, England, and, like other hymns composed for that worshipping community, addresses the author's concern for "making a good transition from worship to service, from celebration to action." (Kaan 1985, 74) "The words 'the sacrament of care' (verse 3, line 2) were used as the theme [becoming the theme song] of the 14th International Assembly of the World Federation of Diaconal Associations . . . Warwick University, Great Britain, in July 1983." (Kaan 1985, 90)

The hymn with this tune was introduced in the USA in *Ecumenical Praise*, 1977.

Deus tuorum militum

See "Bless thou the gifts," page 237.

Now, on land and sea descending (685)

Samuel Longfellow, 1859

This hymn was written in two 87. 87. D stanzas and was first included in the author's *Vespers*, 1859, a collection of hymns for the Second Unitarian Church, Brookline, Massachusetts, where the author was pastor. (Reynolds 1964, 134) The printing of the hymn with the refrain "Jubilate" and the reiterated fourth line of each stanza apparently came with the matching of the text to VESPER HYMN.

This favorite hymn for the opening of evening worship entered our hymnals in *The Methodist Hymnal*, 1935.

Vesper hymn

A Selection of Popular National Airs, 1818

Leonard Ellinwood has traced the source of this tune in *The Hymnal 1940 Companion*:

> [It] first appeared as a glee for four voices in *A Selection of Popular National Airs* . . ., 1818. There it was called *Russian Air*, and an asterisk points out that what is line three of the hymn-tune [*The Hymnal 1940* inverts lines 3 and 4] is added to the original Air by Sir John Stevenson. . . . The original words, by Thomas Moore [87. 87. 86], began: "Hark! the vesper hymn is stealing" [with the final line] . . . "Jubilate, Jubilate, Jubilate, Amen." (Ellinwood 1956, 131)

Stanzas 2 and 3 may be sung by the choir, or alternating male and female voices, with the entire group entering at "Jubilate," sung "you-bee-<u>lah</u>-teh," not "<u>Jew</u>-buh-<u>lah</u>-teh<u>ee</u>."

Now thank we all our God (102)
Nun danket alle Gott

Martin Rinkart, 1663
trans. by Catherine Winkworth, 1858 (Sir. 50:22-24)

The first two stanzas of Martin Rinkart's hymn are based on the doxology from Sirach:

> And now bless the God of all,
>   who everywhere works great wonders,

who fosters our growth from birth,
　　and deals with us according to his mercy.
May he give us gladness of heart,
　　and may there be peace in our days
　　in Israel, as in the days of old.
May he entrust to us his mercy,
　　and may he deliver us in our days! (Sirach 50:22-24)

The hymn was written as a two-stanza family table grace (*Tisch-Gebetlein*, a short table prayer) during the disastrous Thirty Years' War, 1618-48 (see "German Hymns," pages 7-8). It was probably included in the author's *Jesu Herz-Büchlein*, 1636, with a doxological third stanza. Since no copies of that edition have survived, the text is usually dated with that collection's 1663 printing. The earliest surviving texts are in Johann Crüger's *Praxis Pietatis Melica*, 1647. The English text is from the second series of Catherine Winkworth's *Lyra Germanica*, 1858. (Gealy, Lovelace, Young 1970, 298)

Often called the German Te Deum, the hymn is universally sung at local and national thanksgiving festivals. It entered our hymnals in 1881.

Nun danket

Johann Crüger, 1647; harm. by Felix Mendelssohn, 1840

The tune is apparently by Crüger and was first included in his *Praxis Pietatis Melica*, 1647. J. S. Bach evened out the rhythm of the tune in his magnificent setting for full orchestra and chorus in the third movement, "Chorale," in Cantata 79, *Gott, der Herr, ist Sonn und Schild* (*God, the Lord, is Sun and Shield*), 1725. The melody was altered by Mendelssohn for his six-part harmonization in *Lobgesang*, "Hymn of Praise," 1840; it was later reduced in British hymnals to four parts for congregational singing.

Erik Routley has commented on Mendelssohn's setting:

[He] deformed it by obscuring the imitation of the first phrase in the fifth: his raising of the fifth note of the fifth phrase to D (in G major) where the original has B was, one supposes, dictated by the new context he gave it in the *Hymn of Praise*, but it treated the composer's sense of structure rather cavalierly. (Routley 1981, 61)

There is a setting for brass and descants for organ and voice at 251-54 in *The United Methodist Hymnal Music Supplement*. The movement from J. S. Bach's Cantata 79, (see above) is available in several editions in reduction for organ, and organ, brass, and choir.

Now the green blade riseth (311)

J. M. C. Crum, 1928, alt.

This Easter hymn was written to the old French melody associated with the

Christmas carol "Noël nouvelet" and first appeared in *The Oxford Book of Carols,* 1928. It was first included in a USA hymnal in our 1966 edition.

Changes have been made for this hymnal in stanza 1:2, "in" to "in the"; 2:1, "whom men" to "who had"; 2:2, "never he would wake" to "he never would awake"; 3:2, "he that" to "Jesus who"; and 4:2, "thy touch" to "Jesus' touch."

French carol

Trad. French carol; harm. by Martin Shaw, 1928
This harmonization was made for *The Oxford Book of Carols,* 1928. A simpler harmonization may be found at 203 in *Hymns and Psalms,* 1983, and a setting for Orff instruments is at 136 in *The United Methodist Hymnal Music Supplement.*

The hymn may be used as a choral call to praise or as a processional with the choir singing the stanzas in unison accompanied by rhythm instruments, and the congregation and keyboard entering on the refrain.

Now the silence (619)

Jaroslav J. Vajda, 1968
This fourteen-line hymn without punctuation marks first appeared in *This Day,* May 1968. Since its inclusion in *Worship Supplement,* 1969, it has been included in numerous supplements and standard hymnals.

The author has provided this commentary:

> If there was one hymn text that proved a catalyst for my hymn writing, it was "Now the silence." . . . And Carl Schalk must be given the credit for recognizing the potential of this unusual text as a hymn. . . . In the nearly two decades since the text came to me while shaving, I have been discovering roots and hints in past experiences and Scriptural passages and stories. The opening line of one of . . . . [Pavol Országh Hviezdoslav's (1849-1921)] lyrics . . . "Wish me silence, wish me peace," surfaced 25 years later as "Now the silence, now the peace." And the reverse order of the Doxology/Benediction not only expressed the order in which I pictured the Trinity coming to us in worship, but also the order in which the Incarnation took place: the visitation [*sic*] of the Virgin Mary by the Holy Spirit, then the Son's epiphany as the incarnate Word, followed by the universal blessing that is bestowed upon all in whom this same process occurs. (Vajda 1987, 158)

Paul Richardson and Deborah Loftis provide contrasting reflections on the text in "An Interpretation: 'Now the Silence'" in the October 1986 volume of *The Hymn.*

Now

Carl F. Schalk, 1969

The author has made this interesting comment on the role of the composer:

Carl Schalk's collaboration with me on this hymn and others prompts an expression of appreciation to him and to all musicians, without whom's hymn texts, no matter how good, would die. (Vajda 1987, 158)

The hymn may be introduced by groups singing alternate phrases, for example male and female voices, or choir and congregation, with everyone joining on the final six measures. A performance suggestion at 250 in *The United Methodist Hymnal Music Supplement* is to add a handbell on the melody note each time the word "Now" is sung.

Nunc dimittis (225)

See "Canticle of Simeon," pages 263-64.

O beautiful for spacious skies (696)

See "America the beautiful," pages 209-10.

O Breath of life, come sweeping through us (543)

Bessie Porter Head, 1920 (Acts 2; John 20:22)

This prayer to the Holy Spirit to renew the church first appeared in a hymnal in five stanzas in the author's *Heavenly Places and Other Messages*, 1920. The hymn "became widely known from its being sung at the Keswick Convention, held annually (since 1875) in July at Keswick, Cumbria." (Milgate 1985, 137)

The fourth and fifth stanzas follow:

> O heart of Christ, once broken for us,
>   'Tis there we find our strength and rest,
> Our broken contrite hearts now solace,
>   And let Thy waiting Church be blest.
>
> Revive us, Lord! Is zeal abating
>   While harvest fields are vast and white?
> Revive us, Lord, the world is waiting,
>   Equip Thy church to spread the light.

Bishop Powell

David Ashley White, 1987

This tune was commissioned by the Hymnal Revision Committee. Charles H. Webb adapted the original harmonization for our hymnal. The composer's harmonization is found at 44 in *The United Methodist Hymnal Music Supplement*; it may be used as an alternate setting for unison voices. The composer named the tune for Chilton Powell, retired bishop of the Protestant Episcopal Church, who is noted for his support of music through his association with the Evergreen (Colorado) Liturgical Music Conference.

O Christ, the healer (265)

Fred Pratt Green, 1967

Bernard Braley has traced the writing of this five-stanza hymn on healing to the deliberations in 1967 of the committee compiling *Hymns and Songs*:

They had decided to include J. R. Darbyshire's well-known hymn:

> Life and health are in the name
> Of Jesus Christ our Lord.

But even this did not meet the whole need. It was felt there was a major sphere of healing (in which mental healing was the prior necessity) not covered by Darbyshire's writing. So Fred [overnight] produced a first draft. . . . . Brian Frost suggested the line [3:4] "Unconscious pride resists or shelves." . . . This was accepted, and Brian thinks that it is the only time the *unconscious* (in the Freudian sense) appears in a hymn. (Green 1982, 12)

This prayer for wholeness of body, mind, and spirit, a theme often occurring in Green's texts (see stanza 5), affirms the primacy of the worshipping community as the forum and agent for change. The hymn may be prefaced by the reading of the accounts of Jesus' healing ministry—for example, Matthew 15:31, the healing of the mute, maimed, lame, and the blind; and Mark 1:32-34, the casting out of demons.

The hymn was first included in *Hymns and Songs*, 1969. Most hymnals, including our own, have included two changes in the original text: in stanza 4:2, "diagnose" has been changed (and weakened) to "recognize," and 5:4 had euphoniously read "Shall reach, and shall enrich mankind."

Erhalt uns Herr

Geistliche Lieder (Klug), 1543; harm. by J. S. Bach, 1725

The tune was probably derived from the plainsong "Veni, Redemptor gentium," see "Saviour of the nations, come," page 575. Our form of this anonymous melody and the harmonization are from the closing chorale of J. S. Bach's Cantata 6 for the second Easter Festival, *Bleib bei uns, denn es will Abend werden* (*Stay with us, the evening approaches*), 1725. The tune in this form has been included in most British and USA hymnals since *The English Hymnal*, 1906. It is usually found without connecting eighth notes in Lutheran collections.

The name of the tune comes from Martin Luther's hymn "Erhalt' uns, Herr, bei deinem Wort" ("Lord, keep us steadfast in thy Word"). Luther included the text with this tune in Klug's 1543 collection under the inscription "A children's hymn, to be sung against the two arch-enemies of Christ and His holy Church, the Pope and the Turk."

O church of God, united (547)

Frederick B. Morley, 1953 (Acts 2:5-11)

This hymn on our unity in Christ was among nearly 500 hymns submitted for use at the Second Assembly of the World Council of Churches, meeting at Evanston, October 1954. It was first published in the July issue of *The Hymn* and in "Eleven Ecumenical Hymns," 1954. It was one of eleven hymns selected to be offered for use at the assembly. See also "Hope of the world," pages 403-04.

The text was first included in our 1957 hymnal.

Ellacombe

See "Hail to the Lord's anointed," page 385.

O come, all ye faithful (234)
Adeste, fideles

John F. Wade, ca. 1743
trans. by Frederick Oakeley, 1841, and others

One of the most widely sung Christmas hymns, the text may have originated among the "exiled Jacobite Roman Catholics of the 1740s." (Watson and Trickett 1988, 97) Its origins have been traced by Fred D. Gealy:

> Seven manuscripts containing the Latin hymn are known; they are dated 1743-61. All appear to have been written, signed, and dated by John Francis Wade, an Englishman who made his living by copying and selling plainchant and other music. . . . Dom John Stéphan in his extensive study of the manuscripts, *The Adeste Fideles: A Study on Its Origin and Development* [Buckfast Abbey], 1947 [excerpts in Gealy 556/323], concludes that the 1743 manuscript is the *first* and *original* version of the hymn, and that Wade composed the words and music sometime between 1740 and 1743. (Gealy, Lovelace, Young 1970, 302)

Our stanzas 1, 2, 3, and 6 were translated by Frederick Oakeley and first appeared at number 13 under the title "Let us go even unto Bethlehem, and see this thing which is come to pass" in F. H. Murray's *Hymnal for Use in the English Church*, 1852. (Gealy 556/323) Stanzas, 4 and 5 are by Abbé Etienne Jean

François Borderies who upon hearing the hymn wrote three additional stanzas. W. T. Brooke's translation of these appeared in *Altar Hymnal*, 1884.

Portions of all the English texts proved awkward to sing; for example, the first line of William Mercer's translation read "Ye faithful, approach ye, Joyfully triumphant." For the most part these places have been smoothed out by repeated singing. The hymn entered our hymnals in 1905 with Edward Caswall's translation. In 1935 three of Oakeley's stanzas replaced Caswall's. Most British and USA hymnals now use a version of the seven-stanza text from *The English Hymnal*, 1906.

In our hymnal the first stanza and the refrain may be sung concurrently in Latin and English. Stanzas 2, 4, 5, and 6 have been added for an extended processional. Stanza 6 is appropriate for Christmas Eve midnight services and Christmas Day.

Adeste fideles

John F. Wade, ca. 1743

The tune in triple meter is contained in the manuscript from Stonyhurst College, *Cantus Diversi pro Dominicis et Festis per Annum*, prepared by J. F. Wade, 1751. (See Gealy 556/322) While there are antecedents of the tune, scholars generally cite Wade as the composer. It was first arranged for soprano and bass in plainsong notation by Samuel Webbe in *Essay on the Church Plain Chant*, 1782, and also in his *Collection of Motets or Antiphons*, 1792. In the USA it appeared in Benjamin Carr's *Music Journal*, December 1800.

As Leonard Ellinwood notes (1956, 12), the refrain of this tune is an example of the British-USA fuging tune with voices singing in succession, "O come, let us adore him." The refrain was printed in this form in standard nineteenth-century tune books with a variation of voice entrances including *The Sacred Harp*, 1844; *Southern Harmony*, 1854 edition; and Rigdon M. McIntosh's *Hermon*, 1873, where the imitation is sung in sequence by soprano, alto, tenor, and finally by the bass in inversion.

The tune entered our hymnals in 1905 for this text and also for "How firm a foundation" (see page 409). The harmonization for the stanzas was an anonymous adaptation of the settings in *Hymns Ancient and Modern*, 1861, and *Hermon*, 1873, with the "fugue" entrances doubled in the upper and lower voices. Most settings, as our own, spoil the "fugue" by adding either a pedal point or filling in the harmonies, or both. For commentary on fuguing tunes and the singing school tradition, see "USA Hymnody," pages 18-19.

Descants, alternate harmonizations, and an interlude may be found at 7-13 in *The United Methodist Hymnal Music Supplement*.

For a full account of the origins and variants of this hymn and its tune, see Wesley Milgate, *Songs of the People of God*, 1985.

O come and dwell in me (388)

Charles Wesley, 1762 (2 Cor. 3:17; 5:17; Heb. 11:5)
This hymn is a construction by John Wesley that was included in the section "For Believers Groaning for Full Redemption" in his 1780 *Collection*. It was compiled from three single-stanza SMD hymns in Charles Wesley's two-volume *Short Hymns on Select Passages of the Holy Scriptures*, 1762. (Gealy 556/324) The volume and page number, and the scripture for each hymn, respectively, are: 2: 298, 2 Corinthians 3:17; 2:301, 2 Corinthians 5:17; 2:367, Hebrew 11:5. The volume, page number and scripture for each hymn, respectively, are 2:298, 2 Corinthians 3:17; 2:301, 2 Corinthians 5:17; 2:367, Hebrews 11:5.

The text entered our hymnals in A *Selection of Hymns*, 1810. While most of our hymnals have included versions of the text in single SM, the editors for the most part have dropped or softened references to original sin that John Wesley so carefully retained and integrated in his version. For example, we have never included the second quatrain in stanza 2 of his version:

> Th' original offence
>   Out of my soul [Charles: heart] erase;
> Enter thyself, and drive it hence,
>   And take up all the place.

Further, the second quatrain of John's stanza 1, the sinner's prayer to the Spirit for release from the bonds of original sin, was dropped in 1905:

> The seed of sin's disease
>   Spirit of health remove,
> Spirit of finished holiness,
>   Spirit of perfect love.

John Wesley's alterations were few but meaningful. In 1:1 he changed "Come then" to "O come." "Mind" was changed to "will" (our 3:3), "seek" to "ask" (4:1), and "thine" to "my" (4:4). (Gealy, Lovelace, Young 1970, 303) In our hymnal in stanza 4:4, "my" has been changed to "thine."

St. Michael

See "How can we sinners know," pages 407-08.

O come, let us sing unto the Lord (91)

See "Canticle of Praise to God," pages 259-60.

O come, O come, Emmanuel (211)
Veni, veni, Emmanuel

9th cent. Latin; trans. sts. 1, 3, 5ab, 6cd, 7ab, The Hymnal 1940
st. 2, Henry Sloane Coffin, 1916
sts. 4, 5cd, 6ab, 7cd, Laurence Hull Stookey, 1986

In monasteries as early as the ninth century during Advent vespers the eight days before Christmas, seven "O"s (the antiphons on the right facing page to our hymn) and an eighth "O Virgo virginum" ("Virgin of virgins") were sung before and after the Magnificat or "Canticle of Mary" **(199)**. Leonard Ellinwood in *The Hymnal 1940 Companion* writes that "it was customary for each of the principal officers of a monastery to 'keep his O' in turn, by singing his 'Great O' then providing a pittance or feast for the monks." (Ellinwood 1956, 2)

The metrical form of the antiphons was prepared as early as the twelfth century. A version printed in the appendix to *Psalteriolum Cantionum Catholicarum*, 1710, with refrain, was used by John Mason Neale for his translation in *Mediaeval Hymns and Sequences*, 1851. Above the hymn Neale writes, "This Advent Hymn is little more than a versification of some of the Christmas antiphons commonly called the O's." Neale's text was revised and included in Part 2 in his *Hymnal Noted*, (music edition) 1854 music edition, under the heading "The Greater Antiphons, At Even-Song During Eight Days Before Christmas." The balance of the text is set to other chant. At the top of the page the source (of the music?) is cited: "From a French Missal in the National Library, Lisbon." (Gealy 556/325)

The hymn entered our hymnals in 1935 in three stanzas: the first by Neale as altered in *Hymns Ancient and Modern*, 1861; and stanzas 2 and 3 as Henry Sloane Coffin's paraphrase of the first and sixth antiphons in *Hymns of the Kingdom of God*, 1923 edition. Our text is also a composite: stanzas 1, 2, 3, 5ab, 6cd, and 7ab were prepared for *The Hymnal 1940*; stanza 2 is by Henry Sloane Coffin; and Laurence Hull Stookey prepared stanzas 4, 5cd, 6ab, and 7cd for this hymnal.

Stookey has commented on his translation of stanza 6:

[Former] versions do not accurately reflect the Latin text that does not mention Advent but clearly alludes to Messiah as the "sun of justice." My alteration reflects this messianic title. (Correspondence with Carlton R. Young, September 1992)

The English text for the antiphons on the facing page first appeared in *Meditations on the O Antiphons*, 1962. The integrated format of the hymn and antiphons provides for the reading of the antiphon followed by a stanza of the hymn.

Veni Emmanuel

15th cent. French melody; arr. and harm. by Thomas Helmore, 1854

In *The Hymnal Noted*, 1854 edition, Thomas Helmore interlined Neale's first stanza and the refrain "Rejoice, Rejoice" with the chant melody we now call VENI EMMANUEL, credited by Helmore as from a French missal. Later in *Dictionary of Musical Terms*, 1881, he states that it was Neale who had copied the melody from French sources. It is not known who did the copying or the source of what was copied; nevertheless, it is now clear, thanks to the research of Mother Thomas More who found the manuscript in the National Library of Paris, that the tune comes from a fifteenth-century processional of the French Franciscan nuns where it is the setting for the funeral devotional hymn "Libera me," beginning "Bone Jesu dulcis cunctis." (*The Musical Times*, September 1966)

Helmore's block-chord Victorian tune setting in the 1854 edition of *The Hymnal Noted* was modified by the musical editors of both *Hymns Ancient and Modern*, 1861, and *The English Hymnal*, 1906; in the latter it was relegated to the appendix in the 1933 edition and replaced by a plainsong setting. Our version of the tune is from the Presbyterian *Hymnal*, 1933; it entered our hymnals in *The Methodist Hymnal*, 1935. Alternatives to these plodding, heavy harmonies are to sing alternate stanzas in unison without accompaniment, to use an accompaniment with lighter keyboard harmonizations (see 56 in *The Hymnal 1982*), or an arrangement for handbells at 342 in *The United Methodist Hymnal Music Supplement*.

O crucified Redeemer (425)

Timothy Rees, 1946

This hymn that images Christ's crucifixion in our bloody wars first appeared in the *Chronicle of the Community of the Resurrection* (no date). It later appeared in *Sermons and Hymns by Timothy Rees, Bishop of Llandaff*, 1946, headed "Calvary." (Watson and Trickett 1988, 259)

With one exception our version of the text follows *Hymns and Psalms*, 1983, which in turn had included alterations from *BBC Hymn Book*, 1951, and *100 Hymns for Today*, 1969. In 2:4, "our brothers' blood, O Lord" is changed to "our neighbor's blood, O Lord." The second stanza has been omitted:

> Wherever love is outraged,
>   wherever hope is killed,
> Where man still wrongs his brother man,
>   thy Passion is fulfilled.
> We see thy tortured body,
>   we see the wounds that bleed,
> Where brotherhood hangs crucified,
>   nailed to the cross of greed.

Llangloffan

Welsh folk melody; harm. by David Evans, 1927

Alan Luff has traced the sources of this tune:

The first appearance that can be traced of LLANGLOFFAN is in *Llwybrau Moliant* ("The Paths of Praise," Wrexham 1872). This was a collection for the use of Baptists edited by Lewis Jones of Treherbert. . . . A resemblance has been claimed between this tune and the English folk-song "The Jolly Miller of De." This may mean that it was transported from England into Wales in the 18th or 19th century. On the other hand it lives equally well in minor and major mode (in which it is sometimes called LLANFYLLIN), and this is a characteristic of the native Welsh folk melodies which perplexed those who wrote them down by the ambiguity of their tonality. (Luff 1990, 160)

Our harmonization is found without citation at 207 in *The English Hymnal*, 1933 edition, where it appears to be adapted from David Evans's setting in *The Church Hymnary*, 1927, rev. ed.

O day of God, draw nigh (730)

R. B. Y. Scott, 1937

This prayer for the coming of the day of righteousness and peace was written in 1937 for the Fellowship for a Christian Social Order and was first included in *Hymns for Worship*, 1939. (Ellinwood 1956, 314-15) In each stanza the poet succinctly expresses one aspect of the Day of the Lord: judgment, obedience, justice, peace, and light. Scriptural references for the Day of the Lord include Isaiah 2:1, 13:6-16, 22:5-8a; Joel 2:1d, 30-31; Amos 8:9; and Zephaniah 1:14-18 that begins "The great day of the Lord is near, near and hastening fast." Another hymn on the Day of the Lord is "My Lord, what a morning," pages 489-90.

The hymn entered our hymnals in 1966.

St. Michael

See "How can we sinners know," pages 407-08.

O day of peace that dimly shines (729)

Carl P. Daw, Jr., 1982 (Isa. 11:6-7)

The circumstance of the writing of this hymn on peace has been traced by Ray Glover:

[The hymn] was created in response to two special requests received by the Standing Commission on Church Music during its preparation of *The Hymnal 1982* . . . the General Convention's Joint Commission on Peace . . . and an appeal from many sources, request[ing] the inclusion of [Parry's] tune "Jerusalem. . . . To satisfy both of these appeals, the Commission called on the Reverend Dr. Carl P. Daw, Jr., a Consultant to the Text Committee . . . to compose a text on the theme of peace that could be sung to the popular Parry tune. (Glover 1987, 108)

As the poet read *Turning to Christ* by his teacher Urban T. Holmes III, his attention was drawn to Isaiah 11:6-8 and the heart of the hymn: the peaceable kingdom, paradise regained:

> The wolf shall live with the lamb,
>   the leopard shall lie down with the kid,
>   the calf and the lion and the fatling together,
>   and a little child shall lead them.
> The cow and the bear shall graze,
>   their young shall lie down together;
>   and the lion shall eat straw like the ox.
> The nursing child shall play over the hole of the asp
>   and the weaned child shall put its hand on the adder's den.
>   (Isaiah 11:6-8)

The poet writes that he first composed the second stanza as a paraphrase of the Isaiah passage. He continues:

This hymn deals with two aspects of peace: *pax*, an understanding of peace based on the cessation of conflict, and *shalom*, the condition of living abundantly in harmony and mutual goodwill. . . . Although this hymn affirms that peace is always God's gift, it also recognizes the importance of human responsibility in preparing an environment in which peace can flourish. (Daw 1990, 166)

Jerusalem

Charles Hubert Hastings Parry, 1916
harm. by Charles H. Webb, 1987

In either 1915 or 1916 the composer set to music William Blake's poem "And did those feet in ancient time" from the Preface to *Milton*. The suggestion was made by Poet Laureate Robert Bridges "to write suitable simple music to Blake's stanzas—music that an audience could take up and join in." (Dearmer and Jacob 1933, 241)

During the balance of World War I, in the interim between the world wars, and following World War II, the combination of Blake and Parry emerged as an unofficial British national anthem. It was often sung at public and patriotic events and was recently represented in the film score of *Chariots of Fire*.

Charles H. Webb's adaptation and reduction to four parts were made for this hymnal. The first inclusion of this tune in a major USA hymnal was in *The Hymnal 1982*, where the tune is printed one step lower at number 597. An arrangement for organ by G. R. Thalben-Ball is at 578 in *Hymns Ancient and Modern*, revised 1981.

Erik Routley has commented that Parry's tune "is of first-rate excellence which immediately and lastingly receives popular approbation." (Routley 1953, 312) Time will tell how it will wear with United Methodists.

O food to pilgrims given (631)
O Esca viatorum

Maintzisch Gesangbuch, 1661
trans. by John Athelstan Laurie Riley, 1906 (John 6:35-58)

The hymn's central message is from these words of Jesus as he proclaims that he is the bread of life:

I am the living bread that came down from heaven. Whoever eats of this bread will live forever; and the bread that I will give for the life of the world is my flesh. (John 6:51)

The Latin text was probably composed by an anonymous seventeenth-century German Jesuit priest. (Julian 1907, 828) J. A. L. Riley's translation was first included in *The English Hymnal*, 1906, and is our text with the exception that, following *The Hymnal 1982*, the opening couplet of Ray Palmer's translation of 1858 has been adapted and substituted for the original:

O food of men wayfaring,
The bread of angels sharing.

O Welt, ich muss dich lassen

German melody, 15th cent.; adapt. by Heinrich Isaac, 1539
harm. by J. S. Bach, 1729

This melody, also called "Innsbruck," was the setting by Heinrich Isaac for the secular poem "Innsbruck, ich muss dich lassen" in G. Forster, *Ein Augzug guter alter und neuer Teutschen Liedlein*, 1539. Our harmonization is by J. S. Bach from his *St. Matthew Passion*, 1729. There are other harmonizations by J. S. Bach. Johannes Brahms used the tune in an organ prelude that may serve as a hymn intonation, or it may be performed at the beginning or during a communion service designed on the hymn's theme.

The tune name is the first line of the funeral hymn "O world, I now must leave thee," attributed to Johann Hesse, 1490-1547, and set to this melody in the Eisleben *Gesangbuch*, 1598.

O for a heart to praise my God (417)

Charles Wesley, 1742 (Ps. 51:10)

The hymn first appeared in eight stanzas under the scripture heading "Make me a clean Heart, O GOD" in *Hymns and Sacred Poems*, 1742. John Wesley included the slightly altered text in eight stanzas in his 1780 *Collection* in the section "For Believers Groaning for Full Redemption," and it entered our 1786 hymnal in that form.

The commentary in *Companion to Hymns and Psalms* relates how the poet reading the psalm text

> Create in me a clean heart, O God
> and put a new and right spirit within me. (Psalm 51:10)

from a New Testament perspective has transformed its meaning:

> Now the heart is clean because it is set free from sin, and Christ is to reign in it and have his name written on it. . . . With its reference to the indwelling Christ . . . Ephesians 3:14-19 (one of Charles Wesley's most frequently-used passages) ["that Christ may dwell in your hearts through faith, as you are being rooted and grounded in love," verse 17] is an important source for this hymn. (Watson and Trickett 1988, 317)

The gift of the new heart is defined and elaborated in each stanza: 1, free from sin, a feeling heart; 2, a submissive, serving heart; 3, meek, contrite, humble heart; 4, a renewed heart, full of love, perfect, pure, good, a copy of Christ's; 5, a prayer for Christ to write a new name on the heart—the name is love.

Our hymnal includes stanzas 1-4 and 8 of the original. Stanza 1:4 originally read "So freely spilt for me!" and 3:4, "from him that" has been changed to "from Christ who."

Richmond

Thomas Haweis, 1792

The tune was composed for *Carmina Christo*, 1792. It was reduced by four measures to its present length by Samuel Webbe, Jr., in *A Collection of Psalm-Tunes for Four Voices*, 1808. (Watson and Trickett 1988, 424) The tune is named after Leigh Richmond, a friend of the composer and rector at Turvey, Bedfordshire.

RICHMOND entered our hymnals in 1966. The tune along with the text is seldom sung, though many think it easy to sing. There is a descant at 286 in *The United Methodist Hymnal Music Supplement*.

O for a thousand tongues to sing (57)

Charles Wesley, 1739

This is the most characteristic, widely known, and sung hymn of the Wesleyan movement, and with few exceptions it is the opening hymn of Wesleyan collections worldwide. The hymn was composed to celebrate the author's May 21, 1738, conversion, an event that preceded by two days that of his brother's. It first appeared in eighteen stanzas entitled "For the Anniversary Day of One's Conversion" at 120-23 in *Hymns and Sacred Poems*, 1740. The hymn entered our hymnals in 1786.

Our hymn begins with the opening line of stanza 7, "O for a thousand tongues to sing," which may have been prompted by a phrase of Wesley's spiritual mentor Peter Böhler: "Had I a thousand tongues, I would praise him with them all!" (John R. Tyson in "Charles Wesley and the German Hymns," *The Hymn,* reviews Charles's German language skills and his apparent use of German hymns.)

The six stanzas from our previous hymnals are included. In deference to perceived discriminatory language congregations may omit stanza 6. The hymn's concluding stanza is the original stanza 18. In our hymnal the first line is changed from "With me, your chief" to "In Christ, your head," a significant alteration since "chief" is Wesley's characterization of himself, with Paul in 1 Timothy 1:15, as "the chief of sinners." (KJV) See stanza 1:4 in "Depth of mercy!" (**355**) for another inclusion of Paul's description. See also Frank Baker's commentary on the hymn in our hymnal at page 56.

For this hymn in Spanish translation, see "Mil voces para celebrar," page 482. Seventeen of the original eighteen stanzas are included at **58**.

Glory to God, and praise and love (58)

Seventeen stanzas of the original poem are included. With sensitivity to what is now perceived to be racist qualities of stanza 17, the Hymnal Revision Committee omitted it from our hymnal:

> Awake from guilty Nature's Sleep
> And Christ shall give you Light,
> Cast all your Sins into the Deep,
> And wash the *Ethiop* white.

For commentary on hymns considered to be racist, see "The language issue," page 137, and "Have thine own way, Lord," pages 388-89.

Azmon

See "Jesus, thine all-victorious love," page 449.

O gladsome light (686)

φῶς ἱλαρόν ἁγίας δόξης

Ancient Greek hymn; trans. by Robert S. Bridges, 1899

This is one of the oldest Christian hymns extant, dating from a time before St. Basil who late in the fourth century referred to it as an old and anonymous hymn. It is often called "The Candle-lighting Hymn" because of its use in the Greek church at vesper services celebrating God's gift of Jesus Christ, the light of the world. Versions of the printed text date from the twelfth century. By the close of the nineteenth century John Julian in *Dictionary of Hymnody* could account for over twenty English poetic and prose texts. M. Eleanor Irwin provides Julian's 1907 list, those not included by Julian, and recent translations in "Phos Hilaron: The Metamorphoses of a Greek Christian Hymn," *The Hymn*, 1989.

Our version is from *Hymns in Four Parts with English Words for Singing in Church*, 1899 (Milgate 1985, 66); it was included in *The English Hymnal*, 1906, and from there it entered most British and USA hymnals of the twentieth century. Bridges has successfully translated the unrhymed and unmetered Greek text into an expressive rhymed and metered setting that is complemented by the psalm tune.

This is its first inclusion in our hymnals.

Le cantique de Siméon

Louis Bourgeois, 1547; harm. by Claude Goudimel, 1551

Leonard Ellinwood has traced the origins of this tune:

[This] is the melody for the [paraphrase of the] Song of Simeon in the Genevan Psalter. It first appeared in the Lyon Psalter of 1547 [*Pseaulmes cinquante de David*], for which Louis Bourgeois is responsible. The first line is derived from a secular song. . . . [Most of] the harmonization is from Claude Goudimel's choral setting of the Psalter, published in 1551. Its English use is from the Anglo-Genevan Psalter of 1558. (Ellinwood 1956, 129-30)

Our harmonization is taken from *The English Hymnal*, 1906, where Goudimel's setting was probably adapted by Ralph Vaughan Williams. The tune is also called "Nunc Dimittis."

O God in heaven (119)

Words and music: Elena G. Maquiso, 1961
trans. by D. T. Niles, 1964

Becky Asedillo has supplied information concerning this hymn to the Trinity. It was composed in 1961 and translated by D. T. Niles; its first appearance was at 195 in *E.A.C.C. Hymnal*, 1964. (Correspondence with Carlton R. Young, July 1991)

The following changes have been made for our hymnal: in stanza 1:1, "Father in heaven" to "O God in heaven"; and in 3:3, "sonship" has been changed to "kinship."

Halad

Elena G. Maquiso, 1961; harm. by Charles H. Webb, 1987

The music first appeared in *Awitan Ta Ang Dyos*, 1962, with the Cebuano text "Panalangini ang mong halad" ("Bless our offering). The harmonization was prepared for our hymnal.

O God of every nation (435)

William W. Reid, Jr., 1958

This hymn placed first in the search for hymns to be sung at the National Council of Churches' Fifth World Order Study Conference, Cleveland, Ohio, November 1958. The search was cosponsored by the Hymn Society of America who published the hymn in *Twelve New World Order Hymns*, 1958. While the hymn is better written than most social gospel hymns of that decade, we must turn to the poet's later efforts, such as "O God who shaped creation," to discover a more realistic appraisal of human sin.

Llangloffan

See "O crucified Redeemer," pages 506-07.

O God, our help in ages past (117)

Isaac Watts, 1719 (Ps. 90)

This is one of three metrical paraphrases of sections of Psalm 90 that Watts made on pages 228-31 for his *Psalms of David, Imitated*, 1719. (Gealy 56/337) Our hymn is the second paraphrase and appears in nine stanzas under the heading "Man Frail and God Eternal." John Wesley's role in popularizing as well as altering the text began in his *Collection of Psalms and Hymns* (London, 1738) and continued into his 1780 *Collection* where the text was included in seven stanzas in the section "Describing Death." Wesley's alterations have been used by a significant number of hymnal editors. The most compelling alteration has been the first line, rendered by Wesley as "O God" from "Our God." Our own hymnals for the most part followed Wesley's 1780 version until the 1935 Methodist hymnal dropped stanza 7:

The busy tribes of flesh and blood
With all their lives and cares
Are carried downward by thy flood,
And lost in following years.

The commentary in *Companion to Hymns and Psalms* sums up the greatness of this text:

Its great strength comes from the magnificent accommodation of the sense to the lines: the rhythm varies but never falters, and the imagery is simple but striking. Everything conspires to make the hymn a majestic statement of the grandeur and permanence of God compared with the transience and frailty of mankind. (Watson and Trickett 1988, 228)

The Hymnal Revision Committee's alteration of stanza 5:2, "bears all its sons away" to the genderless "bears all who breathe away," exemplifies good intentions corrupting a classic text.

St. Anne

Attr. to William Croft, 1708; harm. by W. H. Monk, 1861
The tune line and bass under the tune name "St. Anne" were anonymously included in *The Supplement to the New Version of the Psalms*, 1708, and set to a metrical paraphrase of Psalm 42. Changes in the tune's rhythm and bass were most likely made by William H. Monk for *Hymns Ancient and Modern*, 1861, the first hymnal to set these words to this tune. This version entered our hymnals in 1905 with slight changes in the bass and tenor respectively in measures 2 and 6.

The opening motif of the tune was used by G. F. Handel in the Chandos anthem "O praise the Lord," and by J. S. Bach in his Triple Fugue in E^b, "The St. Anne Fugue."

There are two alternate harmonizations, a vocal descant, and an organ interlude at 293-96 in *The United Methodist Hymnal Music Supplement*.

O God who shaped creation (443)

William W. Reid, Jr., 1987 (Gen. 1:1-3, 26-27)
When this text was commissioned by the Hymnal Revision Committee, the author was requested to employ alternative metaphors and descriptions for deity. The poet's response may be his best contribution to contemporary USA hymnody.

The first stanza tells of God the creator of heaven and earth who birthed humankind and shared with it the "splendored earth." In stanzas 2 through 4

God's redemptive concern for fallen humanity is seen as a mother anguishing over her child, a woman in search of a treasured coin, and the motherlike compassion of the father of the prodigal. The hymn is complete without the vague and pointless stanza 5.

Tuolumne

Dale Wood, 1968, 1988

This tune was commissioned by the Inter-Lutheran Commission on Worship in 1968, and was included in *Contemporary Worship–1*, 1969. "'Tuolumne' is an American Indian name for a region of the California Sierra Nevada, where the composer wrote the tune." (Stulken 1981, 451)

The tune was originally scored for unison singing. In 1988 the composer rescored it for SATB voices for our hymnal.

O happy day, that fixed my choice (391)

Philip Doddridge, 1755
refrain from The Wesleyan Sacred Harp, 1854 (2 Chr. 15:15)

The hymn first appeared at number 23 in 5 stanzas under the title "Rejoicing in our Covenant Engagements to God. I [actually II] Chron. 15:15" in Job Orton's edition of Doddridge's *Hymns Founded on Various Texts in the Holy Scriptures*, 1755. Showing sensitivity to his evangelical audience, the editor in stanza 2 has footnoted in 2:3, "Anthems" as "Hymns of Praise"; and in 3:4, "Shrine" as "Altar or Place of Worship." (Gealy 557/342) Another version of the text appeared in an edition published in 1839 by Doddridge's great-grandson John Doddridge Humphreys. Our version is from the 1935 *Methodist Hymnal*.

The hymn and tune entered our hymnals in 1867. It was not included in the last hymnal (1957) of the former Evangelical United Brethren Church. Some members of the 1966 *Methodist Hymnal* committee ridiculed the tune's affinity with "How dry I am" and set the hymn to an entirely different tune. Since both these actions removed the hymn from the official repertories, it seemed reasonable to some Hymnal Revision Committee members to ask why it should be restored.

In addition to the restoration of the tune and refrain, in stanza 3:1 "'tis done" is changed to "it's done," and in 3:2, "my Lord's" to "the Lord's."

Happy Day

Anon.; refrain attr. to Edward F. Rimbault, 1854

Robert Guy McCutchan has traced the joining of the anonymous, probable camp-meeting tune with Rimbault's popular refrain "Happy land! Happy land!" to *The Wesleyan Sacred Harp*, 1854. In that volume it was set to John Cennick's hymn "Jesus, my All, to heaven is gone." (McCutchan 1942, 259)

O holy city, seen of John (726)

Walter Russell Bowie, 1909 (Rev. 21:1-22:5)

The commentary in *Guide to the Pilgrim Hymnal* states:

> The hymn was written at the request of Henry Sloane Coffin, who wanted some new hymns that would express the convictions that our hope of the Kingdom of God is not alone some far-off eschatological possibility but in the beginnings, at least, may be prepared for here on our actual earth. (Ronander and Porter 1966, 324)

The hymn first appeared at 187 in *Hymns of the Kingdom of God*, 1910, edited by H. S. Coffin and A. W. Vernon. It entered our hymnals in *The Methodist Hymnal*, 1935. As one of the strongest USA social gospel hymns it has also been included in several British hymnals.

Bowie, a social prophet in the lineage of Walter Rauschenbusch (see "Social Gospel Hymns," pages 30-33), proclaimed in the depths of the great USA depression, "We live in a critical age when only those institutions will deserve to endure which are seeking to fulfill those better possibilities for human life, individual, social, national, and international, which the thought of the Kingdom of God requires." (Bowie at the 125th anniversary of Grace Episcopal Church, New York City, 1933)

In our hymnal in stanza 4:4, "Ways are brotherhood" has been changed to "Crown is servanthood." For additional commentary on hymns of the city see "All who love and serve your city," pages 203-04, and "Where cross the crowded ways of life," page 701.

Morning Song

See "My Master, see, the time has come," page 490.

O how I love Jesus (170)

Frederick Whitfield, 1855

John Julian in *Dictionary of Hymnody* writes that this hymn was titled "The name of Jesus" and was first printed in England "in 1855 in hymn-sheets and leaflets in various languages . . . and was first included in Whitfield's *Sacred Poems and Prose*, 1861." (Julian 1907, 1276) According to William J. Reynolds the text "first appeared in America as early as Goodman's *Village Hymn Book*, 1864." (Reynolds 1976, 220) It is not known when the text was wedded with the melody in our hymnal. For example, Ira Sankey, as late as 1896 in his *Gospel Hymns, Nos. 1 to 6 Complete* set it to another tune without the refrain. It entered our hymnals in 1897.

O how I love Jesus

19th cent. USA melody

This CM tune with refrain may be a combination of two camp-meeting tunes.

Ellen Jane Lorenz has traced the chorus and provides this commentary:

> This chorus, attached to various mother-hymns [by Watts and Wesley and others], was found forty-two times in the present study, but never earlier than 1868. . . . The tune was popular with the blacks. It is part of a tune family of four campmeeting songs, all in 6/8 and with similar melodic outlines and dancelike movement. (Lorenz 1980, 120)

Harry Eskew traces the tune to the 1869 edition of *The Revivalist*. (Adams 1992, (250)

O Jesus, I have promised (396)

John E. Bode, ca. 1866 (Luke 9:57)

The hymn was composed for the confirmation of the writer's daughter and two sons; it began "O Jesus, we have promised." It first appeared in a hymnal in a six-stanza hymn in the first person singular, "I," at 395 as "A Hymn for the Newly Confirmed" with the scripture " 'Lord, I will follow Thee whithersoever Thou goest.'—St. Luke 9:57" in *Psalms and Hymns for Public Worship*, New Appendix, 1869. (Gealy 557/347) Stanley L. Osborne has commented that "throughout the prayer the dominant motif is dedication, and the focus centres upon the word 'servant.' " (Osborne 1976, hymn 304)

The hymn entered our hymnals in 1901. The usually omitted stanza 4 completes the author's connection of the vows of commitment, i.e., confirmation, with human emotion—feeling, hearing, seeing, and loving:

> Oh! let me see Thy features,
>   The look that once could make
> So many a true disciple
>   Leave all things for Thy sake:
> The look that beamed on Peter
>   When he Thy name denied;
> The look that draws Thy lovers
>   Close to Thy pierced side.

Angel's story

Arthur H. Mann, 1881

The tune first appeared in *The Methodist Sunday School Tune-Book*, 1881, (McCutchan 1942, 270) and should have stayed with the text to which it was set, "I love to hear the story which angel voices tell." For almost a century this rambling and pointless tune, devoid of any hint of the challenge of the task or the price that must be paid when living out one's dedication to Christ, has instead fostered pleasant mindless woolgathering, self-satisfaction, and the confidence that Christian commitment is as boring as it is inconsequential. Other more vital and engaging 76.76. D tunes are COMPLAINER **(252)** or LLAN-GLOFFAN **(425)**.

O Jesus, my King and my Sovereign (180)

See "Jesús es mi Rey soberano," page 438-39.

O let the Son of God enfold you (347)

See "Spirit song," pages 605-06.

O little town of Bethlehem (230)

Phillips Brooks, ca. 1868

In 1868 Phillips Brooks, rector of Holy Trinity Church in Philadelphia, presented a timely Christmas gift to the children of the parish's Sunday school, a hymn that had been inspired by his previous Christmas week journey on horseback from Jerusalem to Bethlehem. At Brooks's invitation the parish organist composed a simple *abba* Victorian tune, and the children sang the hymn in their Christmas program. The Dictionary of American Hymnology Project cites the hymn's first appearance in C. L. Hutchins, *The Sunday School Hymnal*, 1871.

Although this vivid and imaginative nativity hymn was written for children, its quintessential poignant fourth stanza according to the composer, Louis H. Redner,

> led to some amusing criticism lest it should smack of the Doctrine of the Immaculate Conception. Brooks then changed that line to "Son of the Mother mild," but he afterwards decided to omit the third verse altogether from the carol. (Correspondence January 1901 with Louis F. Benson. Benson Collection, Speer Library, Princeton Theological Seminary:

Where children pure and happy
   Pray to the blessed Child,
Where misery cries out to thee,
   Son of the Mother mild; [original: Son of the Undefiled;]
Where charity stands watching
   And faith holds wide the door,
The dark night wakes, the glory breaks,
   And Christmas comes once more.

William J. Reynolds has discovered an article in the Richmond *Times-Dispatch* for December 16, 1973, which states that Brooks composed this stanza in 1877 during a visit to Brunswick County, Virginia. (Correspondence with Carlton R. Young, January 1993)

In our hymnal in stanza 2:8, "men" has been changed to "all."

St. Louis

Lewis H. Redner, 1868

According to the composer, "The simple music was written in great haste and under great pressure almost on the Eve of Christmas. It was after midnight that a little angel whispered the strain in my ears and I roused myself and dotted it down as you have it." (Correspondence January 1901 with Louis F. Benson. Benson Collection, Speer Library, Princeton Theological Seminary.)

The tune's name is apparently a homonym of the first name of the composer and was given by the compiler William R. Huntington in *Church Porch*, 1884. In correspondence with Louis F. Benson, October 1904, Redner says, "When the child [his tune] was born it was too humble to name. . . I think the tune was written in 1866." There are additional letters from Redner to Benson in the Benson Collection that elaborate on the circumstances of the tune's composition.

The suggested alternate tune FOREST GREEN **(152)** was set with the text in *The English Hymnal*, 1906, in what Wesley Milgate describes as "one of the many happy inspirations of the music editor, Vaughan Williams." (Milgate 1985, 111) Its listing as an alternate tune is the continuing effort by anglophilic United Methodists to replace ST. LOUIS, a melody ridiculed by Erik Routley as "broken-backed and paralytic." (Routley 1981, 124) Stanley L. Osborne bemoaned the tune as having "nothing of the craftsmanship one associates with great music; [and] the added misfortune of being undeservedly popular." (Osborne 1976, hymn 421)

O Lord, may church and home combine (695)

Carlton S. Buck, 1961

The hymn was written in three CMD stanzas for the North American Conference on Church and Family, 1961, and published that year by the Hymn Society of America under the title "Bless Thou Our Christian Homes, O Lord," in *Thirteen New Marriage and Family Life Hymns*.

The discussion about this hymn by the 1966 hymnal committee centered on whether a hymn on the family should be idealistic or descriptive, i.e., positive or negative. To those preferring optimistic family hymns, such as "Happy the home when God is there" **(445)**, see page 386.

The committee did not include this hymn's original stanza 1:

> Bless thou our Christian homes, O Lord,
>   Come, dwell, thyself, within,
> And keep them by thy holy Word,
>   Protect from blighting sin.
> Thus, save our homes from inner strife,
>   May harmony increase,
> And grant each home abundant life
>   And thine abiding peace.

The Christian focus of the hymn was removed when in line 1 of the second stanza "May Church and Christian home combine" was changed to "O Lord, may church and home combine."

Land of Rest

See "Lord, who throughout these forty days," page 474.

O Lord my God! when I in awesome wonder (77)

See "How great thou art," pages 409-11.

O Love divine, what hast thou done (287)

Charles Wesley, 1742

This contemplation on Jesus' crucifixion is the last of three hymns composed in the same meter under the heading "Desiring to love." It first appeared in four stanzas on pages 26-27 in *Hymns and Sacred Poems*, 1742. (Gealy 556/358) The refrain is a quotation from Ignatius's Letter to the Romans: "amor meus crucifixus est" ("My love is crucified"). The commentary in *Companion to Hymns and Psalms* suggests that "Ignatius's [phrase] means both that Christ (on whom his love is set) is crucified, and that all earthly passion has been quelled within himself. . . . Wesley may have found the phrase in John Mason's *Spiritual Songs*, 1683: 'My Lord, my Love, was crucified.' Wesley characteristically makes this seem more immediate by the use of the present tense." (Watson and Trickett 1988, 130)

The hymn expresses the pathos of the crucifixion scene in John 19:34-35. Stanza 3 echoes Lamentations 1:12a:

> Is it nothing to you, all you who pass by?
>   Look and see
> if there is any sorrow like my sorrow.

The hymn entered our hymnals in 1786 in four stanzas. The 1935 *Methodist Hymnal* reversed the order of stanzas 2 and 3 and dropped stanza 4 with its forceful baroque pietistic imagery:

> Then let us sit beneath His Cross,
>   And gladly catch the Healing Stream,
> All Things for Him account but Loss,
>   And give up all our Heart to Him;
> Of Nothing think, or speak beside:
> My Lord, my Love is Crucified!

In stanza 1:2 and 1:5 the original "immortal God" has been restored; and in 2:2 the original "near to God" has been changed to John Wesley's alteration "back to God" from his 1780 *Collection*, and 3:3 was originally "Come see, Ye worms, Your Maker die."

Selena

Isaac B. Woodbury, 1850

This chordal/choral devotional style gospel hymn tune is similar to William B. Bradbury's OLIVE'S BROW **(282)** and is in contrast to the rousing dance tunes of many gospel hymns, for example, ASSURANCE (369) and the sweet parlor ballads of Stephen Foster, e.g., CONVERSE **(526)**, a step-sibling of "I dream of Jeanie with the light brown hair."

The tune was first included in Woodbury's *Anthem Dulcimer*, 1850. (McCutchan 1942, 172)

O love, how deep, how broad, how high (267)
O amor quam exstaticus

15th cent. Latin
trans. by Benjamin Webb, 1854, alt.

This hymn is a translation from an extraordinary 92-line *aabb* rhymed anonymous fifteenth-century Latin credal and devotional hymn on the incarnation, baptism, ministry, passion, death, resurrection, and exalted reign of Jesus Christ. The complete Latin text, including the added doxology, is in *The Hymnal 1940 Companion*.

Our text is from *The Hymnal 1982*. It is composed of stanzas 2 (beginning with line 5 of the original poem) and 9 through 12 from Benjamin Webb's translation in J. M. Neale's *Hymnal Noted*, 1851, plus an unidentified doxological final stanza. In stanza 1:2 "fantasy" has been changed to Webb's translation "ecstasy" for "exstaticus," and in stanza 4:1 "evil hands" is changed to to "evil power."

Gracia Grindal has commented that "the most striking thing about the entire text is its objectivity. It asks nothing of us, other than our awe. The phrase that repeats and repeats is 'for us.' This was done, God became mortal . . . [and] all of Christ's work was for the sake of the human race." ("An interpretation: 'O Love, How Deep, How Broad, How High,'" *The Hymn 40 (1):33-34*)

Deo Gracias

15th cent. English melody
harm. from Hymns Ancient and Modern, Revised 1950

This stirring fifteenth-century melody was the the victory song "Our King went forth to Normandy" in celebration of Henry V's triumph over the French at Agincourt, October 25, 1415. The tune first appeared with the name AGINCOURT in *The English Hymnal*, 1906. In *Songs of Praise*, it was named DEO GRACIAS, literally "thanks be to God," using the first two words of the melodic embellishment in the fifteenth-century manuscript at Trinity College, Cambridge, included in *Guide to the Pilgrim Hymnal*. The text follows:

> Deo gracias Anglia redde pro victoria.
> Owre kynge went forth to normandy,
> With grace and myght of chyvalry:
> Ther god for him wrought mervelusly.
> Wherefore englonde may calle and cry
> Deo gracias Anglia redde pro victoria.
> (Ronander and Porter 1966, 124)

Wesley Milgate has commented that during the victorious return to London the king was appalled with the pageantry honoring his leadership, and "these words were added in fulfillment of the King's express wish . . . that no honor be paid to him for the victory." (Milgate 1985, 24)

Our harmonization is from *Hymns Ancient and Modern*, Revised 1950, and is presumed to be the work of its musical editors.

O Love that wilt not let me go (480)

George Matheson, 1882

This prayer of thanksgiving and commitment to the God of Love, Light, Joy, and Cross, composed in a matter of minutes, was the fruit of poet's extreme mental distress. (Julian 1907, 1583) Fred D. Gealy has verified that it was first published in the Church of Scotland magazine *Life and Work*, January 1882, and was included in *The Scottish Hymnal*, 1884. (Gealy 556/359)

At the heart of the poem is the sacrificial act of giving one's whole self to Christ, expressed in this commentary in *Handbook to the Church Hymnary* on the poet's use of the words "blossoms red":

> Dr. Matheson used to explain that when he wrote "blossoms red" . . . [in stanza 4:5] he was thinking of the blossom that comes out of sacrifice—of the sacrificial life which blossoms by shedding itself. "White" is the blossom of prosperity, "red" of self-sacrificing love. (Moffatt and Patrick 1951, 146)

The hymn entered our hymnals in 1905.

St. Margaret

Albert L. Peace, 1884

According to the composer his tune for this poem in the unusual meter of 88. 8886, was written at the request of *The Scottish Hymnal*, 1885, committee for which Peace served as music editor. The music was quickly set down so that "the ink of the first note was hardly dry when I had finished the tune." (McCutchan 1942, 345) Several unsuccessful attempts have been made to replace or reconstruct this quintessential Victorian church quartet-style setting.

The tune is named after Margaret of Scotland, 1046-1093, who persuaded her husband Malcolm III to initiate significant reforms in the church and culture. She was canonized in 1249 and is the patroness of Scotland.

O Mary, don't you weep (134)

African American spiritual
adapt. and arr. by William Farley Smith, 1986
(John 20:11-18; Exod. 15:21)

William Farley Smith identifies the masked or double meaning of this spiritual—one for the ears of the slave owner and the other meant for the slaves, a proclamation of freedom. (Sanchez 1989, 61)

For James H. Cone this spiritual proclaims God as liberator:

> Just as God delivered the Children of Israel from Egyptian slavery, drowning Pharoah and his army in the Red Sea, he will also deliver black people from American slavery. It is this certainty that informs the thought of the black spirituals, enabling black slaves to sing: "O Mary, don't you weep, don't you moan." . . . The basic idea of the spirituals is that slavery contra-

dicts God; it is a denial of his will. . . . Here the emphasis [is] on God's liberation of the weak from the oppression of the strong, the lowly and downtrodden from the proud and mighty. (Cone 1972, 34-35)

For additional commentary see "Canticle of Moses and Miriam," pages 258-59, and Jon Michael Spencer, "Promises of Passages" in *Protest and Praise*, 1990.

O Mary

A simpler setting in a higher key is found at 153 in *Songs of Zion*, 1981.

O Master, let me walk with thee (430)

Washington Gladden, 1879

This hymn first appeared in three LMD stanzas under the title "Walking with God" in the author's magazine *Sunday Afternoon*, March 1879. The hymn was discovered by C. H. Edwards, and when the hymn was included in his *Christian Praise*, 1880, he dropped the second stanza:

> O Master, let me walk with thee
> Before the taunting Pharisee;
> Help me to bear the sting of spite,
> The hate of men who hide thy light.

The poet later stated that Edwards had "made a hymn of it by omitting the second stanza, which was not suitable for devotional purposes. It had no liturgical purpose and no theological significance, but it was an honest cry of human need, of the need of divine companionship." (Reynolds 1975, 164)

For over a century the singing of this prayer of petition to God to be present, i.e., to walk with the petitioner in a faith journey, has afforded countless congregations a dutiful response to sermons, offering no-risk and no-fault insurance against life's unexpected Good Fridays.

Maryton

See "How blest are they who trust in Christ," page 405.

O Morning Star, how fair and bright (247)
Wie schön leuchtet der Morgenstern

Words and music: Philipp Nicolai, 1599
trans. by Catherine Winkworth, 1863
st. 3 trans. Lutheran Book of Worship, 1978

The original text of this hymn first appeared with the tune as a seven-stanza acrostic of ten lines in the appendix of Nicolai's *Freuden-Spiegel dess ewigen*

Lebens, 1599. The first line of the text was "Wie herrlich strahlt der Morgenstern" and appeared under the title "A Spiritual bridal song of the believing soul concerning her Heavenly Bridegroom, founded in the 45th Psalm of the Prophet David." The text was written in response to the ravages of the Black Plague. (Julian 1907, 806)

Fred D. Gealy provides this commentary:

> In 1768 J. A. Schlegel radically rewrote the text, providing the new first line "Wie schön leuchtet." . . . Catherine Winkworth made several translations [from Schlegel's revision] which vary considerably from each other. (Gealy, Lovelace, Young 1970, 330)

The hymn, sometimes named the "Queen of the Chorales," entered our hymnals in 1966 with the first two stanzas of Winkworth's translation, appearing at 149 under the title "Love to the Saviour" in her *Chorale Book for England*, 1863. (Gealy 557, 363) Our stanza 3 was prepared by the Inter-Lutheran Commission on Worship for the *Lutheran Book of Worship*, 1978.

The chorale stems from Revelation 21:16, "I am the root and offspring of David, the bright and morning star," and displays a variety of expressive deity metaphors: Morning Star, Sovereign, Root of Jesse, David's Son, Lord, Master, heavenly Brightness, Light divine, and Crown of Gladness.

Wie schön leuchtet der Morgenstern

The version of the tune and harmonization are from the final chorus of part one of J. S. Bach's Advent cantata, *Schwingt freudig euch empor* (*Soar joyfully on high*), ca. 1731.

Ethel K. Porter suggests that the tune may have come from older material including the "melody of 'Jauchzet dem Herren, alle Land,' a setting for Psalm 100 in a 1538 Strasbourg psalter." (Ronander and Porter 1966, 118)

O perfect love (645)

Dorothy B. Gurney, 1883

This widely performed wedding hymn was composed in fifteen minutes in 1883 at the request of the author's sister to be sung to J. B. Dykes's tune "Strength and Stay." (McCutchan 1942, 433) It first appeared at 578 under the title "The Lord do so to me and more also, if ought but death part thee and me" in *Hymns Ancient and Modern*, 1889 Supplement. (Gealy 557/364-B)

The hymn came into prominence when Joseph Barnby set it as an anthem for the marriage of Princess Louise and the Duke of Fife, July 27, 1889. (Julian 1907, 1553) It entered our hymnals in 1905 with Barnby's tune and has remained unaltered.

Perfect love

Joseph Barnby, 1890

The anthem setting was reduced to a hymn tune and appeared in *The Hymnal Companion* (3d musical ed.), 1890. (Milgate 1985, 190)

It remains one of the most durable of Barnby's many tunes.

O sabbath rest of Galilee (499)

See "Dear Lord and Father of Mankind," pages 316-17.

O sacred Head, now wounded (286)
Salve caput cruentatum
O Haupt voll Blut und Wunden

Anon. Latin; trans. by Paul Gerhardt, 1656
and James W. Alexander, 1830
(Matt. 27:27-31; Mark 15:16-20; John 19:1-5)

This compelling hymn on the passion of Jesus Christ comes from the medieval personal devotional practice of viewing and addressing the form of the crucified Christ. This tradition was sustained in German Protestantism in pietistic hymns, painting, and statuary, and found its way into British evangelical use in the hymns of Isaac Watts, "When I survey the wondrous cross" **(298)**, and Charles Wesley, "O love divine, what hast thou done" **(287)**. The precursors of United Methodism and other USA evangelicals have sung these hymns in Maundy Thursday communion services and on Good Friday.

The Latin text has been ascribed to Bernard of Clairvaux, 1091-1153, or to the more probable Arnulf of Louvain, 1200-1251. It is divided into seven parts, one for each day of Holy Week: feet, knees, hands, sides, breast, heart, and head. The sections begin with these lines as translated in John Julian's *Dictionary of Hymnody*, 1907, 991: (1) Jesus, Prince of life, (2) Jesus, source of endless pleasure, (3) Jesus, kind Shepherd, (4) Jesus, caring Savior, (5) Christ, the glory of heaven, (6) O divine heart of Jesus, (7) Christ's head with sharp thorns crowned.

Gerhardt translated the final section that addresses the head of the Crucified. It was first included in ten stanzas in Johann Crüger's *Praxis Pietatis Melica*, 1656.

Crüger's hymn first appeared in our hymnals in the earliest hymnal of the former Evangelical United Brethren Church, *Das Aller Neuste Harfenspiel*, 1795.

Alexander's translation of Crüger's text was made in eight stanzas and first appeared in Joshua Leavitt's *Christian Lyre*, 1830. Alexander later completed the translation, and selections from his total work have been included in our hymnals since 1867. Our three stanzas are Alexander's 1a, 2b, 3, and 6.

Passion chorale

Hans L. Hassler, 1601; harm. by J. S. Bach

This tune is one of the most cited examples of the practice of *contrafactum*, setting a new sacred text to a popular secular melody for the purpose of reaching a wider audience. Its source is the tune for the love song "Mein G'müt ist mir verwirret, Das macht ein Jungfrau zart" ("Confused are all my feelings, A tender maid's the cause"), adapted from a rhythmic medieval melody by Hassler and included in *Lustgarten neuer teutscher Gesäng*, 1601. (McCutchan 1942, 177) For an older example of this practice, as well as one more recent, see commentary on O WELT, ICH MUSS DICH LASSEN, "O food to pilgrims given," page 509, and TRUMPETS, "Weary of all trumpeting," pages 683-84.

The tune was first matched to our text by Johann Crüger in *Praxis Pietatis Melica*, 1656.

Our harmonization was adapted from one of J. S. Bach's settings in *St. Matthew Passion*, 1729, and was included in *Hymns Ancient and Modern*, 1861. Two of Bach's settings for choir from *St. Matthew Passion* are found at 176 in *Hymns and Psalms*, 1983, and Hassler's rhythmic version is included at 169 in *The Hymnal 1982*.

O sing a song of Bethlehem (179)

Louis F. Benson, 1899

Teaching the Bible and doctrine through a graded series of hymnals has been a distinctive contribution to Christian education by Presbyterians in the USA since Benson's time. This hymn is a summary of Jesus' life, passion, death, and resurrection. It was composed in Philadelphia in 1899 and included under the title "Early life of Jesus" in *The School Hymnal*, 1899. The text was reprinted at 23 in the author's *Hymns Original and Translated*, 1925.

Kingsfold

See "Come, let us use the grace divine," pages 293-94. Stanzas of the hymn related to specific seasons may be sung as a choir call to worship. A hymn anthem may also be structured by mixed voices singing stanza 1 in unison, unison women singing stanza 2, four-part harmony or a canon at the octave on stanza 3, and the congregation joining the choir on stanza 4.

O sons and daughters, let us sing (317)
O filii et filiae, Rex coelestis, Rex gloriae

Jean Tisserand, 15th cent.; trans. by John Mason Neale, 1851, alt.
This hymn was originally a nine-stanza Latin poem in the form of a carol with refrain titled "L'aleluya du jour de Pasques," composed by the Franciscan monk Jean Tisserand. It was first discovered in a small untitled booklet between 1518 and 1536, now located in the Paris Bibliothèque Nationale. Stanzas 4, 5, and 8 do not appear in the earliest copies, but are added in later editions. (Ellinwood 1956, 74) The hymn was used in many French dioceses "in the *Salut*, or salutation of the Blessed Sacrament, on the evening of Easter Day." (Julian 1907, 829)

Julian also cites a 1617 German translation and records English texts from the mid-eighteenth century through the late-nineteenth century, the most prominent by J. M. Neale in twelve stanzas at 111-13 in his *Mediaeval Hymns and Sequences*, 1851.

In his preface to the text Neale states that while there has been more than one translation of the text,

> it seemed to me that its rude simplicity might perhaps be more successfully caught by another effort. It is scarcely possible for any one not acquainted with the melody to imagine the jubilant effect of the triumphant *Alleluia* attached to apparently less important circumstances of the Resurrection: e.g., S. Peter's being outstripped by S. John. It seems to speak of the majesty of that event, the smallest portions of which are worthy to be so chronicled. I have here and there borrowed a line from preceding translations. (Gealy 557/370)

The hymn entered our hymnals in 1966 and has been expanded in this edition to included those stanzas appropriate for the Second Sunday of Easter. Our text is the version of Neale's translation from *Hymns Ancient and Modern*, 1861, as revised in the 1950 edition, with stanzas 9 and 5 interchanged.

O filii et filiae

15th cent. French carol; harm. by Charles H. Webb, 1987
According to Leonard Ellinwood this early French melody was probably sung with the original text. The earliest known form is a four-part setting in *Airs sur les hymnes sacrez, odes et noels*, Paris, 1623. (Ellinwood 1956, 74) The tune's name is the first four words of the Latin.

Our tune is adapted from versions in *The English Hymnal*, 1906, and was harmonized for this hymnal. Most hymnals include Alleluias at the beginning of the hymn following the practice at 81 in Neale's *Hymnal Noted*, 2d printing 1856. (Gealy 557/370)

Stanzas may be sung antiphonally accompanied by tambourine and handbells, all joining on the Alleluias.

O Spirit of the living God (539)

Henry H. Tweedy, 1935 (Acts 2)

The author writes that this hymn was composed because "some of the old Pentecostal hymns were to me unsatisfactory, and I was eager to interpret the symbolism of the story in Acts in a way that modern men could understand and sincerely mean." (McCutchan 1942, 228) His friend Halford E. Luccock sent it to the 1935 *Methodist Hymnal* committee who included it in that edition.

The hymn is a prayer for the church to be open once again to receive the fire, wind, and power of the first Pentecost. Stanza 2, with a nod to Isaiah 6:7b, is a petition for Pentecost's tongues of fire to be translated into flaming love and zeal proclaiming the good news of God's commonwealth. The third stanza prays that glossolalia's babble will be replaced by acts of human love that speak loud and clear and need no interpreters. This is one of a few social gospel hymns written in the 1930's that has survived. For additional commentary on this type of hymn see "Social Gospel Hymns," pages 30-33.

In our hymnal in stanza 3:3, "all men" has been changed to "all may"; 3:7, "brotherhood" to "family"; 4:1, "him" to "Christ"; and 4:2, "mankind" to "this world."

Forest Green

See "Come, let us join our friends above," page 293. This innocent tune enhances the hymn's optimistic appraisal of the perfectibility of human endeavor and institutions.

O splendor of God's glory bright (679)
Splendor paternae gloriae

Ambrose of Milan, 4th cent.; trans. by Robert S. Bridges, 1899

This office hymn was composed by Ambrose for lauds, early morning prayer and praise (see Julian 1907, 1080; and "Latin Hymns," pages 5-6).

Our text consists of stanzas 1 through 4 of 8 stanzas from the translator's *Yatten-don Hymnal*, 1899. (Gealy 557/372) It entered our hymnals in 1966.

Wareham

William Knapp, 1738

This tune first appeared in the composer's *Set of New Psalm Tunes and Anthems in Four Parts*, 1738. Robert G. McCutchan in *Our Hymnody*, 1942, pages 66-67, has supplied information on the tune sources and its early variants.

James T. Lightwood in *Hymn-Tunes and Their Story* comments, "There is a special feature about this tune which goes to make it one of the best congregational tunes ever written." Lightwood also includes a poem titled "An Ejaculation" by H. Price about the eccentric Knapp who served as clerk of St. James Church, Poole. It appeared in the London *Magazine*, 1742:

> From pounce and paper, ink and pen,
>   Save me, O Lord, I pray;
> From Pope and Swift and such-like men,
>   And Cribber's annual lay;
> From doctors' bills and lawyers' fees,
>   From ague, gout and trap;
> And what is ten times worse than these,
>   George Savage [the sexton] and Will Knapp.
>   (Lightwood 1905, 147-48)

Wareham is the composer's birthplace. Our harmonization is from the *Presbyterian Hymnal*, 1895, and entered our hymnals in 1935. There is a descant at 137 in *The Hymnal 1982*.

O the depth of love divine (627)

Charles Wesley, 1745 (John 6:35-58)

This hymn first appeared at 57 in *Hymns on the Lord's Supper*, 1745. (Gealy 557/373) There is no record of its use by John Wesley in his collections or by English and USA Methodists in their hymnals until our 1966 edition.

Interest in Wesleyan communion hymns was renewed with the publication of J. E. Rattenbury's *Eucharistic Hymns of John and Charles Wesley*, 1948. Rattenbury comments that this hymn is one of two in the 1745 collection dealing with the mystery of the Eucharist. They face, though they do not attempt to answer the question

> *How* the Bread his Flesh imparts,
> *How* the Wine transmits his Blood.

Two things are indisputable: the fact that God's thoughts are not our thoughts, that He is not only incomprehensible in His methods, but that we should expect Him to be. . . . [While humans] may not presume to know the incomprehensible ways of God, . . . [Wesley] has no doubts that the Sacraments are channels through which the grace of God flows, that virtue works through the Elements although consecration makes no apparent change to them . . . [and] that the Sacramental Elements and action are God-ordained vehicles of His power. They are definite, concrete channels through which blessings came. His only evidence is the typical Methodist appeal to experience; and a joy, the glad and conscious communion with God, of which his *Journals*, as well as the Hymns, give record, are the only evidence he offers or needs. (Rattenbury 1948, 42-43)

For additional commentary see Kathryn Nichols, "Charles Wesley's Eucharistic Hymns: Their Relationship to the *Book of Common Prayer*," *The Hymn*, April 1988, and "The Theology of Christ's Sacrifice and Presence in Charles Wesley's Hymns on the Lord's Supper," *The Hymn*, July 1988.

Our hymn is the original text except in stanza 1:4, "man" is changed to "us"; 2:2, "the" to "thy"; 3:1, "heavenly spirits" to "spirits heavenward"; and in stanza 3:6, "him that" to "Christ who."

Stookey

Carlton R. Young, 1986

According to Frank Baker, Wesley composed 3,500 lines in 76. 76. 77. 76, a meter that is "robust . . . cross-rhymed throughout, but with a group of three consecutive trochaic lines opening the second half and breaking the alternating trochaic-iambic sequence." (Baker 1962, xlvii) There are very few tunes that gracefully accommodate the shifts between trochaic and iambic. The most familiar to United Methodists is the alternate tune AMSTERDAM **(96)**.

The composer's unison pentatonic melody was first included in *Hymnal Supplement II*, (1987). It is named after Laurence Hull Stookey who served as chair of the worship resources subcommittee of the Hymnal Revision Committee.

O the Lamb (300)

Words and music: 19th cent. camp-meeting song
adapt. by Ellen Jane Lorenz, 1980

The adapter, a distinguished composer of church music from the Evangelical United Brethren tradition, has written in her *Glory Hallelujah! The Story of the Campmeeting Spiritual*.

[This] chorus . . . is found frequently in the campmeeting collection with a variety of tunes as well as of mother-hymns. The favorite mother-hymn is "Alas, and did my Savior bleed." "Suffering Savior" [our tune] is the favorite tune, repeated for the chorus. It is also found from 1838 as an independent chorus. (Lorenz 1980, 106)

This melody is from *The Centenary Singer*, 1867, and was included in the composer's unpublished Ph.D. thesis, *A Treasure of Campmeeting Spirituals*. It was included in *Supplement to the Book of Hymns*, 1982, without the melodic variant, a raised leading tone, and the upbeat to the first measure needed when sung with Isaac Watts's "Alas, and did my Savior bleed" **(294)**.

The Lamb

See pages 130-31, for commentary on the inclusion of this hymn in the 1981 hymnal and the contributions of the Lorenz family to USA evangelical hymnody.

O thou, in whose presence (518)

Joseph Swain, 1791 (Ps. 23)

The text, originally entitled "A description of Christ by His Graces and Power," is a paraphrase of portions of the Song of Solomon. It appeared in nine eight-line stanzas in Swain's *Experimental Essays on Divine Subject in Verse*, 1791. (Gealy, Lovelace, Young 1970, 339) William J. Reynolds in *Companion to the Baptist Hymnal* has traced the text with this tune to three early nineteenth-century tune books, including Wyeth's *Repository* (see comment below). All include the hymn in ten four-line stanzas. (Reynolds 1976, 170)

Swain uses imagery from the first three chapters of Song of Solomon in a love song apparently addressed to God in Jesus Christ. The christological vagueness of Swain's text, its greatest virtue, in the nineteenth century prompted numerous anonymous changes; for example, in our stanza 2, "at noontide" was changed to "Shepherd."

This hymn, along with "Amazing grace" and "How firm a foundation," exemplifies the wedding of a British evangelical text with a USA melody, resulting in a folk hymn.

The hymn entered our hymnals in 1859. In our 1878 hymnal it was included in six four-line stanzas, including quatrains that are not Swain's, incorporating imagery from Psalm 23. Our version of the hymn is from our 1905 hymnal.

Davis

Wyeth's Repository of Sacred Music, Part Second, 1813

This melody was apparently first included in Wyeth's *Repository of Sacred Music, Part Second*, where it is identified as a "new tune." Annabel Morris Buchanan in

Folk Hymns of America traces the tune's antecedents and prints a dorian (D to D on the white keys) version of the tune that was "heard in childhood from my father." (Buchanan 1938, 34) Alice Parker in *Creative Hymn Singing* (1976, 43) includes this tune in its dorian and ionian (major) settings to illustrate the nineteenth-century evolution of USA folk tunes from modal to tonal. Variants of the melody appeared in tune books throughout the nineteenth century, including L. R. Rhinehart's *American Church Harp*, 1856, where the melody is stretched two steps beyond the octave. (Gealy 557/376)

Contrary to the citation on the hymn page our harmonization is from our 1878 hymnal where it is credited to Hubert P. Main. Robert G. McCutchan dates Main's setting as 1869. (McCutchan 1942, 368) The tune is also called "Dulcimer," "My Beloved," and "New Salem."

The tune may be sung as a canon at the octave. Alternate stanzas may be sung by the choir using Austin C. Lovelace's choice setting found at 129 in our 1966 hymnal.

O thou who camest from above (501)

Charles Wesley, 1762 (Lev. 6:13)

The text first appeared in vol. 1:57 in *Short Hymns on Select Passages of the Holy Scriptures* 1762, in two stanzas of LMD under the heading from Leviticus 6:13, "The fire shall ever be burning upon the altar, it shall never go out." (Gealy 557/379)

F. Hildebrandt and O. A. Beckerlegge comment on this hymn:

> [It] is the perfect description of "inward religion" as distinct from "formal," yet it appears in the section "For Believers Working." It should not be forgotten that the early Methodist Conferences were "Conversations about the work *of* God," not the work of man for God! The flame of faith can be lit only from outside and above—it is the gift of the Holy Spirit. Christ is the subject and agent. (Wesley 1983, 7:474)

Their commentary also demonstrates that in addition to the Leviticus passage, showing Israel's continual sacrifice and the basis for stanza 2, the hymn is replete with other biblical and literary allusions. Samuel Bradburn in his *Sketch of Mr. Wesley's Character*, 1791, recalls that John Wesley once told him that the first two lines of this hymn expressed his religiious experience.

The hymn was first included in our hymnals in 1793. Several attempts to alter the poet's imaginative "inextinguishable" in stanza 2:2 ignore that one can only sing one syllable at a time. The poet's original text was restored in our 1966 hymnal and is included in this edition. Inexplicably, stanza 1:4 "On the mean altar," has been changed to "Upon the mean altar."

Hereford

Samuel Sebastian Wesley, 1872

This tune was first included in the composer's *European Psalmist*, 1872, a large collection of hymn tunes, anthems, and service music by Wesley and others. It was set to this text in *Hymns Ancient and Modern*, 1904. S. S. Wesley's extraordinary repertory of hymn tunes was introduced to USA hymnal editors by Erik Routley. In his *Musical Wesleys* Routley provides this comment on HEREFORD:

> Its mood . . . is that of a gentle part-song; its inner parts are as melodious as it treble part. Every line, like four of the eight lines of Aurelia, ends with a suspension with a moving treble over a held bass. The style is, in fact, eighteenth century, and to be more precise, it is Handel. (Routley 1968, 204)

The tune is named after Hereford Cathedral where Wesley served as organist 1832-35. This is its first inclusion in our hymnals.

O thou who this mysterious bread (613)

Charles Wesley, 1745 (Luke 24:13-35)

The hymn first appeared at 22-23 in *Hymns on the Lord's Supper*, 1745, and is based on the disciples' Emmaus encounter with the risen Christ, Luke 24:13-35. It also stems from an excerpt from John Wesley's abridgement of Daniel Brevint's *Christian Sacrament and Sacrifice*, 1673, included as an introduction to the 1745 collection:

> Let my heart burn to follow Thee now, when this Bread is broken at this Table, as the hearts of Thy disciples did when Thou didst break it in Emmaus. (Rattenbury 1948, 148)

The poem is an invitation from the faithful to the risen Lord to be present in the eucharistic meal, as at Emmaus, and to speak words of grace and feed their souls with God's gifts of mercy, pardon, and love.

The hymn entered our hymnals in 1786. It was dropped from the 1821 *Collection* and is restored in our hymnal. Changes have been made at stanza 3:1, "we commune still, and mourn" to "communing still, we mourn"; and stanza 4:1, "Inkindle" to "Enkindle."

For commentary on another Emmaus hymn see "On the day of resurrection," page 543.

Land of Rest

See "Lord, who throughout these forty days," page 473-74.

O what their joy and their glory must be (727)
O quanta, qualia sunt illa sabbata

Peter Abelard, 12th cent.; trans. by John M. Neale, 1868

Here the faithful anticipate the joys of the eternal city Jerusalem while living in "exile on Babylon's strand" (stanza 4:4). The hymn was "written [by Abelard] for Saturday at Vespers in Abelard's *Hymnarius Paraclitensis . . .* for his wife Heloise's Convent of the Paraclete, founded at Nogent-sur-Seine in 1129." (Ellinwood 1952, 52, 346)

Abelard's seven-stanza 12 12. 12 12 hymn was translated into 10 10. 10 10 by John M. Neale for *The Hymnal Noted*, 1851. Our text is from *The Hymnal 1982*, which has slightly altered Neale's stanzas 1, 3, 4, 6, and 7.

The Latin text and the plainsong melody are included at 296 in *Historical Companion to Hymns Ancient and Modern*, 1962.

O quanta qualia

Paris Antiphoner, 1681; harm. by John B. Dykes, 1868

For commentary on the source of the tune see "Latin Hymns," page 5. Our harmonization is from *Hymns Ancient and Modern*, 1868 Appendix.

O wondrous sight! O vision fair (258)
Caelestis formam gloriae

Sarum Breviary, 1495; trans. in Hymns Ancient and Modern, 1861
(Matt. 17:1-8; Mark 9:2-8; Luke 9:28-36)

This anonymous text for the Feast of the Transfiguration is one of several brought into common use at Old Sarum late in the fifteenth century. (Frost 1962, 427) Our text is incorrectly cited on the hymn page as John Mason Neale's, though it is stanzas 1 through 5 of the translation by the compilers of *Hymns Ancient and Modern*, 1861, who used only two of Neale's lines: stanza 1:4 and 3:2. A form of the hymn first appeared in our hymnals in 1874.

Our text changes stanza 1:1 from "type" to "sight." For commentary on the Transfiguration see "Christ, upon the mountain peak," pages 282-83.

Wareham

See "O splendor of God's glory bright," page 530.

O Word of God incarnate (598)

William W. How, 1867

This hymn first appeared under Psalm 119:105, "For the commandment is a lamp; and the law is light; and reproofs of instruction are the way of life," in W. W. How and T. B. Morrell's 1867 Supplement to *Psalms and Hymns*, 1854. (Julian 1907, 854) The poet extends the psalm's light motif in a contrived inventory of the Bible's attributes: "Word of God incarnate," "Wisdom from on high," "Truth unchanging," a divine gift, a vessel [originally "casket"] where truth is stored, the picture of Christ, a banner before God's advancing host, and "chart and compass." The final stanza is a petition to Christ to purify and restore the church to its former stature as the light to the nations.

The hymn entered our hymnals in 1882.

Munich

Gesangbuch, Meiningen, 1693; harm. by Felix Mendelssohn, 1847

The tune was constructed from fragments of other tunes for the Meiningen *Gesangbuch*. Our harmonization is from *Elijah*, 1847, where it is Mendelssohn's setting for "Cast thy burden upon the Lord." It was the first tune for "O Sacred Head, now wounded" until our 1935 hymnal where it was matched with How's text.

Wesley Milgate (1985, 86-97) provides a comprehensive coverage of the sources of this tune. There is an alternate harmonization at 234 in *The United Methodist Hymnal Music Supplement*.

O worship the King, all-glorious above (73)

Robert Grant, 1833 (Ps. 104)

This favorite hymn on God's majesty, power, and love is an interpretation of Psalm 104 that was prompted by William Kethe's paraphrase of the psalm from the Anglo-Genevan Psalter, 1560-61, beginning "My Soule, praise the Lord, Speak good of his name." It first appeared in Edward Bickersteth's *Christian Psalmody*, 1833, in the version described as a "more correct and authentic version" and in *Sacred Poems* (new ed. 1839), a collection of the poet's verse compiled by his brother Lord Glenelg. (Both texts are in Gealy 557/382.)

Erik Routley writes that this text is a "good example of the impact on hymnody of the new search for poetic standards which Heber so strongly promoted." (Routley 1979, 70) For commentary on Reginald Heber's influence on hymn writing see "British Hymns," page 14, and the commentary on "Bread of the world in mercy broken," page 244.

The nonsexist deity metaphors, "Shield," "Ancient-of-Days," "Maker," "Defender," "Redeemer," and "Friend," balance the opening line's masculine metaphor "King" and combined with minor alterations—in stanzas 1:2, 2:3, and 2:4, "his" is changed to "God's," and in stanza 2:3, "his" to "whose"— allow this classic text to be included essentially as it entered our hymnals in 1847. Our hymnal includes the first five of the original six stanzas.

Lyons

Attr. to Johann Michael Haydn; arr. by William Gardiner, 1815
Leonard Ellinwood has traced this tune to the second volume of William Gardiner's *Sacred Melodies from Haydn, Mozart and Beethoven*, 1815, where it is set to "O praise ye the Lord, Prepare a new song," scored for instruments and mixed voices. (Ellinwood 1956, 173) The attribution of the tune to either Franz Joseph Haydn or Johann Michael Haydn stems from Gardiner's heading, "Subject Haydn," though never documented. There is no record of the tune's use in British hymnals, owing in part to John Hullah's having set Grant's text to HANOVER **(181)** in *The Book of Praise*, 1868. (Gealy 557/382)

The tune appeared in the USA in Oliver Shaw's *Sacred Melodies*, 1818, and later in Lowell Mason's *Boston Handel and Haydn Society Collection*, 1822. It was popularized among Wesleyan groups through its inclusion in *The Methodist Harmonist*, 1821, revised 1832. The first setting of the tune to this text appears to be in our 1878 hymnal.

There is a keyboard introduction, two alternate harmonizations, and a vocal descant at 223-26 in *The United Methodist Hymnal Music Supplement*.

O young and fearless Prophet (444)

S. Ralph Harlow, 1931
Harlow, a Congregationalist, was a prophet and practitioner of the social gospel. In his letter of July 1963, he comments on the consequences of this activity:

> Years ago, back in 1924, I wrote an article attacking the isolationism, the economic imperialism, the oil scandals of the Republican party. For this I was dropped by the American Board of Missions, who wrote, "One whose attitude toward the Government in Power is what yours is is no longer acceptable to our constituency." SHADES OF THE PILGRIMS! . . . Since 1924 the only committee of the Congregational church to which I have been elected is the Commission on Evangelism which meets in San Francisco [Harlow lived in Massachusetts], and you pay your own expenses. (Correspondence with Carlton R. Young, July 1963)

While Harlow can state that "the only hymn committee to turn [this hymn] down is my own Congregational church, which over 21 years ago said it 'is too radical,'" the fact remains that for half a century our hymnal committees have tempered the blunt prophetic challenge of the hymn. In the 1935 *Methodist Hymnal* the committee changed "race or color" to "race or station" in the original stanza 4:2 because as Harlow relates, "They told me that their Southern congregations would object to the word 'color.'" (Correspondence, July 1963) This stanza is omitted from our hymnal:

> Create in us the splendor that dawns when hearts are kind.
> That knows not race or color as boundaries of the mind;
> That learns to value beauty, in heart, or brain, or soul,
> And longs to bind God's children into one perfect whole.

Our hymnal includes stanza 5, too controversial for the 1935 or 1966 hymnal committees. Harlow has commented that the chair of the former committee

> told me that "the church is not ready to sing that yet." I told him that it was not as radical as the Magnificat in Luke 1:46-55, which is sung in the Methodist service. Later I changed this verse from "unearned wealth" to "the greed of wealth." (Correspondence with Fred D. Gealy, October 1967)

The additional lines of that stanza originally read:

> While men go crushed and hungry who cry for work and health;
> Whose wives and little children are starved for lack of bread,
> Who spend their years o'erweighted beneath a gloomy dread.

The hymn was written on the back of a menu in 1931 during the economic depression. Harlow and his family were driving from Poughkeepsie, New York, to Northampton, Massachusetts. They encountered a man on the side of road. This incident may have inspired stanza five:

> My wife said to me, "If you mean what you say in this poem you would offer him a ride." I stopped the car and went back to the man who was washing his feet in a wayside brook. When I offered him a ride, he said, "Just when you think God has forgotten you, something like this happens. I was thinking of committing suicide." [As we rode he related] . . . that he had walked from Buffalo trying to find work without success; that his wife was sick in Boston. That morning he had sold his razor in order to get food, and he said, "When you sell your razor, you lose your self-respect." (Correspondence with Fred D. Gealy, October 1967; Gealy 557/383)

See Robert G. McCutchan, *Our Hymnody*, page 303, for a variant of this account.

Blairgowrie

John B. Dykes, 1872

Robert G. McCutchan writes that this tune "was written by Doctor Dykes in February, 1872, to the words, 'The voice that breathed o'er Eden,' for the wedding of a friend. It is one of the 'stray tunes found in print,' and listed by his biographer, the Rev. J. T. Fowler." (McCutchan 1942, 304)

The tune is named after a small inland town northwest of Dundee, Scotland. (McCutchan 1957, 49)

O Zion, haste (573)

Mary A. Thomson, 1894

This hymn on Christian missions was written in 1868 to Henry Smart's tune "Pilgrims" for F. W. Faber's "Hark, hark, my soul, angelic songs are swelling." Three years later the refrain was added to the six stanzas. It was first included in *The Church Hymnal*, 1894, and entered our hymnals in 1905. Stanzas 1, 2, 4, and 5 are included in our hymnal.

In stanza 3:4, "man" is changed to "we"; in stanza 4:1, "thy sons" to "thine own."

Tidings

James Walch, 1875

The tune was composed for "Hark, hark, my soul, angelic songs are swelling," and was included in *The Hymnal Companion to the Book of Common Prayer*, 1877. (McCutchan 1942, 462) Its marriage with Thomson's text saved it from certain eclipse since Henry Smart and John B. Dykes had firmly established their tunes with Faber's hymn. Ironically, Faber's hymn is no longer included in hymnals.

Of all the Spirit's gifts to me (336)

Fred Pratt Green, 1979

Bernard Braley has commented on this hymn:

> [It] was written for a United Women's Rally, in Croydon, London, [May 1975], and sung during the session on *The Fruits of the Spirit* [Galatians 5:22] addressed by the Metropolitan Anthony Bloom. (Green 1982, 58)

The hymn was composed to be sung to the tune "Ripponden." It first appeared in *More Hymns for Today*, 1980. In our hymnal stanza 2:1, "He shows me love is at the root" has been changed to "The Spirit shows me love's the root"; and in stanza 3:1, "He shows me that if I possess" to "The Spirit shows if I possess."

Meyer

Geistliche Seelen-Freud, 1692

This tune, also known as "Es ist Kein Tag," first appeared in *Geistliche Seelen-Freud*, published by Johann D. Meyer at Ulm, Germany, in 1692. Meyer contributed fifty-four tunes to the collection.

The tune was introduced to English hymnody in a chorale-like setting, presumably by Ralph Vaughan Williams in *The English Hymnal*, 1906. Our harmonization is from *Rejoice in the Lord*, 1985, where it appeared without citation. Another setting is a realization of the original figured bass by John Wilson in *Hymns and Psalms*, 1983.

Of the Father's love begotten (184)
Corde natus ex parentis ante mundi exordium

Aurelius Clemens Prudentius, 4th cent.
trans. by John Mason Neale, 1854, and Henry W. Baker, 1859

Fred D. Gealy has traced the source of this hymn:

> The text is taken from the *Hymnus omnis horae*, beginning "Da puer plectrum," No. 9 in the *Liber Cathemerinon* of the Spanish poet Prudentius [348-ca. 413], the first great poet of the Latin church. The *Cathemerinon* was a collection of 12 hymns for the daily hours ranging in length from 80 and 220 lines. (Gealy, Lovelace, Young 1970, 345)

J. M. Neale's translation in six stanzas with refrain and doxological stanza was first included in *The Hymnal Noted*, 1854, under the superscription "Evening Hymn from the nativity till Epiphany" and "Rev. 1:6, 'I am Alpha and Omega, the beginning and the ending saith the Lord. Which is, and which was, and which is to come, the Almighty.'" The first line began "Of the Father sole begotten." (Gealy 557/385) A six-stanza version of the text is included at 36 in *Salisbury Hymn-Book*, 1857. *Hymns Ancient and Modern*, 1861, included nine stanzas by Henry W. Baker from the hymnal's draft edition, 1859; only the first is retained from Neale.

There is a parallel printing of the Latin and English texts, a review of the sources of the text and music, and a print of the plainsong melody from *Piae Cantiones*, 1582, at 443-46 in *Historical Companion to Hymns Ancient and Modern*, 1962. Following Neale's version, most translate "Corde natus ex parentis" as "Of the Father's love" rather than "Of the Father's heart."

The hymn entered our hymnal in 1966 using stanzas 1, 6, and 9 from *Hymns Ancient and Modern*, 1861.

Divinum mysterium

11th cent. Sanctus trope; arr. by C. Winfred Douglas, 1940
The tune is from an early vocal embellishment or trope on the word "Sanctus," which most scholars date from eleventh- to fifteenth-century manuscripts where it is a setting for the Latin text *Divinum mysterium*. Thomas Helmore's transcription of the triple-time dance melody from *Piae Cantiones*, 1582, was set to this text at 66 in *The Hymnal Noted*, 1854, Part 2, under the spurious superscription "Melody from Ms. of Wolfenböttel of the XIIIth Century." (Gealy 557/385) For further commentary on *Piae Cantiones* see Erik Routley's *English Carol, The Oxford Book of Carols*, and *Guide to the Pilgrim Hymnal*.

Whatever the criticism (Routley calls it "an excellent example of the limitations of knowledge that attended his zeal for antiquity," Routley 1958, 193), Helmore's transcription of this dance tune into a hymn tune is among the first successful attempts to appropriate ancient melody into mid-nineteenth-century congregational song. Beginning with *Hymns Ancient and Modern*, 1861, isorhythmic versions of the tune with clumsy harmonizations have usually been included in British and USA hymnals, including our setting from *The Hymnal 1940*. An exception is the triple-time version in *The English Hymnal*, 1906.

As a processional hymn, random handbell ringing patterns (see 92 in *The United Methodist Hymnal Music Supplement*) may be used with unaccompanied unison voices singing lines or stanzas in alternatim, with all singing the refrain. *The Hymnal 1982* includes a triple-time version in a simple three-part harmonization.

Oh, fix me (655)

See "Fix me, Jesus," pages 335-36.

Old rugged cross (504)

See "The old rugged cross," pages 642-43.

On a hill far away stood an old rugged cross (504)

See "The old rugged cross," pages 642-43.

On eagle's wings (143)

Words and music: Michael Joncas, 1979 (Exod. 19:4)
This is the refrain of a vocal solo that tells of God's providential care. It first appeared in *On Eagle's Wings*, 1979. In the 1980's it was widely used in ecumenical gatherings. The chorus reflects Exodus 19:4:

Then Moses went up to God; the Lord called to him from the mountain, saying, "Thus you shall say to the house of Jacob, and tell the Israelites: You have seen what I did to the Egyptians, and how I bore you on eagles' wings and brought you to myself.

This is the song's first appearance in a major hymnal.

On eagle's wings

This setting was prepared from the piano vocal version.

On Jordan's stormy banks I stand (724)

Samuel Stennett, 1787

The hymn first appeared in John Rippon, *A Selection of Hymns from the Best Authors*, 1787, in eight four-line stanzas under the heading "The Promised Land." (Gealy 557/387) It entered our hymnals in 1808 (see comment on the tune below) and has appeared in all our collections. Our hymnal includes stanzas 1, 4, 5, and 6.

The British poet composed these apocalyptic lines with an ear towards Exodus and Revelation in another cultural setting. USA evangelicals and their song transformed the text into earthy and vital metaphors of the vision, vigor, enthusiasm, and optimism of frontier life moving on to the promised land of Kentucky or Missouri. In rural areas "Jordan" is frequently pronounced "Jerdan."

Promised land

Southern Harmony, 1835; arr. by Rigdon M. McIntosh, 1874

The tune first appeared in a typical singing-school three-part setting in F$^\sharp$ minor in William Walker's *Southern Harmony*, 1835, with the anonymous refrain "I am bound for the promised land." There the tune is attributed to "Miss M. Durham" and cross-referenced to "H. B. p. 471." The latter is the selection number of the hymn in *A Collection of Hymns*, 1821, suggesting that Walker's collection in the 1830's and after was used in Methodist worship settings, as well as extra-church singing schools, and that in spite of the number of different tunes published with the text in Wesleyan collections, this tune was widely used in the Southern church.

The harmonization in parallel major was made by the Methodist Episcopal Church, South publishing house music editor Rigdon M. McIntosh for *A Collection of Hymns and Tunes*, 1874. (Oswalt 1991, 110) This alteration demonstrates the fate of modal and minor tunes that were either dropped or put into major

keys, reflecting the predominant Sunday school and revival styles of Reconstruction times. The tune did not reappear in our official hymnals until 1966.

On the day of resurrection (309)

Michael Peterson, 1984 (Luke 24:13-35)

The first four stanzas is the story told by Cleopas and another confused and
frightened follower of Jesus of the unknown guest who walked with them on the
road to Emmaus. In stanzas 5 and 6 the risen Christ is made known to them
through the breaking of bread, and they joyously return to Jerusalem to proclaim Christ is risen to the eleven and their companions.

The composer has supplied this information about the hymn:

> The text of the hymn was written by Mike as an exercise in a hymn-writing
> class taught by Gracia Grindal at Luther Northwestern Theological Seminary
> in the fall of 1985. . . . Students were setting narrative texts [and] Mike picked
> the road to Emmaus. I "tuned" the text after his presentation of it to the class.
> (Correspondence of Mark E. Sedio to George H. Shorney, March 1992)

For other Emmaus hymns, see "O thou who this mysterious bread," page 534,
and "Cuando el Pobre," pages 312-14. The text first appeared in *Singing the
Story II*, 1985. It was first included with our tune in *Singing the Story III*, 1986.

Emmaus

Mark Sedio, 1984; harm. by Charles H. Webb, 1987

Two voices may sing stanzas 1 through 4 accompanied by guitar or handbells
using the original accompaniment in *Hymnal Supplement II*, (1984). All may join
on stanzas 5 and 6 using the harmonization prepared for this hymnal.

On this day earth shall ring (248)
Personent hodie voces puerulae

Piae Cantiones, 1582; trans. by Jane M. Joseph
(Luke 2:6-14; Matt. 2:1-12)

This nativity carol was translated from *Piae Cantiones*, a collection of medieval
songs and carols compiled by Theodoric Petri. For commentary on *Piae Cantiones*, see "Of the Father's love begotten," page 541. The original Latin text is
found on pages 171-72 of *The Oxford Book of Carols*.

Personent hodie

Melody from Piae Cantiones, 1582; arr. by Gustav Holst, 1925

Our setting is the popular anthem setting by Gustav Holst for mixed voices, keyboard, and bells. It first appeared as a hymn in *Pilgrim Hymnal*, 1958.

The stanzas may be sung by male or female voices, with everyone singing the refrain's reiterated "Ideo" (ee-deh-oh-oh-oh), meaning "therefore," and the song of the angels' "gloria in excelsis Deo" (glory to God in the highest). Handbells may be added at the refrain; see 267 in *The United Methodist Hymnal Music Supplement*.

Once in royal David's city (250)

Cecil Frances Alexander, 1848 (Luke 2:7)

Included in the poet's *Hymns for Little Children*, 1848, this hymn, as others (see "All things bright and beautiful," pages 201-02), elaborates on an article of the Apostles' Creed. The focus of this text is the tenet "Born of the Virgin Mary." Although it is usually included among Christmas hymns, the hymn concerns the total witness of Jesus' birth, life, and enthronement—"a child and yet a king"—prompting the editors of *The English Hymnal* to preface the hymn "Suitable also for Adults."

The omitted stanzas 3 and 6 follow:

> And through all his wondrous childhood
> he would honor and obey,
> Love, and watch the lowly maiden
> in whose gentle arms he lay.
> Christian children all must be
> mild, obedient, good as he.

> Not in that poor lowly stable,
> with the oxen standing by,
> we shall see him; but in heaven,
> set at God's right hand on high;
> when like stars his children crowned
> all in white shall wait around.

The hymn entered our hymnals in the 1935 *Methodist Hymnal*. It was retained in the 1957 hymnal and dropped from our 1966 hymnal. In our stanza 3:1, "For he is our" has been changed to "Jesus is our."

Irby

Henry J. Gauntlett, 1849

John Wilson and Bernard Massey have established the source of this tune. It was composed for these words and set for voice and piano in the composer's *Christmas Carols*, 1849, and included in the poet's *Hymns for Little Children*, 1858. At the invitation of the proprietors of *Hymns Ancient and Modern*, the composer arranged the tune for SATB voices, and it was included with the text at 361 in the section "For the Young" in the 1868 Appendix. (Correspondence with Carlton R. Young, February 1992)

There are descants and an alternative harmonization by David Willcocks at 182-84 in *The United Methodist Hymnal Music Supplement*. Other harmonizations are by Arthur H. Mann at 102 in *The Hymnal 1982* and at 605 in *The English Hymnal*, 1906.

The practice of a boy soprano singing the first stanza *a cappella* at the beginning of the processional seems to have originated with the annual "Service of Lessons and Carols," Kings College, Cambridge. While appropriate for that production, the practice in other circumstances overstates the poem's simplicity. Of this quality Stanley L. Osborne comments, "Mrs. Alexander possessed the delightful gift of simplicity, but now and then it was marred by fancy and naïveté." (Osborne 1976, hymn 112)

One bread, one body (620)

Words and music: John B. Foley, 1978
(1 Cor. 10:16-17; Gal. 3:28; 1 Cor. 12)

This song with "On eagle's wings" **(143)** was made popular in ecumenical gatherings during the 1980's. It first appeared in *Wood Hath Hope*, 1978. The text comes from 1 Corinthians 10:16-17:

The cup of blessing that we bless, is it not a sharing in the blood of Christ: The bread that we break, is it not a sharing in the body of Christ? Because there is one bread, we who are many are one body, for we all partake of the one bread.

Other metaphors and descriptions of our unity in Christ are from Galatians 3:28, 1 Corinthians 12, and the prayer from the *Didache* that all Christians may be gathered into one body, just as the grain gathered from the harvest that was made into one loaf is shared in the eucharistic rite. See also commentary on "Father, we thank you," pages 332-33.

One bread, one body

harm. by Gary Alan Smith, 1988

This setting was made for our hymnal from the piano vocal score. Bass, guitar, and drums may be added.

Only trust him (337)

Words and music: John H. Stockton, 1874

Paul A. Richardson traces this invitational hymn's first appearance to J. E. Knapp's *Notes of Joy for the Sabbath School*, 1869 (Adams 1992, 109). The first four of five stanzas were reprinted in other collections, including the first inclusion in our hymnal in 1890.

Stockton, who was a minister in the Methodist Episcopal Church, was close to the evangelistic work of Dwight L. Moody and Ira D. Sankey, as were other Wesleyan ministers and musicians of that time. During a trip to England in 1873 while studying the hymn in manuscript, Sankey thought the refrain too hackneyed and changed its first line, "Come to Jesus, Come to Jesus, Come to Jesus just now," to its present form. During the London revival meetings in Her Majesty's Theater in Paul Mall, he also substituted "I will trust him" and "I do trust." (Sankey 1906, 162-63; Gealy 556/85)

Moody and Sankey published the hymn as we have included it in *Sacred Songs and Solos*, 1875, under the scripture "Take my yoke upon you, and learn of me; . . and ye shall find rest unto your souls." (McCutchan 1942, 230)

Stockton

The tune has been included in our hymnals without change except the original dotted quarter- and eighth-note rhythm in the penultimate measure has been smoothed over. In Wesleyan collections the tune was named after the author. It is also called "Invitation" and "Minerva."

Onward, Christian Soldiers (575)

Sabine Baring-Gould, 1864

The hymn was composed in six stanzas for a children's Sunday school procession held in 1864 at Horbury Bridge near Wakefield, Yorkshire, and was first published that year in *Church Times* under the title "Hymn for Procession with Cross and Banners." Low-church Anglicans objected to a processional cross as too Roman and sometimes in derision ended the refrain "with the cross of Jesus left behind the door." Evangelical Dwight L. Moody, in contrast to his contemporaries in the Salvation Army, refused to use the hymn in his revivals because as he wryly protested, "We are a fine lot of soldiers!" Between the two world wars social prophet F. R. Barry in *Relevance of Christianity*, 1931, stated, "There is nothing in the whole world that the church of God should less resemble."

For many, if not most Christians, the hymn still conjures vivid scriptural images of the church's constant and necessary spiritual war with Satan and his host, for example, 2 Timothy 2:3: "Share in suffering like a good soldier of Christ Jesus."

For further commentary on militaristic metaphors see Erik Routley, "Allegory—True and False" in *Hymns Today and Tomorrow*, 1964, Abingdon Press; Anastasia Van Burkalow, "A Call For Battle Symbolism in Hymns," *The Hymn*, 1987; and Samuel J. Rogal, "'Onward Christian Soldiers': A Reexamination," *The Hymn*, 1988.

Of the thousands of letters received in the editor's office in response to the Hymnal Revision Committee's decision to delete the hymn, this excerpt from one made a more positive contribution than most: "My mother, who is a Mennonite, hasn't sung 'Onward Christian Soldiers' for 10 years. She said, however, that if one sings the first two verses of the song while cooking an egg, one will have a perfectly cooked soft-boiled egg." For additional commentary on the Hymnal Revision Committee's consideration of this hymn see *"The United Methodist Hymnal, 1989,"* pages 135-37.

The hymn entered our hymnals in six stanzas in 1878. The original stanza 2, dropped in *The Methodist Hymnal,* 1935, has been restored.

St. Gertrude

Arthur S. Sullivan, 1871

The text was written to "St. Alban," adapted from the Adagio of F. J. Haydn's Symphony in D, no. 15, and included in *Hymns Ancient and Modern,* Appendix 1868. Into the third decade of the twentieth century there was still no fixed tune for this hymn. Other settings ranged from the women's chorus entrance song, act 1, scene 4, of Richard Wagner's *Tannhäuser,* "Freudig begrüßen wir die edle Halle" ("Hail! bright abode where song the heart rejoices"), in the 1895 program booklet of Methodism's Epworth League, to "Prince Rupert's March" in *Songs of Praise,* 1925. The former was traced by Charles H. Webb, dean of the School of Music, Indiana University, and a member of the Hymnal Revision Committee.

Sullivan composed the tune and included it with the text in his *Hymnary,* 1872. It is named after Gertrude Clay-Ker-Seymour in whose house the composer stayed while editing *Church Hymnal,* 1874, and where he apparently was inspired to imitate the first two measures of the melody in the tenor in measures five and six.

Open my eyes, that I may see (454)

Words and music: Clara H. Scott, 1895

The hymn first appeared in *Best Hymns, No. 2,* 1895 (Reynolds 1964, 157) and was first included in our 1921 hymnal.

Open my eyes

Stanzas of the hymn may be sung as a call or response to prayer. The tune was named by the revision committee for the 1966 hymnal. It is also known as "Scott."

OTHER GENERAL SERVICES AND ACTS OF WORSHIP

In addition to recommending these services for our hymnal—"the Basic Pattern of Worship" (2), An Order of Sunday Worship Using the Basic Pattern" (3), A Service of Word and Table (6-32), and "The Baptismal Covenant" (33-54)—the worship resources subcommittee also selected and some instances developed these services and acts of worship. Commentary for each is included in Hoyt L. Hickman, ed., *The Worship Resources of the United Methodist Hymnal*, 1989.

Other General Services

A Service of Christian Marriage (864-69)

See Hickman 1989, 127-44, and hymns 642-47.

A Service of Death and Resurrection (870-75)

See Hickman 1989, 145-76, and hymns 652-56, 700-13.

Orders of Daily Praise and Prayer (876)

See Hickman 1989, 177-85.

An Order for Morning Praise and Prayer (876-78)

See Hickman 1989, 185-90.

An Order for Evening Praise and Prayer (878-79)

See Hickman 1989, 190-95.

Affirmations of Faith (880-89)

See Hickman 1989, 199-203.

The Nicene Creed (880)

The Apostles' Creed

See "All praise to thee, my God, this night," pages 198-99; "All things bright and beautiful," pages 201-02; "Canticle of God's glory" (Glory be to God on high), pages 253-54; "Holy, holy, holy," pages 400-01; and "Rejoice, the Lord is King," pages 565-66; see also "Doxology" and "Gloria Patri" in the "Index of Topics and Categories," **951**, for additional settings.

A Statement of Faith of the United Church of Canada (883)

The Statement of Faith of The Korean Methodist Church (884)

A Modern Affirmation (885)

The World Methodist Social Affirmation (886)

Affirmation from Romans 8:35, 37-39 (887)

Laurence Hull Stookey, 1987

See "Blest be the dear uniting love," pages 240-41.

Affirmation from 1 Corinthians 15:1-6 and Colossians 1:15-20 (888)

Laurence Hull Stookey, 1987

See "Steal away to Jesus," pages 609-10.

Affirmation from 1 Timothy 2:5-6; 1:15; 3:16 (889)

Laurence Hull Stookey, 1987

See "O for a heart to praise my God," page 510.

Prayers of Confession, Assurance, and Pardon (890-93)

See Hickman 1989, 203-04.

The Lord's Prayer (894-96)

See Hickman 1989, 204-05, and "The Lord's prayer," pages 641-42.

Our earth we now lament to see (449)

Charles Wesley, 1758

This text was included at 4 under the title "For peace" in *Hymns of Intercession for All Mankind*, 1758. John Wesley placed it in the section on "Believers interceding for the world" in his 1780 *Collection*. It is printed in our hymnal without change.

In stanza 2 the satanic images from the depths of Sheol are from Revelation 9:11:

> They have as king over them the angel of the bottomless pit; his name in Hebrew is Abaddon [Destruction], and in Greek he is called Apollyon [Destroyer].

The images also express the violent death and destruction of the defilers of God in Jeremiah 7:30-34, prompting this comment from Victor R. Gold and William L Holladay:

> The most gruesome of Israel's aberrations was the the sacrifice of children (19:5; 32:35) on the burning platform (Topheth, 2 Kings 23:10). Strictly forbidden by God (Lev. 18:21), it will eventually be recognized as murder. (Metzger and Murphy 1991, 974 OT)

This reference to Topheth, the sacred place that Jeremiah states will become the burying ground, i.e., the "valley of Slaughter," displays the poet's enormous repertory of scriptural metaphor and detail and demonstrates his consummate skill and apparent ease in placing them most effectively in a line or stanza.

Craig B. Gallaway comments that this "text illustrates how early Methodists made the connection of praying for the world and protesting the evils of war." (Sanchez 1988, 157) This is the first inclusion of the text in our hymnals.

Our Father, which art in heaven (271)

See "The Lord's Prayer," pages 641-42.

Our Father, who art in heaven (271)

See "The Lord's Prayer," pages 641-42.

Our Parent, by whose name (447)

F. Bland Tucker, 1939; alt.

This hymn on the Christian family was originally composed in 66. 66. 88 at the request of the commission preparing *The Hymnal 1940*. The poem was extended to conform to the 66.66.888 tune RHOSYMEDRE. Stanley L. Osborne, apparently quoting the poet, states, "The author had his own 'father and mother in mind as fulfilling those things for which the hymn prays.'" (Osborne 1976, hymn 219)

The text is trinitarian: each stanza addresses a person of the Godhead and ends with a reference to a prayer in the USA *Book of Common Prayer*. For example, the ending of stanza 3 comes from the service of matrimony, "and so live together . . . that their home may be a haven of blessing and of peace." Stanza 2 draws from Luke 2:52: "And Jesus increased in wisdom and in years, and in divine and human favor." The hymn's refreshing objectivity is contrasted with most hymns on this subject that tend to be sentimental and moralizing; see commentary on "Happy the home when God is there," page 386.

Recent hymnal committees have struggled with the hymn's first line and have attempted to balance the invocation to "God the Father" with a neuter description of parentage. Our version, prepared after the author's death but with permission of the copyright holder, is the first to render the line fully nonsexist. Other changes made for this hymnal include stanza 2:4, "thus didst to manhood come" to "did to adulthood come"; 3:1, "O" to "Blest"; and 3:3, "who teachest us to find" to "and teach us so to find."

Rhosymedre

John David Edwards, ca. 1838

This tune first appeared under the tune name "Lovely" in the composer's *Original Sacred Music*, dated 1836 by Alan Luff in *Welsh Hymns and Their Tunes*, 1990. This simple step-wise melody, with a characteristically Welsh repeated final line, was later named after the Welsh parish in northeastern Wales where the composer served as vicar.

Except for the first full measure our harmonization is from *The English Hymnal*, 1906. Another setting, presumably the original, is at 165 in *Welsh Hymns and Their Tunes*. A vocal descant and alternate harmonization are found at 284-85 in *The United Methodist Hymnal Music Supplement*. Ralph Vaughan Williams included an organ prelude on this tune in *Three Preludes Founded on Welsh Hymn Tunes*, 1920.

Out of the deep have I called unto thee (516)

See "Canticle of redemption," pages 261-62.

Out of the depths I cry to you (515)
Aus tiefer Not schrei ich zu dir

Martin Luther, 1524
trans. by Gracia Grindal, 1978 (Ps. 130; 120:1-2)

This free paraphrase of the penitential Psalm 130 (see "Canticle of redemption," pages 261-62) was probably composed in 1523 and was first included in four stanzas in Luther's *Achtliederbuch* (*Hymnal of Eight*), 1524. According to Ulrich S. Leupold it is among the first of Luther's hymns that he was introducing to his congregation at Wittenberg by the end of 1523. (Leupold 1965, 192) The same year a revised five-stanza text appeared in *Geistliches Gesangbüchlein*, 1524. The hymn has long been associated with funeral and memorial services, including Luther's, when in 1546 it was sung at Halle as his body was taken from Eisleben for burial at Wittenberg.

Miles Coverdale's translation in his *Goostly Psalmes*, ca. 1535, is the earliest English text. Many hymnals have used variants of Catherine Winkworth's translation from her *Chorale Book for England*, 1863. Gracia Grindal's translation of four stanzas of Luther's text for *Lutheran Book of Worship*, 1978, restores some of Luther's strong

and rugged metaphors that nineteenth-century English writers tended to domesti-
cate. Changes in Grindal's text are stanza 1:2, "O Father, hear" to "O Lord, now";
2:7, "his" to "God's"; 4:4, "his" to "Christ's"; 4:5, "he" to "who"; and 4:7, "We
praise him for his mercy" to "Praise God for endless mercy."

Aus tiefer Not

Attr. to Martin Luther, 1524; harm. by Austin C. Lovelace, 1963

This phrygian melody (E to E on the white keys) may be the work of Luther.
Lovelace's harmonization retains most of the rhythmic qualities of the original
tune while at the same time providing a fine setting for four-part choir. In this
regard Ulrich S. Leupold has commented on the importance of the choir in
teaching the congregation to sing from Luther's first hymnal, *Geistliches Gesang-
büchlein*, edited by Johann Walther in 1524:

> Actually, this was not a hymn book in the modern sense of the word, but a
> collection of polyphonic motets, based on Lutheran chorales. Primarily it
> was designed not for the congregation but for the choir. But it must be
> remembered that Luther wanted his hymns to be sung by the choir to
> familiarize the whole congregation with them. (Luther 1965, 193)

Because of the encroachment of technological entertainment and the paucity of
trained leaders of congregational song, time is running out to restate the fundamental purpose of the choir in participatory evangelical worship, including
United Methodist forms, as essentially pedagogical rather than exclusively performance oriented.

Pass it on (572)

Words and music: Kurt Kaiser, 1969

This chorus is from the widely performed youth musical *Tell It Like It Is*, one of
the first and most widely imitated attempts to present in a church setting traditional Christian values as alternatives to the life-style of drug and sexual permis-
siveness of the youth counter-culture, embodied in the Haight-Asbury flower
children. Though appearing to express and implement Jesus' great commission
in Matthew 28:19-20, the song is a series of superficial, smug, self-centered, and
antisocial responses to the radical demands and risks of Christian discipleship.

Pass it on

This religious show-biz sophistry remains a favorite of sanctified adolescents of all
ages. The last half of stanza 3 may be repeated ad lib and on beats 4 and 1, following "mountain top," the singers may shout "praise God," point their finger to the
sky, clap their hands, and stomp their feet. Chords for keyboard and guitar are
found at 264 in *The United Methodist Hymnal Music Supplement*.

Pass me not, O gentle Savior (351)

Fanny Crosby, 1868
This hymn first appeared with the tune at number 39 in *Songs of Devotion for Christian Associations*, 1870, compiled by William H. Doane. (Gealy 557/395) William J. Reynolds has traced the writing of the hymn to the spring of 1868 when the poet attended a worship service in a Manhattan prison. "After she had spoken and some of her hymns had been sung, she heard one of the prisoners cry out in a pleading voice, 'Good Lord, do not pass me by.'" (Reynolds 1990, 226) The poet composed the hymn that evening, following Doane's earlier suggestion that she write a hymn using the line "Pass me not, O gentle Savior." Introduced by Dwight L. Moody and Ira D. Sankey in their London revivals, this is Crosby's first hymn to win worldwide acclaim. See also commentary for "Only trust him," pages 545-46. The hymn entered our hymnals in 1874.

The text is apparently based on the blind beggar's plea to Jesus, the "Son of David," to have mercy and restore of his sight. (See accounts in Matthew 20:29-34; Mark 10:46-52; Luke 18:35-43; and a variant in Matthew 9:27-31.) The hymn has been rightly criticized for its faulty exegesis of this scripture since it is not Jesus who is calling, but the beggar; further, it is contrary to the scriptural account to suggest that Jesus Christ, God's universal gift of salvation (John 3:16), could, should, would—and, in this instance did—pass anyone by. These complaints were exacerbated, not diminished, when the poet changed the refrain from "while on others thou art smiling" to "while on others thou art calling."

Pass me not

William H. Doane, 1870
The tune is a paradigm of evangelical minimal music. See the commentary on "Blessed assurance, Jesus is mine," pages 237-38, and "Just as I am without one plea," page 455.

Passion/Palm Sunday (281)

Lutheran Book of Worship, 1978; alt. by Laurence Hull Stookey, 1987
This prayer from the *Lutheran Book of Worship* appears to have been adapted from the collect for Palm Sunday in the *Book of Common Prayer*. Our version omits "to take our flesh upon him" in line 2; and "your Son" in line 6. The prayer is appropriate for Passion/Palm Sunday and other Holy Week services of prayer and praise.

People, look east (202)

Eleanor Farjeon, 1928
This rousing and imaginative proclamation of Christ's coming first appeared in *The Oxford Book of Carols*, 1928. The omitted stanza 3 describes the anticipated Christ as "Love the Bird":

Birds, though ye long have ceased to build,
Guard the nest that must be filled.
Even the hour when wings are frozen
he for fledging-time has chosen.
People, look East, and sing today:
Love the Bird is on the way.

Besançon

Trad. French Carol; harm. by Martin Shaw, 1928

This choir setting is from *The Oxford Book of Carols*, 1928, where the source of the tune is cited:

An old Besançon carol tune, "Chantons, bargiés, Noué, Noué," which appeared with the anonymous words "Shepherds, shake off your drowsy sleep" in Bramley and Stainer's collection [*Christmas Carols New and Old*, ca. 1877]. (*The Oxford Book of Carols* 1964, 273)

A different stanza may be sung by the choir as a call to worship each of the four Sundays in Advent.

Praise and thanksgiving be to God (604)

Frank Whiteley, 1969
versified by H. Francis Yardley; alt. 1989 (Luke 3:21-22)

The circumstances of the writing of this hymn have been traced by Stanley L. Osborne:

[It] grew out of a thesis on "Baptism," submitted by Frank Whiteley to Victoria University in 1970. After completing 5 stanzas in outline, the author sought the assistance of his friend, Harold Francis Yardley, in the versification. By the fall of 1969 the text was ready. The first 3 stanzas are framed as an invocation to the three Persons of the Trinity and are intended to precede the action of baptism. The concluding stanzas constitute a response to that action. (Osborne 1976, hymn 318)

The hymn first appeared using the first three stanzas in the United Church of Canada's, *Hymn Book*, 1971.

Our hymnal omits stanza 4:

Eternal Word, still by the Father spoken,
speak to us now in this baptismal token;
proclaim anew to us, love divine, unceasing,
in us increasing.

Stanza 1:1-2 originally read:

> Praise and thanksgiving be to our Creator,
> source of this sacrament, Father, Mediator.

Other changes for our hymnal occur in stanza 1:3, "make your own these who" to "made your own now we"; and stanza 3:3, "come, O risen Savior" to "strengthen us, O Savior."

Christe sanctorum

See "Christ is the world's light," page 277.

Praise God from whom all blessings flow (94)

Thomas Ken, 1674; adapt. by Gilbert H. Vieira, 1978

This response, or doxology, is comprised of the first two lines of Ken's doxological stanza of his morning and evening hymns, "Awake, my soul, and with the sun," curiously missing from our hymnal, and "All praise to thee, my God, this night" **(682)**; troped Alleluias; and additional lines of praise to the three Persons of the Godhead. The adapter has commented on the response: "[I tried] to create a more acceptable text in the midst of the struggle we were experiencing with sexist language at Mill Valley [California] church." (Correspondence with Carlton R. Young, 1988)

For commentary on "Doxology," see "Glory be to the Father," page 355.

Lasst uns erfreuen

See "All creatures of our God and King," pages 190-91.

Praise God, from whom all blessings flow (95)

Thomas Ken, 1674

This metrical paraphrase of the Lesser Doxology (see "Glory be to the Father," pages 355-56) is the doxological stanza of Thomas Ken's evening hymn "All praise to thee, my God, this night" (see pages 199-201). John Wesley appended it to Isaac Watts's hymn "Praise ye the Lord" at 10 in his Charleston *Collection*, 1737. Its first inclusion in our hymnals as a free-standing act of praise appears to be at 293 in the thirty-sixth edition of the *Pocket Hymn-Book*, 1810. Most of our nineteenth-century hymnals included a selection of doxological stanzas in a section at the end of the collection titled "Doxologies."

The Amen was retained for this doxology, but not for the version at number **94**. See page 139 for a commentary on the deletion of Amens from our hymnal.

Old 100th

See "All people that on earth do dwell," page 197.

Praise, my soul, the King of heaven (66)

Henry F. Lyte, 1834 (Ps. 103)

The author first published this widely sung free paraphrase of Psalm 103 in five stanzas, one for each of the five sections of the psalm, in his *Spirit of the Psalms*, 1834 (Gealy 557/398), a collection with more than 280 psalm paraphrases. This is one of three paraphrases of this psalm.

The omitted stanza 4 is somewhat closer to the psalm text than some other portions of the hymn:

> Frail as summer's flower we flourish;
>   Blows the wind, and it is gone,
> But while mortals rise and perish,
>   God endures unchanging on.
>   Praise Him! Praise Him!
> Praise the high eternal One!

The hymn entered our hymnals in 1878 with the fifth line of each of the first three stanzas substituting "Hallelujah!" for "Praise Him."

Changes have been made for our hymnal in stanza 1:2, "his feet" to "the throne"; 1:4, "his" to "God's"; 2:1, "praise him for his" to "praise the Lord for"; 2:2, "our fathers" to "all people"; 2:3, "him" to "God"; 2:6, "in his" to "now God's"; 3:1-2, "he" to "God"; 3:3, "in his hands he" to "motherlike, God"; 3:6, "his" to "God's"; 4:1, "adore him" to "adoring"; 4:2, "ye behold him" to "you behold God"; 4:3, "bow before him" to "now adoring."

Lauda anima

See "God, whose love is reigning o'er us," page 376.

Praise the Lord who reigns above (96)

Charles Wesley, 1743 (Ps. 150)

This hymn is based on Psalm 150 and first appeared in four eight-line stanzas in the 1743 second edition of *A Collection of Psalms and Hymns*, 1741. John Wesley reduced the hymn to three stanzas by dropping two quatrains, 2b and 3a, and a new 2b was composed of 2a and 3b and included with the hymns and psalms he appended to the 1784 *Sunday Service*, published the same year in London as *A Collection of Psalms and Hymns for the Lord's Day*. (Gealy 557/398) For commentary on Wesley's *Sunday Service* see "The Music of Hymns, Wesleyan Style," page 63, and "Hymnals of The Methodist Church," pages 97, 98, 99.

This appears to be the only psalm paraphrase by Charles Wesley with sustained use in Methodist hymnals. It seems very reserved, if not commonplace, when compared with his earlier hymns, for example, "Christ, from whom all blessings flow" **(550),** and others from *Hymns and Sacred Poems*, 1740. In stanza two the poet's characterization of music as heavenly art and our most powerful music-offering to God as the "music of the heart" is particularly ingratiating.

Although the hymn was included in several nineteenth-century USA tune books, it did not appear in our hymnal until 1966. In our hymnal changes have been made in stanza 2:4, "his" to "this"; 2:5, "him" to "with"; 3:1, "him" to "God"; and 3:5, "his" to "thy."

Amsterdam

Foundery Collection, 1742

The tune is from J. A. Freylinghausen's *Geistreiches Gesangbuch*, 1704, a tune book used by the Moravians on board ship and in the Georgia colony. John Wesley, from his contact with the Moravians in Georgia, included a flawed variant named "Amsterdam Tune" on pages 29-30 in his *Foundery Collection*, 1742, interlined with "I will hearken to what my Lord shall say concerning me," cross-referenced to page 210 in *Hymns and Sacred Poems*, 1742.

Bryan F. Spinney has commented on Wesley's tune book in the introduction to the collection reprinted by him in 1981:

> The Foundery, where cannons had been made until an explosion wrecked the building, stood in Moorfields, London. John Wesley bought it in 1739 and rebuilt it into the first centre of Methodist work in the captial [*sic*], with a preaching-house, school-room and living quarters (later adding a dispensary and alms-house). . . . [In the collection] are many examples of tunes wrongly-barred—although Wesley may have copied these errors from earlier psalm-tune books. The pitch of some tunes is quite incredible. Wesley gathered these tunes from 3 main sources—(1) psalm tunes already in use in churches, (2) German chorales—many from Freylinghausen's *Gesangbuch* of 1704, (3) Contemporary tunes, including a march from a Handel opera. Only the melody is given—Wesley having serious doubts about singing in parts. (Spinney 1981, 2)

Our version of the tune and harmony are from 84 in *The Sacred Harp*, 1844. The tune entered our hymnals at 114 in the 1857 music edition of our 1849 hymnal with the original four-part harmony and alto and tenor notes added to the duet in measures 9-12. There is a descant, an alternate harmonization, and a transposition at 16-18 in *The United Methodist Hymnal Music Supplement*.

Praise to the Lord, the Almighty (139)
Lobe den Herren, den mächtigen

Joachim Neander, 1680
sts. 1, 3, 5, trans. by Catherine Winkworth, 1863
st. 2, S. Paul Schilling, 1986
st. 4 , Rupert E. Davies, 1983 (Ps. 103:1-6; 150)

The German text first appeared in Neander's *Glaub-und Liebes-übung*, 1680. Winkworth's translation is from her *Chorale Book for England*, 1863. (Gealy 557/402) Stanza 2 was translated by S. Paul Schilling, a consultant to the Hymnal Revision Committee, from *Evangelisches Kirchengesangbuch*, 1953; and stanza 4 was translated by Rupert E. Davies for *Hymns and Psalms*, 1983.

S. Paul Schilling has commented on stanza 2:

> I had long been concerned about the theology of the English translation of stanza 2. "How thy desires e're have been granted in what he ordaineth?" We do not regard hopeless poverty, plane crashes, and child abuse as part of God's good plan. . . . I checked Neander's original German text and discovered that the offending passage was a mistranslation. . . . The committee also approved the correction of another error, substituting *who* (Neander's *wer*) for *if* in the last of stanza 3. (Correspondence with Carlton R. Young, July 1992)

The hymn and tune entered our hymnals in 1935.

Lobe den Herren

Ander theil des Erneuerten Gesangbuch, 1665
harm. by William Sterndale Bennett and Otto Goldschmidt, 1863

Neander adapted the tune for his 1680 *Glaub-und Liebes-übung*. Our harmonization is from the music edition of *The Chorale Book for England*, 1863. The hymn is universally sung to this melody, one of the best constructed and singable tunes from the chorale tradition. Unfortunately its vigorous one-to-a-measure pulse is invariably stilted by congregations, abetted by inept accompanists who reduce it to the prance of an elephant dance.

There are a descant, three alternate harmonizations, and a transposition at 218-21 in *The United Methodist Hymnal Music Supplement*.

Praising God of many names (104)

Mechthild of Magdeburg, Germany, 13th cent.
This prayer from the thirteenth century may be recited before singing "God of many names" **(105)** and other hymns with nongender deity metaphors. See for example, "Praise to the Lord, the Almighty" **(139)** or "O worship the King, all-glorious above" **(73)**. The prayer is from George Appleton, ed., *The Oxford Book of Prayer*, 1986.

Prayer for a new heart (392)

Dag Hammerskjöld, Sweden, 20th cent. (Matt. 5:8)
This prayer is seven lines from a nineteen-line prayer composed in 1954 and included at page 83 in *Markings*, a collection of Hammerskjöld's intimate and revealing meditations published in 1964, ten years after his death. Hammerskjöld's prayer for a pure heart is echoed in his other writings in the collection. The poet consistently uses the intimate second person singular "Du" when addressing deity, according to standard English usage faithfully rendered throughout the collection as "thou."

Laurence Hull Stookey has commented that the poem expresses "what it means to have a heart that sees, hears, serves, and abides in God." (Sanchez 1988, 139)

Prayer is the soul's sincere desire (492)

James Montgomery, 1818
This hymn on the all-sufficiency of prayer was written in 1818 at the request of Edward Bickersteth and was first included in broadsheets used by the poet in his Sunday schools in Sheffield. It was included in *Treatise on Prayer*, 1819, and printed as selection 278 in four stanzas of eight lines in the section "Hymns Chiefly Intended for Private Use" under the scripture "'Praying always with all prayer.' Eph. 6. 18," in Thomas Cotterill's *Selection of Psalms and Hymns for Public and Private Use*, 1819 8th ed. (Gealy 557/406)

The hymn entered our hymnals as an eight-stanza CM text in 1837. Since 1878 stanzas 1-3, 5, 4, and 8 have been used. For our hymnal changes have been made in stanza 4:1, "sinner's" to "sinners'"; 4:2, "his ways" to "their way"; 4:4, "he" to "they"; 5:1-2, "Christian's" to "Christians'"; 5:3, "his" to "their"; and 5:4, "he enters" to "they enter."

The omitted stanza 7 links prayers of earth with the activity of the Holy Spirit and the intercession of the enthroned Christ:

> Nor prayer is made on earth alone;
>   The Holy Spirit pleads;
> And Jesus, on the eternal throne,
>   For sinners intercedes.

Campmeeting

USA camp-meeting melody; harm. by Robert G. McCutchan, 1935
According to R. G. McCutchan:

> The tune is also called "Belief," because [it was] used with the familiar revival refrain beginning, "I do believe [I do believe that Jesus died for me]," and to John Newton's hymn beginning: "How sweet the name of Jesus sounds." (McCutchan 1957, 51)

This tune with a slightly different ending and the same basic harmony is named "Morrow" and set to "Alas, and did my Savior bleed," included on page 84 as "Old Melody Arranged" in Rigdon M. McIntosh's *Hermon*, 1873. The collection cites Thomas O. Summers as "assisting in the hymn-tune department."

Prayer of Ignatius of Loyola (570)

Ignatius of Loyola, Spain, 16th cent.
This prayer for guidance in the service of God's people is from Selina Fitzherbert, ed., *A Chain of Prayer Across the Ages*, 1916.

Prayer of John Chrysostom (412)

After the Book of Common Prayer; Greek, 5th cent. (Matt. 18:19-20)
This prayer by Chrysostom, a leader of the Eastern church in the fourth to fifth century, reflects Christ's promise recorded in Matthew 18:20, "For where two or three are gathered in my name, I am there among them." It was adapted by Thomas Cranmer, 1544, and has been included in the *Book of Common Prayer* as the final prayer in "The Order for Daily Morning Prayer." John Wesley maintained it at that place in "The Order for Morning Prayer, Every Lord's Day," in *The Sunday Service of the Methodists in North America*, 1784. The prayer was first printed in our hymnals in the 1935 Methodist hymnal at page 515 in the section "Prayer and Collects." It was also included in *The Book of Worship*, 1944.

Our version in contemporary English first appeared on page 48 under the title "Answer to Prayer" in the *Lutheran Book of Worship*, 1978.

Prayer of Saint Francis (481)

See "The Prayer of Saint Francis," page 643.

Prayer to the Holy Spirit (329)

Trad. Native American prayer
This anonymous prayer from Native American sources is from a longer version in *The United Methodist Book of Worship*, 1992. The prayer identifies and focuses on Native Americans' historic reverence for and affinity with nature.

"Holy Spirit" was included in the title on the hymn page to allay criticism that this is not a Christian prayer; in the fuller form the prayer is addressed to "Great Spirit: Gitchi Manitou or Most Awesome of the Awesome," who may not be considered by some as a person of the one undivided Trinity. For additional commentary on Native American forms of address to deity, see also "'Twas in the moon of wintertime," pages 670-71.

Precious Lord, take my hand (474)

Words and music: Thomas A. Dorsey, 1932

The most celebrated of Dorsey's songs was composed in Chicago in 1932 in the sorrowful aftermath of the death of the composer's wife Nettie during childbirth and shortly thereafter the death of the child. The song of faith came to Dorsey as he quietly fingered at the piano the old Sunday school pentatonic tune MAIT-LAND **(424)**. He sang it for the gospel singer and his friend, Theodore Frye, who the following Sunday introduced it with his choir at Ebenezer Baptist Church. Many years later Dorsey remarked during a filmed interview that the introduction of the song "tore up the church." On April 9, 1968, at the open-air service at Morehouse College following the funeral of Martin Luther King, Jr., at Ebenezer Baptist Church, Atlanta, Georgia, Mahalia Jackson's memorable and compelling rendition introduced this gospel song and the performance practice of African American gospel music to millions worldwide via television and radio.

Precious Lord

Arranged for the 1989 hymnal, this is one of William Farley Smith's best settings for congregational singing. It should be played slowly in qⁱ i-recitative style with warm and intense expression that allows the singerʳ to lean, slide, and glide to and on the blue-notes and the anticipatory and auxiliary notes, and to caress words and phrases with special meaning.

See "Must Jesus bear the cross alone," page 486, for comment on the affinity of Dorsey's tune with the nineteenth-century Sunday school melody MAITLAND **(424)**.

Precious name (536)

Lydia Baxter, 1870 (Phil. 2:9-11)

This text was written in 1870 and was first included with the tune at number 13 under the scripture "'And blessed be his glorious name for ever.' Psalm 72:19" in *Pure Gold for the Sunday School*, 1871. (Gealy 557/447) The hymn is a typical mixture of key evangelical words and phrases such as "child of sorrow" and "when his loving arms receive us." Set to self-confident minimal music, it proclaims simply, if not magically, that in spite of the magnitude and the source of human pain and grief, by taking the Name of Jesus into every situation, all without qualification will enjoy the joy, comfort of Jesus, and his limitless protection from temptation. For comment on other hymns on the name of Jesus, see "At the name of Jesus every knee shall bow," pages 220-21, and "All praise to thee, for thou, O King divine," pages 198-99. The hymn first appeared in our hymnals in 1878. It is included in our hymnal without change.

Precious name

William H. Doane, 1871

Since the hymn is never sung with regard to the original alternation of dotted eighth- and sixteenth- and even eighth-note patterns, these patterns have throughout been printed as the former.

Prepare the way of the Lord (207)

Isaiah 40:3; 52:10

This advent chorus is comprised of Isaiah 40:3b and 52:10b, c. It comes from the Taizé, France, community.

Prepare the way

Jacques Berthier and the Community of Taizé, 1984

This chorus may be sung in unison or as a two-, three-, or four-part round, and can be used as an opening response, call to worship, or processional. The key should be raised to either F or G♭ for more effective singing. Accompany with handbell clusters of the tonic, fourth, and fifth, and tambourine and drums.

For additional commentary on the music of Taizé, see "Eat this bread," pages 324-25.

Psalm 23 (King James Version) (137)

This version of the psalm was included with the hymns and canticles to maintain one language base in the Psalter. In addition, some members of the Hymnal Revision Committee objected to the New Revised Standard Version and before it the Revised Standard Version, in particular the translation of verse 6:8c, "as long as I live," as opposed to the traditional quasi-Christian words "for ever." Other versions of this psalm are found at **23, 128, 136, 518,** and **754.**

Response 1

Words: Psalm 23:1, Grail version, 1963
Music: Joseph Gelineau, 1963

This response by Joseph Gelineau, perhaps his most memorable, is from his musical setting of the complete Grail version text.

Response 2

Words: John 10:10, adapt.
Music: Richard Proulx, 1987

The musical setting was prepared for our hymnal.

Both responses may be used with the version of Psalm 23 at **754**.

Psalm 24 (King James Version) (212)

This version is included with the hymns and canticles to maintain one language base in the Psalter and to make it available to many who prefer the traditional words to those of the New Revised Standard Version.

Response 1

Words: Isa. 6:3
Music: Anon.

The music is taken from Sanctus No. 1, *The Methodist Hymnal*, 1905.

Response 2

Words: Psalm 24:3b, 4a, adapt.
Music: Jane Marshall, 1987

The musical setting was made for this hymnal.

Pues si vivimos (356)
When we are living

St. 1, anon., trans. by Elise S. Eslinger, 1983
sts. 2, 3, 4, Roberto Escamilla, 1983
trans. by George Lockwood, 1987 (Rom. 14:8)

This moving and compelling Mexican folk hymn first appeared in four stanzas in Spanish and English, selection 39 in *Celebremos II*, 1983. Gertrude C. Suppe has traced the discovery of the hymn:

> In February 1980, after a church meeting in La Trinidad United Methodist Church in Los Angeles, CA, I saw a woman standing off to one side by herself. I got acquainted with her and found that she was visiting from Mexico. I asked if she remembered any of the songs they used in her church in Mexico. She did, and her sister, Ana Maria Domingues, sang a number of simple songs, which I taped on the spot. "Pues si vivimos" was one of them, and I later presented it to the Celebremos II Committee for consideration. (Correspondence with Carlton R. Young, July 1991)

The first stanza is based on Romans 14:7-8:

We do not live to ourselves, and we do not die to ourselves. If we live, we live to the Lord, and if we die, we die to the Lord; so then, whether we live or whether we die, we are the Lord's.

The additional stanzas by Roberto Escamilla are elaborations of John 15:8, "My Father is glorified by this, that you bear much fruit and become my disciples," blended with the passage from Romans and composed for *Celebremos*, 1983. Since the English words in *Celebremos* were essentially an independent poem, Escamilla's moving and powerful stanzas were translated for our hymnal by George Lockwood.

The hymn is suitable for times of remembrance and new beginnings, for example graveside committals, baptisms, or weddings. The stanzas may be sung in Spanish and/or English accompanied by a guitar, with the congregation joining on the refrain.

Somos del Señor

Trad. Spanish melody; harm. from Celebremos II, 1983

The tune's name is the first Spanish words of the refrain and the title by which the hymn is widely known. The harmony is probably by Elise S. Eslinger who was music editor of *Celebremos II*, 1983. An alternate harmonization is included in our hymnal at **666**, and a setting for Orff instruments is found at 320 in *The United Methodist Hymnal Music Supplement*.

Quaerite Dominum (125)

See "Canticle of covenant faithfulness," pages 252-53.

Refuge amid distraction (535)

See "A refuge amid distraction," page 185.

Rejoice in God's saints (708)

Fred Pratt Green, 1977

This hymn describes the importance of saints and how they interact in the world. It was composed from two processional hymns that Green had written for the six-hundredth anniversary celebration of Mother Julian's *Revelations of Divine Love*, commissioned by the Dean of Norwich Cathedral. (See **493** for a prayer by Mother Julian.)

Unlike the original hymns that of necessity dealt with the cloistered life of many saints, this text is set in the everyday world. Bernard Braley has commented that the hymn was developed in this regard on the advice of John Wilson, "who was at the time an adviser to the group responsible for *Broadcast Praise*, the supplement to the *BBC Hymn Book*. It was sung for the first time on BBC radio 4 in the Daily Service on Monday 21st September 1981." (Green 1982, 66-67)

The text in *Hymns and Ballads of Fred Pratt Green* at stanza 3:3 reads: "They share our complaining" instead of "They shame our complaining" as found in our hymnal and others including *Broadcast Praise*.

Hanover

Attr. to William Croft, 1708

The tune, similar in its opening to LYONS **(73)**, first appeared anonymously in *The Supplement to the New Version of the Psalms*, 1708 6th ed. (Ellinwood 1956, 190) The collection was edited by William Croft who probably composed the tune. It entered Wesleyan usage at page 6 in John Wesley's *Foundery Collection*, 1742, where it appeared with few blemishes, unlike most tunes, as "Bromswick Tune" set to "Father of mankind, be ever ador'd." The name "Hanover" is apparently from the tune's attribution to G. F. Handel who had served as Kapellmeister to the Elector of Hanover (later George I).

The tune's inclusion in *Hymns Ancient and Modern*, 1861, and *The English Hymnal*, 1906, which used the harmonization without citation, established it as an alternate to LYONS. Our harmonization, unique to USA hymnals, was first included in our 1905 hymnal. It is apparently the work of its musical editors who appear to have adapted it from the the Presbyterian *Hymnal*, 1903. *Rejoice in the Lord*, 1985, includes the *Hymns Ancient and Modern* harmonization with a descant by John Wilson.

Rejoice, the Lord is King (715, 716)

Charles Wesley, 1746 (1 Cor. 15:51-52)

The text first appeared as "Hymn VIII" in *Hymns for Our Lord's Resurrection*, 1746 (1747 3d ed. in Gealy 557/404).

Watson and Trickett have commented that the hymn combines "the first and last verses of Psalm 97: 'The Lord reigneth, let the earth rejoice' and 'Rejoice in the Lord, ye righteous; and give thanks at the remembrance of his holiness.'" (Watson and Trickett 1988, 167)

The text is rich in New Testament and credal imagery of the exalted Christ, for example Hebrews 1:3c-4a: "he sat down at the right hand of the Majesty on high, having become as much superior to angels"; and the Apostles' Creed,

"he ascended into heaven, and sittest at the right hand of God the Father Almighty; from thence he shall come to judge the quick and the dead."

The refrain for the first three stanzas is from the Great Thanksgiving of the Eucharist beginning "Lift up your hearts"; and the final refrain is Paul's resounding affirmation of the Resurrection in 1 Corinthians 15:50-52, particularly 15:51b-52a, "We will not all die, but we will all be changed, in a moment, in the twinkling of an eye, at the last trumpet." The hymn entered our hymnals in 1786 in six stanzas. Our hymnal includes stanzas 1, 2, 3, and 6 with the original words.

Fred D. Gealy comments that since the season of Easter includes seven Sundays, "congregations singing resurrection texts and ministers preaching sermons on the various and difficult aspects of the resurrection faith [could enable] the church to come to a new understanding of itself and be itself raised from the dead." (Gealy 557/406)

Darwall's 148th

John Darwall, 1770
harm. from Hymns Ancient and Modern, 1889, alt.

The tune first appeared in Aaron Williams, *The New Universal Psalmodist*, 1770 (McCutchan 1942, 219), where it was set to a paraphrase of Psalm 148. In nineteenth-century British hymnals it was used with "Ye holy angels bright," and in our hymnals during the nineteenth century it became identified with Wesley's enthronement hymn.

There are instrumental and vocal descants, and an alternate harmonization at 78-80 in *The United Methodist Hymnal Music Supplement*.

Gopsal

G. F. Handel, ca. 1752; arr. by John Wilson, 1964

Between 1749 and 1752 G. F. Handel composed settings for solo voice and figured bass for three texts by Charles Wesley: "On the Resurrection" for this text; "The Invitation" for "Sinners, obey the gospel word"; and "Desiring to Love" for "O Love divine, how sweet thou art." The original manuscript was discovered in 1826 in the Fitzwilliam Museum Library at Cambridge by the poet's son Samuel, who in turn published them as *The Fitzwilliam Music never before Published, Three Hymns, the Words by the late Rev. Charles Wesley . . . Set to Music by George Frideric Handel . . .*, 1826. For additional commentary see John Wilson, "Handel and the Hymn Tune: I, Handel's Tunes for Charles Wesley's Hymns," *The Hymn*, October 1985.

John Wilson realized the tune for four-part singing in *Hymns for Church and School*, 1964, and it is included with his SA descant at 243 in *Hymns and Psalms*, 1983. There is a descant for two trumpets at 147 in *The United Methodist Hymnal Music Supplement*.

The tune is named after Gopsal Hall, Leicestershire, the residence of Charles Jennens, Handel's close friend and the librettist for *Messiah*. This is the tune's first appearance in our hymnals.

Rejoice, ye pure in heart (160, 161)

Edward H. Plumptre, 1865 (Ps. 20:4; 147:1; Phil. 4:4)
This text was composed as an eleven-stanza processional for the annual choir festival at Peterborough Cathedral, England, May 1865, and published that year by Novello and Co. in a musical setting (Julian 1907, 897); and without music in the author's *Lazarus, and Other Poems*, 1868 3d. ed. (Gealy, Lovelace, Young 1970, 359) It was first included as a hymn at 386 in *Hymns Ancient and Modern*, 1868 Appendix.

Erik Routley cites British author and clergyman Nathaniel Micklem's assessment of the hymn as a processional: "He could see why it was necessary to walk about while singing it for otherwise one would fall asleep." (Routley 1977, commentary on hymn 1)

Stanzas 1, 5, 7, 9, and 11 are included in our hymnal. In stanza 1:3, "festal" is changed to "glorious"; and in 5:1, "Him" is changed to "God."

Marion

Arthur H. Messiter, 1883
Leonard Ellinwood has stated that the tune was written for these words in 1883 and was first included in Plumptre's music edition of the *Hymnal*, 1893. (Ellinwood 1956, 339) The composer added a refrain using stanza 1:2.

Vineyard Haven

Richard Wayne Dirksen, 1974
This outstanding contribution to the repertory of twentieth-century USA tunes was composed for the installation of John M. Allin as presiding bishop of the Episcopal Church, Washington Cathedral, June 11, 1974. (Glover 1987, 52-53) The festival setting for choir and congregation is included at 48 in *Ecumenical Praise*, 1977. The composer's refrain is from stanza 2:1 and 1:2. The tune is named after the town in Martha's Vineyard, Massachusetts, to which Francis B. Sayre, dean of Washington Cathedral, retired in 1978.

Dirksen's setting vies with R. Vaughan Williams's SINE NOMINE for saving a maudlin hymn from its deserved place in hymnic obscurity.

Remember me (491)

Trad. (Luke 23:42)
This anonymous prayer response and petition is probably a camp-meeting chorus primarily sung in African American worship. It should be sung very slowly and sustained. For commentary on the prayer of the penitent thief on the cross, see "Do, Lord, remember me," pages 321-22, and "Jesus, remember me," page 445.

Cleveland

Trad; harm. by J. Jefferson Cleveland, 1981
This setting first appeared in *Songs of Zion*, 1981, and is named after its coeditor.

Rescue the perishing (591)

Fanny J. Crosby, 1869
The author has written that this hymn was prompted through her contact with the men of a New York City mission.

> The thought kept forcing itself on my mind that some mother's boy must be rescued that night or not at all. I made a pressing plea that if there were a boy present who had wandered from his mother's home and teaching, he would come to me at the close the service. A young man of eighteen came forward and said, "Did you mean me? I promised my mother to meet her in heaven, but as I am now living that will be impossible." We prayed for him and he finally arose with a new light in his eyes and exclaimed in triumph: "Now I can meet my mother in heaven, for I have found God." When I arrived home I went to work on the hymn at once, and before I retired it was ready for the melody. . . . The next day . . . it was forwarded to Mr. Doane, who wrote the beautiful and touching music. (Crosby 1915, 77)

S. Paul Schilling, the eminent theologian and a consultant to the Hymnal Revision Committee, commented during the deliberation for continuing this hymn in our hymnals that it should be kept because it was one of very few gospel hymns that expressed the gospel imperative to reach out, i.e., "care," "rescue," "weep with," "lift up" and "save" society's despised and rejected. The hymn entered our hymnals in 1882.

Rescue

William H. Doane, 1870
The words and music first appeared at 258 in *Songs of Devotion for Christian Associations*, 1870. (Gealy 557/406)

Righteous and just is the word of our Lord (107)

See "La palabra del Señor es recta," pages 457-58.

Rise, shine, you people (187)

Ronald A. Klug, 1973 (Isa. 60:1)
This powerful advent text was written for and first published in an Augsburg Publishing House bulletin insert. (Stulken 1981, 433)

Each stanza begins with strong active verbs—rise, see, come, and tell—and ends in affirmation of the promised coming in Jesus Christ of the graceful, forgiving, and glorious new creation. For our hymnal changes have been made in stanza 1:3, "He" to "Christ"; 2:2, "he" to "and"; and in 4:5, "His" to "God's."

Wojtkiewiecz

Dale Wood, 1973
The tune was composed for this text and was included with it in the bulletin insert (see above). "[It] bears the composer's family name, Wojtkiewiecz [Polish], which was lost early in this century when an immigration official suggested it be changed to Wood." (Stulken 1981, 433)

Rise to greet the sun (678)
Qing zao qi zan-mei Shen

Chao Tzu-ch´en, 1931; trans. by Mildred and Bliss Wiant, 1946
This morning hymn with the tune first appeared at 425 in *Hymns of Universal Praise*, 1936, "[a volume of] more than four hundred hymns of Western Christendom translated into Chinese. It also included sixty-two hymns written by Chinese Christians and seventy-two tunes of Chinese origin or composition." (Ronander and Porter 1966, 367)

It was translated by Mildred and Bliss Wiant and included in their *Pagoda*, ca. 1946, a small collection of Asian music used by them to teach and celebrate the Asian heritage of Christian song upon their return to the USA following the Chinese Communist revolution.

The hymn describes in simple, almost childlike words, phrases, and metaphors the sun's summons to a new day and the responses of nature and humans. Stanza 2 is a prayer for safekeeping and, reflecting Confucian teaching, a petition to be a worthy example by good conduct, restrained actions, and veneration of parents and elders. The hymn concludes with words of trust and thanksgiving to Jesus.

Le p'ing

Te-ngai Hu; arr. by Bliss Wiant, 1936

The tune name means "Happy peace." It was arranged for *Hymns of Universal Praise*, 1936, for which Wiant served as music editor. Wiant recounted in his lectures, attended by this writer, that the composer told him that he first heard the tune in a marketplace played on a flute by a street musician.

As with most indigenous Asian melody, it is desirable to sing only the melody. Accompany the singers with a recorder or four-foot organ flute, adding a light tambourine tap on beats 1 and 3. The melody may also be sung as a canon at the octave one measure apart. See additional commentary on the performance practice of Asian music in "Asian American Hymns," pages 35-36.

For a discussion of the styles of Chinese hymn tunes see Bliss Wiant, "What Music Means to the Chinese," *The Hymn*, 1974.

Rise up, O men of God (576)

William P. Merrill, 1911

Fred D. Gealy has commented on the origin of the hymn:

> [It] was prompted by a suggestion of Nolan R. Best, editor of the *Continent*, that a brotherhood hymn was needed by the Presbyterian Brotherhood Movement. About that time Merrill saw an article by S. Lee entitled "The Church of the Strong Men," which furnished the inspiration for the hymn. While on a steamer on Lake Michigan, returning to Chicago for a Sunday at his own church, he suddenly thought of the words. (Gealy, Lovelace, Young 1970, 362)

The poem was published in the *Continent* on February 16, 1911, and was included with the music in the *Pilgrim Hymnal*, 1912. It was included in all major hymnals, entering our hymnals in 1935.

While the hymn has recently and rightly been criticized because of its "men only" invitation to Christian service (note the suggested change to "ye saints"), the fundamental objection is in its unqualified call to whomever it pleases to rise up, i.e., leave or forsake undesignated lesser things. Further objections are to its fuzzy teaching that God's kingdom of righteousness, having already been set before us in the life, death, and resurrection of Christ Jesus, is yet to be brought in rather than joined to, and its sexist and phallic characterization of the Christian church (her) as inadequate, patiently waiting to be fulfilled with an infusion of masculine endeavor. Finally, it closes with military marching metaphors that divert dealing with human societal systemic evil and substitute personal feel-good sentiment and gang eroticism for reality.

That the hymn has remained the theme song of United Methodist Men is as disquieting as is its continued use in local settings.

Festal song

William H. Walter, 1894

The tune first appeared in *Hymnal Revised and Enlarged*, 1894, and was first set to this text in the *Pilgrim Hymnal*, 1912. The shortcomings of the hymn are enhanced by Walter's platitudinous tune.

Rock of ages, cleft for me (361)

Augustus M. Toplady, 1776

The imagery in this famous hymn bears close resemblance to two hymns in Charles Wesley's *Hymns on the Lord's Supper*, 1745: number 27, "Rock of Israel, cleft for me"; and number 31, especially the later stanzas 1:1, 5-6, "O Rock of our salvation, see By water and by blood redeem, And wash us in the mingled stream"; 2:1-2, "The sin-atoning blood apply, And let the water sanctify"; and 3:1, "The double stream in pardons rolls."

The summary of these hymns and Toplady's is found in this excerpt from John Wesley's abridgement of Daniel Brevint's *Christian Sacrament and Sacrifice*, 1673, included as an introduction to the 1745 collection:

O Rock of *Israel*, Rock of Salvation, Rock struck and cleft for me, let those two streams of *Blood and Water*, which once gushed out of Thy side, bring down *pardon* and *holiness* into my soul. And let me thirst after them now, as if I *stood upon the mountain whence sprung this Water*; and near the *cleft* of that Rock, the wounds of my Lord, whence gushed this sacred *Blood*. All the distance of time and countries between *Adam* and me doth not keep his sin and punishment from reaching me, any more than if I had been born in his house. *Adam* descended from above, let Thy Blood reach as far, and come as freely to save and sanctify me as the blood of my first father did both destroy and to defile me. (Rattenbury 1948, 148)

Toplady's hymn, composed in 1775, was included on page 308 under the title "A Prayer, living and dying" in his *Psalms and Hymns for Public and Private Worship*, 1776. (Gealy 557/411) A three-stanza version was included by Thomas Cotterill in his *Selection of Psalms and Hymns*, 1815 (Gealy 557/411), and this version entered our hymnals in 1831. Our hymnal restored Toplady's original text for stanzas 2 and 3. See Julian 1907, 971-72, for a discussion of the sources and variances of this hymn. Erik Routley has provided a penetrating commentary in *Hymns and the Faith*, 1956, and he includes at 113 in *An English-Speaking Hymnal Guide* a transcription of the article from *The Gospel Magazine*, March 1776, that precedes the first printing of the text.

Research by H. J. Wilkins, *An Enquiry Concerning Toplady and His Hymn "Rock of Ages" and its Connection with Burrington Combe, Somerset*, 1938 (Gealy 557/411), has connected the hymn to the theology of its flinty author, including his running battle with John Wesley on matters of predestination and election. Notwithstanding Wilkins's strong and convincing case to discourage such action, there are those, including this writer, who have climbed the steep wall of the gorge near Burrington Combe in order to have their picture taken as they stand, more likely stoop, in the cleft of the rock that was supposed to have sheltered the author and prompted this hymn.

Toplady

Thomas Hastings, 1830

The tune was first included in *Spiritual Songs for Social Worship*, 1832. (Reynolds 1976, 187) Countless generations of USA congregations and organists have attempted in vain to establish and maintain a suitable tempo for this hymn, described by Erik Routley "as the only popular and universal hymn about sin." (Routley 1956, 146)

Rock-a-bye, my dear little boy (235)
Najej, nynej

Czech carol; trans. by Jaroslav J. Vajda, 1987

The translator of this charming nativity carol has commented that it had captivated him for many years:

> I was, however, disappointed in the lightness of its content, pretending as it does to be sung by the maiden who composed the Magnificat. Wondering what kind of lullaby the mother of the Savior might have sung to "that holy thing" she had borne, [at the invitation of Carlton R. Young whom I met at the Hymn Society meeting in Fort Worth] I wrote a new text moving the content of the carol closer to a hymn while trying to keep the simplicity and intimacy of the traditional carol. (Vajda 1987, 172)

Rocking

Czech carol; melody collected by Martin Shaw, 1928

This harmonization was first included at 87 in *The Oxford Book of Carols*, 1928. Unlike the setting in *The Oxford Book of Carols*, the translator has placed each syllable under one note. Erik Routley has noted the tune's similarity to "Twinkle, twinkle, little star." (Routley 1958, 203)

When performed by a choir or as a solo accompanied by guitar, measure 2 may be echoed in measure 3, and 7-8 in 9-10.

¡Santo! ¡santo! ¡santo! (65)

Reginald Heber, 1826; trans. by Juan Bautista Cabera (Rev. 4:8-11)

This is one of many translations of classic English hymns that Cabera made for evangelical hymnals in Spain during the late-nineteenth and early-twentieth centuries. Sixty-nine of his hymns were included in *El Himnario para el Uso de las Englesias Evangélicas de Todo el Mundo,* New York, 1931, a collection of 491 hymns whose content influenced most North American, Mexican, and Caribbean evangelical Spanish language hymnals. Cecilio M. McConnell has commented that Cabera's translation of Heber's trinitarian hymn is greatly beloved and widely sung in Spanish language churches. (McConnell 1987, 120)

For commentary on this hymn see "Holy, holy, holy! Lord God Almighty," pages 400-01.

Nicaea

See "Holy, holy, holy! Lord God Almighty," pages 401-02.

Saranam, Saranam (523)
I take refuge

Trad. Pakistani; trans. by D. T. Niles, 1963 (Ps. 61; Heb. 13:8)

The English text first appeared at 163 in the *E.A.C.C. Hymnal,* 1964. I-to Loh has noted that "the key word *saranam* is repeated many times, almost like a mantra [Hindu incantation], to reinforce the central idea. (Sanchez 1988, 179)

Punjabi

Arr. Shanti Rasanayagam, 1962

This version of a popular Punjabi mantra-like melody is arranged in the style of a Sunday school song and first appeared in the *E.A.C.C. Hymnal,* 1964. For our hymnal the first beat in each measure of the refrain has been changed to an upbeat.

Savior, again to thy dear name we raise (663)

John Ellerton, 1866; alt.

The text was composed in six stanzas as the closing hymn for the 1866 Festival of the Malpas, Middlewich, and Natwich Choral Association. It was revised by the author and reduced to four stanzas for *Hymns Ancient and Modern,* 1868 Appendix. (Ellinwood 1956, 300) This shorter version entered our hymnals in 1878 and was set to W. H. Monk's EVENTIDE **(700).**

Stanley L. Osborne has nicely summarized the hymn: "The central theme is peace: the peace of evening, the peace of night, and peace throughout our life." (Osborne 1976, hymn 370)

Ellerton's manuscript of his reduction of the hymn to four stanzas, titled "Evening (After Services, Sundays or Festivals)," is reproduced at 92 in *Historical Companion to Hymns Ancient and Modern*, 1962.

Ellers

Edward J. Hopkins, 1869
This tune was set for this text and first appeared in Robert Brown-Borthwick, *Supplemental Hymn and Tune Book*, 1869 3d ed., with a different organ accompaniment for each stanza. The composer adapted one harmonization for SATB voices for *Appendix to the Bradford Tune Book*, 1872. This version entered our hymnals in 1905 and has been included in all our editions. (See *Pilgrim Hymnal*, 1958, for the original harmonies.)

Relief from this harmonization is found in *The Hymnal 1982*, a sturdy harmonization by Arthur Sullivan from *Church Hymns with Tunes*, 1874; and in *Hymns for Church and School*, 1964, where two additional adaptations from the composer's extended setting are included. *The United Methodist Hymnal Music Supplement* includes a descant at 117.

Savior, like a shepherd lead us (381)

Attr. to Dorothy A. Thrupp, 1836 (John 10:1-29)
The hymn first appeared in the poet's *Hymns for the Young*, ca. 1830. Its authorship is uncertain, a dilemma for the hymnologist, aptly expressed by John Julian:

The most that we can say is that the evidence is decidedly against Miss Thrupp and somewhat uncertain with regard to [Henry F.] Lyte as the writer of the hymn. (Julian 1907, 996)

The hymn was first included in our hymnals in 1867.

Bradbury

William B. Bradbury, 1859
This tune was set to these words and appeared in the composer's *Oriola*, 1859. The refrain was abridged for the 1966 hymnal, and because of many complaints, the original version is included in our hymnal (see commentary on "God be with you till we meet again," pages 361-62).

Savior of the nations, come (214)
Nun komm, der Heiden Heiland
Veni, Redemptor gentium

Sts. 1, 2, Martin Luther, 1523
trans. by William M. Reynolds, 1851; sts. 3-5, Martin L. Seltz, 1969
The Latin text is usually ascribed to Ambrose of Milan. For commentary on this hymn and Ambrose, see Julian 1907, 56-57; "Latin Hymns," page 5; and the commentary on "O splendor of God's glory bright," pages 529-30. Martin Luther's translation was made in 1523. In 1524 it was included in both *Enchiridion Oder handbüchlein* and Johann Walther's *Geistliches Gesangbuchlein*. W. M. Reynold's translation is from the Evangelical Lutheran Church hymnal, *Hymns, Original and Selected*, 1851. M. L. Seltz's stanzas 3-5 were included in the *Worship Supplement*, 1969. (Stulken 1981, 127) See 55 in *The Hymnal 1982* for Ambrose's hymn translated in LM.

This hymn is one of the most simple lyrical restatements of God's saving and reclaiming grace in Jesus' sonship with the Father, his virgin birth, death, and ascension. The final stanza proclaims Christ as the Light of the world. This is the first appearance of this hymn in our hymnals.

Nun komm, der Heiden Heiland

Enchiridion Oder handbüchlein, 1524; harm. by J. S. Bach; alt.
Erik Routley traces the chorale melody to the plainsong "Jesu Dulcedo Cordium." (Routley 1981, 23; X28) Two more early forms of the melody are shown at pages 190-91 in *Historical Companion to Hymns Ancient and Modern*, 1962. Konrad Ameln reprints six Reformation tunes derived from the plainsong "Veni Redemptor gentium" (55, *The Hymnal 1982*) in *The Roots of German Hymnody of the Reformation Era*, 1964 (reprinted at 296 in *The Hymnal 1982 Companion*, vol. 1, 1990).

The chorale melody was shaped by either Johann Walther or Martin Luther and appeared with Luther's text in *Enchiridion Oder handbüchlein*, 1524. Our setting is adapted from J. S. Bach's harmonization in *The English Hymnal*, 1906; it seems to be a composite setting from Bach's harmonization. There are many organ settings of this chorale including three by J. S. Bach in *Clavierübung* and one in *Orgelbüchlein*.

The hymn may be performed in cantional style (see "German Hymns," pages 7-8) with stanzas accompanied or performed without singing from the above resources and other harmonizations from *Lutheran Book of Worship*, 1978, and *The Hymnal 1982*.

See how great a flame aspires (541)

Charles Wesley, 1749 (Luke 12:49; 1 Kings 18:44-45)
This hymn was written for coal miners whose exhausting twelve to fourteen-hour workplace by day was the dark and filthy mines, and whose nights were

endured in the stench and glow of the colliery fires (the imagery of stanza 1), burning refuse, and the roar of the furnaces. It is the last of four hymns under the title "After Preaching to the Newcastle Colliers," and was included at 315-16 in *Hymns and Sacred Poems*, 1749. (Gealy 557/419) Frank Baker states that the hymn "was actually written for the coalminers in Staffordshire, probably in 1743 or 1744, and taken up with enthusiasm by those in Newcastle. (Baker 1962, 110) John Wesley included it in his 1780 *Collection* in the section "For Believers Rejoicing." The hymn first appeared in our hymnals in *A Selection of Hymns*, 1810.

Craig B. Gallaway comments that each stanza mirrors powerful scriptural images, including the outpouring of the Holy Spirit in Acts 1:8; 2:3, 17, and "'I came to cast fire upon the earth; and would that it were already kindled' (Lk., 12:49); God's 'word runs swiftly' (Ps. 147:15); God's 'call into existence the things that do not exist' (Rom. 4:17); and Elijah's victory over the prophets of Baal (1 Kg. 18:36-46)." (Sanchez 1988, 185) See F. Hildebrandt and O. A. Becker-legge (Wesley 1983, 7:341-42), for additional scriptural references.

Changes for our hymnal have been made in stanza 3:1, "sons" to "saints"; and in 3:2 and 3:6, "he" to "who."

Arfon (Major)

Welsh hymn melody; harm. by Carlton R. Young, 1963, alt.
This sturdy tune is a variant of the French tunes "Je sais, Vierge Marie" and "Un nouveaux présent des Cieux." (Routley 1958, 210) Alan Luff has traced its first appearance in Welsh sources to Edward Jones's *Relicks of the Welsh Bards*, 1784, reprinted 1794. (Luff 1990, 151) The tune received its name in *Caniadau y Cyssegr*, 1878 (Gealy, Lovelace, Young 1970, 375), and was brought into common use through *The English Hymnal*, 1906.

For additional commentary on this tune, see C. Louis Fouvy, "The Hymn Tune 'Arfon,'" *Bulletin: The Hymn Society of Great Britain and Ireland*, 1988.

The major form of the melody in our hymnal has been included in recent Canadian and USA hymnals. The harmonization was prepared for our 1966 hymnal.

See the morning sun ascending (674)

Charles Parkin, 1953 (Rev. 5:11-14; 7:11-12)
This hymn connects morning worship to the imagery from Revelation of heavenly hosts singing praises to the Lamb on the throne. It was written for the May 1953 session of the Maine Annual Conference of the former Methodist Church and entered our hymnals in 1966.

Changes have been made for our hymnal in stanza 2:4, "praising God for his" to "praising thee for thy"; and in 3:1, 3, 4, "for his" to "for thy."

Unser Herrscher

The matching of this hymn with this tune exemplifies how our hymn singing can be and often is basically a musical experience. For commentary on this tune, see "God of love and God of power," pages 367-68.

Seek the Lord (124)

Fred Pratt Green, 1986 (Isa. 55:6-11)

The hymn was written at the request of the Hymnal Revision Committee to complement the "Canticle of Covenant Faithfulness" **(125)**. The author has written about its composition:

> I was delighted to be asked to try to write a paraphrase of my favourite O. T. passage. It surprised me that no one else, at least in the hymn books I possess, had done it. But when I started on the work I soon found how difficult it is to turn such a magnificent passage into rhymed verse. I have done my best, deciding not to try to do a thorough paraphrase but to concentrate on certain ideas. You will see I have added a final verse in the form of a personal commentary. If you like it, and are willing to include it (providing, of course, you accept the text), I suggest it should be either printed in italics or separated from the main text, as I have done.

> You will be amused to know I finished my rough draft between 3 and 4 a.m. this morning! (Correspondence with Carlton R. Young, October 1986)

A comparison of the hymn with the canticle on the facing page will reveal the author's faithful yet refreshing paraphrase of this call to repentance and reminder of God's unfailing grace. For additional commentary see "Canticle of Covenant Faithfulness," page 252.

Since our hymnal's editor neglected to follow the author's wishes in regard to the final stanza, it is here included in the requested form:

> *God is love! How close the prophet*
> *To that vital gospel word!*
> *In Isaiah's inspiration*
> *It is Jesus we have heard!*

In stanza 1:6 "he" has been changed to "God."

Geneva

George Henry Day, 1940

The tune was "composed in 1940 . . . and named in honor of Geneva, New York, where the composer . . . served as organist and choirmaster of Trinity Church [from 1935 until his death in 1966]. (Ellinwood 1956, 105) The author suggested that the hymn be sung to an 87. 87 tune, for example STUTTGART **(611)**. The Hymnal Revision Committee chose GENEVA, an 87. 87. D tune, with the view that its midpoint change from minor to major would allow equal expression for each stanza, especially the final stanza, and a summary in a New Testament context.

Seek the Lord who now is present (125)

See "Canticle of covenant faithfulness," page 252.

Seek ye first (405)

Words and music: Karen Lafferty, 1971 (Matt. 6:33)
st. 2 anon., 1980 (Matt. 7:7)

This devotional scripture song was written in 1971 following a Bible study on Matthew 6:33. It was shared informally and soon became a standard song of the "Jesus movement," whose music became to be known as "Contemporary Christian." It was first included in *Praise 1*, 1971. The second stanza and the "Alleluia" descant were included in *Songs for Celebration*, 1980.

For a discussion of scripture song see Carol Doran, "Popular Religious Song" in vol. 1 of *The Hymnal 1982 Companion*, 1990.

Seek ye

There is an accompaniment for singing the stanzas with the descant and as a round at 711 in *The Hymnal 1982*.

Send me, Lord (497)
Thuma mina Somandla

Words and music: Trad. South African (Isa. 6:8)

This prayer-song was transcribed from recordings of South African worship and included in *Freedom Is Coming*, published by the Iona Community, Scotland.

Thuma mina

Sing this traditional call-and-response song very slowly and freely without accompaniment. Some editions cite A. Nyberg as arranger.

Send your word (195)
Mikotoba o kudasai

Yasushige Imakoma, 1965; trans. by Nobuaki Hanaoka, 1983 (Gen. 10, 11; Matt. 7:7)
Toshiharu Motomura of the Hymnal Committee of the United Church of Christ in Japan has provided this information: "This text was selected from invited contributions and included in *Sambika* (*Hymns of Praise*), 1967, published by the United Church of Christ in Japan." (Correspondence with Carlton R. Young, June 1992) It was translated for *Hymns from the Four Winds*, 1983, whose editor, I-to Loh, has commented that the text is a prayer that the Incarnate Word may be sent to free us from chaos and strife and lead us into a new world. (Sanchez 1988, 78)

Mikotoba

Shozo Koyama, 1965
The music was composed for this text and appeared in *Sambika* (*Hymns of Praise*), 1967.

Toshiharu Motomura, a member of the Hymnal Committee of the United Church of Christ in Japan, has provided this information:

> The tune was also a winning piece when the Hymnal Committee invited new hymn tunes for Rev. Imakoma's hymn. The composer was deeply impressed by the colloquial expressions of the hymn, in which the author speaks of God directly, and [this] was his first experience of composing a tune in a colloquial Japanese verse. [The] original tune had a more complicated rhythm in the middle part; it was simplified in accordance with the committee's request. (Correspondence with Carlton R. Young, June 1992)

The tune may be doubled by recorder, and the second stanza may be sung by the choir. The tune's name is from the first line of the hymn in English sounds.

Sent forth by God's blessing (664)

Omer Westendorf, 1964
Marilyn Stulken has noted that the hymn was included "under the pseudonym 'J. Clifford Evers' . . . in the *People's Mass Book*, 1964. Several alterations were made in the text when it entered *Contemporary Worship-4: Hymns for Baptism and Holy Communion*, 1972." (Stulken 1981, 301)

Changes in the text were made for the *Lutheran Book of Worship*, 1978. Our hymnal makes additional changes that complete the change of this joyous hymn from a dismissal song at the Eucharist to a general closing hymn that bids the worshipper to tell of God's grace and our unity in Christ. These changes also remove the remaining sexist pronouns: stanza 1:4, "supper" to "service"; 1:6, "this service" to "our worship"; 1:7, "his" to "the"; 1:10, "His" to "God's"; 1:11, "his" to "and"; 1:12, "his" to "call"; 2:4, "his" to "God's"; 2:7, "feast" to "grace"; and 2:12 "his" to "that."

The Ash Grove

Welsh folk tune; harm. by Leland Sateren, 1972

Alan Luff has traced this tune to the harp melodies that were made popular

> outside Wales by a succession of harpists who became very popular in England in the 17th, 18th and 19th centuries. . . . These were melodies mainly of Welsh origin, some of them published with variations in the fashion of the time. The earlier Welsh harpists played the 'triple harp,' a form of the instrument in which there were three rows of strings, the outer rows tuned in unison and the inner row giving the semitones to make a full chromatic scale possible. . . . The instrument has had a clear influence on the melodies, however ancient in origin many of them may be. Most of these melodies are in the modern major and minor keys. The harp plays chords easily, and the melodies are built strongly around notes of the basic chords of the key, tonic, dominant and sub-dominant. The well-known *Ash Grove* makes this quite clear. . . .
>
> [When the tunes were recovered in the nineteenth century, they were set to themes] of wistful love and longings for home, with much reference to the hills and valleys of Wales. . . . [When] *Ash Grove* is sung in English, [it is] a celebration of the delights of the country lover; in Welsh it is called *Llwyn Onn* and is the tragic story of an accidental shooting while out hunting with the bow. (Luff 1990, 26-29)

Luff also includes a form of the melody from John Owen's *Gems of Welsh Melody*, 1873. Our harmonization is from *Contemporary Worship-4*, 1972.

Serenity (499)

John Greenleaf Whittier, 1872

See "Dear Lord and Father of mankind," pages 316-17.

Serenity

Charles E. Ives, ca. 1909

This impressionistic setting of stanzas 3 and 4 of our text (358) was scored by Ives for muted strings and soprano. The gentle dissonant ostinato in the accompaniment against the chant-like solo line effectively combine to characterize the poet's mystical "silence of eternity." Each stanza ends with a typically Ivesian quotation of a Victorian harmonic cliché. The subtle raise of the vocal line in the second stanza by one step and the final concluding clusters demonstrate the composer's genius and uniqueness in early twentieth-century USA music.

Our keyboard version should be played at the organ using light strings and tremulant to accompany either a soprano solo, or soli treble voices, preferably middle-school-age voices.

Serenity prayer (459)

See "The serenity prayer," page 643.

SERVICE MUSIC

Amen

A Hebrew word meaning "so let it be" or "truly," amen (Deuteronomy 27:15-26) is by far the most important [liturgical] acclamation. (Werner 1959, 265) In Christian worship it has been used as a response of the congregation to prayer: "All the people shall say, 'Amen!'" as a shouted individual response to preaching and sung to a variety of choral settings ranging from the monumental final chorus of G. F. Handel's *Messiah* to a two-chord cadence for a church choir.

The decision by the Hymnal Revision Committee to recommend dropping the amens from all but a few of the hymns in our hymnal elicited a grumble of dissatisfaction from United Methodists. The committee's rationale for the deletion came from the position that Erik Routley had so convincingly set forth in *Church Music and the Christian Faith*, 1976, reprinted at pages 269-71 in *The Hymns of the United Hymnal*, 1988.

In brief, Routley viewed the practice of joining amen with hymn singing as originating in Ambrosian and monastic performance practice whereby the final doxological stanza to the triune God ends, as does its spoken version, with "amen." For an example of a doxological stanza, see stanza three of "Father, we praise thee" (**680**).

There is no precedent for this practice in Lutheran, Reformed, seventeenth- and eighteenth-century Anglican, or evangelical worship. (John Wesley would have thought it particularly absurd to have concluded his brother's hymns this way.) In the mid-nineteenth century the inclusion of Anglican translations of ancient hymns into congregational hymnals included amens—and with it a major problem. While plainsong can accommodate an extra two syllables at the end of the hymn, the standard English hymn tune composed for parish congregational singing cannot accommodate it without being rewritten. Therefore the "amen" was placed outside the tune and at the end of the doxological stanza and sung to a plagal cadence, IV-I. The practice soon got out of hand.

So eager were the Tractarians to make it clear that the medieval culture alone was the pure religious culture, and medieval hymnody the proper norm for all other hymnody, that at a number of points in their hymnals they appended doxologies with amens to existing hymns. . . . Doxology or no, amen was added to every hymn, and since every non-plainsong tune in that book ended with a perfect cadence the amens were set uniformly to a plagal cadence. The hymnal [that set this precedent] was the most famous of all hymnals, the 1861 edition of *Hymns Ancient and Modern.* (Routley 1978, 96-99)

By the turn of the century some, not all, non-Anglican USA hymnals had adapted this unnecessary yet comforting practice that marked for some the conclusion of hymns played and sung "as if you were half dead, or half asleep." (John Wesley's "Directions for Singing," **vii**) Presbyterians led the way for appending the amen in their 1895 hymnal: "It is the usage of many of our churches to sing the Amen at the close of each hymn, and the proper chords have been provided for such purpose." (Preface, *The Hymnal* 1885, iv) Amen was added to each hymn in our 1905 and 1935 hymnals. Our 1957 and 1966 hymnals selectively excluded it from some hymns, for example, "The first Noel" and "How great thou art."

By the mid-twentieth century the amen was an anachronism to British Anglicans and nonconformist worship leaders alike. USA Protestant Episcopal Church hymnals faithfully maintained it until *The Hymnal 1982*, when it was dropped. Most recent hymnals have dropped the amen and join with Southern Baptist hymnals who have never included it.

To assist those United Methodist musicians and clergy who have made the amen the eleventh commandment, the plagal cadence is set in all major and minor keys in all positions at 904 B-C in *The United Methodist Hymnal Music Keyboard Edition.*

(897) *Dresden*

This amen may have been composed by Johann Gottlieb Naumann, 1741-1801. (Gealy, Lovelace, Young 1970, 441) Felix Mendelssohn used it in his *Reformation Symphony*, 1830, and Richard Wagner employed it as the Grail theme in *Parsifal*, 1882.

(898) *Danish*

A Scandinavian breakfast pastry in G major for sleepy choirs, this amen is of Danish origin according to tradition.

(899) (900) *Vincent Persichetti*

These were included in *Hymns and Responses for the Church Year*, 1956. In the preface the composer describes each as a "musical entity, complete but compressed." They were first included in *the Pilgrim Hymnal*, 1958.

(901) *Carl Wiltse*

This was first included in the Service Music Project published in 1983 by the Section on Worship of the General Board of Discipleship.

(902)   *John Rutter*

This is the final section of the widely performed anthem "The Lord Bless You and Keep You," 1981. At the editor's request the composer adapted it for our hymnal, lowering it one-half step. It is the only composition in our hymnal with dynamic and expression marks—a condition insisted on by the composer.

(903)   *Philip E. Baker*

The composer appended this amen to "Let us now depart in thy peace" (**668**). It may be performed as a coda to the hymn or as an amen. The full setting of the hymn with the amen is found at 1 in *The United Methodist Hymnal Music Supplement*.

(904)   *Peter Christian Lutkin*

This is the amen from the composer's famous benediction response that was published in octavo as "The Lord Bless You and Keep You," 1900. The first section of the setting appeared in the 1905 hymnal without this amen, "as Dean Lutkin did not feel it was suitable for congregational use." (McCutchan 1942, 555) The complete setting is included in *The Baptist Hymnal*, 1991.

Musical Responses for Baptismal Covenant (53-54)

Many congregations have a tradition of congregation singing of responses that extends back to the mid-nineteenth century and beyond that to the camp-meeting chorus. In providing these congregational musical settings for Baptismal Covenant and Word and Table, as well as the psalm responses, the Hymnal Revision Committee affirms that vital tradition. The music for a liturgy conceived and convened as the people's work is music for the primary choir—that is, the congregation. The purpose of other choirs is to assist the primary choir.

> [Therefore] when congregations encourage or permit a choir to take over their own responses and hymns by elaborate musical settings beyond the reach of the average worshipper, they are forfeiting their privileges and responsibilities. They no longer participate in a liturgy; they are listening to a performance. (Shepherd 1952, 55)

In "The Baptismal Covenant" 1, 2, and 3, these are the congregational responses within the "Thanksgiving Over the Water." Response 1 is 1 Chronicles 16:23; response 2 is from 2 Chronicles 16:24; and the final response a doxology. Both settings were composed for our hymnal.

1987   *Charles H. Webb,*

This setting was composed in a nineteenth-century harmonic idiom to complement the sections from Franz Schubert's *Deutsche Messe* (**21**). The four-part harmony is found in *The United Methodist Hymnal Keyboard Edition*.

1987   *Carlton R. Young,*

These are set in a leader-and-response pattern to be accompanied by guitar and/or piano.

For commentary on the services of the Baptismal Covenant see pages 86-109 in Hoyt L. Hickman, ed., *The Worship Resources of the United Methodist Hymnal*, 1989.

Musical Responses for the Psalms

The Psalter of the 1966 hymnal proved controversial. Fifty psalms from the Revised Standard Version of the Bible were included in whole or part, but they were printed in short phrases that for the most part destroyed their characteristic parallelism. Further, its language for the worshipping assembly was more exclusive and sexist than the majority of the hymns. Reflecting this widely held negative opinion as well as the renewed use of the psalms in United Methodist worship, the 1980 General Conference instructed the Section on Worship of the General Board of Discipleship to develop and test a new version of the Psalter. The result was the commissioning of a new translation of the Psalms by Gary Chamberlain, published by The Upper Room in *The Psalms: A New Translation for Prayer and Worship* (1984) and *Psalms for Singing* (1984).

The 1984 General Conference in authorizing the hymnal's revision called for a combination hymnal and worshipbook but did not explicitly call for the development of a new Psalter, leaving it to the Hymnal Revision Committee to make that determination. The committee's Psalter subcommittee formed the psalms text subcommittee, comprised of Charles M. Smith, chair, Harrell Beck, John Holbert, S T Kimbrough, Jr., Alan Luff, and editor, Carlton R. Young, who developed the responses for the psalms and canticles and their musical settings.

For further commentary on the work of the psalms text subcommittee see "*The United Methodist Hymnal*, 1989: Worship Resources," page 154. A description of the committee's formation and task, and the content of The United Methodist Liturgical Psalter are described by Charles M. Smith in *The Worship Resources of the United Methodist Hymnal* (Hickman 1989, 110-26).

The purpose of The United Methodist Liturgical Psalter is described in its preface:

> The book of Psalms is the hymn book of the Bible. At the heart of Judeo-Christian worship and prayer, the psalms express the rich spectrum of human emotions, attitudes, and needs in relation to God, God's family, and the world. . . . Psalms, spoken and sung, were early on the foundation of Christian worship. [See Massey H. Shepherd, Jr., *The Psalms in Christian Worship*, 1976.] The church in reform and renewal has turned to the psalms. [See Walter Brueggemann, *The Message of the Psalms*, 1984, and *Israel's Praise*, 1988.]

> This liturgical psalter, prepared for use in public worship, is based upon the new Revised Standard Version of the book of Psalms. It is faithful to the

biblical text and its message and is more readable, singable than any of our previous psalters. Metaphors and forms of address for people and deity are, with few exceptions, inclusive. (Preface 1989, 736)

Because of space limitations only 100 psalms and their responses out of the 114 from the *Report of the Hymnal Revision Committee* are included in our hymnal. These are included with the remaining fifty psalms and the omitted portions of other psalms, referenced to the common lectionary, in *Psalms for Praise and Worship: A Complete Liturgical Psalter*, 1992, edited by John Holbert, S T Kimbrough, Jr., and Carlton R. Young, with a foreword by Walter Brueggemann.

The psalms in The United Methodist Liturgical Psalter may be read in unison or in a call-and-response style. They may also be sung. Reading and singing may be combined.

Singing the psalms and responses

The psalms and responses may be sung with or without accompaniment in a variety of ways:

1. The verses may be chanted by a soloist/cantor, choir or congregation using the five psalm tones that are included from the *Lutheran Book of Worship*, 1978, as shown in the hymnal at **737**; or the responses may be sung with the chanted verses. Pitch adjustments may have to be made when using a sung response with a psalm tone. The five psalm tones are transposed to seven adjacent keys for ease in making the appropriate adjustments in pitch in order to accommodate the sung response and the sung text at 367-70 in *The United Methodist Hymnal Music Supplement*.

2. The verses may be chanted with accompaniment using the harmonizations for all responses, and the psalm tones are included in the *Keyboard Edition of The United Methodist Hymnal*. The responses may be accompanied either in octaves or with the harmony that is provided. Handbells may be used for intonations, and may double the keyboard at the response. Guitar, Orff instruments, or additional keyboards may also be used.

3. The psalms may be sung in variants of 1 and 2; for example, the verses may be sung without accompaniment, and the responses sung with accompaniment; or the verses may be sung in alternation by male and female soloists or soli choir and the response sung by all.

4. Be sure to take sufficient time to introduce the congregation properly to new tones, responses, or when altering the performance practice.

5. Worship leaders are encouraged to use phrases from other familiar hymns as sung responses.

Combinations of reading and singing the psalms

Combining the reading and singing of psalms is particularly useful when the performance practice of psalm reading and singing is new to a congregation. When introducing combinations of reading or singing, it is important to remain flexible to avoid establishing one format as normative for all occasions. Performance directions should be explicitly stated and in some instances reviewed in a brief rehearsal.

There are two basic ways to combine reading and singing:

1. The psalm, or portions thereof, may be read in unison or in responsorial styles by a leader or leaders, or by the congregation. The choir, soloist/cantor sings the response.

2. The psalm may be read in unison or responsorial styles by a leader or leaders, or the congregation. Everyone sings the response.

The scriptural references of the responses are included at the top of the psalm. Some responses were written by members of the psalms text subcommittee whose contributions are noted in the "Biographies," pages 714-866. Many sung responses were drawn from familiar hymns, spirituals, and songs. Six composers were commissioned to supply settings for the remaining responses: Alan Luff, Jane Marshall, Richard Proulx, Don E. Saliers, Gary Alan Smith, and Carlton R. Young. The composers are included in "Biographies," pages 714-866.

The sources of the musical responses are listed below by psalm and response number. The responses adapted from Charles Wesley's verse have been traced by S T Kimbrough, Jr., and citations to "Fish" refer to Henry Fish, *The Wesleyan Psalter*, 1854, originally published in 1854 as *A Poetical Version of Nearly the Whole of the Psalms of David. By The Rev. Charles Wesley, M. A., 1854.* The musical responses commissioned by the Hymnal Revision Committee are identified "C."

1-1	C
1-2	Excerpt from an African American spiritual at 35 in *Songs of Zion*, 1981.
2-1	C
2:2	See "Lift up your heads, ye mighty gates," page 466.
3	C
4	See "There is a balm in Gilead," pages 645-46.
5	C
8-1	See "Sing praise to God," pages 597-98.
8:2	See "Many and great," pages 480-81.
9	C
10	"King's Lynn," trad. English melody harm. by Ralph Vaughan Williams, 1906; see 485, *The Methodist Hymnal*, 1966.
13	See "Be still, my soul," pages 227-28.
14	C, 15; C, 16-1; C, 16-2 C

17	Excerpt from an anthem published in 1986.
19	See "The God of Abraham praise," pages 636-37.
19-2	C
22	See "O sacred head, now wounded," pages 526-27.
22-2	C
23	See "Psalm 23," King James Version, page 562.
23-2	C
24-1	Excerpt from anon. "Tersanctus," 439 in our 1878 hymnal.
24-2	C, 25-1, C
25-2	See "Lead me, Lord," page 458.
27	C, 28 C
29	Words: stanza 2:1-2 from Charles Wesley's metrical paraphrase of Psalm 29. The first line originally read "Extol the great Jehovah's name." (Fish, 78); music: see "Forth in thy name," (DUKE STREET), pages 348-49.
30	See "Let all mortal flesh keep silence," page 460.
31-1	See "A mighty fortress is our God," pages 182-84.
31-2	See "All creatures of our God and King," pages 189-91.
32	C, 33-1 C
33-2	Words: stanza 1:5, 7 from Charles Wesley's metrical paraphrase of Psalm 33. (Fish 89) Music: see "Hail the day that sees him rise," page 382.
34-1	C, 34-2 C
36	See "Jesus, joy of our desiring," page 440.
37	See "What does the Lord require, page 689.
39	C, 40 C
41	See "Out of the depths I cry to you," pages 551-52.
42	See "O Word of God incarnate," page 536.
43	Excerpt from *La Rédemption*, 1882.
44	C
46-1	See "A mighty fortress is our God," pages 182-84.
46-2	C
47	Words: stanza 13:3, 4 of Charles Wesley's metrical paraphrase of Psalm 47. (Fish 119) Music: see "Hail the day that sees him rise," page 382.
48	See page 461.
50	C, 51-1 C, 51-2 C, 62 C
63	From *Worship II*, 1975.
65	See "Now thank we all our God," pages 497-98.
66	C, 67C
68	From *Hymns for the People*, 1931, and *The Pagoda*, ca. 1946.
70	See "Out of the depths I cry to you," pages 551-52.
71	See "Blow ye, the trumpet, blow," pages 242-43.
72-1	C
72-2	"King's Lynn," trad. English melody harm. by Ralph Vaughan Williams, 1906; see 485, *The Methodist Hymnal*, 1966.
76	C, 77C
78	Submitted to the psalms text subcommittee in 1987.
80-1	C

80-2   See "The God of Abraham praise," pages 636-37.
81   From *Worship III*, 1986.
82   C, 84 C, 85 C, 89-1 C, 89-2 C, 90 C, 91 C
92   See "Now thank we all our God," pages 497-98.
93   C, 95-1 C, 95-2 C, 96 C, 97-1 C
97-2   See "Lift every voice and sing," page 465.
98   C, 99 C
100-1   Words: stanza 1:1-2 of Charles Wesley's metrical paraphrase of Psalm 100. The first line originally read "Ye sons of men, lift up your voice." (Fish 188) Music: see "Rejoice, ye pure in heart," page 567.
100-2   Submitted to the psalms text subcommittee in 1987.
102   C, 103 C
104   See "Praise to the Lord, the Almighty," page 558.
105   C
106   See "For the beauty of the earth," 341-42.
107   C, 111-1 C, 111-2 C, 112 C, 113 C, 114 C, 115 C, 116-1 C, 116-2 C, 117 C
118-1   From the composer's full service composed in 1976. See "Word and Table Musical Setting 'E.'"
118-2   From *Worship II*, 1975.
119-1   C, 119-2 C
119-3   See "Thy word is a lamp unto my feet," page 662.
121-1   C
121-2   From "Morning Praise" in *Praise God in Song*, 1979.
121-3   Submitted to the psalms text subcommittee in 1987.
122-1   See "Hail to the Lord's Anointed," pages 384-85.
122-2   C
124   See "Stand by me," page 607.
126-1   See "Come, let us join friends above," pages 292-93.
126-2   See "Let all mortal flesh keep silence," page 460.
130   C, 132 C
133   See "Thy holy wings, O Savior," page 661.
1345   The response was inspired during Night Prayer at St. Meinrad's Abbey, St. Meinrad's, Indiana. It was composed at a psalms workshop, Emory University, Atlanta, October 1980, and included in *Alive Now*, July-August, 1981.
135   See "Sing praise to God," pages 597-98.
137   C, 138 C
139   See "Out of the depths I cry to you," pages 551-52.
143-1   C
143-2   From *Cancionero Abierto*, 1978, and *Canciones de Fe y Compromiso*, 1978; see also number 6 in *Celebremos II*, 1983.
145   See "Christian people, raise your song," page 284.
146   See "Let all mortal flesh keep silence," page 460.
147   Words: stanza 1:1 of Charles Wesley's metrical paraphrase of Psalm 150, with Alleluia added. (Fish 280) Music: see "Hail the day that sees him rise," page 382.
148   See "All creatures of our God and King," pages 189-91.

150-1   See "The strife is o'er," page 644.
150-2   See "Cantemos al Señor," page 251.

Musical Settings for Word and Table I, II, III (17-25); IV (28-31)

In the service of Word and Table I, II, and III, there are musical settings for the congregational responses "Holy, Holy, Holy," "Memorial Acclamation," and "Great Amen." These appear in the order of very easy to moderately difficult.

In Word and Table IV there are settings for "Holy, Holy, Holy" and "O Lamb of God." For commentary on the services of Word and Table, see pages 11-85 in Hoyt L. Hickman, ed., *The Worship Resources of The United Methodist Hymnal*, 1989, 11-85.

Holy, holy, holy

This first section of this hymn of praise, echoed in Revelation 4:8-11, is from the vision of Isaiah 6:3:

> And one [seraph] called to another and said:
> "Holy, holy, holy is the Lord of hosts;
> the whole earth is full of his glory."

The second part is the crowd's greeting to Jesus as he enters Jerusalem, "Hosanna to the Son of David! Blessed is the one who comes in the name of the Lord" ("Benedictus qui venit"), Matthew 21:9, that reflects Psalm 118: 25-26a. (Werner 1959, 267) This was not included in John Wesley's communion text "The Order for the Administration of the Lord's Supper" that he adapted from the 1552 *Book of Common Prayer* and printed with *The Sunday Service*, 1784. It was included in our liturgies in the 1957 hymnal and in *The Sacrament of the Lord's Supper: an Alternate Text*, 1972, revised 1980. Our text is from *Prayers We Have in Common*, 1975 2d. rev. ed. Under the guise of inclusivity the words in our liturgy "Blessed is he" are often changed to "blessed is the One," a practice that disregards the historic contexts of the gospel and the psalm.

Settings of the "Holy, holy, holy" have been included in our hymnals since Reconstruction times, and until this hymnal they were printed in the back of the volume where they were quickly perceived by the congregation as belonging to the choir. Each of our five sets of musical responses is printed with the "Great Thanksgiving" for ease of learning and singing. A song leader is imperative in the teaching and directing of these responses. A brief rehearsal of the congregation at the time of their gathering is desirable.

Memorial Acclamation

This is an affirmation and remembrance of God's great salvific act in Jesus Christ's death, rising, and expected return.

Great Amen

See "Amen," page 581, for commentary on the concluding act of "The Great Thanksgiving."

Musical Setting A (17-18)

Elise S. Eslinger, 1985, alt. 1989

These settings are based on the tune NICAEA **(64)**. They first appeared in *The Upper Room Worshipbook*, 1985, and have been slightly modified for our hymnal. The composer has commented that the responses were written to fill the need "for accessible and singable service music for congregations and choirs as we were beginning to introduce the singing of both psalms and music for the communion liturgy . . . . It was first performed in the Claremont [School of Theology, Claremont, California, 1980] summer school worship." (Correspondence with Carlton R. Young, August 1992)

Musical Setting B (18-20)

James A. Kriewald, 1985

These are set in leader/response style and first appeared as parts of a fuller setting of the liturgy in *Alive Now!* July/August 1985. The "Lord, have mercy" (Kyrie Eleison) section is hymn **482**. They can be sung with or without guitar and keyboard accompaniment.

Musical Setting C (20-22)

Holy, holy, holy

Franz Schubert, Deutsche Messe, 1827
adapt. by Richard Proulx, 1985

This and the two other responses are adapted from Franz Schubert's F major *Deutsche Messe*, ca. 1827 (D. 872), arranged in two settings: choir and organ; and choir, organ, and orchestra. Schubert wrote this remarkably expressive and singable setting of the vernacular text for congregations to sing in four-part harmony supported by organ. It is still a favorite of Austrian parishes. Additional portions of the mass have been adapted by Richard Proulx and are included in *The Hymnal 1982 Service Music*.

The adaptation of the "Sanctus" was first included in *The German Mass*, 1985. The original score was replete with expression marks and a tempo indication of *sehr langsam* (very slow).

Memorial Acclamation and Great Amen

Franz Schubert, Deutsche Messe, 1827
arr. by Charles H. Webb, 1987

These arrangements were made for our hymnal.

Musical Setting D (23-24)

Carlton R. Young, 1981, 1987

The "Holy, holy, holy" was composed for organ, brass, and congregation and was first performed at the opening of Cannon Chapel, Emory University, September 1981. The two additional responses are derived from the former. The minor tonality should not be interpreted as nonfestive, and the responses may be accompanied by full organ and brass quartet.

Musical Setting E (25)

William Mathias, 1976

These responses are from the composer's full service composed in 1976. In the "Holy, holy, holy" the phrase "Blessed is he who comes in the name of the Lord" was originally scored for unison treble voices. The two additional responses were adapted from other portions of the service and approved by the composer. The composer's "Glory to God in the highest" and "Jesus, Lamb of God" are included in *The Hymnal 1982 Service Music*.

Musical Settings for Word and Table IV (28-31)

John Merbecke, 1550

This setting of "Holy, holy, holy" from *Booke of Common Praier Noted*, 1550, was first included in our hymnals in 1966. In *The Hymnal 1982 Service Music* it was extended to include "Blessed is he who comes in the name of the Lord" by repeating material from the last phrase.

"O Lamb of God" was first included in a musical setting in our hymnals in *The Methodist Hymnal*, 1935.

Additional musical responses and acts of praise appropriate for Holy Communion are found at "Lord, have mercy" (Kyrie eleison), **482-85**; "Glory be to God on high" (Gloria in excelsis), **82-83**, and the "Lord's Prayer," **270-71**. See also appropriate hymns to be sung at the distribution and the dismissal in "Index of Topics and Categories" under "Holy Communion," **943**, and "Following Communion," **952**.

Serving the poor (446)

Mother Teresa of Calcutta, Yugoslavia, 20th cent.

Written by one of the most compelling Christian leaders of our time, this prayer is to strengthen the hands of those who serve those in hunger and poverty. The prayer is from George Appleton, ed., *The Oxford Book of Prayer*, 1986.

Shackled by a heavy burden (367)

See "He touched me," page 393.

Shall we gather at the river (723)

Words and music: Robert Lowry, 1864 (Rev. 22:1-5)

The poem entitled "Mutual Recognition in the Hereafter" was first published in *Happy Voices*, 1865, in five four-line stanzas with refrain. The text reflects these apocalyptic visions of Revelation 22:1-2:

> Then the angel showed me the river of the water of life, bright as crystal, flowing from the throne of God and of the Lamb through the middle of the street of the city. On either side of the river is the tree of life with its twelve kinds of fruit, producing its fruit each month; and the leaves of the tree are for the healing of the nations.

John Julian provides this information about the composition of the hymn from E. W. Long's *Illustrated History of Hymns and their Authors*:

> On a very hot summer day in 1864, a pastor was seated in his parlour in Brooklyn, N .Y. It was a time when an epidemic was sweeping through the city, and draping many persons and dwellings in mourning. All around friends and acquaintances were passing away to the spirit land in large numbers. The question began to arise in the heart, with unusual emphasis, "Shall we meet again? We are parting at the river of death, shall we meet at the river of life?" "Seating myself at the organ," says he, "simply to give vent to the pent of emotions of the heart, the words and music of the hymn began to flow out, as if by inspiration." (Julian 1907, 699-700)

In stanza 4:1, "shining" was originally "silver." Most hymnals use four stanzas, omitting stanza 4:

> At the smiling of the river,
> Mirror of the Saviour's face,
> Saints, whom death will never sever,
> Lift their songs of saving grace.

The hymn was sung by the United States Army Chorus at the memorial service for William O. Douglas, social prophet and Associate Justice of the United States Supreme Court, January 23, 1980, National Presbyterian Church, Washington, DC. (Reynolds 1990, 246) The hymn entered our hymnals in 1867.

Hanson Place

The tune was named for the Hanson Place Baptist Church in Brooklyn, New York, where Lowry was pastor 1861-69, by the committee that prepared the

Baptist Hymnal, 1956. Aaron Copland included this hymn in a setting for solo voice and keyboard in *Old American Songs*, 1954.

Shalom (667)
Shahlohm

Trad. Hebrew blessing; trans. by Roger N. Deschner, 1982
This translation was prepared for *Supplement to the Book of Hymns*, 1982.

Shalom

The blessing may be sung as a closing response in either or both English and Hebrew as a two- or four-part round, with voices entering as indicated by the numbers.

Shalom to you (666)

Elise S. Eslinger, 1980
The words are the English stanza 4 of "Pues si vivimos," number 39 in *Celebremos II*, 1983. They have become a favorite benediction response that may be repeated several times while persons exchange parting greetings and words of peace.

The author has supplied this information: "The four-stanza English text, not a translation of 'Pues si vivimos,' was composed for the tune SOMOS DEL SEÑOR and is a summary of the concept of shalom. It was first sung at the 1981 South Indiana Conference Youth Annual Conference of The United Methodist Church, and was included in *Songs of Shalom*, 1983." (Correspondence with Carlton R. Young, August 1992)

Somos del Señor

Trad. Spanish melody; harm. by Carlton R. Young, 1989
See "Pues si vivimos" **(356)** for another setting of this melody, and page 564 for commentary and suggested performance practice.

Sheaves of summer (637)

See "Una espiga," pages 671-72.

Silence, frenzied, unclean spirit (264)

Thomas H. Troeger, 1984 (Mark 1:21-28; Luke 4:31-37)
The hymn was first included in *New Hymns for the Lectionary*, 1986. In the preface to that collection the author and composer comment on the words and the musical setting:

[The hymn] first retells the story of Jesus exorcising a demon, then probes the meaning of demons today, and concludes with a prayer for wholeness. This spiritual unfolding of the passage is highlighted by the music, which moves from percussive repetition into a songful melody that heralds Christ's healing power. (Doran and Troeger 1986, vi)

The poet and musician comment on their combined efforts in composing this and other hymns in "Writing Hymns as a Theologically Informed Artistic Discipline," *The Hymn*, 1985.

Authority

Carol Doran, 1984

The composer relates that the first half of the tune expresses "the strength [that] Christ brought to bear in the exorcism of the unclean spirit, [and] the second, more lyric, half of the hymn tune describes the wonder of the consequences of Christ's action." (Correspondence with Carlton R. Young, September 1992)

The tune should be taught to the congregation without accompaniment in two-measure phrases in a call-and-response pattern. The sometimes dissonant and expressive harmony may then be added under the voices. The hymn may prelude or follow a sermon on Christ's battle with the demons.

The alternate tune EBENEZER may be used by the faint of heart but will diminish the impact of the words of terror and prayer.

Silent night, holy night (239)
Stille Nacht, heilige Nacht

Joseph Mohr, 1818, alt.; sts. 1, 2, 3, trans. by John F. Young
st. 4, trans. anon. (Luke 2:6-20)

The carol's origin has been traced to Christmas Eve, 1818, at St. Nicholas's Church, Oberndorf, Austria, when the organ broke down and Joseph Mohr, the parish priest, and the village music teacher and organist Franz Gruber composed it for the traditional service. The carol quickly spread in manuscript form and by Tyrolese singers to other parishes, but it was not published until 1838 in *Leipziger Gesangbuch*. It first appeared with an English text with a free paraphrase by J. W. Warner at 373 in the Methodist *Devotional Harmonist*, 1849 (Gealy 557/432), with this first stanza:

> Silent night! hallow'd night!
> Land and deep silent sleep,
> Softly glitters bright Bethlehem's star,

> Beck'ning Israel's eye from afar,
> Where the Saviour is born—
> Where the Saviour is born.

John R. Young's text, of which we use stanzas 1 through 3, first appeared in *The Sunday School Service and Tune Book*, 1863.

The most interesting aspect of the universal popularity of the carol is that for the most part, like other deeply felt and simple religious songs, i.e., the gospel hymn and African American spiritual, it was set aside by English hymnal compilers as not worthy to be placed in the common repertory, and it was not even included with other non-English texts in *The Oxford Book of Carols*, 1928. It did not enter our hymnals and most British collections until after the turn of the century.

As late as 1958 Erik Routley presented this condescending view of the carol, characteristically and skillfully disguised as historic comment:

> The real force in "Stille nacht" is, without doubt, the manner in which historically and stylistically it epitomizes the German Christmas, cozy and child-centered, which was first becoming part of the English scene just when it was being composed. . . . [This] evangelical hymn of the Incarnation and Atonement . . . is at least as much a carol of the nineteenth-century revival movement as "Hark the herald" was of the Wesleyan. (Routley 1958, 202)

The German text is the first stanza that has been included in many post-World War II hymnals and pictures the holy family quietly attending the holy child who has lovely curly hair, "Holder Knabe im lockingen Haar." This description of the child has caused some to alter the line to "das im Stalle zu Bethlehem war." Its last line should read "schlaf in himmlischer Ruh" instead of "schlaf im."

In 1897 a plaque observing the collaboration of church musician and pastor in the composition of the carol was placed on the schoolhouse in Arnsdorf where Gruber served as schoolmaster. The text follows in a translation from W. G. Polack (1942, 460):

> Silent night! Holy night!
> Who composed thee, hymn divine?
> Mohr it was who wrote each line,
> Gruber found my tune sublime,—
> Teacher together with priest.

Stille Nacht

Franz Gruber, 1818

The carol was apparently first performed with Mohr on tenor lead with Gruber singing bass and playing the guitar. It was first included in a USA collection in *The Devotional Harmonist*, 1849. (Gealy, Lovelace, Young 1970, 372)

For the carol's inherent simplicity and tender piety to be expressed, it should be performed with a guitar strumming two slow counts per 6/8 measure and filling in the afterbeats; and the first stanza sung by two male voices in German, with the final two lines answered in four-part harmony. The congregation may respond by singing this stanza in English or German. Allow the singers to establish and maintain the tempo. There are guitar chords and a descant at 322-23 in *The United Methodist Hymnal Music Supplement*.

Sing, my tongue, the glorious battle (296)
Pange, lingua, gloriosi praelium certaminis

Venantius Honorius Fortunatus, 6th cent.
trans. by Percy Dearmer, 1925

Our text is a portion of a ten-stanza Latin hymn attributed to Fortunatus and traditionally divided into two passion hymns. The hymn retells God's design for our salvation and extols Jesus' victory over death through allusions to medieval myth—for example, Christ's cross, fashioned from a tree of Eden—and strong metaphors from Hebrew scripture and the Gospels. The final doxological stanza was added later.

Percy Dearmer in *Songs of Praise*, 1925 1st ed., provided a single text by selecting stanzas from his translation in *The English Hymnal*, 1906, writing new verse and adapting portions of John M. Neale's translation in *Mediaeval Hymns and Sequences*, 1851. (See page 67 in *A Panorama of English Hymnody* for the eleven-stanza text in parallel Latin and English with their sources.)

The objective and universal qualities of this hymn are distinct from, yet complement, the evangelical subjectivity of Isaac Watts's "When I survey the wondrous cross" **(298)** or Charles Wesley's "O Love divine, what hast thou done" **(287)**, these hymns in continuity with the seventeenth-century German pietistic hymn, such as, "O sacred Head, now wounded" **(286)**. The hymn is new to our hymnals and provides another alternative to the ephemeral, vague, and escapist qualities of hymns such as "Beneath the cross of Jesus" **(297)**, stanza 3, "I take, O cross, thy shadow for my abiding place . . . content to let the world go by," and "The old rugged cross," whose final stanza and refrain portray the cross with the force of a college alma mater.

Changes for our hymnal are stanza 2:3, "He" to "Christ"; 2:5, "showed to men the perfect manhood" to "showed us human life made perfect"; and 4:2, "men" to "us."

Picardy

See "Let all mortal flesh keep silence," page 460.

Sing of Mary, pure and lowly (272)

Roland Ford Palmer, 1938
Stanley L. Osborne has commented on this hymn:

[It] was written . . . in order to fill the gap for a more suitable hymn about the mother Jesus than was otherwise available to the committee preparing HB [*The Hymn Book*]. It was accepted at the last meeting of the committee and appeared anonymously when the book was printed. With characteristic modesty the author comments: "It is just a jingle, but jingles often make better hymns." (Osborne 1976, hymn 494)

Stanza 1:2 originally read "virgin mother, undefiled." Our version of the text is from *The Hymn Book*, 1972, without the doxological stanza.

Raquel

Skinner Chávez-Melo, 1985
The music was composed for this text and was first included in *The Hymnal 1982*. The composer supports this carefully constructed simple, plaintive, and expressive melody with judiciously selected Broadway ballad harmonies. The tune is named after Raquel Gutiérrez-Achon, vice-chair of the Hymnal Revision Committee who brought the tune in manuscript to the tunes subcommittee. She and the composer were consultants to the Standing Commission on Music that during 1982-85 selected the musical settings for texts in *The Hymnal 1982*, approved by the 1982 General Assembly of the Protestant Episcopal Church.

The composer just prior to his death composed a descant and edited the tune for organ, found at 274-75 in *The United Methodist Hymnal Music Supplement*.

Sing praise to God who reigns above (126)
Sei Lob und Ehr dem Höchsten Gut

Johann J. Schütz, 1675
trans. by Frances E. Cox, 1864 (Deut. 32:3)
The hymn was composed in nine stanzas with the refrain "Gebt unserm Gott die Ehre" (Give to our God the praise) and first appeared in *Christliches Gedenckbüchlein*, 1675. It was translated by Frances E. Cox in eight stanzas for *Hymns from the German*, 1864, where it was printed in parallel German and English. (Gealy 557/426) The translator has skillfully maintained the hymn's balance between the strong and powerful biblical metaphors for God and the warm pietistic "Mit Mutterhänden leitet Er," translated "As with a Mother's tender hand." Fred D. Gealy has commented that this "is a hymn to aspire to: it both demands and releases power." (Gealy 557/426)

This hymn of praise entered our hymnals with stanzas 1, 3, 5, and 7 in *The Methodist Hymnal*, 1935, but it was placed where few could find it in the section "The Christian Life" between the hymns "Peace, perfect peace" and "O how happy are they who their Saviour obey." In the 1966 hymnal stanza 8 was added, and the hymn was placed as number 4 in the front of the book in the section "The praise of God."

The former stanza 2, the original stanza 3, has been dropped because of the perceived ambiguity if not contradiction in lines 5 and 6 between God's powerful establishment of the kingdom and its attributes of justice and righteousness:

> What God's almighty power hath made,
> His gracious mercy keepeth;
> By morning glow or evening shade,
> His watchful eye ne'er sleepeth;
> Within the kingdom of his might,
> Lo! all is just and all is right:
> To God all praise and glory.

Other changes for our hymnal are in stanzas 1:5, "he fills" to "is filled"; 2:6, "He leads his own, his" to "God gently leads the"; 3:3, "that men" to "that earth"; 4:1, "O ye" to "let all"; 4:5, "he" to "its"; 4:6, "the Lord is God, and he alone" to "for Christ is Lord, and Christ alone."

Mit Freuden zart

Kirchengesänge, 1566
harm. by Maurice F. Bell, 1906

Erik Routley in examples 84, 85 A-B in *The Music of Christian Hymns* shows the similarities of this tune with other psalm and hymn tunes. Our harmonization is from *The English Hymnal*, 1906; it was included without citation in our 1935 and 1966 Methodist hymnals. The original harmonization is a unison setting with organ accompaniment that was apparently the first to reduce our four-part harmony, again without citation, for *The Hymnbook*, 1955. There is a vocal descant at 237 in *The United Methodist Hymnal Music Supplement*.

Sing the wondrous love of Jesus (701)

See "When we all get to heaven," pages 699-700.

Sing them over again to me (600)

See "Wonderful words of life," page 708.

Sing we now of Christmas (237)
Noël nouvelet

Trad. French carol (Luke 2:8-20; Matt. 2:1-12)

This is a translation of five of the six stanzas of this charming traditional French carol. It first appeared at 28 arranged for SA voices in *Christmas Carols from Many Countries*, 1934, compiled by Satis N. Coleman and Elin K. Jörgensen.

French Carol

Trad. French carol; harm. by Martin Shaw, 1928

For suggested performance practice see "Now the green blade riseth," pages 498-99. The carol may be sung in conjunction with a tableau or projected images of the Nativity. Ours is the first hymnal to include this carol.

Sing with all the saints in glory (702)

William J. Irons, 1873 (1 Cor. 15:20)

This hymn first appeared at 75 under the heading "Now is Christ Risen from the dead" in the author's *Psalms and Hymns for the Church*, 1873, 2d ed. 1875. (Gealy 557/429) It has been included in our hymnals since 1878. Its longevity, one could say immortality since it appears in no other hymnal, is credited to its association with Beethoven's HYMN TO JOY.

Hymn to joy

See "Joyful, joyful, we adore thee," page 459.

Sinners, turn: why will you die (346)

Charles Wesley, 1742

This invitation hymn was first printed in sixteen 77. 77. D stanzas under the heading "Why will ye die, O House of Israel! Ezek. 18:31" at 43-46 in *Hymns on God's Everlasting Love*, second series, 1742. John Wesley printed stanzas 1-4 in his 1780 *Collection* in the section "Exhorting, and beseeching [Sinners] to return to God." Our hymnal includes stanzas 1-3, 6-8, 13, and 16. F. Hildebrandt and O. A. Beckerlegge (Wesley 1983, 7:86-87) provide an interesting commentary on John Wesley's changing "ye" to "you" for his 1780 *Collection*. The text was first included in our hymnals in 1786.

Our change in 8:2, "If to All His Bowels move?" to "If to all his mercies move?", presents the case for making sensible changes although others uncritically urge, "Give us the texts exactly as they were written."

Softly and tenderly Jesus is calling (348)

Words and music: Will L. Thompson, 1880

This invitation hymn first appeared in J. Calvin Bushey's *Sparkling Gems,* 1880, Nos. 1 and 2 Combined. (Adams 1992, 233) It entered our hymnals in 1897.

Thompson

This is a typical lullaby in the gospel hymn tradition that characterizes Jesus as a mother, gently rocking and comforting a child. This attribute contributes to the continuing popularity of this genre of religious song that presents Jesus as waiting, caring, and forgiving in intimate—and for many, compelling—metaphors. For additional commentary see "Gospel Hymns," pages 28-29.

Sois la semilla (583)
You are the seed

Words and music: Cesareo Gabaráin, 1979
trans. by Raquel Gutiérrez-Achon
and Skinner Chávez-Melo (Matt. 28:19-20)

Gertrude C. Suppe has identified the first publication of this hymn as apparently in a small booklet, *Dios con nosotros*, published in Madrid, Spain, between 1973 and 1979. (Correspondence with Carlton R. Young, July 1991)

The hymn is an elaboration of Jesus' images and characterizations of his and his disciples'ministry as seed (Matthew 13:37), salt, and light (Matthew 5:13-14). The refrain is a commission for all to take the message of Christ to the world. It is an ideal commissioning and ordination or renewal hymn. The translation was made for our hymnal.

Id y enseñad

Harm. by Skinner Chávez-Melo, 1987

The name means literally "Go and teach"; it is the hymn's common title. Chávez-Melo's setting was prepared for our hymnal.

Soldiers of Christ, arise (513)

Charles Wesley, 1749 (Eph. 6:13-18)

This extraordinary treatise on individual courage in the struggle against the forces of evil was first published in sixteen CMD stanzas at the end of John Wesley's *Character of a Methodist*, 1742, and later at 236-39 in *Hymns and Sacred Poems*,

1749, under the heading "The Whole Armour of God; Ephesians 6." (Gealy 557/433) John Wesley in his 1780 *Collection* spread twelve stanzas of the hymn over three selections in the section "For believers fighting."

The hymn moves at several points beyond personal protection from the forces of evil to their demise. The former is the central theme of Ephesians 6:13-18: "Therefore take up the whole armor of God, so that you may be able to withstand on that evil day, and having done everything, to stand firm" (6:13). At some points, however, Charles Wesley urges the destruction of evil in verses that John chose not to include in his *Collection*, as shown in stanza 10:

> Brandish in Faith 'till then [the heavenly Marriage Feast]
> The Spirit's two-edg'd Sword,
> Hew all the Snares of Fiends and Men
> In Pieces with the Word;
> *'Tis written:* This applied
> Baffles their Strength and Art;
> Spirit and Soul with this divide,
> And Joints and Marrow part.

These metaphors from the horrors of the battlefield and the Tower of London are contrasted in this moving penultimate stanza, a prayer for the peace of Sion and humankind:

> Pour out your Souls to God,
> And bow them with your Knees,
> And spread your Hearts and Hands abroad
> And pray for *Sion's* Peace;
> Your Guides and Brethren, bear
> Forever on your Mind;
> Extend the Arms of mighty Prayer
> Ingrasping all Mankind.

The hymn was included in our first *Pocket Hymn Book,* ca. 1786, and has appeared in all our hymnals, sometime reduced to as few as three militant stanzas. Our hymnal includes stanzas 1, 2, 12, and 16.

These severe reductions, when combined with the marching tune DIADEMATA, tend to reduce this classic exegesis of the epistle's assurance to the faithful that they will be strengthened in daily conflicts by God's Word, to the implicit call for holy war in "Onward Christian soldiers" **(575)** and "The battle hymn of the Republic" **(717)**. The poet's contrasting call to personal prayer in our stanza 3 relieves this problem to some extent. The reader is urged to examine the entire text in Frank Baker (1962, 45-48). Pages 21-35 of the same volume provide a brief introduction to Charles Wesley's vocabulary, literary allusions, and rhetorical style.

See also Elizabeth Hart, "Whither the Wily Fiends?: A Case Study in Editing Charles Wesley's 'Soldiers of Christ,'" *The Hymn*, October 1988.

Diademata

The tune is a near perfect matching of melody, harmonic climax, musical phrase and form with the overall militant spirit of the abridged hymn. For additional commentary on the tune see "Make me a captive, Lord," page 478.

The tune that John Wesley suggested for this hymn in his 1780 *Collection* was "Handel's Tune" from the composer's Italian opera *Ricardo Primo*, 1727, a tune called "Jericho Tune" in Wesley's *Foundery Collection*, 1742. O. A. Beckerlegge states that this was "the earliest example of a popular tune being seized on by Wesley." (Wesley 1983, 7:778)

Something beautiful (394)

Gloria Gaither, 1971

Gloria and William J. Gaither have provided this commentary on this chorus:

> This song was born on a Monday morning when our children were quite small. We were watching them play and have such a good time expressing their delight in life. We thought of how good God has been to us and simply had to conclude that he had certainly done something beautiful in our lives. What a marvel it is that no matter what we have to bring to Jesus, no matter how much pain and dysfunction, no matter how much confusion and broken-ness, Jesus takes us as we are then makes us truly new. He doesn't just patch up and make the best of a fractured past; he truly makes "something beauti-ful" of our lives. (Correspondence with Carlton R. Young, October 1992)

Something beautiful

William J. Gaither, 1971

The hymn was first published in 1971 in piano/vocal sheet music. *Hymns for the Family of God*, 1976, was the first hymnal to include it.

Soon and very soon (706)

Words and music: Andraé Crouch, 1978 (Rev. 21:3-4)

William Farley Smith writes that "John's comforting prediction [revelation] has been set in highly spirited music with accented syncopations. It is customarily used in procession and should sound and look like a 'snappy' religious march.'" (Sanchez 1989, 235) William B. McClain has commented that "the tempo can be march-like, signifying the march of Christians into the promised land, or a little faster, signifying the jubilation of going home." (McClain 1990, 138)

Other stanzas and phrases may be improvised.

Very soon

Adapt. by William Farley Smith, 1987

This adaptation of stanzas 1-4 for four-part singing was made for our hymnal. The entire song is included at 198 in *Songs of Zion*, 1981.

Source and Sovereign, Rock and Cloud (113)

Thomas H. Troeger, 1987

This hymn was commissioned by the Hymnal Revision Committee who extended an invitation to thirteen writers for texts using alternative metaphors and descriptions of deity. Each was sent a list of over 200 alternative words and phrases. Upon receiving the invitation and the list, Thomas H. Troeger included thirty-nine of them in his hymn.

The poet has provided a catalog of human and natural attributes of God in a cleverly framed text with alliterated, rhymed, and juxtapositioned metaphors tied together with a compelling refrain.

God's names

Carol Doran, 1987

The composer supplied this tune for this text as was the practice of this writing team. After hearing that the Hymnal Revision Committee perceived her tunes as unsingable, the composer apparently, and uncharacteristically, placed the text in a setting devoid of melody in a generally accepted harmonic idiom to ensure acceptance.

The composer comments that she "formed a melody line for the stanzas which contains little movement so that the list of God's names might be highlighted sounding on the near-monotone." (Correspondence with Carlton R. Young, September 1992)

Spirit of faith, come down (332)

Charles Wesley, 1746

The hymn first appeared at 30-31 in *Hymns of Petition and Thanksgiving for the Promise of the Father*, 1746. (Gealy 557/436-A) John Wesley included four of the five stanzas in the section "Praying for a Blessing" in his 1780 *Collection*, changing 3:3 from "My dear atoning Lamb" to "the dear atoning Lamb," and omitting the original stanza 3:

> O know my Saviour lives,
> He lives, who died for Me,
> My inmost Soul his Voice receives
> Who hangs on yonder Tree:
> Set forth before my Eyes
> Ev'n Now I see Him bleed,

> And hear his Mortal Groans, and Cries,
> While suffering in my Stead.

The commentary in *Companion to Hymns and Psalms* points to the phrase in stanza 1:5, "Tis thine the blood to apply," as frequently occurring in Charles Wesley's works and "vital to the understanding of his theology: it suggests that the work of the Holy Spirit is to bring salvation to the individual." (Watson and Trickett 1988, 211)

Our hymnal includes stanzas 1, 2, 4, and 5 of the original text. Changes have been made in stanzas 3:7, "all mankind" to "humankind"; 4:2, "receives" to "receive," "the witness in himself he hath" to "the witness in themselves they have"; and stanza 4:4, "believes" to "believe." The hymn entered our hymnals in *A Selection of Hymns*, 1810, bound with the 36th ed. of *The Pocket Hymn Book*.

Bealoth

The Sacred Harp (Mason), 1840

The tune first appeared in *The Sacred Harp, or Beauties of Church Music*, vol. 2, 1840, collected by Timothy B. Mason. (Gealy, Lovelace, Young 1970, 378) It was first included in our hymnals in 1905.

The tune originally opened with an interval of a rising sixth that was smoothed over in our 1966 hymnal to avoid a false accent in stanza 1. Austin C. Lovelace's harmonization for that hymnal may be used on alternate stanzas with the choir. The tune name is a town in south Judah, perhaps the same as cited in Joshua 15:24. (*The Interpreter's Dictionary of the Bible*, 1:367)

Spirit of God, descend upon my heart (500)

George Croly, 1867 (Gal. 5:25)

The hymn first appeared in *Lyra Britannica*, 1867. (Gealy, Lovelace, Young 1970, 379) It entered our 1901 hymnal in four stanzas, and in 1905 the full five stanzas were included and have been maintained in subsequent hymnals without change.

Morecambe

Frederick C. Atkinson, 1870

The tune was first named "Hellespont" and was the setting for "Abide with me" in *Congregational Church Hymnal*, 1887. (Gealy, Lovelace, Young 1970, 379) The tune is named after a watering place on Morecambe Bay in western England near Bradford, where the composer served as church organist. (McCutchan 1957, 105)

The tune's warm, considered, and restrained Victorian harmonies are a perfect match for this elegant text. Alternate stanzas may be sung by solo or soli voices, or SATB choir.

Spirit of the living God (393)

Words and music: Daniel Iverson, 1926 (Acts 11:15)
William J. Reynolds has provided this information concerning the writing of this chorus:

> During January and February of 1926, the George T. Stephans Evangelistic Party conducted a city-wide revival in the tabernacle in Orlando, Florida. Daniel Iverson, a Presbyterian minister from Lumberton, North Carolina, spent several days in Orlando visiting with the Stephans' team. The day he arrived, he was greatly impressed by a message on the Holy Spirit given by Dr. Barron, a physician from Columbia, South Carolina. Later that day Iverson went to the First Presbyterian Church in Orlando, sat down at the piano, and wrote this song. Miss Birdie Loes, the pianist for the Stephans' team, wrote it out on manuscript paper. E. Powell Lee, the team song leader, was immediately impressed, and taught it to the people that evening in the tabernacle, and used it throughout the campaign. (Reynolds 1976, 199)

The chorus was widely used in Stephans's revivals, and its use soon spread to other evangelical groups, many times taught by rote rather than from a printed version. It was first included in *Revival Songs*, 1929, in a revised version without the author's permission. In 1937 B. B. McKinney included that version with slight changes under his name as arranger in his *Songs of Victory*. This version entered the 1956 *Baptist Hymnal* and other evangelical collections. Through the efforts of E. Powell Lee, Iverson's name was restored as the author in early 1960 printings of the *Baptist Hymnal*. (Reynolds 1976, 199)

The popularity of the revised version established it as the standard version. Another version of the chorus, presumed to be the first, may be found at 297 in *The Worshiping Church*.

Living God

This chorus may be used as a call to prayer, a prayer response, or a prayer for illumination before reading scripture.

Spirit Song (347)

Words and music: John Wimber, 1979
This song of surrender of oneself to Jesus, the Son of God, is characterized in the phrase in the second stanza, "Lift your hands in sweet surrender to his name.

O give him all your tears and sadness." Composed as an altar call, it is the type of song used in charismatic communities, some of which are composed of former United Methodists who claimed they were not spiritually fulfilled in their own local church worship and song.

The author has related that the "lyrics and melody came to me while stopped at a stop sign." (Correspondence with Carlton R. Young, August 1992)

Spirit song

This is one of the best constructed tunes in the contemporary gospel repertory. The harmonic realization, ample for most accompanists, may be enhanced by adding passing chords and arpeggios. The three-part SSA harmonies have been retained in the refrain. The song may be sung as a choral response.

Stand by me (512)

Words and music: Charles Albert Tindley, ca. 1906
(Matt. 8:23-27; Mark 4:35-41; Luke 8:22-25)

This is one of the most enduring of Tindley's hymns. It was included in the group of hymns that he published in 1905 (Jones 1982, 40) and may be found in *New Songs of Paradise*, No. 6. In 1966 it became the first hymn by an African American author to appear in our hymnals.

The themes of Tindley's sermons and verse tend to center on transforming the evil world for Christ through love, personal holiness, the apocalyptic hope, and those of our hymn: the suffering of this world, "the storms of life"; the loneliness of discipleship, "when my friends misunderstand"; and the daily need for companionship with Jesus, "O thou Lily of the Valley, stand by me."

Jon Michael Spencer has commented on this genre:

> Tindley claims that those who are already in heaven are the little ones who "lived and suffered in the world." . . .They were the poor and often despised. . . . However, until the "morning" comes ushered in by the Christ Liberator Jesus, those who suffer in this world are exhorted to endure, a charge attainable only if Christ Friend and Protector Jesus is standing by. (Spencer 1990, 214)

In this as in his other hymns Tindley employs "proverbs, folk images, biblical allusions well-known to black Christians . . . that [universally] appeal to the human heart with words of hope, grace, love and pity" (McClain 1990, 75): for example, in stanza 1, Jesus' calming the storm, Matthew 8:23-27; and in stanza 5, approaching death as nearing the River Jordan. For additional commentary on Tindley's hymns see "Beams of heaven as I go," pages 229-30, and "Leave it there," page 459.

Stand by me

Arr. by William Farley Smith, 1989

William Farley Smith's setting maintains the original gospel-quartet style, while introducing chromatic alterations that may cause congregations to stumble. F. A. Clark's simpler arrangement at number 2 in *New Songs of Paradise*, No. 6, may be used throughout or sung by the choir, quartet, or soloist in alternation with our setting. In either arrangement the dotted eighth and sixteenth figure is performed throughout as a triplet.

Stand up and bless the Lord (662)

James Montgomery, 1824 (Neh. 9:5)

The hymn was written for the Red Hill Wesleyan Sunday School anniversary, and it was published in six stanzas at 558 under the title "Exhortation to praise and thanksgiving" in the author's *Christian Psalmist*, 1825. (Gealy 557/439) It entered our hymnals in 1837. Our hymnal includes the text without alteration and omits the original stanza 4.

With the exception of the sturdy call to praise in the first and last stanzas and the arresting paraphrase of Isaiah 6:5-7 in stanza 3, this hymn illustrates why Erik Routley can state:

> [Montgomery's name] would not appear in anybody's list of the half-dozen greatest hymns. But it is just this touch of the commonplace, this avoidance of the extreme, this solidity of doctrine and catholicity of experience that gives Montgomery this pivotal place in hymnody. His work is good, sound, hard-wearing stuff with a touch of the genuinely inspired here and there that makes us able to regard him as the typical English hymn-writer. (Routley 1959, 124)

St. Michael

See "How can we sinners know," pages 407-08.

Stand up, stand up for Jesus (514)

George Duffield, Jr., 1858 (Eph. 6:10-17)

The hymn was written during a revival in Philadelphia in 1858 in the aftermath of the tragic accidental death of the brilliant Episcopal abolitionist preacher Dudley A. Tyng. It was printed in leaflets and subsequently in the *Church Psalmist*, 1859. (Ellinwood 1956, 330)

One account of the writing of the hymn was provided by the author's son, Samuel A. W. Duffield, in his *English Hymns. Their Authors and History*, 1886. (Gealy 557/440) It is not clear from other accounts whether Tyng uttered the first words of the hymn on his death bed or as part of a final sermon. The Sunday following Tyng's death Duffield preached on Ephesians 6:14, "Stand therefore, and fasten the belt of truth around your waist, and put on the breastplate of righteousness," and wrote a concluding hymn on that theme.

The hymn entered our hymnals in 1867. The cento in our hymnal is made up of stanzas 1, 3, 4, and 6. Changes were made for our hymnal in stanza 1:7, "is" to "be"; 2:5, "men" to "brave"; 4:5, "him that overcometh" to "those who vanquish evil"; and 4:7, "he" to "they."

Most hymnals omit stanzas 2 and 5. The latter has an allusion to the death of Tyng in lines 4-6:

> Stand up!—stand up for Jesus!
>   Each soldier to his post;
> Close up the broken column,
>   And shout through all the host!
> Make good the loss so heavy,
>   In those that still remain,
> And prove to all around you
>   That death itself is gain!

For other hymns with prevalent militaristic imagery, see "Soldiers of Christ, arise" **(513)** and "Onward, Christian soldiers" **(575)**.

Webb

George J. Webb, 1830

Webb composed this tune in 1830 as he sailed from England to Boston, and it was included in *The Odeon*, 1837, a collection of secular songs he co-published with Lowell Mason. The first use of the tune for a hymn was for "The morning light is breaking" in *The Wesleyan Psalmist*, 1842. William B. Bradbury in *The Golden Chain*, 1861, appears to be the first to wed this tune and text. (McCutchan 1942, 471)

Standing in the need of prayer (352)

See "It's me, it's me, O Lord," pages 435-40.

Standing on the promises (374)

Words and music: R. Kelso Carter, 1886 (Eph. 6:14-17)

This hymn was first published in *Songs of Perfect Love*, 1886, compiled by John R. Sweney and the author. (Reynolds 1964, 185)

As in other single-theme evangelical hymns and songs of this period the biblical source of the hymn is not clear. "Stand firm" from Ephesians 6:14 has often been cited as the theme of the hymn, although the word "promise" tends to be reenforced as well. In this latter regard there are several scriptural references including 2 Samuel 22:31, "This God—his way is perfect; the promise of the Lord proves true; he is a shield for all who take refuge in him"; Ephesians 3:6, "partakers of the promise in Christ Jesus"; and Hebrews 6:12c, " so that you may not become sluggish, but imitators of those who through faith and patience inherit the promises"; and Hebrews 6:17, "In the same way, when God desired to show even more clearly to the heirs of the promise the unchangeable character of his purpose, he guaranteed it by an oath."

The author's evangelical Wesleyan roots—a belief in Christian perfection, holiness, and freedom from the bondage of sin—are reflected in stanza 3, omitted from most hymnals:

> Standing on the promises I now can see
> Perfect, present cleansing in the blood for me;
> Standing in the liberty where Christ makes free,
> Standing on the promises of God.

The hymn first appeared in our hymnals in 1897, but it was never included in an authorized Methodist hymnal and was not included in the 1957 *Hymnal* of the Evangelical United Brethren. Its place in our hymnal came from its inclusion in a list of hymns determined to be widely used by evangelical United Methodists. See *"The United Methodist Hymnal*, 1989," pages 159-60, for a discussion of the process that brought a number of these hymns into our hymnal.

Promises

William J. Reynolds has commented that the hymn's "martial rhythm reflects life on the campus of the military academy where the composer-author was a student and later taught." (Reynolds 1990, 262)

The tune was named by the committee who produced the *Baptist Hymnal*, 1956.

Steal away to Jesus (704)

African American Spiritual
adapt. and arr. by William Farley Smith, 1986

John Lovell, Jr., writes that this spiritual illustrates the double meanings in some slave songs: "Perry Bradford quotes Grandma Betsy Bradford, a former slave, to the effect that 'Steal Away to Jesus' always meant to go up north to the promised land," [and] "Nat Turner used 'Steal Away' to call his conspirators together." (Lovell 1972, 191, 196)

The spiritual also affirms that God's judgment speaks to the trembling sinner through the mystery and fear of wind, thunder, and lightning. The slave's departure for the North or from this life is anticipated in the reiterated words "I ain't got long to stay here," and it will be as clearly signaled as "the sound of the trumpet" in 1 Corinthians 15:51-52.

In the *Supplement* to *The Story of the Jubilee Singers*, F. J. Loudin tells the moving story of how the singers on their world tour in 1886 introduced this spiritual to the Aborigines in Australia:

> After a drive of fourteen miles through thickly wooded forests . . . we found these black people far from cordial, in fact they gave us to understand by their actions that they did not wish to have anything to do with us. After we had spent about an hour inspecting their schools, homes, etc., the church bell rang, and when they had assembled we took our places and began to sing that sweetly pathetic song evolved from the crushed hearts of the enslaved black people of America, "Steal Away to Jesus." [No. 24 in the *Supplement*] Up to this time they seemed like unwilling children forced to go to Sabbath school; but what a change of expression the tones of the old slave song awoke! First, wonder, which seemed to say, "What strange sounds are these which for the first time fall upon our ears?" then joy, as the full volume of the melody filled the humble little church. . . . Long before the "Benediction" . . . they were weeping like children, tears of joy; and when we had finished they gathered about us, and, with tears still flowing, they clasped our hands and in broken accents exclaimed, "O! God bless you! we have never heard anything like that before!" (Marsh 1897, 141)

Steal away

The setting in our hymnal may be sung by the choir in alternation with the simpler harmonization at 134 in *Songs of Zion*, 1981. The spiritual may also be performed in call-and-response style with the one-line stanzas sung by a soloist without accompaniment and the congregation and choir answering in four-part harmony.

Stille Nacht, heilige Nacht (239)

See "Silent night, holy night," pages 594-96.

Sufficiency of God (495)

See "The sufficiency of God," page 643.

Sundays of Easter (321)

Lutheran Book of Worship, 1978

This prayer celebrating the joys of the Resurrection is appropriate for the Sundays after Easter and other occasions celebrating the glorious victory of Christ over death and our promise of eternal life.

Surely the presence of the Lord (328)

Words and music: Lanny Wolfe, 1977

This chorus on the presence of the Holy Spirit is a standard gathering song and call to worship.

Wolfe

For commentary on choruses see "Spirit Song," pages 605-06.

Sweet hour of prayer (496)

William Walford, 1845

Armin Haeussler in *The Story of Our Hymns*, 1952, Fred D. Gealy (Gealy, Lovelace, Young 1970, 384), and William J. Reynolds in *Companion to the Baptist Hymnal*, 1976, have provided extensive research on the authorship of this hymn. Gealy's research files (557/446) are the basis for his opinion that the hymn should be attributed only to William Walford. William J. Reynolds (1976, 203-05) continuing his coverage of the problem of authorship from *Hymns of Our Faith*, 1964, believes that Thomas Salmon, whose account of the authorship of the hymn was first included in the New York *Observer*, September 13, 1845, may have misattributed the text to W. W. Walford. In May 1992, Reynolds supplied this writer with copies of his research.

Information from reel 137 in Dictionary of American Hymnology Project indicates the hymn was first included in *Conference Hymns, a new collection of hymns, designed especially for use in Conference and prayer Meetings and family worship, E. H. Fletcher, 1849*, edited by John Dowling, 1807-78. Reynolds states that the first hymnal to include the hymn with a tune was *Church Melodies*, 1858.

This most familiar of all hymns on prayer and trust entered our hymnals in 1867. Most of our editions have used three of the four stanzas. In 1935, before the rigors of scheduled air travel, the original stanza 4 was dropped from *The Methodist Hymnal*.

> Sweet hour of prayer, sweet hour of prayer,
> May I thy consolation share,
> Till, from Mount Pisgah's lofty height,
> I view my home, and take my flight:

> This robe of flesh I'll drop, and rise
> To seize the everlasting prize;
> And shout, while passing through the air,
> Farewell, farewell, sweet hour of prayer!

Sweet hour

William B. Bradbury, 1861

The tune was composed for this text and apparently first appeared in the composer's *Golden Chain*, 1861.

Sweet, sweet Spirit (334)

Words and music: Doris Akers, 1962

This chorus was written while Akers served as choir director for the Sky Pilot Radio Church in Los Angeles. One Sunday morning as the the choir prepared for worship, the author prayed:

> "I know there's a sweet, sweet spirit in this place." The phrase stayed with her throughout the worship service, and the next day she wrote both words and music of this hymn, which praises the sweetness and goodness of the Holy Spirit known to Christians as they worship together. (Sanchez 1989, 121)

Sweet, sweet Spirit

The music first appeared in solo sheet music form in 1965. (Reynolds 1976, 224) Our arrangement is from *Hymns for the Family of God*, 1976, and is apparently by its editor Fred Bock who probably provided the tune's name.

Swing low, sweet chariot (703)

African American spiritual
adapt. and arr. by William Farley Smith, 1987 (2 Kings. 2:11)

This spiritual personalizes the account of the ascension of Elijah in 2 Kings 2:11, "As they continued walking and talking, a chariot of fire and horses of fire separated the two of them, and Elijah ascended in a whirlwind into heaven."

John Lovell, Jr., comments on the spiritual's dual theme:

> Of course, the slave could be referring to the Underground Railroad which had taken to glory (free land) many of his friends and fellow workers. Assume he it not. This is one of a family of songs in which a great golden vehicle, powered and directed by God, manned by angels, comes down

from heaven through the skies to pick up and elevate a particular individual. (Lovell 1972, 247)

William B. McClain provides John W. Work, Jr.'s, account of the origin of this spiritual:

> A slave mother had been sold and was to be separated from her baby daughter and taken "down South." Choosing rather to die and to take her child's life, rather than to be eternally separated, the young mother went to throw herself over into the Cumberland River [Tennessee]. An old "mammy" knowing the woman's intentions stopped her with the words, "Don't you do it, honey; wait, let de chariot of de Lord swing low." (McClain 1990, 98)

The spiritual is often sung at funerals.

Swing low

There is another setting at 104 in *Songs of Zion*, 1981, similar to one of the first arrangements at no. 2 in F. J. Loudin's *Supplement* to *The Story of the Jubilee Singers*, 1897. Both more fully reflect the slow and expressive call-and-response performance practice from the oral tradition of this spiritual, identified by John W. Work in his paper "The Negro Spiritual," 1962, 24. Our setting may also be sung in a call-and-response pattern with the soloist singing the lead-in line, and the stanzas, with or without accompaniment, answered by the group.

Take my life, and let it be (399)

Frances R. Havergal, 1874 (Rom. 12:1)
In *Our Hymnody* Robert G. McCutchan included the author's account of the writing of this hymn:

> [In December 1873] I went for a little visit of five days [to Areley House, Worcestershire]. There were ten persons in the house; some unconverted and long prayed for, some converted but not rejoicing Christians. He [God] gave me the prayer, "Lord, give me all in this house!" and He just *did*. Before I left the house every one had got a blessing. The last night of my visit I was too happy to sleep, and passed most of the night in renewal of my consecration, and those little couplets formed themselves and chimed in my heart one after another till they finished with *"Ever*, only, ALL for Thee." (McCutchan 1942, 269)

The text was included in six 77.77 stanzas at 1072 under the heading "2 Sam. 19:30. 'Yes, let Him take all'" in *Songs of Grace and Glory*, 1876 ed., edited by the poet and Charles B. Snepp. (Gealy 557, 446) It was suggested that the last two lines of each stanza may be repeated to make each stanza 77.77.77.

The poet provides an interesting insight into her creative process:

> [Hymn-writing] is praying . . . for I never seem to write even a verse by myself, and [I] feel like a little child writing: you know a child would look up at every sentence and say, "And what shall I say next." (Price 1911, 64)

This writer has the indelible impression from his youth of occasions when this hymn, particularly stanza 2:5-6, "take my silver and my gold; not a mite would I withhold," was sung with great determination by affluent worshippers in vocal response to the annual appeal for financial support of the church where his father served as pastor. Their financial response to the challenge was to pledge a small fraction of the interest income from their considerable inherited wealth— pledges that reportedly were often among the last to be paid at the end of the fiscal year.

The hymn entered our hymnals in 1881. In our 1905 edition it was reduced to three stanzas of 77. 77 D with MESSIAH as the second tune.

Messiah

Arr. from Louis J. F. Hérold by George Kingsley, 1839

The tune first appeared in George Kingsley, *The Sacred Choir*, 1839. (McCutchan 1942, 269) The 1957 Evangelical United Brethren hymnal set this text to a slightly more solid and interesting tune, HENDON **(163)**.

Take our bread (640)

Words and music: Joe Wise, 1966

This hymn was first included at page 18 in the author's *Gonna Sing My Lord*, 1966. It was widely used in the 1970's by Roman Catholics who sang it at the offertory and during the serving of Holy Communion. It entered United Methodist repertory in *Supplement to the Book of Hymns*, 1982.

Take our bread

The keyboard accompaniment is adapted from Carlton R. Young's setting in *Songbook for Saints and Sinners*, 1971.

Take the name of Jesus with you (536)

See "Precious name," pages 561-62.

Take time to be holy (395)

William D. Longstaff, ca. 1882 (1 Pet. 1:16)
The writing of this hymn was apparently suggested by the words from 1 Peter 1:16, "Be ye holy; for I am holy," from the King James Version of the Bible, spoken by Griffith John at a missionary conference held in China. They were repeated at a meeting in Keswick, England, ca. 1882, and inspired Longstaff to write the hymn one evening. It was first included in *Hymns of Consecration*, a collection used at the Keswick meeting. (McCutchan 1942, 290) The hymn entered our hymnals in 1901.

This hymn's invitation to holiness is devoid of the mandate for radical change of heart and the resulting release from the bonds of sin as embodied in Wesleyan precepts of entire sanctification, perfecting grace, perfect love, and Christian perfection. Contrast, for example, stanza 2:5-8 in Charles Wesley's "Love divine, all loves excelling" **(384)**:

> Take away our bent to sinning;
>   Alpha and Omega be;
> end of faith as its beginning,
>   set our hearts at liberty.

Holiness

George C. Stebbins, 1890
Robert G. McCutchan has traced the writing of this tune to India, where the composer, who was assisting George F. Pentecost and Methodist Bishop James Mills Thoburn in evangelistic and conference activity, had received several hymns from a friend who had clipped them from a periodical. Stebbins "decided to set the music to them and in a short time had made the setting and sent it on to Mr. Sankey in New York." (McCutchan 1942, 290)

The tune and text were first published in Ira Sankey's *Winnowed Songs for Sunday School*, 1890, and a year later in *Gospel Hymns, No. 6*. (Reynolds 1964, 190)

There is an alternate harmonization at 159 in *The United Methodist Hymnal Music Supplement*.

Take up thy cross, the Savior said (415)

Charles W. Everest, 1833
(Matt. 16:24-25; Mark 8:34-35; Luke 9:23-24)
This hymn is based on Mark 8:34-35, mirrored in Matthew and Luke, "If any want to become my followers, let them deny themselves and take up their cross ["daily"

in Luke 9:23] and follow me." It first appeared in six LM stanzas in the poet's *Visions of Death, and Other Poems*, 1833 (Julian 1907, 358); it was first included in a hymnal in the Dutch Reformed Church's *Sabbath School and Social Hymns*, 1843. (Reynolds 1976, 208)

Hymns Ancient and Modern, 1861, included the hymn with significant changes from the original, particularly those by Earl Nelson for his *Salisbury Hymn-Book*, 1857. The hymn entered our hymnals in 1878 with stanzas 1-5 from the 1861 version. In 1889 stanza 4 was dropped:

> Take up thy cross, then, in his strength,
> And calmly every danger brave;
> 'Twill guide thee to a better home,
> And lead to victory o'er the grave.

Our hymnal includes stanzas 1, 2, 3, and 5. In stanza 4:3, "he who bears" has been changed to "those who bear."

Percy Dearmer comments that this is "one of those hymns of poor quality which have to be always changed in order to make them possible for use." (Dearmer and Jacob, 1933, 76) Setting it to strong LM tunes has contributed to this hymn's longevity and popularity. It continues to be one of the most sung "cross and discipleship" hymns.

Germany

William Gardiner's Sacred Melodies, 1815

This is one of the most singable LM tunes in the repertory. While the melody was attributed by Gardiner to Beethoven ("Subject from Beethoven") in his 1838 memoirs he could not clearly identify its source. (Watson and Trickett 1988, 207) Erik Routley (1953, 65) traced a phrase of the tune to "O Isis und Osiris" from Mozart's *Die Zauberflöte* (*The Magic Flute*). Others, including Ellinwood (1956, 305), have attributed it to portions of Beethoven's Piano Trio, op. 70, no. 2. The more likely prospect is that Gardiner pieced together several memorable melodic fragments into his tune and harmonized it.

Our harmonization has remained unaltered since its first inclusion in our hymnals in 1878. There is a descant, alternative harmonization, and transposition at 142-43 in *The United Methodist Hymnal Music Supplement*.

In a moment of practical concern Erik Routley remarks at the conclusion of his essay "A Note on Hymns and the Classics" that when this tune and others adapted from classical musical sources are included in our hymnals, "musical purists have to bear in mind . . . that when musicians are dealing with the needs of the Church's aesthetic standards [they] have to come to terms with the discipline imposed by the unmusical condition of the ordinary worshipper." (Routley 1953, 66)

Te Deum Laudamus (80)

See "Canticle of the Holy Trinity," pages 265-67.

Tell me the stories of Jesus (277)

William H. Parker, ca. 1885 (Matt. 19:13-15; 21:8-9)
This song about Jesus' life and ministry was written following a request by the children of the poet's Sunday school class at Chelsea Street Baptist Church, Nottingham, "Teacher, tell us another story." (Martin 1962, 146) It was printed in six stanzas on a hymn sheet and was first included in *The Sunday School Hymnary*, 1905.

The song entered our hymnals in the 1935 *Methodist Hymnal* in three stanzas in the section "Hymns for Children." The stanzas on Jesus' miracles and passion, thought by Christian educators to be beyond children's comprehension, were dropped: for example, stanza 3:

> Tell me, in accents of wonder,
>   How rolled the sea,
> Tossing the boat in a tempest
>   On Galilee;
> And how the Master,
>   Ready and kind,
> Chided the billows,
>   And hushed the wind;

and the original stanza 6:

> Show me that scene in the garden,
>   Of bitter pain;
> and of the cross where my Saviour
>   For me was slain:
> Sad ones or bright ones,
>   So that they be
> Stories of Jesus,
>   Tell them to me.

Most of the deleted stanzas and a new stanza on the Resurrection are included in British hymnals.

Stories of Jesus

Frederick A. Challinor, 1903
William J. Reynolds has written that this tune was the prizewinning tune in a competition sponsored by the national Sunday School Union, London, in its

centennial year, 1903. Frederick Bridge, organist at Westminster Abbey and judge of the contest, acclaimed, "This is the best. A fine hymn, too. In a few years both will be sung all over the kingdom." *The Sunday School Hymnary*, 1905, was the first hymnal to include it. (Reynolds 1964, 505)

Tell out, my soul, the greatness of the Lord (200)

Timothy Dudley-Smith, 1961 (Luke 1:46b-55)

This metrical paraphrase of the Song of Mary (Magnificat) is the first and most widely sung of the author's hymns. Its composition is recounted by the poet:

> I did not think of myself . . . as having in any way the gifts of a hymn-writer when in May 1961 I jotted down a set of verses, beginning "Tell out, my soul, the greatness of the Lord." I was reading a review copy of the New English Bible New Testament, in which that line appears exactly as I have put it above; I saw in it the first line of a poem, and speedily wrote the rest. I cannot now recall how it came to the hands of the editors of the *Anglican Hymn Book* [1965], then in the early stages of compilation, but they told me that they would like to use it as a hymn. (Dudley-Smith 1984, 12)

Commentary on the circumstances whereby the Hymnal Revision Committee changed "his" to "God" in stanzas 1:3, 2:1, 2:2, 2:3, 2:4, 3:1, 4:1, and 4:2 is found in the section on "God Language," pages 138-43. While the author and others view these changes as infelicitous, the hymn would not have not been included without them.

For commentary on the biblical text, see "Canticle of Mary," pages 257-58.

Woodlands

Walter Greatorex, 1919

After its first marriage with "Tidings" in *The Anglican Hymnal*, 1965, this text had the good fortune to be rematched by the editors of *100 Hymns for Today*, 1969, with this tune, described as "irresistible" by Cyril Taylor. (Taylor 1984, 27)

The tune first appeared in *Public School Hymn Book*, 1919. It is named after one of the schoolhouses at Gresham's School, Holt, Norwich, where the composer served as director of music 1911-36. The composer's expanded harmonization is included at 438 in *The Hymnal 1982 Accompaniment Edition*; it may be used with a descant by John Wilson, 86 in *Hymns and Psalms*, 1983.

Thank you, Lord (84)

Trad. chorus adapt. and arr. by William Farley Smith, 1986

The arranger has commented, "Afro-American slaves knew well the products of 'sowing' righteous seeds. They also learned to say, 'thank you, Lord,' before a blessing was returned." (Sanchez 1989, 46)

Thank you, Lord

This chorus may be used as a response in Holy Communion or before and following prayer. This arrangement was made for our hymnal. There is another setting at 228 in *Songs of Zion*, 1981.

That boy-child of Mary (241)

Tom Colvin, 1969 (Luke 2:7)

The story of Jesus' birth and the significance of his life for us is told in this call-and-response song from Malawi. Tom Colvin comments that the song is patterned after the African practice and understanding that "the name that is given to a child is very important expressing often the hopes for the child or the 'events' associated with its birth." (*Fill Us with Your Love* 1983, 43)

Blantyre

Trad. Malawi melody; adapt. by Tom Colvin, 1969

This is a traditional dance tune of Malawi. (*Fill Us with Your Love* 1983, 43) The tune is named after the Blantyre Synod of the Church of Central Africa, Presbyterian. The opening interval has been inverted from a descending third, C to A, to an ascending sixth, C to A.

Our setting was adapted from the arrangement in *Fill Us with Your Love*, 1983. In the preface Tom Colvin discusses hymn singing style and performance practice in African worship:

> These are not simply a new body of hymns: they imply a different style of singing and even a different approach to worship. The sharing of the hymn between leader and people, or the passing of the melody back and forth between two groups of singers, introduces an element of drama and a greater excitement into the Church's praise. The repetitive character of the melodies and the habit these hymns have of expanding to a climax elicit a more spontaneous response from and a fuller participation by the worshippers. The customary overlap between verses, and between leader and people, contributes to this cumulative effect. Common in the African Church also are the spontaneous improvisation of harmonies (say in thirds or fifths, with treble and bass voice often richly doubling at the octave) and the use of percussion instruments for accompaniment.

> Those who sing these hymns are encouraged to interpret them in their own way, in the overlap of voices, the addition of harmonies, and the use of percussion and rhythms. Although the melodies are written in modes which appear similar to the scales used generally, they are not necessarily identical.

In a sense the hymns have been "frozen" by being put on paper. It is up to the singers to "thaw them out" in the singing, and so make them their own. Some of them are alive only when they are danced to because they started life as dance tunes. Others were wedding songs, boating songs, work songs, welcoming songs, praise songs and the like. These are tunes which accompany village life and are now used to assist worship, supplied as they are with words which arise out of African present-day life. (*Fill Us with Your Love* 1983, 4-5)

The Apostolic Blessing (669)

2 Cor. 13:14

Called the Apostolic Blessing because it is the apostle Paul's closing of his second letter to the church at Corinth, the text was recommended for use by USA Methodists beginning in 1824. Nolan B. Harmon has traced its origins:

[The Benediction] was added in [the] 1661 [*Book of Common Prayer*] with a "free" translation, as Dr. Summers terms it, as against the "literal" translation (Authorized Version) which the Methodist Episcopal Churches hold now (except Holy *Spirit* in place of Holy *Ghost*, in the M. E.). In the English Book it was "our Lord" for "the Lord"; *fellowship* for *communion*; *with us all evermore* for *with you all*—"the last change having been made," so Summers quotes Bishop Bownell, "that the priest may implore a blessing for himself as well as the congregation." We, however, have dropped the English form here for that of the Authorized Version. (Harmon 1926, 306)

The Order of Worship on the inside front cover of the 1896 printing of the 1878 hymnal recommended its use, but did not include the text. In the 1905 and 1935 hymnals it was included as the benediction at the conclusion of the burial services. In our 1957 and 1966 hymnals it was included in the section of "Benedictions." In our hymnal it appears with "fellowship" changed to "communion" at page 11 in the "Service of Word and Table" and at the conclusion of "An Order for Morning Praise and Prayer," page 878.

Laurence Hull Stookey suggests that "this act of blessing is suitable for use by a leader of worship at the close of any service" or at the conclusion of baptism, confirmation, or the installation of church officers. (Sanchez 1989, 225)

The Ascension (323)

Laurence Hull Stookey, 1987

The author provides this commentary on the prayer for the fortieth day of the Easter season, Ascension Day:

[It] embodies the meaning of the ascension: The living Christ, who before his resurrection was bound to a few hundred square miles for roughly thirty years, is present with us at all times and in all places. The ascension declares Christ's dominion and power throughout creation and beyond. We pray for the faith to live by these truths. (Sanchez 1989, 118)

This prayer, which reflects the theology of Brian Wren's hymn "Christ is alive" (**318**), was first used from this hymnal at the "Service of Thanksgiving and Consecration," May 4, 1989. (See "Dedication," pages 174-77.)

The Battle Hymn of the Republic (717)

Sts. 1-4, Julia Ward Howe, 1861; st. 5, anon.
According to the author's account in *The Century Magazine*, August 1887 (Gealy 556/302), this hymn was written after she and her husband and several friends, including their pastor James Freeman Clark, had visited the Union troops on review near Washington, DC. On their return to the city they were caught in the congestion of troops, horses, and battlewagons that were counterattacking the Southern forces. To spend the time her group began to sing favorite war choruses, among them "John Brown's body," about the militant abolitionist folk hero who was court-marshalled and hanged in 1859, including stanzas such as "We will hang Jeff Davis to a sour apple tree." The tune they sang was called "John Brown's Tune":

Someone remarked upon the excellence of the tune, and I said that I had often wished to write some words which might be sung to it. [James Freeman Clark also suggested she write a hymn to the camp-meeting tune.] We sang, however, the words which were already well known as belonging to it, and our singing seemed to please the soldiers, who surrounded us like a river, and who themselves took up the strain in the intervals crying to us "Good for You."

I slept as usual that night, but awoke before dawn to the next morning, and soon found myself trying to weave together certain lines which, though not entirely suited to the John Brown music, were yet capable of being sung to it. I lay still in the dark room, line after line shaping itself in my mind, and verse after verse. . . . I sprang out of bed and groped about in the dim twilight to find a bit of paper and the stump of a pen which I remembered to have had the evening before. Having found these articles, and having long been accustomed to scribble with scarcely any sight of what I might write in a room made dark for the repose of my infant children, I began to write the lines of my poem in like manner. (I was always careful to decipher these lines within twenty-four hours, as I had found them perfectly illegible after a long period.) . . . I completed my writing, went back to bed, and fell fast asleep. (Howe 1887, 690)

Upon her return to Boston the author shared the poem with James T. Fields, editor of the *Atlantic Monthly* who added the title "Battle Hymn of the Republic" and published it in five stanzas on the front page of the February 1862 issue. (Gealy 556/302) Although it is often stated that the author withdrew the sixth stanza, it is not known who wrote a sixth stanza, our fifth, or when it was first included with the original five. While the 15.15.15. 6 tune was the basis for the text, it is not known who adapted the chorus to accommodate the verses, but it appears that the text was first interlined with the tune in John Dadman's *Aeolian Harp Collection*, 1862.

Most hymnals omit the original stanza 3:

> I have read a fiery gospel writ in burnished rows of steel:
> "As ye deal with my contemners, so with you my grace shall deal;
> Let the Hero, born of woman, crush the serpent with his heel,
> Since God is marching on."

The hymn entered our hymnals in 1921. Its inclusion in our 1966 hymnal was met with opposition from some in the South where tradition teaches that General Sherman's army sang it as they razed Atlanta and pressed on to the Atlantic coast.

Since its introduction during the USA Civil War and after the war by Charles Cardwell McCabe, the 122nd Ohio Volunteers' chaplain who was elected a Methodist bishop in 1896, the hymn has become the USA's second and more singable national anthem. It has been associated with various nationalistic and political causes including women's suffrage, temperance, two world wars, the Vietnam war, the 1960's USA civil rights movement, most political gatherings at every level, and it has been sung in many churches on the Sunday nearest the Fourth of July. It has been used at the funerals and memorial services of politicians, war heros, and heads of state. Its use with the USA tune, by directive of the deceased's will, in Winston Churchill's memorial service in 1965 at St. Paul's Cathedral caused no end to handwringing on the part of English church musicians and hymnal editors who for half a century had deemed the tune inappropriate for use in worship.

Julia Ward Howe's military and apocalyptic rhetoric forcefully presented by this marching tune is often programmed by beguiling politicians, sports entrepreneurs, and religious leaders to galvanize their audiences in solidarity of purpose and a feeling of moral superiority. In light of its action on "Onward, Christian Soldiers" (see pages 135-37), the Hymnal Revision Committee at one point deleted the more militaristic stanzas 2 and 3 of this hymn. These were restored, and our stanzas 1 through 4 appear without change from the author's version in *The Century Magazine*, August 1887. (Gealy 556/302)

The hymn has been published in a wide variety of choral and instrumental settings, the most famous being Roy Ringwald's arrangement in 1944 for choir and orchestra that after World War II became a showcase for Fred Waring's Pennsylvanians and thousands of school and church choirs. As guest conductor of hundreds of choral festivals, Waring, disregarding McCarthyism and other despotic manifestations of patriotic zeal, including some evangelical Christian crusades, changed stanza 4:3 to "let us live to make men free." The text that was approved by the 1988 General Conference included Waring's change; nevertheless, the alteration inexplicably has not been included in our hymnal.

Battle hymn of the Republic

USA Camp-meeting tune, 19th cent.

Ellen Jane Lorenz (1980, 121) has traced this *aaab* form camp-meeting chorus to *Songs of Zion*, 1851:

> Say brothers, will you meet us, (repeat twice)
> In Canaan's happy land.
>
> Say sisters, will you meet us,
> In Canaan's happy land.
>
> By the grace of God we'll meet you,
> In Canaan's happy land.

Following the execution of John Brown in 1859 the tune was parodied in the North as "John Brown's body lies a-mouldering in the grave, but his soul goes marching on." In New England it was performed by military bands as "John Brown's Tune," not named, according to tradition, after the abolitionist folk hero but after an affable Scotsman soldier from Boston, John Brown.

Other parodies included in *The Revivalist*, 1872, are "Ye soldiers of the cross arise" and "Now I know what makes me happy." Later secular parodies are "John Brown's Baby," "Little Peter Rabbit," and "It isn't any trouble just to S-M-I-L-E." (Lorenz 1980, 63)

Eileen Southern has written that the tune was a favorite of African Americans who improvised this parody while serving in the Northern army:

> We are done with hoeing cotton, we are done with hoeing corn,
> We are colored Yankee soldiers, as sure as you are born;
> When Massa hears us shouting, he will think 'tis Gabriel's horn,
> As we go marching on.

Southern continues her commentary:

> John Brown's body came to be the unofficial theme song of black soldiers. Early in the war it was invested with a special sentiment for them. Historians

report, for example, that when the band of the Fifth-fourth of Massachusetts, one of the first black regiments to go South, played the melody
as the soldiers marched down State Street in Boston en route to Battery
Wharf, tears came to the eyes of the proud black women watching the
parade and the mother of the white commanding officer, Mrs. Shaw.
(Southern 1971, 232)

Other nineteenth-century attempts to use the tune with other texts include Frederick L. Hosmer's antislavery hymn:

> From age to age they gather, all the brave of heart and strong;
> In the strife of truth with error, of the right against the wrong.
> (Hughes 1980, 152)

The music of the chorus was included at 899 in the 1889 hymnal of the Methodist
Episcopal Church, South. Some Spanish language hymnals have used the music
of the chorus with a five-stanza hymn, beginning:

> ¡Gloria a Ti, Jesús divino!
> ¡Gloria a Ti por tus bondades!
> ¡Gloria eterna a tus piedades,
> Queredo Salvador!

There is an arrangement by J. Jefferson Cleveland for SATB voices with descant
at 213 in *Songs of Zion*, 1981, and a vocal or instrumental descant at 40 in *The
United Methodist Hymnal Music Supplement*.

The bread of life for all is broken (633)
Jiu shi zhe shen, wei zhong shengij bokai

Timothy Ting-fang Lew, 1936
trans. by Walter Reginald Oxenham Taylor, 1943
phonetic transcription from the Chinese by I-to Loh, 1988

This is one of fifty indigenous hymns included in *Hymns of Universal Praise*, a
landmark union hymnal published in 1936 for the Protestant groups of China.
Most of the hymns were translated from Western collections. The translation
was first included in the *BBC Hymn Book*, 1951, a collection of standard and new
hymns and tunes that were used in the Daily Service of Worship, and special
programs featuring hymns and hymn singing that were broadcast for many
years on Radio 4 UK.

I-to Loh has written that the hymn is written in semiclassical Chinese and
employs specific Buddhist terms and images with which traditional Chinese can
easily identify.

The translator has commented:

> The original meter of the text is preserved in the English. Each line is a pair of phrases, of four and five characters each. . . . There seemed to be a special poignancy in Dr. Lew's words, written during the times of acute suffering the Chinese people were going through during the war [with Japan]. (Correspondence with Carlton R. Young, 1968)

Bliss Wiant told this writer that Chinese Christians who were inmates of Japanese prison camps in the late 1930's and in World War II, not being able to celebrate Holy Communion, would sing or chant in a call-and-response style this hymn of Christian unity on Christ's suffering, death, and promised presence.

Sheng En

Su Yin-Lan, 1934; harm. by Robert C. Bennett, 1988

The tune name means literally "God's, or holy, grace." This harmonization was made for our hymnal. Other harmonizations may be found at 157 and 157b in *Cantate Domino*, 1980.

The first printing of this tune in *Hymns of Universal Praise*, 1936, included a fermata at the end of each two measures. This writer observed Bliss Wiant teach this hymn in two-measure phrases with a light gong or handbell sounded at the fermatas. A flute or recorder may introduce and accompany the voices. The first stanza may be sung by a soloist using the transcription of the Chinese sounds. Alternate stanzas may be sung by female and male voices.

The care the eagle gives her young (118)

R. Deane Postlethwaite, 1980 (Deut. 32:11)

This hymn is based on the compelling metaphor in Deuteronomy 32:11, where God's saving relationship with Jacob is like an eagle, characteristically the mother, caring for its young:

> He sustained him in a desert land,
>   in a howling, wilderness waste;
> he shielded him, cared for him,
>   guarded him as the apple of his eye.
>
> As an eagle stirs up its nest,
>   and hovers over its young;
> as it spread its wings, takes them up,
>   and bears them aloft on its pinions,
> The Lord alone guided him;
>   no foreign god was with him.   (Deuteronomy 32:10-12)

The hymn was first included in the author's *Eight Hymns, In Context*, 1980, under the title "For a Recognition of God's Feminine Attributes." It was one of the first hymns to use female imagery and metaphors in descriptions and forms of address to God. In his commentary on the hymn the poet writes:

> I was disappointed to learn, after the hymn had been written, that the Revised Standard Version (which is noncommittal as to the sex of the eagle) or the Jerusalem Bible (which says it is a <u>father</u> eagle) may be better translations of the original Hebrew. . . . I do not claim an exhaustive knowledge of the nesting habits of eagles, nor do I know how to evaluate the male chauvinist inclinations of ancient Hebrew writers; but I still would maintain that I find a deep meaning and power in the image of a God who, like a mother eagle, pushes me from her nest, but who catches me, bears me up, when I fall. (Postlethwaite 1980, commentary on the hymn)

God as a mother eagle is one of many female deity metaphors and descriptions in scripture and tradition. S. Paul Schilling has commented:

> Our main words for God are the deposit of a still-powerful patriarchal tradition. Theologically, however, the mother symbol is no less warranted than the father image. Certainly the woman's role in giving birth to new life gives her a firm and important place in our thought of God as Creator. The Bible often uses feminine imagery to refer to God, as in Deut. 32:18 [giving birth]; Isa. 42:14 [woman in labor]; Isa. 46:3-4 [birthing Israel]; 66:13 [comforting a child]; Matt. 23:37 [a mother hen]; Luke 15:8-10 [woman who finds lost coin]. Hymns likewise extol qualities in God frequently thought of as feminine, such as mercy, patience, gentleness. These traits are not peculiarly male or female, but both, and we can recognize this by allowing both sexes to symbolize our understanding of the divine Spirit. Then we shall be able to address God the Father also as Mother. (Schilling 1983, 23)

For commentary on another hymn with female metaphors see "God of many names," pages 369-70.

Crimond

Jesse Seymour Irvine, 1872; harm. by TCL Pritchard, 1929

Apparently the tune was composed by the youthful Irvine and sent to David Grant to be harmonized. It first appeared in the Northern Psalter, 1872, William Carnie, ed., where the preface suggests that the tune was composed by David Grant, a citation that continued into this century.

Our harmonization is by TCL Pritchard from the Scottish Psalter, 1929. The tune was matched with this text and widely performed by the Glasgow Orpheus Choir, Hugh Roberton, conductor. Its popularity spread when it was used at the wedding of Princess Elizabeth and Prince Philip in 1947 and at the silver wedding anniversary of King George and Queen Elizabeth in 1948.

The tune's name is the village near Peterhead, Grampian, Scotland, where Irvine's father was minister of the parish. (Information on this tune is from Watson and Trickett 1988, 74.)

Erik Routley writes:

> [This] is the only Scottish psalm tune known to have been written by a woman, and did not see print until it had been harmonized (indifferently) by an Aberdeen tobacconist named David Grant who was also a precentor. One way and another this now exceedingly popular tune is the most anomalous and unusual of all Scottish tunes; and it is musically unusual in being the only one in the repertory to make use of "sequence"—which it does in its third line. (Routley 1981, 85)

This is the first appearance of this tune in our hymnals.

The church of Christ, in every age (589)

Fred Pratt Green, 1969

This hymn calls the church to be the agent of change and reconciliation in the struggle against injustice and hunger. It was composed in six stanzas and was first included under the title "The Caring Church" in the poet's *26 Hymns*, 1971. It came into prominence with its publication in *New Church Praise*, 1975. The text was slightly modified and the stanzas reordered for the *Lutheran Book of Worship*, 1978, to become the approved form of the hymn. Our hymnal follows the poet's text in *The Hymns and Ballads of Fred Pratt Green*, 1982, in stanza 2:4, "until they die," rather than "before they die," as printed in the earlier versions.

In the omitted stanza 4 the poet counters the social gospel's optimistic view of human nature:

> And all men suffer deeper ills:
>   for there's fever in our blood
> that prostitutes our human skills
>   and poisons all our brotherhood.

Dickinson College

Lee Hastings Bristol, Jr., 1962

This tune, a splendid piece of four-part writing in the style of Eric Thiman, was adapted by the composer from a section of his hymn-anthem "Lord of All Being Throned Afar," 1962. It was first included in *More Hymns and Spiritual Songs*, 1971, where it was named after Dickinson College, Carlisle, Pennsylvania.

The church's one foundation (545)

Samuel J. Stone, 1866

In 1866 the author wrote twelve hymns on the twelve articles of the Apostles' Creed **(882)** and published them in *Lyra Fidelium. Twelve Hymns on the Twelve Articles of the Apostles' Creed.* (Gealy 557/454) These hymns were composed in support of the Bishop of Capetown Robert Gray's defense of traditional means of dating and tracing the authorship of the Pentateuch. Gray's criticism centered on the activity of his popular colleague Bishop John William Colenso of Natal, the author of several commentaries on scripture, including *The Pentateuch and Book of Joshua, Critically Examined*, 1866, that used source-criticism, a then-new scholarly method of biblical criticism for dating and establishing the authorship of scripture. This method uses, though not exclusively as recent opponents errantly proclaim, scientifically derived evidence from the findings of medicine, geography, language, archeology, sociology, and history.

Stone's hymn is based on article nine, "The Holy Catholic Church: The Communion of Saints," composed in seven stanzas of 76.76 D, with a parallel commentary in the right margin for each stanza. It is prefaced by a "Summary of Truths Confessed in Article IX."

> I believe that the Church of Christ is, has been, and will be one and the same: that it is holy in respect of (1) its Author and End, (2) the vocation of all the baptized, (3) the true saints within it: that it is One, by unity of origination, of faith, of hope, of charity, of sacraments, of discipline: that it is Catholic, as being universally disseminated, as teaching all truth, as possessing all graces: that its truly sanctified members have communion with the holy Trinity, the angels, and with all Saints on earth and in Paradise.

Erik Routley's brilliant exegesis of the text in "How Long," pages 237-46 in *Hymns and the Faith*, 1956, begins with this outline:

> First: the Church is directly derived from Jesus Christ, and has a duty to Jesus Christ. Second: the Church directly emerges from history, and has a duty to history. Third: Jesus Christ loved and loves the Church. Fourth: the Church is in schism. (We might add for completeness a fifth proposition: the Church is a company of travellers in time.) (Routley 1956, 237-38)

The hymn entered our hymnals in 1901 using four stanzas of the unimpassioned composite text from *Hymns Ancient and Modern*, 1868 Appendix, constructed from the original stanzas 1, 2, 5, and the first 4 lines of stanzas 6 and 7. Our hymnal restores the original stanza 4, the touchstone of the debate but omits stanza 3 as do most hymnals:

> The Church shall never perish!
> Her dear Lord to defend,

To guide, sustain, and cherish,
  Is with her to the end;
Though there be those who hate her,
  And false sons in her pale,
Against or foe or traitor
  She ever shall prevail.

Also omitted are lines 5-8 of stanzas 6 and 7:

With all her sons and daughters
  Who, by the Master's Hand
Led through the deathly waters,
  Repose in Eden land.

There past the border mountains,
  Where in sweet vales the Bride,
With Thee by living fountains
  For ever shall abide.

The church's one foundation (546)

Samuel J. Stone, 1866; adapt. by Laurence Hull Stookey, 1983
This sensitive adaptation of the classic hymn in contemporary English renders it inclusive, ecumenical, and nonsexist. It was first included in *The Upper Room Worshipbook*, 1983; it is the only instance in our hymnal that implements the mandate of the 1988 General Conference that significantly altered texts could be placed side-by-side with the original. This occurrence speaks well for the Hymnal Revision Committee's middle-ground approach to mending texts so that in most instances they do not interrupt the singer's recall—one of the most compelling and useful attributes of congregational song.

Aurelia

Samuel Sebastian Wesley, 1864
One of the most popular Victorian hymn tunes in the repertory, this tune is a musical metaphor for the church militant: its unity and global and heavenly company of Christians. It is a model of conservative part-writing: a memorable tune, balanced chromaticism, and harmonic suspensions with a durability that has allowed it to be sung for more than a century by a variety of congregations in as many buildings with or without organ and choir—the accompanying ensemble for which it was composed.

The tune was first performed in the composer's home, sung to Bernard of Cluny's "Urbs Sion aurea" ("Jerusalem the golden"). At that time the composer predicted the tune would be popular, and according to tradition, his wife named it *aurelia* ("magnificent" or "splendid") from *aurea* ("golden"). It was included in Charles Kemble's and the composer's *Selection of Hymns*, 1864, and was first set to this text in *Hymns Ancient and Modern*, 1868 Appendix.

There is a descant and alternative harmonization at 25-26 in *The United Methodist Hymnal Music Supplement*.

The day is past and over (683)
Τὴν 'ημέραν διελθών

Anon. Greek, prob. 6th cent.
trans. by John Mason Neale, 1853

This Greek hymn from the sixth or seventh century was included by John Mason Neale in *The Ecclesiastic and Theologian*, 1853. A revised text appeared in Neale's *Hymns of the Eastern Church*, 1862. (Gealy 557/455) In the preface he favorably compares this lovely evening hymn to Thomas Ken's "All praise to thee, my God, this night" **(682)**. The hymn was first included in our hymnals in the 1935 *Methodist Hymnal* with stanza 4 omitted:

> Lighten mine eyes, O SAVIOUR,
>   Or sleep in death shall I;
> And he, my wakeful tempter,
>   Triumphantly shall cry:
> "He could not make their darkness light,
> Nor guard them through the hours of night!"

Our text is the version from that hymnal with the exception in stanza 4:5, "lover of men" has been changed to "Lord Jesus Christ."

Du Friedensfürst, Herr Jesu Christ

Bartholomäus Gesius, 1601, attrib. to J. S. Bach

The tune was included in *Geistliche deutsche Lieder*, 1601, and it was used by J. S. Bach in the first movement of his chorale Cantata 116, *Du Friedensfürst, Herr Jesu Christ*, 1724. R. G. McCutchan cites Bach as the source of the harmony without a date. While our setting is similar to sections of Bach's harmonization of O WELT, ICH MUSS DICH LASSEN **(631)** in the *St. Matthew Passion*, 1729, the source of our harmonization has not been determined.

The day of resurrection (303)
'Αναστάσεως ημέρα

John of Damascus, 8th cent., trans. by John Mason Neale, 1862

This text and "Come, ye faithful, raise the strain" **(315)** (see page 305) are hymns of praise freely translated from the Easter "Golden Canon," also called the

"Queen of Canons," linking the mighty acts of God: the Hebrews' exodus (see "Canticle of Moses and Miriam," page 258) and Jesus' resurrection.

Fred D. Gealy has provided this commentary:

> In the introduction to his translation, Neale in *Hymns of the Eastern Church*, 1862, [Gealy 557/457] recounts how a modern writer describes the way the hymn is used at Athens. At 12:00 midnight on Easter Eve a cannon shot announces that Easter Day has begun. At that moment the Archbishop, elevating the cross, cries out, "Christ is risen." Instantly the vast multitude, waiting in long silence, bursts forth in a shout of indescribable joy, "Christ is risen! Christ is risen!" Then the oppressive darkness is succeeded by a blaze of light from a thousand tapers. Bands of music strike up their gayest strains. Everywhere men clasp each other's hands and embrace with countenances beaming with delight. And above the mingling of many sounds the priests can be heard chanting, "The day of resurrection/Earth, tell it out abroad." (Gealy, Lovelace, Young 1970, 391)

The hymn entered our hymnals in 1878 with Neale's translation slightly altered from *The Parish Hymn Book*, 1863 (Gealy 557/457). In our hymnal stanza 3:2, "her" has been changed to "the."

Lancashire

See "Go, make of all disciples," page 359.

The day thou gavest, Lord, is ended (690)

John Ellerton, 1870 (Ps. 113:2-3)
This hymn on missionary outreach was written for *A Liturgy for Missionary Meetings*, 1870. It was slightly revised and included under the heading "'Their office was to stand every morning to thank and praise the Lord, and likewise at even.' 1 Chron. 23:30," at 32 in *Church Hymns and Tunes*, 1874. (Gealy 557/458) The text appeared in *Hymns Ancient and Modern*, 1875 Supplement, under the heading "From the rising of the sun to its setting the name of the Lord is to be praised, Psalm 113:3."

The hymn is a carefully wrought prayer of thanksgiving and intercession that likens the constancy and universality of the church's witness through prayer and song to her Lord, the Light of the world, to the sun's daily rising in our land and every land. It is also an expression of late-nineteenth-century British Victorian military and cultural imperialism that could not have been written in any other time and sung in any other church. Concerning this aspect of the hymn Erik Routley has commented:

It was written as a missionary hymn, and it celebrates that bright and heroic story of missionary expansion [during] the . . . nineteenth century . . . expansion of the British Empire. "An empire on which the sun never sets" is precisely the thought that is here adapted to Christian use. The whole setting is geographical; each verse invites the singer to contemplate the territorial extent of Christendom. That is almost certainly what has made the hymn so attractive in the remotest hamlets of the country—that and its boldly attractive tune. . . . To be reminded of the vastness of the distances and achievements within the Christian fold is as good for the ordinary urban or rural Christian. . . . But the danger, of course, is that contemplation of the Christian empire may encourage a cosy detachment.

It [also] appears that the great popularity of [the hymn] dates from the year 1897, in which Queen Victoria chose it for the Diamond Jubilee . . . a prodigious festival of thanksgiving for all that Victorian England had meant. (Routley 1956, 258-59)

The hymn entered our hymnals in the heyday of foreign missionary activity in 1905 using the 1875 version, omitting stanza 4:

> The sun, that bids us rest, is waking
> Our brethren 'neath the western sky,
> And hour by hour fresh lips are making
> Thy wondrous doings heard on high.

St. Clement

Clement Cotterill Scholefield, 1874

This tune was composed for these words and first appeared in the music edition of *Church Hymns with Tunes*, 1874, where it was named after the composer by the collection's music editor Arthur Sullivan.

For ease of unison singing the pitch has been dropped one step to F major. Performing the hymn in the original key of A^b major, number 54 in *The Methodist Hymnal*, 1935, will brighten the singing, secure the inner harmonies, and make it more consistent with the hymn's central themes of light, continuity, and promise. There is an alternative harmonization in G major with a descant at 648 in *Hymns and Psalms*, 1983, and an alternative harmonization at 297 in *The United Methodist Hymnal Music Supplement*.

The 1966 hymnal match of this text to the psalter tune "Commandments," combined with a decrease in evening worship services and the reconstruction of United Methodist and other world missions along less imperialistic modes, has almost caused the loss of this classic Victorian missionary text.

The earth is the Lord's (212)

See "Psalm 24 (King James Version)," page 563.

The first Noel (245)

Trad. English carol (Luke 2:8-14; Matt. 2:1-12)

This carol is apparently from the latter part of the seventeenth century and first appeared at 28-29 in nine stanzas in Davies Gilbert, *Some Ancient Christmas Carols*, 1823 2d ed. (Gealy 557/459) It was altered and included in William Sandys, *Christmas Carols, Ancient and Modern*, 1833. The Sandys text is included at 55 in *The Oxford Book of Carols*, 1964. The carol is more appropriate as an Epiphany processional than as a nativity hymn. Without regard to the carol's probable folk origins some hymnals have adjusted the second stanza to show it is the Wise Men in Matthew 2:2c, not the shepherds in Luke 2:8-20, who see and follow the star to the manger.

The carol entered our hymnals in the 1935 *Methodist Hymnal* with stanzas 1, 2, 3, 4, and 6 of the Sandys text. Robert G. McCutchan, probably following the practice of H. Augustine Smith in *The New Hymnal for American Youth*, 1930, altered the Old English "Nowell" to its Old French form "Nouel" ("Noël"), printed "Noel." (McCutchan 1942, 133)

The first Noel

Trad. English carol
harm. from Christmas Carols New and Old, 1871

The melody, apparently from England's West Country, first appeared in William Sandys, *Christmas Carols, Ancient and Modern*, 1833. The compiler also included it with one stanza at 318, the full text at 202-03, in his *Christmastide, Its History, Festivals, and Carols*. Fred D. Gealy includes these pages in his research with the notation "no date, before 1884." (Gealy 557/449)

Our harmonization is included at pages 6-7 in John Stainer's and H. R. Bramley's *Christmas Carols New and Old*, 1871, and is the standard setting for most USA hymnals. The stanzas are marked to be sung "*mf*" and the refrain "*fff*." Percy Dearmer in the preface to *The Oxford Book of Carols*, commenting on the late nineteenth-century renewal of interest in the carol, states that it is "mainly to Bramley and Stainer that we owe the restoration of the carol; and if they obscured as well as restored, the age must be blamed rather than the editors." (*The Oxford Book of Carols* 1964, xiii) Erik Routley provides extended coverage of the tune's origins and variants at 96-99 in *The English Carol*, 1958.

The mesmerizing effect of singing five stanzas and the refrain to three almost identical phrases can be relieved by alternating the stanzas between groups, some without accompaniment, with all singing the refrain. This carol, as other dance tunes, should be accompanied without stopping. To this end interludes may be added or improvised between the ending of the refrain and the beginning of each stanza. A descant, alternate harmonization, and keyboard interlude are at 328-30 in *The United Methodist Hymnal Music Supplement*. Additional settings are included in *The Oxford Book of Carols*, 1964, *Hymns and Psalms*, 1983, and *The Hymnal 1982*.

The first one ever (276)

Words and music: Linda Wilberger Egan, 1980, alt.
(Luke 1:26-38, 45; John 4:7-26; Luke 24:1-11)

This folk-style hymn retells the Gospel's accounts of several of the women who were the first to know or experience significant events in the life and ministry of Jesus. Stanza 1 is about Jesus' mother, Mary; 2, the Samaritan woman at the well; and 3, Mary, Joanna, and Magdalene, the first ones to experience and spread the news of his resurrection.

The author has related the hymn's origin:

> The ballad was written after the first year of a three year study of the Gospels with Mary Morrison. . . . That year I was reading to discover Jesus's relationships with the women he encountered, and their function in his ministry. That year was also the first year of the Rev. Elaine Kebba's ministry at Trinity Episcopal Church, Swarthmore, Penn. Because of their contact with her, many women here had begun to expand their views of their own ministries. This song is a simple explication of three of the texts I had been thinking about. . . . It is an effort to remind people of what they already know about three famous events in Jesus's life. . . . Later in that year I became a musician for the Well Woman Project [of] the Diocese of Pa. Venture in Mission. Among its purposes is a search for liturgical expression consistent with the spiritual experience of women as well as men. . . .We take the woman at the well [stanza 2] as a symbol because she listened to Jesus, she perceived that he was a prophet, she talked theology with him, and she preached about him so convincingly to the people of her city that they all came to see him. (Correspondence between the author and John E. Williams, Jr., the Church Hymnal Corporation, February 1982)

The hymn was altered from a 1980 version for inclusion in *The Hymnal 1982*.

Ballad

The hymn was printed in *The Hymnal 1982* with tune-line and chord symbols. In 1983 the author completed the realization that is included in our hymnal. She has indicated that it is "to be sung slowly and emphatically (the dotted half note

= 46) with a single guitar strum to each measure." (Correspondence with Carlton R. Young, June 1992) The hymn may be effectively sung by solo or soli voices and interpreted in dance. For comment on accompanying "dance tunes," see "The first Noel," page 633.

The friendly beasts (227)

12th cent. French carol; trans. anon. (Luke 2:7)

This nativity carol was set to the tune ORIENTIS PARTIBUS and was included in Clarence Dickinson's cantata *The Coming of the Prince of Peace*, published in the USA in 1920 by H. W. Gray. It has become a favorite carol for children. The text later appeared at 588 in the "Section for Younger Children" in the British Methodist *School Hymn-Book of the Methodist Church*, 1950. The *Companion* to that hymnal states on page 426, "Robert Davis wrote this hymn. More particulars concerning it and him are desired." (Kelynack 1950, 426)

The carol may be performed by individual singers dressed in appropriate costumes to portray the three animals and the dove. The congregation may join in stanzas 1 and 8. Let the singers enter and circle-dance as a recorder plays the tune several times. The recorder may also play an interlude between the stanzas as the individual singer portrays the particular animal or the dove and as the singers circle-dance. The singers may exit while the tune is repeated. Add hand-drum, sticks, and rattles. For additional comment on accompanying "dance tunes," see "The first Noel," page 633.

Orientis partibus

Medieval French melody; harm. by Carlton R. Young, 1987

Archibald Jacob has provided this information about the tune:

> [It] is derived from a medieval French melody. In some parts of France, notably at Beauvais, during the Middle Ages, there was celebrated on 14 Jan. a church festival known as the Feast of the Ass, commemorating the flight into Egypt. A young woman holding a child in her arms and seated upon an ass was led in procession through the streets of the town and, finally, into the principal church, where mass was celebrated while the ass with its burden stood beside the high altar. During the service a hymn (*conductus*) written in a mixture of medieval Latin and old French was sung, of which the first lines were 'Orientis partibus adventavit asinus' ["from the Eastern regions the ass is now come"], to which a form of the present melody was sung. (Dearmer and Jacob 1933, 100-01)

It is not known when this tradition began to incorporate the nativity sequence of the donkey's carrying Mary to Bethlehem, or when the other animals and the dove were included. Another version of this tune is found at "There's a spirit in the air," page 649.

The gift of love (408)

Hal Hopson, 1972 (1 Cor. 13:1-3)

The author's compelling, brief paraphrase of Paul's "treatise on love" (1 Corinthians 13:1-3) first appeared in his widely sung anthem "The Gift of Love," 1972.

Gift of love

Trad. English melody; adapt. by Hal Hopson, 1972

This lovely folk melody was collected by Cecil Sharp and named "O Waly, Waly" for his *Folk Songs from Somerset*, 1906 series 3. It has been used in recent British and Australian hymnals in its original triple-meter form as a setting for 98.98 and LM hymns. Hal Hopson's adaptation of the melody for his quadruple-meter anthem "The Gift of Love," 1972, is unique and very singable with the composer's interesting, flowing accompaniment.

As the result of many requests for its use as a hymn, particularly for weddings, the anthem was reduced to strophic form by the composer and distributed as a songsheet. It was included in *Hymnal Supplement II*, (1984). Unfortunately, the tune tends to flounder without the support of the anthem's accompaniment, recommended as an alternative to the setting in our hymnal. The optional descant for flute and/or voice from the anthem for stanza 3 is included at number 145 in *The United Methodist Hymnal Music Supplement*. The second stanza may be sung in canon at the octave. There is a four-part choral setting of this form of the tune by Alice Parker at 623 in *Hymnal: A Worship Book*, 1992, for the Brian Wren text "When love is found" **(643)**.

The publisher, stating that the tune and text are one, would not accede to the Hymnal Revision Committee's request for permission to set the text to a triple-meter LM form of the melody. In an assertion of free will over predestination *The Presbyterian Hymnal*, 1990, included the text with a triple-meter form of the tune.

The God of Abraham praise (116)
Yigdal Elohim Hai

From the Yigdal of Daniel ben Judah, ca. 1400
para. by Thomas Olivers, 1760; alt.

The thirteen articles of the Jewish creed were codified in the twelfth century by the Jewish scholar Moses Maimonides and formed into the *Yigdal* or doxology in the fourteenth century by Daniel ben Judah, a judge in Rome. Tradition indicates that our English metrical paraphrase was made ca. 1770 by the Welsh Wesleyan preacher Thomas Olivers after he heard the *Yigdal* chanted by the cantor and congregation of London's Great Synagogue. John Julian in his *Dictionary of Hymnody* includes the Hebrew text, an English paraphrase of each article, Olivers's twelve stanzas, and the tune LEONI in responsorial style for leader and congregation. In this latter form it has been traditionally sung in synagogues on the Sabbath eve and other services. Olivers's stanzas 9, 11, and 12 are explicitly Christian, fulfilling the the poet's purpose to give the paraphrase "a Christian character." (Julian 1907, 1149)

Our hymn, with several minor changes to avoid sexist language, is made up of stanzas 1, 4, 6, and 10 in the version found at 127 under the heading "The God of Abraham" in Augustus Toplady's *Psalms and Hymns for Public and Private Worship*, 1776. (Gealy 557/401) Fred Gealy's research includes pages from nine additional hymnals with variants of the text including the translation made ca. 1885 by Unitarian minister Newton Mann and Jewish rabbi Max Landsberg that appeared in *The Union Hymnal for Jewish Worship*, 1914, and was the text for our 1966 hymnal.

The hymn in various selections of stanzas has been included in our hymnals since the *Pocket Hymn Book*, 1786, where it was probably taken from either Spence's *Pocket Hymn Book*, ca. 1785, or John Wesley's *Pocket Hymn Book*, 1785.

Leoni

Hebrew melody, Sacred Harmony, 1780
harm. from Hermon, 1873, alt.

The tune was named by Olivers after Meyer Lyon, known as Leoni, the chief musician of London's Great Synagogue. Tradition has it that ca. 1770 Lyon transcribed it for the author after the latter had heard it sung in a Sabbath eve service. John Wesley included the melody with the text in *Sacred Harmony*, 1780, "and [it] has ever since been associated with Olivers's hymn." (Watson and Trickett 1988, 67)

Because the hymn has appeared in all our hymnals, it is presumed that USA Methodists may have sung Olivers's text to LEONI. Yet it was not included in our hymnals with the text until 1878, when it replaced the bright and forceful A-major tune "God of Abraham." Our harmonization is slightly altered from the one in R. G. McIntosh's *Hermon*, 1873, where it was based on a version in common use in the USA and was first included in our 1905 hymnal.

The melody is common to Jewish, Spanish-Basque, and Russian folk traditions. Bedrich Smetana used the melody in his orchestral masterpiece *Vltava* (*The Moldau*), 1874. There is an alternate harmonization at 211 in *The United Methodist Hymnal Music Supplement*. Another harmonization is found in *Hymns and Psalms*, 1983.

The head that once was crowned with thorns (326)

Thomas Kelly, 1820 (Heb. 2:9-10)
The text was first published in six stanzas at page 251 under the heading "Perfect through sufferings, Hebrews 2:10" in the poet's *Hymns on Various Passages of Scripture*, 1820 5th ed. (Gealy 557/460) This collection was first published in 1804 and periodically revised so that by 1853 it contained 765 texts. This hymn is one of the author's two hymns from that collection that are still in common use. At its final meeting, October 1987, the Hymnal Revision Committee voted not to include the other, Kelly's companion ascension hymn "Look, ye saints! the sight is glorious," because of anticipated space limitations and the perceived similarity of the two texts.

The hymn's opening stanza may have been prompted by John Bunyan's poem published ca. 1664, "One Thing is Needful, or Serious Meditations upon the Four last Things, Death, Judgement, Heaven and Hell":

> The head that once was crowned with thorns
>   Shall now with glory shine;
> That heart that broken was with scorns
>   Shall flow with life divine.

The hymn has been cited for its forceful yet carefully chosen and placed metaphors and descriptions of Christ's enthronement and reign contrasted with his rejection, passion, and death.

In *The Gospel in Hymns*, Albert E. Bailey comments on the Irish poet's evangelical fervor demonstrated in this hymn:

> [His ideas] are collected from passages such as 2 Timothy 2:12; Ephesians 3:18-19; and Revelation 3:12. Such an intertwining of Biblical ideas is characteristic of an eighteenth-century rather than of the nineteenth-century preacher's mind. (Bailey 1950, 153)

Erik Routley in his concluding words in *Hymns and Human Life* states:

> [The hymn is] perhaps the finest of all hymns; Thomas Kelly has here comprehended the whole Gospel, and he tells of the Good News and of the mysterious mercy by which we may lay hold on it. (Routley 1959, 315)

The hymn entered our hymnals in 1849 in five stanzas. The complete hymn, with the accumulated slight alterations, was included in our 1966 hymnal.

St. Magnus

Attr. to Jeremiah Clark, 1707; harm. by W. H. Monk, 1868
This tune, known also as "Nottingham," "Birmingham," and "Greenock," first appeared anonymously in Henry Playford, *The Divine Companion, or David's*

Harp New Tun'd, 2d. ed. 1707. Its attribution to Clark comes from the statement on preceding pages: "The three following psalms sett by Mr. Jer. Clark." (Ellinwood 1956, 78) The tune was named in William Riley's *Parochial Harmony*, 1758, after the Church of St. Magnus the Martyr near London Bridge.

The tune and harmonization entered our hymnals in the 1935 *Methodist Hymnal* with an uncited harmonization from the 1933 Presbyterian *Hymnal*, there included without citation from *Hymns Ancient and Modern*, 1868 Appendix, where the text and tune were apparently first joined.

There is a vocal descant at 209 in *Hymns and Psalms*, 1983, and at 305 in *The United Methodist Hymnal Music Supplement*. A faux-bourdon version is included at 175 in *Songs of Praise*, 1931.

The King of love my shepherd is (138)

Henry W. Baker, 1868 (Ps. 23)

This metrical paraphrase of Psalm 23 first appeared at 330 in *Hymns Ancient and Modern*, 1868 Appendix. It entered our hymnals in 1901 and is included in our hymnal with the original text.

Baker's first line is a parody of George Herbert's "The God of love my shepherd is." The hymn's first three stanzas are a psalm paraphrase in the tradition of Isaac Watts. Beginning with stanza four the text is Christianized to include "cross," chalice," and "Good Shepherd," and, as Erik Routley suggests, the hymn effectively moves hospitality from the duty of the pastorale shepherd to the church's priests, ministers, members, and officers. (Routley 1956, 68)

Other scriptural and hymnic versions of Psalm 23 are found at **128, 136, 137, 518,** and **754**.

St. Columba

Irish melody; harm. from The English Hymnal, 1906

Leonard Ellinwood has traced this tune to the *Irish Church Hymnal*, 1873 (1877 ed.) where it was marked "Hymn of the Ancient Irish Church." It was included by Charles Villiers Stanford in his *Complete Collection of Irish Music as noted by George Petrie*, 1902. (Ellinwood 1956, 224-25) According to *Companion to Psalms and Hymns*, 1988, Stanford harmonized it for *Hymns Ancient and Modern*, 1904, and prepared another harmonization with the distinctive melodic triplets for *The English Hymnal*, 1906. (Watson and Trickett 1988, 284)

The tune is named for the sixth-century Celtic saint who according to tradition brought the gospel to Scotland. It is sometimes called ST. COLUMBA (Erin or Irish) to distinguish it from H. S. Irons's tune with the same name.

Alternate stanzas may be sung by the choir with or without accompaniment, and solo or soli voices may sing the melody with the harmonization. There are alternative harmonizations at 298-99 in *The United Methodist Hymnal Music Supplement*. A setting in CM by H. Walford Davies is included at 349 in *Rejoice in the Lord*, 1985.

The kingdom of God (275)

Gracia Grindal, 1985 (Matt 13:31-32; Mark 4:30-32)
This paraphrase of Jesus' parable of the kingdom was first published in *Singing the Story II*, 1985. In stanza 3 the metaphor of the tree as a home for birds is cleverly expanded in imagery to which children can relate, a haven from the predator. Another unrhymed paraphrase of scripture by this author is "To a maid engaged to Joseph" **(215)**.

Mustard seed

Austin C. Lovelace, 1985
This charming setting is ideal for children to learn the parable and share it with others. It first appeared in *Hymnal Supplement II*, (1987). Stanzas may be sung by individual or soli voices, with everyone joining on the refrain and on stanza 4. The parable may be read before stanza 1.

The left-hand notes on the downbeat of the third measure from the end are F and A. There were incorrectly printed as D and F in early editions of the hymnal.

The Lord is my shepherd (137)

See "Psalm 23 (King James Version)," page 562.

The Lord's my shepherd, I'll not want (136)

Scottish Psalter, 1650 (Ps. 23)
Millar Patrick in *Four Centuries of Scottish Psalmody*, 1949, has traced the sources of this famous metrical psalm to lines and phrases from seven psalters beginning with the "Old Version" of 1564. The imagery of the paraphrase may be compared with the King James Version printed on the facing page, "Psalm 23 (King James Version)." Other scriptural and hymnic versions of Psalm 23 are included in the hymnal at **128, 518,** and **754.**

For commentary on the early development of English language metrical psalms see "Genevan/Anglo Metrical Psalmody," page 9; and Robin A. Leaver, "English Metrical Psalmody," vol. 1, 321-33 in *The Hymnal 1982 Companion*,1990.

Crimond

Since the psalm entered our hymnals in 1878, credited in error to Francis Rous, several CM tunes have been set to the words, but none as compelling as its present setting to CRIMOND. In the 1930's and 1940's the psalm apparently became associated with CRIMOND through the concerts and broadcasts of the Glasgow Orpheus Choir, Hugh T. Roberton, director. For further commentary on this tune, see "The care the eagle gives her young," pages 626-27.

The Lord's prayer (270, 271)

Matt. 6:9-11; Luke 11:2-4

The gospel writers provide two forms of our Lord's prayer for the kingdom. A concluding doxology from 1 Chronicles 29:11 was added to the prayer by the early church and came into English use with the *Scottish Book of Common Prayer*, 1637, and the 1662 *Book of Common Prayer*. (Gealy, Lovelace, Young 1970, 461)

Geoffrey Wainwright has commented that the prayer is the pattern for Christian prayer:

> It begins with 'Abba,' and it brings out, in the fourth, fifth and sixth petitions, the fact that God is the provider, preserver and redeemer of his children. The opening clauses reveal that the glory of God involves the achievement of his will, the coming of his kingdom. For humanity, this means salvation; for that is precisely God's intention for mankind. On the human side, the active aspect of salvation is obedience to God; this 'service' is 'perfect freedom,' for humanity is thus achieving its vocation and fulfilling its nature. (Wainwright 1980, 22)

The prayer is included in all the rituals in our hymnal, except for "Baptismal Covenant." Three versions of the text are provided for speaking: the "Ecumenical Text," ELLC, 1975 (**894**); "From the Ritual of the Former Methodist Church" (**895**) with Tyndale's "trespasses" and doxology from the 1662 *Book of Common Prayer* that John Wesley included as a postcommunion congregational prayer in his *Sunday Service*, 1784, and without doxology said at the opening by the minister; and "From the Ritual of the Former Evangelical United Brethren Church" (**896**), where it was included in the Lord's Supper after the invocation, with "debts" from the Great Bible, 1539.

Two sung versions are included:

Gregorian (270)

Lowell Mason, 1824

This setting appeared in the 1935 *Methodist Hymnal* where it was cited "Gregorian." It was apparently arranged from Lowell Mason's tune HAMBURG; see "When I survey the wondrous cross," page 692. It bears some similarity to a single chant at page 445 in our 1878 hymnal.

This sung version of the Lord's Prayer and the OLD SCOTTISH CHANT setting for the "Canticle of God's glory" (Gloria in Excelsis) **(82)** from the 1935 *Methodist Hymnal* were used by congregations with a tradition of the sung communion service. This setting of the prayer is sung every Sunday in a number of churches, including those that are predominantly African American in membership. Apparently reflecting its use by African Americans in the nineteenth century, F. L. Loudin included a variation of Mason's setting at page 256 in "Jubilee Songs," in the *Supplement* to *The Story of the Jubilee Singers*, 1896.

West Indian (271)

West Indian folk tune; arr. by Carlton R. Young, 1988

Duke Ellington included this setting of the Lord's Prayer in his "Sacred Concert, II" and performed it in call-and-response style with the congregation joining on "halloweda be thy name."

The arrangement in our hymnal is from the version by J. Jefferson Cleveland and Verolga Nix in *Songs of Zion*, 1981. Add a calypso beat and rhythm instruments. A setting for leader without accompaniment and four-part harmony for the congregation is found at 632 in *AMEC Bicentennial Hymnal*, 1984.

The old rugged cross (504)

Words and music: George Bennard, 1913 (1 Cor. 1:22-25)

The author began writing this hymn in the fall of 1912 and probably completed it the following January while conducting a revival at a Friends' church in Sturgeon Bay, Wisconsin. "Charles H. Gabriel, well-known gospel-song composer, helped Bennard complete the manuscript of the music and 'fix up the harmonies.'" (Reynolds 1990, 219) Its introduction by Homer Rodeheaver was apparently responsible for its immediate success. The hymn was first included in *Heart and Life Songs, for the Church, Sunday School, Home and Campmeeting*, 1915. (Reynolds 1976, 174) For almost half a century it was widely sung in Methodist and Evangelical United Brethren churches, but it was not included in their hymnals until 1957.

The reluctance of our hymnal editors prior to 1957 to include the hymn stemmed from not only its prohibitive permission fee, but primarily its central message on which Erik Routley has commented:

> [It is] a monstrous blasphemy, but I can give my reason, which is theological. I believe it to be wrong, misleading, and spiritually wicked to treat the Cross as affectionately as that lyric does. I believe there is all the difference in the world between that lyric and the old Latin hymn "Faithful cross, above all other, one and only noble tree" [paraphrased from "Sing, my tongue, the glorious battle" **(296)**] and that the difference is fatal. But even

so, I do not regard myself as having come to the end of the evidence; I may yet learn that with all its unspeakable vulgarity it has said something authentic to somebody. (Routley 1967, 96)

Routley's conclusion is the reason that this hymn and others like it are included in this hymnal. For additional commentary on hymns on the cross, see "Beneath the cross of Jesus," pages 235-36; "O Love divine, what hast thou done," pages 520-21; and "Sing, my tongue, the glorious battle," page 596.

The old rugged cross

This writer's understanding of the compelling witness for the gospel in this hymn, despite its perceived theological and musical shortcomings, began to be formed in 1974 after hearing it requested and then performed in Preservation Hall, New Orleans.

The prayer of St. Frances (481)

Attr. to Francis of Assisi, Italy, 13th cent.

Laurence Hull Stookey comments that "this set of petitions, attributed to Francis of Assisi, is one of the most beloved prayers in the Christian tradition." (Sanchez 1989, 166) In 1949 the prayer was set by Olive Dungan as a vocal solo, "Eternal Life," and gained popularity as the theme song of several local and regional Roman Catholic radio programs. It was arranged as a hymn by Fred Bock and included in his *Hymns for the Family of God*, 1976. Sebastian Temple included a variant of the prayer in another musical setting in *Happy the Man*, 1967. The author of the English text has not been determined.

The serenity prayer (459)

Anonymous

This prayer for serenity, courage, and wisdom is drawn from traditional sources. It has been attributed to the theologian and teacher Reinhold Niebuhr since he made use of it in his writing, lectures, and teaching at Union Theological Seminary, New York City.

The sufficiency of God (495)

Juliana of Norwich, England, 15th cent.

This is a prayer for the all-sufficiency of God's presence in our lives. See also "Rejoice in God's saints," pages 564-65.

The souls of the righteous (652)

See "Canticle of remembrance," pages 262-63.

The strife is o'er, the battle done (306)
Alleluia! Alleluia! Finita jam sunt praelia

Anon. Latin, 1695; trans. by Francis Pott, 1861, alt.
Leonard Ellinwood has traced this anonymous Latin hymn to *Symphonia Sirenum Selectarum ex quatuor vocibus composita, Ad commodiorem usum Studiosae Juventutis*, 1695. (Ellinwood 1956, 69) John M. Neale included the Latin text with his translation in *Mediaeval Hymns and Sequences*, 1851. (Gealy 557/475) Francis Pott translated the hymn for inclusion in his *Hymns Fitted to the Order of Common Prayer*, 1861. Each stanza is composed of three statements proclaiming the victory of Christ's resurrection over the reign of sin and death, followed by an Alleluia. Pott's text was altered for inclusion in *Hymns Ancient and Modern*, 1861, and subsequent editions. (Gealy 557/475) The original text may be found in *The English Hymnal*, 1906.

Stanza 4, given here in its original form, is usually omitted:

> He brake the age-bound chains of hell:
> The bars from heaven's high portals fell
> Let songs of joy his triumph tell.
> > Alleluia!

The hymn entered our hymnals in 1921 with versions of stanzas from *Hymn Ancient and Modern*.

Victory

Giovanni P. da Palestrina, 1591; arr. by W. H. Monk, 1861
This setting is an arrangement by W. H. Monk of the first two lines, "Gloria Patri Et Filio," from the "Gloria Patri" of Palestrina's *Magnificat Tertii Toni*, 1591. Alleluias were added at the beginning and end. Palestrina's SATB choral score is included in *Hymnal Companion to the Lutheran Book of Worship* (1981, 233).

The matching of these lines with this tune demonstrates the skill of the editors of *Hymns Ancient and Modern*, 1861, in providing singable hymns for parish congregations, supported by choir and organ. The hymn may be sung antiphonally between choir and congregation. The melody of the Alleluias and the final stanza may be played on a trumpet, or the harmonies may be doubled by a brass quartet.

The voice of God is calling (436)

John Haynes Holmes, 1913; alt. 1987 (Isa. 6:8)
This social gospel hymn was written on board ship in September 1913 as the author was returning from travel in England, Scotland, and Wales. It is based on

Isaiah's response to God's calling, Isaiah 6:8, and was first sung at the 1913 convention of the Young People's Religious Union (Haeussler 1954, 405). It was first included in *New Hymn and Tune Book*, 1914, and entered our hymnals in the 1935 *Methodist Hymnal*.

The hymn is an explicit call to minister to those living in the squalor of urban slums, to abolish child labor, and to establish a decent wage and a safer workplace. See "Social Gospel Hymns," pages 30-33, for commentary on early twentieth-century hymns of social protest.

Changes were made for our hymnal in stanza 1:2, "unto men" to "in our day"; 1:3, "as once he spake" to "Isaiah heard"; 1:4, "he speaks again" to "we hear today"; 2:2, "cot and mine and slum" to "slum and mine and mill"; 2:4, "dumb" to "still"; 3:1, "thy" to "your"; 3:3, "thine" to "your"; 3:4, "thy" to "your"; 3:7, "thou canst" to "you can"; and 3:8 and 4:6, "thy" to "your."

Meirionydd

William Lloyd, 1840

Alan Luff has traced this tune by William Lloyd, 1786-1852, to *Caniadau Seion* (*Songs of Sion, that is a Collection of Tunes suitable to be sung in the worship of God . . . for Welsh church music*), 1840. (Luff 1990, 174) Luff also includes Lloyd's version of the tune and his harmonization. Our harmonization is apparently from *The English Hymnal*, 1906, and it entered our hymnals with the text in *The Methodist Hymnal*, 1935.

Stanzas may be sung without accompaniment. The dotted quarter and eighth upbeats must not be rushed, but given full value so as to preserve the tune's strength and unique character. The tune is named after the composer's home south of Carnarvon in northwest Wales.

Then Moses and the people (135)

See "Canticle of Moses and Miriam," page 258.

There is a balm in Gilead (375)

African American spiritual
adapt. and arr. by William Farley Smith, 1986

There are two references to "balm in Gilead" in Jeremiah:

> Is there no balm in Gilead?
> Is there no physician there?
> Why then has the health of my poor people
> not been restored? (8:22)

> Go up to Gilead, and take balm,
>   O virgin daughter Egypt!
> In vain you have used many medicines;
>   there is no healing for you. (46:11)

William Farley Smith has commented:

> Slave-poets, with the assurance of knowing, acquired from Christian learn-
> ing and experience, responded to Jeremiah's despairing [and negative]
> queries with profound conviction. Indeed, "Doctor" Jesus is alive and well
> and does heal the sin-sick soul. (Sanchez 1989, 133)

James H. Cone believes that this spiritual exemplifies African Americans' hope
in the midst of oppression:

> Hope, in the black spirituals, is not a denial of history. Black hope accepts
> history, but believes that the historical is in motion, moving toward a
> divine fulfillment. It is the belief that things can be radically otherwise than
> they are: that reality is not fixed, but is moving in the direction of human
> liberation. (Cone 1972, 95-96)

Our version, as in most collections, is adapted from *Folk Songs of the American
Negro*, 1907, compiled and edited by Frederick J. Work and John W. Work, Jr. The
text with another tune entered our hymnals at 856 in *The Methodist Hymnal*, 1889.

Balm in Gilead

There is an alternate setting in call-and-response style at 123 in *Songs of Zion*,
1981. It was prepared for its 1982 edition at the request of William Dawson who
demonstrated that the version included in the first edition was derived from his
standard choral setting.

There is a fountain filled with blood (622)

William Cowper, ca. 1771 (Zech. 13:1)
On that day a fountain shall be opened for the house of David and the
inhabitants of Jerusalem, to cleanse them from sin and impurity.
(Zechariah 13:1)

This meditation on the saving power of the blood of Jesus Christ was probably
written in 1771 and was first included in R. Conyers, *Collection of Psalms and
Hymns from Various Authors*, 1772 (the page from the 1774 New Edition is in
Gealy 557/478). "Blood" is the metaphor for life, and the shed blood of Jesus is
the symbol of sacrifice whereby God's only son was crucified for the sins of

humankind. The poet links Zechariah's prophecy to God's universal redemptive act in Christ's suffering and death (no mention of his resurrection). Particularly compelling is the poet's comparison of his sinful plight with the thief on the cross. The final stanza is reminiscent of stanza 4:1 in "What wondrous love is this" (**292**) "And when from death I'm free, I'll sing on." The several attempts to alter the first stanza to soften its "offensive" imagery "have proved disastrous failures." (Moffatt 1951, 235) The hymn entered our hymnals in 1849.

Cleansing Fountain

19th cent. USA camp-meeting melody

This rousing nineteenth-century camp-meeting tune has been in our hymnals since 1878, where only the melody was included as an alternate tune to Lowell Mason's similar tune "Cowper." In our 1905 hymnal the tune was harmonized with credit to Mason, a citation that William J. Reynolds has commented "is, in all probability, erroneous." (Reynolds 1976, 219) The tune's refrain extends each stanza of the solid CM text into CMD, not without some amusing results.

Dena J. Epstein cites William Francis Allen's *Journal* for December 13, 1863, that describes African Americans singing this hymn at a praise meeting on St. Helena Island where it was "deaconing out" to William Tansur's "St. Martin's." (Epstein 1981, 351) She also includes the witness of the war correspondent Charles Carleton Coffin who in 1863 in an African Baptist church in Port Royal, South Carolina, heard "St. Martin's" performed by African Americans "not reading the music exactly as good old Tansur composed it, for there were crooks, turns, slurs, and appoggiaturas, not to be found in any printed copy. It was sung harshly, nasally, and dragged out in long, slow notes." (Epstein 1981, 302)

There is a name I love to hear (170)

See "O how I love Jesus," pages 516-17.

There is a place of quiet rest (472)

See "Near to the heart of God," page 492.

There's a song in the air (249)

Josiah G. Holland, 1874

This Christmas hymn was included in W. T. Giffe's Sunday school collection *The Brilliant*, 1874. (Reynolds 1976, 222) It was first included in a hymnal at 112 in

The Methodist Hymnal, 1905, with three musical settings. The text has never been altered. Our hymnal appears to be the last to include this simple, expressive Christmas hymn. Stanza 3 reflects the optimism of early social gospel hymns that heralded the emerging twentieth century as the Christian century and the fulfillment of Jesus' great commission, Matthew 28:19-20.

Christmas song

Karl P. Harrington, 1904

The tune was composed in July 1904 while the composer was vacationing in North Woodstock, New Hampshire. It first appeared in the 1905 *Methodist Hymnal* as one of three settings for Holland's hymn. Karl P. Harrington, with Peter Lutkin, served as music editors for that hymnal.

The composer's suggested tempos included in the 1905 hymnal were the first two lines *Andante con moto*, closing with a *ritard*; the next two lines *piu mosso*, closing each stanza with a three-measure ritard. R. G. McCutchan remarks that during the life of the 1905 hymnal Harrington's tune "was the only one sung." (McCutchan 1942, 134)

There's a Spirit in the air (192)

Brian Wren, 1969

The poet has commented about this hymn:

[It] was written for Pentecost at Hockley, to try and celebrate the Holy Spirit "Working in Our World." The alternating repetition of two choruses is a device borrowed from Isaac Watts' "Give to Our God Immortal Praise." (Wren "Notes" in *Faith Looking Forward*, hymn 44)

This hymn extends the images of Pentecost—"Spirit in the air," "find your tongue," "change our ways," and "tell the world"—into a call for Christians to feed the hungry, house the homeless, and set right society's wrongs.

Even though the author's original text and British hymnals in stanza 1:1 lower case "s" in "spirit," most USA hymnals capitalize it as "Spirit." Other changes for our hymnal include stanza 2:4, "We can see his power today" to "Live tomorrow's life today"; 4:1, "Still his spirit" to "Still the Spirit"; 4:4, "We can see his power today" to "Live tomorrow's life today"; 6:1, "May his Spirit" to "May the Spirit." To reduce the hymn to six stanzas the original stanza 7 becomes a repeat of stanza 1, and "telling" is questionably substituted for "calling."

The hymn first appeared in *Praise for Today*, 1974. (Watson and Trickett 1988, 211)

Orientis partibus

Medieval French melody; harm. by Richard Redhead, 1853
This is a version of the traditional melody used for "The friendly beasts," pages 635-36. Richard Redhead's setting was published in *Church Hymn Tunes, Ancient and Modern*, 1853.

There's a sweet, sweet Spirit in this place (334)

See "Sweet, sweet, Spirit," page 612.

There's a wideness in God's mercy (121)

Frederick W. Faber, 1854
While nine of Faber's hymns were included in our 1878 hymnal, only this hymn and "Faith of our fathers" **(710)** are still included in recent USA hymnals. This hymn was first included in eight stanzas under the heading "Come to Jesus" in the author's *Oratory Hymns*, 1854, and expanded to thirteen stanzas in later collections. (Gealy, Lovelace, Young 1970, 405) The full text with the original first lines "Souls of men, why will ye scatter Like a crowd of frightened sheep?" was included in *Hymns Selected from F. W. Faber*, 1867, and may be found at 557/482 in the research files of Fred D. Gealy. The usually omitted stanzas 5 and 7 elaborate the hymn's theme of God's unmeasurable mercy and grace, and demonstrate Faber's affinity with eighteenth-century evangelical writers such as Charles Wesley:

> There is no place where earth's sorrows
> Are more felt than up in heaven;
> There is no place where earth's failings
> Have such kindly judgment given.
>
> There is grace enough for thousands
> Of new worlds as great as this;
> There is room for fresh creations
> In that upper home of bliss. (Gealy 557/482)

The hymn entered our hymnals in 1872 made up of quatrains 4, 6, 8, and 13. Since then it has been included with various alterations including these for our hymnal: stanza 1:3, "his" to "God's"; 3:2, "Man's" to "our"; 4:2, "take him at his" to "rest upon God's"; and 4:4, "all sunshine in the sweetness" to "illumined by the presence."

Wellesley

Lizzie S. Tourjée, 1877; harm. by Charles H. Webb, 1988
This tune was "composed by Lizzie S. Tourjée for her graduation from high school at Newton, Massachusetts." (Reynolds 1976, 224) It first appeared at 55 in

our 1878 hymnal with three 87. 87 texts, including our hymn. The tune was apparently included in that collection by her father who with J. P. Holbrook was one of its music editors.

The tune is named after Wellesley College where the composer was a student 1877-78. (McCutchan 1942, 108) The wideness of God's mercy is more fully expressed in the alternate tune IN BABILONE **(325)**.

There's something about that name (171)

Gloria Gaither and William J. Gaither, 1970
The authors have shared that this one-stanza hymn was inspired by "many experiences of joy and sorrow—the birth of their first child, the death of Bill's grandmother, and others. . . . [Experiences that confirmed it is] the name of Jesus that brings reason and meaning to all the confusing passages of our own lives. The sweetest and most amazing force to impact our days and infuse the mundane with glory is still the same." (Correspondence with Carlton R. Young, October 1992)

That name

William J. Gaither, 1970
The hymn was first included in *Hymns for the Family of God*, 1976, where the tune received its name.

There's within my heart a melody (380)

Words and music: Luther B. Bridgers, 1910
For many years it was believed the hymn had been written in the aftermath of a tragic fire in Kentucky in which the author's wife and children perished. Reynold's recent research establishes that there is no relationship.

In addition to sharing his research, William J. Reynolds has provided this additional information:

[The hymn] was first published in [*The Revival* No. 6] 1910 by Charlie D. Tillman, a well-known publisher in Georgia. When [Bridgers] had finished the words, [he] picked out the melody on the piano, and his wife's sister wrote down the notes he played to complete the song. (Correspondence with Carlton R. Young, January 1991)

Sweetest name

The tune's name was first included in the 1956 *Baptist Hymnal*.

They crucified my Lord (291)

See "He never said a mumbalin' word," pages 391-92.

They crucified my Savior (316)

See "He rose," pages 392-93.

Thine be the glory, risen, conquering Son (308)
A toi la gloire ô Ressuscité

Edmond L. Budry, 1904; trans. by R. Birch Hoyle, 1923

The origin of this joyous Easter hymn has been traced by Liya Steuffel Huie:

> The original hymn was written by Pastor Edmond Budry of the Free
> Church, Canton of Vaud, Switzerland. It first appeared in *Chants Evan-*
> *geliques*, 1885, that was published in Lausanne and intended for evangelis-
> tic use. Budry was often asked to make translations of favorite German or
> English hymns, but he preferred to re-write the texts, often improving on
> the original, and often freely adapting old Latin hymns. Paul Laufer, a
> friend of Budry, believed that the author drew his inspiration from the
> words of Friedrich-Heinrich Ranke (1798-1876), which were first published
> in 1908 to Handel's melody and are found in the *Evangelisches Gesangbuch*
> *fur Elsass-Lothringen*—"Daughter of Zion, rejoice." Budry freely adapted
> this Advent hymn for use as an Easter hymn, and thus emphasized still
> more the triumphal nature of Handel's music. (Correspondence with
> Sylvia Mills, January 1969, in Gealy 557/484).

The hymn was translated into English in 1923 by Richard Birch Hoyle and
appeared at 28 in *Cantate Domino*, 1925. The stanzas recount the Resurrection
images of angels rolling the stone away, the women at the tomb, and doubting
Thomas, with Handel's rousing refrain as a response. The hymn entered our
hymnals in 1957. Changes made for our hymnal include: stanza 1:1, "is" to "be";
2:5, "His" to "the"; and 2:7, "her" to "our."

Fred Pratt Green provided a new translation, "Yours be the glory," that the poet
indicates is more nearly Budry's original, for *Cantate Domino*, 1974.

Judas Maccabeus

Harmonia Sacra, ca. 1753; arr. from G. F. Handel, 1747

The tune is adapted from Othniel's victorious procession from G. F. Handel's
oratorio *Joshua*, 1747, used by the composer in later versions of *Judas Maccabeus*,
1746. It first appeared as a hymn tune in Thomas Butts's *Harmonia Sacra*, ca.
1753, "in which it was given in three parts and set to 'Christ the Lord is risen

today.'" (Watson and Trickett 1988, 149) The tune was one of John Wesley's favorites as he notes in his *Journal* for March 29, 1774, and March 30, 1787.

There is an arrangement for handbells, two trumpets, and organ at 190 in *The United Methodist Hymnal Music Supplement*. A slightly different realization and melody with a descant are found at 212 in *Hymns and Psalms*, 1983.

This is a day of new beginnings (383)

Brian Wren, 1978; alt. 1984 (Rev. 21:5)

[This hymn was] written for a New Year's Day service [1978] at Holy Family Church, Blackbird Leys, Oxford. In itself, the new year is an arbitrary convention, its "newness" a mere mark on the calendar. The recurrent awakening of life in nature is not a strong enough foundation for hope of real change. Yet by faith in the *really* new events of the Christian story, a day, or a month, or an hour can become charged with promise, and be a springboard to a changed life. For stanza 3, see 2 Corinthians 5, 16-17. (Wren Notes in *Faith Looking Forward*, hymn 34)

The editors of *Hymnal Supplement II*, (1984), expressing the problem of singing a question-and-response—the original began with a question, "Is this a day of new beginnings?"—requested that the poet unify the text on one theme.

To accommodate this request the poet omitted the original stanza 2,

> How can the seasons of a planet
>   mindlessly spinning round its sun
> with just a human name and number
>   say that some new thing has begun?

and composed a new stanza, our stanza 4. Our stanza 2 was altered, "Yet through" to "For by"; and stanza 5:1, "So let us" was changed to "In faith we'll."

The result is an elaboration on 2 Corinthians 5:17, "So if anyone is in Christ, there is a new creation: everything old has passed away; see, everything has become new!" God in Christ makes all things new. Everyday has the potential for new life, i.e., new beginnings, in Christ because each day God in Christ precedes us and joins us in proclaiming the victory of life over death: "Christ is alive, and goes before us to show and share what love can do." Stanza 5 is an alternate text for Holy Communion. The author has stated that "the revision is an improvement, a more economical and widely usable hymn." (Comment to Carlton R. Young, July 1992.)

The text first appeared in this form at 65 in *Hymnal Supplement*, 1984.

Beginnings

Carlton R. Young, 1984

The tune's parallel and altered harmonies are in the style of a 1930's warm Broadway ballad. It was written in 1983 for Wren's original text in which the first two stanzas are questions. To accommodate the questions as well as the answers, the composer ended all stanzas except the last on the dominant V. The tune should not be sung any faster than quarter note = 110. At the last ending the singers may choose to sing any note in the E^b chord, holding it indefinitely without accompaniment.

This is my Father's world (144)

Maltbie D. Babcock, 1901

In this hymn the singer joins with "rocks," "trees," "skies," "seas," "birds," "light," "lilies," and "rustling grass" in the praise of God who is creator, sustainer, and ruler.

The original poem was in sixteen CM stanzas and first appeared at 180 in the author's *Thoughts for Every-Day Living*, 1901. (Gealy 557/485) The text and tune were evidently first brought together as a three-stanza SMD hymn in a cento of stanzas 2-3, 4-5, 14, and 16 in Franklin L. Sheppard's hymnal *Alleluia*, 1915. It entered our 1935 hymnals in this form.

Terra beata

Trad. English melody; adapt. by Franklin L. Sheppard, 1915

An alternate harmonization to Franklin L. Sheppard's was made in 1926 by Edward Shippen Barnes and was included with this text in the Presbyterian *Hymnal*, 1933. His setting appeared with slight modification in the third line without his name in *The Hymnbook*, 1955, and it is included essentially in that form in *The Presbyterian Hymnal*, 1990. For additional commentary on this tune, see "How can we name a love," pages 405-07.

This is my song (437)

Sts. 1, 2, Lloyd Stone, 1934; st. 3, Georgia Harkness, ca. 1939

Stanzas 1 and 2 were first included in *Sing a Tune*, 1934. They were written between the great world wars during the brief period of international peace and are an expression of love of country and aspirations for peace that can be shared and expressed by all of the human family.

Georgia Harkness has commented on the writing of the third stanza:

> I wrote [it] expressly for the Wesleyan Service Guild [of the Methodist Church] at the request of Miss Marion Norris, then the Executive Secretary.

She wrote me that they had been using the first two verses but wanted something with a more distinctly religious note as a supplement to them. I cannot tell you exactly how long ago this was, but since I can recall writing the stanza at my desk when I was teaching at Mount Holyoke 1937-39, it was within this period.

I think it never occurred to Miss Norris or the Wesleyan Service Guild that they needed to get permission to use the copyrighted Stone material [in their publications]. This came up when the [1966] hymnal was being compiled, and after some uncertainty as to how to handle it the Lorenz Company paid me something—$20 or $25, I forget which, for the verse, and Mr. Young [the hymnal editor] paid Mr. Lorenz $200 for permission to use the three stanzas. I should gladly have contributed my small effort, but not to enrich his [the publisher's] coffers. I thought his fee exorbitant, but this, of course, was not my business. (Correspondence with Fred D. Gealy, November 1967, Gealy 557/486)

The hymn was adopted as the official hymn of the Wesleyan Service Guild and was widely sung throughout the former Methodist Church. It is appropriate for occasions that celebrate our commonality as equally created by God, the planet earth as our shared home and resources, and our unity in Christ. The hymn entered our hymnals in 1966. In stanza 3:3 "men" has been changed to "shall."

Finlandia

See "Be still, my soul," page 227-28.

This is our prayer (487)

These traditional words may be said or sung by the congregation after each petition or at the conclusion of prayer, thus allowing individual prayers to be prayed by all.

Our prayer

Sally Ahner, 1983

This response first appeared in the Service Music Project, 1983, sponsored and distributed by the Section on Worship of the General Board of Discipleship of The United Methodist Church.

This is the day (657)

Psalm 118:24; adapt. by Les Garrett, 1967

This call-and-response gathering scripture song was first included in *Scripture in Song*, 1967. In *Companion to Hymns and Psalms* it is cited as "From *Sound of Living*

Waters, 1974." (Watson and Trickett 1988, 339) *Hymns and Psalms*, 1983, includes two additional stanzas for Easter and Pentecost: "This is the day when he rose again" and "This is the day when the Spirit came."

This is the day

Les Garrett, 1967

Scotty W. Gray in *Handbook to the Baptist Hymnal* recounts Garrett's account of the origin of this song:

> [It] was given to us in Brisbane, Australia, in 1967 at the time we were having a very hard time really going through a valley. Then one morning, the Lord gave this song to us from Psalm 118:24. (Adams 1992, 256)

In *Hymns and Psalms*, 1983, the tune is described as a "Fiji Folk Melody," arranged by Ivor H. Jones who, according to the hymnal's *Companion*, "was particularly concerned to produce a standard version from the various settings which have appeared in hymn books of all kinds." (Watson and Trickett 1988, 339) Singing measures 2 and 3 of the third line as they appear in our hymnal may pose a problem since the song's middle phrases in most hymnals are identical.

Bass, melody, and percussion instruments may join with the keyboard. Some musicians will resist raising the key on each repeat of the song.

This is the day the Lord hath made (658)

Isaac Watts, 1719 (Ps. 118:24)

This call to worship and praise make up the first stanza of Watts's paraphrase of Psalm 118:24-26, titled "Hosanna, the Lord's Day; or, Christ's Resurrection and our Salvation," in *The Psalms of David*, 1719. The poet's notes on the hymn page for this stanza are included in *Companion to Hymns and Psalms*:

> This is the day wherein Christ fulfilled his sufferings, and rose from the dead, and has honoured it with his own name. Rev. i 10 *The Lord's Day*. (Watson and Trickett 1988, 339)

Twenty-Fourth

Attr. to Lucius Chapin, ca. 1813

This tune, probably adapted from a folk melody, first appeared on page 20 in John Wyeth's *Repository of Sacred Music, Part Second*, 1813. Irving Lowens on pages xii-xiii of his introduction to the 1964 reprint describes the problems that scholars have had in attempting to establish the composer of the six tunes cited as "Chapin" in this collection's index.

Austin C. Lovelace's stirring four-part vocal harmonization written for our 1966 hymnal has been harmed on its way to inclusion in our hymnal.

This is the feast of victory (638)

Revelation 5:12-13; trans. by John W. Arthur, 1970

This unrhymed paraphrase is taken from hymns in Revelation 5:9-10, 12-14, and 7:10b-13. The antiphon appears to be an allusion to the marriage feast of the Lamb and the church in Revelation 19:7, 9b:

> Let us rejoice and exult
>   and give him the glory,
> for the marriage of the Lamb has come,
>   and his bride has made herself ready. (19:7)

Blessed are those who are invited to the marriage supper of the Lamb. (19:9b)

It first appeared in *Contemporary Worship 2*, 1970, and was included with the music as indicated below.

Festival Canticle

Richard Hillert, 1975, alt.

The canticle was adapted by the composer from his *Festival Canticle: Worthy Is Christ*, a setting for one or more choirs with brass, timpani, and organ accompaniment, first performed at Grace Lutheran Church, River Forest, Illinois, Easter Sunday, March 30, 1975. It was published in that form in 1976. In that year the composer prepared a unison congregational version for the Liturgical Music Committee of the Inter-Lutheran Worship Commission with organ accompaniment, that he included as an alternate hymn of praise in his setting of "Holy Communion Setting One." The service first appeared at 56-76 in the *Lutheran Book of Worship*, 1978. Hillert made slight alterations to the harmony for our hymnal. (The above information has been reduced from the Hymnal Revision Committee correspondence files, April 1986)

The canticle is suitable as an opening or an offertory hymn or response. The stanzas should be sung antiphonally with all joining on the antiphon. In the original setting our stanzas 3 and 4 were combined. The melody of the antiphon may be doubled by a solo organ reed or single trumpet.

This is the Spirit's entry now (608)

Thomas E. Herbranson, 1972 (Rom. 6:3-4)

Marilyn K. Stulken has traced the writing of this hymn:

[It was] written at White Bear Lake, Minnesota, [and] was partly inspired by the upcoming baptism of the author's child in 1965, and was included as a part of his master's thesis (a study of Christology and the Sacraments in the [1958] hymnal) at Luther Theological Seminary [St. Paul, MN]. It was first published [with slight alteration] in *Contemporary Worship-4*, 1972. . . . The hymn [with Leo Sowerby's tune "Perry"] was first published in 1979 as a chorale concertato by Kevin Norris. (Stulken 1981, 279)

The hymn is based on Romans 6:3-4, a section of Paul's fuller commentary on the new life in Christ in chapters 5:1–8:29—we are baptized in Christ's death, burial, and rising. His teaching may be reflected in a fragment of an early Christian hymn that is included in his letter to the church at Ephesus:

> Sleeper, awake!
> > Rise from the dead,
> > > and Christ will shine on you.   (Ephesians 5:14b)

Our hymnal omits stanza 3:

> This miracle of life reborn
> > Comes from the Lord of breath;
> The perfect man from life was torn;
> > Our life comes through his death.

> © 1972 by Thomas E. Herbranson. Used by permission.

Azmon

The author has commented on the appropriate musical setting for his text:

In the 1958 *Service Book and Hymnal* there were six hymns on baptism, all set to sad and doleful tunes. Therefore, after I had written this hymn, I intended it to be sung to a joyful and spritely tune, which Sowerby's "Perry" [321 in our 1966 hymnal] is not." (Conversation with Carlton R. Young, July 1992)

For commentary on AZMON, see "Jesus, thine all-victorious love," page 449.

This little light of mine (585)

African American spiritual (Matt. 5:14-16)

John Lovell, Jr., has commented that the composing of spirituals about the reflective light of stars demonstrates the slave poet's "determination to borrow a creative function of stars, and just shine. . . . One reason for shining is that you worship a Deity who created light and who deals in it. . . . [In this spiritual] the poet is fully aware that his is a modest talent . . . . Though it is just a *little* light, any bit of light can penetrate a mighty lot of darkness. He is proud to be a light and to know that he has the gift of shining." (Lovell 1972, 287)

Long a favorite parting hymn in African American worship (McClain 1990, 110) and the source of countless choral settings, this spiritual took on new meaning in the freedom movement of the 1960's. As a consequence the movement's leaders and singers contributed additional stanzas:

> Up and down this street, Lord, I'm going
>   to let it shine . . .
> Every time I'm bleeding . . .
> Voting for my Freedom . . . (Lovell 1972, 535)

Other spirituals in this genre are "Shine for Jesus," "Oh rise an' shine an' give God de Glory," and "Oh, rise, shine, for thy light is a-coming."

Lattimer

African American spiritual;
adapt. by William Farley Smith, 1987
William Farley Smith, who composed this modest and expressive setting, named the tune after Louis Lattimer, the African American inventor and developer who with Thomas Edison and others developed the incandescent light bulb. There is a delightful choral setting for SAT voices in E^b at 132 in *Songs of Zion*, 1981. The text is set to another traditional African American melody at 190 in *Lead Me, Guide Me*, 1987.

Thou hidden love of God (414)
Verborgne Gottesliebe du

Gerhard Tersteegen, 1729; trans. by John Wesley, 1736 (Gal. 2:20)
The original text appeared in ten stanzas in *Geistliches Blumen-Gärtlein*, 1729, under the title "The Longing of the soul quietly to maintain the secret drawings of the love of God." (Julian 1907, 1216) This translation was made by John Wesley in 1736-37 from the eight-stanza version in the Herrnhut *Gesangbuch*, 1735, that Wesley sang and translated from in Savannah, Georgia. Probably because of space limitations this text was not included with his other translations in his *Collection of Psalms and Hymns*, published in Charleston in 1737. For commentary on this collection, see "Give to the winds thy fears," pages 352-53, and "John Wesley and the Music of Hymns," page 49. The full German text is included at 287 in *The Hymnal 1940 Companion*, 1956.

The hymn first appeared in eight 8.8.8.8.88 stanzas in *A Collection of Psalms and Hymns*, 1738, titled "From the German, Verborgne Gottesliebe du," a collection similar in format to the 1737 *Collection* (see Wesley 1983, 7:22-23). It was also included at 78-80 in *Hymns and Sacred Poems*, 1739, under the title "Divine Love. From the German." "As usual with his translations, it is a free handling of the German. The echo in stanza 1:5 of Augustine's *Confessions*, 'Fecisti nos ad te; et irrequietum est cor nostrum, donec requiescat in te,' ('Thou hast made us for thyself; and our heart cannot rest till it rests in thee'), is not in the German original." (Wesley 1983, 7:491-92) This text is included as "Finding rest in God" **(423)**.

The text appeared in subsequent Wesleyan hymnbooks including the the 1780 definitive *Collection* where in the 1786 edition Wesley placed over the hymns the tune names he deemed appropriate—in this instance "Carey's," in our hymnal CAREY'S (SURREY) **579**.

Centos of 5, 8, or 4 stanzas have been included in our our hymnals since the 1786 *Pocket Hymn Book*. Our version is stanzas 1, 3, 4, 6, and 8. Changes for our hymnal have been made in stanza 1:2, "man" to "one"; 1:4, "Only I sigh" to "And inly sigh"; 2:2, "her peace" to "its peace"; 2:3, "And while" to "but while"; 4:3, "through all my" to "from all my"; and stanza 4:4, "through all its latent" to "from all its hidden."

Vater unser

Geistliche Lieder, 1539; harm. from J. S. Bach, 1726

Martin Luther's version of this tune with his translation of the Lord's Prayer was included in Valentin Schumann's *Geistliche lieder auffs new gebessert und gemehrt*, 1539. The tune came into the British collections via the Anglo-Genevan Psalter, 1560-62, where it was set to metrical versions of the Lord's Prayer and Psalm 112; from the latter it received its alternate name. (See commentary on "All people that on earth do dwell," pages 196-97; "British Hymns," pages 9-10; and Robin Leaver, "English Metrical Psalmody," Vol. 1, *The Hymnal 1982 Companion*.)

Wesley first heard the tune sung by Moravians either on board ship on the way to Georgia or in Georgia. On page 33 in his *Foundery Collection*, 1742, it is set to "Father, if thou my Father art" in a version from *Psalms and Hymns in Solemn Musick*, 1671, appropriately named after the compiler, "Playford's tune." It remained a favorite, and in his 1780 *Collection* Wesley called for it to be sung with ten hymns.

Our harmonization is adapted from the seventh section of J. S. Bach's 1726 Cantata 102, *Herr, deine Augen sehen nach dem Glauben!*

Thou hidden source of calm repose (153)

Charles Wesley, 1749

This hymn was first included in vol. 1:245-46 in *Hymns and Sacred Poems*, 1749. (Gealy 557/489-A) The opening line may have been suggested by the first line of

John Wesley's translation of Anastasius Freylinghausen's "Wer ist wol, wie du," "O Jesu, source of calm repose," included in the 1737 Charleston *Collection*. John Wesley included Charles's hymn without alteration in the 1780 *Collection* in the section "For Believers Rejoicing."

Key words in stanzas 1 and 2 are "rest" or "repose," and "name." The former may be from Matthew 11:28, "Come to me, all you that are weary and are carrying heavy burdens, and I will give you rest"; the latter is in reference to Jesus' saving and mighty name. See "Jesus! the name high over all," **193**, and the commentary on hymns on the name of Jesus: "At the name of Jesus every knee shall bow," pages 220-22, and "All praise to thee, for thou, O King divine," pages 198-99. Wesley's brilliant exposition of contrasting metaphors, e.g., "rest in toil" and "ease in pain," begins in stanza 3 and escalates to a veritable shout at the hymn's climax: "My life in death, my heaven in hell."

The text entered our hymnals in *A Selection of Hymns*, 1810. It appears in our hymnal with one variant from the original that was made for *The Methodist Hymnal*, 1935: stanza 3:3, "the Med'cine of my broken heart" is changed to "the healing of my broken heart."

St. Petersburg

Attr. to Dimitri S. Bortniansky, 1825

This tune first appeared as a hymn tune attributed to Bortniansky in *Choral-buch*, 1825, edited by Johann Heinrich Tscherlitzky. Our hymnal uses the form of the tune and harmonization from our 1878 hymnal where it apparently first appeared in our hymnals. The tune is named for the city in Russia where Tscherlitzky was organist.

There is a more interesting harmonization at 113 in *Rejoice in the Lord*, 1985.

Thou my everlasting portion (407)

See "Close to thee," page 285.

Though I may speak with bravest fire (408)

See "The gift of love," page 636.

Three things we pray (493)

Richard of Chichester, England, 13th cent.

This petition is offered in response to Christ's sacrifice and example. The closing lines were the lyrics of the song "Day by day" from the 1970's musical *Godspell*. The prayer was included in J. Manning Potts, *Prayers of the Middle Ages*, 1954.

Through it all (507)

Words and music: Andraé Crouch, 1971

This popular gospel song of thanksgiving and trust in God's word reflects the assurance of Romans 8:28: "We know that all things work together for good for those who love God, and are called according to his purpose." It was written when the composer was in deep disappointment and discouragement while on a concert tour with Andraé Crouch and the Disciples. The song was completed "just minutes before an earthquake shook the San Fernando Valley—where Crouch was composing." (Stanislaw and Hustad 1992, 156)

The song has been characterized by Jon M. Spencer as applying "the customary means of consoling the disconsolate by heralding the virtues of cross-bearing . . . [placing] greater emphasis on the joy of 'crown-wearing' than on the sorrow of 'cross-bearing.' . . . There is neither a sense of anticulturalism being radical in his music nor of urgency to get to heaven at the earliest opportunity." (Spencer 1990, 219-20)

Through it all

The first hymnal to include this song was *Hymns for the Family of God*, 1976, where it is printed in its entirety. The chorus in our hymnal may be sung as a response to a soloist or choir singing the verses.

Thy holy wings, O Savior (502)

Caroline V. Sandell-Berg, 1865; trans. by Gracia Grindal, 1983
(Ps. 91:4; 73:26; 119:114; 51:10; 1 Pet. 3:18-22)

The hymn was first included as "Children's Evening Prayer" in *Korsblomman*, 1866. This translation and harmonization were first included at 11 in *Songs of the People*, 1986. The second stanza is appropriate for use as a response in the "Baptismal Covenant," **32-52**.

Bred Dina Vida Vingar

Swedish folk tune; harm. by LaRhrae Knatterud, 1983

The tune is thought to be a folk melody from the Skane region in Southwestern Sweden. It has been associated with this text since *Sionstoner* (*Melodies of Zion*), 1889, a hymn that Sandell-Berg helped to produce when she joined the editorial staff of the Evangeliska Fosterlandssiftelson (the Evangelical National Foundation). Gracia Grindal has provided the information for this text and tune. The pianistic harmonies in lines 1, 2, and 4 were reduced to chordal style for our hymnal. The tune name literally means "Spread your wide wings."

There is an introduction for two flutes and unison treble voices, and a flute descant at 47-49 in *The United Methodist Hymnal Music Supplement*.

Thy word is a lamp unto my feet (601)

Amy Grant, 1984 (Ps. 119:105)

The celebrated contemporary Christian recording artist has used Psalm 119:105 as a refrain to her song that witnesses to God's faithful guiding light and Jesus' companionship in daily life. The song first appeared as a hymn with stanzas and refrain in *Songs of the People*, 1986.

Thy word

Michael W. Smith, 1984; arr. by Keith Phillips

The refrain may be used as a response to prayer. It is also included at **841** as a psalm response.

'Tis finished! the Messiah dies (282)

Charles Wesley, 1749-51; 1762 (John 19:30)

Stanzas 1 and 3 of this hymn for Good Friday first appeared as stanzas 1:1-4 and 2:1-4 of a two-stanza LMD hymn under the heading "It is finished—John 19:30" at 2:234 in *Short Hymns on Select Passages of Holy Scriptures*, 1762. (Gealy 557/493) The LMD hymn appeared in some collections with a slight change in stanza 2:4 in 4 LM stanzas, including *A Select Collection of Hymns, Universally sung in all the Countess of Huntingdon's Chapels*, 1786. (Gealy 557/493) Stanzas 2 and 4 are from *MS Richmond*, which includes some unpublished Charles Wesley verse composed 1749-51. (Baker 1962, 390)

A version of the hymn appeared in eight CM stanzas at number 614 in *A Supplement to the Collection of Hymns*, 1831. (See Frank Baker 1962, 385, for commentary on this supplement to the 1780 *Collection*.) This version entered our hymnals in 1847 in six stanzas. The hymn was dropped in 1905 but returned in our 1966 edition in three stanzas. The 1904 British Methodist hymnal was the last to include the hymn, and our hymnal alone appears to sustain the text. The complete text is included in O. A. Beckerlegge and S T Kimbrough, Jr., *The Unpublished Poetry of Charles Wesley* (1990, 2:277-79).

Stanza 3:4 was originally "And I am more than justified," and for our hymnal stanza 2:4, "all mankind" was changed to "all the world."

Stanzas 1:5-8 and 2:5-8 from *Short Hymns* provide insight on Wesley's developing theology of the universal atonement of humankind in Jesus' suffering and death:

Finished the first transgression is,
  And purged the guilt of actual sin,
And everlasting righteousness
  Is now to all the world brought in.

Sin, death, and hell are now subdued,
  All grace is now to sinners given,
And lo, I plead th' atoning blood,
  For pardon, holiness, and heaven.

S T Kimbrough, Jr., has commented on stanza 3:

> It is an important addition for the sequence of the hymn and wholeness of
> Wesley's presentation of a theology of atonement. Stanzas 1, 2, and 4 are
> written in the third person and are descriptive of the power and effect of
> Christ's death. Stanza 3 is in the first person and emphasizes the personal
> experience of the atonement: "For me, for me the Lamb is slain," a recur-
> rent theme in Wesley's hymns and sacred poems, e.g., "And can it be that I
> should gain." In other words, stanzas 1 and 2 are Christ's story, stanza 3 is
> my story, and stanza 4 is everyone's story." (Correspondence with Carlton
> R. Young, September 1992)

Olive's Brow

William B. Bradbury, 1853

The tune was composed for this hymn in 1822 but did not appear in print until
its inclusion with the text in *The Shawm*, 1853. R. G. McCutchan describes the
importance of this tune book in accommodating the unique meters of Charles
Wesley's hymns:

> This book, which was a "Library of Church Music, embracing about one
> thousand pieces, consisting of psalm and hymn tunes adapted to every
> meter in use," included a special index for "all the Peculiar Metres of the
> Methodist hymnbooks as used in the North, these hymns being differently
> marked from those of the other religious denominations." (McCutchan
> 1942, 167)

Our tune is one of several by William B. Bradbury, Lowell Mason, and other
USA composers of the early- and middle-nineteenth century that were written
in a modest expressive unaccompanied SATB chordal devotional style. Besides
our tune, SELENA (287) and HAMBURG (298) have also survived the onslaught of
toe-tapping dance tunes and parlor love-ballads that became normative Wes-
leyan-evangelical style, Reconstruction-day congregational song.

'Tis so sweet to trust in Jesus (462)

Louisa M. R. Stead, 1882

This hymn, a series of loosely connected key evangelical words and phrases, was first published in *Songs of Triumph*, 1882. (Reynolds 1964, 216) No one knows the exact circumstances of the writing of the text, but many believe that the hymn was composed 1880-82 in the author's sorrow occasioned by the death of her husband in 1880.

Trust in Jesus

William J. Kirkpatrick, 1882

The tune was written for the text and first appeared with it in *Songs of Triumph*, 1882.

'Tis the old ship of Zion (345)

African American spiritual

George Pullen Jackson in pages 198-99 and 211-13 in *Spiritual Folk-Songs of Early America* and pages 257-58 in *White Spirituals of the Southern Uplands* has demonstrated that a mother text (from English seafaring traditions?) is the source of two distinct songs and their variants in African American worship and the shaped-note songbooks of the singing schools. He comments: "How old the American versions of the 'Ship of Zion' songs are I have not been able to learn. Newman I. White points to a version since the 1820's (*American Negro Folk-Songs*, p. 94)." (Jackson 1937, 212)

Dena J. Epstein quotes Fredrika Bremer from *Homes of the New World*, describing her visit to two black churches in Cincinnati on November 27, 1850:

> In the morning she attended "a negro Baptist Church belonging to the Episcopal creed" where the "negro aristocracy of the city" conducted a service that was "quiet, very proper and a little tedious. The hymns were beautifully and exquisitely sung." But in the afternoon the service at the African Methodist church in a black neighborhood was quite different. "I found in the African Church African ardor and African life. The church was full to overflowing, and the congregation sang their own hymns. The singing ascended and poured forth like a melodious torrent, and the heads, feet and elbows of the congregation moved all in unison with it . . . . The hymns and psalms which the negroes have themselves composed have a peculiar *naive* character, childlike, full of imagery and life." (Epstein 1981, 223)

Bremer cites "'Tis the old ship of Zion" as a favorite hymn of this church with this variant:

What kind of Captain does she have on board?
O, glory halleluiah!
King Jesus is the Captain, halleluiah!

A variant of the text with another tune was included at 914 in *The Methodist Hymnal*, 1889. A variant of the text of the spiritual with another melody was included at page 186 in "Jubilee Songs," a supplement with 139 selections compiled by F. J. Loudin for *The Story of the Jubilee Singers*, 1896.

John Lovell, Jr., places this spiritual within the category of "Occupational singing," coming from the slave poet's experience with boats, the ships, the rivers, and the sea that link back to roots in African waterways. (Lovell 1972, 161) James H. Cone has commented on the unique meaning of this spiritual for African American slaves: "[The ship] was a symbol that their life had meaning. . . . It was an affirmation . . . that they would triumph over life's contradictions, because they had met the Captain of the 'Old Ship of Zion' and were already on board." (Cone 1972, 56) William B. McClain relates the line in the spiritual "Git on board, git on board" to the code names that slaves used for their escape to the North. . . . In recent years the coded message of this song has somehow faded into non-use and the other worldly message has been emphasized, making [it] a common funeral selection." (McClain 1990, 109)

The alternate words for our refrain, "Give me that old time religion," come from a traditional folk song of the nineteenth-century USA rural South. George Pullen Jackson recalls "hearing it sung at meetings of both negroes and whites." (Jackson 1937, 218) Cecil Sharp cites the tune as the setting for "Sinner Man" that "Mrs. Boone [of Shoal Creek, North Carolina] heard at a negro service." (Sharp 1933, 291) F. J. Loudin (Marsh 1897, 192) includes a variant as "This old time religion." There is a setting of the traditional melody with a variant of the text by A. M. Townsend at number 2 in *Spirituals Triumphant Old and New*, 1926, edited by Edward Boatner. J. Jefferson Cleveland's arrangement at 89 in *Songs of Zion*, 1981, appears to be based on Townsend's version of the tune. The melody and words of "'Tis the old ship of Zion" and "Give me that old time religion" are frequently interchanged.

Yarmouth

African American spiritual
adapt. and arr. by William Farley Smith, 1986

As with most spirituals, this spiritual is sung too fast by non-African American congregations. In the African American worship tradition it is usually performed in a slow, devotional style with a good deal of freedom. There is an alternate harmonization at 131 in *Songs of Zion*, 1981.

To a maid engaged to Joseph (215)

Gracia Grindal, 1983 (Luke 1:26-38)

This is an unrhymed paraphrase of Gabriel's announcement to Mary that she had been chosen by God to become pregnant by "the Power of the Most High" and the virgin's ready acceptance of her role as the mother of Jesus. The words and music first appeared at 55 in *Hymnal Supplement*, 1984.

Annunciation

Howard M. Edwards, III, 1983

The composer has written about the origin of the hymn:

> The words and music were written November 1982 at Luther Northwestern Seminary, St. Paul, Minnesota, and first sung in an Advent hymn sing. It was the second of twenty hymns that Grindal and Edwards wrote together during the early 1980's. It first appeared in *Singing the Story*, 1983. On the night of composition, both writers had laryngitis, [and] the hymn was first "sung" by an alto recorder and a guitar with only two strings. (Correspondence with Carlton R. Young, July 1992)

The first two lines of the stanzas may be sung in alternation by choir, congregation and soloists, with everyone singing four parts on the last line.

To God be the glory (99)

See "My tribute," pages 491-92.

To God be the glory, great things he hath done (98)

Fanny J. Crosby, 1875

The words and music first appeared under the title "Praise for Redemption" in *Brightest and Best*, 1875. It came to be used by British churches during the Moody and Sankey revivals and was included by Sankey in editions of *Sacred Songs and Solos*, 1875 1st ed. It appeared in some British collections including *Methodist Hymn Book*, 1933.

William J. Reynolds in *Hymns of the Faith*, 1964, was the first to document the introduction of this hymn to USA congregations as a result of the 1952 Billy Graham Crusades in Great Britain. Reynolds quotes the crusade's music director Cliff Barrows about its introduction: "I believe the first crusade we used this hymn in America upon our return was in Nashville in 1954." (Reynolds 1964, 217)

Reynolds provides this additional commentary:

> It is most extraordinary that this long forgotten American gospel song should have been imported from England and become immensely popular during the last decade. . . . [The hymn is] an expression of objectivity not usually found in gospel hymnody. Here is a straight-forward voicing of praise to God, not simply personal testimony nor sharing some subjective aspect of Christian experience. (Reynolds 1964, 217)

To God be the glory

William H. Doane, 1875

The tune is a perfect match for these words of glory and praise to God in Christ Jesus. Some British editors have attempted to stifle the tune by reharmonizing it as in *The Anglican Hymnal*, 1965, or by deleting the refrain and setting the text to another tune—for example, it appears with ST. DENIO in *The Church Hymnary*, 1973 3d. ed.

To mock your reign, O dearest Lord (285)

Fred Pratt Green, 1972 (Matt. 27:27-31; Mark 15:16-20; John 19:1-5)

At the suggestion of Francis Westbrook this Holy Week hymn was written to be sung to Thomas Tallis's "Third Mode Melody." (Green 1982, 44) It first appeared in that setting in *Sixteen Hymns of To-day for Use as Simple Anthems*, edited by John Wilson, 1978. The poem effectively contrasts Jesus' crown of thorns with the crown of triumph, the snatched purple cloak a robe for our naked shame. The reed mockingly thrust in the victim's hand becomes the Sovereign's scepter. The text is included in our hymnal without alteration.

Kingsfold

English melody, arr. by Ralph Vaughan Williams, 1906

Tallis's "Third Mode Melody" was set aside by the Hymnal Revision Committee for KINGSFOLD, perceived as more singable. The original setting (see 170 in *The Hymnal 1982*), may be used by the choir as a call to worship or as a response to the reading of the passion narrative.

For commentary on KINGSFOLD, see "Come, let us use the grace divine," pages 293-94.

Toda la tierra espera al Salvador (210)
All earth is waiting to see the Promised One

Catalonian text by Alberto Taulé, 1972
English trans. by Gertrude C. Suppe, 1987 (Isa. 40:3-5)

This advent hymn was first included in *Cantoral de Missa Dominical Centre de Pastoral Liturgica*, 1972. It was brought to the attention of the Hymnal Revision

Committee in a Spanish version in *Cancionero para la Iglesia Joven*, number 28, no date. An English text was apparently prepared from the Catalonian text in *Himnos y Cantios de la Iglesia*, no date, for our hymnal and approved by the author. For commentary on Catalonian language and culture, see "En el frío invernal," pages 326-27.

Gertrude C. Suppe has provided this information about the author and the hymn:

> I attended a workshop Taulé helped lead two years ago. . . . He was absolutely delighted to have us choose "Toda la tierra" for the United Methodist *Hymnal,* as it was the first time he had had a song published in the United States. . . . In Taulé's introduction to his book of songs, *El Señor es mi luz*, no date, . . . he refers to the new type of songs [including our hymn] which were beginning to appear in the [Spanish Roman Catholic] church about 1967. (Correspondence with Carlton R. Young, June 1991)

Taulé

Alberto Taulé, 1972; harm. by Skinner Chávez-Melo, 1988
The harmonization was made for our hymnal.

Transfiguration (259)

Laurence Hull Stookey, USA, 20th Cent.
(Matt. 17:1-8; Mark 9:2-8; Luke 9:28-36)
This prayer was written for our hymnal and combines the transfiguration theme, Jesus the fulfillment of Hebrew scripture, with the petition that we might share in Christ's suffering and therefore his glory. For commentary on the Transfiguration, see "O wondrous sight! O vision fair," page 535 and, "Christ, upon the mountain peak," pages 282-83.

Trinity Sunday (76)

After the Book of Common Prayer; alt.
This prayer for the First Sunday after Pentecost and general use addresses God whom the church worships both as Unity and Trinity. It first appeared in this form at 24 in the *Lutheran Book of Worship*, 1978, adapted from the longer prayer for Trinity Sunday in the *Book of Common Prayer*.

For commentary on the Holy Trinity, see "Canticle of the Holy Trinity," pages 265-67; "Holy, holy, holy! Lord God Almighty," pages 400-02; "Praise and thanksgiving be to God," page 554-55; and "We believe in one true God," page 676.

Trust and obey (467)

John H. Sammis, 1887 (1 John 1:7)
Ira D. Sankey tells the story of this hymn in *My Life and the Story of the Gospel Hymns*:

> "Some years ago," says Professor [Daniel Brink] Towner, musical director of the Moody Bible Institute, "Mr. Moody was conducting a series of meetings in Brockton, Massachusetts, and . . . one night a young man rose in a testimony meeting and said, 'I am not quite sure—but I am going to trust, and I am going to obey.'" I just jotted that sentence down, and sent it with the little story to the Rev. J. H. Sammis, a Presbyterian minister. He wrote the hymn, and the tune was born. The chorus . . . was written before the hymn was. (Sankey 1907, 290)

The hymn, including the usually omitted stanza 2,

> Not a shadow can rise,
> Not a cloud in the skies
> But His smile quickly drives it away;
> Not a doubt or a fear,
> Not a sigh nor a tear
> Can abide while we trust and obey,

is concerned with the rewards of trusting God's word and obeying God's will, but its simple and direct text bears little resemblance to 1 John 1:7, from which it is said to stem. The hymn was first included in *Hymns Old and New*, 1887, (Reynolds 1964, 260) and entered our hymnals in 1897.

Trust and obey

Daniel B. Towner, 1887
The tune was composed as described above. The chorus may be used as a response to prayer or witness.

Tú has venido a la orilla (344)
Lord, you have come to the lakeshore

Cesáreo Gabaráin; trans. by Gertrude C. Suppe, George Lockwood and Raquel Gutiérrez-Achon, 1987 (Matt. 4:18-22)
This hymn personalizes the story of Jesus' call to Peter and Andrew to become fishers of people (Matthew 4:19). According to Gertrude C. Suppe, "The first publication of this hymn was apparently in a small booklet, *Dios con nosotros*, published in Madrid, Spain, between 1973 and 1979. [It] is generally known by

the title 'Pescador de Hombres' ('Fishers of Men'). Sister Andrea Johnson reports that Gabaráin told her that [the song] had been translated into 80 languages." (Correspondence with Carlton R. Young, July 1991)

Two English texts were independently developed by Lockwood and Suppe. When they were brought to the Hispanic Consultation, Gutiérrez-Achon was requested to combine them into one. The result was so successful that it was agreed that all three names should appear with this classic translation of one of the most popular songs to emerge from the 1970's revival of religious song in Spain.

Pescador de Hombres

Cesareo Gabaráin; harm. by Skinner Chávez-Melo, 1987
This setting first appeared at 28 in *Albricias*, 1987, Chávez-Melo, editor, developed by the Spanish Hymnal Commission of the Protestant Episcopal Church.

Turn your eyes upon Jesus (349)

Words and music: Helen H. Lemmel, 1922
This is the refrain of the three-stanza poem "The Heavenly Vision," published in Great Britain with the first line "O soul, are you weary and troubled" in the poet's *Glad Songs*, 1922. William J. Reynolds has traced the origin of the hymn: "The text was inspired by a sentence in a missionary pamphlet by Lillias Trotter, 'So then, turn your eyes upon Him. Look full into His face, and you will find that the things of earth will acquire a strange, new dimness.'" (Adams 1992, 210)

Lemmel

The entire hymn is included at 320 in *The Baptist Hymnal*, 1991.

'Twas in the moon of wintertime (244)
Estennialon de tsonue Iesus ahatonnia

Jean de Brébeuf, ca. 1643; trans. by Jesse Edgar Middleton, 1926
This, the earliest of Native North American nativity carols, stems from the early seventeenth-century activity of Jesuit missionary Jean de Brébeuf among the Canadian Huron Indians. Stanley L. Osborne has written:

> Father de Villeneuve, a Jesuit missionary stationed at Lorette from 1747, in 1794 wrote down the words as he heard them. A translation into French was made by Paul Picard, an Indian notary. . . . The first printed version

was in Ernest Myrand's *Noel Anciens de la Nouvelle France* [1899]. (Osborne 1976, commentary on hymn 412)

Hugh D. McKellar comments on the meaning of the carol in "The Huron Carol—JESOUS AHATONHIA."

[Brébeuf] does not present Christ's birth as an event which happened far away and long ago, nor linger on its details; what matters for him, as well it might for every Christian, is the immediacy of the Incarnation and the difference it can make in the lives not just of Hurons . . . but of believers in any culture. He mentions the wise men rather than the shepherds because, as the *Relations* [a missionary periodical] often attests, converted Indians made a point of reaching a church at Christmas even if they had to travel for days. (McKellar 1992, 203)

Middleton's poem extends beyond the original French text and tells the story of Jesus' birth into Huron everyday life and its retelling in their folk symbols, such as "rabbit skin" for "swaddling clothes" and "gifts of fox and beaver pelt" for the Magi's presents. His version was set to a traditional French melody and first appeared in the December 22, 1926, issue of *New Outlook*, where it was described as a "charming little Christmas song . . . [in which] the devoted missionary has adapted the story of the infant Christ to the minds of the Indian children, . . . [an] "interpretation . . . not a translation, written to provide English-speaking Canadians with an opportunity to sing the first Christmas carol ever heard in the Province of Ontario." (McKellar 1992, 200)

The carol was included with Healy Willan's setting in the Canadian Anglican Church's *Hymn Book*, 1938. An arrangement of the carol by Walter Ehret at 76-77 in *The International Book of Christmas Carols*, 1963, has been widely used in public and church school music education. The carol entered our hymnals in *Supplement to the Book of Hymns*, 1982.

Jesous Ahatonhia

French Canadian melody; arr. by H. Barrie Cabena, 1970
Stanley L. Osborne has traced this melody to an old French folk song entitled "Une Jeune Pucelle." Our arrangement was made for *The Hymn Book*, 1971. The concluding phrase of the melody is slightly different from the two settings at 114 in *The Hymnal 1982*.

Una espiga (637)
Sheaves of summer

Cesáreo Gabaráin, 1973; trans. by George Lockwood, 1987
This hymn on the unity of Christians everywhere who gather at Christ's table was first included in *Alabemos al Señor*, 1976, published by Seminario Regional

de Veracruz. Concerning this collection Gertrude C. Suppe comments: "Someone evidently came from Spain with a suitcase full of the exciting new music that was emerging after Vatican II." (Correspondence with Carlton R. Young, July 1991)

Our translation faithfully transmits the hymn's subtle and powerful Spanish images and metaphors of grain, water, grapes, wine, bread, the body and blood of Christ, and the common table.

Una espiga

Cesareo Gabaraín, 1973; harm. by Skinner Chávez-Melo, 1985

Our harmonization first appeared at 22 in *Albricias*, 1987. For comment on accompanying "dance tunes," see "The first Noel," pages 633-34.

Up from the grave he arose (322)

Words and music: Robert Lowry, 1874

This favorite Easter hymn was written while Lowry was pastor of the First Baptist Church of Lewisburg, Pennsylvania. It first appeared at 113 under the heading "He is not here, but risen—Luke 24:5" in *Brightest and Best*, 1875 (Gealy 556/293), and quickly became very popular in the USA. In Great Britain its inclusion by Ira D. Sankey in editions of *Sacred Songs and Solos*, 1875 1st ed., led to its wide use in the Moody-Sankey revivals and its inclusion in a number of late nineteenth-century evangelical hymnals including those for British Methodists.

The hymn entered our hymnals in 1921, but it was not included in a Methodist hymnal until 1966.

Christ arose

In the first printing of the hymn the refrain is marked "faster," a performance practice that is still followed. The refrain may be used as a call to worship during the Easter season.

Venite exultemus (91)

See "Canticle of praise to God," pages 259-60.

Victory hymn (478)

See "Jaya ho," pages 436-37.

Victory in Jesus (370)

Words and music: Eugene M. Bartlett, 1939

This rousing gospel song was first included in *Gospel Choruses*, 1939 (Reynolds 1976, 101), and was made popular in the rural South at the "singings" that use the eight-shaped-note songbooks published by Stamps-Baxter Music Company of Dallas, Texas, and in concerts by professional male gospel quartets. The majority of the Hymnal Revision Committee had never heard of it until Charles M. Smith, a member of the committee and a district superintendent from North Carolina, introduced it with the comment: "This is the most requested recent gospel hymn from my district." After singing it, many of the committee simply shook their heads as they confessed their distance from this type of evangelical repertory sung in many United Methodist congregations. For additional commentary on this repertory, see "Consultations to the Hymnal Revision Committee: Gospel Hymns," pages 159-60.

Hartford

This hymn should be sung in a strong two-beat pulse with gospel-style piano accompaniment. The tune was named by the composer's son, Gene Bartlett, "for the Arkansas town where he [the composer] lived and the music publishing firm that he founded." (Reynolds 1976, 101)

Wake, awake, for night is flying (720)

Philipp Nicolai, 1599; trans. by Catherine Winkworth, 1858
(Rom. 13:11-12; Matt. 25:1-13)

This advent hymn is sometimes called the king of the chorales and the author's counterpart, "O Morning Star, how fair and bright" **(247)**, the queen of the chorales. It is based on Matthew 25:1-13, Jesus' parable of the wise and foolish bridesmaids, appointed for the Twenty-seventh Sunday after Trinity, and contains images of the watchman calling to the children of light from Isaiah 52:8 and Ezekiel 3:17, and the Lamb's marriage feast in Revelation 19:6-9. The text first appeared with the tune in the appendix to Nicolai's *Freuden-Spiegel des ewigen lebens* (*The Mirror of the joy of eternal life*), 1599.

The hymn entered our hymnals in 1966 slightly altered from Winkworth's translation on page 290 under the title "The Final Hour" in *Lyra Germanica*, 1858 2d series. (Gealy 557/501) For our hymnal there is a change in stanza 1:2, "men" to "saints."

Wachet auf

Philipp Nicolai; harm. by J. S. Bach, 1731

Our harmonization is Bach's isorhythmic setting of the chorale for the conclusion, "Gloria sei dir gesungen mit Menschen-und englischen Zungen" ("Gloria be to Thee, sung with men's and angels' tongues") of Cantata 140, *Wachet auf, ruft uns die Stimme*, 1731.

Walk on, O people of God (305)

See "Camina, pueblo de Dios," pages 249-50.

Wash, O God, our sons and daughters (605)

Ruth Duck, 1987 (John 3:3-8)

This baptismal hymn was commissioned by the Hymnal Revision Committee; see *"The United Methodist Hymnal*, 1989: Hymns Subcommittee," page 155. It is a tightly constructed singable 87. 87. D text that elaborates on the biblical and traditional promises of baptism as the rebirthing, cleansing, anointing, nurturing, recreating, and transforming rite of initiation into the Christian family. The hymn is appropriate for services of infant and adult baptism and the renewal of the baptismal covenant.

Stanza 2:2, "by your milk may we be fed," originally read "at your breast may we be fed." Discussion about the change, among others supplied by the poet upon request of the hymns subcommittee, came late at the final meeting of the full committee, October 1987, and resulted in the painful reopening of the language debate, specifically female metaphors (for example, "Womb") that describe God's nature (see commentary on "God of many names," pages 369-70; and pages 131-35 in *"The United Methodist Hymnal*, 1989: The Language Issue"). One committee member almost resigned in protest over the perceived sexually explicit metaphor of a child's feeding at a mother's breast that described and addressed God as mother. Another member of the committee who voted against the change stated, "It appears that only Jesus is allowed to have breasts," citing the Charles Wesley hymn that begins "Jesus, lover of my soul, let me to thy bosom fly" **(479)**.

Beach Spring

See "Lord, whose love through humble service," page 474.

We are climbing Jacob's ladder (418)

African American spiritual (Gen. 28:10-17)

Miles M. Fischer (1953, 56) believes the ladder theme to have been included in African American spirituals as early as 1824. (Gealy 557/504) Cecil J. Sharp cites two songs that are probably variants of the original spiritual: the refrain of "'Sinner Man,' sung by Mrs. Sina Boone at Shoal Creek, Burnsville, North Carolina, Oct. 1, 1918, 'as heard by [her] at a negro service. She said that only. . . three verses were sung there'" (Sharp 1932, 1:291); and another song that begins "We'll climb up Jacob's Ladder, and it's higher up and higher; Hallelujah," "sung by Mrs. June Gentry at Hot Springs, North Carolina, Sept. 15, 1916." (Sharp 1932, 2: 396) There are similar images in other spirituals: "Do you think I'd make a soldier," "Rise, shine, give God the glory," "To see God's bleeding Lamb," and "You go, I'll go with you."

John B. Lovell, Jr., comments that in this spiritual the slave poet is expressing "his determination to rise from his low estate and to progress up the material and spiritual ladder, 'round by round.'" (Lovell 1972, 119) But "the climbing . . . is a fighting operation, not a sports activity." (Lovell 1972, 371) It is this writer's recollection that the spiritual's military image, "soldiers of the cross," was never an issue in the Hymnal Revision Committee's debate on language; see "The Language Issue," pages 131-35.

For commentary on the spiritual's central image, Jacob's dream at Bethel in Genesis 28:10-17, see "Nearer, my God, to thee," page 493. The spiritual was apparently first included in H. Augustine Smith's *American Student Hymnal*, 1928. It entered our hymnals in 1966.

Jacob's ladder

African American spiritual
adapt. and arr. by William Farley Smith, 1986
Space limitations did not allow for both the 3/4 and our 2/2 variant of the spiritual to be included in our hymnal. The arranger has suggested that the 2/2 variant be played "as a bright march, changing key each succeeding stanza up a half step as an effective means of variation to highlight the spiritual's meaning." (Sanchez 1989, 147) His harmonies can be adapted and incorporated into the 3/4 version, or the spiritual may be sung from memory without accompaniment, allowing the congregation to supply the basic three-chord I, IV, V harmonies, adding 7's where appropriate.

R. Nathaniel Dett's standard choral setting is included at 205 in *Songs of Zion*, 1981.

We are the church (558)

Word and music: Richard K. Avery and Donald S. March, 1972
This song has proved useful as an intergenerational lesson on the nature of the church and can be led effectively by children. It first appeared in the authors' *Songs for the Easter People*, 1972, and since then it has often been included in United Methodist church school publications for children. The song's direct language, relevant message, limited vocal range, simple harmonies, and chorus are typical of this creative duo's early songs that proved so compelling as alternatives to standard hymnody.

Port Jervis

The tune's name is the city where the authors serve respectively as pastor and musician in the First Presbyterian Church, Port Jervis, New York.

We are tossed and driven on the restless sea of time (525)

See "We'll understand it better by and by," pages 684-85.

We believe in one true God (85)

Tobias Clausnitzer, 1668; trans. by Catherine Winkworth, 1863

This metrical version of the trinitarian articles of the Apostles' Creed **(881, 882)** first appeared in the Culmbach-Bayreuth *Gesangbuch*, 1668. It entered our hymnals in 1878 with Catherine Winkworth's text included at 75 in her *Chorale Book for England*, 1863. (Gealy 557/506) It was dropped from our 1905 hymnal and restored in the 1966 hymnal, using an altered version of Winkworth's text from *The Lutheran Hymnal*, 1941. The 1966 revision committee deleted the second word "all" from each stanza, rendering it a 77. 77. 77 text, and set this hymn of praise to RATISBON.

For additional commentary on hymns and tunes composed with reference to the Apostles' Creed, see "All things bright and beautiful," pages 201-02, "Holy, holy, holy! Lord God Almighty," pages 400-02, "Once in royal David's city," pages 544-45, and "The church's one foundation," pages 628-29.

Ratisbon

See "Christ, whose glory fills the skies," pages 283-84.

We do not know how to pray as we ought (406)

See "Canticle of prayer," pages 260-61.

We gather together to ask the Lord's blessing (131)
Wilt heden nu treden voor God den Heere

Nederlandtsch Gedenckclanck; trans. by Theodore Baker, 1894

Leonard Ellinwood first established the sources of this hymn and musical setting in *The Hymnal 1940 Companion*. (1956, 205-06) This anonymous late sixteenth-century text celebrating the freedom of the Netherlands from Spanish oppression was first published in Haarlem in Adrianus Valerius's *Nederlandtsch Gedenckclanck*, 1626. It was included by Edward Kremser in his *Sechs Altniederländische Volkslieder*, 1877, all drawn from Valerius's collection. The English translation by Theodore Baker was made for the anthem setting "Prayer of Thanksgiving," published in 1894.

Baker's text, faithful to the spirit of the original nationalistic hymn, was introduced to the church and the general public in patriotic celebrations of thanksgiving extolling the USA, who with God's help and favor, vanquished its various enemies and became the haven for the oppressed while at the same time affirming the manifest destiny and duty of those elected and protected by God to govern. This use of the text apparently prompted Julia Cady Cory in 1902 to compose for her church, Brick Presbyterian, New York City, "We praise thee, O God, our Redeemer, Creator," a general hymn of praise and thanksgiving using the Dutch tune. For many it became a more appropriate hymn for annual community interdenominational Thanksgiving services convened without regard to racial, national, or ethnic histories.

Kremser

16th cent. Dutch melody; arr. by Edward Kremser, 1877

Paul G. Hammond has written that in 1877 Kremser arranged the Dutch melody "Heij wilder dan wild" from the 1626 collection in a setting for male voices and orchestra using his German text. (Adams 1992, 264) His setting was published by G. Schirmer with Baker's English words in 1894 as "Prayer of Thanksgiving" for mixed voices and instruments.

According to the Dictionary of American Hymnology Project (1978, reel 162), Baker's text with the Dutch tune was first included in *Chautauqua Hymnal and Liturgy*, 1903. *The Methodist Hymnal*, 1935, was the first denominational hymnal to include it. There is an alternate harmonization and vocal and trumpet descants at 192-93 in *The United Methodist Hymnal Music Supplement*.

We know that Christ is raised (610)

John Brownlow Geyer, 1969 (Rom. 6:3-11)

The writing of this hymn was prompted by considerations of the ethical and religious ramifications of research to produce human living cells, i.e., the baby in the test tube. The poet writes, "The hymn attempted to illustrate the Christian doctrine of baptism in relation to those experiments. Originally intended as a hymn for the Sacrament of Baptism, it has become popular as an Easter hymn" (Stulken 1981, 274), no doubt owing to its arresting first line taken from Romans 6:9: "We know that Christ, being raised from the dead, will never die again; death no longer has dominion over him."

The text was written for ENGELBERG; it was first included in *Hymns and Songs*, 1969. The original second stanza appropriately read:

> We share by water in his saving death;
> this union brings to being one new cell,
> a living and organic part of Christ.
> Alleluia!

For our hymnal stanza 3:3, "our saving Christ" has been changed to "a living Christ." A trinitarian third stanza, omitted from our hymnal, was included in *Supplement to the Book of Hymns*, 1982:

> The Father's splendor clothes the Son with life;
> the Spirit's fission shakes the church of God;
> baptized, we live with God, the Three-in-One:
> Alleluia!

Engelberg

Charles Villiers Stanford, 1904

The composer provided five harmonizations for *Hymns Ancient and Modern*, 1904, set to "For all the saints." "There it languished for over fifty years in the shadow of 'Sine Nomine,' Vaughan Williams' now classic tune." (Glover 1987, 37)

Stanford's settings are included with optional brass and timpani at 118-26, and a transposition to F major at 127 in *The United Methodist Hymnal Music Supplement*. *The Hymnal 1982* includes the tune with the composer's amen.

Contrary to the original setting, at the suggestion of Philip R. Dietterich, in our hymnal the dotted quarter and eighth notes on the downbeat of measures 2 and 5 are repeated in measure 8.

We look for light (205)

See "Canticle of light and darkness," pages 255-56.

We meet you, O Christ (257)

Fred Kaan, 1966

The poet has supplied this information about this hymn:

> [It] was born when I was preparing the script for a BBC television programme in the series "Seeing and Believing" in 1966. The programme was broadcast on Passion Sunday that year when it coincided with the 25th anniversary of the destruction of the city of Plymouth in the German air raid. The theme caption for the programme (which was called "The Tree Springs to Life") [the title of the poem] was a photograph of the bombed church of Saint Andrew's where out of a heap of stones and rubble in the nave, a small apple tree had miraculously pushed its way through and won in blossom. It was sung in the broadcast by the folksinger Len Pearcy. (Kaan 1985, 140)

The hymn first appeared in a USA collection in *Ecumenical Praise*, 1977.

Stanley Beach

Carl F. Schalk, 1987
This tune was commissioned by the Hymnal Revision Committee for this text. It is named after the street in Hong Kong where the composer's daughter, Jan Schalk Westrick, resides.

We praise you, O God (80)

See "Canticle of the Holy Trinity," pages 265-67.

We shall overcome (533)

African American spiritual
Two possible sources have been set forth for this anthem of the USA civil rights movement of the 1960's and 1970's. The first and most widely held view is that it is adapted from the optimistic refrain of stanza 1 of Charles Albert Tindley's hymn composed in 1901, "I'll overcome some day," titled "Ye shall overcome if ye faint not," number 18 in *New Songs of Paradise*, 1941. A unique quality of this hymn is the summary refrain that follows each stanza; for example:

> 1. This world is one great battlefield,
>   With forces all arrayed;
>   If in my heart I do not yield
>   I'll overcome some day.
>
> Refrain: I'll overcome some day,
>   I'll overcome some day;
>   If in my heart I do not yield
>   I'll overcome some day.

The difficulty with this view is that in Tindley's 66.76 chorus in 3/4 time, apart from four words "overcome some day" and "heart," two occurrences of the stepwise tune moving from the fifth to the sixth of the scale, there is no similarity with the 55. 7. 54. 7 meter and 4/4 melody of "We shall overcome." Furthermore, and most important for this study, the poet apparently took the key words and central liberation theme from the slave song "We shall overcome" and created a typically Tindleyan hymn that C. Eric Lincoln and Lawrence H. Mamiya characterize as "not simply other-worldly. [It is] also addressed to helping the oppressed to survive *this* world." (Lincoln and Mamiya 1990, 360)

Wesley Milgate writes that a source of the spiritual is *The European Magazine and London Review* (November 1792, 355 and 385-86), where "there is 'We shall overcome' a Negro spiritual, to the tune 'The Sicilian Mariner's Hymn to the Virgin.'"

(Milgate 1985, 84) A review of these pages in *The European Magazine and London Review*, however, reveals no connection with the African American song, except a single reference to "A Hymn to the Blessed Jesus," presumably the "The Sicilian Mariner's Hymn to the Virgin" interlined at 385-86 with SICILIAN MARINERS in SA parallel thirds and keyboard bass.

Since the first eight measures of SICILIAN MARINERS are strikingly similar to MARTIN, and the former apparently had a seafaring origin (see "Lord, dismiss us with thy blessing," page 470), our tune may have entered the slave song tradition as a worksong onboard slave ships going from Africa via England to the USA. A variant of the tune may be the call-and-response rowing song "Michael, row the boat ashore." William Farley Smith suggests the tune resembles "No more auction block for me." (Sanchez 1989, 182) While its roots in slavery can be affirmed, "it is not known exactly how many or which of the verses of this song originated with the slaves." (McClain 1990, 108)

In the 1940's the song emerged from the African American oral tradition and became a protest song of both segregated and integrated labor unions. "[It] was sung in 1946 on picket lines in Charleston, South Carolina, by members of Local 15 of the Food and Tobacco Workers Association. They were striking to increase their wages of forty-five cents an hour. Two members of this union [introduced it] to the Highlander Folk School." (Reynolds 1990, 315) In the next decade it "was first introduced to the civil rights movement by Guy Carawan, a white songwriter who learned it at the Highlander Folk School." (Spencer 1990, 84-85) As the movement spread into both rural and urban settings, particularly by Martin Luther King, Jr., and his followers, additional lines were added "not for artistic variety, but out of the need blacks had to express the complexity of complaints and rebuttals regarding their oppression. For example, additional verses . . . include "The truth shall make us free/ . . . someday," "We are not afraid." (Spencer 1990, 84)

For those in the African American community who remain impatient with the slow progress of equal rights or others who are pledged to separatism as the only solution to continuing discrimination, how long it will be to "someday" has became a point of criticism and conjecture as to the relevancy of the song's continued use as a sign and song of protest. Some others still sing it, as they do any song that links them with their vital heritage, as a means of passing along the ethos of protest and change to their children. Others outside that tradition, including some African Americans born since the 1970's and non-African Americans of all ages, sing it as an expression of their unity with all who have in the past and presently affirm God's will that someday soon all persons will be free from racial, sexual, physical, and age discrimination, violence, hunger, homelessness, loneliness, and poverty.

Martin

African American spiritual
adapt. by William Farley Smith, 1986

The song's name is the first name of the martyred social prophet and preacher Martin Luther King, Jr.

We shall see a new heaven and and earth (734)

See "Canticle of hope," pages 254-55.

We three kings (254)

Words and music: John H. Hopkins, Jr., 1857 (Matt. 2:1-12)
This carol was written ca. 1857 and first appeared at pages 12-13 in the author's *Carols, Hymns, and Songs*, 1863. (Gealy 557/513) Because the wealth of USA Appalachian and other folk carols was yet to be discovered, this carol for almost a century was regarded by hymnal editors as the sole USA contribution to the repertory of English language carols.

Kings of Orient

The first printing of this carol included a brief interlude that modulated from G major to E minor, and the footnote supplied these performance suggestions: /

> Each of verses 2, 3, and 4, is sung as a solo [Kings Gaspard, Melchior and Balthazar] to the music of Gaspard's part to the 1st and 5th verses, the accompaniment and chorus being the same throughout. Only verses 1 and 5 are sung as a trio. Men's voices are best for the parts of the Three Kings, but the music is set in the G clef for the accommodation of children. (Hopkins 1863, 12)

Additional performance suggestions and an interlude for winds are included at 195 in *The Oxford Book of Carols*, 1964.

We, thy people, praise thee (67)

Kate Stearns Page, 1932
The words were composed as a school song for the Diller-Quaile School of Music, New York City (Gealy 557/514), and it was published with Franz Joseph Haydn's tune in *Selected Hymns for Use in School or Home*, 1922. Its appearance in Edith Lovell Thomas's *Singing Worship*, 1935, bought it into church school curricula where it was set as a children's choir anthem. The hymn entered our hymnals in 1966.

St. Anthony's Chorale

Franz Joseph Haydn, ca. 1780
arr. by Edith Lovell Thomas, 1935; alt.
The arranger's setting has been slightly adjusted to conform to the melody as found in Franz Joseph Haydn's unpublished "Chorale St. Antoni" for winds and

serpent. (Gealy, Lovelace, Young 1970, 423) Johannes Brahms used Haydn's theme in his *Variations on a Theme by Joseph Haydn*, op. 56a, 1873, but Nicolas Slonimsky warns that it may not be Haydn's tune. (Baker 1984, 326)

The melody is often used as a wedding processional.

We utter our cry (439)

Fred Kaan, 1983

The hymn was written for the 1983 Christian World Conference on Life and Peace held in Uppsala, Sweden, attended by representatives of sixty-two counties. "The hymn was sung several times during the Conference, and was finally included in the official Message." (Kaan 1985, 150) It was included in the poet's collected verse, *The Hymn Texts of Fred Kaan*, 1985, and the songbook *Singing for Peace*, 1986.

The Hymnal Revision Committee, having found few hymns of quality that spoke with force on the issues of world peace and ecology, voted to include Kaan's hymn, but dropped stanzas 4 and 5. Behind this proposal was a twofold concern: the reluctance of some committee members in the wake of the "Onward Christian soldiers" controversy (see *"The United Methodist Hymnal*, 1989," pages 135-38) to appear to encourage "unpatriotic" peace and anti-nuclear arms protests and marches; and the poem's length, which tended to lessen the impact of the hymn's superb climax, "choose Christ before Caesar and life before death!"

This excerpt from the author's response provides commentary on his under-standing of the hymn's central theme:

> I cannot agree to you leaving out verses that commit us to protest and demonstration, and to following our (usually) mealy-mouthed church reso-lutions on peace with an active involvement in the peace-movement. Peace is something that has to be *pursued*.

> The hymn also contains that feeling of awareness that the leaders of the world need to be prayed for, so that they may lose their deviousness and their bloody-mindedness in the power struggle.

> No, Sam, no, the hymn must go in completely, or not at all. What your com-mittee has done is take the teeth out of the text. All that is left is prayer, and I believe that prayer is no good without action. There are in fact many things we should not pray for because we should jolly well do, or work toward, them ourselves. (Correspondence with Carlton R. Young, December 1988)

The author permitted three changes: stanza 5:1, the deity metaphor "Lord-Love" was diminished to "Lord; love"; 3:3, "earth" to "Earth"; and 4:3, "statesmen" to "leaders." Stanzas 4 and 5 are asterisked "may be omitted." *The Baptist Hymnal*, 1991, includes stanzas 1, 2, 4, and 6.

Paderborn

See "Because thou hast said," pages 232-33.

We would see Jesus (256)

J. Edgar Park, 1913
The hymn, whose first line was taken from Anna B. Warner's hymn "We would see Jesus, for the shadows lengthen," was written to express "youth, promise and sunshine and an inner glimpse of the Young Man of Nazareth living and moving among us." (Ronander and Porter 1966, 124) It was apparently prompted by this scripture that has spawned countless somnolent sermons: "Now among those who went up to worship at the festival were some Greeks. They came to Philip, who was from Bethsaida in Galilee, and said to him, 'Sir, we would see Jesus.'" (John 12:20-21, KJV)

In stanza 4:4, "of God and man" is changed to "of God made flesh." The hymn and tune first appeared at 93 in *Worship and Song*, 1913. (Gealy 557/515) Both entered our hymnals in 1935.

Cushman

Herbert B. Turner, 1907
The retention of this hymn perpetuates this befittingly tedious and clichéd tune.

Weary of all trumpeting (442)

Martin Franzmann, 1971
This hymn was written at the request of Jan Bender for the tune by Hugo Distler. Bender related the story of the writing of the tune and the text to Erik Routley who included it in *Companion to Westminster Praise*, 1977. Routley used a reduced form of the story in *The Music of Christian Hymns*, 1981:

> [After the Nazis] invaded Austria in 1939 [sic] . . . poets enough lauded the annexation . . . . [The] Nazis looked for a composer and found the young, gifted Distler [who composed the setting]. The words were printed on a postcard and distributed for sale. (Routley 1981, 180)

After the war Bender, still remembering the tune from his youth, set it in *Six Variations*, 1966, while looking for a poet to write new words. In 1970 he asked Martin Franzmann for a text to the tune, and Franzmann completed it the following year. It was first included at 301 in *Worship II*, 1975.

Like "Onward, Christian soldiers," this hymn employs military metaphors to call and spur on the faithful, but in Franzmann's audience, unlike the Victorian children for whom the processional was written, there are many who remember and felt the demonic and destructive force of Nazi Germany and fear the present threat of nuclear holocaust. The poet transforms the shrill sounds of martial trumpets, the symbols and metaphors of violence, hate, and war, into God's clarion call to celebrate Christ's triumph over death in a life of self-denial as partners in Christ's splendor. The hymn's theme of questioning the USA post-Vietnam global militaristic policies combined with the slight prospect of Roman Catholics singing Distler's angular tune probably merits its selection for *Worship II* as one of the most curious if not courageous feats by hymnal editors since G. K. Chesterton's prophetic "O God of earth and altar" entered *The English Hymnal*, 1906, the hymnic paradigm of establishment Anglo-Catholic propriety.

Trumpets

Hugo Distler, 1938; harm. by Richard Proulx, 1975
The tune may be more easily learned if the first two lines are taught as identities in call-and-response style, and lines 3 and 4 in half phrases. This setting was first included in *Worship II*, 1975.

We'll understand it better by and by (525)

Charles Albert Tindley, ca. 1906 (1 Cor. 13:12)
This is one of eight hymns, including "Stand by me" **(512)**, written during a difficult period of Tindley's life when negotiations were underway for the purchase of Westminster Presbyterian Church on Broad Street. It reflects that aspect of Tindley's ministry through preaching that aimed to lift the spirits of turn-of-the-century urban African Americans. This type of Tindley hymn is described by C. Eric Lincoln and Lawrence H. Mamiya as "not simply other-worldly. [These hymns] are also addressed to helping the oppressed to survive *this* world." (Lincoln and Mamiya 1990, 360) These qualities were part and parcel of his sermons. An excerpt from his famous sermon "Heaven's Christmas Tree" demonstrates how this gifted preacher-poet "would punctuate a point in his sermon with a familiar hymn from camp meetings, gospel songfests, or prayer sessions" (Jones 1982, 38) and impart hope and encouragement to his congregation:

I may be speaking to some parents who have come here hopeless of ever making anything worthwhile out of their son or daughter, or ever having their children become what they had hoped and prayed that they might be. I have a song for you:

'Tho' the cloud may hide your sun,
Ere your battle has been won,

If you still will watch and pray,
Soon will come a brighter day. (Jones 1982, 149)

This is one of Tindley's most popular hymns. It appears to have been first published in *Soul Echoes*, number 1, no date, and was included at 26 in *New Songs of Paradise*, 1941.

By and by

Charles Albert Tindley; arr. by F. A. Clark, 1906
The music for the stanzas is similar to "Leave it there" (**522**) and "God will provide for me," number 3 in *New Songs of Paradise*, 1941.

Wellspring of Wisdom (506)

Words and music: Miriam Therese Winter, 1987
This hymn was commissioned by the Hymnal Revision Committee. The poet creatively transforms water, light, and soil into fresh deity metaphors and images—Wellspring of Wisdom, Dawn of a New Day, Garden of Grace, and Call to Compassion—that enhance and facilitate our prayers for meaning, hope, and direction in a world that may be parched, dark, barren, and uncaring.

Wellspring

Harm. by Don McKeever, 1987
The poem can more effectively be used as a litany or prayer.

Were you there (288)

African American spiritual
The slave poet in this moving and solemn spiritual recasts the events of the Crucifixion in questions that bring the singer close to the anguish and shame of Jesus' death on the cross, a "death [that] was a symbol of [black slaves'] suffering, trials, and tribulation in an unfriendly world. They knew the agony of rejection and the pain of hanging from a tree." (Cone 1972, 53)

George Pullen Jackson compares lines and phrases of this Good Friday spiritual in *White Spirituals of the Southern Uplands* (1933, 276-77), and he cites a "white" version from the upper Cumberland plateau of Tennessee, "Have you heard how they crucified our Lord," in chapter 15 of *White and Negro Spirituals*, 1943. Apparently the music and words were first included in one setting in William E. Barton, *Old Plantation Hymns*, 1899. (Ronander and Porter 1966, 144) It was also included in *Songs of Evangelism for Revival and Evangelistic Services*, 1911, compiled by H. R. Christie.

The spiritual entered our hymnals in three stanzas in 1957. Our text includes stanzas from the version in John W. Work, Jr., and Frederick J. Work, *Folk Songs of the American Negro*, 1907. Other variants include another crucifixion stanza,

> I uz dere win dey took 'im down, took im,
> I uz dere when dey took 'im down,
> Oh-o! how it maes miah spirit trimble, trimble, win
> r'calls how dey took him down,   (Lovell 1972, 304)

and a resurrection stanza,

> Were you there when he rose up from the dead?
> Were you there when he rose up from the dead?
> Oh! Sometimes I feel like shouting glory, glory, glory.
> Were you there when he rose up from the dead?

Were you there

African American spiritual
adapt. and arr. by William Farley Smith, 1986

Other settings in *Songs of Zion*, 1981, and *The Methodist Hymnal*, 1966, may be used in alternation with the 1989 hymnal version.

We've a story to tell to the nations (569)

Words and music: H. Ernest Nichol, 1896

This hymn, long on preaching and short on action, is typical of hundreds that were written to express the determined, dynamic, energetic, and expansive attributes of late nineteenth-century Christian missions. It first appeared in *The Sunday School Hymnary*, 1896. (McCutchan 1942, 482) Many of these hymns have an underlying theme of condescension whereby in preaching our superior story about our superior religion and civilization we will render their inferior story, hearts, and civilization as ours—superior. Most of these hymns have been dropped from our hymnals; for example, there were twenty-eight hymns included in the section "Missions" in our 1905 hymnal.

The hymn has been retained because of its essential message of global peace and unity in Christ, notwithstanding that it suggests, as do many social gospel hymns, that God's kingdom of righteousness, having already been set before us in the life, death, and resurrection of Christ Jesus, will arrive when our telling, singing, and showing have turned the darkness to light. A more adequate hymn on the mission and witness of the church is "We utter our cry" **(439)**.

Message

This is a typical nineteenth-century Sunday school marching song.

What a fellowship, what a joy divine (133)

See "Leaning on the everlasting arms," pages 458-59.

What a friend we have in Jesus (526)

Joseph M. Scriven, ca. 1855
The poet composed the text ca. 1855 to comfort his mother "in a time of special sorrow, not intending that anyone else should see it." (Sankey 1907, 295) The hymn was first included in *Spirit Ministrel: A Collection of Hymns and Music*, 1857. (Reynolds 1976, 238) The hymn was also anonymously included at 242 in *Social Hymns, Original and Selected*, 1865 (Gealy 557/522), where a fourth stanza describes heaven as a place where praise will replace prayer:

> Blessed Jesus, thou hast promised
> Thou wilt all our burdens bear,
> May we ever, Lord, be bringing
> All to thee in earnest prayer.
> Soon in glory, bright, unclouded,
> There will be no need for prayer;
> Rapture, praise, and endless worship
> Shall be our sweet portion there.

This hymn in its warm musical setting extends the intimate characterization of Jesus as a mother, gently rocking and comforting a child, to a friend who shares and bears our sorrows, hears our prayers, and carries them to God. For additional commentary, see "Softly and tenderly Jesus is calling," page 600, and "Gospel Hymns," pages 27-30. Our 1878 hymnal was the first Methodist hymnal to include the hymn, and this appears to be among the first USA collections to match this text to our tune.

According to David Graber, editor of *Cheyenne Spiritual Songs*, the native American hymn "Jesus our friend and brother" **(659)** may have been adapted from this hymn.

Converse

Charles C. Converse, 1868
This melody is like the pentatonic folk tune that Stephen Foster could mold into a love-ballad, for example, "I dream of Jeanie with the light brown hair," that,

coincidently, bears some similarity to our tune. Converse's masterpiece of simplicity is composed for ease of learning in bar-form *aaba* and is further strengthened by the quasi antiphon "Take it to the Lord in prayer." There have been several attempts to improve the harmonies of this tune, including a fateful and futile attempt by Van Denman Thompson, who added secondary-sevenths and altered harmonies that were included in the 1935 *Methodist Hymnal*. At the 1939 uniting conference of The Methodist Church, in an unparalleled action responding to thousands of complaints from church members, the conference voted to remove that harmonization and restore the original. The tune was first included in *Silver Wings*, 1870 (McCutchan 1942, 280)

What can wash away my sin (362)

See "Nothing but the blood of Jesus," page 496.

What child is this (219)

William C. Dix, 1871 (Luke 2:6-20; Matt. 2:1-12)
Erik Routley states in *An English-Speaking Guide,* page 94, in opposition to Ellinwood (1956, 30) and others who copy Ellinwood without citation, that this nativity carol is not from *The Manger Throne*, ca. 1865, but that it first appeared at number 14 in Henry R. Bramley's and John Stainer's *Christmas Carols New and Old*, 1871, where it was apparently written for the tune GREENSLEEVES. It entered our hymnal in 1935.

Greensleeves

16th cent. English melody
Ellinwood (1956, 30) documents the sixteenth-century sources of this tune and its mention by William Shakespeare twice in his *Merry Wives of Windsor*: Falstaff's letter to Mrs. Ford in act 2 and again in act 5, scene 5. In *New Christmas Carols*, 1642, it was used to the words of the new year Waits' carol, "The old year now away is fled," included at number 28 in *The Oxford Book of Carols*, 1964. Erik Routley includes a variant of the tune from the eighteenth-century *Beggar's Opera* at 102 in the hymnal *Rejoice in the Lord*, 1958. Our setting is number 14 in Henry R. Bramley's and John Stainer's *Christmas Carols New and Old*, 1871, except the fourth step has been raised in the refrain as in *The Oxford Book of Carols*.

The stanzas of this carol may be sung by a treble voice or voices accompanied by guitar. All voices may enter on the refrain. The carol may be preceded by the reading of one of the accounts of the birth of Jesus in Matthew 2:1-12 or Luke 2:6-20. Dancers may interpret the story and the refrain.

What does the Lord require (441)

Albert F. Bayly, 1949; alt. (Micah 6:6-8)
Cyril Taylor has commented on this hymn:

> Early in his long hymn-writing career Albert Bayly wrote a series of seven-teen hymns to interpret the message of each of the Hebrew Prophets in the Old Testament, "viewing them in the light of the climax and fulfillment of the Old Testament revelation in the coming of Christ." (Taylor 1984, 30)

This hymn was first included in the poet's *Rejoice, O People*, 1950. It is one of two of Bayly's hymns that were at the front of the British hymnic explosion (the other, "O Lord of every shining constellation") and mark the transition in English language hymnody to a resurgence of the social gospel hymn and hymns embodying space-age imagery and warnings of nuclear destruction. In this regard he is widely heralded as the father of the late twentieth-century English hymn. See Fred Pratt Green, "Albert F. Bayly," *The Hymn*, 1984, for a review of Bayly's contributions to recent English hymnody.

Our text follows with slight variation the revisions that have been made since 1969 including those in *Hymns and Psalms*, 1983. The omitted stanza 4 is included to complete Micah's indictment and challenge to the powerful:

> Still down the ages ring
> the prophet's stern commands:
> To merchant, worker, king,
> he brings God's high demands:
> Do justly;
> Love mercy;
> Walk humbly with your God.

Sharpthorne

Erik Routley, 1968
Erik Routley set this text to "Tyes Cross" in the poet's *Rejoice, O People*, 1950. Routley has written that when the text was selected for *100 Hymns for Today*, 1969, its music editor, John Dykes-Bower

> having seen my tune . . . gently pointed out that I had duplicated a phrase from John Ireland's immortal tune "Love Unknown" and asked whether I would consider altering it. My immediate answer was to write a new tune, which will be seen to be a paraphrase of the old one in the minor mode. I think it was right to judge that E flat is not the key for the prophet Micah. This was included as #99 in that book and has travelled a bit since then. (Routley 1990, xxii)

The tune is named for a village near East Grinstead, Sussex, one mile from Tyes Cross.

What gift can we bring (87)

Words and music: Jane Marshall, 1980

This hymn was composed in three stanzas for the twenty-fifth anniversary of the Northaven United Methodist Church, Dallas, Texas. It was first included at 970 in *Supplement to the Book of Hymns*, 1982, where the first stanza was adapted as a summary and affirmation.

In this carefully wrought hymn the worshipper's tokens, words, and songs are called to remember and celebrate the vision and effort of those who made possible the church's worship and mission. Stanza 3 gives thanks for the future and the promise of God's guiding presence.

Anniversary song

The composer's melodic gift and her sure counterpoint are combined to produce one of the sturdiest tunes to come from the USA hymnic explosion of the 1970's and 1980's.

What wondrous love is this (292)

USA folk hymn

Marion Hatchett has found that this anonymous text appeared in print as early as Stith Mead's *General Selection of the Newest and Most Admired Hymns and Spiritual Songs Now in Use*, 1811 2d enlarged ed. (Correspondence with Carlton R. Young, May 1992) William J. Reynolds has traced a variant of the text to *Hymns and Spiritual Songs, Original and Selected*, probably published in the same year, 1811, by Starke Dupuy. (Reynolds 1976, 239) George Pullen Jackson and others have suggested that the structure of the text may have been borrowed from the English ballad "Captain Kidd." See Ellen Jane Porter and John F. Garst, "More Tunes in the Captain Kidd Meter," *The Hymn*, 1979, for the conclusion of a two-year exchange across the Atlantic; see also Alan Luff, "More on Two Early American Tunes," *The Hymn*, 1978.

The hymn entered our hymnals in a six-stanza variant with the melody in the soprano at 871 in the seventy-two selection supplement that is unindexed and appended to *The Methodist Hymnal*, 1889. It did not appear in succeeding hymnals until 1966 when two stanzas were included. Three stanzas have been added in our hymnal. The theme of the final stanza, "And when from death I'm free, I'll sing on," is similar to stanza 5 in "There is a fountain filled with blood" **(622)**.

Native American Methodists have recorded that on the third day of the 1906 Indian Mission Conference William Jimboy, the acclaimed Creek Indian Methodist evangelist, "although the last hours of his life are full of pain . . . died singing 'What wondrous love is this, oh my soul.'" (Noley 1991, 243)

Wondrous love

USA folk hymn; harm. by Paul J. Christiansen, 1955

According to Harry Eskew the tune first appeared "in the appendix of the 1840 [2d] edition of William Walker's *The Southern Harmony, and Musical Companion*, 1835." (Adams 1992, 271) In nineteenth-century shaped-note tunebooks the tune-line is printed as a mixolydian melody, C-C on the white keys with a B^b; but in performance it is invariably sung as a dorian melody, D-D, with a half-step between the seventh and eighth note of the scale. This writer, while attending his first Sacred Harp singing at Loretto, Tennessee, in 1960, noted this inconsistency and pointed it out to an elder of the singing school, who responded with a smile, "We don't always sing them as written."

Alternatives to the 1989 hymnal's SATB choral setting, which groans from having been dropped one step for unison singing, are found at 439 in *The Hymnal 1982*, 143 in *The Baptist Hymnal*, 1991, and 347 in *The United Methodist Hymnal Music Supplement*. For additional commentary on this tune, see "Wondrous Love: Three Settings with Composers' Commentaries," *The Hymn*, October 1982.

When Christmas morn is dawning (232)
När Juldagsmorgon glimmar

Attr. to Elisabeth Ehrenborg-Posse, 1856
trans. by Joel W. Lundeen, 1978 (Luke 2:7)

Marilyn Stulken has traced the origins of this hymn to *Andelig Örtegård för Barn*, 1851, where the text is credited to the German author Abel Burckhardt. The translation was prepared for the *Lutheran Book of Worship*, 1978. (Stulken 1981, 161)

In this simple pietistic children's nativity hymn the singers wish to be at Jesus' manger to see him, express their love, and ask for his guidance.

Wir hatten gebauet

German folk hymn

The tune's name is the first line of August von Binzer's text to which it was sung. It is "considered by some to be a Thuringian folksong . . . known at least as early as 1819." (Stulken 1981, 161) Our harmonization is from *The Service Book and Hymnal*, 1958. Johannes Brahms used the tune in op. 80, *Academic Festival Overture*, 1880.

When I survey the wondrous cross (298, 299)

Isaac Watts, 1707

The hymn first appeared at 189 in the section for the Lord's Supper under the inscription "VII. Crucifixion to the World by the Cross of Christ; Gal. 6:14" in the poet's *Hymns and Spiritual Songs*, 1707, Book 3. (Gealy 557/529)

Stanza 1:2 originally read "Where the young Prince of Glory died," and 4:2, "present." In the 1709 2d ed. the author bracketed the omitted stanza 4 for optional use:

> His dying Crimson like a Robe
>   Spread o'er his Body on the Tree,
> Then am I dead to all the Globe,
>   And all the Globe is dead to me. (Gealy 557/529)

Watts's hymn is especially appropriate for Maundy Thursday and Good Friday services, joining Jesus' memorial meal, passion, and death and celebrating his sacrificial redemption of humankind, described by Erik Routley as the "reckless pouring out of divine love [that] demands a reckless abandonment of earthly defences against it. The very last thing the Cross demands is an increase of specialized and fugitive holiness. The very first thing it demands is the throwing down of the barriers." (Routley 1956, 116)

Watts's passion-communion hymn, included by George Whitefield in the normative four-stanza version in his 1757 *Supplement* and subject to endless tampering in the nineteenth century, did not appear in Wesleyan collections until the 1831 British supplement, and USA Methodist collections until 1847. Yet today it is widely acclaimed as the paradigm of eighteenth-century British evangelical pastor-poet hymns.

Hamburg

Lowell Mason, 1824

This setting first appeared in *The Boston Handel and Haydn Society Collection of Church Music*, 1825 3d ed., where "Mason indicated his source as: Gregorian Chant: 'Benedictus'—see Novello's Evening Service [!]" (Ellinwood 1956, 152) There are many similar settings of Tone I and ending I in nineteenth-century tune books and our own hymnals. See also "The Lord's prayer," "Gregorian," pages 641-42.

Rockingham

Anon.; arr. by Edward Miller, 1790

This tune was derived from "Tunbridge," a 55.11 D tune in Aaron William's *Second Supplement to Psalmody in Miniature*, 1780, and Miller included his setting in *The Psalms of David for the Use of Parish Churches*, 1790. (Watson and Trickett 1988, 133) *Hymns Ancient and Modern*, 1861, was the first to match our tune to Watts's text and elicited this response from Robert Bridges in *The Small Hymn Book*: "This hymn stands out at the head of the few English hymns which can be held to compare with the best old Latin hymns of the same measure. Its true

grandeur has been almost obscured by an unfortunate musical association."
(Gealy 557/529) The tune was named after Miller's friend, the Marquis of Rockingham. (McCutchan 1957, 122) It entered our hymnals in 1889.

There is another harmonization "mostly from S. Webbe" at 292 in *Rejoice in the
Lord*, 1985, and a descant at 180 in *Hymns and Psalms*, 1983.

When in our music God is glorified (68)

Fred Pratt Green, 1972 (Mark 14:26)

This hymn, titled "Let the people sing!", celebrates the Judeo-Christian tradition
of sacred song from its roots in creation through its unique and traditional identification with worship, its potential for faithful, prophetic, and global witness to
the truth, and the disciples' song after the memorial meal and ours heralding
Jesus' resurrection. The poet's use of "Alleluia" at the conclusion of each stanza
and the paraphrase of Psalm 150 in the final stanza allude to the limitations that
mere words, even inspired words such as these, place upon the faithful to
describe adequately and express the joys of inclusion in God's creation and
redemptive act in Christ. It was included in *New Church Praise*, 1975, and all
major hymnals and supplements since that time. This text has probably been set
in anthem form more than any other of the late twentieth century.

The alteration of the opening line, "When in man's music God is glorified," to
our present form occurred in the *Lutheran Book of Worship*, 1978. That change
tends to weaken the affirmation that mere mortal musicians and their music
may and often do glorify God; and it sets aside the poet's imaginative and sure
instinct for alliteration: "**m**an's" - "**m**usic," "**G**od" - "**g**lorified." Hymnal committees are often forced to chose between aesthetics and social witness. See commentary on "Tell out, my soul," page 618.

Engelberg

Charles Villiers Stanford, 1904

The text was written for John Wilson who asked the poet for a text that might be
sung to ENGELBERG, set to "For all the saints" in the 1904 edition of *Hymns
Ancient and Modern*, but set aside by the lavish acclaim proffered Vaughan
Williams's SINE NOMINE, composed for *The English Hymnal*, 1906. "John points
out that the tune ENGELBERG should never be sung without the composer's special 'Amen,' which contains the climax of the melody." (Green 1982, 52)

Although it is often used as the opening hymn for festival gatherings of church
musicians and worship leaders, by the third stanza the hymn tends to flounder
when sung in local settings without the support of choir and organ. For additional commentary, see "We know that Christ is raised," pages 677-78.

When Israel was in Egypt's land (448)

See "Go down, Moses," pages 356-57.

When Jesus came to Jordan (252)

Fred Pratt Green, 1973 (Matt. 3:13-17; Mark 1:9-11
Luke 3:21-22; John 1:29-34)

This hymn was prompted by the poet's extended correspondence with Dirk van Dissel about the anticipated absence of liturgical office hymns in *The Australian Hymn-Book*, 1977, in particular a hymn on the baptism of Jesus. (Green 1982, 34) The development of the hymn demonstrates the poet's ability to write within strict guidelines and his generous and engaging willingness to exchange several drafts of this text with the hymnal committee or other individuals who ask for the hymn, the end result being a new conduit for transmitting a facet of the Christian faith.

In our hymnal stanza 1:4, "but as his Father's Son," has been changed to "but as the sinless one"; the change accentuates the poet's apparent contradictory references in stanza 1:3-6 to Jesus, sinful as well as sinless:

> He did not come for pardon
> but as the sinless one.
> He came to share repentance
> with all who mourn their sins.

The hymn is appropriate for the First Sunday (baptism of the Lord) after the Epiphany, or the Baptism Covenant and congregational reaffirmation of the covenant, **32-56**. Read one or more of the four accounts of Jesus' baptism before singing.

Complainer

Attr. to William Walker, 1835; harm. by Carlton R. Young, 1988

This is a setting of an upbeat major-key tune on page 18 in *Southern Harmony*, 1835, that, curiously, is set to "I am a great complainer, that bears the name of Christ," a five-stanza, blue-side-of-life hymn from which the tune's name is derived. This appears to be the only use of this tune in a denominational hymnal. It entered our hymnals in 1966 in another harmonization by the composer.

When Jesus the healer passed through Galilee (263)

Words and music: Peter D. Smith, 1975

The hymn is based on accounts of healing: stanza 1, Luke 4:31-41; stanza 2, Mark 2:3-12; stanza 3, Mark 5:22-24, 35-43; stanza 4, Mark 10:46-52; stanzas 5 and 6,

Matthew 10:5-15, Isaiah 35:6. It was written in 1975 when the author was leading a course on contemporary worship for the Iona community. (Watson and Trickett 1988, 117) The song was included at 55 in *Partners in Praise*, 1979, as one of ten contributions by the author who also served on its editorial committee.

Stanza 5:4 originally read: "Now lame leap for joy and the dumb laugh and shout," but with sensitivity to issues of discriminatory language, it was rewritten by the Hymnal Revision Committee. The original stanza 4 was also omitted:

> A deaf and dumb spirit had made a boy mad,
> Heal us, heal us today!
> His father had faith—Jesus healed the young lad,
> Heal us, Lord Jesus.

For additional commentary on hymns with perceived discriminatory language, see *"The United Methodist Hymnal*, 1989: The Language Issue," pages 131-37.

Healer

A soloist or soloists may sing the stanzas and all respond, "Heal us, heal us today." This song should be performed as a joyful dance. For comment on accompanying "dance tunes," see "The first Noel," pages 633-34.

When love is found (643)

Brian Wren, 1978

This wedding text first appeared as "Love Song," 25 in the poet's *Mainly Hymns*, 1980. It was also included at 28 in *Faith Looking Forward: The Hymns & Songs of Brian Wren with Many Tunes by Peter Cutts*, 1983. The companion text, "As man and woman we were made" **(642),** is placed on a facing page in the 1989 hymnal to facilitate the use of both hymns as weddings hymns or readings.

The poet has described both texts:

> [These] show different aspects of love between man and woman, and were both written for friends or relatives, in March 1973 and October 1978 respectively. One ["As man and woman"] is exuberant, the other more reflective. It is important that verse 2 of "When love is found" asks that love may reach out *beyond* the nuclear family, rather than the more cosy and familiar theme of inviting others *into* "home's warmth and light." (Wren "Notes" in *Mainly Hymns*, 1980)

This is one of Wren's most consistent, thoughtful, and useful texts from his early period, ca. 1968-78, attested by its rare unaltered state. Stanzas 3-4 challenge lovers to show patience and forbearance awaiting an Easter of reconciliation.

The concluding stanza tenderly links praise, love, life, and death with liturgy. The hymn is a welcome addition to the repertory of wedding and family hymns.

Gift of Love

For commentary on this tune, see "The gift of love," page 636.

When morning gilds the skies (185)
Beim frühen Morgenlicht

Katholisches Gesangbuch, 1828
sts. 1, 2, 4, trans. by Edward Caswall, ca. 1854
st. 3 by Robert S. Bridges, 1899

Leonard Ellinwood includes the German text of this hymn of praise at 237 in *The Hymnal 1940 Companion*, 1956. "Caswall's translation . . . probably . . . a third version . . . first appeared in six stanzas in Henry Formby, *Catholic Hymns*, 1854." (Gealy 557/530) (Gealy, Lovelace, Young 1970, 431) Caswall's other translation in twenty-eight 666. stanzas, included in his *Masque of Mary*, 1858 (Gealy 557/530), appears to be based on an earlier text than the 1828 version.

Hymns Ancient and Modern, 1868 Appendix, included sixteen stanzas from the 1858 version and reduced them to eight 666.D stanzas, and four stanzas of that version entered our 1901 hymnal. Stanza 3:1-2 is from Robert Bridges's five-stanza 666. 666.D translation in his *Yattendon Hymnal*, 1899 (Gealy 557/530), a text more faithful to the spirit and sense of the German hymn. Selections from it are included in most hymnals.

Caswall's departure from the German may be seen in these quaint lines from his 1858 text in our 1905 hymnal:

> My tongue shall never tire
> Of chanting with the choir; [original "in the choir"]
>   May Jesus Christ be praised:
> This song of sacred joy
> It never seems to cloy; [satiate; filled to satisfaction]
>   May Jesus Christ be praised.

Laudes Domini

Joseph Barnby, 1868

Barnby's tune is a joyous and well-constructed Victorian part-song. It first appeared at 314 in *Hymns Ancient and Modern*, 1868 Appendix, with the performance note "In quick time" and dynamic markings at the beginning, *mf* building to *f* and midpoint decreasing to *p*, followed by a long crescendo to the end. For a discussion of Barnby's compositional technique, see Erik Routley (1981, 101-02).

The tune's name means "praising" or "praises of the Lord." An introduction and interlude are included at 208-09 in *The United Methodist Hymnal Music Supplement*.

When our confidence is shaken (505)

Fred Pratt Green, 1971

This hymn titled "A Mature Faith" was included in the poet's *26 Hymns*, 1971. It affirms a God active in our doubts and the source where questions of faith return full circle. A mature faith stems from our discipline, prayer, and acceptance of God's redemptive act in Christ.

Although it was composed in the post-honest-to-God era (see page 46 in "Recent USA Hymnody"), the hymn continues to express the difficulties in addressing the disturbing questions that arise from life's experiences. As with some other topical hymns, it may be more useful in a discussion of faith. For example, the adequacy of the hymn text can be compared with biblical definitions: "Now faith is the assurance of things hoped for, the conviction of things not seen" (Hebrews 11:1), or "For just as the body without the spirit is dead, so faith without works is also dead" (James 2:26).

Grafton

From Chants Ordinaires de l'Office Divin, 1881
harm. by Basil Harwood, 1908

Our harmonization, incorrectly cited as from *The English Hymnal*, 1906, "is by the late Basil Harwood, who arranged it for *The Oxford Hymn Book*, 1908, and who also wrote a beautiful chorale prelude for organ on it (op. 58, no. 2)." (Routley 1953, 58). This tune, as PICARDY **(626)**, may have been adapted from a French folk tune (see "Let all mortal flesh keep silence," page 460, and "Latin Hymns," pages 5-6).

Because Harwood's setting was made for the solemn passion hymn "Pange lingua," "Sing, my tongue, the glorious battle" **(296)**, matters of phrasing and articulation should be carefully considered when establishing a tempo appropriate for this hymn.

When peace, like a river (377)

See "It is well with my soul," page 435.

When the church of Jesus (592)

Fred Pratt Green, 1968 (James 2:14-17)

This hymn, written in 1968 for the Stewardship Renewal Campaign of Trinity Methodist Church, London, was the poet's first effort in an amazing retirement career as a hymn writer.

698 COMPANION TO THE HYMNAL

The text embodies the 1960's controversy concerning urban churches who distanced themselves within their church buildings and liturgy from the realities and challenges of a decaying urban society. The first stanza exploits the metaphor of the closed door insulating the congregation from human suffering and need—a congregation preoccupied with hearing its own prayers. Stanza 2 the poet's call for relevance in worship, including hymn singing, adroitly draws on the Marx-Lenin's critique of religion as the opiate of the people, "lest our hymns should drug us to forget its needs." Stanza 3, the hymn's weakest and least convincing yet essential point, is directed at those who through their giving, even tithing, may attempt to salve their guilty consciences.

The story of the rewriting of the final four lines demonstrates the poet's remarkable flexibility and pastoral instincts:

> John Wilson asked questions about the last four lines of the draft and so led Fred to add a touch of encouragement in his revision. They first read:

> > Let the world rebuke us
> > By the way it gives;
> > Teach us, dying Saviour,
> > How a Christian lives!

> Fred also felt the new version avoided the difficulty that the words . . . contradicted the saying of Jesus, "Not as the world gives, give I unto you." (Green 1982, 2-3)

The hymn first entered our collections in *Supplement to the Book of Hymns*, 1982, and prompted a defensive letter from the pastor and staff of a United Methodist church with the query: "How else can you have worship unless you close the doors of the church?" (Correspondence with Carlton R. Young, 1984) Only Southern Baptists and United Methodists have included this hymn in their hymnals.

King's Weston

The poet could find no suitable tune for his hymn, described by one friend as "abrasive." Therefore, "he wrote his own tune 'Sutton Trinity' with help of musician friends. This experience taught him the value of having a tune in mind when writing a hymn." (Green 1982, 3)

For commentary on KING'S WESTON, see "At the name of Jesus every knee shall bow," page 222.

When the poor ones (434)

See "Cuando el pobre," pages 312-13.

When the storms of life are raging (512)

See "Stand by me," pages 606-07.

When we all get to heaven (701)

Eliza E. Hewitt, 1898

This hymn on anticipating heaven elaborates on the promise of Jesus, "In my Father's house there are many dwelling places. If it were not so, would I have told you that I go to prepare a place for you?" (John 14:2), with images from John's revelation: a home, "mansions bright and blessed" (Revelation 15:18), a place with "pearly gates" and "streets of gold" (Revelation 21:21), where there are no shadows (Revelation 21: 23 and 22:5) or sighs (Revelation 21:4).

Visioning life and Christian witness through these restricted though compelling biblical metaphors exemplifies the union of revivalism and adventism in much of post-Civil War Wesleyan preaching and worship, an ethos that was celebrated in seasonal and annual protracted meetings. Ocean Grove, New Jersey, where the author and composer "regularly attended the Methodist camp meetings" (Reynolds 1976, 194), is typical of the Wesleyan campgrounds that were formed, some continuing from earlier in the century, to embody indoors the spirit of the camp meeting. Participants, many with families, could experience the rigors of the original camp meeting by sparse living in huts and cottages, sometimes sleeping on the ground.

At Ocean Grove the author and composer viscerally, visually, and audibly experienced the thrilling, though carefully staged, anticipation of Paul's promise to members of the Thessalonian congregation. "[We] will be caught up in the clouds together with them to meet the Lord in the air; and so we will be with the Lord forever." (1 Thessalonians 4:17) These first-century Christians, like the Ocean Grovers after days of hearing perdition preached, had an elevated anxiety about their status at Christ's imminent return.

To sing this hymn is to remember and distinguish that part of the Wesleyan tradition that simplistically still is rejected as otherworldly and detached from the gospel's social dimensions. For additional commentary see "Gospel Hymns," pages 27-30; and "Social Gospel Hymns," pages 30-33.

The hymn was first included in *Pentecostal Praises*, 1898.

Heaven

Emily D. Wilson, 1898

This Sunday school marching tune portrays the church, its mission, and the role of the faithful Christian progressing towards a goal. In this regard for many, singing "Onward Christian soldiers" may invoke the same positive images of the church and its future as "For all the saints." It is a useful genre of Christian music whereby the faithful are assured the church is on the move, irrespective of reality. It is not unlike the practice of playing "Happy days are here again" at every Democratic national convention, a tradition that began in the 1930's with the second advent of the corner saloon, a campaign promise of Franklin Delano Roosevelt.

The original quartet version of the tune is included in *The Baptist Hymnal*, 1991.

When we are living (356)

See "Pues si vivimos," pages 563-64.

When we walk with the Lord (467)

See "Trust and obey," page 669.

Where charity and love prevail (549)
Ubi caritas et amor

9th cent. Latin; trans. by Omer Westendorf, 1961 (1 John 4:16)
This is one of several English translations completed in the 1960's, the last hymn in the Latin rite *Mandatum novum (New Commandment)* that commemorates Jesus' washing the disciples' feet. H. Myron Braun has commented on this ancient hymn:

> [It] is said to date from the ninth century . . . with its emphasis on community within the faith, on Christians holding one another in love and concern. . . . It is appropriate for. . . [Maundy Thursday] when we note the "new commandment" that we love one another, and also several times in Eastertide when the lectionary leads us to reading on love from the Gospel and epistles of John. (Braun 1982, 83)

The hymn also reflects Jesus' words to his disciples: "I give you a new commandment, that you love one another. Just as I have loved you, you also should love one another." (John 13:34) In this regard it complemented the inclusive and outgoing gestures of the post-Vatican II church and was often sung at large outdoor gatherings. Our version was first included in *The People's Hymnal*, 1961. William J. Reynolds (1976, 244-45) has included an extended and interesting commentary by Westendorf on the development of post-Vatican II Roman Catholic music. Another version of the hymn in a plainsong setting was included in *Supplement to the Book of Hymns*, 1982.

This hymn joins other standard hymns in the section of our hymnal "United in Christ" that celebrating our unity within the reality and inevitability of Christ's broken body.

St. Peter

Alexander R. Reinagle, ca. 1830
harm. from Hymns Ancient and Modern, 1861

The tune was first included in Reinagle's *Psalm Tunes for the Voice and Pianoforte,* published between 1830 and 1836. "In his *A Collection of Psalm and Hymn Tunes, Chants, and Other Music as sung in the Parish Church of St. Peter-in-the-East, Oxford,* 1840, it was named "St. Peter" after that Church, where Reinagle was organist." (Watson and Trickett 1988, 175) It apparently first entered our hymnals in 1905 in the harmonization from *Hymns Ancient and Modern,* 1861, called "St. Peter's Oxford," to distinguish it from "St. Peter," an LM version of Nikolaus Decius's "Allein Gott in der Höh," included in our previous hymnals.

Where cross the crowded ways of life (427)

Frank Mason North, 1903 (Matt. 22:9)

This is among the first of the social gospel hymns about the city and its peoples. It was composed at the suggestion of Caleb T. Winchester of the committee that prepared our 1905 hymnal and first appeared under the title "A Prayer for the Multitudes" in the June 1903 issue of *The Christian City.* In the 1905 hymnal the text was set to GERMANY to which it is usually sung in the USA.

The poet's images of wretchedness and inhumanity in stanzas 1-4 spring from his long ministry in New York City among the poor and neglected whose human needs and civil rights were constantly ignored by racist slumlords, corrupt and self-serving politicians, and greedy and union-busting business entrepreneurs. Fred D. Gealy has commented on this hymn:

> North's long intimacy with the crowds of New York's teeming streets . . . together with his Christian concern for all . . . has come to poignant and powerful expression in this hymn, based on Matthew 22:9 ["Go ye therefore unto the partings of the highways" (ARV)]. (Gealy, Lovelace, Young 1970, 433)

Stanzas 5 and 6, reflecting Revelation 22:20b, "Amen. Come, Lord Jesus," are a prayer for Jesus' return. The hymn has been included in most hymnals of this century. The author's manuscripts and library are housed at Drew University, Madison, New Jersey.

For additional commentary on hymns of the city, see "O holy city, seen of John," page 516, and "All who love and serve your city," pages 203-04.

Germany

See "Take up thy cross, the Savior said," pages 615-16.

Where he leads me (338)

E. W. Blandy, 1890 (Matt. 8:19)

This hymn calls us to obey the call of Jesus, Matthew 8:19, go with him in his passion (skipping death and resurrection), and be rewarded with grace and glory (see Matthew 7:6). It first appeared in *Pearls of Paradise*, 1891. (Reynolds 1976, 96)

Norris

John S. Norris, 1890

This tune that bears some similarity to HAPPY DAY (391) was composed for this text and first appeared with it in 1891. The chorus may be used as a prayer response.

Where shall my wondering soul begin (342)

Charles Wesley, 1738

The text is generally thought to be Charles Wesley's eight-stanza conversion hymn that was first included under the title "Christ, the Friend of Sinners" at 101-03 in part 2 of *Hymns and Sacred Poems*, 1739. (Gealy 557/534) Frank Baker has commented:

> This hymn . . . is probably the hymn to which Charles Wesley refers [Wesley 1849, 94] in his *Journal* for Tuesday 23rd May, 1738, where he speaks of his experience on Whitsunday, two days earlier, an experience which seems to have released his power of evangelical verse: 'At nine I began an hymn upon my conversion, but was persuaded to break off, for fear of pride. Mr. Bray coming, encouraged me to proceed in spite of Satan. I prayed Christ to stand by me, and finished the hymn. . . . In his name, therefore, and through His strength, I will perform my vows unto the Lord, of not hiding His righteousness within my heart.' [See the *Journal of Charles Wesley*, 1:94-95](With this last phrase cf. lines 17-18 of the hymn.)

> The following evening, 24th May, John Wesley's heart was "strangely warmed" and Charles records in his *Journal*: 'Towards ten, my brother was brought in triumph by a troop of our friends, and declared, "I believe." We sang the hymn [probably the tune: "Crucifixion Tune," 706 in *Hymns and Psalms*] with great joy, and departed with prayer.' (Baker 1962, 3)

The hymn opens with three stanzas of responses that S T Kimbrough, Jr. has commented "express the awestruck openness and vulnerability which characterized the humble, yet confident, acknowledgement of both Charles and John Wesley that they had been claimed by the gospel of Christ." (Correspondence with Carlton R. Young, August 1992)

> That I, a child of wrath and hell,
> I shall be called a child of God!

Others are questions:

> Shall I, the hallowed cross to shun,
> Refuse his righteousness to impart,
> by hiding it within my heart?

That question introduced a primary goal of the Wesleyan revival: telling everyone who would listen the good news of redemption in Christ. The balance of the hymn, also echoed in "Glory to God, and praise and love" **(58)**, composed for the first anniversary of Charles's conversion, is a call to all to believe "for you the Prince of Glory died." "Believe, and all your guilt's forgiven."

Stanzas 4 and 6 are omitted from our hymnal:

> No—tho' the Ancient Dragon rage
>   And call forth all his Hosts to War,
> Tho' Earth's self-righteous Sons engage;
>   Them, and their God alike I dare:
> Jesus the Sinner's Friend proclaim,
> Jesus, to Sinners still the same.

> Come all ye *Magdalens* in Lust,
>   Ye Ruffians fell in Murders old;
> Repent, and live: despair and trust!
>   Jesus for you to Death was sold;
> Tho' Hell protest, and Earth repine,
> He died for Crimes like Yours—and mine.

The hymn is one of a trilogy of Charles Wesley's early spiritual-autobiographical hymns in 88. 88. 88; see also "And can it be that I should gain" **(363)** and "Come, O thou Traveler unknown" **(386)**. For additional commentary on Charles Wesley's conversion and this hymn see 70-73 in Frederick C. Gill, *Charles Wesley: the First Methodist*, 1964; 400-01 in *Companion to Hymns and Psalms*, 1988; and 116-17 in John Wesley's 1780 *Collection* with commentary by F. Hildebrandt and O. Beckerlegge, 1983.

S T Kimbrough, Jr., provides additional commentary:

What a picture of the beginning of the Wesley revival: the two brothers with friends in Charles's sickroom singing stanza 4:

> Out cast of men, to you I call,
>   harlots and publicans and thieves;
> he spreads his arms to embrace you all,
>   sinners alone his grace receive.
> No need of him the righteous have;
>   he came the lost to seek and save.

This inclusive, universal summons, particularly to the dispossessed, would become the hallmark of their ministry for half a century. (Correspondence with Carlton R. Young, August 1992)

The hymn entered our hymnals in *A Selection of Hymns,* 1810, without stanza 4 and the invitation to "harlots and publicans and thieves,"—Jesus's words in Matthew 21:31-32 that appear to have offended the sensitivities of USA Methodists. It was dropped in 1849 and restored in 1966 using stanza 4. The 1966 hymnal version included two variants from the original: stanza 4:4, "receives" to "receive," which misstates Wesley theology of grace whereby it is God's grace that receives sinners; and 6:2 "in pardons" was mistakenly printed "in pardon." It may be sung to CAREY'S (SURREY) (**579**), a tune used by early Methodists for 8.8.8.8.88 hymns, or ST. CATHERINE (**710**).

Whether the Word be preached or read (595)

Charles Wesley, 1783 (2 Cor. 3:5-6)

This poem is from *MS Scriptural Hymns,* 1783, 254 items on the Old and New Testaments. (Baker 1962, 393) It appears to be an expansion of 1 Corinthians 3:6: "The letter killeth, but the spirit giveth life" (KJV). With "Come, divine interpreter" (**594**), the text prefaces the section of our hymnal designated as "The Book of the Church: Holy Scripture."

S T Kimbrough, Jr., has commented that Charles Wesley often articulated the futility of reliance merely upon the "letter of the law" as seen in this poem from *Short Hymns,* 1762, 2:337.

> Thy word in the bare *literal* sense,
>   Tho's read ten thousand times, and read,
> Can never of itself dispense
>   The saving power which wakes the dead;
> The meaning *spiritual* and true
>   The learned expositor may give,
> But cannot give the virtue too,
>   Or bid his own dead spirit live.

(Correspondence with Carlton R. Young, September 1992)

While shepherds watched their flocks by night (236)

Nahum Tate, 1700 (Luke 2:8-14)

This metrical paraphrase of Luke's nativity story is the sole contribution to survive of Nahum Tate. It was included with five other hymns for Christmas, Easter, and Holy Communion in *A Supplement to the New Version of Psalms by Dr. Brady and Mr. Tate*, 1700. (Watson and Trickett 1988, 103) In the 1717 eighth edition of the *Supplement* (Gealy 557/535), the hymn appeared under the title "Song of the Angels, at the Nativity of our Blessed Saviour, Luke II ver. 3 to ver. 14; To St. James's tune or any of the tunes of common measure printed towards the end of this Supplement." John Arnold included it at pages 4-5 in a triple meter four-part setting in A minor titled "Anthem for Christmas Day" in book 4 of *The Complete Psalmodist*, 1741. (Gealy 557/535) The hymn was apparently first included in our hymnals in 1793.

Christmas

Harmonia Sacra, 1812; arr. from G. F. Handel, 1728

This tune is based on the soprano aria "Non vi piacque ingiusti Dei," act 2 in Handel's Italian opera *Siroe* (McCutchan 1942, 122), produced by Handel in London in 1728. It first appeared as a hymn tune in *The Psalms of David for the use of Parish Churches*, 1791, ed. S. Arnold and J. W. Callcott (see John Wilson, "Handel and the Hymn Tune: II, Some Hymn Tune Arrangements," *The Hymn*, 1986). It was assured popularity when Lowell Mason included the setting from James Hewitt's *Harmonia Sacra*, 1812, in his *Boston Handel and Haydn Society Collection of Church Music*, 1821. Austin C. Lovelace suggests that the tune INNOCENTS (**675**) may also be from Handel's aria. (Gealy, Lovelace, Young 1970, 107)

Leonard Ellinwood first cited the possible influence of the fuguing tune between the soprano and tenor in measures seven and eight. (Ellinwood 1956, 107) This writer has traced that possibility to measures 23-24 at 124 in Wyeth's *Repository of Sacred Music, Part Second*, 1813, where our text is set to "Bethlehem."

The hymn entered our hymnals in *The Pocket Hymn-Book*, 1793, 13th ed., and was set to a fuguing tune in most nineteenth-century shaped-note songbooks. The tune with this text was included in our hymnals beginning with the 1859 tune edition of our 1849 hymnal. There is an interlude at 65 in *The United Methodist Hymnal Music Supplement*.

Who is he in yonder stall (190)

Words and music: Benjamin R. Hanby, 1866

This hymn on the birth, life, passion, death, resurrection, and enthronement of Jesus Christ was first included in eight stanzas at 38 in *The Dove: A Collection of*

Music for Day and Sunday Schools, Juvenile Singing Classes, and the Social Circle, 1866. It was also included in *The Amaranth*, 1872, the first Sunday school songbook that was authorized by the General Conference of the Methodist Episcopal Church, South.

Our hymnal includes stanzas 1 and 5-8 of the original and omits 2, 3, and 4:

> Who is He in yonder cot,
> Bending to His toilsome lot?
>
> Who is He who stands and weeps
> At the grave where Laz'rus sleeps?
>
> Who is He in deep distress,
> Fasting in the wilderness?

Who is he

A soloist or quartet may sing the stanzas with all joining on the refrain. Those singing this hymn for the first time invariably attempt to continue the harmonic and melodic sequence at the chorus.

Paul A. Richardson has shared information on this hymn and composer.

Whom shall I send? (582)

Fred Pratt Green, 1970 (Isa. 6:8)

This hymn was commissioned by the Presyterian Church in Canada "for a hymn which could be used in meetings challenging youth to consider the Christian ministry as a vocation." (Green 1982, 16) It was first included in the author's *26 Hymns*, 1971.

In our hymnal in stanzas 1:2, 3:1, and 4:1, "his" and "he" have been changed to "God's" and "God." The hymn may be paired with "Here I am, Lord" **(593)** in a service of commitment.

Deus tuorum militum

See "Bless thou the gifts," pages 236-37.

Wind who makes all winds that blow (538)

Thomas H. Troeger, 1983 (Acts 2: 1-13)

The text was written for Father Sebastian Falcone, dean of St. Bernard Institute, for a mass celebrating the gift of the Holy Spirit. It first appeared in *The Christian Ministry*, May 1983. The tune and text appeared together in *New Hymns for the Liturgy*, 1985.

The poet represents in striking metaphors, powerful images, and descriptive phrases the power of the wind-driven, tongues-of-fire first Pentecost in an extraordinarily well crafted prayer for the church's renewal in the Spirit.

Falcone

Carol Doran, 1985

This tune, apparently written after the text, exemplifies how to compose a hymn tune to complement the text's general statement or feeling rather than just an impressive opening line or thought. The tune typifies the composer's use of pre-pared and unprepared harmonic dissonance found in her prophetic but occasionally uneven settings of this poet's texts. This setting begins with eight measures of not-so-simple melody riding uneasily over shifting harmonies. At measure 9 the reiterated B in the melody supported by steadier harmony prepares the singer for the scale-wise ending for each stanza. The result is a perfect setting for an outstanding text.

At one point the Hymnal Revision Committee asked the poet through the editor to consider allowing the text to be set to ABERYSTWYTH **(479)** instead of FALCONE. He said "no." The text is set to ABERYSTWYTH in *The Presbyterian Hymnal*, 1990. For additional commentary on this composer's tunes see "Source and Sovereign, Rock and Cloud," page 603, and "Silence, frenzied, unclean spirit," pages 593-94.

The tune is named for Father Sebastian Falcone.

Woman in the night (274)

Brian Wren, 1982

The poet has commented that the text was prompted by an abortive Christmas carol "which I abandoned because it was stale and secondhanded" that started him thinking about "the women around Jesus . . . and the song grew from there. Having just written *The Horrors of Our Century* ['Christ is alive! Let Christians sing' **(318)**], I thought it was high time I wrote something joyful." (Wren "Notes" in *Faith Looking Forward*, 1983)

The stanzas are eight glimpses where the lives of women intersect Jesus' life and ministry: the birth of Jesus, Luke 2:6-7; a woman touches his garment, Mark 5:24-34; a woman at the well, John 4:7-30; a woman at the feast bathing his feet with her tears, Luke 7:36-50; visiting Martha in her house, Luke 10:38-42; women on the road, joining the women standing near his cross, John 19:25; and the women at the empty tomb who first tell the resurrection story, Luke 23:55-24:10.

The hymn first appeared at 15 in *Faith Looking Forward*, 1983. For another hymn that focuses on the women in Jesus' life and ministry, see "The first one ever, oh, ever to know" **(276)**.

Haiz

Charles H. Webb, 1987

The tune, following the form of the hymn, is structured like a medieval carol with the story in the stanzas. It may be sung by solo female and male voices, with the group responding on the dance-like refrain.

The composer named the tune after his mother's family name.

Wonderful words of life (600)

Words and music: Philip P. Bliss, 1874

This hymn first appeared in *Words of Life*, 1874 (Reynolds 1964, 179), and entered our hymnals in 1890. It was successfully used by Bliss in numerous evangelistic campaigns beginning in Connecticut in 1878.

Words of life

The author and his wife often performed this hymn as a duet.

Word of God, come down on earth (182)

James Quinn, 1969

The poet skillfully expands John 1:14, "And the Word became flesh and lived among us, and we have seen his glory," into a hymn that describes Jesus Christ, his life and ministry, and that prays for his return that we may hear once more his saving Word of love, his healing Word for a broken world, and the Word of life in the one Bread of the Eucharist. It may effectively be used in Advent with other hymns on the nature of Christ who is to come, for example, "O come, O come, Emmanuel" **(211)**.

The hymn was first included in *Hymns for All Seasons*, 1969.

Liebster Jesu

See "Blessed Jesus, at thy word," page 240.

Ye servants of God (181)

Charles Wesley, 1744 (Rev. 7:9-11)

This hymn of six stanzas was included at 43 and first appeared in the section entitled "Hymns to be sung in a Tumult" in *Hymns for Times of Trouble and Persecution*, 1744. (Gealy 557/537) It was composed against the background of anti-

Methodist persecution, when the followers of the Wesleys were slandered, plun-
dered, and mobbed . . . [and] often dubbed Papists and [anti-crown] Jacobites,
just as John Wesley was reputed to be the Young Pretender in disguise. (Baker
1962, 50)

The intense feelings of the wrongly accused Wesleys are expressed in the omitted stanza 4:

> Men, Devils engage, The billows arise,
> And horribly rage, And threaten the Skies:
> Their Fury shall never Our Steadfastness shock,
> The weakest Believer is built on a Rock,

and in stanza 2 of the adjoining hymn, "Omnipotent King, Who reignest on high":

> The Reprobates dare Their Master proclaim,
> And loudly declare Their Sin and their Shame;
> Presumptuous in Evil, Their God they avow,
> Their Father the Devil; And worship him Now.

While Wesley did not include the hymn in his 1780 *Collection*, it was added in
the 1797 edition using stanzas 1, 2, 4, 5, 6, and a spurious final stanza.

Shorn of two stanzas that affirm God as our refuge in struggle, "The waves of the
sea have lift up their voice . . . he always is near," the hymn was included in a number of eighteenth-century evangelical collections. In this form it entered our hymnals
in 1849 and has been maintained in them as a hymn of praise and dedication.

Hanover

See "Rejoice in God's saints," pages 564-65.

Ye watchers and ye holy ones (90)

John Athelstan Laurie Riley, 1906

This hymn was written to the tune LASST UNS ERFREUEN. The author served as
one the compilers of *The English Hymnal*, 1906, and the text first appeared there.
"Much of it is suggested by phrases from the Greek liturgies. Stanza 2 is a direct
paraphrase of the Theotokion, 'Hymn to the Mother of God,' sung at the close of
the choir office." (Ellinwood 1956, 352) The text also includes metaphors and
phrases from the fourth- and fifth-century Te Deum Laudamus. For commentary on this ancient hymn, see "Canticle of the Holy Trinity," pages 265-67, and
"Holy God, we praise thy name," pages 399-400.

The hymn entered our hymnal in the 1935 *Methodist Hymnal*.

Lasst uns erfreuen

See "All creatures of our God and King," pages 189-91.

Ye who claim the faith of Jesus (197)

Sts. 1-3, Vincent Stucky Stratton Coles, 1906
st. 4, F. Bland Tucker, 1982 (Luke 1:26-55)

The hymn first appeared in *The English Hymnal*, 1906, in seven stanzas at 218 in the section "Saints' Days: St. Mary The Virgin." *The Hymnal 1982* included the first 3 stanzas slightly altered and added F. Bland Tucker's remarkable paraphrase of lines 1, 2, 5, 11, and 12 of "Canticle of Mary" **(199)**.

The hymn is appropriate for the season of Advent and the Annunciation, March 25. See also commentary on "To a maid engaged to Joseph," page 666, and Luke 1:26-38.

Julion

David Hurd, 1983

The tune, referred to by the composer as "a generic tune," was written in 1974 and appeared with this text in *The David Hurd Hymnary*, 1983, and in *The Hymnal 1982* at its publication in 1985. A four-measure introduction, which also serves as an interlude following stanzas 2 and 3, sets the tune's gentle rocking lyrical style.

The tune is named after John Julion Mann, a friend of the composer. The composer has included a descant for stanza 4 at 191 in *The United Methodist Hymnal Music Supplement*.

You are the seed (583)

See "Sois la semilla," page 600.

You have put on Christ (609)

From the Rite of Baptism for Children, ICEL, 1969 (Gal. 3:27)

As many of you as were baptized into Christ have clothed yourself with Christ. (Gal. 3:27)

Robert Batastini comments, "This baptismal acclamation was composed to be sung following the immersion of the candidate or pouring of water upon the head of the candidate and the proclamation of the trinitarian formula." (Correspondence with Carlton R. Young, August 1992) This response may also be sung following the pastor's invitation for the parent or parents with the child, family, friends, and sponsors to gather at the font. It may also be sung after the dismissal. Teach it to the children of the congregation first; then have them share it with the adults. It is, of course, also appropriate for adult baptism and the renewal of "The Baptismal Covenant" **(32-54)**.

The response was first included in the Canadian *Catholic Book of Worship II*, 1980.

Baptized in Christ

Howard Hughes, 1977

The composer has commented that the response "should be a jaunty little procession, sort of a skipping up the aisle. By having the cantor first sing 'We have put on Christ' . . . it opens the piece up to use by the entire assembly." (Correspondence with Carlton R. Young, August 1992)

This setting first appeared in *Music for Rite of Funerals and Rite of Baptism for Children*, 1977. Bells, flute, and tambourine may also be used with keyboard as accompaniment. The tune also whistles nicely. Try it with treble and male voices alternating singing and whistling. Instructions for singing this response in canon and instrumental patterns are found at 39 in *The United Methodist Hymnal Music Supplement*.

You satisfy the hungry heart (629)

Omer Westendorf, 1977 (John 6:34; 10:1-5; 1 Cor. 10:16-17)

The poet and composer collaborated on this hymn entitled "Gift of Finest Wheat," chosen from 200 entries as the official hymn of the 41st International Eucharistic Congress, Philadelphia, 1976. It was first included in *We Celebrate with Song*, 1979, where the hymn's first line was apparently substituted for the title.

One of the most widely used communion hymns, the text is rich in biblical eucharistic imagery: stanza 1, the great shepherd of the sheep, John 10:1-5; 2, and our worthiness to partake this heavenly food, John 6:33-35; stanza 3, a paraphrase of 1 Corinthians 10:16-17; stanza 4, the mystery of the sacrament of the memorial meal; and stanza 5, the sending forth from the table to serve the world in truth and charity in the name of Jesus Christ.

Gift of finest wheat

Robert E. Kreutz, 1977

Austin C. Lovelace has supplied this information: "The composer named the tune "Bicentennial," but it was apparently changed to GIFT OF FINEST WHEAT by the editors of *Songs of the People*, 1986." (Correspondence with Carlton R. Young, September 1992)

The ingratiating refrain has been formatted for SATB voices and may be used as a response.

Your love, O God, has called us here (647)

Russell Schulz-Widmar, 1981

This hymn was written in 1981 for *The Hymnal 1982*. "The author's purpose was to write a marriage hymn that declared clearly that all love is derived from God's love and asked God's blessing not only on the person being married, but on all married couples . . . including . . . the renewal of marriage vows." (Glover 1993, 2)

Cornish

M. Lee Suitor, 1984

This gracious and flowing tune first appeared in *The Hymnal 1982*. It is a welcome alternative to the repertory of LM tunes, many of which are either too stodgy or too strident. The tune is set with this text for the first time in our hymnal.

Your love, O God (120)
Guds kärlek

Anders Frostenson, 1968; trans. by Fred Kaan, 1972

This hymn contrasts the breadth and depth of God's love with our narrow self-serving structures of mistrust and envy. It first appeared in *Psalmer och*, 1975, trial edition 1971. Fred Kaan's translation was made for *Cantate Domino*, text edition 1972, under the title "The love of God." The Swedish text was also included. For our hymnal Kaan's text with his approval was recast in inclusive language by using "you" and "your" instead of "he," "him," and "his."

The hymn was first included in a USA collection in *Ecumenical Praise*, 1977, and also appeared in *Supplement to the Book of Hymns*, 1982.

Guds kärlek

Lars Åke Lundberg, 1968; harm. by Carlton R. Young, 1988

The composer, who is also a pastor, has commented that he started writing tunes after he discovered

> that many people, especially young people, could not join in the singing of the traditional hymns to the accompaniment of organ. Their music and that of the church were miles apart. I therefore started setting texts by Anders Frostenson [and others]. (Correspondence with Carlton R. Young, 1988)

The harmonization was prepared for our hymnal. Fill in the warm pop harmonies, add bass and light brushes on a snaredrum. Do not even think of singing this to the suggested alternate tune FINLANDIA.

BIOGRAPHIES

Abelard, Peter, born Pallet, France, 1097; died Priory of St. Martel, 21 April 1142. He was known as the "first of the modernists" for his critical appraisal of scripture and the church fathers; lecturer at Notre Dame Cathedral at age twenty-two. Abelard suffered emasculation for his romance and marriage to Héloise, the daughter of Canon Fulbert, after which both joined orders. He died on the way to Rome to appeal his conviction for heresy. Author: "O what their joy and their glory must be," **727.**

Achon, Rachel. See **Gutiérrez-Achon, Rachel.**

Ackley, Alfred Henry, born Spring Hill, PA, 21 January 1887; died Whittier, CA, 3 July 1960. He studied composition and harmony under Hans Kronald in New York and at the Royal Academy of Music in London, where he became an accomplished cellist. Graduated from Westminster Theological Seminary, Ackley was ordained in 1914, serving churches in Pennsylvania and California. He compiled hymnals and songbooks for Rodeheaver Publishing Company. Of Ackley's 1,500 hymns, gospel songs, children's songs, secular, and college glee club songs, "He Lives" remains the most popular. Ackley was awarded an honorary Doctor of Sacred Music degree by John Brown University, Siloam Springs, Arkansas. Author and composer: "He Lives" (ACKLEY), **310.**

Adams, Sarah Fuller Flower, born Harlow, Essex, England, 22 February 1805; died London, England, 14 August 1848. Born into a literary family, she was a poet and Shakespearian actress. Her poems were published in *Unitarian Monthly Repository* and later in *Hymns and Anthems,* 1840-41. Other writings include a children's catechism and dramatic poetry. Author: "Nearer, my God, to thee," **528.**

Adebesin, Biodun Akinremi Olvsoji, born Lagos, Nigeria, 1 January 1928. Adebesin began the study of piano at age nine and earned a Cambridge certificate. He is an associate of the Royal College of Music. As a jazz musician he has performed in and led many groups, including his Hot Shots and the African Cultural Group Band. Translator: "Jesus, we want to meet," **661.**

Adkins, Leon McKinley, born Ticonderoga, NY, 14 July 1896; died Nashville, TN, 11 October 1986. A Methodist pastor and administrator, serving congregations (1921-55) and the Board of Education of The Methodist Church (1955-66), he was the author of many poems on the life and work of the church. Author: "Go make of all disciples," **571.**

Ahle, Johann Rudolf, born Mülhausen, Thuringia, 24 December 1625; died Mühlausen, 8 July 1673. He studied at Göttingen and Erfurt, and later became organist at St. Blasius' Church in Mülhausen (1649) and mayor (1661). Ahle was a composer of sacred arias in the Italian style, cantatas, organ and instrumental music, and spiritual songs. Composer: LIEBSTER JESU, **182, 596.**

Ahner, Sally, born Christiansburg, VA, 11 July 1948. A lyric soprano and teacher, she received the B.A. in music from Salem College, North Carolina

(1970), M.A. in music theory, Eastman School of Music (1974), diploma, cum laude, Franz Schubert Institut, Austria (1988), with further study with Sharon Mabry. Composer: "Hear us, O God," **490;** "This is our prayer," **487.**

Akers, Doris Mae, born Brookfield, MO, 21 May 1922. Akers wrote her first gospel song at the age of ten, and despite the lack of formal musical training, she has conducted choirs throughout the nation. According to William J. Reynolds, Akers has described her ability to capture the attention of the congregation as "just letting go and releasing the Spirit of God." (Adams 1992, 284) Author and composer: "There's a sweet, sweet Spirit in this place" (SWEET, SWEET SPIRIT), **334.**

Albright, William Hugh, born Gary, IN, 20 October 1944. Educated at the Juilliard Preparatory Department, University of Michigan (B.A. 1966, M.A. 1967, Ph.D. 1970), and Paris Conservatoire, he has taught at the University of Michigan since 1970, serving as associate director of the electronic music studio there. His teachers included Finney, Rochberg, and Messiaen for composition and Marilyn Mason for organ. He has written prolifically for instruments and voices and has received numerous awards, including two Koussevitzky composition awards, a Fulbright Fellowship, an American Academy of Arts and Letters award and the Queen Marie-Jose Prize. Composer: ALBRIGHT, **563.**

Alexander, Cecil Frances, born Redcross, County Wicklow, England, 1818 or 1823; died Londonderry, Ireland, 12 October 1895. The author of over 400 hymns, many for children, Alexander published her works in *Hymns for Little Children,* 1848, containing paraphrases of articles from the Apostles' Creed. Author: "All things bright and beautiful," **147;** "Jesus calls us o'er the tumult," **398;** "Once in royal David's city," **250.**

Alexander, James Waddell, born Hopewell, VA, 13 March 1804; died Sweetsprings, VA, 31 July 1859. A graduate of Princeton Seminary, Alexander served Presbyterian congregations in New Jersey and New York City and on the faculties of the College of New Jersey and Princeton Seminary. He translated Latin and German hymns. Translator: "O sacred Head, now wounded," **286, 752** (Antiphon).

Alford, Henry, born London, England, 7 October 1810; died Canterbury, England, 12 January 1871. He was educated at Trinity College, Cambridge, was ordained in 1833, and served in parishes and as dean of Canterbury. Although he was from a long line of Anglican clergy, Alford maintained close ties with evangelicals and independents. He was famous for his commentary on the Greek New Testament, a standard work in his time. Author: "Come, ye thankful people, come," **694.**

Allen, George Nelson, born Mansfield, MA, 7 September 1812; died 9 December 1877. He was a graduate and faculty member of Oberlin College where he established choral and instrumental music education programs that lead to the Conservatory of Music. Nelson also wrote hymn texts. Composer: MAITLAND, **424**.

Alves, Rubem. A twentieth-century theologian and teacher from Brazil, he is the author of *I Believe in the Resurrection of the Body*, 1986. Author: "Bread and Justice," **639**; "Freedom in Christ," **360**.

Ambrose of Milan, born Treves [Germany], ca. 337-40; died Milan, Italy, 4 April 397. A staunch supporter of the Nicene faith against the Arians, Ambrose was elected bishop of Milan at age 34. Most famous for his organization of the Milan liturgy, which became known as Ambrosian chant, he brought hymn singing to congregations, especially through antiphonal psalmody. His texts are notable for their artistic simplicity and mark a departure in Western hymnody from nonmetrical to metrical. Author: "O spendor of God's glory bright," **679**.

Anderson, Boris. No information is available on Anderson. Co-translator: "God created heaven and earth," **151**.

Anderson, Clare. No information is available on Anderson. Co-translator: "God created heaven and earth," **151**.

Antes, John, born Frederickstownship, near Bethlehem, PA, 24 March 1740; died Bristol, England, 17 December 1811. He was educated in his father's boys' school, became a watchmaker and a clock maker, and invented a device that would turn pages while the violinist was playing. Antes composed twenty-five short anthems in the style of Michael Haydn with both English and German texts. In 1769 he went to Egypt as a Moravian missionary where he was beaten and crippled. He moved to Germany in 1781, and in 1783 he settled in England. Antes's three string trios were discovered in 1949 and are considered the first chamber music by a USA-born composer. Attributed composer: MONKLAND, **194**.

Arne, Thomas Augustine, born London, England, 12 March 1710; died London, 5 March 1778. One of the most important native English composers of the eighteenth century, Arne wrote dramatic works and many instrumental compositions, including the famous "Rule Britannia!" He was among the first to introduce women's voices into choral writing. Composer: ARLINGTON, **511**.

Arthur, John W., born Mankato, MN, 25 March 1922; died Palo Alto, CA, 15 August 1980. Educated at Gustavus Adolphus College, St. Peter, Minnesota (B.A., B.M. 1944), he also studied at Wartburg Theological Seminary, Augustana Theological Seminary, Rock Island, Illinois (B.D.), and Western Theological Seminary in Pittsburgh, Pennsylvania (M.Theo.). Ordained in 1946, Arthur served in Pennsylvania, New York, and California. He was western regional secretary for the Division of College and University Work of the National Lutheran Council (1960-67) and a professor at Lutheran School of Theology, Chicago, where he served on many worship committees and published, with Daniel Moe, *Contemporary Liturgy*, 1963, among other works. Translator: "This is the feast of victory," **638**.

Asuncion, Francisca, born Manila, Philippines, 1 November 1927. She was educated at Union Theological Seminary (B.S.M.), Union Theological Seminary, Philippines, and at Westminster Choir College (M.Mus.). Asuncion has served as choral conductor and accompanist in Manila, head of the music department at Philippine Christian College, and as a faculty member at Union Theological Seminary (Philippines). In addition to adapting Philippine folk songs, she has published *The Seed of Life Is Sown*. Author and arranger: "Dear Lord, lead me day by day" (COTTAGE GROVE), **411**.

Atkinson, Frederick Cook, born Norwich, England, 21 August 1841; died East Dereham, England, 1897. He served as organist and choirmaster in various English parishes, and composed services, anthems, songs, and piano pieces. Composer: MORECAMBE, **500**.

Augustine of Hippo, born Tagaste (Souk-Ahras), 354; died 430. He was one of the four Latin fathers and bishop of Hippo. Augustine's influence on Christianity is considered second only to that of the apostle Paul's. Roman Catholics and Protestants consider him the founder of theology. He is the author of *City of God* and *Confessions*. Author: "Finding rest in God," **423**.

Avery, Richard Kinsey, born Visalia, CA, 26 August, 1934. A member of "Avery and Marsh," contemporary worship leaders since the late 1960's, he was educated at the University of Redlands (B.A.) and Union Theological Seminary (M.Div.). He composed more than 100 hymns and with Donald Marsh cofounded Proclamation Productions, Inc. Co-author and co-composer: "We are the church" (PORT JERVIS), **558**.

Avila, Rubén Ruíz. See Ruíz, Rubén Avila.

Babcock, Maltbie Davenport, born Syracuse, NY, 3 August 1858; died Naples, Italy, 18 May 1901. A gifted and effective preacher, Babcock was educated at Syracuse University (1879) and Auburn Theological Seminary (1882) where he was known as an athlete and musician. He served congregations of the Presbyterian Church including the Brick Presbyterian Church in New York City, where he succeeded Henry Van Dyke. His hymns appear in *The School Hymnal*, 1899, and the posthumous *Thoughts for Every-Day Living*, 1901. Author: "This is my Father's world," **144**.

Bach, Johann Sebastian, born Eisenach, Thuringia, 21 March 1685; died Leipzig, 28 July 1750. Bach's career marks the culmination of the baroque era and may be divided into three major periods: Weimar, 1708-17 (earlier works also from Mühlhausen), Cöthen, 1718-23, and Leipzig, 1723-50. His music lay dormant after his death until revived in the nineteenth century by Felix Mendelssohn and others, including Samuel Wesley. The chorale cantatas of Bach, written according to the church year, combine harmonizations of the classic sixteenth-century chorale with settings of devotional texts from various sources, including Bach himself. The harmonizations included in our hymnal are primarily extracted from the passions and cantatas. See also Karl Geiringer, *J. S. Bach: The Culmination of an Era*, 1966. Harmonizer: CHRIST LAG IN TODESBANDEN, **319;** DU FRIEDENSFÜRST, HERR JESUS CHRIST, **683;** ERHALT UNS HERR, **265;** ERMUNTRE DICH, **223;** JESUS, JOY OF MAN'S DESIRING, **644;** JESU, MEIN FREUDE, **532;** NUN KOMM, DER HEIDEN HEILAND, **214;** O WELT, ICH MUSS DICH LASSEN, **631;** PASSION CHORALE, **286;** RESPONSE, **771;** VATER UNSER, **414;** WACHET AUF, **720;** WIE SCHÖN LEUCHTET DER MORGENSTERN, **247.**

Baker, Henry Williams, born Belmont House, Vauxhall, England, 21 June 1821; died, Monkland, England, 12 February 1877. Educated at Trinity College, Cambridge (1844, 1847), he was ordained in 1844 and knighted in 1859. Baker was a composer, author, translator, and chairman of the committee that prepared *Hymns Ancient and Modern*, 1861. Translator: "Of the Father's love begotten," **184;** author: "The King of love my shepherd is," **138**.

Baker, Philip Eldridge, born Burkburnett, TX, 27 November 1934. Educated at Midwestern University, Wichita Falls, Texas (B.A. 1957), and Southern Methodist University, Dallas, Texas (M.M. 1966), he has served Highlands Park United Methodist Church in Dallas, Texas, since 1959. He received the distinguished alumni award from Midwestern University and has published several anthems, including "Easter Anthem," "Isaiah's Song," and "O Savior Sweet." Composer: "Amen," **903**.

Baker, Theodore, born New York, NY, 3 June 1851; died Dresden, Germany, 13 October 1934. Author, translator, and musicologist, he was educated in Leipzig (Ph.D. 1882). Baker is most famous for his *Biographical Dictionary of Music and Musicians* (1900 first edition, continuing to the present). He was influential in the promotion of USA music and composers. Translator: "Lo, how a Rose e'er blooming," **216;** "We gather together," **131."**

Bakewell, John, born Brailsford, Derbyshire, England 1721; died Lewisham, England, 18 March 1819. Bakewell was an early itinerant preacher and advocate of the Wesleyan movement in London. He is buried near John Wesley at City Road Chapel. Attributed author: "Hail, thou once despised Jesus," **325**.

Baring-Gould, Sabine, born Exeter, England, 28 January 1834; died Lew-Trenchard, Devonshire, England, 2 January 1924. An Anglican choir master, deacon, and rector educated at Clare College, Cambridge (1854, 1856), he had a variety of interests, including folk music, poetry, fiction, biography, and history, and was influential in the English folk music movement. In this latter regard he set the stage for the work of Cecil J. Sharp. His most famous hymns were written for children. Author: "Onward, Christian soldiers," **575**.

Barnby, Joseph, born York, England, 12 August 1838; died London, England, 28 January 1896. A precocious Anglican choirmaster and organist who began his musical contributions to the church at age seven as a choirboy, he became organist at Yorkminster at the age of twelve. Among the many positions he held was principal of the Guildhall School of Music. He was knighted in 1892. In addition to hymn tunes, his compositions include an oratorio, services, motets, anthems, and organ and piano pieces. Composer: LAUDES DOMINI, **185**; PERFECT LOVE, **645**.

Barnes, Edward Shippen, born Seabright, NJ, 14 September, 1887; died Idyllwild, CA, 14 February, 1958. An American organist and composer, he studied under Horatio Parker and David Stanley Smith at Yale University. Barnes served as organist at St. Stephen's Episcopal Church, Philadelphia, and at the First Presbyterian Church, Santa Monica, California. He composed two organ symphonies, much sacred music, and books of organ arrangements. Arranger: "Angels we have heard on high," **238**.

Bartlett, Eugene Monroe, Sr., born Waynesville, MO, 24 December 1885; died Siloam Springs, AR, 25 January 1941. Bartlett was educated at Hall-Moody Institute, Martin, Tennessee, and at the William Jewell Academy, Independence, Missouri (1913-14). From 1918 to 1935 he published many songbooks and edited a music magazine, *Herald of Song*, as president of Hartford Music Company, Hartford, Arkansas. According to Paul Hammond, Bartlett was later affiliated with the Stamps-Baxter Music Company, Dallas, Texas, and the James D. Vaughan Music Company, Lawrenceburg, Tennessee. (Adams 1992, 293) Known also as a gospel singer and composer, Bartlett is best known for his song "Victory in Jesus." He was inducted as a member of the Gospel Music Hall of Fame in 1979. Author and composer: "I heard an old, old story" (HARTFORD), **370**.

Batastini, Robert J., born Chicago, IL, 1 January 1942. Bastastini is the current vice-president and senior editor of GIA Publications, Inc., Chicago, Illinois. He received his music education and church music degrees from De Paul University, School of Music, Chicago. While serving as director of music at St. Barbara Parish, Brookfield, Illinois, he received the 1981 Outstanding Parish Award from the National Association of Pastoral Musicians. Since 1991 he has served as director of music at St. Joseph Parish, Downers Grove, Illinois. Bastastini has been active in the Hymn Society in the United States and Canada as a member of the executive committee (1982-88) and as president (1986-88). As executive editor and project director, he published the *Worship* hymnal series and the *Gather* hymnal. He is the author of numerous articles for *The Hymn, The American Organist*, and other publications. Author (in conjunction with the Community of Taizé): "Eat this bread," **628**; harmonizer: PETITIONS LITANY, **485**.

Bateman, Christian Henry, born Wyke, near Halifax, Scotland, 9 August 1813; died Carlisle, England, July 1889. He was a Congregational minister, was ordained into the Church of England, and his hymns were contained in two widely published children's hymnals. Author: "Come, Christians, join to sing," **158**.

Bates, Katharine Lee, born Falmouth, MA, 12 August 1859; died Wellesley, MA, 28 March 1929. Educated at Wellesley College and later head of the that college's English department, Bates was the author or co-author of over twenty collections and books. Author: "America the beautiful," **696**.

Baxter, Lydia, born Petersburg, NY, 8 September 1809; died New York, NY, 22 June 1874. Baxter was converted through the preaching of Baptist missionary Eben Tucker. She formed the Baptist church at Petersburg and later moved to New York where her home was a center for preachers and evangelists. Author: "Precious name," **536**.

Bayly, Albert Frederick, born Bexhill on Sea, Sussex, England, 6 September 1901; died Chichester, 26 July 1984. Bayly was educated for the ministry at Mansfield College, Oxford (1925-28), and served as a Congregational minister in England. His best known book of verse is *Again I Say Rejoice*, 1967. His later hymns mark the beginning of the British hymnic explosion. In 1968 he was named an honorary fellow of Westminster Choir College, Princeton, New Jersey. Author: "Lord, whose love through humble service," **581**; Response, **772**; "What does the Lord require," **441**.

Beck, Harrell Frederick, born Lyons, NE, 2 March 1922; died Lexington, MA, 10 December 1987. A celebrated lecturer, preacher and teacher who was educated at Boston University School of Theology (M.A. 1945, Ph.D. 1954). Beck was dean of the School of Oriental Studies, American University, Cairo, Egypt (1945-54); professor, Boston University School of Theology (1954-87); and visiting professor at several universities. He is the author of numerous articles on religion, including "The History of Israel" in *The Interpreter's One-Volume Commentary of the Bible*, 1971. Beck, with John Holbert, S T Kimbrough, Jr., and Alan Luff, was a member of the Psalms text committee that prepared The United Methodist Liturgical Psalter. Adapter: "Canticle of Wisdom," **112**; author: Responses, **832**, **849**.

Beck, John Ness, born Warren, OH, 16 February 1930; died Columbus, OH, 25 June 1987. A graduate of Ohio State University (B.A., B.S. 1952), Beck later taught music theory and directed musicals there. He also served as music director at University Baptist Church and operated the University Music House. He was president and co-founder of Beckenhorst Press and chairman of the board of the John Ness Beck Foundation, established in memory of Randall Thompson and Joseph Clokey for composers and arrangers of traditional American choral music. A well-known composer of anthems, hymns, and vocal solos, Beck has published 120 works. Composer: ACCEPTANCE, **560**.

Beethoven, Ludwig van, born Bonn, Germany, 16 December 1770; died Vienna, Austria, 1827. Beethoven brought to full maturity the classical sonata, concerto, string quartet, and symphony. His sacred works include Mass in C, Mass in D (*Missa Solemnis*), and *Christus am Oelberg* (*Christ on the Mount of Olives*). Several of his themes have been adapted as hymn tunes. See also *Baker's Biographical Dictionary of Music and Musicians*. Composer: HYMN TO JOY, **89, 702**.

Bell, Maurice Frederick, born London, England, 1862; died ca. 1931. Educated at Hertford College, Bell served as vicar of St. Mark's Church, Regent's Park,

London, from 1904 to his death. He contributed to *The English Hymnal*. His book *The Art of Church Music*, 1909, was based on his experiences in the church as a chorister, precentor, organist, and priest. Harmonizer: MIT FREUDEN ZART, **126**.

Bennard, George, born Youngstown, OH, 4 February 1873; died Reed City, MI, 10 October 1958. As the sole supporter of his widowed mother and family he never received a formal education. He became a Salvation Army worker and later worked as a Methodist evangelist in the northern Middle West and Canada. Bennard wrote some 300 hymns. Author and composer: "The old rugged cross" (THE OLD RUGGED CROSS), **504**.

Bennett, Robert Charles, born Houston, TX, 10 November 1933. Diaconal minister of music at St. Luke's United Methodist Church in Houston since 1954 and organ instructor at St. Thomas University in Houston, Bennett holds degrees from the University of Houston, Trinity College, London, and Southwestern University (D.Mus.). He has been active in the American Guild of Organists and has served as dean and convention chair numerous times. A past president of the Fellowship of United Methodists in Worship, Music, and Other Arts, Bennett has taught organ, hymnody, hymn arranging, voice, conducting, cantata and choral repertoire. He served as chair of the tunes subcommittee for the Hymnal Revision Committee of *The United Methodist Hymnal*, 1989. He has concertized in Europe, Mexico, the USA, Great Britain, and the Orient. In 1979 he received the Music Leadership award of Sigma Alpha Iota. Harmonizer: SHENG EN, **633**.

Bennett, William Sterndale, born Sheffield, England, 13 April 1816; died London, England, 1 February 1875. Bennett was a distinguished English pianist, conductor, and composer, and friend of Robert Schumann and Felix Mendelssohn. As professor of music at Cambridge University and principal of the Royal Academy of Music (1866), he amassed many honors and was knighted by Queen Victoria in 1871. With Jenny Lind's husband, he edited Catherine Winkworth's *Choral Book for England*, 1863. Bennett was buried in Westminster Abbey. Harmonizer: LOBE DEN HERREN, **139**.

Benson, Louis FitzGerald, born Philadelphia, PA, 22 July 1855; died Philadelphia, 10 October 1930. He was educated at the University of Pennsylvania in law, admitted to the bar in 1877, and later entered Princeton Theological Seminary and ordained in 1886. His vast hymnological collection is housed in the library at Princeton Seminary. His monumental *English Hymn*, 1915, established him as one of the most renowned hymnologists in the USA. Besides his editing of numerous hymnals, included the paradigmatic Presbyterian *Hymnal*, 1895, Benson's *Hymnody of the Western Church*, 1930, stands as a major work on the history of Western hymnody. Author: "For the bread which you have broken," **614**, **615**; "O sing a song of Bethlehem," **179**.

Bernard of Clairvaux, born Castle Fountaines, near Dijon, France, 1090 or 1091; died Clairvaux, 20 August 1153. The greatest religious force of his age, he founded in 1115 the Cistercian monastery of Clairvaux where he was abbot until his death. He was canonized twenty-one years after his death and declared a doctor of the church in 1830. Attributed author: "Jesus, the very thought of thee," **175**.

Berthier, Jacques, born 1923. Organist of Saint-Ignace in Paris, composer, accompanist, and recitalist, he lives in Paris and maintains a close relationship with the Taizé community near Cluny in Burgundy. Co-composer: "Gloria, gloria," **72**; "Jesus, remember me," **488**; "Kyrie eleison," **484**; "Prepare the way of the Lord," **207**; composer: "Eat this bread," **628**.

Bianco of Siena, born Anciolina, in the Val d'Arno, date unknown; died Venice, Italy, ca. 1434. He was a member of the Order of Jesuits, an Augustine order that was abolished in 1668. His *Laudi Spirituali* is a collection of vernacular devotional hymns. Author: "Come down, O Love divine," **475**.

Blanchard, Richard Eugene, born Chungking, China, 14 March 1925. Son of Methodist missionaries to China, he received the B.A. from Mercer University (1947) and the B.D. from Emory University (1949); he was ordained in 1950. Blanchard served as senior pastor of many large United Methodist churches in Florida, including Conway Methodist Church in Orlando and First Methodist Church in Jacksonville. His published works include books, articles, and twenty-three songs. At least thirty hymnals include "Fill my cup, Lord." Author and composer: "Fill my cup, Lord," **641**.

Blandy, E. W., nineteenth century. No information is available on Blandy. Author: "I can hear my Savior calling," **338**.

Bliss, Philip Paul, born Clearfield County, PA, 9 July 1838; died Ashtabula, OH, 29 December 1876. An itinerant Baptist music teacher who gained some formal training during summers at the Normal Academy of Music in Genesco, New York, Bliss was influenced by Dwight L. Moody to become a singing evangelist. Bliss led music in revivals in the South, Middle West, and East, including those led by Major D. W. Whittle. He and his wife died in a train wreck near Ashtabula. Author: "Hallelujah! What a Savior," **165**; composer: VILLE DU HAVRE, **377**; author and composer: "Wonderful words of life" (WORDS OF LIFE), **600**.

Bode, John Ernest, born St. Pancras, England, 23 February 1816; died Castle Camps, Cambridgeshire, England, 6 October 1874. An Anglican priest educated at Eton, Charterhouse, and Christ Church, Oxford (1837, 1840), Bode was an important literary figure of his day, giving the 1855 Bampton Lectures at Oxford and producing a large output of poetry, including *Hymns from the Gospel of the Day, for Each Sunday and the Festivals of Our Lord*, 1860. Author: "O Jesus, I have promised," **396**.

Bonar, Horatius, born Edinburgh, Scotland, 19 December 1808; died Edinburgh, 31 July 1889. Bonar was educated at the University of Edinburgh, where he was influenced by Thomas Chalmers. A visit to the Holy Land (1855-56) directed his preaching and writing toward fulfillment of Jewish prophecy and the Second Coming. He was editor of the *Journal of Prophecy* and wrote many hymns that appeared in Scottish, English, and USA hymnals. Author: "Here, O my Lord, I see thee," **623**.

Bonhoeffer, Dietrich, born Breslau, Germany, 4 February 1906; died Flossenburg, Germany 9 April 1945. A skillful athlete and pianist in his youth and the son of a noted physician, Bonhoeffer studied theology at Tübingen in 1923 and obtained his doctorate from the University of Berlin in 1927. He spent a year at Union Theological Seminary, New York, learning of the inequality of African Americans and studying their spirituals. He returned to Germany in 1931 to teach systematic theology, and in 1933 he publicly spoke against Hitler. He wrote *Ethics*, 1935, *Life Together*, 1938, and *The Cost of Discipleship*, 1959. On April 5, 1943, following the unsuccessful plot to assassinate Hitler, he was imprisoned at Tegel. At his execution by hanging, his parting words to his fellow prisoners were,"This is the end, but for me it is the beginning of life." Author: "At the close of Day," **689**; "By gracious powers," **517**.

Borthwick, Jane Laurie, born Edinburgh, Scotland, 9 April 1813; died Edinburgh, 7 September 1897. With her sister, Sarah Findlater, she translated German hymns into English. Besides her work in hymnody she actively supported missions and social agencies throughout her life. Translator: "Be still, my soul," **534, 746**.

Bortniansky, Dimitri Stepanovitch, born Glukhov, Ukraine, 28 October 1752; died St. Petersburg, 10 October 1825. He was educated in both Russia and Italy. Bortniansky was a prolific composer of choral and vocal music and in 1776 became the director of vocal music at the court chapel in St. Petersburg. His choral music has been widely performed in Europe and the USA. The collected choral works, edited and published ca. 1884 by Tschaikowsky, comprise ten volumes. Attributed composer: ST. PETERSBURG, **153**.

Bourgeois, Louis, born Paris, France, ca. 1510; died ca. 1561. Bourgeois was the cantor and choirmaster at St. Peter's Church in Geneva where John Calvin gave him responsibility for the musical editorship of the Genevan Psalter from 1542 to 1557. He was a skillful composer and adapter of existing melodies with many compositions attributed to him. Composer: LE CANTIQUE DE SIMÉON, **686**; attributed composer: OLD 100TH, **75, 95, 621**; RENDEZ À DIEU, **565**;

Bowie, Walter Russell, born Richmond, VA, 8 October 1882; died Alexandria, VA, 23 April 1969. He was educated at Harvard (1904, 1905) and Virginia Theological Seminary (1909) and served as an Episcopal priest, hospital chaplain in France during World War I, and professor at the Protestant Episcopal Seminary in Virginia. His distinguished career as a scholar, teacher, and social prophet includes membership on the committee preparing the Revised Standard Version of the Bible. Hymns by Bowie appear in both USA and British hymnals. Author: "O holy city, seen of John," **726**.

Bowring, John, born Exeter, England, 17 October 1792; died, Exeter, 23 November 1872. One of the world's outstanding linguists, he claimed to read 200 and speak 100 languages. Bowring was active in social and economic reforms, became a member of Parliament in 1835, and later served in diplomatic positions in China. Queen Victoria knighted him in 1854. His writings, including hymns, comprise thirty-six volumes. Author: "In the cross of Christ I glory," **295**.

Boyce, William, born London, England, 7 February 1710; died Kensington, London, 16 February 1779. One of England's most important eighteenth-century composers, Boyce studied with Maurice Greene and served in several parishes, including Chapel Royal. Increasing deafness turned his career from performing to editing and composing. Boyce's great work, begun by Maurice Greene, is *Cathedral Music*, three volumes of sixteenth-, seventeenth-, and eighteenth-century English church music. His works include instrumental, organ, choral, and incidental theatrical music. Composer: "Canticle of Praise to God (Venite Exultemus)," **91**.

Boynton, Charles, born Carnegie, OK, 24 January 1943; died Anadarko, OK, 9 September 1988. Educated at Southwestern Oklahoma University in piano and voice, Boynton became the music director and organist of the Oklahoma Indian Missionary Conference. He was the son of Libby Littlechief Ahtone. Arranger: KIOWA, **330**.

Bradbury, William Batchelder, born York, MD, 6 October 1816; died Montclair, NJ, 7 January 1868. Born into a musical family, Bradbury moved to Boston to study with Summer Hill and came under the influence of Lowell Mason. In Brooklyn and New York City, he played the organ and organized singing classes. After studying in England and Germany, he returned to New York to devote his time to teaching, music conventions, normal institutes, composing, and editing. Composer: BRADBURY, **381**; HE LEADETH ME, **128**; HUDSON, **359**; JESUS LOVES ME, **191**; OLIVE'S BROW, **282**; SWEET HOUR, **496**; THE SOLID ROCK, **368**.

Brébeuf, Jean de, born Condé-sur-Vire, France, 25 March 1593; died Saint-Ignace, Quebec, 16 March 1649. A Jesuit priest who began a mission among the Hurons in the early seventeenth century, he wrote the earliest Canadian carol in existence. De Brébeuf taught at the Collège in Rouen and was steward, minister, and confessor at the Collège in Eu. In 1626 and 1633 he traveled 800 miles by canoe from Quebec to live with the Bear tribe. He suffered a torturous death during an Iroquois massacre. Author: "'Twas in the moon of wintertime," **244**.

Bridgers, Luther Burgess, born Margaretsville, NC, 14 February 1884; died Atlanta, GA, 27 May 1948. He began to preach at the age of seventeen, and after attending Asbury College, Wilmore, Kentucky, Bridgers served as a Methodist pastor for more than twelve years. While he was conducting a revival meeting in 1910, his wife and three sons died in a fire at his father-in-law's home in Harrodsburg, Kentucky. In 1914 he remarried and became a general evangelist for the Methodist Episcopal Church, South. Briefly engaging in mission work in Belgium, Czechoslovakia, and Russia after World War I, he later served pastorates in Georgia and North Carolina. Author and composer: "There's within my heart a melody," **380**.

Bridges, Matthew, born Malden, Essex, England, 14 July 1800; died Devonshire, England, 6 October 1894. He grew up in the Church of England but became a Roman Catholic in 1848 under the influence of the Oxford movement. He spent the latter part of his life in Quebec, Canada. His poems were introduced in the USA through Henry Ward Beecher's *Plymouth Collection*, 1855. Author: "Crown him with many crowns," **327**.

Bridges, Robert Seymour, born Walmer, Kent, England, 23 October 1844; died Boar's Hill, Abingdon, Berkshire, England, 21 April 1930. Bridges was an English poet laureate, scholar, hymnologist, musician, and physician. He was educated at Eton and Corpus Christi College, Oxford, and St. Bartholomew's Hospital, London, but he gave up medicine because of ill health and devoted himself to literature and hymnody. *The Yattendon Hymnal*, 1899, named after the Berkshire town where he lived, was published in reaction to *Hymns Ancient and Modern*, 1861, and previews of the literary quality of *The English Hymnal*, 1906. In 1924 he received an LL.D. from the University of Michigan and was awarded the Order of Merit in 1929. Translator: "Ah, holy Jesus," **289**; "O gladsome light," **686**; "O splendor of God's glory bright," **679**; "When morning gilds the skies," **185**.

Briggs, George Wallace, born Kirkby, Nottingham County, England, 15 December 1875; died Hindhead, Surrey, England, 30 December 1959. He was educated at Emmanuel College, Cambridge, and was a chaplain to the Royal Navy and served English parishes as vicar or canon. A prolific writer of hymns, Briggs was a founder of the Hymn Society of Great Britain and Ireland. He also lectured briefly in the United States in 1950 at Berkeley, New Haven, and the Hymn Society of America in New York. Author: "God has spoken by the prophets," **108**.

Bristol, Lee Hastings, Jr., born Brooklyn, NY, 9 April 1923; died Syracuse, NY, 10 August 1979. A multitalented businessman, educator, administrator, and musician, he graduated from Hamilton College, Clinton, New York (A.B. 1947), studied organ at Trinity College of Music, London, and pursued graduate work at the Institute of International Studies, Geneva, Switzerland, and the Conservatoire de Musique (1947-48). He is the recipient of eleven honorary doctorates. Having held several positions at the Bristol-Myers Company, New York City (1948-62), he became president of Westminster Choir College at Princeton (1962-69). He was vice-chair and executive secretary of the Joint Commission on Church Music of the Protestant Episcopal Church and a Fellow of the Royal School of Church Music and of the Hymn Society of America. Both an author and composer, he was general editor of the Joint Commission's hymnal supplements published in 1972, *Songs for Liturgy* and *More Hymns and Spiritual Songs*. Composer: DICKINSON COLLEGE, **589**; adapter: "Let us now depart in thy peace" (A LA PUERTA), **668**.

Brooks, Phillips, born Boston, MA, 13 December 1835; died Boston, 23 January 1893. One of the USA's greatest preachers, Brooks was educated at Harvard University (1855) and Virginia Theological Seminary, and was ordained in 1859. He served as rector of congregations in Philadelphia and Trinity Church, Boston. From 1891 until his death, he was bishop of Massachusetts. Oxford conferred upon him the D.D. degree in 1885. Author: "O little town of Bethlehem," **231**.

Buchanan, Annabel Morris, born Groesbeck, TX, 22 October 1888; died Paducah, KY, 6 January 1983. She studied music at the Landon Conservatory, Dallas, Texas, and at the Guilmant Organ School, New York City. Buchanan was honored in 1955 for her work with American folk music. Her publications include *Adventures in Virginia Folkways, American Folk Music, Folk Hymns of America,* 1938, and numerous journal articles. Her valuable collection of books, photographs, recordings, and manuscripts was donated in 1978 to the University of North Carolina at Chapel Hill. Arranger: LAND OF REST, **269**, **613**, **695**.

Buck, Carlton C., born Salina, KS, 31 August 1907. Buck was educated at Biola Institute, California Christian College, Whittier College, and San Gabriel College. He began his career in church music and was ordained in 1934 into the Christian Church (Disciples of Christ), and retired in 1974 after serving congregations in California and Oregon. He has written numerous hymns, poems, meditations, librettos, and books. Author: "O Lord, may church and home combine," **695**.

Budry, Edmond Louis, born Vevey, Switzerland, 30 August 1854; died Vevey, Switzerland, 12 November 1932. Budry was a pastor for thirty-five years of the Free Evangelical Church of the Canton of Vevey, Switzerland, and studied theology at Lausanne. In addition to writing original poetry, he freely translated and adopted German, English, and Latin hymns. Author: "Thine be the glory," **308**.

Burleigh, Henry Thacker, born Erie, PA, 2 December 1866; died Stamford, CT, 12 September 1949. Burleigh was a distinguished African American singer and songwriter who served as baritone soloist at St. George's Episcopal Church, New York City, from 1894 to 1946. Tradition holds that Burleigh provided Anton Dvorák with the themes for the *New World Symphony.* Burleigh was a noted composer and arranger of popular songs, anthems, and spirituals, including *Deep River* and *Little Mother of Mine,* and was a charter member of the American Society for Composers, Authors and Publishers (ASCAP). Adapter and harmonizer: McKEE, **548**.

Bushyhead, Robert Henry, born Cherokee, Jefferson City, Tennessee, 29 October 1914. Son of a minister, he attended Carson-Newman College and received a ministerial diploma from the Harrison Chilhowie Baptist Academy. He served on the home mission board of the Southern Baptist Conference in Atlanta, Georgia. Translator: "Jesus loves me!" **191**.

Butts, Thomas. Wesley's bookkeeper and steward at the Foundery, London, between 1742 and 1753, who compiled *Harmonia Sacra,* no date, ca. 1754. See footnote on page 738 in John Wesley's *Collection of Hymns for the Use of the People called*

Methodists, volume 7 *in The Works of John Wesley,* edited by Franz Hildebrandt and Oliver A. Beckerlegge. Source: CHRISTMAS, **236**; JUDAS MACCABEUS, **308**.

Buyers, Norah (Cruz, Luiza), born Los Angeles, CA, 11 April 1919. Educated at the University of Southern California (1964, 1987, 1988) and Westminster Choir School, she was commissioned, along with her husband, as a fraternal worker to Brazil from 1950 to 1975. There she was the first missionary teacher in the Methodist Institute of Higher Education, San Paulo, Brazil (1972-75). Buyers has been an organist/choirmaster since 1975, serving Mt. Soledad Presbyterian; First Baptist, La Jolla; and First United Presbyterian, San Francisco. She has published *Vamos Cantar,* *Musica Sacra Brasileira* (an album), and *A Nova Cancão,* first and second editions, 1974, 1978. Author and composer: "¡Canta, Débora, Canta!" (DÉBORA), **81**.

Byrne, Mary Elizabeth, born Dublin, Ireland, 1 July 1880; died Dublin, 19 January 1931. She was a linguist educated at the Dominican convent in Dublin and the University of Ireland (1905), and her published works include contributions to dictionaries of the Irish language and an award-winning treatise on *England in the Age of Chaucer.* Translator: "Be thou my vision," **451**.

Cabena, Harold Barrie, born Melbourne, Australia, 12 August 1933. He enrolled at the Royal College of Music in London, England, in 1954 and studied under John Dykes-Bower, Herbert Howells, Eric Harrison, and W. E. Lloyd Webber. Honors include the senior organ prize, FTCL, and FRCO. From 1957 to 1975 he held the position of director of music at First-St. Andrew's United Church, London, Ontario, Canada. Since 1970 he has been professor of organ and church music at Wilfrid Laurier University in Waterloo. His works include *Cabena's Homage, The Dorian Mass,* and many liturgical settings in the *Catholic Book of Worship,* 1972. Cabena is well known for his organ recitals over the CBC. Arranger: JESOUS AHATONHIA, **244**.

Cabera, Juan Bautista, born Alicante, Spain, 1837; died 1916. Educated at Escuelas Pías, later he was converted at Gibraltar. He formed an evangelical congregation and served five years in prison for illegal religious activity. In 1880 he was elected the first bishop of the Spanish Reformed Church. As bishop he initiated and maintained a dialogue between evangelicals and Roman Catholics, stimulated interest in early congregational models of Christian worship including the Mozarabic rite, and was a pioneer in Spanish language hymnody. For commentary on Cabera's hymns, see Cecilio McConnell, *Comentario Sobre Los Himnos Que Cantamos.* Translator: "¡Santo! ¡santo! ¡santo!" **65**.

Cameron, Catherine Arnott, born St. John, New Brunswick, Canada, 27 March 1927. Educated at McMaster University, Canada (B.A. 1949), and the University of Southern California (Ph.D. 1971), she is professor of sociology at the University of La Verne, La Verne, California. Harry Eskew in *Handbook to the Baptist Hymnal* has quoted Cameron about her interest in writing hymns: "As a child and teenager with a gift for writing poetry, I was troubled by the mismatch between words and music in some of the hymns sung in our church. . . . I thought that one day I might write a hymn that was a harmony of poetry and music." (Adams 1992, 310) Author: "God, who stretched the spangled heavens," **150**.

Campbell, Thomas, born 1777; died 1844. Little is known of Thomas Campbell. It is believed that he was a native of Sheffield, England, and that he was in some way related to the Methodist movement. Composer: SAGINA, **363**.

Card, Michael, born Madison, TN, 11 April 1957. A recording artist of nine contemporary Christian music recordings, a video, and the author of several books, Card has received the Moody Monthly award for songwriter and artist of the year (1983) and several Dove awards for "Praise and Worship Album of the Year" (1987), "Songwriter of the Year" (1983), and "Song of the Year"(1983). Co-author and co-composer: "El Shaddai" (EL SHADDAI), **123**.

Carey, Henry, born Rothwell, Yorkshire, England, ca. 1687; died London, England, 1743. Carey was wrongly purported to be the illegitimate son of the Marquis of Halifax Primarily a writer, Carey wrote very little church music but many ballads, some to his own music, of which "Sally in our alley" is best known. His poem "Namby Pamby" added a phrase to the English language. He also wrote plays, musical dramas, and burlesques and produced operas with J. F. Lampe that were the equivalent in their day of Gilbert and Sullivan operas. He published *Poems on Several Occasions* (London, 1713) and a collection of his songs in *The Musical Century: One Hundred English Ballads on various important occasions* (London, 1740). Composer: CAREY'S (SURREY), **579**.

Carmichael, Amy Wilson, born Millisle, North Ireland, 16 December 1867; died January 1951. A missionary to India, in 1901 she founded the Dohnavur Fellowship, an institution for unwanted and exploited children, especially for those about to be sold to Hindu temples as prostitutes. Later a hospital was added, and the institution continues to serve the needy. She was the author of sixty-five collections of devotions and poetry, fifteen of which were written from the time of a crippling accident in 1931 until her death. Her life story is included in Elizabeth Elliot's *Bright Legacy: Portraits of Ten Outstanding Christian Women.* Author: "Dear Lord, for all in pain," **458**.

Carmines, Alvin Allison, Jr., born Hampton, VA, 25 July 1936. A graduate of Swarthmore College (B.A. 1958), he earned degrees from Union Theological Seminary (B.D. 1961, S.T.M. 1963) and was ordained into the ministry in 1960. Currently pastor of Rauschenbusch United Church of Christ in New York City and adjunct-professor of musical theater at Columbia University, he was associate pastor of Judson Memorial Church in Greenwich Village for twenty years where he founded the Judson Poets' Theater and administered the Judson Dance Theater and the Judson Art Gallery. Awarded the Obie five times, he has received the Drama Desk award, the New York State award, and his collaboration with Gertrude Stein won him the Vernon Rice award in 1968. His works include *Promenade* and *A Look at the Fifties*, musical plays; *The Duel*, an opera; and *Christmas Rappings*, a dance-oratorio. Composer, playwright, director, stage and television actor, musical performer, singer, and pianist, he has also been commissioned to write hymns by The United Methodist Church, the United Presbyterian Church, and the United Church of Christ. Author and composer: "Many gifts, one Spirit" (KATHERINE), **114**.

Carr, Benjamin, born London[?], England, 12 September 1768; died Philadelphia, PA, 24 May 1831. He received his musical training from Samuel Arnold, publisher of Handel's works, and Charles Wesley. In 1793 he moved to Philadelphia and continued his father's trade of music publishing and opened one of the United States' first music stores, Carr's Musical Repository, a leader in publishing patriotic music, including "The Star Spangled Banner," 1814. Carr was one of the most influential and versatile musicians of his day and is an important figure in the transmission of European performance practice and repertory. Besides his influence on USA music as a Roman Catholic church musician and teacher, publisher, and performer, he also composed an opera, ballads, songs, keyboard works, two sacred collections of liturgical music, and hymns. Arranger: SPANISH HYMN, **158**.

Carter, Russell Kelso, born Baltimore, MD, 18 November 1849; died Catonsville, MD, 23 August 1926. Carter's highly eclectic professional life included teaching, sheep-raising, publishing, writing, editing, composing gospel hymns, and practicing medicine. He was an ordained Methodist minister active in the holiness and camp-meeting movements. With A. B. Simpson, he edited *Hymns of the Christian Life*, 1891. Author and composer: "Standing on the promises" (PROMISES), **374**.

Carter, Sydney Bertram, born Camden Town, London, England, 6 May 1915. Educated at Christ's Hospital and Balliol College, Oxford, he became a schoolmaster at Frensham Heights School. He served with the Friends' Ambulance Unit during World War II (1940-45). An author with Quaker sympathies, he wrote for the School of Southwark Cathedral, London, lectured for the British Council for two years, and was a free-lance writer and broadcaster. During the late 1950's and into the 1960's Carter composed pop-style congregational song as an alternative to traditional church hymns. For a discussion of this movement see Erik Routley, *Twentieth Century Church Music*. Author: "I danced in the morning," **261**.

Caswall, Edward, born Yately, Hampshire, England, 15 July 1814; died Edgbaston, Birmingham, England, 2 January 1814. Born into a clerical family, Caswall was educated at Marlborough and Brasenose College, Oxford (1836, 1838), and he was ordained a priest in 1839. Under the influence of Cardinal Newman, he became a Roman Catholic, and after the death of his wife, was reordained in 1852. He is second only to John Mason Neale as a translator of Latin hymns, with over 200 translations to his credit that are notable for their faithfulness to Latin textual rhythms. Translator: "Jesus, the very thought of thee," **175**; "My God, I love thee," **470**; "When morning gilds the skies," **185**.

Cennick, John, born Reading, Berkshire, England, 12 December 1718; died London, England, 4 July 1755. He was born into a Quaker family but was brought up in the Church of England. In 1739, he gave up surveying to join the Wesleys, who appointed him the first local preacher; he preached in the villages around

Bristol and became a teacher at Kingswood School. After doctrinal differences with the Wesleys, he became a follower of George Whitefield, and later joined the Moravians, preaching in Germany and Ireland. His published hymns comprise three collections. Author: "Be present at our table, Lord," 621.

Chadwick, George Whitefield, born Lowell, MA, 13 November 1854; died Boston, MA, 4 April 1931. A noted organist, teacher, composer, conductor, and conservatory director, he attended the Boston Conservatory of Music, later working in his father's insurance office and teaching music. After working at Olivet College, Michigan, he studied in Europe and returned to Boston to teach privately. He joined the faculty of the New England Conservatory of Music in 1882 and became director in 1887. Composer: PEACE, **341**.

Challinor, Frederic Arthur, born Longston, Staffordshire, England, 12 November 1866; died Paignton, England, 10 June 1952. After spending his earlier years as a laborer in a brickyard, coal mine, and china factory, Challinor pursued a musical education, earning a diploma from the Royal College of Music, plus a B.M. and Mus.D. from the University of London (1897, 1903). His over 1,000 published works include cantatas, hymns, part-songs, and several poems. Composer: STORIES OF JESUS, **277**.

Chao, T. C. (Tzu-ch´en), born Hso-tsun, China, 14 February 1888; died 1979. A brilliant twentieth-century Chinese theologian, Chao was educated at Soochow University (B.S.) and Vanderbilt University (M.A. 1916, B.D. 1917), and attended the interdenominational Missionary Council in Jerusalem, 1928, and Madras, 1939, delivering a major address at the latter conference. Elected a vice-president of the World Council of Churches in 1948, he was also dean of the School of Religion of Yenching University (1928-53), and although suffering considerable persecution, he was allowed to continue on the faculty when the Communist regime reorganized it as the Yenching Union Theological Seminary. In addition to his significant contributions to Chinese-Christian philosophy, Chao published fifty indigenous Christian hymns in *Hymns for the People*, 1931. There has been no information from China about Chao since 1950. Author: "Rise to greet the sun," **678**.

Chapin, Lucius, born Springfield, MA, 1760; died Hamilton County, OH, 1842. Chapin was one of a family of musicians from Massachusetts cited in Southern tune books. After serving as a fifer in the Revolutionary army, he became a singing master in the Shenandoah Valley of Virginia. For a discussion of the Chapin family, see Irving Lowens, *Music and Musicians in Early America*. Attributed composer: TWENTY-FOURTH, **658**.

Chávez-Melo, Skinner, born Mexico City, Mexico, 1944; died New York City, NY, 26 January 1992. Chávez-Melo completed music studies in the USA, earning degrees from the School of Sacred Music, Union Theological Seminary, Juilliard School of Music, and Manhattan School of Music, with further study at the Royal School of Church Music, Croydon, Surrey, England. He was a well-known organ recitalist in the United States, Central and South Americas, England, and Canada, and represented Mexico at the Tenth International Organ Festival in Morelia, Michoacan, Mexico. He served as choral director and instructor at the Manhattan School of Music and Mannes College of Music, New York City, and was organist/choirmaster at Union Theological Seminary and the Church of the Intercession, New York City. A conductor and composer of hymns, choral, orchestral, and organ works, he contributed tunes and arrangements to *The Hymnal 1982*. Chávez-Melo served as chairperson of the National Hispanic Music Committee of the Protestant Episcopal Church, editor of *Albricias*, 1987, and as music editor of *Songs of Hope and Peace*. He is also represented in *Worship III* and *Canticos de Gracia y Alabanza II*. At his death he was serving on the committee for the forthcoming United Methodist Spanish language hymnal *Himnario Metodista*. Author: "En el frío invernal," **233**; composer: RAQUEL, **272**; translator: "Sois la semilla," **583**; harmonizer: ID Y ENSEÑAD, **583**; LO DESEMBRE CONGELAT, **233**; PESCADOR DE HOMBRES, **344**; TAULE, **210**; UNA ESPIGA, **637**.

Chisholm, Thomas Obediah, born near Franklin, Simpson County, KY, 29 July 1866; died Ocean Grove, NJ, 29 February 1960. Despite a lack of formal education, at twenty-one he became the associate editor of the Franklin *Advocate*, his hometown paper. In 1893 he was invited by the founder of Asbury College and Theological Seminary to become editor of the *Pentecostal Herald* in Louisville, Kentucky. Ordained a Methodist minister in 1903, he served only one year because of failing health and spent the following five years near Winona Lake, Indiana, where he later became a life insurance agent. He wrote over 1,200 poems, many of which were published in religious periodicals. Author: "Great is thy faithfulness," **140**.

Christiansen, Paul J., born Northfield, MN, 31 July 1914. Educated at St. Olaf College, Northfield, Minnesota (B.M. 1934), Oberlin College, Oberlin, Ohio, and Eastman School of Music (M.M. 1938), he served as director of music and director of the Concordia Choir, Concordia College, Moorhead, Minnesota, from 1937 to 1986. His annual Concordia Christmas Concerts have attracted audiences totaling over 30,000 people. The recipient of several honorary doctorates, he has written hundreds of choral compositions and arrangements, and he continues to direct choral schools in the summer. Harmonizer: WONDROUS LOVE, **292**.

Chrysostom, John, born Antioch, ca. 347; died near the Black Sea, 407. Doctor of the church and the greatest of the Greek Fathers, John studied Greek classics and became an Anchorite monk in 374. After ordination as a priest in 386, he preached brilliantly in Antioch for twelve years. Appointed patriarch of Constantinople in 398 and loved by the people for his charity, asceticism, and eloquence, he was condemned by the Roman emperor for denouncing rampant immorality. Though persecuted and exiled, he continued through sermons and letters to exert influence until his death. He is credited with writing many prayers in the *Liturgy of John Chrysostom* and for shaping the liturgy's beautiful eucharistic rite. Attributed author: "Prayer of John Chrysostom," **412**.

Chun, Ivy Grace, born Delaware, OH, 29 March 1969. She attended Boston University and the University of Tennessee, College of Dentistry, Memphis,

Tennessee. She is the daughter of the Reverend Sang E. Chun. Co-translator: "Come back quickly to the Lord," **343**.

Chun, Sang Eui, born Seoul, Korea, 10 June 1938. He earned the B.A., M.Div., and D.Min. degrees and was graduated from Yonsei University, College of Theology, Seoul, Korea, and the Methodist Theological School in Ohio, Delaware. After serving as a minister in the East Ohio Conference of The United Methodist Church (1969-82), he became director of Evangelism Ministries, General Board of Discipleship. He is the son of the Reverend Young Tack Chun, author of "Come back quickly to the Lord." Co-translator: "Come back quickly to the Lord," **343**.

Chun, Young Taik, born Pyung Yang, Korea, 18 January 1894; died Seoul, Korea, 16 January 1968. He received degrees from Aoyama Gakuin University, Toyko, Japan, and Pacific School of Religion, Berkeley, California. During the Japanese occupation of Korea (1910-45) he was the editor and publisher of a Korean Christian literary journal, *New Person.* Chun was ordained a minister in the Korean Methodist Church in 1923 and became editor of the Korean Christian Literature Society in 1954. Honors include the Cultural Mayoral award of Seoul, Special City, Korea (1961), and the Cultural Presidential award, Republic of Korea (1963). Author: "Come back quickly to the Lord," **343**.

Clark, Eugene. No information is available on Clark. Arranger: FILL MY CUP, **641**.

Clark, Francis Alfred, born 1851; died 1933. Although he was extremely popular in Philadelphia as an organist and choir director during the first half of the twentieth century, little is known about Clark including his musical education. In 1905 he gained prominence as the arranger of Charles Albert Tindley's second group of published gospel hymns and became the staff arranger for Tindley's Soul Echoes Publishing Company, arranging twelve of Tindley's songs between 1905 and 1913. He probably added the harmonies since Tindley could neither read music nor play the piano. Clark became chorister of the Wesley African Methodist Episcopal Zion Church in 1913. Arranger: BY AND BY, **525**; NOTHING BETWEEN, **373**.

Clark, Jeremiah, born London, England, ca. 1669-73; died London, 1 December 1707. As an English baroque organist, choirmaster, and composer, he succeeded John Blow in 1693 as choirmaster of St. Paul's Cathedral, becoming organist in 1695. Clark and William Croft were made joint organists of the Chapel Royal in 1704. Sometimes called the "father of the modern English hymn tune," Clark also composed incidental music for plays, a cantata, an ode, anthems, and songs. Attributed composer: ST. MAGNUS, **326**; composer: UFFINGHAM, **450**.

Clausnitzer, Tobias, born Thum, Saxony, ca. 5 February 1619; died Weiden, 7 May 1684. He was educated at the University of Leipzig (1643), and after serving as a chaplain to the Swedish army, after the Peace of Westphalia in 1649 he spent the rest of his life as a pastor in Weiden in Upper Palatine. Author: "We believe in one true God," **85**; "Blessed Jesus, at thy Word," **596**.

Clephane, Elizabeth Cecilia, born Edinburgh, Scotland, 18 June 1830; died Melrose, Roxburghshire, Scotland, 19 February 1869. She was a member of the Free Church of Scotland and in her time a legendary humanitarian and poet known as "Sunbeam" by the poor of Melrose. Her eight poems were published in *Family Treasury* by Free Church minister William Arnot. Author: "Beneath the cross of Jesus," **297**.

Cleveland, Judge Jefferson, born Elberton, GA, 21 September 1937; died Washington, DC, 20 June 1986. Graduated from Clark College, Atlanta, Georgia, and Illinois Wesleyan University, Cleveland received the D.Ed. from Boston University. He taught at Claflin College, Orangeburg, South Carolina; Langston University, Langston, Oklahoma; Jarvis Christian College, Hawkins, Texas; University of Massachusetts, Boston; and Wesley Theological Seminary, Washington, DC. Cleveland served with great distinction as co-editor, with Verolga Nix, of the United Methodist hymnbook *Songs of Zion*, 1981, contributing numerous arrangements and important historical essays and notes on performance practice. He was a consultant in hymnody with the General Board of Discipleship of The United Methodist Church. As a teacher, lecturer, and performer, he toured the United States, Africa, and Europe. Co-adapter: "Our Father, which art in heaven," **271**; harmonizer: CLEVELAND, **491**.

Coffin, Henry Sloane, born New York, NY, 5 January 1877; died Lakeville, CT, 25 November 1954. A distinguished clergyman, social prophet, hymnologist, scholar, teacher, and administrator, Coffin was educated at Yale University (1897, 1900) with additional study at New College, Edinburgh, and Union Theological Seminary. Ordained a Presbyterian minister in 1900, he was pastor of Madison Avenue Presbyterian Church and then became president of Union Theological Seminary, 1926-45. His published works include fifteen books, plus the co-editing of *Hymns of the Kingdom of God*, 1910. Translator: "Canticle of wisdom," Response 2, **112**; "O come, O come, Emmanuel," **211**.

Cole-Turner, Ronald S. Born Logansport, IN, 22 December 1948. Cole-Turner received the M.Div. and Ph.D. from Princeton Theological Seminary and is an ordained minister in the United Church of Christ. He has been an associate professor of theology at Memphis Theological Seminary since 1985, and is the author of *The New Genesis: Theology and the Genetic Revolution*. Author: "Child of blessing, child of promise," **611**.

Coles, Vincent Stucky Stratton, born Shepton Beauchamp, Somerset, England, 25 March 1845; died Shepton Beauchamp, 19 June 1929. Educated at Eaton and Balliol College, Oxford, England, and ordained in 1869, he served as assistant curate of Wantage (1869-72), rector of Shepton Beauchamp (1872-84), librarian, Pusey House, Oxford (1884-1909), and as principal and warden of the Community of the Epiphany, Truro (1910-20). He contributed to various editions of *Hymns Ancient and Modern, The English Hymnal*, and *Church Hymns*. Author: "Ye who claim the faith of Jesus," **197**.

Colvin, Tom (Thomas Stevenson), born Glasgow, Scotland, 16 April 1925. Trained and employed as an engineer, he left his position as lieutenant with the Royal Indian Engineers to become a divinity student at Trinity College, Glasgow University. He became a member of the Iona community (where Scottish Christianity began in 653) and was ordained by the Church of Scotland in 1954. Colvin served as missionary in Malawi (then Nyasaland) in Northern Ghana (1959-64) and as development advisor to the Blantyre Synod of the Church of Central Africa (1964-74). His work in Africa included community development projects, refugee rehabilitation, famine and flood relief, and long-term settlement programs. Encouraging the African citizens to write original hymn texts to traditional folk melodies, he published two collections, *Free to Serve*, 1976, and *Leap My Soul*, 1976. Another collection, *Fill Us with Your Love*, was published by Hope Publishing Company in 1983. After ten years as a minister in Lewisham, South London, he returned in 1985 to Africa as a training consultant to the Zimbabwe Christian Council. Author: "Jesu, Jesu," **432**; "That boy-child of Mary," **241**; adapter: BLANTYRE, **241**; arranger: CHEREPONI, **432**.

Conkey, Ithamar, born Shutesbury, MA, 15 May 1815; died Elizabeth, NJ, 30 April 1876. He was a singer, choral conductor, organist, and composer known widely for his work as a church and oratorio soloist. He served churches in Norwich, Connecticut, and in New York City where from 1861 until his death he was the bass soloist and quartet director of Madison Avenue Baptist Church. Composer: RATHBUN, **295**.

Converse, Charles Crozat, born Warren, MA, 7 October 1832; died Highwood, NJ, 18 October 1918. Educated at the Leipzig Conservatory (1855-59), he returned to the United States to study law and was graduated from Albany University in 1861. He worked most of his life in Erie, Pennsylvania, retiring to Highwood, New Jersey. He was an associate of William B. Bradbury and Ira D. Sankey in Sunday school and revival activity. His compositions include both large-scale and chamber works for instruments as well as vocal solos, hymns, and chorales, often written under the pen names "Redan," "Nevers," or "Revons." Composer: CONVERSE, **526**.

Cooper, Joseph Thomas, born 25 May 1819; died 17 November 1879. London, England, organist and writer on church music, Cooper collaborated with E. H. Bickersteth in the 1877 revision of *The Hymnal Companion to the Book of Common Prayer*, 1858. Harmonizer: DOLOMITE CHANT, **455**.

Copenhaver, Laura Scherer, born Marion, VA, 29 August 1868; died Marion, 18 December 1940. She was a leader of southern mountain missionary work under the sponsorship of the United Lutheran Church in America. In addition to teaching English literature at Marion College, she wrote pageants and articles that were widely circulated. Author: "Heralds of Christ," **567**.

Copes, Vicar Earle, born Norfolk, VA, 12 August 1921. He was educated at Davidson College, Davidson, North Carolina (1940), and received music and theology degrees from Union Theological Seminary (1944, 1945). As a composer, teacher, performer, and editor, Copes has been an important force in the development of Methodist and ecumenical hymnody, church music repertory and performance practice, and the development of professional standards. He served as minister of music at Highland Park Methodist Church, Dallas, Texas (1946-49), as professor of organ and church music at Hendrix College, Conway, Arkansas (1949-56), and at Cornell College in Mount Vernon, Iowa (1956-58). From 1958 to 1967 he was music editor of the General Board of Education of the former Methodist Church, where he developed Methodism's first Sunday school music curriculum and hymn studies, and edited the acclaimed monthly *Music Ministry*. He was a consultant to the Hymnal Committee that developed *The Methodist Hymnal*, 1966. In 1967 he was named head of the department of organ and church music at Birmingham Southern College. From 1973 to 1986 he was minister of music at Christ United Methodist Church, Kettering, Ohio. Copes is an ordained elder, retired, in the West Ohio Conference of The United Methodist Church. Harmonizer: OLD 113TH, **60**; composer: FOR THE BREAD, **331, 508, 614**; VICAR, **178**.

Cosin, John, born Norwich, England, 30 November 1594; died Westminster, England, 15 January 1672. After attending Caius College, Cambridge, Cosin was ordained as chaplain to the bishop of Durham in 1624. He was archdeacon of East Riding (Yorkshire), master of Peterhouse, Cambridge, and vice-chancellor of the university. Driven from his position by the Puritan Long Parliament, he served as chaplain to the exiled royal family in France. After the 1660 Restoration, he was appointed dean and then consecrated bishop of Durham and participated in the 1662 revision of the *Book of Common Prayer*. Translator: "Come, Holy Ghost, our souls inspire," **651**.

Cowper, William, born Berkhampstead, Hertfordshire, England, 15 November 1731; died East Dereham, Norfolk, England, 25 April 1800. The son of a clergyman, Cowper studied law at Westminster School, and although admitted to the bar, he never practiced. Beginning with his childhood he periodically suffered depressions, and in his final years he felt that he was eternally damned. His most lucid productive years were spent with John Newton, curate at Olney, with whom he collaborated on the famous *Olney Hymns* of 1779, containing sixty-seven of Cowper's hymns. As a poet, Cowper is considered one of the finest of his day, marking the transition from Pope to Burns and Wordsworth. Author: "Heal us, Emmanuel, hear our prayer," **266**; "There is a fountain filled with blood," **622**.

Cox, Frances Elizabeth, born Oxford, England, 10 May 1812; died Headington, England, 23 September 1897. Cox contributed fifty-six translations from the German in *Sacred Hymns from the German*, 1841, a second edition of which appeared in 1864 (*Hymns from the German*). Translator: Responses, **80, 743, 851**; "Sing praise to God, who reigns above," **126**.

Croft, William, baptized Nether Eatington (now Ettington), Warwickshire, England, 30 December 1678; died Bath, England, 14 August 1727. Croft was one of the most important composers of English hymn tunes. He was a chorister in John

Blow's choir at Chapel Royal and co-organist with Jeremiah Clark until Clark's death, when he became organist. In 1708 he succeeded John Blow at Westminster Abbey while continuing as composer and master of the children at Chapel Royal. Croft's most significant sacred publication is the two-volume *Musica Sacra*, 1724, the first church music engraved in score on plates. Many of his psalm tunes appear in *The Divine Companion or David's Harp New Tun'd*, 1707, and its 1708 Supplement. Attributed composer: HANOVER, **181, 708**; ST. ANNE, **117**.

Croly, George, born Dublin, Ireland, 17 August 1780; died Holborn, England, 24 November 1860. Croly was educated at the University of Dublin (M.A. 1804), and ordained into the Church of Ireland, serving until 1810, when he moved to London to pursue a successful literary career. He was politically and theologically conservative, and sharply critical of the notion of free thought and behavior (latitudinarianism) within the church. As rector of St. Bene't Sherehog and St. Stephen's Walbrook, through his preaching he attracted large numbers of people from all strata of society. Author: "Spirit of God, descend upon my heart," **500**.

Cropper, Margaret Beatrice, born Kendal, Westmorland (now Cumbria), England, 29 August 1886; died Woodland, Kendal, Westmorland, 27 September 1980. The daughter of Charles James Cropper and the author of plays, poems, and prayers reflecting her interest and activity in Sunday school work with children, she wrote *Flame Touches Flame*, 1949, *Sparks Among the Stubble*, 1955, and *Life of Evelyn Underhill*, 1959. Her dramatic works include *Christ Crucified*, 1932, and *Country Cottage*, 1939. Most of her hymns are in *Hymns and Songs for the Church Kindergarten*, ca. 1930. Author: "Jesus' hands were kind hands," **273**.

Crosby, Fanny Jane, born Southeast Putnam County, NY, 24 March 1820; died Bridgeport, CT, 12 February 1915. The author of over 8,500 gospel hymns, including 1,000 unpublished manuscripts found in 1972 by Hope Publishing Co., Crosby set the standard for "successful" writing of gospel hymns. Blind at the age of six weeks, by age six she began writing verse and at age twelve entered the New York School for the Blind, where she later served on the faculty. She supplied texts for the most popular gospel hymn composers of her day, including Bradbury, Doane, Lowry, Sankey, and Kirkpatrick. Through the Moody-Sankey revivals her work also reached England. Many of her songs were published under pen names including "Ella Dale," "Mrs. Kate Gringley," and "Miss Viola V. A." Living most of her life in New York City, she was a lifelong Methodist and the wife of blind musician Alexander Van Alstyne. British hymnologists inexplicably distinguish the poet by her married name. Author: "Blessed assurance," **369**; "Close to thee," **407**; "I am thine, O Lord," **419**; "Jesus, keep me near the cross," **301**; "Pass me not, O gentle Savior," **351**; "Rescue the perishing," **591**; "To God be the glory," **98**.

Crotch, William, born Green's Lane, Norwich, England, 5 July 1775; died Taunton, England, 29 December 1847. A child prodigy who at the age of four gave public recitals in London, at age eleven he began studies at Cambridge with John Randall, and at age thirteen entered Christ Church, Oxford, to study theology. He was a professor at Cambridge and later was the first principal of the Royal Academy of Music (1822-32). His catalogue of works includes oratorios, anthems, organ and piano works, and various vocal compositions. He also wrote theoretical works on composition and thorough bass. Crotch is best known, however, for his chants, of which he wrote seventy-four. Arranger: ST. MICHAEL, **372, 388, 662, 730.**

Crouch, Andraé, born Los Angeles, CA, 1 July 1945. Gospel singer and songwriter, he began as a child accompanist for his father's worship services. As a teenager he organized a singing group, the COGICS (acronym for Church of God in Christ Singers). He attended Valley Junior College, California, and later formed the Disciples, a group that has toured nationally and internationally for twenty-five years. The recipient of several Grammy and Dove awards for his accomplishments as a composer and recording artist, he has written more than 300 songs and published an autobiography, *Through It All* (with Nina Bell), 1974. Author and composer: "Soon and very soon" (VERY SOON), **706;** "Through it all" (THROUGH IT ALL), **507;** "To God be the glory" (MY TRIBUTE), **99.**

Crüger, Johann, born Gross-Breesen near Frankfurt-am-Oder, 9 April 1598; died Berlin, 23 February 1662. One of the most important chorale composers of the seventeenth century, he was educated at the Jesuit College of Olmütz and the poet's school at Regensburg. From 1622 to 1662 he was cantor of St. Nicholas' Church in Berlin, where he was an ardent promoter of congregational singing. In addition to his *Praxis Pietatis Melica*, 1647, Crüger compiled, edited, and contributed to four other volumes of tunes and texts, as well as theoretical works and compositions in typical genres of the seventeenth century. Composer: GRÄFENBERG, **193, 266;** HERZLIEBSTER JESU, **289;** NUN DANKET, **102;** Response, **789, 811;** SCHMÜCKE DICH, **612.**

Crum, John Macleod Campbell, born Mere Old Hall, Cheshire, England, 12 October 1872; died Farnham, Surrey, England, 19 December 1958. Educated at Eton and New College, Oxford (1895, 1901), Crum served as a chaplain to the bishop of Oxford, vicar at Mentmore, and from 1929 to 1943 as canon of Canterbury. He is the author of biblical, architectural, and historical works, and books for children. Author: "Now the green blade riseth," **311.**

Cruz, Luiza. See **Buyers, Norah**.

Cummings, William Hayman, born Sidbury, Devonshire, England, 22 August 1831; died London, England, 6 June 1915. A chorister of St. Paul's Cathedral and later at Temple Church, London, at the age of sixteen he sang in the chorus of the first London performance of Mendelssohn's *Elijah* with the composer conducting. Cummings was an internationally celebrated oratorio tenor and the Evangelist in J. S. Bach's Passions. He was also instrumental in the founding of the Purcell Society and wrote Purcell's biography in 1882. His compositions include a cantata, church music, glees, and part-songs. Arranger: MENDELSSOHN, **240.**

Currie, Randolph Newell, born Atmore, Alabama, 5 April 1943. Educated at Birmingham-Southern College and Ohio State University, he has served as director of music at St. Joseph Church, Sylvania, Ohio, since 1981. Currie is also an instructor at Lourdes College in Sylvania. His compositions, including hymns, psalms, choral and organ works, have been published in *Worship, Gather, The Organist's Companion*, and the journal *Bach*. Composer: Response, **803**.

Cutts, Peter Warwick, born Birmingham, England, 4 June 1937, was educated at Clare College, Cambridge (B.A. 1961, M.A. 1965), and read theology at Mansfield College, Oxford (B.A. 1963). He served as organist in several United Reformed churches and has taught music in Huddersfield's College of Technology and Oastler College, and Bretton Hall College, Wakefield. At Oxford he was encouraged by Erik Routley to try his hand at writing hymn tunes, and in 1963 Routley introduced them to the committee responsible for *The Methodist Hymnal*, 1966. They included his magnificent "Wylde Green." Cutts's successful collaboration with Brian Wren, particularly in *Faith Looking Forward*, 1983, brought his work to the attention of hymnal committees in Great Britain and the USA, and his well-crafted tunes have been included in most recent collections. He is presently the organist and music director at the First United Methodist Church, Watertown, Massachusetts, and serves on the faculty of Andover Newton Seminary. Composer: SHILLINGFORD, **260**; BRIDGEGROOM, **544**.

Daniel ben Judah, Rome, mid-fourteenth century. He is the presumed arranger of the Hebrew *Yigdal*, or doxology, for use by precentor and congregation in antiphonal singing. Attributed author: Response, **801**; "The God of Abraham praise," **116**.

Daniel, D. M. No information is available on Daniel. Author: "Jaya ho," **478**.

Dare, Elkanah Kelsay, born 1782; died 1826. A Methodist minister, Freemason, and sometime dean of boys at Wilmington College, Wilmington, Delaware, he was probably the music editor of John Wyeth's *Repository of Sacred Music, Part Second*, 1813. The introduction to the collection is based on a theoretical work on music that Dare authored, and he contributed at least thirteen tunes to it. Irving Lowens states that "if Dare was the main musical figure behind *Part Second*, he must be considered most important in the foundation of the Southern singing tradition." (Lowens 1964, 152) Probable composer: KEDRON, **109**.

Darwall, John, born Haughton, Staffordshire, England; baptized 13 January 1731; died Walsall, England, 18 December 1789. Darwall was an English cleric who, in addition to serving the pastoral offices of curate and vicar of St. Matthew's, Walsall, wrote two volumes of piano sonatas and tunes for the entire Psalter (*New Version*, 1696). Composer: DARWALL'S 148TH, **715**.

Davies, Rupert Eric, born London, England, 29 November 1909. Educated at Balliol College, Oxford, and the University of Tübingen, Germany, he became a Methodist pastor after preparation at Wesley House, Cambridge, and later was chaplain of Kingswood School and a minister in the Bristol area. He held the position of principal of Wesley College, Bristol, from 1967 until 1973, and president of the Methodist Conference, 1970-71. Translator: "Praise to the Lord, the Almighty," **139**.

Davis, Frances Mina Wheeler, born Winnipeg, Manitoba, Canada, 18 November 1936. A graduate of the University of Manitoba and the University of Toronto, she has served as a teacher and has written a number of poems and stories. Author: "Let there be light," **440**.

Daw, Carl Pickens, Jr., born Louisville, KY, 18 March 1944. Educated at Rice University (B.A. 1966), the University of Virginia (M.A. 1967, Ph.D. 1970), and the University of the South, Sewanee, Tennessee (M.Div. 1981), Daw was ordained in 1982. He has served as vicar-chaplain of St. Mark's Chapel in Storrs, Connecticut, since 1984 and as lecturer in English at the University of Connecticut since 1988. He was assistant rector at Christ and Grace Church, Petersburg, Virginia (1981-84), associate professor at the College of William and Mary (1970-78), and member of the text committee of the Standing Commission on Church Music for *The Hymnal 1982* (1980-82). His work on the hymnal committee during his years at Sewanee led to his becoming a hymn writer. He served on the Committee for Spirituality and Lay Ministry (1981-84), on the Ecumenical Committee (1982-84), as a delegate to the Virginia Council of Churches (1982-84), and as secretary (1986) and chair (1989-91) of the Protestant Episcopal Church Standing Commission on Church Music. He is author of *A Year of Grace,* 1990, numerous hymns and articles, and a contributor to *The Hymnal 1982 Companion,* Vol. 1. Author: "God the Spirit, guide and guardian," **648**; "Like the murmur of the dove's song," **544**; "O day of peace that dimly shines," **729**.

Day, George Henry, born New York, NY, 13 September 1883; died Geneva, NY, 23 November 1966. A choir boy at Trinity Chapel, New York, and the organist/choirmaster at St. Peter's Episcopal Church in Chelsea Square in 1911, Day prepared at New York University for a career in accounts and commercial law only to choose music instead. He graduated from the New York College of Music in 1913 and studied with G. Edward Stubbs, Edward Shippen Barnes, and Orlando Mansfield. In 1923 he received his doctorate from Lincoln-Jefferson University. Day served as organist/choirmaster of Christ Church, Rochester, New York (1925-35), and at Trinity Church, Geneva, New York, from 1935 until his death. He was active in the American Guild of Organists, a director of the American Organ Players' Club, and the composer of some 400 works. Composer: GENEVA, **124**.

Dearle, Edward, born Cambridge, England, 2 March 1806; died Camberwell, London, England, 20 March 1891. The composer of hymn tunes, anthems, oratorios, and service music, Dearle received his education at Cambridge (Mus.D. 1842), and served as organist and master of the song school for most of his career (1835-64) at the parish church at Newark-upon-Trent. Composer: PENITENTIA, **623**.

Dearmer, Percy, born Somerset House, Kilburn, Middlesex, England, 27 February 1867; died Westminster, England, 29 May 1936. One of the most influential leaders in twentieth-century English hymnody, Dearmer was educated at Westminster School and Christ Church, Oxford. He was chaplain during World War I to the British Red Cross in Serbia and earned a Red Cross decoration, professor of ecclesiastical art at King's College, London, and canon of Westminster. With Ralph Vaughan Williams he edited *The English Hymnal*, 1906, and with Martin Shaw and Vaughan Williams, he produced *Songs of Praise*, 1925, *The Oxford Book of Carols*, 1928, and *Songs of Praise Enlarged*, 1931. His wide-ranging interests are reflected in over fifty publications covering history, language, and the arts. Author: "Draw us in the Spirit's tether," **632**; translator: "Father, we praise thee," **680**; "Sing, my tongue, the glorious battle," **296**.

Deschner, Roger Neil, born, San Antonio, TX, 1 December 1927; died, Richardson, TX, 23 October 1991. Educated at the University of Texas at Austin, Union Theological Seminary, New York City, and Yale University, New Haven, Connecticut, he was ordained an elder in The Methodist Church in 1962. Deschner served as minister of music at Epworth United Methodist Church, Chickasha, Oklahoma (1958-61), minister of music at First United Methodist Church, Houston (1961-75), and as director of the sacred music program at Perkins School of Theology, Southern Methodist University (1975-87). He was associate professor of church music and director of the Seminary Singers at Perkins (1975-91). A charter member of the Charles Wesley Society, Deschner was a leading scholar on Wesleyan hymnody and Methodist church music. He served as secretary of the Hymnal Revision Committee for *The United Methodist Hymnal*, 1989, and published *Hallelujah - a Guide to Christian Worship*, 1975, and *Your Ministry of Singing in the Church Choir*, 1990. Translator: "Shalom, chaverim," **667**.

DeVenter, Judson W. Van. See **Van Deventer, Judson W.**

Dimitri of Rostov (Dmitriy Rostovskiy), born 1651; died 1709. An ecclesiastical writer and preacher, he entered a monastery in 1668 and wrote a polemic against the *Old Believers*, a manuscript of the Bible, and *Chet'u-Minei* (biographies of saints). Author: "An invitation to Christ," **466**.

Dirksen, Richard Wayne, born Freeport, IL, 8 February, 1921. Educated at the Peabody Conservatory, Baltimore, Maryland, Dirksen is one of the Protestant Episcopal Church's most distinguished musicians and composers. Organist/choirmaster of the Washington Cathedral, Washington, DC (1977-88), he has served there for over four decades as assistant and associate organist/choirmaster, director of the advanced program, director of music for the cathedral schools, and assistant musical director of the Cathedral Choral Society. In 1969 he was the first lay person in an American cathedral to be appointed precentor; he continues in that position. Awarded honorary doctorates from George Washington University (1980) and Mt. Union College, Alliance, Ohio (1986), he is the composer of many anthems, an oratorio, five operettas, and several extended works in free form. Composer: VINEYARD HAVEN, **161**.

Distler, Hugo, born Nuremberg, Germany, 24 June 1908; died Berlin, Germany, 1 November 1942. Distler studied at the Leipzig Conservatory and became organist at the St. Mary Church in Lübeck where Buxtehude had served, and taught at the Lübeck Conservatory. From 1933 to 1937 he taught church music at the lay-academy in Spandau, and from 1937 to 1940 he was on the faculty of the Hochschule für Musik in Wurttemberg. His compositions are marked by a strong sense of polyphony and cross-rhythms. A decade of harassment by the Nazi regime resulted in his suicide. Composer: TRUMPETS, **442**.

Dix, William Chatterton, born Bristol, England, 14 June 1837; died Cheddar, Somersetshire, England, 9 September 1898. Dix, whose avocations were languages and poetry, was a businessman in Glasgow in marine insurance. His works include original hymns published in *Hymns of Love and Joy*, 1861, and *Altar Songs, Verses on the Holy Eucharist*, 1867, and translations from Greek and Ethiopian. Author: "What child is this," **219**.

Doan, Gilbert Everett, Jr., born, Bethlehem, PA, 14 September 1930. After receiving a B.A. in geology at Harvard College (1952), he completed the D.B. at the Lutheran Theological Seminary, Philadelphia (1955), and the M.A. at the University of Pennsylvania (1962). He served as campus pastor (1955-61) and northeastern director for the National Lutheran Campus Ministry (1961-84). Doan chaired the hymn texts committee of the Inter-Lutheran Commission on Worship (1967-78). Since 1984 he has been pastor of the Lutheran Church of the Holy Communion, Philadelphia. His publications include *Preaching to the College Students* and *Worship in Campus Ministry*, devotional guides, numerous articles, reviews, and sermons in Lutheran journals. Co-author: "Come, let us eat," **625**.

Doane, William Howard, born Preston, CT, 3 February 1832; died South Orange, NJ, 24 December 1915. Doane collaborated with Fanny Crosby in providing musical settings for gospel hymns, and was active with Robert Lowry and others in editing and publishing collections for use in various Sunday school and evangelistic enterprises. He composed over 2,200 with over 30 still in use. He was noted as a benefactor of charitable and educational causes. Denison University, Ohio, in recognition of his generosity conferred on him the Mus.D. degree in 1875. Composer: I AM THINE, **419**; MORE TO LOVE THEE, **453**; NEAR THE CROSS, **301**; PASS ME NOT, **351**; PRECIOUS NAME, **536**; RESCUE, **591**; TO GOD BE THE GLORY, **98**.

Doddridge, Philip, born London, England, 26 June 1702; died Lisbon, Portugal, 26 October 1751. Educated at one of the dissenting academies at Kibworth in Leicestershire, Doddridge began preaching at age twenty-one and later became the head of an academy in Northampton. He wrote some 400 hymns, published posthumously, which, like Watts's, were based on the scripture and sermon of the day. Author: "O happy day, that fixed my choice," **391**.

Doran, Carol, born Philadelphia, PA, 11 November 1936. In 1970 Doran received the D.M.A. from the Eastman School of Music, University of Rochester, and is associate professor of worship and pastoral music, Colgate Rochester Divinity

School/Bexley Hall, Crozer Theological Seminary, Rochester. She is the composer of music for hymns and the co-author, with Thomas H. Troeger, of two hymn collections: *New Hymns for the Lectionary*, 1986, and *New Hymns for the Life of the Church*, 1992. Composer: AUTHORITY, **264**; FALCONE, **538**; GOD'S NAMES, **113**.

Dorsey, Thomas Andrew, born Villa Rica, GA, 1 July 1899; died Chicago, IL, 23 January 1993. The son of a Baptist preacher, Dorsey played, accompanied, and arranged for Tampa Red, Ma Rainey, and Bessie Smith. He became known as "Georgia Tom" and "Barrelhouse Tom." Dorsey's contribution to sacred music, with more than 200 songs to his credit, is an amalgam of African American "worldly music" (rhythm and blues) and the religious devotion of Charles Albert Tindley's hymns and songs. Dorsey's music was popularized largely through the founding of the National Convention of Gospel Choirs and Choruses in 1932, and gospel singers such as Mahalia Jackson, Sallie and Roberta Martin, Theodore Frye, Kenneth Morris, Lillian Bowles, J. Herbert Brewster, Sr., and Clara Ward. Author and composer: "Precious Lord, take my hand" (PRECIOUS LORD), **474**.

Douglas, Charles Winfred, born Oswego, NY, 15 February 1867; died Santa Rosa, CA, 18 January 1944. Eminent church musician and clergyman of the Protestant Episcopal Church, Douglas received his B.M. from Syracuse University where he taught vocal music. In 1892 he was appointed organist-choirmaster of the Church of Zion and St. Timothy's Church, New York City. He attended St. Andrew's Divinity School in Syracuse and was ordained a deacon in 1893. Because of ill health, he moved to Colorado, where he founded the Mission of the Transfiguration at Evergreen, and continued theological study at St. Matthew's Hall in Denver and was ordained a priest in 1899. Further study of music and liturgics was undertaken in England, France, and Germany, 1930-36. From 1937 to 1943 he was vicar of the Mission of the Transfiguration at Evergreen and was named honorary canon of cathedrals in Colorado and Wisconsin. His influence is most widely felt through his work as music editor of the *New Hymnal*, 1916, and its successor *The Hymnal 1940*. Douglas was widely known for his work with plainsong, liturgics, linguistics, and American Indian culture. Besides his work on hymnals, Douglas's important 1935 Hale Lectures at Seabury-Western Seminary were published as *Church Music in History and Practice*, 1937. Arranger: DIVINUM MYSTERIUM, **184**; harmonizer: CONDITOR ALME, **692**; GENEVA 124, **670**.

Draper, William Henry, born Kenilworth, Warwickshire, England, 19 December 1855; died Clifton, Bristol, England, 9 August 1933. Educated at Cheltenham College and Keble College, Oxford, and ordained in 1880, Draper served as a curate, vicar, and rector in various churches, becoming master of the Temple Church in London, 1919-30. He is the author of two collections of hymns and the translator of many Greek and Latin hymns. Translator: "All creatures of our God and King," **62**; Responses, **764, 861**.

Drury, Miriam, born, CA, 1900; died CA, 1985. An organist at a Congregational church in her youth, Drury married a Presbyterian minister in 1922 and pursued her musical interests and education wherever he pastored, including China and

Scotland. She was an award-winning composer for the Hymn Society of America and had several of her hymns published by that organization. She composed many complete hymns, anthems, and poems for adults and children. Author: "Become to us the living bread," **630**.

Duba, Arlo D., born Brule County, SD, 12 November 1929. Educated at the University of Dubuque (B.A. 1952), Princeton Theological Seminary (B.D. 1955, Ph.D. 1960), Duba served Westminster Choir College as chaplain and professor of religion (1960-68) and was director of the chapel, director of admissions, and a lecturer in liturgical studies at Princeton Theological Seminary (1969-82). Since 1992 he has been dean and professor of worship at the University of Dubuque Theological Seminary. He co-authored with Mary Faith Carsons *Praise God: Worship Through the Year* and has published several articles and the words and music for many psalms. Author: Response, **850**.

Duck, Ruth C., born, Washington, DC, 21 November 1947. Educated at Southwestern University, Memphis, Tennessee (B.A. 1969), Chicago Theological Seminary (M.Div. 1973), University of Notre Dame (M.A. 1987), and Boston University School of Theology (Ph.D. 1989), she also received an honorary D.D. from Chicago Theological Seminary. Ordained by the United Church of Christ, she is currently assistant professor of worship at Garrett-Evangelical Theological Seminary, Evanston, Illinois. She served as pastor of St. John's United Church of Christ, Hartford, Wisconsin (1975-79), and Bethel-Bethany United Church of Christ, Milwaukee, Wisconsin (1979-84). Co-editor of an early inclusive language hymn collection, *Because We Are One People*, 1974, she has also edited *Everflowing Streams: Songs for Worship*, 1981, *Becoming One*, 1986, and *Touch Holiness: Resources for Worship*, 1990. Author: "Wash, O God, our sons and daughters," **605**.

Dudley-Smith, Timothy, born Manchester, England, 26 December 1926. Educated at Pembroke College and Ridley Hall, Cambridge, he served as curate of St. Paul's, Rochester (1950-53), and was ordained an Anglican priest in 1950. His positions include head, Cambridge University Mission, Bermondsey (1953-55); honorary chaplain to the bishop of Rochester (1953-60); editorial secretary of the Evangelical Alliance and first editor of *Crusade* (1955-60), founded in the wake of the 1955 Billy Graham Crusade; assistant secretary and secretary of the Church Pastor-Aid Society (1959-73); archdeacon of Norwich (1973-81); and bishop of Thetford, Norfolk, from 1981 until his retirement in 1992. Having inherited a love of poetry from his father, he began writing at Cambridge. He has written 199 texts and is the author of *A Collection of Hymns, 1961-1981*, 1981, *Lift Every Heart*, 1983, *A Flame of Love*, 1987, *Songs of Deliverance*, 1988, *Praying with the English Hymn Writers*, 1989, and *A Voice of Singing*, 1993. Author: "Behold a broken world, we pray," **426**; "Tell out, my soul, the greatness," **200**.

Duffield, George Jr., born Carlisle, PA, 12 September 1818; died Bloomfield, NJ, 6 July 1888. The son of a prominent Presbyterian minister, Duffield was educated at Yale (1837) and Union Theological Seminary and served congregations in New Jersey, Pennsylvania, Illinois, and Michigan. He was independently wealthy and used his means to establish small congregations and to support evangelistic endeavors. Author: "Stand up, stand up for Jesus," **514**.

Dwight, Timothy, born Northampton, MA, 14 May 1752; died Philadelphia, PA, 11 January 1817. The grandson of Jonathan Edwards, Dwight became the foremost hymnologist of his day. He graduated at age seventeen from Yale, served as a tutor at Yale, was a Congregational minister in Fairfield, Connecticut, and later became president of Yale. His alteration of Isaac Watts's *Psalms of David*, to which Dwight added his versified psalms for those omitted by Watts, was published in 1801. Author: "I love thy kingdom, Lord," **540**.

Dykes, John Bacchus, born Kingston-upon-Hull, Yorkshire, England, 10 March 1823; died Ticehurst, Sussex, England, 22 January 1876. Dykes was educated at Cambridge (1847) and ordained the same year, serving as priest at Malton, Yorkshire. He moved to Durham in 1849 where he became minor canon and precentor. He received the Mus.D. from University of Durham, 1861. He served the parish of St. Oswald's until the year of his death. Dykes's musical output includes 300 hymn tunes, a setting of Psalm 23, anthems, and part-songs. His hymn tunes, some of the most successful of all settings composed in the popular Victorian style, are remarkable for their durability and strong musical sense. Composer: BLAIRGOWRIE, **444**; NICEA, **64**, **65**; ST. AGNES, **175**, **445**, **561**; harmonizer: O QUANTA QUALIA, **727**.

Edson, Lewis, Sr., born Bridgewater, MA, 22 January 1748; died Mink Hollow (Woodstock), CT, 1820. Lewis Edson is of the second generation of a musical family in the "Yankee tunesmith" tradition. A blacksmith by trade, he probably learned music from his brother Obed and became famous for his singing voice. He led music in a local singing school and congregational music in an Anglican parish in Lanesboro, Massachusetts, where he also began writing tunes. Three of his tunes, BRIDGEWATER, LENOX, and GREENFIELD, were very popular and widely published. Edson's later life was spent in mysterious seclusion. Irving Lowens devotes a chapter to a discussion of the Edson family in *Music and Musicians in Early America*. Composer: LENOX, **379**; Response, **794**.

Edwards, Howard M., III (Rusty), born Dixon, IL, 22 January, 1955. A graduate of Interlochen Arts Academy, University of Nebraska, and Lutheran Northwestern Seminary, he earned his doctorate in creative ministry from the Graduate Theological Foundation, Notre Dame, Indiana. He is senior pastor of Gloria Dei Lutheran Church, Rockford, Illinois, and pastoral advisor for Rockford Lutheran High School. His hymns have appeared in over three dozen publications, including *Sing to the Lord, Christian Worship: A Lutheran Hymnal*, and *The Presbyterian Hymnal*, 1990. Hope Publishing Company has collected his works in *The Yes of the Heart*, 1993. Composer: ANNUNCIATION, **215**.

Edwards, John David, born Penderlwyngoch, Gwnnws, Cardiganshire, Wales, 19 December 1806; died Llanddoget Rectory, Denbighshire, North Wales, 24

November 1885. Educated at Oxford University (B.MA.), he was ordained deacon and priest in 1832. Edwards was vicar after 1843 at the parish of Rhosymedre, near Ruabon, Clwyd, North Wales. He was a composer of a considerable amount of music and author of *Original Sacred Music*, 1836. Composer: RHOSYMEDRE, **447**.

Egan, Linda Wilberger, born Washington, DC, 16 December 1946. Raised in Maryland, she received the B.S. and Mus.Ed. degrees in voice and organ from Gettysburg College, Gettysburg, Pennsylvania (1968), and the S.M.M. from Union Theological Seminary School of Sacred Music, New York City. Her composition teachers included Robert Crandall and Alice Parker. She was director of music at Trinity Church, Swarthmore, Pennsylvania (1979-84), and a musician for the Well Woman Project, a project of Venture in Mission (1980-82). She presently serves as minister of music at the Episcopal Church of the Redeemer, Springfield, Pennsylvania, and teaches voice at Darlington Fine Arts Center, Wawa, Pennsylvania. She is active as an organ recitalist and composer. Author and composer: "The first one ever" (BALLAD), **276**.

Ehrenborg-Posse, Elisabeth. According to Marilyn Kay Stulken in *Hymnal Companion to the Lutheran Book of Worship*, attributing "When Christmas morn is dawning" to Ehrenborg-Posse resulted from its appearing in volume two of her *Andliga sanger för barn* in 1856. (Stulken 1981, 161) Nothing further is known about the author. Attributed author: "When Christmas morn is dawning," **232**.

Ehret, Walter Scarsdale. Ehret is a native of New York City and was educated at Juilliard School of Music (B.M.Ed.) and Teacher's College, Columbia University (M.A.). He has been a music teacher and choral director in New Jersey and New York, and for thirty-five years was the district coordinator of music for the Scarsdale Public Schools, Scarsdale, New York. Ehret has lectured and directed choral festivals and has published over 1,500 choral arrangements. Arranger: LO DESEMBRE CONGELAT, **233**.

Ellerton, John, born London, England, 16 December 1826; died Torquay, Devonshire, England, 15 June 1893. Educated at King William's College on the Isle of Man and Trinity College, Cambridge (1849, 1854), and ordained a priest in 1851, Ellerton was a prominent Victorian hymn writer. His first hymns were for children while he was curate at St. Nicholas' Brighton (1850-52), with his work continuing through the 1889 edition of *Hymns Ancient and Modern*. His works are contained in two collections, *Church Hymns*, 1871, and *The London Mission Hymn Book*, 1884. Most of his sixty-eight hymns and some translations are for special days and observances. Ellerton's hymns are widely regarded as some of the finest from this period of English hymnody. Author: "Savior, again to thy dear name," **663**; "The day thou gavest, Lord, is ended," **690**.

Ellington, Edward Kennedy ("Duke"), born Washington, DC, 29 April 1899; died New York, NY, 24 May 1974. African American pianist, bandleader, and composer, Ellington revolutionized jazz by integrating his "big band" style into his complex scores and innovative arrangements. He was known as "The Duke" because his graceful style and eloquence inspired respect. He toured Europe, Latin America, Japan, Australia, and Africa; inaugurated an annual jazz concert series at Carnegie Hall in New York; and established a tradition of sacred jazz concerts. Ellington was a prolific composer with over 1,000 compositions to his credit. He received sixteen honorary doctorates, including those from Yale and Columbia, the President's Gold Medal, the Presidential Medal of Freedom, and the French Legion of Honor. Author and composer: "Come Sunday," (ELLINGTON), **728**.

Elliott, Charlotte, born Clapham, London, England, 18 March 1789; died Brighton, East Sussex, England, 22 September 1871. The author of some 150 hymns, she was an invalid for the last 50 years of her life. Her works, contained in six volumes, are characterized by their simplicity, devotion, and particular relevance to those in sickness or sorrow. "Just as I am" is undoubtedly one of the most popular English hymns sung in the USA. Author: "Just as I am, without one plea," **357**.

Ellor, James, born Droylsden, Lancashire, England, 1819; died Newburgh, NY, 27 September 1899. Ellor was a hatter by trade and choir director in the Wesleyan chapel at Droylsden; he migrated to the USA in 1843. Composer: DIADEM, **155**.

Elvey, George Job, born Canterbury, England, 27 or 29 March 1816; died Windlesham, Surrey, England, 9 December 1893. Organist of St. George's Chapel from 1835 to 1882, Elvey was awarded the Mus.D. from New College, Oxford, by special action of the chancellor, and knighted in 1871. His compositions include two oratorios, odes, glees, anthems, and service music. Composer: DIADEMATA, **88, 327, 421, 513**; ST. GEORGE'S WINDSOR, **694**.

Emerson, Luther Orlando, born Parsonfield, ME, 29 September 1820; died Hyde Park, MA, 1 October 1915. Educated in both music and medicine, Emerson gave up a medical career to study music with I. B. Woodbury. After serving eight years as a teacher and choirmaster in Salem, Massachusetts, he took a position with the publishing firm of Oliver Ditson Company in Boston. Emerson's works are published in over seventy collections. For his distinguished work in music he was awarded the honorary Mus.D. degree from Findlay College in Ohio. Harmonizer: AR HYD Y NOS, **688**.

Escamilla, Roberto, born Sabinas Hidalgo, Mexico, 29 August 1931. Educated at Parsons College, Iowa Wesleyan College, Southern Methodist University, and Trinity University, he was ordained an elder in 1956. After pastoring several Methodist churches in Texas, he joined the Board of Missions in New York City in 1964. He received further education from Union Theological Seminary (1967) and Vanderbilt University (1985). Escamilla served on the Board of Education, the Board of Pensions, the National Council of Churches, and the Board of Discipleship, and taught at Southern Methodist University and McCormick Theological Seminary. He edited the Spanish edition of *The Upper Room* and *Celebremos I* and *II*, and in 1965 translated

One Witness in One World. Escamilla is the recipient of the De Journett award in homiletics (1955), several citations, and two honorary doctorates. Author: "Pues si vivimos," **356**; translator: "Cantemos al Señor," **149**.

Eslinger, Elise, born Hattiesburg, MS, 2 December 1942. Educated at Millsaps College, Jackson, Mississippi (B.A. 1963), she is a United Methodist church musician, composer, writer, organist, and vocalist. The director of worship and culture for The United Methodist Church General Board of Discipleship (1978-81) and founder of *Worship Alive* series, she served on the hymn supplement projects, *Songs of Zion* and *Hymns from the Four Winds,* and edited *Songs of Shalom,* 1983, *Celebremos II*, 1982, and *The Upper Room Worshipbook,* 1985. Twice named to Outstanding Young Women of America, she has been a consultant in music and spiritual formation for The Upper Room since 1981. Author: "Shalom to you," **666**; composer: "Musical Setting A," **17, 18**; co-translator: "Cantemos al Señor," **149**; "Pues si vivimos," **356**.

Espinosa, Juan Antonio. No information has been received about this person. Composer: Response, **856**.

Est(e), Thomas, born London, England, ca. 1540; died London, January 1608. The most famous publisher of his day, Est was the assignee of the printing patent for William Byrd. His publication of the *Whole Booke of Psalmes,* 1592, was the first to be printed in full score and to identify tunes by specific names. Other publishing efforts include *Triumphs of Oriana,* 1603, a collection of madrigals honoring Queen Elizabeth, the works of Tudor composers, and the introduction to England of music from the Italian school. Source: WINCHESTER OLD, **470, 603**.

Evans, David, born Resolven, Glamorganshire, Wales, 6 February 1874; died Rhosllannerchrugog, near Wrexham, Denbighshire, Wales, 17 May 1948. Educated at Arnold College, Swansea, University College, Cardiff, and Oxford University, he served as organist for the Jewin Street Welsh Presbyterian Church in London, and from 1930 to 1939 he was professor of music at the University College in Cardiff. He was editor of *Y Cerddor* (1916-21), the Welsh music periodical, and chief musical editor for *The Church Hymnary,* 1927. His harmonizations from this latter work have been widely used in British and USA hymnals. Evans composed cantatas, anthems, services, and works for chorus and orchestra. Harmonizer: CHRISTE SANCTORUM, **188, 604, 680**; GARTAN, **242**; LLANFAIR, **312**; LLANGLOFFAN, **425, 435**.

Evans, George K. born Clinton, KY, 26 August 1917. Educated at Rice University (B.A.), the University of Texas (M.A.), and George Peabody College (Ph.D.), he served as music editor at Prentice-Hall from 1958 to 1966. Translator: "From a distant home," **243**.

Everest, Charles William, born East Windsor, CT, 27 May 1814; died Waterbury, CT, 11 January 1877. Everest was a graduate of Trinity College, Hartford, and was ordained in 1842, serving for thirty-one years as rector of the Episcopal church in Hampden, Connecticut. His collection of poems, published when he was nineteen, *Visions of Death and Other Poems*, is the source of the hymn for which he is most remembered. Author: "Take up thy cross," **415**.

Excell, Edwin Othello, born Stark county, OH, 13 December 1851; died Louisville, KY, 10 June 1921. Excell studied with George F. Root and was an important revival song leader, composer, and music publisher. He was a leader in the Sunday school movement and with Methodist Bishop John H. Vincent founded the International Sunday School Lessons. Arranger: AMAZING GRACE, **378**.

Faber, Frederick William, born Calverley, Yorkshire, England, 28 June 1814; died London, England, 26 September 1863. Faber was an Oxford-educated Anglican priest. In 1835 under the influence of John Henry Newman he seceded to Rome and established a branch of the priests of the Congregation of St. Philip Neri. He wrote 150 hymns with strong popular appeal, all of which were published after he became a Roman Catholic. They are contained in *Jesus and Mary - Catholic Hymns for Singing and Reading*, 1849, 1852, *All for Jesus, or the Easy Ways of Divine Love*, 1853, and *Oratory Hymns*, 1854. Author: "Faith of our fathers," **710**; "There's a wideness in God's mercy," **121**.

Farjeon, Eleanor, born Westminster, London, England, 13 February 1881; died Hampstead, London, 5 June 1965. The daughter of a novelist her works number approximately eighty, including *Nursery Rhymes of London Town, The Glass Slipper, Silversand and Snow*, and *The Two Bouquets*. She received the Carnegie Medal, the Hans Anderson International Medal, and the Regina Medal. *Morning Has Broken: A Biography of Eleanor Farjeon* was written by her niece Annabel Farjeon in 1987. Author: "Morning has broken," **145**.

Fawcett, John, born Lidget Green, near Bradford, Yorkshire, England, 6 January 1740; died Hebden Bridge, Yorkshire, England, 25 July 1817. Fawcett was moved to join the Methodists through the preaching of George Whitefield. After a time he united with the Baptists at Bradford (1758) and began preaching in 1763. At Hebden Bridge he converted part of his home into a school for neighborhood children. His best-known hymns are contained in the collection *Devotional Commentary on the Holy Scriptures*, published in 1811, the same year Brown University, Providence, Rhode Island, honored him with the D.D. degree. Author: "Blest be the tie that binds," **557**; "Lord, dismiss us with thy blessing," **671**.

Featherstone, William Ralph, born Montreal, Quebec, Canada, 23 July 1846; died Montreal, 20 May 1873. Little is known about Featherstone except his parentage and that he was a member of the Wesleyan Methodist Church in Montreal. Author: "My Jesus, I love thee," **172**.

Fettke, Thomas Eugene, born Bronx, New York, NY, 24 February 1941. Educated at Oakland City College and California State University, Hayward, he served as a minister of music and schoolteacher for thirty-three years. Fettke was senior editor of *The Hymnal for Worship and Celebration*, 1986. He is an arranger, producer, clinician, and composer, best known for his anthem "The Majesty and Glory of Your Name." Arranger: HE IS LORD, **177.**

Fischer, William Gustavus, born Baltimore, MD, 14 October 1835; died Philadelphia, PA, 12 August 1912. Influenced by the music instruction and singing in singing schools attended during his boyhood, Fischer became widely acclaimed as a teacher of theory and conductor of choral festivals, one of which, an 1876 Moody-Sankey revival, had a chorus of over 1,000 voices. After serving ten years (1858-68) as professor of music at Girard College in Philadelphia, Fischer and John E. Gould established a retail piano business and music store. He wrote 200 tunes, publishing some Sunday school songs under the name of his business, Fischer and Gould. Composer: HANKEY, **156.**

Fishel, Donald Emry, born Hart, MI, 1 November 1950. Educated at the University of Michigan (B.M. 1972) and a flutist from age ten, he joined The Word of God, a charismatic Catholic community, and was a music leader and orchestral conductor at one of its main centers in Ann Arbor, Michigan (1969-81). As publications editor for the *The Word of God* and *Servant Music* (1973-81), he typeset music and produced record albums. He later studied computer science and became a systems programmer in 1983, discontinuing his work in music. Author and composer: "Alleluia, alleluia" (ALLELUIA NO. 1), **162.**

Fleming, Robert James Berkeley, born Prince Albert, Saskatchewan, Canada, 12 November 1921; died Ottawa, Ontario, Canada, 28 November 1976. After early music training in Saskatoon, he entered the Royal College of Music, London, England (1937), studying with Arthur Benjamin and Herbert Howells, and made his debut in Regina in 1940. In 1941 he enrolled at the Royal Conservatory of Music, Toronto. Fleming served as composer, conductor, and music director for the National Film Board (1946-58), taught at Carleton University (1970-76), and served as choirmaster/organist for churches in Toronto, Montreal, and Ottawa. His works, written in almost all forms, have been widely performed in Canada. Composer: CONCORD, **440.**

Foley, (William) Brian, born Waterloo, near Liverpool, Lancashire, England, 28 November 1919. Educated at the Christian Brothers' School, Crosby, and Upholland Diocesan Roman Catholic Seminary (1945), he was ordained to the priesthood in 1945. After serving as a priest in the diocese of Liverpool, he has been parish priest at Clayton Green, Chorley, Lancashire, since 1971. He was an important figure in the compilation of the *New Catholic Hymnal*, 1971, contributing fourteen texts himself. His hymns are also published in several other hymnals, including a Japanese hymnal. Author: "Holy Spirit, come, confirm us," **331.**

Foley, John B., born Peoria, IL, 14 July 1939. Educated at St. Louis University (two M.A.'s 1968, 1974; Ph.D. 1968) in theology, philosophy, and liturgical theory, Foley has also received extensive formal musical training, including study at Wichita State University (1962), Washington University, St. Louis (1966), and the Royal Conservatory of Music in Toronto (1979). A Jesuit priest since 1972, Foley has received numerous awards and an honorary doctorate from the University of Scranton (1980). He has been composer-in-residence at Seattle University (1981-84) and at the Colleges of St. Catherine and St. Thomas, St. Paul, Minnesota (1986-88). He has taught at St. Louis University, Regis College, Denver, and is vice-president of the Liturgical Conference Board. As a composer he has published sixty-three religious pieces, including *Mass of Thanksgiving*, numerous concert pieces, and four musicals. As a member of the St. Louis Jesuits, he has recorded seven albums of liturgical music. Author and composer: "One bread, one body" (ONE BREAD, ONE BODY), **620**.

Fortunatus, Venantius Honorius, born Treviso, Italy, ca. 530; died Poitiers, France, ca. 609. According to tradition, Fortunatus recovered his sight from near blindness by the anointing of his eyes with oil from a lamp that burned before the altar of St. Martin of Tours in Ravenna. While on a pilgrimage to the tomb of the saint, Queen Rhadegonda persuaded him to come to Poitiers near a convent she had founded, where he later became bishop. He is the author of over 250 poems. Author: "Hail thee, festival day," **324**; "Sing, my tongue, the glorious battle," **296**.

Fosdick, Harry Emerson, born Buffalo, NY, 24 May 1878; died New York, NY, 5 October 1969. Educated at Colgate College (B.A. 1900), Union Theological Seminary (B.D. 1904), and Columbia University (M.A. 1908), this distinguished American clergyman was also the recipient of numerous honorary degrees. He was ordained a Baptist minister in 1903, becoming the pastor of First Baptist Church, Montclair, New Jersey, 1904-15. On the faculty of Union Theological Seminary, he taught homiletics and later occupied the chair of practical theology (1915-46). While at Union, he also served the First Presbyterian Church and was chosen as the first minister of the racially inclusive nondenominational Riverside Church. His famous hymn "God of grace and God of glory" was written as the processional hymn for the opening service of Riverside Church, New York City, October 5, 1930. Through his teaching, preaching, and radio broadcasts from Riverside Church, and thirty-two books, Fosdick influenced an entire generation of USA Protestantism. His autobiography, *The Living of These Days*, was published in 1956. Author: "God of grace and God of Glory," **577**.

Frances, Esther, born Keokuk, IA, 23 May 1955. Graduated from Southwestern College, Winfield, Kansas, and Perkins School of Theology, Dallas, Texas (M.S.M.), she has made a special study of the music of the Hispanic Protestants of the Southwest, arranging and translating many hymns and coritos. Her work appeared in *Celebremos I*, published by Discipleship Resources of The United Methodist Church. Translator: "Jesús es mi Rey soberano," **180**.

Francis of Assisi, born Assisi, Italy, ca. 1182; died Assisi, 4 October 1226. The onset of a serious illness in his youth caused Francis to renounce his earlier frivolous life and dedicate his life to the imitation of Christ through prayer, poverty, and service to society, all of which led to the founding of the monastic order bearing his name. He was at home in the natural world of flowers, birds, and animals. Author: "All creatures of our God and King," **62**; Responses, **764**, **861**; attributed author: "The prayer of Saint Francis," **481**.

Franck, Johann, born Guben, Brandenburg, 1 June 1618; died Guben, 18 June 1677. Franck was a German lawyer and civil servant who, in addition to his highly successful and respected public career, was a hymnologist and compiler, and translated hymns from Latin. He wrote over 100 pietistic hymns that were published in *Teutsche Deutsche Gedichte, bestehend im geistlichen Sion*, 1674. Author: "Deck thyself, my soul, with gladness," **612** ; "Jesus, priceless treasure," **532**.

Franz, Ignaz, born Protzau, Silesia, 12 October 1719; died 1790. German Roman Catholic hymnologist, compiler, and priest who studied at Glaz and Breslau, Franz was ordained in 1742 at Olmütz. His published works, important in the study of eighteenth-century Catholic hymnody, include the *Katholisches Gesangbuch*, ca. 1774, and a 1778 tune book. Attributed author: "Holy God, we praise thy name," **79**.

Franzmann, Martin Hans, born Lake City, MN, 29 January 1907; died Cambridge, England, 28 March 1976. Educated at Northwestern College, Watertown, Wisconsin (1928), and Wisconsin Lutheran Seminary, Thiensville, Wisconsin, he returned in 1936 to teach at Northwestern. In 1946 he became a professor at Concordia Seminary, St. Louis, Missouri, and department head of exegetical theology there nine years later. He studied in Greece, received an honorary D.D. in 1958, and was ordained into the Evangelical Lutheran Church of England, 1969. From 1952 to 1956 Franzmann chaired the synodical conference, was a representative to the Lutheran World Federation (1962), and a member of the Commission on Theology and Church Relation (1962-69). Author of numerous theological and devotional books, he began translating German hymns as well as writing original hymns in the late 1930's. Author: "Weary of all trumpeting," **442**.

Frazier, Francis Philip, born Santee, NE, 2 June 1892; died Yankton, SD, 29 September 1964. A third generation full-blooded Sioux minister and missionary, Frazier was educated at the Santee Mission, Yankton Academy, Mt. Herman School in Massachusetts, and Dartmouth College. After military service in World War I in France and Germany, he continued his education at Oberlin College, Garrett Seminary, and Chicago Theological Seminary. As a Quaker missionary, he dedicated his ministry to Native American missions. Oberlin College honored him with the D.H.L. degree in 1960, and Dartmouth College the D.D. degree in 1964. The June 1968 edition of *Music Ministry* contains an extensive article on Frazier's life and work. Author: "Many and great, O God," **148**.

Friedell, Harold, born Jamaica, NY, 1905; died Hastings-on-Hudson, New York, 17 February 1958. He served as organist at Calvary Episcopal Church, New York City (1928-31), St. John's Episcopal, Jersey City (1931-39), and St. Bartholomew's

Church, New York City (1946-58). He also taught at the Guilmant Organ School, Juilliard School of Music, and Union Theological Seminary School of Sacred Music. A Fellow of the American Guild of Organists and composer of anthems, carols, hymn tunes, and service music, Friedell received an honorary doctorate from Missouri Valley College and was a delegate to the International Congress of Organists, London, 1957. Composer: UNION SEMINARY, **632**.

Frostenson, Anders, born 1906. He studied theology at Lund and has been a leading figure in the movement to revise Swedish hymnody. After not writing for a quarter of a century, he resumed writing in 1960. Frostenson has been pastor of the Isle Lovî beyond Stockholm including service there at the royal castle of Drottningholm, where he was preacher for three Swedish kings. Author: "Faith, while trees are still in blossom," **508**; "Your love, O God," **120**.

Gabaráin, Cesáreo, born Hernani (Guipúzkoa), Spain, 16 May 1936; died Mondragón, Spain, 30 April 1991. After the completion of basic theological studies, he received postgraduate degrees in theology, journalism, and musicology from the University of Madrid. He became a parish priest and was known for his work among youth, including many tours with cyclists who in appreciation named him the "priest of the cyclists." Gabaráin served as president of the Spanish liturgical music association Associación para la promoción de la música religiosa and was a leading composer of congregational music. His many works and recordings are included in the catalog of Oregon Catholic Press. In 1990 he traveled to the USA and conducted workshops in twenty-two cities. His most popular songs, in addition to those included in our hymnal, are "Juntos Como Hermanos," "Cristo Te Necesita Para Amar," and "La Muerte No Es Final De La Vida." Author and composer: "Camina, pueblo de Dios" (NUEVA CREACIÓN), **305**; "Sois la semilla" (ID Y ENSEÑAD), **583**; "Tú has venido a la orilla" (PESCADOR DE HOMBRES), **344**; "Una espiga" (UNA ESPIGA), **637**.

Gabriel, Charles Hutchinson, born Wilton, IA, 18 August 1856; died Los Angeles, CA, 15 September 1932. A prolific composer of gospel music, he was active in Chicago as a poet, composer, and editor from 1892 until his retirement. Gabriel composed 7,000 songs, anthems, and cantatas, and was associated with the publishing firms of Homer Rodeheaver, Hope, and E. O. Excell. Author and composer: "I stand amazed in the presence" (MY SAVIOR'S LOVE), **371**.

Gaither, Gloria, born Battle Creek, MI, 4 March 1942. Educated at Anderson College in Indiana, she married William J. Gaither while in college. They established the Gaither Music Company, co-writing many songs, and have become successful as recording and concert artists. Author: "Something beautiful," **394**; co-author: "God sent his Son," **364**; "Jesus, Jesus, Jesus," **171**.

Gaither, William James, born Alexandria, IN, 28 March 1936. Interested in gospel music even as a child, Gaither graduated from Anderson College (B.A.) and Ball State University in Muncie, Indiana (M.A.), and taught high school English while he formed the Gaither Music Company and the Bill Gaither Trio.

He and his wife Gloria have been highly successful gospel songwriters and recording artists. He received an honorary D.Mus. from Anderson and was named Gospel Songwriter of the Year, 1974, by the Gospel Music Association and ASCAP. Author and composer: "Shackled by a heavy burden" (HE TOUCHED ME), **367**; co-author and composer: "God sent his son" (RESURRECTION), **364**; "Jesus, Jesus, Jesus" (THAT NAME), **171**; composer: SOMETHING BEAUTIFUL, **394**.

García, Juan Luís, born Matanzas, Cuba, 26 March 1935. Educated at St. Thomas University (1976) and the University of Miami (1979), he served as organist/choir director and cantor for Sts. Peter and Paul Catholic Church (1962-70), St. Jude Greek Catholic Church (1970-75), and Our Lady of Lebanon Maronite-Catholic Church (1988-), all in Miami, Florida. He was a member of the diocesan commission on the production of a hymnal for the Spanish-speaking communities of South Florida (1979-86) and a member of the international commission on the production of a Spanish hymnal for the Protestant Episcopal Church to be used in Latin America, Spain, and the United States (1979-87). His publications include *La Palabra del Señor, ¿Como Pagarle al Señor?* and *El Señor Es Mi Pastor*, all published in 1990. Author and composer: "La palabra del Señor es recta" (NELSON), **107**; harmonizer: NUEVA CREACIÓN, **305**.

Gardiner, William, born Leicester, England, 15 March 1770; died Leicester, 16 November 1853. A hosier by trade, Gardiner devoted much of his time to music, especially the introduction into England of the music of Beethoven, Haydn, and Mozart. His business travels brought him in contact with many of the important musicians of his day and are chronicled in his three-volume *Music and Friends* (1838-53). In addition to writing on the science of acoustics and translating, he also adapted classic eighteenth-century melodies into hymn tunes in *Sacred Melodies* (1812-15), a collection that greatly influenced Lowell Mason's *Boston Handel and Haydn Society Collection of Church Music*, 1822. Arranger: LYONS, **73**; composer: GERMANY, **415, 427**.

Garrett, Les. Born 1944. The copyright holder has not made additional information available. Adapter and composer: "This is the day" (THIS IS THE DAY), **657**.

Gastoldi, Giovanni Giacomo, born Caravaggio, Italy, ca. 1556; died ca. 1622. An eminent Italian composer and priest, he was maestro di cappella at the church of Santa Barbaras, Mantua. Especially known for his balletos (light-hearted, dance-like pieces with a fa-la-la refrain), his music influenced Monteverdi, Hassler, and Morley. Composer: IN DIR IST FREUDE, **169**.

Gauntlett, Henry John, born Wellington, Shropshire, England, 9 July 1805; died Kensington, London, England, 21 February 1876. Educated in both law and music, Gauntlett is the composer of over ten thousand hymn tunes. He was active as a church organist and as a reformer in organ construction. The most important source of his tunes is *The Congregational Psalmist* (1858 1st ed.). Composer: IRBY, **250**; adapter: STUTTGART, **611**.

Gealy, Fred Daniel, born Oil City, PA, 13 May 1894; died Dallas, TX, 15 December, 1976. A distinguished New Testament scholar, preacher, hymnologist, and seminary professor, Gealy served as a missionary in Japan, taught at Iliff School of Theology, Denver, Colorado (1937-39), Perkins School of Theology, Dallas, Texas (1939-59), and Methodist Theological School, Delaware, Ohio (1960-1970). He served as consultant on liturgical music for the 1964 Methodist hymnal and as co-author with Austin C. Lovelace and Carlton R. Young on *Companion to the Hymnal*, 1970. Gealy contributed to *The Interpreter's Bible* and was author of *Let Us Break Bread Together*, 1960, a collection of sermons preached at Perkins Chapel. His hymnological research files from *Companion to the Hymnal*, 1970, were used by the author of this companion. Author: "For true singing," **69**.

Geer, E. Harold, born Tabor, IA, 1886; died 25 December 1957. An organ recitalist, choral conductor, and teacher, Geer was educated at Doane College, Crete, Nebraska (B.A., M.A.), and Oberlin College, Oberlin, Ohio (Mus.B.), and he studied with Charles Widor and T. Tertius Noble. He taught at Lake Erie College for Women, Ohio, and later at Albion College, Michigan. From 1916 to 1952 he was assistant professor at Vassar College, Poughkeepsie, New York. He received an honorary doctorate from Doane in 1949. Geer wrote over 100 choral works for women's voices, toured his Vassar choir throughout the USA, edited *Hymnal for Colleges and Schools*, 1956, and published *Organ Registration in Theory and Practice*, 1957. Adapter: THE CALL, **164**.

Gelineau, Joseph, born Champ-sur-Layon, Maine-et-Loire, France, 31 October 1920. A Jesuit priest, Gelineau studied composition and organ at the École César-Franck in Paris. He also received a doctorate in theology from Lyon-Fourviere. He has been a leader in the recovery of singing the psalms and widely acclaimed for his musical settings of texts from the Jerusalem Bible, now translated into many languages. He founded the "Hosanna" choir in 1956 to sing the liturgy at the Church of Saint-Ignace, Paris. In 1959 the Catholic Institute of Paris conferred upon Gelineau a doctorate for his work in Rome on liturgical singing. He has lectured on liturgical music, published several books, including *Chant et musique dans le culte Chrétien*, 1962, and *The Liturgy Today and Tomorrow*, 1978, recorded his compositions, and founded in 1966 *Universa Laus*, an international study group for research on liturgical music. Composer: Response: **137, 754**.

Gerhardt, Paul, born Gräfenhainichen, Saxony, 12 March 1607; died Lübben, Saxe Merseburg, 27 May 1676. The son of a Burgermeister, Gerhardt ranks along with Martin Luther as one of Germany's greatest hymn writers. His hymns are the expression of a faith tested by the Thirty Years' War, personal tragedy, and religious persecution; they mark the transition from the Confessional to the Pietistic eras. Gerhardt was educated at the University of Wittenberg and in 1642 moved to Berlin to be a tutor in the home of Andreas Barthold, whose daughter, Anna Maria, he married in 1655. Ordained in 1651, he served as pastor in Mittenwalde (1651-57), deacon at St. Nicholas' Church (1657-66), and as archdeacon and pastor of the church in Lübben, where he remained until his death. In 1666 Gerhardt was deposed from his office as a result of his refusal to sign an edict by the Reformed Elector Frederick William I, which sought to stop Lutheran pastors from preaching on doctrinal differences between the Lutherans and the Reformed. His 132 hymns appeared in Johann Crüger's 1648 *Praxis Pietatis Melica* and in Johann Ebeling's *Das andere Dutzend geistlicher Andachtslieder Herrn Paul Gerhardts mit neuen Melodien*, 1666-67. The first English translations of Gerhardt's hymns are by John Wesley in Georgia, with some of the most famous by Catherine Winkworth who held his work in high regard. Author: "Give to the winds thy fears," **129**; "Jesus, thy boundless love to me," **183**; translator: "O sacred Head, now wounded," **286**; Response, **752**.

Gesius, Barthölomäus, born near Frankfurt, ca. 1555; died Frankfurt, ca. 1613. Trained as both a theologian and a musician, Gesius was a prolific composer of Lutheran liturgical music, including ten collections of hymns and a setting of the *St. John Passion*, 1588. From 1592 until his death, he was the cantor of Frankfurt, where he also wrote the theoretical work *Synopsis musicae practicae*, 1609, 1615, 1618. Composer: DU FRIEDENSFÜRST, HERR JESU CHRIST, **683**.

Geyer, John Brownlow, born Wakefield, Yorkshire, England, 9 May 1932. A student at Queen's College, Cambridge, England (1953-56), and Mansfield College (1956-59), he was ordained by the Congregational Union of Scotland in 1959 and became chaplain at the University of St. Andrews. He has served congregations in Fife and Glasgow, held the position of tutor at the colleges of Westminster and Cheshunt, Cambridge, served the United Reformed Church at Little Baddow, and since 1980 has served at Weoley Hill, Birmingham, and as chaplain to United Reformed Church students at the University of Birmingham. A member of the Society for Old Testament Study, he is a respected theologian and author of numerous articles, hymn texts, and a commentary on *The Wisdom of Solomon*, 1963. His hymns have appeared in *Dunblane Praises I*, 1964, and *New Songs for the Church*, 1969. Author: "We know that Christ is raised," **610**.

Giardini, Felice de, born Turin, Italy, 12 April 1716; died Moscow, 8 June 1796. Giardini began his musical life as a choir boy at the Cathedral of Milan. He was best known, however, as a violinist, conductor, and opera impresario, performing in Germany, England, Italy, and Russia, where he died. He was a prolific composer of operas, chamber music, concertos, and overtures. Composer: ITALIAN HYMN, **61**, **568**.

Gibbons, Orlando, baptized Oxford, England, 25 December 1583; died 8 June 1625. The outstanding organist of his time, Gibbons began his musical career as organist of the Chapel Royal in 1601. From Cambridge he earned his B.M. (1606) and the honorary Mus.D. (1622). In 1623 he was named organist of Westminster Abbey, where in the year of his own death he conducted the funeral music for King James I. His compositions include forty anthems and services, noteworthy for their beautiful melodic lines and straightforward contrapuntal texture. Gibbons's most well known hymn tunes were written for George Wither's *Hymns and Songs of the Church* (1623), as tunes with bass lines, and are designated today by their number in that collection. Composer: CANTERBURY, **355**, **465**, **550**, **699**.

Gilmore, Joseph Henry, born Boston, MA, 29 April 1834; died Rochester, NY, 23 July 1918. Educated at Phillips Andover Academy, Brown University (1858), and Newton Theological Seminary where he also taught Hebrew (1861-62), Gilmore was an ordained Baptist minister who turned to teaching and writing after serving churches in Philadelphia, New Hampshire, and New York. From 1868 to 1908 he was professor of English at the University of Rochester. Besides writing for newspapers and periodicals, he is the author of three books, including *He Leadeth Me, and Other Religious Poems*, 1877. Author: "He leadeth me: O blessed thought," **128**.

Gladden, Washington, born Pottsgrove, PA, 11 February 1836; died Columbus, OH, 2 July 1918. An early advocate for the church's role in issues of social justice, Gladden was educated at Owego Academy and Williams College, and was ordained into the Congregational ministry in 1860. After serving churches in New York and Massachusetts, he accepted a call to the First Congregational Church, Columbus, Ohio, where he served from 1882 to 1914. From 1904 to 1907 he was the moderator of the National Council of Congregational Churches. He was one of the editors of the *Pilgrim Hymnal*, 1904, and the editor of the *Independent*, a significant contributor to the writing of social protest, and the author of *Recollections*, 1909. Author: "O Master, let me walk with thee," **430**.

Gläser, Carl Gotthelf, born Weissenfels, 4 May 1784; died Barmen, 16 April 1829. Gläser studied violin with his father at St. Thomas' School, Leipzig, and was a chorister at St. Thomas' Church. He was known as a violinist, teacher, choral conductor, and the composer of numerous choral and instrumental works. Composer: AZMON, **57, 59, 422, 608**.

Gordon, Adoniram Judson, born New Hampton, NH, 19 April 1836; died Boston, MA, 2 February 1895. Gordon was educated at Brown University and Newton Theological Seminary, and was ordained a Baptist minister in 1863. He served congregations in Jamaica Plain and Boston, Massachusetts. Active in evangelistic music and a close friend of Dwight L. Moody, he edited two hymnals: *The Service of Song for Baptist Churches*, 1871, and *The Vestry Hymn and Tune Book*, 1872. Composer: GORDON, **172**.

Goss, John, born, Fareham, England, 27 December 1800; died London, England, 10 May 1880. The son of a parish organist, Goss was a leading figure in the history and reform of English cathedral music and hymnody. He studied with John Stafford Smith at the Chapel Royal and later with Thomas Attwood. He was organist of Stockwell Chapel (1821-24), St. Luke's, Chelsea (1824-37), and St. Paul's London (1838-72), where he succeeded Attwood. From 1827 to 1874 he was professor of harmony at the Royal Academy of Music. Upon his retirement, he was knighted and in 1876 honored with the Mus.D. degree from Cambridge. Besides composing anthems and glees, Goss published *Parochial Psalmody*, 1826; *257 Chants, Ancient and Modern*, 1841; a two-volume collection of services and anthems with James Turle, 1854. He edited William Mercer's *Church Psalter and Hymn Book*, 1854, and wrote *Introduction to Harmony and Thorough-Bass*, 1833. Composer: LAUDA ANIMA, **66, 100**.

Goudimel, Claude, born Besançon, France, ca. 1505; died Lyons, France, 27 August 1572. Goudimel composed polyphonic settings of liturgical music and Genevan psalm tunes for use in both Roman Catholic and Protestant churches until their use was banned by Rome. He joined with the Huguenots in the early 1560's, and when the St. Bartholomew's Day massacres spread to Lyons, he was among those killed. His settings of Genevan tunes formed the basis for later adaptations. *Les CL Pseaumes David* (Paris, 1564) was the first entirely homophonic harmonization of the complete Psalter and the base for later harmonizations. Harmonizer: LE CANTIQUE DE SIMÉON, **686**.

Gould, John Edgar, born Bangor, ME, 1822; died Algiers, Africa, 4 March 1875. Composer, publisher, and merchant in New York City, Gould moved to Philadelphia around 1868 to open a music business with William G. Fischer. With Edgar L. White, he compiled four collections of gospel songs, along with his own *Harmonia Sacra*, 1851, and *Songs of Gladness for the Sabbath School*, 1869. Composer: PILOT, **509**.

Gounod, Charles François, born Paris, France, 17 June 1818; died St. Cloud, France, 18 October 1893. This famous French composer received his musical training at the Paris Conservatory and won the Grand Prix de Rome in 1839. Best known for his five-act opera *Faust*, 1859, he wrote many operas, including *Mireille*, 1864, and *Roméo et Juliette*, 1867, several masses, cantatas, the oratorio *La Rédemption*, 1882, first performed at the Birmingham Festival, and the popular "Ave Maria" for soprano, originally called "Méditation sur le Prélude de Bach." Composer: Response, **778**.

Graber, David, born Wayland, IA, 22 November 1942. Educated at Goshen College, Goshen, Indiana (B.A.), and the University of Iowa, Iowa City (M.A.), he has been a band and choral music instructor in public schools on Indian reservations in Montana since 1973. He served as editor and transcriber of the *Tsese Ma'heone-Nemeototse*, 1982, the Cheyenne hymnbook, and the *Chiuahiçwalaxuua*, 1991, the Crow spiritual hymnal. Transcriber: ESENEHANE JESUS, **659**.

Grant, Amy, born Nashville, TN, 1960. Grant's recording career began with sweeping floors and demagnitizing tape heads in a Nashville recording studio where she made her first album singing her original, contemporary Christian music at the age of seventeen. She has produced twelve albums, sold over ten million recordings worldwide, won multiple Dove and Grammy awards, had her own TV special, and toured the world several times. Author: "Thy word is a lamp unto my feet," **601**; Response, **841**.

Grant, Robert, born Bengal, India, 1779; died Dalpoorie, India, 9 July 1838. Educated at Magdalen College, Cambridge (1801, 1804), and admitted to the bar in 1807, Grant led a distinguished public life as a lawyer, member of Parliament, judge advocate general, and governor of Bombay. He was knighted in 1834. His hymns were published in the *Christian Observer* (1806-15), H. V. Elliot's *Psalms and Hymns*, 1835, and in a collection compiled by his brother, Lord Glenelg, *Sacred Poems*, 1839. Author: "O worship the King," **73**.

Greatorex, Henry Wellington, born Burton-on-Trent, Staffordshire, England, 24 December 1813; died Charleston, SC, 18 September 1858. After early training from his father who was organist at Westminster Abbey, he moved to Hartford, Connecticut, in 1839. There he was organist of Center Church and later St. John's Church. Around 1846 he went to St. Paul's Church in New York City and was later organist-choirmaster of Calvary Church. He moved to Charleston in 1853. His work is contained in his *Collection of Psalm and Hymn Tunes, Chants, Anthems and Sentences for the use of the Protestant Episcopal Church in America*, 1851. Composer: GREATOREX, **71**.

Greatorex, Walter, born Mansfield, Nottinghamshire, England, 30 March 1877; died Bournemouth, Hampshire, England, 29 December 1949. An Anglican church musician, he was educated at Derby School and St. John's College, Cambridge. Greatorex was assistant music master at Uppingham School and later was music master at Gresham's School, Holt, Norfolk (1911-49). Composer: WOODLANDS, **200**.

Green, Fred Pratt, born Roby, near Liverpool, England, 2 September 1903. Educated at Huyton High School, Wallasey Grammar School, Rydal School, and Didsbury College, Manchester, Green was ordained to the Methodist ministry in 1928 and served circuits in the north and south of England (1927-69). During this time he wrote plays and hymns, greatly encouraged by his poet friend Fallon Webb, and he assembled three collections of his poems: *This Unlikely Earth*, 1952, *The Skating Parson*, 1963, and *The Old Couple*, 1976. His poems are in *The Oxford Book of Twentieth-Century English Verse* as well as many periodicals. After his retirement, Green began writing prolifically, creating over 300 hymns and Christian songs, many for the supplements to the British Methodist *Hymns and Songs*, 1969, and *Partners in Praise*, 1979, as well as commissioned texts for special occasions. He is considered by his colleagues to be the leader of the "hymnic explosion" in England and by Erik Routley as the most important hymnist in Methodism since Charles Wesley. In 1982 he received an honorary doctorate in Humane Letters from Emory University, Atlanta, Georgia, and was made a Fellow in the Hymn Society of America. His works include *26 Hymns*, 1971, *The Hymns and Ballads of Fred Pratt Green*, 1982, and *Later Hymns and Ballads, Fifty Poems*, 1989. His hymns have been included in all recent USA hymnals. Author: "Christ is the world's light," **188**; "For the fruits of this creation," **97**; "God is here!" **660**; "How blest are they who trust in Christ," **654**; "O Christ, the healer," **265**; "Of all the Spirit's gifts to me," **336**; "Rejoice in God's saints," **708**; "Seek the Lord who now is present," **124**; "The church of Christ, in every age," **589**; "To mock your reign, O dearest Lord," **285**; "When in our music God is glorified," **68**; "When Jesus came to Jordan," **252**; "When our confidence is shaken," **505**; "When the church of Jesus," **592**; "Whom shall I send?" **582**; co-author: "Break forth, O beauteous heavenly light," **223**; translator: "All my hope is firmly grounded," **132**; "By gracious powers," **517**.

Gregory the Great, born Rome, Italy, 540; died Rome, 604. Born of wealthy parents, Gregory became a monk and turned his fortune to monastic work. Elected pope in 590, he was influential in spreading the Roman Catholic faith to England by way of Augustine at Canterbury in 597. He had an enormous influence on the standardization of hymns and liturgical chants. His system, under the name of Gregorian chant, by the eighth century had displaced or accommodated other chants and was the norm in the Western church until the late twentieth century. Attributed author: "Father, we praise thee," **680**.

Greiter, Matthäus, born Aichach, Bavaria, ca. 1500; died Strassburg, 20 December 1550. Greiter studied to be a singer and monk in the monastery in Strassburg Minster and in 1524 became a Lutheran pastor there. Before his death by the plague, Greiter recanted and returned to the Roman Catholic Church. He composed seven melodies for his *Strassburger Kirchenamt*, 1525, and John Calvin included four of Greiter's melodies in his first psalter, *Aulcuns pseaulmes et cantiques mys en chant* (Strassburg, 1539). Attributed composer: OLD 113TH, **60**.

Griffiths, Thomas Vernon, born West Kirby, Cheshire, England, 22 June 1894; died Christchurch, New Zealand, 23 November 1985. Educated at Pembroke College, Cambridge (M.A., Mus.B.), and the University of New Zealand, Griffiths studied with Charles Stanford and Charles Wood, and was organist/choirmaster at Pembroke (1919-22), senior music master at Downside School, Somerset (1922-23), and taught at St. Edmund's School, Canterbury (1923-26). Moving to New Zealand in 1927, he was music lecturer at Christchurch Teachers' College. In 1933 he became music director at the Dunedin Technical College and from 1942 to 1962 was professor of music at Canterbury University. Griffiths received honorary degrees from the University of New Zealand and the University of Canterbury. Internationally known for his book on imaginative teaching methods, *An Experiment in School Music Making*, he was awarded the Officer of the British Empire by Queen Elizabeth II in 1957. Composer: DUNEDIN, **725**.

Grindal, Gracia, born Powers Lake, ND, 4 May 1943. After graduating from Augsburg College (1965), she lived one year in Oslo, Norway, then attended the University of Arkansas (1969). She taught English and poetry at Luther College, Decorah, Iowa (1968-84), and published many poems and articles in Christian journals. Since 1984 Grindal has been associate professor of pastoral theology and ministry-communications at Luther Northwestern Theological Seminary, St. Paul, Minnesota. She has served on the hymn text committee of the Inter-Lutheran Commission on Worship, helping to produce the *Lutheran Book of Worship*. She has authored *Pulpit Rock* and *Sketches Against the Dark*, books of poetry; she edits *Wellwoman*, the newsletter of the Lutheran Women's Caucus, and writes the column "Hymn Interpretation" in *The Hymn: A Journal of Congregational Song*. Grindal was a valued and good-humored consultant in language to the Hymnal Revision Committee. During one debate she commented, "The reason why denominational revision committees come up with such wooden and dry phraseology is that English is their second language!" Author: "The Kingdom of God," **275**; "To a maiden engaged to Joseph," **215**; translator: "Out of the depths I cry to you," **515**; "Thy holy wings, O Savior," **502**.

Grove, William Boyd, born Johnstown, PA, 24 April 1929. Educated at Bethany College (1951), Drew University (1954), and Pittsburgh Theological Seminary (1978), Grove pastored churches in the Western Pennsylvania Conference (1954-80). In 1980 he became the bishop of the West Virginia Conference of The United Methodist Church and later received honorary degrees from Allegheny, Bethany, and West Virginia Wesleyan colleges. Author: "God, whose love is reigning o'er us," **100**.

Gruber, Franz Xaver, born Unterweizberg, near Hochburg, Upper Austria, 15 November 1787; died Hallein, 7 June 1863. Although his father wanted him to stay in the family trade of linen weaving, Gruber secretly studied violin and in 1805 went to Burghausen for organ study under Georg Hartdobler. He was a teacher at Arnsdorf (1807-29), serving frequently as organist at St. Nicholas' Church, a Roman Catholic parish in neighboring Oberndorf. From 1833 until his death, he was headmaster at Berndorf and organist at Hallein. His "Stille Nacht," one of over ninety compositions, alone is remembered and held in such regard that in many parts of the world Christmas would not be complete without its singing. Composer: STILLE NACHT, **239**.

Gurney, Dorothy Frances Blomfield, born London, England, 4 October 1858; died Kensington, England, 15 June 1932. The daughter of a rector of the Church of England, she and her husband, Gerald Gurney, converted to Roman Catholicism in 1919. Her poetry is published in two volumes. Author: "O perfect Love," **645**.

Gutiérrez-Achon, Raquel, born Central Preston, Oriente, Cuba, 5 May 1927. She holds degrees from the Instituto Santiago and the Conservatorio Provincial, Santiago de Cuba, Oriente, Cuba; Martin College, Pulaski, Tennessee; and George Peabody College for Teachers, Nashville, Tennessee. She was the task group chair of *Celebremos II*, a publication of the General Board of Discipleship, and served as vice-chair of the Hymnal Revision Committee, the editorial production, and the tunes subcommittees of *The United Methodist Hymnal*, 1989. Having done extensive research in Hispanic hymnology for over thirty-five years, she served as a consultant to the commission of the National Hispanic Music Committee of the Protestant Episcopal Church that produced *Albricias*, 1987. Translator: "¡Canta, Débora, canta!" **81**; co-translator: "Tú has venido a la orilla," **344**; "Sois la semilla," **583**.

Hammarskjöld, Dag Hjalmar Agne Carl, born Jönköping, Sweden, 29 July 1905; died near Ndola, Northern Rhodesia, 18 September 1961. The son of the prime minister of Sweden, he studied law and economics at the universities of Uppsala and Stockholm. Hammarskjöld was a Swedish statesman who served as secretary-general of the United Nations (1953-61). He was killed in an airplane crash over the Congo en route on a United Nations peacekeeping operation to negotiate a cease-fire between the United Nations and Katanga forces. He was posthumously awarded the Nobel Peace Prize for 1961. Author: "Prayer for a new heart," **392**.

Hanaoka, Nobuaki, born Saga, Japan, 25 December 1944. He received degrees in theology from Kanto Gakuin University, Yokohama, Japan, and Colgate Rochester Divinity School, Bexley Hall, and became an American Baptist minister in 1972. Hanaoka became an ordained elder in The United Methodist Church in 1978 and is the pastor of the Sacramento (California) Japanese United Methodist Church. He is author of *Nihilism and Nothingness*, 1968, and many articles on theology published in Japanese and English, and his translations of hymns were included in *Hymns from the Four Winds*, 1983. Translator: "Send your Word," **195**.

Hanby, Benjamin Russell, born Rushville, OH, 22 July 1833; died Chicago, IL, 16 March 1867. He was the son of Bishop William Hanby, whose antislavery sentiments greatly influenced him. Educated at Otterbein University (1858), he became a United Brethren minister and musician after traveling as an agent for his alma mater. Encountering resistance to his progressive views in ministry, he turned his musical avocation into a profession, becoming a composer, arranger, and editor with the music companies of John Church and Root & Cady and publishing *Our Song Birds*, 1866, a collection containing sixty of his own compositions. Hanby composed patriotic, day school, and Sunday school songs, including "Darling Nelly Gray" and "Ole Shady," but he is most remembered for "Up on the Housetop." Author and composer: "Who is he in yonder stall" (WHO IS HE), **190**.

Handel, George Frederick, born Halle, 23 February 1685; died London, England, 14 April 1759. Although Handel was born in Germany, he is considered at the top of the ranks of English composers. He moved to England in 1712, was made a British subject in 1727, and remained until his death. His output includes Italian operas, oratorios, instrumental chamber and orchestral works, psalm settings, anthems, and a Te Deum. His oratorios defined a style that was to remain until the Victorian era, with *Messiah*, 1741, being the most performed and universally admired of all his works. Between 1749 and 1752 Handel wrote three hymn tunes, one of which (GOPSAL) appears in this hymnal. These were discovered 1826 in the Fitzwilliam Museum Library at Cambridge by Wesley's son Samuel, who in turn published them as *The Fitzwilliam Music never before Published, Three Hymns, the Words by the late Rev. Charles Wesley . . . Set to Music by George Frideric Handel . . .* , 1826. Adaptations of melodies from his operas and oratorios for hymn settings were encouraged by John Wesley, who included them in his tune collections. For more extensive biography and bibliographical information, see *Baker's Biographical Dictionary of Music and Musicians*. Composer: ANTIOCH, **246**; CHRISTMAS, **236**; GOPSAL, **716**; JUDAS MACCABEUS, **308**.

Hankey, Arabella Katherine, born Clapham, London, England, 1834; died Westminster, England, 9 May 1911. At an early age, Hankey came under the influence of the Clapham sect of Anglican evangelicals led by William Wilberforce through her father's membership in the sect. After a trip to Africa, she became a benefactor to foreign missions and gave all proceeds from her literary work to this cause. Her most famous collection of poems, *Heart to Heart*, was published in 1870. Author: "I love to tell the story," **156**.

Harkness, Georgia Elma, born Harkness, NY, 21 April 1891; died Claremont, CA, 21 August 1974. Harkness was an important and highly educated author, educator, and theologian. She studied at Cornell University (1912), Boston University (M.A. 1920, M.R.E. 1920, Ph.D. 1923), with additional work at Harvard University, Yale Divinity School, and Union Theological Seminary. She was also the recipient of numerous honorary degrees. Harkness held professorships in philosophy at Elmira College (1922-37), in religion at Mount Holyoke College (1937-39), and in applied theology at Garrett School of Theology (1939-50) and the Pacific School of Religion (1950-61). From 1956 to 1957, she taught at the Japanese International Christian University. Her hymns, many of which have won awards from the Hymn Society of America, are contained in three collections of prayers and poems. Author: "Hope of the world," **178**; "In time of illness," **460**; composite author: "This is my song," **437**.

Harlow, Samuel Ralph, born Boston, MA, 20 July 1885; died Northampton, MA, 21 August 1972. Educated at Harvard, Columbia, and Hartford Theological Seminary (Ph.D.), and an ordained minister of the Congregational Christian Church, Harlow spent the early part of his career as a teacher and chaplain at International College, Smyrna, Turkey, and during World War I as religious director of the French YMCA through the American Expeditionary Force. From 1919 to 1922 he served as general director of the Student Volunteers Movement for the Near East. He was professor of religion and social ethics at Smith College from 1923 until his retirement. Author: "O young and fearless Prophet," **444**.

Harrington, Karl Pomeroy, born Somersworth, NH, 13 June 1861; died Berkeley, CA, 14 November 1953. Widely known as a teacher of Latin, Harrington was on the faculties of Wilbraham Academy, Wesleyan University, the University of North Carolina, and the University of Maine, with Wesleyan University conferring on him the Mus.D. degree in 1946. He served as organist in churches near or in schools where he taught and was very active as a choral conductor, founding the Chapel Hill Choral Society and directing the Middlesex Musical Association. Along with Peter Lutkin, he was musical editor of the 1905 Methodist hymnal; it contained twelve of his tunes and responses. He was a member of the committee that produced the 1935 Methodist hymnal, the music editor of six other hymn and song collections, and the author of *Education in Church Music*, 1931. Much of his choral works remains unpublished. Composer: CHRISTMAS SONG, **249**.

Harrison, Ralph, born Chinley, Derbyshire, England, 10 September 1748; died Manchester, Lancashire, England, 4 November 1810. Harrison was an independent minister trained at the Unitarian Warrington Academy who served the independent chapel at Shrewsbury (1769-71) and from 1771 until his death, the Cross Street Chapel, Manchester, where he established a boys' school and Manchester Academy. Among his publications, *Sacred Harmony* in two volumes, 1784 and 1791, exerted a considerable influence on independent hymn and psalm tune collections. Arranger: ARLINGTON, **511**.

Hart, Joseph, born London, England, 1712; died London, 24 May 1768. Hart was a strict Calvinist independent preacher who was converted at a Moravian chapel in Fetter Lane, London, on Whitsunday, 1757. In 1741 he castigated one of John Wesley's sermons by publishing a tract, "The Unreasonableness of Religion, Being Remarks and Animadversion on the Rev. John Wesley's Sermon on Romans 8:22." He served the Jewin Street Independent Chapel from 1759 until his death. His hymns, ranked with those of Isaac Watts in popularity among independent hymn writers, are contained in *Hymns Composed on Various Subjects, with the Author's Experience*, 1759. Author: "Come, ye sinners, poor and needy," **340**.

Harwood, Basil, born Woodhouse, Olveston, Gloucestershire, England, 11 April 1859; died London, England, 3 April 1949. Educated at Trinity College, Oxford (D.M. 1896), and Leipzig Conservatory, Germany, he was organist at Trinity College (1878-81), St. Barbabas, Pimlico (1883-87), Ely Cathedral (1887-92), and Christ Church, Oxford (1892-1909). He served as precentor of Keble College, where he conducted the Oxford Bach Choir, and as choragus of the University of Oxford. Harwood edited *The Oxford Hymn Book*, 1908, and composed about ninety hymn tunes and much sacred music. Harmonizer and adapter: DEUS TUORUM MILITUM, **582**, **587**, **634**.

Hassler, Hans Leo, born Nuremberg, 25 October 1564; died Frankfurt-am- Main, 8 June 1612. A pupil of Andrea Gabrieli and a friend of Giovanni Gabrieli, Hassler is one of the most important German composers to mold the Italian influence into an idiomatic German style. He held positions as both court and church organist, including at Nuremberg's Frauenkirche and to the Elector of Saxony. His collections include *Cantiones Sacrae*, 1591, *Neue Deutsche Gesang*, 1596, *Kirchengesänge, Psalmen und Geistliche Lieder*, 1608, as well as masses, motets, litanies, and organ works. Composer: PASSION CHORALE, **286**; Response, **752**.

Hastings, Thomas, born Washington, Litchfield County, CT, 15 October 1784; died New York, NY, 15 May 1872. Hastings was a self-taught musician who ranks with Lowell Mason in the establishment of USA church and public school music in the "European norm" of theory, notation, repertory, and taste. In this effort, with the exception of Native American tunes, Hastings and Mason branded as "nonscientific" other indigenous music such as shaped-note music and notation. At an early age he began directing choirs and compiling collections of hymns. His work culminated in the *Utica Collection*, 1816, later titled *Musica Sacra*. Hastings became the editor of the religious weekly *Western Recorder* in 1828 and later moved to New York where he joined Lowell Mason in publishing *Spiritual Songs for Social Worship*, 1833. New York University conferred the Mus.D. in 1858. His output includes over 600 hymns, 1,000 tunes, and 50 collections, including the *Mendelssohn Collection*. Composer: CONSOLATOR, **510**; Response, **125**; TOPLADY, **361**.

Hatch, Edwin, born Derby, England, 4 September 1835; died Oxford, England, 10 November 1889. Hatch received his education from King Edward's School, Birmingham, and Pembroke College, Oxford. In 1853 he was confirmed into the

Church of England and was ordained a priest in 1859. After serving briefly as a priest in East London, he moved to Toronto, Canada, where he taught at Trinity College, and later served as rector in a Quebec high school. In 1867 he returned to England and served as vice-principal of St. Mary's Hall, Oxford, rector of Purleigh, Essex, and university reader in ecclesiastical history in 1885. Author: "Breathe on me, Breath of God," **420**.

Hatton, John, born Warrington, England, ca. 1710; died, St. Helen's, England, December 1793. Nothing is known of Hatton, except that he lived "in a street whose name he gave to the one tune by which his name is known." (Dearmer and Jacob 1933, 435) Composer: DUKE STREET, **101**, **157**, **438**; Response, **761**.

Havergal, Frances Ridley, born Astley, England, 14 December 1836; died Oystermouth, Glamorganshire, Wales, 3 June 1879. Frances was the youngest child of William Henry Havergal. In spite of chronic poor health, she wrote verse from the age of seven and mastered the modern languages, Greek, and Hebrew through travel and private study. In addition to writing poetry, she composed several hymn tunes. Author: "Take my life, and let it be," **399**; "Lord, speak to me," **463**.

Havergal, William Henry, born Chipping Wycombe, Buckinghamshire, England, 18 January 1793; died Leamington, Warwickshire, England, 19 April 1870. Havergal was a Church of England clergyman and hymnologist who graduated from St. Edmund's Hall, Oxford (1815, 1819), was ordained a priest in 1817, and served as curate and rector at Astley until a serious accident forced him to inactive status. During the time of recuperation, he devoted himself to the study of church music, reissuing in 1845 Ravenscroft's *Whole Booke of Psalms*, 1621, adding an introduction. His own compilation, *Old Church Psalmody*, was issued in 1847. When his health was restored, he became rector of St. Nicholas', Worcester, honorary canon of Worcester Cathedral (1845), and vicar of Shareshill, Wolverhampton (1860). Other publications include *A History of the Old Hundredth Psalm Tune*, 1854, and *A Hundred Psalm and Hymn Tunes*, 1859. Arranger: RATISBON, **85**, **173**; composer: EVAN, **566**.

Haweis, Thomas, born Redruth, Cornwall, England, 1 January 1733 (Old Calendar Style); died Bath, Somersetshire, England, 11 February 1820. Although he started his training as a surgeon, Haweis (pronounced "Haw-iss") entered Christ Church, Oxford, and Magdalen Hall in 1755, and was ordained in 1757. He served parishes in various places, but was attracted to Methodism, becoming Martin Madan's assistant at the Lock Hospital Chapel in London. From 1764 until his death, he was rector of All Saints', Aldwinkle, Northamptonshire. A champion of interdenominational missions, he helped found the London Missionary Society. In 1768 he became chaplain to the Countess of Huntingdon and an administrator of her college at Trevecca, Wales. Several hymn tunes and texts are published in *Carmina Christo, or Hymns to the Saviour*, 1792. Composer: RICHMOND, **417**.

Hawhee, Howard, born Cresco, IA, 27 July 1953. He was a student of Gracia Grindal at the Luther College, Decorah, Iowa, when he translated hymn texts. He later pursued a doctoral degree in comparative literature at the University of Iowa. Translator: "Cold December flies away," **233**.

Hawkes, Annie Sherwood, born Hoosick, NY, 28 May 1835; died Bennington, VT, 3 January 1918. Encouraged by her pastor, Robert Lowry of Hanson Place Baptist Church to write hymns, Hawkes composed over four hundred hymn texts, only one of which remains in common use; its tune was composed by Lowry. The hymn, common in USA hymnals, has been translated into many languages. Author: "I need thee every hour," **397**.

Hawkins, Ernest, born Lawrence End, Herts, England, 25 January 1802; died Dean's Yard, Westminster, England, 5 October 1868. Fellow of Exeter College, Oxford, England (1831-52), he was prebendary of St. Paul's (1844), minister of Curzon Chapel, Mayfair (1850-68), and canon of Westminster (1864-68). He published *A Book of Family Prayers*, 1856, *The Book of Psalms with explanatory notes*, 1857, and contributed tunes and arrangements to Novello's *Psalmist*. Adapter: WESTMINSTER ABBEY, **559**.

Haydn, Franz Joseph, born Rohrau, Austria, 31 March 1732; died Vienna, Austria, 31 May 1809. Kapellmeister in the court of Prince Paul Esterhazy, Haydn was one of the great creative geniuses of the eighteenth century, whose work defined the classical period of music. He is the composer of over one hundred symphonies, twenty-two operas, four oratorios, masses, songs, and much vocal and instrumental chamber music. Although he composed six hymn tunes for Tattersall's *Improved Psalmody*, 1794, most of the melodies associated with hymns in modern hymnals are adapted from larger choral and instrumental works. See *Baker's Biographical Dictionary of Music and Musicians* for more complete biographical and bibliographical information. Arranger: AUSTRIA, **731**; probable composer: ST. ANTHONY CHORALE, **67**.

Haydn, Johann Michael, born Rohrau, Austria, 16 September 1737; died Salzburg, Austria, 10 August 1806. The younger brother of Franz Joseph, Johann Michael became Kapellmeister as Grosswardein in 1757, and from 1762 until his death he was the musical director to Archbishop Sigismund of Salzburg. His musical career was devoted to writing music, much of it still unpublished, for the Roman Catholic Church, including hymn tunes, oratorios, large and small scale choral works, and organ concertos. Composer: LYONS, **73**.

Hayford, Jack William, born Los Angeles, CA, 25 June 1934. A graduate of L.I.F.E. Bible College, Los Angeles, California (1956), Azusa Pacific University, Azusa, California (1970), and the recipient of several honorary doctorates, Hayford served as national youth director for the International Church of the Foursquare Gospel (1956-73). From 1965 to 1982 he was associated with L.I.F.E. Bible College, first as a faculty member, then as dean of students, and after 1977 as president. Since 1969 he has pastored The Church on the Way, which has grown from 18 to 7,000 members. Widely known as an author and speaker, he has written over 400 hymns, songs, and other musical works. Author and composer: "Majesty, worship his majesty" (MAJESTY), **176**.

Head, Bessie Porter, 1850-1936. The identity of this author is unknown. Author: "O Breath of life," **543**.

Heber, Reginald, born Malpas, Cheshire, England, 21 April 1783; died Trichinopoly, India, 3 April 1826. Educated at Brasenose College, Oxford, Heber was named a fellow of All Souls' College in 1805, and from 1807 to 1823 he served his family's parish of Hodnet, Shropshire, as rector. During this time his hymns were written and appeared in the *Christian Observer* beginning in 1811. Heber was influenced by the vital congregational singing of the Methodists and Baptists and began to compile a hymnbook according to the Christian Year and special days. He enlisted the aid of poets such as Sir Walter Scott, Henry Milman, and Robert Southey. The effort to have the collection authorized was halted by the bishop of London's refusal, by Heber's election as the bishop of Calcutta, and by his untimely death on a visit to Trichinopoly. It was published by his wife in 1827 as *Hymns Written and Adapted to the Weekly Service of the Church Year* and became one of the most influential collections of nineteenth-century Anglican hymnody. Heber's hymns represent a movement away from the evangelical style of Wesley and others to those authored by participants in the Oxford group, culminating in *Hymns Ancient and Modern*, 1861. His hymns also prompted the composition of tunes in meters such as 98. 98. 84 or 1112. 1210. Author: "Bread of the World," **624**; "God that madest earth and heaven," **688**; "Holy, holy, holy! Lord God Almighty," **64**; "¡Santo! ¡Santo! ¡Santo!" **65**.

Hedge, Frederick Henry, born Cambridge, MA, 12 December 1805; died Cambridge, 21 August 1890. A Unitarian minister and educator, Hedge spent several years studying in Germany and Holland. He was ordained in 1829, serving congregations in Maine and Massachusetts. While serving as minister of Brookline Unitarian Church (1857-72), he also was professor of ecclesiastical history (1857-76) and German (1872-84) at Harvard. Hedge was an important Transcendentalist and a brilliant scholar of German literature and biography. With F. Dan Huntington he compiled *Hymns for the Church of Christ*, 1853. Translator: "A mighty fortress is our God," **110**; Responses, **764**, **780**.

Heerman, Johann, born Raudten, Silesia, 11 October 1585; died Lissa, Posen, 17 February 1647. Heerman received his education in Wohlau, Fraustadt, Breslau, and Brieg, after which he became a teacher until ill health caused him to quit and become a pastor at Koeben (1611-34). A witness to much of the horror of the Thirty Years' War, he came close to death several times and lost all his possessions. He is considered the most important German hymn writer between Martin Luther and Paul Gerhardt, and like Gerhardt, his poetry is an expression of faith amidst deep personal and social tragedy. Author: "Ah, holy Jesus," **289**.

Helmore, Thomas, born Kidderminster, Worcestershire, England, 7 May 1811; died Westminster, England, 6 July 1890. Helmore was an important figure in the nineteenth-century restoration of plainsong. Educated at Magdalen Hall, Oxford (1840, 1845), he served most of his career as vice-principal at St. Mark's College, Chelsea, besides being master of the choristers of the Chapel Royal at St. James. He was the musical editor of John Mason Neale's translations of Latin hymns, wrote an important article on plainsong for the *Dictionary of Musical Terms*, 1881, and edited numerous collections. Through his efforts in both music and text translations, the rich tradition of plainsong hymnody was rediscovered for English language churches with mixed results. Adapter and harmonizer: VENI EMMANUEL, **211**.

Hemy, Henri Frederick, born Newcastle-upon-Tyne, England, 12 November 1818; died Hartlepool, Durham, England, 1888. With an early career as organist of St. Andrew's Roman Catholic Church at Newcastle, he later became professor of music at St. Cuthbert's College in Ushaw, Durham. Besides his popular collections of sacred music, including *The Crown of Jesus Music*, 1864, Hemy also wrote *Royal Modern Tutor for the Pianoforte*, 1858, a popular piano method that had several reprints. Composer: ST. CATHERINE, **710**.

Henderson, Richard Alan. No information is available on Henderson. Author and composer: "Move me" (MOVE ME), **471**.

Herbert, George, born Montgomery Castle, England, 3 April 1593; died Bemerton, near Salisbury, England, 1 March 1633. Herbert was educated and taught at Trinity College, Cambridge. He also served two parishes for three years each. His most famous work, *The Temple*, 1633, was popular for a time, then ignored until John Wesley made use of its poems in various collections, including the 1737 Charleston *Collection*, where he altered their meters and subdued their humor. Ralph Vaughan Williams's *Five Mystical Songs from George Herbert*, 1911, also used poetry from *The Temple*. Herbert's biography was published by his friend Izaak Walton. Author: "Come, my Way, my Truth, my Life," **164**; "Let all the world in every corner sing," **93**.

Herbranson, Thomas Edmond, born Bagley, MN, 3 December 1933. Educated at St. Olaf College, Luther Theological Seminary (B.A. 1960, M.Th. 1969), and the University of Minnesota (M.A.), Hebranson served as campus minister at Winona State College, Winona, Minnesota (1960-62), following an internship with a trilingual congregation in Venezuela. After working with a home mission church at White Bear Lake, Minnesota (1963-67), he worked in Mexico City, Mexico, with a bilingual church serving poor Mexicans. In 1971 he joined Lutheran Brotherhood in Minneapolis and worked in public relations. In 1979 he worked for the governor of Minnesota as a special projects coordinator. Author: "This is the Spirit's entry now," **608**.

Herklots, Rosamond Eleanor, born Masuri, North India, 22 June 1905; died Bromley, Kent, England, 21 July 1987. Trained as a teacher at the University of

Leeds, she chose instead to be a secretary to an eminent neurologist. She had written verse for several years, but began writing hymns about 1940 and was encouraged by the Hymn Society of Great Britain and Ireland and by Oxford University Press. Two of her hymns reached the finals in the Hymns for Britain contest in 1968 and were sung on television. Herklots has written seventy hymns and considers her texts to be ecumenical and according to *Hymnal Companion to the Lutheran Book of Worship*, "intended to express in simple words the faith, hope, and dedication of the ordinary Christian." (Stulken 1981, 366) Author: "Forgive our sins as we forgive," **390**.

Hernaman, Claudia Frances Ibostson, born Addlestone, Surrey, England, 19 October 1838; died Brussels, Belgium, 10 October 1898. The daughter of a clergy-man of the Church of England and married to a minister/inspector of schools, she was vitally interested in the religious education of children and conse-quently prepared 150 hymns, some original compositions, and some translations from Latin for children. Among her published work were *A Child's Book of Praise*, 1873, *Christmas Carols for Children*, 1885, and *Lyra Consolationis from the Poets of the 17th, 18th and 19th centuries*, 1890. She also jointly compiled the *Altar Hymnal*, 1884. Author: "Lord, who throughout these forty days," **269**.

Hérold, Louis Joseph Ferdinand, born Paris, France, 28 January 1791; died Thernes, France, 19 January 1833. Hérold entered the Paris conservatory at age fifteen and won first prize in the piano competition four years later. While he is known primarily as an opera composer and chorusmaster, he also wrote much music for the piano in all the major forms. Composer: MESSIAH, **399**.

Hewitt, Eliza Edmunds, born Philadelphia, PA, 28 June 1851; died Philadelphia, PA, 24 April 1920. Quite interested in the Sunday school movement, Hewitt spent much of her life working with Philadelphia's Northern Home for Friend-less Children and was active in her home church, Olivet Presbyterian Church. After moving across the city, she joined Calvin Presbyterian Church and served as superintendent of the primary department until her death. Her poems were set to music by John R. Sweney, B. D. Ackley, Charles H. Gabriel, E. S. Lorenz, and Homer Rodeheaver. Her poems were published by Sweney and William J. Kirkpatrick. Author: "Sing the wondrous love of Jesus," **701**.

Hillert, Richard, born Granton, WI, 14 March 1923. Educated at Concordia Teachers College, River Forest, Illinois (B.S. 1951), and Northwestern Univer-sity, Evanston, Illinois (M.M. 1955, D.M. 1968), he studied composition with Matthew Lundquist, Anthony Donato, and at the Berkshire School of Music, Tanglewood, Massachusetts, with Goffredo Petrassi. He served as teacher and parish musician in St. Louis, Missouri, Wausau, Wisconsin, Chicago and Westchester, Illinois. Since 1959 he has been professor of music at his alma mater, Concordia, and is currently serving as head of the music department. His compositions include choral works, gospel motets, hymn tunes, carols, piano, organ, and chamber works. As music editor for *Worship Supplement*, 1969, and a member of the committee that produced the *Lutheran Book of*

Worship, 1978, he has composed numerous liturgical and hymnic settings. He has written many articles and served as associate editor of *Church Music* (1966-80). Composer: FESTIVAL CANTICLE, **638**.

Hine, Stuart Wesley Keene, born London, England, 25 July 1899. Although he passed the entrance examination for Oxford, Hine did not continue his education, serving instead in the army in World War I in France. From 1923 to 1932 he and his wife were missionaries in east Poland, and from 1932 to 1939 in east Czechoslovakia. In Britain they have worked with displaced persons, producing evangelical literature in various languages as well as a number of popular hymns. Author and composer: "How great thou art" (HOW GREAT THOU ART), **77**.

Hodges, Edward, born Bristol, Gloucestershire, England, 20 July 1796; died Clifton, Gloucestershire, England, 1 September 1867. Hodges was a composer and organist who received the Mus.D. degree from Cambridge in 1825. He moved to Canada to serve as organist of the Toronto Cathedral in 1838 and after one year moved to New York City where he was organist of St. John's Episcopal Church (1839-46) and Trinity Episcopal Church (1846-63). In addition to his writing hymn tunes and anthems, he is the author of *An Apology for Church Music and Musical Festivals*, 1834, and *An Essay on the Cultivation of Church Music*, 1841. His library and manuscripts are housed in the Library of Congress. Arranger: HYMN TO JOY, **89, 702**.

Hodges, John Sebastian Bach, born Bristol, Gloucestershire, England, 1830; died Baltimore, MD, 1 May 1915. The son of Edward Hodges, he came to the United States in 1845, was educated at Columbia University (1850, 1853), and was ordained priest in 1855. After serving Episcopal churches in Pittsburgh, Chicago, and Newark, he spent thirty-five years as rector at St. Paul's, Baltimore, where he reestablished the men and boys' choir and parish choir school, the first, according to some, in the USA. In addition to composing some 100 hymns and anthems, he compiled the *Book of Common Praise*, 1869, and the revised edition of *Hymn Tunes*, 1903. He was influential in the revision of the 1874 Episcopal *Hymnal* and served on the joint commission preparing the 1892 *Hymnal*. Composer: EUCHARISTIC HYMN, **624**.

Hoffman, Elisha Albright, born Orwigsburg, PA, 7 May 1839; died Chicago, IL, 25 November 1929. The son of an Evangelical Association minister, Hoffman was educated at Union Bible Seminary at New Berlin, Pennsylvania, and was connected with the Board of Publications of the Evangelical Association for eleven years (1868-79). He also served Evangelical, Congregational, and Presbyterian churches in Ohio, Illinois, and Michigan as an ordained Evangelical minister. He was the first music editor of Hope Publishing Company (1894-1912), editing over fifty hymnals and songbooks and writing texts or tunes for at least 1,000 gospel hymns. Author: "What a fellowship," **133**.

Holbert, John, born New Castle, IN, 8 July 1946. He attended Grinnell College, Grinnell, Iowa (B.A. 1968), Perkins School of Theology (M.Th. 1971), and Southern Methodist University (Ph.D. 1975). He has been associate professor of religion, Texas Wesleyan University (1976-79), associate pastor, University United Methodist Church, Lake Charles, Louisiana (1978-79), and associate professor of preaching, Perkins School of Theology since 1979. Holbert, with Harrell F. Beck, S T Kimbrough, Jr., and Alan Luff, was a member of the Psalms text committee that prepared The United Methodist Liturgical Psalter. His publications include *Preaching Old Testament*, 1991, *Storyteller's Companion: Genesis*, 1991, and with S T Kimbrough Jr. and Carlton R. Young, *Psalms for Praise and Worship*, 1992. Author: Response: **822**.

Holden, Oliver, born Shirley, MA, 18 September 1765; died Charlestown, MA, 4 September 1844. A man of great professional versatility, Holden was a carpenter, musician, minister, congressman, merchant, and realtor. He built and was the minister of the Puritan church in Charlestown and served in the Massachusetts House of Representatives. His publications include nine hymn collections during the years 1792 through 1803. Composer: CORONATION, **154**.

Holland, Josiah Gilbert, born Belchertown, MA, 24 July 1819; died New York, NY, 21 October 1881. After a short career in medicine, Holland turned to writing, joining the Springfield *Republican* as the author of the "Timothy Titcomb" letters. He later assisted in the establishment of *Scribner's Magazine* and served as its editor until his death. His *Complete Poetical Writings* was published in 1879. Author: "There's a song in the air," **249**.

Holmes, John Haynes, born Philadelphia, PA, 29 November 1879; died New York, NY, 3 April 1964. A noted pacifist and advocate for civil rights, Holmes was educated at Harvard, ordained a Unitarian minister, and served forty-two years as minister of the Church of the Messiah, New York City, renamed Community Church after it withdrew from the denomination. His life and written works proclaim an urgent need for direct social action on the part of the church. Publications include his biography, *I Speak for Myself*, 1959, and *Collected Hymns*, 1960. Author: "The voice of God is calling," **436**.

Holst, Gustav Theodore, born Cheltenham, Gloucestershire, England, 21 September 1874; died Ealing, near London, England, 25 May 1934. One of the great figures in twentieth-century English music, Holst, a colleague of Ralph Vaughan Williams, represents through his music the intense interest in the early part of the century in indigenous folk music, as well as the urge to find a fresh musical expression apart from romanticism. His principal teacher was C. V. Stanford at the Royal College of Music, 1893-98. He taught music at James Allen Girls' School, St. Paul's Girls' School (for which the *St. Paul's Suite* was written), the Morley College for Working Men and Women, and, during World War I, to troops in Asia Minor where he often performed sixteenth-century choral music. His travels also brought him to the USA on two occasions: the Ann Arbor Festival, 1923, and Harvard, 1932. Holst's music was compiled and cataloged by his daughter, Imogen, in

The Music of Gustav Holst, 1951. She also wrote his biography, *Gustav Holst*, 1938. In addition to hymn tunes and arrangements his compositions include five operas, instrumental suites, choral hymns, vocal and instrumental chamber music, folk song settings, and the large chorus and orchestral work *Hymn of Jesus*, 1917. Composer: CRANHAM, **221**; arranger: PERSONENT HODIE, **248**.

Hopkins, Edward John, born Westminster, England, 30 June 1818; died St. Pancras, London, England, 4 February 1901. Hopkins's musical career began as a choir boy at the Chapel Royal and continued from 1843 to 1898 as organist for the Mitcham Parish Church, St. Luke's, Berwick Street, and the Temple Church. He received honorary degrees from the Archbishop of Canterbury and Trinity College, Toronto. With Edward F. Rimbault, he published *The Organ: Its History and Construction*, 1855. Hopkins's church music, including anthems, hymn tunes, and chant settings, have been widely used in England and the United States. Composer: ELLERS, **663**.

Hopkins, John Henry, born Burlington, VT, 17 September 1861; died Grand Isle, VT, 1 November 1945. Hopkins, the nephew of John Henry Hopkins, Jr., was educated at the University of Vermont and General Theological Seminary, New York City, where he was organist and supervised the installation of the organ in 1888. He was ordained priest in 1891 and served churches in Chicago and the Middle West, returning to Vermont where he retired. He served on the tunes committee for the commission that produced *The Hymnal 1940*. Composer: GRAND ISLE, **711**.

Hopkins, John Henry, Jr., born Pittsburgh, PA, 28 October 1820; died Hudson, NY, 14 August 1891. Theologian, musician, artist, and teacher, Hopkins was a leader in mid-nineteenth-century Episcopal church music. Educated at University of Vermont (1839, 1845) and General Theological Seminary in New York City (1850), he was the first instructor in church music at General Theological Seminary and the founding editor of the *Church Journal*, 1853-68. After his ordination in 1872, he served as rector of Trinity Church, Plattsburg, New York (1872-76), and Christ Church, Williamsport, Pennsylvania (1876-87). Author and composer: "We three kings" (KINGS OF ORIENT), **254**.

Hopper, Edward, born New York, NY, 17 February 1816; died New York, 23 April 1888. A graduate of Union Theological Seminary, Hopper was a Presbyterian minister who served congregations in New York, including his last pastorate at Church of the Sea and Land, New York City. He was honored with the D.D. degree from Lafayette College in 1871. Author: "Jesus, Savior, pilot me," **509**.

Hopson, Hal Harold, born Mound, TX, 12 June 1933. After attending Baylor University (B.A. 1954) and the Southern Baptist Theological Seminary (M.S.M. 1956), he did additional study with Lloyd Pfautsch, Dora Barclay, and Helmut Schuller. He taught church music at Westminster Choir College (1983-84) and Scarritt Graduate School (1984-88), and also served as music director for several congregations, principally in Nashville, Tennessee. The writer of more than 800 published compositions and arrangements, Hopson is a highly respected conductor, clinician, and workshop leader. Author: "Though I may speak," **408**; composer: MERLE'S TUNE, **209**; adapter: GIFT OF LOVE, **408, 643**.

Horn, Johann, born Domaschitz, Bohemia, ca. 1490; died Jungbunzlau, Bohemia, 11 February 1547. He went with Michael Weisse to Wittenberg in 1522 to discuss the Brethren views with Martin Luther and was consecrated a bishop of the Bohemian Brethren in 1933. He published a Czech hymn collection, *Písne chval bozskych*, 1541, containing 481 hymns, 300 melodies, and surpassing all contemporary songbooks in size. In 1544 Horn revised Weisse's 1531 *New Gesengbuchlen*, containing thirty-two new hymns, and presented *Ein Gesangbuch der Brüder im Behemen und Merherrn*, which also included hymns from his own 154-hymn collection. Composer: AVE VIRGO VIRGINUM, **636**.

Hosmer, Frederick Lucian, born Framingham, MA, 16 October 1840; died Berkeley, CA, 7 June 1929. Educated at Harvard (1862, 1869), Hosmer was ordained into the Unitarian ministry where he was a leader for hymnic and liturgical renewal. He served congregations in Massachusetts, Illinois, Ohio, Missouri, and California, with fifty of his hymns appearing in *The Thought of God in Hymns and Poems*, 1918. Author: "Forward through the ages," **555**; "God, that madest earth and heaven," **688**.

How, William Walsham, born Shrewsbury, Shropshire, England, 13 December 1823; died Leenane, County Mayo, Ireland, 10 August 1897. How was a graduate of Wadham College, Oxford (1845, 1847), and was ordained in 1847. After serving three parishes, he was suffragan bishop of East London, where he was called the "poor man's bishop." Later he became the first bishop of Wakefield (1888). He is the author of fifty-four hymns, *Daily Prayers for Churchmen*, 1852, *Psalms and Hymns*, 1854, with Thomas Morrell, and chaired the committee for *Church Hymns*, 1871, edited by John Ellerton and Arthur Sullivan. Author: "For all the saints," **711**; "O Word of God incarnate," **598**.

Howe, Julia Ward, born New York, NY, 27 May 1819; died Newport, RI, 17 October 1910. Deeply involved in humanitarian causes, Howe was a poet and social worker who attempted to organize a worldwide campaign among women to end war and preparations for war, and through her Unitarian church, she preached for the cause of abolition. Her published works include *Passion Flowers*, 1854, *Words of the Hour*, 1856, and *Later Lyrics*, 1866. Author: "Mine eyes have seen the glory," **717**.

Howells, Herbert, born Lydney, Gloucestershire, England, 17 October 1892; died London, England, 24 February 1983. An apprentice with Herbert Brewer at Gloucester Cathedral (1909-11) and self-taught in music composition, he earned a scholarship in composition in 1912 at the Royal College of Music in London, where he studied with Charles V. Stanford. He served as sub-organist at Salisbury Cathedral for only a short time because his health failed. He later taught composition at the Royal College of Music (1920), succeeded Gustav Holst as director of music at St. Paul's Girls' School (1936), and received a Doctor of Music degree from Oxford in 1937. His extensive list of musical compositions includes choral, organ, piano, and chamber ensemble works, songs, and much liturgical music. He was a guest conductor on tours throughout South Africa, Canada, and the United States and was a well-known adjudicator and music critic. Composer: MICHAEL, **132**.

Hoy, (Jay) James Edward Matthew, born Avondale, PA, 9 October 1920. The son of a pastor, Hoy attended the Philadelphia Musical Academy and Temple University, Philadelphia, Pennsylvania, where he received the B.A. degree. He has served Tindley Temple United Methodist Church, Philadelphia, Pennsylvania, since 1955 as the organist/director. He chaired the organ department at the Settlement Music School from 1964 to 1988 and received an honorary doctorate from Grambling University, Grambling, Louisiana. Hoy served on the Hymnal Revision Committee. Arranger: SOMEDAY, **524**.

Hoyle, Richard Birch, born Cloughfold, Lancashire, England, 8 March 1875; died London, England, 14 December 1939. Hoyle was a Baptist minister and scholar who, after serving several churches in England, came to the United States in 1934 to teach at Western Theological Seminary (1934-36). Translator: "Thine be the glory," **308**.

Hu Te-ngai, born China, ca. 1900. No information is available on this person, according to Bliss Wiant in *Companion to the Hymnal* (Gealy, Lovelace, Young 1970, 580), except that her given name, Te-ai, means "virtuous love" and is representative of names given to Chinese Christians, especially young women. Composer: LE P'ING, **678**.

Hudson, Ralph E., born Napoleon, OH, 9 July 1843; died Cleveland, OH, 14 June 1901. During the Civil War he served in the 39th Pennsylvania Volunteers and from 1862 to 1863 was a nurse at the General Hospital, Annapolis, Maryland. Later he taught music at Mount Vernon College, Alliance, Ohio, and became active as a composer, singer, and music publisher. A Methodist Episcopal Church minister and a strong prohibitionist, he spent much time preaching and publishing works including *Salvation Echoes*, 1882, *Gems of Gospel Songs*, 1884, *Songs of Peace, Love and Joy*, 1885, *The Temperance Songster*, 1886, and *Songs of the Ransomed*, 1887. Arranger: BLESSED BE THE NAME, 63; HUDSON, **359**.

Hughes, Donald Wynn, born Southport, Lancashire, England, 25 March 1911; died Welwyn Garden City, Hertfordshire, England, 12 August 1967. He was educated at Perse School and Emmanuel College, Cambridge, England. Hughes was teacher at the Leys School, Cambridge, from 1934 until 1967, when he became headmaster at Rydal School, a residential school in North Wales founded by English Methodists. He began writing hymns in later life, but died in a car accident, leaving many hymns in manuscript form. Author: "Creator of the earth and skies," **450**.

Hughes, Howard, born Baltimore, MD, 28 June 1930. He earned a B.S. in education from the University of Dayton in 1951 and became a Marionist brother in 1952. Further studies were at the University of Fribourg, Switzerland (1957-59), Case-Western Reserve University, Cleveland (M.A. 1965), the Institut Catholique de Paris, and New York University. He taught in high schools and served as organist/choir director in Marionist communities until 1989 when he began teaching liturgical music at St. Mary's University in San Antonio. He is a prolific composer of liturgical music, a member of ASCAP, the Marionist Writers' Guild, and the National Association of Pastoral Musicians. His compositions have been commissioned by the International Commission on English in the Liturgy. Composer: BAPTIZED IN CHRIST, **609**.

Hughes, John, born Dowlais, Wales, 1873; died Fardre, Pontypridd, Wales, 14 May 1932. Hughes was a product of the the South Wales coal fields. At the age of twelve he worked as a doorboy at the mine in Llantuit Fardre, and in 1905 he was appointed clerk at the Great Western Colliery, Pontypridd, remaining there until his death. A lifelong member of Salem Baptist Chapel, serving as deacon and precentor, he composed Sunday school marches, anthems, and hymn tunes. Composer: CWM RHONDDA, **127, 428, 577**.

Hull, Eleanor Henrietta, born Manchester, England, 15 January 1860; died London, England, 13 January 1935. As an author and promoter of Gaelic culture, Hull was founder and honorary secretary of the Irish Text Society, president of the Irish Literary Society of London, and author of several books on Irish literature and history. Versed: "Be thou my vision," **451**.

Hunter, John, born Aberdeen, Scotland, 12 July 1848; died Hampstead, London, England, 15 September 1917. Hunter was a draper's apprentice, who under the influence of the revival of 1859-61 entered the ministry and attended Mansfield College, Oxford. He was a celebrated Congregational minister, serving churches in York, Hull, Glasgow, and London before returning to Trinity House in 1904. His *Services for Public Worship*, 1886, was highly influential, along with *Hymns for Faith and Life*, 1899, which contained radically altered classic hymn texts. Author: "Dear Jesus, in whose life I see," **468**.

Hurd, David, born Brooklyn, New York, 27 January 1950. Educated at the High School of Music and Art of the Juilliard School, New York, Oberlin College, Oberlin, Ohio (B.M.), and the University of North Carolina, Chapel Hill, North Carolina, Hurd has received honorary doctorates from Berkeley Divinity School, New Haven, Connecticut; the Church Divinity School of the Pacific, Berkeley, California; and Seabury-Western Theological Seminary, Evanston, Illinois. In 1976 he became professor of music and organist at General Theological Seminary, New York, and in 1985 director of music for All Saints Episcopal Church, New York. He was visiting lecturer at the Institute of Sacred Music, Yale University, from 1982 to 1983. A member of the organ faculty of Manhattan School of Music, New York, and an internationally known concert organist, he has received first prize for organ playing and improvisation from the International

Congress of Organists (1977) and the diploma for improvisation from Siching International Organconcours (1981). Hurd is a composer of organ, choral, and instrumental works, and his liturgical compositions and arrangements are in several hymnals. He has served on the Hymn Music and Service Music committees of the Protestant Episcopal Church's Standing Commission on Church Music. Composer: JULION, **197**; MIGHTY SAVIOR, **684**.

Ignatius of Loyola, St., born Spain, 1491; died 1556. Of noble birth, he became a religious leader and in 1539 was one of the founders of the Society of Jesus (Order of the Jesuits) with its worldwide mission to educate youth. Author: "Prayer of Ignatius of Loyola," **570**.

Imakoma, Yasushiga, born Tokyo, Japan, 10 March 1926. He graduated from the Japan Biblical Seminary in 1957 and became an ordained minister of the United Church of Christ in Japan, serving from 1960 to retirement in 1989. He published *Shiroi Tsue no Hitobito* (*People with White Sticks*) in 1970. Author: "Send your Word, O Lord," **195**.

Irons, William Josiah, born Hoddesdon, Hertfordshire, England, 12 September 1812; died London, England, 18 June 1883. Irons earned his B.A., M.A., B.D., and D.D. degrees from Queen's College, Oxford. One of his parishes, St. Mary-Woolnoth, was also served by John Newton. From 1860 until his death, he was prebendary of St. Paul's Cathedral. His hymns and translations are contained in four collections, one of which went through three printings, *Psalms and Hymns for the Church*, 1873, 1875, 1883. Author: "Sing with all the saints in glory," **702**.

Irvine, Jessie Seymour, born Donnottar, Kincardineshire, Scotland, 26 July 1836; died Aberdeen, 2 September 1887. She is the daughter of a minister who served parishes in Dunnottar, Perterhead, and Crimond near Grampian, between 1908 and 1911. Irving is considered the composer of CRIMOND because of a letter written by her sister to William Carnie, a well-known conductor and teacher, who was preparing the Northern Psalter, 1872, for publication. Composer: CRIMOND, **118, 136**.

Isaac, Heinrich, born Flanders, ca. 1450; died Florence, Italy, 26 March 1517. An important Flemish composer, he served Lorenzo de'Medici in Florence (1485-92), became court composer to the Emperor Maximillian I at Vienna (1497), and resettled in Florence in 1514 when the Medicis regained power, living there until his death. His *Choralis Constantinus*, 1550, containing fifty-eight offices for the liturgical year, profoundly influenced German music. Composer: O WELT, ICH MUSS DICH LASSEN, **631**.

Iverson, Daniel, born Brunswick, GA, 26 September 1890; died Asheville, NC, 3 January 1977. Educated at the University of Georgia, Athens, Georgia; Moody Bible Institute, Chicago, Illinois; Columbia Theological Seminary, Decatur, Georgia; and the University of South Carolina, he became a Presbyterian minister in

1914 and served churches in Georgia, South Carolina, and North Carolina. He organized the Shenandoah Presbyterian Church, Miami, Florida, in 1927, ministering there until his retirement in 1951. Author and composer: "Spirit of the living God" (LIVING GOD), **393**.

Ives, Charles Edward, born Danbury, CT, 20 October 1874; died New York, NY, 19 May 1954. Greatly influenced by his experimentally musical father and graduated from Yale University, he created innovative, iconoclastic music that used atonal, polytonal, arhythmic, and polyrhythmic procedures. A successful insurance agent during the week and a reclusive composer in the evenings and on the weekends, he wrote 114 songs, 4 symphonies, piano and violin sonatas, among many other works. He seldom attended concerts and did not own a radio or record player. Belated recognition came when he received the Pulitzer Prize in music in 1947 for his Third Symphony, 1901-04. Composer: SERENITY, **499**.

Jackson, Francis Alan, born Malton, Yorkshire, 2 October 1917. Educated at the University of Durham, he became organist of Malton Parish Church at the age of sixteen and in 1946 succeeded his teacher, Sir Edward Bairstow, as master of the music, York Minster, remaining there until 1982. He also was conductor of the York Musical Society (1947-82) and of the York Symphony Orchestra (1947-80). A notable recitalist in England, Europe, Canada, Australia, and the USA, he received wide acclaim for his 1990 compact disk of the complete organ works of Bairstow. He has written several organ works, much church music, four sonatas, a symphony, and an overture. Two monodramas for speaker, chorus, and organ, *Daniel in Babylon* and *A Time of Fire*, were collaborations with John Stuart Anderson. He is an honorary fellow of both the Royal College of Church Music and of Westminster Choir College, Princeton, New Jersey. Composer: EAST ACKLAM, **97**.

Jackson, Robert, born Oldham, Lancashire, England, 1842; died Oldham, 1914. The son of a parish musician, Jackson studied music at the Royal Academy of Music. After a time, he succeeded his father at St. Peter's in Oldham in a combined tenure that spanned a record ninety-six years. He directed the Oldham Musical Society and the Werneth Vocal Society. Composer: TRENTHAM, **420**.

Jackson-Miller, Jill, born Kansas City, MO, 25 August 1913. She is a radio and motion-picture actress and children's songwriter. Co-author: "Let there be peace on earth," **431**.

James, William Marceus, born Meadville, MS, 4 June 1915. Educated at Mt. Beulah College (A.A.), Butler University, Indianapolis, Indiana (B.S.L. 1938), and Drew University, Madison, New Jersey (B.D. 1942, M.A. 1945), he pastored East Calvary United Methodist Church (1940-44), Trinity Methodist Church of the Bronx (1944-52), and Metropolitan Community United Methodist Church (1952-85), all in New York City. He assisted in organizing the East Harlem Triangle Housing Program and founded the Ministerial Interfaith Association of Harlem, ministering to street gangs and homeless people. James became director of the

Multi-Ethnic Center for Ministry of the northeastern jurisdiction of the United Methodist Church at Drew University and was awarded an honorary doctorate from the university in 1985. Author: "Easter people, raise your voices," **304**.

Janus (Jahn), Martin, born Silesia, ca. 1620; died Ohlau, Silesia, ca. 1682. He was precentor of two churches at Sorau, Silesia, rector of the Evangelical School at Sagan in 1653, and pastor of the church near Eckersdorf Gate, 1664. When the imperial edict of 1668 drove all evangelical pastors and teachers out of the principality, it is believed he became precentor at Ohlau. Author: "Jesus, joy of our desiring," **644**.

John of Damascus, born ca. 675; died ca. 749. The most important dogmatic theologian of the Eastern church, John also played a major role in the regulation of Byzantine chant, parallel to the work initiated by Gregory I, through a new type of hymn, the canon, initiated by Andrew of Crete. John composed six canons for the major festivals and set them to music. His influence spread into the thirteenth-century Latin church through the scholastics, and into nineteenth-century English church music via the translations of John Mason Neale. He was an advocate for the use of pictures and images as aids to the worshiper. Author: "Come, ye faithful, raise the strain," **315**; "The day of resurrection," **303**.

John Paul II, born Wadowice, Poland, 18 May 1920. Originally named Karol Wojtyla, Pope John Paul II became the first Polish, as well as the first non-Italian, pope in 456 years when he was elected in 1978. A conservative pope who has endorsed traditional Catholic views, he has been a vigorous defender of human rights and economic justice. Author: "Litany for Christian unity," **556**.

Johnson, James Weldon, born Jacksonville, FL, 17 June 1871; died Wiscasset, ME, 26 June 1938. African American lyricist, librettist, anthologist, writer on music, and teacher, he studied literature at Atlanta University (M.A. 1904). A self-taught lawyer, Johnson was the first African American to pass the bar examinations in Florida. He collaborated with his brother J. Rosamond Johnson in forming the song-writing team of Cole and Johnson Brothers. His poetic sermons *God's Trombones* were published in 1927. (See biography by Eugene Levy, *James Weldon Johnson: Black Leader, Black Voice*, 1973.) Author: "Lift every voice and sing," **519**.

Johnson, John Rosamond, born Jacksonville, FL, 11 August 1873; died New York City, NY, 11 November 1954. African American composer and vocalist, he studied at Atlanta University and the New England Conservatory of Music, Boston. Collaborating with his brother James in the song-writing team of Cole and Johnson Brothers, he wrote lyrics and music to over 200 songs and edited several important collections of African American music. Composer: LIFT EVERY VOICE, **519**.

Johnston, Julia Harriette, born Salineville, OH, 21 January 1849; died Peoria, IL, 6 March 1919. Daughter of a Presbyterian pastor, she was a Sunday school superintendent and a teacher for forty-one years, as well as president for twenty years of the Presbyterian Missionary Society, founded by her mother. She wrote Sunday school lesson material, about 500 hymn texts, and published several books. Author: "Marvelous grace of our loving Lord," **365**.

Joncas, Jan Michael, born Minneapolis, MN, 20 December 1951. A Roman Catholic priest, musician, and scholar, he was educated at the College of St. Thomas, St. Paul, Minnesota, the University of Notre Dame, and the Pontificio Istituto Liturgico, Collegio Sant'Anselmo (Rome, 1989, 1991). He has served as associate pastor, Church of the Presentation of the Blessed Virgin Mary, Maplewood, Minnesota (1980-84), chaplain, Newman Community, University of Minnesota (1984-87), and since 1991 he has been assistant professor of theology, University of St. Thomas, and parochial administrator, St. Cecilia's Parish, St. Paul, Minnesota. Joncas has written numerous articles on liturgical music, prayer, and the psalms. He has composed and recorded collections of liturgical music and was co-editor of *Gather*. Author and composer: "And God will raise you up" (ON EAGLE'S WINGS), **143**; Response, **844**.

Joseph, Jane M., born London, England, 1894; died London, England, 1929; Educated at St. Paul's Girls' School, Brook Green, and Cambridge, she was a gifted student of Gustav Holst, a composer and conductor. Translator: "On this day earth shall ring," **248**.

Jude, William Herbert, born Westleton, Suffolk, England, September 1851; died London, 8 August 1922. Jude was the organist at the Blue Coat Hospital in Liverpool and later at the Stretford Town Hall near Manchester. He was an active recitalist and lecturer in England and Australia and the editor of several important musical periodicals and two hymn collections: *Mission Hymns*, 1911, and *Festival Hymns*, 1916. He wrote songs, anthems, and an operetta, *Innocents Abroad*. Composer: GALILEE, **398**.

Julian or **Juliana of Norwich**, born England, 1342; died England, ca. 1416. During the Hundred Years' War and the Black Death in Europe, she was an English mystic and theologian whose experiences of the healing and vision of Christ and the Virgin Mary are recounted in her *Revelations of Divine Love*. Author: "The sufficiency of God," **495**.

Kaan, Fred (Frederik Herman), born Haarlem, The Netherlands, 27 July 1929. He attended the University of Utrecht; Western College, Bristol, England; and received the B.A. degree from the University of Bristol (1954). Ordained by the United Reformed Church, he served Windsor Road Congregational Church, Barry, South Wales (1955-63), and Plymouth Church, Plymouth (1963-68). From 1968 to 1978 he first served as minister-secretary of the International Congregational Council, Geneva, Switzerland, and then was named the executive secretary of the World Alliance of Reformed Churches. Having returned to England in 1978 as moderator of the Western Midlands Province of the United Reformed Church, from 1985 to 1989 he was on the ministerial team at Central Church in Swindon and pastor of Penhill United Reformed

Church. He received an honorary Th.D. degree from the Reformed Seminary in Debrecen, Hungary (1978), and earned a Ph.D. degree from Geneva Theological College in 1984 for his dissertation "Emerging Language in Hymnody." His linguistic ability, ecumenical service, and fervent concern for the powerless are apparent in his hymns, numbering more than 200. His works have been published in *The Hymn Texts of Fred Kaan*, 1985, and *Planting Trees and Sowing Seeds*, 1989, and have been translated into more than fifteen languages. (See also Wallace 1980.) Author: "For the healing of the nations," **428**; "Help us accept each other," **560**; "Now let us from this table rise," **634**; "We meet you, O Christ," **257**; "We utter our cry," **439**; translator: "Christ is risen," **313**; "Faith, while trees are still in blossom," **508**; "Your love, O God," **120**.

Kagawa, Toyohiko, born Kobe, Japan, 1888; died 1960. A Japanese social reformer, pacifist, and evangelist, he was disinherited at age fifteen for converting to Christianity. Having graduated from Princeton Theological Seminary (1917), he returned to Japan to become influential in the women's suffrage and peace movements. He was the author of 150 books on religious subjects and two novels, *Across the Death Line*, 1920, and *Before the Dawn*, 1924. Author: "For our country," **429**.

Kaiser, Kurt Frederic, born Chicago, IL, 17 December 1934. Educated at the American Conservatory of Music and Northwestern University (B.M. 1958, M.M. 1959), he was vice-president and music director for many years of Word, Incorporated. He is now a free-lance composer and arranger. Author and composer: "It only takes a spark" (PASS IT ON), **572**.

Kawashima, Hope C. Omachi, born Auburn, CA, 2 April 1937. Graduated from California State University and San Francisco Theological Seminary, with further study at Juilliard School of Music, New York, she is a registered music therapist and a diaconal minister of music in The United Methodist Church, and served on the Hymnal Revision Committee. Versed: "Mountains are all aglow,"**86**; "Lonely the boat," **476**.

Kawashima, Mas, born Yokosuka, Japan, 12 March 1936. Graduated from Tokyo Christian College, Fuller Theological Seminary, San Francisco Theological Seminary, and Claremont Graduate School, he has pastored United Methodist churches in New York and California. Transcriber: "Jesus loves me," **191**.

Kelly, Thomas, born Kellyville, Stradbally, County Queens, Ireland, 13 July 1769; died Dublin, Ireland, 14 May 1855. Educated at Trinity College, Dublin, for the bar, Kelly instead took holy orders in 1792. He was banned from preaching by the archbishop of Dublin because of his friendship with Walter Shirley, a cousin of lady Huntingdon, and his sympathies for the evangelical movement. Kelly was considerably wealthy, and when he became an independent minister, he used his money and time for the benefit of the poor and in building churches at Athy, Portarlington, and Wexford. He is the author of 765 hymns contained in three collections and the composer of several tunes written for use with his hymns. Author: "The head that once was crowned," **326**.

Ken, Thomas, born Little Berkhampstead, Hertfordshire, England, July 1637; died Longleat, Wiltshire, England, 19 March 1710. Orphaned at the age of nine, Ken grew up under the guardianship of Izaak Walton, who was married to Ken's sister, Ann. He was educated at Winchester College and Hart Hall, Oxford, and became a fellow of New College in 1657, where he earned his B.A. and M.A. (1661, 1664). After his ordination in 1662, he was rector of Little Easton, returning to Winchester as chaplain to Bishop Morley. In 1679 he was appointed chaplain to Princess Mary at the Hague, and in 1865 he was consecrated bishop of Bath and Wells. Because he refused to subscribe to James II's Declaration of Indulgence, he was sent to the Tower in 1688. He was acquitted but resigned his bishopric in 1691. Ken was the author of many hymns, but he is most famous for the three hymns for morning, evening, and midnight that conclude with the "doxology." His most well known hymns are found in *A Manual of Prayers for Use of the Scholars at Winchester College*, 1674. Author: "All praise to thee, my God, this night," **682;** "Praise God, from whom all blessings flow," **94, 95**.

Kennedy, Benjamin Hall, born Summer Hill, England, 6 November 1804; died Torquay, Devonshire, England, 6 April 1889. Kennedy was an influential nineteenth-century educator, hymn writer, minister, compiler, and translator, who wrote texts for the study of Latin as well as hymns. His *Hymnologia Christiana*, 1863, an important source for nineteenth-century hymnody, contains several of his original hymns and translations, many from the German. Translator: "Ask ye what great thing I know," **163**.

Kennedy, Gerald Hamilton, born Benzonia, MI, 30 August 1907; died Laguna Hills, CA, 17 February 1980. Educated at the College of the Pacific, the Pacific School of Religion, and Hartford Theological Seminary, Kennedy was ordained a Methodist minister in 1932, serving his first pastorate at the First Congregational Church in Collinsville, Connecticut (1932-36). He then served Methodist congregations in California and Nebraska. In 1948 he was elected bishop and was assigned the Portland, Oregon area, followed by the Los Angeles area from 1952 to 1972. Kennedy served on the texts subcommittee for the 1964 *Methodist Hymnal* in a self-acclaimed role as "the resident lowbrow." Besides authoring seventeen books, he delivered the Lyman Beecher Lectures at Yale in 1954. Author: "God of love and God of power," **578**.

Kethe, William, died ca. 1594. Although nothing is known of Kethe's birth and early life, it is believed he was a Scotsman who during the Marian persecutions of 1555-58 was in exile on the continent, serving as a messenger to other exiles in Basel and Strassburg. It is believed that he may have worked with the scholars who remained in Geneva after Mary's death to complete the Geneva Bible, published in 1560. From 1561 until his death, he was the rector of the church of Childe Okeford, while in 1563 and 1569 he served as chaplain to the English troops under the Earl of Warwick. Some of his twenty-five metrical psalms appear as early as 1559. Author: "All people that on earth do dwell," **75**.

Kim, Dao. No information is available on Kim. Author and composer: "My prayer rises to heaven" (VIETNAM), **498**.

Kim, Hae Jong, born Seoul, Korea, 18 July 1935. Educated at the Methodist Theological Seminary, Seoul, Korea (Th.B. 1961), and the Methodist Theological School in Ohio (B.D. 1964), with additional study at Drew University, he was ordained elder in 1965. He was pastor of Basking Ridge United Methodist Church and district superintendent in the Northern New Jersey Conference before his election in July 1992 as United Methodism's first Korean American bishop. Translator: "Mountains are all aglow," **86**; "Lonely the boat," **476**.

Kim, Helen, born Inchon, Korea, 27 February 1899; died Seoul, Korea, 10 February 1970. Educated at Ewha College, Seoul, Ohio Wesleyan University, Boston University, and Columbia University Teachers College, she returned to Korea to be vice-president and later president of Ewha College. As a Methodist educator and world Christian leader, she was a delegate to forty international gatherings, including the International Missionary Council and the World Council of Churches. She was an ambassador-at-large to the United Nations and served on world councils for the YWCA, the Red Cross, and many other ecumenical and international organizations. Author: "Lonely the boat," **476**.

Kimbrough, S T, Jr., born Athens, AL, 17 December 1936. Internationally known scholar, musician, and Old Testament specialist, Kimbrough holds the doctorate in Old Testament and Semitic languages from Princeton Theological Seminary, where he taught Hebrew and biblical studies. He also did postgraduate study at Hebrew University in Jerusalem and has taught Hebrew Bible and Judiac studies in universities in middle and western Europe. From 1985 to 1990 he was a member of the Center of Theological Inquiry in Princeton, New Jersey. Kimbrough is the author of *Israelite Religion in Sociological Perspective*, *Lost in Wonder*, and with John Holbert and Carlton R. Young, *Psalms for Praise and Worship*, 1992. With Harrell F. Beck, John Holbert, and Alan Luff, he was a member of the psalms text committee that prepared The United Methodist Liturgical Psalter. He is a specialist in Charles Wesley studies and has edited *The Unpublished Poetry of Charles Wesley* in three volumes and is the founding president of the Charles Wesley Society. Adapter: "Canticle of love," **646**; "Canticle of hope," **734**; author: Responses, **747**, **850**; adapter: Responses, **745**, **795**, **807**, **814**, **833**.

Kimbrough, Timothy Edward, born Birmingham, AL, 12 August 1952. Educated at Duke University, Durham, North Carolina, and the General Theological Seminary, New York (1984), he was vicar at St. David's Episcopal Church, Laurinburg, North Carolina (1984-89), and is rector at the Church of the Holy Family, Chapel Hill, North Carolina (1989-). A jazz pianist and arranger, he has published *Sweet Singer*, 1987. Composer: Responses, **74**, **652**, **799**, **821**, **844**.

King, Martin Luther, Jr., born Atlanta, GA, 15 January 1929; died Memphis, TN, 4 April 1968. African American civil rights leader and eloquent Baptist preacher, he led the movement against racial segregation from the mid-1950's until his death by assassination. (See Lincoln 1970.) Author: "God is able," **106**.

Kingsley, George, born Northampton, MA, 1811; died Northampton, 13 March 1884. A self-taught musician, Kingsley was organist of the Old South Church and Hollis Street Church in Boston, a music teacher at Girard College, Philadelphia, and music supervisor for the Philadelphia public schools. His hymn tunes appear in Charles Everest's *Sabbath*, 1873. Arranger: MESSIAH, **399**.

Kirkpatrick, William James, born Duncannon, PA, 27 February 1838; died Philadelphia, PA, 20 September 1921. At the age of seventeen Kirkpatrick moved to Philadelphia where he joined the Wharton Street Methodist Episcopal Church. By the age of twenty-one he had published a collection of camp-meeting songs, *Devotional Melodies*, 1859. After serving as a fife major in the Civil War, he went into the furniture business until his wife's death in 1878, when he devoted all his time to music, serving at Grace Methodist Episcopal Church, Philadelphia. From 1880 to 1921 he collaborated on some 100 collections of gospel songs, many of which were published by his own Praise Publishing Company. His chief collaborators were John R. Sweney, H. L. Gilmour, John Stockton, and J. Howard Entwhistle. Composer: TRUST IN JESUS, **462**.

Kitchin, George William, born Naughton, Suffolk, England, 7 December 1827; died Durham, England, 13 October 1912. He was educated at Christ Church, Oxford, and served as dean of Winchester Cathedral and Durham Cathedral, and was chancellor of Durham University. Co-author: "Lift high the cross," **159**.

Klug, Ronald Allan, born Milwaukee, WI, 26 June 1939. After receiving the B.S. degree from Martin Luther College, New Ulm, Minnesota (1962), he taught at St. Matthew Lutheran School, Oconomowoc, Wisconsin. He was a graduate student in English at the University of Wisconsin, Milwaukee (1965-68), while he was a teaching assistant. He has been an advertising copywriter at Concordia Publishing House and a book editor at Augsburg Publishing House. Since 1976 Klug has taught English for the American School in Fort Dauphin, Madagascar. He is the author of several articles, texts for music, poetry, and two books, *The Strange Young Man in the Desert*, 1970, and *Lord, I've Been Thinking*, 1978. Author: "Rise, shine, you people," **187**.

Knapp, Phoebe Palmer, born New York, NY, 8 March 1839; died Poland Springs, ME, 10 July 1908. The daughter of the Methodist evangelist William C. Palmer, and wife of Fairfield Knapp, the founder of Metropolitan Life Insurance Company, Knapp's musical abilities were recognized early in her singing and composition of songs for children. Following her husband's death in 1891, she shared her fortune with various charitable causes. She was a close friend and collaborator of Fanny Crosby. Of the over 500 gospel hymns and tunes she wrote, many of which were used in the USA and England, only two remain in common use today. Composer: ASSURANCE, **369**.

Knapp, William, born Wareham, Dorsetshire, England, 1698; buried Poole, Dorsetshire, England, 26 September 1768. Believed to be of German descent, Knapp was the parish clerk of St. James's Church, Poole, for thirty-nine years. His work is contained in two collections: *New Psalm Tunes and Anthems*, 1738, and *New Church Melody*, 1753. Composer: WAREHAM, **258, 679**.

Knatterud, LaRhae Anne Grindal, born Rugby, ND, 5 May 1948. Educated at Augsburg College, Minneapolis, MN (B.A. 1970), and University of Minnesota (M.A.P.A. 1977), she is planning coordinator for the Metropolitan Council of St. Paul, Minnesota. From 1972 to 1990 she was involved with the aging program for the council. She has also directed and sung in choirs since 1966. Harmonizer: BRED DINA VIDA VINGAR, **502**.

Knight, Gerald Hocken, born Par, Cornwall, England, 27 July 1908; died London, 16 September 1979. He was educated at Truro Cathedral School, Peterhouse, Cambridge, and the Royal College of Music where he served as its director 1952-72. A distinguished organist, composer, and educator, Knight was joint musical editor of *Hymns Ancient and Modern Revised*, 1950 and a member of the committee for its two supplements, *100 Hymns for Today*, 1969, and *More Hymns for Today*, 1980. Harmonizer: DETROIT **390**.

Kocher, Conrad, born Ditzingen, Württemberg, 16 December 1786; died Stuttgart, 12 March 1872. Pianist, composer, church musician, and choral conductor who studied in St. Petersburg and Italy, Kocher founded a sacred vocal music society in Stuttgart in 1821. His study of Palestrina prompted his leadership in the early nineteenth-century reform of German church music, particularly its emphasis on four-part singing. In 1827 he became the music director in the collegiate church in Stuttgart, and in 1852 he was awarded an honorary doctorate by the University of Tübingen. His compositions include two operas, an oratorio, and smaller works, plus a piano method and a treatise on church music, *Die Tonkunst in der Kirche*, 1823, and a collection of chorales, *Zionsharfe*, 1855. Composer: DIX, **92**; Response, **829**.

Koizumi, Isao, born Osaka, Japan, 3 November 1907. He studied composition and organ privately while also earning the bachelor of economics degree from the Osaka University of Commerce (1932). He lectured at his alma mater until 1942 and at the same time was an organist in Tokyo. In 1951 he became minister of music at the United States Far East Air Force Chapel Center in Tokyo and was also appointed as the music editor of *The Hymnal 1954* for the United Church of Christ in Japan. A leading figure in Japanese hymnody, Koizumi has composed and arranged many hymn tunes, published many collections, and has been appointed music editor for several subsequent hymnals, including *The Sunday School Hymnal*, 1954, and *Hymns of Praise*, 1967 2d ed. He has been a director at the Christian Music Seminary, Tokyo, since 1967. James Siddons, editor of *Dictionary of Contemporary Japanese Music*, has provided information about Koizumi and other Japanese composers. Composer: TOKYO, **552**.

Koyama, Shozo, born Nagano-ken, Japan, 3 October 1930. Having received his degree in music education from the Kunitachi College of Music, Koyama has been professor of music at his alma mater since 1970. He was awarded the West-minster Choir College prize in 1965 and has published *Gassho to Kyoìku* [*Chorus and Education*], 1980, and *Yama, to Kawa to Ai to* [*Mountain, River and Love*], 1967, among other works. Composer: MIKOTOBA, **195**.

Kremser, Edward, born Vienna, 10 April 1838; died Vienna, 26 November 1914. The conductor of the Vienna Männergesangverein, Kremser published a collec-tion of six anonymous Dutch patriotic songs from Adrian Valerius's collection, *Nederlandtsche Gedenckclank*, 1626, for his men's chorus entitled *Sechs altnieder-ländische Volkslieder*, 1877. Through the choir's performance of this music, the melodies became popular and have found wide acceptance in many hymnals. Arranger: KREMSER, **131**.

Kreutz, Robert Edward, born LaCrosse, WI, 21 March 1922. A development engineer, music composer, teacher, and choral director, Kreutz was educated at Loras College, Dubuque, Iowa; UCLA, Los Angeles, California; American Conservatory, Chicago, Illinois (B.M. 1949); and the University of Denver, Colorado (M.A. 1970). He studied composition with Arnold Schoenberg, Leo Sowerby, and Normand Lockwood. Kreutz has published over 300 works and received numerous honors and commissions for his compositions, including the winner of the 41st International Eucharistic Congress Hymn Competition (1976) and commissioning for *Laudate Dominum*, papal mass at Dodger Stadium, Los Angeles, California, in 1987. Composer: GIFT OF FINEST WHEAT, **629**.

Kriewald, James A., born Platteville, WI. An educator, composer, and church musician, Kriewald was educated at the University of Wisconsin, (B.S., M.M., Ph.D) and is presently vice-president for International Programs and Enrollment Management, Shenandoah University, Winchester, Virginia. Composer: "Word and Table Musical Setting B," **19**; KRIEWALD KYRIE, **482**.

Kwillia, Billema, born Liberia, ca. 1925. As a young man, Kwillia learned to read his own language, Loma, through the church's literary program. He became a liter-acy teacher in the early 1960's, serving in that role for several years. During this time he was baptized a Christian and became an evangelist and church leader in his home town. Author and composer: "Come, let us eat" (A VA DE), **625**.

Lafferty, Karen, born Alamagordo, NM, 29 February 1948. Educated at Eastern New Mexico University (BME. 1970) with private study in New Mexico and at the University of Texas. In 1971 she became worship leader and concert artist at Calvary Chapel, Costa Mesa, California, since 1971. Currently founder/director of Musicians for Mission and Youth with a Mission in the Netherlands, Lafferty is also a recording artist involved in concert performances and leading music seminars. Author and composer: "Seek ye first" (SEEK YE), **405**.

Lathbury, Mary Artemisia, born Manchester, Ontario County, NY, 10 August 1841; died East Orange, NJ, 20 October 1913. A professional artist, Lathbury contributed to periodicals of the Methodist Sunday School Union. She was the founder of the Look-Up Legion, a Methodist Sunday school organization. She was called the "Poet Laureate of Chautauqua" for her literary activity in the summer assemblies at Lake Chautauqua, New York. Author: "Break thou the bread of life," **599**; "Day is dying in the west," **687**.

LeCroy, Anne Kingsbury, born Summit, NJ, 21 January 1930. She was educated at Bryn Mawr College, University of Cincinnati, Duke University, and University of the South, Sewanee, Tennessee. Professor of English at East Tennessee State University, Johnson City, Tennessee, LeCroy was a member of the Southern Leadership Conference (1974-82), contributing material to *Lesser Feasts and Fasts*, 1980, and working as a language consultant for inclusive language in the constitution and canons of the Protestant Episcopal Church and hymn texts for *The Hymnal 1982*. Revision: "Christ, mighty Savior," **684**.

Lee, Dong Hoon. No information is available on Lee. Composer: BAI, **476**.

Lees, John. Organist of the Moravian church at Leominster, Lees was the editor of *Hymn Tunes of the United Brethren*, Manchester, England, 1824. Arranger: MONKLAND, **194**.

Lemmel, Helen Howarth, born Wardle, England, 14 November 1863; died Seattle, WA, 1 November 1961. Brought to the USA at the age of nine, she became a gifted singer who organized a women's quartet that traveled the Chautauqua circuit. In 1904 she moved to Seattle, traveled as a concert singer, and led religious services for children. She composed more than 400 hymns. Author and composer: "Turn your eyes upon Jesus," **349**.

Lew, Timothy Ting-fang, born Wenchau, Chekiang, China, 1891; died Albuquerque, NM, 5 August 1947. A leading Chinese author, educator, and editor, Lew studied in China and the United States, earning his B.D. from Yale and the M.A. and Ph.D. degrees from Columbia University, with additional study at Union Theological Seminary. He taught and lectured at leading schools and colleges and was the commission chairman for *Hymns of Universal Praise*, 1936, the hymnbook of the Chinese Union, and co-editor of the *Union Book of Common Prayer*. He was the Chinese delegate to three sessions of the World Council of Churches and a member of the national legislative body of the Chinese government from 1936 to 1941. Known for his work with Chinese Christian organizations, Lew resided in the United States from 1941 to 1947 and died while teaching at the University of New Mexico. Author: "The bread of life for all is broken," **633**.

Lewis-Butts, Magnolia, born Kansas City, MO, date of birth unknown; died Chicago, IL, December 1949. She taught bookkeeping in Kansas City before moving to Chicago. There she became secretary of the Metropolitan Community Church and private secretary to Professor J. Wesley Jones, the minister of music at Metropolitan. She served as secretary of the Biennial Council of Community Churches in the USA for over twenty years. In addition to composing, she arranged many African American spirituals and gospel songs. Author and composer: "Let it breathe on me" (LET IT BREATHE), **503**.

Lim, Ok Im, born Korea, 1 June 1915. Lim graduated from Nora Teacher's College, Japan, becoming professor of literature and dean of home economics of Kunkook University. She has received the award of Asian Freedom and Korean Women's Literature award, and has published nine books. Author: "Mountains are all aglow," **86**.

Lincoln, Charles Eric, born Athens, AL, 23 June 1924. African American scholar and teacher, educated at Le Moyne College, Syracuse, New York (A.B. 1947); Fisk University, Nashville, Tennessee (M.A. 1954); University of Chicago (B.D. 1956); and Boston University (M.Ed., Ph.D. 1960), Lincoln taught at Clark College (1954-64), Union Theological Seminary (1966-73), Fisk University (1973-76), and Duke University (1976-). He has received thirteen honorary degrees and the William Kenan Rand Distinguished Professor citation. His publications include *The Black Masking in America; Race, Religion and the Continuing American Dilemma; The Black Church Since Frazier; This Road Since Freedom: Profile of Martin Luther King;* and *The Black Church in the African American Experience.* Author: "How like a gentle spirit," **115**.

Lindemann, Johann, born Thuringia, Germany, 1549; died Gotha, 6 November 1631. Son of a burgess of Gotha, he attended the University of Jena (M.A. 1570), later became cantor at Gotha and remained there until his death. In 1598 he published *Amorum Filii Dei Decades Duae.* Author: "In thee is gladness," **169**.

Littlechief (Ahtone), Libby, born Lawton, OK, 10 September 1917. Daughter of United Methodist pastors, she attended Haskell Institute, graduating in 1938. She was a United States Civil Service clerical employee in the Bureau of Indian Affairs until her retirement in 1979. She served three terms as secretary of the Kiowa tribe of Oklahoma, a tribe numbering more than 8,000 persons. Paraphrased: "Daw-Kee, Aim Daw-Tsi-Taw," **330**.

Littledale, Richard Frederick, born Dublin, Ireland, 14 September 1833; died London, England, 11 January 1890. Educated at Trinity College, Dublin, where he was a distinguished scholar and ordained in 1857, Littledale served parishes in Norwich and London before devoting his time to writing because of ill health. Though he was active in the Oxford movement, he warned against a return to Rome in *Plain Reasons for Not Joining the Church of Rome,* 1880. He is the author of some fifty publications, most of which treat theological, historical, liturgical, and hymnological subjects, plus translations from Danish, Swedish, Greek, Latin, Syriac, German, and Italian. Translator: "Come down, O Love divine," **475**.

Lloyd, William, born Rhos Goch, Llaniestyn, Caernarvonshire, Wales, 1786; died Caernarvonshire, Wales, 1852. Lloyd, a cattleman and farmer, was a self-taught musician and conductor of Welsh singing societies. His home was a popular gathering place for singing schools. Composer: MEIRIONYDD, **436**.

Lockwood, George F., IV, born Chicago, IL, 3 April 1946. The son of a Methodist minister and a musically talented mother who began his music training early, he graduated from Indiana University, Bloomington (B.M.E. 1968). After college he spent time as a missionary to Costa Rica, where in 1969 he participated in the first week-long church music workshop for Protestants ever held in Central America. This sparked his interest in the new Hispanic music emerging from Roman Catholic and Protestant musicians following Vatican II. He graduated from the School of Theology, Claremont, California (D.M. 1981), and was ordained in 1984. While pastoring in Arizona and California, Lockwood has translated thirty new Hispanic hymns, led workshops on new Hispanic hymnology and hymn translation, served as a consultant for *Celebremos II*, and was a member of the Hispanic Consultation of the Hymnal Revision Committee. Translator: "Camina, pueblo de Dios," **305**; "Cantemos al Señor," **149**; "Cuando el pobre," **434**; "Jesús es mi Rey soberano," **180**; "La palabra del Señor es recta," **107**; "Niño lindo," **222**; "Pues si vivimos," **356**; "Tú has venido a la orilla," **344**; "Una espiga," **637**.

Loh, I-to, born Tamsui, Taipei, Taiwan, 28 September 1936. Educated at Tainan Theological College, Taiwan, Union Theological Seminary, New York, and the University of California, Los Angeles, Loh has since the early 1960's actively pursued the contextualization of church music of Taiwan and other Asian countries. In 1972 he compiled *New Songs of Asian Cities*, 1972, for the Christian Conference of Asia. In the USA he directed the Asian American Hymnbook Project, which published *Hymns from the Four Winds*, 1983, a supplement to *The Methodist Hymnal*, 1966, reflecting the effort of Chinese, Filipino, Japanese, Korean, and Taiwanese groups in the National Federation of the Asian-American United Methodists (NFAAUM). He has taught at his alma mater in Taiwan, directed many church and collegiate choirs, and published over fifty anthems and hymns. Currently a professor of church music and ethnomusicology at the Asian Institute for Liturgy and Music, Manila, and at Tainan Theological College, Taiwan, Loh also serves the World Association for Chinese Church Music as associate general secretary. Composer: BENG-LI, **615**; harmonizer: TOA-SIA, **151**; transcriber: "For the bread which you have broken," **615**; "Here, O Lord, your servants gather," **552**; "Jaya ho," **478**; "The bread of life for all is broken," **633**.

Longfellow, Samuel, born Portland, ME, 18 June 1819; died Portland, ME, 3 October 1892. The brother of Henry Wadsworth Longfellow, Samuel received his B.A. degree from Harvard University (1839) and the B.D. from Harvard Divinity School (1846). Besides serving Unitarian congregations in Massachusetts, New York, and Pennsylvania, he edited, with Samuel Johnson, *A Book of Hymns for Public and Private Devotions*, 1846, and *Hymns of the Spirit*, 1864.

Additional publications include *Vespers*, 1859, *A Book of Hymns and Tunes*, 1860, and the biography of his poet brother in 1866. Author: "Bless thou the gifts," 587; "Holy Spirit, Truth divine," 465; "Now, on land and sea descending," 685.

Longstaff, William Dunn, born Sunderland, England, 28 January 1822; died Sunderland, 2 April 1894. When his friend Arthur A. Reese left the Anglican Church to establish Bethesda Free Chapel, Longstaff, a man of independent means, followed and became its treasurer as well as benefactor and friend of well-known evangelical preachers Dwight L. Moody, Ira D. Sankey, and William Booth. Author: "Take time to be holy," 395.

Lorenz (Porter), Ellen Jane, born Dayton, OH, 3 May 1907. Distinguished composer, church music historian, and educator, she was educated at Wellesley College (B.A. 1929), Wittenberg University (M.S.M. 1972), and Union Graduate School (Ph.D. 1978). For most of her career she was an editorial partner with Lorenz Publishing Co. (1931-62). She was music editor for the 1957 hymnal of the Evangelical United Brethren Church and a consultant to *Supplement to the Book of Hymns*, 1982, and the Hymnal Revision Committee. Her publications include many anthems, organ pieces, cantatas, handbell compositions, and *Glory, Hallelujah: the Story of the Campmeeting Spiritual*. Adapter and arranger: "O the Lamb" (THE LAMB), 300.

Lovelace, Austin Cole, born Rutherfordton, NC, 26 March 1919. Lovelace is one of the most important and influential figures in USA church music in the twentieth century, and his music and books are used in the worship and hymnody of every major Protestant denomination. He holds degrees from High Point College, High Point, North Carolina (A.B. 1939), Union Theological Seminary (M.S.M., 1941, D.S.M., 1950), and the Mus.D. degree from High Point College. Besides serving congregations in North Carolina, Evanston, Illinois, New York City, Dallas and Denver, he has taught at the University of Nebraska, Queens College, Charlotte, and Davidson College, Davidson, North Carolina, Garrett Theological Seminary, Union Theological Seminary, Iliff School of Theology, and Temple Buell College. He was the first president of the National Fellowship of Methodist Musicians, a past president and a fellow of the Hymn Society in the United States and Canada, and has served as vice-president of the Choristers Guild. As chair of the tunes committee he greatly influenced the content of *The Methodist Hymnal*, 1966. Lovelace is active as an organ recitalist and lecturer and has been prominent in the national and local leadership of the American Guild of Organists. He was organist for the Second Assembly of the World Council of Churches, Evanston, 1954. He is the composer of over 700 compositions, including hymns, hymn arrangements, and music for choir, organ, and solo voice. Books include *The Organist and Hymn Playing*, 1962, *The Anatomy of Hymnody*, 1965; with William C. Rice, *Music and Worship in the Church*, 1960, and *Hymn Notes for Church Bulletins*, 1987. He was a contributing author to *Companion to the Hymnal*, 1970. Lovelace prepared the Metrical Index for *The United Methodist Hymnal*, 1989. Composer: MUSTARD SEED, 275; harmonizer: ARMENIA, 554; AUS TIEFER NOT, 515; DAVIS, 518; GLORIA, 238; SPANISH HYMN, 158; versed: "Jesus, we want to meet," 661.

Lowry, Robert, born Philadelphia, PA, 12 March 1826; died Plainfield, NJ, 25 November 1899. Popular Baptist preacher, orator, and educator who served churches in Pennsylvania, New York City, Brooklyn, and Plainfield, New Jersey, Lowry was a graduate of Bucknell University and also taught there, receiving the D.D. degree in 1875. While in Brooklyn, he became interested in writing and composing gospel hymns. He collaborated with William H. Doane in producing a dozen collections and succeeded William B. Bradbury as music editor for songbook publishers Biglow and Main. Author and composer: "Nothing but the blood" (PLAINFIELD), **362**; "Shall we gather at the river" (HANSON PLACE), **723**; "Up from the grave he arose" (CHRIST AROSE), **322**; composer: MARCHING TO ZION, **733**; NEED, **397**.

Luff, Alan Harold Frank, born Bristol, England, 6 November 1928. Educated in the classics and theology at University College, Oxford, England, and Westcott House, Cambridge, he was ordained in 1956 and served parish churches in Manchester, becoming precentor of Manchester Cathedral. In 1968 he moved to the parish of Dwygyfylchi (Penmaenmawr). He was precentor of Westminster Abbey from 1979 to 1992, and is presently canon residentiary of Birmingham Cathedral. Luff is one of the leading commentators on church music in Britain and an expert on Welsh hymnology. (See his *Welsh Hymns and Their Tunes.*) He served as secretary (1973-86) and is currently the chair of the Hymn Society of Great Britain and Ireland. He has served on the committee that produced the British Methodist *Hymns and Psalms*, 1983, and with Harrell F. Beck, John Holbert, and S T Kimbrough, Jr., he served on the Psalms text committee that prepared The United Methodist Liturgical Psalter. He has contributed to the preparation of *The Hymnal 1982 Companion*. Adapter: "Canticle of light and darkness," **205**; "Canticle of prayer," **406**; Response: **746, 785, 809, 814, 838, 856**.

Lundberg, Lars Åke, born Sweden, 1935. From a musical family, he studied theology at the University of Uppsala and worked summers as a restaurant musician. Upon becoming a clergyman in 1960, he "discovered that many people could not join in the singing of traditional hymns" because "their music and that of the church were miles apart." (Correspondence with Carlton R. Young, July 1992) Thus he began setting texts as well as composing songs for children. His recording "Let us form a ring" was awarded with the "Golden Record" as the best-selling children's recording. He is currently editor at the official publishing house of the Church of Sweden. Composer: GUDS KÄRLEK, **120**.

Lundeen, Joel Waldemar, born Yuhsien, Honan, China, 24 May 1918; died 12 April 1990. The son of missionaries and educated at Augustana College, Rock Island, Illinois (B.A. 1940), and Augustana Theological Seminary, Rock Island (M.Div. 1945), he has served as associate archivist for the Lutheran Church in America since 1967. A musician, pastor, professor, and archivist, he also teaches hymnology and worship courses at the Lutheran School of Theology and is a member of the Hymn Society in the United States and Canada. Translator: "When Christmas morn is dawning," **232**.

Luther, Martin, born Eisleben, Saxony, 10 November 1483; died Eisleben, 18 February 1546. Educated at Magdeburg and Erfurt, Luther became a monk in the Augustinian order at Erfurt. He was ordained in 1507 and earned his Th.D. from Wittenberg University where he also taught. As a result of his teaching, study, and deep dismay over corruption within the church at Rome, on All Saints' Eve, October 31, 1517, he posted his famous Ninety-Five Theses on the church door at Wittenberg as a basis for debate. After refusing to retract his writings before the Diet of Worms, 1521, particularly those on the sale of indulgences, he openly broke with Rome and became the leader of the German Reformation. Luther was a skilled dilettante musician and an articulate writer, translator, and preacher. In addition to producing a large volume of theological writing, Luther translated the Bible into German, 1521-34, wrote several original hymns and melodies, revised many Latin hymns to German texts set to adaptations of plainsong and folk melodies, and encouraged the composition of new texts and rhythmic hymn melodies. His thirty-seven hymns and paraphrase are cast in simple, plain, and sometimes rough phrases and striking metaphors, qualities that are for the most part lost in English translations. He was a leader in liturgical reform, particularly through his *Formulae Missae*, 1523, and *Deutsche Messe*, 1526. His creation of the *chorale* embodied the essence of this reform. Author: "Christ Jesus lay in death's strong bands," **319**; "Savior of the nations, come," **214**; author and attributed composer: "Out of the depths I cry to you" (AUS TIEFER NOT), **515**; author and composer: "A mighty fortress is our God" (EIN' FESTE BURG), **110**; Response, **764, 776, 780, 793, 854.**

Lutkin, Peter Christian, born Thompsonville, WI, 27 March 1858; died Evanston, IL, 27 December 1931. Having studied at the St. James' Cathedral Choir School and in Europe from 1881 to 1884, he returned as organist/choirmaster at St. Clements (1884-91), at St. James' (1891-96), and as music theory teacher at the American Conservatory of Music. The first dean of Northwestern University's School of Music, Evanston, Illinois (1896), Lutkin was a founder of the American Guild of Organists, president of the Music Teachers' National Association, and a member of the editorial boards of the 1905 Methodist hymnal and the 1918 Protestant Episcopal hymnal. A composer of anthems, hymn tunes, and works for instruments, he was an important leader in the development of USA twentieth-century church music and music education. Composer: "Amen," **904.**

Lvov, Alexis Feodorovich, born Reval, now Tallinn, Estonia, 5 June 1798; died near Kovno, now Kaunas, Lithuania, 28 December 1870. Lvov received his first musical training from his father, director of the imperial court chapel at St. Petersburg. After serving in the Russian army, in 1837 he succeeded his father, a post he held for twenty-four years. A violin virtuoso, Lvov performed Mendelssohn's Violin Concerto at the Leipzig Gewandhaus in 1840 with the composer conducting. He edited a collection of music for the Eastern Orthodox liturgical year, composed an opera and a violin concerto, and toured with his own string quartet until deafness forced his retirement in 1867. He is chiefly remembered for the music of the Russian national anthem, *Bozhe, tsarya khrani* (*God save the Tsar*) composed in 1833, included as a hymn tune in many English-language hymnals. Composer: RUSSIAN HYMN, **653.**

Lyte, Henry Francis, born Kelso, Scotland, 1 June 1793; died Nice, France, 20 November 1847. Educated at Enniskillen and Trinity College, Dublin (1814), Lyte was honored three times for his poetry. After his ordination in 1815, his longest appointment was as perpetual curate at Lower Brixham, Devonshire, where he served twenty-four years, retiring and moving to Nice and the continent because of ill health. His published works include *Tales on the Lord's Prayer in Verse*, 1826, *Poems, Chiefly Religious*, 1833, 1845, and *The Spirit of the Psalms*, 1834. Author: "Abide with me," **700**; "Praise, my soul, the King of heaven," **66**.

McAfee, Cleland Boyd, born Ashley, MO, 25 September 1866; died Jaffrey, NH, 4 February 1944. Educated at Park College, Parksville, Missouri (1884), and Union Theological Seminary, New York, he returned to Park College to teach while he pastored the campus church and directed the choir. He later served churches in Chicago and Brooklyn (1901-12), was professor of systematic theology at McCormick Theological Seminary, Chicago (1912-30), and served as secretary of the Presbyterian Board of Foreign Missions (1930-36). Author and composer: "There is a place of quiet rest" (McAFEE), **472**.

McCoy, Helen Beth Perkinson, born Chattanooga, TN, 11 May 1947. Educated at Emory and Henry College, Emory, Virginia (B.A. 1969), and Peabody of Vanderbilt (M.M.E. 1971), she is diaconal minister of music at Pleasant View United Methodist Church, Abingdon, Virginia, and a member of and adjudicator for the National Guild of Piano Teachers. She researched and drafted the new biographical entries for this volume and is a published author and composer.

McCutchan, Robert Guy, born Mt. Ayr, IA, 13 September 1877; died Claremont, CA, 15 May 1958. One of the USA's most distinguished hymnologists, McCutchan played a major role in shaping Methodist church music practice during the first half of the twentieth century. He was educated at Park College, Parkville, Missouri, and Simpson College, Indianola, Iowa (B.M. 1904). He taught voice at Baker University, Baldwin, Kansas, where in 1910 he established the conservatory of music. After study in Berlin and Paris, he became dean of the school of music at DePauw University, Greencastle, Indiana, serving from 1911 to 1937. Honorary degrees were bestowed on him from Simpson College (Mus.D.), Southern Methodist University (D.Sac.Litt.), Southwestern University (D.Litt.), and DePauw University (Mus.D.). McCutchan began work on the 1935 Methodist hymnal as chairman of the subcommittee on tunes, and in 1931 he was elected editor. Because of the constraints of the depression years, he single-handedly saw the book through its publication. At the same time he acquired information that was included in the first significant hymnal handbook in the United States, *Our Hymnody*, 1937. The hymn tunes and responses he wrote for the hymnal were published under the pseudonym "John Porter." McCutchan's work on behalf of church music is marked by his deep love and concern for local congregations and a strong desire for typical worshipers to experience the joy of singing great hymns. Other publications include *American Junior and Church School Hymnal*, 1928; *Aldersgate, 1738-1938*, 1938; *Hymns in the Lives of Men*, 1945; and *Hymn Tune Names: Their Sources and Significance*, 1957. He lectured at several colleges and universities including Perkins School of Theology at Southern Methodist University, 1954-55. Throughout his life he collected songbooks and hymnbooks from all over the country, assembling a library of more than 3,000 volumes. The collection is now housed in the Honald Library of the associated colleges of Claremont. See also Helen Cowles McCutchan, *Born to Music: The Ministry of Robert Guy McCutchan*, 1972. Arranger: CAMPMEETING, **492**.

McDougall, Alan G., born 1895; died 1964. Translator: "Christ, mighty Savior," **684**.

McGee, Bob, born Vancouver, British Columbia, Canada, 18 June 1949. Graduated from Glad Tidings Bible College, Vancouver (1971), he is pastor for the Vineyard Churches. Author and composer: "Emmanuel, Emmanuel" (McGEE), **204**.

McGranahan, James, born near Adamsville, PA, 4 July 1840; died Kinsman, OH, 7 July 1907. McGranahan was encouraged by P. P. Bliss to become a mass evangelist, gospel song leader, and composer. He taught and directed George F. Root's National Normal Institute for three summers, then joined with D. W. Whittle, touring the USA and Great Britain (1877-88). A tunes writer for Whittle's texts, he became an editor with Ira D. Sankey and George Stebbins of *Gospel Hymns and Sacred Songs*, 1878-91. His compilations include *The Gospel Male Choir*, 1878, 1883, *The Choice, Harvest of Song* (with C. C. Case), and *Gospel Choir* (with Ira D. Sankey). Composer: EL NATHAN, **714**.

McGuire, David Rutherford, born St. Catharines, Ontario, Canada, 22 July 1929; died Richmond Hill, Ontario, 13 November 1971. Educated at the University of Toronto (B.A. 1951) and Wycliffe College (B.A. 1954), he was an Anglican priest, a member of the committee for *The Hymn Book*, 1971, and the editor of *Sing I*, 1971. Co-author: "Jesus loves me," **191**.

McIntosh, Rigdon McCoy, born Maury County, TN, 3 April 1836; died Atlanta, GA, 4 July 1899. Educated at Jackson College, Columbia, Tennessee (1854), he was a member of the faculty of Vanderbilt University, Nashville, from 1875 to 1876. McIntosh moved to Emory College, Oxford, Georgia, and from 1877 to 1895, he earned his living through fees paid directly by students, by plying his trade as a "singing school master," licensing copyrights, and publishing a number of Sunday school songbooks and hymnals. Sunday school songbooks, including *Tabor*, 1866, *Glad Tidings*, 1867, *Emerald*, 1872, *The Gem*, 1873, *A Collection of Hymns and Tunes for Public, Social, and Domestic Worship*, 1874. He also was editor for a number of collections for the Methodist Episcopal Church, South. Information about McIntosh has been supplied by Lewis E. Oswalt from his unpublished doctoral dissertation about the composer. Arranger: PROMISED LAND, **724**.

McKeever, Don. No information is available about McKeever. Harmonizer: WELLSPRING, **506**.

Madan, Martin, born Hertingfordbury, England, 1726; died Epsom, Surrey, England, 2 May 1790. Madan earned his B.A. from Christ Church, Oxford (1746), and in 1748 he was admitted to the bar. Sent to hear John Wesley preach in order to caricature him for a group of friends, he instead was converted and ordained for the ministry. He became the chaplain to Lock Hospital, an institution for disturbed women, and through his social standing he gathered funds for the building of a chapel. His treatise, *Thelyphthora*, 1780, which advocated polygamy as a possible solution to the problems he observed, caused an outrage that forced his retirement to Epsom. Though not the author of any original hymns, Madan altered and compiled the works of others in *A Collection of Psalms and Hymns Extracted from Various Authors*, 1760, to which he added an appendix in 1763. He also was known as a composer and a scholar of Latin classics. Attributed alterer: "Hail, thou once despised Jesus," **325**

Maker, Frederick Charles, born Bristol, England, 1844; died Bristol, 1 January 1927. Maker trained as a chorister in Bristol Cathedral and with organist Alfred Stone, and later contributed to Stone's *Supplement* to the *Bristol Tune Book*, 1881. A teacher, conductor, and composer, he served as organist in Free Methodist and Congregational churches. Composer: ST. CHRISTOPHER, **297**; REST, **358**.

Malan, Henri Abraham César, born Geneva, Switzerland, 7 July 1787; died Vandoeuvres, Switzerland, 18 May 1864. Malan was a popular preacher in the French language evangelical Calvinistic movement of Switzerland. He wrote about 1,000 hymns that are almost identical in spirit to those springing from the English Calvinistic reaction to the Wesleyan movement. Malan composed the tunes for most of his hymns. Composer: HENDON, **163**.

Mann, Arthur Henry, born Norwich, England, 16 May 1850; died Cambridge, England, 19 November 1929. He was educated at Norwich Cathedral and New College, Oxford. It is said that while a chorister at Norwich, he was capable of playing the cathedral service when he was only eight years old. Mann served as organist at King's College, Cambridge, from 1875 until 1928. Composer: ANGEL'S STORY, **396**.

Manzano, Miguel. Nothing is known about this person except he is thought to be a Spanish Roman Catholic priest. Co-author and co-composer: "Cuando el pobre" (EL CAMINO), **434.**

Maquiso, Elena G. Born Guindulman, Bohol, Philippines, 7 October, 1914. She was educated in the Philippines and the USA, and received the Doctor of Religious Education from the Hartford Theological Foundation in 1960. She is a member of the faculty of Silliman University in Dumaguete, Philippines, and the director of its Ulahingan Research Project. Her significant contributions to indigenous folk lore and hymnody began with *Awitan Ta Ang Dyos*, 1962, and include *Mga Sugilanon Sa Negros*, 1980, and *Ulahingan: Epic of the Southern Philippines*, 1992. Author and composer: "O God in heaven" (HALAD), **119.**

Marlatt, Earl Bowman, born Columbus, IN, 24 May 1892; died Winchester, IN, 13 June 1976. The son of a Methodist minister, Marlatt was educated at DePauw University (1912) and Boston University (1922, 1929) with further study at Harvard, Oxford, and the University of Berlin. From 1925 to 1938 he taught philosophy and from 1938 to 1945 served as dean at Boston University. He was professor of philosophy of religion and religious literature at Perkins School of Theology, Southern Methodist University, from 1946 to 1957, and 1960 to 1962 was curator of the Treasure Room and Hymn Museum, Interchurch Center, New York City. Besides writing several volumes of poetry, Marlatt was the associate editor of *The American Student Hymnal*, 1928. Author: "Are ye able," **530**.

Marsh, Donald Stuart, born Akron, OH, 5 September 1923. He attended Western Maryland University, the University of Houston (B.S., M.S.), and the Theodora Irvine School of Drama. He and Richard Avery, well known for their worship workshops, co-founded Proclamation Productions, Inc., writing approximately 100 hymn texts and tunes. Marsh was director of music at Port Jervis Presbyterian Church. Co-author and co-composer: "I am the church" (PORT JERVIS), **558**.

Marshall, Jane Manton, born Dallas, TX, 5 December 1924. A distinguished composer, educator, conductor, and author, Marshall was educated at Southern Methodist University (B.M. 1945, M.M. 1968) and serves on the faculty of church music at Perkins School of Theology, Southern Methodist University (1969-present). She is active in the areas of music and worship in The United Methodist Church, the American Guild of Organists, the American Choral Directors Association, and the Choristers Guild. The recipient of the 1965 Woman of Achievement award from Southern Methodist University and the 1974 award for distinguished service to church music from the Southern Baptist Church Music Conference, Marshall has published many anthems and collections, served as a clinician, lecturer, and contributor to church music journals, as well as chair of the hymnal supplement task force of The United Methodist Church. Author and composer: "What gift can we bring" (ANNIVERSARY SONG), **87**; composer: HIGH STREET, **590**; Response, **212, 516, 652, 739, 749, 750, 755, 758, 760, 783, 806, 813, 816, 819, 832, 837, 840, 845, 848, 852.**

Martin, Civilla Durfee, born Jordan, NJ, 21 August 1866; died Atlanta, GA, 9 March 1948. A schoolteacher with some formal training in music, she wrote gospel songs for evangelistic campaigns in collaboration with her husband, Walter Stillman Martin. Author: "Be not dismayed," **130**.

Martin, Walter Stillman, born Rowley, MA, 1862; died Atlanta, GA, 16 December 1935. Martin was a Harvard-educated Baptist minister who later became a member of the Disciples of Christ. After teaching at Atlantic Christian College, he moved in 1919 to Atlanta, which became the base for evangelistic meetings he held across the country. His hymn tunes were often set to texts by his wife, Civilla Durfee Martin. Composer: MARTIN, **130**.

Martínez, Nicholás, born Buenos Aires, Argentina, 7 October 1917; died 19 August 1972. Born into a Roman Catholic family, he converted as a youth to evangelical Christianity and studied at the Evangelical Faculty of Theology in Buenos Aires, doing postgraduate work in Puerto Rico. Ordained by the Disciples of Christ (1948), Martínez pastored in Argentina and Paraguay, became active in ecumenical cultural activities, and served as one of the editors of *Cantico Nuevo*, 1962. Author: "Christo vive," **313**.

Martínez, Raquel Mora, born Allende, Coahuila, Mexico, 17 January 1940. A composer and arranger of Hispanic songs and hymns, Martinez was educated at the University of Texas at El Paso (B.M.) and Perkins School of Theology and the School of the Arts, Southern Methodist University (M.S.M), with further study at the Manhattan School of Music, New York. She is the editor of the forthcoming revision of *Himnario Metodista*. Arranger: ROSAS, **149**.

Mason, Harry Silverdale, born Gloversville, NY, 17 October 1881; died Torrington, CT, 15 November 1964. Educated at Syracuse University (1911) with further study at Boston University, Mason was organist and instructor of music for Auburn Theological Seminary. He also served First and Second Presbyterian Churches in Auburn, the latter for twenty-seven years. Composer: BEACON HILL, **530**.

Mason, Lowell, born Medfield, MA, 8 July 1792; died Orange, NJ, 11 August 1872. Preeminent USA composer, hymnologist, church musician, conductor, and music educator, Lowell began directing choirs and singing schools at the age of sixteen, following training by local musicians. When he was twenty, he moved to Savannah, Georgia, to work as a bank clerk but also served as the organist and choir director for First Presbyterian Church and studied music theory with F. L. Abel. In order to secure a publisher for his hymn tunes and a book on church music, he returned to Boston and influenced G. K. Jackson of the Boston Handel and Haydn Society to sponsor publication of the *Boston Handel and Haydn Society Collection of Church Music*, 1821, according to Eric Routley, the "most influential publication in the history of American hymnody." (Routley 1953, 459) With the success of the collection, Mason moved permanently to Boston, becoming the president and later conductor of Boston Academy of Music and the Handel and Haydn Society, and serving as music director of the Bowdoin Street Church. As his interests broadened to include music education, he resigned from the Handel and Haydn Society to devote more time to music and instructional methods for children. With Thomas Hastings, for more than half a century he was the dominant force that established USA church and public school music in the "European norm" of theory, notation, repertory, and taste. In 1832 he went to Europe to study the Pestalozzian method of music instruction and brought back to the USA many publications of English, German, and French music through his association with Johann Nägeli, Beethoven's publisher. Mason devoted considerable time to lectures, teacher-training classes, and conventions, and inaugurated a music curriculum for the Boston public schools in 1838, the official beginning of public school music education in the USA. His lecturing took him back to Europe from 1851 to 1853, and in 1855 New York University honored him with the Mus.D.

degree. Mason's publications include at least eighty compilations and collections, the most important being *New Carmina Sacra*, 1852. His grandson, Henry L. Mason, lists 1,126 original hymn tunes and 497 arrangements in his *Hymn Tunes of Lowell Mason*, 1944. Arranger: ANTIOCH, **246**; AZMON, **57, 59, 422, 608**; DENNIS, **553, 557**; EVAN, **566**; composer: BETHANY, **528**; BOYLSTON, **413**; GREGORIAN, **270**; HAMBURG, **298**; OLIVET, **452**; harmonizer: HENDON, **163**.

Massie, Richard, born Chester, Cheshire, England, 18 June 1800; died Pulford Hall, Coddington, England, 11 March 1887. Self-taught in German, Massie, the son of the rector of St. Bride's Church, Chester, became an important translator of German hymns, particularly those of Spitta, Gerhardt, and Luther. His published volumes of translations include Luther's spiritual songs, 1854, *Lyra Domestica*, from Spitta's *Psalter und Harfe*, 1860, and a second volume of Spitta's texts with an appendix of works from other German sources. Translator: "Christ Jesus lay in death's strong bands," **319**.

Masters, J. The only information about this person is in regard to the Latin hymn "Matutinus altiora," which he apparently translated into English and published as "King Alfred's Hymn" (see Julian 1907, 1579). Translator: "As the sun doth daily rise," **675**.

Matheson, George, born Glasgow, Scotland, 27 March 1842; died North Berwick, Scotland, 28 August 1906. Although nearly blind by the age of eighteen, Matheson was an outstanding student, graduating from Glasgow Academy (1852) and Glasgow University (1861, 1862). After attending Glasgow's Divinity School, he was licensed to preach in the Presbyterian Church and served churches in Glasgow, Innellan, Argylshire, and from 1866 to 1899 at St. Bernard's in Edinburgh, where he retired because of ill health. Matheson received honorary doctorates from Edinburgh University (1879) and Aberdeen University (1902) in recognition of his outstanding preaching and theological writing. His sole volume of poetry, *Sacred Songs*, was published in 1890. Author: "Make me a captive, Lord," **421**; "O Love that will not let me go," **480**.

Mathias, William, born Whitland, Dyfed, Wales, 1 November 1934; died Anglesey Island, Wales, 29 July 1992. A Welsh composer, pianist, and teacher, he studied at the University College of Wales, Aberystwyth (B.Mus. 1956), and the Royal Academy of Music in London, earning a doctorate in music from the University of Wales (1966) one year after his election as a fellow of the Royal Academy. He was professor and music department chair at the University College of North Wales, Bangor (1970-88). A prolific composer of instrumental and vocal music in a sophisticatedly modern yet tonal style, he was commissioned to write "Let the People Praise Thee, O God" for the wedding of Prince Charles and Lady Diana, 1981. See also *Baker's Biographical Dictionary of Music and Musicians*. Composer: "Musical Setting," **25**; Response, **839**.

Maurus, Rhabanus, born Mainz, 776; died Winkel, on the Rhine, 4 February 856. After becoming a monk, Maurus studied in Tours in 802. One year later he was made director of the Benedictine school at Fulda. Following his ordination in 814, he made a pilgrimage to the Holy Land. Maurus was named abbot at Fulda (822-42) and archbishop of Mainz (847). His writings include poetic and theological works. Attributed author: "Come, Holy Ghost, our souls inspire," **651**.

Mechthild of Magdeburg, born Saxony, ca. 1209; died Halfta, ca. 1283. A German mystical writer, she led a life of prayer and penance for forty years as a Beguine at Magdeburg. Her collection of spiritual poems, *Das fliessende Licht der Gottheit [The Flowing Light of the Godhead]*, 1250-70, reflects her understanding of the mystery of Christ's love and mercy. See also *New Catholic Encyclopedia*, page 546. Author: "Praising God of many names," **104**.

Meier, Margret S. No information has been received about this person. Harmonizer: VIETNAM, **498**.

Meineke, Charles (Christoph), born Oldenburg, Germany, 1 May 1782; died Baltimore, MD, 6 November 1850. The son of the organist to the duke of Oldenburg, Meineke moved to England around 1810. In 1820 he moved to Baltimore, where he was organist at St. Paul's Episcopal Church until his death. He is the author of *Music for the Church . . . Composed for St. Paul's Church, Baltimore*, 1844. Composer: MEINEKE, **70**.

Mendelssohn, Jakob Ludwig Felix, born Hamburg, 3 February 1809; died Leipzig, 4 November 1847. Mendelssohn was the son of a Jewish banker and a grandson of the philosopher Moses Mendelssohn. He received his earliest musical training from his mother, Lea. After moving to Berlin in 1811, the family converted to Lutheranism, and the name "Bartholdy" was added. A prodigious and prolific composer, Mendelssohn had composed five symphonies by the age of twelve; in addition to his works for orchestra, piano, voice, chorus, organ, concerti, and chamber music, he is well known for the revival of the music of J. S. Bach with the 1829 performance of Bach's *St. Matthew Passion*, the first since Bach's death. The influence of Bach is seen in Mendelssohn's own oratorios, *St. Paul*, 1836, from which his chorale harmonizations in many hymnals are derived, and *Elijah*, 1846. He also built the Leipzig Gewandhaus Orchestra into the first of the great modern symphony orchestras and founded the Leipzig Conservatory in 1843. For more complete biography and bibliography, see *Baker's Biographical Dictionary of Music and Musicians*. Composer: MENDELSSOHN, **240**; harmonizer: MUNICH, **598**; NUN DANKET, **102**.

Mendoza, Vicente (Polanco), born Guadalajara, Mexico, 1875; died 1955. A first-generation Mexican Methodist, he was a pioneer of Methodism in Mexico through his preaching and evangelizing. Mendoza was educated at the Seminario Presbiteriano and the Instituto Methodista in Puebla, and served as professor at the Seminary Centro Evangélico Unido in the Federal District of Mexico. He began his ministry in 1897 in Puebla, Mexico. From 1915 to 1921 he served Methodist churches in California, returning to Mexico where he continued to teach and serve churches until his death. In 1901 Mendozo began writing and translating hymns that he included in *Himnos Selectos*, now in its tenth edition. Several of his 300 hymns and translations are included in Spanish language hymnals. Author and composer: "Jesús es mi rey sobrano" (MI REY Y MI AMIGO), **180**.

Merbecke, John, born England, 1523; died England, ca. 1585. Although he began his career as a clerk and organist of St. George's, Windsor, Merbecke (variously spelled Marbeck and Marbecke) is known chiefly as the compiler of the first concordance to the English Bible, 1550, his musical settings in the *Book of Common Praier Noted*, 1550, and his close connection with Calvinist theology for which he was tried for heresy but escaped death through the intervention of Bishop Gardiner of Winchester and the pardon of Henry VIII. His settings for morning prayer and Holy Communion were made according to the instructions of Thomas Cranmer: "not full of notes, but, as near as may be, for every syllable a note, so that it may be sung distinctly and devoutly." (Leaver 1982, 29-30). Merbecke is also the author of several tracts promoting the Reformed position, written during the reign of Queen Elizabeth. Composer: "Word and Table" Responses: "Holy, holy, holy," **28**; "O Lamb of God," **30**.

Merrill, William Pierson, born East Orange, NJ, 10 January 1867; died New York, NY, 19 June 1954. Educated at Rutgers College (B.A. 1887, M.A. 1890) and Union Theological Seminary (B.D. 1890), Merrill was ordained a Presbyterian minister in 1890, serving congregations in Pennsylvania, Illinois, and from 1911 to 1938 at the Brick Presbyterian Church in New York City. He was a prominent preacher and the author of ten books. Columbia University honored him with the S.T.D. degree in 1927. Author: "Rise up, O men of God," **576**.

Messiter, Arthur Henry, born Frome, Somersetshire, England, 12 April 1834; died New York, NY, 2 July 1916. After receiving his early training from private tutors and four years of musical study at Northampton, Messiter moved to the United States in 1863 and began to sing in the choir at Trinity Church in New York City. He served briefly as organist in Poultney, Vermont, and Philadelphia before returning to Trinity Church as organist, serving from 1866 to 1897, and maintaining the high standards of the English men's and boys' choir tradition. Messiter is the author of *A History of the Choir and Music of Trinity Church*, 1906, and editor of a music edition of the Protestant Episcopal *Hymnal*, 1893, *Psalter*, 1889, and *Choir Office Book*, 1891. Composer: MARION, **160**; Responses, **74**, **821**.

Meyer, Johann David, born Schwäbisch Hall, Ulm, 15 June 1636; died Schwäbisch Hall, 23 December 1696. A director of music and town councillor, he collected *Geistliche Seelen-Freud: oder Davidische Hausse-Capell . . .*, Ulm, 1692. Composer: MEYER, **336**.

Middleton, Jesse Edgar, born Pilkington Township, Wellington Co., Ontario, Canada, 3 November 1872; died Toronto, 27 May 1960. With training in elementary school teaching, he instead became a correspondent in Quebec for the Montreal *Herald*. He returned to Toronto as a special writer for *The Mail and Empire* newspaper, and in 1942 for *The Saturday Night* he collaborated with leading scholars, producing books on Ontario history. He also directed the choir for forty years for Toronto's Centennial United Church and published several books. Translator: "'Twas in the moon of wintertime," **244**.

Mieir, Audrey Mae, born Leechburg, PA, 12 May 1916. Educated at L.I.F.E. Bible College and ordained to the gospel ministry in the International Church of Foursquare Gospel (1937), Mieir was an evangelical pianist for radio programs and personal appearances from 1937 to 1945. The organizer of various choirs, in 1959 she became director of Mieir Choir Clinics in Hollywood, California; in 1960 she became vice-president of Mieir Music Foundation, Incorporated. Author and composer: "His name is wonderful" (HIS NAME IS WONDERFUL), **174**.

Miles, C. Austin, born Lakehurst, NJ, 7 January 1868; died Pitman, NJ, 10 March 1946. Educated at the Philadelphia College of Pharmacy and the University of Pennsylvania, he became a pharmacist but left his profession for music publishing after submitting his first gospel song to the Hall-Mack Publishing Company of Philadelphia. Miles was employed there for thirty-seven years as editor and manager and continued as editor when the firm merged with Rodeheaver. He was a popular music director for camp meetings, conventions, and churches. Author and composer: "I come to the garden alone" (GARDEN), **314**.

Miller, Edward, born Norwich, England, 1731; died Doncaster, England, 12 September 1807. Apprenticed as a paver for his father, he ran away to study music with Charles Burney and played flute in George Frederick Handel's orchestra. Organist for Doncaster Parish Church (1756-1807), he also published *The Psalms of David Set to new Music*, 1774, *Thoughts on the Present Performance of Psamody*, 1791, *The Psalms of Watts and Wesley*, 1801, *Sacred Music*, 1802, and *Elements of Thorough-bass and Composition*, 1787. Miller's most important work was *The Psalms of David for the Use of Parish Churches*, 1790, in which he collaborated to provide a course of psalms for the church year. In 1786 he received a doctorate from Cambridge. In addition to writing numerous hymn tunes, he composed six sonatas for harpsichord. Arranger: ROCKINGHAM, **299**.

Miller, Margaret D., born Clifton Springs, NY, 23 March 1927. Educated at Wilson College, Chambersburg, Pennsylvania (B.A. 1949), she joined her mother's missionary work in Liberia in 1950 to serve on the Committee on World Literacy and Christian Literature. Since her commissioning in 1954, she has served at the literacy center in Wozi and edited the Loma *Weekly*, a bilingual newspaper. Translator: "Come, let us eat," **625**.

Miller, Max, born 21 October 1927. Educated at the University of Redlands, California (B.M. 1950, M.M. 1957), Boston University, Boston, Massachusetts (Ph.D. 1955), the Akademie der Music, Vienna, Austria, and King's College, Cambridge, England, Miller was organist/choirmaster for Grace Cathedral, Topeka, Kansas, while he taught at Washburn University. He is now university organist and chair of the organ department at the School of the Arts and the School of Theology, Boston University. He has been active in the American Guild of Organists as dea national convention chair, and examination committee member and is also founder and director of the Geneva Point Conference on Church Music for the National Council of Churches. Miller was the editor of *Sing of Life and Faith*, a hymnal of the United Church of Christ and has written numerous articles and recorded for the Musical Heritage Society and Boston Records. Composer: MARSH CHAPEL, **426, 551**.

Miller, Sy, born Brooklyn, NY, 9 February 1908; died Beverly Hills, CA, 17 August 1971. Miller collaborated with Jill Jackson-Miller in writing eighty-five songs. Author and composer: "Let there be peace on earth" (WORLD PEACE), **431**.

Mills, Sylvia Anne Jenkins, born Laurel, MS, 24 April 1940. Educated at Belhaven College, Jackson, Mississippi; Winthrop College, Rock Hill, South Carolina; and the University of Tennessee (B.S. 1968), she has held positions in radio broadcasting, radio and newspaper advertising, and from 1964 to 1968 at The Methodist Publishing House, Nashville, copyediting *The Methodist Hymnal*, 1966. As a freelance copyeditor she edited *Companion to the Hymnal*, 1970, and *Companion to the United Methodist Hymnal*, 1993. She resides in Chattanooga, Tennessee, where she works for Provident Life and Accident Insurance Company as an underwriter.

Milner-White, Eric. No information is available on Milner-White. Author: "An invitation to the Holy Spirit," **335**.

Mohr, Joseph, born Salzburg, Austria, 11 December 1792; died Wagrein, Austria, 4 December 1848. Because his father was a mercenary soldier and away much of the time, Mohr was raised by the Salzburg Cathedral vicar, J. N. Hiernle, and sang in the cathedral choir. He was ordained a Roman Catholic priest in 1815 and served in the diocese of Salzburg. When he was assistant priest at St. Nicholas' Church, Oberndorf (1817-19), he wrote his famous Christmas carol. Author: "Silent night, holy night," **239**.

Monk, William Henry, born Brompton, London, England, 16 March 1823; died London, 1 March 1889. Monk was a leading nineteenth-century hymnologist, editor, and composer who, after early positions as organist in London churches, was successively choir director (1847), organist (1849), and professor of vocal music (1874) at King's College. He also served as organist of St. Matthias' Church, Stoke Newington, and as professor of music at the School for the Indigent Blind, National Training School for Music, and Bedford College. His most significant contributions were as editor of *The Parish Choir*, 1840-51, music editor of *Hymns Ancient and Modern*, 1861, Appendix 1868, and collaborator on the 1875 and 1880 editions of the same hymnal to which he contributed fifty tunes and arrangements. Arranger: DIX, **92**; VICTORY, **306**; composer: EVENTIDE, **700**; harmonizer: ELLACOMBE, **203, 278**; INNOCENTS, **675**; ST. ANNE, **117**; ST. MAGNUS, **326**; ST. THEODULPH, **280**.

Montgomery, James, born Irvine, Ayrshire, Scotland, 4 November 1771; died Sheffield, Yorkshire, England, 30 April 1854. One of the most important writers of hymns in the English language, Montgomery was the son of Moravian missionary parents who intended for him to enter the Moravian ministry. His parents, having left him with the Moravian settlement at Bracehill, died while doing mission work in the West Indies when Montgomery was nineteen. He attended school at Fulneck but was dismissed for his preoccupation with writing poetry. After running away in 1787, he worked in a chandler's shop at Mirfield, near Wakefield. Looking for a publisher of his poetry, he went to London without success, but found a friend in Joseph Gales, publisher and owner of the Sheffield *Registrar*, who made him his assistant. When Gales left the country to avoid prosecution for his anti-Tory writings, Montgomery assumed ownership, changing the name to the Sheffield *Iris*. For his writings he was twice imprisoned, once for a song celebrating the fall of the Bastille and again for reporting a political riot in Sheffield. The *Iris* was also a vehicle for the publication of some of his early hymns. Although closely associated with Methodism, Montgomery had a keen interest in the promotion of congregational hymn singing in Anglican worship. He eventually became a communicant at St. George's, where William Mercer was the vicar. His output includes many articles and poems, as well as some 400 hymns collected in 1853. Author: "Angels from the realms of glory," **220**; "Go to dark Gethsemane," **290**; "Hail to the Lord's Anointed," **203**; "Prayer is the soul's sincere desire," **492**; Response, 208, 845; "Stand up and bless the Lord," **662**.

Moore, Thomas, born Dublin, Ireland, 28 May 1779; died London or Sloperton, Devizes, Wiltshire, 25 February 1852. Educated at Trinity College, Dublin, Moore studied law in London and in 1803 was appointed admiralty registrar in Bermuda. In 1840 he traveled to New York, touring the United States and Canada. His popular and versatile works include his collected poems, among them "Believe me, if all those endearing young charms" and "The last rose of summer," and the editing of Lord Byron's letters, 1830. His only contribution to hymnody is thirty-two texts set to national airs contained in *Sacred Songs*, 1816. Author: "Come, ye disconsolate," **510**.

Moore, William. Little information is known about this composer. He published a four-shaped-note tune book, *The Columbian Harmony*, in 1825, registering it in Wilson County, West Tennessee. Moore claimed authorship to eighteen of the tunes, several of which became widely used by subsequent compilers in the South. Composer: HOLY MANNA, **150**.

More, Thomas, born London, England, 1478; died London, England, 1535. One of the most eminent Renaissance humanists, statesmen, and scholars, More was lord chancellor of England (1529-32) and author of *Utopia*, 1516. King Henry VIII beheaded him for treason when More refused to recant the pope's authority and uphold the king's divorce from Catherine of Aragon. Author: "For grace to labor," **409**.

Morley, Frederick B. Born Saskatchewan, Canada, 24 March 1884; died St. Petersburg, FL, 19 October 1969. Educated at Syracuse University (A.B.) and Boston University School of Theology (S.T.B.), Morley was ordained in the

Methodist ministry in 1915, and served churches in New Jersey and New York, including the First Methodist Church, Oceanside, New Jersey. Author: "O church of God, united," **557**.

Mote, Edward, born London, England, 21 January 1797; died Horsham, Sussex, England, 13 November 1874. Mote was the son of a tavern owner and grew up in the streets without religious training. After being apprenticed to a cabinet-maker, he began attending church and came under the influence of John Hyatt. When he settled in Southwark near London, he became a cabinetmaker and reporter and in 1852 a Baptist minister. Mote was the first to use the term "gospel hymn" in his collection *Hymns of Praise, A New Selection of Gospel Hymns*, 1836. Author: "My hope is built," **368**.

Moultrie, Gerard, born Rugby, England, 16 September 1829; died Southleigh, England, 25 April 1885. Known chiefly for his excellent translations of hymns from Greek, Latin, and German, Moultrie also had strong ancestral ties to the United States. His great-grandfather left South Carolina for England during the Revolution, and his great-grand-uncle was General William Moultrie, elected governor of South Carolina in 1875. He received his education from Exeter College, Oxford (1851, 1856), and was ordained an Anglican priest. Positions include master and chaplain of Shrewsbury School, vicar of Southleigh, and warden of St. James's College, Southleigh. Among his publications are *Hymns and Lyrics for the Seasons and Saints' Days of the Church*, 1867, and the preface to *Cantica Sanctorum*, 1880. Translator: "Let all mortal flesh keep silence," **626**.

Murray, James Ramsey, born Andover, MA, 17 March 1841; died Cincinnati, OH, 10 March 1905. Murray was a student of Lowell Mason, George F. Root, William B. Bradbury, and George J. Webb. He also studied at the Musical Institute in North Reading, Massachusetts. After serving in the Civil War as a Union soldier, he worked for the publishing firm of Root & Cady, editing the monthly *Song Messenger* until the Chicago fire destroyed the business. From 1881 until his death he worked for the Cincinnati firm of John Church Company, heading the publishing department and editing the monthly *Musical Visitor*. Murray is the composer of many Sunday school songs, gospel songs, and the editor of numerous collections. His work is researched in William J. Reynolds's *Hymns of Our Faith*, 1964. Composer: AWAY IN A MANGER, **217**.

Nägeli, Johann Georg, born Wetzikon, near Zurich, Switzerland, 26 May 1772; died Wetzikon, 26 December 1836. Nägeli was a writer, teacher, composer, and publisher. Beginning in 1803 his firm published the op. 31 sonatas of Beethoven in *Répertoire de clavecinistes*. He was an exponent of the Pestalozzian method of music teaching and was a significant influence on Lowell Mason. Composer: DENNIS, **553, 557**.

Neale, John Mason, born London, England, 24 January 1818; died Grinstead, Sussex, England, 6 August 1866. Born to evangelical parents and named for his maternal grandfather, John Mason Good, Neale was one of the most important translators of Greek and Latin hymnody with his work included in virtually all English-language hymnals. He graduated from Trinity College, Cambridge, in 1840, becoming a fellow, chaplain, and acting tutor of Downing College. In spite of his evangelical background, he became identified with the Oxford movement and was a founder of the Cambridge Camden Society. Although he was ordained a priest in 1842, chronic lung disease and his strong Anglo-Catholic leanings kept him out of the parish priesthood. In 1846 he became warden of Sackville College, East Grinstead, a home for elderly men. Besides researching and writing, he also founded a nursing sisterhood, promoted social welfare, and expanded the ministry of Sackville College to orphans and young women. His primary publications include *Hymns of the Eastern Church*, 1862, *Mediaeval Hymns and Sequences*, 1851, 1863, and *Hymns, Chiefly Mediaeval, on the Joys and Glories of Paradise*, 1865. *The Hymnal Noted*, 1851, 1854, contains many original hymns as well as translations, and his work appeared in the trial edition of *Hymns Ancient and Modern*, 1859. For a more complete biography and listing of works, see John Julian's *Dictionary of Hymnology*. Translator: "All glory, laud, and honor," **280**; "Christ is made the sure foundation," **559**; "Come, ye faithful, raise the strain," **315**; "Good Christian friends, rejoice," **224**; "O sons and daughters, let us sing," **317**; "O what their joy and their glory must be," **727**; "O wondrous sight! O vision fair," **258**; "Of the Father's love begotten," **184**; "The day is past and over," **683**; "The day of resurrection," **303**.

Neander, Joachim, born Bremen, 1650; died Bremen, 31 May 1680. Although Neander was the son of a long line of clergymen, he studied at the Pädagogium and Gymnasium Illustre where he joined in the rebellious, wanton student life of seventeenth-century Germany. In 1650 he attended St. Martin's Church, Bremen, to ridicule Pastor Theodore Under-Eyck, but was instead converted and later through Under-Eyck's influence was appointed rector of the Latin school at Düsseldorf in 1674. Neander became closely associated with Pietism and P. J. Spener. Under Spener's influence he started private Bible studies, absenting himself from regular services and communion for fear of communing with the unconverted. Altering the schedules and routine of the school lead to his suspension. In 1679 he returned to St. Martin's as rector; he died at the age of thirty from tuberculosis. John Julian calls him Germany's most important German Reformed Church hymn writer of the seventeenth-century. (Julian 1907, 790) Author: "All my hope is firmly grounded," **132**; "Praise to the Lord, the Almighty," **139**; Response, **826**; composer: UNSER HERRSCHER, **578**, **674**.

Nelson, Horatio Bolton, born Brickworth House, Wiltshire, England, 7 August 1823; died Trafalgar House, 1 March 1913. Educated at Trinity College, Cambridge (M.A. 1844), as Thomas Bolton he succeeded to the title of earl in 1835 and assumed the name of his renowned uncle Admiral Viscount Nelson. He was assisted by his intimate friend John Keble in editing the *Salisbury Hymn-Book*, 1857, revised as the *Sarum Hymnal* in 1868. He also published two devotional books, *A Form of Family Prayer, with Special Offices for the Seasons*, 1852, and *A Calendar of Lessons for Every Day of the Year*, 1857. Adapter: "As the sun doth daily rise," **675**.

Nelson, Ronald Axel, born Rockford, IL, 29 April 1927. Nelson was educated at St. Olaf College (1949) and the University of Wisconsin (1959). He began his career as a public school music teacher and later served as the full-time director of music at Tabor Lutheran Church in Rockford and director of music at Westwood Lutheran Church, St. Louis Park, Minnesota. His work is marked by a strong emphasis on children's choirs and the pursuit and composition of quality liturgical music for children, adults, and congregations. Besides lecturing frequently at Lutheran colleges and seminaries, Nelson has been active in the American Guild of Organists and served on the Inter-Lutheran Commission of Worship, composing for it a setting of the communion service used in *Lutheran Book of Worship* and *Lutheran Worship*. St. Olaf College honored him with the Distinguished Alumnus award in 1967. Harmonizer: BEACH SPRING, **581, 605**.

Neumark, Georg, born Langensalza, Thuringia, 16 March 1621; died Weimar, 18 July 1681. Neumark's early education was in the gymnasia of Schleusingen and Gotha. As he was on his way to study law at Königsberg, his caravan was robbed by highwaymen, leaving him with only a prayerbook and a few coins. After searching for employment, he secured a tutorship in the family of Judge Stephan Henning. After two years he returned to Königsberg to study law. Following another period of unemployment, he became court poet, librarian, and registrar at Weimar, and later became secretary of the ducal archives. Blind during the last year of his life, Neumark wrote most of his hymns during times of trial and suffering. Author: "If thou but suffer God to guide thee," **142**.

Newbolt, Michael Robert, born Dymock, Gloucestershire, England, 1874; died Bierton, Buckinghamshire, England, 7 February 1956. Educated at St. John's College, Oxford, England (B.A. 1895, M.A. 1912), and ordained in 1900, he served in Wantage and Iffley and as principal of the Missionary College in Dorchester from 1910 to 1916. He then became perpetual curate of St. Michael and All Angels in Brighton (1916-27) and canon of Chester Cathedral (1927-46). In 1946 he was licensed to officiate in the diocese of Oxford. Co-author: "Lift high the cross," **159**.

Newton, John, born London, England, 24 July 1725; died London, 21 December 1807. The son of a shipmaster, Newton was at sea by the age of eleven. After being imprisoned on a man-of-war, he escaped and later became the master of a slave-trading ship. In Liverpool the influence of George Whitefield, the Wesleys, and Thomas à Kempis's *Imitation of Christ* influenced him to give up sea duty and become an ardent abolitionist. Newton studied Greek and Hebrew, became curate at Olney, and was ordained in 1764. With William Cowper he produced the 1779 *Olney Hymns* (containing 281 hymns by Newton), the first and most important Anglican hymnbook printed for parish use. In 1780 he became rector of St. Mary's, Woolnoth, where he served until he was eighty. Newton wrote his own epitaph, which he requested might be put up on a plain marble tablet near the vestry of his church in London:

John Newton, Clerk.
Once an Infidel and Libertine,
A servant of slaves in Africa,
Was, by the rich mercy of our Lord and
Saviour
JESUS CHRIST
Preserved, restored, pardoned,
And appointed to preach the Faith
He had long labored to destroy,
Near 16 years at Olney in Bucks
And twenty-six years in this church.
On Feb. 1, 1750, he married
Mary,
Daughter of the late George Catlett
Of Chatham, Kent.
He resigned her to the Lord who gave her
On 15th of December, 1790

Author: "Amazing grace," **378**; "Glorious things of thee are spoken," **731**.

Nichol, Henry Ernest, born Hull, Yorkshire, England, 10 December 1862; died Aldborough, Skirlaugh, Yorkshire, 30 August 1926. After beginning a career in civil engineering, Nichol began to study music and earned a B.M. from Oxford in 1888. The majority of his 130 tunes were written for Sunday school anniversaries, with those for which he also wrote texts written under the pen name "Colin Sterne." Author and composer: "We've a story to tell to the nations" (MESSAGE), **569**.

Nicholson, Sydney Hugo, born London, England, 9 February 1875; died Ashford, Kent, England, 30 May 1947. Educated at Rugby and New College, Oxford (M.A., D.M.), he also studied under Walter Parratt and Charles V. Stanford at the Royal College of Music, and at Frankfurt am Main. He served as organist for Carlisle Cathedral, Eton College, and Manchester Cathedral. After nine years as organist for Westminster Abbey, Nicholson resigned in 1927 to found the School of English Church Music at St. Nicholas College, Chislehurst (renamed the Royal School of Church Music by George VI in 1945), which he directed until his death. Following World War II the school was moved to Canterbury, and in 1954 it was permanently located at Addington Palace, Croydon. Nicholson was music editor of *Hymns Ancient and Modern*, 1916-47, as well as the first layman to hold the chair, 1938-47. Knighted in 1938 for his services to church music, he composed anthems, hymn tunes, and operettas. Composer: CRUCIFER, **159**; harmonizer: PADERBORN, **439, 635**.

Nicolai, Philipp, born Mengeringhausen, Waldeck, 10 August 1556; died Hamburg, 26 October 1608. The son of a Lutheran pastor, Nicolai was educated at Erfurt and Wittenberg and ordained in 1576, first assisting his father and then becoming pastor at Herdecke. He served congregations in Niederwildungen,

Altwildungen, Unna (a town devastated by the plague), and in 1601 at St. Katherine's in Hamburg where he died from a fever. Nicolai was a strong supporter of Lutheran sacramental orthodoxy and often became embroiled in controversies with Catholics (particularly through Spanish invasions), Calvinists, and Sacramentarians. He is known for only two hymns, both published in the appendix of his *Freuden-Spiegel dess ewigen Lebens* (*The Mirror of the joy of eternal life*), 1599, the texts of which, if centered when printed, form the shape of a chalice. Author and composer: "O Morning Star, how fair and bright" (WIE SCHÖN LEUCHTET DER MORGENSTERN), **247**; "Wake, awake, for night is flying" (WACHET AUF), **720**.

Niles, Daniel Thambyrajah, born Telipallai, Ceylon, August 1908; died Vellore Christian Medical College, India, 17 July 1970. Niles was greatly influenced by a devout Hindu warden in his Ceylon University dormitory and changed his course of study from law to the Christian ministry. He was ordained by The Methodist Church in 1932, serving as superintendent of the Point Pedro and Jaffna circuits, and secretary and later as chair of the North Ceylon district of The Methodist Church. In 1968 he was elected president of the Ceylon Methodist Conference. Highly regarded in the World Council of Churches, he was president of the East Asia Christian Conference, evangelism secretary of the World YMCA in Geneva, and a gifted administrator and author. He contributed forty-four hymns, translations, and adaptations to the *E.A.C.C. Hymnal*, 1963. Translator: "O God in heaven," **119**; "Jesus, Savior, Lord," **523**.

Nix-Allen, Verolga, born Cleveland, OH, 6 April 1933. Educated at the New England Conservatory, Boston, Massachusetts, and Oberlin Conservatory of Music, Oberlin, Ohio (B.M., M.M.), she is the founder, arranger, and music director of the Intermezzo Choir Ministries in Philadelphia, Pennsylvania. She co-edited *Songs of Zion*, 1981, with J. Jefferson Cleveland and is the founder and president of the Foundation for the Preservation of African American Music in Philadelphia. Co-adapter: "Our Father, which art in heaven," **271**.

Noel, Caroline Maria, born London, England, 10 April 1817; died London, 7 December 1877. Although she wrote hymns at an early age, she stopped at age twenty but resumed writing in 1857. In 1861 *The Name of Jesus and Other Verses for the Sick and Lonely* was published; other poetry was published posthumously in 1878. Author: "At the name of Jesus," **168**; Response, **167**.

Norris, John Samuel, born West Cowes, Isle of Wight, England, 4 December 1844; died Chicago, IL, 23 September 1907. Educated and ordained into the Methodist ministry (1868) while living in Canada, he served Methodist churches in Canada, New York, and Wisconsin. He became a Congregationalist in 1878, pastoring in Wisconsin and Iowa and also serving as conference evangelist in Iowa. Norris published one collection of hymns, *Songs of the Soul*. Composer: NORRIS, **338**.

North, Frank Mason, born New York, NY, 3 December 1850; died Madison, NJ, 17 December 1935. North was educated at Wesleyan University (1872, 1875) and ordained into the ministry of the Methodist Episcopal Church in 1872. Besides serving churches in Florida, New York, and Connecticut, he was editor of the *Christian City*, corresponding secretary of the New York Church Extension and Missionary Society, secretary of the Board of Foreign Missions, 1892-1912, and president of the Federal Council of Churches of Christ in America, 1916-20. His writings are housed at Drew University, Madison, New Jersey. Author: "Where cross the crowded ways of life," **427**.

O'Driscoll, Thomas Herbert, born Cork, Ireland, 17 October 1928. Educated at Trinity College, Dublin, Ireland, he took Holy Orders in 1953 and held posts in Dublin, Ottawa, and the Royal Canadian Navy. O'Driscoll was appointed dean of Christ Church Cathedral, Vancouver, British Columbia, 1968, warden of the College of Preachers, Washington, DC, 1982, and rector of Christ Church, Calgary, Alberta, 1984. He was an Anglican member of the committee that compiled *The Hymn Book*, 1971, for the Anglican Church of Canada and the United Church of Canada. Author: "Let my people seek their freedom," **586**.

Oakeley, Frederick, born Shrewsbury, Worcester, England, 5 September 1802; died Islington, London, England, 29 January 1880. Educated at Christ Church, Oxford, Oakeley became a fellow of Balliol in 1827 and served as prebendary of Lichfield Cathedral, preacher at Whitehall, and minister of Margaret Chapel (All Saints', Margaret Street). While at Margaret Chapel, he translated Latin hymns and became associated with the Oxford group, especially John Henry Newman. In 1845 he became a Roman Catholic and spent many years ministering to the poor of Westminster; in 1852 he was made canon of Westminster Procathedral. Translator: "O come, all ye faithful," **234**; Response, **205**.

Olivar, José Antonio. Nothing is known about this person except he is thought to be a Spanish Roman Catholic priest. Co-author: "Cuando el pobre" (EL CAMINO), **434**.

Olivers, Thomas, born Tregynon, near Newtown, Montgomeryshire, Wales, 1725; died London, England, March 1799. Orphaned at the age of four, Olivers received little nurture or education from the various relatives who kept him. While apprenticed to a shoemaker in 1743, he left Tregynon at eighteen because of his unruly behavior and happened to hear George Whitefield preaching in Bristol. He joined the Methodist Society at Bradford-on-Avon, and while he continued as a cobbler, in 1753 he became an evangelist under John Wesley, preaching throughout England and Ireland. From 1775 until 1789 he was supervisor of the Methodist publications. His body was buried in Wesley's tomb at City Road Chapel. Paraphraser: "The God of Abraham praise," **116, 801**.

Olson, Ernst William, born Skane, Sweden, 1870; died Chicago, IL, 6 October 1958. Olson came to the United States with his family at the age of five. After graduating from Augustana College, he served as editor for several Swedish weeklies. He possessed unusual literary gifts and was made office editor for the Engberg-Holmberg Publishing Company (1906-11) and held a similar post with the Augustana Book Concern from 1911 to 1949. Besides several prose works, Olson contributed twenty-eight translations and four original hymns to the *Augustana Hymnal*, 1925, and served on the committee for the *Service Book and Hymnal*, 1958. Translator: "Children of the heavenly Father," **141**.

Olude, Abraham Taiwo Olajide, born Ebute-Mette, Lagos, Nigeria, 16 July 1908. Educated at Wesley College, Ibandan, and at the Mindola training school, Olude has been a pioneer in the use of indigenous African music, including the use of native drums and instruments in congregational and choral music in worship. He formed and toured with his own choir in Nigeria to demonstrate church music in an African style and has written many hymns in the folk idiom. His honors include the Order of the Niger, and the Mus.D. degree from the University of Nigeria. Letters mailed by the hymnal editor to Olude in 1989 were returned marked "deceased." Author and composer: "Jesus, we want to meet" (NIGERIA), **661**.

Ova'hehe, Mrs. Bear Bow, born Oklahoma Indian Territory, ca. 1880; died Oklahoma, 1934. No information is available on this author/composer. Attributed author and composer: "Jesus our friend and brother" (ESENEHANE JESUS), **659**.

Owens, Carol, born El Reno, OK, 30 October 1931. Educated at San Jose State College, Owens has received Grammy and Dove nominations for various works. Her publications include the musicals *Come Together*, *Show Me*, *If My People*, and *The Glory of Christmas*, among others. Author and composer: "God forgave my sins" (FREELY, FREELY), **389**.

Oxenham, John, born Cheetham, Manchester, England, 12 November 1852; died High Salvington, Sussex, England, 23 January 1941. Born with the given name William Arthur Dunkerly, Oxenham took his pen name from the Elizabethan sea dog in *Westward Ho!* After his education at Old Trafford School and Victoria University in Manchester, he went into business with his father, traveling in Europe and the United States. Because of the success of his publications, he turned to writing full time, producing novels, short stories, poems, and eleven volumes of religious works. A devout Congregationalist, he edited the *Christian News-Letter* and served as a deacon and taught a Bible class at Ealing Congregational Church, London. Author: "In Christ there is no east or west," **548**.

Page, Kate Stearns, born Brookline, MA, 21 August 1873; died New York, NY, 19 January 1963. Page was a music educator who taught at the Dennison House Settlement School in Boston, the Parke School in Brookline, and from 1933 to 1941 at the Diller-Quaile School of Music in New York City. With Angela Diller she collaborated in the writing of six music books for children. Author: "We, thy people, praise thee," **67**.

Pagura, Federico José, born Arroyo Seco, Argentina, 9 February 1923. Educated at Facultad Evangélica de Teologia, Buenos Aires, Argentina, he has served as Methodist bishop of Costa Rica and Panama (1969-73) and as bishop of Argentina (1977-89). He received an honorary doctorate from DePauw University, Indiana, and has been president of the Latin American Council of Churches (1972-92), as well as co-president of the Ecumenical Movement for Human Rights in Argentina. Pagura is the author of several books, including *ABC of the Biblical Doctrine*, 1959, hymns, and translations. He was a moving force in the production of hymnals that incorporated indigenous folk tunes and rhythms as well as songs in popular styles. He translated seventy-one hymns for *Cántico Nueva*. Translator: "Mil voces para celebrar," **59**.

Palestrina, Giovanni Pierluigi Sante da, born Palestrina, Italy, 1525; died Rome, Italy, 2 February 1594. One of the most important composers of sixteenth-century music, whose compositional style became the standard for post-Trent music in the Roman Catholic Church, in 1544 he was appointed organist and choirmaster in Palestrina. When his bishop, Julius III, ascended to the papacy in 1551, Palestrina was called to Rome where he spent the rest of his life. His complete works, including masses, motets, and madrigals, comprise thirty-three volumes. Composer: VICTORY, **306**.

Palmer, Ray, born Little Compton, RI, 12 November 1808; died Newark, NJ, 29 March 1887. A graduate of Yale University (B.A. 1830), Palmer was ordained into the Congregational ministry in 1835, serving churches in Bath, Maine, and Albany, New York. In 1865 he became corresponding secretary of the American Congregational Union, a position he held until his retirement. His translations compare favorably with J. M. Neale's, and original hymns appear in *Sabbath Hymn Book*, 1858, *Hymns and Sacred Pieces*, 1865, *Hymns of My Holy Hours*, 1868, and the complete *Poetical Works*, 1876. Author: "My faith looks up to thee," **452**.

Palmer, Roland Ford, born London, England, 12 December 1891; died Victoria, British Columbia, Canada, 24 August 1985. Educated at Skinner's Company School, in 1905 Palmer moved to Canada where he attended the Peterborough Collegiate Institute and Trinity College, Toronto (L.Th. 1914, B.A. 1916). Ordained in 1917, he served Englehart, and St. George's, Port Arthur, Ontario. In 1919 he joined the Society of St. John the Evangelist at Cambridge, Massachusetts, and later was appointed superior of the society's house in San Francisco. In 1927 as provincial superior, he opened a society house at Bracebridge, Canada. Palmer served on the committee that compiled the Canadian hymnal of 1938, *The Book of Common Praise*, and the committee to revise the Prayer Book. He received an honorary doctorate from Trinity College in 1941. Author: "Sing of Mary, pure and lowly," **272**.

Park, Jae (Chai) Hoon, born Kangwondo, Korea, 4 November 1922. Park was educated at Tokyo Music School; Central Theological Seminary, Seoul, Korea; Christian Theological Seminary, Indianapolis, Indiana; and Westminster School of Music, Princeton, New Jersey. He served as professor at the College of Music, Hangyang University, Seoul, Korea (1952-73), and as director of music at Young-nak Presbyterian Church, Seoul. He has lectured at the Presbyterian Seminary, Seoul Seminary, Seoul, Korea, and the Methodist Theological Seminary in Ohio.

Awarded the Doctor of Humanities from Agusa University, Agusa, California, Park has published the oratorios *Esther* and *The Passion of Mark* and written the *Handbook on the Korean Hymnal*. Composer: KAHM-SAH, **86**; KOREA, **343**.

Park, John Edgar, born Belfast, Ireland, 7 March 1879; died Cambridge, MA, 4 March 1956. Park received an international education, studying at Queens College, Belfast, Royal University, Dublin, and the universities of Edinburgh, Leipzig, Munich, Oxford, and Princeton. As a Presbyterian minister, he worked in the Adirondacks lumber camps. After changing to the Congregational Church, he served the Second Congregational Church in West Newton, Massachusetts. He taught at Boston University School of Theology in 1925 and in 1926 became president of Wheaton College, Newton, Massachusetts. Author: "We would see Jesus," **256**.

Parker, William Henry, born New Basford, Nottingham, England, 4 March 1845; died Nottingham, 2 December 1929. Parker was an insurance executive who was active in the Sunday school work of Chelsea Street Baptist Church in Nottingham. Most of his hymns are for Sunday School anniversaries, fifteen of which appear in the *Sunday School Hymnary*, 1905. Author: "Tell me the stories of Jesus," **277**.

Parkin, Charles, born Felling on Tyne, England, 25 December 1894; died Portland, ME, 3 March 1981. After serving in the British army in World War I, Parkin was secretary of the British Poetry Society. In 1922 he came to the USA, where he was ordained an elder in the Maine Conference of the Methodist Episcopal Church. His career in the USA is marked by his interest in missions. He served from 1952 to 1964 as director of the Advance Department, Division of National Missions in Philadelphia, and in 1961 as a delegate to the World Methodist Conference in Oslo, Norway. His hymns have been published by the Hymn Society of America and in various denominational publications. Author: "See the morning sun ascending," **674**.

Parry, Charles Hubert Hastings, born Bournemouth, England, 27 February 1848; died King's Croft, Rustington, Littlehampton, Sussex, England, 7 October 1918. He received the B.M. degree from Eton College and graduated from Exeter College, Oxford (B.A. 1870). After attempting to please his father by working at Lloyd's, he returned to music, becoming professor of composition and music history at the Royal College of Music in 1883 and director in 1894. Parry was honored with doctorates from Cambridge (1883), Oxford (1884), Dublin (1891), and Durham University (1894). Knighted in 1898 and made a baronet soon after, this multitalented musician was a squire, magistrate, amateur scientist, play critic, and yachtsman. He was a gifted lecturer on musical subjects and wrote *The Art of Music*, 1893, volume 2 of *The Oxford History of Music*, 1902, *Style in Musical Art*, 1911, and a work on Bach. Partially responsible for the renaissance of English music in the late-nineteenth century, Parry composed five symphonies, an opera, cantatas, organ works, and many hymn tunes. Composer: INTERCESSOR, **517**; JERUSALEM, **729**.

Parry, Joseph, born Merthyr Tydfil, Wales, 21 May 1841; died Cartref, Penarth, Wales, 17 February 1903. Born into poverty, Parry began work puddling furnaces before he was ten. He received his first music instruction from a class conducted by other iron workers. After winning a prize for composition in 1860, he enrolled in a normal music school in Genesco, New York, and returning to Wales, he won additional prizes in Eisteddfods. From 1868 to 1871 he studied at the Royal Academy of Music then came again to the United States to run a private music school in Pennsylvania. He became professor of music at the Welsh University College at Aberystwyth, later teaching at the University College in Cardiff from 1888 until his death. Parry is the composer of *Blodwen*, 1880, the first Welsh opera, two oratorios, cantatas, and some 400 hymn tunes. He greatly influenced a generation of early twentieth-century Welsh composers. Composer: ABERYSTWYTH, **479**.

Paton, Alan (Stewart), born Pietermaritzburg, Natal, South Africa, 11 January 1903; died near Durban, Natal, 12 April 1988. One of the foremost authors in South Africa, he wrote *Cry, the Beloved Country*, 1948, bringing international focus on the issue of apartheid. He was involved in South African politics and served as national president of the Liberal Party of South Africa until its forced dissolution in 1968. Author: "For courage to do justice," **456**.

Peace, Albert Lister, born Huddersfield, Yorkshire, England, 26 January 1844; died Liverpool, Lancashire, England, 14 March 1912. A child prodigy, Peace took his first organ position at Holmfirth, Yorkshire, at the age of nine. After his graduation from Oxford (B.M. 1870, Mus.D. 1875) he served as organist at St. George's Hall, Liverpool, until his death. He played inaugural recitals at numerous churches, including Canterbury Cathedral, and was known for his brilliant pedal technique. Peace served as editor for *The Scottish Hymnal*, 1844, *Psalms and Paraphrases with Tunes*, 1886, *The Psalter with Chants*, 1888, and *The Scottish Anthem Book*, 1891. Composer: ST. MARGARET, **480**.

Peacey, John Raphael, born Hove, Brighton, Sussex, England, 16 July 1896; died Brighton, Sussex, 31 October 1971. Having attended St. Edmund's School, Canterbury, he served the armed forces in France during World War I and received the Military Cross. He graduated from Selwyn College, Cambridge (1921), was ordained, and served Wellington College and Selwyn College. Headmaster at Bishop Cotton School, Simla, India, from 1927 to 1945, he returned to England to be canon residentiary at Bristol Cathedral until his retirement in 1966. He was rural dean at Hurstpierpoint in Sussex until his death. His first hymn texts, which he began writing in retirement, were published in *100 Hymns for Today*, 1969. Author: "Filled with the Spirit's power," **537**; "Go forth for God," **670**.

Peloquin, C. Alexander, born Northbridge, near Worcester, MA, 16 June 1918. A church organist at age eleven, he won first prize in an organists' contest at age seventeen and appeared with the Rhode Island WPA Symphony. Educated at the New England Conservatory, Boston, Massachusetts (1940), and the Berkshire Music Center, Tanglewood, Massachusetts (1941), he studied with Isidor Philipp in New York. Entering the US Air Force in 1943, he served as a bandmaster and soloist in Algeria, Italy, France, Germany, and Belgium. In 1950 Peloquin became organist/music director at the Cathedral of St. Peter and St. Paul, Providence, Rhode Island, and in 1955 he joined the faculty of Boston College. He founded the Peloquin Chorale and the Boston College University Chorale. The author of journal articles and a contributor to the *New Catholic Encyclopaedia*, he has received numerous awards, including the BBC Golden Bell award and several honorary degrees. His sacred works total more than 135 and include "Gloria of the Bells," *Songs of Israel*, "I Give You a New Commandment," and *Lyric Liturgy*. Composer: "Canticle of God's glory," **83**.

Perronet, Edward, born Sundridge, Kent, England, 1726; died Canterbury, England, 2 January 1792. The Perronet family, Huguenots from Switzerland, was closely associated with and esteemed by the Wesleys. Edward was educated by private tutors and entered the ministry, and against John Wesley's wishes, he advocated the administration of the Lord's Supper by Methodist preachers. He also angered the Wesleys and the Countess of Huntingdon with his satire on the established church, *The Mitre*. He left the countess's chapel to become the minister of an independent chapel in Canterbury. Author: "All hail the power of Jesus' name," **154, 155**.

Perry, Michael Arnold, born Beckenham, Kent, England, 8 March 1942. An Anglican priest and hymn writer, he was educated at Dunwich and University College, London, Oak Hill Theological College and Ridley College, Cambridge, and the University of Southhampton. Perry served as curate of St. Helens, Lancashire, and Bifferne, Southampton, and as rector of Eversley, Hampshire. He is now vicar of Tonbridge, Kent. A prolific and influential hymnist, he was editor of *Hymns for Today's Church*, 1982, *Carols for Today*, 1986, and *Come Rejoice!* 1989. His quarterly *Word and Music*, "a galley for new writing," later merged with the journal *Music in Worship*. Honorary secretary of Jubilate Hymns, Ltd., he organizes writers for encouragement, critical appraisal, and hymn festivals. Author: "Blessed be the God of Israel," **209**; "Heal me, hands of Jesus," **262**; "How shall they hear the word of God," **649**.

Persichetti, Vincent, born Philadelphia, PA, 6 June 1915; died Philadelphia, PA, 13, August 1987. An outstanding twentieth-century USA composer, he played the piano in local orchestras at the age of eleven and was organist/choir director at Arch Street Presbyterian Church, Philadelphia, for twenty years (1931-51). Persichetti was graduated from Combs College (B.Mus. 1936), Curtis Institute of Music (1938), where he studied with Fritz Reiner and the Philadelphia Conservatory of Music (M.M. 1939, D.M. 1945). He taught theory and composition for the Philadelphia Conservatory. In 1947 he joined the faculty of the Juilliard School of Music, teaching composition. From 1952 until his death he was a director director of the Elkan-Vogel music publishing firm. Known for his commissioned works for orchestra, band, and chamber ensemble, he is the author of *Twentieth Century Harmony*, 1961, and *Hymns and Responses for the Church Year*, 1956. Composer: "Amen," **899**; "Amen," **900**.

Peterson, Michael L., born New Auburn, WI, 24 October 1954. Peterson was educated at Winona State University, Winona, Minnesota, where he received degrees in vocal music, music education, and theater arts, and at Luther-Northwestern Theological Seminary, St. Paul. He has served as associate pastor of Lutheran churches in Shawano and Menomonie, Wisconsin. Author: "On the day of resurrection," **309**.

Phillips, Keith. No information is available on Phillips. Arranger: THY WORD, **601**.

Pierpoint, Folliot Sandford, born Bath, Somersetshire, England, 7 October 1835; died Newport, England, 10 March 1917. Educated at Queen's College, Cambridge, Pierpoint was classical master at Somersetshire College. He contributed to *Lyra Eucharistica*, *The Hymnal Noted*, and published several volumes of poems. Author: "For the beauty of the earth," **92**; Response, **829**.

Plumptre, Edward Hayes, born London, England, 6 August 1821; died Wells, Somersetshire, England, 1 February 1891. An esteemed scholar, theologian, author, and preacher, Plumptre was educated at King's College, London, and University College, Oxford. He held academic and pastoral positions at King's College, Queen's College, Oxford, St. Paul's, Kent, and as dean of Wells. His literary works include a biography of Bishop Thomas Ken, 1888, several volumes of poetry, and translations from the classics. He was a member of the Old Testament Company for the revision of the Authorized Version of the Bible. Author: "Rejoice, ye pure in heart," **161**, **162**; Response, **74**, **821**.

Pollard, Adelaide Addison, born Bloomfield, IA, 27 November 1862; died New York, NY, 20 December 1934. Active in evangelistic work, Pollard taught in girls' schools in Chicago in the 1880's. She became an assistant to Alexander Dowie's healing crusades and taught at the Missionary Training School, Nyack-on-the-Hudson. She was a missionary in Africa prior to World War I and during the war worked in Scotland. In her last years she was attracted to extreme sects, living the life of a mystic. Author: "Have thine own way, Lord," **382**.

Pond, Sylvanus Billings, born Milford, VT, 5 April 1792; died Brooklyn, NY, 12 March 1871. Pond was a composer, conductor, editor, and publisher who composed Sunday school songs and was conductor of both the New York Sacred Music Society and the New York Academy of Sacred Music. He edited and published *Union Melodies*, 1838, *United States Psalmody*, 1841, and for the Reformed Dutch Church in America, *The Book of Praise*, 1866. Composer: ARMENIA, **554**.

Pongnoi, Sook. No information is available for this person. Author: "Come, all of you," **350**.

Porter, Ellen Jane Lorenz. See **Lorenz, Ellen Jane**.

Postlethwaite, R. Deane, born Concordia, KS, 16 March 1925; died Annandale, MN, 7 October 1980. Educated at the University of Kansas (B.A. 1947, M.A. 1948), Union Theological Seminary (M.Div. 1956), United Theological Seminary of the Twin Cities, New Brighton, Minnesota (D.Min. 1979), he taught political science at Baker University, Baldwin, Kansas (1948-51). As an ordained deacon in 1956 and elder in 1958 in the Minnesota Annual Conference of The United Methodist Church, he was pastor of churches in Kansas, New York, and Minnesota, including Minnehaha United Methodist Church, Minneapolis, where he served from 1972 until his death. Postlethwaite typifies the poet-pastor who writes hymns that are "related both to the lives of the people who sing [them] and to the acts of prayer, praise, preaching and Bible reading that precede or follow." (Preface to *Eight Hymns, in Context*) Author: "The care the eagle gives her young," **118**.

Pott, Francis, born Southwark, London, England, 29 December 1831; died Speldhurst, England, 26 October 1909. Pott was a translator of Latin hymnody and a member of the committee that prepared the original edition of *Hymns Ancient and Modern*, 1861. He was ordained in 1856 and served as rector at Norhill, Ely (1866-91), when deafness and ill health forced his resignation, causing him to turn his talents to study and translations. His works include *Hymns Fitted to the Order of Common Prayer*, 1861, and the *Free Rhythm Psalter*, 1898, both works reflecting his interest in a return to chant. Translator: "The strife is o'er, the battle done," **306**.

Praetorius, Michael, born Creutzburg an der Werra, near Eisenach, 15 February 1571; died Wolfenbüttel, 15 February 1621. Educated at the Latin school of Torgau and the University of Frankfurt-on-Oder, Praetorius was a major figure in the early baroque period in both secular and sacred music. In 1589 he was organist of the Castle Church in Groningen, and in 1594 he became court organist and Kappelmeister in Wolfenbüttel, where he served until his death. His church music ranges from settings for two voices to massive polychoral works set to Lutheran chorales and liturgical texts. His treatise on musical instruments is a primary source for contemporary study of baroque performance practice. Praetorius was a prolific composer, author, theorist, and editor, and his collections include *Musae Sioniae*, 1605-19, and *Syntagma Musicum* in four parts, 1614-19, which explains to church musicians how to perform in various contemporary styles. Harmonizer: ES IST EIN ROS, **216**.

Prentiss, Elizabeth Payson, born Portland, ME, 26 October 1818; died Dorset, VT, 13 August 1878. By the age of sixteen, Elizabeth began contributing poetry and prose to *Youth's Companion*. After teaching in Maine, Massachusetts, and Virginia, she married George Lewis Prentiss who became a professor of homiletics and polity at Union Theological Seminary, New York. Her best-known work is *Stepping Heavenward*, 1869. Author: "More love to thee, O Christ," **453**.

Prichard, Rowland Huw (Hugh), born Graienyn, near Bala, North Wales, 14 January 1811; died Holywell, Flintshire, Wales, 25 January 1887. A worker in the textile industry, Prichard was an amateur precentor and the composer of a number of powerful, but simple tunes published in Welsh periodicals. He spent most of his life in Bala, moving to Holywell in 1880 to be an assistant loomtender. His *Cyfaill y Cantorion (The Singer's Friend)* was published in 1844. Composer: HYFRY-DOL, **196, 648**.

Pritchard, Thomas Cuthbertson Leithead, born Glasgow, 1885; died 1960. Educated at the University of Glasgow and Trinity College, Dublin, Pritchard also studied music at York Minster. He served as organist/choirmaster in Irvine, Glasgow, and Bearsden, and was a professor at the Athenaeum School of Music. He was a well-known recitalist, lecturer, author of music and articles on music, and an associate member of the revision committee for *The Church Hymnary*. Harmonizer: CRIMOND, **118, 136**.

Proulx, Richard, born St. Paul, MN, 3 April 1937. Educated at the University of Minnesota, MacPhail College of Music, Columbus Boychoir School, St. John's Abbey, Collegeville, Minnesota, and the Royal School of Church Music, England, he was organist/choir director at St. Thomas' Episcopal Church, Seattle, Washington, where he established a tradition of liturgical handbell ringing. As organist/choir director since 1980, he has developed an extensive music program at Holy Name Cathedral, Chicago, Illinois. A composer of more than 250 works for piano, organ, solo voice, chorus, orchestra, documentary films, and commercials, Proulx was commissioned by the American Guild of Organists in 1978 to write *The Pilgrim,* a chamber opera. The National Endowment for the Arts commissioned his opera *Beggar's Christmas* in 1989. He was an editorial consultant for *The Hymnal 1982, The United Methodist Hymnal, 1989, A New Hymnal for Colleges and Schools,* 1992, and *Worship II and III.* Adapter: "Musical Setting C," **21**; composer: Responses, **137, 199, 205, 225, 738, 744, 746, 754, 767, 788, 804, 824, 830, 835, 839, 856**; harmonizer: LACQUIPARLE, **148**; TRUMPETS, **442**.

Prudentius, Aurelius Clemens, born Spain, 348; died ca. 410. Born into a prominent Spanish family, Prudentius practiced law and served as a judge and chief of the imperial bodyguard of the Emperor Honorius. At the age of fifty-seven, he joined a monastery and devoted his time to meditation and writing sacred poems and hymns. His chief works were *Liber Cathemerinon* (hymns for the hours of the day), and *Liber Peristephanon* (fourteen hymns praising important martyrs). Author: "Of the Father's love begotten," **184**.

Purcell, Henry, born London(?), England, 1659; died Dean's Yard, Westminster, London, 21 November 1695. The greatest English composer of the late seventeenth century, Purcell was a chorister of the Chapel Royal in 1669 and appointed organist of Westminster Abbey in 1679. Known for the opera *Dido and Aeneas,* stage works, church music, and chamber works, Purcell displayed through his compositions a mastery of form and harmony, melodic originality, and rich inventiveness. Composer: WESTMINSTER ABBEY, **559**.

Quinn, James, born Glasgow, Scotland, 21 April 1919. Educated at St. Aloysius' College, Glasgow, and Glasgow University (M.A. 1939), he joined the British province of the Society of Jesus and was ordained priest in 1950. He was spiritual director for Beda College, Rome (1976-80). An active member of the Commission on Christian Doctrine and Unity for the Bishop's Conference of Scotland, he is also a consultant for the International Commission on English in the Liturgy. Quinn is the author of *New Hymns for All Seasons*, 1969, and *The Theology of the Eucharist*, 1973. His hymn texts are published in all major English-language hymnals. Author: "Word of God, come down on earth," **182**.

Rankin, Jeremiah Eames, born Thornton, NH, 2 January 1828; died Cleveland, OH, 28 November 1904. Rankin was educated at Andover Theological Seminary and ordained into the Congregational ministry in 1855, serving churches in New York, Vermont, Massachusetts, Washington, DC, and New Jersey. In 1889 he became president of Howard University. He published three volumes of poems and translations and collaborated with E. S. Lorenz in producing *Gospel Temperance Hymnal*, 1878, and with J. W. Bischoff and Otis F. Presbrey in *Gospel Bells*, 1880. Author: "God be with you till we meet again," **672, 673**.

Rasanayagam, Shanti, of Pakistan, was a member of the committee that produced the *E.A.C.C. Hymnal*, 1963, and, according to the hymnal preface, prepared the musical score for publication. No additional information has been found. Arranger: PUNJABI, **523**.

Redhead, Richard, born Harrow, Middlesex, England, 1 March 1820; died Hellingly, England, 27 April 1901. Redhead received his early musical training as a chorister at Magdalen College, Oxford, and as an organ student of Walter Vicary. He conducted daily choral services from 1839 to 1864 at Margaret Street Chapel (after 1859, All Saints' on Margaret Street, known as the "Tractarian Cathedral") and served as organist of St. Mary Magdalene, Paddington, from 1864 to 1894. Chiefly known for his part in the Tractarian revival of plainsong, he contributed to *Laudes Diurnae*, 1843, with H. S. Oakley, *Church Hymn Tunes, Ancient and Modern*, 1853, edited choir, organ, and hymn tune collections, and was the composer of numerous vocal compositions. Composer: REDHEAD, **290**; harmonizer: ORIENTIS PARTIBUS, **192**.

Redner, Lewis Henry, born Philadelphia, PA, 15 December 1830; died Atlantic City, NJ, 29 August 1908. Redner was a wealthy real estate broker who was also very active in church work both in church music and Sunday school activities. He served as organist for four different Philadelphia churches and increased Sunday school attendance at Holy Trinity Episcopal, where Phillips Brooks was rector, from thirty-six to over one thousand during his nineteen years as superintendent. There is an interesting exchange of correspondence between the composer and Louis F. Benson in the Benson Collection, Speer Library, Princeton Theological Seminary. Composer: ST. LOUIS, **230**.

Reed, Edith Margaret Gellibrand, born Islington, Middlesex, England, 31 March 1885; died Barnett, Hertfordshire, 4 June 1933. Reed was a student at St. Leonard's School in St. Andrew's and the Guildhall School of Music in London.

She was also an associate of the Royal College of Organists, assisting Percy Scholes in editing *The Music Student, Music and Youth,* and *Panpipes.* Original works include two Christmas mystery plays and *Story Lives of the Great Composers,* 1825. Translator: "Infant holy, infant lowly," **229**; arranger: W ZLOBIE LEZY **229, 307**.

Rees, Timothy, born Trefeglwysm Llanon, Cardiganshire, Wales, 15 August 1874; died Llandaff, Glamorganshire, Wales, 29 April 1939. Educated at St. David's College, Lampeter (B.A. 1896), and St. Michael's College, Aberdare, he was ordained by the Church of England in 1897, serving as curate of Mountain Ash, Glamorganshire (1897-1901), and as chaplain to St. Michael's College (1901-06). He became a member of the Community of the Resurrection, Mirfield, Yorkshire, in 1907, traveling to New Zealand, Canada, and Ceylon as a missionary. Rees received the Military Cross for his service as a chaplain during World War I. Appointed warden of the College of the Resurrection in 1922, he remained there until he was consecrated bishop of Llandaff in 1931. Author: "O crucified Redeemer," **425**.

Reid, William Watkins, Jr., born New York, NY, 12 November 1923. Educated at Oberlin College, Oberlin, Ohio (B.A.), and Yale Divinity School (B.Div.), he served in the United States Army Medical Corps from 1943 to 1945, earning three battle stars and suffering eight months of imprisonment in Germany. Since 1949 he has pastored Congregational and Methodist churches in North Dakota and Pennsylvania, and was appointed as Wilkes-Barre district superintendent by The United Methodist Church in 1978. Active in the Hymn Society in the United States and Canada, he has published several hymns and articles and won national hymn-writing contests. Author: "O God of every nation," **435**; "O God who shaped creation," **443**.

Reinagle, Alexander Robert, born Brighthelmstone, East Sussex, England, 21 August 1799; died Kidlington, Oxfordshire, England, 6 April 1877. Reinagle's grandfather was "trumpeter to the king," his father an accomplished cellist, and his uncle a leading conductor, composer, teacher, and manager in the USA. Reinagle was organist at St. Peter's-in-the-East, Oxford, and published string method books as well as two collections of hymn tunes, *Psalm Tunes, for the Voice and Pianoforte,* 1836, and *A Collection of Psalm and Hymn Tunes,* 1840. Composer: ST. PETER, **549**.

Remenschneider, Thomas A., born Fort Wayne, IN, 12 September 1949. Educated at Indiana State University, St. Francis College (B.A. 1978), Indiana University (M.S. 1982), and Westminster Choir College (M.M. 1989), he has been active in music education, church music, community choral groups, and as a clinician and conductor for choral festivals. Remenschneider has served as music director for several Lutheran churches, including Redeemer Lutheran Church in Fort Wayne, as well as churches in Pennsylvania and New Jersey. He presently teaches vocal music at Wayne High School in Fort Wayne, is conductor of the Fort Wayne Philharmonic Chorus, and music director of the

Fort Wayne Männerchor. At Westminster Choir College, he studied Lutheran liturgical practice and hymnody with Robin A. Leaver. He researched the German youth music movement and the practical applications of liturgical choral music for parish, translated articles from the German, and published articles in several journals. He contributed to *The Hymnal 1982 Companion* and condensed and updated the biographies from *Companion to the Hymnal*, 1970, for inclusion in *Companion to the United Methodist Hymnal* [1989], 1993.

Renville, Joseph R., born, St. Paul, MN, 1779; died 1846. A French-Dakota Indian guide and fur trader, he was the son of a French-Canadian trader and a Dakota mother and was educated by a Roman Catholic priest. He encouraged Native Americans to plant corn and grain and was an interpreter whose language skills allowed him to help translate the Bible into Dakota. He suggested the establishment of the Native American mission site at Lac qui Parle. Author: "Many and great, O God," **148**.

Reynolds, William Morton, born Fayette County, PA, 1812; died 1876. He attended Jefferson College, and the Lutheran Gettysburg Seminary. A professor at Pennsylvania College (1833-50), president of Capital University, Columbus, Ohio (1850-53), and president of Illinois State University (1857-60), he edited a hymnal for the General Synod of the Evangelical Lutheran Church in 1854. He was ordained in the Episcopal Church in 1864 and founded the journal *Evangelical Review*. Translator: "Savior of the nations, come," **214.**

Richard of Chichester, born Droitwich, Worcestershire, England, 1197; died Dover, England, 1253. Educated at Oxford and Paris, Richard became chancellor of Oxford University about 1235 and later chancellor of Canterbury under Archbishop St. Edmund Rich, going into exile with the archbishop. Despite Henry III's opposition, he was elected and consecrated bishop of Chichester in 1245. Author: "Three things we pray," **493**.

Riley, John Athelstan Laurie, born London, England, 10 August 1858; died Isle of Jersey, England, 17 November 1945. Educated at Eton and Pembroke College, Oxford, Riley traveled to Persia, Turkey, and Kurdistan to gain material on various Eastern Christian churches published in articles and in the book *Athos, or the Mountain of the Monks*, 1887. He was prominent in the preparation of the 1906 *English Hymnal*. The hymnal committee met in his house where most of their work was done. At its publication "the book was heavily attacked on doctrinal grounds . . . but eventually it made its way, partly due to the excellence of the music that had been edited by Ralph Vaughan Williams, and partly to the many illustrated lectures that Riley himself gave, with the assistance of a group of singers." (Osborne 1976, commentary on hymn 7) *The English Hymnal* includes three of Riley's hymns and nine translations. Author: "Ye watcher and ye holy ones," **90**; translator: "O food to pilgrims given," **631**.

Rimbault, Edward Francis, born Soho, London, England, 13 June 1816; died Soho, 26 September 1876. The son of the organist and composer Stephen Francis

Rimbault, Rimbault was a music scholar, composer, and organist of the Swiss Church, Soho. Attributed composer: HAPPY DAY, **391**.

Rinkart, Martin, born Eilenburg, Saxony, 23 April 1586; died Eilenburg, 8 December 1649. An accomplished musician, theologian, and prolific writer, Rinkart was educated at Eilenburg and the St. Thomas' School in Leipzig, and studied theology at the University of Leipzig. He was cantor and later deacon at Eisleben, pastor at Ardeborn, and archdeacon at Eilenburg in 1617. With the onset of the Thirty Years' War, many people flocked to the walled city of Eilenburg, severely smitten by the plague. Rinkart became the only pastor left in the city, presiding over nearly five thousand funerals, including his wife's, sometimes numbering fifty to sixty a day. He belongs to the ranks of the great Pietistic German hymn writers who out of their experience of severe personal and social tragedy produced lasting expressions of faith and trust in God. Author: "Now thank we all our God," **102**; Response, **789**.

Rippon, John, born Tiverton, Devonshire, England, 29 April 1751; died London, England, 17 December 1836. After joining the Baptist Church at the age of sixteen, Rippon studied for the Baptist ministry at Bristol Baptist College. In 1772 he was named interim pastor at the Baptist church at Carter Lane, London. After the post became permanent the next year, he held it for sixty-three years. As a pastor and the editor of the *Baptist Annual Register,* 1790-1802, Rippon became one of the most influential Baptist ministers of his time in both Great Britain and the USA. An authority on the hymns of Isaac Watts, Rippon compiled two collections, *Hymns from the Best Authors. . .,* 1787, and *A Selection of Psalms and Hymn Tunes,* 1791, standard sources for early nineteenth-century hymnals in England and the USA, in spite of the fact that he failed to identify his alterations of texts or, in some cases, the authors or composers of hymns. Alterer: "All hail the power of Jesus' name," **154, 155**; source: "How firm a foundation," **529**.

Rist, Johann, born Ottensen, Holstein, 8 March 1607; died Wedel, Holstein, 31 August 1667. Rist was both a pastor and physician in Wedel who during the Thirty Years' War lost all his personal property. He wrote on many religious subjects and was named poet laureate by Emperor Ferdinand III in 1645. His hymns, though not widely used in his lifetime, number 680, most of which were published in 6 collections issued from 1641 to 1656. Author: "Break forth, O beauteous heavenly light," **223**.

Roberts, Daniel Crane, born Bridgehampton, Long Island, NY, 5 November 1841; died Concord, NH, 31 October 1907. An 1857 graduate of Kenyon College, Gambier, Ohio, and a private in the 84th Ohio volunteers during the Civil War, Roberts was ordained a deacon in 1865 and a priest in 1866, serving parishes in Vermont, Massachusetts, and for twenty-nine years, St. Paul's Church in Concord, New Hampshire. He was president of the New Hampshire State Historical Society, chaplain of the Grand Army of the Republic, and active in the Knights Templar. Author: "God of the ages, whose almighty hand," **698**.

Roberts, John (Gwyllt, Ieuan), born Tanrhiwfelen, Penllwyn, near Aberystwyth, Wales, 22 December 1822; died Vron, Caernarvon, Wales, 6 May 1877. He is also known by the pen name that he gave himself, Ieuan Gwyllt (John Wild). Roberts was a Welsh musician, editor, teacher, composer, and Calvinistic Methodist minister. He received his musical training as a pupil of Richard Mills, began preaching in 1856, was ordained in 1859, serving churches in Aberdare and Capel Cock, and edited the Calvinistic Methodist hymnal *Llyfr Tonau Cynulleidfaol*, 1859. "His main work was with the music of the church: he collected and edited hymn tunes; he produced periodicals for musicians; he lectured and preached to raised the people's consciousness of the need for better standards in worship; he judged *eisteddfodau* and conducted musical festivals; indeed [in 1859] he created the 'Cymanfa Ganu' as it is now known." (Luff 1990, 196-97) For additional information about this composer and his work, see Alan Luff, *Welsh Hymns and Their Tunes*. Source: ST. DENIO, **103**.

Robinson, Robert, born Swaffham, Norfolk, England, 27 September 1735; died Birmingham, England, 9 June 1790. Robinson was a barber's apprentice who was influenced by the preaching of George Whitefield. Following his conversion in 1755, he began preaching in the Calvinistic Methodist chapel at Mildenhall, Suffolk, and later founded an independent congregation at Norwich. He adopted Baptist views and was rebaptized in 1759. He started to preach at Stone Yard Baptist Church, Cambridge, and was its pastor from 1761 to 1790. In his later years, Robinson was influenced by the Unitarian theologian Joseph Priestly. His publications include *A History of Baptism*, 1790. For additional information see Paul A. Richardson's article "Robert Robinson" in *Companion to the Baptist Hymnal*. Author: "Come, thou Fount of every blessing," **400**.

Roentgen, Julius, born Leipzig, Germany, 9 May 1855; died Utrecht, 13 September 1932. Roentgen (Röntgen) studied with some of the most important teachers of his day, including Moritz Hauptmann and Carl Reinecke. He was the conductor of the Society for the Advancement of Musical Art in 1866 and became professor, later director, of the Amsterdam conservatoire. Highly regarded as a performer, composer, musicologist, and editor, he was a friend of Liszt, Brahms, and Grieg. Arranger: IN BABILONE, **325**.

Rohrbough, Katherine F., born Hunter, NY, 9 July 1896; died Delaware, OH, 21 October 1971. A graduate of Wellesley College and Boston University School of Theology, she and her husband Lynn founded Cooperative Recreation Service, Delaware, Ohio, a publisher of recreational sources and songbooks. From the end of World War II until the early 1970's, Cooperative Recreation Service, also known as Informal Songs, produced most of the songbooks for use in church camping and recreational ministries. Many third-world songs and hymns appeared in translation for the first time in their publications. Translator: "Jaya ho," **478**.

Rosas, Carlos, born Linares, Nuevo Leon, Mexico, 4 November 1939. Music director and liturgy coordinator at San Juan de los Lagos parish, San Antonio, Texas, since 1970, Rosas attended Seminario Arquidiocesano de Monterrey,

Mexico (1951-58); Instituto de Liturgia, Musica y Arte Cardenal Dario Miranda, Mexico City, Mexico; San Antonio College, San Antonio, Texas; and the Mexican American Cultural Center, San Antonio. He has directed choirs in Mexico and Texas, and served as director of music and liturgy coordinator at the Mexican American Cultural Center, San Antonio (1976-80). He conducts workshops in music and liturgy throughout the United States. His parish choir was invited to sing at St. Peter's Basilica, Rome, Italy, in 1990. The author of numerous articles and the composer of a large volume of music, he received first place in the Concurso Canción del Papa competition for the song "San Antonio y Roman Cantan," performed for Pope John Paul II in 1987. Author and composer: "Cantemos al Señor" (ROSAS), **149**; Response, **862**.

Rossetti, Christina Georgiana, born St. Pancras, London, England, 5 December 1830; died St. Giles, London, 29 December 1894. Rossetti was the daughter of Gabriele Rossetti, professor of Italian at King's College, London. She had an exceptionally beautiful face and was a model for portraits of the Madonna by such artists as Millais and her brother Dante Gabriel who was a leader of the Pre-Raphaelite movement of British artists and poets. She was in poor health from the age of sixteen, finding solace in prolific writing of prose and poetry and through intense religious devotion. She published three collections of poems and four devotional books. In 1904 her brother collected her other verse that had appeared in periodicals. Author: "In the bleak midwinter," **221**; "Love came down at Christmas," **242**; "Open wide the window of our spirits," **477**.

Routley, Erik Reginald, born Brighton, Sussex, England, 31 October 1917; died Nashville, TN, 8 October 1982. Educated at Lancing College, Sussex (1931), Magdalen College, Oxford (B.A. 1936), Mansfield College, Oxford (1939), and Oxford University (B.A. 1940, B.D. 1946, Ph.D. 1952), he was ordained as a Congregational minister in 1943, serving two pastorates, Trinity Congregational Church, Wednesbury, and Dartford Congregational Church, Kent, before returning to Mansfield College as a tutor. He continued at Mansfield, becoming a lecturer in church history, chaplain, librarian, and director of music (1948-59). From 1959 to 1967 he pastored Augustine-Bristo Congregational Church, Edinburgh, and St. James' United Reformed Church, Newcastle-upon-Tyne. Routley was elected president of the Congregational Church in England and Wales (1970-71), the denomination's highest honor, and was appointed first chair of the Doctrine and Worship Committee of the new United Reformed Church, the result of the 1972 unification of the Congregationalist with the Presbyterian Church of England. Coming to the USA as a visiting professor and director of music at Princeton Theological Seminary, he joined the faculty at Westminster Choir College, Princeton, in 1975 as professor of church music and director of the chapel.

Routley was considered the most influential hymnologist of his generation, and his works, in addition to those on page 875, include the following: *The Church and Music*, 1950, *The English Carol*, 1958, *Church Music and Theology*, 1959, *Music Sacred and Profane*, 1960, *Hymns Today and Tomorrow*, 1964, *Exploring the Psalms*, 1975, and his final volume, *Christian Hymns Observed*, 1982, an eloquent, brief, and characteristically opinionated history of congregational song. He was editor of *Bulletin: The Hymn Society of Great Britain and Ireland*, 1948-74, and co-edited *Hymns for Celebration*, 1974, *Ecumenical Praise*, 1977, and *Companion to Congregational Praise*, 1953. He was secretary of the committee for *Congregational Praise*, 1951, editorial consultant of *Cantate Domino*, 3d ed. 1974, and editor of *Rejoice in the Lord*, 1985.

Caryl Micklem describes Routley as a fine pianist and organist, given to frequent laughter, deeply committed to pastoral care, "incandescently" swift as a typist, and "perpetually awestruck; devoting all his energy and skill . . . so that thanks to his testimony we might look past him and see what he had seen." (Leaver and Litton 1985, 14)

Upon the death of Routley, Fred Pratt Green composed the following memorial:

>He was, of all of us, the most alive.
>He lived his life *allegro*, let us say,
>Even con brio; yet he could contrive,
>In his untiring and warm-hearted way,
>To play it *con amore*. To each friend
>He was most loyal, lovable, and kind;
>As author, teacher, his exciting mind
>Instructed us how wit and wisdom blend.
>
>His many gifts made debtors of us all:
>His love of hymnody, his dedication.
>But, as God's servant, was he apt to be,
>In giving of himself, too prodigal?
>Be sure of this: he needs no threnody;
>What he deserves of us is celebration.

(Green 1991, 162)

Author: "All who love and serve your city," **433**; composer: AUGUSTINE, **93**; PRAYER CANTICLE, **406**; Response, **772**; SHARPTHORNE, **441**.

Rowan, William Patrick, born San Diego, CA, 30 November 1951. A graduate of Southern Illinois University (B.A., M.M.) and the University of Michigan (M.M.), Rowan is the director of music ministries at St. Mary Cathedral in Lansing and the liturgical music consultant for the diocese of Lansing. He has composed over thirty-five hymn tunes, anthems, and organ works. His hymn settings have been sung at hymn festivals throughout the USA, in Great Britain, and Europe and are included in most recent hymnals. Composer: MANY NAMES, **105**.

Rowthorn, Jeffery William, born Gwent, Wales, 9 April 1934. Educated at Cambridge University, Oxford University, Union Theological Seminary, New York, and Cuddeson Theological College, Oxford, he was ordained a priest in 1963, serving as curate of Woolwich Parish Church, London, 1962-65, and as rector of St. Mary's Church, Garsington, Oxford, 1965-68. After an appointment as dean of instruction and chaplain at Union Theological Seminary, he went to Yale University in 1973 as a founding faculty member of the Institute of Sacred Music. While at Yale he was chapel minister of the Divinity School and first holder of the Bishop Percy Goddard Chair in Pastoral Theology at Berkeley Divinity School, where he also received an honorary doctorate. Consecrated as bishop suffragan of Connecticut in 1987, he has edited two hymnals, *Laudamus: Services and Songs of Praise*, 1980, and *A New Hymnal for Colleges and Schools* [*The Yale Hymnal*], 1989, and with Russell Schulz-Widmar, *A New Hymnal for Colleges and Schools* [The Yale Hymnal], 1992. His hymn texts are published in numerous hymnals. Author: "Creating God, your fingers trace," **109**; "Lord, you give the great commission," **584**.

Ruíz, Rubén (Avila), born in Cuautla, Morelos, Mexico, 12 November 1945. His mother a homemaker and his father a Methodist minister, he was educated at the instituto Mexicano Madero, where he also served as choir director. Ruíz and his two sons lived in Covington, Virginia, for a brief time. Author and composer: "Mantos y palmas" (HOSANNA), **279**.

Runyan, William Marion, born Marion, NY, 21 January 1870; died Pittsburg, KS, 29 July 1957. A church organist at the age of twelve, he taught music as a teenager. Runyan was ordained by the Methodist Church in 1891 and held pastorates in Kansas for twelve years. He served the Central Kansas Methodist Conference as an evangelist for twenty years before becoming pastor of the Federated Church at John Brown University, Sulphur Springs, Arkansas, as well as editor of the *Christian Workers Magazine*. Associated with Moody Bible Institute after his retirement to Chicago, Runyan was also music editor and advisor for Hope Publishing Company, where he reviewed all manuscripts for twenty-two years. Composer: FAITHFULNESS, **140**.

Rutter, John, born London, England, 1945. Educated at Clare College, Cambridge University (M.A., Mus.B. 1968), he received his first musical training as a boy chorister at Highgate School. During his undergraduate studies, he wrote his first published compositions and conducted his first recording. Sir David Willcocks invited him to co-edit the second volume of the *Carols for Choirs* series, a collaboration that later included the third and fourth volumes. From 1975 to 1979 he was the director of music at Clare College, but resigned to spend more time composing. He later formed the Cambridge Singers and has recorded many albums, winning the Gramophone award for the Fauré *Requiem* in its 1893 version. A frequent leader of USA music clinic and festivals, in 1980 he became an honorary fellow of Westminster Choir College, Princeton, New Jersey. Composer and adapter: Amen, **902**.

Saliers, Don E., born Fostoria, OH, 11 August 1937. Educated at Ohio Wesleyan University (B.A. 1959), Yale Divinity School (B.D. 1962), and St. John's College,

Cambridge University (Fulbright fellow 1964-65), he served as organist/choirmaster at First Presbyterian Church, New Haven (1966-72), while professor of theology and worship at Yale Divinity School (1966-74). Since 1974 he has been professor of theology and worship and organist/choirmaster for university worship at Emory University, Atlanta, Georgia. The recipient of the 1992 Berakah award from the North American Academy of Liturgy, the Tew and Hooker prizes from Yale, and the Emory Williams Distinguished Teaching award, he is the author of *Word and Table*, 1976, *From Ashes to Fire*, 1979, and *From Hope to Joy*, 1983. He was co-author of the *Handbook of the Christian Year*, 1980, 1986, and *Christian Spirituality III*, 1989. He also has written *Worship and Spirituality*, 1984, and *The Soul in Paraphrase: Prayer and the Religious Affections*, 1980, 1992. Composer: Responses: **740, 756, 769, 774, 807, 828, 832, 836, 841**.

Sammis, John H., born Brooklyn, NY, 6 July 1846; died Los Angeles, CA, 12 June 1919. Sammis moved to Logansport, Indiana, where he was a successful businessman. His work with the YMCA prompted him to enter the ministry. After study at McCormick and Lane seminaries, he was ordained into the Presbyterian ministry in 1880, holding pastorates in Iowa, Indiana, Michigan, and Minnesota. Toward the end of his life he was on the faculty of Los Angeles Bible Institute. Author: "When we walk with the Lord," **467**.

Sandell-Berg, Caroline V., born Fröderyd, Småland, Sweden, 3 October 1832; died Stockholm, Sweden, 26 July 1903. Also known as Lina Sandell, she was the daughter of a Lutheran minister who leaned toward the *pietists* and the Moravians. Sandell-Berg suffered temporary paralysis at an early age, followed by the tragic death of both parents, and she turned to writing poems, some 650 in all. She joined the editorial staff of the Evangelical National Foundation, working with the foremost Swedish lay preacher of the day, Carl Rosenius. Settings of her poems were provided by his musical associate, Oskar Ahnfelt. Called the "Fanny Crosby of Sweden," she had many hymns published in *Andeliga daggdroppar*, *Sionstoner*, and *Ahnfelt's Sanger*, personally underwritten by Jenny Lind. Author: "Children of the heavenly Father," **141**; "Thy holy wings, O Savior," **502**.

Sateren, Leland Bernhard, born Everett, WA, 13 October 1913. Educated at Augsburg College (B.A. 1935) and the University of Minnesota (M.A. 1943), he became professor of music, choral director, and chair of the music department at Augsburg College (1950). An adjudicator, teacher, and music festival director, he has received several honorary doctorates and the St. Olaf Medal, given by King Olav of Norway in 1971. Sateren is a composer of more than 300 choral works and has served on the Inter-Lutheran Commission on Worship (1967-78). Harmonizer: A VA DE, **625**; THE ASH GROVE, **664**.

Savonarola, Girolamo, born Ferrara, Italy, 1452; died Florence, Italy, 23 May 1498. A monk who was greatly concerned by the immorality of Pope Alexander VI during the Italian Renaissance, Savonarola wrote *Laudi spirituali* "to replace the objectionable secular songs in use during his time." (Stulken 1981, 193) His stand against indecent books, paintings, and song collections caused him to be declared a heretic, hanged, and his body was burned. Author: "For overcoming adversity," **531**.

Schalk, Carl Flentge, born Des Plaines, IL, 26 September 1929. Educated at Concordia Teachers College, River Forest, Illinois (B.S. 1952), Eastman School of Music, Rochester, New York (M.M. 1957), Concordia Theological Seminary, St. Louis, Missouri (M.A.), with honorary doctorates from Concordia College, Seward, Nebraska, and Concordia College, St. Paul, Minnesota, Schalk served as teacher and director of music at Zion Lutheran Church, Wausau, Wisconsin (1952-56), and was director of music for the International Lutheran Hour, St. Louis (1958-65). He has been professor of church music at Concordia Teachers College since 1965. Schalk has served on the editorial advisory committee of Concordia Publishing House, the hymn music committee of the Inter-Lutheran Commission on Worship (1967-78), and has edited *Church Music* since 1966. He was editor of *Key Words in Church Music*, 1978, and is author of *Luther on Music: Paradigms of Praise*, 1988. His fifty hymn tunes and carols are collected in *The Carl Schalk Hymnary*, 1989. Composer: ROEDER, **122**; STANLEY BEACH, **257**; NOW, **619**.

Schiavone, John, born Los Angeles, CA, 27 March 1947. A 1982 graduate of the Rensselaer Program of Church Music and Liturgy, holding the M.M. from St. Joseph's College, Rensselaer, Indiana, he is music and liturgy consultant to the Los Angeles archdiocese office for worship, who commissioned him to compose three pieces for the visit of Pope John Paul II to Los Angeles in 1987. He has served as assistant pastor in several parishes in California. Adapter: "Chant Mode VI."

Schilling, Sylvester Paul, born Cumberland, MD, 7 February 1904. Graduate of St. John's, Annapolis, Maryland (B.S. 1923), Boston University (A.M. 1927, S.T.B. 1929, Ph.D. 1934), with additional study at Harvard University and the University of Berlin, he was ordained in the Methodist ministry in 1930. After pastoring churches in Virginia, Maryland, and Washington, DC (1932-45), he became professor of systematic theology and philosophy of religion at Westminster Theological Seminary, Maryland (1945-53), and professor of systematic theology at Boston University (1953-69). He is a fellow in the National Society for Values in Higher Education and was the Lowell Institute lecturer for Boston University in 1968. He was editor of *Methodism and Society in Theological Perspective*, 1960, and the author of *Contemporary Continental Theologians*, 1966, *God in an Age of Atheism*, 1969, *God Incognito*, 1974, *God and Human Anguish*, 1977, and *The Faith We Sing*, 1983. He was a consultant in language and theology to the Hymnal Revision Committee. Co-translator: "Praise to the Lord, the Almighty," **139**.

Schlegel, Katharina Amalia Dorothea von, born 22 October 1697. Little is known of this writer. She was probably attached to the little ducal court at Cöthen and was one of the eighteenth-century Pietists of the younger Halle School who compiled the *Cöthnische Lieder*, 1744 complete edition. Twenty-six hymns have been attributed to her. (Julian 1907, 50, 1009) Author: "Be still, my soul," **534**; Response, **746**.

Scholefield, Clement Cotterill, born Edgbaston, Birmingham, England, 22 June 1839; died Godalming, England, 10 September 1904. A self-taught musician and tune writer, he graduated from St. John's College, Cambridge University (M.A. 1867), and served as curate at St. Peter's Church, South Kensington, and as chaplain of Eton College, Windsor. Composer: ST. CLEMENT, **690.**

Schop, Johann, born Hamburg[?], Holstein, Germany, ca. 1595; died Hamburg, ca. 1667. A noted performer on the lute, trumpet, violin, and zinke, Schop was a friend of Johann Rist, a member of the court orchestra at Wolfenbüttel, and later director of "Ratsmusik" in Hamburg. He was music editor of Rist's *Himmlische Lieder*, 1641-43. Composer: ERMUNTRE DICH, **223;** JESU, JOY OF MAN'S DESIRING, **644.**

Schubert, Franz Peter, born Lichtenthal, near Vienna, Austria, 31 January 1797; died Vienna, Austria, 19 November 1828. Schubert is considered the creator of the modern German *lied*, writing 634 songs for solo voice and piano accompaniment. He was also a prolific composer of opera, church music, chamber music, and orchestral music. Composer: "Musical Setting C," **21, 22.**

Schulz-Widmar, Russell, born Hebron, IL, 29 July 1944. A church musician and teacher, he graduated from Valparaiso University in Indiana (B.Mus. 1966), the School of Sacred Music, Union Theological Seminary, New York (S.M.M. 1968), and the University of Texas, Austin (D.M.A. 1974). In 1970 he became co-director of music at the University United Methodist Church, Austin, and in 1974 became adjunct professor of church music at the Episcopal Theological Seminary of the Southwest, Austin. From 1975 to 1991 he was visiting lecturer in church music at the Austin Presbyterian Theological Seminary. He is the author of many articles on church music, notably hymnody, and the composer of over 100 published works. Past president of the Hymn Society in the United States and Canada, he was editor of *Songs of Thanks and Praise*, 1980, chair of the music committee for *The Hymnal 1982*, and co-editor of *A New Hymnal for Colleges and Schools*, 1992. Author: "Your love, O God, has called us here," **647.**

Schumann, Robert Alexander, born Zwickau, Saxony, 8 June 1810; died Endenich, near Bonn, 29 July 1856. Schumann began composing at the age of seven and studied with Friedrich Wieck, the father of Clara, an accomplished pianist and composer who later became Schumann's wife, chief exponent, and performer of his impressive piano repertory. The composer of symphonies, piano, chamber, and vocal music, Schumann was also a founder and editor of *Die neue Zeitschrift für Musik*, a significant publication in the young field of musicology. His masses and compositions for male voice choirs are standard literature. He was instrumental in launching the careers of Brahms and Chopin. In 1854 after an attempted suicide by drowning, Schumann was committed to an asylum in Bonn where he died. For a more complete biography, see *Baker's Biographical Dictionary of Music and Musicians*. Composer: CANONBURY, **463.**

Schutmaat, Alvin L., born 1921; died Bogota, Colombia, 1 May 1987. Latin American missionary, educator, ecumenist, artist, and scholar, Schutmaat received a doctorate in theology from Edinburgh University and did extensive graduate work in Latin American literature and education. With his wife he lived in Colombia during "La Violencia," a treacherous time of persecution and political tension. He was principal of several large Presbyterian schools in Colombia and Venezuela and was a delegate from Colombia to the first Evangelical Conference of Latin America, 1949. Primarily an artist who sought to use the arts to communicate the gospel, he served as a consultant in the arts for Central American churches and for the International Christian Center for the Arts in Mexico City. He taught theology and music at the Presbyterian Seminary of Bogota and was a consultant and teacher at the Latin American Biblical Seminary in Costa Rica. Arranger: HOSANNA, **279;** EL CAMINO, **434.**

Schutte, Daniel L., born Neenah, WI, 28 December 1947. Educated at St. Louis University (B.S. 1973), Jesuit School of Theology, Berkeley, California (M.Div. 1979), and Graduate Theological Union, Berkeley, California (M.L.T. 1980), he joined the Jesuits, serving as director of liturgy on the campus ministry staff at Marquette University (1982-86). From 1986 to 1987 he was director of music at Immaculate Heart of Mary parish, Milwaukee, when he became director of music for Our Lady of Lourdes parish, Milwaukee. He received an honorary doctorate from the University of Scranton. Author and composer: "I, the Lord of sea and sky" (HERE I AM, LORD), **593.**

Schütz, Johann Jacob, born Frankfurt-am-Main, Germany, 7 September 1640; died Frankfurt-am-Main, 22 May 1690. Schütz studied at Tübingen and was licensed to practice civil and canon law; he worked in Frankfurt as a Rath, or counselor, all his life. He was influenced by his friends Johann Wilhelm Petersen, and Philipp Jakob Spener. In 1680 Schütz suggested to Spener that he begin the famous *Collegia Pietatis* (prayer meetings). These are considered the beginning of the Pietist movement in Germany.

Under the influence of J. S. Petersen, Schütz became a Separatist, leaving the Lutheran Church in 1686. In 1683, through the Frankfurt company, he bought land in Germantown, Pennsylvania, from William Penn. His many hymns were published in *Christliches Gedenckbüchlein*, 1675, and *Christliche Lebensregeln*, 1677. From this latter collection the hymn "Sei Lob und Ehr dem höchsten Gut" has remained in common use in English language hymnals through Frances E. Cox's translation. Author: Responses, **80, 743, 851;** "Sing praise to God who reigns above," **126.**

Schwedler, Johann Christoph, born Krobsdorf, Silesia, 21 December 1672; died Niederweise, 12 January 1730. Educated at the University of Leipzig, Schwedler was a powerful preacher, hymn writer, and humanitarian. He went to Niederweise, near Greiffenberg, in 1698 and served there successively as assistant, deacon, and pastor until his death. Besides writing hundreds of hymns, he also founded an orphanage in Niederweise. Author: "Ask ye what great thing I know," **163.**

Scott, Clara H., born Elk Grove, IL, 3 December 1841; died Dubuque, IA, 21 June 1987. She attended the first musical institute in Chicago taught by C. M. Cady and taught music in the Ladies' Seminary at Lyons, Iowa. With the encouragement of Horatio R. Palmer she contributed many songs to his collections. Her *Royal Anthem Book,* 1882, was the first collection of anthems published by a woman. Author and composer: "Open my eyes, that I may see" (OPEN MY EYES), **(454).**

Scott, Lesbia, born London, England, 11 August 1898; died Pershore, Worcestershire, England, 1986. Scott was graduated from Raven's Croft School, Sussex, and was active in amateur theater and religious drama, compiling *Everyday Hymns for Little Children*, 1929, for her own children. In 1931 she wrote and produced the Malta Cathedral Nativity play. After her husband became a rector of a parish near Dartmoor, Devon, she joined the Religious Drama Society. Six of her plays have been published. Author: "I sing a song of the saints of God," **712.**

Scott, Robert Balgarnie Young, born Toronto, Canada, 16 July 1899; died Toronto, 1 November 1987. Educated at Knox College (B.D.) and the University of Toronto (B.A., M.A., Ph.D.), he became a minister of the United Church of Canada and served in Ontario. He taught Old Testament at Union College, Vancouver, and United Theological College, McGill University, Montreal. In 1955 he joined the faculty of Princeton Theological Seminary where he became chair of the department of religion and Danforth Professor of Religion, retiring in 1965. Scott was active in social reform. For four years he served as president of the Fellowship for a Christian Social Order, and during this time he wrote hymns for the group's use and with Gregory Vlastos edited *Toward the Christian Revolution*, 1936. His best-known book is *The Relevance of the Prophets*, 1945, revised 1968. During World War II he served as chaplain of the Royal Canadian Air Force. His hymns are found in most English language hymnals. Author: "O Day of God, draw nigh," **730.**

Scriven, Joseph Medlicott, born Seapatrick, County Down, Ireland, 10 September 1819; died Bewdley, Rice Lake, Ontario, 10 August 1886. After entering Trinity College, Dublin, he decided on an army career, but poor health forced him to give up the idea, and he returned to Trinity, graduating in 1842. His Irish fiancée accidently drowned the evening before their wedding. He moved to Canada, and similarly his fiancée died after a brief illness. Scriven joined the Plymouth Brethren and devoted his life to doing menial volunteer work for the physically handicapped and poor. Toward the end of his life he suffered from depression, and his death by drowning may have been suicide. His poems were included in *Hymns and Other Verses*, 1869. Author: "What a friend we have in Jesus," **526.**

Sears, Edmund Hamilton, born Sandisfield, MA, 6 April 1810; died Weston, MA, 16 January 1876. Sears was educated at Union College, Schenectady, New York, and Harvard Divinity School. He was ordained into the Unitarian ministry in 1839 and held pastorates in Wayland, Lancaster, and Weston, Massachusetts. His theological position was Swedenborgian in that he saw a direct mystical union between the world and spirituality and strongly affirmed the divinity of Christ. John Julian calls his two Christmas hymns some of the best in the English language. (Julian 1907, 1036) Most of his hymns were published in the *Monthly Religious Magazine* when he was co-editor. Author: "It came upon the midnight clear," **218**.

Sedio, Mark Edward, born Minneapolis, MN, 16 November 1954. Currently cantor for Mount Olive Lutheran Church, St. Paul, Minnesota, he attended Augsburg College (B.A.) and the University of Iowa (M.A.) with graduate studies at Luther Northwestern Theological Seminary. He has won various composition competitions, including hymn-related contests, and is active in the Association of Lutheran Church Musicians as director for ecclesiastical concerns. Composer: EMMAUS, **309**.

Seiss, Joseph August, born Graceham, MD, 18 March 1823; died Philadelphia, PA, 20 June 1904. Son of an Alsatian coal miner who discouraged his son's call to the ministry, Seiss received guidance from his Moravian pastor, attended Pennsylvania College and Seminary, Gettysburg, and was licensed by the Evangelical Lutheran Synod of Virginia (1842). After pastorates in Virginia and Maryland, he served St. John's Lutheran Church, Philadelphia, for sixteen years. He later established the Church of the Holy Communion in western Philadelphia. Among his eighty works are *The Last Times*, 1856, *The Evangelical Psalmist*, 1859, *Lectures on the Gospels*, 1868-72, and *Lectures on the Epistles*, 1885. Translator: "Fairest Lord Jesus," **189**.

Seltz, Martin Louis, born near Gibbon, MN, 20 December 1909; died St. Paul, MN, 5 October 1967. A graduate of Concordia College, St. Paul, Minnesota (1928), and Concordia Seminary, St. Louis, Missouri (1934), he was an instructor at Concordia College from 1928 to 1932. He served Lutheran churches in New Jersey, Minnesota, Iowa, and Illinois (1933-67). As an active musician, he edited *The North Star Song Book*, 1945, 1956, and was a member of the Commission on Worship and the Inter-Lutheran Commission on Worship. Translator: "Savior of the nations, come," **214**.

Shaw, Martin Fallas, born Kensington, London, England, 9 March 1875; died Southwold, Suffolk, England, 24 October 1958. Born into a musical family, Shaw studied at the Royal College of Music under Charles V. Stanford, C. H. H. Parry, and Walford Davies. He was organist of Primrose Hill, London, 1908, St. Martin's in the Fields, 1920, and Guildhouse in London. Besides being a cofounder of the Summer School of Church Music, later the Royal Society of Church Music, and serving as director of music for the diocese of Chelmsford (1935-45), he published *Additional Tunes*, 1915, with Percy Dearmer and Ralph Vaughan Williams, edited *The Oxford Book of Carols*, 1928, and with Ralph Vaughan Williams, he co-edited *Songs of Praise*, 1925, 1931. His own compositions include songs, anthems, and service music. In 1932 he and his brother, Geoffrey, were awarded the Lambeth Mus.D. degree. Arranger: ROCKING, **235**; ROYAL OAK, **147**; harmonizer: BESANÇON, **202**; FRENCH CAROL, **237, 311**.

Shepherd, Thomas, born England, 1665; died Bocking, Essex, England, 29 January 1739. Although ordained into the Church of England, Shepherd left the church in 1694 to become an independent pastor, first in Nottingham and in 1700 at Bocking. Of his thirty-nine years at Bocking, the first seven were spent preaching in a barn before a chapel was built. Composite author: "Must Jesus bear the cross alone," **424**.

Sheppard, Franklin Lawrence, born Philadelphia, PA, 7 August 1852; died Germantown, PA, 15 February 1930. An honors graduate and charter member of the Phi Beta Kappa chapter of the University of Pennsylvania (1872), Sheppard moved to Baltimore in 1875 to take charge of his father's foundry business and also served as organist for Zion Protestant Episcopal Church. He later joined Second Presbyterian Church, Baltimore, and became the music director. Besides serving in many capacities within the Presbyterian Church, including president of the Board of Publication, he served on the editorial committee of the 1911 Presbyterian *Hymnal* and edited the Presbyterian Sunday school songbook *Alleluia*, 1915. Adapter: TERRA BEATA, **111, 144**.

Sherring, Victor C., born Kanpur, U.P., India, 9 July 1919. Raised in the Methodist schools at Mathura, U.P., India, he attended Southwestern College, Winfield, Kansas (A.B. 1941), Garrett Biblical Institute, Evanston, Illinois (B.D. 1943), and Northwestern University, Evanston, Illinois (M.A. 1945). Currently the superintendent of Howard Plested Girls' Intermediate College, Meerut, U.P., India, he toured the India Centenary Choir throughout India and in seventy cities in the USA, 1955-56. He has been instrumental in popularizing Indian church music by arranging texts and music for publication. Arranger: VICTORY HYMN, **478**.

Sherwin, William Fiske, born Buckland, MA, 14 March 1826; died Boston, MA, 14 April 1888. Sherwin, who was renowned for his ability to work with amateur singers, studied with Lowell Mason and served on the faculty of the New England Conservatory of Music. Though a Baptist, he was invited by John H. Vincent to be musical director of the Methodist Chautauqua Assembly in western New York State. Composer: BREAD OF LIFE, **599**; CHAUTAUQUA, **687**.

Showalter, Anthony Johnson, born Cherry Grove, Rockingham County, VA, 1 May 1858; died Chattanooga, TN, 16 September 1924. He was trained by his musical father, who was a singing school teacher in the Shenandoah Valley. Showalter's later musical instruction came from B. C. Unseld, George F. Root, H. R. Palmer, and F. W. Root. After teaching music for the Ruebush-Kieffer Company of Dayton, Virginia, he founded his own firm in Dalton, Georgia, 1884, and reportedly sold millions of copies of his collections of songs. He also published a monthly periodical, *The Music Teacher*, 1884-1924, and conducted singing schools in many southern states. Composer: SHOWALTER, **133**.

Shurtleff, Ernest Warburton, born Boston, MA, 4 April 1862; died Paris, France, 29 August 1917. Shurtleff was a Congregational minister who studied at Harvard University, New Church Theological Seminary, and Andover Theological Seminary. While at Andover, he was organist for the Stone Chapel of Phillips Academy. He served congregations in California, Massachusetts, and Minnesota and organized the American Church in Frankfurt, Germany. In 1906 he became director of student activities at the Academy Vitti in Paris, and during World War I he and his wife were active in relief work. Author: "Lead on, O King eternal," **580**.

Sibelius, Jean, born Tavastehus, Finland, 8 December 1865; died Järvenpää, Finland, 20 September 1957. Regarded as Finland's greatest composer, Sibelius composed symphonic poems, seven symphonies, eighty-six songs, twenty choral works, and sacred music in *Musique religieuse*, 1927, and *Christmas Songs*, 1895. The music of Sibelius is the culmination of nineteenth-century nationalistic music, evoking the mythic and epic ethos of Finland. He ceased composing in 1929. For a more complete biography, see *Baker's Biographical Dictionary of Music and Musicians*. Composer: FINLANDIA, **437**, **534**; Response, **746**.

Sinclair, Jerry, born Calais, ME, 25 March 1943. He began writing songs as a teenage preacher and traveled with a religious singing group during the Jesus movement. Today he owns a music publishing company, Southern California Music, and is a telephone company executive. Author and composer: "Alleluia" (ALLELUIA), **186**.

Singh, Sundar. No information has been found on this twentieth-century poet from India. Author: "Finding rest in God," **423**.

Sleeth, Natalie Allyn Wakeley, born Evanston IL, 29 October 1930; died Denver, CO, 21 March 1992. The daughter of musical parents, she began piano lessons at the age of four and majored in music theory at Wellesley College (B.A. 1952). She married Ronald E. Sleeth, a Methodist clergyman and professor of homiletics, and lived in university communities in Nashville, Dallas, Evanston, and Denver. She served as music secretary at Highland Park United Methodist Church, Dallas (1969-76), and during that time she audited a course taught by Lloyd Pfautsch at Southern Methodist University. At his recommendation, the Choristers Guild published her first work, "Canon of Praise," in 1969. Her subsequent choral works have received wide publication. Author of *Adventures for the Soul*, 1987, and the subject of a videotape, *Words and Music*, 1990, she received honorary doctorates from West Virginia Wesleyan College (1989) and Nebraska Wesleyan College (1990). Author and composer: "Go now in peace" (GO IN PEACE), **665**; "In the bulb there is a flower" (PROMISE), **707**.

Smart, Henry Thomas, born London, England, 26 October 1813; died London, 6 July 1879. Although Smart studied with his father and W. H. Kerns, he was essentially self-taught in organ playing and composition. He held several positions in London, including appointments at St. Philip's and St. Pancras from 1865 until his death. He championed congregational singing and was noted for his improvisations. He designed organs and composed an opera, cantatas, songs, part-songs, anthems, a morning and evening service, organ music, and hymn tunes. He edited the music of *The Choral Book*, 1858, and *The Presbyterian Psalter and Hymnal*, 1877-78. Composer: LANCASHIRE, **303, 571, 580**; REGENT SQUARE, **220, 304**.

Smith, Alfred Morton, born Jenkintown, PA, 20 May 1879; died Brigantine, NJ, 26 February 1971. A graduate of the University of Pennsylvania (B.A. 1901) and the Philadelphia Divinity School (B.Div. 1905, B.S.T. 1911), he was ordained an Episcopal priest in 1906 and served in Pennsylvania and California. He spent ten years at St. Matthias' Church, Los Angeles, before becoming an army chaplain during World War I. Returning from France and Germany in 1919, he served the Episcopal City Mission, the Eastern State Penitentiary, Sleighton Farm School, and the city hospital as chaplain. As an adult Smith studied harmony and composed two eucharistic masses, some hymn tunes, and carols, several of which have been published in *The Hymnal 1940* and *The Hymnal 1982* of the Protestant Episcopal Church. Composer: SURSUM CORDA, **115**.

Smith, Gary Alan, born Milwaukee, WI, 4 August 1947. Educated at the University of Wisconsin, Milwaukee (B.F.A. 1971), and Perkins School of Theology, Southern Methodist University, Dallas (M.Th. and M.S.M. 1975), he served as director of music for churches in Memphis and Johnson City, Tennessee (1975-85), prior to becoming hymnal revision project manager for The United Methodist Publishing House, Nashville. Smith has been music editor of Abingdon Press, Nashville, since 1989, and has written more than forty published choral compositions and arrangements. Composer: Responses, **167, 646, 748, 752, 766, 771, 779, 787, 795, 804, 815, 822, 834, 838, 853**; harmonizer: IN DULCI JUBILO, **224**; LORD OF THE DANCE, **261**; ONE BREAD, ONE BODY, **620**.

Smith, Henry Percy, born Malta, December 1825; died Bournemouth, England, 28 January 1898. Educated at Balliol College, Oxford, Smith was curate to Charles Kingsley at Eversley, 1849-51, perpetual curate of St. Michael's York Town, Camberley, Surrey, 1851-68, vicar of Great Barton, Suffolk, 1868-82, chaplain of Christ Church, Cannes, France, 1882-95, and in 1892 canon of the cathedral of Gibraltar. Although he is the author of two books, little is known of his activities as a musician. Composer: MARYTON, **430, 654**.

Smith, Kenneth Donald, born Manchester, England, 1928. Educated at Keble College, Oxford (M.A.), he was assistant director of music for Wrekin College, Shropshire (1953-58), head of the music department for Sir Thomas Rich's School, Gloucester (1958-63), and later for St. Matthias College of Education,

Bristol (1964-78). He currently is director of music at All Saints, Clifton, Bristol. The composer of much unpublished church music, he has also had hymn tunes included in *Sunday School Praise*, 1958, the *Anglican Hymnal*, 1965, the *New Catholic Hymnal*, 1971, and *The Church Hymnary*, 1973 3d ed. Composer: RAPHAEL, **458**.

Smith, Michael Whitaker, born Kenova, WV, 7 October 1957. A contemporary Christian songwriter, performer, and recording artist/producer, he moved to Nashville, Tennessee, in 1978 and joined a gospel singing group, Higher Ground, in 1980. He has written songs for television and produced recordings of his own performances. Composer: THY WORD, **601**; Response, **841**.

Smith, Peter David, born Weybridge, Surrey, England, 26 April 1938. Educated at Farnham Grammar School, he served as an apprentice in the aircraft industry. Later he became a Methodist minister, serving in various circuits. While trained as a classical pianist, he chose to be a folksinger and guitarist. He led courses on contemporary worship for the Iona community in 1975. He edited *Faith, Folk and Clarity*, 1968, *Faith, Folk and Nativity*, 1969, *Faith, Folk and Festivity*, 1969, *New Orbit*, 1972, and contributed to *Partners in Praise*, 1979. Author and composer: HEALER, **263**.

Smith, Robert Archibald, born Reading, Berkshire, Scotland, 16 November, 1780; died Edinburgh, Scotland, 3 January 1829. A violinist, cellist, composer, and editor of church music, he is noted for compiling the impressive six-volume *Scottish Minstrel*, 1820-24, and *Sacred Music sung at St. George's Church*, 1825. The latter was completed at St. George's Church, Edinburgh, where he was an associate of Andrew Thomson. Smith also set a number of poems by Robert Tannahill. Arranger: MARTYRDOM, **359**.

Smith, Samuel Francis, born Boston, MA, 21 October 1808; died Boston, 16 November 1895. Smith was educated at the Boston Latin School, Harvard University, and Andover Theological Seminary. Stimulated by the mission work of Adoniram Judson, Smith attempted to enter the mission field but was prevented because of poor health. He became a prominent Baptist pastor, teacher, and served as editor of the *Baptist Missionary Magazine* before becoming pastor of the Baptist church in Waterville, Maine, where he also taught modern languages at Waterville (now Colby) College. Following twelve years as pastor of the Newton, Massachusetts, Baptist church, he became editorial secretary of the American Baptist Missionary Union and devoted much of his time to mission-related travel and writing. A close friend of Lowell Mason and Oliver Wendell Holmes, Smith helped compile *The Psalmist*, 1843, contributed to Mason's *Juvenile Lyre*, and wrote 100 hymns, most of which were for special occasions. There are interesting exchanges of correspondence between Smith and Louis F. Benson in the Benson Collection, Speer Library, Princeton Theological Seminary. Author: "My country, 'tis of thee," **697**.

Smith, Walter Chalmers, born Aberdeen, Scotland, 5 December 1824; died Kinbuck, Perthshire, Scotland, 20 September 1908. Educated at the University of Aberdeen and New College, Edinburgh, Smith was a Free Church pastor who served parishes in London, Milnathort, Glasgow, and from 1876 to 1894 in Edinburgh at the Free High Church of Scotland. In 1893 he was elected moderator of the Free Church of Scotland. His published works include *Hymns of Christ and the Christian Life*, 1867, and *Poetical Works*, 1902. Author: "Immortal, invisible, God only wise," **103**.

Smith, William Farley, born Durham, NC, 23 April 1941. A graduate of Manhattan School of Music (B.A. 1962, M.A. 1963), Columbia University (Ed.M. 1982, Ed.D. 1984), with certification in music therapy, and music ministry in The United Methodist Church, Smith has taught in the New York City schools and at Montclair State College. He is presently a faculty member at Drew University, music director at Harlem's St. Mark's United Methodist Church, and organist/music director for the New York Annual Conference of The United Methodist Church. He has traveled, lectured, and performed in Europe, West Africa, the West Indies, and the USA. Smith served as a consultant in African American music and worship to the Hymnal Revision Committee. He is the recipient of the Crusader Scholar award and has published numerous articles on slave songs and spirituals. Adapter: I'M GOIN' A SING, **333**; LATTIMER, **585**; MARTIN, **533**; SOJOURNER, **521**; VERY SOON, **706**; arranger: O MARY, **134**; PENITENT, **352**; STAND BY ME, **512**; THANK YOU, LORD, **84**; adapter, arranger: ASCENSIUS, **316**; BALM IN GILEAD, **375**; BURLEIGH, **719**; DITMUS, **527**; DUBOIS, **520**; FIX ME, JESUS, **655**; GO TELL IT ON THE MOUNTAIN, **251**; I WANT TO BE A CHRISTIAN, **402**; I WANT TO BE READY, **722**; I WILL TRUST, **464**; JACOB'S LADDER, **418**; LET US BREAK BREAD, **618**; PENTECOST, **404**; STEAL AWAY, **704**; SUFFERER, **291**; SWING LOW, **703**; TUBMAN, **448**; TURNER, **416**; WERE YOU THERE, **288**; YARMOUTH, **345**.

Sojo, Vicente E., born Guatire, Venezuela, 8 December 1887; died Caracas, 11 August 1974. Eager to bring music to his people in Venezuela, Maestro Sojo studied music history, taught music, and became an organist and composer. He founded the Orquesta Sinfónica Venezuela and the choral ensemble Orfeón Lamas, and they made significant contributions to the development of the nation's music and culture. Sojo was active in ethnomusicology and collected and adapted Venezuelan folk songs and hymns of the colonial period. Arranger: CARACAS, **222**.

Sosa, Pablo D., born Chivilcoy, Argentina, 16 December 1933. Born the son and nephew of Methodist pastors, Sosa also studied theology and music in Argentina, the USA, and Germany. He has served as a coordinator in the department of communication of the Interconfessional Association of Theological Studies and as a professor at the National Conservatory of Music in Buenos Aires. The composer, author, and translator of numerous hymns, he promotes Latin-American religious folk songs and is internationally recognized as an authority and leader in Hispanic music and worship. He served as the music leader for the United Methodist Global Gathering, Louisville,

1988, and the United Methodist Women's Assembly, Kansas City, 1990. He is an editor, conductor, and professor of communication at the Instituto Superior Evangélico de Estudios Teológicos de Buenos Aires. Co-leader of music for the sixth assembly of the World Council of Churches, Vancouver, 1983, he has led global workshops on third world music and liturgy in Denmark, Zimbabwe, the Philippines, Costa Rica, and Toronto. Composer: CENTRAL, **313**.

Spafford, Horatio Gates, born North Troy, NY, 20 October 1828; died Jerusalem, 16 October 1888. After establishing a successful legal practice in Chicago in 1856, he became a professor of medical jurisprudence at Lind University (later Chicago Medical College), and was an active layman and Sunday school teacher in the Presbyterian Church. From 1871 to 1880 he suffered repeated personal tragedies: heavy real estate losses in the Chicago fire, four daughters drowned in the Atlantic Ocean, and the death of his son soon after. In 1881 Spafford and his wife pursued their interest in the Holy Land by moving to Jerusalem where they established the American colony. *Our Jerusalem*, written by his daughter, Bertha Spafford Vester, vividly describes their experiences. Author: "When peace, like a river," **377**.

Spohr, Louis (baptized **Ludwig**), born Brunswick, 5 April 1784; died Cassel, 22 October 1859. Spohr, who was born into a musical family, showed early musical talent and was one of the most popular composers and violin virtuosos of his day. He was highly critical of the music of Beethoven and Weber, but championed the music of Wagner and produced two of his operas in Cassel over opposition from the court. Although he was a prolific composer of oratorios, operas, violin concerti, and chamber music, his works are largely forgotten, except for some of the chamber music for unusual combinations of instruments. Composer: GERALD, **410**.

Stanford, Charles Villiers, born Dublin, Ireland, 30 September 1852; died Marylebone, London, England, 29 March 1924. Showing early musical talent, he was a choral scholar at Queen's College, Cambridge (1870), and he was appointed organist of Trinity College, Cambridge, in 1873, where he graduated (B.A. 1874, M.A. 1877). After studies in Leipzig and Berlin (1874-76), Stanford became professor of composition and orchestra at the Royal College of Music and professor of music at Cambridge. His students included Ralph Vaughan Williams and Gustav Holst. He conducted the Cambridge Musical Society, the London Bach Choir, and the Leeds Festival, and was the recipient of several honorary doctorates. He was knighted in 1902. Stanford, with C. H. H. Parry and W. Walford Davies, introduced the unison hymn tune as an alternative to Victorian four-part tunes, and he was active in the revival of English folk songs. Composer: ENGELBERG, **68, 610**.

Stead, Louisa M. R., born Dover, England, ca. 1850; died Penkridge, near Umtali, Southern Rhodesia, 18 January 1917. Converted at age nine, Louisa came to the United States in 1871. At a camp meeting in Urbana, Ohio, she offered her life as a missionary but could not serve because of ill health. After the death of her husband by drowning while trying to rescue a child, she and her daughter went to South Africa where she worked in the Cape Colony for fifteen years and married Robert Wodehouse. In 1895 they returned to America, and Robert became a Methodist minister. After her health improved, they returned to Africa in Southern Rhodesia where she retired in 1911. Author: "'Tis so sweet to trust in Jesus," **462**.

Stebbins, George Coles, born East Carlton, NY, 26 February 1846; died Catskill, NY, 6 October 1945. After early musical experience in a singing school, Stebbins studied music in Buffalo, Rochester, and New York. He moved to Chicago in 1869 where he worked for Lyon & Healy Music Company and was music director of the First Baptist Church. In 1874 he went to Boston and was music director of the Clarendon Baptist Church and later Tremont Temple. Stebbins joined the Moody-Sankey revival team in 1876 as a song leader, and with Sankey and James McGranahan, he compiled three editions of *Gospel Hymns*, 1878-91. He composed hundreds of songs, his last tune at the age of 98, and edited and compiled many other gospel song collections. The music and musicians of the urban revival are recalled in his *Reminiscences and Gospel Hymn Stories*, 1924. Composer: ADELAIDE, **382**; HOLINESS, **395**.

Stennett, Samuel, born Exeter, Devonshire, England, 1727; died Muswell Hill, Middlesex, England, 25 August 1795. The son of a Seventh-Day Baptist pastor, Stennett was not able to attend any university because his family was nonconformist. Instead, he studied with distinction under John Hubbard of Stepney and John Walker of the academy at Mile End. He became assistant to his father at Little Wild Street, Lincoln's Inn Fields, in 1747, becoming pastor in 1758 at his father's death. In 1767 he was called to the Sabbatarian Baptist church where his grandfather had served as pastor. Although he declined the call, he preached there every Saturday for twenty years while continuing his other position. Stennett was awarded the D.D. degree from King's College, Aberdeen. He was a friend of King George III and John Howard and contributed thirty-eight hymns to Rippon's *Selection of Hymns*, 1787. Author: "On Jordan's stormy banks I stand," **724**.

Stimpson, O. James, born 1820; died 1886. Arranger: GERALD, **410**.

Stockton, John Hart, born New Hope, PA, 19 April 1813; died Philadelphia, PA, 25 March 1877. Although born into a Presbyterian family, Stockton converted to Methodism at a camp meeting when he was twenty-one. He became licensed as an exhorter and preacher, 1844-46, and was made a full member of the New Jersey Conference of the Methodist Episcopal Church in 1857. He left the active ministry in 1874 because of ill health but was active in evangelical work. Stockton provided assistance to the Moody-Sankey meetings in Philadelphia, writing several songs that were published in *Salvation Melodies No. 1*, 1874, and *Precious Songs*, 1875. Author and composer: "Come, every soul by sin oppressed" (STOCKTON), **337**.

Stone, Lloyd, born Coalinga, CA, 29 June 1912. Educated at the University of Southern California, Stone moved to Hawaii in 1936 and taught in public schools and at the University of Hawaii. He is the author of ten books of poetry, two children's books, and has served as chapter president of the National Society of Arts and Letters. Composite author: "This is my song," **437**.

Stone, Samuel John, born Whitmore, Staffordshire, England, 25 April 1839; died Charterhouse, England, 19 November 1900. Stone earned both his B.A. and M.A. from Pembroke College, Oxford (1862, 1872), and was ordained into the Church of England in 1862. He was curate at Windsor, succeeded his father at St. Paul's Church, Haggerston, London, and was rector of All Hallows on the Wall, London, from 1890 until his death. He is the author of several books and served on the committee that prepared *Hymns Ancient and Modern*, 1904. Stone's *Collected Poems and Hymns* were published posthumously by F. G. Ellerton. Author: "The church's one foundation," **545, 546**.

Stookey, Laurence Hull, born Belleville, IL, 4 August 1937. Educated at Swarthmore College (B.A. 1959), Wesley Theological Seminary (M.Div. 1962), and Princeton Theological Seminary (Ph.D. 1971), he served as a United Methodist pastor in Maryland and Delaware from 1957 to 1973, and has been professor of preaching and worship at Wesley Theological Seminary since 1973. He has been a consultant in worship to the Board of Global Ministries and the Board of Discipleship of The United Methodist Church and served as chair of the worship resources subcommittee of the Hymnal Revision Committee. Stookey has guest lectured at numerous universities and written many articles and books, including *Living in a New Age: Sermons for the Season of Easter*, 1978, *Baptism: Christ's Act in the Church*, 1982, *Handbook of the Christian Year* (joint-author), 1992, and *Eucharist: Christ's Feast with the Church*, 1993. Adapter: "The church's one foundation," **546**; alterer: "Advent," **201**; "Christmas," **231**; "For help for the forthcoming day," **681**; "For the sick," **457**; "For true singing," **69**; "Passion/Palm Sunday," **281**; author: "Ash Wednesday," **353**; "Day of Pentecost," **542**; "Epiphany," **255**; "For those who mourn," **461**; "In Christ there is no east or west," **548**; "O come, O come, Emmanuel," **211**; "The Ascension," **323**; "Transfiguration," **259**.

Stowe, Everett McKinley, born Clinton County, OH, 18 November, 1897; died Wilmington, OH, 1 July, 1979, was educated at Boston Univ. and Columbia Univ. (Ed.D.), taught in China and served on the World Council of Christian Education. Translator: "Here, O Lord, your servants gather," **552**.

Su Yin-lan. Born Tientsin, China, 1915; died Tientsin, 1937. Su Yin-lan was a student of Bliss Wiant and graduated in music from Yenching University in 1935 with honors. She was married soon after and returned to Tientsin to live. When the Japanese army of occupation bombed the city in the summer of 1937, she had just given birth to a son. Being of an exceedingly timid and sensitive nature, she was literally frightened to death by the terrible noise of the bombs. She contributed two tunes to *Hymns of Universal Praise*, 1936. Composer: SHENG EN, **633**.

Sugano, Doug. No information has been received about this person. Versed: "Lonely the boat," **476**.

Sugano, Linda. No information has been received about this person. Versed: "Lonely the boat," **476**.

Suitor, M. Lee, born San Francisco, CA, 1942. Educated at the University of Redlands, California, and the School of Sacred Music, Union Theological Seminary, New York, Suitor began piano lessons at the age of three and was a chorister at Grace Cathedral, San Francisco, California. While at Union Seminary he studied composition and organ with Alec Wyton and conducting with Abraham Kaplan. He taught at the University of Utah and served as director of music for All Saints Episcopal Church and Congregation Kol Ami, Salt Lake City, Utah. He was also active in concert management, broadcasting, and music criticism. In 1987 Union Theological Seminary commissioned him to compose *God's Promises,* an extended work for chorus, soloists, organ, and other instruments. Composer: CORNISH, **647**.

Sullivan, Arthur Seymour, born Bolwell Terrace, Lambeth, England, 13 May 1842; died Westminster, England, 22 November 1900. Best known for his operettas, Sullivan maintained an intense interest in church music, even though he wrote little. His musical training began as a chorister in the Chapel Royal and continued with Sterndale Bennett, Goss, Moritz Hauptmann, David, and Moscheles. He was the musical editor of *The Hymnary,* 1872, *Church Hymns with Tunes,* 1874, and he composed several large choral works. His international fame stems from his collaboration with W. S. Gilbert in their operettas, masterpieces of satire of Victorian English court, church, and common life. Queen Victoria knighted him in 1883, and both Cambridge and Oxford gave him honorary doctorates in music. Composer: ST. GERTRUDE, **555**, **575**; ST. KEVIN, **315**.

Suppe, Gertrude C., born Los Angeles, CA, 6 November 1911. Educated at Pomona College, Claremont, California (B.A. 1933), and Claremont Graduate School (M.A. 1934), she taught public school briefly before her marriage. In 1976 she took a class in worship for Spanish churches, and her interest in the field blossomed into the only computer database of all Hispanic church music in current use. Her translations were first included in *Celebremos II.* Translator: "¡Canta, Débora, canta!" **81**; "Mantos y palmas," **279**; "Toda la tierra," **210**; "Tú has venido a la orilla," **344**.

Swain, Joseph, born Birmingham, England, 1761; died Walworth, London, England, 14 April 1796. Swain was an orphan apprenticed to an engraver. After purchasing a Bible, he began serious study and was converted under the preaching of John Rippon. In 1791 he was given charge of a Baptist mission in Walworth, England, and in 1792 published his *Walworth Hymns.* Author: "O Thou, in whose presence," **518**.

Tallis, Thomas (also **Tallys** and **Talys**), born probably Kent, England, ca. 1505; died Greenwich, Kent, 23 November 1585. Thomas Tallis is one of the towering figures of sixteenth-century English music. He successfully survived the changes in the political-religious climate of the reigns of Henry VIII, Edward VI, Mary, and Elizabeth I, writing music for both the Catholic mass and settings of the second Prayer Book of Edward VI. Known as the father of English cathedral music, Tallis along with William Byrd was granted exclusive rights to print music and music paper for twenty-one years by Elizabeth. Together they published *Cantiones quae ab argumento sacrae vocantur*, 1575. His tunes, in four-part harmony, were included in Parker's *Whole Psalter Translated into English Metre*, 1561-67. In 1577 he and Byrd were named joint organists of the Chapel Royal. The music of Tallis includes anthems, masses, motets, magnificats, and other service music ranging from simple settings to the massive *Spem in alium non habui* for eight five-part choirs. Composer: TALLIS' CANON, **682**.

Tate, Nahum, born Dublin, Ireland, 1652; died Southwark, London, England, 12 August 1715. Educated at Trinity College, Dublin, Tate moved to London in 1688 to write for the stage, chiefly adapting the work of others, notably Shakespear's *King Lear* to give it a happy ending. He was made poet laureate in 1692 and royal historiographer in 1702. His chief contribution to hymnody is in *The New Version of the Psalms of David*, 1696, produced with Nicolaus Brady as an alternative to the "Old Version" of Sternhold and Hopkins, along with supplements in 1698 and 1700. The 1698 supplement includes the Apostles' Creed, the Lord's Prayer, *Veni Creator*, and six additional hymns; the 1700 supplement includes the Christmas hymn in our hymnal. The work, bound with the *Book of Common Prayer*, was influential well into Victorian times. Author: "While shepherds watched their flocks," **236**.

Taulé, Alberto Viñas, born Sabadell, Spain, 2 December 1932. Educated at the Pontificio Istituto di Musica Sacra S. Pio X. Roma (B.S.M.), he is a priest of a small parish and director of music publications in Centre de Pastoral Liturgica, Barcelona, Spain. He has written several books, including *El Señor es mi luz* and *Cantoral de Missa Dominical*, produced records and tapes of church music, and has had more than thirty-five of his hymns published in *Cantoral Litúrgico Nacional*, the official hymnal of the Roman Catholic Church in Spain. Author and composer: "Toda la tierra" (TAULÉ), **210**.

Taylor, Cyril Vincent, born Wigan, Lancashire, England, 11 December 1907; died Petersfield, England, 20 June 1992. Educated at Magdalen College School, Oxford, where he was a chorister at Magdalen College Chapel (1918-23), Christ Church, Oxford (B.A. 1929), with graduate studies at Westcott House in Cambridge, Taylor became a priest in 1932, serving at St. Mary's, Hinckley (1931-33), and St. Andrew's, Kingswood (1933-36). From 1936 to 1939 he was precentor at Bristol Cathedral and beginning with World War II he was employed as assistant to the head of religious broadcasting for fourteen years. Appointed warden and chaplain of the Royal School of Church Music in 1953, and in 1958 perpetual curate of Cerne Abbas, he served as precentor and residentiary canon at Salisbury Cathedral from

1969 to 1975. After retirement he continued his activities as a writer, hymnal editor, and member of the board of *Hymns Ancient and Modern*. He was an editor of the *BBC Hymnbook*, 1951, *100 Hymns for Today*, 1969, and *More Hymns For Today*, 1980. Author of *Hymns for Today Discussed*, 1984, he was chair of the Hymn Society of Great Britain and Ireland (1975-80). Composer: ABBOT'S LEIGH, **584, 660**; SHELDO-NIAN, **537**.

Taylor, Walter Reginald Oxenham, born Portsmouth, Hampshire, England, 1 August 1889; died Sevenoaks, Kent, England, 14 November 1973. Educated at the school of the China Inland Mission, Chefoo, North China, and at the University of Durham in England, Taylor was ordained into the Church of England and served with the Church Missionary Society of China, 1924-49, remaining in occupied China during World War II. He served on the committee that prepared the Chinese Union hymnal *Hymns of Universal Praise*, 1936, and had an interest in introducing translated Chinese hymns into the English hymnal repertoire. Upon his retirement, he moved to Sevenoaks, Kent, England. Translator: "The bread of life for all is broken," **633**.

Teresa of Avila, born Avila, Spain, 28 March 1515; died Alba de Tormes, Spain, 4 October 1582. A Spanish nun, religious reformer of the Roman Catholic Church, and author of spiritual classics, Teresa is considered one of history's great authorities on mysticism. She originated the Carmelite reform, which reemphasized fasting, silence, and austere living. In 1970 Pope Paul VI declared her a doctor of the church, calling her the "light of the universal church." Author: "For true life," **403**.

Teresa of Calcutta (Mother Teresa), born Skopje, Macedonia, 27 August 1910. Founder of the Order of the Missionaries of Charity, a Roman Catholic congregation of women who minister to the destitute outcasts of India, she was the recipient of the 1979 Nobel Peace Prize. Author: "Serving the poor," **446**.

Tersteegen, Gerhardt, born Mörs, Netherlands, 25 November 1697; died Mühlheim, Rhenish Prussia, 3 April 1769. His parents intended him to be a Reformed minister, but the death of his father when Tersteegen was six left his mother unable to support a university education. Instead, he attended the Latin school at Mörs and apprenticed as a silk weaver. He entered a five-year spiritual depression from 1719 to 1724, ending on Maundy Thursday with his signing a covenant with God in his own blood. In 1719 he quit attending the Reformed services and absented himself from Holy Communion because he did not want to commune with open sinners, choosing instead to establish a retreat center for prayer meetings, an illegal action that brought increased pressure from civil authorities. Attracted to mysticism, Tersteegen translated the works of medieval mystics and wrote 111 hymns, the most important collection being *Geistliches Blumen-Gärtlein*, 1729. Author: "Thou hidden love of God," **414**.

Teschner, Melchior, born Fraustadt, Silesia, 29 April 1584; died Oberpritschen, Posen, 1 December 1635. Teschner was appointed cantor and schoolmaster at

Zum Kripplein Christi, Fraustadt, in 1609. In 1614 he became the pastor at Ober-pritschen and was succeeded in this position by his son and grandson. Composer: ST. THEODULPH, **280**.

Theodulph of Orleans, born probably Spain, ca. 750; died Angers, 18 September 821. Theodulph became abbot of a monastery in Florence and in 781 was taken to France by Charlemagne where he served as abbot of Fleury, bishop of Orleans, and the king's chief theologian. At the death of Charlemagne in 818 he was accused of conspiring against Louis I, imprisoned, and after three years died from probable poisoning. It is likely that his hymns were written while he was in prison and unlikely that he was ever canonized, even though the tune ST. THEODULPH was named for him. Author: "All glory, laud, and honor," **280**.

Thomas, Edith Lovell, born Eastford, CT, 11 September 1878; died Claremont, CA, 17 March 1970. A pioneer in the field of music education for churches and church schools, Edith Thomas studied at Boston University (B.R.E., S.R.E., M.Ed.), the School of Sacred Music at Union Theological Seminary, New York, and Wellesley College. She held positions as professor of music and worship at Boston University, minister of music in New York, New Jersey, and Connecticut, including director of church school music at Christ Church Methodist in New York City. Her publications include *Singing Worship*, 1935, *Sing, Children, Sing*, 1939, *The Whole World Singing*, 1950, and *Music in Christian Education*, 1953. Through her books and extensive lecturing on music education, she introduced many musicians and teachers in the church to the vast potential of the arts in education and worship. Thomas provided her philosophy of church music education in "Music Remembered," *The Hymn*, April and July, 1969. Arranger: ST. ANTHONY'S CHORALE, **67**.

Thomas, Eugene, born 1941. This is a pen name for a composer who wishes to remain anonymous. Arranger: MAJESTY, **176**.

Thomerson, Kathleen Armstrong, born Jackson, TN, 18 February 1934. Educated at the University of Texas (B.M., M.M.) and Syracuse University, and the Flemish Royal Conservatory, Antwerp, she studied with E. W. Doty, John Boe, Jean Langlais, Flor Peeters, Arthur Poister, and Everett Jay Hilty. She is currently the director of music at University United Methodist Church, St. Louis, Missouri, and a member of the organ faculty of the St. Louis Conservatory and Southern Illinois University at Edwardsville. Active in the American Guild of Organists and a recitalist, Thomerson is the author of *Jean Langlais/A Biography*, 1988. She has served on the music committee of the Episcopal diocese of Springfield. Author and composer: "I want to walk as a child of the light" (HOUSTON), **206**.

Thompson, Colin Peter, born Exeter, England, 1945. Graduated from Oxford and ordained as a Congregational minister in 1971, he is a minister in the United Reformed Church in England and a linguist of considerable accomplishment. In

1978 he was appointed university chaplain at the University of Sussex, Falmer, Brighton, where he also taught European studies. Author: "Christian people, raise your song," **636**.

Thompson, John. The copyright owner has not provided information about this person. Co-author and co-composer: "El Shaddai" (EL SHADDAI), 123.

Thompson, Will Lamartine, born Smith's Ferry, PA, 7 November 1847; died New York, NY, 20 September 1909. A composer and publisher much admired by Dwight L. Moody, Thompson studied at Mount Union College (Ohio), New England Conservatory of Music, Boston, and Leipzig, Germany. Besides founding Will L. Thompson & Company, East Liverpool and Chicago, he also wrote numerous secular, patriotic, and gospel songs. Author and composer: "Jesus is all the world to me" (ELIZABETH), **469**; "Softly and tenderly Jesus is calling" (THOMPSON), **348**.

Thomson (also **Thompson**), **Mary Ann**, born London, England, 5 December 1834; died Philadelphia, PA, 11 March 1923. The author of over forty hymns, Mary Ann Thomson described herself as follows: "I am an English woman and was born, baptized, and confirmed in London, and I am, and for many years have been, a member of the Church of the Annunciation, Philadelphia. I am the wife of John Thompson, the librarian of the Free Library of Philadelphia, and he is the Accounting Warden of the Church of the Annunciation." (Haeussler 1954, 942) Author: "O Zion, haste, thy mission high fulfilling," **573**.

Threlfall, Jeanette, born Blackburn, Lancashire, England, 24 March 1821; died Westminster, Middlesex, England, 30 November 1880. Born into a prominent family, but orphaned at an early age, Threlfall lived with an aunt and uncle. An accident left her an invalid for life. Her verses were collected in *Woodsorrel, or Leaves from a Retired Home*, 1856, and *Sunshine and Shadow*, 1873. Author: "Hosanna, loud hosanna," **278**.

Thring, Godfrey, born Alford, Somersetshire, England, 25 March 1823; died Shamley Green, Guilford, Surrey, England, 13 September 1903. Educated at Shrewsbury School and Balliol College, Oxford, Thring was ordained deacon in 1846, priest in 1847, and after serving several curacies, succeeded his father as rector of Alford in 1858. In 1876 he was named prebendary of Wells. His publications include several collections, the most important being *Hymns and Sacred Lyrics*, 1874, *Daily Services of the Church Throughout the Year*, 1880, revised in 1882 as *The Church of England Hymn Book*. Author: "Crown him with many crowns," **327**.

Thrupp, Dorothy Ann, born London, England, 20 June 1799; died London, 14 December 1847. She was the author of many hymns, most written under pseudonyms. Her work appeared in *The Friendly Visitor, Children's Friend*, and *Selection of Hymns and Poetry for Use of Infants and Juvenile Schools and Families*. She was the editor of *Hymns for the Young*, ca. 1830, in which all the hymns were unsigned. Attributed author: "Savior, like a shepherd lead us," **381**.

Thurman, Howard, born Daytona Beach, FL, 18 November 1900; died San Francisco, CA, 10 April 1981. Author and Baptist clergyman, Thurman was educated at Morehouse College (A.B. 1923), Rochester Theological Seminary (B.D. 1926), and Wesleyan College (D.D. 1946). The recipient of numerous honorary doctorates, he was a professor of theology at Morehouse College (1928-31), Howard University (1932-44), and Boston University (1953-67). Thurman was a prolific author, and his commentaries on spirituals included *Deep River*, 1945, and *The Negro Spiritual Speaks of Life and Death*, 1947. Author: "For God's gifts," **489**; "For holiness of heart," **401**.

Tindley, Charles Albert, born Berlin, MD, 7 July 1851; died Philadelphia, PA, 26 July 1933. This famous African American Methodist preacher and hymn writer was the son of slave parents. His mother died when he was four, and he was separated from his father at age five. By the age of seventeen he had taught himself to read and write and moved to Philadelphia where he worked as a hod carrier and janitor for Calvary Methodist Episcopal Church. During this time he attended night school and took correspondence courses from Boston University School of Theology. He was ordained into the Methodist ministry and served congregations in South Wilmington, Odessa, Ezion, and Wilmington, Delaware, and May, New Jersey. From 1899 to 1902 he was presiding elder of the Wilmington district. In 1902 he returned to Calvary Methodist, this time as its pastor. His highly successful ministry saw the building of a new church, the name changed over his protest to Tindley Temple Methodist Church, and the development of a worshipping community that grew to more than 7,000 members and included African Americans, Europeans, Jews, and Hispanics. For additional commentary see William B. McClain, *Come Sunday*, 1990, and the biography by Ralph H. Jones, *Charles Albert Tindley*. A portion of one of Tindley's many gospel songs, "I'll overcome some day," was used in forming the civil rights anthem "We shall overcome." Author and composer: "Beams of heaven as I go" (SOMEDAY), **524**; "If the world from you withhold" (LEAVE IT THERE), **522**; "Nothing between my soul and my Savior" (NOTHING BETWEEN), **373**; Response, **846**; "We are tossed and driven" (BY AND BY), **525**; "When the storms of life are raging" (STAND BY ME), **512**.

Tisserand, Jean, died Paris, France, 1494. Little is known of this writer except that he was a preaching friar in the Franciscan Order in Paris, the founder of an order for penitent women, and the author of some hymns and liturgical texts. Author: "O sons and daughters, let us sing," **317**.

Tomer, William Gould, born 5 October 1833; died NJ, 26 December 1896. Tomer, a Civil War veteran who served under General Oliver O. Howard, received his musical training in singing schools and through singing in a choir at Finesville, New Jersey. He worked in Washington, DC, as a federal employee where he also served as music director for Grace Methodist Episcopal Church. His last years were spent in New Jersey as a schoolteacher. Composer: GOD BE WITH YOU, **672**.

Toplady, Augustus Montague, born Farnham, Surrey, England, 4 November 1740; died London, England, 11 August 1778. Educated at Trinity College, Dublin (1760), Toplady was converted by lay Methodist minister James Morris. Although he was ordained into the Church of England in 1762, he was strongly Calvinistic and engaged in a long public feud with John Wesley, both from the pulpit and in print. He attacked Wesley in *The Gospel Magazine* in three articles: *A Caveat against Unsound Doctrines*, 1770; *A Letter to the Rev. Mr. John Wesley relative to his pretended Abridgment of Zanchius on Predestination*, 1770; and *More Work for Mr. John Wesley*, 1772. In 1775 he moved to London where he preached in the French Calvinist church in Leicester Fields. His *Psalms and Hymns for Public and Private Worship*, 1776, was published while he served as curate in Blagdon and Farleigh. He died from tuberculosis. Author: "Rock of Ages, cleft for me," **361**.

Torrey, Bradford, born Weymouth, MA, 9 October 1843; died Santa Barbara, CA, 7 October 1912. Torrey was an ornithologist and naturalist, and his publications include *Birds in the Bush, Nature's Invitation*, and *Thoreau's Journal*, for which he served as editor. Author: "Not so in haste, my heart," **455**.

Tourjée, Lizzie Shove, born Newport, RI, 9 September 1858; died Auburndale, MA, 28 December 1913. A student at the New England Conservatory of Music, which her father founded, and Wellesley College for one year, she became a music teacher and organist for Centenary Methodist Church, Auburndale, Massachusetts. Composer: WELLESLEY, **121**.

Towner, Daniel Brink, born Rome, PA, 5 March 1850; died Longwood, MO, 3 October 1919. Towner's first teacher was his musician-father J. G. Towner. He later studied with John Howard, George F. Root, and George J. Webb. After serving Methodist Episcopal congregations in New York, Cincinnati, and Kentucky, he joined with Dwight L. Moody, becoming head of the music department of Moody Bible Institute in 1893. He composed over two thousand songs and was associated with the publication of fourteen collections. The University of Tennessee awarded him the Mus.D. degree in 1900 for his contributions to evangelistic music. He died while leading a revival in Longwood, Missouri. Composer: MOODY, **365**; TRUST AND OBEY, **467**.

Troeger, Thomas H., born Suffern, NY, 30 January 1945. A Presbyterian minister, teacher, and writer, he graduated from Yale University (B.A. 1967) and Colgate-Rochester Divinity School (B.D. 1970). He served as associate pastor of New Hartford Presbyterian Church, New York, for seven years, before joining the faculty of Colgate Rochester Divinity/Bexley Hall/Crozer Theological Seminary, Rochester, New York. Since 1991 he has been Peck Professor of Preaching and Communication at Iliff School of Theology, Denver, Colorado. A prolific author and highly regarded preacher and lecturer, he has written more than eighty hymns, many in collaboration with Carol Doran. His hymns are collected in *New Hymns for the Lectionary: To Glorify the Maker's Name*, 1986, and *New Hymns for the Life of the Church: To Make Our Prayer and Music One*, 1992. Author: "Silence, frenzied, unclean spirit!" **264**; "Source and Sovereign, Rock and Cloud," **113**; "Wind who makes all winds that blow," **538**.

Troutbeck, John, born Blencowe, Cumberland, England, 12 November 1833; died London, England, 11 October 1889. Troutbeck was a graduate of Oxford, precentor of Manchester Cathedral, and a chaplain and priest in ordinary to the queen. His translations for Novello music editions of German, French, and Italian oratorio and opera set the standard for nineteenth-century English texts, particularly those that he translated from the works of J. S. Bach. Translator: stanza 1, "Break forth, O beauteous heavenly light," **223**.

Tsosi, Albert, born Tolikai, NM, 1903; died Ft. Defiance, AZ, 1968. His parents were sheepherders. Fred Vazzi has supplied this information. Transcriber: "Amazing grace," **378**.

Tucker, Francis Bland, born Norfolk, VA, 6 January 1895; died Savannah, GA, 1 January 1984. Educated at the University of Virginia (B.A. 1914) and Virginia Theological Seminary (B.D. 1920, D.D. 1942), Tucker was ordained a deacon in 1918 and priest in 1920, serving parishes in Virginia, Washington, DC, and Christ Church, Savannah, Georgia, where John Wesley served as missionary priest. He was a member of the joint commission that produced the Protestant Episcopal *Hymnal 1940* and a consultant in language for *The Hymnal 1982*. Erik Routley has written in *A Panorama of Christian Hymnody*, "There is no better twentieth-century writing in either of our countries than is to be found in Tucker." (Routley 1979, 205) Author: "All praise to thee, for thou, O King divine," **166**; "Awake, O sleeper," **551**; "Our Parent, by whose name," **447**; composite author: "Ye who claim the faith of Jesus," **197**; translator: "Father, we thank you," **563**, **565**; "Holy God, we praise thy name," **79**.

Turner, Herbert Barclay, born Brooklyn, NY, 17 July 1852; died Washington, CT, 1 May 1927. Following his education at Amherst College and Union Theological Seminary in New York, Turner entered the Congregational ministry, serving congregations in Massachusetts and Connecticut. From 1892 to 1925 he was chaplain of Hampton Normal and Agricultural Institute. He is the editor of *Hymns and Tunes for Schools*, 1907, with William Bindle, and two other collections for use in Sunday schools. Amherst College honored him with the D.D. degree in 1905. Composer: CUSHMAN, **256**.

Turner, Jet E., born Monrovia, CA, 3 March 1928. Educated at Pomona College (B.A. 1949), Andover Newton Theological School (B.D.), and Union Theological Seminary (M.S.M.), he has pastored Baptist churches in New Jersey and New Hampshire. He has served as minister of education and music at First Baptist Church, Peoria, Illinois, and on the faculty of Bradley University. Turner is founder and chair of the Fellowship of American Baptist Musicians, editor of its newsletter, and dean of the conference for church musicians, American Baptist Assembly, Green Lake, Wisconsin. An author, organ recitalist, and workshop leader, he served on the Baptist-Disciples hymnbook committee as chair of the tunes and service music subcommittee. Adapter: UNION SEMINARY, **632**.

Tweedy, Henry Hallam, born Binghamton, NY, 5 August 1868; died Brattlebury, VT, 11 April 1953. A descendant of William Bradford and William Pratt on his mother's side, Tweedy was educated at Phillips Andover Academy, Yale University (B.A., M.A.), Union Theological Seminary, and the University of

Berlin. He was ordained into the Congregational ministry in 1898, serving congregations in Utica, New York, and Bridgeport, Connecticut. From 1909 to 1937 he was professor of practical theology at Yale Divinity School. Besides authoring many books, he compiled *Christian Worship and Praise*, 1939, and won several hymn contests sponsored by the *Homiletic Review* and the Hymn Society of America. Author: "O Spirit of the living God," **539**.

Vail, Silas Jones, born Brooklyn, NY, 6 October 1818; died Brooklyn, 20 May 1884. A hatter and clerk and later a successful businessman, Vail was also an amateur composer. He compiled *The Athenaeum Collection*, 1863, containing unpublished songs by Stephen Foster, and was engaged by Horace Walters and W. F. Sherwin to compile *Songs of Grace and Glory*, 1874, for the prohibitionist movement. Composer: CLOSE TO THEE, **407**.

Vajda, Jaroslav John, born Lorain, OH, 28 April 1919. Educated at Concordia Junior College (1938) and Concordia Theological Seminary, St. Louis, Missouri (B.A., B.D. 1944), he served as vicar of several bilingual churches in Pennsylvania and Indiana. He was editor of the *Lutheran Beacon* of the Synod of Evangelical Lutheran Churches (1959-63), and in 1963 he became editor of *This Day*, a monthly family religious/cultural magazine. From 1971 until his retirement he was book editor and developer for Concordia Publishing House, St. Louis. A poet from the age of eighteen, he found his interest in poetry and music led to his work on the Commission on Worship of the Lutheran Church (1960-78) and on the Inter-Lutheran Commission on Worship (1967-78). The recipient of an honorary L.L.D. from Concordia College (1987), he became a fellow of the Hymn Society of the United States and Canada in 1988. Vajda led workshops in hymn writing and recorded his reflections on the subject in *Now the Joyful Celebration*, 1987. With his texts published in twenty-five hymnals, he is also the author of *They Followed the King*, 1965, *Follow the King*, 1977, and numerous translations. Author: "God of the sparrow," **122**; "Now the silence," **619**; translator: "Rock-a-bye, my dear little boy," **235**.

Van Deventer, Judson W., born near Dundee, MI, 5 December 1855; died Tampa, FL, 17 July 1939. He received his musical training in singing schools and studied art by touring Europe in 1885. Van Deventer taught art and penmanship for ten years before entering the ministry as a local preacher of the Methodist Episcopal Church. An evangelistic preacher in the USA, England, and Scotland, he was assisted by evangelistic singer W. S. Weeden. He was influential in Billy Graham's development as an evangelist. Author: "All to Jesus I surrender," **354**.

Van Dyke, Henry, born Germantown, PA, 10 November 1852; died Princeton, NJ, 10 April 1933. Educated at Brooklyn Polytechnic Institute, Princeton University, and Princeton Theological Seminary, Van Dyke was ordained into the Presbyterian ministry and served the United Congregational Church, Newport, Rhode Island, and Brick Presbyterian Church in New York City. From 1899 to 1922 he was Murray Professor of English Literature at Princeton. He was appointed United States minister to the Netherlands and Luxemburg by his friend President Woodrow Wilson, and was a lieutenant-commander in the United States Navy Chaplain Corps during World War I. Besides writing some twenty-five books, he was chairman of the committee that prepared the Presbyterian *Book of Common Worship*, 1905, and a member of the committee that prepared the 1932 revision. Author: "Joyful, joyful, we adore thee," **89**.

Vang, Cher Lue. No information is available on Vang. Translator: "Come, all of you," **350**.

Vanstone, William Hubert, born Mossley, Manchester, England, 9 May 1923. Educated at Balliol College, Oxford (B.A.), St. John's College, Cambridge (B.A.), Union Theological Seminary, New York City (S.T.M.), and Westcott House, Cambridge, he was ordained priest in 1951 and served as curate at Kirkholt (1955-64), incumbent at Kirkholt (1964-76), and honorary canon at Manchester Cathedral from 1968 to 1976. He then became incumbent at Hattersley, diocese of Chester (1977-78). Author: "Morning glory, starlit sky," **194**.

Vaughan Williams, Ralph, born Down Ampney, Gloucestershire, England, 12 October 1872; died St. Marylebone, England, 26 August 1958. The greatest English composer since Purcell, Vaughan Williams was the son of the vicar of Christ Church, Down Ampney, and his mother, a descendant of Josiah Wedgewood, was a cousin of Charles Darwin. His early musical training was in piano, violin, and theory, with continued study at Charterhouse School, the Royal College of Music, 1890-92, and Trinity College, Cambridge (B.M. 1894, B.A. 1895, Mus.D. 1901). He also studied with Max Bruch in Berlin and Maurice Ravel in Paris. From 1895 to 1898 he was organist of St. Barnabas,' South Lambeth, where he directed the choir, gave recitals, and formed a choral and orchestral society. He served in the Royal Army Medical Corps in World War I. In his music and in his contributions to hymnody and church music, Vaughan Williams was deeply influenced by and involved in the study of folk music of the British Isles and established folk tunes as an integral part of congregational song. He joined the Folk-Song Society in 1904, collecting a vast body of indigenous folk music. Many of these tunes appeared in *The English Hymnal*, 1906, for which Vaughan Williams was the musical editor and author of its famous preface with the premise that the choice of tunes is a "moral rather than a musical issue." He was music editor of *The Oxford Book of Carols*, 1928, and with Martin Shaw and Percy Dearmer, he edited *Songs of Praise*, 1925 and 1931. He was inspired by the music of the Tudor composers, particularly Thomas Tallis, and the music of Henry Purcell. His harmonizations and original tunes show a strength and melodic integrity that have set a standard for twentieth-century hymnody. Vaughan Williams's prolific output includes six symphonies, fantasias for strings, operas, ballets, film music, chamber music, choral works, and organ music. For additional information, see *Baker's Biographical Dictionary of Music and Musicians*. Adapter: DEUS TUORUM MILITUM, **582, 587, 634**; arranger: FOREST GREEN, **152, 539, 709**; KINGSFOLD, **179, 285, 606**; SUSSEX CAROL, **642**; composer: DOWN AMPNEY, **475**; KING'S WESTON, **168, 592**; Response, **167**; RANDOLPH, **673**; THE CALL, **164**; SALVE FESTA DIES, **324**; SINE NOMINE, **166, 711**; harmonizer: LASST UNS ERFREUEN, **62, 90, 94**.

Vieira, Gilbert H., born Lawrence, MA, 27 May 1926. He graduated from the University of California, Berkeley (B.A.), Boston University (M.A.), and Pacific School of Religion (B.D.), then pastored Methodist churches in the San Francisco Bay area of California. Adapter: "Praise God, from whom all blessings flow," **94**.

Wade, John Francis, born ca. 1710; died Douay, France, 16 August 1786. Born in England, Wade went to Douay, France, a Roman Catholic center with an English college, to escape the Jacobean rebellion of 1745. He taught music and specialized in copying plainchant and hymn collections for use in the private chapels of English Roman Catholic families. Composer: ADESTE FIDELES, **234**, and Response, **205**.

Walch, James, born Edgerton, near Bolton, England, 21 June 1837; died Llandudno, Caernarvonshire, Wales, 30 August 1901. Walch received his musical training from his father and Henry Smart. He was organist for Duke's Alley Congregational Church, Bolton, Walmsley Church, Bridge Street Wesleyan Chapel, and St. George's Parish Church, Bolton. From 1870 until 1874 he was conductor of the Bolton Philharmonic Society, and from 1877 until his death he was a music dealer. Composer: TIDINGS, **573**.

Walford, William, born Bath, Somersetshire, England, 1772; died Uxbridge, England, 22 June 1850. Educated at Homerton Academy, Walford was ordained into the Congregational ministry, serving congregations in Suffolk, Norfolk, and Uxbridge. He also was a classical tutor at Homerton where he suffered from mental illness during the year 1831-33. Author: "Sweet hour of prayer," **496**.

Walker, William, born near Martin's Mills, near Cross Keys, SC, 6 May 1809; died Spartanburg, SC, 24 September 1875. He was of Welsh descent, showed early musical talent, and at the age of eighteen led congregational singing in the First Baptist Church of Spartanburg and began collecting and arranging folk tunes. He and his brother-in-law, Benjamin Franklin White, were active in singing schools and became partners in collecting traditional southern Appalachian tunes and camp-meeting melodies. Walker went to New Haven, Connecticut, with the manuscript of *Southern Harmony and Musical Companion* and published it in 1835 without any credit to White. In 1844 White published the equally significant collection *The Sacred Harp*, thus setting up a rivalry between the two books and those who sang from them. Both books used the four-shaped-note system of notation. Walker expanded the four shaped-note system to one of seven shaped notes in his *Christian Harmony*, 1867. For further commentary on Walker and his collections, and shaped-note notation, see Harry Eskew's 1990 article, "Southern Harmony and Its Era," *The Hymn*. Composer: COMPLAINER, **252**.

Walter, William Henry, born Newark, NJ, 1 July 1825; died New York, NY, 1893. He studied with Edward Hodges and became the organist of the Church of the Epiphany, St. John's Chapel, St. Paul's Chapel, and Trinity Chapel, New York City. In 1864 Columbia University conferred on Walter an honorary

Mus.D., and the following year he was appointed university organist. His publications include *Manual of Church Music*, 1860, *The Common Prayer, with Ritual Song*, 1868, and numerous anthems, masses, and services. Composer: FESTAL SONG, **129, 596**.

Walton, James George, born Clitheroe, Lancashire, England, 1821; died Bradford, York, 1905. Little is known about Walton except that he edited *Plain Song Music for the Holy Communion Office*, 1874. Adapter: ST. CATHERINE, **710**.

Walworth, Clarence Alphonsus (Augustus), born Plattsburg, NY, 30 May 1820; died Albany, NY, 19 September 1900. Admitted to the bar in 1841, Walworth studied for the Episcopal ministry at General Theological Seminary in New York in 1845 and was ordained a Roman Catholic priest. Besides serving as rector of St. Mary's in Albany, he helped found the Order of Paulists in the United States and took the name Alphonsus. He was blind the last ten years of his life. Translator: "Holy God, we praise thy name," **79**.

Ward, Samuel Augustus, born Newark, NJ, 28 December 1847; died Newark, 28 September 1903. After study in New York City, Ward operated a successful music store in Newark. In 1880 he followed Henry S. Cutler as organist at Grace Episcopal Church in Newark and founded the Orpheus Club of Newark in 1889, serving as its director until 1900. Composer: MATERNA, **696**.

Ware, Henry, Jr., born Hingham, MA, 21 April 1794; died Framingham, MA, 25 September 1843. Ware graduated from Harvard in 1812 and was appointed to the faculty of Exeter Academy in New Hampshire. He was ordained a Unitarian minister in 1817 at Second Unitarian Church, Boston, but because of ill health he was assigned Ralph Waldo Emerson as an assistant. From 1830 to 1842 he was a professor at Cambridge Theological School and served as editor of the *Christian Disciple*, later the *Christian Examiner*. His collected works comprise four volumes. Harvard University awarded him the D.D. degree in 1834. Author: "Happy the home when God is there," **445**.

Warner, Anna Bartlett, born Long Island, NY, 1820; died Constitution Island, near West Point, NY, 1915. Some time after 1837, she and her sister Susan moved to Constitution Island near the United States Military Academy at West Point with their father Henry W. Warner, a New York lawyer. The sisters collaborated on novels under the pen names of Amy Lothrop (Anna) and Elizabeth Wetherell (Susan). Having conducted Sunday school classes for the West Point cadets for years, the sisters willed their home, "Wood Crag," to the academy. It is now a national shrine. Anna Warner published two collections, *Hymns of the Church Militant*, 1858, and *Wayfaring Hymns, Original and Translated*, 1869. Co-author: "Jesus loves me! This I know," **191**.

Warren, George William, born Albany, NY, 17 August 1828; died New York, NY, 17 March 1902. Educated at Racine College, Wisconsin, and largely self-taught as an organist, Warren held positions in Albany, Brooklyn, and from 1870 to 1890 at St. Thomas' in New York City. He collected *Warren's Hymns and Tunes as Sung at St. Thomas' Church*, 1888, the source for his only surviving hymn tune. Composer: NATIONAL HYMN, **567, 698**.

Warren, Norman Leonard, born London, England, 19 July 1934. He was educated at Dulwich College and Corpus Christi College, Cambridge, was ordained, and became vicar of St. Paul's Church, Leamington Spa. Warren is the author of several books, including *Journey into Life*, and he was member of the committee that produced *Hymns for Today's Church*, 1982. Composer: SUTTON COMMON, **262**.

Watts, Isaac, born Southampton, England, 17 July 1674; died Stoke Newington, England, 25 November 1748. The first of nine children of dissenter parents, Watts received his early education in Greek, Latin, and Hebrew in grammar school at Southampton. He declined an opportunity to study for the Anglican priesthood, choosing instead to attend the nonconformist academy at Stoke Newington, 1690-94. For six years he was tutor to the family of Sir John Hartopp. During this time he devoted intense study to theology and philosophy, leading to his ordination and installation as pastor of Mark Lane Independent Chapel, London, in 1702. Because of failing health he entered semiretirement in the home of Sir Thomas Abney. While serving as chaplain to Abney's family, he wrote some sixty books and carried on an active correspondence with religious leaders. Besides writing many theological and philosophical books, among them *Logic*, used as a text at Oxford for many years. His 600 hymns are found in 7 collections including *Hymns and Spiritual Songs*, 1707, 1709; *Horae Lyricae*, 1706, 1709; *The Psalms of David, Imitated in the Language of the New Testament*, 1719; and *Sermons with Hymns*, 1721-27. As the "father of English hymnody," Watts, through his work, broke away from the strict settings of psalm and scripture texts and pointed to hymns with relationships to preaching, worship, and the education of children. Most of his texts use simple meters, have a single theme, and are relatively short. Watts was largely responsible for breaking the dull psalm-singing tradition and establishing the foundation of English hymnody, and his work marks the beginning of the golden era of English hymnody that includes Charles Wesley and continues through James Montgomery. He is to English hymnody what Ambrose was to the Latin office hymn, and Luther to the German chorale. Author: "Alas! and did my Savior bleed," **294, 359**; "Am I a soldier of the cross," **511**; "Come, we that love the Lord," **732, 733**; "From all that dwell below the skies," **101**; "I'll praise my Maker while I've breath," **60**; "I sing the almighty power of God," **152**; "Jesus shall reign where'er the sun," **157**; "Joy to the world," **246**, Response, **818**; "O God, our help in ages past," **117**; "This is the day the Lord hath made," **658**; "When I survey the wondrous cross," **298, 299**.

Webb, Benjamin, born London, England, 28 November 1819; died London, England, 27 November 1885. Educated at St. Paul's School, Trinity College, Cambridge (B.A. 1842, M.A. 1845), he was ordained by the Church of England in 1843 and became assistant curate of Kemeston, Gloucestershire (1843-44), Christ Church, St. Pancras (1847-49), and Brasted, Kent (1849-51). He became perpetual curate of Sheen, Staffordshire, in 1851 and vicar of St. Andrew's, Well's Street, London, in 1862. He edited *The Ecclesiologist* (1842-68) and *Church Quarterly Review* (1881-85), and he collaborated with his friend John Mason Neale on *An Essay on Symbolism* and *A Translation of Durandus*. He contributed to *The Hymnal Noted*, 1852, and *The Hymnary*, 1872, as an editor and translator. Translator: "O love, how deep," **267**.

Webb, Charles Haizlip, born Dallas, TX, 14 February 1933. Educated at Southern Methodist University, Dallas, Texas (A.B. and M.Mus. 1955), and Indiana University, Bloomington, Indiana (D.Mus. 1964), Webb joined the faculty of Indiana University School of Music in 1960, was appointed assistant dean in 1964, associate dean in 1969, and dean in 1973. In addition to his administrative duties, he is conductor of the Indianapolis Symphonic Choir as well as a guest conductor throughout the USA, concert pianist with the Dallas and Indianapolis Symphony Orchestras and at Carnegie Recital Hall, and currently he is organist of the First Methodist Church in Bloomington. He has made several recordings and written two collections of free harmonizations and descants. Named in 1983 to the prestigious Indiana Academy and the recipient of numerous awards, he has served as judge for many international music competitions. He has served on the boards of the International Festivals, Inc., Indiana Arts Commission, Busoni Foundation, and the Van Cliburn Piano Competition. Webb served on the Hymnal Revision Committee and was the chair of the service music subcommittee. Arranger: "Musical Setting C," **22**; composer: "Baptismal Covenant Musical Responses," **53**; transcriber: HELELUYAN, **78**; harmonizer: HALAD, **119**; WELLESLEY, **121**; MORNING SONG, **198, 226, 726**; EMMAUS, **309**; O FILII ET FILIAE, **317**; RESTORATION, **340**; WORLD PEACE, **431**; CHEREPONI, **432**; LAND OF REST, **613, 695**; DOVE OF PEACE, **617**; JERUSALEM, **729**; composer: HAIZ, **274**; adapter: GARDEN, **314**.

Webb, George James, born Wiltshire, England, 24 June 1803; died Orange, NJ, 7 October 1887. Although his father wanted him to enter the ministry, Webb chose the study of music under Alexander Lucas at Salisbury. After a short period as organist in Falmouth, he emigrated to Boston, where in 1830 he was named organist for the Old South Church, a position he held for forty years. He was appointed professor at the Boston Academy of Music, served as president of the Boston Handel and Haydn Society in 1840, and joined with Lowell Mason in musical ventures in New York and New Jersey. Webb was widely known and respected as a choral director and teacher of voice. Besides editing periodicals, he published *The Massachusetts Collection of Psalmody*, 1840, *The American Glee Book*, 1841, with Lowell Mason, *The Psaltery*, 1845, *The National Psalmist*, 1848, *Cantica Laudis*, 1850, and *Cantica Ecclesiastica*, 1859. Composer: WEBB, **514**.

Webbe, Samuel, Sr., born London, England, 1740; died London, 25 May 1816. Webbe began work as an apprentice to a cabinet maker, but around the age of twenty decided to study music. His job as a music copyist for the London publisher Welcker brought him to the attention of organist Carl Barbandt, who became his teacher. He was employed as the organist for the Roman Catholic chapels at the Sardinian and Portuguese embassies, and from 1784 to 1816, he was secretary of the Catch Club, winning twenty-seven prizes in the club's composition contests. His published works include *A Collection of Sacred Music as Used in the Chapel of the King of Sardinia in London*, ca. 1793, *A Collection of Masses for Small Choirs*, 1792, *Antiphons in Six Books of Anthems*, 1818, catches, glees, a harpsichord concerto, music for wind band, and hymn tunes and adaptations. Composer: CONSOLATOR, **510**.

Weeden, Winfield Scott, born Middleport, OH, 29 March 1847; died Bisby Lake, NY, 31 July 1908. Weeden taught singing schools before entering evangelistic work. A gifted song leader, he was associated with Judson W. Van Deventer for many years. He was the compiler of several collections, including *The Peacemaker*, 1894, *Songs of Sovereign Grace*, 1897, and *Songs of the Peacemaker*, 1895. He moved to New York City late in life and owned a small hotel. His tombstone in Woodlawn Cemetery is engraved with "I Surrender All." Composer: SURRENDER, **354**.

Weissel, Georg, born Domnau, Prussia, 1590; died Königsberg, Prussia, 1 August 1635. Educated at the University of Königsberg and at Wittenberg, Leipzig, Jena, Strassburg, Basel, and Marburg, Weissel became pastor of the newly erected Altrossgart Church in Königsberg in 1623, where he remained until his death. His hymns were written for the greater festivals of the liturgical year. Author: "Lift up your heads, ye mighty gates," **213**.

Wesley Family. Wesley originally was Welswe from the Somerset region in the the mid tenth century. It continued as Westley of Westleigh, Devonshire. The present spelling evolved through Wellesley. The following chart traces four generations of the better-known Wesleys:

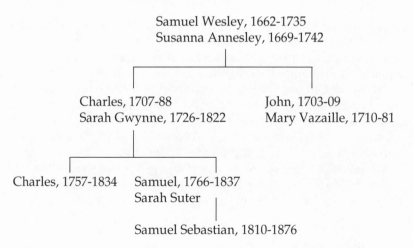

Samuel Wesley, 1662-1735
Susanna Annesley, 1669-1742

Charles, 1707-88
Sarah Gwynne, 1726-1822

John, 1703-09
Mary Vazaille, 1710-81

Charles, 1757-1834
Samuel, 1766-1837
Sarah Suter

Samuel Sebastian, 1810-1876

Wesley, Charles, born Epworth, Lincolnshire, England, 18 December 1707; died Marylebone, London, England, 29 March 1788. Charles was the eighteenth child and youngest son of Samuel and Susanna Wesley, and the brother of John. He received his earliest education from his parents and in 1716 enrolled in the Westminster School with his room and board paid by his brother Samuel. In 1721 he was elected a king's scholar and allowed free board and education. With the assistance of a Westminster studentship, he attended Christ College, Oxford (B.A. 1730, M.A. 1732), where he, John, and George Whitefield formed the Oxford Holy Club. The club's disciplined approach to Bible study, worship, and visitation to the sick and imprisoned, along with the frequent observance of Holy Communion, led to the members being known as the first "Methodists." Charles was ordained a deacon and an elder in the Church of England in 1735. Shortly after that time, his brother John influenced him to go to the Georgia colony as a missionary. He served as secretary to General James Edward Oglethorpe at St. Simon's Island, but he quickly became disillusioned and went back to England via Boston where he preached in several churches, including what is now Old South Church. Back in England, he became associated with William Law, Count Zinzendorf, and Peter Böhler, and was converted on May 21, 1738, Whitsunday, three days prior to his brother. He served, without license from the bishop, as curate of St. Mary's Islington, a center of early Methodist activity. In 1749 he moved to Bristol where he married Sarah Gwynne with whom he had eight children; three of whom survived, including Charles and Samuel, who were musicians. He moved back to London in 1771. It is incorrect to name Charles the poet of the Wesleyan revival and John the preacher and organizer, since it is clear that Charles no less than his brother began, spread, and sustained the revival in Great Britain. Throughout his life he remained faithful to the Church of England and on occasion took exception to John's increasing separation.

Charles Wesley's life is summarized in this memorial in John Wesley's City Road Chapel, London:

> "God buries his workmen, but carries on His work."
> Sacred to the Memory
> of THE REV. CHARLES WESLEY, M.A.
> Educated at Westminster School
> And sometime Student at Christ-Church, Oxford.
> As a preacher
> He was eminent for ability, zeal, and usefulness,
> Being learned without pride,
> And pious without ostentation;
> The sincere, diffident Christian,
> A son of Consolation
> But to the vain boaster, the hypocrite, and the profane,
> A Son of Thunder.
>
> He was the first who received the Name of Methodist;
> And, uniting with his Brother, the Rev. John Wesley,
> In the plan of Itinerant Preaching,
> Endured hardship, persecution, and disgrace
> As a good Soldier of Jesus Christ;

Contributing largely, by the usefulness of his labours,
To the first formation of the Methodist Societies,
In these Kingdoms.

As a Christian Poet he stood unrivalled;
And his hymns will convey instruction and consolation,
To the faithful in Christ Jesus,
As long as the English language shall be understood.
He was born the IVIII of December, MDCCVIII,
And died the XXIX of March, MDCCLXXXVIII,
A firm and pious believer in the doctrines of the Gospel,
And a sincere friend to the Church of England.

The hymns of Charles Wesley are notable for their use of over forty-five different meters, their subjective expression of the Christian experience, and their heavy reliance on scripture. All but four books of the Bible are cited in his hymns. The unusual meter of his poetry inspired the composition of new music. His hymns number over 6,500 and are contained in sixty-four collections published in his lifetime. The collected works of Charles and John, compiled by George Osborn, comprise thirteen volumes. See Frank Baker, *The Representative Verse of Charles Wesley*; and Frederick Gill, *Charles Wesley, The First Methodist*. Author: "A charge to keep I have," **413**; "All praise to our redeeming Lord," **554**; "And are we yet alive," **553**; "And can it be that I should gain," **363**; "Because thou hast said," **635**; "Blest be the dear uniting love," **566**; "Blow ye the trumpet, blow," **379**; "Christ, from whom all blessings flow," **550**; "Christ the Lord is risen today," **302**; "Christ, whose glory fills the skies," **173**; "Come, and let us sweetly join," **699**; "Come, Holy Ghost, our hearts inspire," **603**; "Come, let us join our friends above," **709**; "Come, let us use the grace divine," **606**; "Come, sinners, to the gospel feast," **339, 616**; "Come, O thou Traveler unknown," **386**; "Come, thou-long expected Jesus," **196**; "Depth of mercy," **355**; "Forth in thy name, O Lord, I go," **438**; "Give me the faith which can remove," **650**; "Glory to God, and praise and love," **58**; "Hail the day that sees him rise," **312**; "Hark! the herald angels sing," **240**; "How can we sinners know," **372**; "I want a principle within," **410**; "Jesus, Lord, we look to thee," **562**; "Jesus, lover of my soul," **479**; "Jesus! the name high over all," **193**; "Jesus, thine all-victorious love," **422**; "Jesus, united by thy grace," **561**; "Lo, he comes with clouds descending," **718**; "Love divine, all loves excelling," **384**; "Let us plead for faith alone," **385**; "Maker, in whom we live," **88**; "Mil voces para celebrar," **59**; "O come and dwell in me," **388**; "O for a heart to praise my God," **417**; "O for a thousand tongues to sing," **57**; "O Love divine, what hast thou done," **287**; "O the depth of love divine," **627**; "O thou who camest from above," **501**; "O thou who this mysterious bread," **613**; "Praise the Lord who reigns above," **96**; "Rejoice, the Lord is King," **715, 716**; "See how great a flame aspires," **541**; "Soldiers of Christ, arise," **513**; "Spirit of faith, come down," **332**; "Thou hidden source of calm repose," **153**; "'Tis finished! the Messiah dies," **282**; "Ye servants of God," **181**.

Wesley, John, born Epworth, Lincolnshire, England, 17 June 1703; died London, England, 2 March 1791. John was the son of Anglican priest Samuel and Susanna, and brother of Charles. When he was six, he was dramatically pulled from a rectory fire. His mother believed that John's life was saved for God's purposes. He attended Charterhouse School and Christ College, Oxford (B.A. 1724, M.A. 1726-27), and was a fellow of Lincoln in 1727. Ordained in 1728 he became a curate to his father and in 1729 returned to Oxford as a tutor. There he joined with Charles in the activities of the Holy Club. Through the Society for the Propagation of the Gospel, John went to Savannah, Georgia, as a priest. He came in contact with the Moravians, whose influence and hymnody were to have a strong impression on his life and work. Embroiled in controversy in Georgia, he returned to England in February 1738. On May 24, 1738, he attended a meeting of the Moravians on Aldersgate Street where he heard Peter Böhler reading Martin Luther's preface to the Epistle to the Romans, where he "felt his heart strangely warmed." From this point, he purchased an old foundery building in London, converted it to a chapel, and spent the rest of his life as an itinerant minister, traveling thousands of miles, preaching, and writing many books, hymns, and translations.

John Wesley can be credited with compiling the first English hymnbook meant to be used in worship, *A Collection of Psalms and Hymns*, 1737, published at Charleston. The book is an amazing collection of psalm paraphrases, English devotional poetry, English hymnody, and German hymns, the latter coming from his contact with the Moravians. His translations from the German are considered among the best of the eighteenth century and equal the standard of the great nineteenth-century translators. He was keenly interested in vital congregational singing, as exemplified in his "Directions for Singing," found on page vii of *The United Methodist Hymnal*, 1989. His influence and active role in hymnody belie the old notion that John did all the preaching and Charles wrote the hymns. The 1780 *Collection* is the supreme hymnbook of the eighteenth century, containing the best of earlier collections and his significant preface (see pages 12-14). Alterer: "I'll praise my Maker while I've breath," **60**; author: "I am no longer my own, but thine," **607**; translator: "Give to the winds thy fears," **129**; "Jesus, thy boundless love to me," **183**; "Thou hidden love of God," **414**.

Wesley, Samuel Sebastian, born London, England, 14 August 1810; died London, 19 April 1876. The son of Samuel, Charles's son, Samuel Sebastian was educated first by his musician-father and later as a chorister in the Chapel Royal. He served in several London churches as organist from 1826 to 1832, and at Hereford Cathedral, Exeter Cathedral, and Gloucester Cathedral until his death. He was excused from the Oxford bachelor's exam, and the university conferred upon him the Mus.D. degree in 1839. He held several organ positions, including professor of organ at the Royal Academy of Music. As a church musician, he was a leader in reforms in church music; he was one of the first cathedral organists to insist on a full pedal board. His views are contained in *A Few Words on Cathedral Music and the Musical System of the Church, with a Plan of Reform*, 1849. He was famous as a performer and composer and is credited with some 131 hymn tunes, notable for their innovation and unconventional writing, four church services, works for the organ, two psalm settings, anthems, glees, and *Ode to Labor*, 1864. Composer: AURELIA, **545**; HEREFORD, **501**; LEAD ME, LORD, **473**; Response, **756**.

Wesley, Samuel, born Winterborne, Whitchurch, Dorsetshire, England, 1662; died Epworth, Lincolnshire, England, 25 April 1735. Both Samuel and his wife, Susanna, were children of nonconformist parents. After study, he forsook the dissenting position and received his degrees from Exeter College, Oxford. He was ordained in 1869, and after a short time at South Ormsby, he became rector at Epworth where he remained until his death. His tenure at Epworth included two rectory fires and time spent in a Lincoln debtors' prison. Samuel's own works have been overshadowed by those of his sons John and Charles. His deep interest in congregational song, especially in moving away from the stilted "Old Version" of the psalter, was undoubtedly an inspiration to his children. His attacks on boring singing can be found in his *Athenian Oracle* and *Advice to a Young Clergyman*. Other works include *An Epistle to a Friend Concerning Poetry* (espousing the use of contemporary poetic works), *Heroic Poem on the Life of Our Blessed Lord and Saviour Jesus Christ*, 1693, and *History of the Old and New Testament*. Author: "Behold the Savior of Mankind," **293**.

Westerdorf, Omer, born Cincinnati, OH, 24 February 1916. Educated at the University of Cincinnati (M.M. 1950), he has been organist/choirmaster at St. Bonaventure Church, Cincinnati, since the age of twenty. His Bonaventure Choir, a free-lance chorale, concertizes and records sacred music. Founder of the World Library of Sacred Music, 1950, and World Library Publications, 1957, he also has established a consultation agency on liturgical music, lecturing and conducting seminars. He has written over thirty-five hymn texts, compiled four hymnals, and was a consultant on the *Armed Forces Hymnal*. His *People's Mass Book*, 1964, 1966, 1970, 1976, was the first vernacular hymn and service book to implement the Catholic liturgies decreed by Vatican Council II. He wrote *Music Lessons for the Man in the Pew* to teach the art of sight reading choral music. Translator: "Where charity and love prevail," **549**; "You satisfy the hungry heart," **629**; "Sent forth by God's blessing," **664**.

White, Benjamin Franklin, born near Spartanburg, SC, 20 September 1800; died Atlanta, GA, 5 December 1879. The youngest of fourteen children and later the father of fourteen, he was self-taught in music with almost no formal education. In 1844 he co-edited *The Sacred Harp* with E. J. King, and the book's popularity increased with his success as a singing school teacher. Editor of the Harris County, Georgia, weekly newspaper, he was elected mayor of his town in 1865. (For more information, see Cobb 1989.) Attributed composer: BEACH SPRING, **581, 605**.

White, David Ashley, born San Antonio, TX, 11 December 1944. Currently professor of theory and composition at the University of Houston's School of Music, he was educated at Del Mar College, Corpus Christi, the University of Houston, and the University of Texas at Austin. With graduate studies in composition under William Schroeder and Eugene Kurtz, among others, he is the recipient of various composition prizes and awards. White's activity in both secular and sacred music is reflected in his extensive catalog of chamber music and works for band, orchestra, choir, and solo voice. His *Evening Service* was premiered in Westminster Abbey in 1989. Composer: BISHOP POWELL, **543.**

Whitefield, George, born Gloucester, England, 16 December 1714; died Newburyport, MA, 30 September 1770. Educated at St. Mary le Crypt School and Pembroke College, Oxford, Whitefield, along with the Wesleys, joined the Oxford Holy Club in 1735. He was ordained into the Church of England in 1736. One year later, he began preaching for the Methodists, and in 1738 he made the first of seven trips to the colonies, where his powerful preaching initiated "The Great Awakening." Whitefield, like the Wesleys, made effective use of hymn singing, introducing the hymns of Isaac Watts to the colonies and publishing his *Collection of Hymns for Social Worship*, used in both England and the colonies. He is buried under the pulpit of Old South Presbyterian Church in Newburyport. Alterer: "Hark! the herald angels sing," **240.**

Whiteley, Frank J., born Sheffield, England, 22 December 1914. Whiteley's family immigrated to Dryden, Ontario, in 1919. Educated at Peterborough Normal School (1941), Queen's University (B.A. 1944), and Queen's Theological College (B.D. 1946), he was ordained a minister by the United Church of Canada, serving churches in Ontario, Oshawa, and Sarnia. Author: "Praise and thanksgiving be to God," **604.**

Whitfield, Frederick, born Threapwood, Shropshire, England, 7 January 1829; died Lower Norwood (S.E. London), England, 13 September 1904. Educated at Trinity College, Dublin, Ireland (B.A. 1859), he was ordained by the Church of England in 1859 and served appointments in Yorkshire, London, Kent, and Wimbledon. Whitfield served twenty-four years as vicar of St. Mary-in-the-Castle, Hastings. His poems and hymns were published in *Sacred Poems and Prose*, 1859, and *The Christian Casket; or Sacred Poems and Prose*, 1864. Author: "There is a name I love to hear," **170.**

Whittier, John Greenleaf, born Haverhill, MA, 17 December 1807; died Hampton Falls, NH, 7 September 1892. Largely self-educated, Whittier was of Quaker background and was an important USA poet and abolitionist. His earliest poems were published by William Lloyd Garrison. Besides editing publications including the *American Manufacturer*, the *New England Review*, and serving on the staff of the abolitionist *National Era*, he wrote many devotional poems from which some fifty hymns have been drawn. Author: "Dear Lord and Father of mankind," **358;** "O sabbath rest of Galilee," **499.**

Whittle, Daniel Webster, born Chicopee Falls, MA, 22 November 1840; died Northfield, MA, 4 March 1901. A cashier of the Wells Fargo Bank, in 1861 he joined the 72nd Illinois Infantry, Company B. He became provost marshal, participating in Sherman's march to the sea. He was wounded and imprisoned during the battle of Vicksburg and received a brevet promotion to major after the war. Whittle returned to Chicago to be treasurer of the Elgin Watch Company, but Dwight L. Moody's influence caused him to enter evangelistic work in 1873. Under the pseudonym "El Nathan," he wrote almost 200 hymn texts, with many set to music by his associates P. P. Bliss, James McGranahan, and George C. Stebbins. Author: "I know not why God's wondrous grace," **714.**

Wiant, Bliss, born Dalton, OH, 1 February 1895; died Delaware, OH, 1 October 1975. Educated at Wittenberg College, Ohio Wesleyan University (B.A. 1920), Boston University (M.A. 1936), Peabody College (Ph.D. 1946), Harvard, and Union Theological Seminary, Wiant was ordained an elder in the Methodist Episcopal Church in 1923. From 1923 to 1951 he was the head of the music department at Yenching University in Peking, China. One of Wiant's remembrances is having served as organist at the funeral of Sun Yat-sen in 1925. Upon his return to the USA, he was pastor of St. Paul's, Delaware, Ohio, minister of music at Mahoning Methodist Church, Youngstown, and executive director of the National Fellowship of Methodist Musicians from 1957 to 1961. He served as director of music at Scarritt College, director of music for the Ohio Council of Churches, professor at Chung Chi College, Chinese University of Hong Kong, director of music programming for the National Council of Churches of Christ in the USA in Hong Kong, and lectured at theological schools in Southeast Asia. Wiant was music editor of *Hymns of Universal Praise*, 1936, and with his wife Mildred, he provided many translations of Chinese hymns. His lectures on Chinese culture and music included performance on indigenous instruments. His doctoral thesis, *Character and Function of Music in Chinese Culture*, was privately published in 1966. Harmonizer: LE P'ING; adapter: Response, **792**; translator: "Rise to greet the sun," **678.**

Wiant, Mildred Kathryn Artz, born Lancaster, OH, 8 June 1898. A Phi Beta Kappa graduate of Ohio Wesleyan University, Wiant was a singer and educator who also studied in Boston and as a special student of Metropolitan Opera singer Marie Sundelius. In the fall of 1922 she married Bliss Wiant and went with him to Yenching University in Peking, China, where she served as associate professor of voice. She was on the faculty of Scarritt College, Chung Chi College, and the Chinese University of Hong Kong. Wiant was a teacher for the biennial convocations of the National Fellowship of Methodist Musicians and a translator of some fifty indigenous Chinese hymns contained in *Worship Materials from the Chinese*, 1969. She lives in retirement in Delaware, Ohio. Translator: "Rise to greet the sun," **678.**

Wilkes, John Bernard, born London, England, 1785; died London, England, 1869. Having studied at the Royal Academy of Music in London, he became organist at St. David's Church, Merthyr Tydfil, and later at Llandaff Cathedral. He became organist for the Monkland church near Leominster, 1860, where Henry W. Baker, the chairman of the compiling committee of *Hymns Ancient and Modern*, 1861, was vicar. Wilkes was a contributor to the original edition of this collection. Harmonizer: MONKLAND, **194.**

Williams, Aaron, born London[?], England, 1731; died London, 1776. Music teacher, publisher, and music engraver, Williams also served as clerk for Scots Church, London Wall. His publications include *The Universal Psalmodist*, 1763 (also published in the colonies in 1769 by Daniel Bailey as *The American Harmony or Universal Psalmodist*), *The Royal Harmony*, 1766, *The New Universal Psalmodist*, 1770, *Harmonia Coelestis*, 1175 6th ed., and *Psalmody in Miniature*, 1778. Source: ST. THOMAS, **540, 732**.

Williams, Peter, born Llansadurnin, Carmarthenshire, Wales, 7 January 1722; died Llandyfeilog, Wales, 8 August 1796. Converted under George Whitefield and ordained in 1744, Williams served the parish of Eglwys Cymmyn and began a school there. In 1746 he left the Church of England and joined the Calvinistic Methodists, becoming a leader in the Welsh Methodist revival. In 1791 he was expelled by the Methodists for heresy and started his own chapel on Water Street, Carmarthen. His publications include a Welsh hymnal, a Welsh Bible with concordance, 1773, and *Hymns on Various Subjects*, 1771. Composite translator: "Guide me, O thou great Jehovah," **127**.

Williams, Robert, born Mynydd Ithel, Anglesey County, North Wales, ca. 1781; died Mynydd Ithel, 1821. A blind basketmaker on the island of Anglesey, Williams was unusually gifted musically; he possessed a fine singing voice and the ability to write out a tune after one hearing. Composer: LLANFAIR, **312**; Responses, **767, 781, 859**.

Williams, Thomas John, born Ynysmeudwy, Swansea Valley, Glamorganshire, Wales, 1869; died near Llanelly, Wales, 1944. Williams was a pupil of David Evans and the organist-choirmaster of Zion Church, Llanelly, and Calfaria Church, Llanelly, from 1913 until his death. Composer: EBENEZER, **108, 586**; Response, **782**.

Williams, William, born Cefn-y-Coed, Llanfair-y-bryn, Carmarthenshire, Wales, 11 February 1717; died Pantycelyn, near Llandovery, Carmarthenshire, Wales, 11 January 1791. The most famous hymn writer of Welsh Methodism, he was known as the "sweet singer of Wales" and is equated with Paul Gerhardt in Germany and Isaac Watts in England. Converted by Howel Harris, one of George Whitfield's Methodist preachers, he deserted his background as an independent and his intention to become a doctor. Because of his Methodist views, he was refused ordination as a priest but became a deacon, serving Llanwrtyd and Llanddewi Abergwesyn. In 1744 he joined the Calvinistic Methodists and the evangelistic work of Howel Harris and Daniel Rowland. A noted preacher and leader of the "society" meetings, he is best known for his 800 Welsh hymns and 100 English hymns. Alan Luff calls him the "first Welsh romantic poet" and notes his well-developed theory of hymnody, which emphasized the need to be scriptural, to center on Christ, to remove the word "I," and to meet the conditions of the congregation. (Luff 1990, 93-103). Author: "Guide me, O thou great Jehovah," **127**.

Willis, Richard Storrs, born Boston, MA, 10 February 1819; died Detroit, MI, 7 May 1900. Composer, critic, and publisher educated at Chauncey Hall and Yale University, Willis also studied in Germany with Xavier Schnyder and Moritz Hauptmann and established a friendship with Felix Mendelssohn. In 1848 he was music critic for the New York *Tribune*, the *Albion*, and the *Musical Times*, and served as editor for several publications. Other published works include *Church Chorals and Choir Studies*, 1850, *Our Church Music*, 1856, *Waif of Song*, 1876, and *Pen and Lute*, 1833. Arranger: ST. ELIZABETH, **189**; composer: CAROL, **218**.

Wilson, Emily Divine, born Philadelphia, PA, 24 May 1865; died Philadelphia, 23 June 1942. She was the wife of a Methodist minister, and both she and her husband were well known at the Methodist camp meetings at Ocean Grove, New Jersey. Composer: HEAVEN, **701**.

Wilson, Hugh, born Fenwick, Ayrshire, Scotland, ca. 1764 or 1766; died Duntocher, 14 August 1824. The son of a shoemaker and apprenticed in the same trade, Wilson studied music and mathematics in his spare time and made sundials as an avocation. He was part-time precentor at the Secession Church in Fenwick where he also taught writing, mathematics, and music to the villagers. He moved to Pollokshaws to work as a draughtsman and calculator and was active in the church there. Through his and other laymen's efforts, the first Sunday school in Duntocher was established. He is the presumed composer of many hymn tunes, but the manuscripts are believed to have been destroyed. Only the present tune survives. Composer: MARTYRDOM, **294**.

Wilson, John Whitridge, born Bournville, suburb of Birmingham, Warwickshire, England, 21 January 1905; died Guildford, England, 16 July 1992. A noted hymnist and music historian, Wilson was educated at Cambridge University with honors in physics and mathematics, but he chose a profession in music, studying at the Royal College of Music and living with his noted uncle Sir Walford Davies. He taught at the Royal College of Music (1965-80) and was director of music at England's famous Charterhouse School from 1947 to 1965. He was organist of Guildford Methodist Church, Surrey, treasurer of the Hymn Society of Great Britain and Ireland (1965-90), and a highly regarded scholar/teacher of English hymnody. Best known as the organizer and director of Westminster Abbey's hymn singing event known as Come and Sing, he served on the editorial committees of *The Clarendon Hymn Book*, 1936, *Hymns for Church and School*, 1964, *Hymns and Songs*, 1969, *Broadcast Praise*, 1981, and *Hymns and Psalms, A Methodist and Ecumenical Hymn Book*, 1983. He was co-editor with Erik Routley of *Hymns for Celebration*, 1974, and compiler of *Sixteen Hymns of Today for Use as Simple Anthems*, 1978, and *Twenty-one Hymns Old and New for Use as Simple Anthems*, 1985. In 1985 at Bethlehem, Pennsylvania, Wilson was named a fellow of the Hymn Society of America. "Warm of spirit, self-effacing, possessed of a great sense of humor and dignity, he did not suffer fools lightly." (Unpublished tribute to John Whitridge Wilson by George H. Shorney, September 1992) Arranger: GOPSAL, **716**.

Wilste, Carl, born Grand Rapids, MI, 21 October 1944. Educated at Western Michigan University (B.M. 1967), he has been an elementary music specialist for Holland Public Schools since 1969. Prior to this position he was a vocal music teacher in Portage, Michigan (1967-69), and director of music for Holland First United Methodist Church (1967-92). He has received several awards in composition, including the Western Michigan University Sophomore Composition award in 1966, Advent Hymn Competition winner, San Diego, 1983, and the AGEHR handbell composition contest winner twice, 1981 and 1988. His articles have been featured in *The Church Musician* and *Handbells,* and his compositions are included in several catalogs. Composer: Amen, **901**.

Wimber, John, born February, 1934. Educated at Fuller Theological Seminary and Azusa Pacific University (B.A.), he became pastor to the Society of Friends, Yorba Linda, California, in 1970, moving to Calvary Chapel, Costa Mesa, California, in 1978. He has been senior pastor of Vineyard Christian Fellowship since 1983. His publications include *Power Evangelism, Power Healing,* and the *Kingdom of God* series. Author and composer: "O let the Son of God enfold you" (SPIRIT SONG), **347**.

Winkworth, Catherine, born London, England, 13 September 1827; died Monnetier, Savoy, 1 July 1878. Winkworth is the foremost translator of German hymns into English. Though her life was spent near Manchester, she moved to Clifton with her father in 1862. Her interest in education and social work is shown in the translations from German of biographies of two founders of sisterhoods for the poor and the sick: *Life of Pastor Fliedner,* 1861, and *Life of Ameilia Sieveking.* Publications of hymn translations include *Lyra Germanica,* 1855, 1858, and *The Chorale Book for England,* 1863. Her original book, *Christian Singers of Germany,* was published in 1869. Margaret T. Shaen edited a biography of Catherine and her sister Susannah entitled *Memorials of Two Sisters.* Translator: "Blessed Jesus, at thy word," **596**; "Deck, thyself, my soul, with gladness," **612**; "If thou but suffer God to guide thee," **142**; "In thee is gladness," **169**; "Jesus, priceless treasure," **532**; "Lift up your heads, ye mighty gates," **213**; "Now thank we all our God," **102**; Response, **789**; "O Morning Star, how fair and bright," **247**; "Out of the depths I cry to thee" (Response), **793**; "Praise to the Lord, the Almighty," **139**; Response, **826**; "Wake, awake, for night is flying," **720**; "We believe in one true God," **85**.

Winter, Miriam Therese (Gloria Frances), born 14 June 1938. A medical mission Sister who has been writing biblical songs since Vatican II, she is best known for *Joy Is Like the Rain,* the first of thirteen albums, and for "Mass of a Pilgrim People," which premiered at Carnegie Hall. Educated at Catholic University, Washington, DC (B.A. 1964), McMaster Divinity College, Hamilton, Ontario (M.R.E. 1976), and Princeton Theological Seminary, New Jersey (Ph.D. 1983), she is also the recipient of an honorary doctorate from Albertus Magnus College, New Haven, Connecticut. A member of the North American Academy of Liturgy, she is a professor at Hartford Seminary, Hartford, Connecticut. In addition to articles on liturgy and music, she has published *Preparing the Way of the Lord,* 1978,

God-With-Us, An Anthology of Scripture Songs, 1982, *Why Sing? Toward a Theology of Catholic Church Music*, 1984, *Woman Prayer, Woman Song*, 1987, resources for ritual from a feminist perspective, *Woman Word*, 1990, *Woman Wisdom*, 1991, and *Woman Witness*, 1992, works that feature women of the Bible. She has traveled internationally to share her ministry of liberation, justice, and peace. Author: "My soul gives glory to my God," **198**; Author and composer: "Wellspring of Wisdom" (WELLSPRING), **506**.

Wise, Joseph Edward, born Louisville, KY, 19 August 1939. Wise is a folk-pop style songwriter who in the 1960's and 1970's was in the forefront of the revitalization of Roman Catholic congregational song. His songs were included in most songbooks of that period, and he recorded them in nineteen albums. Wise did graduate theological study at the Catholic University of America, Washington, DC. Author and composer: "Take our bread" (TAKE OUR BREAD), **640**.

Witt, Christian Friedrich, born Altenburg, Germany, ca. 1660; died Altenburg or Gotha, Germany, 13 April 1716. Musically trained by his father, an Altenburg court organist, Witt later studied counterpoint and composition with Georg Kaspar Wecker in Nuremberg, becoming chamber organist at the Gotha court in 1686 and Kapellmeister in 1713. A composer of vocal and instrumental music, as well as sixty-five church cantatas, he is considered the compiler of one of the most important German hymnals of the early eighteenth century, *Psalmodia sacra*, 1716, which included 774 chorales, with 356 melodies using over 100 new tunes, most attributed to Witt himself. Attributed composer: STUTTGART, **611**.

Wojtyla, Karol. See **John Paul II.**

Wolcott, Samuel, born South Windsor, CT, 2 July 1813; died Longmeadow, MA, 24 February 1886. Educated at Yale and Andover Theological Seminary, Wolcott was a missionary to Syria but returned to the United States because of ill health. He also served Congregational churches in Rhode Island, Massachusetts, Chicago, Cleveland, and for several years was secretary of the Ohio Home Missionary Society. Of his two hundred hymns, all written after he was fifty-six, one remains in common use. Author: "Christ for the world we sing," **568**.

Wolfe, Lanny Lavon, born Columbus, OH, 2 February 1942. Educated at Ohio State University (B.A., M.A.), San Jose State University (B.S.), and Southern Illinois University, Edwardsville (M.A.), he served as dean of music for Christian Life College, Stockton, California (1965), and for Gateway College of Evangelism, St. Louis, Missouri (1968-74), before joining the Jackson College of Ministries, Jackson, Mississippi, as dean of music since 1974. He also is minister of music at First Pentecostal Church, Jackson, and director of the Lanny Wolfe Singers and Band. Composer of over 400 songs and 10 musicals, Wolfe has been nominated best gospel composer by the Gospel Music Association and has twice received SESAC's Gospel Composer of the Year award. In 1984 he received the Dove award for "More than Wonderful." Author and composer: "Surely the Presence" (WOLFE), **328**.

Wood, Dale, born Glendale, CA, 13 February 1934. With no formal music training, he won a national hymn-writing contest at the age of thirteen. In 1951 he
was organist/choirmaster at Hope Lutheran Church, Hollywood, California,
when his first anthem was published. He attended Los Angeles City College and
the Los Angeles Institute for the Arts. Wood was organist of Eden Lutheran
Church, Riverside, California, before becoming organist/choirmaster at the
Episcopal Church of St. Mary the Virgin in San Francisco in 1968 and also music
director for the San Francisco Cathedral School for Boys (1973-74). Author of
numerous articles and a frequent conductor for festival choirs, he has been a
consultant for the Inter-Lutheran Commission on Worship, the international
Choristers Guild, and several hymnals. He has composed over 300 published
works, including a major music drama scored for symphony orchestra. Composer: TUOLUMNE, **443;** WOJTKIEWIECZ, **187.**

Woodbury, Isaac Baker, born Beverly, MA, 23 October 1819; died Charleston,
SC, 26 October 1858. Woodbury studied in Boston, Paris, and London and
taught music in Boston. After moving to New York, he directed music at Rutgers
Street Church. He edited the *New York Musical Review, The Musical Pioneer*,
assisted in compiling the 1857 music edition of the 1845 *Methodist Hymn Book*,
and also edited many popular tune books. When his health broke in 1858, he
moved to Charleston and died there three days after his move. Composer:
SELENA, **287.**

Work, John Wesley, Jr., born Nashville, TN, 6 August 1872; died Nashville, TN,
7 September 1925. Educated at Fisk University, Nashville (A.B. 1895, M.A. 1898),
he eventually became chair of the history and Latin department there. He was a
leader in the preservation, study, and performance of African-American spirituals, and with his brother, Frederick Jerome Work (1879-1942), he published collections of slave songs and spirituals, including *New Jubilee Songs as Sung by the
Fisk Jubilee Singers*, 1901, and *Folk Songs of the American Negro*, 1907. For eighteen
years he trained the Jubilee Singers, performing as a tenor soloist with them, and
in 1909 he organized the Fisk Jubilee Quartet, which toured the country and
recorded commercially. In 1923 he resigned from Fisk to become president of
Roger Williams University, Nashville. Adapter: "Go, tell it on the mountain,"
251.

Wren, Brian Arthur, born Romford, Essex, England, 3 June 1936. Educated at New
College, Oxford (B.A. 1960), and Mansfield College, Oxford (B.A. 1962), he was
ordained as a Congregational minister in 1965, pastoring at Hockley and Hawk-
well, Essex, 1965-70. He then spent five years as secretary to Churches' Committee
for World Development of the British Council of Churches with the mission of
communicating the tragedy and causes of world poverty. He later worked for
Third World First and was chair of the Council of War on Want. Having begun
writing at Mansfield with the encouragement of Erik Routley, by 1983 Wren chose
to pursue hymn writing on a full-time basis, serving as a workshop leader and visiting professor for numerous colleges and universities in the USA, Canada, Australia, and New Zealand. His hymns are collected in *Faith Looking Forward*, 1983,

Praising a Mystery, 1986, *Bring Many Names,* 1989, *New Beginnings,* 1992, and *Faith Renewed,* 1992. Additional works such as *Contemporary Prayers for Public Worship,* 1967, *Education for Justice,* 1977, and *What Language Shall I Borrow?* 1989, reflect his work in education and in worship and social issues. Author: "Arise, shine out, your light has come," **725;** "As man and woman we were made," **642;** "Christ is alive," **318;** "Christ is risen," **307;** "Christ loves the church," **590;** "Christ, upon the mountain peak," **260;** "God of many names," **105;** "How can we name a Love," **111;** "I come with joy," **617;** "Lord God, your love has called us here," **579;** "There's a Spirit in the air," **192;** "This is a day of new beginnings," **383;** "When love is found," **643;** "Woman in the night," **274.**

Wyeth, John, born Cambridge, MA, 31 March 1770; died Philadelphia, PA, 23 January 1858. Though not a musician, Wyeth was an important printer and publisher who spent most of his life in Harrisburg, Pennsylvania, as editor of the federalist *Oracle of Dauphin.* His interest in folk and fuguing tunes led to his publishing two significant volumes in USA folk hymnology: *Repository of Sacred Music,* 1810, and *Repository of Sacred Music, Part Second,* 1813. Though a Unitarian, his interests were cross-denominational and included tunes from German-speaking sects active in Pennsylvania in the early nineteenth century. See also Irving Lowens, *Music and Musicians in Early America.* Source: DAVIS, **518;** MORNING SONG, **198, 226, 726;** NETTLETON, **400.**

Yamaguchi, Tokuo, born Tomie-cho, Nagasaki Prefecture, Japan, 13 July 1900. Educated at the Aoyama Gakuin Theological Seminary (1924), he became a minister of the Methodist church, serving in Sahara, Chiba Prefecture; Tanimura, Yamanashi Prefecture; Fujieda, Shizuoka Prefecture; and Asahikawa, Hokkaido. From 1937 to 1979 he was pastor of the Toyohashi Church, Aichi Prefecture, which in 1941 became the United Church of Christ in Toyohashi. Since 1979 he has been the pastor emeritus of the Toyohashi church. The translator of *The Journal of John Wesley,* 1961, he won official commendation from the Christian Literature Society of Japan in 1983. Author: "Here, O Lord, your servants gather," **552.**

Yardley, Harold Francis, born Salford, Lancashire, England, 11 March 1911. He immigrated to Canada in 1929 and graduated in arts and theology from Victoria University, becoming a lay supply minister and later ordained by the United Church of Canada, where he has served churches in Saskatchewan, Ontario, Sarnia, and Alberta. According to Stanley L. Osborne, "His writing of hymns began partly as a reaction against what he terms 'morbidity of the Moody and Sankey era.'" (Osborne 1976, commentary on hymn 318) Author: "Praise and thanksgiving be to God," **604.**

Yin-lan, Su. See **Su Yin-lan.**

Young, Carlton Raymond, born Hamilton, OH, 25 April 1926. Educated at the Cincinnati College-Conservatory of Music (B.M.E.) and Boston University School of Theology (S.T.B.), he did further study at Union Theological Seminary,

New York, Vienna, and Prague. In 1969 he received the D.Mus. degree (h.c.) from Ohio Northern University. Young has served on the faculties and directed graduate studies in church music at Perkins School of Theology, Southern Methodist University, and Scarritt College and is emeritus professor of church music at Candler School of Theology, Emory University. He has taught at other seminaries and schools of church music in the USA and England. From 1969 to 1972 he was choral director and lecturer in music for ACUIS, Graz University, Graz, Austria, and from 1980 to 1990 he directed the United Methodist Youth Chorale in concert tours of England, Wales, France, Switzerland, Austria, East and West Germany. He is presently the director of programs in music and other arts at the Scarritt-Bennett Center, Nashville. He is an ordained elder in The United Methodist Church, East Ohio Conference, and has served as director of music in churches in Massachusetts, Ohio, Texas, and Georgia. From 1966 to 1988 he was the director of music for nine General Conferences of the former Methodist Church and The United Methodist Church.

Young has the unique distinction of serving as editor of two revisions of hymnals for Methodists: *The Methodist Hymnal*, 1966, and *The United Methodist Hymnal*, 1989. He is co-author with Fred D. Gealy and Austin C. Lovelace of *Companion to the Hymnal*, 1970 (*The Methodist Hymnal*, 1966); executive editor of *Ecumenical Praise*, 1977; *Duty and Delight (Routley Remembered)*, 1985; *Our Lives Praise: The Hymn Tunes, Carols, and Texts of Eric Routley)*, 1990; *Supplement to the Book of Hymns*, 1982; *Hymnal Supplement I*, 1984; *Hymnal Supplement II*. He is co-author with John Holbert and S T Kimbrough, Jr., of *Psalms for Praise and Worship: A Complete Liturgical Psalter*, 1992, and author of *Companion to the United Methodist Hymnal* [1989], 1993. He has written many articles in the field of church music and hymnody, including "Hymn" for *Evangelischen Kirchenlexikon* (*EKL*), 1989, and 150 published compositions. The American Society of Composers and Publishers (ASCAP) has recognized Young's work with twenty-three awards presented by the standard awards panel. Since 1971 he has been a consultant and editor with Hope Publishing Co. Young is a past president and Fellow of the Hymn Society in the United States and Canada and the first American to be named an honorary member of the British Methodist Church Music Society. Composer: "Word and Table Musical Setting D," **23**; "Baptismal Covenant Musical Responses," **54**; BEGINNINGS, **383**; STOOKEY, **627**; Responses, **112**, **135**, **205**, **734**, **742**, **747**, **769**, **773**, **776**, **780**, **785**, **790**, **791**, **797**, **798**, **801**, **810**, **814**, **818**, **833**, **837**, **844**, **849**, **854**; adapter: HERE I AM, LORD, **593**; arranger: ON EAGLE'S WINGS, **143**; BUNESSAN, **145**; ORIENTIS PARTIBUS, **227**; IL EST NÉ, **228**; COMPLAINER, **252**; WEST INDIAN, **271**; AU CLAIR DE LA LUNE, **273**; CANDLER, **386**; CHARLESTOWN, **433**; SLANE, **451**; DESMOND, **494**; ARFON (MAJOR), **541**; SOMOS DEL SEÑOR, **666**.

Young, John Freeman, born Pittston, ME, 30 October 1820; died New York, NY, 15 November 1885. Educated at Wesleyan University and Virginia Theological Seminary, Young was ordained in 1845 and pastored churches in Florida, Texas, Mississippi, Louisiana, and New York, besides serving eighteen years as the second Protestant Episcopal bishop of Florida. He published *Hymns and Music for the Young*, 1860-61, and *Great Hymns of the Church*, published posthumously by

John Henry Hopkins in 1887. Young maintained active interests in education and architecture. Translator: "Silent night, holy night," **239**.

Zundel, John, born Hochdorf, Germany, 10 December 1815; died Cannstadt, Germany, July 1882. Educated in Germany, Zundel spent seven years in St. Petersburg as organist of St. Anne's Lutheran Church and as a bandmaster before coming to the USA in 1847. He was organist at First Unitarian, Brooklyn, St. George's, New York, and Plymouth Congregational Church, Brooklyn, where Henry Ward Beecher was pastor. After retiring for the third time, he still spent a few months as organist of Central Methodist Episcopal Church in Detroit. With Henry and Charles Beecher, he prepared the *Plymouth Collection of Hymns*, 1855, supplying twenty-eight tunes, and he also edited various collections and instructional books for organ playing and harmony. Composer: BEECHER, **384**.

REFERENCES

Works Cited

Adams, Jere V., ed. 1992. *Handbook to the Baptist Hymnal* [1991]. Nashville: Convention Press.

Adey, Lionel. 1988. *Class and Idol in the English Hymn.* Vancouver: Univ. of British Columbia Press.

Alexander, Ruth W. 1914. "Music and Religion." *Methodist Quarterly Review* 63: 60-63.

Andrews, Edward Deming. 1940. *The Gift to Be Simple: Dances and Rituals of the American Shakers.* New York: J. J. Augustine.

Arnold, Denis, ed. 1983. *The New Oxford Companion to Music.* 2 vols. Reprint. London and New York: Oxford Univ. Press.

Bailey, Albert E. 1950. *The Gospel in Hymns.* New York: Charles Scribner's Sons.

Baker, Frank. 1962. *Representative Verse of Charles Wesley.* New York and Nashville: Abingdon Press.

Baker, Theodore. 1984. *Baker's Biographical Dictionary of Music and Musicians.* 7th ed. Edited by Nicolas Slonimsky. New York: G. Schirmer.

Beckerlegge, Oliver A., and S T Kimbrough, Jr. 1990. 3 vols. *The Unpublished Poetry of Charles Wesley.* Nashville: Kingswood Books.

Behney, J. Bruce, and Paul H. Eller. 1979. *The History of the Evangelical United Brethren Church.* Nashville: Abingdon Press.

Benson, Louis Fitzgerald. 1915. *The English Hymn: Its Development and Use in Worship.* Reprint. Richmond: John Knox Press, 1962.

———. 1930. *The Hymnody of the Christian Church.* New York: George H. Doran.

Bett, Henry. 1945. *The Hymns of Methodism.* 3d ed. London: Epworth Press.

Bloesch, Donald G. 1985. "The Battle of the Trinity." *The Debate over Inclusive God Language.* Ann Arbor: Servant Books.

Boehm, R. T. 1981. "Spanish Chant: An Intruder's Adventures into Hymnology." *The Hymn* 32 (1): 17-24.

Braley, Bernard. 1991. *Hymn Writers 3.* Oxford: Alden Press.

Braun, H. Myron. 1982. *Companion to the Book of Hymns Supplement* [1982]. Nashville: Discipleship Resources.

Brueggemann, Walter. 1984. *The Message of the Psalms.* Minneapolis: Augsburg.

———. 1988. *Israel's Praise.* Minneapolis: Augsburg.

Buchanan, Annabel Morris. 1938. *Folk Hymns of America.* New York: J. Fischer and Bro.

Bucke, Emory S., ed. 1964. *The History of American Methodism.* 3 vols. Nashville: Abingdon Press.

Burkalow, Anastasia Van. 1987. "A Call for Battle Symbolism in Hymns." *The Hymn* 38 (2): 14-17.

Buttrick, George A., ed. 1962. *The Interpreter's Dictionary of the Bible.* 4 vols. New York and Nashville: Abingdon Press.

Christenson, Donald E. 1988. "A History of the Early Shakers and Their Music." *The Hymn* 39 (1): 17-22.

Claghorn, Charles Eugene. 1974. *Battle Hymn: The Story Behind the Battle Hymn of the Republic*. New York: Hymn Society of America.

Cobb, Buell E., Jr. 1978. *The Sacred Harp: A Tradition and Its Music*. Athens: Univ. of Georgia Press.

Collier, James Lincoln. 1987. *Duke Ellington*. New York: Oxford Univ. Press.

Cone, James H. 1972. *The Spirituals and the Blues: An Interpretation*. New York: Seabury Press.

Coverdale, Myles. 1846. *The Remains of Myles Coverdale*. Edited by George Pearson. London: Cambridge Univ. Press.

Covert, William C., and Calvin W. Laufer. 1935. *Handbook to the Hymnal* [1933]. Philadelphia: Presbyterian Board of Education.

Crafts, Wilbur Fisk. 1875. *Trophies of Song: Articles and Incidents on the Power of Sacred Music*. Boston: D. Lothrop.

Crosby, Fanny. 1903. *Fanny Crosby's Life-Story*. New York: Everywhere.

Curnock, Nehemiah. 1909. *The Journal of the Rev. John Wesley, A.M.* Vol. 1. Reprint. London: Epworth Press, 1938.

Daw, Carl R., Jr. 1990. *A Year of Grace: Hymns for the Church Year*. Carol Stream, IL: Hope Publishing.

Day, Thomas. 1990. *Why Catholics Can't Sing*. New York: Crossroad Publishing.

Dearmer, Percy, and Archibald Jacob. 1933. *Songs of Praise* [1931] *Discussed*. London: Oxford Univ. Press.

Dearnley, Christopher. 1970. *English Church Music, 1650-1750*. London: Oxford University Press.

Dett, R. Nathaniel, ed. 1927. *Religious Folk-Songs of the Negro*. Hampton, VA: Friends United.

Dickinson, Edward. 1908. *Music in the History of the Western Church*. New York: Charles Scribner's Sons.

Dictionary of American Hymnology Project. Coordinated by Mary Louise Van Dyke. Oberlin, OH: Oberlin College Library.

Doran, Carol, and Thomas H. Troeger. 1985. "Writing Hymns as a Theological Informed Artistic Discipline." *The Hymn* 36 (2): 7-11.

Douglas, Paul F. 1939. *The Story of German Methodism*. New York: Methodist Book Concern.

Dunkle, William F., and Joseph D. Quillian. 1970. *Companion to the Book of Worship*. Nashville: Abingdon Press.

Ellinwood, Leonard. 1953. *The History of American Church Music*. New York: Morehouse-Gorham.

_____. 1956. *The Hymnal 1940 Companion*. 3d ed. New York: Church Pension Fund.

Elliot, Elizabeth. 1983. *Bright Legacy: Portraits of Ten Outstanding Christian Women*. Grand Rapids: Servant Books.

Emurian, Ernest K. 1980. "Take Me Home at the Cross." *The Hymn* 31 (3): 195.

Epstein, Dena J. 1981. *Sinful Tunes and Spirituals: Black Folk Music to the Civil War.* Urbana and Chicago: Univ. of Illinois Press.

Eskew, Harry. 1990. "Southern Harmony and Its Era." *The Hymn* 41 (4): 28-34.

Ferguson. John. 1989. "Hymns in the Early Church." *Bulletin: Hymn Society of Great Britain and Ireland* 12 (7): 114-23.

Filbert, Alan Mark. 1989. "An Analysis of 'All Praise to Thee, For Thou, O King Divine' and 'At the Name of Jesus' in Relation to Philippians 2:6-11." *The Hymn* 40 (3): 12-15.

Fisher, Miles Clark. 1953. *Negro Slave Songs in the United States.* New York: Citadel Press.

Fouvy, C. Louis. 1988. "The Hymn Tune 'Arfon.'" *Bulletin: Hymn Society of Great Britain and Ireland* 12 (2): 22-24.

Frost, Maurice. 1953. *English and Scottish Psalm and Hymn Tunes, ca. 1543-1677.* London: Oxford University Press.

_____, ed. 1962. *Historical Companion to Hymns Ancient and Modern.* London: William Clowes and Sons.

Gaither, Gloria. 1984. *Fully Alive.* Alexandria, IN: Gaither Music.

Gealy, Fred. D. Research Files for the 1970 *Companion to the Hymnal* [1966]. Dallas: Bridwell Library, Special Collections, Southern Methodist Univ.

Gealy, Fred D., Austin C. Lovelace, and Carlton R. Young, 1970. *Companion to the Hymnal* [1966]. Nashville: Abingdon Press.

Gebauer, Victor E. 1990. "Problems in the History of American Church Music." *The Hymn* 41 (4): 45-48.

Geiringer, Karl. 1966. *J. S. Bach: The Culmination of an Era.* New York: Oxford Univ. Press.

Gill, Frederick C. 1965. *Charles Wesley: The First Methodist.* Nashville: Abingdon Press.

Glover, Ray. 1987. *A Commentary on New Hymns.* New York: Church Hymnal Corporation.

_____, ed. 1990. *The Hymnal 1982 Companion.* Vol. 1. New York: Church Hymnal Corporation.

_____, ed. 1993. *The Hymnal 1982 Companion.* Vol. 2. New York: Church Hymnal Corporation.

"Go Forth for God." 1987. *Bulletin: Hymn Society of Great Britain and Ireland* 11 (10): 223.

Gonzales, Justo L., ed. 1991. *Each in Our Own Tongue: A History of Hispanic Methodism.* Nashville: Abingdon Press.

Graham, Fred Kimball. 1988. "John Wesley's Choice of Hymn Tunes." *The Hymn* 39 (4): 29-37.

Green, Fred Pratt. 1982. *The Hymns and Ballads of Fred Pratt Green.* Edited by Bernard Braley. Carol Stream, IL: Hope Publishing.

_____. 1984. "Albert F. Bayly." *The Hymn* 35 (4): 246.

_____. 1989. *Later Hymns and Ballads, and 50 Poems.* Edited by Bernard Braley. Carol Stream, IL: Hope Publishing.

Grindal, Gracia. 1988. "An Interpretation: 'Come Down, O Love Divine.'" *The Hymn* 39 (2): 28.

_____. 1988. "An Interpretation: 'Children of the Heavenly Father.'" *The Hymn* 39 (4): 52-53.

_____. 1989. "An Interpretation: 'O Love, How Deep, How Broad, How High.'" *The Hymn* 40 (1): 33-34.

Guillermo, Artemio, ed. 1991. *Churches Aflame: Asian Americans and United Methodism.* Nashville: Abingdon Press.

Haeussler, Armin. 1952. *The Story of Our Hymns* [*The Hymnal* of the Evangelical and Reformed Church, 1941]. 3d ed. St. Louis: Eden Publishing House.

Harmon, Nolan B. 1926. *The Rites and Rituals of Episcopal Methodism.* Nashville: Publishing House of the Methodist Episcopal Church, South.

_____, ed. 1974. *The Encyclopedia of World Methodism.* 2 vols. Nashville: United Methodist Publishing House.

Harrington, Karl Pomeroy. 1931. *Education in Church Music.* New York: Century.

Hart, Elizabeth. 1988. "Whither the Wily Fiends?: A Case Study in Editing Charles Wesley's 'Soldiers of Christ.'" *The Hymn* 39 (4): 16-19.

Hatchett, Marion J. 1991. "Benjamin Shaw's and Charles H. Spilman's *Columbian Harmony or Pilgrim's Music Companion.*" *The Hymn* 42 (1): 20-23.

Heisey, Terry. 1990. "Singet Hallejah! Music in the Evangelical Association, 1800-1894." *Methodist History* 28 (4): 237-51. Madison, NJ: General Commission on Archives and History, The United Methodist Church.

Hewitt, Theodore Brown. 1976. *Paul Gerhardt as a Hymn Writer and His Influence on English Hymnody.* 2d ed. St. Louis: Concordia Publishing House.

Hickman, Hoyt L., ed. 1989. *Worship Resources of the United Methodist Hymnal* [1989]. Nashville: Abingdon Press.

Higginson, J. Vincent. 1954. *Hymnody in the American Indian Missions.* New York: Hymn Society of America.

_____. 1982. *History of American Catholic Hymnals: Survey and Background.* Springfield, OH: Hymn Society of America.

Hine, Stuart K. 1958. *The Story of How Great Thou Art.* London: Stuart K. Hine.

Hopkins, John H., Jr., 1863[?]. *Carols, Hymns, and Songs.* New York. Church Book Depository.

Hostetler, Lester. 1949. *Handbook to the Mennonite Hymnary* [1940]. Newton, KS: General Conference of the Mennonite Church of North America.

Hughes, Charles W. 1980. *American Hymns Old and New.* New York: Columbia Univ. Press.

Hustad, Don P. 1978. *Dictionary-Handbook to Hymns for the Living Church* [1974]. Carol Stream, IL: Hope Publishing.

_____. 1983. "In the Garden." *The Hymn* 34 (4): 244-45.

_____. 1986. "An Interpretation: 'Come, Holy Ghost, Our Souls Inspire.'" *The Hymn* 37 (2): 37.

_____. 1986. "An Interpretation: 'Now the Silence.'" *The Hymn* 37 (4): 27.

Hutchins, Charles L. 1916. *Carols Old and Carols New.* Boston: Parish Choir.

Ingram, Robert D. 1992 *Scriptural and Seasonal Indexes of The United Methodist Hymnal.* Nashville: Abingdon Press.

Irwin, M. Eleanor. 1989. "Phos Hilaron: The Metamorphosis of a Greek Christian Hymn." *The Hymn* 40 (2): 7-11.

Jackson, George Pullen. 1933. *White Spirituals of the Southern Uplands.* Chapel Hill: Univ. of North Carolina Press. Reprint. New York: Dover Publications, 1956.

_____. 1964. *Spiritual Folk-Songs of Early America.* New York: J. J. Augustine. Reprint. New York: Dover Publications.

_____. 1944. *The Story of the Sacred Harp, 1844-1944.* Nashville: Vanderbilt Univ. Press.

Johansen, J. H. 1956. "The Olney Hymns." Hymn Society Papers, 10. New York: Hymn Society of America.

_____. 1979. "Moravian Hymnody." Hymn Society Papers, 32. Fort Worth: Hymn Society of America.

Jones, Ralph H. 1982. *Charles Albert Tindley.* Nashville: Abingdon Press.

Julian, John, ed. 1907. *A Dictionary of Hymnody.* 2 vols. Reprint. New York: Dover Publications, 1957.

Kaan, Fred. 1985. *The Hymn Texts of Fred Kaan.* Carol Stream, IL: Hope Publishing.

Kelynack, William S. 1950. *Companion to the School Hymn-Book of the Methodist Church.* London: Epworth Press.

Lawrence, T. E. 1935, 1937. *Seven Pillars of Wisdom: A Triumph.* Garden City: Doubleday, Doran.

le Huray, Peter. 1967. *Music and the Reformation in England, 1549-1660.* London: Oxford Univ. Press.

Leaver, Robin A. 1987. "Dykes' 'Nicea': An Original Hymn Tune or the Reworking of Another?" *The Hymn* 38 (2): 21-24.

_____. 1988. "English and German Hymnody: Imports and Exports." *Bulletin: Hymn Society of Great Britain and Ireland* 12 (4): 62-69.

_____. 1991. *'Goostly Psalmes and Spirituall Songes': English and Dutch Metrical Psalms from Coverdale to Utenhove, 1535-1566.* London: Oxford Univ. Press.

Leaver, Robin A., and James A. Litton, eds. 1985. *Duty and Delight, Routley Remembered.* Carol Stream, IL: Hope Publishing.

Levy, Eugene. 1973. *James Weldon Johnson: Black Leader, Black Voice.* Chicago: Univ. of Chicago Press.

Lightwood, James T. 1905. *Hymn-Tunes and Their Story.* London: Charles H. Kelly.

_____. 1927. *Methodist Music in the Eighteenth Century.* London: Epworth Press.

_____. 1935. *The Music of the Methodist Hymn-Book* [1933]. London: Epworth Press.

Lincoln, C. Eric, ed. 1970. *Martin Luther King, Jr.: A Profile.* New York: Hill and Wang.

Lincoln, C. Eric, and Lawrence H. Mamiya. 1990. *The Black Church in the African American Experience.* Durham: Duke Univ. Press.

Lorenz, Edmund S. 1909. *Practical Church Music.* New York: Fleming H. Revell.

Lorenz, Ellen Jane. 1980. *Glory Hallelujah! The Story of the Campmeeting Spiritual.* Nashville: Abingdon Press.

Lovelace, Austin C. 1965. *The Anatomy of Hymnody.* Nashville: Abingdon Press. Reprint. Chicago: GIA Publications, 1982.

Lovell, John B., Jr. 1972. *Black Song: The Forge and the Flame.* New York: Macmillan.

Lowens, Irving. 1964. *Music and Musicians in Early America.* New York: W. W. Norton.

Luff, Alan. 1978. "More on Two Early American Tunes." *The Hymn* 29 (4): 222-23.

_____. 1990. *Welsh Hymns and Their Tunes.* Carol Stream, IL: Hope Publishing.

Luther, Martin. *Luther's Works.* 1965. General editor Helmut T. Lehmann. vol. 53. *Liturgy and Hymns.* Edited by Ulrich S. Leupold. Philadelphia: Fortress Press.

Lutkin, Peter Christian. 1910. *Music in the Church.* Milwaukee: Young Churchman.

_____. 1930. *Hymn-Singing and Hymn-Playing.* Chicago: Univ. of Chicago Press.

McClain, William B. 1984. *Black People in the Methodist Church. Whither Thou Goest?* Nashville: Abingdon Press.

_____. 1990. *Come Sunday: The Liturgy of Zion.* Nashville: Abingdon Press.

McConnell, Cecilio. 1985. *Comentario Sobre Los Himnos Que Cantamos.* El Paso: Casa Bautista de Publicaciones.

_____. 1987. *La Historia del Himno en Castellano.* 3d ed. El Paso: Casa Bautista de Publicaciones.

McCutchan, Helen Cowles. 1972. *Born to Music: The Ministry of Robert Guy McCutchan.* New York: Hymn Society of America.

McCutchan, Robert Guy. 1942. *Our Hymnody: A Manual of the Methodist Hymnal* [1935]. 2d ed. Nashville: Abingdon-Cokesbury Press.

_____. 1957. *Hymn Tune Names: Their Sources and Significance.* New York and Nashville: Abingdon Press.

McDonald, J., ed. 1967. *New Catholic Encyclopedia.* New York: McGraw Hill.

McKellar, Hugh D. 1992. "The Huron Carol - 'JESOUS AHATONHIA.'" Part 3 of *Hymn Texts in the Aboriginal Language of Canada: Three Historical Bibliographic Studies. The Hymnology Annual.* vol. 2. 1992. Berrien Springs, MI: Vande Vere Publishing.

Manning, Bernard Lord. 1942. *The Hymns of Wesley and Watts.* London: Epworth Press.

Marbeck, John. 1982. *Marbeck's "Booke of Common Praier Noted [1550]."* Edited by Robin A. Leaver. Appleford: Courtenay Facsimiles.

Marsh, J. B. T. 1897. *The Story of the Jubilee Singers.* With Supplement and Songs by F. J. Loudin. London: Hodder and Stoughton.

Massey, Bernard S. 1987. "John Wilkes and Monkland." *Bulletin: Hymn Society of Great Britain and Ireland* 11 (10): 210-13.

Mason, Henry L., comp. 1944. *Hymn-Tunes of Lowell Mason.* Cambridge, MA: Univ. Press.

Meredith, William Henry. 1909. *Jesse Lee: a Methodist Apostle.* New York: Eaton and Mains. Cincinnati: Jennings and Graham.

Metcalf, Frank J. 1925. *American Writers and Compilers of Sacred Music.* New York and Cincinnati: Abingdon Press.

———. 1928. *Stories of Hymn Tunes.* New York, Chicago, and Nashville: Abingdon Press.

Metzger, Bruce M., and Roland E. Murphy, eds. 1991. *The New Oxford Annotated Bible* [New Revised Standard Version]. New York: Oxford Univ. Press.

Milgate, Wesley. 1985. *Songs of the People of God: A Companion to the Australian Hymn Book/With One Voice* [1979]. Rev. ed. Sydney: Collins Liturgical Publications.

———. 1988. *A Companion to Sing Alleluia.* New improved ed. Sydney: Australian Hymn Book Pty.

Minutes of the Methodist Conference [1744-1824]. 1862-64. London: John Mason. 5 vols. The "Large" Minutes are in 1: 443-675.

Moffatt, James, and Millar Patrick. 1951. *Handbook to the Church Hymnary* [1927 Supplement]. London: Oxford Univ. Press.

Mountain, Charles M. 1993. "The New Testament Christ Hymn." *The Hymn* 44 (1): 20-28.

Murray, Charlotte W. 1966. "The Story of Harry T. Burleigh." *The Hymn* 17 (4): 101-11.

Music, David W. 1988. "Wesley Hymns in Early American Hymnals and Tunebooks." *The Hymn* 39 (4): 37-42.

Myers, Kenneth. 1989. *All God's Children and Blue Suede Shoes: Christians and Popular Culture.* Westchester, IL: Crossway Books.

Náñez, Alfredo. 1981. *Historia de la Conferencia de Río Grande de la Iglesia Metodista Unida* (Eng. ed. *The History of the Rio Grande Conference of the United Methodist Church*). Dallas: Bridwell Library, Southern Methodist Univ.

Njieden, Hans-Jörg. 1989. "Zur Beurteilung neuer Kirchenliedmelodian." *Music und Kirche* 6: 292-99.

Nichols, Kathryn. 1988. "Charles Wesley's Eucharistic Hymns: Their Relationship to the *Book of Common Prayer.*" *The Hymn* 39 (2): 13-21.

———. 1988. "The Theology of Christ's Sacrifice and Presence in Charles Wesley's Hymns on the Lord's Supper." *The Hymn* 39 (3): 19-29.

Noley, Homer, 1991. *First White Frost: Native Americans and United Methodism.* Nashville: Abingdon Press.

Noyes, Morgan Phelps. 1955. *Louis F. Benson, Hymnologist.* New York: Hymn Society of America.

Nutter, Charles S. 1897. *Hymn Studies.* 3d ed. New York: Eaton and Main.

Osborne, Stanley. 1976. *If Such Holy Song: The Story of the Hymns in the Hymn Book* [1971]. Whitby, Ont.: Institute of Church Music.

Oswalt, Lewis E. 1991. "Rigdon McCoy McIntosh: Teacher, Composer, Editor, and Publisher." Unpublished DMA diss., New Orleans Baptist Theological Seminary.

Outler, Albert C. 1984. *John's Wesley's Sermons. An Introduction.* Foreword by Richard P. Heitzenrater. Nashville: Abingdon Press.

Parker, Alice. 1976. *Creative Hymn Singing.* Chapel Hill, NC: Hinshaw Music.

Parry, K. L., ed. 1953. *Companion to Congregational Praise* [1951]. London: Independent Press.

Paterson, Daniel. 1979. *The Shaker Spiritual.* Princeton: Princeton Univ. Press.

Patrick, Millar. 1927. *The Story of the Church's Song.* Edinburgh: Scottish Churches Joint Committee on Youth. Reprint. Richmond: John Knox Press, 1962.

Peacey, J. R. 1991. *Go Forth for God. The Hymns of J. R. Peacey.* Carol Stream, IL: Hope Publishing.

Petry, Ray C. 1957. *Late Medieval Mysticism.* Vol. 13. Philadelphia: Library of Christian Classics.

Pierce, Alfred M. 1948. *Giant Against the Sky, the Life of Bishop Warren Akin Candler.* Nashville: Abingdon Cokesbury Press.

Pilkington, James. 1968. *The History of the Methodist Publishing House.* Vol. 1. Nashville: United Methodist Publishing House.

Polack, W. G. 1942. *The Handbook to the Lutheran Hymnal* [1941]. St. Louis: Concordia Publishing House.

Porter, Ellen Jane Lorenz. 1987. "The Hymnody of the Evangelical United Brethren Church." *Journal of Theology* 91 (Spring 1987): 74-80. (United Theological Seminary, Dayton)

Porter, Ellen Jane Lorenz, and John F. Garst. 1979. "More Tunes in the Captain Kidd Meter." *The Hymn* 30 (4): 252-62.

Postlethwaite, R. Deane. 1980. *Eight Hymns, In Context.* Minneapolis: Guy's Printing.

Pratt, Waldo Selden. 1901. *Musical Ministries in the Church.* New York: F. H. Revell.

Price, Carl Fowler. 1926. *Curiosities of the Hymnal* [1905]. New York: Methodist Book Concern.

_____. 1911. *The Music and Hymnody of the Methodist Hymnal* [1905]. New York: Eaton and Mains. Cincinnati: Jennings and Graham.

Ralston, Jack L. 1965. "Come, Thou Fount of Every Blessing." *The Hymn* 16 (1): 5-12, 24.

Rattenbury, J. Ernest. 1941. *The Evangelical Doctrines of Charles Wesley's Hymns.* London: Epworth Press.

_____. 1948. *The Eucharistic Hymns of John and Charles Wesley.* London: Epworth Press. Text reset. Cleveland: OSL Publications, 1990.

Rauschenbusch, Walter. 1908. *Christianity and the Social Crisis.* New York: Macmillan.

The Report of the Hymnal Revision Committee to the 1988 General Conference of the United Methodist Church. 1988. Nashville: United Methodist Publishing House.

Revision of the Hymn Book of the Methodist Episcopal Church [Report of the Committee to the Bishops]. 1878. New York: Nelson and Phillips. Cincinnati: Hitchcock and Walden.

Reynolds, William J. 1964. *Hymns of Our Faith* [Companion to the *Baptist Hymnal*, 1956]. Nashville: Broadman Press.

_____. 1976. *Companion to the Baptist Hymnal* [1975]. Nashville: Broadman Press.

_____. 1987. *A Joyful Sound. Christian Hymnody.* 2d ed. edited by Milburn Price. New York: Holt, Rhinehart and Winston.

_____. 1990. *Songs of Glory: Stories of 300 Great Hymns and Gospel Songs.* Grand Rapids: Zondervan Books.

Reynolds, William J., and Milburn Price. 1987. *A Survey of Christian Hymnody.* Carol Stream, IL: Hope Publishing.

Rice, William C. 1953. "A Century of Methodist Music: 1859-1950." Unpublished Ph.D. diss., Univ. of Iowa.

Richardson, Paul, and Deborah Loftis. 1986. "An Interpretation: 'Now the Silence.'" *The Hymn* 37 (4): 27.

Robb, John Donald. 1980. *Hispanic Folk Music of New Mexico and the Southwest: A Self-Portrait of a People.* Norman, OK: Univ. of Oklahoma Press.

Rogal, Samuel J. "'Onward Christian Soldiers': A Reexamination." *The Hymn* 39 (1): 23-30.

Ronander, Albert C., and Ethel K. Porter. 1966. *Guide to the Pilgrim Hymnal* [1958]. Philadelphia and Boston: United Church Press.

Routley, Erik. 1951. *I'll Praise My Maker.* London: Independent Press.

_____. 1953. "Notes on the Music." *Companion to Congregational Praise* [1951]. London: Independent Press.

_____. 1956. *Hymns and the Faith.* Greenwich, CT: Seabury Press.

_____. 1957. *The Music of Christian Hymnody.* London: Independent Press.

_____. 1958. *The English Carol.* London: Oxford Univ. Press.

_____. 1959. *Hymns and Human Life.* Grand Rapids: Wm. B. Eerdmans.

_____. 1964, 1966. *Twentieth Century Church Music.* London: Jenkins. Reprint. Carol Stream, IL: Agape, 1984.

_____. 1967. *Music Leadership in the Church.* Nashville: Abingdon Press. Reprint. Carol Stream, IL: Agape, 1984.

_____. 1968. *The Musical Wesleys.* New York: Oxford Univ. Press.

_____. 1968. *Words, Music, and the Church.* Nashville: Abingdon Press.

_____. 1976. *Church Music and the Christian Faith.* Carol Stream, IL: Hope Publishing.

_____. 1977. *Companion to Westminster Praise.* Chapel Hill, NC: Hinshaw Music.

_____. 1979. *An English-Speaking Hymnal Guide.* Collegeville, MN: Liturgical Press.

_____. 1979. *A Panorama of Christian Hymnody.* Collegeville, MN: Liturgical Press.

_____. 1979. "Sexist Language: A View from a Distance." *Worship* 53: 2-11; reprinted *The Hymn* 31 (1980): 26-32.

_____. 1981. *The Music of Christian Hymns.* Chicago: GIA Publications.

_____. 1982. "Hymnody 1981-82: A Quiet Year." *Worship* 56 (6): 508-10.

_____. 1990. *Our Lives Be Praise: The Hymn Tunes, Carols, and Texts of Erik Routley.* Edited by Carlton R. Young. Carol Stream, IL: Hope Publishing.

Rowe, Kenneth E. 1991. "Authorized United Brethren Hymnals." Previously unpublished research. Madison, NJ: Drew Univ. General Commission on Archives and History, The United Methodist Church.

Rowe, Kenneth E. 1993. "Redesigning Methodist Churches: Auditorium-Style Sanctuaries and Akron-Plan Sunday-Schools in Romanesque Costume 1875–1925." Unpublished paper, Drew University, Madison NJ.

Sadie, Stanley, ed. 1980. *New Grove's Dictionary of Music and Musicians.* 20 vols. London: Macmillan.

Sailor's Magazine and Seamen's Friend, The, 43, (April 1871):119. NY: American Seamen's Friend Society.

Sanchez, Diana, ed. 1989. *The Hymns of the United Methodist Hymnal* [1989]. Nashville: Abingdon Press.

Sankey, Ira D. 1907. *My Life and the Story of the Gospel Hymns.* Rev. ed. NY: Harper and Brothers.

Schalk, Carl, ed. 1978. *Key Words in Church Music.* St. Louis: Concordia Publishing House.

Schilling, S. Paul. 1983. *The Faith We Sing.* Philadelphia: Westminster Press.

Scholes, Percy. 1954. *God Save the Queen.* London: Oxford Univ. Press.

Sharp, Cecil. 1932. *English Folk Songs from the Southern Appalachians.* 2 vols. Rev. ed. London: Oxford Univ. Press.

Sharp, Eric. 1991. "Developments in English Hymnody in the Eighties." *The Hymn* 42 (2): 7-11.

Shepherd, Massie H., Jr. 1955. *Oxford American Prayer Book Commentary.* London and NY: Oxford Univ. Press.

_____, ed. 1963. *Worship in Scripture and Tradition.* NY: Oxford Univ. Press.

_____. 1976. *The Psalms in Christian Worship.* Collegeville, MN: Liturgical Press.

Shockley, Grant S., ed. 1991. *Heritage and Hope: The African American Presence in United Methodism.* Nashville: Abingdon Press.

Slabey, Andrew P. 1965. "John Hus and Congregational Singing." *The Hymn* 16 (3): 69-74, 87.

Sleeth, Natalie. 1987. *Adventures for the Soul.* Carol Stream, IL: Hope Publishing.

Smith, H. Augustine. 1931. *Lyric Religion.* NY: Century.

Smith, William Farley. 1991. "Charles Wesley and African American Hymnody." *Charles Wesley Society Newsletter* 1 (3): 7. Madison, NJ: Drew Univ.

Southern, Eileen. 1971. *The Music of Black Americans: A History.* NY: W. W. Norton.

Spencer, Jon Michael. 1990. *Protest and Praise: Sacred Music of Black America.* Minneapolis: Fortress Press.

_____. 1990. "The Hymnody of Black Methodists." *Theology Today* 46: 373-85.

_____. 1992. *Black Hymnody: A Hymnological History of the African-American Church.* Knoxville: Univ. of Tennessee Press.

Stanislaw, Richard J., and Donald P. Hustad. 1992. *Dictionary-Handbook to the Worshiping Church: A Hymnal* [1990]. Carol Stream, IL: Hope Publishing.

Stevenson, Arthur L., 1931, *The Story of Southern Hymnology.* Salem, VA: Arthur L. Stevenson. Reprint 1975, NY: AMS Press.

Stevenson, George John. 1883. *The Methodist Hymn Book Illustrated with Biography, Incident, and Anecdote.* London: Charles H. Kelley.

Stevenson, Robert M. 1953. *Patterns of Protestant Church Music.* Durham: Duke Univ. Press.

_____. 1968. *Music in Aztec and Inca Territory.* Berkeley: Univ. of CA. Press.

Stulken, Marilyn Kay. 1981. *Hymnal Companion to the Lutheran Book of Worship* [1978]. Philadelphia: Fortress Press.

_____. 1982. "The Hymn Tunes of Orlando Gibbons." *The Hymn* 33 (4): 221-34.

Sydnor, James R., ed. 1962. *Addresses at the International Hymnological Conference.* New York: Hymn Society of America.

_____. 1979. "Hymns of the Social Gospel, Including Such Concerns as Ecology, Non-Sexist Language, and Elimination of Hunger and Poverty." Paper presented to Hymn Society of America, Dallas, April 1979.

Taylor, Cyril. 1984. *Hymns for Today Discussed.* Croyden, England: Royal School of Church Music.

Temperley, Nicholas. 1979. *The Music of the English Parish Church.* 2 vols. Cambridge: Cambridge Univ. Press.

Thomas, Edith Lovell. 1969. "Music Remembered." *The Hymn* 20 (2): 36-40; 20 (3): 84-88.

Thurman, Howard. 1975. *Deep River and the Negro Spiritual Speaks.* Hampton, VA: Friends United.

Thust, Karl Christian. 1898. "Das Kirchen-Lied der Gegenwart." *Music und Kirche* 6: 292-99.

Tourjée, Eben. 1884. "Introduction," *Tribute of Praise and Methodist Protest Hymn Book.* Pittsburgh: Wm. McCracken, Jr. Baltimore: W. J. C. Dulany.

Tripp, David. 1969. *The Renewal of the Covenant in the Methodist Tradition.* London: Epworth Press.

Tyson, John R. 1984. "Charles Wesley and the German Hymns." *The Hymn* 35 (3): 153-57.

Underwood, Byron E. 1973, 1974. "'How Great Thou Art' (More Facts About Its Evolution)." *The Hymn* 24 (4): 105-08; 25 (1): 4-8.

Vajda, Jaroslav, Jr. 1987. *Now, the Joyful Celebration.* St. Louis: Morning Star Music Publishers.

_____. "Translations of 'Ein' Feste Burg.'" 1983. *The Hymn* 34 (3): 134-40.

Vernon, Walter Newton. 1988. *The History of the United Methodist Publishing House.* Vol. 2. Nashville: United Methodist Publishing House.

Wade, William N. 1981. "A History of Public Worship in the Methodist Episcopal Tradition." Ph.D. diss., Univ. of Notre Dame.

Wainwright, Geoffrey. 1980. *Doxology. The Praise of God in Worship, Doctrine, and Life: A Systematic Theology.* New York: Oxford Univ. Press.

Walker, John M., ed. 1923. *Better Music in Our Churches.* New York: The Methodist Book Concern.

Walker, Wyatt Tee. 1979. *Somebody's Calling My Name.* Valley Forge: Judson Press.

Wallace, Robin Knowles. 1980. "The Hymns of Fred Kaan." Master's thesis, Emory Univ.

Ward, John Owen, ed. 1970. *The Oxford Companion to Music.* London: Oxford University Press.

Warren, James L., Jr. 1988. *O for a Thousand Tongues.* Grand Rapids: Zondervan Books.

Warrington, James. 1898. *Short Titles of Books Relating to or Illustrating the History and Practice of Psalmody in the United States, 1620-1820.* Philadelphia: James Warrington. Reprint. New York: Burt Franklin, 1971.

Watson, Richard, and Kenneth Trickett, eds. 1988. *Companion to Hymns and Psalms* [1983]. Peterborough, England: Methodist Publishing House.

Watts, Isaac. 1707. *Hymns and Spiritual Songs. In Three Books. With an Essay.* London: Printed by F. Humfreys, for John Lawrence, at the Angel in the Poultrey.

Wellesz, Egon. 1949. *History of Byzantine Music and Hymnography.* London: Oxford Univ. Press.

Werner, Eric. 1959. *The Sacred Bridge, The Interdependence of Liturgy and Music in Synagogue and Church During the First Millenium.* New York: Columbia Univ. Press.

Wesley, Charles. *Journal of the Rev. Charles Wesley, M.A.* 1849. An Introduction and Occasional Notes by Thomas Jackson. 2 vols. Reprint. Grand Rapids, MI: Baker Book House, 1980.

Wesley, John. 1983-87. *The Works of John Wesley.* Editor-in-Chief Frank Baker. Vols. 1-4: *Sermons: "An Introduction,"* edited by Albert C. Outler with a foreword by Richard P. Heitzenrater. Nashville: Abingdon Press, 1984; and Vol. 7: *A Collection of Hymns for the Use of the People called Methodists,* edited by Franz Hildebrandt and Oliver A. Beckerlegge. New York: Oxford Univ. Press, 1983.

Whalum, Wendell P. 1973. "Black Hymnody." *Review and Expositor* 70: 347-48.

Wiant, Bliss. 1974. "What Music Means to the Chinese." *The Hymn* 25 (3): 37-40.

_____. 1974. "Chinese Artifacts Inspire Christian Hymns." *The Hymn* 25 (4): 115-22.

White, James F. 1989. *Protestant Worship. Traditions in Transition.* Louisville: John Knox Press.

_____. 1990. *Introduction to Christian Worship.* Rev. ed. Nashville: Abingdon Press.

_____, ed. 1991. *John Wesley's Prayer Book.* Chicago: OSL Publications.

Wilson, John. 1962. "The Sources of the 'Old Hundreth' Paraphrase." *Bulletin: Hymn Society of Great Britain and Ireland* 95: 96-104.

_____. 1981. "The Tune 'Lasst uns erfreuen' as We Know It." *Bulletin: Hymn Society of Great Britain and Ireland* 9 (January 1981): 194-200.

_____. 1985. "Handel and the Hymn Tune: I, Handel's Tunes for Charles Wesley's Hymns." *The Hymn* 36 (4): 18-23.

_____. 1986. "Handel and the Hymn Tune: II, Some Hymn Tune Arrangements." *The Hymn* 37 (1): 25-31.

_____. 1987. "Response to Leaver." *The Hymn* 38 (3): 33-34.

_____. 1987. "The Tune 'Monkland' and John Antes." *Bulletin: Hymn Society of Great Britain and Ireland* 11 (12): 260-64.

_____. 1992. "And Can It Be." *Bulletin: Hymn Society of Great Britain and Ireland* 13 (5): 104-06.

Wilson, Ruth M. 1980. "The Old Scottish Chant." *The Hymn* 31 (3): 174-82.

"'Wondrous Love': Three Settings with Composers' Commentaries." 1982. *The Hymn* 33 (4): 206-08.

Work, John W. 1940. *American Negro Songs and Spirituals.* New York: Bonanza Books.

Wren, Brian. 1980. *Mainly Hymns.* Leeds, England: John Paul the Preacher's Press.

_____. 1983. *Faith Looking Forward: The Hymns and Songs of Brian Wren with Many Tunes by Peter Cutts*. Carol Stream, IL: Hope Publishing.

_____. 1986. *Praising a Mystery, 30 New Hymns by Brian Wren*. Carol Stream, IL: Hope Publishing.

_____. 1987. "Onward Christian Rambos? The Case Against Battle Symbolism in Hymns." *The Hymn* 38 (3): 13-15.

_____. 1989. "What Language Shall I Borrow?" *God Talk in Worship: A Male Response to Feminist Theology*. New York: Crossroad Publishing.

Wyeth, John. *Wyeth's Repository of Sacred Music. Part Second*. 1813. With a New Introduction by Irving Lowens. Reprint. New York: Da Capo Press, 1964.

Yoder, Don. 1961. *Pennsylvania Spirituals*. Lancaster: Pennsylvania Folklife Society.

Young, Carlton R. 1990. "John Wesley's 1737 Charlestown *Collection of Psalms and Hymns*." *The Hymn* 41 (October 1990): 19-27.

_____. 1993. *Music of the Heart: Church Music from a Wesleyan Perspective*. Carol Stream, IL: Hope Publishing.

Zahn, Johannes. 1889-93. *Die Melodien der deutschen evangelischen Kirchenlieder*. 6 vols. Reprint. Hildesheim, 1962.

Hymnals and Collections

For collections of the former Evangelical United Brethren Church, see pages 81-89; for collections of the former Methodist Church, see the chart on pages 94-95.

Albricias. Colección de 38 Himnos para Congregaciones de Habla Hispana. 1987. Edited by Skinner Chávez-Melo. New York: Episcopal Church Center.

Alive Now. 1985. Edited by Mary Ruth Coffman. Vol. 15. Nashville: Upper Room.

Anglican Praise: A Hymn Book Supplement. 1987. London: Oxford Univ. Press.

The Australian Hymn Book/With One Voice: A Hymn Book for All Churches. 1979. Sydney: Collins Liturgical Publications.

Baptist Hymnal. 1975. Edited by William J. Reynolds. Nashville: Convention Press.

The Baptist Hymnal. 1991. General editor Wesley L. Forbis. Nashville: Convention Press.

Book of Common Prayer [Protestant Episcopal Church]. 1944. New York: Harper and Brothers.

Book of Common Prayer [Protestant Episcopal Church]. 1990. New York: Oxford Univ. Press.

The Book of Discipline of The United Methodist Church. 1988. Nashville: United Methodist Publishing House.

The Book of Worship [The United Methodist Church]. 1992. Nashville: United Methodist Publishing House.

The Book of Worship for Church and Home [The Methodist Church]. 1945. 1952 ed. Nashville: Methodist Publishing House.

The Book of Worship for Church and Home [The Methodist Church]. 1965. Nashville: Methodist Publishing House.

Broadcast Praise [A Supplement to the *B.B.C. Hymn Book*, 1955]. 1981. London: Oxford Univ. Press.

Cantate Domino [World's Student Christian Federation Hymnal]. 1924. Geneva: World's Student Christian Federation.

Cantate Domino [World Council of Churches]. 1974. Music ed. 1980. Music editor Erik Routley. London: Oxford Univ. Press.

Celebremos. Primera Parte, Colección de Coritos. 1979. Edited by Roberto Escamilla, Elise Shoemaker, and Esther Frances. Nashville: Discipleship Resources.

Celebremos. Segunda Parte, Colección de Himnos, Salmos y Cánticos. Rev. disiembre 1983. Edited by Roberto Escamilla and Elise S. Eslinger. Nashville: Discipleship Resources.

Christian Harmony. 1873. Compiled by William Walker. Philadelphia: Miller's Bible and Publishing House. Reprint 1979. Columbia, SC: A. Press.

The Church Hymnary. 1927. Rev. ed. with music. Music editor David Evans. London: Oxford Univ. Press.

The Cokesbury Hymnal. 1923. Edited by Harold Hart Todd. Nashville: Cokesbury Press.

The Cokesbury Worship Hymnal. 1938. Nashville: Abingdon Press.

A Collection of Hymns for the Use of the People called Methodists. 1831. London: Wesley Conference Office.

A Collection of Tunes Set to Music, As they are commonly Sung at the Foundery. 1742. Edited by John Wesley. London: A. Pearson. Reprint 1981. Bristol, England: Bryan F. Spinney.

Congregational Praise. 1951. London: Independent Press.

E.A.C.C. Hymnal [East Asia Christian Conference hymnal]. 1964. 2d. ed. Edited by John Milton Kelly and Daniel Thambyrajah Niles. Tokyo: East Asia Christian Conference.

Ecumenical Praise. 1977. Edited by Austin C. Lovelace, Erik Routley, Alec Wyton, and Carlton R. Young. Carol Stream, IL: Agape.

The English Hymnal. 1906. New ed. 1933. London: Oxford Univ. Press.

The English Hymnal with Tunes. 1906. New ed. 1933. General editor Percy Dearmer, music editor Ralph Vaughan Williams. London: Oxford Univ. Press.

English Praise. A Supplement to the English Hymnal [rev. ed. 1933]. 1975. London: Oxford Univ. Press.

Fill Us with Your Love, and other Hymns from Africa. 1983. Edited by Tom Colvin. Carol Stream, IL: Agape.

Gospel Hymns Nos. 1 to 6 Complete. 1896. Compiled by Ira D. Sankey, James McGranahan, and Geo. C. Stebbins. Chicago: Biglow and Main.

The Harvard University Hymn Book. 1964. Cambridge: Harvard Univ. Press.

Hermon, A New Collection of Sacred Music. 1873. Edited by R. M. McIntosh and Thomas O. Summers. New York: F. J. Huntington.

El Himnario. 1964. Edited by George P. Simmonds and Elizabeth R. de Donald-son. Albuquerque, NM: Canticos Escogidos.

Himnario Methodista. Himnal de la Conferencia Río Grande de La Iglesia Metodista Unida. 1973. Edited by Alfredo Náñez. Music editor Robert O. Hoffelt. Nashville: United Methodist Publishing House.

The Hymnal [Presbyterian Church in the United States of America]. 1895. Edited by Louis F. Benson and William W. Gilchrist. 1903 impression. Philadel-phia: Presbyterian Board of Publication and Sabbath-School Work.

The Hymnal [Presbyterian USA]. 1933. Edited by Clarence Dickinson and Calvin Weiss Laufer. Philadelphia. Presbyterian Board of Christian Education.

Hymnal for Colleges and Schools [The Yale Hymnal]. 1956. Edited by E. Harold Geer. New Haven and London: Yale Univ. Press.

Hymnal for Worship and Celebration. 1986. Edited by Tom Fettde. Waco, TX: Word Music.

The Hymnal 1940 [The Protestant Episcopal Church]. 1943. New York: Church Pension Fund.

The Hymnal 1982 [The Protestant Episcopal Church]. 1985. General editor Ray-mond F. Glover. New York: Church Hymnal Corporation.

The Hymnal 1982. Service Music [The Protestant Episcopal Church]. 1985. General editor Raymond F. Glover. New York: Church Hymnal Corporation.

Hymnal of the United Church of Christ. 1974. Edited by John Ferguson and William Nelson. Philadelphia: United Church Press.

Hymnal Supplement. 1984. Edited by Carlton R. Young. Carol Stream, IL: Agape.

Hymnal Supplement II. 1987. Edited by Austin C. Lovelace, Jane Marshall, W. Thomas Smith, and Carlton R. Young. Carol Stream, IL: Agape.

Hymnal: A Worship Book [Church of the Brethren, General Conference Mennonite Church, Mennonite Church in North America]. 1992. Managing editor Rebecca Slough. Elgin, IL: Brethren Press.

The Hymnary [The United Church of Canada]. 1930. Toronto: United Church Publishing House.

Hymnary for Use in [Canadian] Baptist Churches. 1936. Toronto: Ryerson Press.

The Hymnbook [Presbyterian]. 1955. Edited by David Hugh Jones. Philadelphia: Westminster Press.

The Hymn Book [Anglican Church of Canada and the United Church of Canada]. 1971. Reprint with corrections 1974. Toronto: United Church of Canada.

Hymns III [Supplement to *The Hymnal 1940*]. 1979. New York: Church Hymnal Corporation.

Hymns Ancient and Modern. 1916. 2d. supp. to the Old Edition. London: William Clowes and Sons.

Hymns Ancient and Modern Revised. 1981. [Organ edition] London: Hymns Ancient and Modern.

Hymns and Psalms. A Methodist and Ecumenical Hymn Book. 1983. 1984 ed. Lon-don: Methodist Publishing House.

Hymns for Church and School. 1964. London: Novello.

Hymns for the Family of God. 1976. Edited by Fred Bock. Nashville: Paragon Asso-ciates.

Hymns for the Living Church. 1974. Edited by Donald P. Hustad. Carol Stream, IL: Hope Publishing.

Hymns for Today's Church. 1982. Edited by Michael Baughen. London: Hodder and Stoughton.

Hymns from the Four Winds. 1983. Edited by I-to Loh. Nashville: Abingdon Press.

Hymns of Universal Praise [Union hymnal of Chinese Protestant churches]. 1936. 6th ed. 1961. Music editor Bliss Wiant. Hong Kong: Council on Christian Literature for Overseas Chinese.

Hymns on the Great Festivals and Other Occasions. 1746. John F. Lampe. London: M. Cooper.

John Wesley's First Hymn-Book [A facsimile of John Wesley's *Collection of Psalms and Hymns*, Charles-Town, 1737]. Edited with additional material by Frank Baker and George Walton Williams. Charleston: Dalcho Historical Society.

Laudamus: Gesangbuch Für Den Lutherischen Weltbund [Hymnal for the Lutheran World Federation]. 1984. 5th ed. Budapest/Geneva: Lutheran World Federation.

Lead Me, Guide Me: The African American Catholic Hymnal. 1987. Chicago: GIA Publications.

Lift Every Heart. 1984. Edited by Timothy Dudley-Smith. Carol Stream, IL: Hope Publishing.

Lift Every Voice. 1953. Delaware, OH: Cooperative Recreation Service.

Lutheran Book of Worship. 1978. Minneapolis: Augsburg Publishing House.

The Lutheran Hymnal [Missouri Synod]. 1941. St. Louis: Concordia Publishing House.

Methodist Hymn-Book, with tunes. 1904. Music editor Frederick Bridge. London: Wesleyan Conference Office.

Methodist Hymn-Book, with tunes. 1933. London: Wesleyan Conference Office.

More Hymns and Spiritual Songs [Supplement to *The Hymnal 1940*]. General editor Lee H. Bristol, Jr. New York: Walton Music.

More Hymns for Today. A Second Supplement to Hymns Ancient and Modern. 1980. London: Hymns Ancient and Modern.

New Church Praise [United Reformed Church]. 1975. Edinburgh: Saint Andrew Press.

New Hymns for the Lectionary. 1986. Edited by Carol Doran and Thomas H. Troeger. New York: Oxford Univ. Press.

100 Hymns for Today [A Supplement to *Hymns Ancient and Modern*]. 1969. London: Hymns Ancient and Modern.

The Original Sacred Harp. 1971. Denson Rev. Cullman, AL: Sacred Harp Publishing.

The Oxford Book of Carols. 1928. Re-engraved and reset with some changes 1964. Edited by Percy Dearmer, R. Vaughan Williams, and Martin Shaw. London: Oxford Univ. Press.

Partners in Praise [Supplement to *The Methodist Hymn Book*, 1933]. 1979. Great Yarmouth, England: Galliard.

Pilgrim Hymnal. 1958. Music editors Ethel and Hugh Porter. Boston: Pilgrim Press.

Praise God in Song. 1979. Edited by John Allyn Melloh and William G. Storey. Chicago: GIA Publications.

The Presbyterian Hymnal. 1990. Edited by LindaJo McKim. Louisville: Westminster/John Knox Press.

Psalter Hymnal. 1987. Edited by Emily R. Brink. Grand Rapids: CRC Publications.

Rejoice in the Lord [Reformed Church in America]. 1985. Edited by Erik Routley. Grand Rapids: Wm. B. Eerdmans Publishing.

Scots Musical Museum: Consisting of Six Hundred Scots Songs with Proper Basses for the Piano Forte. 1787-1803. 6 vols. Edinburgh: P J. Johnson.

The Service Book and Hymnal [Lutheran Church in America]. 1958. Minneapolis: Augsburg Publishing House.

A Shaker Hymnal [A facsimile ed. of the 1908 hymnal of the Canterbury Shakers]. 1990. Intro. by Cheryl P. Anderson. Woodstock, NY: Overlook Press.

Sing Alleluia [Supplement to *The Australian Hymn Book/With One Voice*]. 1987. Sydney: Australian Hymn Book Pty.

The Small Hymn Book. 1914. Edited by Robert Bridges. Oxford: Clarendon Press.

Songs of Deliverance. 1988. Edited by Timothy Dudley-Smith. Carol Stream, IL: Hope Publishing.

Songs of Praise. 1925. 1931 Enlarged ed. London: Oxford Univ. Press.

Songs of Zion. 1981. Rev. 1982. Edited by J. Jefferson Cleveland and Verolga Nix. Nashville: Abingdon Press.

Sound the Bamboo [CCA Hymnal, trial edition]. 1990. Edited by I-to Loh. Manila: Asian Institute for Liturgy and Music and the Christian Conference of Asia.

Southern Harmony and Musical Companion. 1835. Philadelphia: E. W. Miller. 1954. 4th ed. reprinted 1987. Lexington, KY: Univ. Press of Kentucky.

Sunday School Praise. 1958. London: National Sunday School Union.

Supplement to the Book of Hymns. 1982. Edited by Carlton R. Young. Nashville: United Methodist Publishing House.

Tabor. The Richmond Collection of Sacred Music. 1867. Edited by R. M. McIntosh. Columbia, SC: W. J. Duffie.

Tsese-Ma'heone-Nemeototse (Cheyenne Spiritual Songs). 1982. Edited by David Graber. Newton, KS: Faith and Life Press.

The United Methodist Hymnal. 1989. Edited by Carlton R. Young. Nashville: United Methodist Publishing House.

The United Methodist Hymnal Music Supplement. 1991. Vol. 1. Edited by Gary Alan Smith. Nashville: Abingdon Press.

The Upper Room Worshipbook: Music and Liturgies for Spiritual Formation. 1985. Edited by Elise S. Eslinger. Nashville: Upper Room.

Voices: Native American Hymns and Worship Resources. 1992. Edited by Marilyn M. Hofstra. Nashville: Discipleship Resources.

Wesley's Hymns: A New Supplement with Tunes. 1877. London: Wesleyan Conference Office.

Worship II. 1975. Edited by Robert J. Batastini, Robert H. Oldershaw, Richard Proulx, and Daniel G. Reuning. Chicago: GIA Publications.

Worship III. 1986. Edited by Robert J. Batastini. 3d ed. Chicago: GIA Publications.

Worshiping Church, The. 1990. Edited by Donald P. Hustad. Carol Stream, IL: Hope Publishing.

Worshipbook [Presbyterian]. 1972. Philadelphia: Westminster Press.

GENERAL INDEX

(Biographies and major comments are noted by bold face numbers.)

Abelard, Peter, 5, 535, **714**
Achon, Rachel; *see* Gutiérrez-Achon, Raquel
Achtliederbuch (Luther, 1524), 7, 551
Ackley, Alfred Henry, 391, **714**
Adams, Sarah Fuller Flower, 493, **714**
Addison, Joseph, 352
Adebesin, Biodun Akinremi Olvsoji, 450, **714**
Adey, Lionel, 14, 137
Adkins, Leon McKinley, 116, 358, **714**
Adventures for the Soul (Sleeth, 1987), 412, 831
Aeolian Harp Collection (Dadman, 1862), 622
African American Consultation; *see* Hymnal Revision Committee
African American Episcopal Church, 23
African American hymnody, **21-27**; bibliographical listings for, 26-27; chants as part of tradition, 21-22; contributions of, 23-24; hymnbooks, 23; language in 1989 Methodist hymnal, 392-93; in the Methodist church, 23-26; in 1989 Methodist hymnal, 162, 167; in official hymnals of the Methodist church, 26-27; origins of, 21-22; performance practice of, 24, 26; *spirituals*, 25-26; language of, 490, 494; origins of, 356-57, 422-23; themes of, 296, 299, 327-28, 336, 523-24
African worship, performance practice of, 619-20
Agnus Dei, 7, 253
Aguinaldos Populares Venozolanos, 494
Ahle, Johann Rudolf, 240, **714**
Ahner, Sally, 146, 395, 654, **714-15**
Ahnfelt, Oskar, 824
Ahtone, Libby Littlechief; *see* Littlechief, Libby

Ail Lyfr Tonau ac Emynau (1897), 442
Airs sur les hymnes sacrez, odes et noels (1623), 528
Akers, Doris Mae, 612, **715**
alabados, 38
Alabemos al Señor (1976), 671
Albricias (1987), 327, 670, 672, 731, 760
Albright, Jacob, 76
Albright, William Hugh, 170, 333, **715**
Alexander, Cecil Frances, 201, 438, 544, **715**
Alexander, James Waddell, 526, **715**
Alexander, Ruth, 73
Alford, Henry, 307, **715**
Alive Now, 457, 588, 590
Alleine, Joseph, 184
Alleine, Richard, 184
Alleluia, use of, 204-05
Alleluia (Sheppard, 1915), 406, 653, 830
Alleluia (W. Williams, 1745), 380
Allen, George Nelson, 486, **715-16**
Allen, Richard, 23, 24, 56, 207, 384, 489
Allen, William Francis, 647
Allon, Henry, 247, 388, **391**
Along This Way (Johnson, 1933), 465
Alpha und Omega, Glaub-und Liebesübung (Neander, 1680), 369
Altar Hymnal (1884), 503, 768
Altdorffisches Gesang-Büchlein (1663), 240
Alte Catholische Geistliche Kirchengesang (1599), 469
alternatum, 7, 8
Alves, Rubem, 243, 350, **716**
Amaranth, The (1872), 705
Ambrose of Milan, 5, 529, 575, **716**, 850
Ambrosian chant, Ambrosian performance practice, 581, 716

English, 217, 633, 688; French, 214-
15, 389, 498-99, 528, 553-54, 599,
635; German, 377, 594-96; Huron,
20, 670-71; Latin, 541; macaronic
(German-Latin), 377; Pakistani, 167;
Puerto Rican, 315; Polish, 275-76,
433-34; USA, 223-24; Venezuelan,
493-94; *see also* folk music
Carols, Hymns, and Songs (Hopkins,
1863), 681
Carols for Christmas-tide (Neale, 1853),
377
*Carols for Use in the Church During
Christmas and Epiphany* (Chope,
1875), 214
Carr, Benjamin, 57, 288, 509, 567, 503,
729
Carr's Musical Repository, 729
Carter, Russell Kelso, 608, **729**
Carter, Sydney Bertram, 16, 169, 472,
729
Casaview United Methodist Church,
487
Casad, Mary Brooke, 146, 150, 155
Case, Riley B., 138, 146, 160, 496
Caswall, Edward, 6, 448, 487, 503,
696, **729**
cathedral music, 169, 756, 839
Cathedral Music (Boyce, 1760), 274, 724
Catholic Book of Worship I (1972), 727
Catholic Book of Worship II (Canadian,
1980), 711
Catholic Hymns (Formby, 1854), 696
Catholisches Gesangbuch (Beuttner,
1602), 232
Catholisch-Paderbornisches Gesangbuch
(1765), 232
Celebrate with Song (1979), 721
Celebremos I and *II* (1979, 1883), 42,
43, 123, 125, 166, 251, 313, 563, 564,
588, 593, 747, 750, 760, 787, 838
Celebremos project, 42, 43, 479, 563
Cennick, John, 14, 226-27, 467, 516,
729-30
Centenary Singer, The (1867), 532
Century Magazine, The, 621, 622
Chadwick, George Whitefield, 420, **730**

Chain of Prayer Across the Ages, A
(1916), 340, 560
Challinor, Frederic Arthur, 617, **730**
Chamberlain, Gary, 126, 584
Chang, Jonah, 146
chants, African American, 22, 356-57;
Anglican, 6, 62, 168, 254, 257, 266;
Byzantine, 457, 777; canticles per-
formed as, 260; for congregational
and choir use in Wesleyan tradi-
tions, 70; early Christian, 3; Gre-
gorian, 64, 68, 70, 759; in 1872
Methodist hymnal, 64; in 1878
Methodist hymnal, 111; in 1989
Methodist hymnal, 166; perfor-
mance practice in singing psalms
and responses, 586; *see also* Angli-
can chant and Psalm tones
Chants de Zion (Malan, 1827), 220
Chants Evangeliques (1855), 651
Chants Ordinaires de l'Office Divin
(1881), 697
Chao, T. C. (Tzu-ch'en), 569, **730**
Chapel Conference Songbook (USAF,
ca. 1955), 463
Chapel Royal, 10, 308, 724, 732, 736,
755-56, 767, 771, 815, 838-39, 855
Chapin, Lucius, 655, **730**
Character of a Methodist, The (J. Wes-
ley, 1742), 600
Charleston *Collection* (J. Wesley); *see
Collection of Psalms and Hymns, A*
(J. Wesley, Charleston, 1737)
Charles Wesley Society, 740, 781
Chautauqua Carols, The (1877), 246
Chautauqua Hymnal and Liturgy
(1903), 677
Chautauqua Literary and Scientific
Circle, 246
Chautauqua movement, 246, 830;
worship forms of, 314
Chávez-Melo, Skinner, 161, 180, 326-
27, 597, 600, 668, 670, 682, **730-
31**
Chesterton, Gilbert K., 117, 684
Cheyenne Spiritual Songs (1982), 443,
444, 687, 769

Church, John, 352, 761

Church Chorals and Choir Studies (Willis, 1850), 328-29, 435, 860

Church Hymnal (Sullivan, 1874), 547

Church Hymnal, The (1894), 539

Church Hymnal (Irish, 1919), 229, 484

Church Hymnal, The (United Brethren, 1935), 82, 85, 492, 496

Church Hymnary, The (1927 rev.), 15, 165, 269, 277, 382, 476, 484, 507, 747, 815; (1973) 667, 833

Church Hymns (Ellerton & Sullivan, 1871), 277, 733, 745, 772

Church Hymns with Tunes (Sullivan, 1874), 399, 405, 574, 631, 632, 838; (1903) 305

Church Hymn Tunes, Ancient and Modern (Redhead, 1853), 361, 649, 816

Churchman's Choral Companion to his Prayerbook, The (W. Smith, 1809), 254

Church Melodies (1858), 611

Church Music, 769, 825

Church Music Publishers Association, 173

Church Porch (1884), 519

Church Psalmodist (1859), 607

Church of England Hymn Book, The (Thring, 1882), 277, 842

Church School, 358

Church Times, 546

City Road Chapel (London), 51, 718, 807, 853

Clarendon Hymn Book, The (1936), 195, 860

Clark, Eugene, 334, **732**

Clark, Francis Alfred, 496, 607, 685, **732**

Clark, James Freeman, 621

Clark, Jeremiah, 168, 310, 638, **732**, 736

Clarke, Adam, 385

Clarke, James F., 493

Clausnitzer, Tobias, 240, 676, 493, 676, **732-33**

Clavierübung (J. S. Bach), 575

Clephane, Elizabeth Cecilia, 15, 235-36, **733**

Cleveland, Judge Jefferson, 26, 568, 624, 642, 665, **733**, 806

Cobb, Buell, 19

Coeleste Palmetum (1669), 487

Coffin, Henry Sloane, 268, 342, 505, 516, **733**

Coke, Thomas, 63; influence on early Methodist hymnbooks, 97, 98, 99, 101, 105, 107, 453; role in educating clergy, 54

Cokesbury Hymnal, The (1923), 97

Cokesbury Worship Hymnal, The (1938), 97, 166, 472

Cole and Johnson Brothers, 777

Cole-Turner, Ronald S., 268, **733**

Coleman, Rivert H., 375

Coleman, Satis N., 599

Colenso, John William, 628

Coles, Vincent Stucky Stratton, 710, **733**

Collection of Hymn and Psalm Tunes, A (Madan, 1769), 468

Collection of Hymns, A (1821), 542

Collection of Hymns, A (Kemble, 1864), 207

Collection of Hymns Addressed to the Holy, Holy Triune God, A (1757), 383

Collection of Hymns and Spiritual Songs Selected from Various Authors, A (Allen, 1801), 23, 55-56, 207, 489

Collection of Hymns and Tunes, A (1874), 542

Collection of Hymns for Social Worship (Whitefield), 299, 387, 857

Collection of Hymns for the Use of Native Christians of the Mohawk Language, A, 21

Collection of Hymns for the use of the Church of Christ, A (1759), 300

Collection of Hymns for the Use of the Methodist Episcopal Church, A (J. Wesley, 1821), 98, 549

129-32, 380; merger with the
Methodist Church, 120-21, 129
Evangelische Gemeinschaft, 76
Evangelisches Gesangbuch (1850), 77,
81, 87
*Evangelisches Gesangbuch fur Elsass-
Lothringen*, 651
Evangelisches Kirchengesangbuch
(1953), 558
Evans, David, 269, 277, 382, 507, **747**
Evans, George K., 315, 389, **747**
Evans, James, 20
Evely, Louis, 467
Everest, Charles William, 615, **747-
48**, 782
Everett, A. B., 241
Everett, Lemuel C., 110-11
Everflowing Streams (1981), 268, 743
Everyday Hymns for Little Children
(1929), 419, 828
Excell, Edwin Othello, 207-08, 420,
748, 752
*Experimental Essays on Divine Subjects
in Verse* (Swain, 1791), 532

Faber, Frederick William, 6, 329, 539,
649, **748**
Fair, Agnes H., 146
Fair, Harold, 146
Faith Looking Forward (Wren, 1983),
217, 406, 471, 648, 652, 695, 707,
738, 863
Falconer, Keith, 7
Fallersleben, A. H. Hoffman von,
328-29
Family Treasury (1872), 235, 733
Fanshaw, Daniel, 198
Fantasia on Christmas Carols
(Vaughan Williams, 1912), 217
Farjeon, Eleanor, 484, 553, **748**
Farr, Edward, 272
Favorite Catholic Melodies (1854), 400
Fawcett, John, 242, 470, **748**
Feaster, Robert K., viii, xiv, 146, 152,
174
Featherstone, William Ralph, 489,
748

Fécamp, Jean de, 186
Fellowship for a Christian Social
Order, 507, 828
Fellowship of the Saints, The (1948), 335
Fellowship of United Methodists in
Worship, Music, and Other Arts,
128, 721
Fenner, T. P., 490
Ferguson, John, 5
Festgesang (Mendelssohn, 1840), 391
Festival Canticle: Worthy Is Christ
(Hillert, 1975), 656
Fettke, Thomas Eugene, 390, **748-49**
Fifty Sacred Leaflets (1888), 248
File, J. C., 224
Fill Us with Your Love (1983), 619, 734
Filson, Floyd V., 263
Findlater, Sarah, 723
Finlandia, 228
Finlay, Kenneth, 116
Fish, Henry, 586, 587, 588
Fischer, Alice, 173
Fischer, Miles Clark, 463, 674
Fischer, William Gustavus, 418, **749**,
757
Fishel, Donald Emry, 205, **749**
Fisk (Univ.) Jubilee Singers, 25, 863
Fitzherbert, Selina, 340, 560
*Fitzwilliam Music never before Pub-
lished, Three Hymns, the words by
the late Rev. Charles Wesley . . ., The*
(1826), 566, 761
Fleming, Daniel, 339
Fleming, Robert James Berkeley, 462,
749
Foley, John B., 47, 545, **749-50**
Foley, (William) Brian, 16, 402, **749**
folk carols; in 1989 Methodist hym-
nal, 166-67; *see also* carols
Folk Hymns of America (1938), 474, 533
folk music, in 1989 Methodist hymnal, 166-67, 533; Catalonian, 326-
27; Croatian, 354; English, 217,
636, 770; Fiji, 655; French, 671;
German, 232-33, 377, 691; Ghana,
437; Philippine, 318; Spanish, 464;
Swedish, 270, 410-11, 661; USA,

166-67, 239, 309, 424, 474, 532-33, 690-91; Welsh, 507, 580; West Indian, 642; *see also* African American hymnody, carols, Native American hymnody

Folk Songs from Somerset (Sharp, 1906), 636

Folk Songs of the American Negro (1907), 471, 646, 686

Fong, Ben, 146

Ford, Don, 146

"For Editors and Committees of a New Hymn Book" (Green, 1985), 134

Formby, Henry, 696

Forster, G., 509

Fortgepflanzter musikalisch-poetischer Lustwald (Neumark, 1657), 426

Fortunatus, Venantius Honorius, 5, 383, 596, **750**

Fosdick, Harry Emerson, 33, 366-67, 368, **750**

Foster, Stephen, 18, 27, 28, 687, 846

Foundery Collection (Wesley, 1742), 49, 50, 108, 201, 281, 310, 426, 428, 441, **557**, 565, 602, 659

Fox, William J., 493

Frances, Esther, 42, 438-39, **750**

Francis of Assisi, 6, 189-90, 643, **750-51**

Franck, Johann, 8, 321, 444, **751**

Franz, Ignaz, 400, **751**

Franzmann, Martin Hans, 8, 47, 683, **751**

Fraser, Ian M., 204

Frazier, Francis Philip, 480, **751**

Freedom Is Coming, 575

Free to Serve (Colvin), 437, 734

French-Genevan Psalter; *see* Genevan Psalter

Freuden-Spiegel dess ewigen Lebens (Nicolai, 1599), 524, 673, 806

Freylinghausen, J. A., 8, 352, 369, 557, 660

Friedell, Harold William, 323, 463-64, **751-52**

Frost, Brian, 501

Frost, Maurice, xii, 183, 468, 470

Frostenson, Anders, 9, 331, 383, 712, **752**

Frye, Theodore, 561

Fuenfzig geistliche Lieder und Psalmen (Osiander, 1585), 7

fuguing tune, 17, 18, 56, 62, 108, 243, 503, 705, 864; definition of, 56; J. Wesley's views on, 56, 453

Funeral Hymns (1759), 292

Funk, Joseph, 409

Fyfe, Lois, 269

Gabaráin, Cesáreo, 44, 249-50, 600, 669, 670, 671-72, **752**

Gabriel, Charles Hutchinson, 225, 420, 642, **752**, 768

Gabriel's Vineyard Songs (1892), 225

Gagaku, 398

Gaither, Gloria, 230-31, 393, 602, 650, **752**

Gaither, William James, 125, 170, 230-31, 393, 602, 650, 738, **752-53**

Gallaway, Craig B., 146, 156, 159, 198, 235, 242-43, 479, 550, 576

Gallaway, Ira, 146

García, Juan Luís, 250, **753**

García, Thomás, 40

Gardiner, William, 537, 616, **753**

Garrett, Les, 654-55, **753**

Garrett-Evangelical Theological Library (Evanston, IL), xiii

Garst, John F., 690

Gastoldi, Giovanni Giacomo, 433, **753**

gatha, 3

Gather, 719, 778

Gauntlett, Henry John, 269, 388, 544, **753**

Gealy, Fred Daniel, xi, xii, xiii, 19, 487, **754**; author, 346-47, 865; comments and research on hymns and hymnody, 4, 10-11, 31, 44, 182, 185, 189, 191, 196-97, 200, 201, 208, 223-24, 246, 247, 253, 257, 259, 261-62, 264, 265, 268, 274, 287, 291, 303, 304, 314, 328, 329, 332, 355, 358-59, 368,

Gill, Frederick C., 703
Gilmore, Joseph Henry, 390, **756**
Gladden, Washington, 30, 524, **756**
Glad [Song] Evangel for Revival, Camp and Evangelistic Meetings, The (1887), 457
Glad Songs (Lemmel, 1922), 670
Gläser, Carl Gotthelf, 449, **756**
Glaub-und Liebes-übung (Neander, 1680), 558
Glehn, Manfred von, 410
Gloria in Excelsis, 65-68, 253-54, 266, 353, 456, **461**, 543, 591, 642
Gloria Patri, 65, 66, 68, 266, 268, 291, 356, 644
Glory of God, The (1943), 433
Glover, Ray, 146, 173, 204, 222, 249, 279, 308-09, 357, 399, 424, 467, 474-75, 483, 507-08
Gnegy, Bill, 146, 177
Gnostics, Gnosticism, 4, 5, 253
God of a Hundred Names (1962), 346
God's Trombones (Johnson, 1927), 467
God with Us, Resources for Prayer and Praise (1979), 491
Gold, Victor R., 550
Goldbeck, Robert, 67
"Golden Canon," 305, 630
Golden Censer, The (1864), 390
Golden Chain, The (Bradbury, 1861), 608, 612
Golden Shower (1862), 443
Goldschmidt, Otto, 558
Gollancz, Victor, 346
Gonna Sing My Lord (Wise, 1966), 614
González, Anita, 41, 146
González, Justo L., 43
González, Noé, 41
Goostly Psalmes and Spirituall Songes (Coverdale, ca. 1535), 9, 183, 196, 551
Gordon, Adoniram Judson, 489, **756**
Gospel Bells (1880), 362, 816
Gospel Choruses (1939), 672
gospel hymnody, **28-30**; in British hymnals, 15-16; commercial influence on, 28-30; criticism of, 29;

development of in the USA, 27-30; in hymnals of the Methodist church, 28, 30; in 1989 Methodist hymnal, 159-60, 170; origins of, 27, 802; recent developments in, 29-30
Gospel Hymns, 1-6 (Sankey), 238, 306, 385, 409, 416, 435, 615, 836
Gospel Hymns and Sacred Songs (Bliss & Sankey, 1875), 418, 792
Gospel Light, The (1895), 549
Gospel Magazine The (Toplady, ed.), 192, 488, 571, 844
Gospel Message No. 2, The (1912), 432
Gospel Music (Doane & Lowry, 1876), 496
Gospel Music Association, 753, 862
Gospel Music Hall of Fame, 719
Gospel Songs (Bliss, 1874), 28, 306, 418
Gospel Songs of Grace and Glory (1896), 421
Goss, John, 169, 376, **756**
Go to Galilee (Carmines, 1974), 481
Gott, der Her, ist Sonn und Schild (J. S. Bach), 498
Goudimel, Claude, 512, **757**
Gould, John Edgar, 446, 749, **757**
Gounod, Charles François, **757**
Go with Us, Resources for Prayer and Praise (Winter, 1979), 497
Graber, David, 443, 687, **757**
Graham (Billy) Crusades, 28, 409-10, 455, 666, 743, 846
Graham, Fred Kimball, 50
Grant, Amy, 30, 166, 170, 325, 662, **757**
Grant, David, 626, 627
Grant, Robert, 536, **757**
Gray, Gladys E., 246, 314
Gray, Robert, 628
Gray, Scotty W., 655
Great Awakening, 17, 27, 28, 857
Greater Doxology, 253, 266
Greatorex, Henry Wellington, 356, 432, 618, **758**
Greatorex, Walter, **758**

Meditations (Kagawa, 1956), 340
Meditations of the Heart (Thurman, 1950), 339, 340
Meier, Margret S., 491, **797**
Meineke, Charles (Christoph), 356, **797**
Mendelssohn, Jakob Ludwig Felix, 388, 498, 536, 582, 717, 721, 737, **797**, 860
Mendelssohn Collection, or Third Book of Psalmody (1849), 455, 763
Mendoza, Vicente (Polanco), 40, 438-39, **797-98**
Mennonite Hymnal, The (1969), 398
Mennonite Indian Leaders' Council, 21
Merbecke, John, 117, 153, 591, **798**
Mercer, William, 503, 756, 801
Merrill, William Pierson, 570, **798**
Merritt, Frances, 146, 173
Messenger, Ruth, 383
Messiah (Handel), 453, 567, 581, 761
Messiter, Arthur Henry, 265, 567, **798**
Metcalf, Frank J., 18
meters of tunes and texts, 57-60
Méthode de Plain-Chant (La Feillée), 237
Methodist Harmonist, The (1821, rev. 1832), 108, 303, 349, 470, 537
Methodist Hymnal, The (1905), 91, **112-13**; critique of, 113; format of, 112-13;
Methodist Hymnal, The (1935), 28, 91, **113-15**; format of, 114; marketing of, 118-20; revision committee of, 113-14, 118, 120
Methodist Hymnal, The (1966) (*The Book of Hymns*), 61, **115-22**, 123; acceptance of, 119; African American hymns in, 21; contents of, 117; critique of, 116, 119; funding of, 118; printing and distribution of, 119-20; Psalter of, 117, 584; revision committee of, 116; use of Native American hymns, 21; Wesley hymns, 117

Methodist Hymn Book (British, 1933), 427, 675
Methodist hymnals, authorized; **96-180; chart of, 94-95;** German, 92; Methodist Episcopal, 61-64, **97-108,** 61-61, 109; Methodist Episcopal South, **110-12**; Methodist Protestant, **109-10**; 1905 Methodist, 112-13; 1935 Methodist, **113-15**; 1966 Methodist, **115-22**; 1989 United Methodist, **123-80**; Portuguese, 93; *see also* United Methodist Hymnal, 1989
Methodist Hymnology (Creamer, 1848), xi, 107, 110
Methodist Recorder, 343, 405
Methodist Reporter, 413
Methodists Associated Representing Concerns of Hispanic Americans (MARCHA), 42
Methodist Societies, 96, 231, 352, 807, 853, 859
Methodist Sunday School Tune-Book, The (1881), 518
metrical psalmody, Genevan-Anglo, 9; English, 9-10
Metrical Psalter (1855), 297
Mevis, Floyd, 146, 173
Meyer, Johann David, 540, **798**
Micklem, Nathaniel, 567
Middleton, Jesse Edgar, 670, **798-99**
Mieir, Audrey Mae, 399, **799**
Miles, C. Austin, 432, **799**
Milgate, Wesley, xii, 17, 217, 248, 266, 275-76, 284, 287, 400, 402, 420, 433, 465, 468, 470, 503, 519, 522, 536, 679
militaristic language (United Meth. hymnal 1989), 32, 135-36, 138, 250, 293, 330, 338, 340, 367, 465-66, 546, 608, 622
Miller, Edward, 354, 692, **799**
Miller, Margaret D., 292, **799**
Miller, Max, 170, 223, **799-800**
Miller, Sy, 462, **800**
Mills, Sylvia Anne Jenkins, xiv, 651, **800**
Milner-White, Eric, 210, **800**

Robinson, Charles S., 246, 314
Robinson, John, 46
Robinson, Robert, 300, **820**
Robson, George B., 184
Rodeheaver, Homer, 642, 768
Rodeheaver Publishing Company, 714, 752, 799
Rodenmayer, Robert N., 340
Rodríguez, Primitivo A., 40
Roeder, Paul J., 372
Roentgen, Julius, 384, **820**
Rogers, James A., 124
Rohr, Philip, 400
Rohrbough, Katherine F., 436, **820**
Rohrbough, Lynn, 820
Roman Catholic hymnody, bibliographical listings for, 47; congregational singing as part of, 6, 9, 329, 862; as a contributor to the 1989 Methodist hymnal, 165, 173; history, 5, 6; influence on *The English Hymnal,* 15, 190; influence on Hispanic American hymnody, 36-37; hymnals, 6, 16, 344, 839; hymns of in 1989 Methodist hymnal, 385, 500, 668, 502, 700; revival of earlier forms of worship, 291; revival movement of, 330
Roman breviary, 261, 264
Ronander, Albert C., 187, 218, 236, 371, 373, 390, 406, 444-45, 516, 522, 525, 529, 683, 685
Root, George F., 830, 748, 844
Root & Cady (publishers), 761, 802, 831
Rosas, Carlos, 251, **820-21**
Rosas Del Tepeyac (Rosas, 1976), 251
Rose from Briar (Carmichael), 317
Rosenius, Carl, 824
Rossetti, Christina Georgiana, 343, 430-31, 475, **821**
Rous, Francis, 641
Rousseau, W. W., 353, 371
Routley, Erik Reginald, **16**, **821-22**; author, 203-04, 278, 413; comments on hymns, authors, composers, 186, 188, 190, 194, 203-04,

213, 215, 221, 232, 249, 272, 274, 289, 305-06, 309, 310, 330, 348, 361, 365, 372, 376, 394, 409, 413, 442, 458, 461, 468, 472, 493, 498, 509, 519, 534, 541, 567, 572, 595, 607, 616, 627, 628, 638, 639, 642-43, 683, 688, 689, 692, 795; composer, 169, 229, 261, 278, 461, 470, 689; editor, 173, 237, 248, 262, 311, 410, 860; general comments on hymnody, 15, 44, 62, 116, 125, 139, 190, 582, 758, 795, 845; influence on hymnody, 16, 45, 204, 275, 467, 738, 821-22, 863; works cited, 18, 52, 166, 170, 294, 546, 571, 572, 581, 598, 633, 729, 860
Royal School of Church Music, 725, 730, 805, 815
Rowan, William Patrick, 275, 370, **822**
Rowe, Kenneth E., xiii, 75, 80
Rowthorn, Jeffery William, 47, 308, 373, 474, **822-23**
Royal Diadem for the Sunday School (1873), 418
Royal Praise for the Sunday School (1888), 225
Rudiments of Music (ca. 1763), 254
Rufty, Hilton, 309
Ruíz, Rubén (Avila), 479-80, **823**
Runyan, William Marion, 131, 379-80, **823**
Runyon, Cindy G., xiii
Rutter, John, 169, 583, **823**

Sabbath Hymn and Tune Book (1859), 493, 809
Sabbath School and Social Hymns (1843), 616
Sacred Choir, The (Kingsley, 1839), 614
Sacred Harmony (J. Wesley, 1780), 49, 281, 352, 441, 637
Sacred Harmony (Harrison, 1784), 206, 762
Sacred Harmony (1825), 188
Sacred Harmony (1848), 108

Turning to Christ (Holmes), 514

Tweedy, Henry Hallam, 529, **845-46**

Twelve New World Order Hymns (1958), 513

26 Hymns (Green), 627, 697, 706, 758

Tyng, Dudley A., 607

Under the Surface (Havergal, 1874), 473

Underwood, Byron E., 410

Union Harmony or Universal Collection of Sacred Music (1793), 17, 194

Union Hymnal for Jewish Worship, The (1914), 637

Union Theological Seminary (NYC), 323, 644, 717, 723, 728, 730-31, 733, 735, 740, 743, 745-46, 750, 762, 771, 785-88, 791, 798, 814, 822, 826, 838, 841, 845, 847, 858, 864

United Brethren in Christ hymnody, 75-76; hymnbooks, 82-85

United Evangelical Church hymnals, 88-89

United Korean Hymnal (1989), 484

United Methodist Book of Worship, The (1992), 560

United Methodist Hymnal, The (1989); **123-80**; approval by 1988 General Conference, 172-74; classification structure of, 156-58; dedication service of, 174-77; distribution of, 177-79; Enabling Petition as establishing guidelines for, 127-28; Evangelical United Brethren in determining contents of, 129-31; language issues in, 131-43, 622 (*see also* separate entries under inclusive language, militaristic language, racist language, sexist language); liturgy in, 152-53; music of, 164-70; production of, 172-73; Psalter in, 154; structure of revision process, 144-52; Wesleyan focus in structure of, 157-58; *see also* Hymnal Revision Committee; General Conference (1984), (1988)

United Methodist Hymnal Music Supplement, The (1991), xiv, 148; *see*

also cross-references in the commentaries

United Methodist Liturgical Psalter, **584-85**, 720, 770, 781, 789; language guidelines, 142-43; *see also* Psalter

United Methodist Publishing House; *see* publishing houses, official Methodist

United Methodist Reporter, The, 409

United States Psalmody (1841), 198, 813, 824

United States Sacred Harmony, The (Pilsbury, 1799), 204, 309

United Theological Seminary (Dayton, OH), xiii

Upper Room, The (publisher), 126, 584, 744

Upper Room, The, 746

Upper Room Worshipbook, The (1985), 239, 375, 590, 629, 747

USA hymnody, bibliographical listings for, 18-19; early, 17-19; influence on 1989 Methodist hymnal, 169; language controversy in, 46-47; recent, 44-47, 169-70; *see also* African American hymnody, Asian American hymnody, gospel hymns, Hispanic hymnody, Native American hymnody, and social gospel hymns

Vail, Silas Jones, 285, **846**

Vajda, Jaroslav John, 6, 47, 183, 371, 499-500, 572, **846**

Valdés, Pedro Grado, 40

Valerius, Adrianus, 676, 784

Van Alstyne, Alexander, 736

Van Deventer, Judson W., 421, **846**, 852

Van Dyke, Henry, 453-54, 717, **846-47**

Vanderbilt University (Nashville, TN), 40, 119, 730, 746, 791-92

Vang, Cher Lue, 285-86, **847**

Vanstone, William Hubert, 483, **847**

Vasey, Thomas, 63

TUNES INDEX

(Major comments are noted by bold face numbers.)